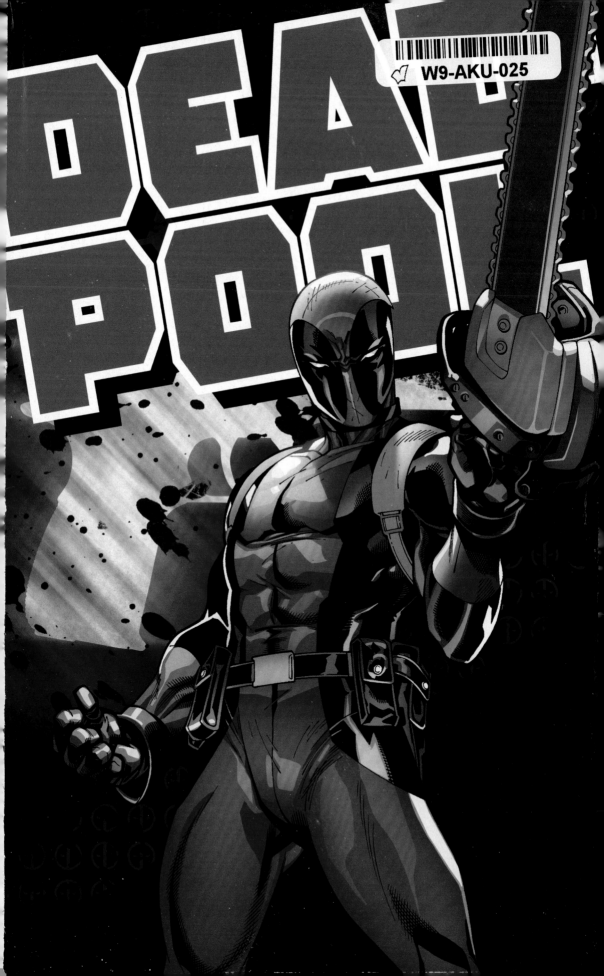

W9-AKU-025

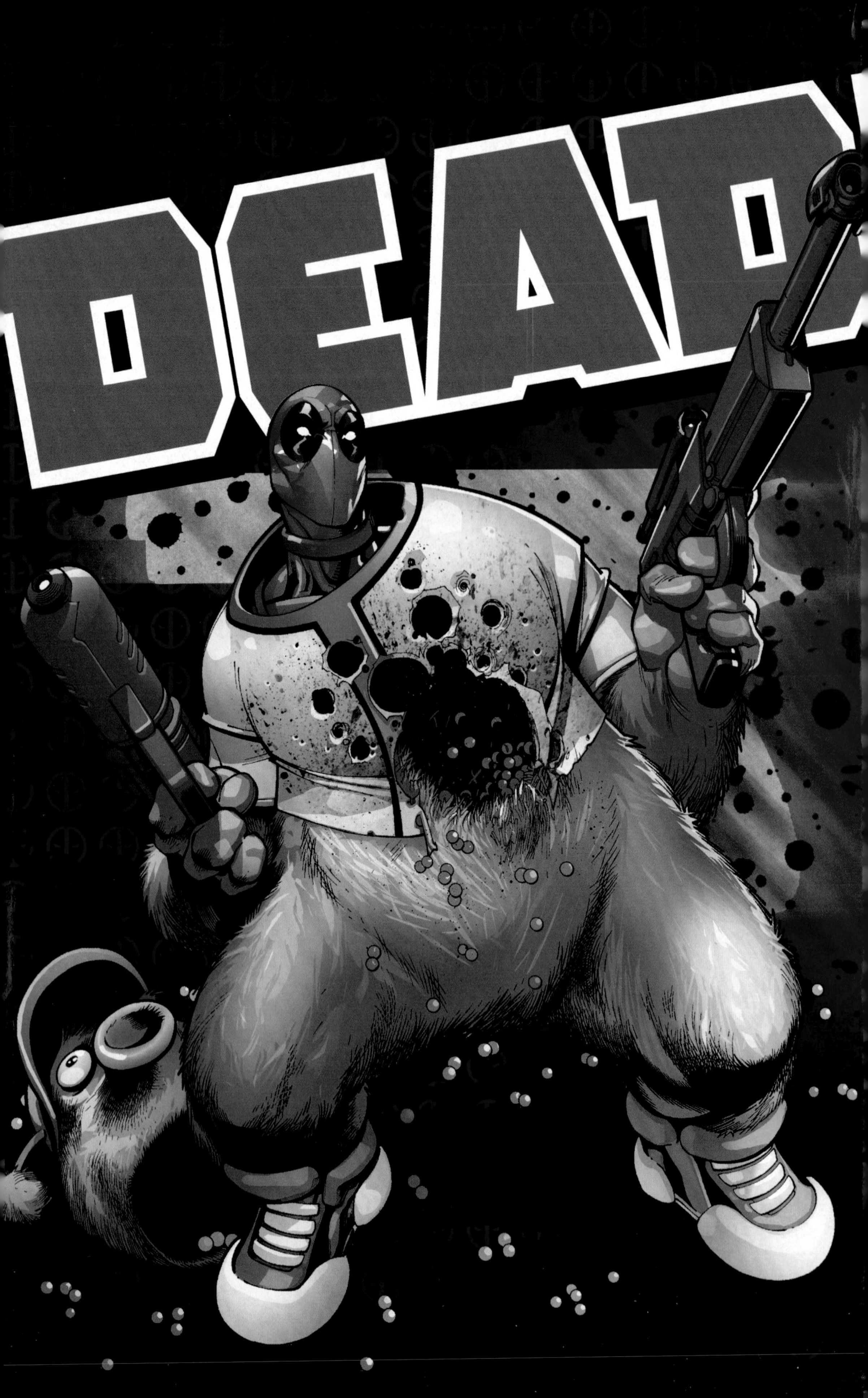
DEAD

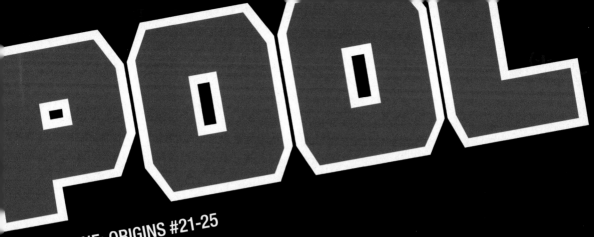

WOLVERINE: ORIGINS #21-25
WRITER: **DANIEL WAY**
ART: **STEVE DILLON**
COLORS: **MATT MILLA**
LETTERS: **VIRTUAL CALLIGRAPHY'S CORY PETIT**
COVER ART: **SIMONE BIANCHI** & **SIMONE PERUZZI**
ASSISTANT EDITOR: **AUBREY SITTERSON**
EDITOR: **JOHN BARBER**
GROUP EDITOR: **AXEL ALONSO**

DEADPOOL #1-12
WRITER: **DANIEL WAY**
PENCILS: **PACO MEDINA** (#1-4 & #6-12) & **CARLO BARBERI** (#4-5)
INKS: **JUAN VLASCO** WITH **SANDU FLOREA** (#5 & #7)
COLORS: **MARTE GRACIA** WITH **RAÚL TREVIÑO** (#4-5 & #7)
LETTERS: **VIRTUAL CALLIGRAPHY'S CORY PETIT** & **CHRIS ELIOPOULOS** (#1)
COVER ART: **CLAYTON CRAIN** (#1-3) & **JASON PEARSON** (#4-12)
ASSISTANT EDITORS: **JODY LEHEUP** & **DANIEL KETCHUM**
EDITOR: **AXEL ALONSO**

THUNDERBOLTS #130-131
WRITER: **ANDY DIGGLE**
PENCILS: **BONG DAZO**
INKS: **JOE PIMENTAL**
COLORS: **FRANK MARTIN** & **GIOVANNI KOSOKI** (#131)
LETTERS: **RICHARD STARKINGS & COMICRAFT'S**
ALBERT DESCHESNE
COVER ART: **FRANCESCO "MATT" MATTINA**
ASSISTANT EDITOR: **MICHAEL HORWITZ**
EDITOR: **BILL ROSEMANN**

COLLECTION EDITOR: **MARK D. BEAZLEY**

DIGITAL TRAFFIC COORDINATOR: **JOE HOCHSTEIN**

ASSISTANT EDITOR: **SARAH BRUNSTAD**

ASSOCIATE MANAGING EDITOR: **ALEX STARBUCK**

EDITOR, SPECIAL PROJECTS: **JENNIFER GRÜNWALD**

SENIOR EDITOR, SPECIAL PROJECTS: **JEFF YOUNGQUIST**

SVP PRINT, SALES & MARKETING: **DAVID GABRIEL**

BOOK DESIGN: **RODOLFO MURAGUCHI**

EDITOR IN CHIEF: **AXEL ALONSO**

CHIEF CREATIVE OFFICER: **JOE QUESADA**

PUBLISHER: **DAN BUCKLEY**

EXECUTIVE PRODUCER: **ALAN FINE**

1 0 9 8 7 6 5

DEADPOOL BY DANIEL WAY: THE COMPLETE COLLECTION VOL. 1. Contains material originally published in magazine form as WOLVERINE: ORIGINS #21-25, DEADPOOL #1-12 and THUNDERBOLTS #130-131. Fifth printing 2015. ISBN# 978-0-7851-8532-1. Published by MARVEL WORLDWIDE, INC., a subsidiary of MARVEL ENTERTAINMENT, LLC. OFFICE OF PUBLICATION: 135 West 50th Street, New York, NY 10020. Copyright © 2013 MARVEL. No similarity between any of the names, characters, persons, and/or institutions in this magazine with those of any living or dead person or institution is intended, and any such similarity which may exist is purely coincidental. **Printed in Canada.** ALAN FINE, President, Marvel Entertainment; DAN BUCKLEY, President, TV, Publishing and Brand Management; JOE QUESADA, Chief Creative Officer; TOM BREVOORT, SVP of Publishing; DAVID BOGART, SVP of Operations & Procurement, Publishing; C.B. CEBULSKI, VP of International Development & Brand Management; DAVID GABRIEL, SVP Print, Sales & Marketing; JIM O'KEEFE, VP of Operations & Logistics; DAN CARR, Executive Director of Publishing Technology; SUSAN CRESPI, Editorial Operations Manager; ALEX MORALES, Publishing Operations Manager; STAN LEE, Chairman Emeritus. For information regarding advertising in Marvel Comics or on Marvel.com, please contact Jonathan Rheingold, VP of Custom Solutions & Ad Sales, at jrheingold@marvel.com. For Marvel subscription inquiries, please call 800-217-9158. **Manufactured between 11/11/2015 and 12/14/2015 by SOLISCO PRINTERS, SCOTT, QC, CANADA.**

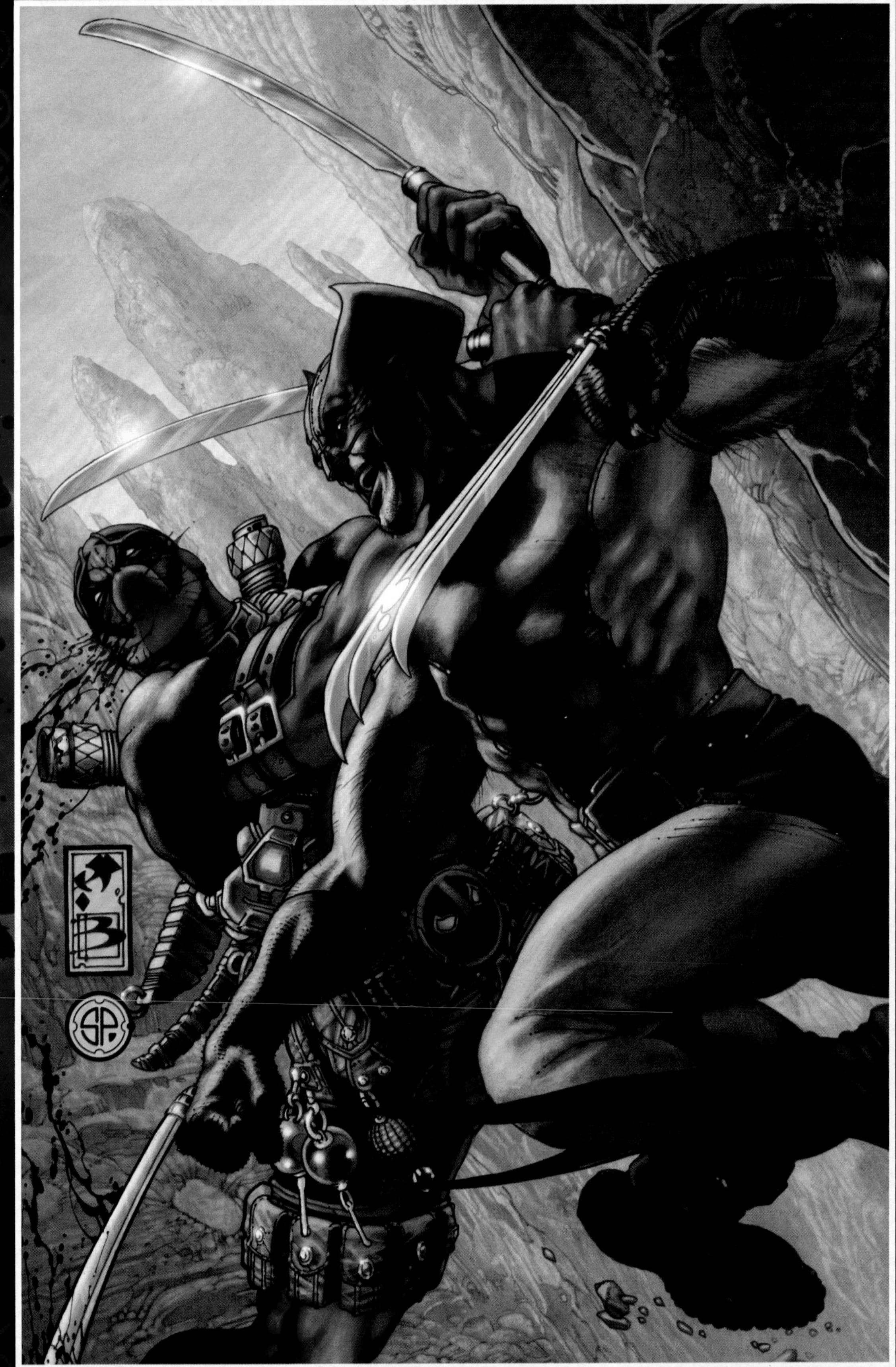

WOLVERINE ORIGINS

The mutant Wolverine has spent a century fighting those who would manipulate him for his unique powers—savage claws, heightened senses, and a healing factor capable of miracles. After repeated brainwashing, torture, and reprogramming, Wolverine's past was as much a mystery to him as to anyone. With those long-lost memories finally returned to him, Wolverine has set out on a mission to punish the conspirators who have wronged him.

Recently, a shadowy figure hired a killer to hunt down and take out Wolverine. The name of that killer? None other than the Merc with the Mouth, Deadpool.

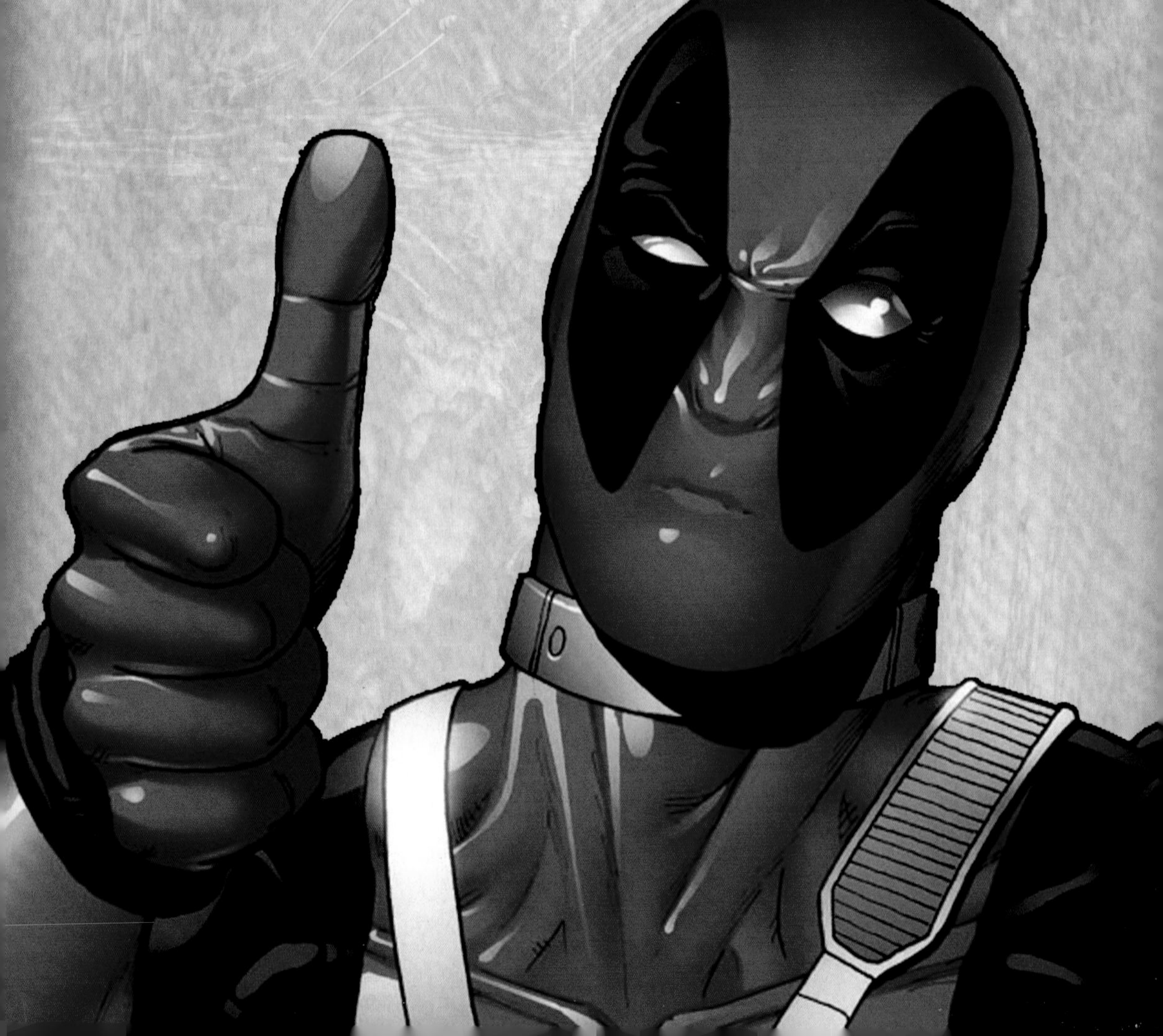

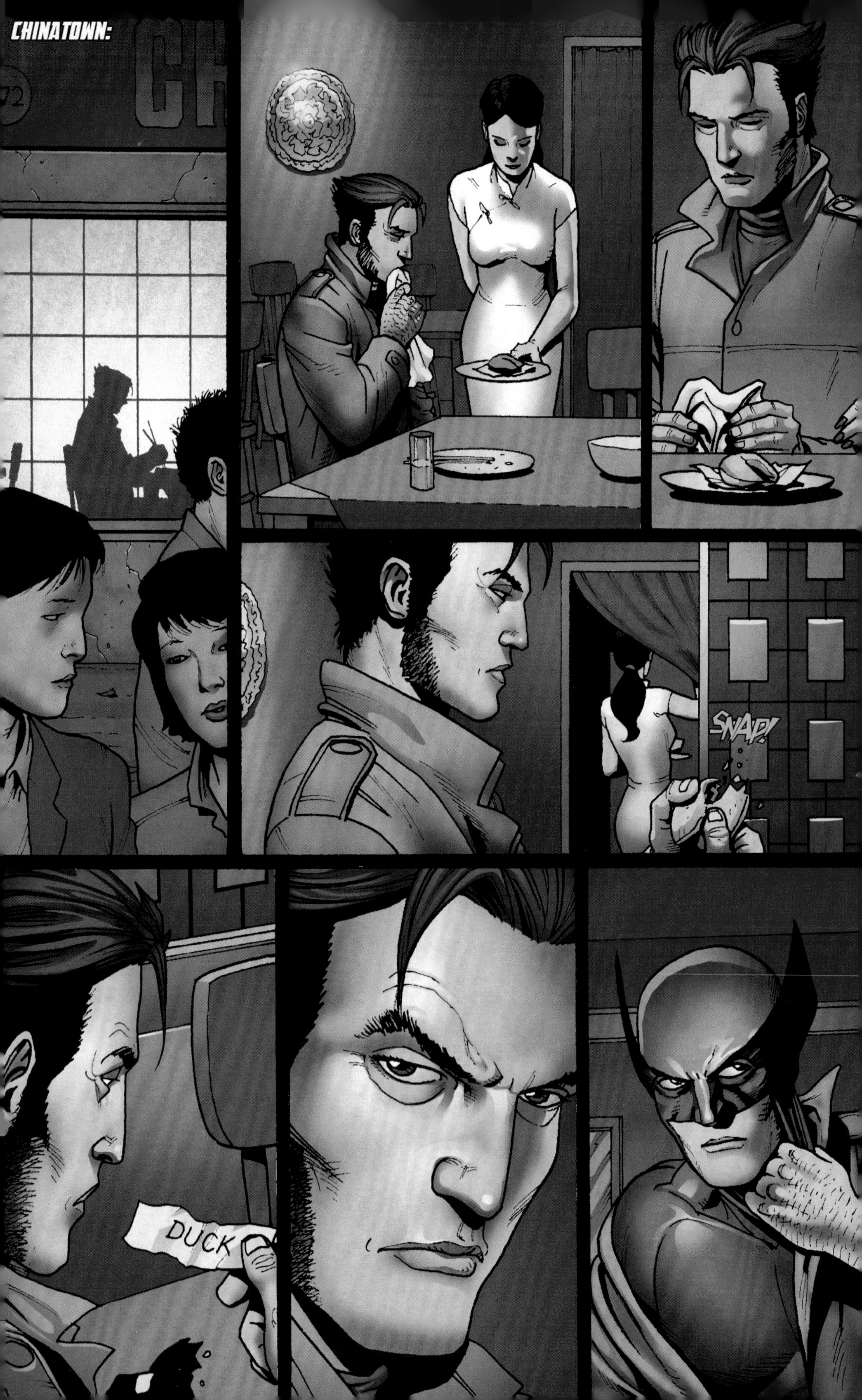
CHINATOWN:
SNAP!
DUCK

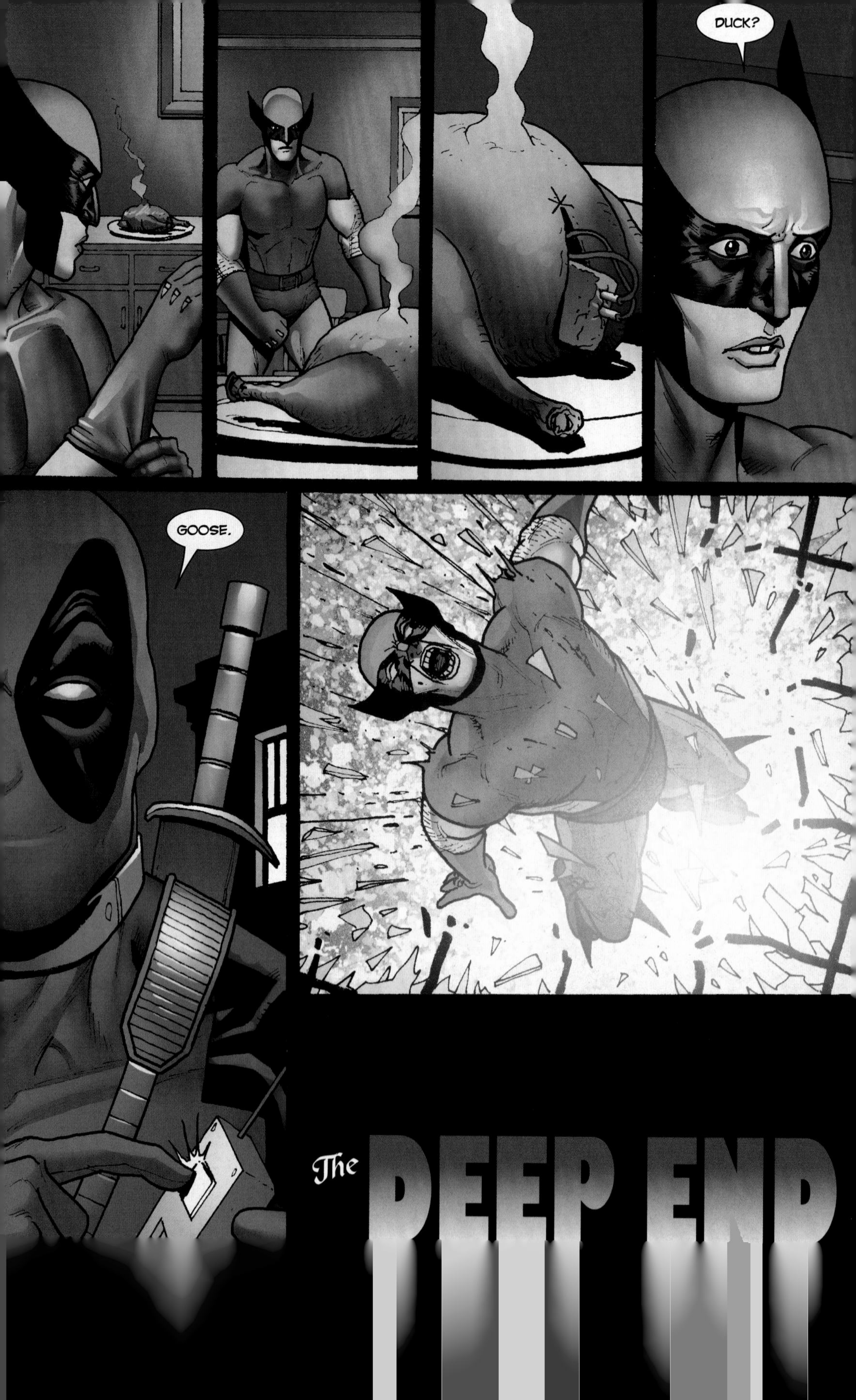
DUCK?
GOOSE.
The DEEP END

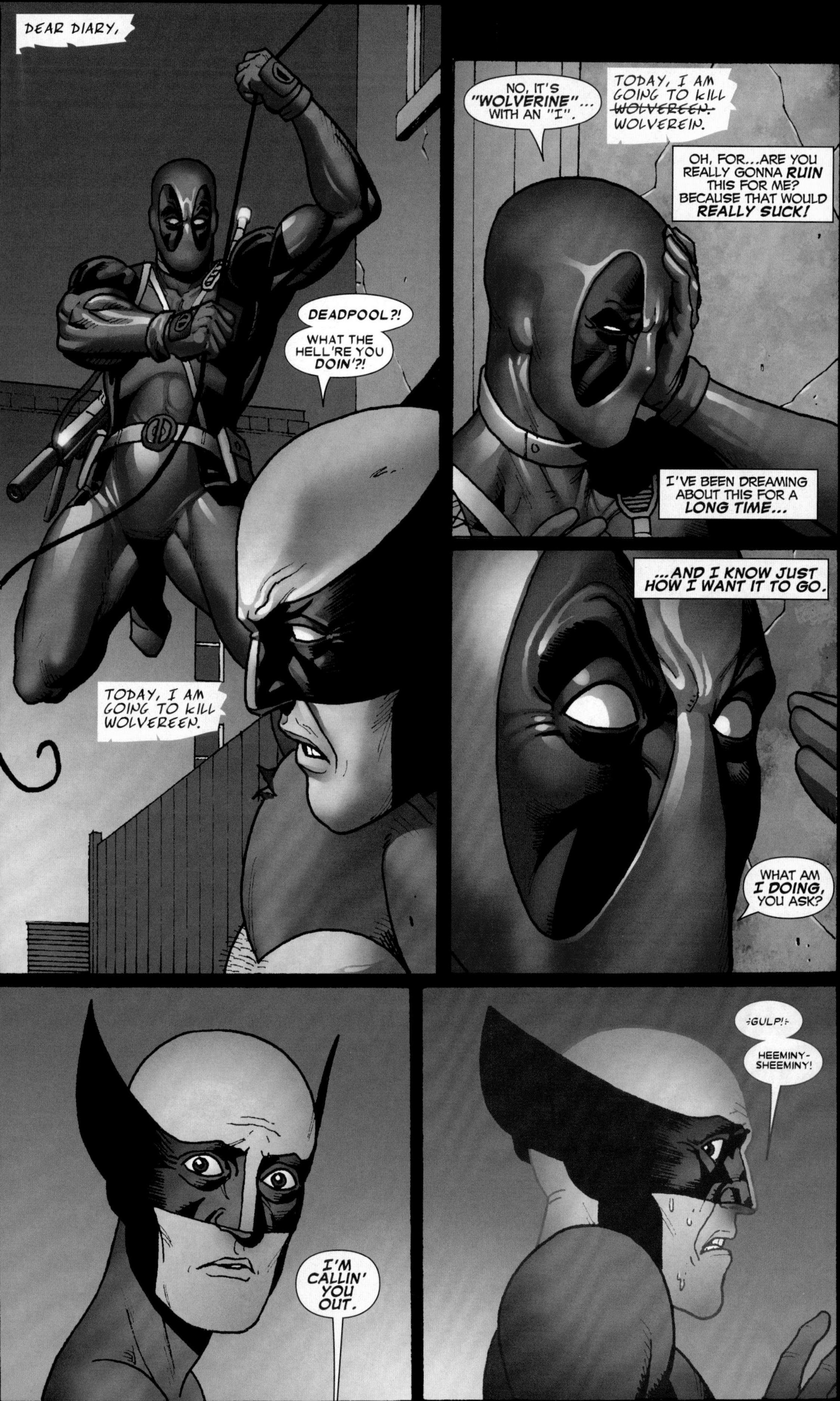

DEAR DIARY,
DEADPOOL?!
WHAT THE HELL'RE YOU DOIN'?!
TODAY, I AM GOING TO KILL WOLVEREEN.
NO, IT'S "WOLVERINE"... WITH AN "I".
TODAY, I AM GOING TO KILL ~~WOLVEREEN~~. WOLVEREIN.
OH, FOR...ARE YOU REALLY GONNA RUIN THIS FOR ME? BECAUSE THAT WOULD REALLY SUCK!
I'VE BEEN DREAMING ABOUT THIS FOR A LONG TIME...
...AND I KNOW JUST HOW I WANT IT TO GO.
WHAT AM I DOING, YOU ASK?
I'M CALLIN' YOU OUT.
-GULP!-
HEEMINY-SHEEMINY!

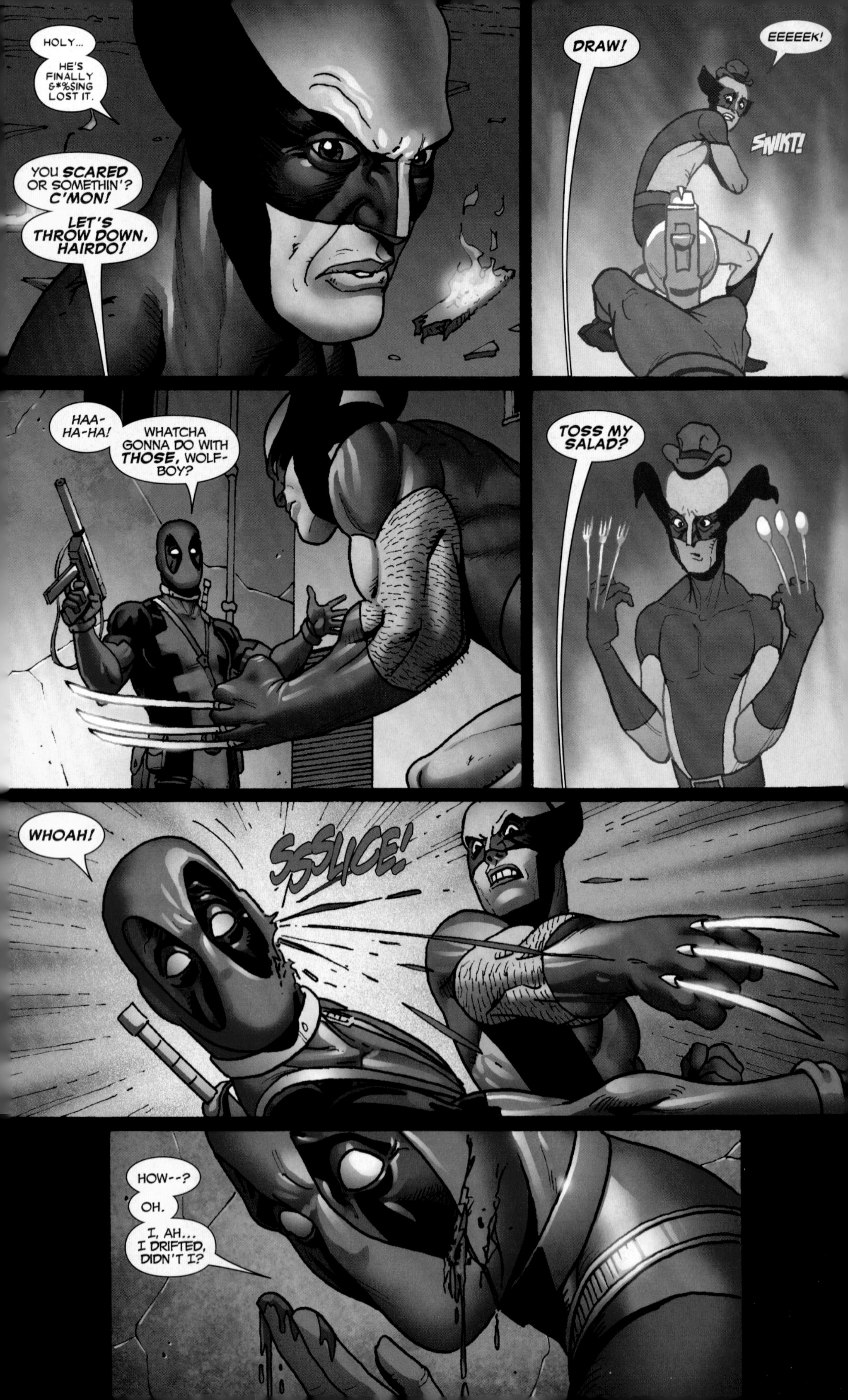
HOLY...
HE'S FINALLY &*%$ING LOST IT.
YOU SCARED OR SOMETHIN'? C'MON!
LET'S THROW DOWN, HAIRDO!
DRAW!
EEEEEK!
SNIKT!
HAA-HA-HA!
WHATCHA GONNA DO WITH THOSE, WOLF-BOY?
TOSS MY SALAD?
WHOAH!
SSSLICE!
HOW--?
OH.
I, AH... I DRIFTED, DIDN'T I?

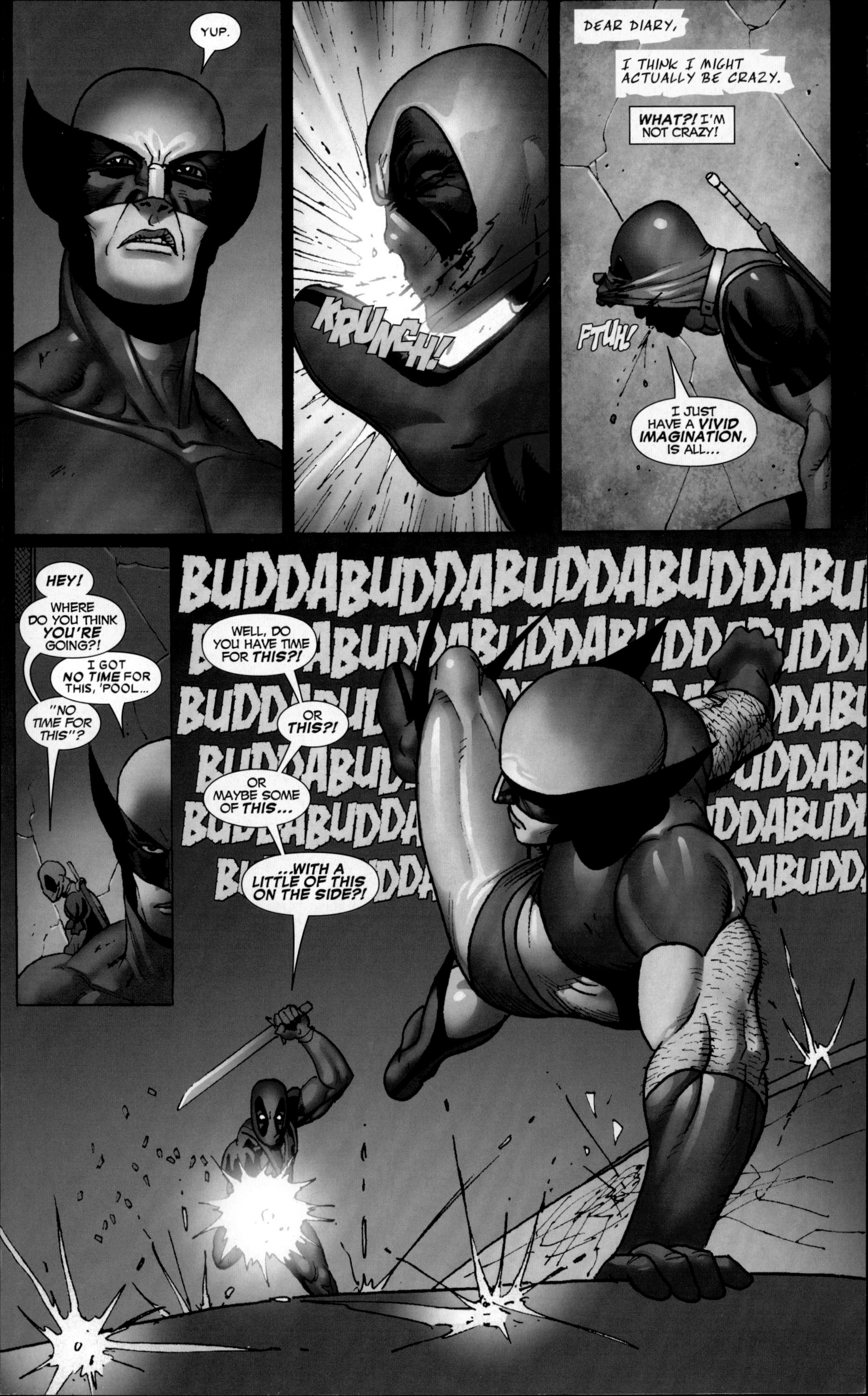
YUP.
KRUNCH!
DEAR DIARY,
I THINK I MIGHT ACTUALLY BE CRAZY.
WHAT?! I'M NOT CRAZY!
FTUH!
I JUST HAVE A VIVID IMAGINATION, IS ALL...
HEY! WHERE DO YOU THINK YOU'RE GOING?!
I GOT NO TIME FOR THIS, 'POOL...
"NO TIME FOR THIS"?
BUDDABUDDABUDDABUDDABU
WELL, DO YOU HAVE TIME FOR THIS?!
OR THIS?!
OR MAYBE SOME OF THIS...
...WITH A LITTLE OF THIS ON THE SIDE?!

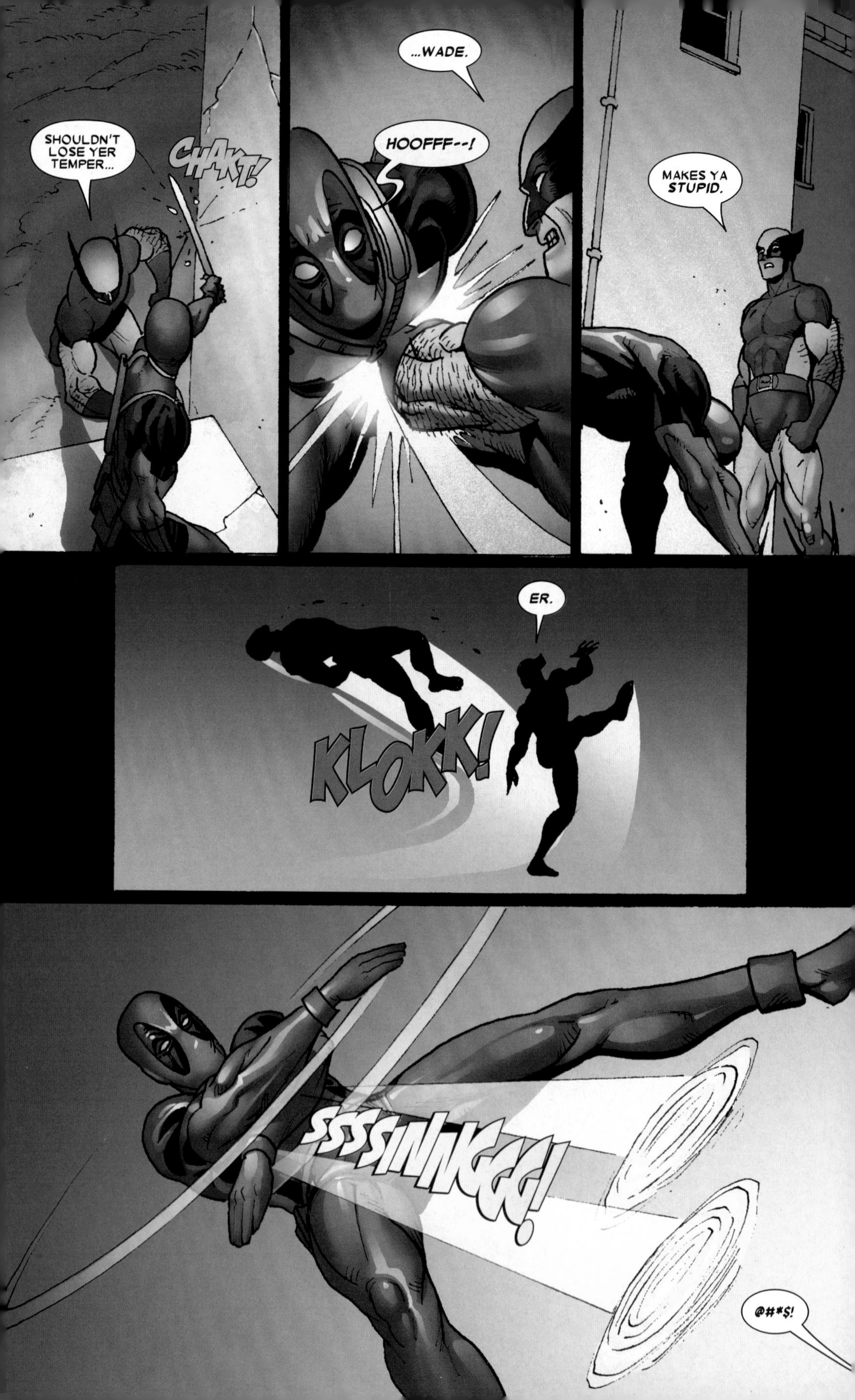
SHOULDN'T LOSE YER TEMPER...
CHAKT!
...WADE.
HOOFFF--!
MAKES YA STUPID.
ER.
KLOKK!
SSSSINNGG!
@#*$!

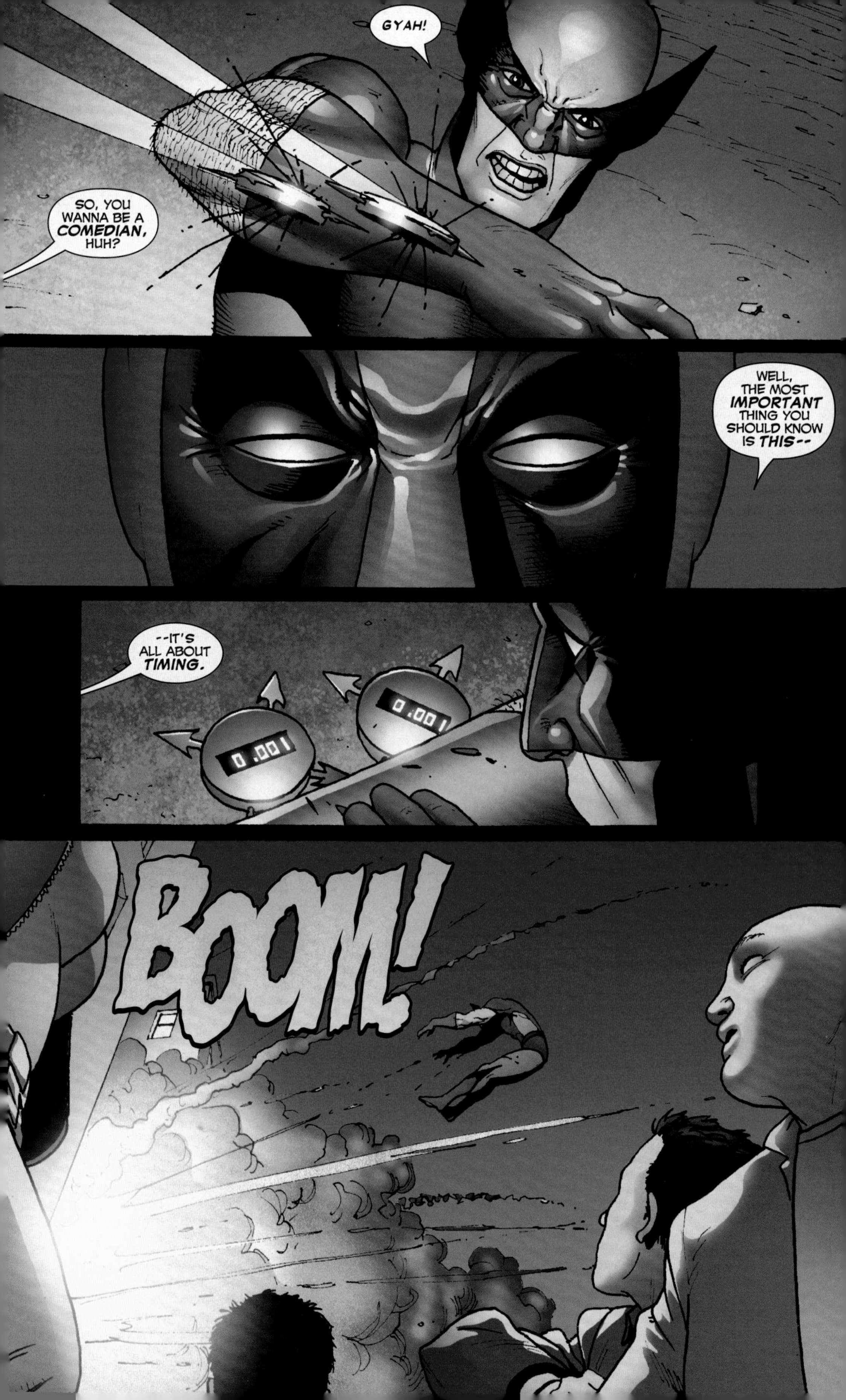
GYAH!
SO, YOU WANNA BE A COMEDIAN, HUH?
WELL, THE MOST IMPORTANT THING YOU SHOULD KNOW IS THIS--
--IT'S ALL ABOUT TIMING.
0.001
0.001
BOOM!

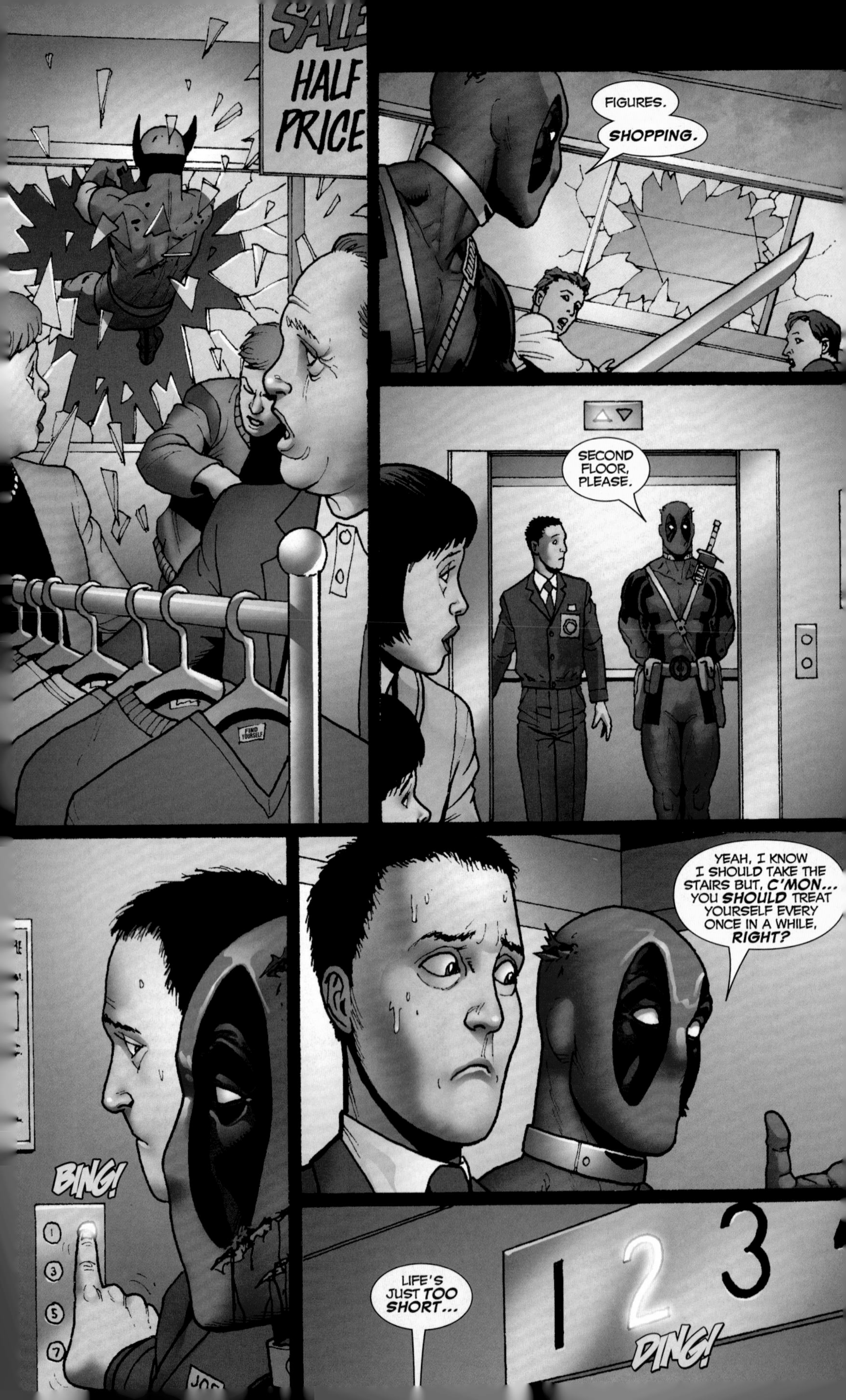
SALE
HALF PRICE
FIND YOURSELF
FIGURES.
SHOPPING.
SECOND FLOOR, PLEASE.
YEAH, I KNOW I SHOULD TAKE THE STAIRS BUT, C'MON... YOU SHOULD TREAT YOURSELF EVERY ONCE IN A WHILE, RIGHT?
BING!
LIFE'S JUST TOO SHORT...
1 2 3
DING!

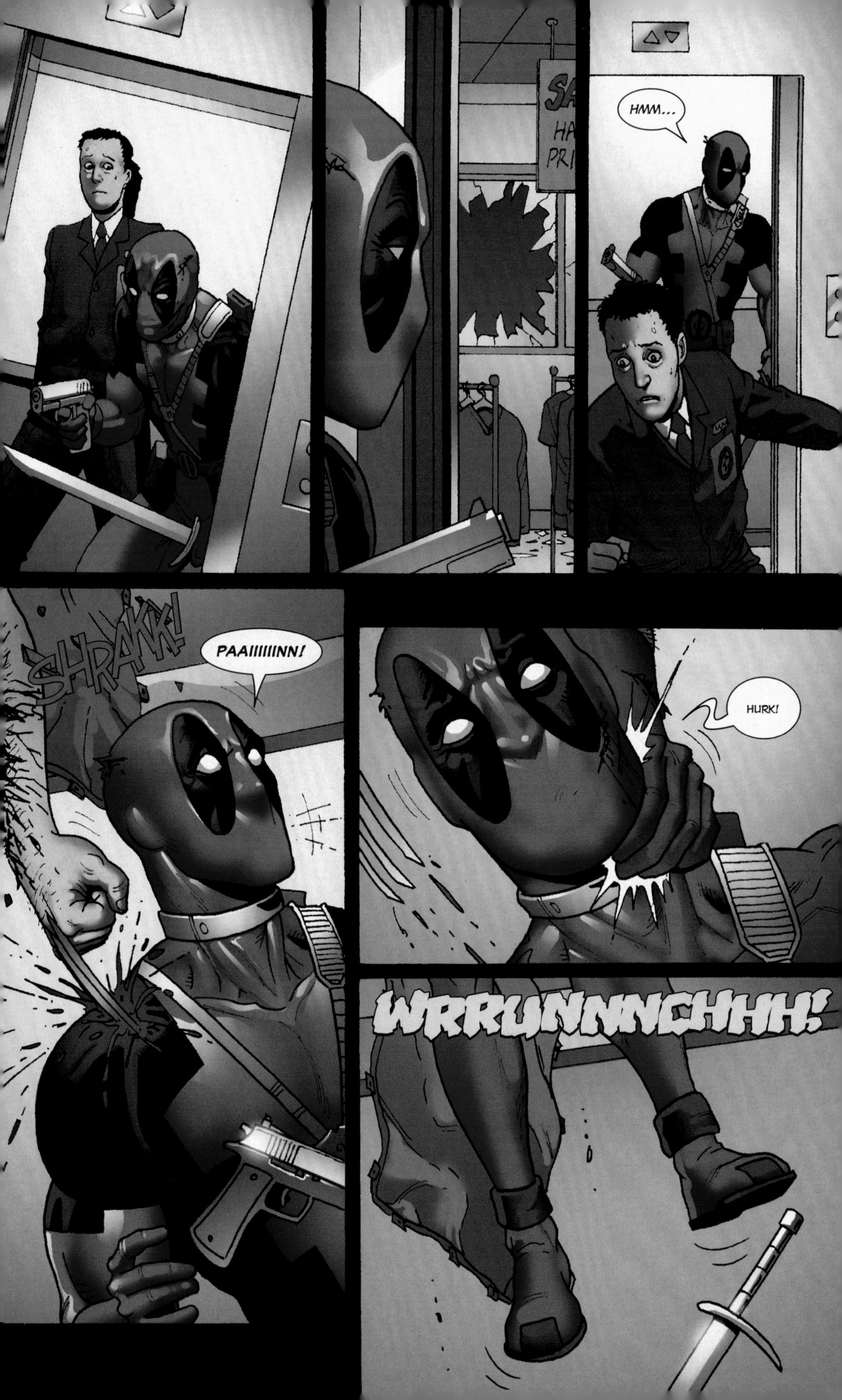
HMM...
SHRAKK!
PAAIIIIIINN!
HURK!
WRRUNNNCHHH!

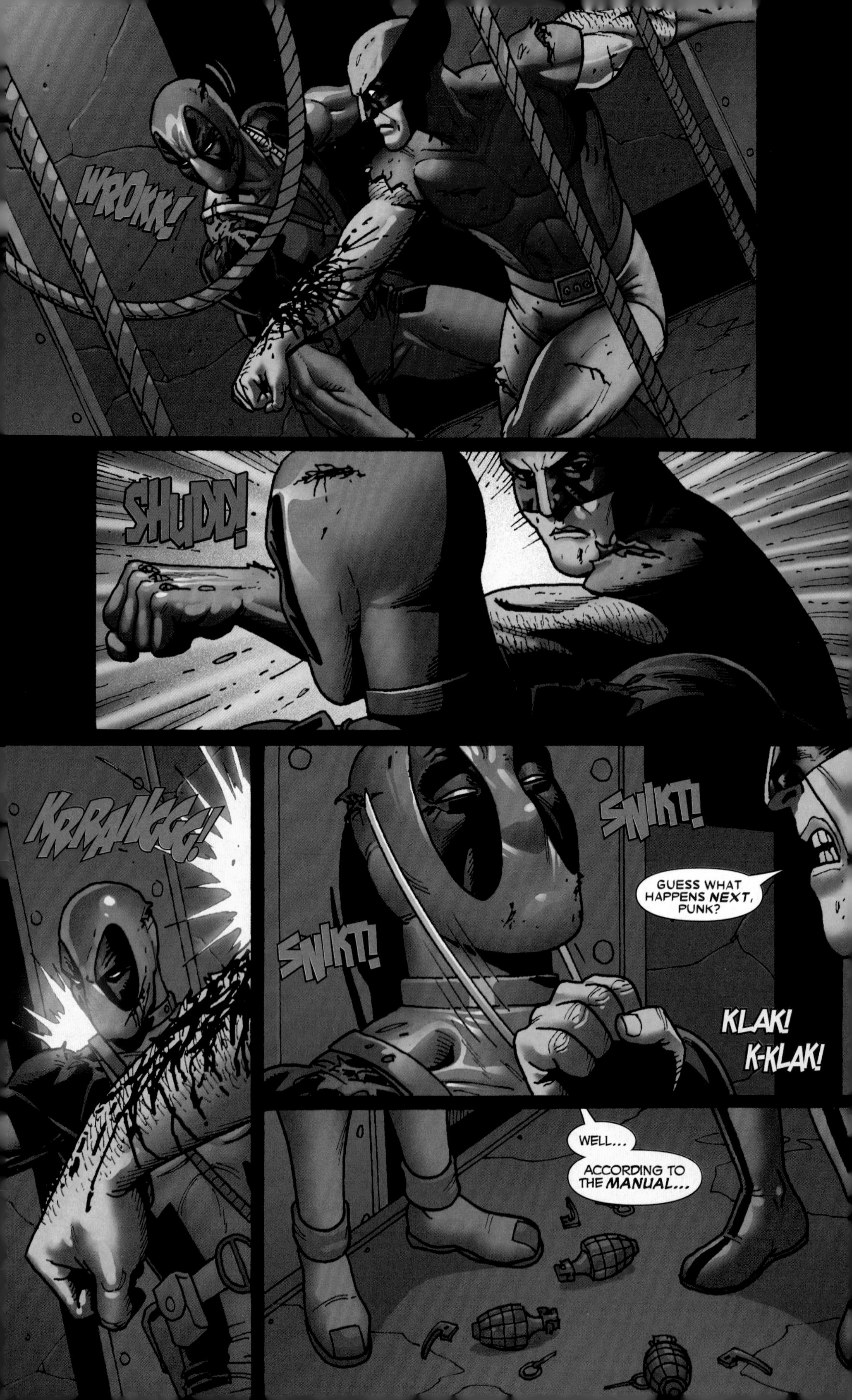
WROKK!
SHUDD!
KRRANGG!
SNIKT!
SNIKT!
GUESS WHAT HAPPENS NEXT, PUNK?
KLAK!
K-KLAK!
WELL...
ACCORDING TO THE MANUAL...

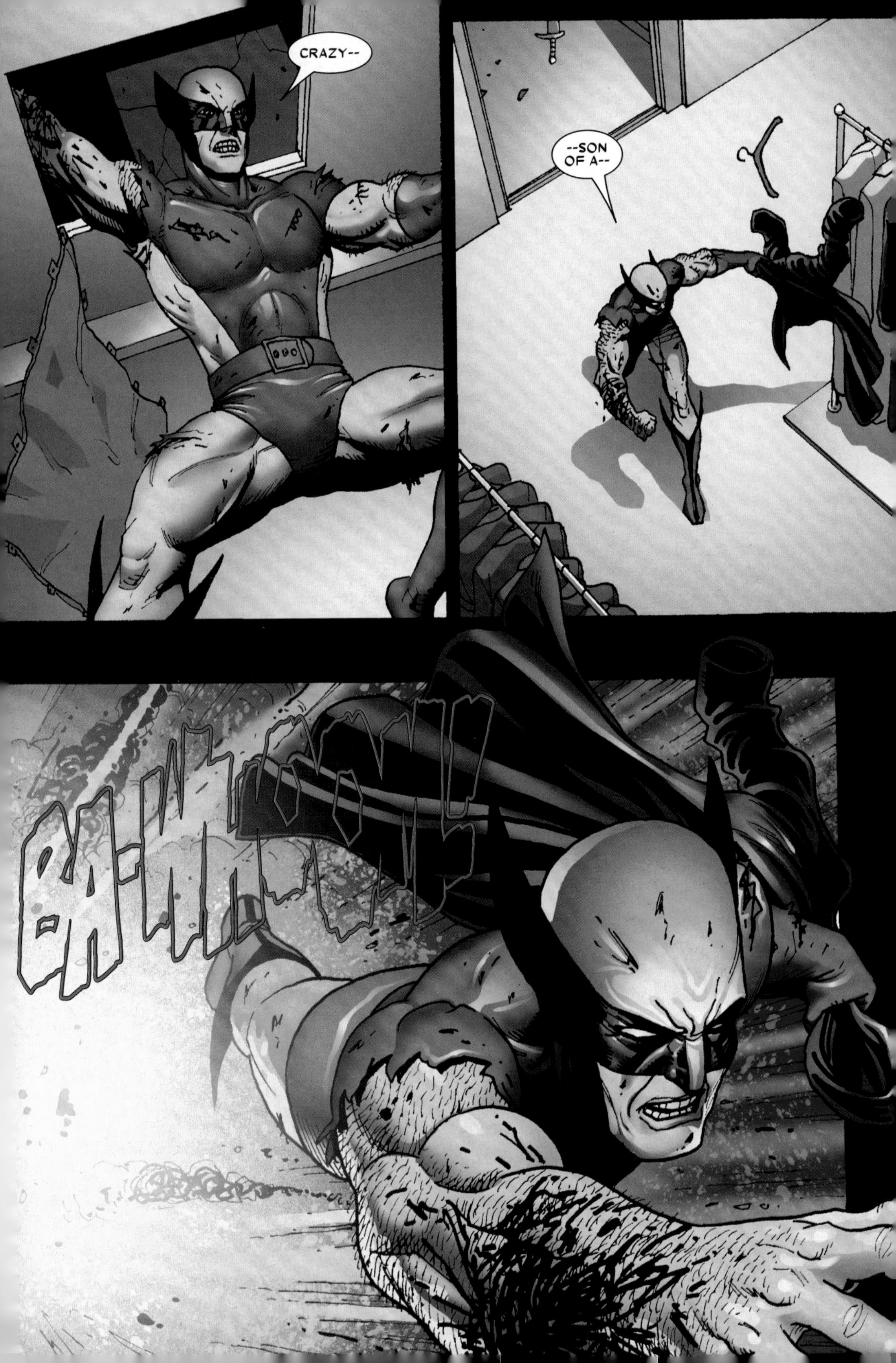
CRAZY--
--SON OF A--

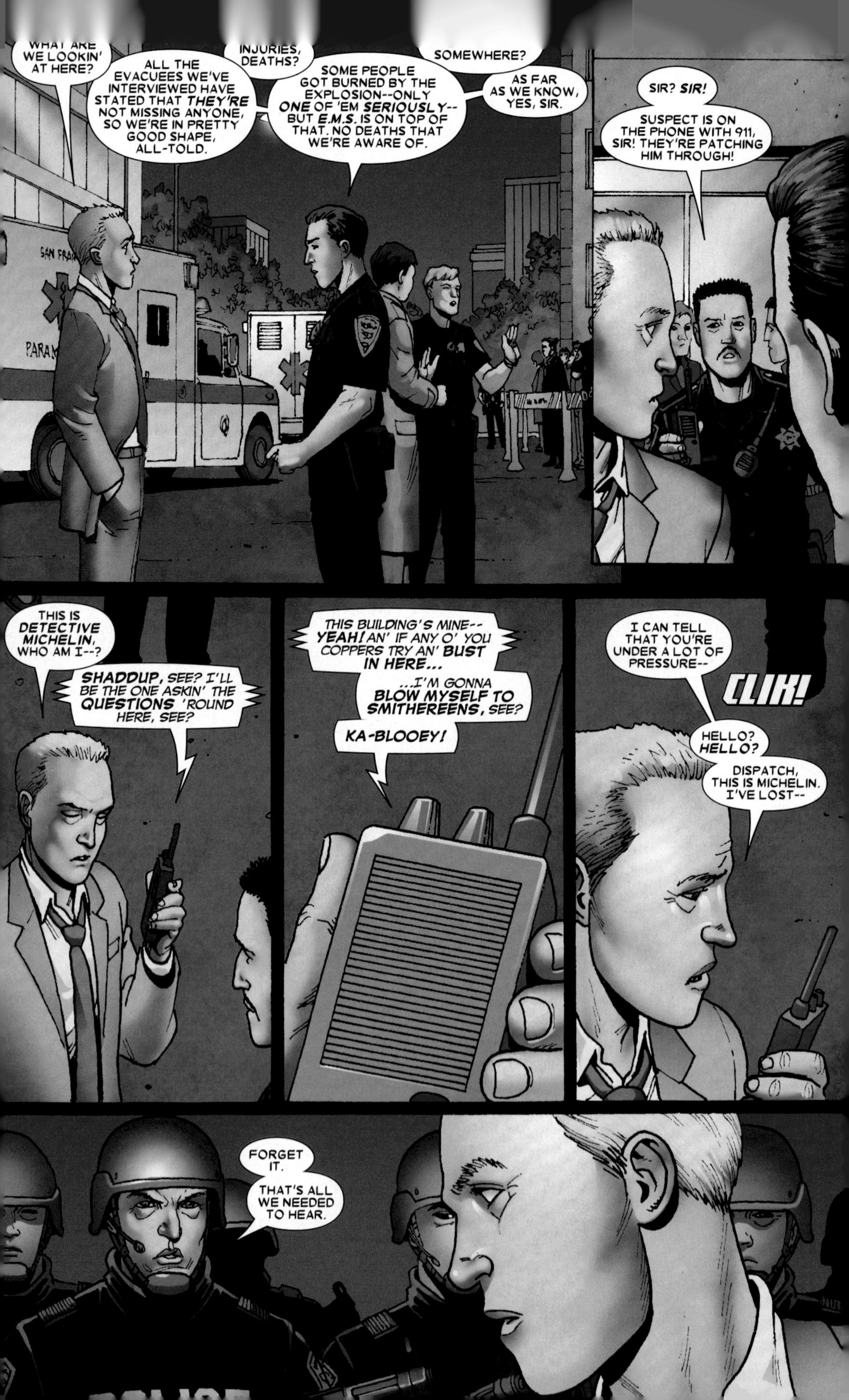
WHAT ARE WE LOOKIN' AT HERE?
ALL THE EVACUEES WE'VE INTERVIEWED HAVE STATED THAT THEY'RE NOT MISSING ANYONE, SO WE'RE IN PRETTY GOOD SHAPE, ALL-TOLD.
INJURIES, DEATHS?
SOME PEOPLE GOT BURNED BY THE EXPLOSION--ONLY ONE OF 'EM SERIOUSLY--BUT E.M.S. IS ON TOP OF THAT. NO DEATHS THAT WE'RE AWARE OF.
SOMEWHERE?
AS FAR AS WE KNOW, YES, SIR.
SIR? SIR!
SUSPECT IS ON THE PHONE WITH 911, SIR! THEY'RE PATCHING HIM THROUGH!
THIS IS DETECTIVE MICHELIN. WHO AM I--?
SHADDUP, SEE? I'LL BE THE ONE ASKIN' THE QUESTIONS 'ROUND HERE, SEE?
THIS BUILDING'S MINE--YEAH! AN' IF ANY O' YOU COPPERS TRY AN' BUST IN HERE...
...I'M GONNA BLOW MYSELF TO SMITHEREENS, SEE?
KA-BLOOEY!
I CAN TELL THAT YOU'RE UNDER A LOT OF PRESSURE--
CLIK!
HELLO? HELLO?
DISPATCH, THIS IS MICHELIN. I'VE LOST--
FORGET IT.
THAT'S ALL WE NEEDED TO HEAR.

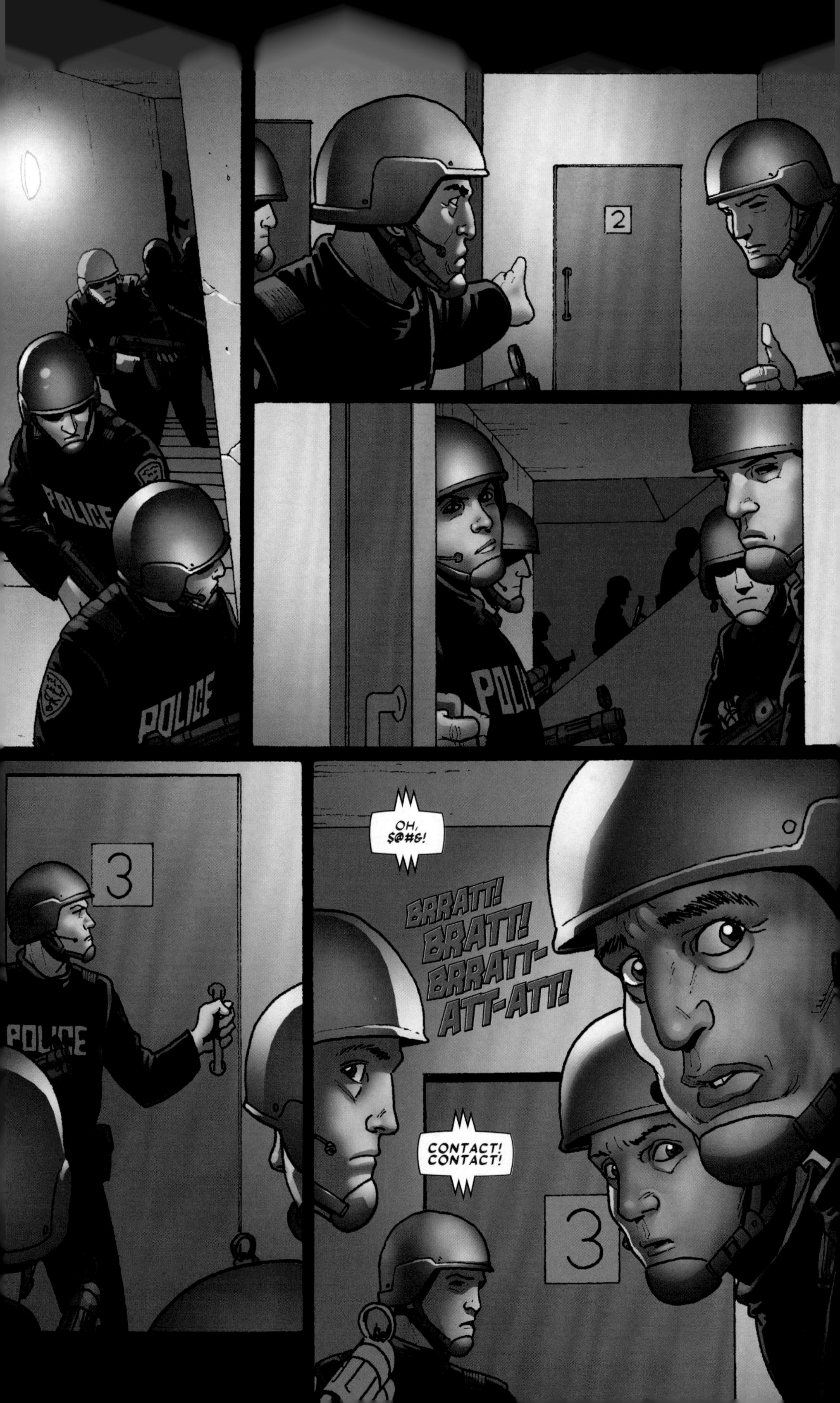
POLICE
POLICE
2
POLICE
3
POLICE
OH, $@#&!
BRRATT! BRATT! BRRATT-ATT-ATT!
CONTACT! CONTACT!
3

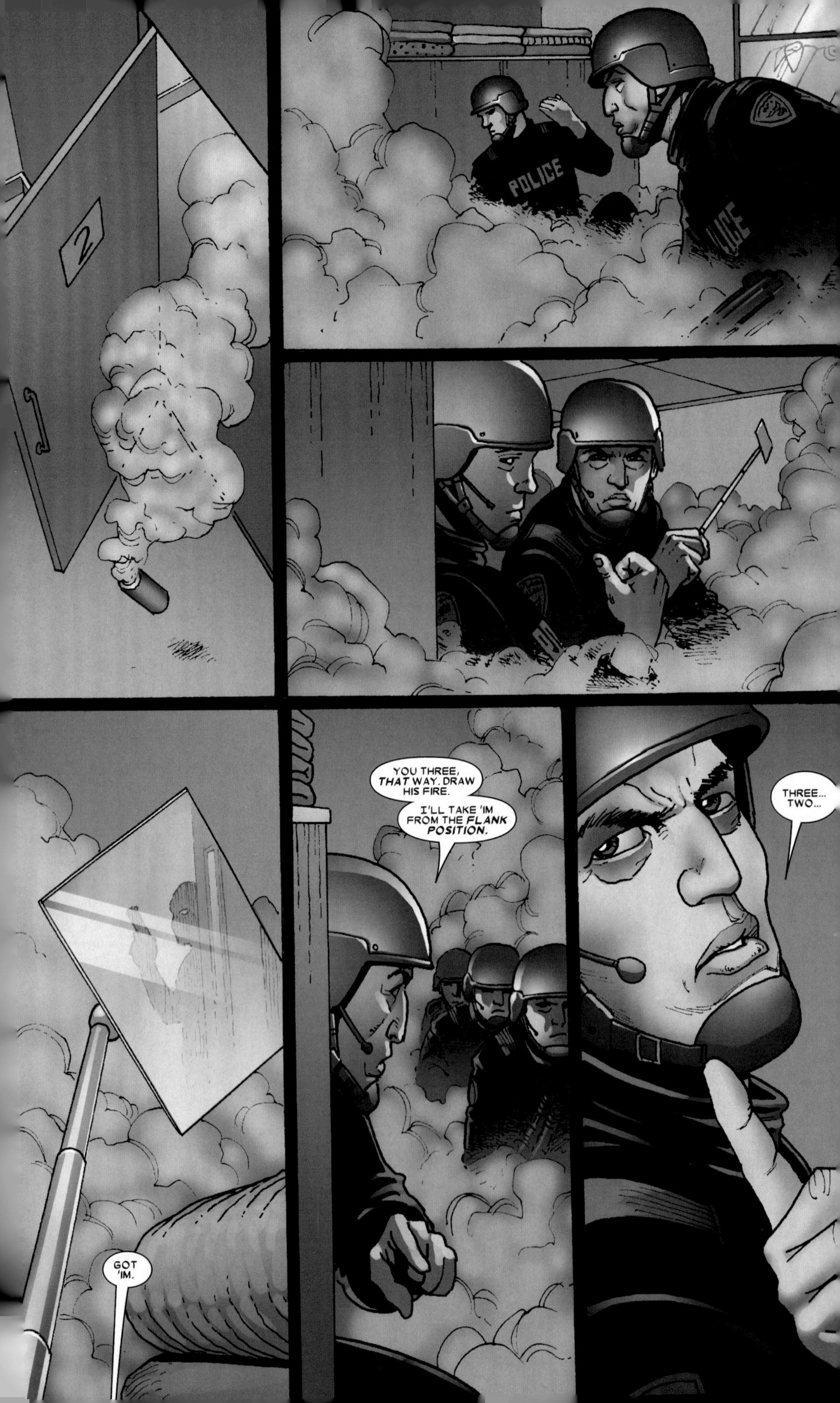
YOU THREE, THAT WAY. DRAW HIS FIRE.
I'LL TAKE 'IM FROM THE FLANK POSITION.
THREE... TWO...
GOT 'IM.

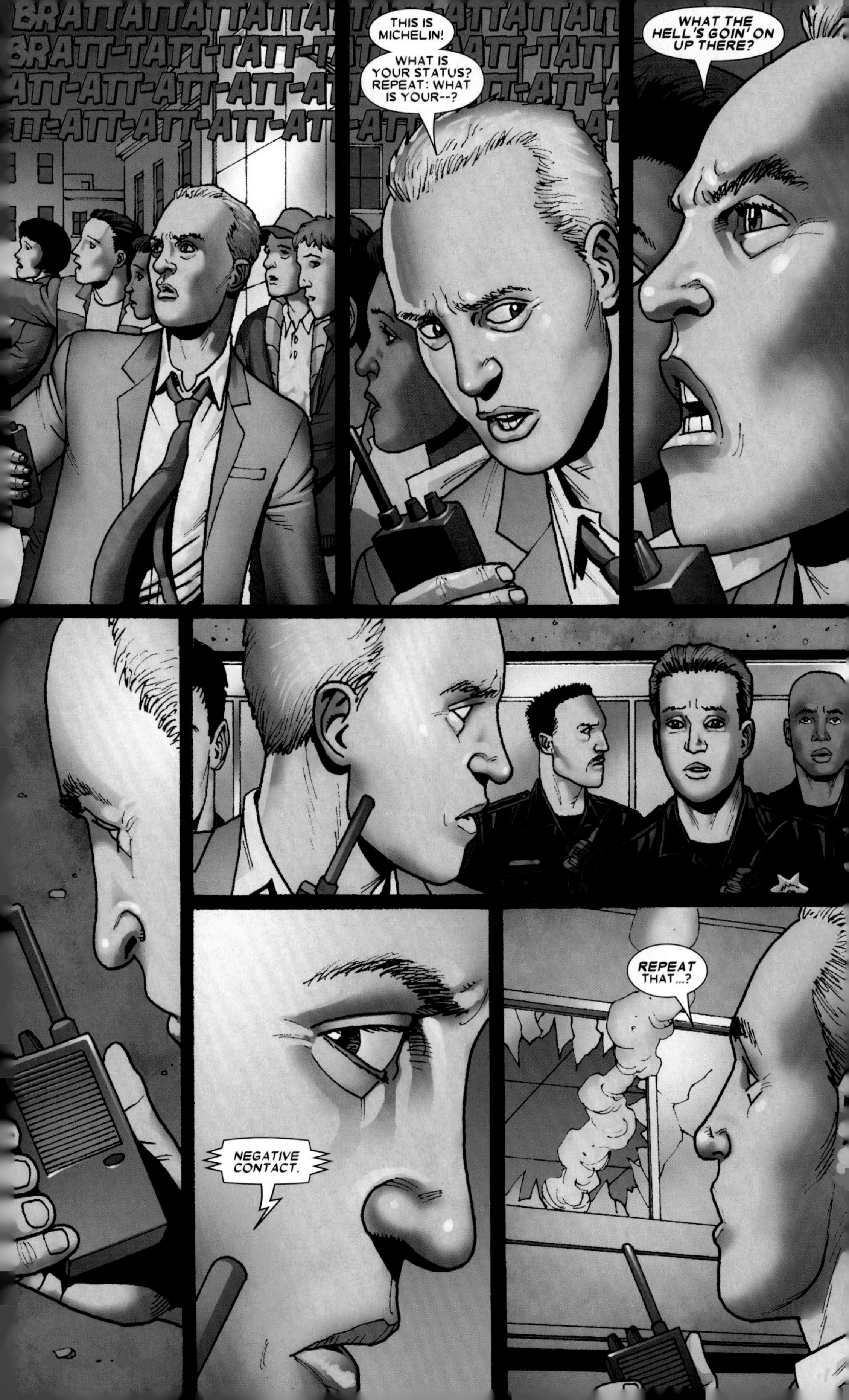
BRATTATTATTATTATTATTATTATT
BRATT-TATT-TATT-TATT-TATT-TATT
ATT-ATT-ATT-ATT-ATT-ATT-ATT-ATT
ATT-ATT-ATT-ATT-ATT-ATT
THIS IS MICHELIN!
WHAT IS YOUR STATUS? REPEAT: WHAT IS YOUR--?
WHAT THE HELL'S GOIN' ON UP THERE?
NEGATIVE CONTACT.
REPEAT THAT...?

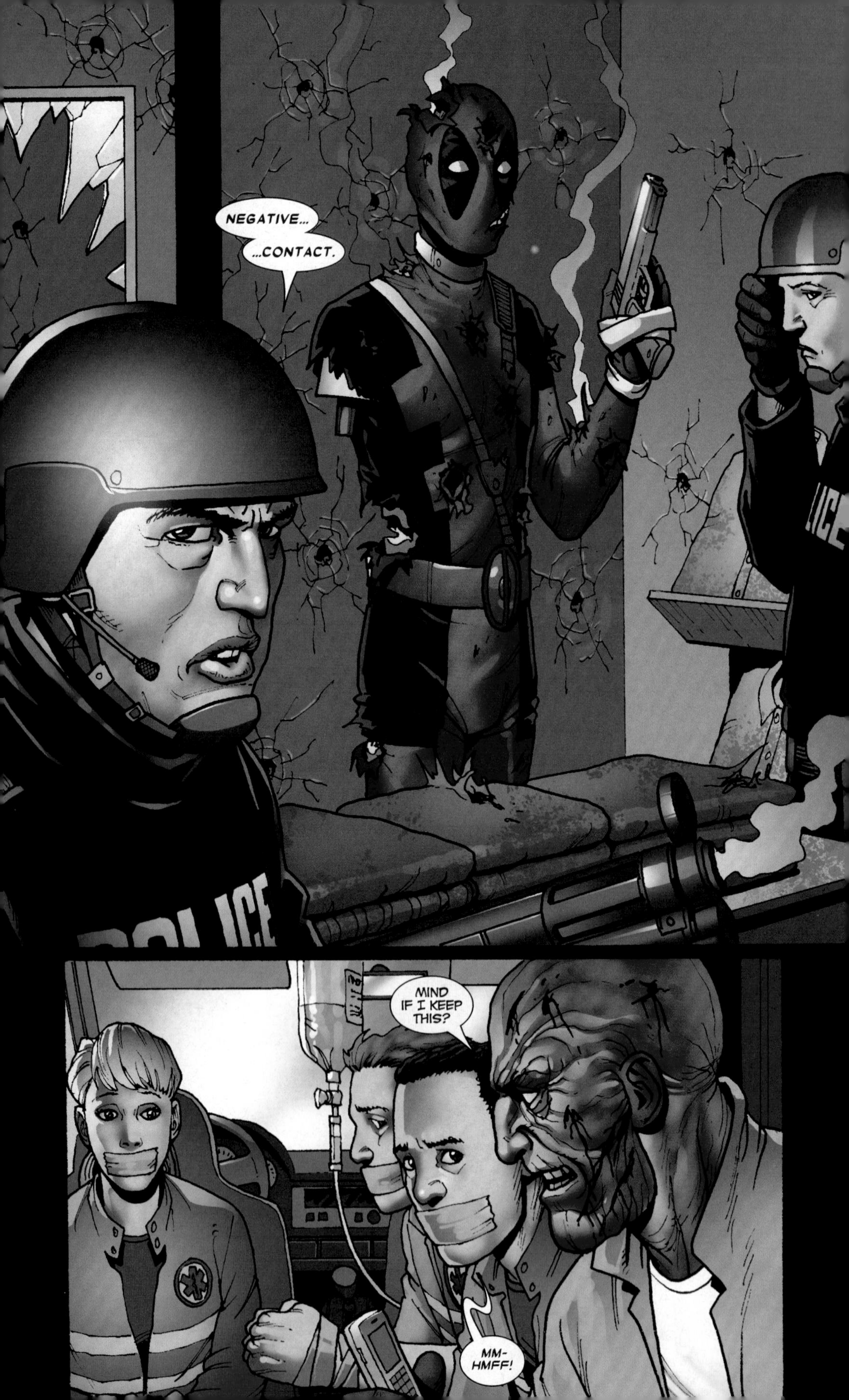
NEGATIVE...
...CONTACT.
MIND IF I KEEP THIS?
MM-HMFF!

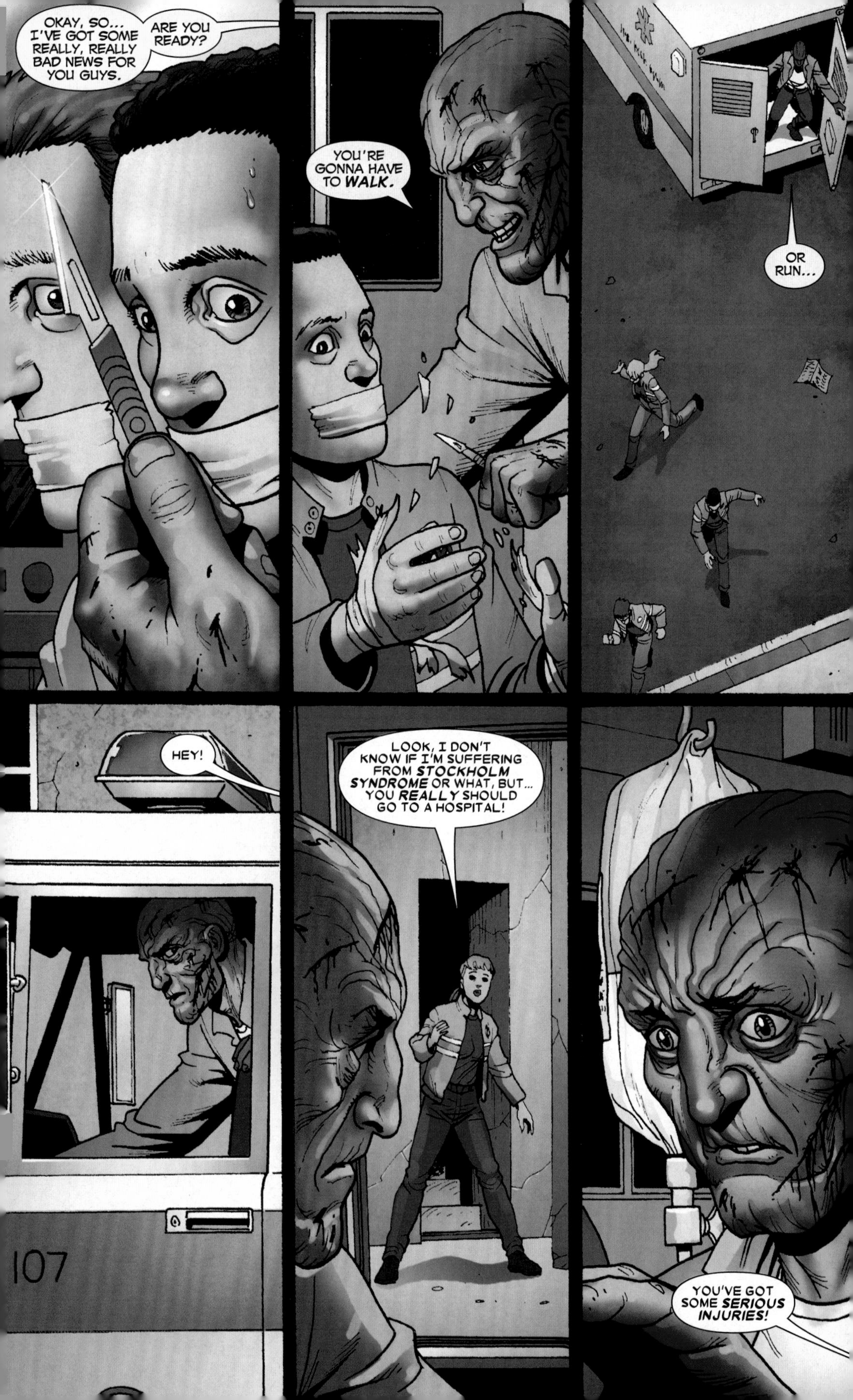
OKAY, SO... I'VE GOT SOME REALLY, REALLY BAD NEWS FOR YOU GUYS.
ARE YOU READY?
YOU'RE GONNA HAVE TO WALK.
OR RUN...
HEY!
107
LOOK, I DON'T KNOW IF I'M SUFFERING FROM STOCKHOLM SYNDROME OR WHAT, BUT... YOU REALLY SHOULD GO TO A HOSPITAL!
YOU'VE GOT SOME SERIOUS INJURIES!

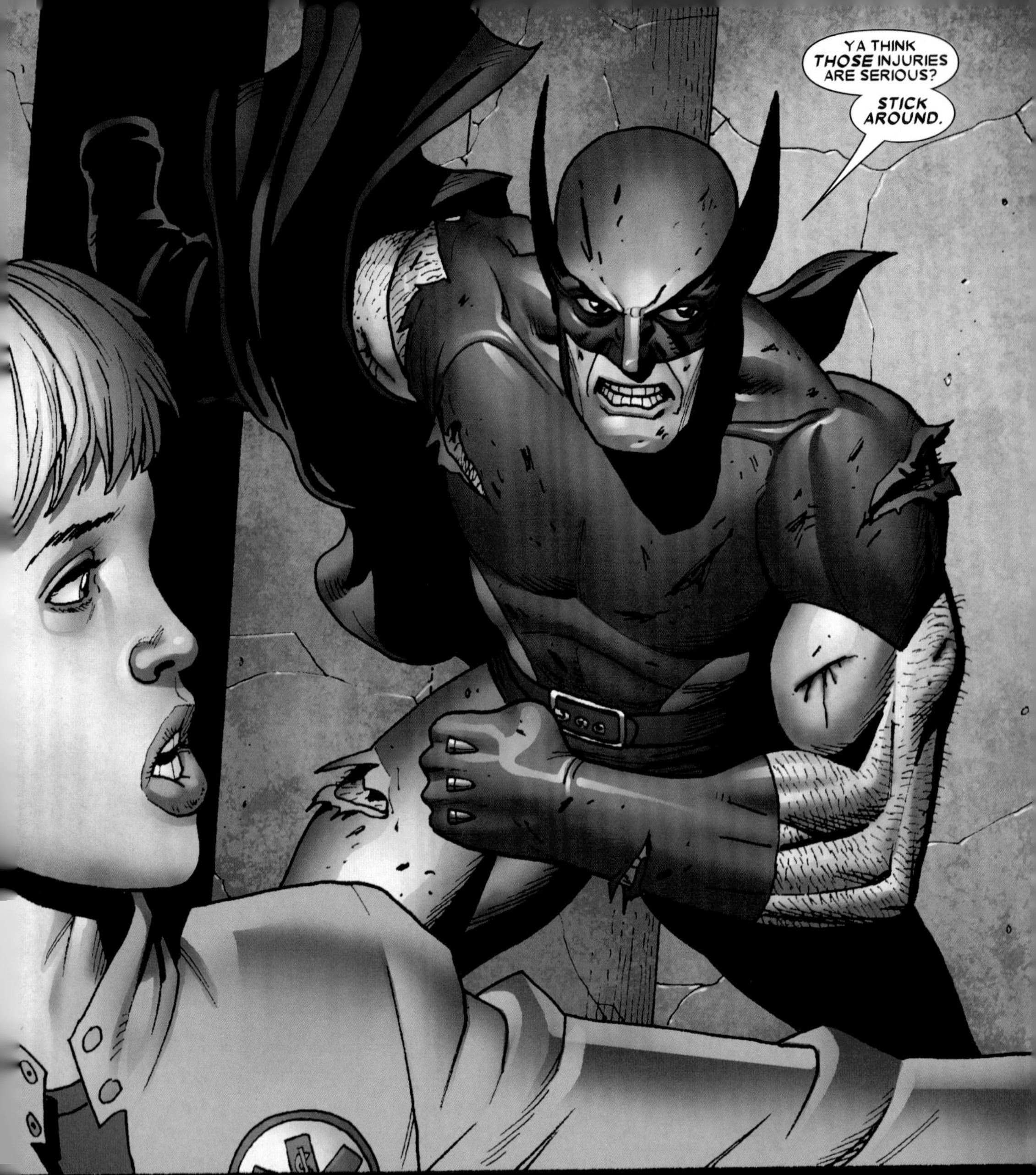
YA THINK THOSE INJURIES ARE SERIOUS?
STICK AROUND.

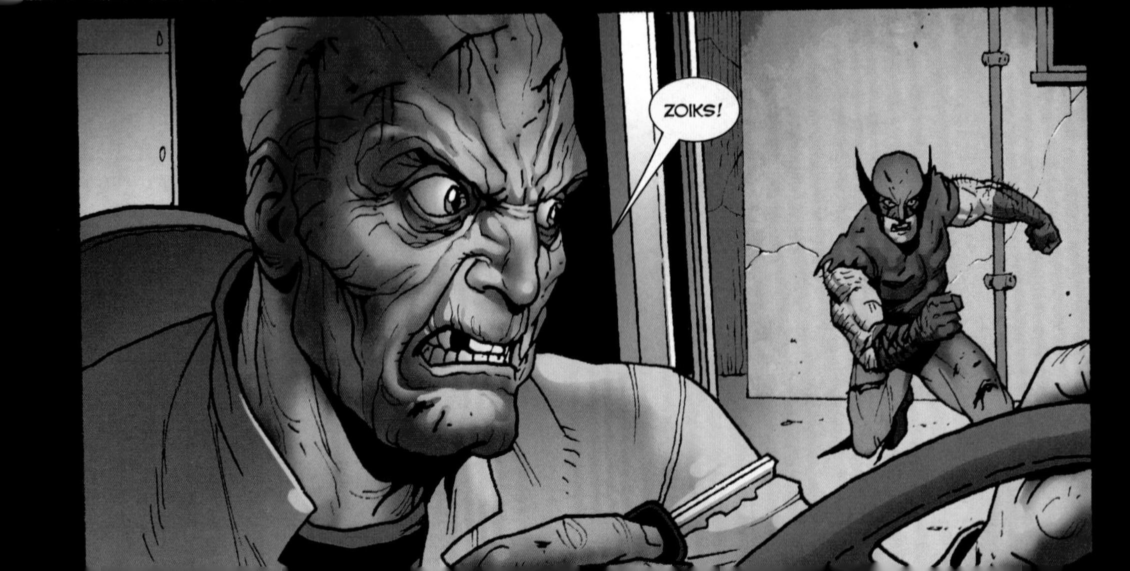
ZOIKS!

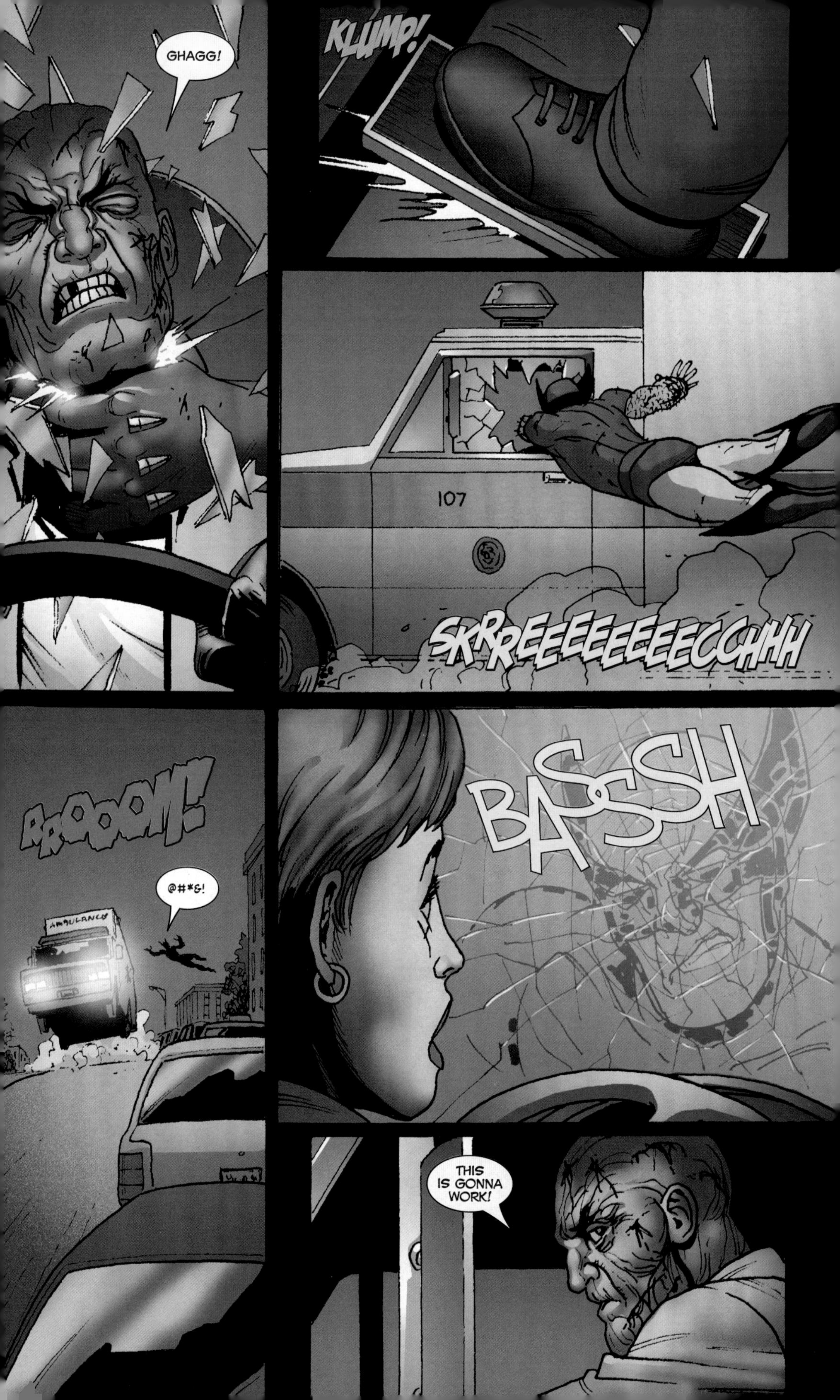
GHAGG!
KLUMP!
107
SKRREEEEEEEEEECCHHH
RRROOOM!
@#*&!
BASSSH
THIS IS GONNA WORK!

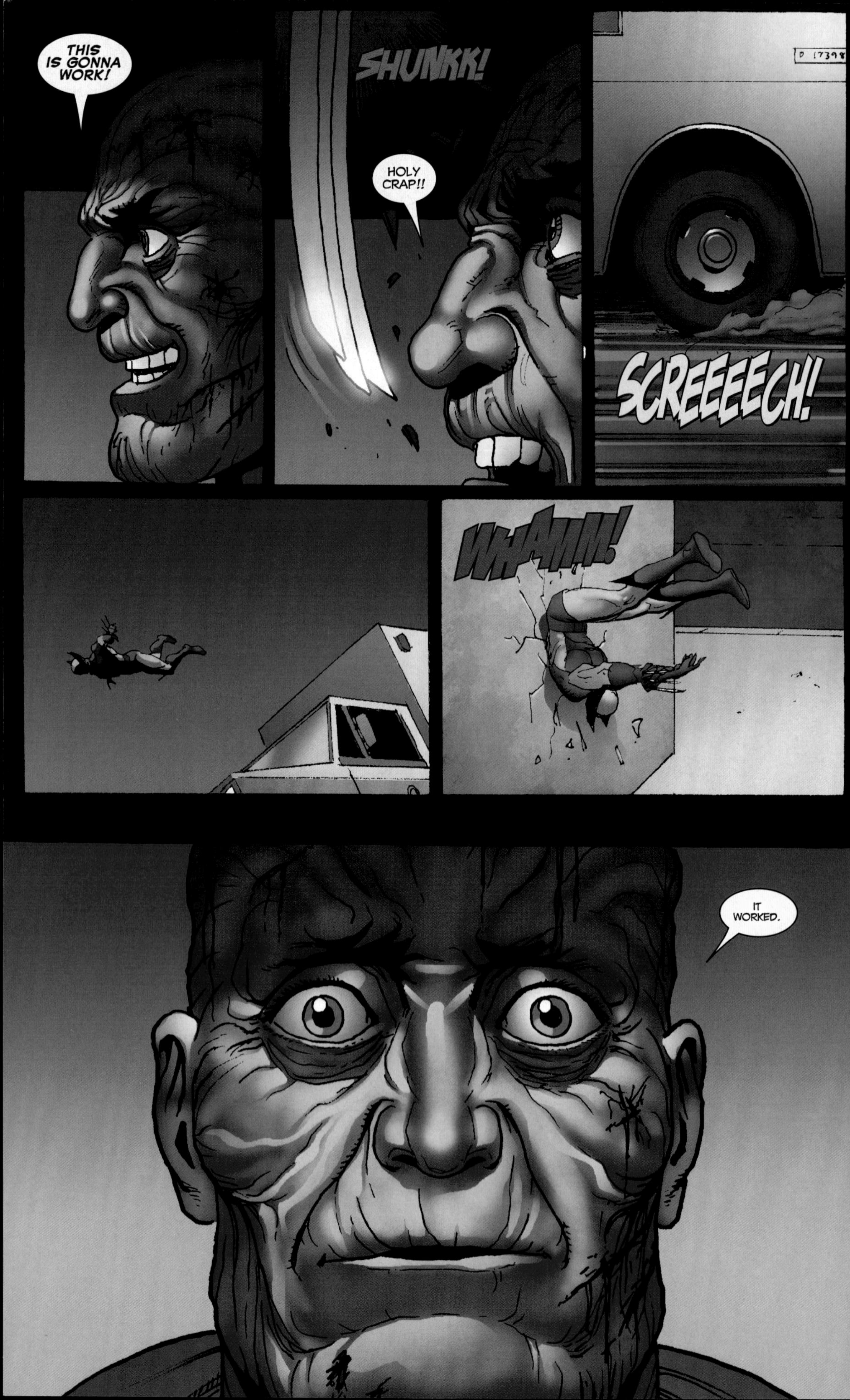
THIS IS GONNA WORK!
SHUNKK!
HOLY CRAP!!
SCREEEECH!
WHAMM!
IT WORKED.

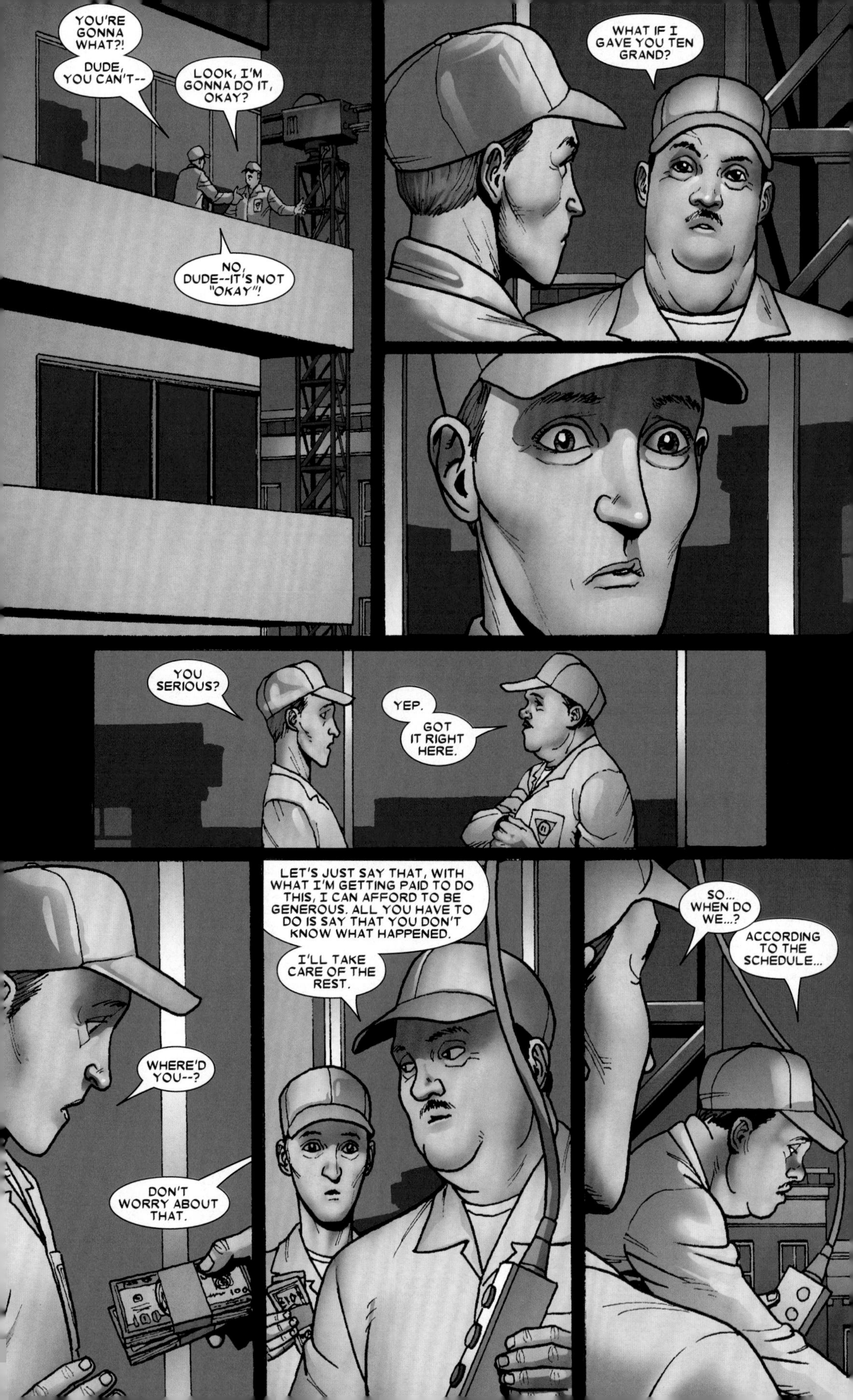
YOU'RE GONNA WHAT?!
DUDE, YOU CAN'T--
LOOK, I'M GONNA DO IT, OKAY?
NO, DUDE--IT'S NOT "OKAY"!
WHAT IF I GAVE YOU TEN GRAND?
YOU SERIOUS?
YEP.
GOT IT RIGHT HERE.
WHERE'D YOU--?
DON'T WORRY ABOUT THAT.
LET'S JUST SAY THAT, WITH WHAT I'M GETTING PAID TO DO THIS, I CAN AFFORD TO BE GENEROUS. ALL YOU HAVE TO DO IS SAY THAT YOU DON'T KNOW WHAT HAPPENED.
I'LL TAKE CARE OF THE REST.
SO... WHEN DO WE...?
ACCORDING TO THE SCHEDULE...

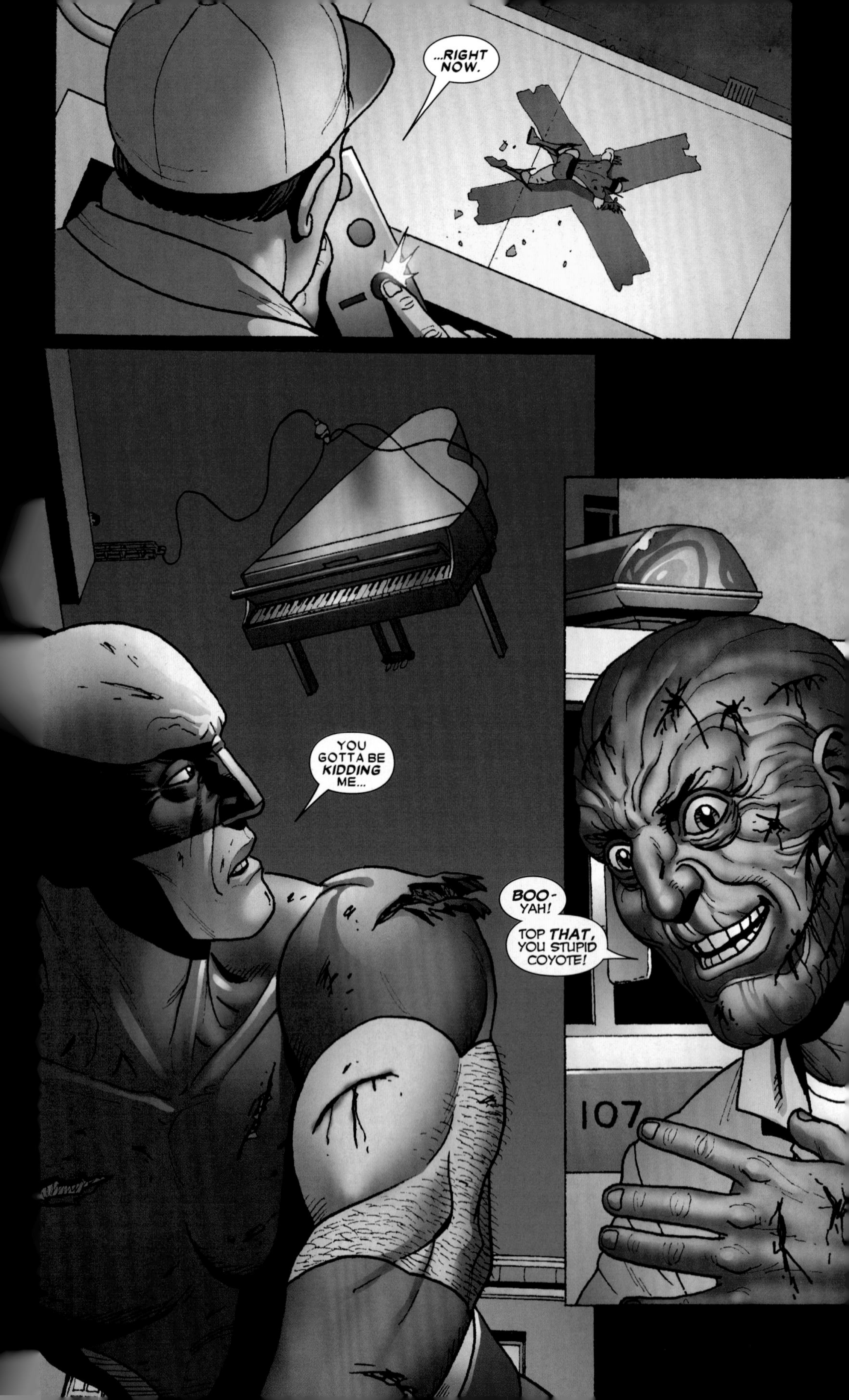
...RIGHT NOW.
YOU GOTTA BE KIDDING ME...
BOO-YAH!
TOP THAT, YOU STUPID COYOTE!
107

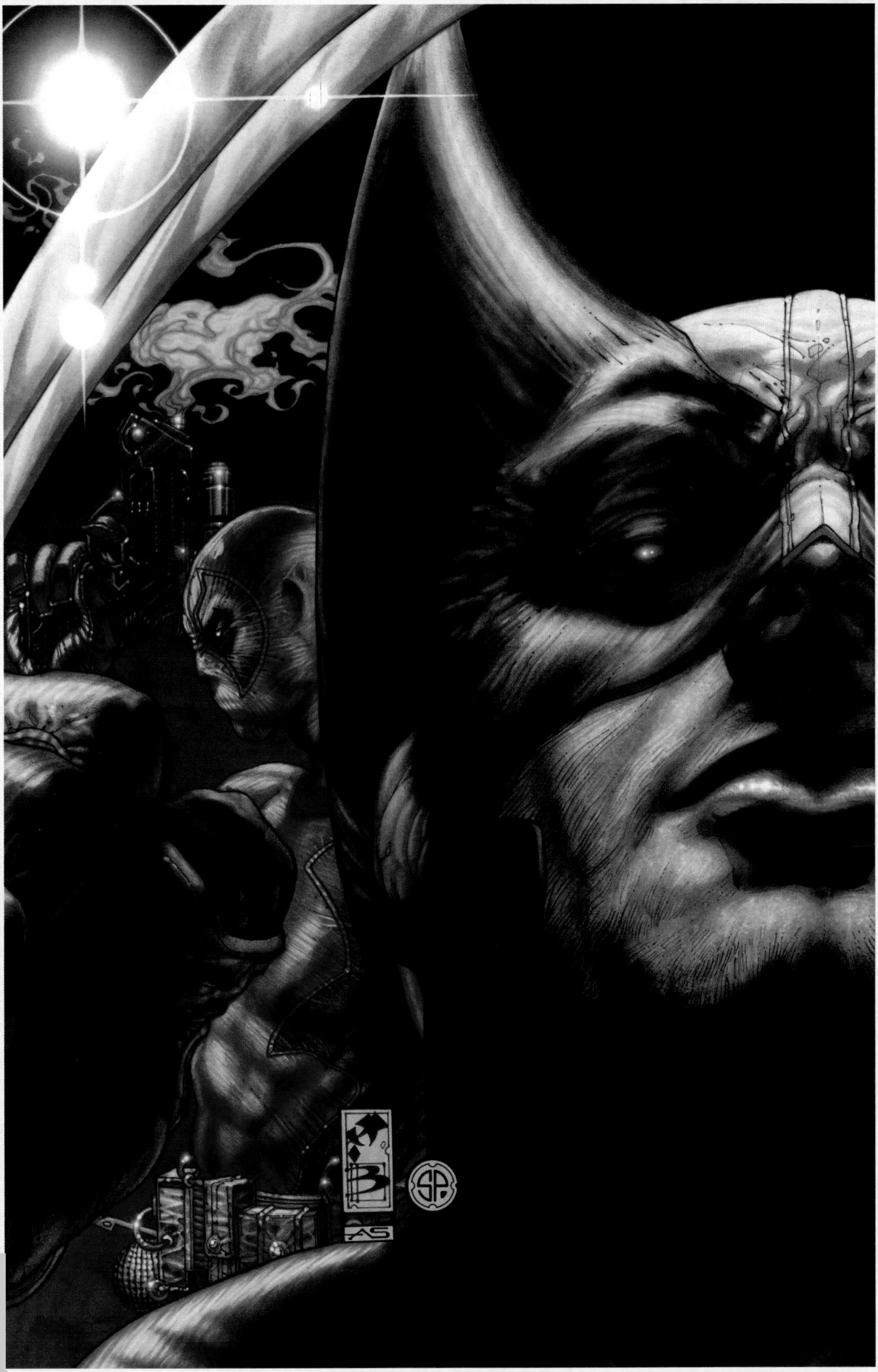

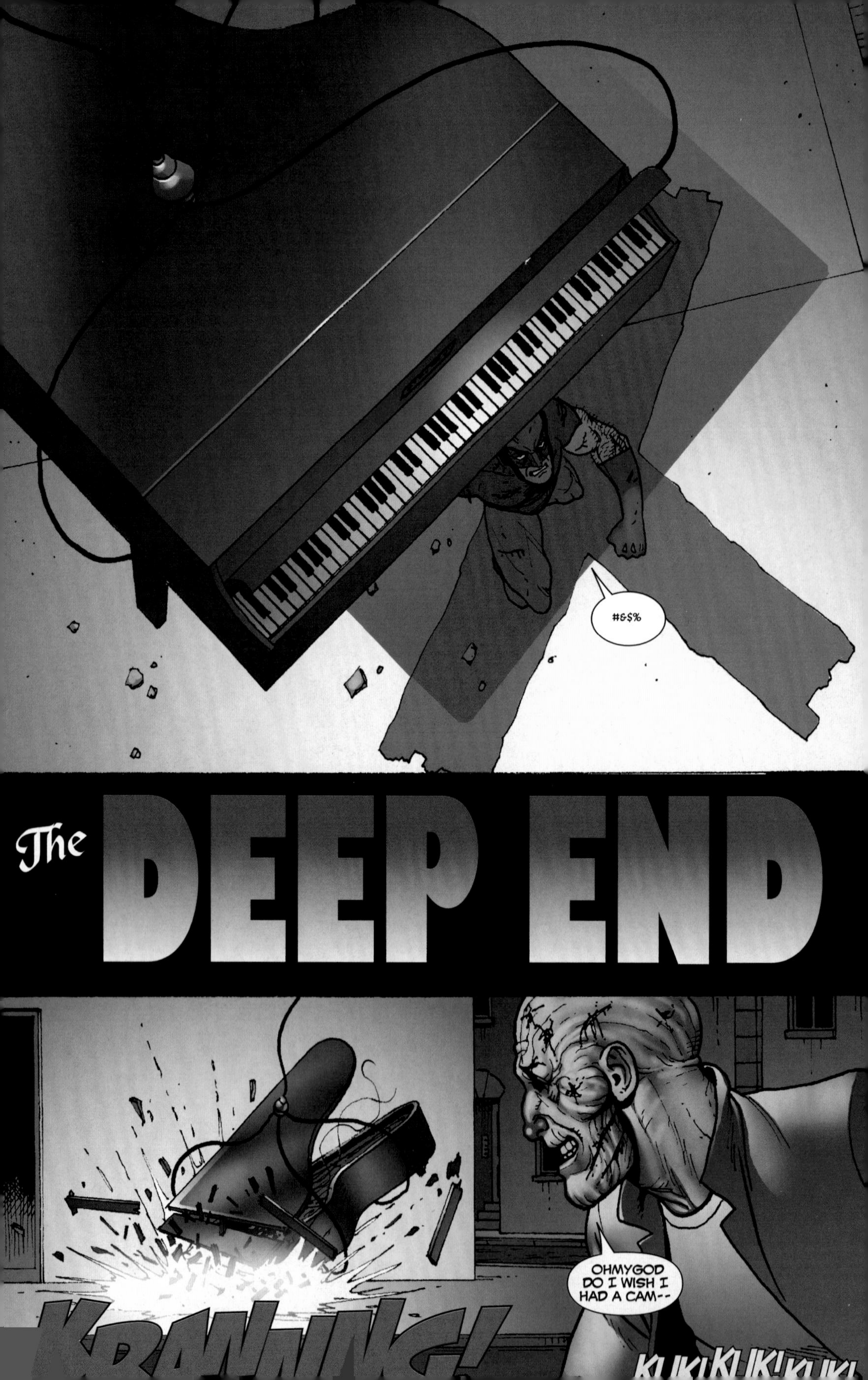
#&$%
The DEEP END
OHMYGOD DO I WISH I HAD A CAM--

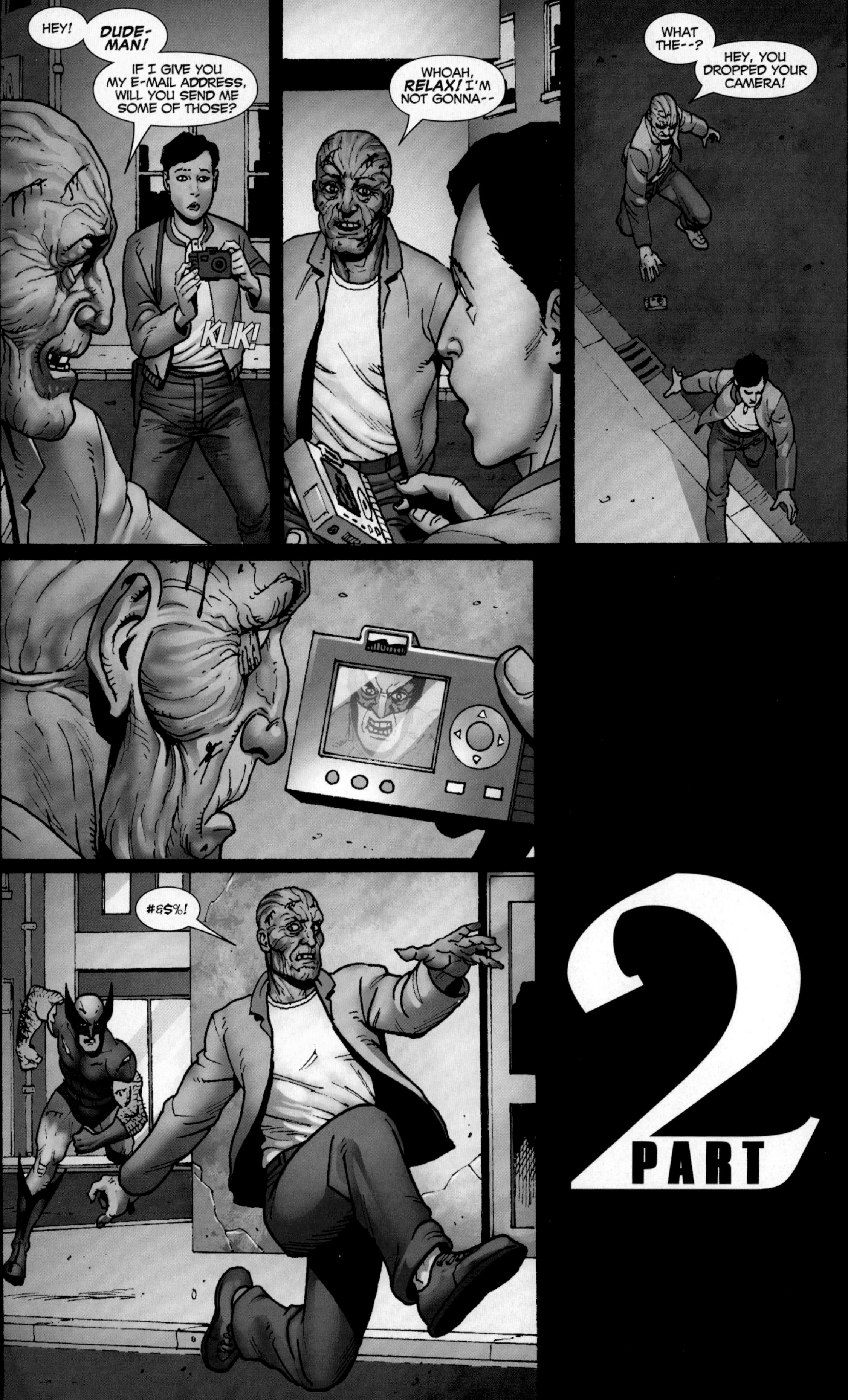
HEY!
DUDE-MAN!
IF I GIVE YOU MY E-MAIL ADDRESS, WILL YOU SEND ME SOME OF THOSE?
KLIK!
WHOAH, RELAX! I'M NOT GONNA--
WHAT THE--?
HEY, YOU DROPPED YOUR CAMERA!
#&$%!
2
PART

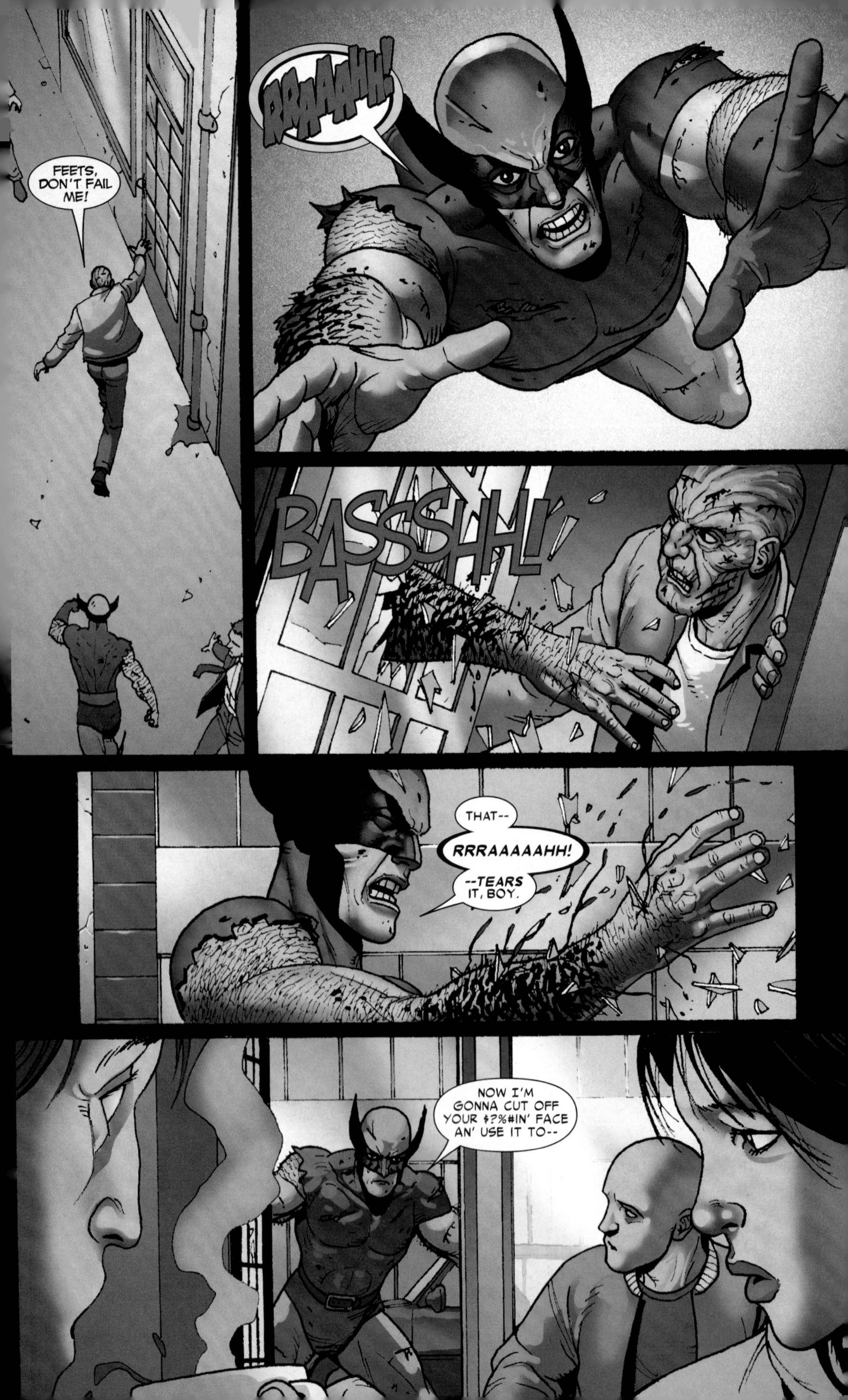
FEETS, DON'T FAIL ME!
RRAAAHH!
BASSSHHL!
THAT--
RRRAAAAAHH!
--TEARS IT, BOY.
NOW I'M GONNA CUT OFF YOUR $?%#IN' FACE AN' USE IT TO--

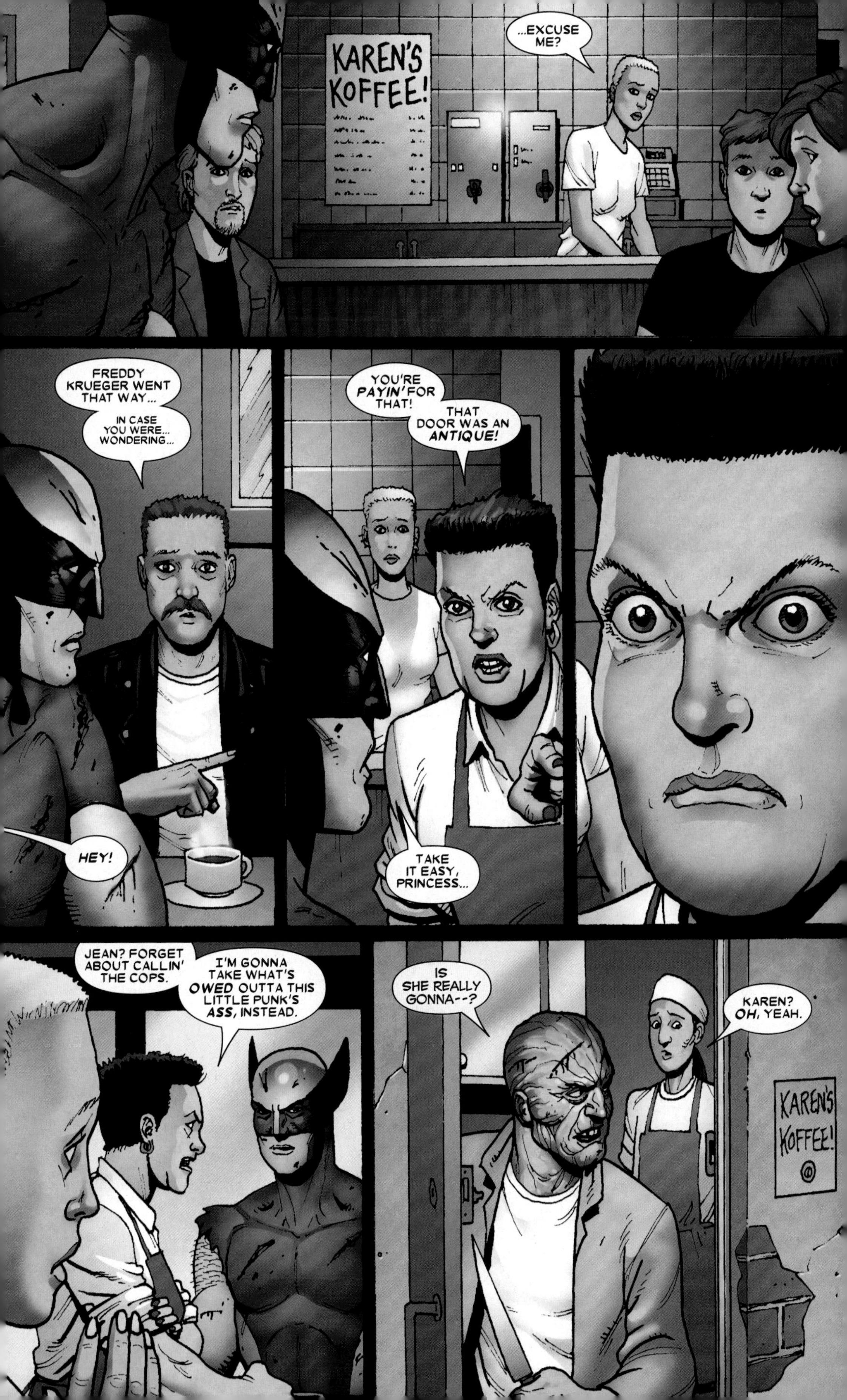
...EXCUSE ME?
KAREN'S KOFFEE!
FREDDY KRUEGER WENT THAT WAY...
IN CASE YOU WERE... WONDERING...
HEY!
YOU'RE PAYIN' FOR THAT!
THAT DOOR WAS AN ANTIQUE!
TAKE IT EASY, PRINCESS...
JEAN? FORGET ABOUT CALLIN' THE COPS.
I'M GONNA TAKE WHAT'S OWED OUTTA THIS LITTLE PUNK'S ASS, INSTEAD.
IS SHE REALLY GONNA--?
KAREN? OH, YEAH.
KAREN'S KOFFEE!

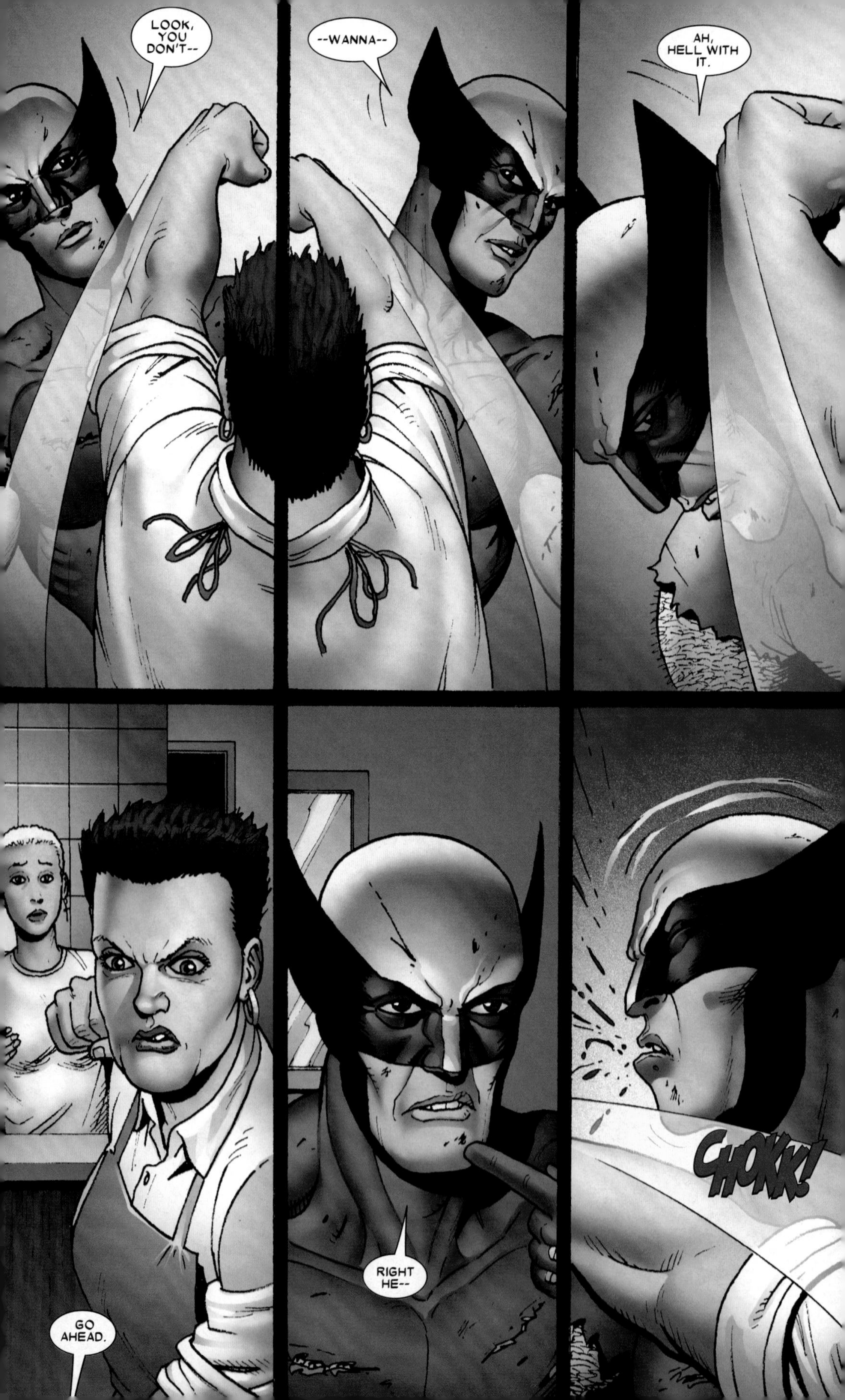
LOOK, YOU DON'T--
--WANNA--
AH, HELL WITH IT.
GO AHEAD.
RIGHT HE--
CHOKK!

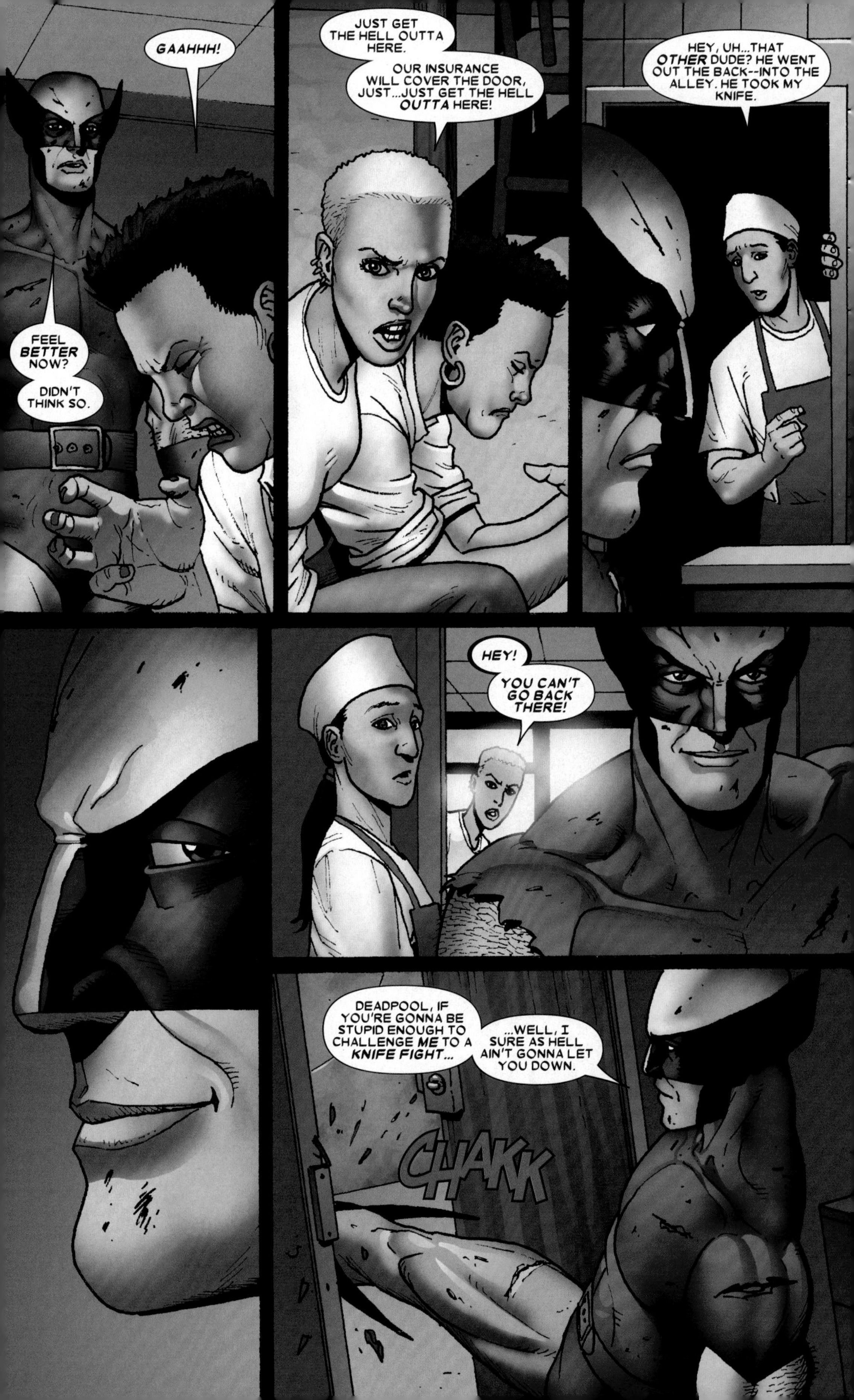
GAAHHH!
FEEL BETTER NOW?
DIDN'T THINK SO.
JUST GET THE HELL OUTTA HERE.
OUR INSURANCE WILL COVER THE DOOR, JUST...JUST GET THE HELL OUTTA HERE!
HEY, UH...THAT OTHER DUDE? HE WENT OUT THE BACK--INTO THE ALLEY. HE TOOK MY KNIFE.
HEY!
YOU CAN'T GO BACK THERE!
DEADPOOL, IF YOU'RE GONNA BE STUPID ENOUGH TO CHALLENGE ME TO A KNIFE FIGHT...
...WELL, I SURE AS HELL AIN'T GONNA LET YOU DOWN.
CHAKK

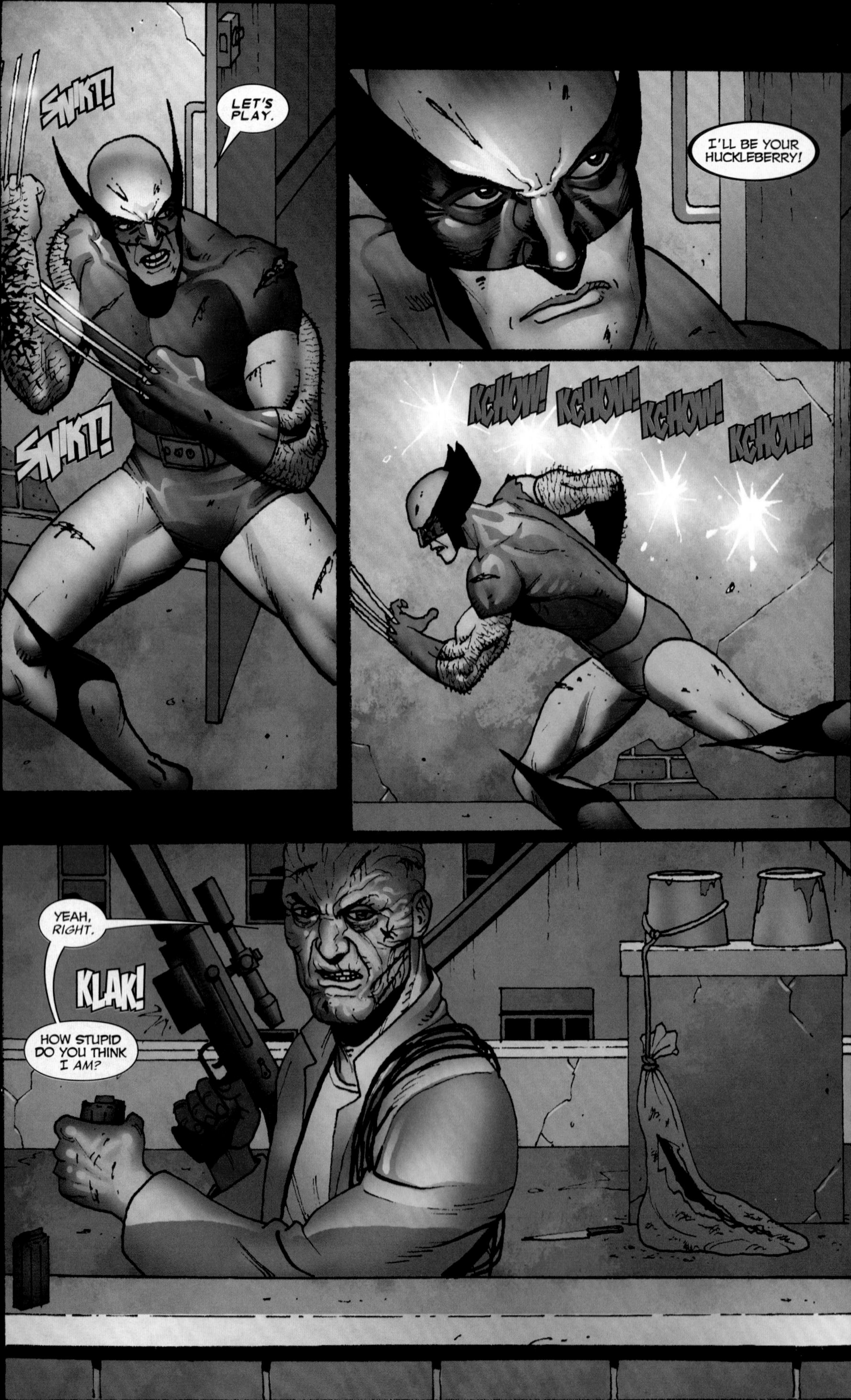
SNIKT!
LET'S PLAY.
SNIKT!
I'LL BE YOUR HUCKLEBERRY!
KCHOW! KCHOW! KCHOW! KCHOW!
YEAH, RIGHT.
KLAK!
HOW STUPID DO YOU THINK I AM?

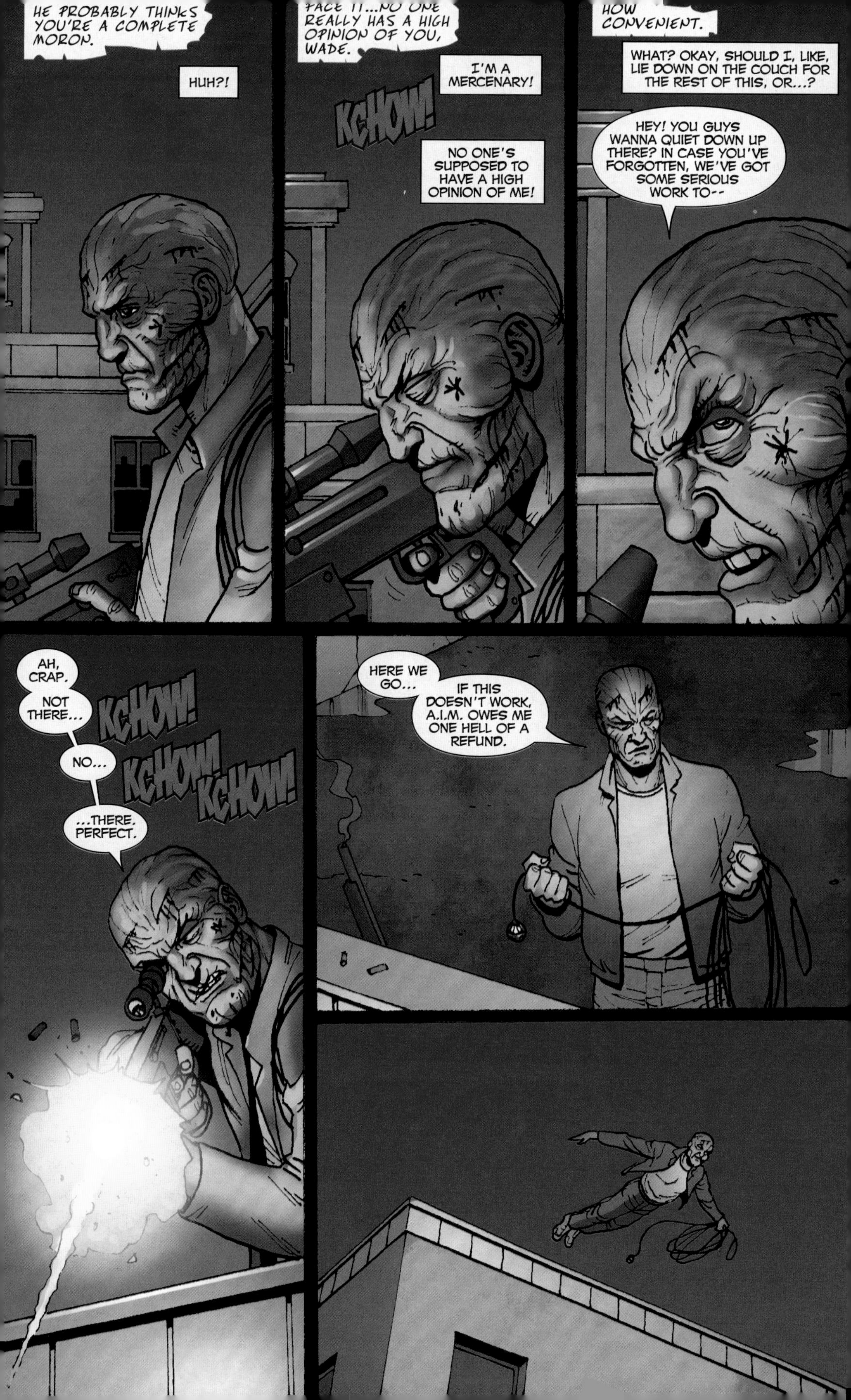
HE PROBABLY THINKS YOU'RE A COMPLETE MORON.
HUH?!
FACE IT...NO ONE REALLY HAS A HIGH OPINION OF YOU, WADE.
I'M A MERCENARY!
KCHOW!
NO ONE'S SUPPOSED TO HAVE A HIGH OPINION OF ME!
HOW CONVENIENT.
WHAT? OKAY, SHOULD I, LIKE, LIE DOWN ON THE COUCH FOR THE REST OF THIS, OR...?
HEY! YOU GUYS WANNA QUIET DOWN UP THERE? IN CASE YOU'VE FORGOTTEN, WE'VE GOT SOME SERIOUS WORK TO--
AH, CRAP.
NOT THERE...
KCHOW!
NO...
KCHOW! KCHOW!
...THERE. PERFECT.
HERE WE GO...
IF THIS DOESN'T WORK, A.I.M. OWES ME ONE HELL OF A REFUND.

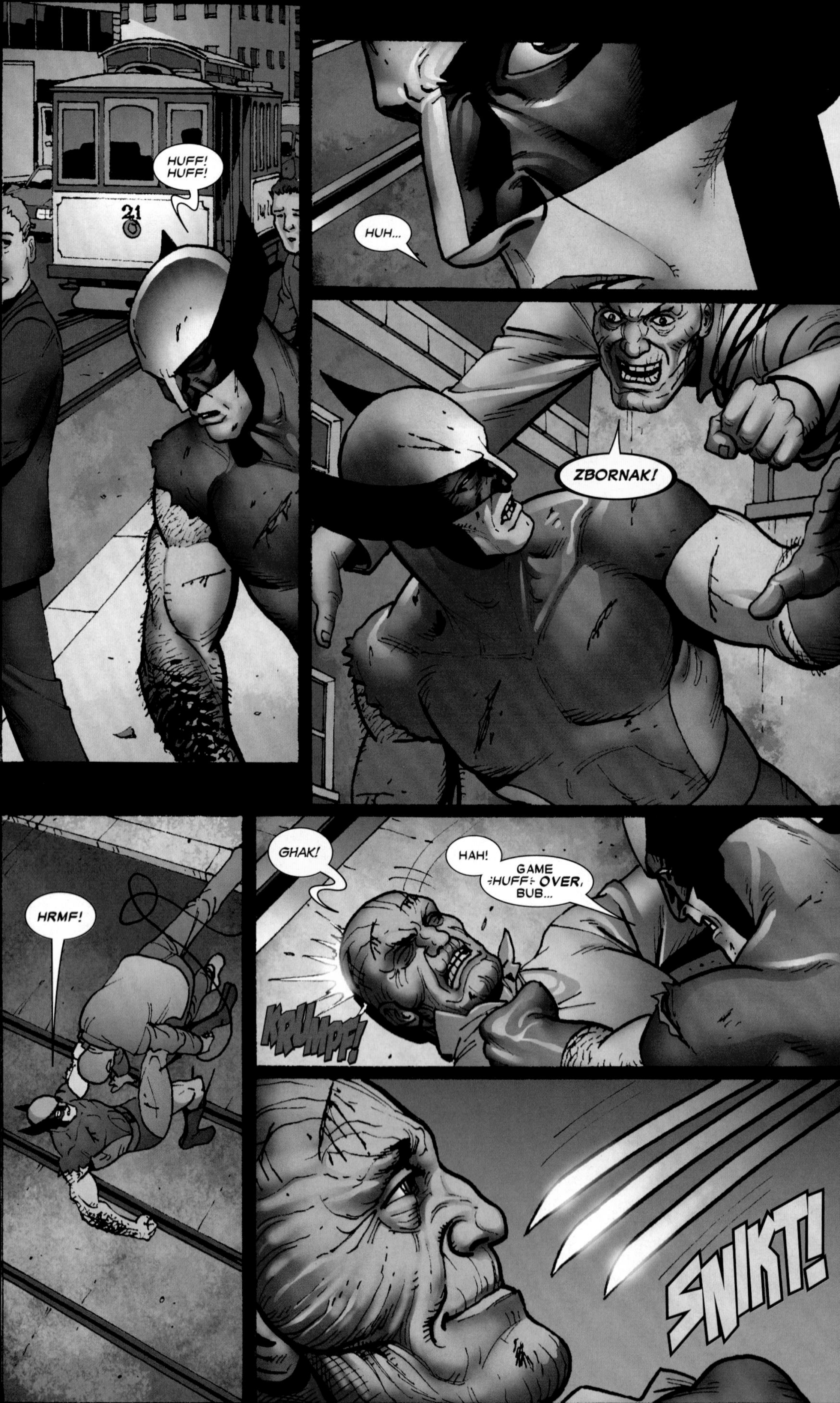
HUFF! HUFF!
HUH...
ZBORNAK!
HRMF!
GHAK!
KRUMPF!
HAH!
GAME -HUFF- OVER, BUB...
SNIKT!

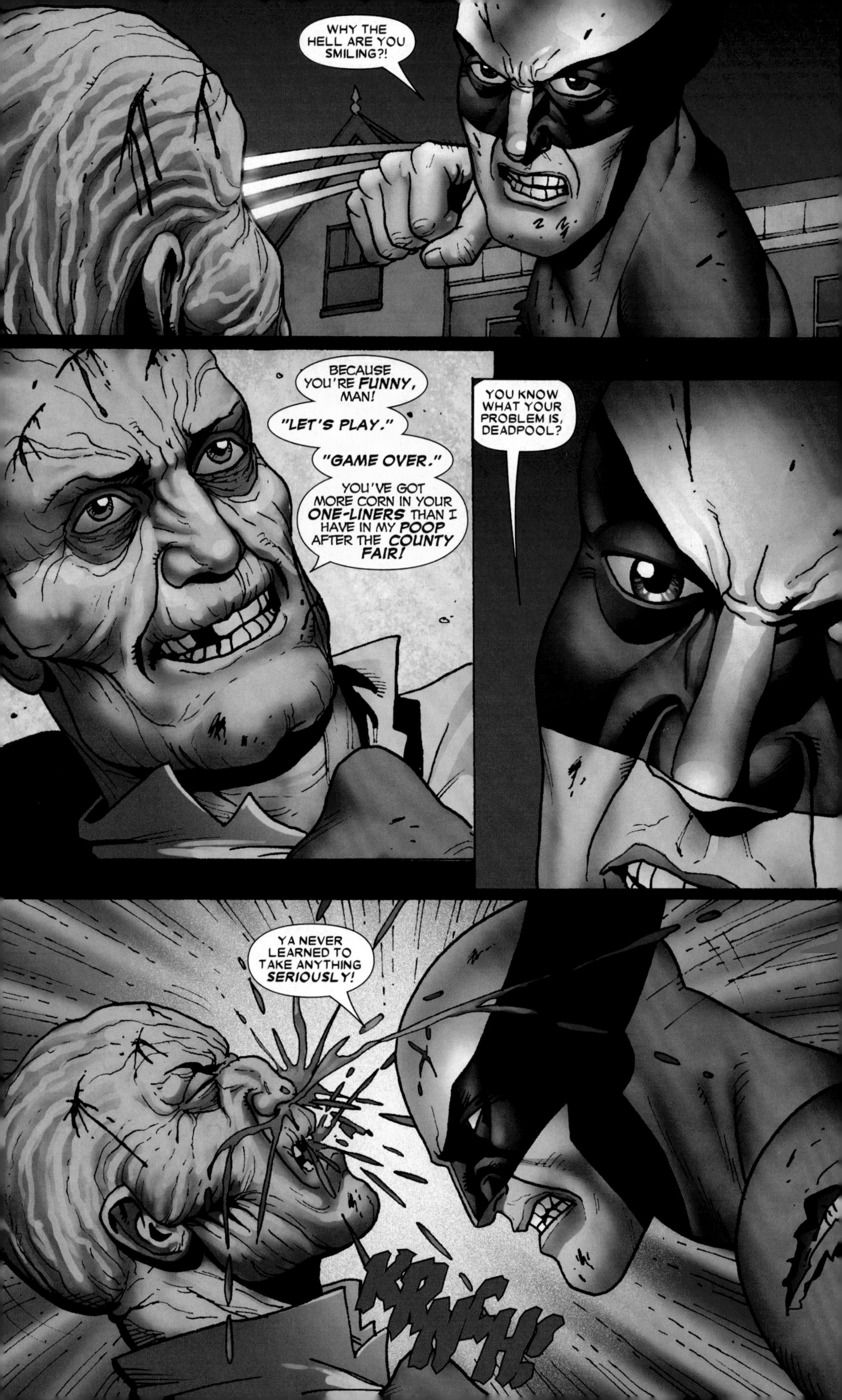
WHY THE HELL ARE YOU SMILING?!
BECAUSE YOU'RE FUNNY, MAN!
"LET'S PLAY."
"GAME OVER."
YOU'VE GOT MORE CORN IN YOUR ONE-LINERS THAN I HAVE IN MY POOP AFTER THE COUNTY FAIR!
YOU KNOW WHAT YOUR PROBLEM IS, DEADPOOL?
YA NEVER LEARNED TO TAKE ANYTHING SERIOUSLY!
KRNCH!

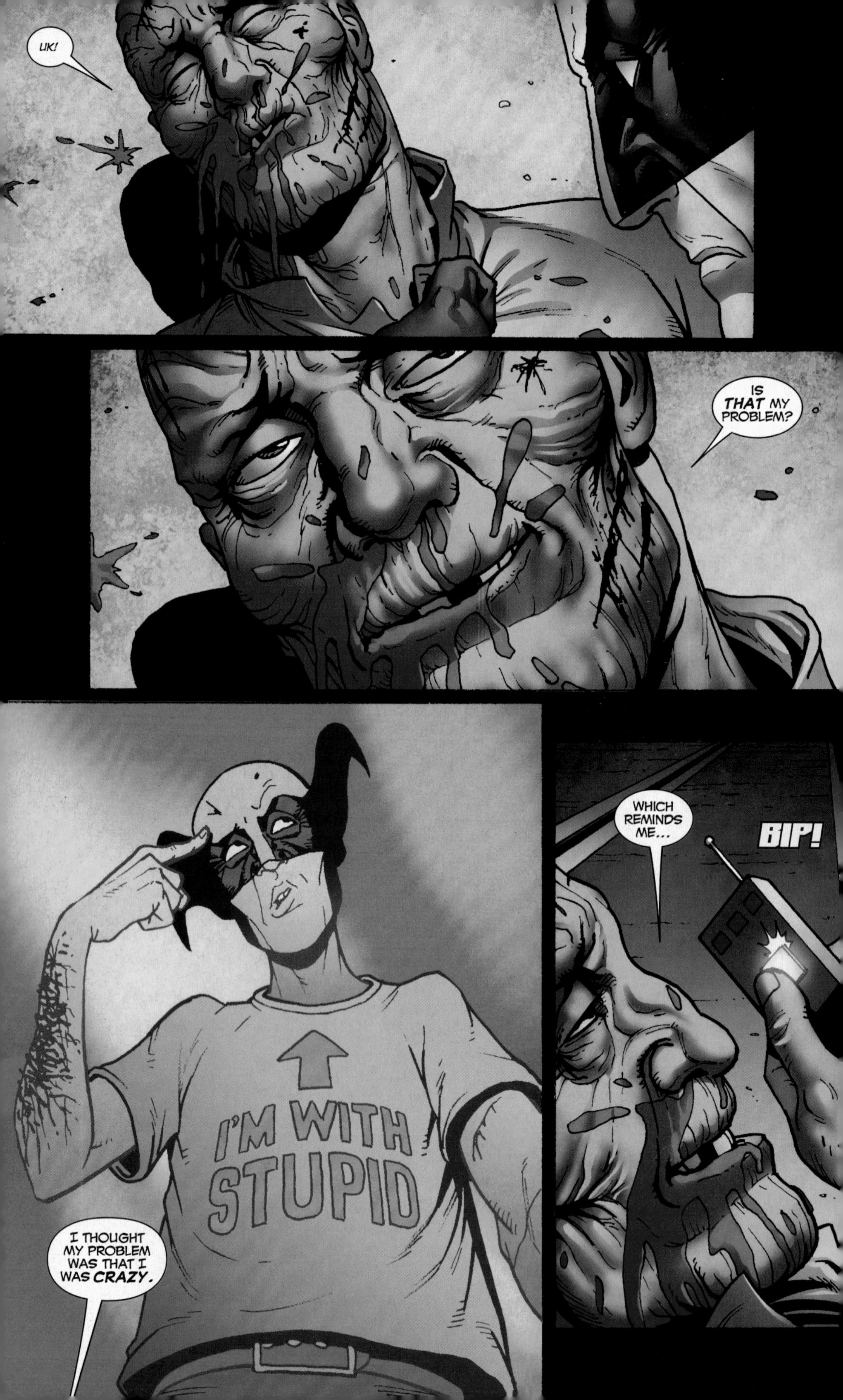
UK!
IS THAT MY PROBLEM?
I'M WITH STUPID
I THOUGHT MY PROBLEM WAS THAT I WAS CRAZY.
WHICH REMINDS ME...
BIP!

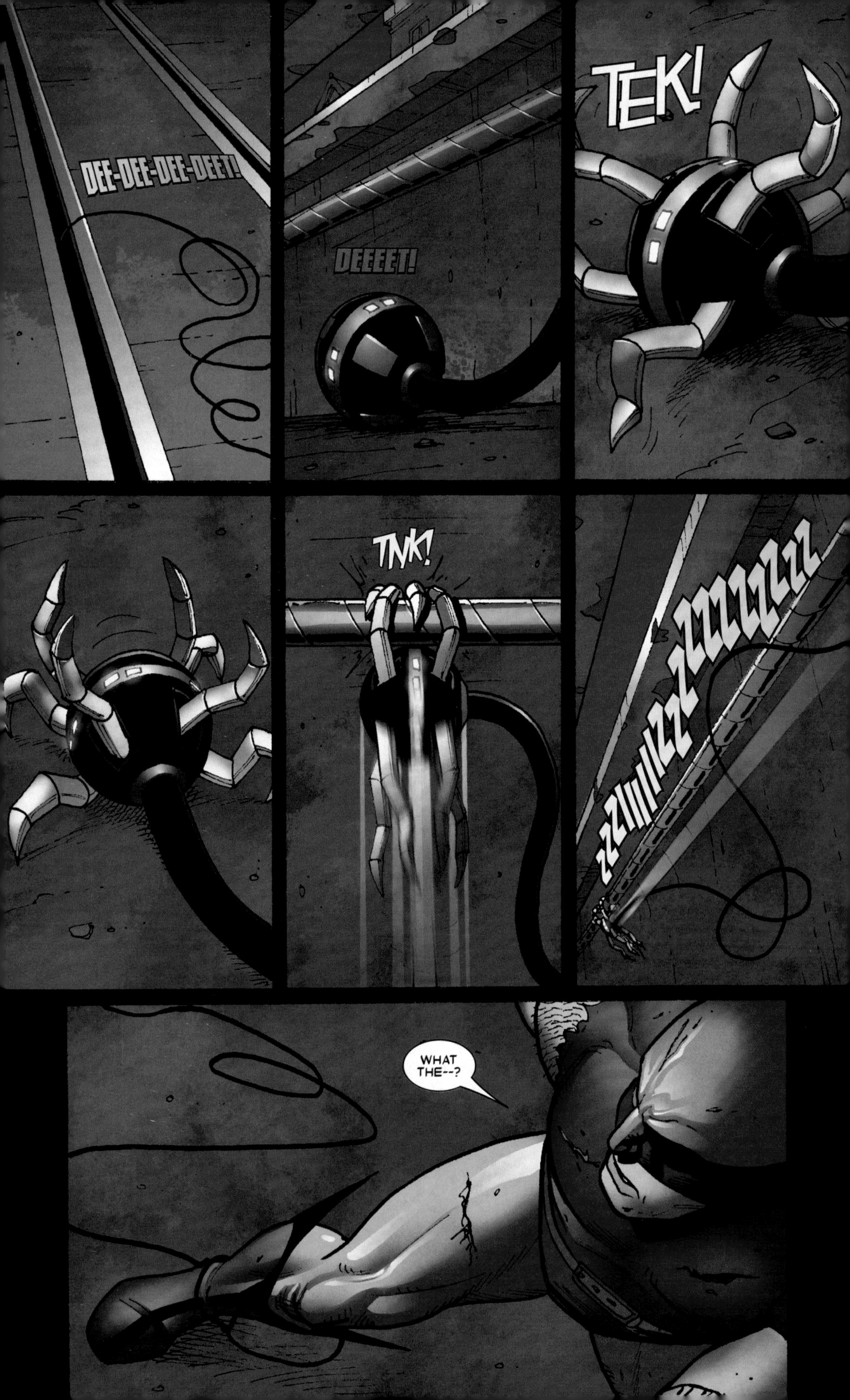
DEE-DEE-DEE-DEET!
DEEEET!
TEK!
TNK!
WHAT THE--?

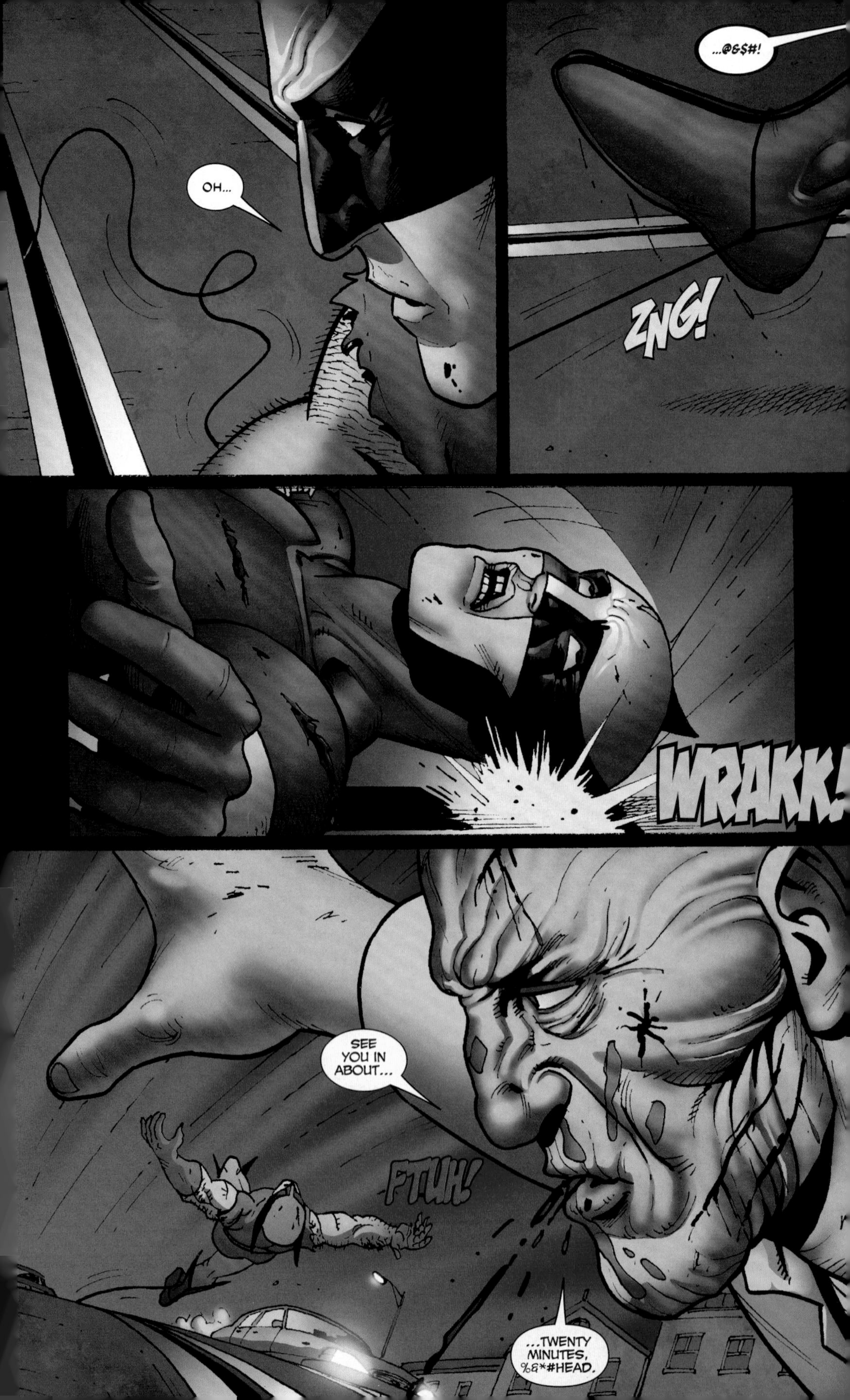
OH...
...@&$#!
ZNG!
WRAKK!
SEE YOU IN ABOUT...
FTUH!
...TWENTY MINUTES, %&*#HEAD.

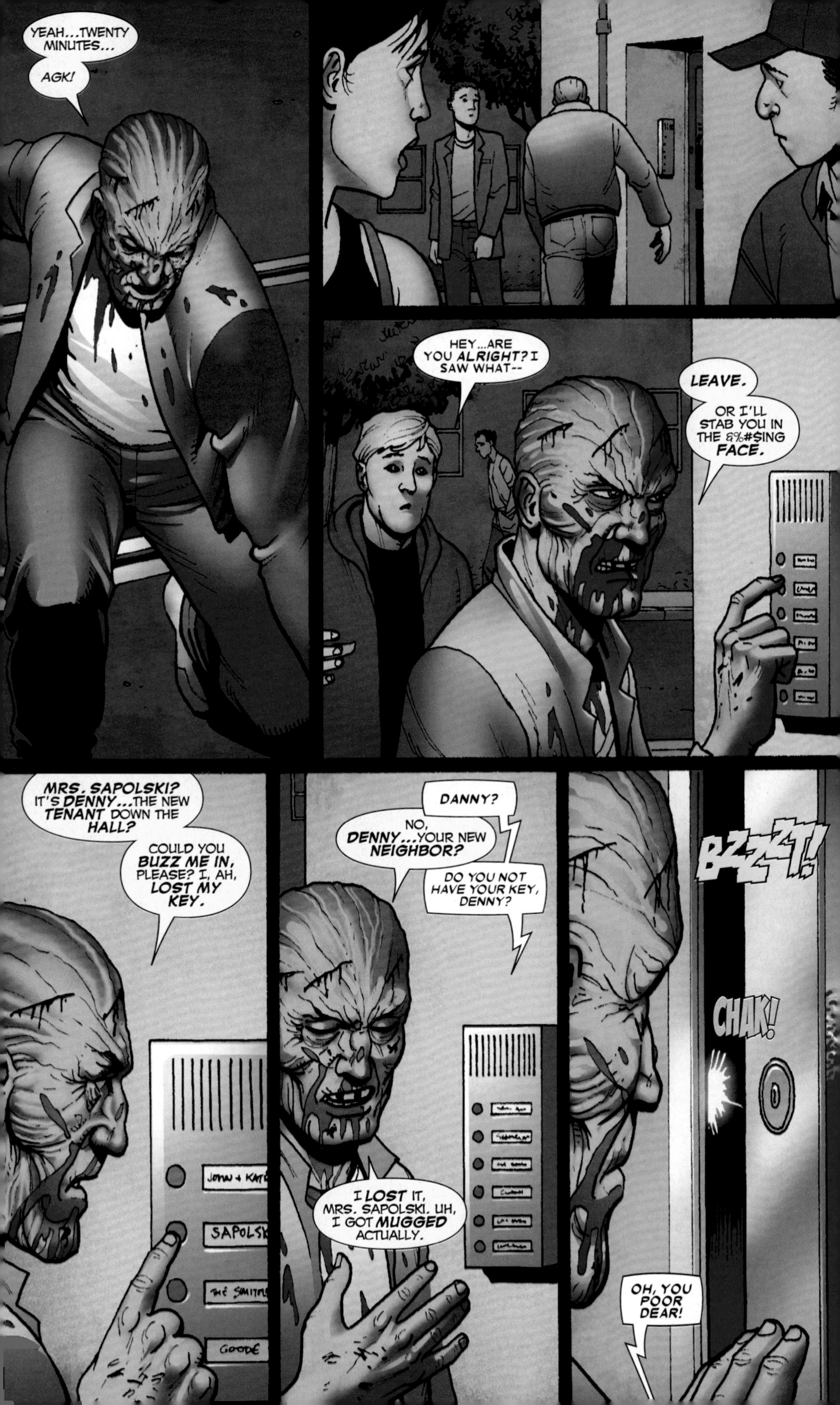

YEAH...TWENTY MINUTES...
AGK!
HEY...ARE YOU ALRIGHT? I SAW WHAT--
LEAVE.
OR I'LL STAB YOU IN THE &%#$ING FACE.
MRS. SAPOLSKI? IT'S DENNY...THE NEW TENANT DOWN THE HALL?
COULD YOU BUZZ ME IN, PLEASE? I, AH, LOST MY KEY.
JOHN + KATE
SAPOLSKI
THE SMITHS
GOODE
DANNY?
NO, DENNY...YOUR NEW NEIGHBOR?
DO YOU NOT HAVE YOUR KEY, DENNY?
I LOST IT, MRS. SAPOLSKI. UH, I GOT MUGGED ACTUALLY.
BZZZT!
CHAK!
OH, YOU POOR DEAR!

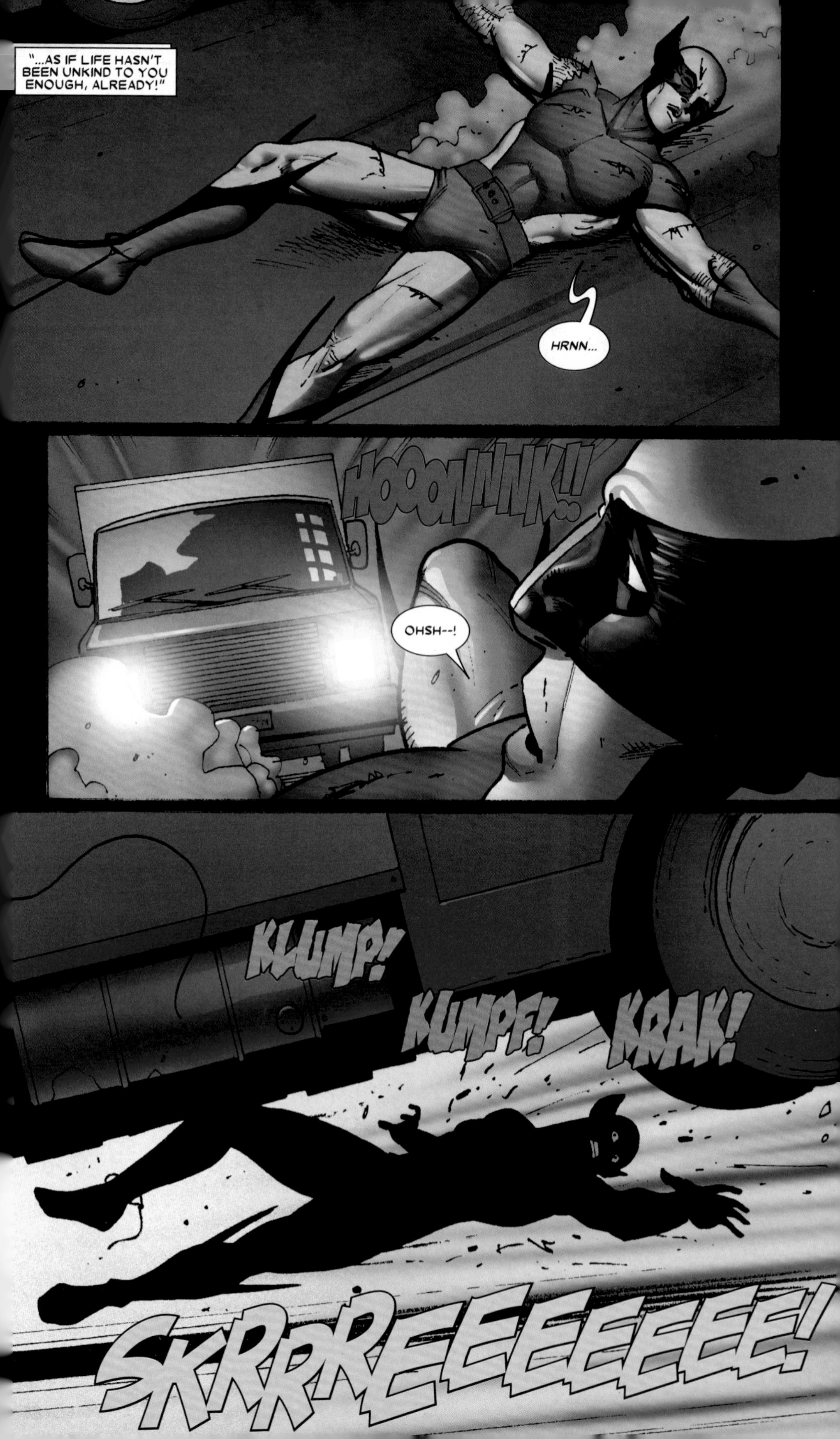
"...AS IF LIFE HASN'T BEEN UNKIND TO YOU ENOUGH, ALREADY!"
HRNN...
HOOONNNK!!
OHSH--!
KLUMP!
KUMPF!
KRAK!
SKRRREEEEEEE!

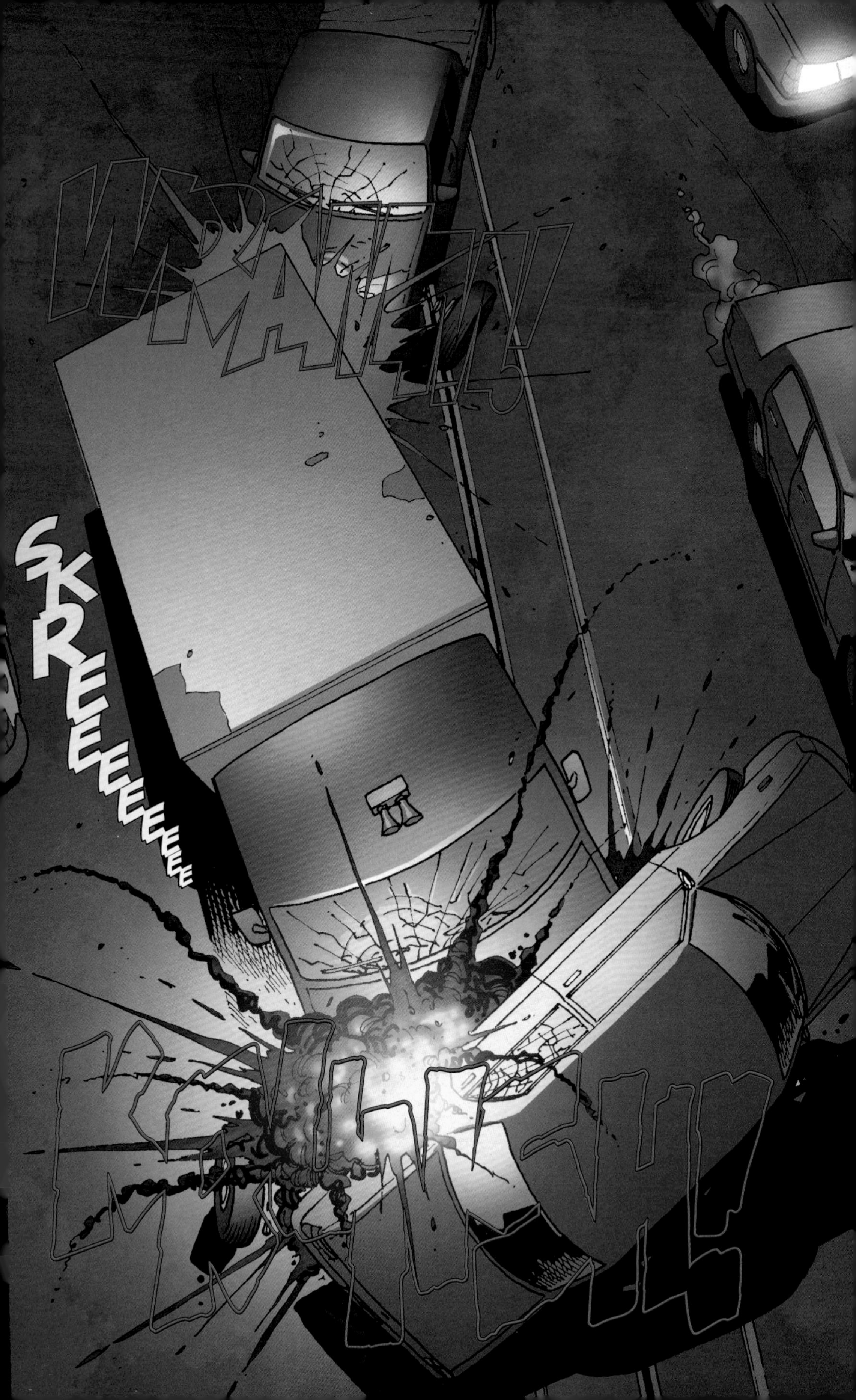
SKREEEEEEEEEE

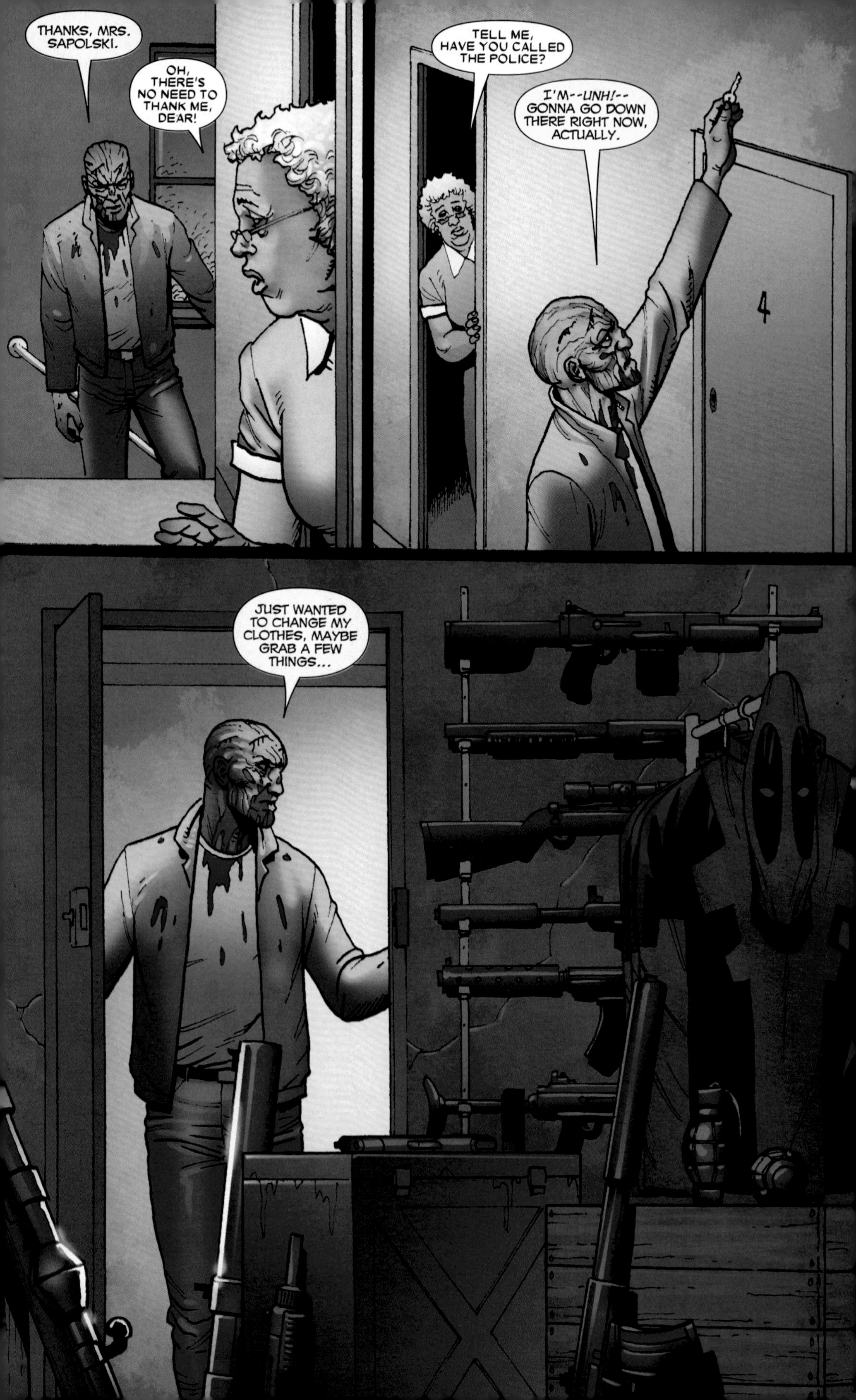
THANKS, MRS. SAPOLSKI.
OH, THERE'S NO NEED TO THANK ME, DEAR!
TELL ME, HAVE YOU CALLED THE POLICE?
I'M--UNH!--GONNA GO DOWN THERE RIGHT NOW, ACTUALLY.
4
JUST WANTED TO CHANGE MY CLOTHES, MAYBE GRAB A FEW THINGS...

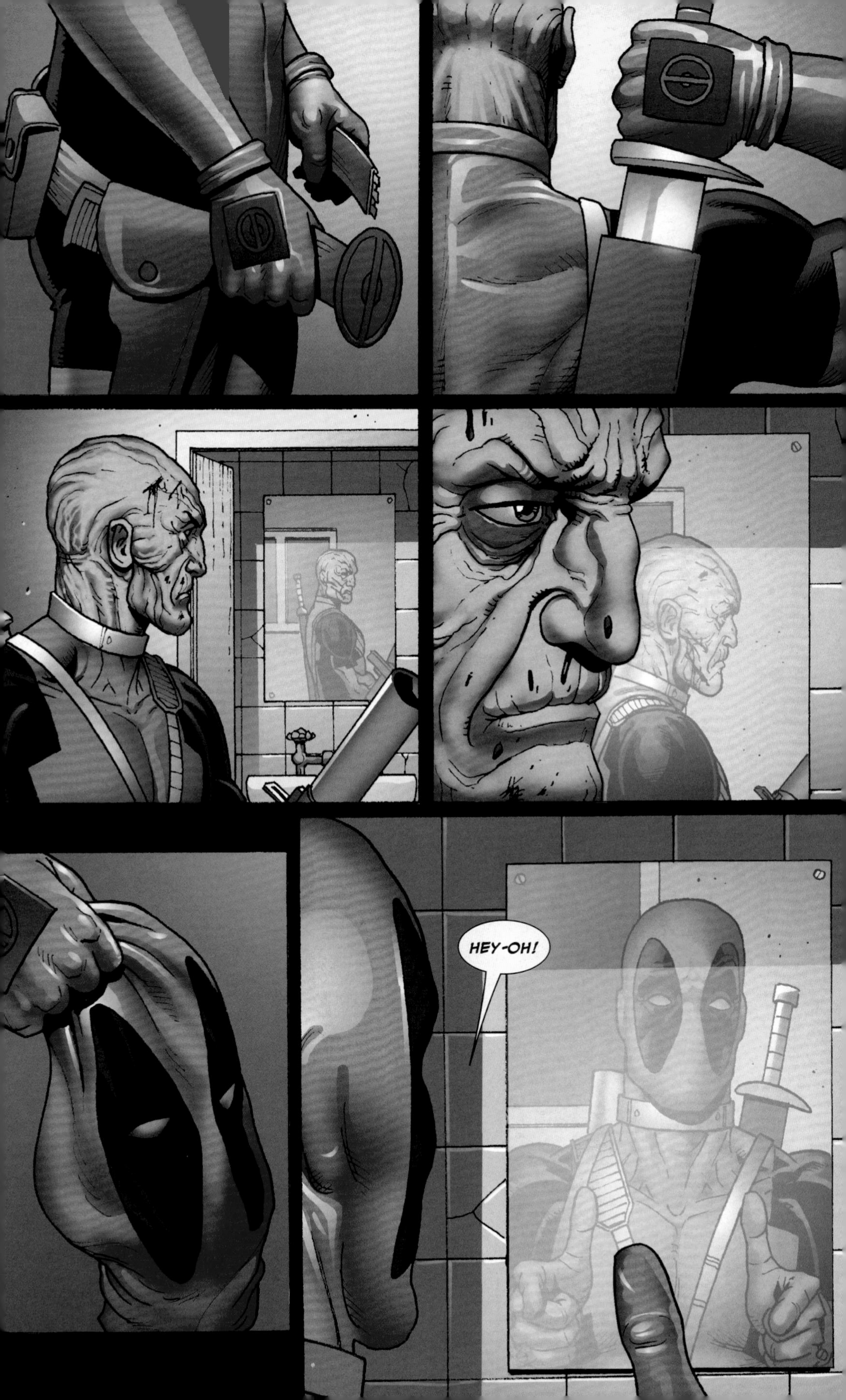
HEY-OH!

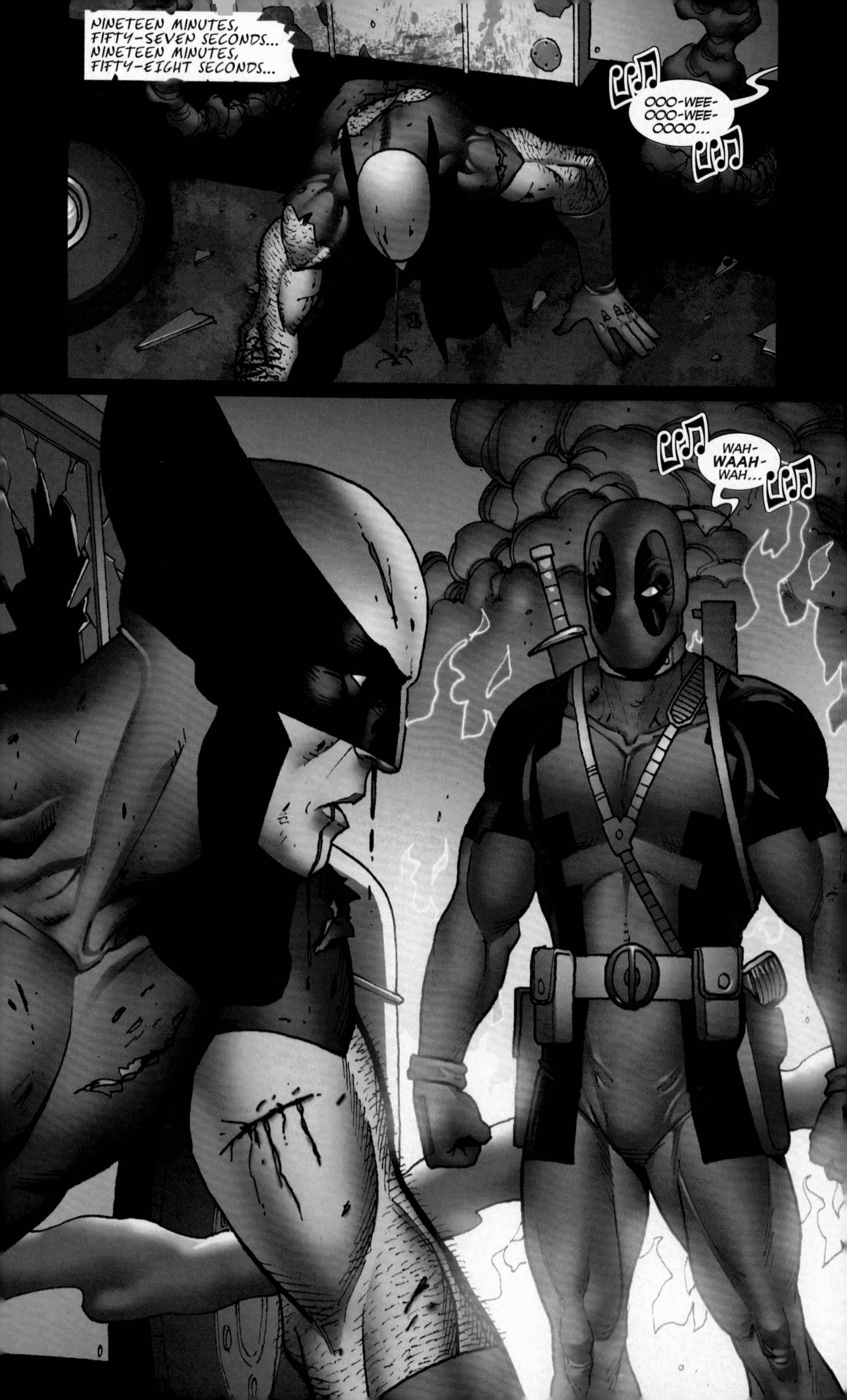
NINETEEN MINUTES, FIFTY-SEVEN SECONDS... NINETEEN MINUTES, FIFTY-EIGHT SECONDS...
OOO-WEE-OOO-WEE-OOOO...
WAH-WAAH-WAH...

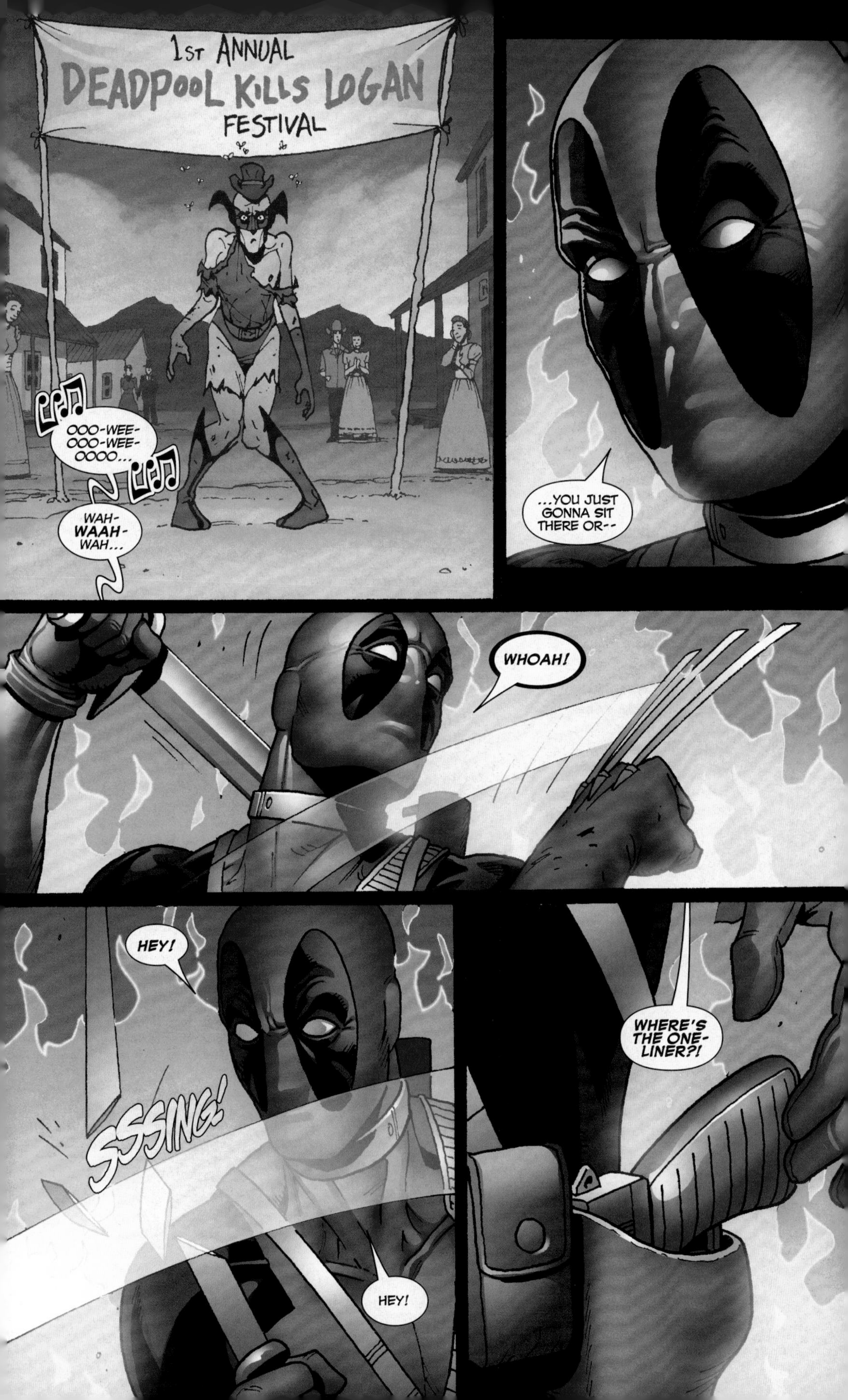
1st ANNUAL
DEADPOOL KILLS LOGAN
FESTIVAL
OOO-WEE-OOO-WEE-OOOO...
WAH-WAAH-WAH...
...YOU JUST GONNA SIT THERE OR--
WHOAH!
HEY!
SSSING!
HEY!
WHERE'S THE ONE-LINER?!

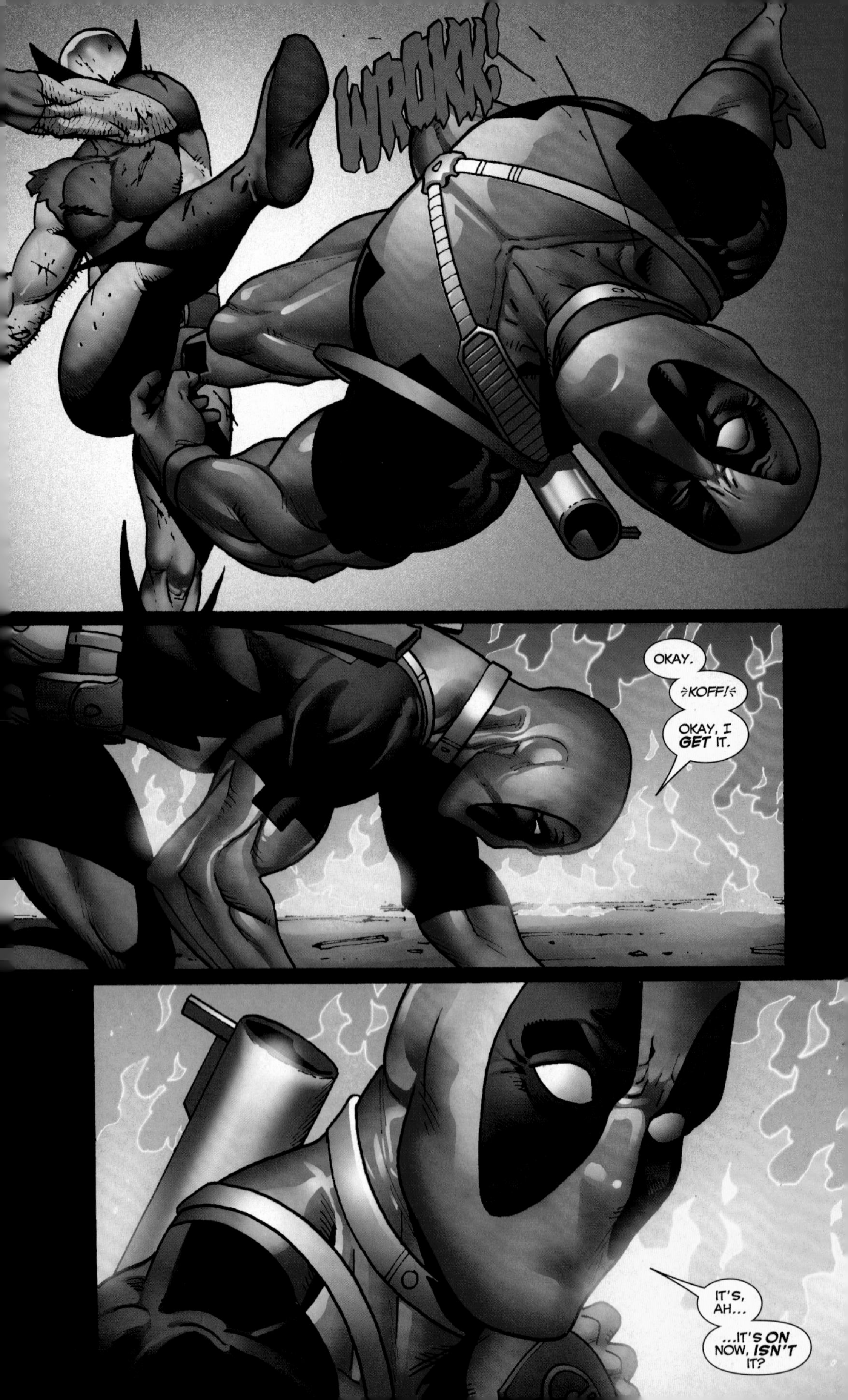
WROKK!
OKAY.
KOFF!
OKAY, I GET IT.
IT'S, AH...
...IT'S ON NOW, ISN'T IT?

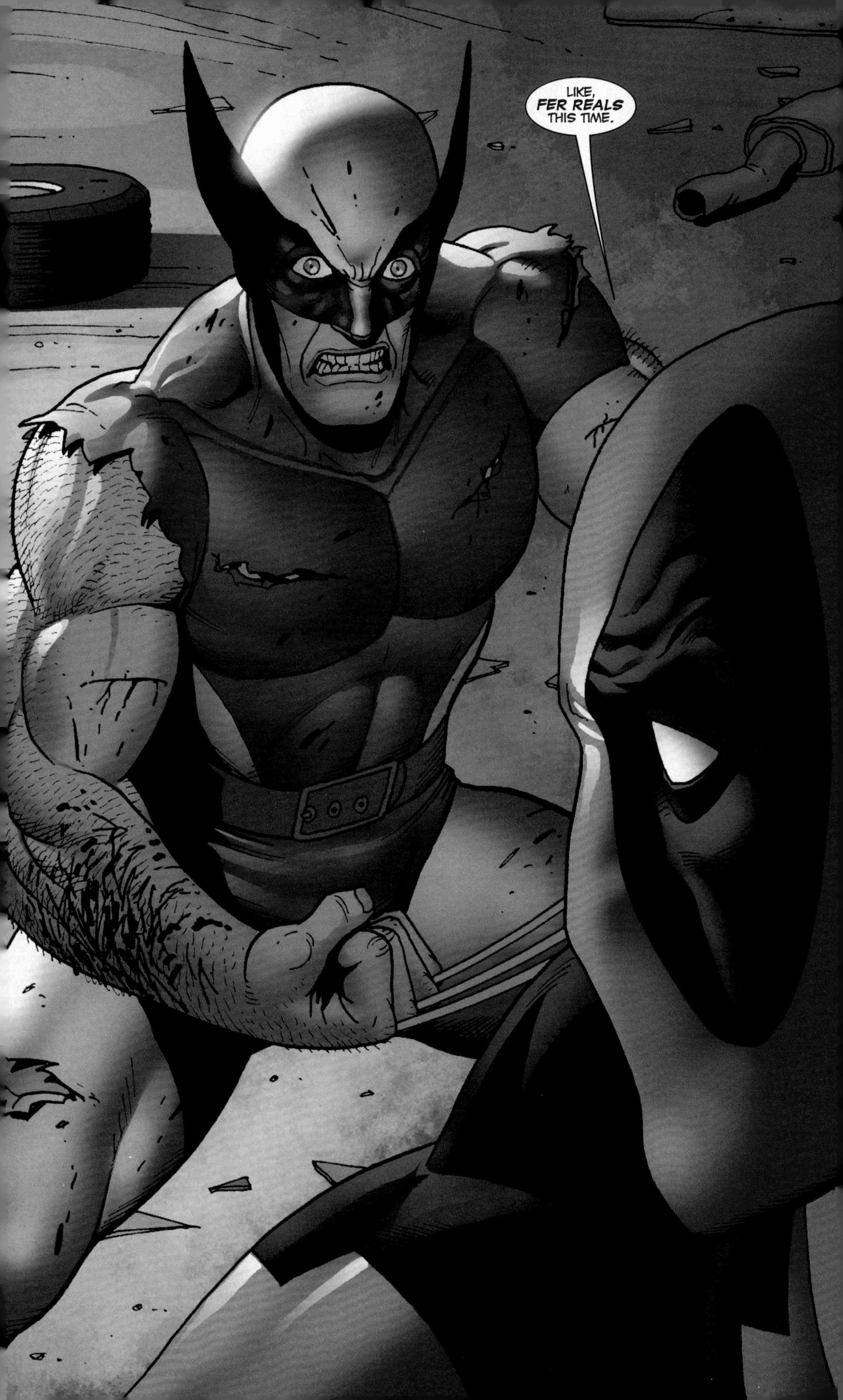
LIKE, FER REALS THIS TIME.

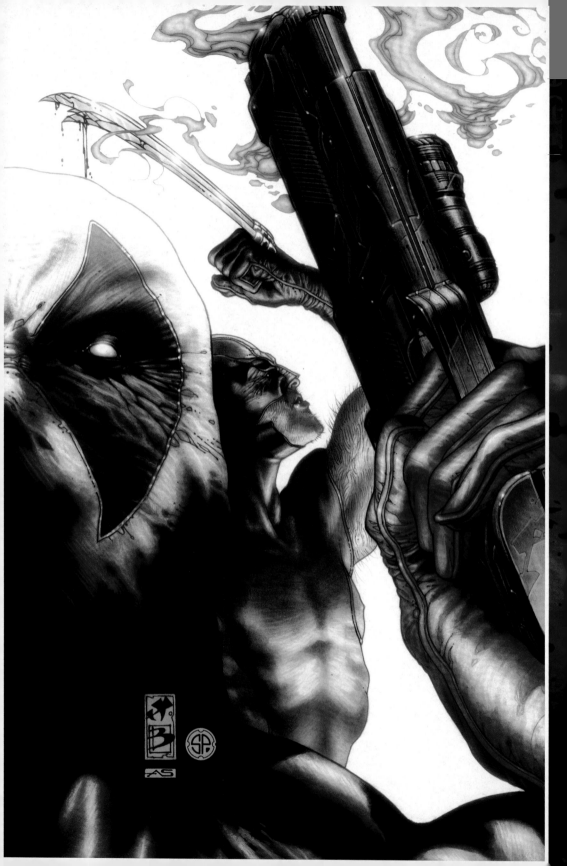

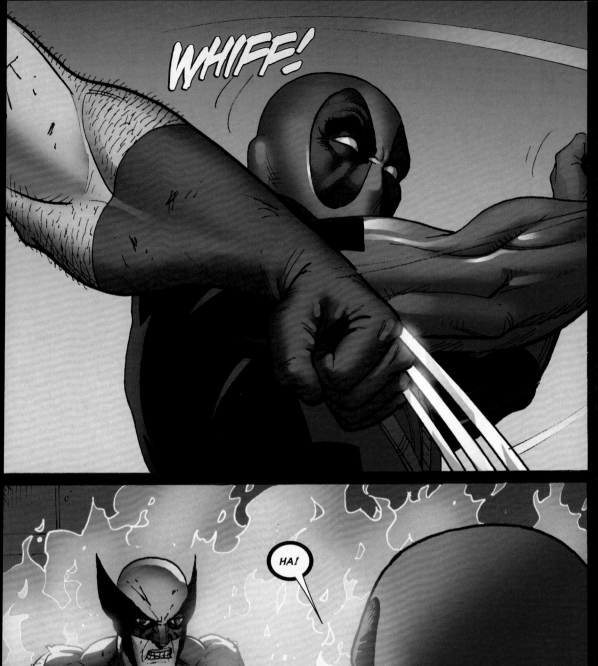

WHIFF!

HA!

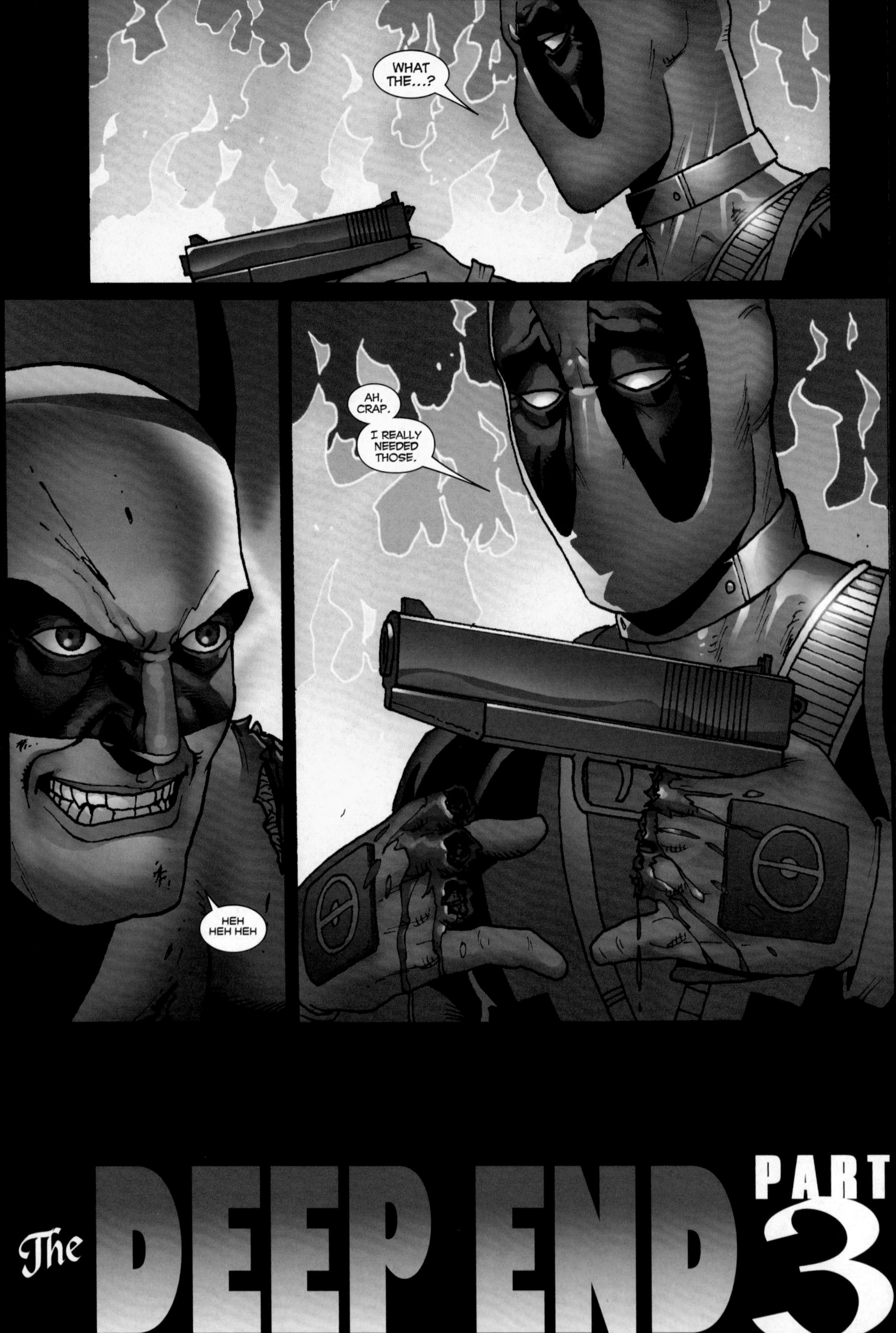
WHAT THE...?
HEH HEH HEH
AH, CRAP.
I REALLY NEEDED THOSE.
The DEEP END PART 3

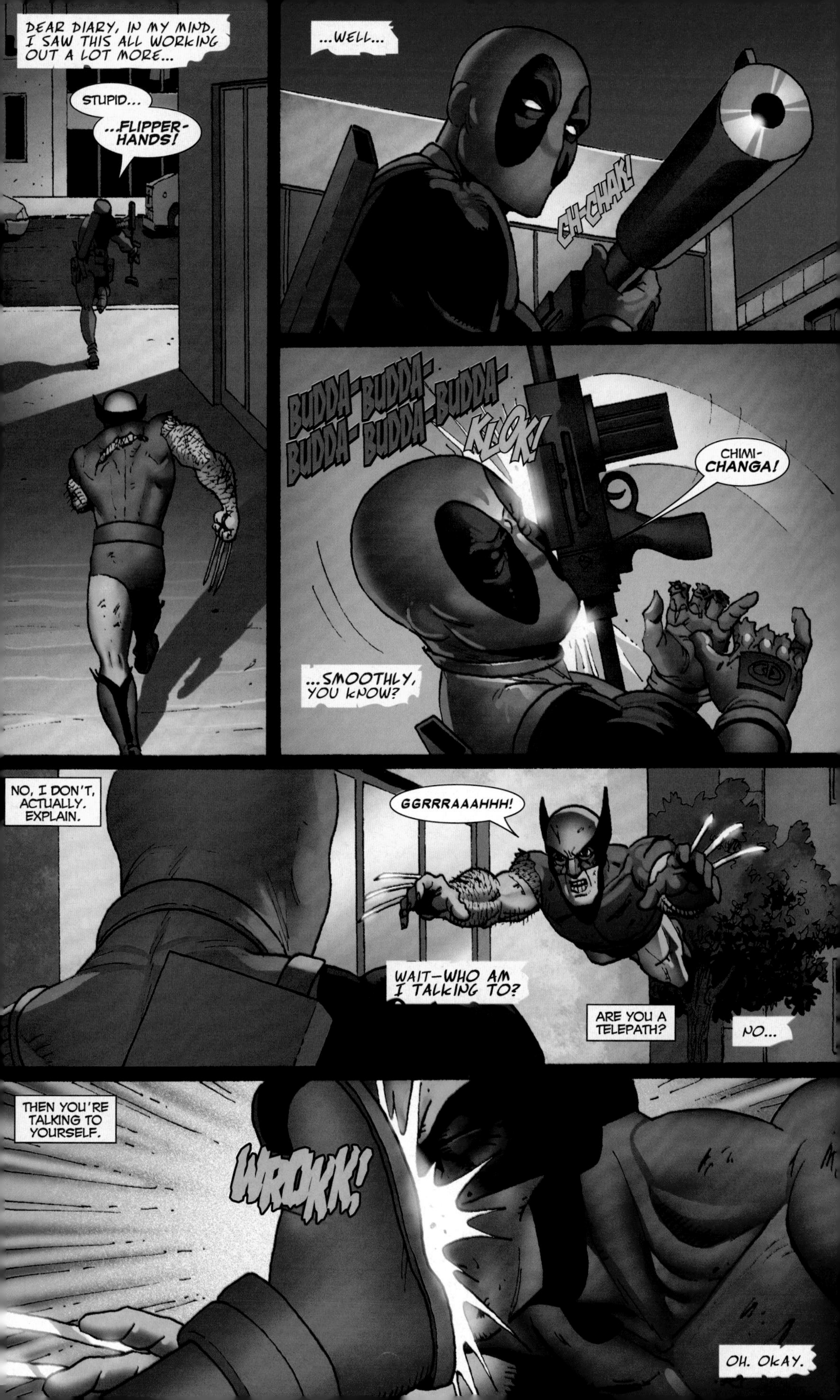
DEAR DIARY, IN MY MIND, I SAW THIS ALL WORKING OUT A LOT MORE...
STUPID...
...FLIPPER-HANDS!
...WELL...
CH-CHAK!
BUDDA-BUDDA-BUDDA-BUDDA-BUDDA-BUDDA-
KLOK!
CHIMI-CHANGA!
...SMOOTHLY, YOU KNOW?
NO, I DON'T, ACTUALLY. EXPLAIN.
GGRRRAAAHHH!
WAIT—WHO AM I TALKING TO?
ARE YOU A TELEPATH?
NO...
THEN YOU'RE TALKING TO YOURSELF.
WROKK!
OH. OKAY.

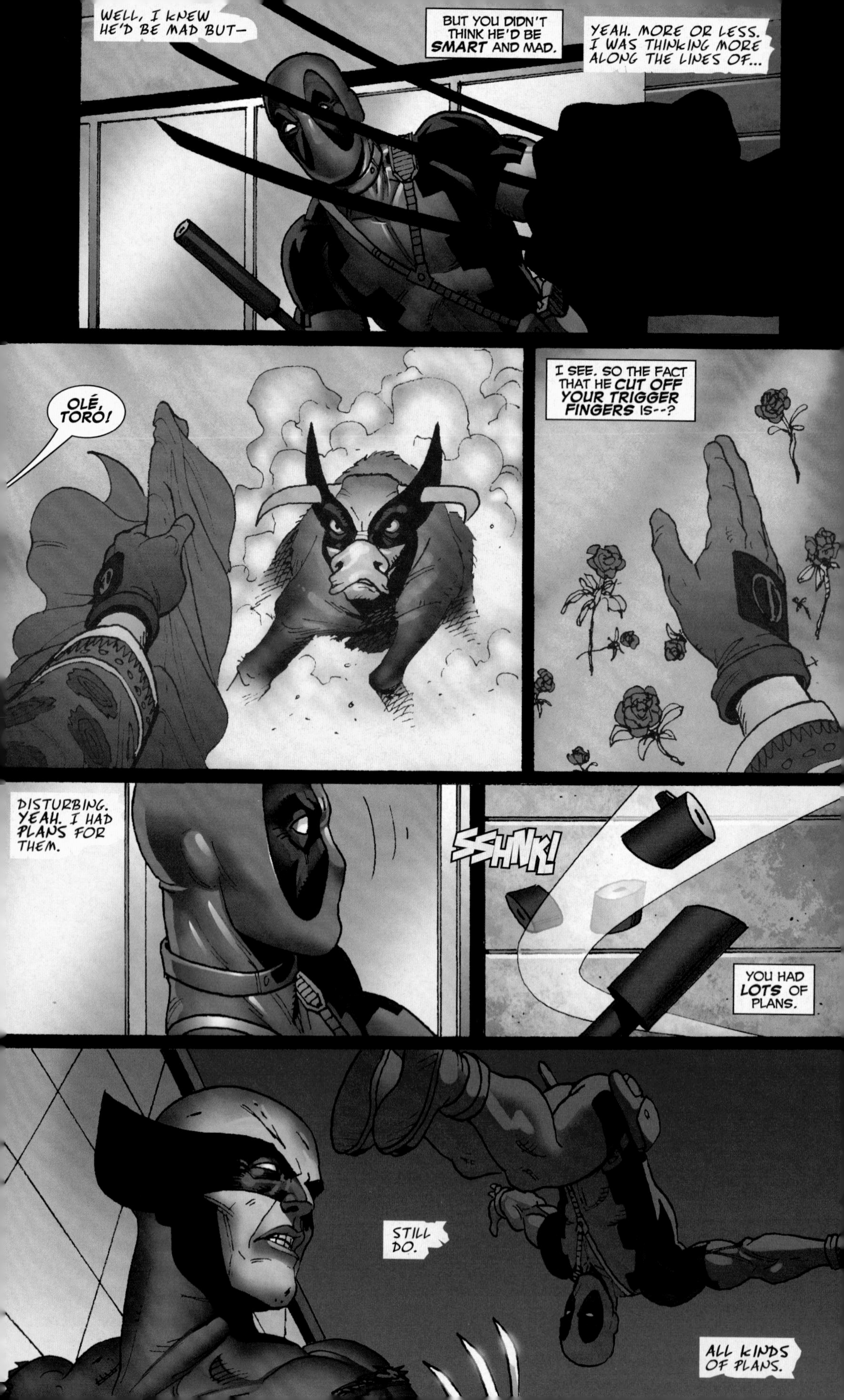
WELL, I KNEW HE'D BE MAD BUT—
BUT YOU DIDN'T THINK HE'D BE SMART AND MAD.
YEAH. MORE OR LESS. I WAS THINKING MORE ALONG THE LINES OF...
OLÉ, TORO!
I SEE. SO THE FACT THAT HE CUT OFF YOUR TRIGGER FINGERS IS--?
DISTURBING. YEAH. I HAD PLANS FOR THEM.
SSHNK!
YOU HAD LOTS OF PLANS.
STILL DO.
ALL KINDS OF PLANS.

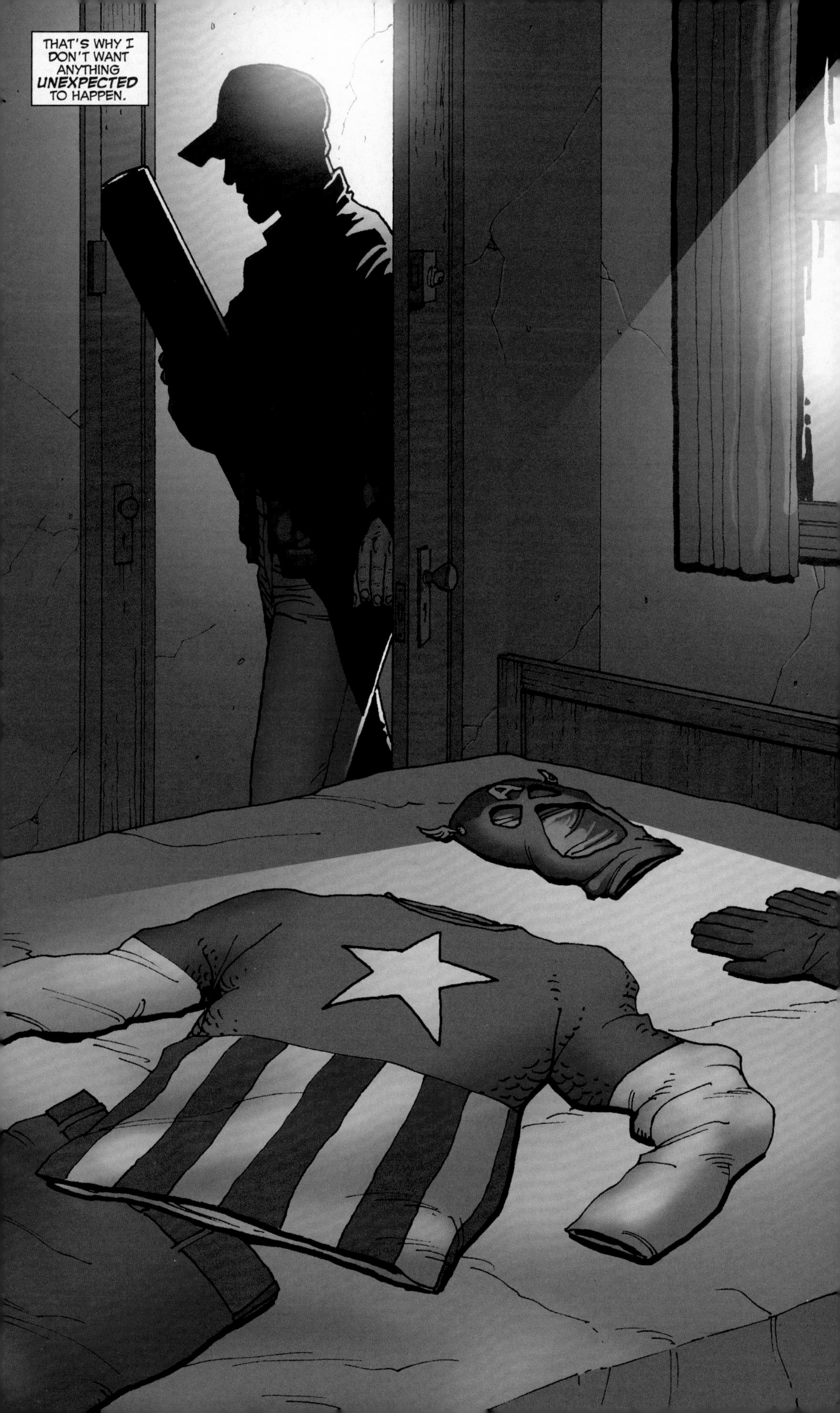
THAT'S WHY I DON'T WANT ANYTHING *UNEXPECTED* TO HAPPEN.

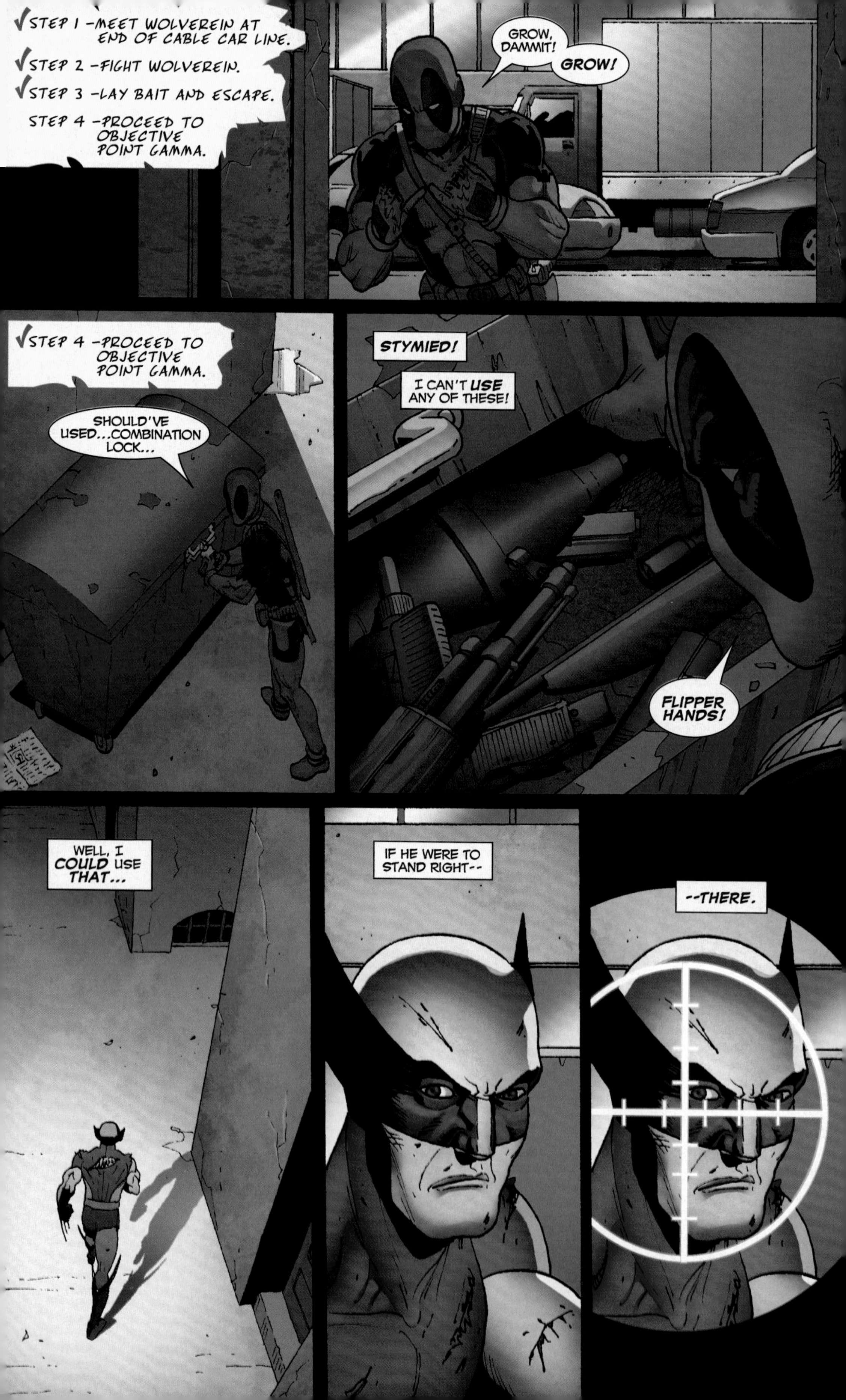

√STEP 1 -MEET WOLVEREIN AT END OF CABLE CAR LINE.
√STEP 2 -FIGHT WOLVEREIN.
√STEP 3 -LAY BAIT AND ESCAPE.
STEP 4 -PROCEED TO OBJECTIVE POINT GAMMA.
GROW, DAMMIT!
GROW!
√STEP 4 -PROCEED TO OBJECTIVE POINT GAMMA.
SHOULD'VE USED...COMBINATION LOCK...
STYMIED!
I CAN'T USE ANY OF THESE!
FLIPPER HANDS!
WELL, I COULD USE THAT...
IF HE WERE TO STAND RIGHT--
--THERE.

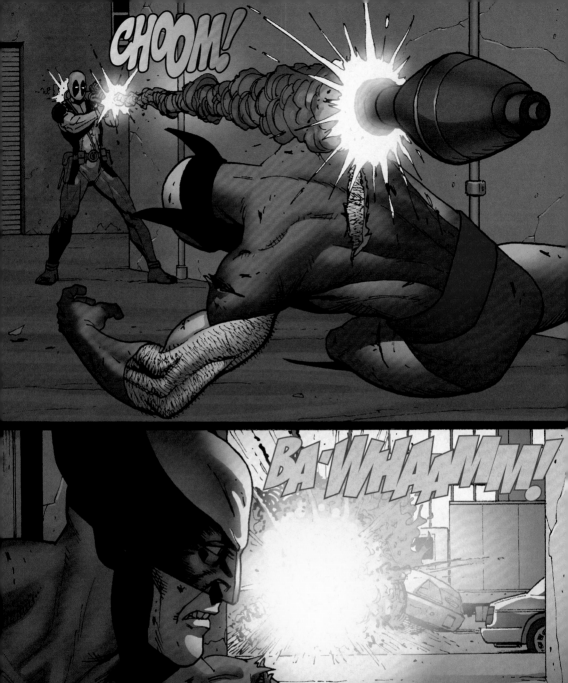

CHOOM!

BA-WHAMM!

✓ STEP 17 - BLOW UP CAR (MAKE IT LOOK COOL).

FINGERS! WHO NEEDS 'EM!?

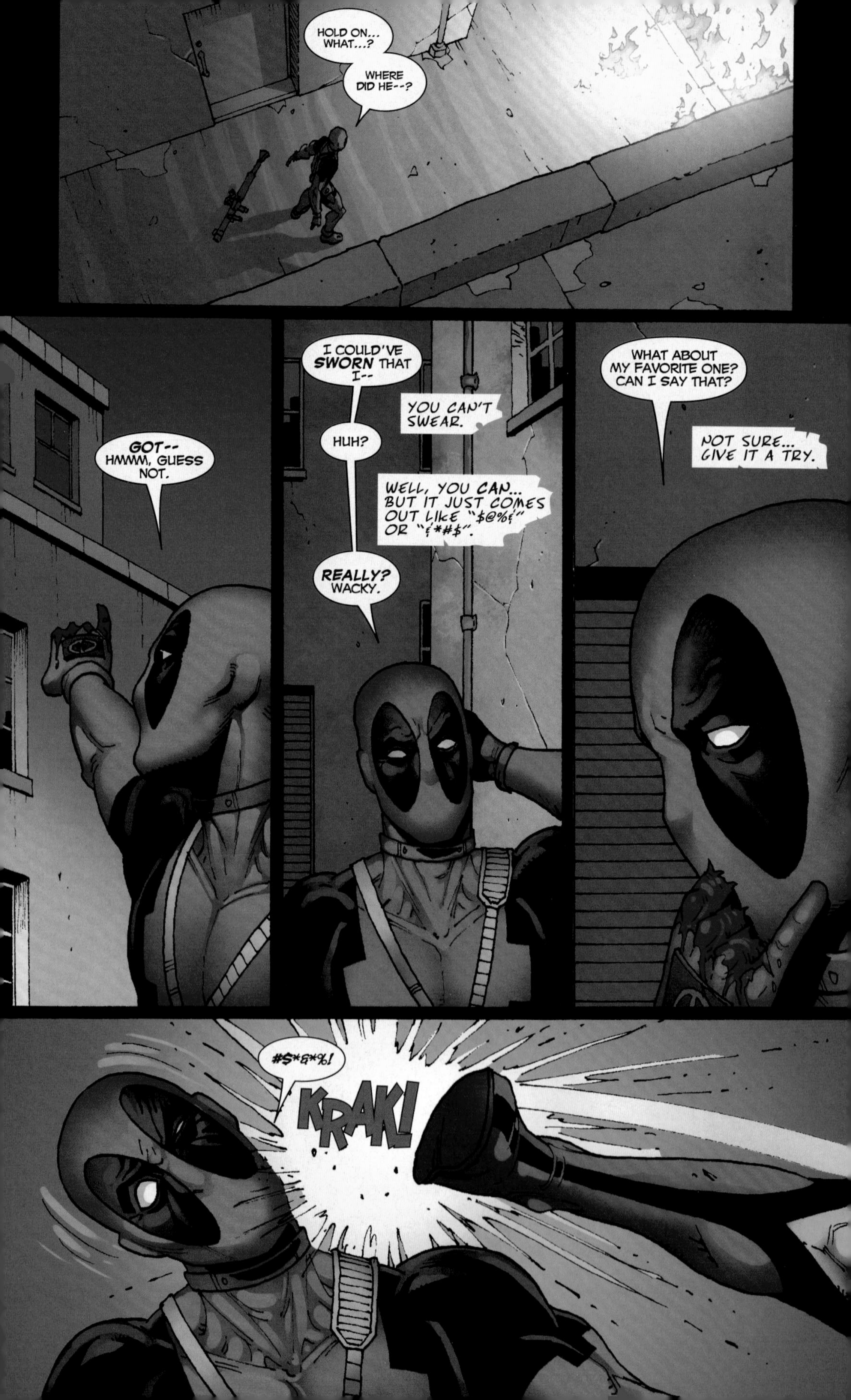

HOLD ON... WHAT...?
WHERE DID HE--?
GOT-- HMMM, GUESS NOT.
I COULD'VE **SWORN** THAT I--
YOU CAN'T SWEAR.
HUH?
WELL, YOU **CAN**... BUT IT JUST COMES OUT LIKE "$@%¢" OR "¢*#$".
REALLY? WACKY.
WHAT ABOUT MY FAVORITE ONE? CAN I SAY THAT?
NOT SURE... GIVE IT A TRY.
#$*&*%!
KRAK!

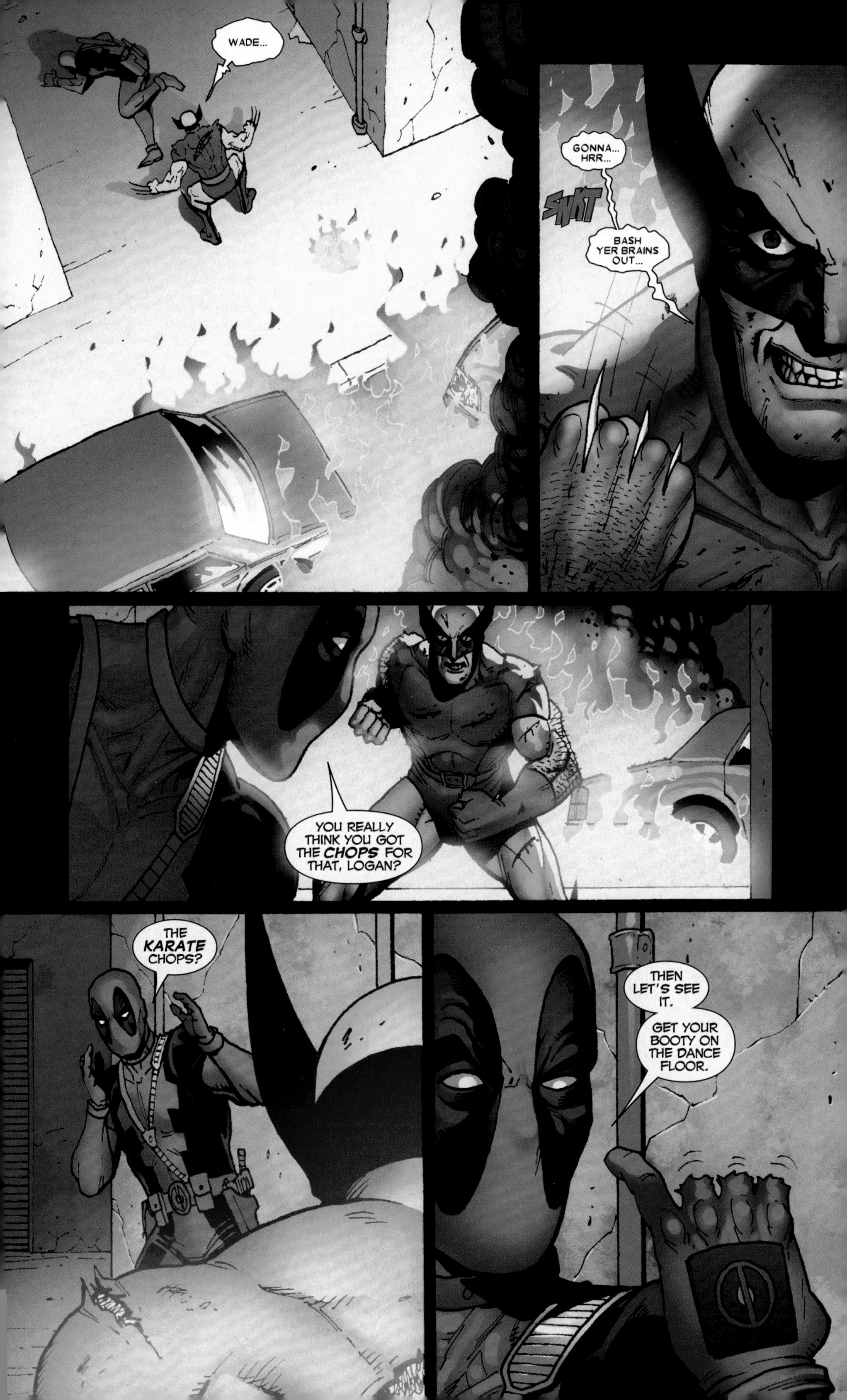
WADE...
GONNA... HRR...
SNIKT
BASH YER BRAINS OUT...
YOU REALLY THINK YOU GOT THE CHOPS FOR THAT, LOGAN?
THE KARATE CHOPS?
THEN LET'S SEE IT.
GET YOUR BOOTY ON THE DANCE FLOOR.

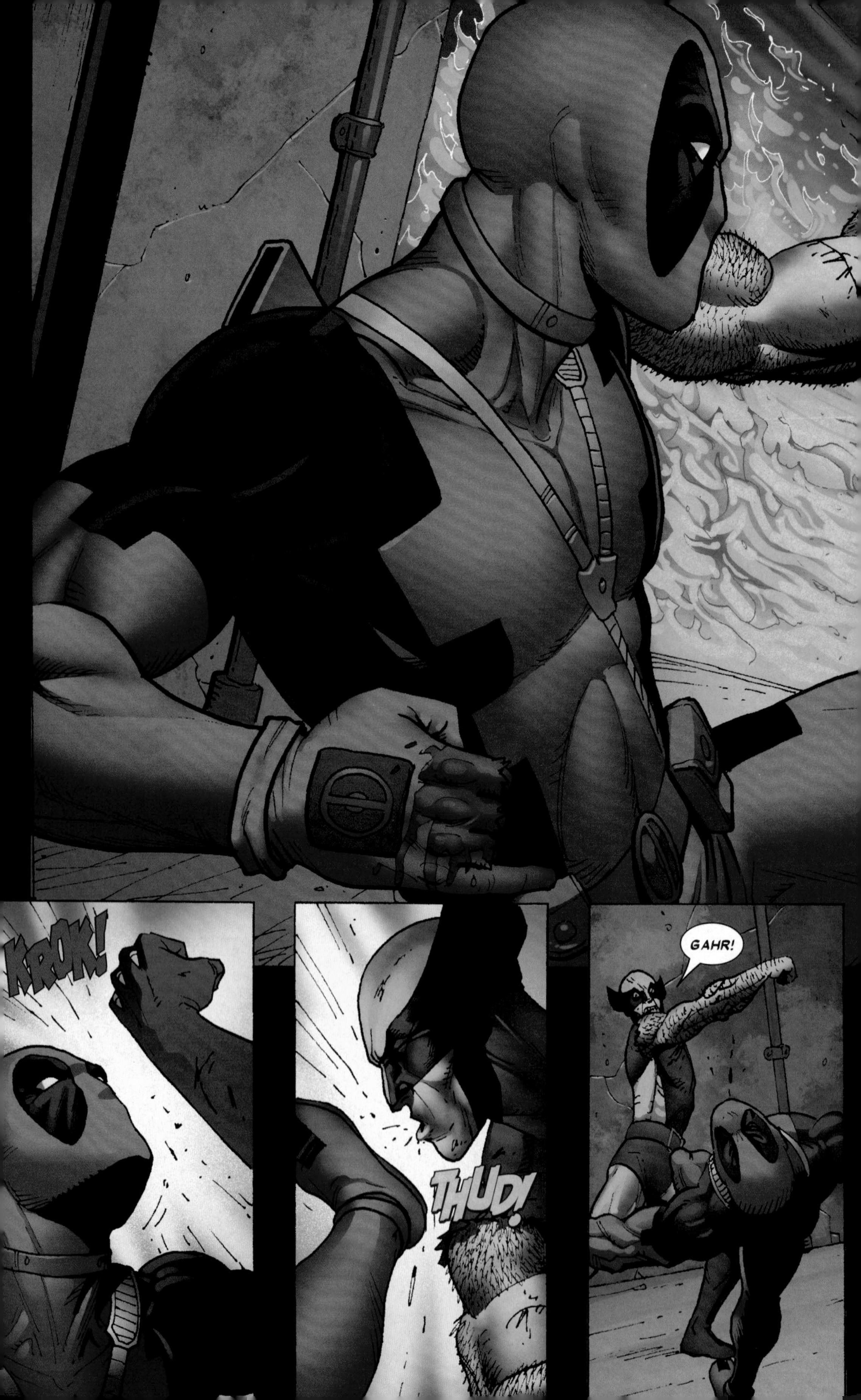

KROK!
THUD!
GAHR!

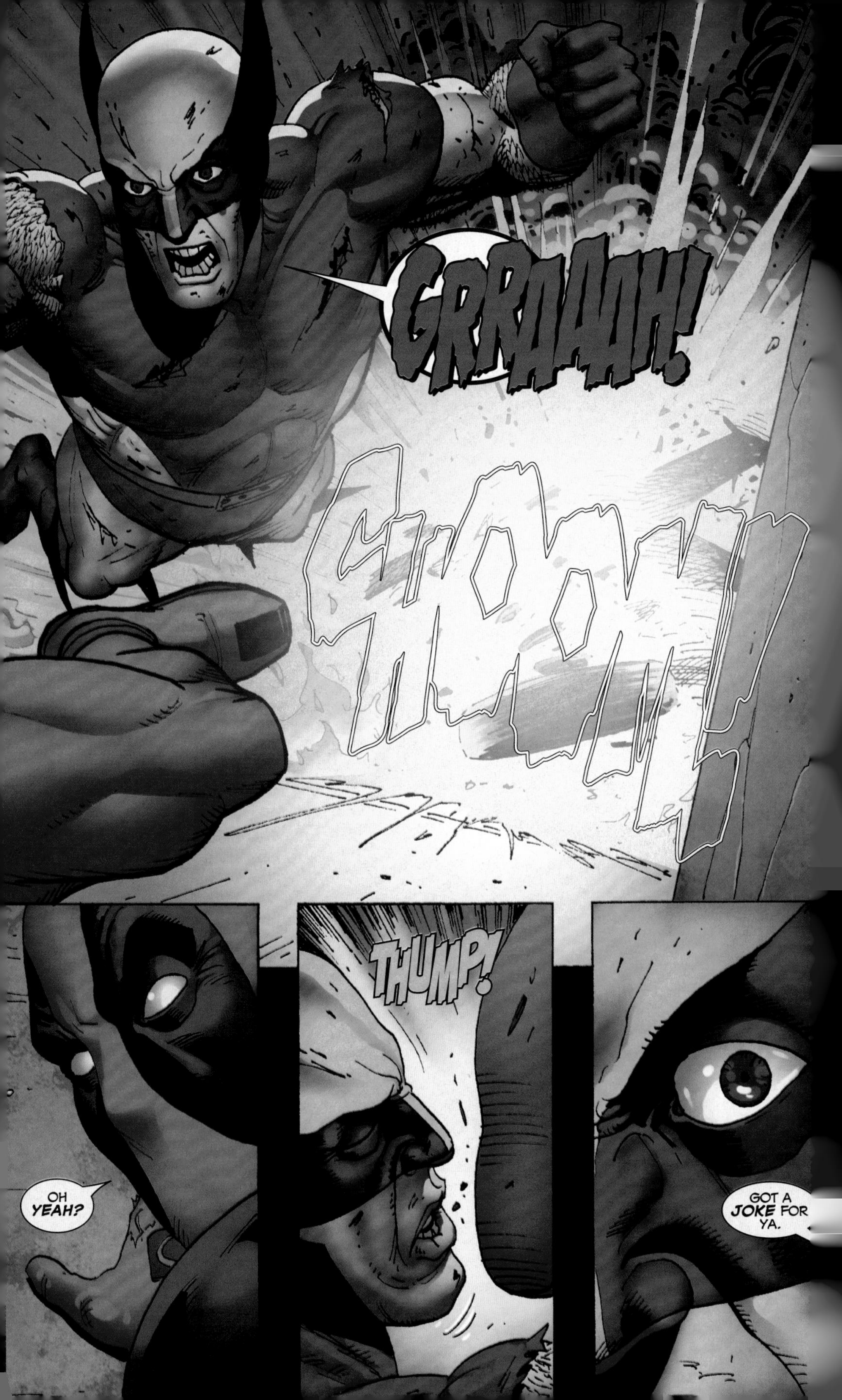
GRRAAAH!
SHOOM!
THUMP!
OH YEAH?
GOT A JOKE FOR YA.

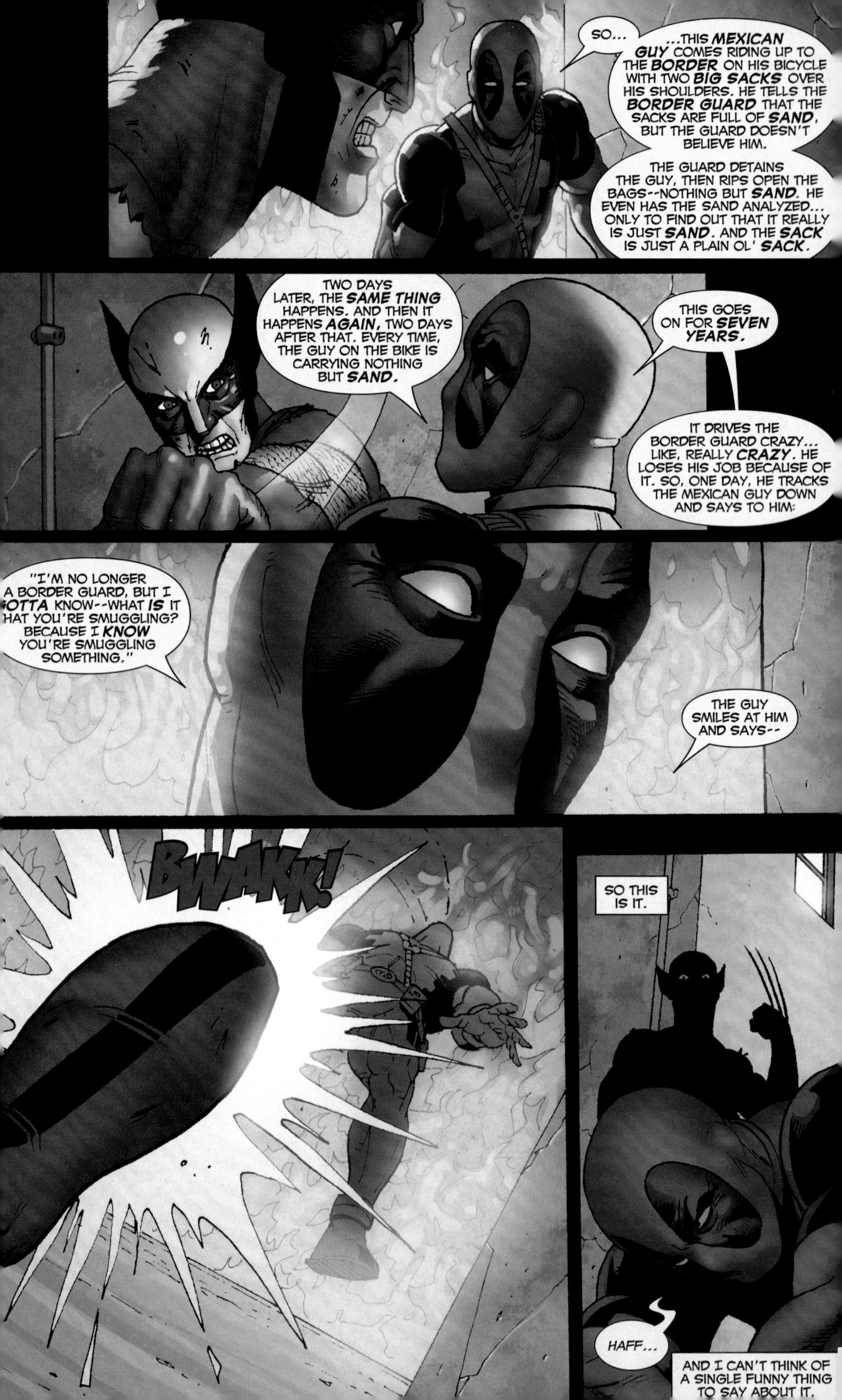

SO...
...THIS MEXICAN GUY COMES RIDING UP TO THE BORDER ON HIS BICYCLE WITH TWO BIG SACKS OVER HIS SHOULDERS. HE TELLS THE BORDER GUARD THAT THE SACKS ARE FULL OF SAND, BUT THE GUARD DOESN'T BELIEVE HIM.
THE GUARD DETAINS THE GUY, THEN RIPS OPEN THE BAGS--NOTHING BUT SAND. HE EVEN HAS THE SAND ANALYZED... ONLY TO FIND OUT THAT IT REALLY IS JUST SAND. AND THE SACK IS JUST A PLAIN OL' SACK.
TWO DAYS LATER, THE SAME THING HAPPENS. AND THEN IT HAPPENS AGAIN, TWO DAYS AFTER THAT. EVERY TIME, THE GUY ON THE BIKE IS CARRYING NOTHING BUT SAND.
THIS GOES ON FOR SEVEN YEARS.
IT DRIVES THE BORDER GUARD CRAZY... LIKE, REALLY CRAZY. HE LOSES HIS JOB BECAUSE OF IT. SO, ONE DAY, HE TRACKS THE MEXICAN GUY DOWN AND SAYS TO HIM:
"I'M NO LONGER A BORDER GUARD, BUT I GOTTA KNOW--WHAT IS IT THAT YOU'RE SMUGGLING? BECAUSE I KNOW YOU'RE SMUGGLING SOMETHING."
THE GUY SMILES AT HIM AND SAYS--
BWAKK!
SO THIS IS IT.
HAFF...
AND I CAN'T THINK OF A SINGLE FUNNY THING TO SAY ABOUT IT.

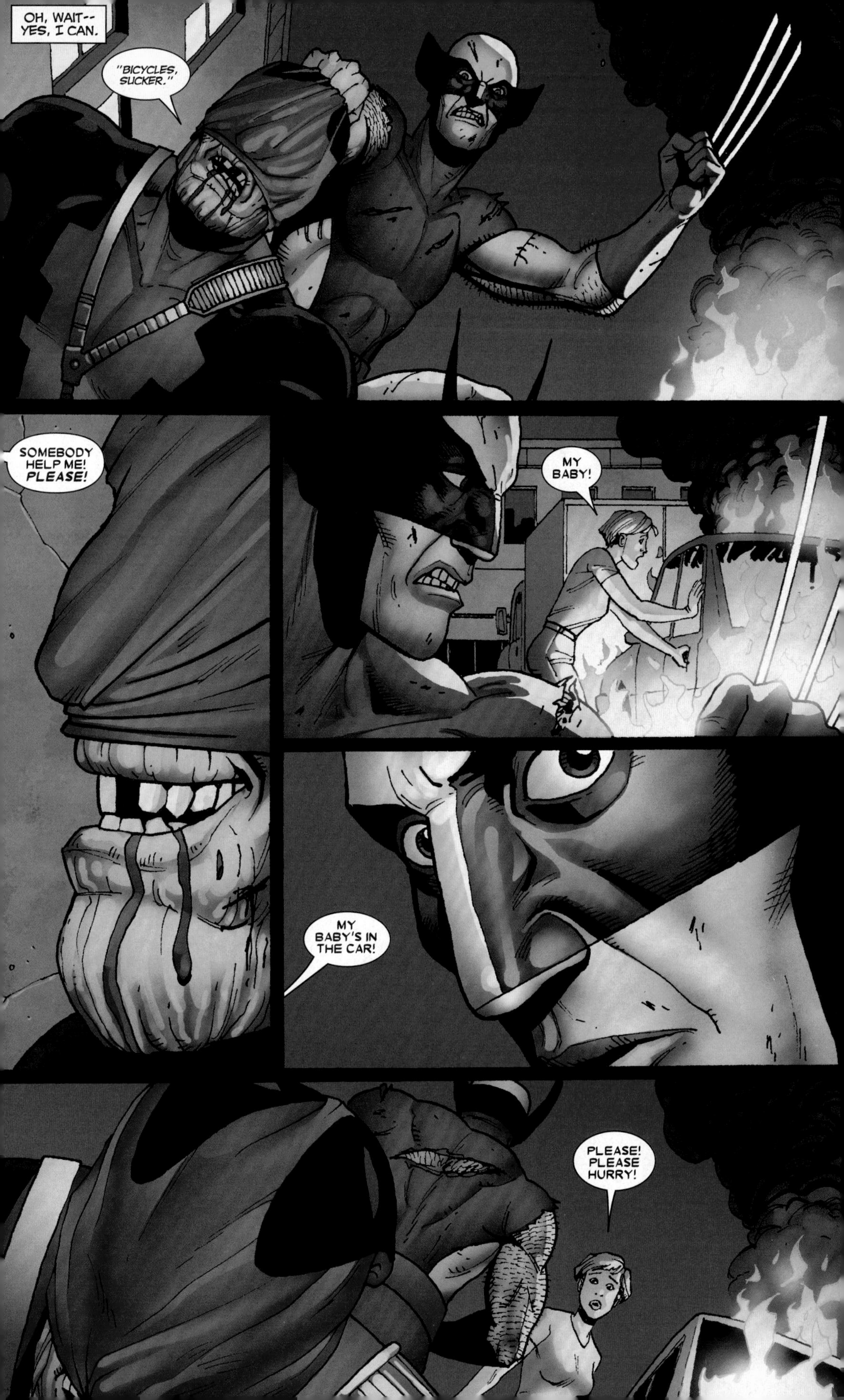
OH, WAIT--
YES, I CAN.
"BICYCLES, SUCKER."
SOMEBODY HELP ME! PLEASE!
MY BABY!
MY BABY'S IN THE CAR!
PLEASE! PLEASE HURRY!

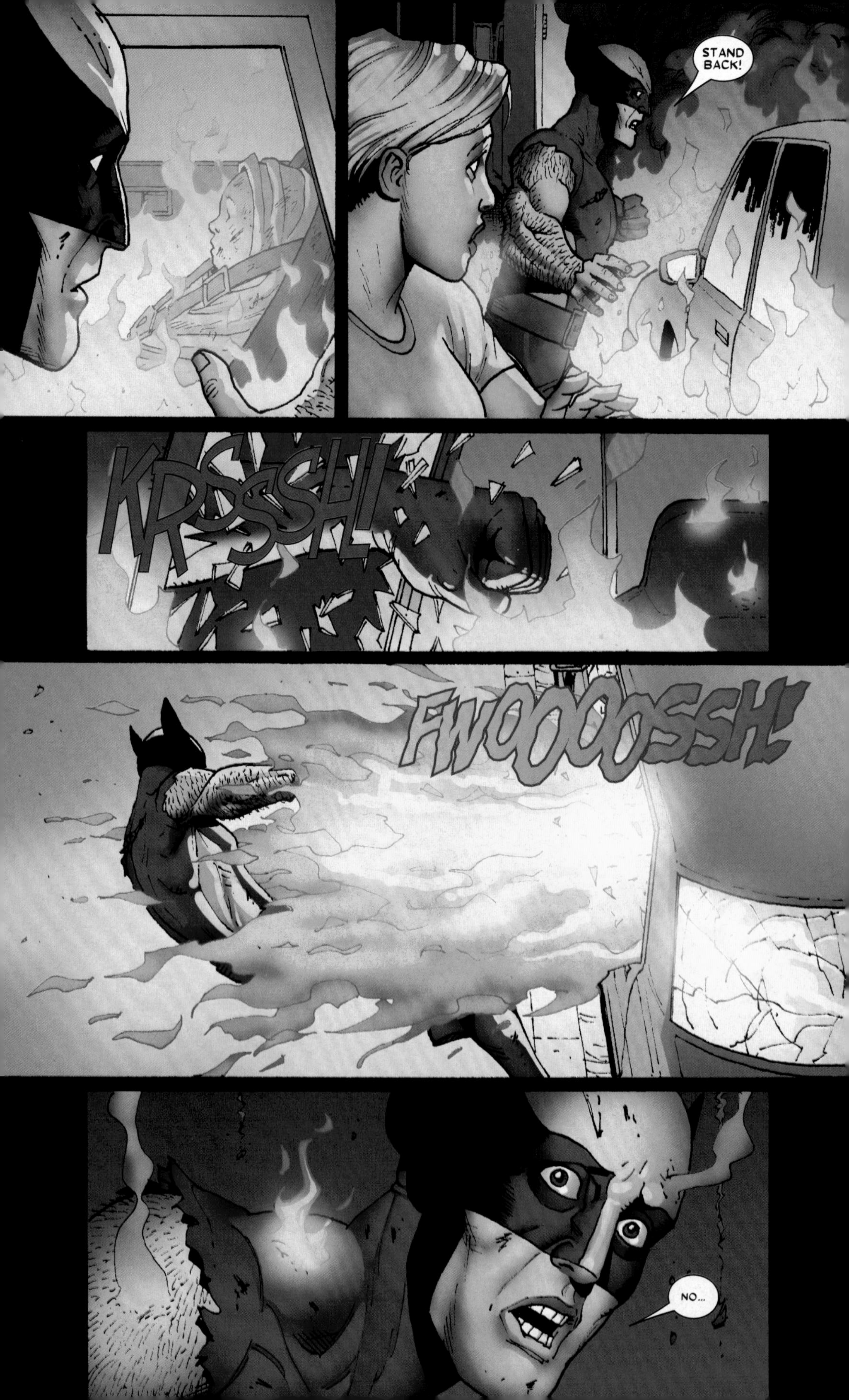
STAND BACK!
KRSSSH!
FWOOOOSSH!
NO...

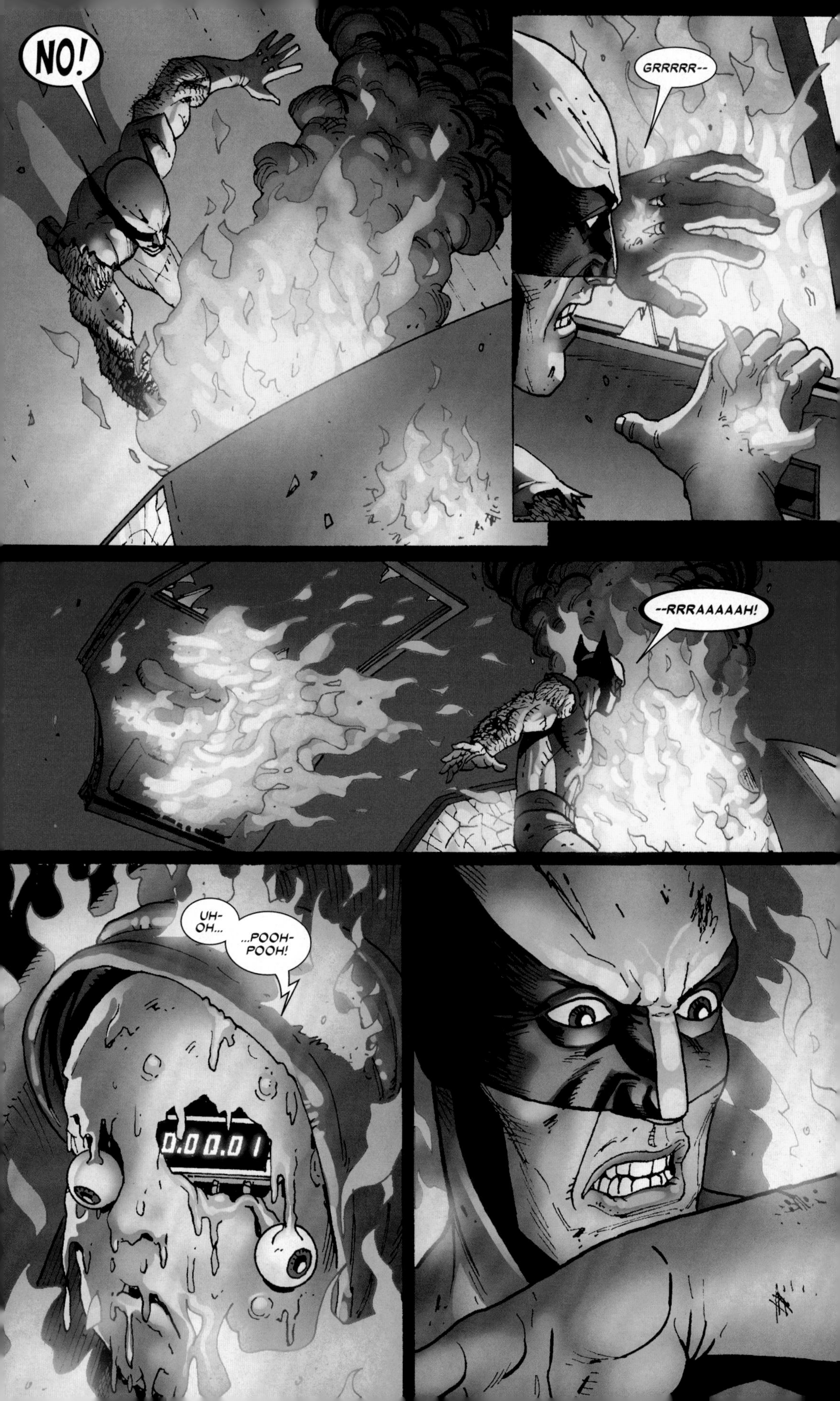
NO!
GRRRRR--
--RRRAAAAAH!
UH-OH...
...POOH-POOH!
0.00.01

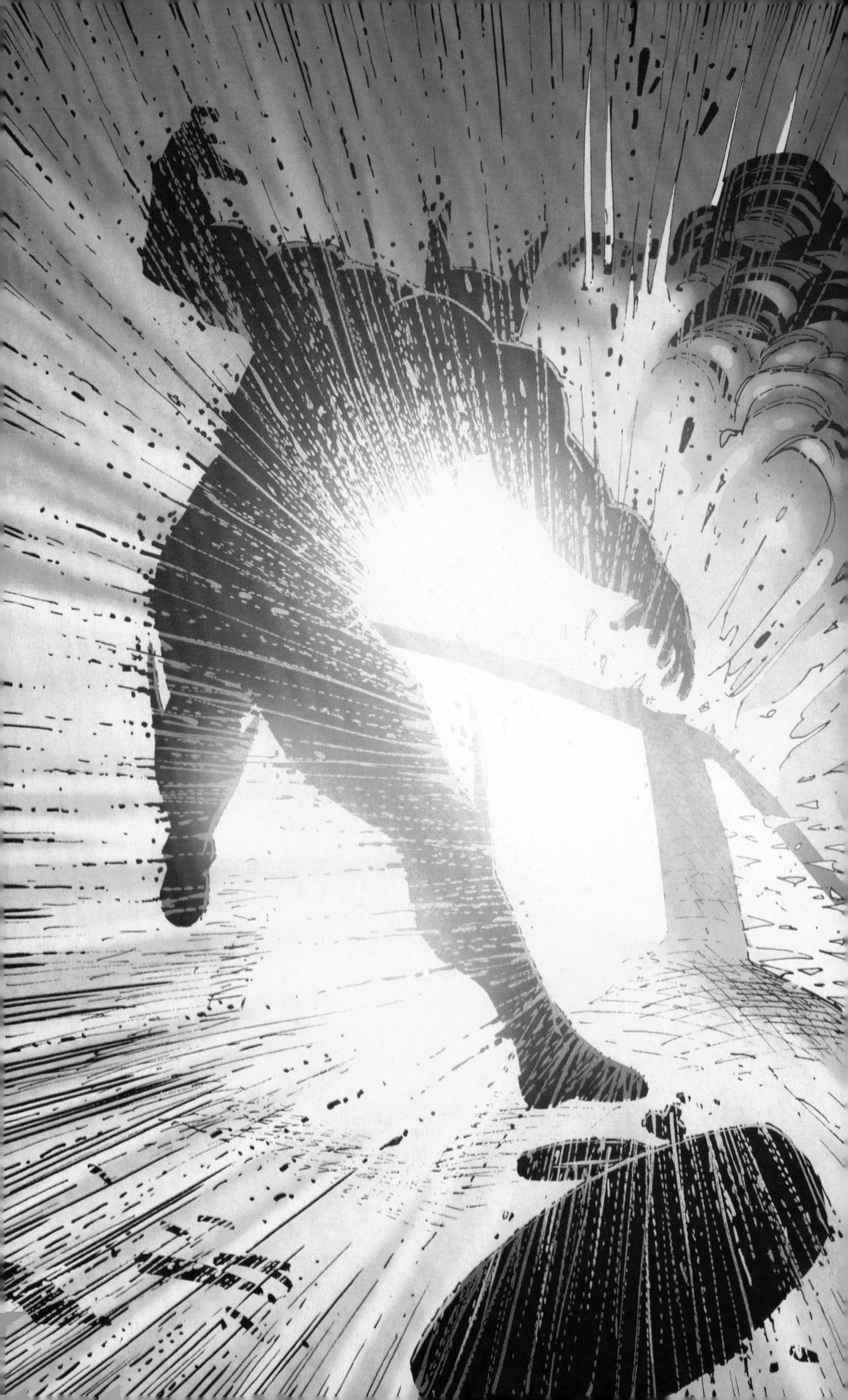

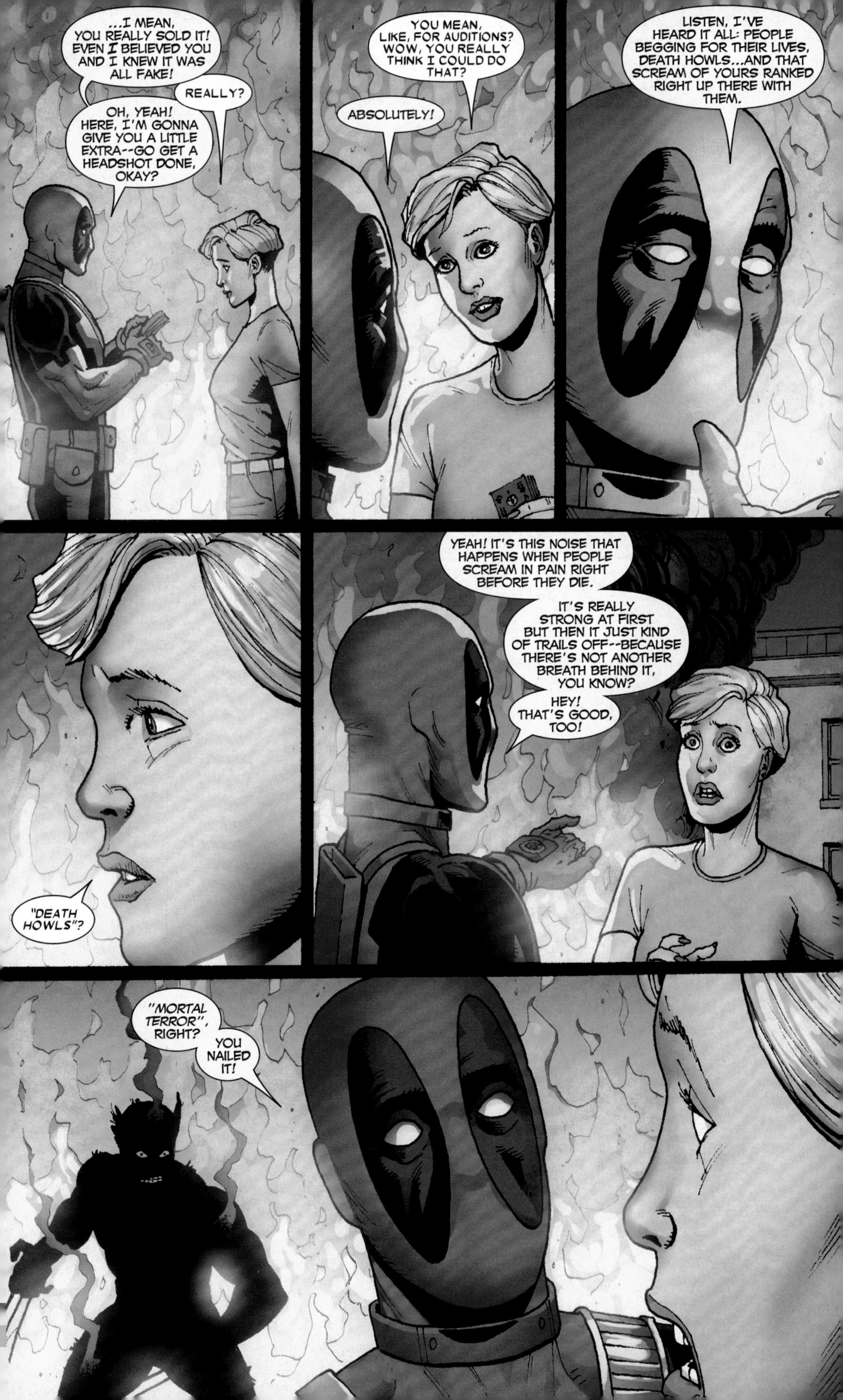
...I MEAN, YOU REALLY SOLD IT! EVEN I BELIEVED YOU AND I KNEW IT WAS ALL FAKE!
REALLY?
OH, YEAH! HERE, I'M GONNA GIVE YOU A LITTLE EXTRA--GO GET A HEADSHOT DONE, OKAY?
YOU MEAN, LIKE, FOR AUDITIONS? WOW, YOU REALLY THINK I COULD DO THAT?
ABSOLUTELY!
LISTEN, I'VE HEARD IT ALL: PEOPLE BEGGING FOR THEIR LIVES, DEATH HOWLS...AND THAT SCREAM OF YOURS RANKED RIGHT UP THERE WITH THEM.
"DEATH HOWLS"?
YEAH! IT'S THIS NOISE THAT HAPPENS WHEN PEOPLE SCREAM IN PAIN RIGHT BEFORE THEY DIE.
IT'S REALLY STRONG AT FIRST BUT THEN IT JUST KIND OF TRAILS OFF--BECAUSE THERE'S NOT ANOTHER BREATH BEHIND IT, YOU KNOW?
HEY! THAT'S GOOD, TOO!
"MORTAL TERROR", RIGHT?
YOU NAILED IT!

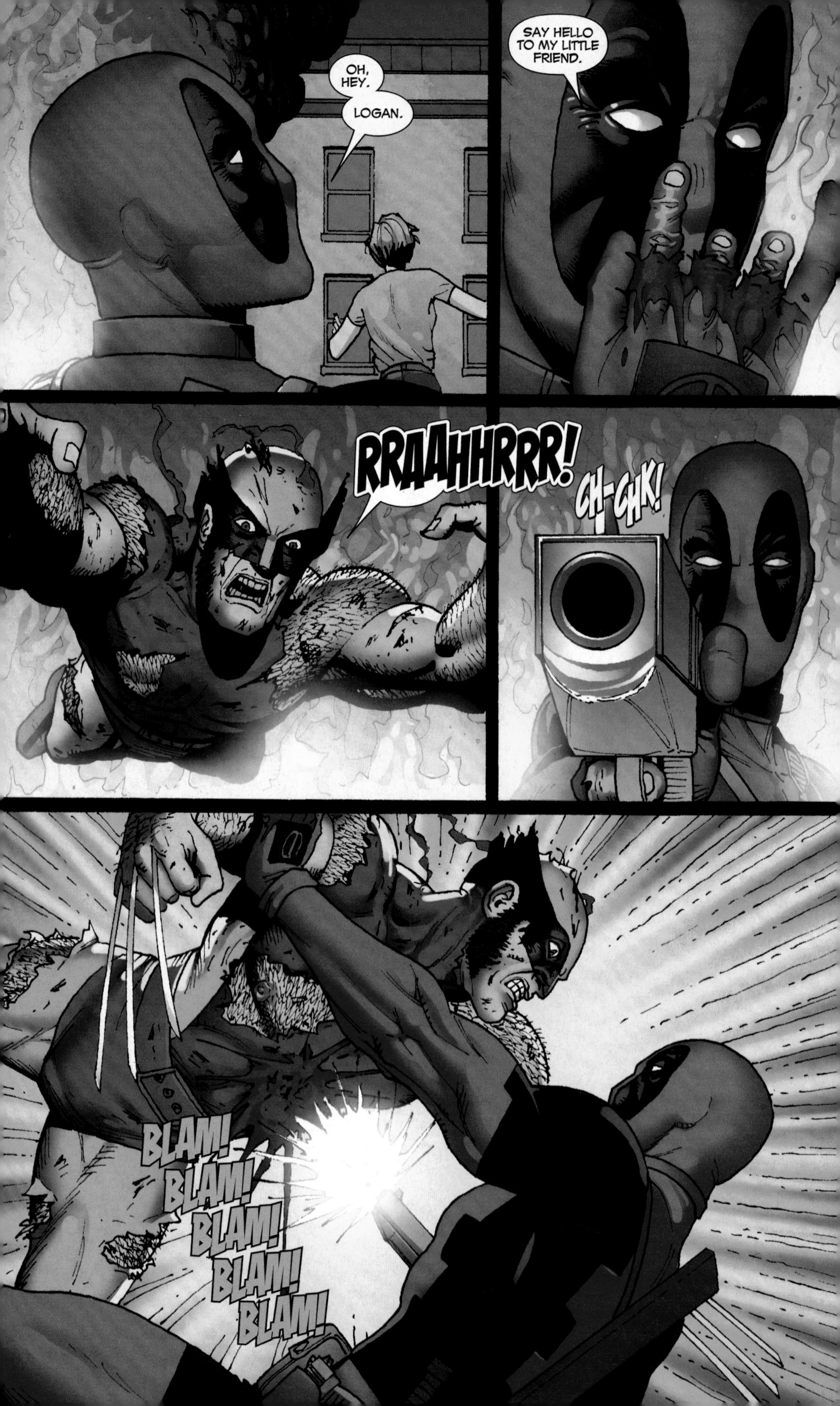
OH, HEY.
LOGAN.
SAY HELLO TO MY LITTLE FRIEND.
RRAAHHRRR!
CH-CHK!
BLAM! BLAM! BLAM! BLAM! BLAM!

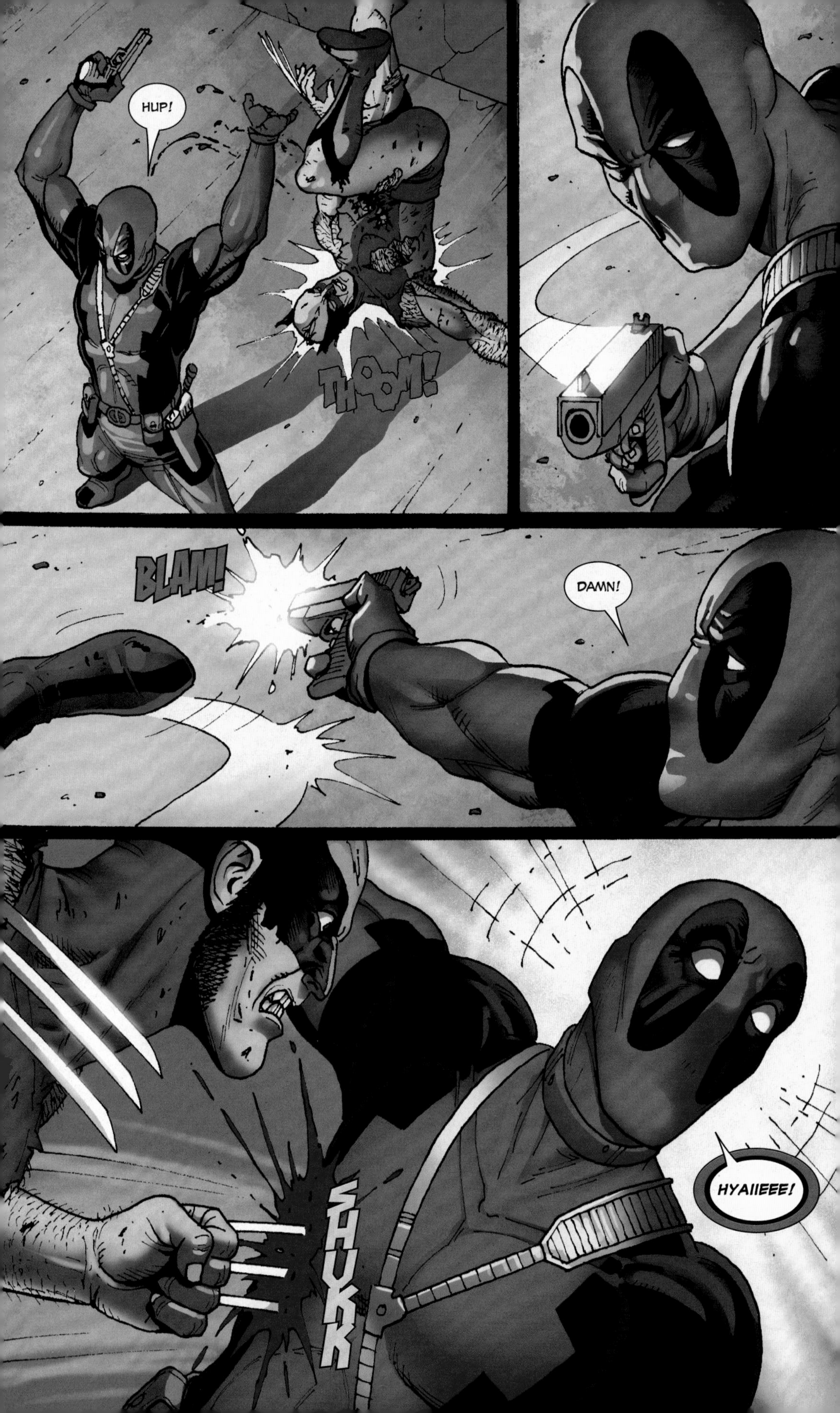
HUP!
THOOM!
BLAM!
DAMN!
HYAIIEEE!
SHUKK

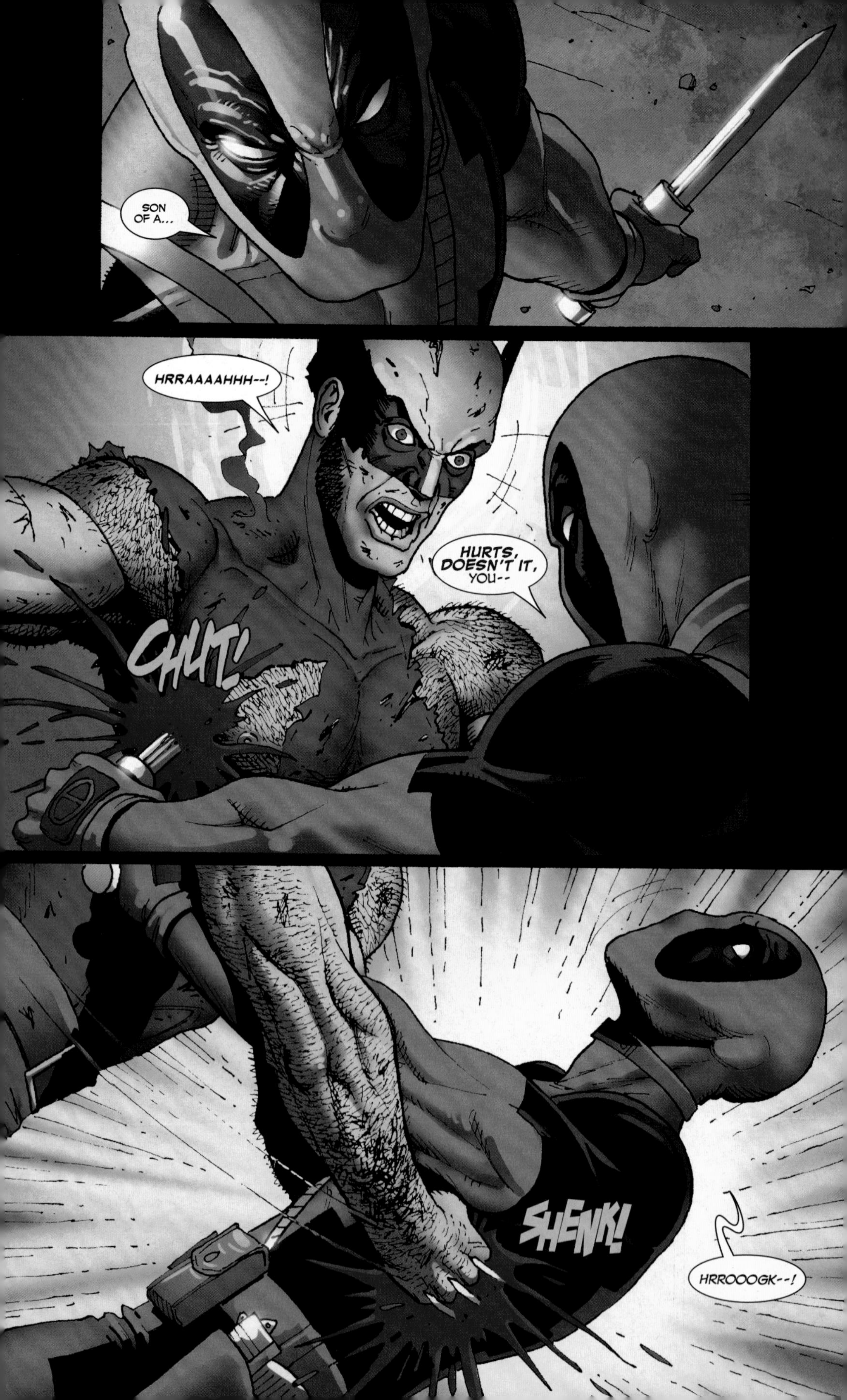
SON OF A...
HRRAAAAHHH--!
HURTS, DOESN'T IT, YOU--
CHUT!
SHENK!
HRROOOGK--!

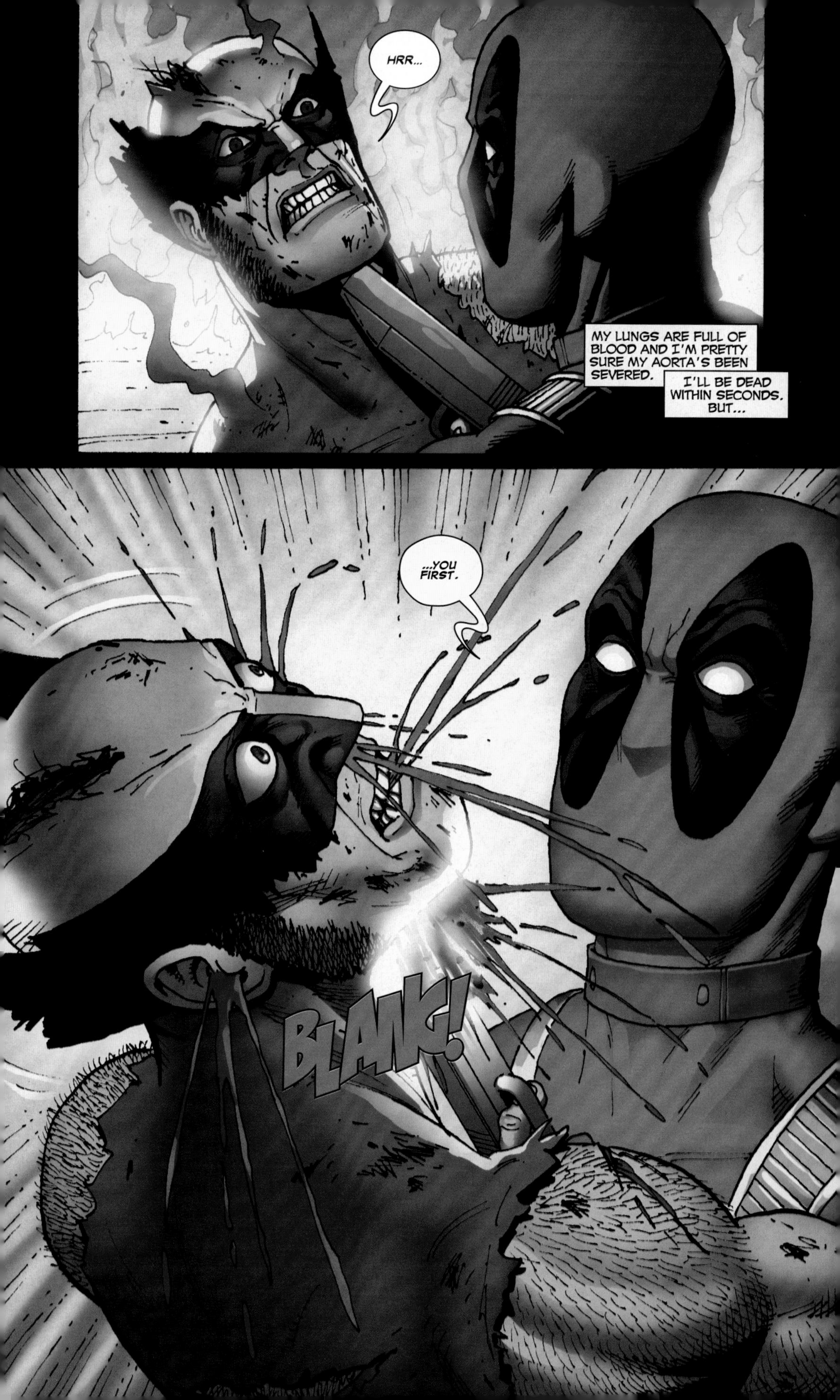
HRR...
MY LUNGS ARE FULL OF BLOOD AND I'M PRETTY SURE MY AORTA'S BEEN SEVERED.
I'LL BE DEAD WITHIN SECONDS. BUT...
...YOU FIRST.
BLANG!

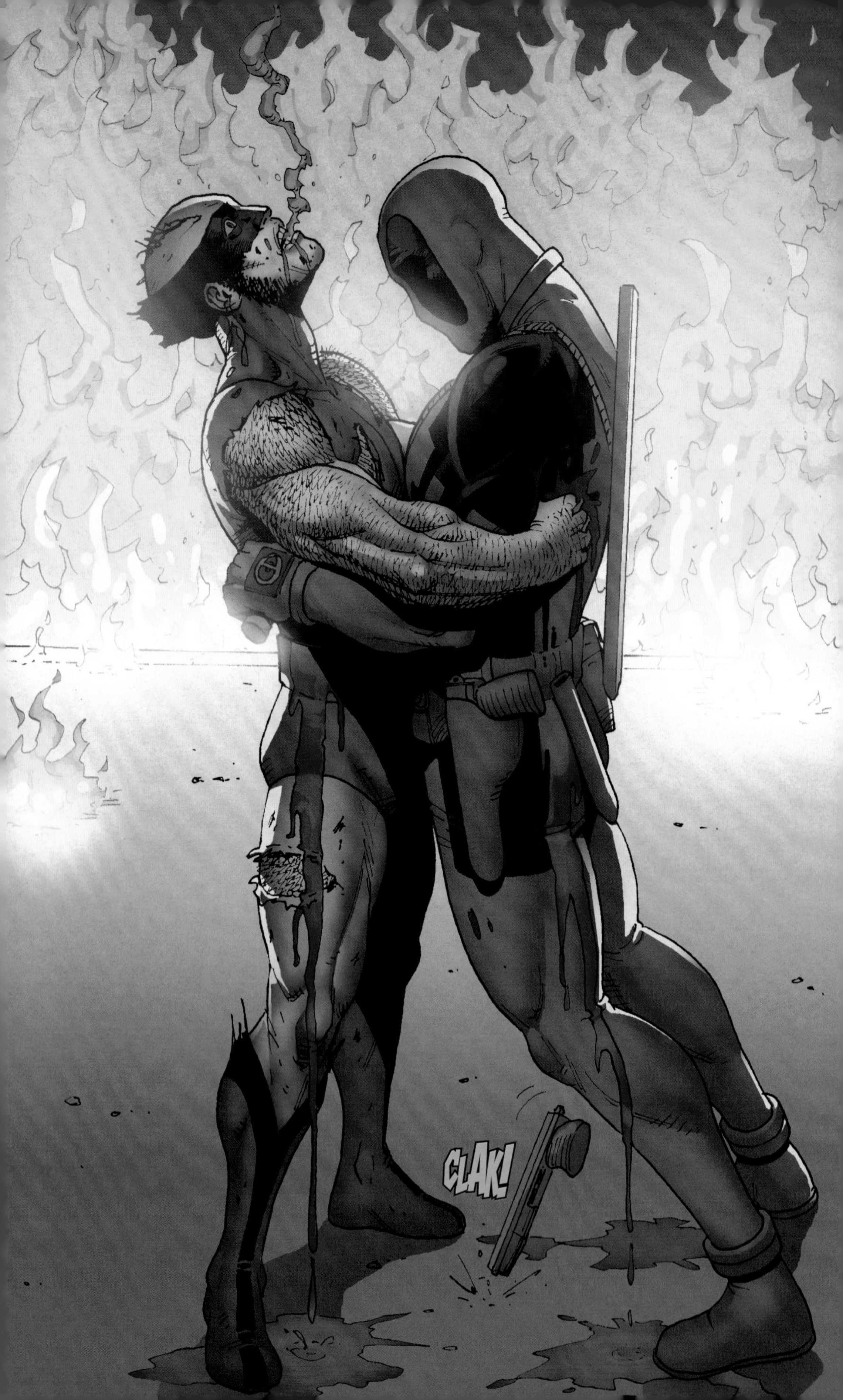
CLAK!

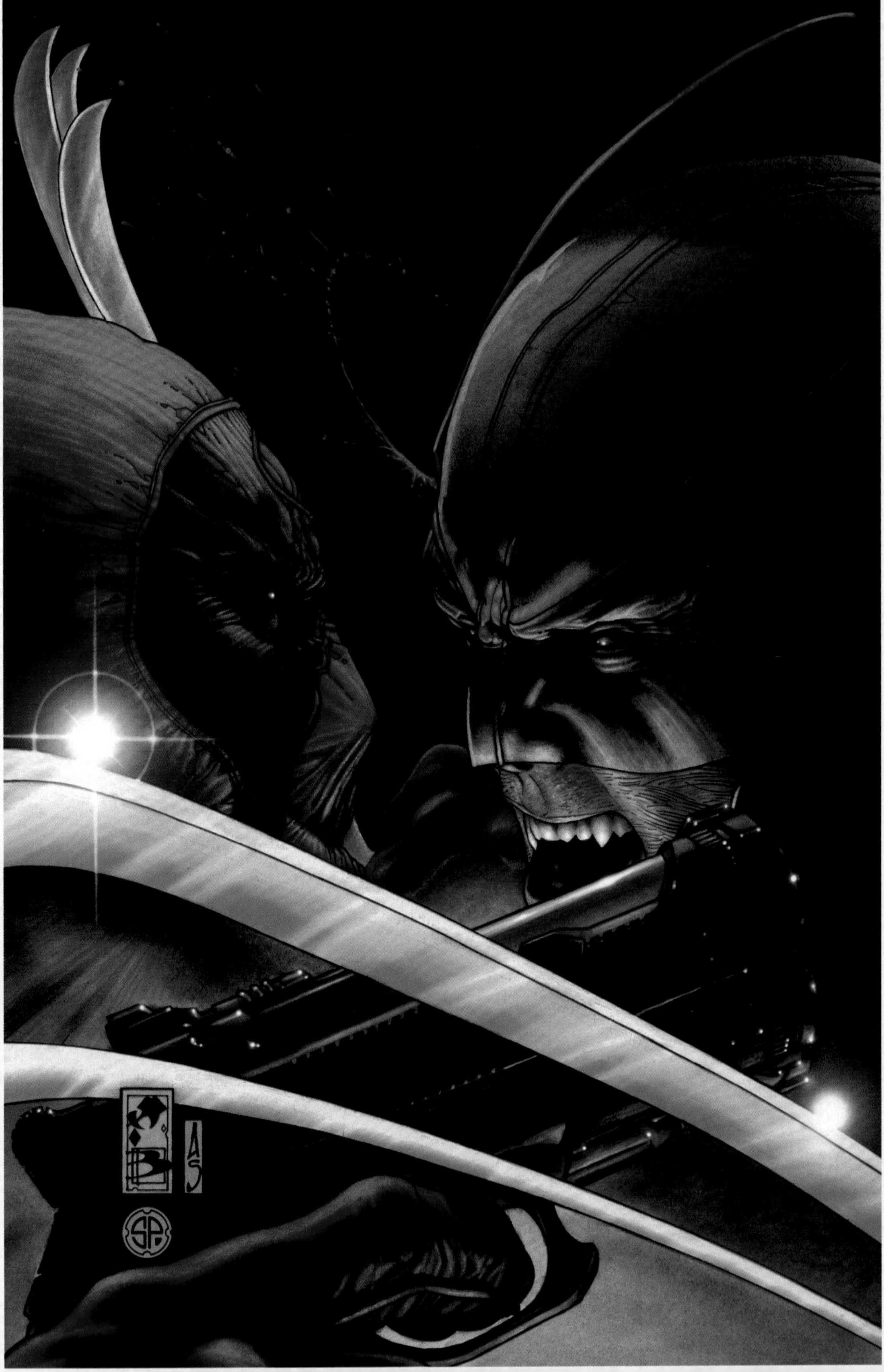

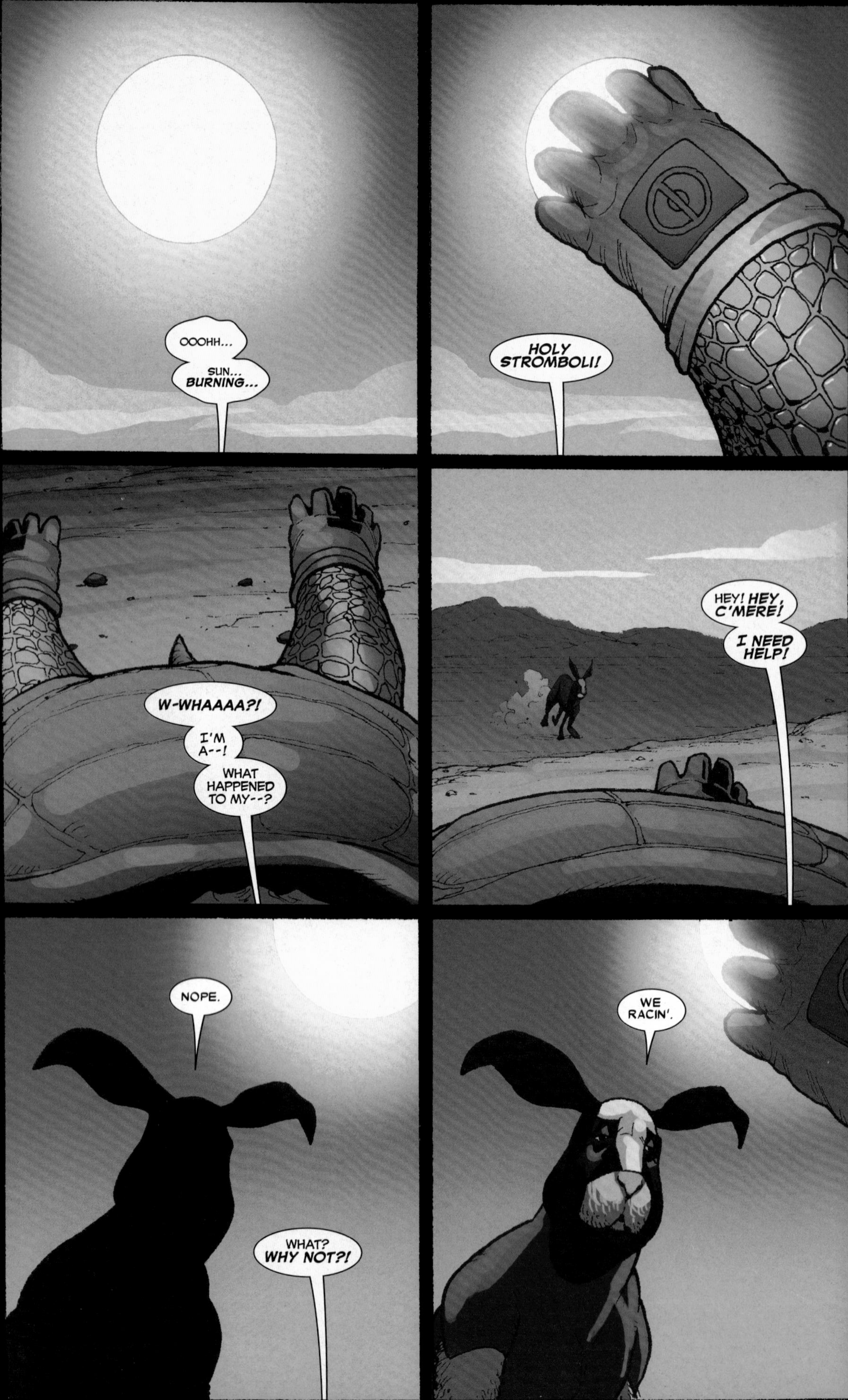
OOOHH...
SUN... BURNING...
HOLY STROMBOLI!
W-WHAAAA?!
I'M A--!
WHAT HAPPENED TO MY--?
HEY! HEY, C'MERE!
I NEED HELP!
NOPE.
WHAT? WHY NOT?!
WE RACIN'.

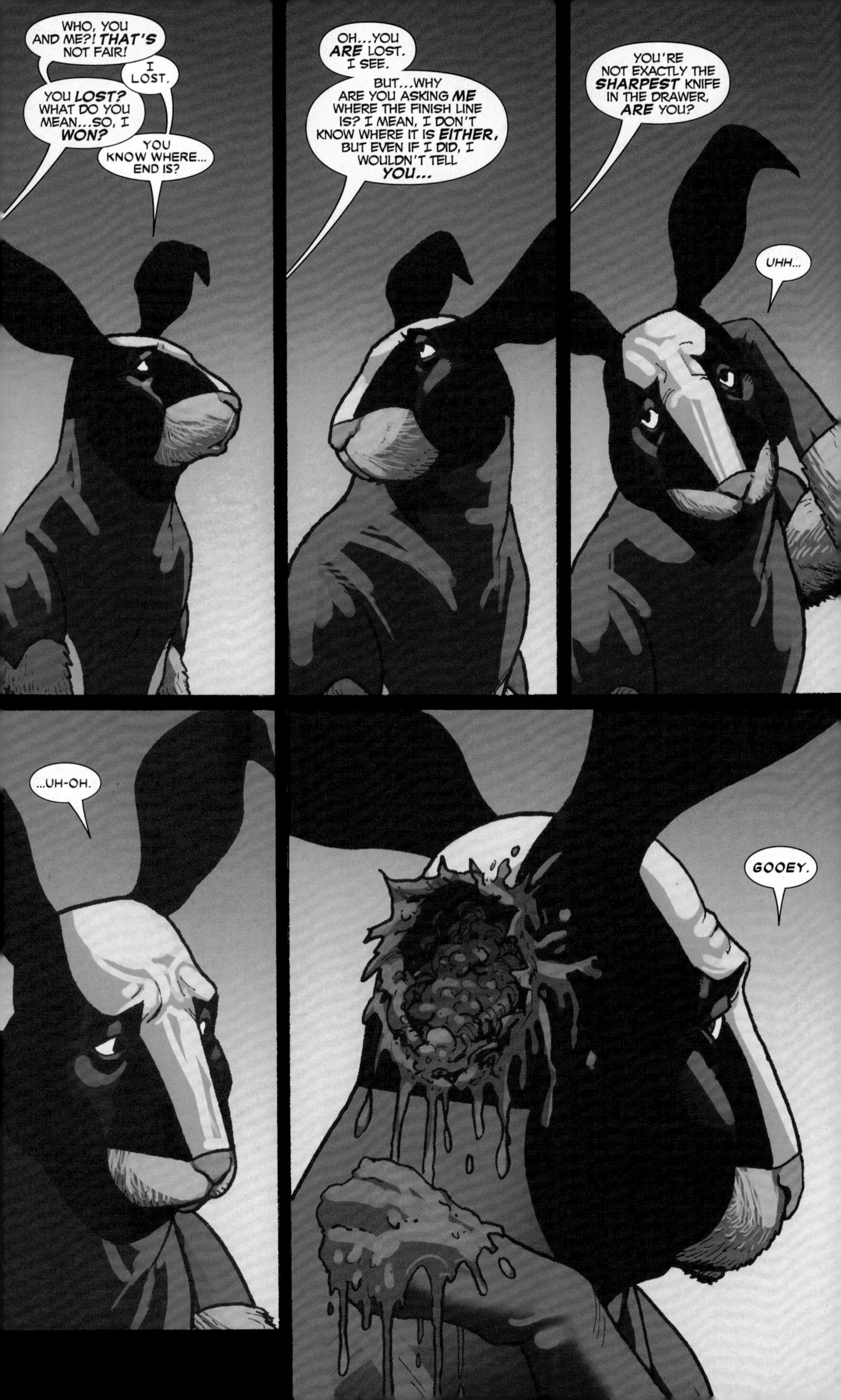
WHO, YOU AND ME?! THAT'S NOT FAIR!
I LOST.
YOU LOST? WHAT DO YOU MEAN...SO, I WON?
YOU KNOW WHERE... END IS?
OH...YOU ARE LOST. I SEE.
BUT...WHY ARE YOU ASKING ME WHERE THE FINISH LINE IS? I MEAN, I DON'T KNOW WHERE IT IS EITHER, BUT EVEN IF I DID, I WOULDN'T TELL YOU...
YOU'RE NOT EXACTLY THE SHARPEST KNIFE IN THE DRAWER, ARE YOU?
UHH...
...UH-OH.
GOOEY.

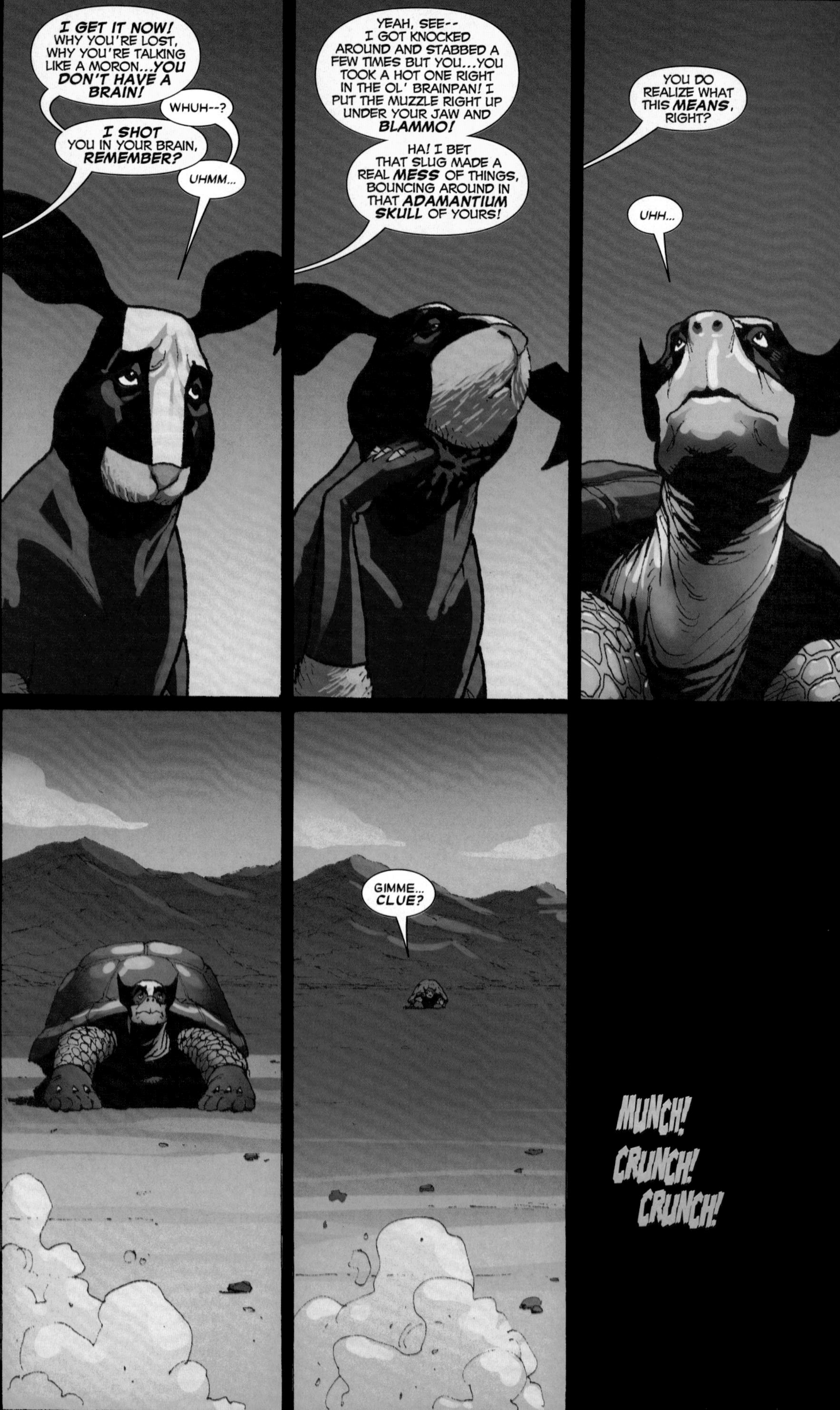
I GET IT NOW! WHY YOU'RE LOST, WHY YOU'RE TALKING LIKE A MORON...YOU DON'T HAVE A BRAIN!
WHUH--?
I SHOT YOU IN YOUR BRAIN, REMEMBER?
UHMM...
YEAH, SEE-- I GOT KNOCKED AROUND AND STABBED A FEW TIMES BUT YOU...YOU TOOK A HOT ONE RIGHT IN THE OL' BRAINPAN! I PUT THE MUZZLE RIGHT UP UNDER YOUR JAW AND BLAMMO!
HA! I BET THAT SLUG MADE A REAL MESS OF THINGS, BOUNCING AROUND IN THAT ADAMANTIUM SKULL OF YOURS!
YOU DO REALIZE WHAT THIS MEANS, RIGHT?
UHH...
GIMME... CLUE?
MUNCH!
CRUNCH!
CRUNCH!

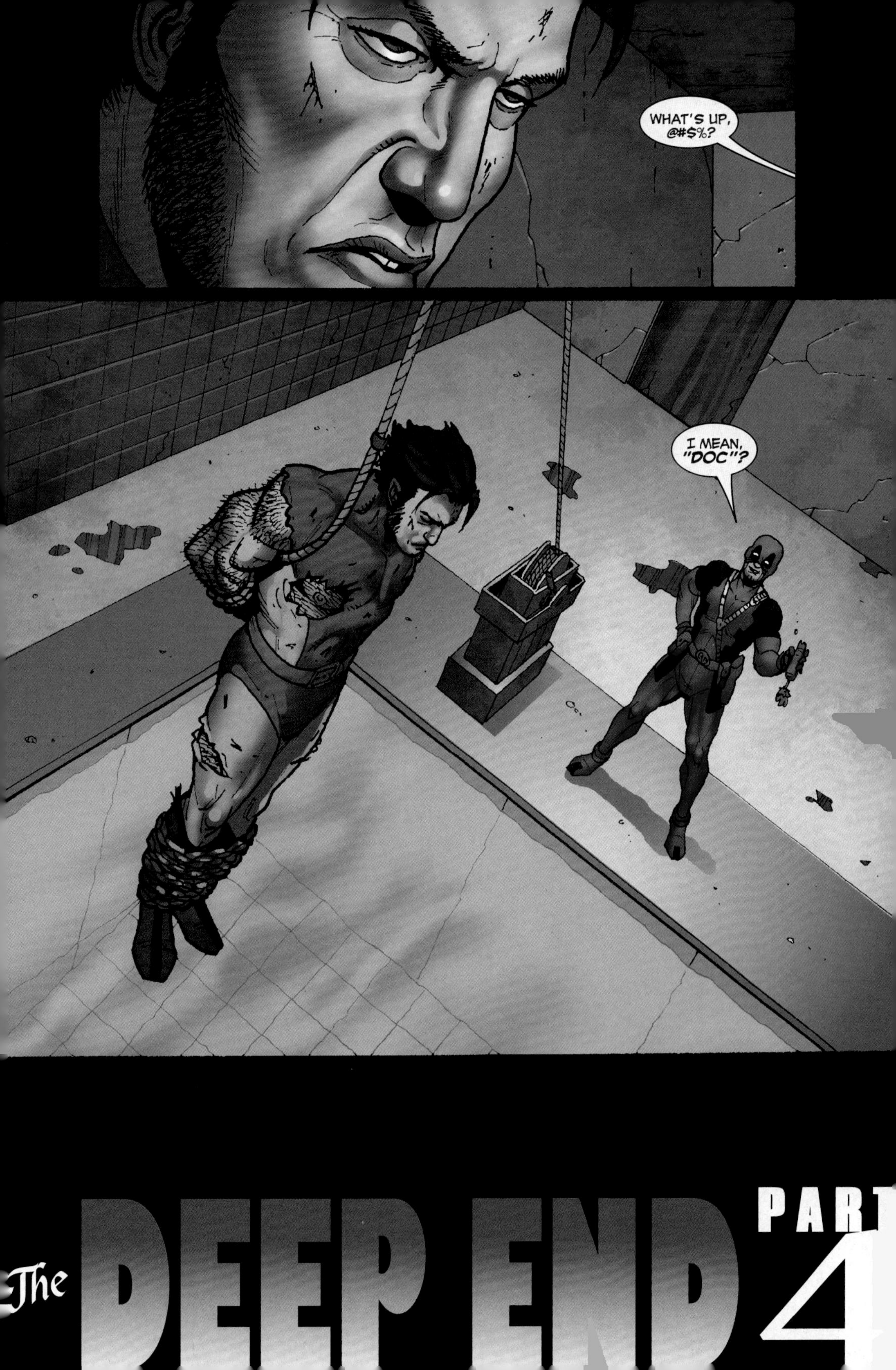
WHAT'S UP, @#$%?
I MEAN, "DOC"?
The DEEP END PART 4

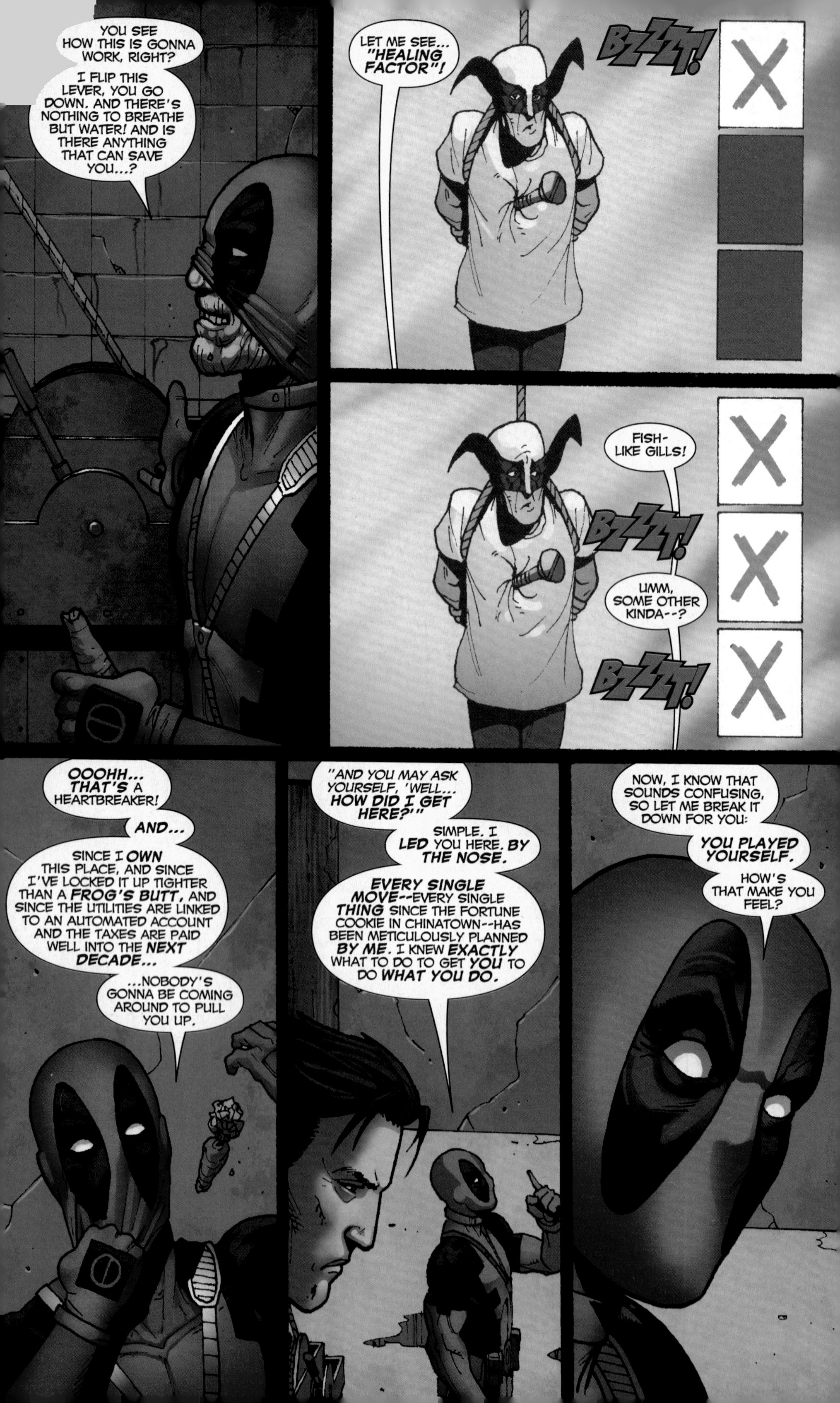
YOU SEE HOW THIS IS GONNA WORK, RIGHT?
I FLIP THIS LEVER, YOU GO DOWN. AND THERE'S NOTHING TO BREATHE BUT WATER! AND IS THERE ANYTHING THAT CAN SAVE YOU...?
LET ME SEE... "HEALING FACTOR"!
BZZZT!
FISH-LIKE GILLS!
BZZZT!
UMM, SOME OTHER KINDA--?
BZZZT!
OOOHH... THAT'S A HEARTBREAKER!
AND...
SINCE I OWN THIS PLACE, AND SINCE I'VE LOCKED IT UP TIGHTER THAN A FROG'S BUTT, AND SINCE THE UTILITIES ARE LINKED TO AN AUTOMATED ACCOUNT AND THE TAXES ARE PAID WELL INTO THE NEXT DECADE...
...NOBODY'S GONNA BE COMING AROUND TO PULL YOU UP.
"AND YOU MAY ASK YOURSELF, 'WELL... HOW DID I GET HERE?'"
SIMPLE. I LED YOU HERE. BY THE NOSE.
EVERY SINGLE MOVE--EVERY SINGLE THING SINCE THE FORTUNE COOKIE IN CHINATOWN--HAS BEEN METICULOUSLY PLANNED BY ME. I KNEW EXACTLY WHAT TO DO TO GET YOU TO DO WHAT YOU DO.
NOW, I KNOW THAT SOUNDS CONFUSING, SO LET ME BREAK IT DOWN FOR YOU:
YOU PLAYED YOURSELF.
HOW'S THAT MAKE YOU FEEL?

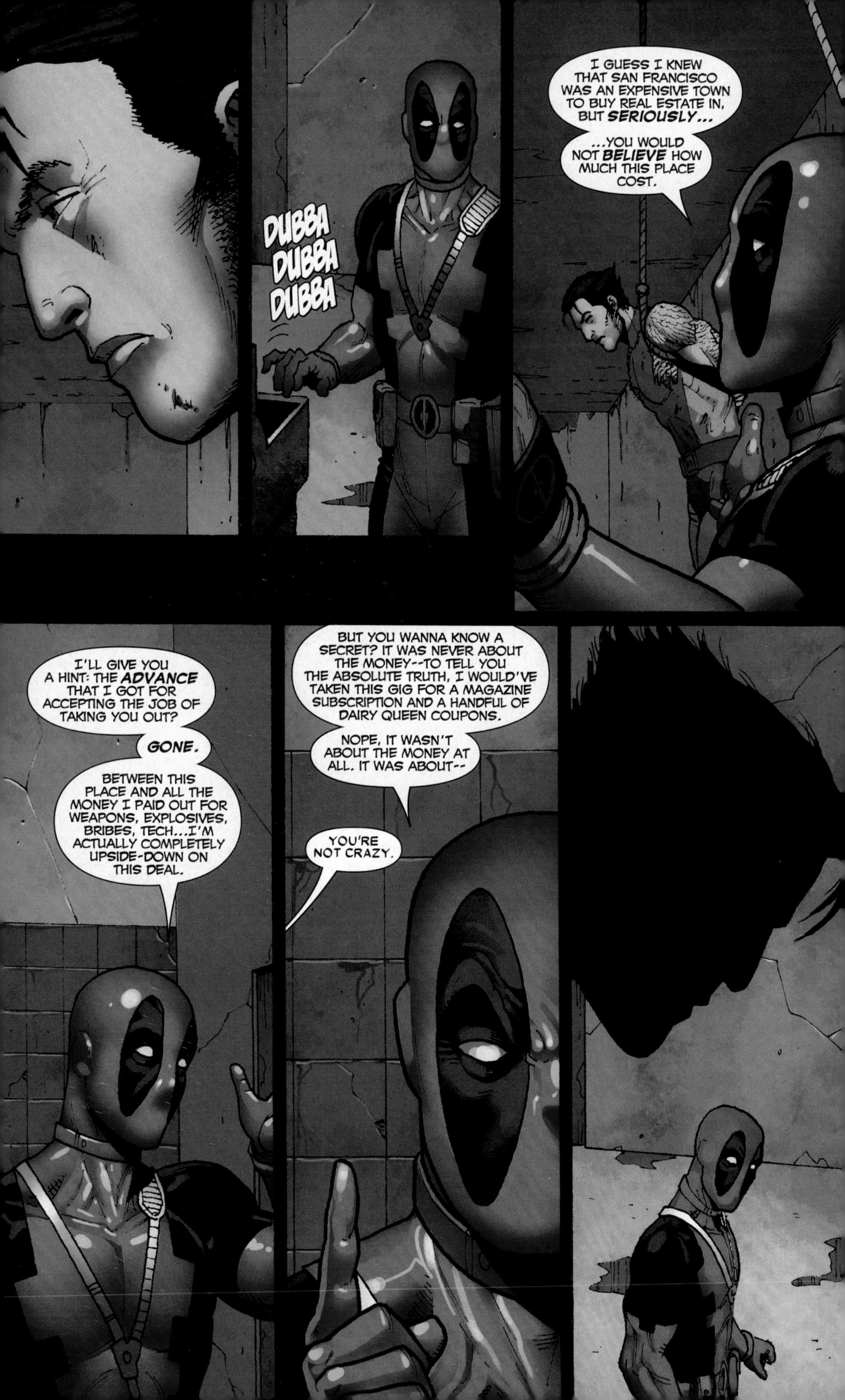
DUBBA DUBBA DUBBA
I GUESS I KNEW THAT SAN FRANCISCO WAS AN EXPENSIVE TOWN TO BUY REAL ESTATE IN, BUT SERIOUSLY...
...YOU WOULD NOT BELIEVE HOW MUCH THIS PLACE COST.
I'LL GIVE YOU A HINT: THE ADVANCE THAT I GOT FOR ACCEPTING THE JOB OF TAKING YOU OUT?
GONE.
BETWEEN THIS PLACE AND ALL THE MONEY I PAID OUT FOR WEAPONS, EXPLOSIVES, BRIBES, TECH...I'M ACTUALLY COMPLETELY UPSIDE-DOWN ON THIS DEAL.
BUT YOU WANNA KNOW A SECRET? IT WAS NEVER ABOUT THE MONEY--TO TELL YOU THE ABSOLUTE TRUTH, I WOULD'VE TAKEN THIS GIG FOR A MAGAZINE SUBSCRIPTION AND A HANDFUL OF DAIRY QUEEN COUPONS.
NOPE, IT WASN'T ABOUT THE MONEY AT ALL. IT WAS ABOUT--
YOU'RE NOT CRAZY.

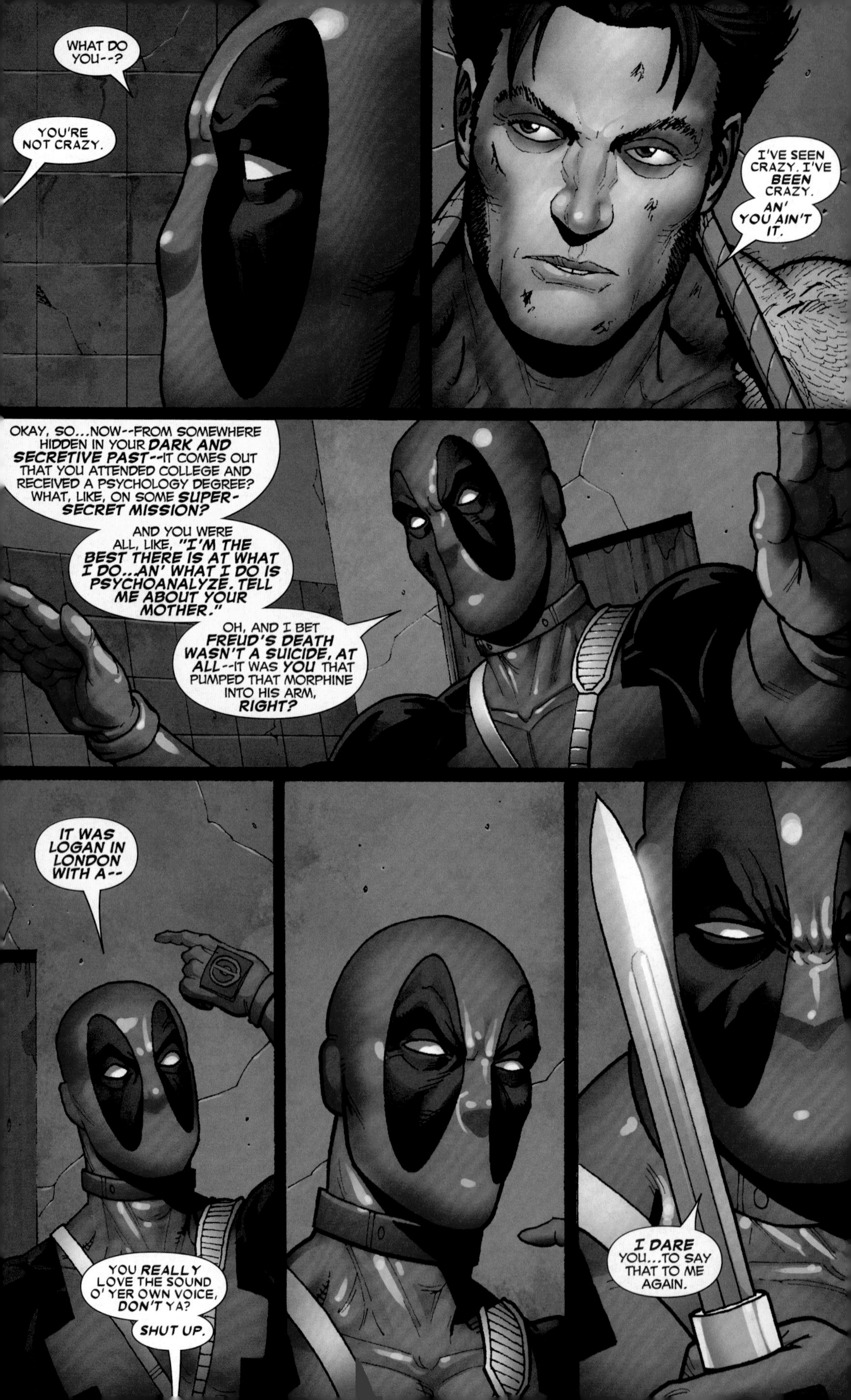
WHAT DO YOU--?
YOU'RE NOT CRAZY.
I'VE SEEN CRAZY. I'VE BEEN CRAZY.
AN' YOU AIN'T IT.
OKAY, SO...NOW--FROM SOMEWHERE HIDDEN IN YOUR DARK AND SECRETIVE PAST--IT COMES OUT THAT YOU ATTENDED COLLEGE AND RECEIVED A PSYCHOLOGY DEGREE? WHAT, LIKE, ON SOME SUPER-SECRET MISSION?
AND YOU WERE ALL, LIKE, "I'M THE BEST THERE IS AT WHAT I DO...AN' WHAT I DO IS PSYCHOANALYZE. TELL ME ABOUT YOUR MOTHER."
OH, AND I BET FREUD'S DEATH WASN'T A SUICIDE, AT ALL--IT WAS YOU THAT PUMPED THAT MORPHINE INTO HIS ARM, RIGHT?
IT WAS LOGAN IN LONDON WITH A--
YOU REALLY LOVE THE SOUND O' YER OWN VOICE, DON'T YA?
SHUT UP.
I DARE YOU...TO SAY THAT TO ME AGAIN.

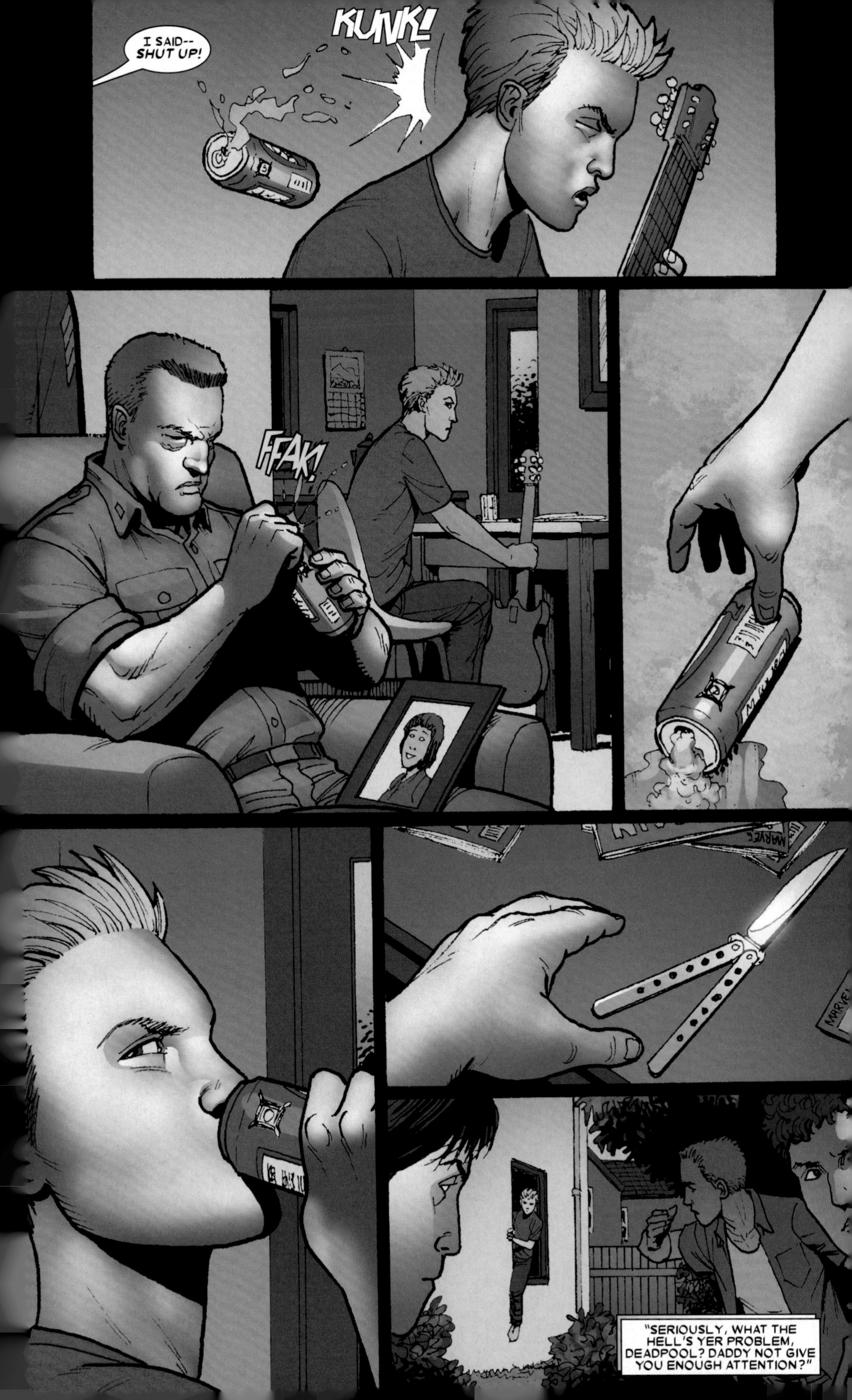
I SAID--
SHUT UP!
KUNK!
FFAK!
"SERIOUSLY, WHAT THE HELL'S YER PROBLEM, DEADPOOL? DADDY NOT GIVE YOU ENOUGH ATTENTION?"

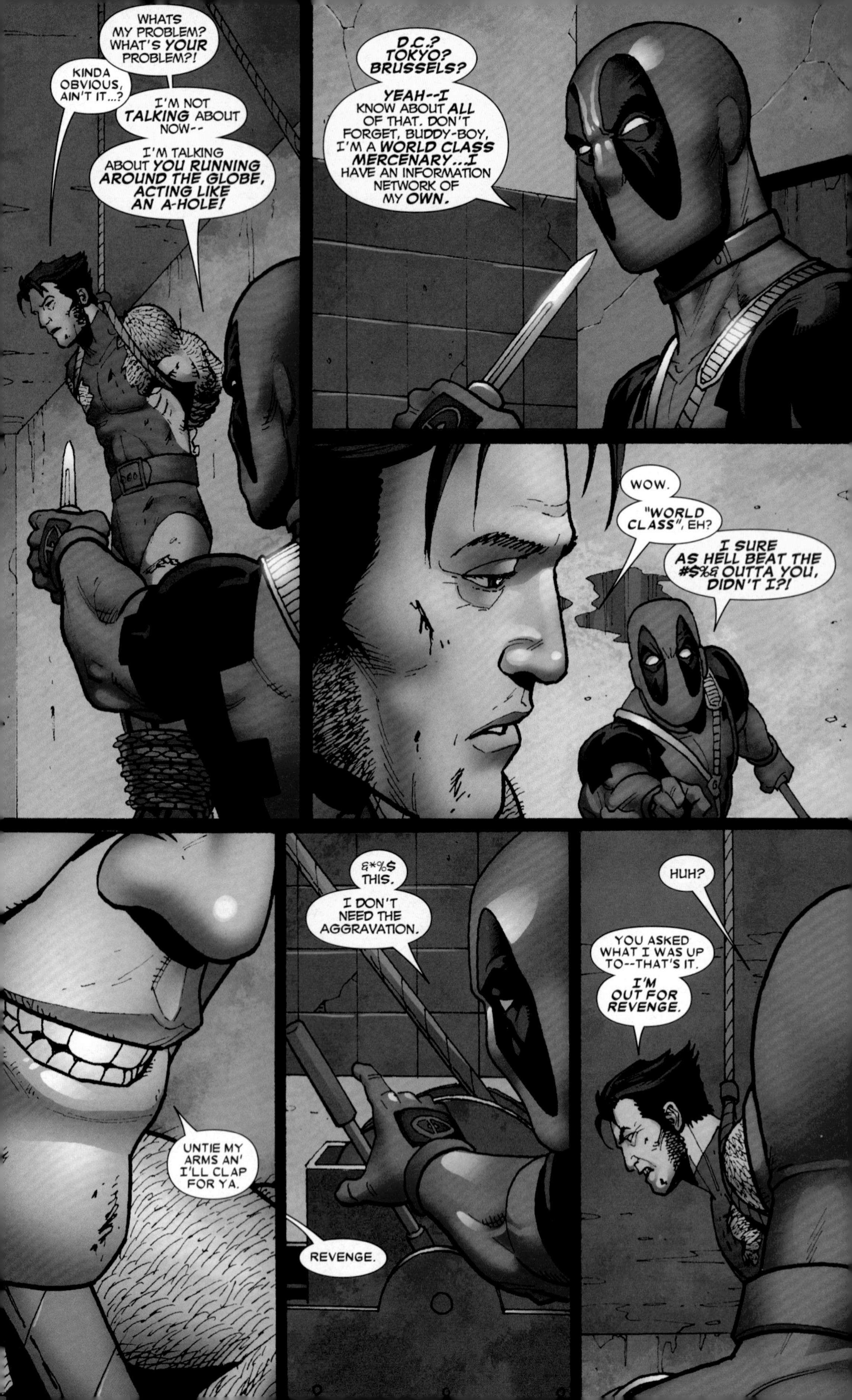
WHATS MY PROBLEM? WHAT'S YOUR PROBLEM?!
KINDA OBVIOUS, AIN'T IT...?
I'M NOT TALKING ABOUT NOW--
I'M TALKING ABOUT YOU RUNNING AROUND THE GLOBE, ACTING LIKE AN A-HOLE!
D.C.? TOKYO? BRUSSELS?
YEAH--I KNOW ABOUT ALL OF THAT. DON'T FORGET, BUDDY-BOY, I'M A WORLD CLASS MERCENARY...I HAVE AN INFORMATION NETWORK OF MY OWN.
WOW.
"WORLD CLASS", EH?
I SURE AS HELL BEAT THE #$%& OUTTA YOU, DIDN'T I?!
UNTIE MY ARMS AN' I'LL CLAP FOR YA.
&*%$ THIS.
I DON'T NEED THE AGGRAVATION.
REVENGE.
HUH?
YOU ASKED WHAT I WAS UP TO--THAT'S IT.
I'M OUT FOR REVENGE.

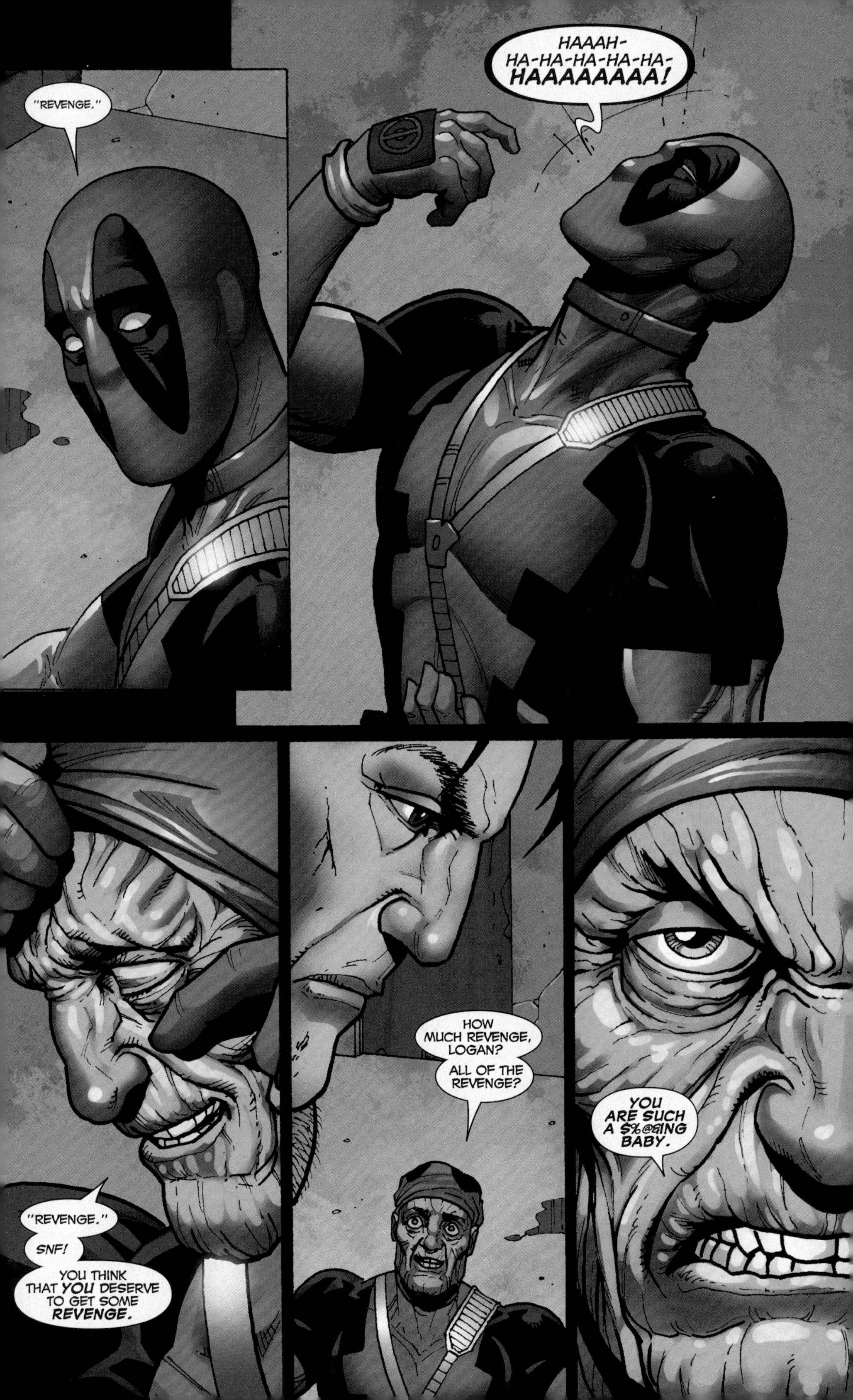
"REVENGE."
HAAAH-HA-HA-HA-HA-HA-HA-HAAAAAAAA!
"REVENGE."
SNF!
YOU THINK THAT YOU DESERVE TO GET SOME REVENGE.
HOW MUCH REVENGE, LOGAN?
ALL OF THE REVENGE?
YOU ARE SUCH A $%@&ING BABY.

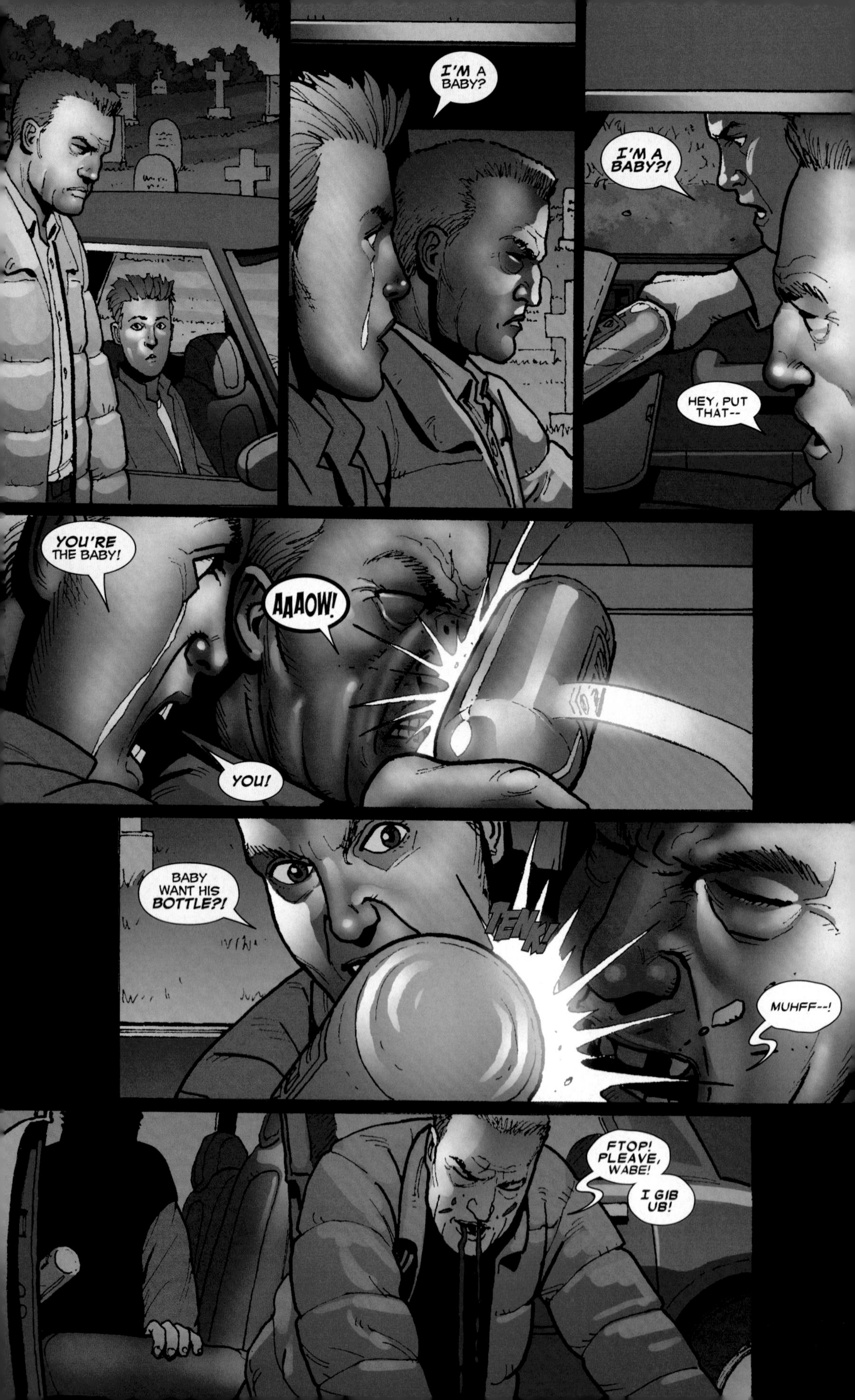
I'M A BABY?
I'M A BABY?!
HEY, PUT THAT--
YOU'RE THE BABY!
AAAOW!
YOU!
BABY WANT HIS BOTTLE?!
TENK!
MUHFF--!
FTOP! PLEAVE, WABE!
I GIB UB!

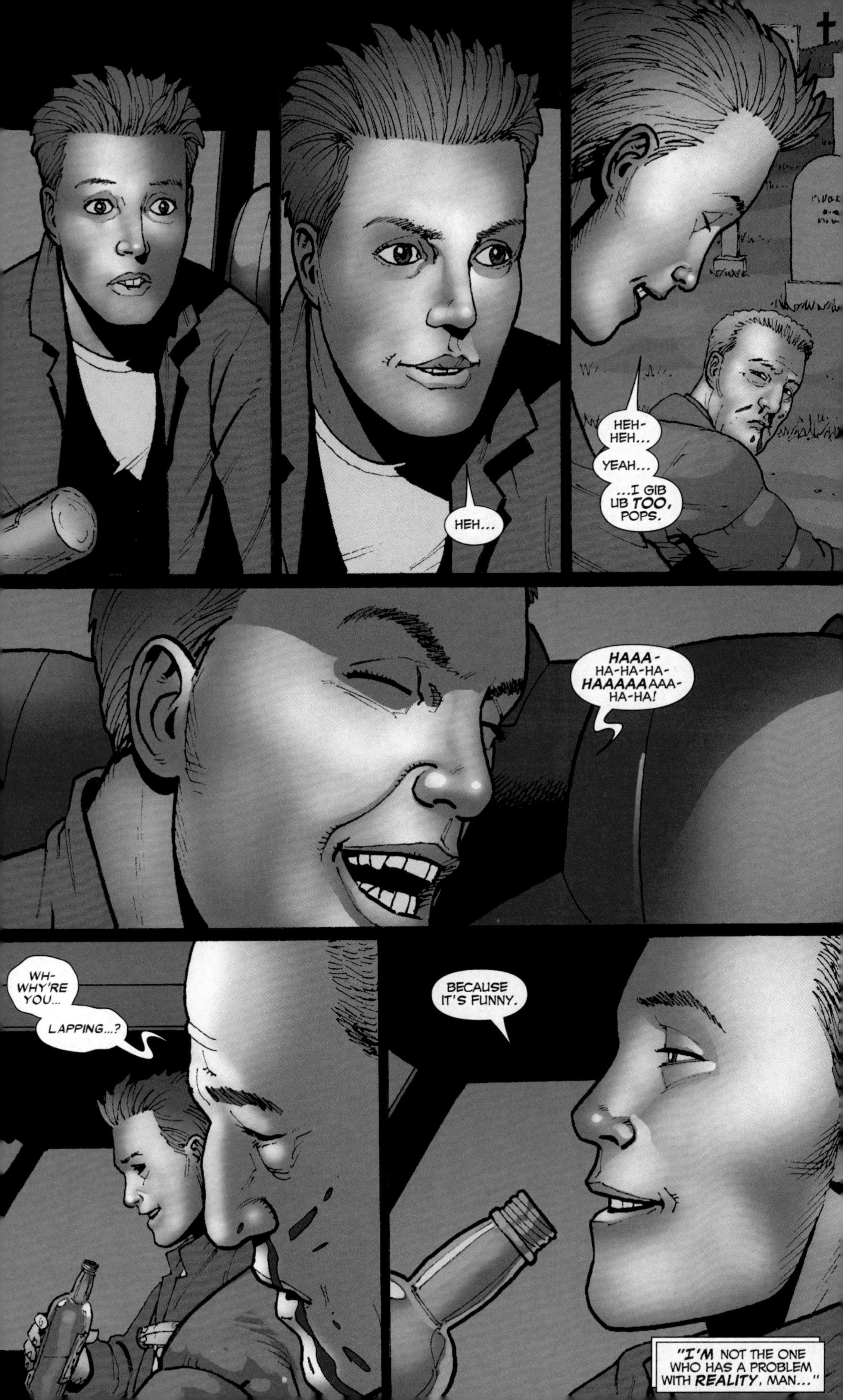
HEH...
HEH-
HEH...
YEAH...
...I GIB UB TOO, POPS.
HAAA-HA-HA-HA-HAAAAAAAA-HA-HA!
WH-WHY'RE YOU...
LAPPING...?
BECAUSE IT'S FUNNY.
"I'M NOT THE ONE WHO HAS A PROBLEM WITH REALITY, MAN..."

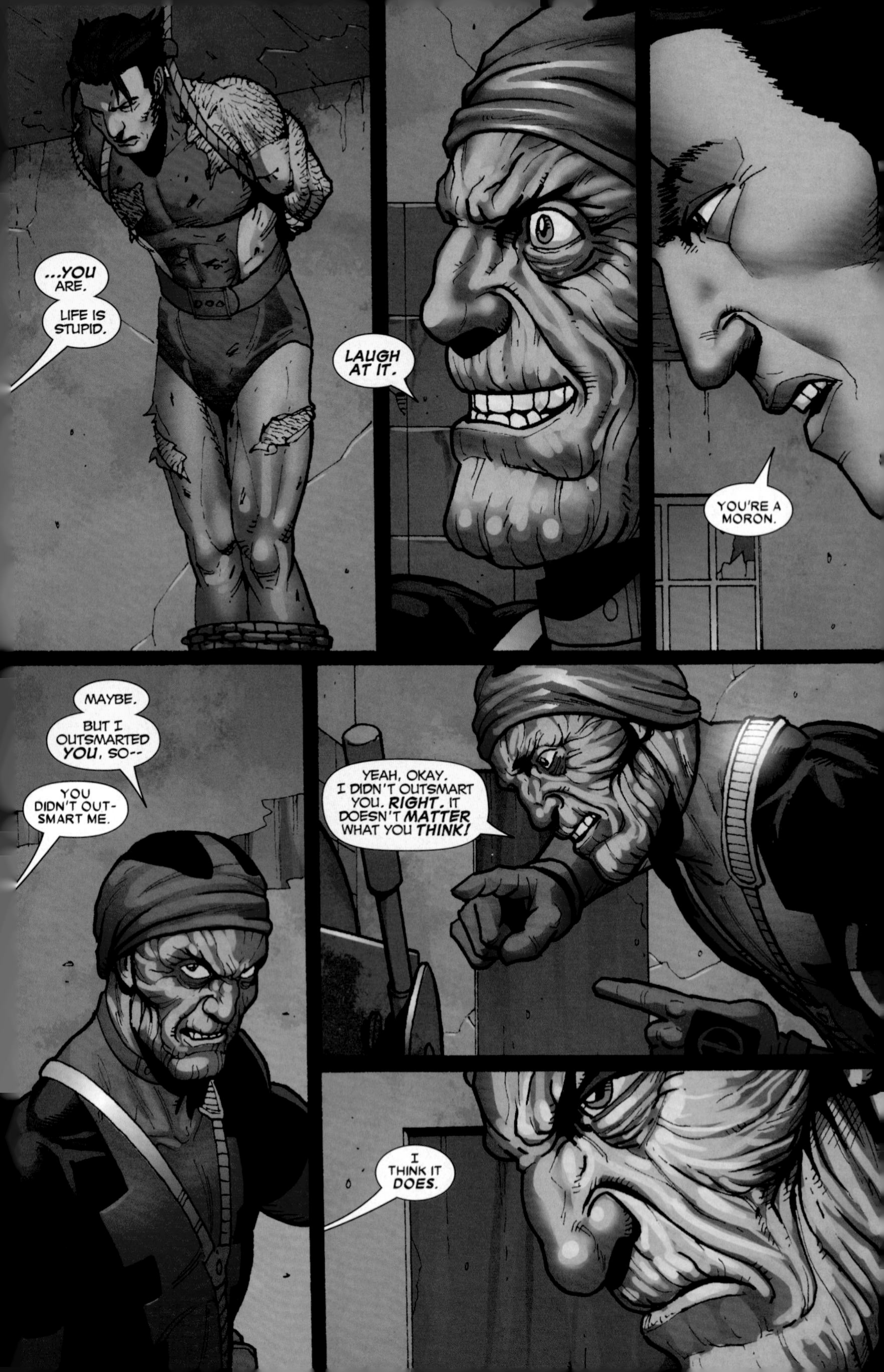

...YOU ARE.
LIFE IS STUPID.
LAUGH AT IT.
YOU'RE A MORON.
MAYBE.
BUT I OUTSMARTED YOU, SO--
YOU DIDN'T OUT-SMART ME.
YEAH, OKAY. I DIDN'T OUTSMART YOU. RIGHT. IT DOESN'T MATTER WHAT YOU THINK!
I THINK IT DOES.

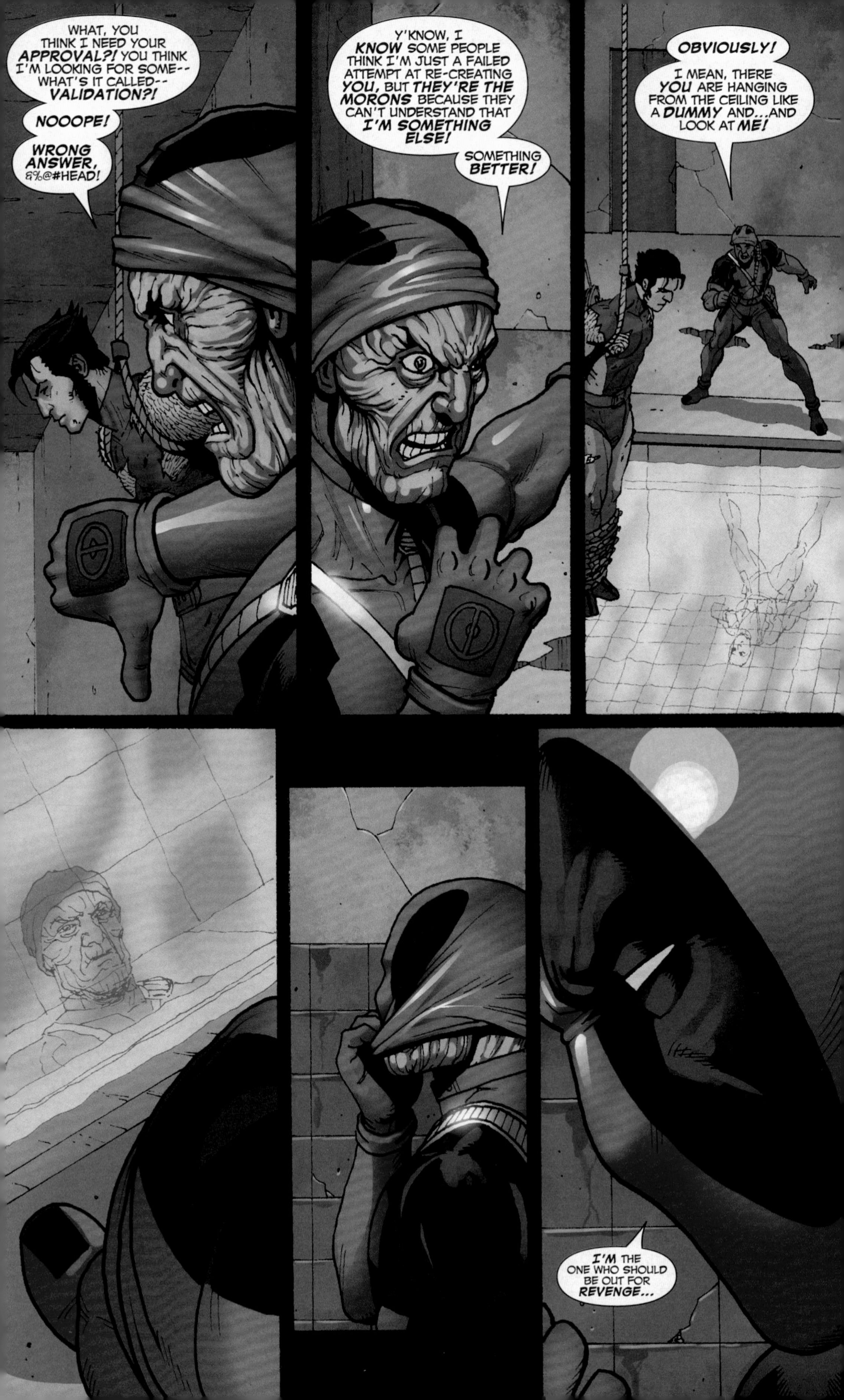
WHAT, YOU THINK I NEED YOUR APPROVAL?! YOU THINK I'M LOOKING FOR SOME--WHAT'S IT CALLED--VALIDATION?!
NOOOPE!
WRONG ANSWER, &%@#HEAD!
Y'KNOW, I KNOW SOME PEOPLE THINK I'M JUST A FAILED ATTEMPT AT RE-CREATING YOU, BUT THEY'RE THE MORONS BECAUSE THEY CAN'T UNDERSTAND THAT I'M SOMETHING ELSE!
SOMETHING BETTER!
OBVIOUSLY!
I MEAN, THERE YOU ARE HANGING FROM THE CEILING LIKE A DUMMY AND...AND LOOK AT ME!
I'M THE ONE WHO SHOULD BE OUT FOR REVENGE...

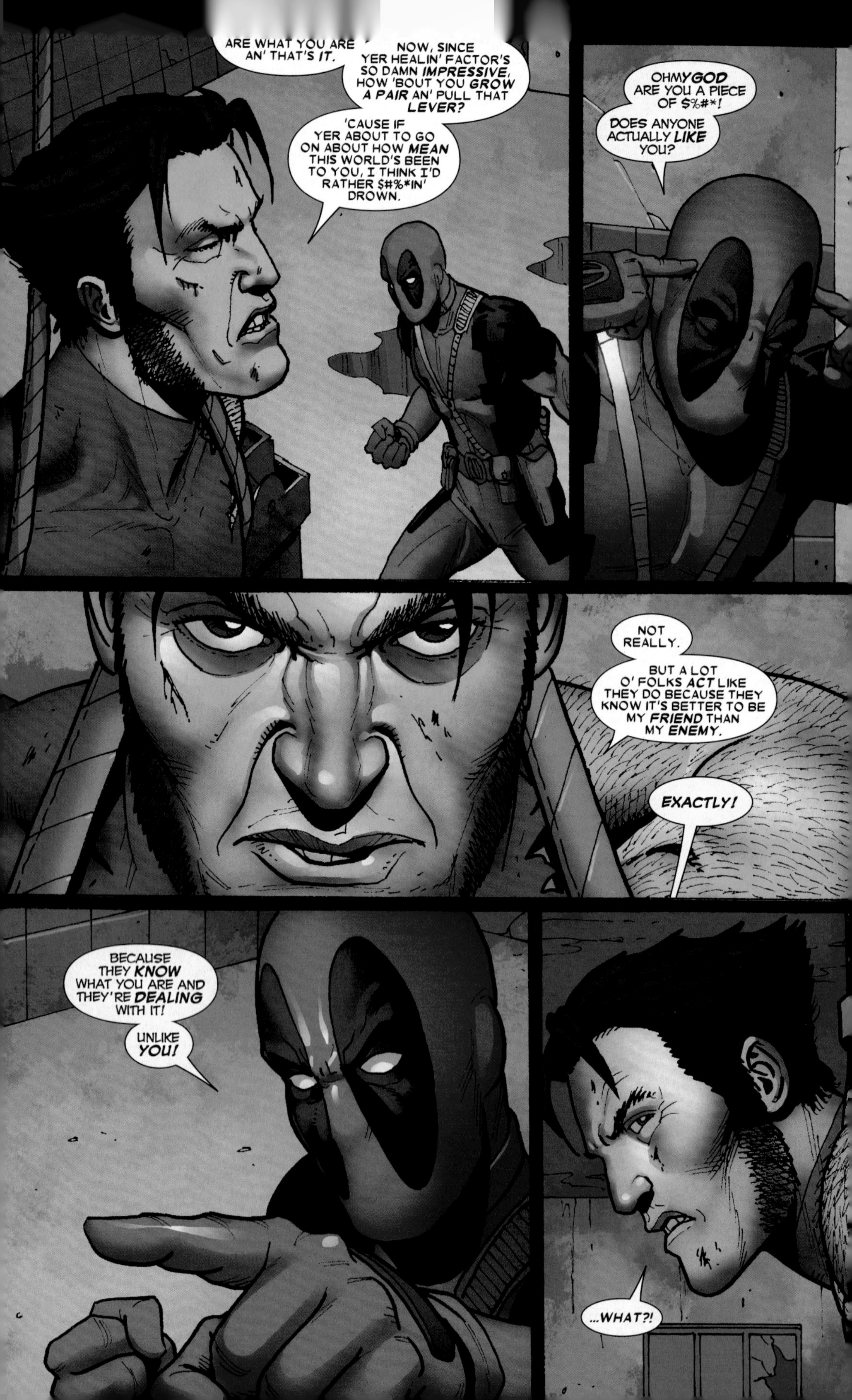
ARE WHAT YOU ARE AN' THAT'S IT.
NOW, SINCE YER HEALIN' FACTOR'S SO DAMN IMPRESSIVE, HOW 'BOUT YOU GROW A PAIR AN' PULL THAT LEVER?
'CAUSE IF YER ABOUT TO GO ON ABOUT HOW MEAN THIS WORLD'S BEEN TO YOU, I THINK I'D RATHER $#%*IN' DROWN.
OHMYGOD ARE YOU A PIECE OF $%#*!
DOES ANYONE ACTUALLY LIKE YOU?
NOT REALLY.
BUT A LOT O' FOLKS ACT LIKE THEY DO BECAUSE THEY KNOW IT'S BETTER TO BE MY FRIEND THAN MY ENEMY.
EXACTLY!
BECAUSE THEY KNOW WHAT YOU ARE AND THEY'RE DEALING WITH IT!
UNLIKE YOU!
...WHAT?!

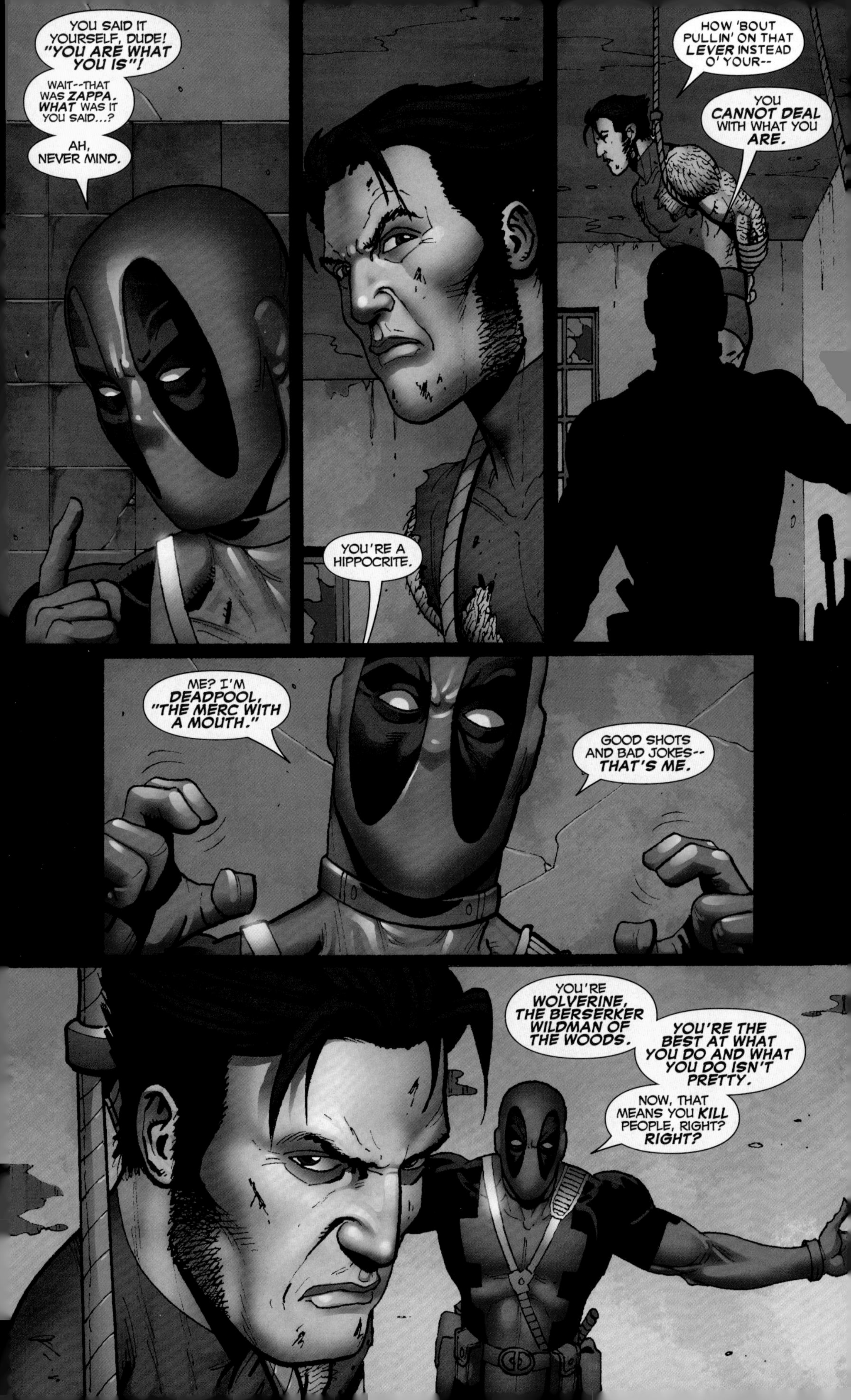
YOU SAID IT YOURSELF, DUDE! "YOU ARE WHAT YOU IS"!
WAIT--THAT WAS ZAPPA. WHAT WAS IT YOU SAID...?
AH, NEVER MIND.
YOU'RE A HIPPOCRITE.
HOW 'BOUT PULLIN' ON THAT LEVER INSTEAD O' YOUR--
YOU CANNOT DEAL WITH WHAT YOU ARE.
ME? I'M DEADPOOL, "THE MERC WITH A MOUTH."
GOOD SHOTS AND BAD JOKES-- THAT'S ME.
YOU'RE WOLVERINE, THE BERSERKER WILDMAN OF THE WOODS.
YOU'RE THE BEST AT WHAT YOU DO AND WHAT YOU DO ISN'T PRETTY.
NOW, THAT MEANS YOU KILL PEOPLE, RIGHT? RIGHT?

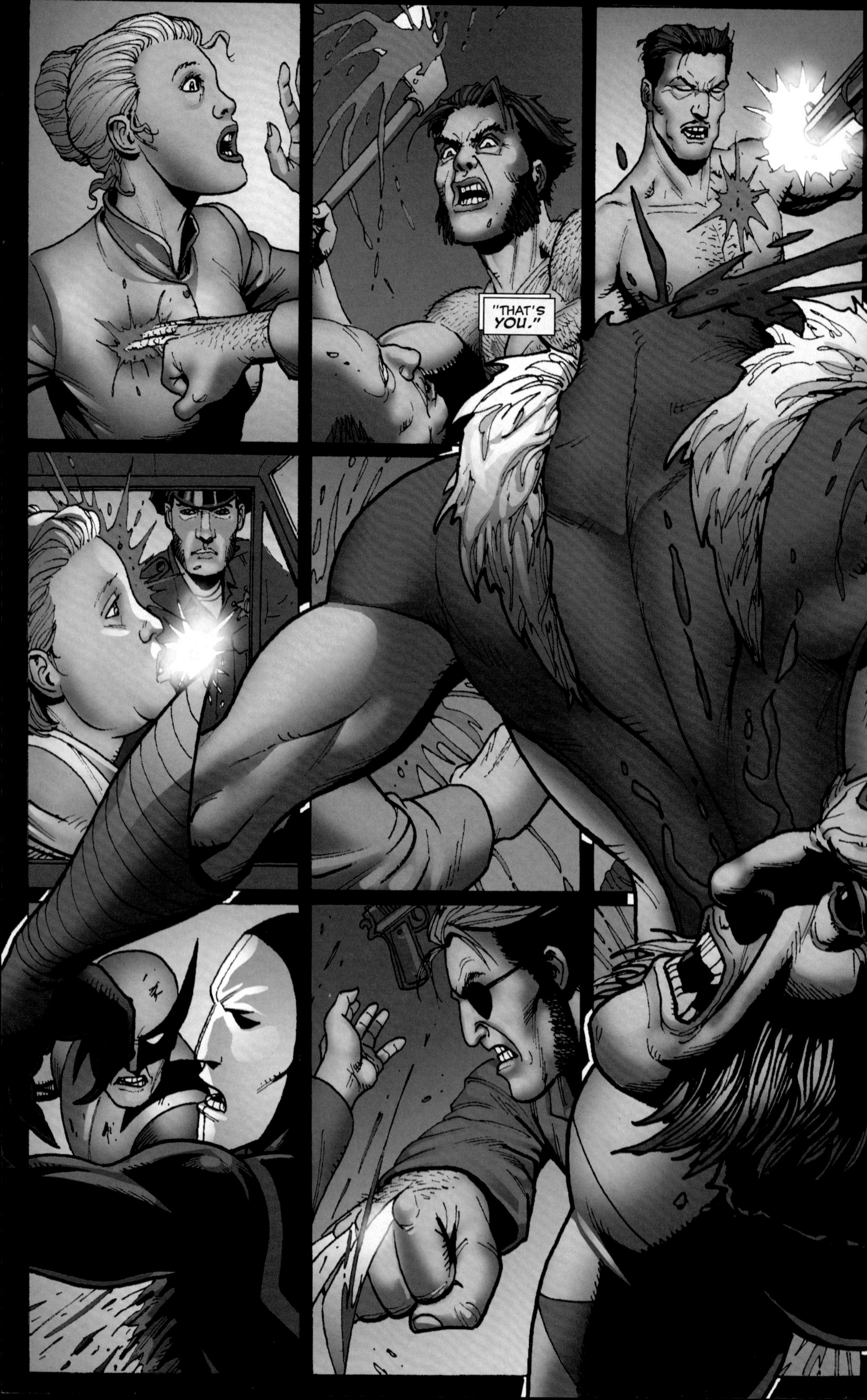
"THAT'S YOU."

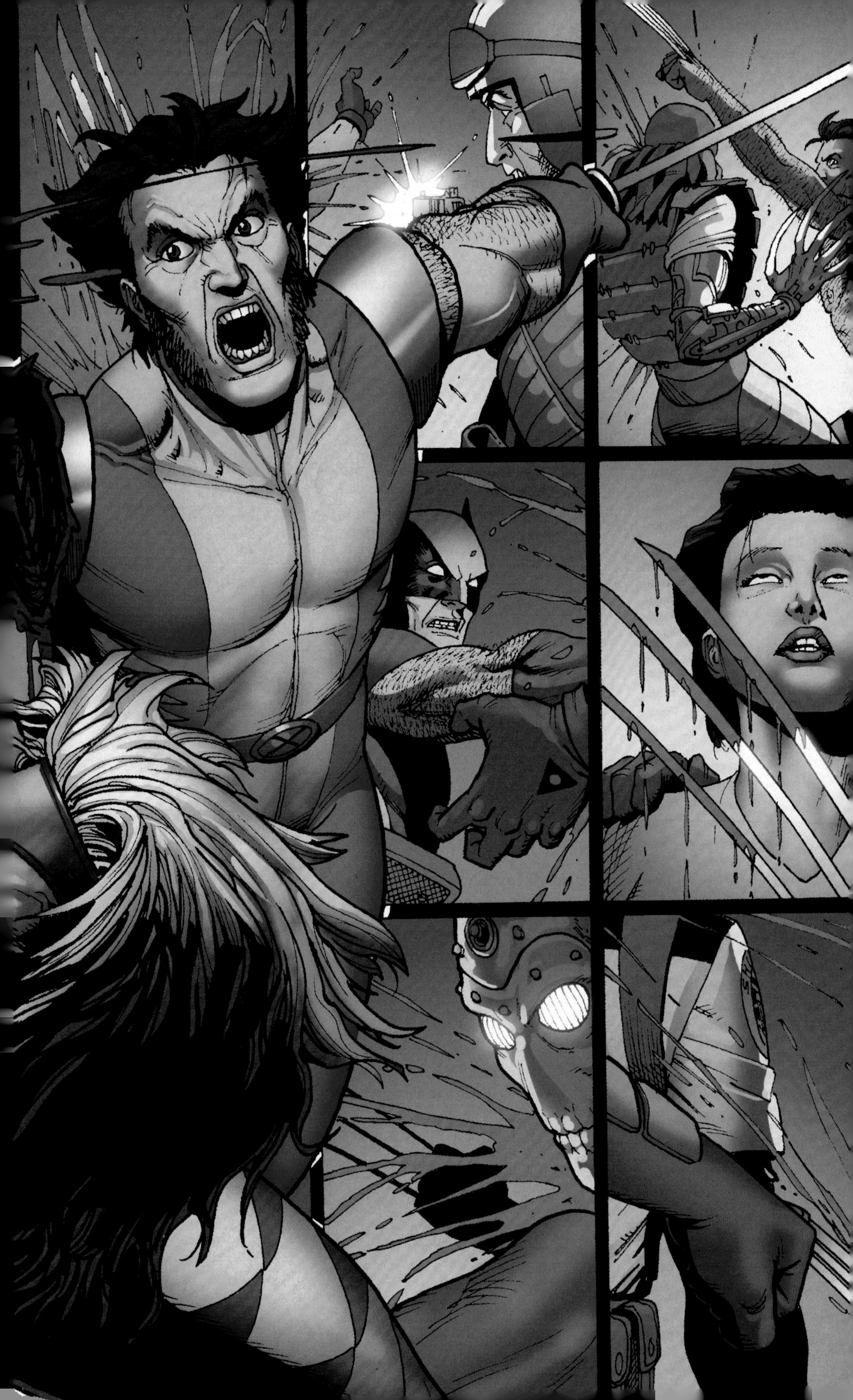

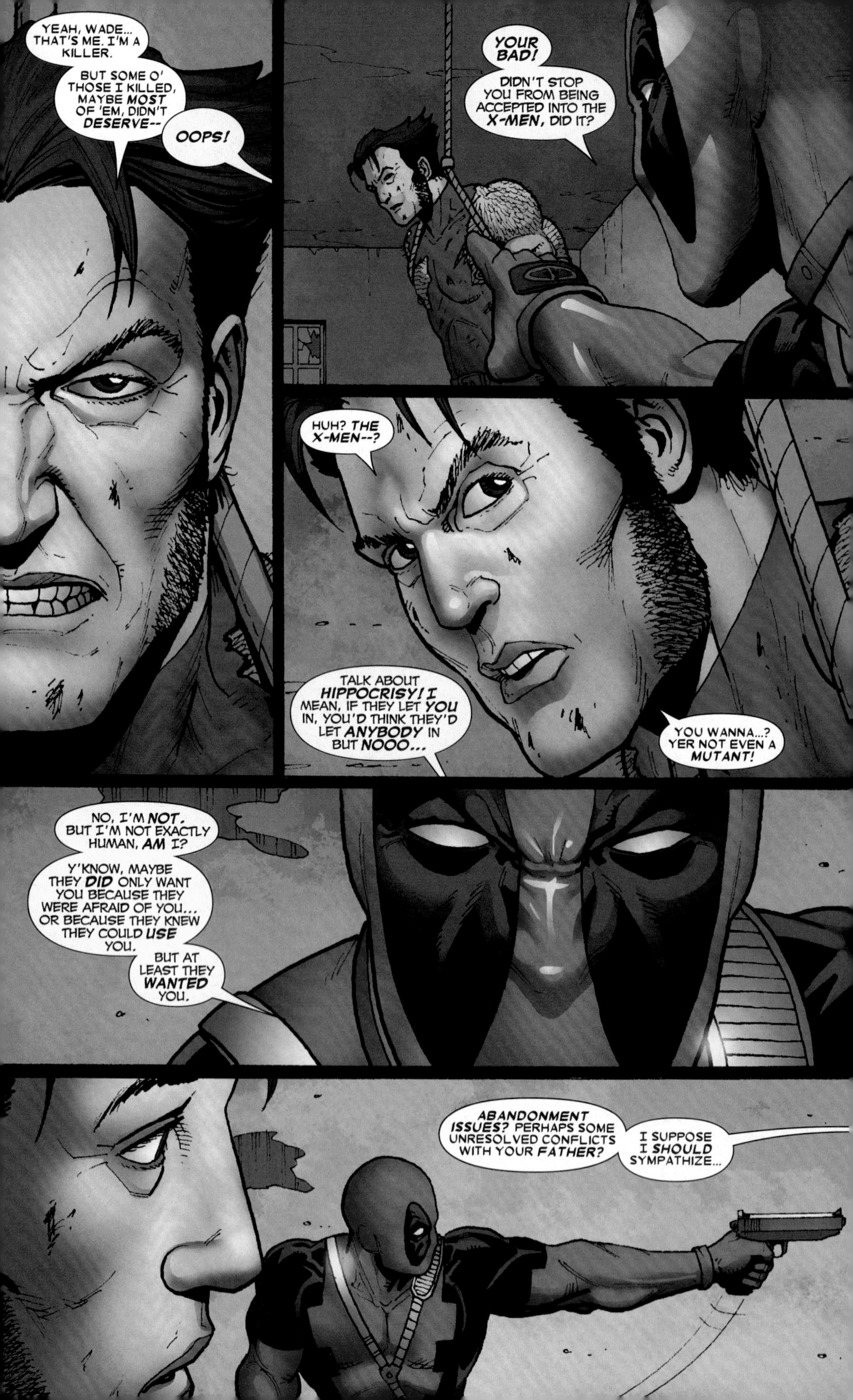
YEAH, WADE... THAT'S ME. I'M A KILLER.
BUT SOME O' THOSE I KILLED, MAYBE MOST OF 'EM, DIDN'T DESERVE--
OOPS!
YOUR BAD!
DIDN'T STOP YOU FROM BEING ACCEPTED INTO THE X-MEN, DID IT?
HUH? THE X-MEN--?
TALK ABOUT HIPPOCRISY! I MEAN, IF THEY LET YOU IN, YOU'D THINK THEY'D LET ANYBODY IN BUT NOOO...
YOU WANNA...? YER NOT EVEN A MUTANT!
NO, I'M NOT. BUT I'M NOT EXACTLY HUMAN, AM I?
Y'KNOW, MAYBE THEY DID ONLY WANT YOU BECAUSE THEY WERE AFRAID OF YOU... OR BECAUSE THEY KNEW THEY COULD USE YOU.
BUT AT LEAST THEY WANTED YOU.
ABANDONMENT ISSUES? PERHAPS SOME UNRESOLVED CONFLICTS WITH YOUR FATHER?
I SUPPOSE I SHOULD SYMPATHIZE...

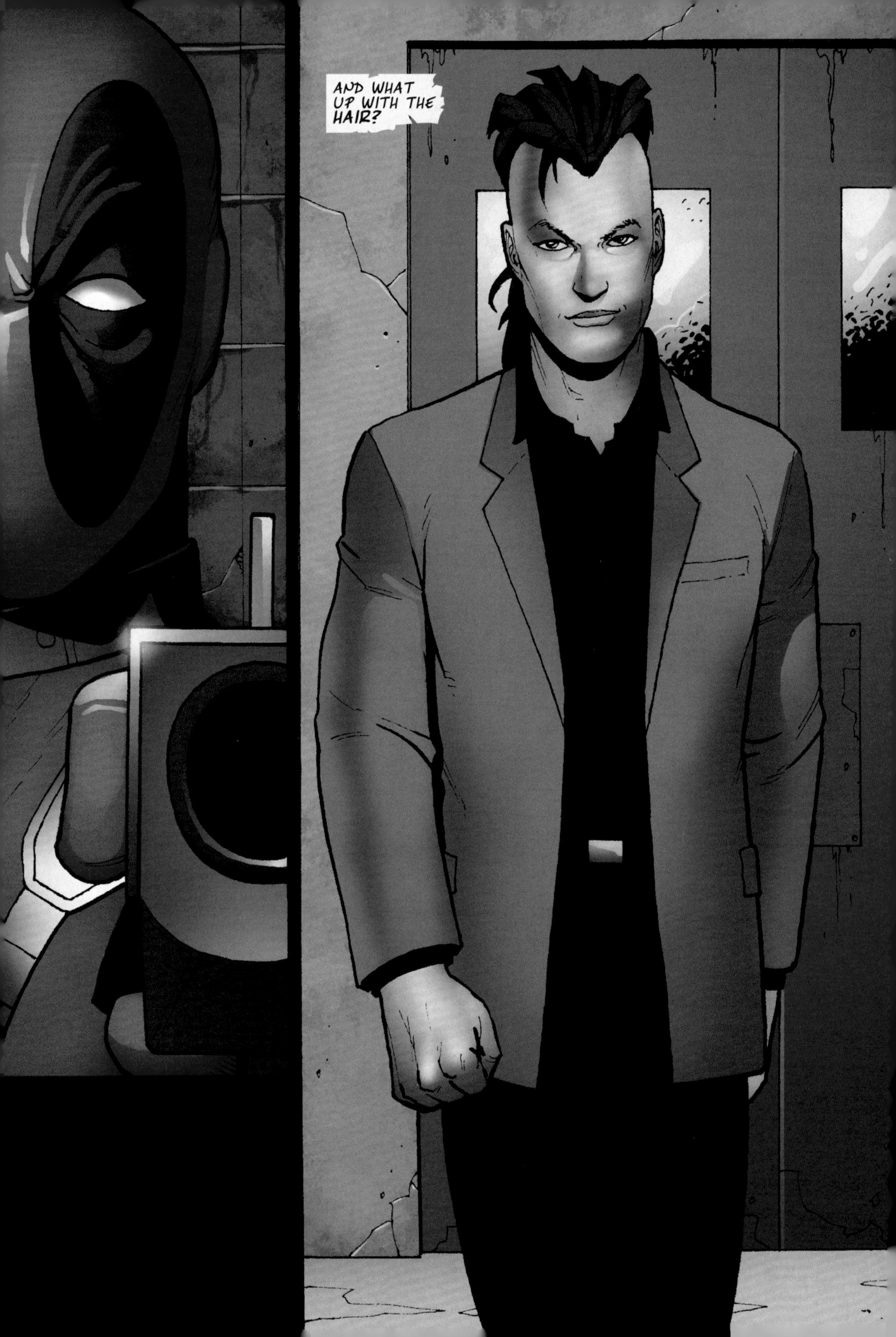
AND WHAT UP WITH THE HAIR?

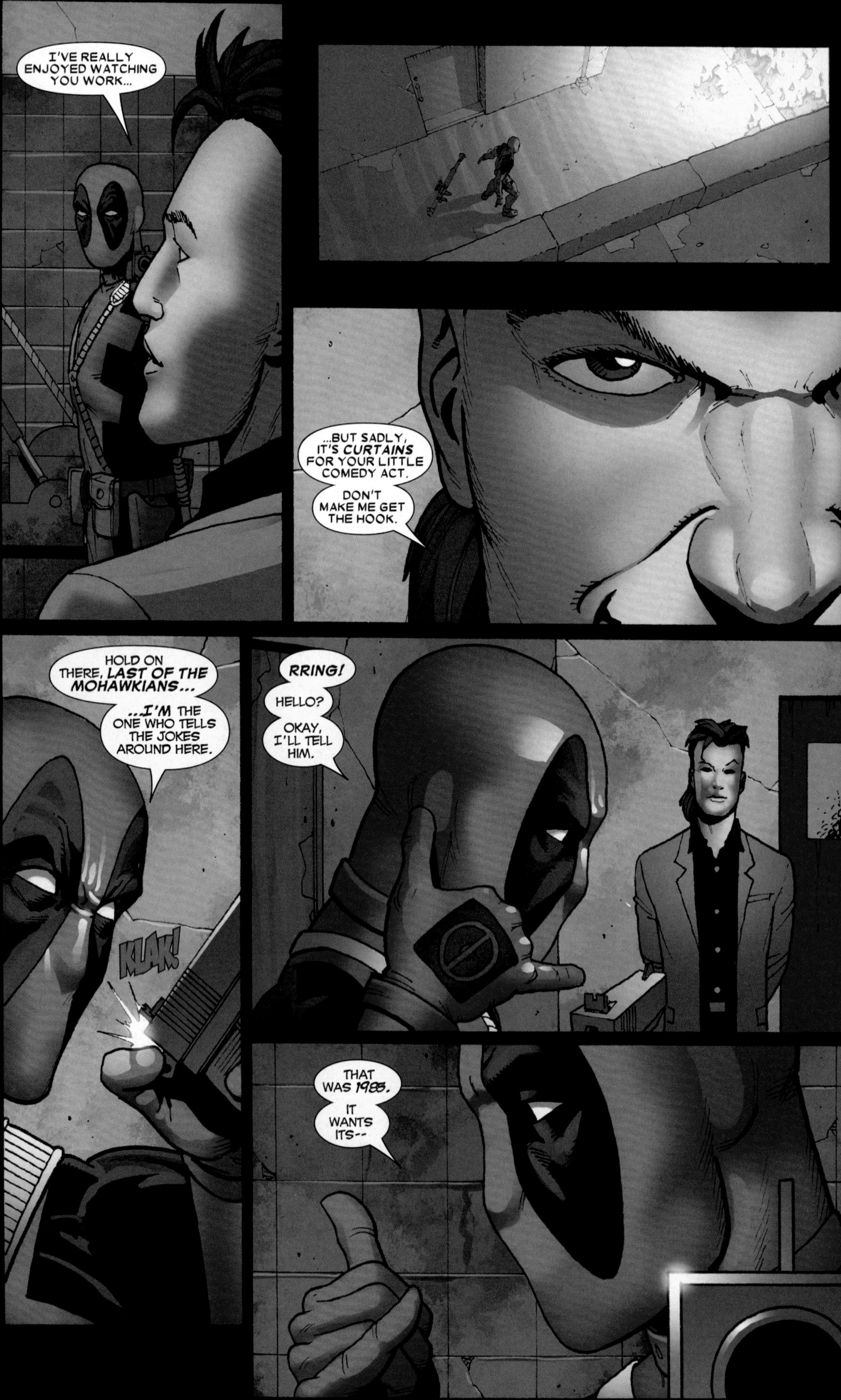

I'VE REALLY ENJOYED WATCHING YOU WORK...
...BUT SADLY, IT'S CURTAINS FOR YOUR LITTLE COMEDY ACT.
DON'T MAKE ME GET THE HOOK.
HOLD ON THERE, LAST OF THE MOHAWKIANS...
...I'M THE ONE WHO TELLS THE JOKES AROUND HERE.
KLAK!
RRING!
HELLO?
OKAY, I'LL TELL HIM.
THAT WAS 1985.
IT WANTS ITS--

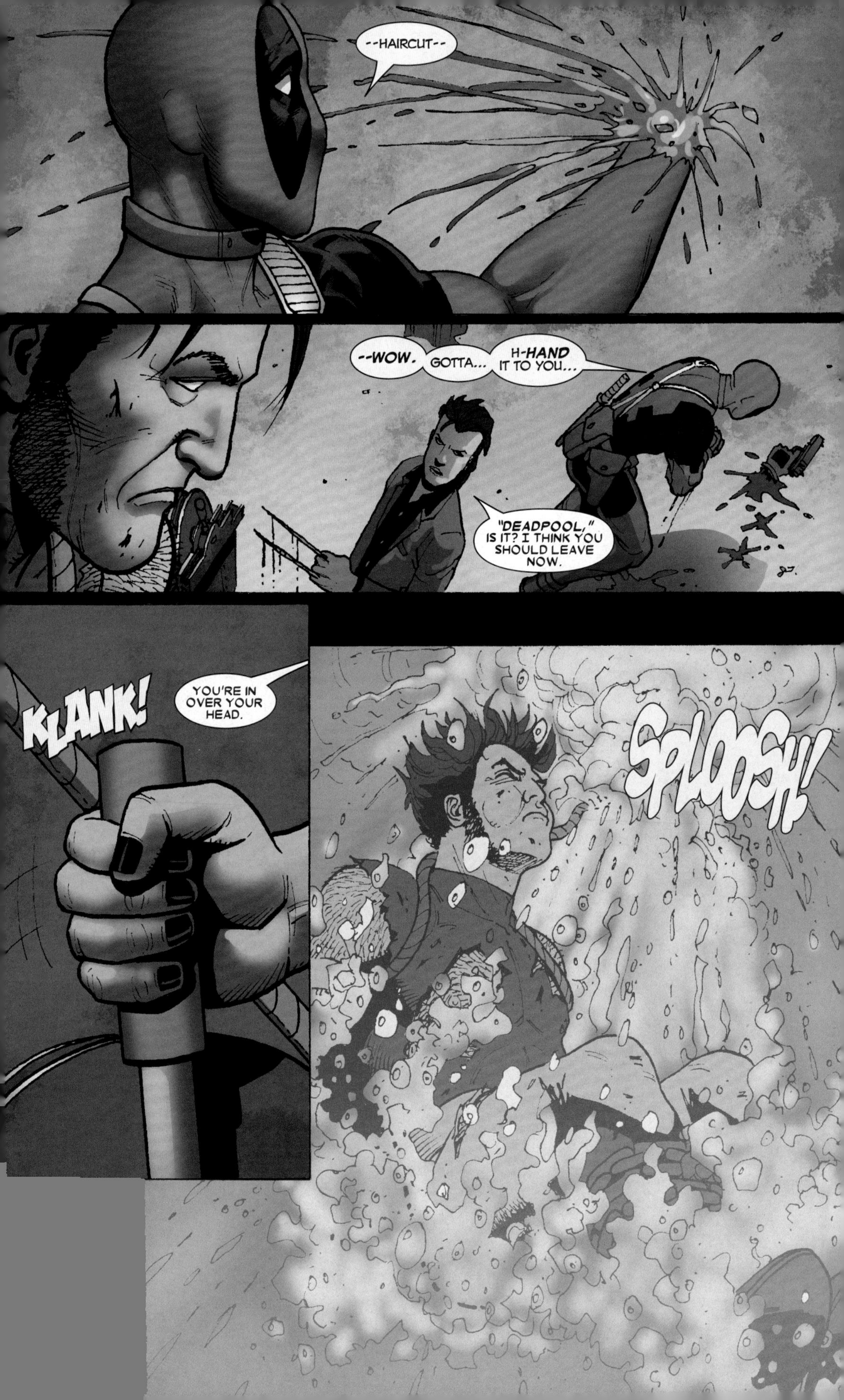
--HAIRCUT--
--WOW.
GOTTA...
H-HAND IT TO YOU...
"DEADPOOL," IS IT? I THINK YOU SHOULD LEAVE NOW.
KLANK!
YOU'RE IN OVER YOUR HEAD.
SPLOOSH!

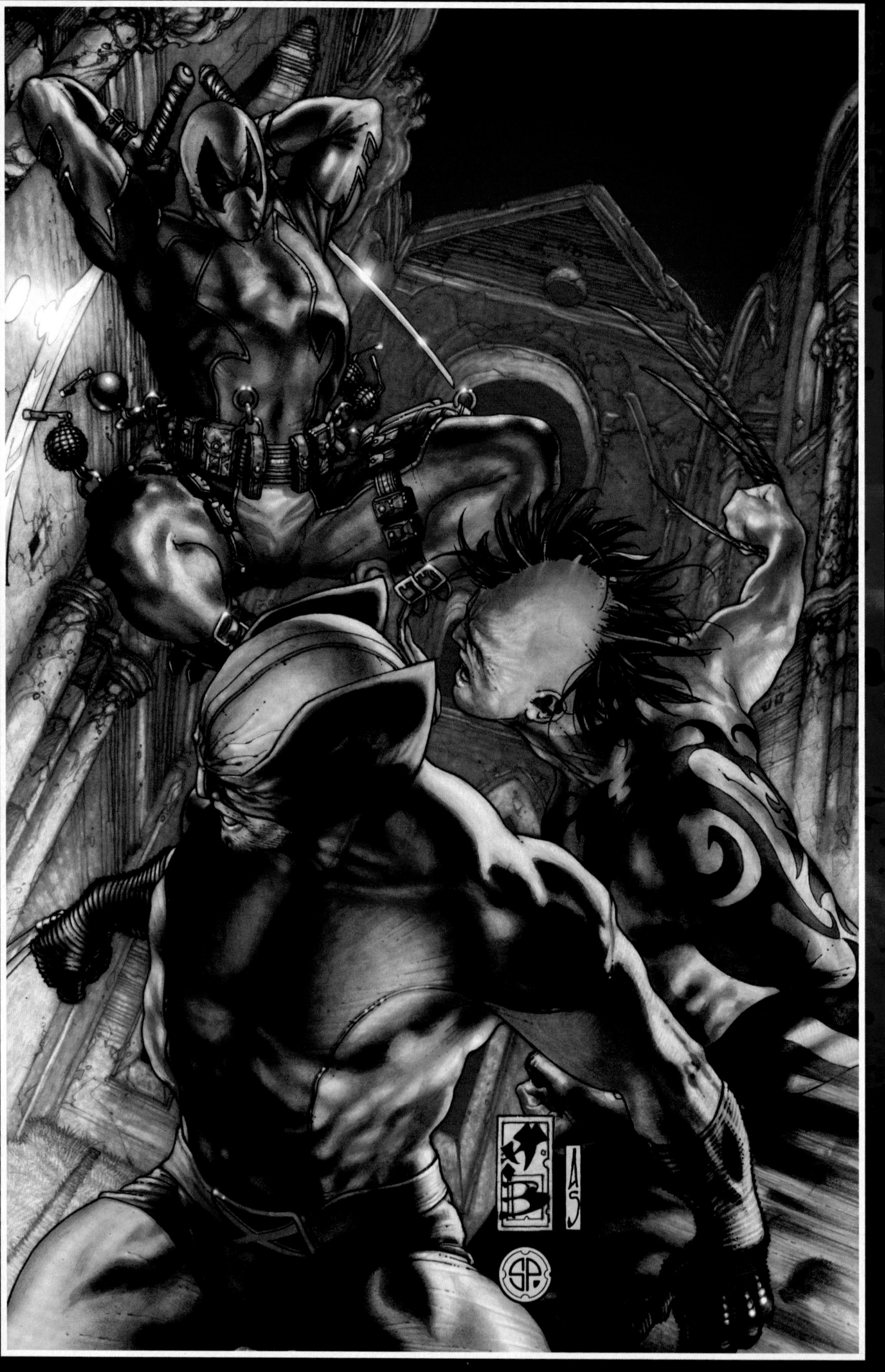

WOLVERINE: ORIGINS #25

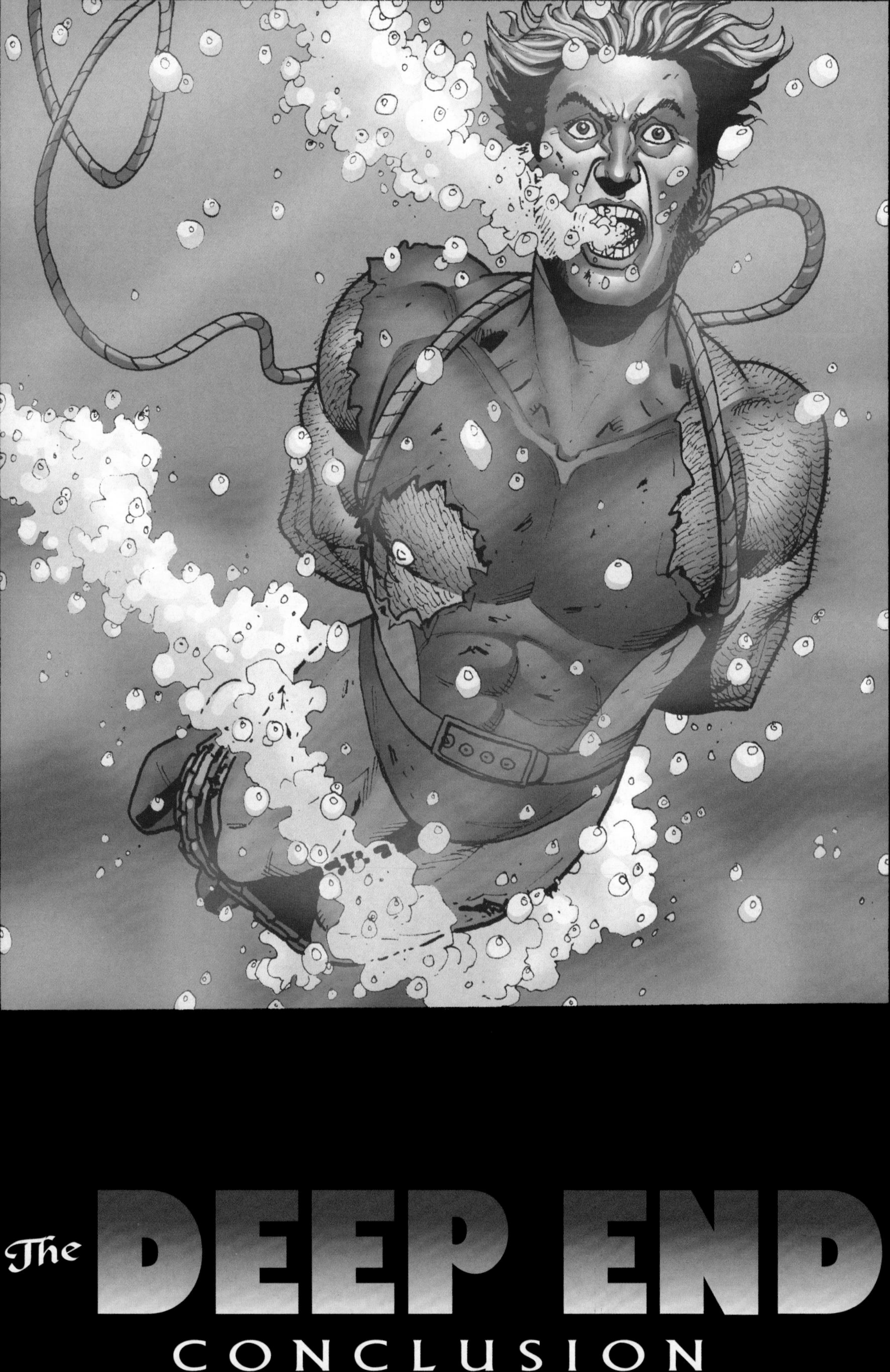

The DEEP END

CONCLUSION

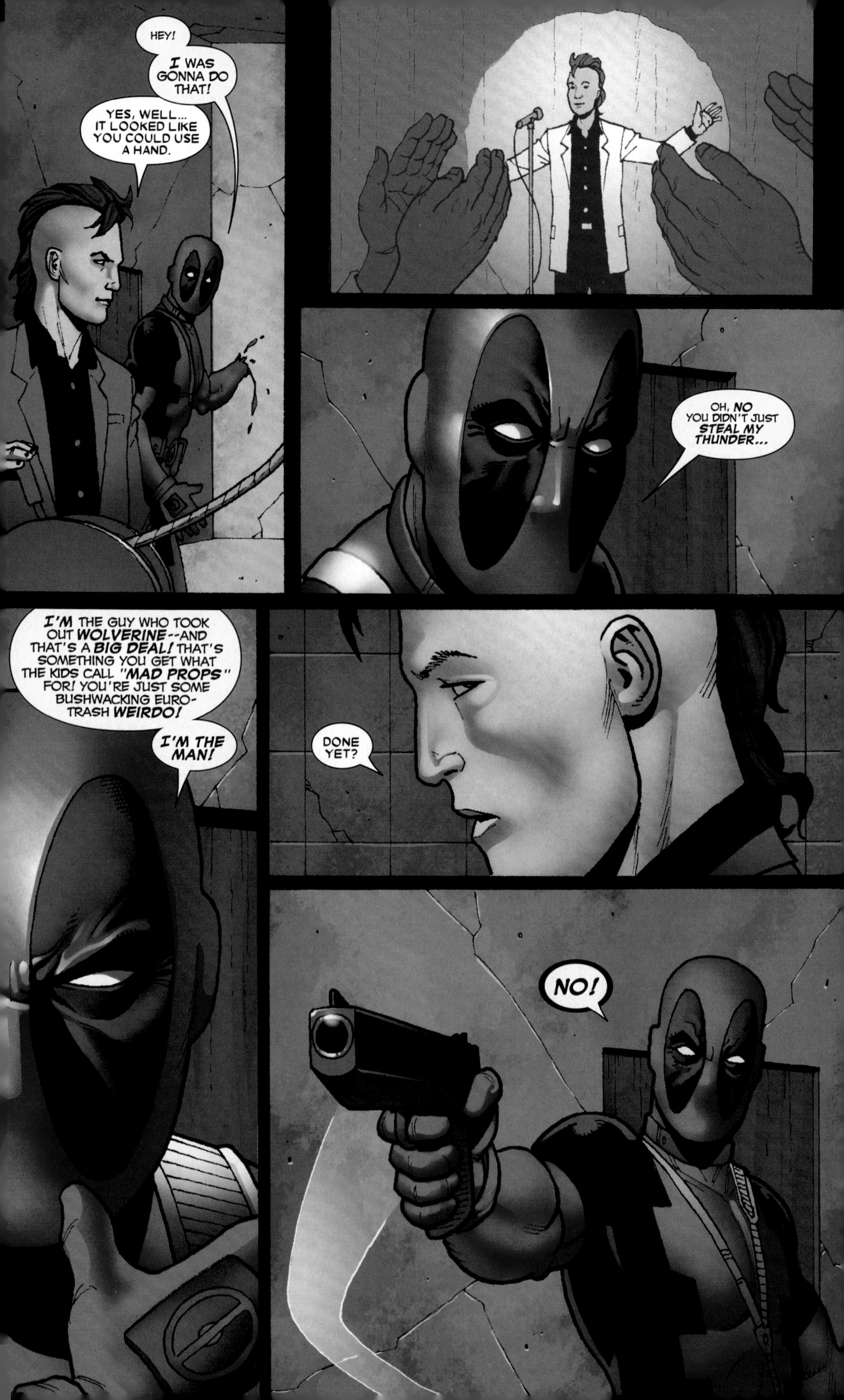
HEY!
I WAS GONNA DO THAT!
YES, WELL... IT LOOKED LIKE YOU COULD USE A HAND.
OH, NO YOU DIDN'T JUST STEAL MY THUNDER...
I'M THE GUY WHO TOOK OUT WOLVERINE--AND THAT'S A BIG DEAL! THAT'S SOMETHING YOU GET WHAT THE KIDS CALL "MAD PROPS" FOR! YOU'RE JUST SOME BUSHWACKING EURO-TRASH WEIRDO!
I'M THE MAN!
DONE YET?
NO!

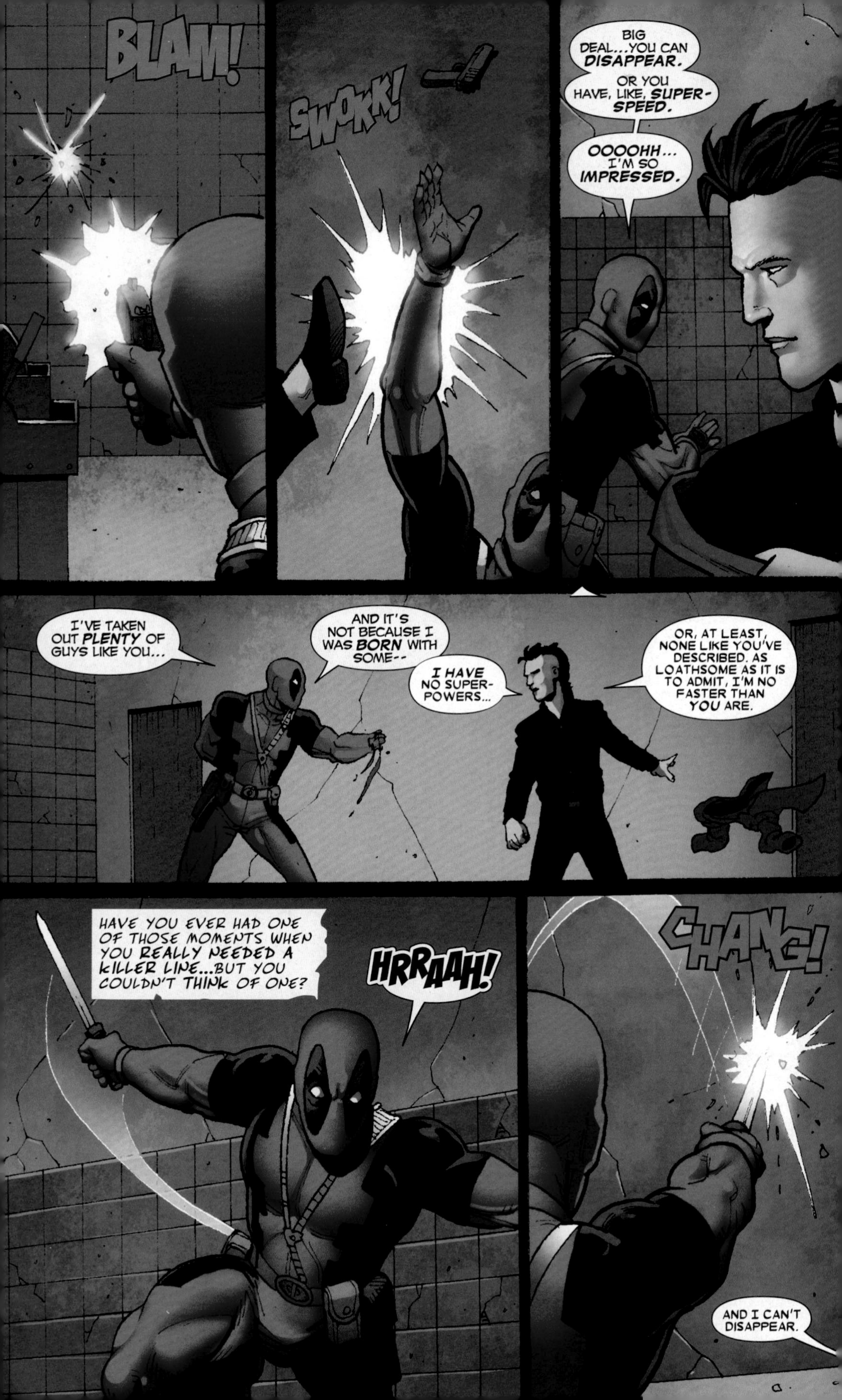
BLAM!
SWOKK!
BIG DEAL...YOU CAN DISAPPEAR.
OR YOU HAVE, LIKE, SUPER-SPEED.
OOOOHH... I'M SO IMPRESSED.
I'VE TAKEN OUT PLENTY OF GUYS LIKE YOU...
AND IT'S NOT BECAUSE I WAS BORN WITH SOME--
I HAVE NO SUPER-POWERS...
OR, AT LEAST, NONE LIKE YOU'VE DESCRIBED. AS LOATHSOME AS IT IS TO ADMIT, I'M NO FASTER THAN YOU ARE.
HAVE YOU EVER HAD ONE OF THOSE MOMENTS WHEN YOU REALLY NEEDED A KILLER LINE...BUT YOU COULDN'T THINK OF ONE?
HRRAAH!
CHANG!
AND I CAN'T DISAPPEAR.

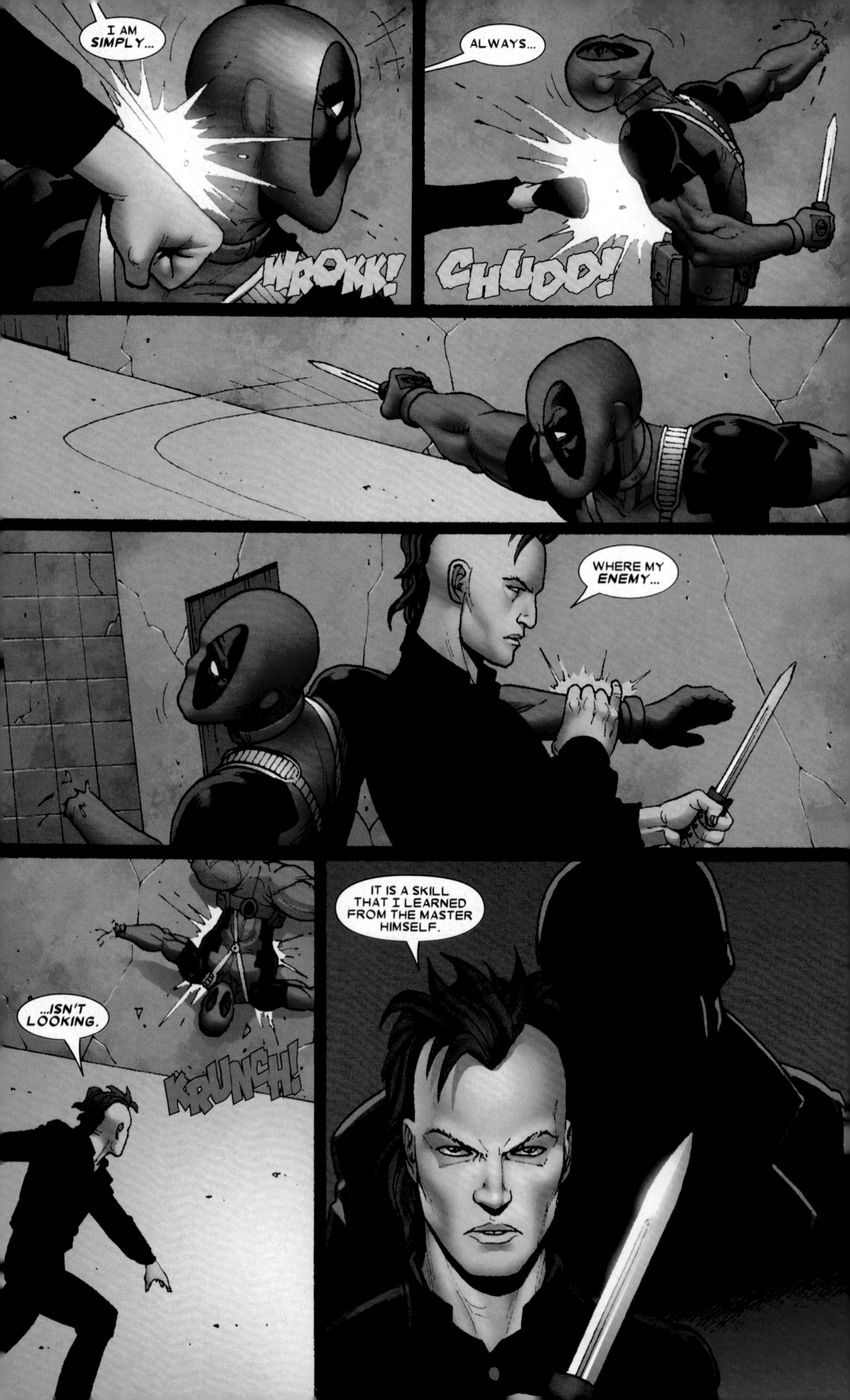
I AM SIMPLY...
WROKK!
ALWAYS...
CHUDD!
WHERE MY ENEMY...
...ISN'T LOOKING.
KRUNCH!
IT IS A SKILL THAT I LEARNED FROM THE MASTER HIMSELF.

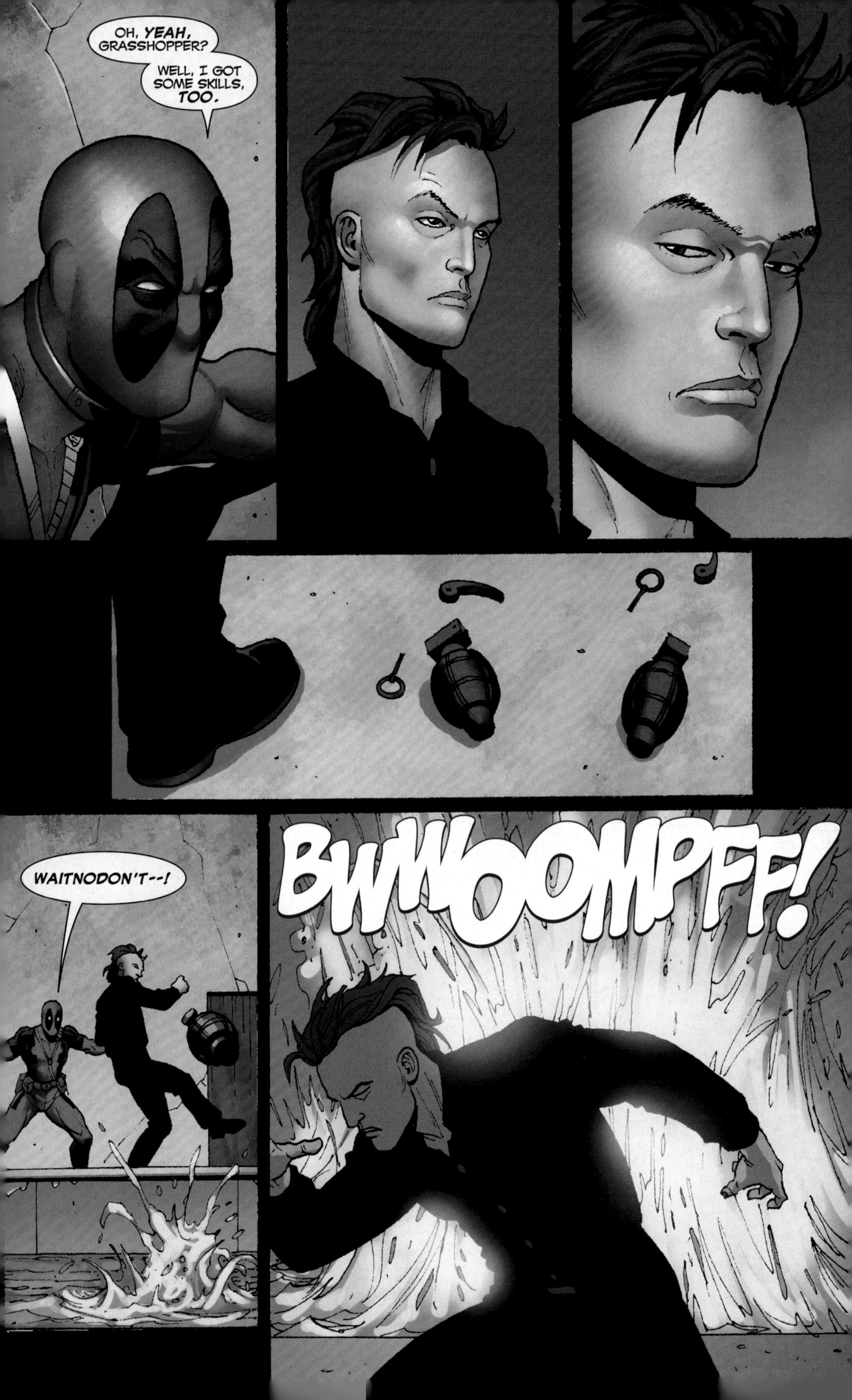
OH, YEAH, GRASSHOPPER?
WELL, I GOT SOME SKILLS, TOO.
WAITNODON'T--!
BWWOOMPFF!

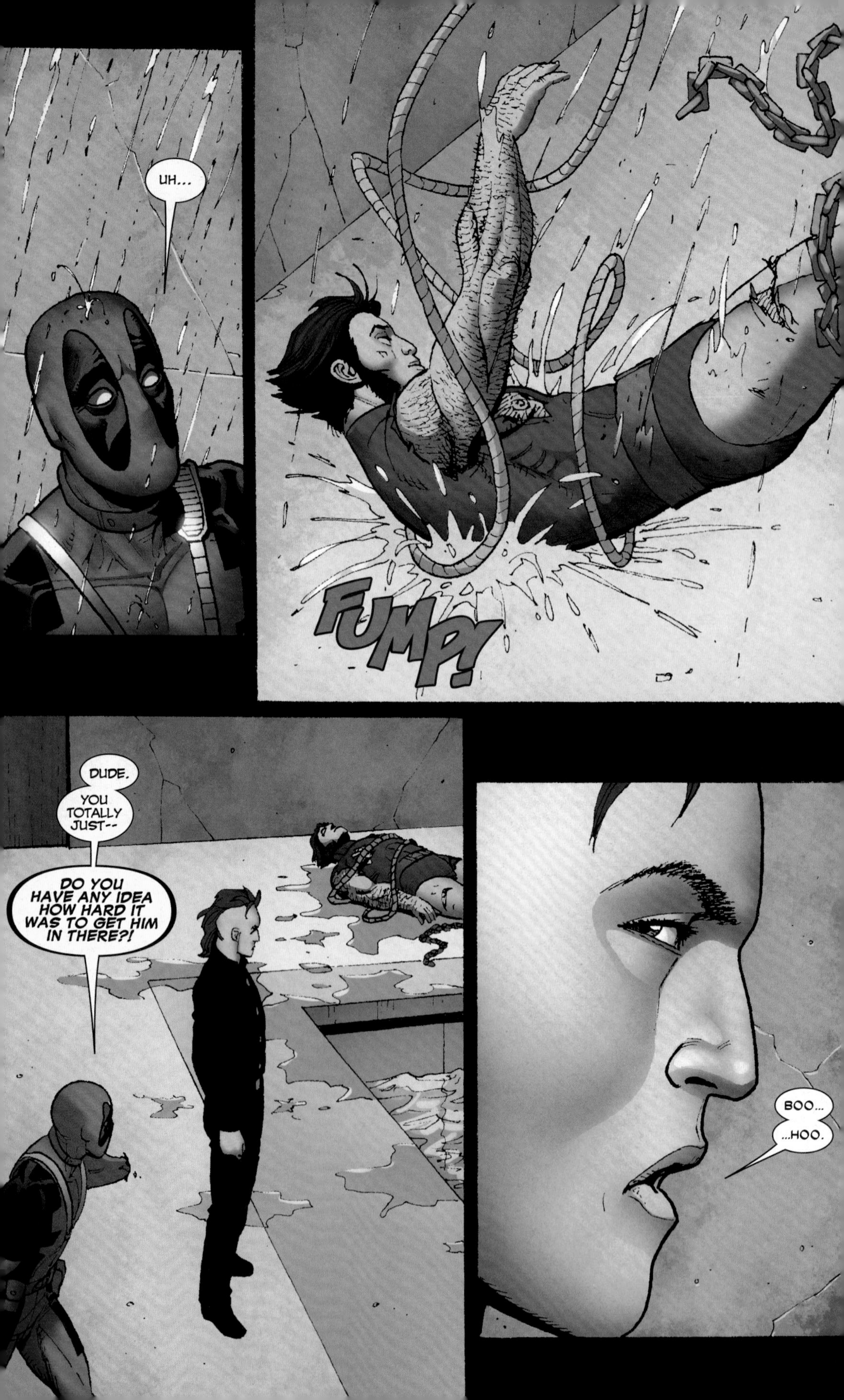
UH...
FUMP!
DUDE.
YOU TOTALLY JUST--
DO YOU HAVE ANY IDEA HOW HARD IT WAS TO GET HIM IN THERE?!
BOO...
...HOO.

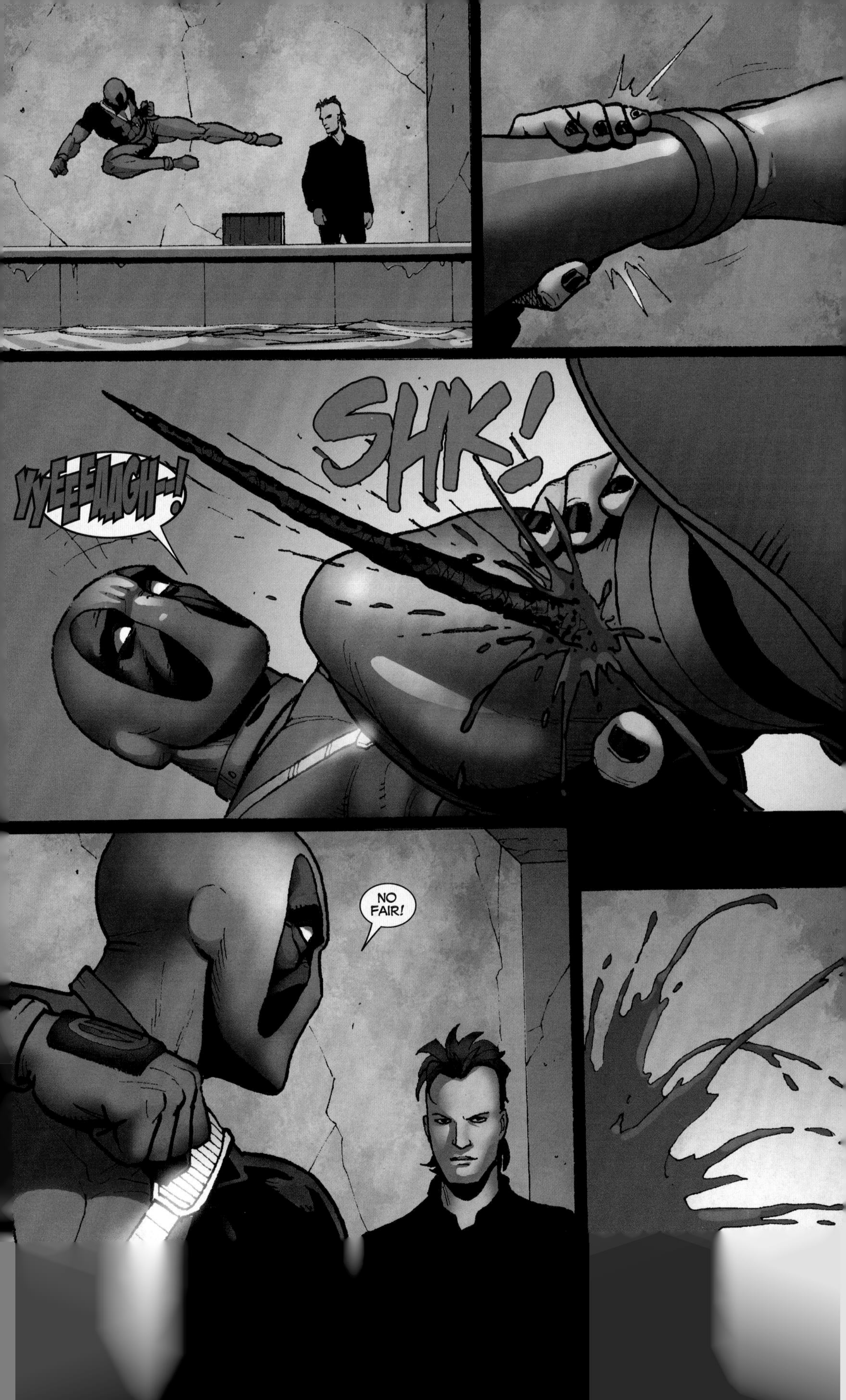
SHK!
YyEEEAAGH--!
NO FAIR!

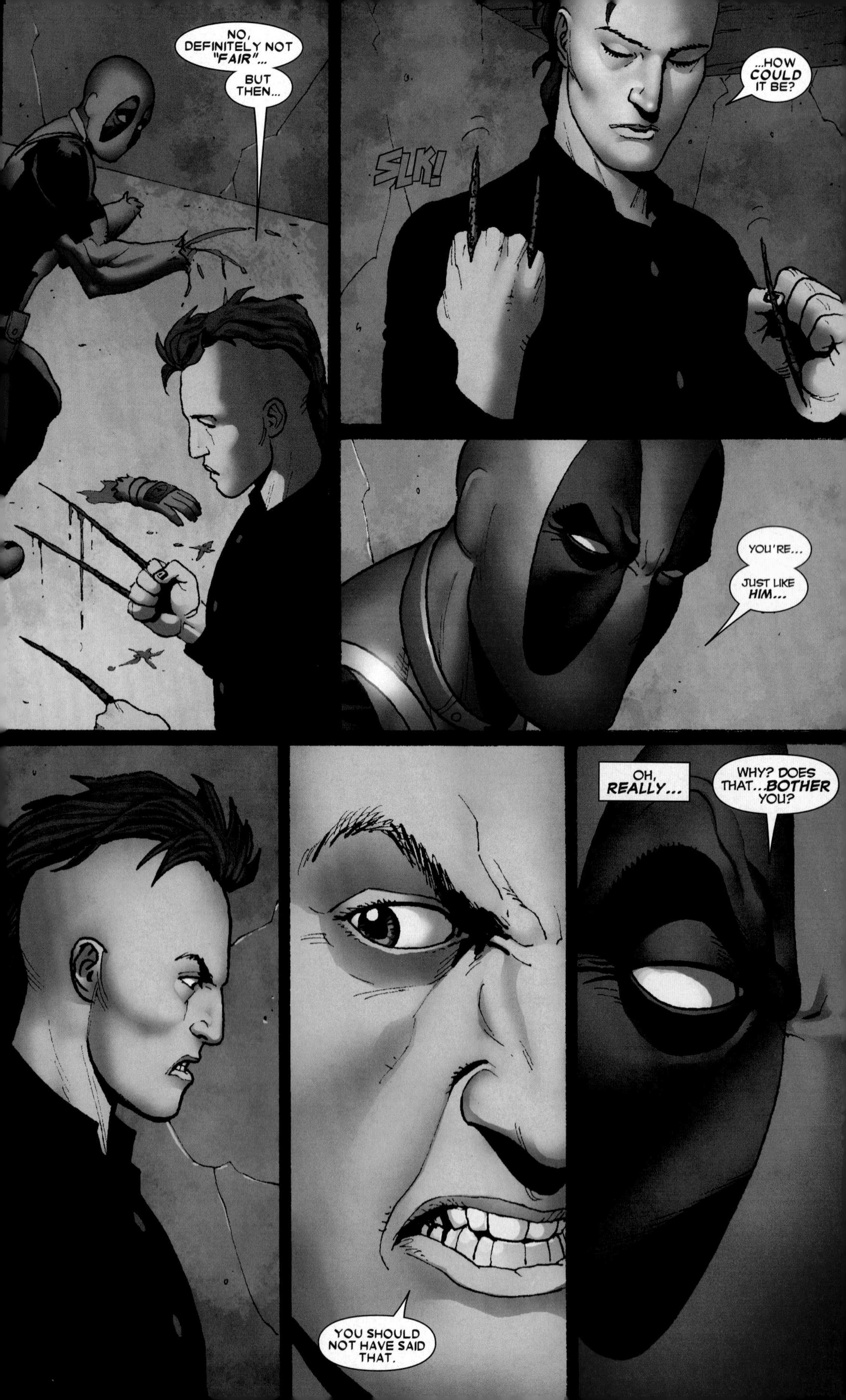
NO, DEFINITELY NOT "FAIR"...
BUT THEN...
...HOW COULD IT BE?
SLK!
YOU'RE...
JUST LIKE HIM...
YOU SHOULD NOT HAVE SAID THAT.
OH, REALLY...
WHY? DOES THAT...BOTHER YOU?

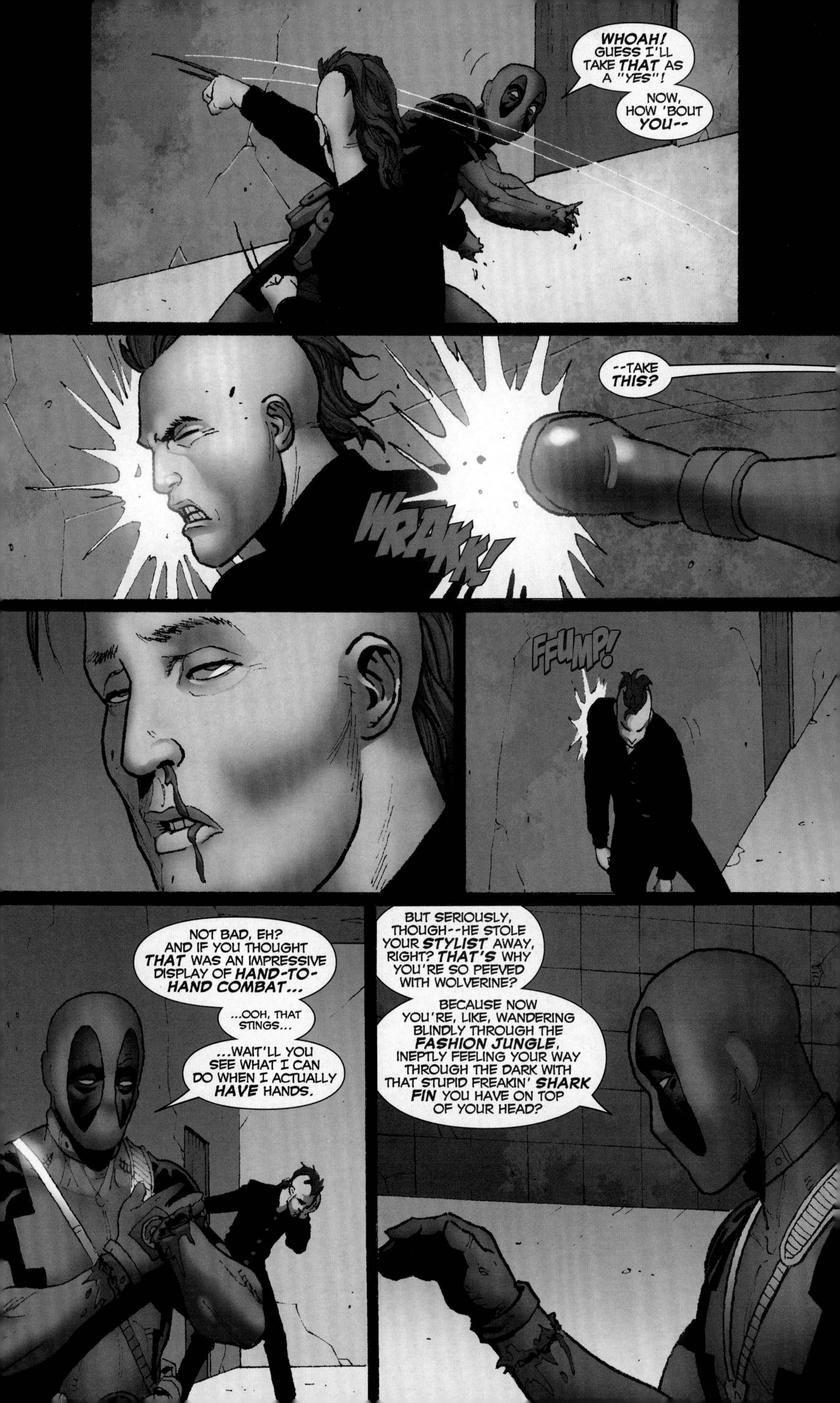
WHOAH! GUESS I'LL TAKE THAT AS A "YES"!
NOW, HOW 'BOUT YOU--
--TAKE THIS?
WRAKK!
FFUMP!
NOT BAD, EH? AND IF YOU THOUGHT THAT WAS AN IMPRESSIVE DISPLAY OF HAND-TO-HAND COMBAT...
...OOH, THAT STINGS...
...WAIT'LL YOU SEE WHAT I CAN DO WHEN I ACTUALLY HAVE HANDS.
BUT SERIOUSLY, THOUGH--HE STOLE YOUR STYLIST AWAY, RIGHT? THAT'S WHY YOU'RE SO PEEVED WITH WOLVERINE?
BECAUSE NOW YOU'RE, LIKE, WANDERING BLINDLY THROUGH THE FASHION JUNGLE, INEPTLY FEELING YOUR WAY THROUGH THE DARK WITH THAT STUPID FREAKIN' SHARK FIN YOU HAVE ON TOP OF YOUR HEAD?

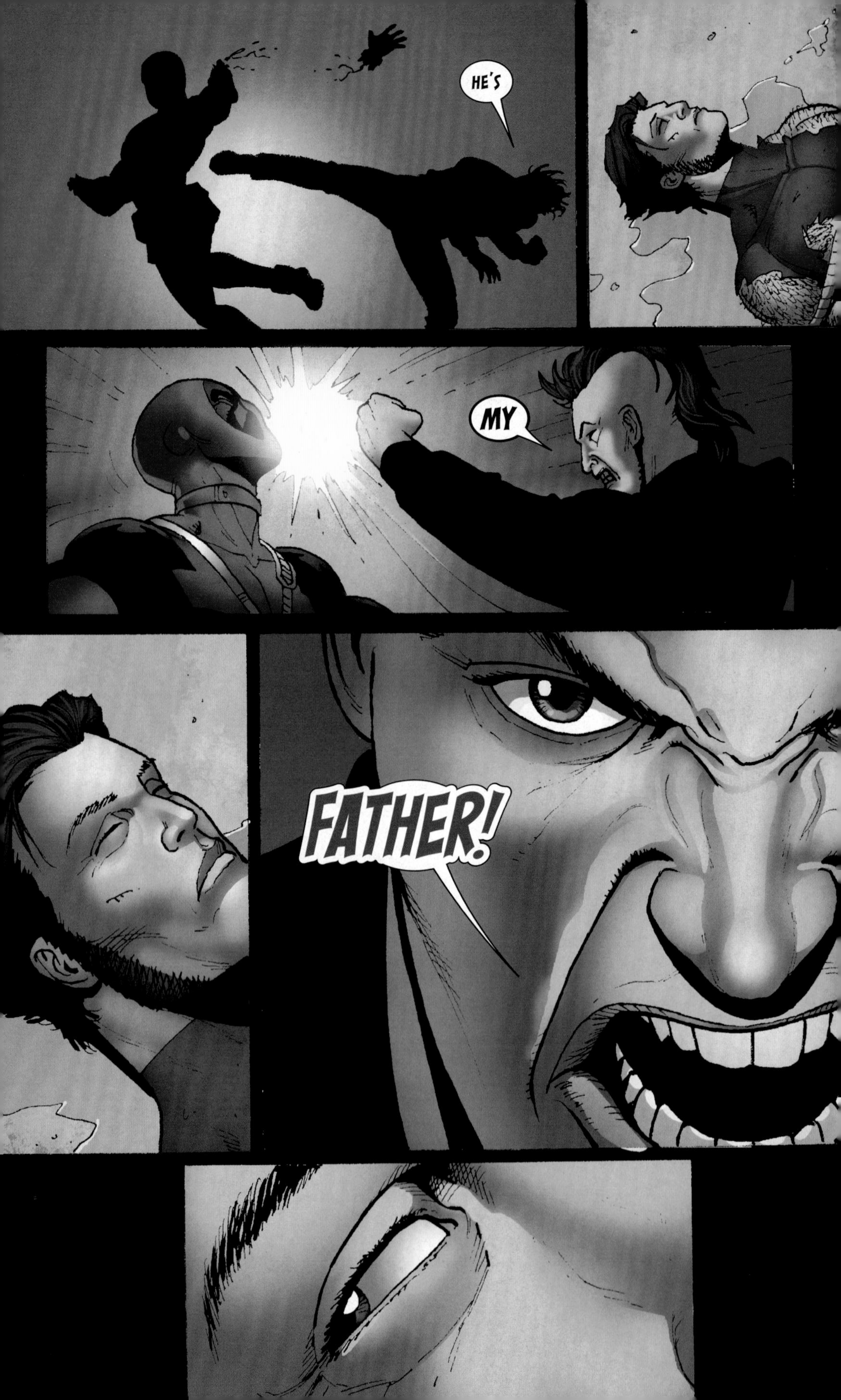
HE'S
MY
FATHER!

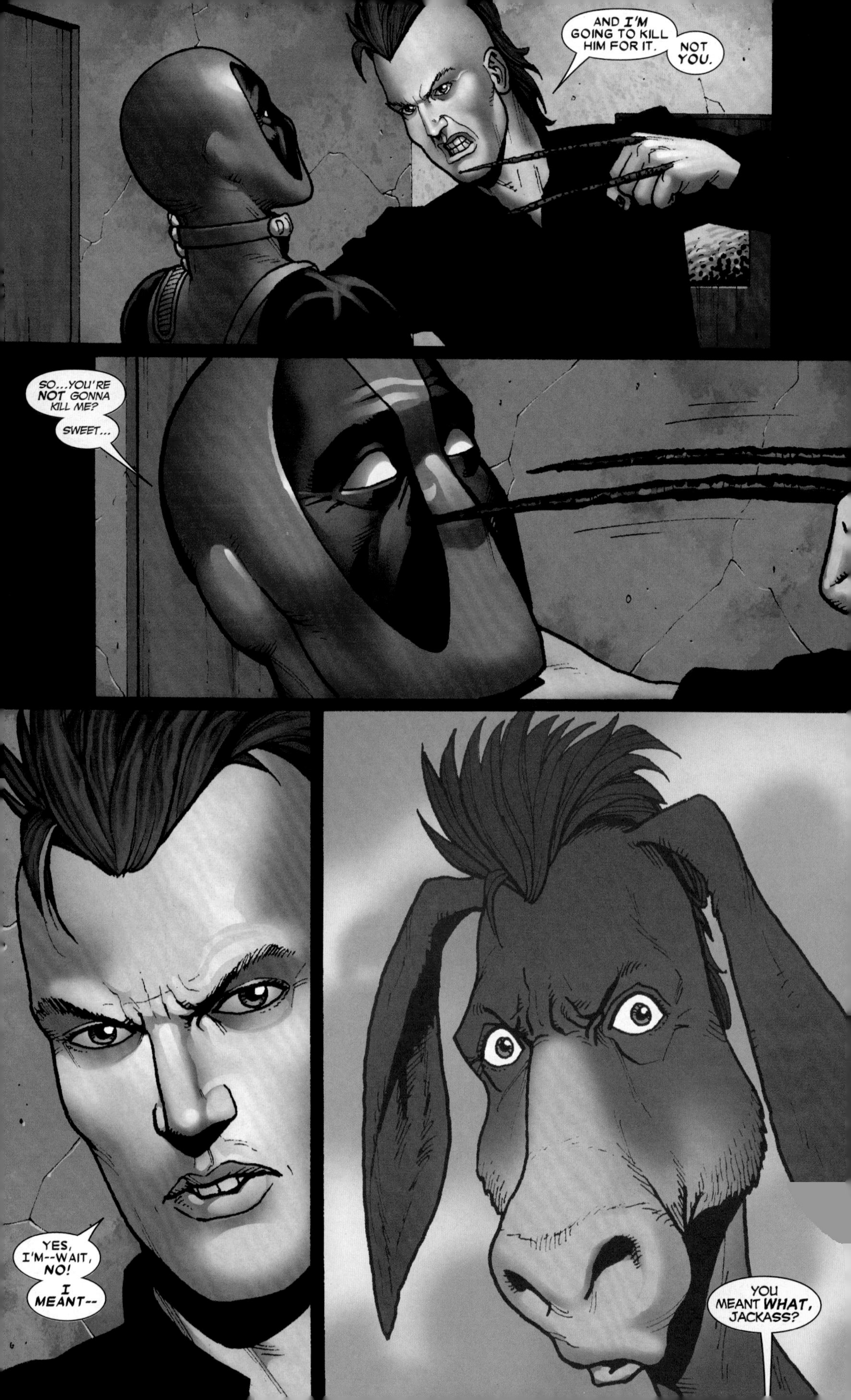
AND I'M GOING TO KILL HIM FOR IT.
NOT YOU.
SO...YOU'RE NOT GONNA KILL ME?
SWEET...
YES, I'M--WAIT, NO!
I MEANT--
YOU MEANT WHAT, JACKASS?

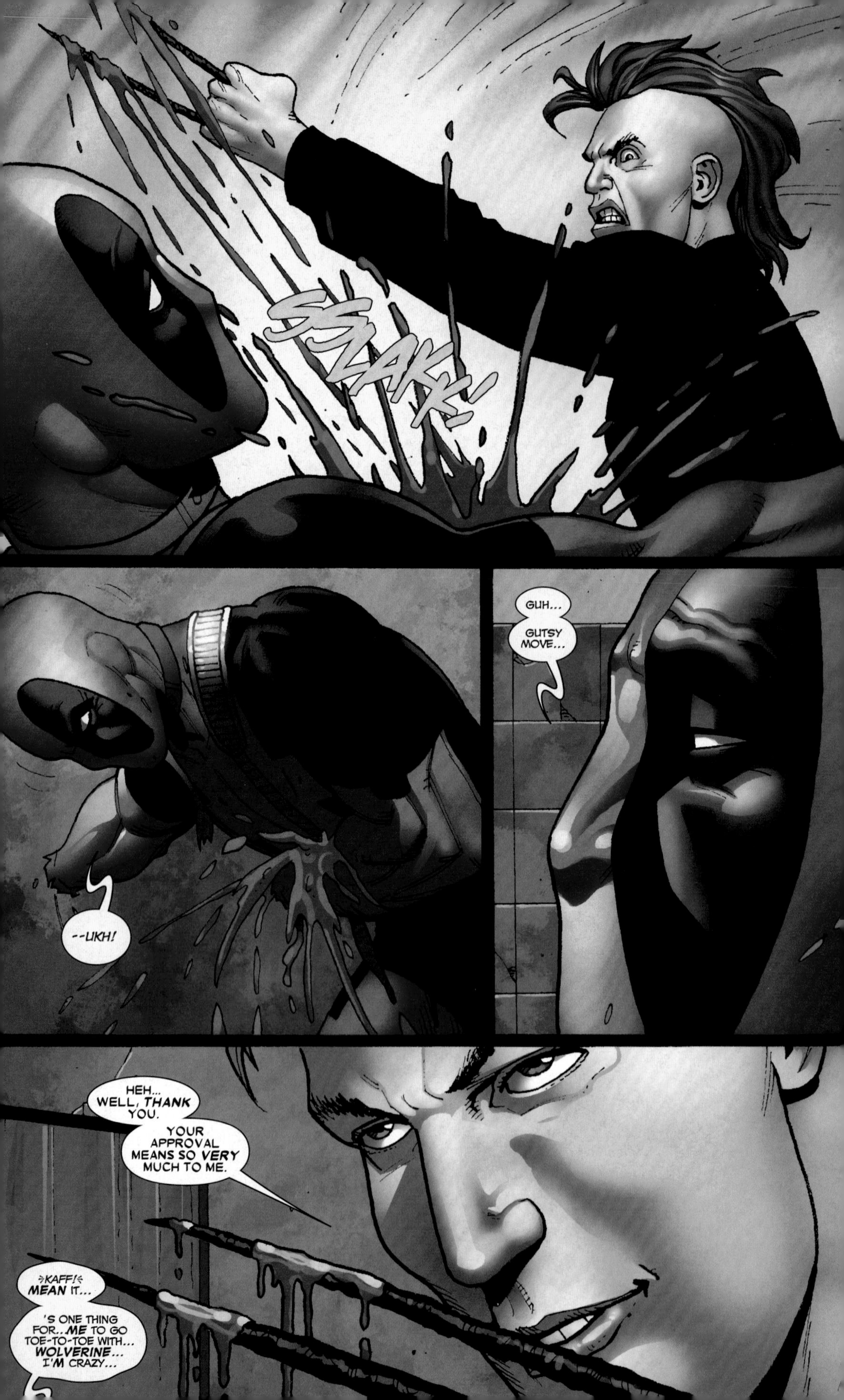
SSNAKT!
GUH...
GUTSY MOVE...
--UKH!
HEH... WELL, THANK YOU.
YOUR APPROVAL MEANS SO VERY MUCH TO ME.
KAFF! MEAN IT...
'S ONE THING FOR.. ME TO GO TOE-TO-TOE WITH... WOLVERINE... I'M CRAZY...

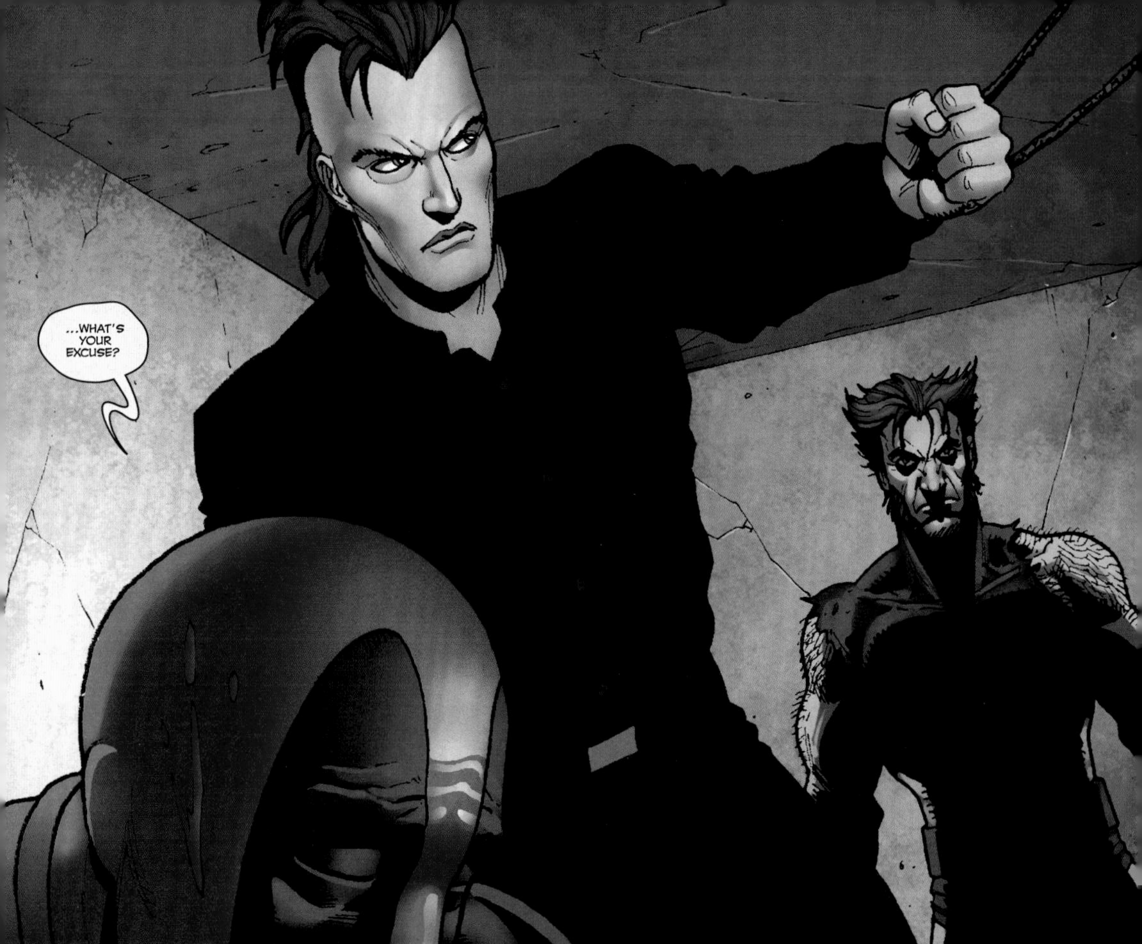
...WHAT'S YOUR EXCUSE?

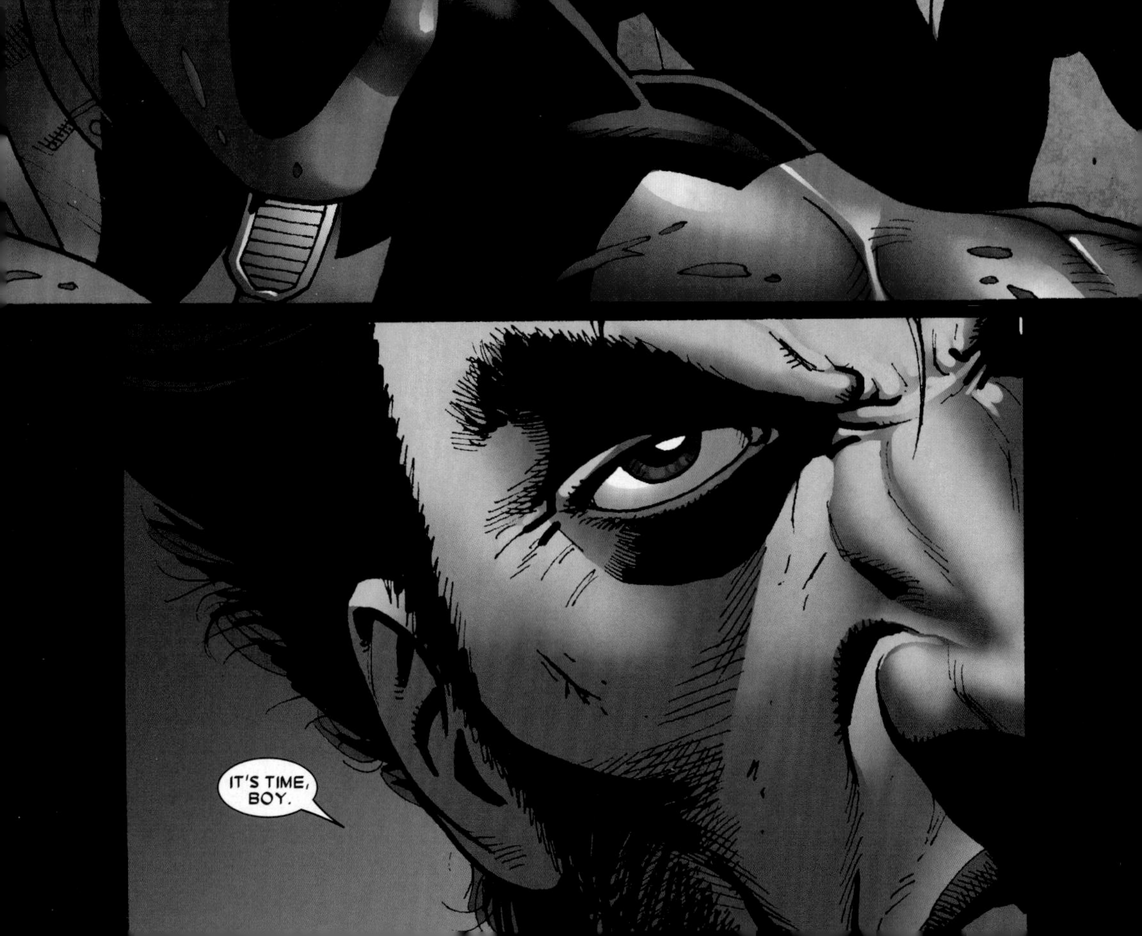
IT'S TIME, BOY.

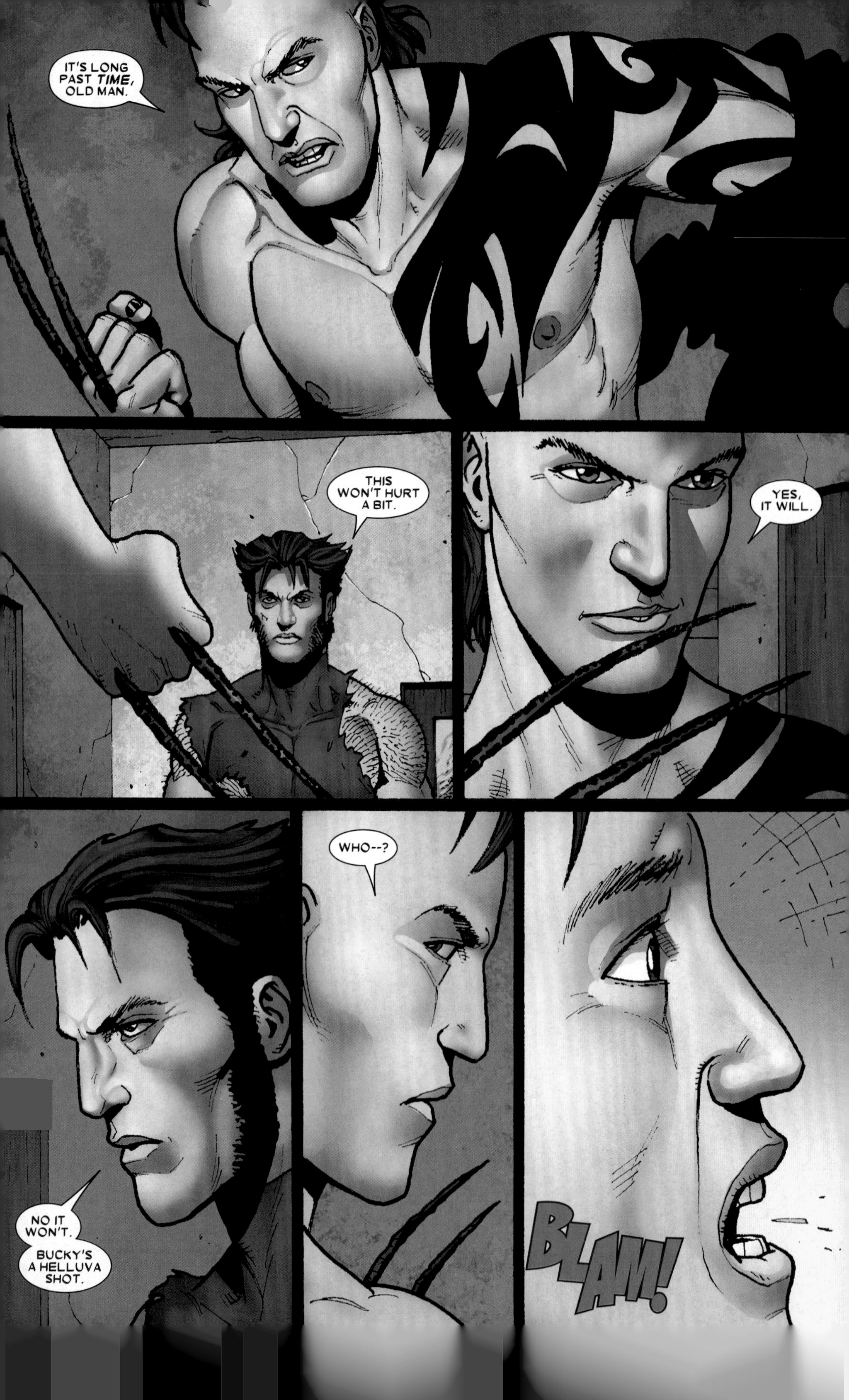
IT'S LONG PAST TIME, OLD MAN.
THIS WON'T HURT A BIT.
YES, IT WILL.
NO IT WON'T.
BUCKY'S A HELLUVA SHOT.
WHO--?
BLAM!

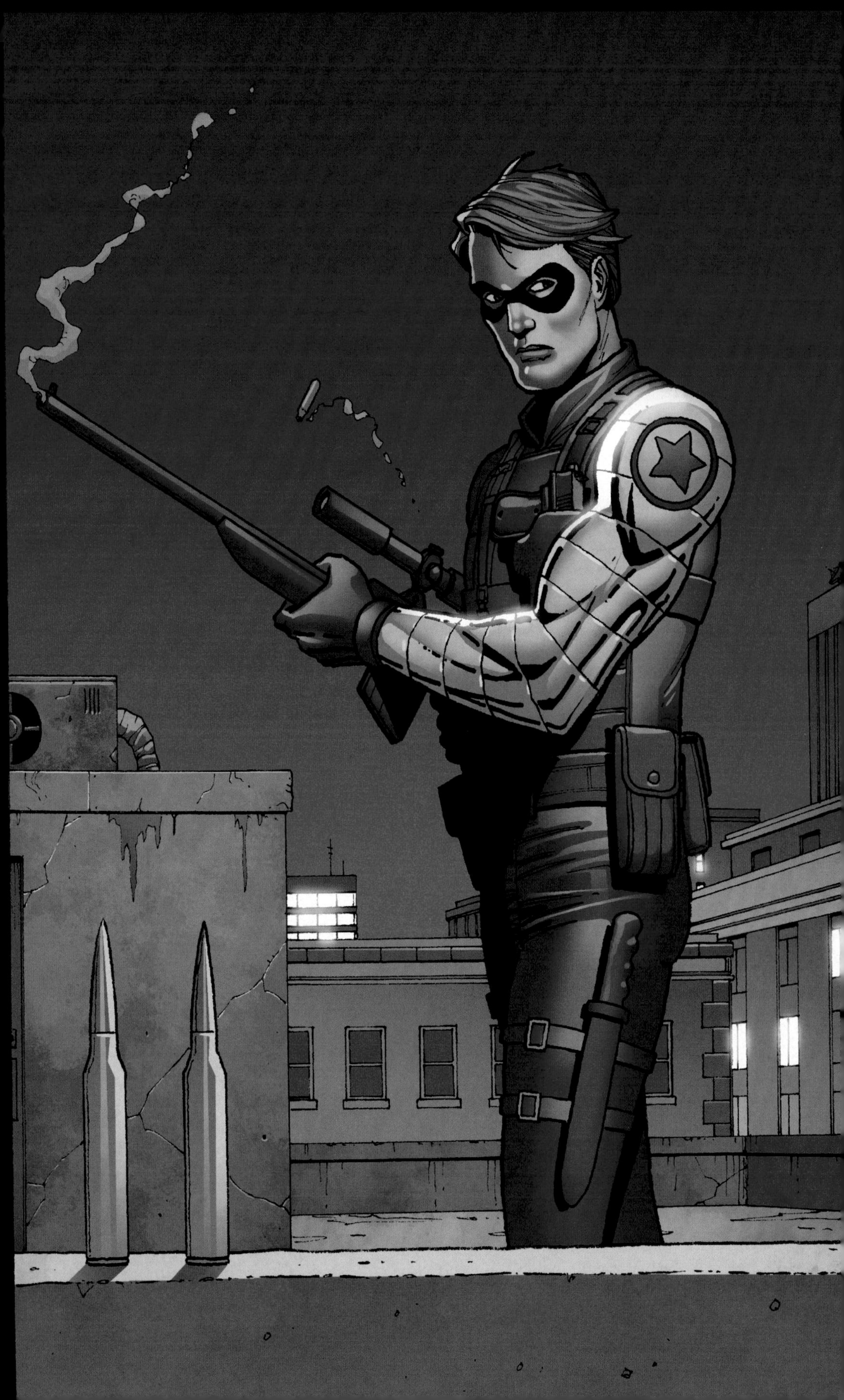

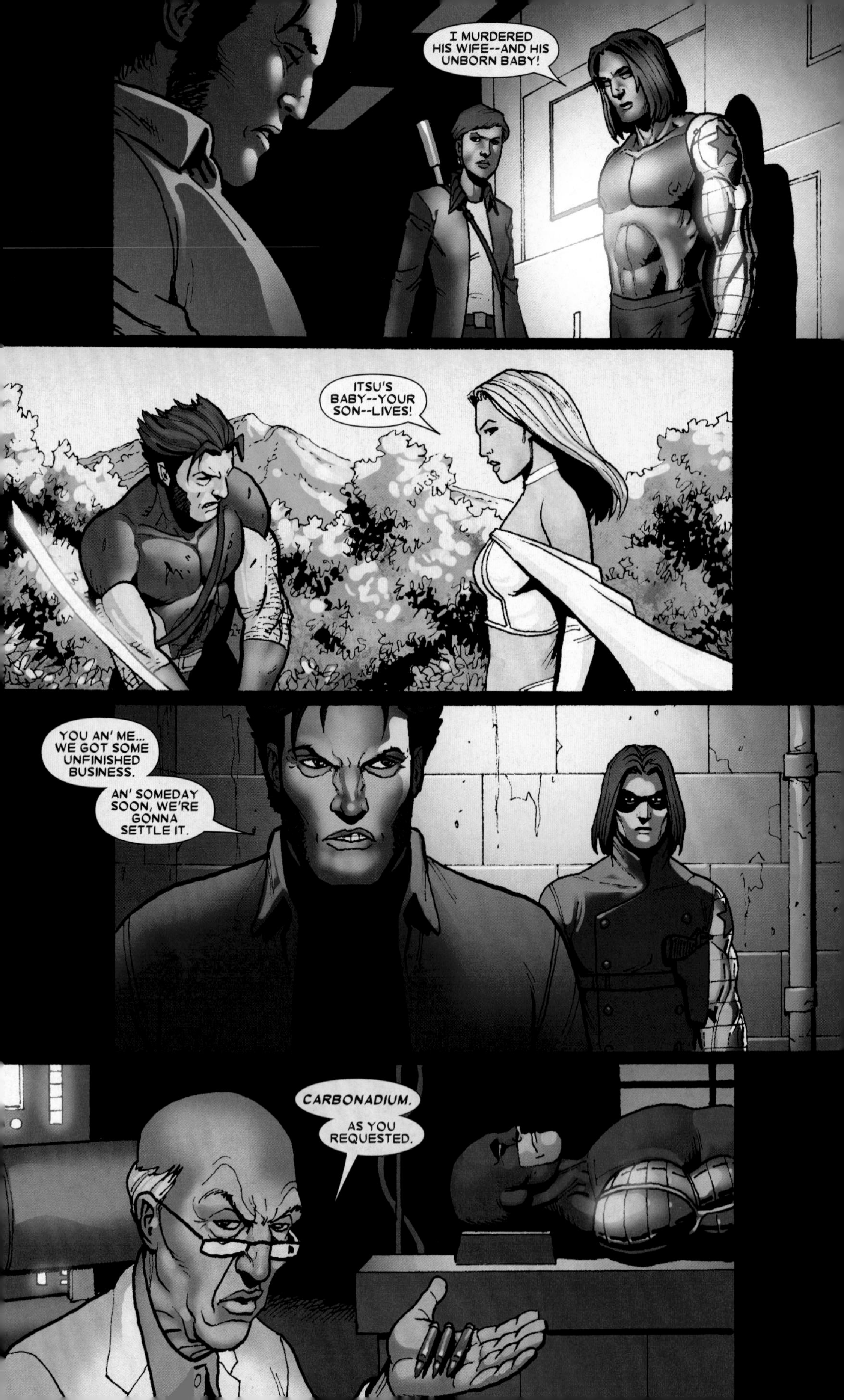
I MURDERED HIS WIFE--AND HIS UNBORN BABY!
ITSU'S BABY--YOUR SON--LIVES!
YOU AN' ME... WE GOT SOME UNFINISHED BUSINESS.
AN' SOMEDAY SOON, WE'RE GONNA SETTLE IT.
CARBONADIUM.
AS YOU REQUESTED.

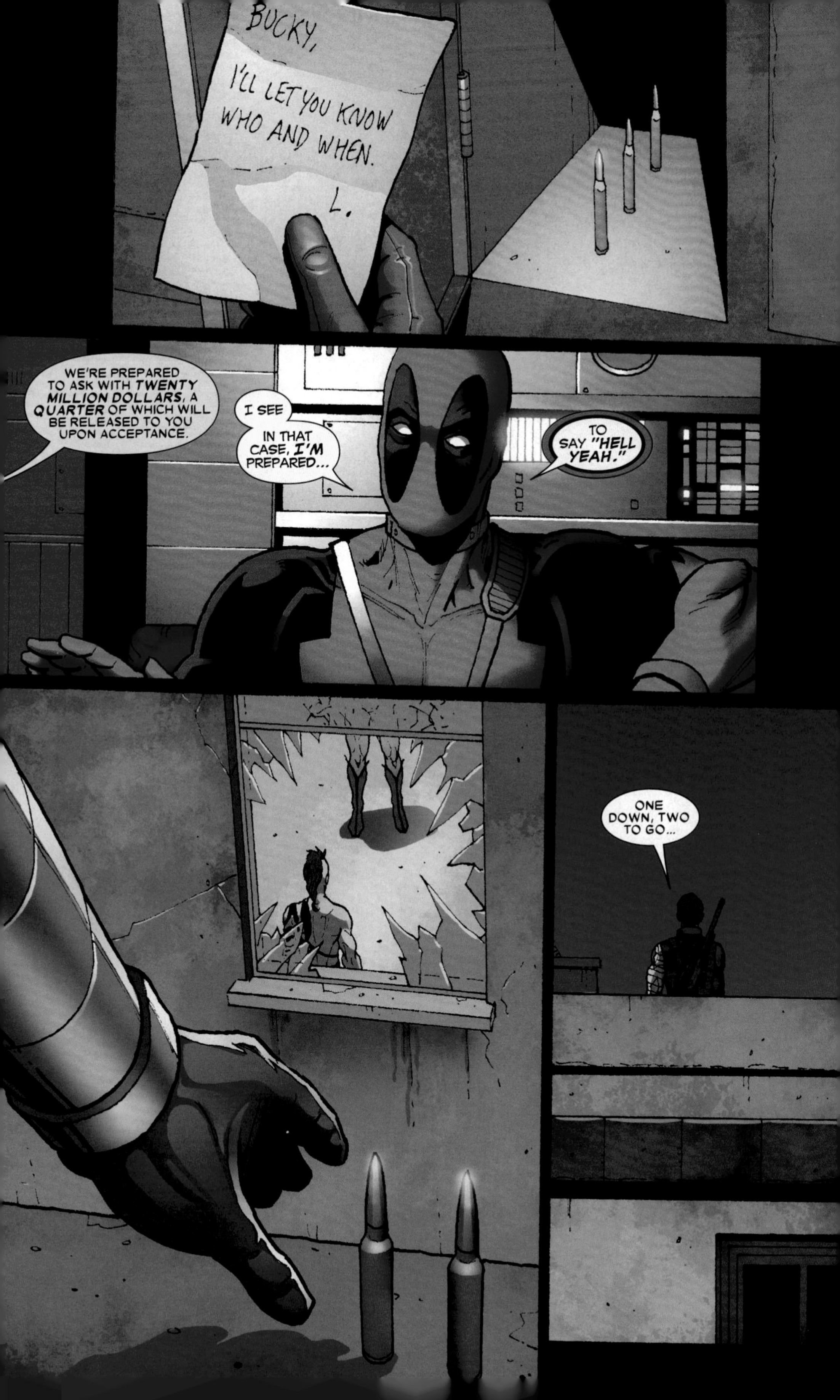
BUCKY,
I'LL LET YOU KNOW WHO AND WHEN.
L.
WE'RE PREPARED TO ASK WITH **TWENTY MILLION DOLLARS**, A **QUARTER** OF WHICH WILL BE RELEASED TO YOU UPON ACCEPTANCE.
I SEE
IN THAT CASE, **I'M** PREPARED...
TO SAY **"HELL YEAH."**
ONE DOWN, TWO TO GO...

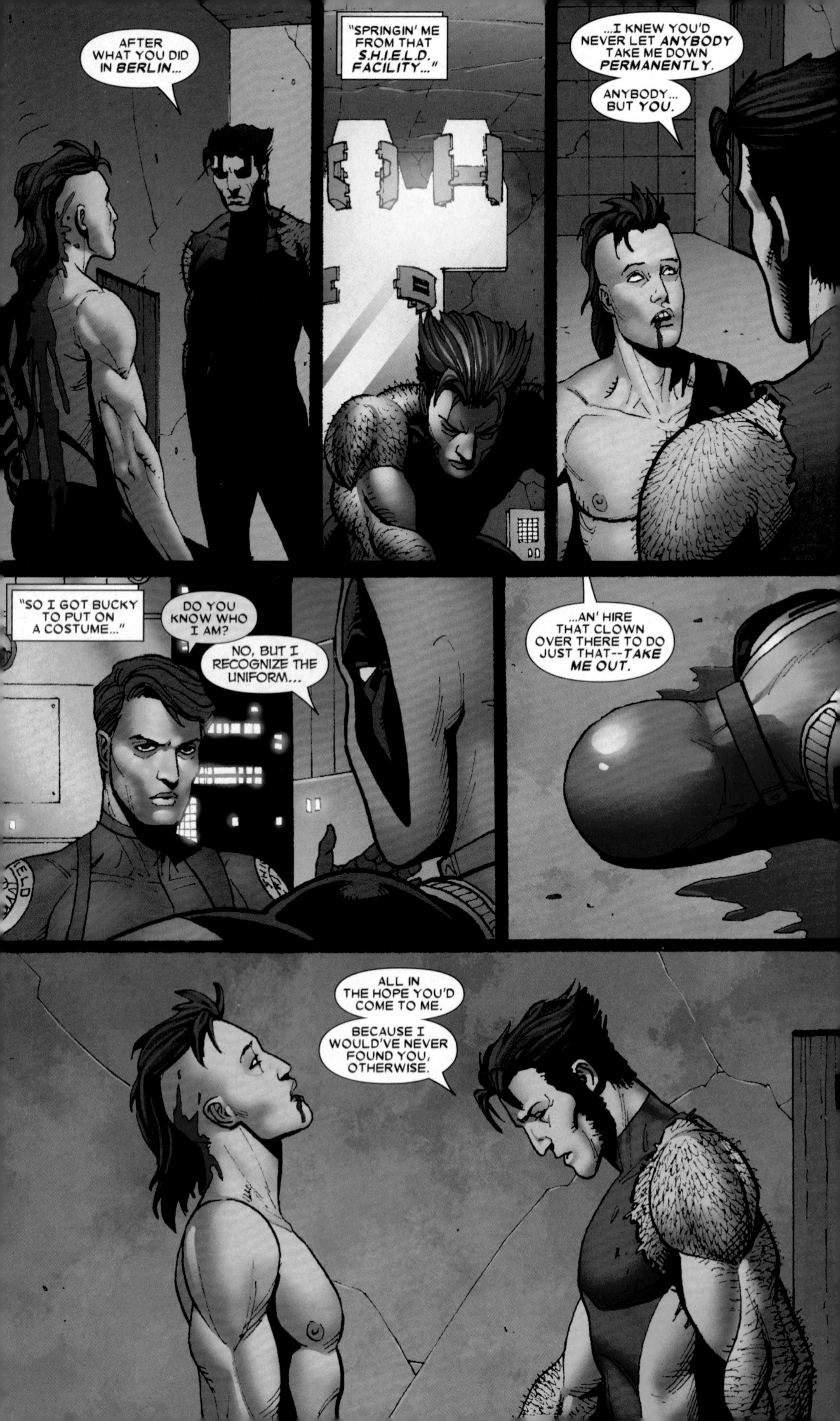
AFTER WHAT YOU DID IN BERLIN...
"SPRINGIN' ME FROM THAT S.H.I.E.L.D. FACILITY..."
...I KNEW YOU'D NEVER LET ANYBODY TAKE ME DOWN PERMANENTLY.
ANYBODY... BUT YOU.
"SO I GOT BUCKY TO PUT ON A COSTUME..."
DO YOU KNOW WHO I AM?
NO, BUT I RECOGNIZE THE UNIFORM...
...AN' HIRE THAT CLOWN OVER THERE TO DO JUST THAT--TAKE ME OUT.
ALL IN THE HOPE YOU'D COME TO ME.
BECAUSE I WOULD'VE NEVER FOUND YOU, OTHERWISE.

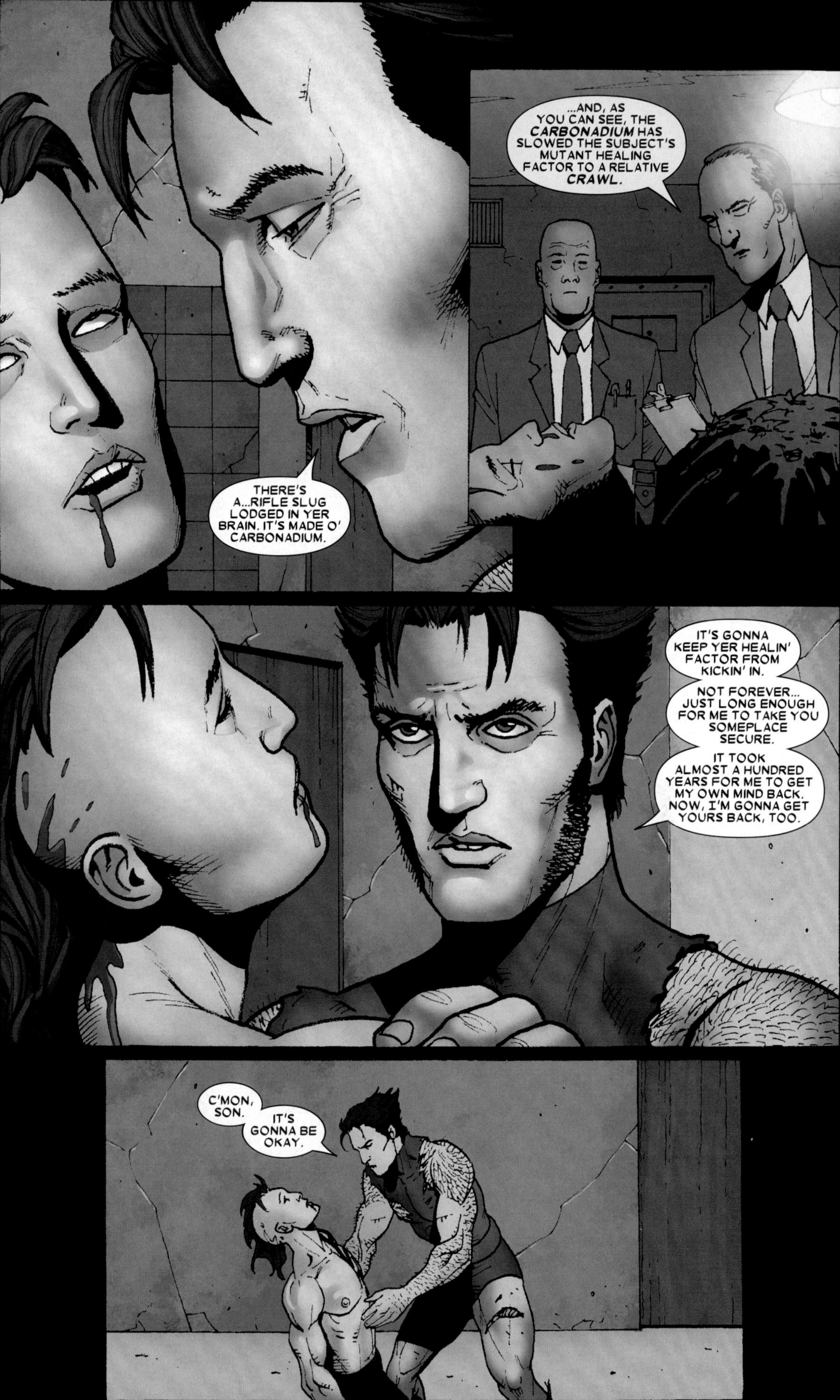
...AND, AS YOU CAN SEE, THE CARBONADIUM HAS SLOWED THE SUBJECT'S MUTANT HEALING FACTOR TO A RELATIVE CRAWL.
THERE'S A...RIFLE SLUG LODGED IN YER BRAIN. IT'S MADE O' CARBONADIUM.
IT'S GONNA KEEP YER HEALIN' FACTOR FROM KICKIN' IN.
NOT FOREVER... JUST LONG ENOUGH FOR ME TO TAKE YOU SOMEPLACE SECURE.
IT TOOK ALMOST A HUNDRED YEARS FOR ME TO GET MY OWN MIND BACK. NOW, I'M GONNA GET YOURS BACK, TOO.
C'MON, SON.
IT'S GONNA BE OKAY.

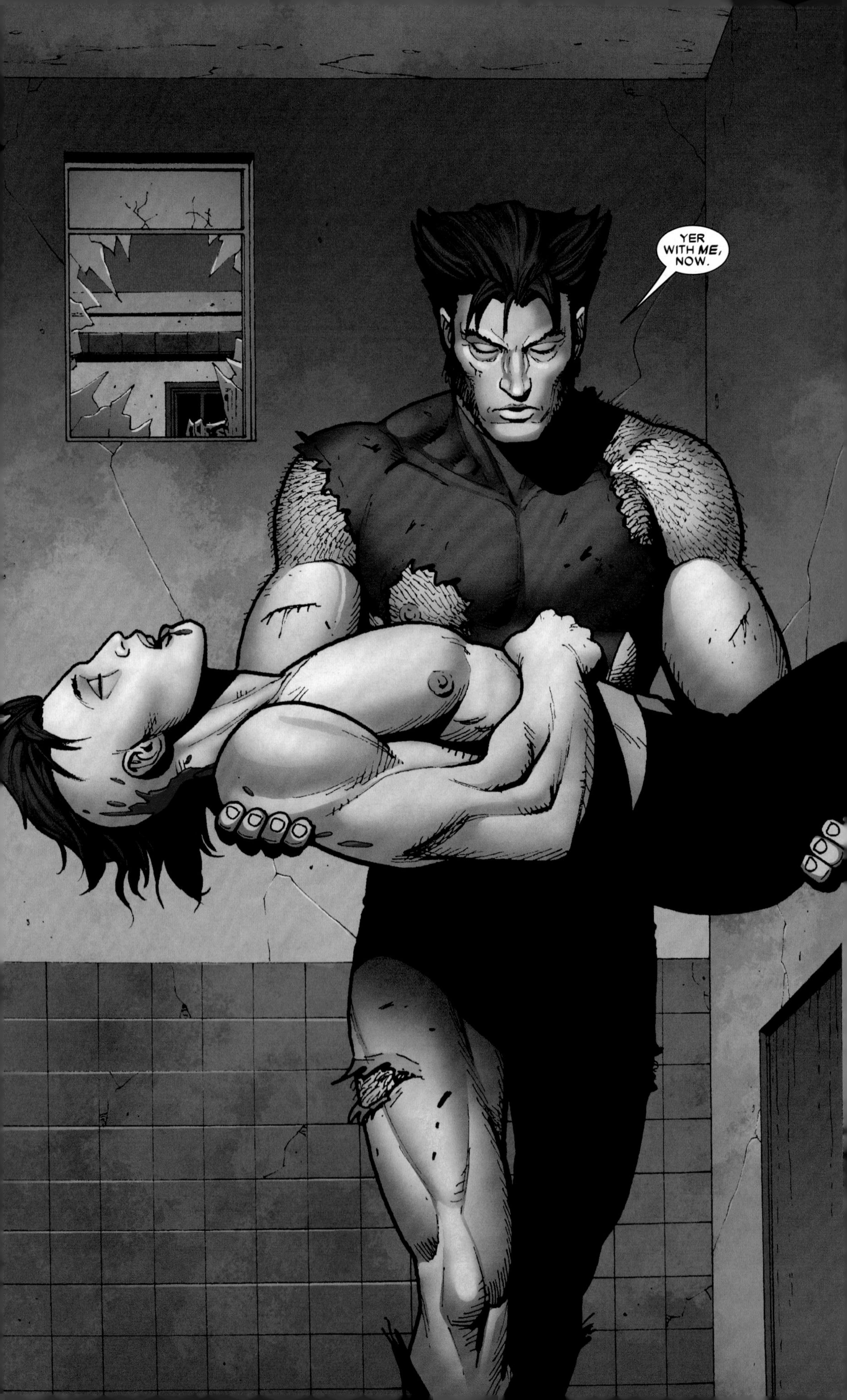
YER WITH ME, NOW.

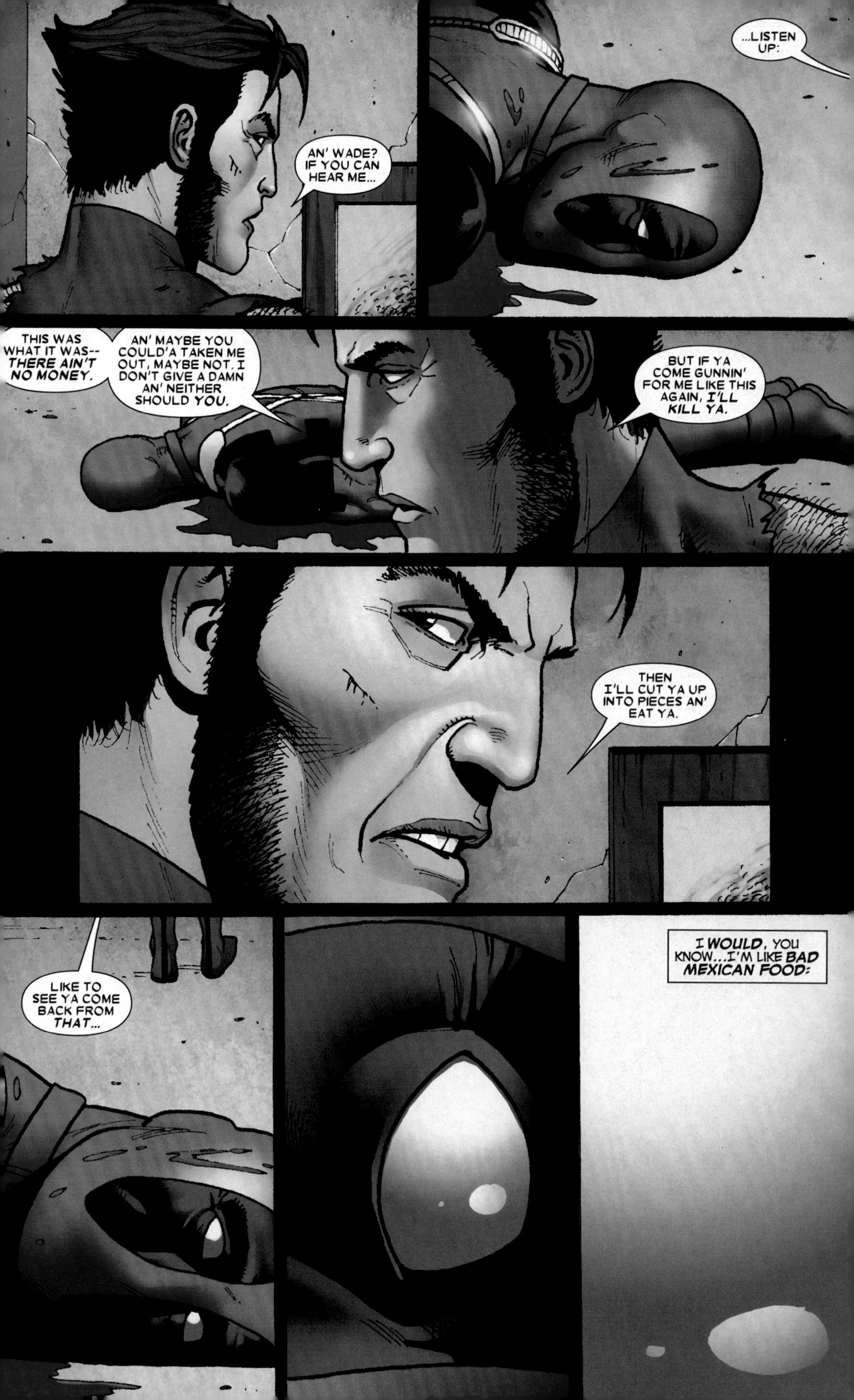
AN' WADE? IF YOU CAN HEAR ME...
...LISTEN UP:
THIS WAS WHAT IT WAS-- THERE AIN'T NO MONEY.
AN' MAYBE YOU COULD'A TAKEN ME OUT, MAYBE NOT. I DON'T GIVE A DAMN AN' NEITHER SHOULD YOU.
BUT IF YA COME GUNNIN' FOR ME LIKE THIS AGAIN, I'LL KILL YA.
THEN I'LL CUT YA UP INTO PIECES AN' EAT YA.
LIKE TO SEE YA COME BACK FROM THAT...
I WOULD, YOU KNOW...I'M LIKE BAD MEXICAN FOOD:

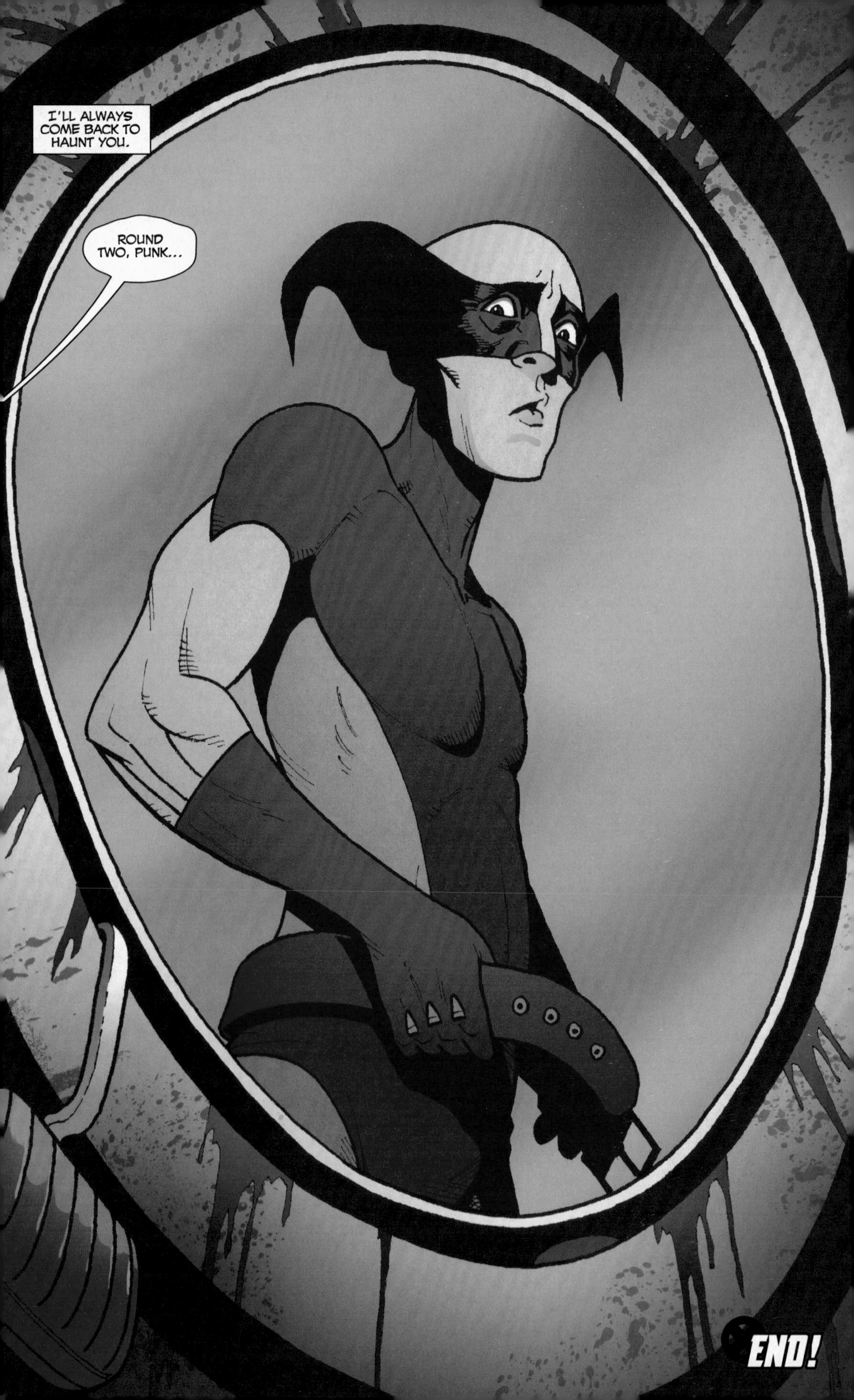
I'LL ALWAYS COME BACK TO HAUNT YOU.
ROUND TWO, PUNK...
END!

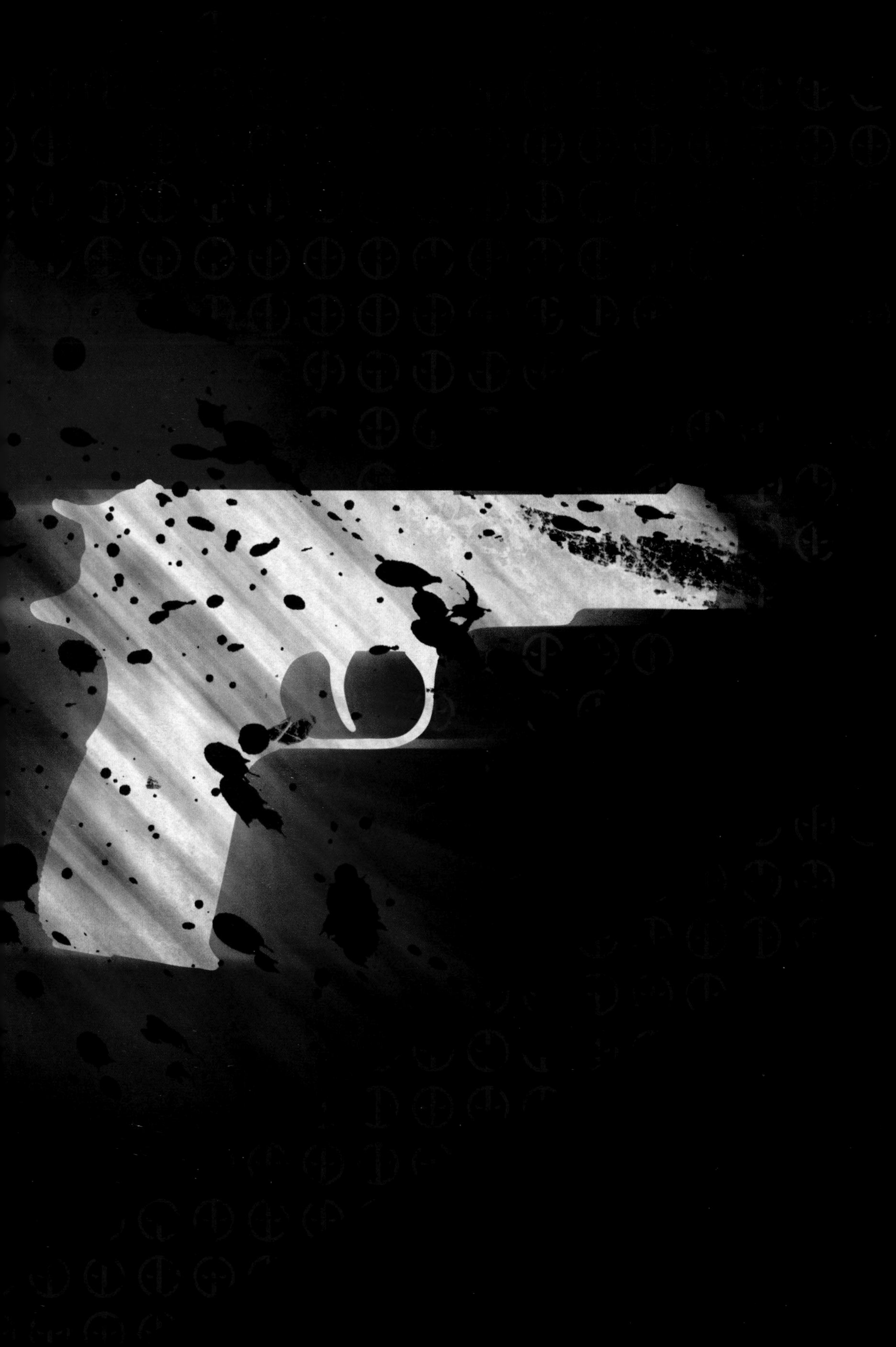

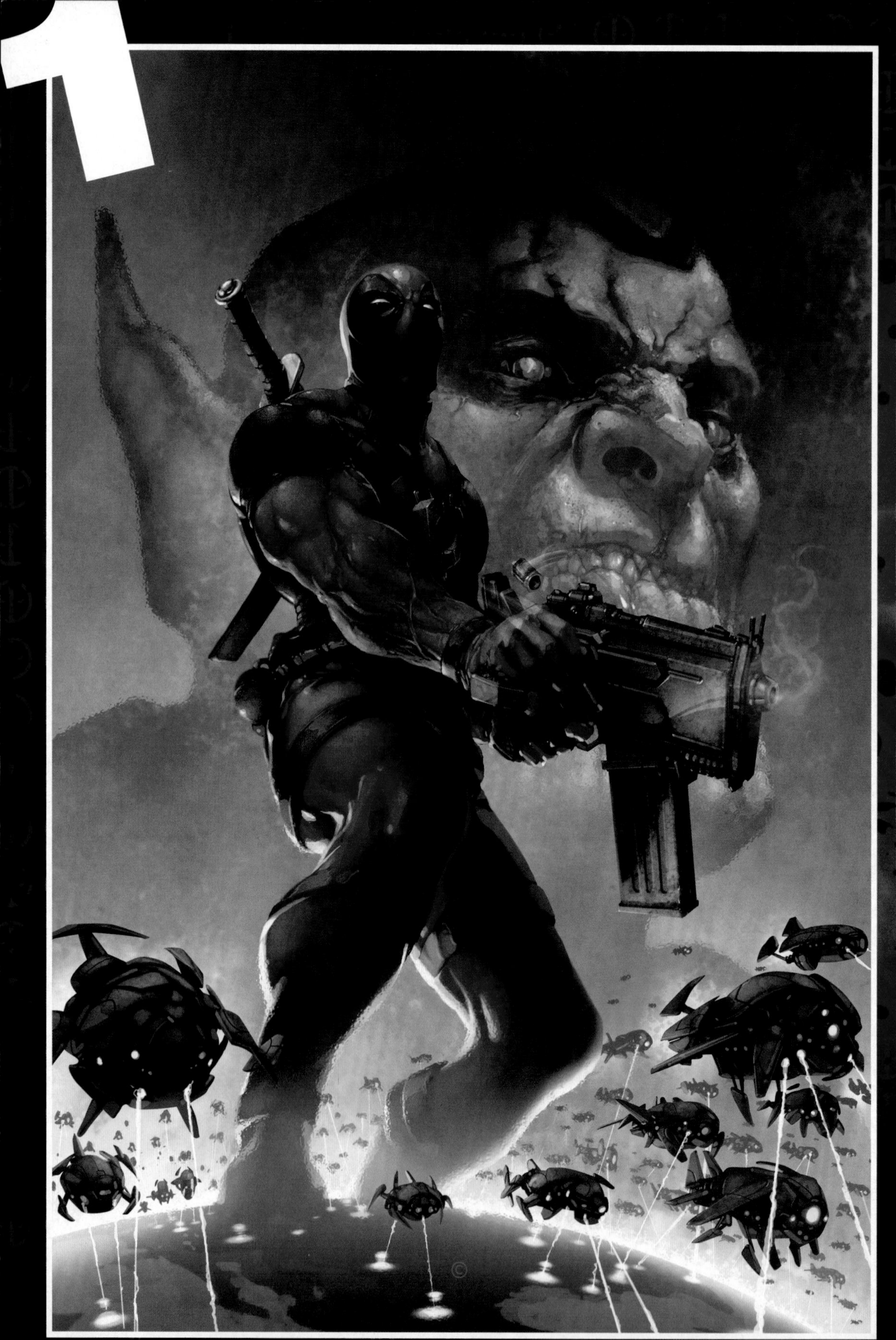
1

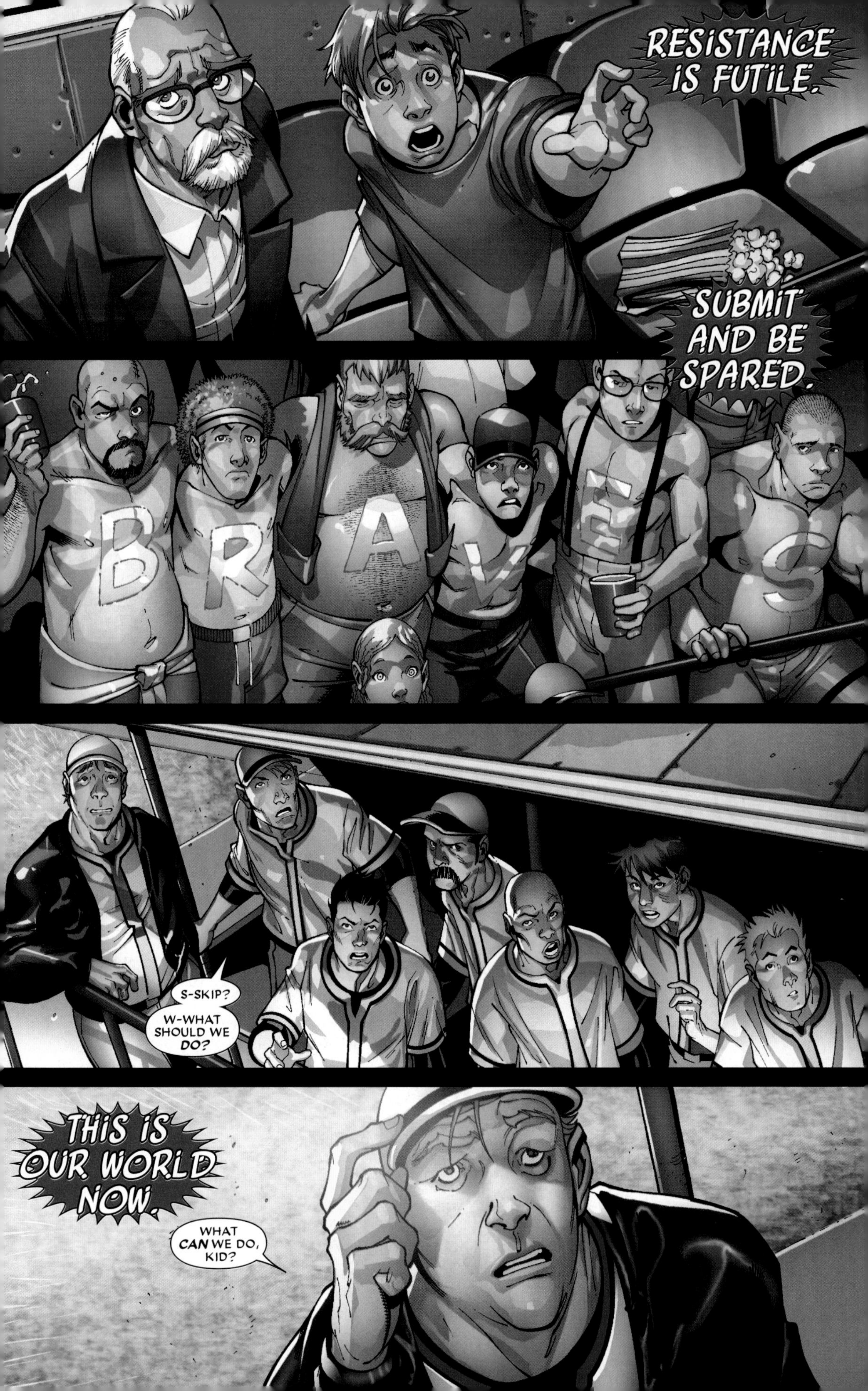
RESISTANCE IS FUTILE.
SUBMIT AND BE SPARED.
BRAVES
S-SKIP?
W-WHAT SHOULD WE DO?
THIS IS OUR WORLD NOW.
WHAT CAN WE DO, KID?

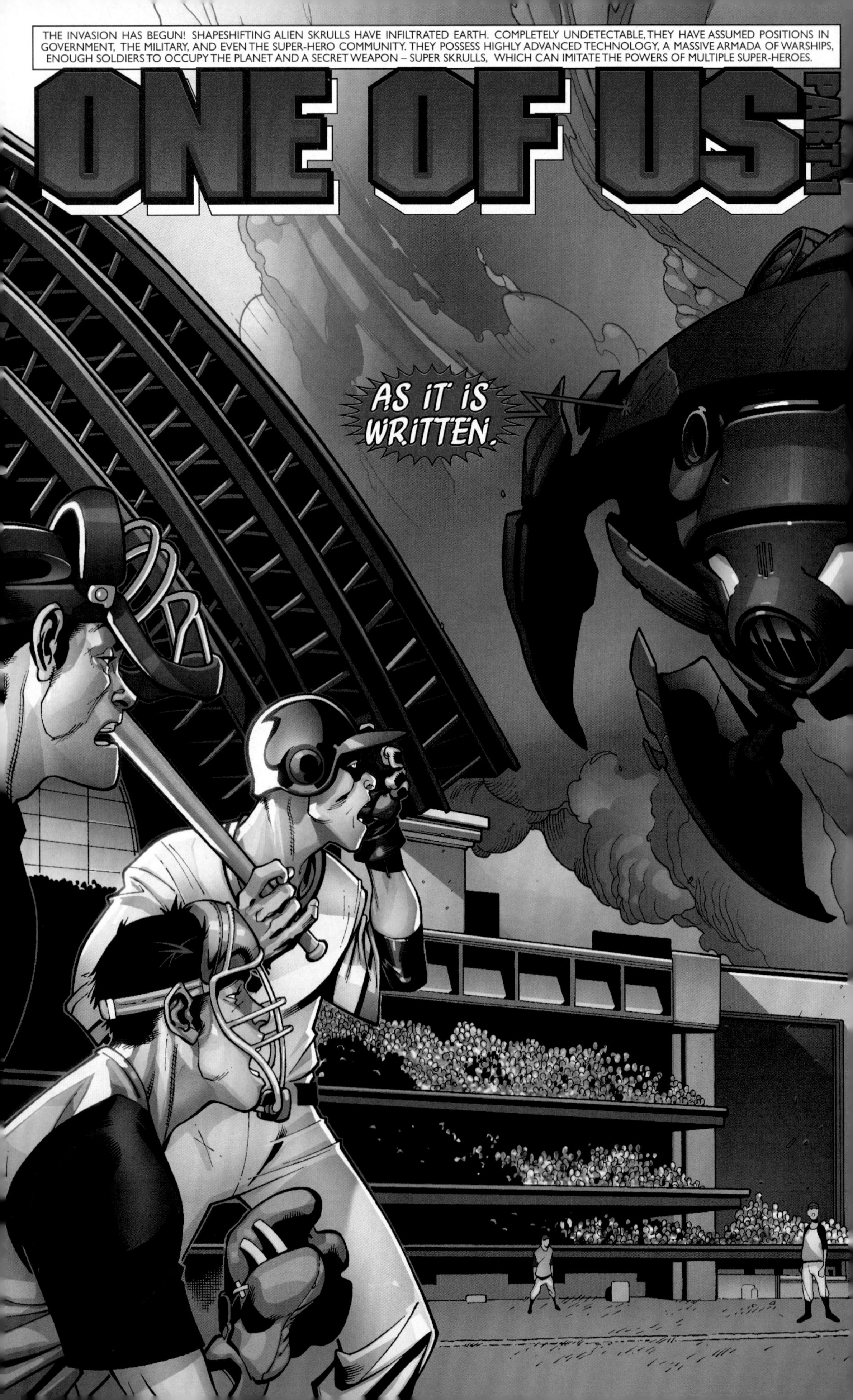
THE INVASION HAS BEGUN! SHAPESHIFTING ALIEN SKRULLS HAVE INFILTRATED EARTH. COMPLETELY UNDETECTABLE, THEY HAVE ASSUMED POSITIONS IN GOVERNMENT, THE MILITARY, AND EVEN THE SUPER-HERO COMMUNITY. THEY POSSESS HIGHLY ADVANCED TECHNOLOGY, A MASSIVE ARMADA OF WARSHIPS, ENOUGH SOLDIERS TO OCCUPY THE PLANET AND A SECRET WEAPON – SUPER SKRULLS, WHICH CAN IMITATE THE POWERS OF MULTIPLE SUPER-HEROES.
ONE OF US
PART 1
AS IT IS WRITTEN.

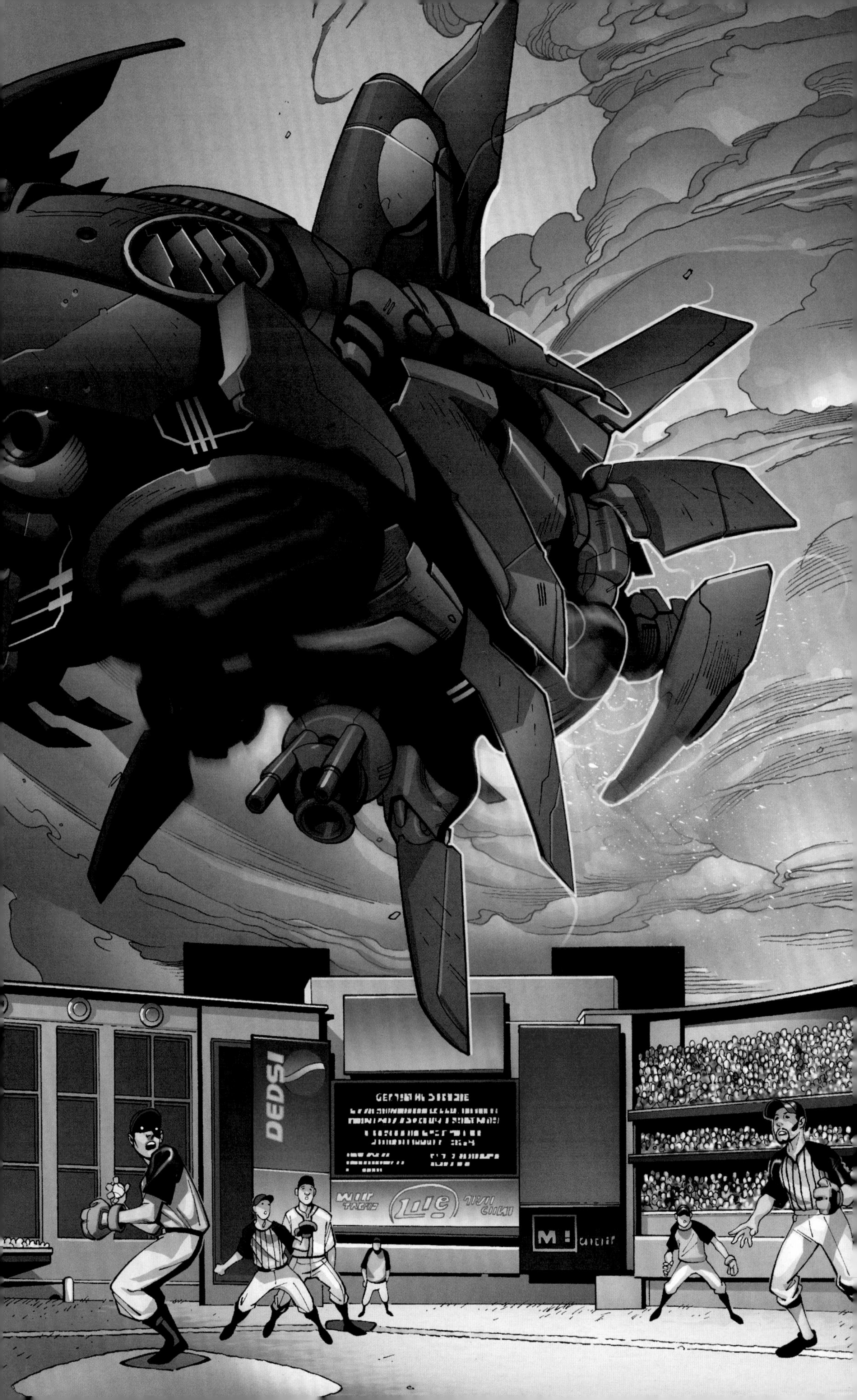
DEDSI

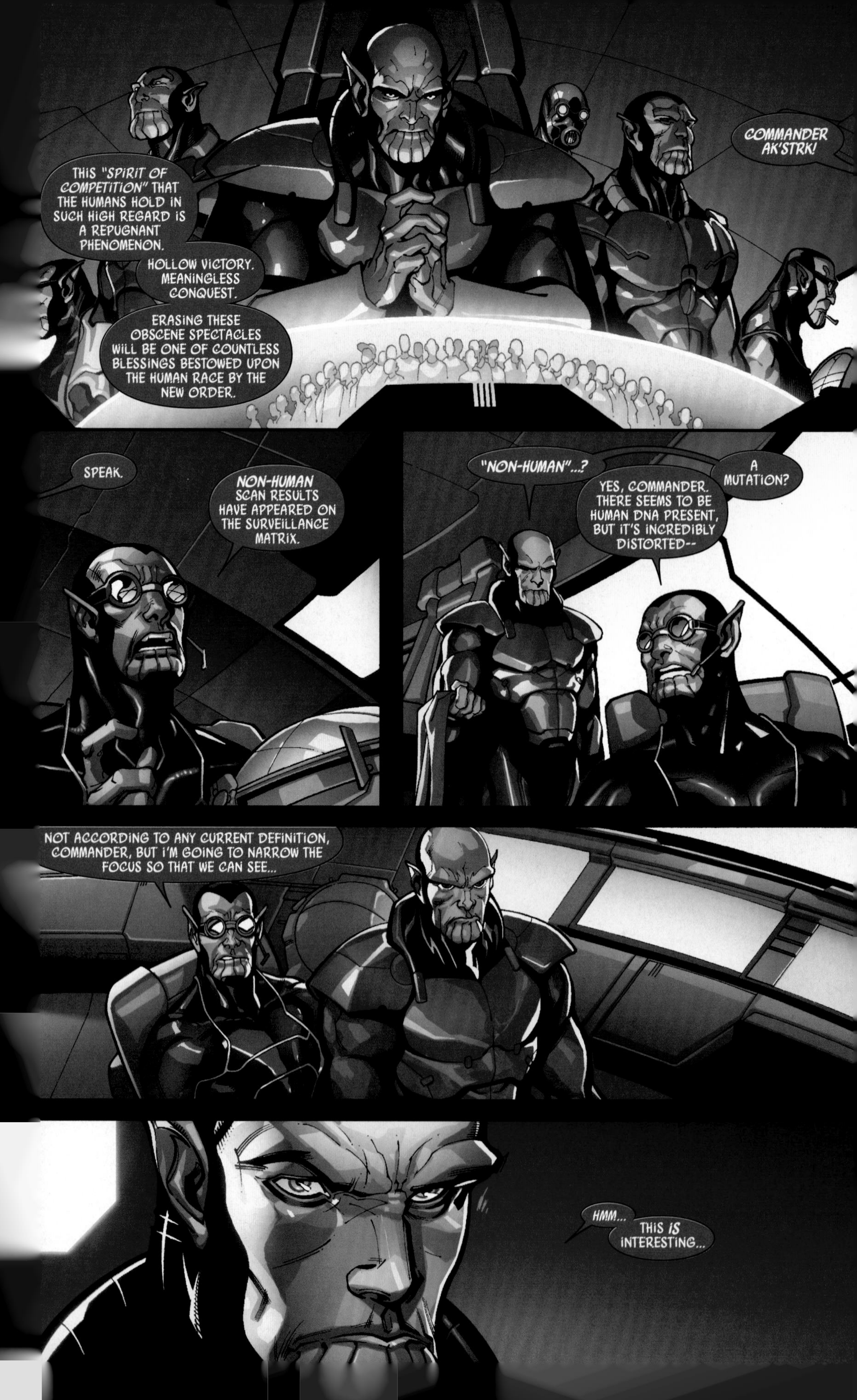

THIS "SPIRIT OF COMPETITION" THAT THE HUMANS HOLD IN SUCH HIGH REGARD IS A REPUGNANT PHENOMENON.
HOLLOW VICTORY. MEANINGLESS CONQUEST.
ERASING THESE OBSCENE SPECTACLES WILL BE ONE OF COUNTLESS BLESSINGS BESTOWED UPON THE HUMAN RACE BY THE NEW ORDER.
COMMANDER AK'STRK!
SPEAK.
NON-HUMAN SCAN RESULTS HAVE APPEARED ON THE SURVEILLANCE MATRIX.
"NON-HUMAN"...?
YES, COMMANDER. THERE SEEMS TO BE HUMAN DNA PRESENT, BUT IT'S INCREDIBLY DISTORTED--
A MUTATION?
NOT ACCORDING TO ANY CURRENT DEFINITION, COMMANDER, BUT I'M GOING TO NARROW THE FOCUS SO THAT WE CAN SEE...
HMM...
THIS IS INTERESTING...

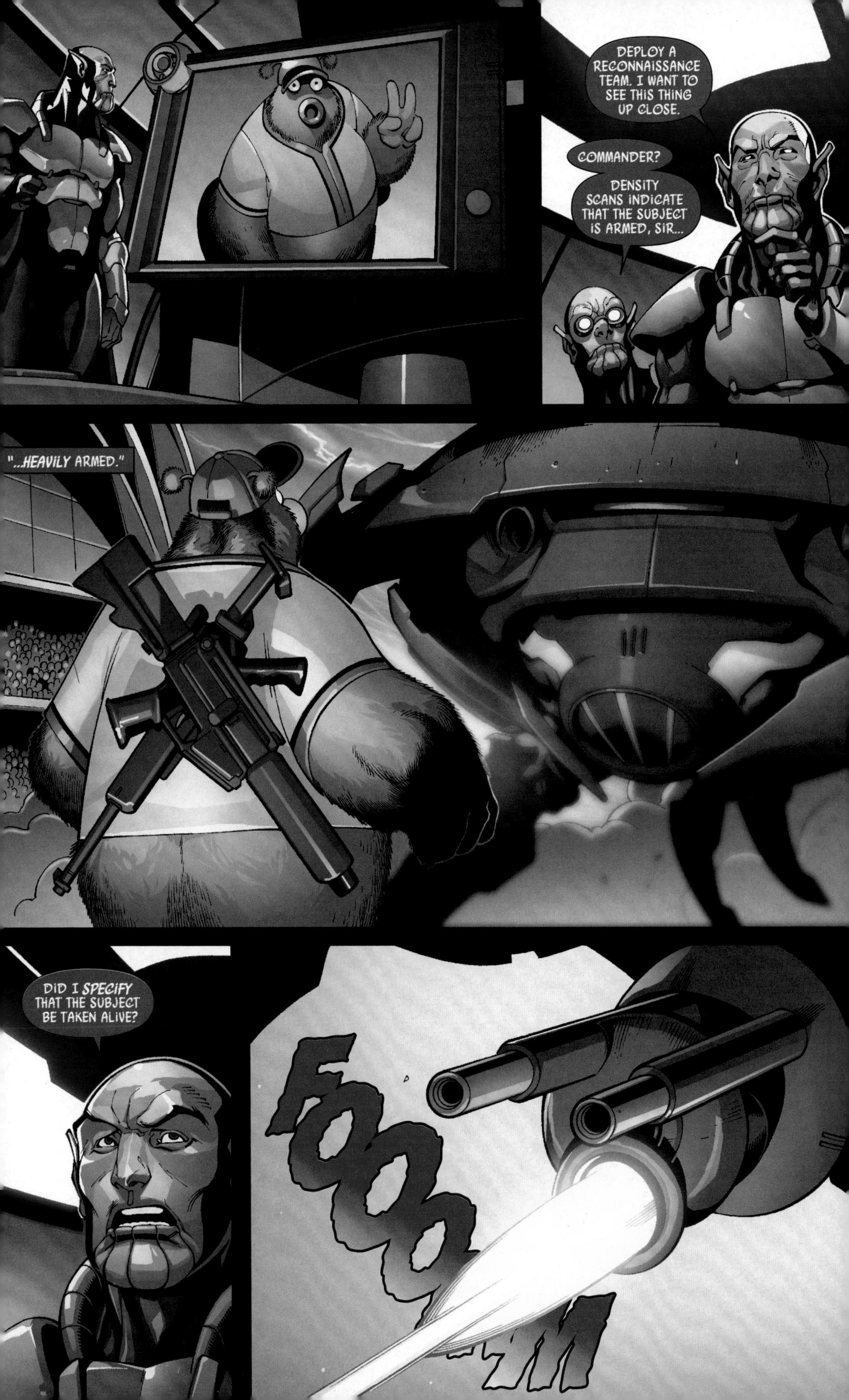
DEPLOY A RECONNAISSANCE TEAM. I WANT TO SEE THIS THING UP CLOSE.
COMMANDER?
DENSITY SCANS INDICATE THAT THE SUBJECT IS ARMED, SIR...
"...HEAVILY ARMED."
DID I SPECIFY THAT THE SUBJECT BE TAKEN ALIVE?
FOOOOM

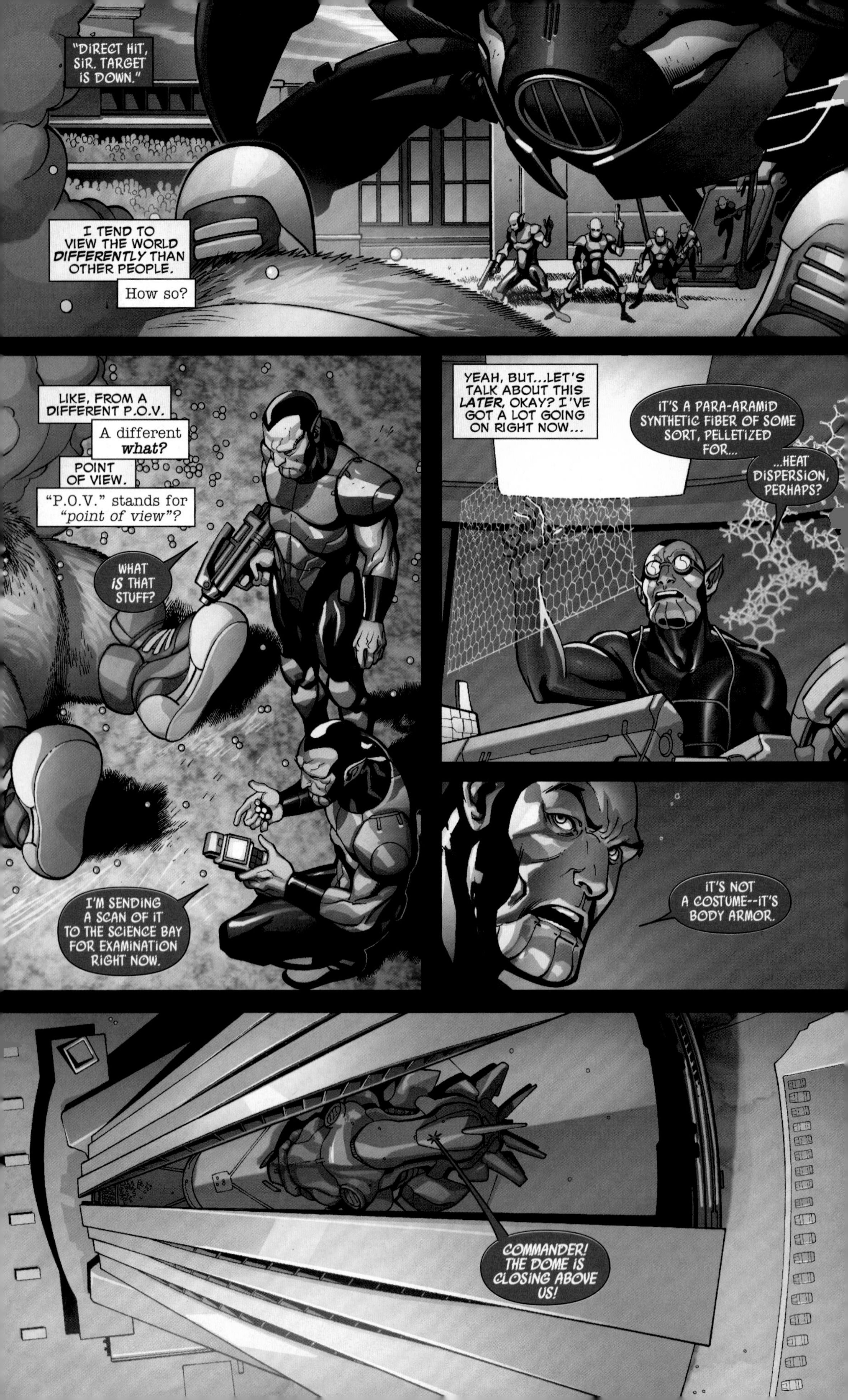
"DIRECT HIT, SIR. TARGET IS DOWN."
I TEND TO VIEW THE WORLD *DIFFERENTLY* THAN OTHER PEOPLE.
How so?
LIKE, FROM A DIFFERENT P.O.V.
A different ***what?***
POINT OF VIEW.
"P.O.V." stands for *"point of view"*?
WHAT *IS* THAT STUFF?
I'M SENDING A SCAN OF IT TO THE SCIENCE BAY FOR EXAMINATION RIGHT NOW.
YEAH, BUT...LET'S TALK ABOUT THIS *LATER*, OKAY? I'VE GOT A LOT GOING ON RIGHT NOW...
IT'S A PARA-ARAMID SYNTHETIC FIBER OF SOME SORT, PELLETIZED FOR...
...HEAT DISPERSION, PERHAPS?
IT'S NOT A COSTUME--IT'S BODY ARMOR.
COMMANDER! THE DOME IS CLOSING ABOVE US!

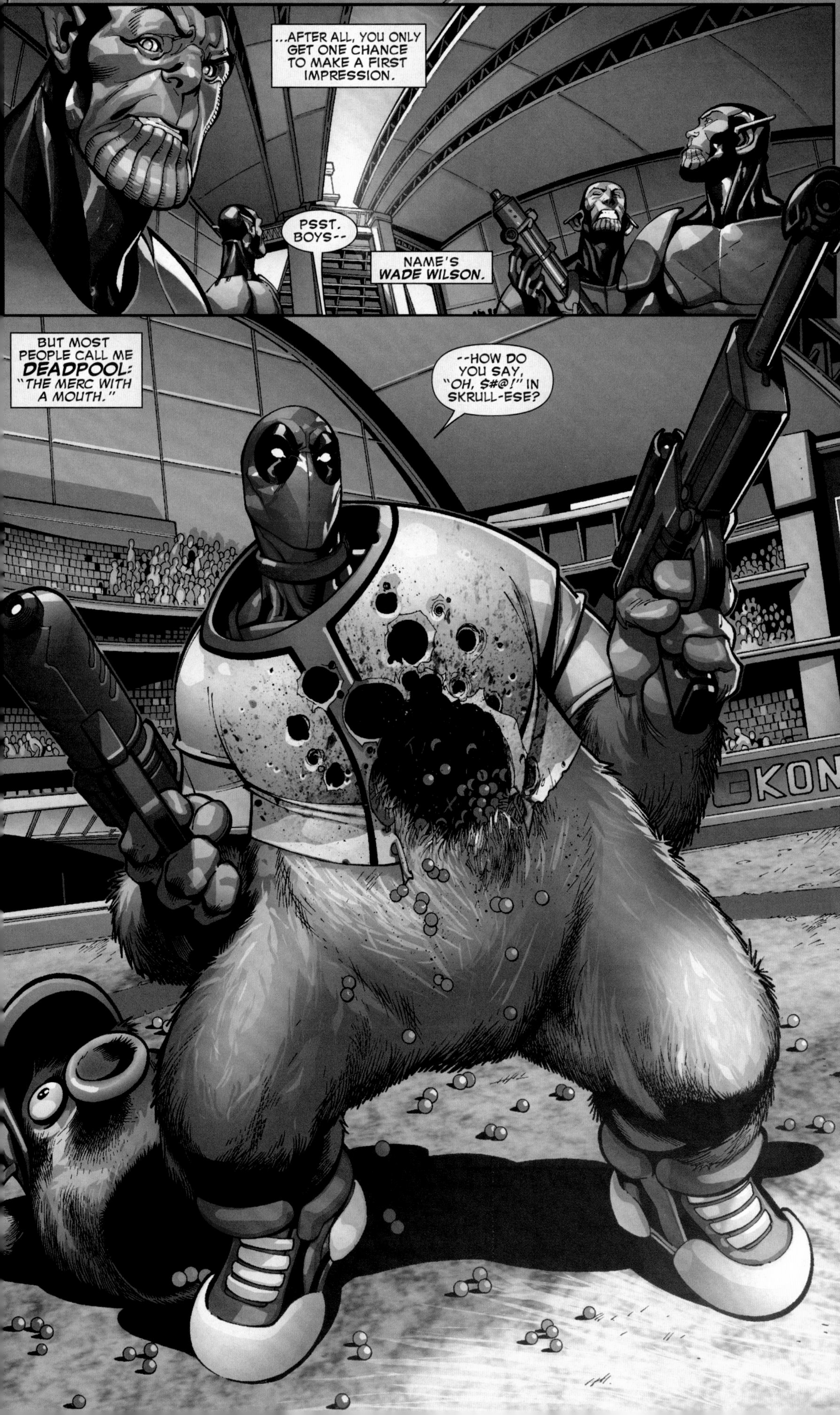
...AFTER ALL, YOU ONLY GET ONE CHANCE TO MAKE A FIRST IMPRESSION.
PSST. BOYS--
NAME'S WADE WILSON.
BUT MOST PEOPLE CALL ME DEADPOOL: "THE MERC WITH A MOUTH."
--HOW DO YOU SAY, "OH, $#@!" IN SKRULL-ESE?
KONI

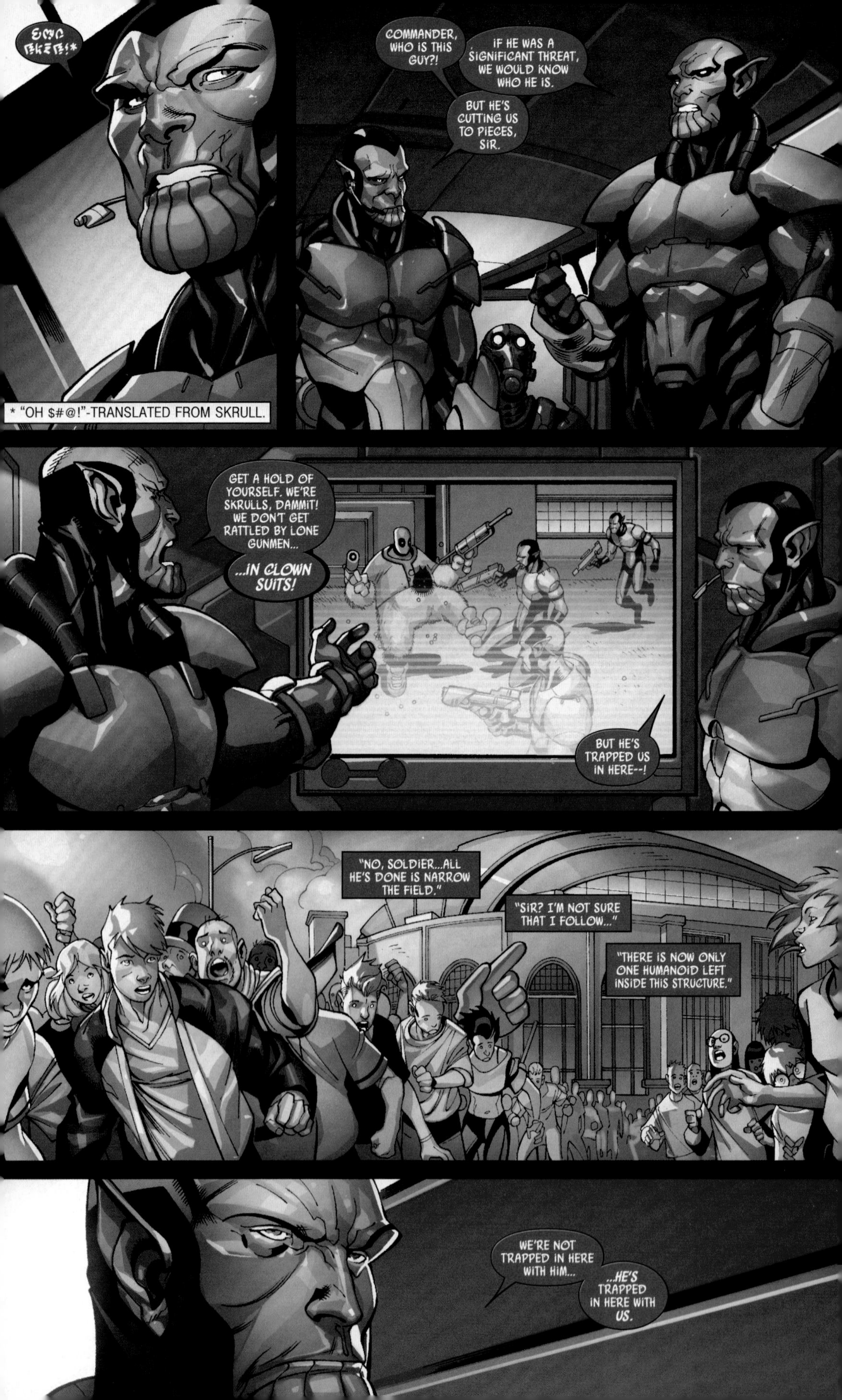

COMMANDER, WHO IS THIS GUY?!
IF HE WAS A SIGNIFICANT THREAT, WE WOULD KNOW WHO HE IS.
BUT HE'S CUTTING US TO PIECES, SIR.
* "OH $#@!"-TRANSLATED FROM SKRULL.
GET A HOLD OF YOURSELF. WE'RE SKRULLS, DAMMIT! WE DON'T GET RATTLED BY LONE GUNMEN...
...IN CLOWN SUITS!
BUT HE'S TRAPPED US IN HERE--!
"NO, SOLDIER...ALL HE'S DONE IS NARROW THE FIELD."
"SIR? I'M NOT SURE THAT I FOLLOW..."
"THERE IS NOW ONLY ONE HUMANOID LEFT INSIDE THIS STRUCTURE."
WE'RE NOT TRAPPED IN HERE WITH HIM...
...HE'S TRAPPED IN HERE WITH US.

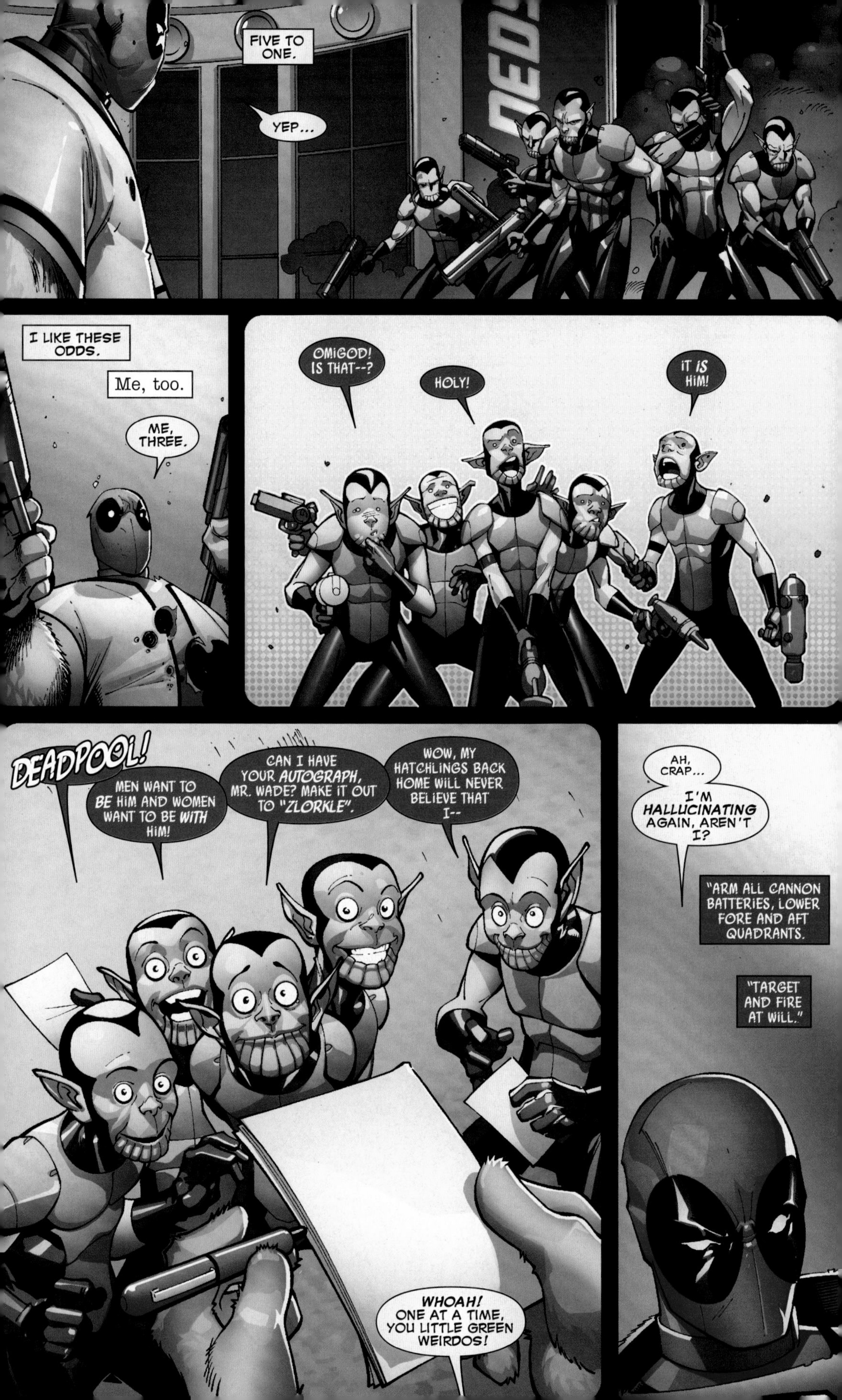
FIVE TO ONE.
YEP...
I LIKE THESE ODDS.
Me, too.
ME, THREE.
OMIGOD! IS THAT--?
HOLY!
IT IS HIM!
DEADPOOL!
MEN WANT TO BE HIM AND WOMEN WANT TO BE WITH HIM!
CAN I HAVE YOUR AUTOGRAPH, MR. WADE? MAKE IT OUT TO "ZLORKLE".
WOW, MY HATCHLINGS BACK HOME WILL NEVER BELIEVE THAT I--
WHOAH! ONE AT A TIME, YOU LITTLE GREEN WEIRDOS!
AH, CRAP...
I'M HALLUCINATING AGAIN, AREN'T I?
"ARM ALL CANNON BATTERIES, LOWER FORE AND AFT QUADRANTS.
"TARGET AND FIRE AT WILL."

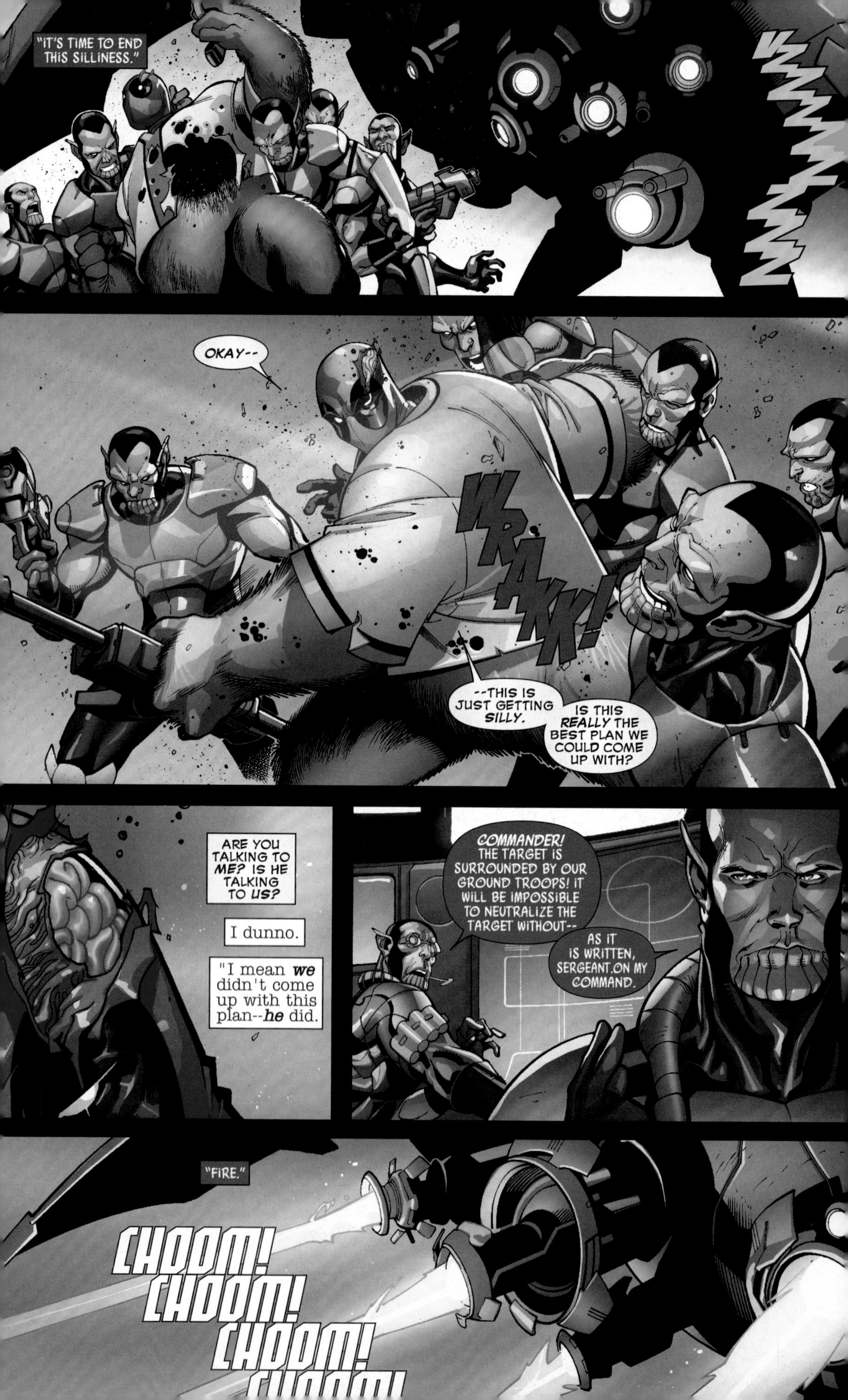
"IT'S TIME TO END THIS SILLINESS."
VMMMMMMM
OKAY--
WRAKK!
--THIS IS JUST GETTING SILLY.
IS THIS REALLY THE BEST PLAN WE COULD COME UP WITH?
ARE YOU TALKING TO ME? IS HE TALKING TO US?
I dunno.
"I mean we didn't come up with this plan--he did.
COMMANDER! THE TARGET IS SURROUNDED BY OUR GROUND TROOPS! IT WILL BE IMPOSSIBLE TO NEUTRALIZE THE TARGET WITHOUT--
AS IT IS WRITTEN, SERGEANT. ON MY COMMAND.
"FIRE."
CHOOM! CHOOM! CHOOM!

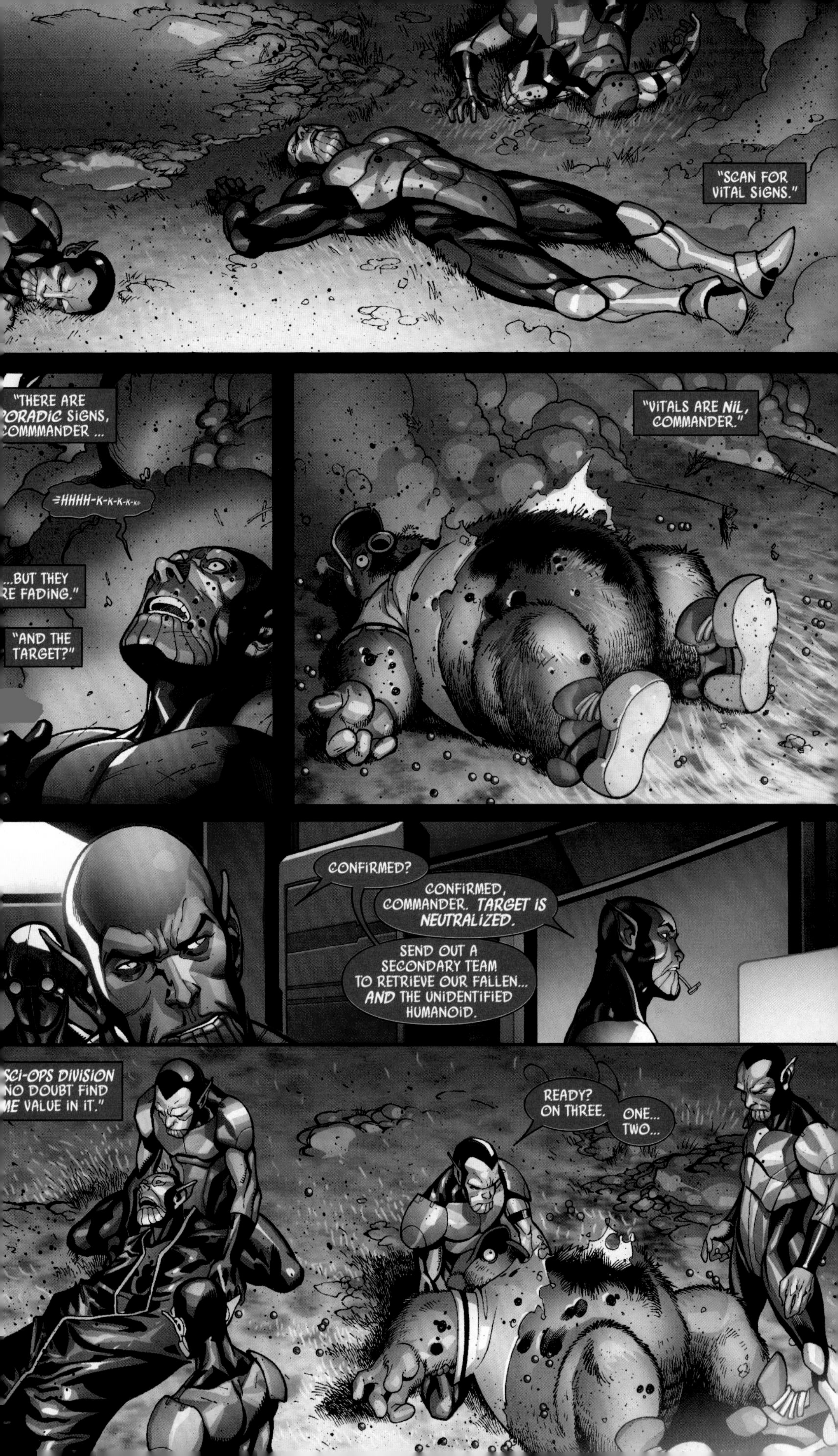
"SCAN FOR VITAL SIGNS."
"THERE ARE SPORADIC SIGNS, COMMMANDER ...
HHHH-K-K-K-K-K
...BUT THEY ARE FADING."
"AND THE TARGET?"
"VITALS ARE NIL, COMMANDER."
CONFIRMED?
CONFIRMED, COMMANDER. TARGET IS NEUTRALIZED.
SEND OUT A SECONDARY TEAM TO RETRIEVE OUR FALLEN... AND THE UNIDENTIFIED HUMANOID.
SCI-OPS DIVISION NO DOUBT FIND ME VALUE IN IT."
READY? ON THREE.
ONE... TWO...

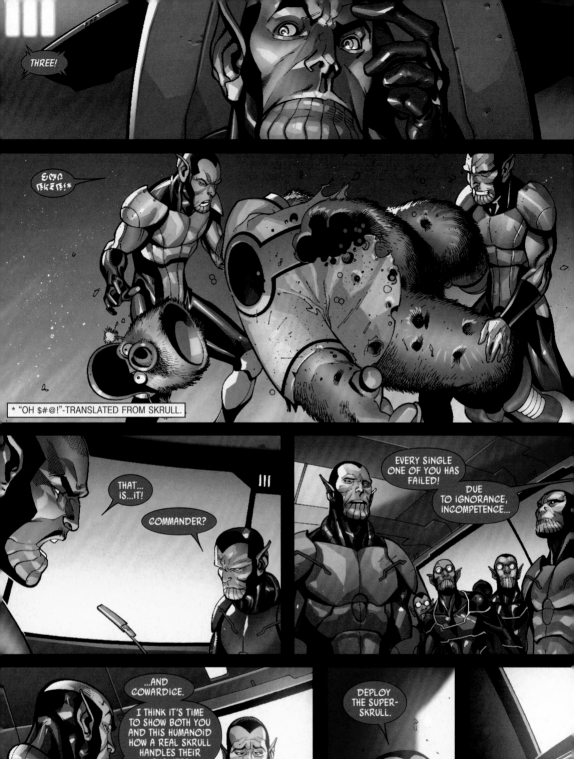

THREE!

EYC BKEB!

* "OH $#@!"-TRANSLATED FROM SKRULL.

THAT... iS...iT!

COMMANDER?

EVERY SINGLE ONE OF YOU HAS FAILED!

DUE TO IGNORANCE, INCOMPETENCE...

...AND COWARDICE.

I THINK IT'S TIME TO SHOW BOTH YOU AND THIS HUMANOID HOW A REAL SKRULL HANDLES THEIR BUSINESS.

DEPLOY THE SUPER-SKRULL.

KLIK

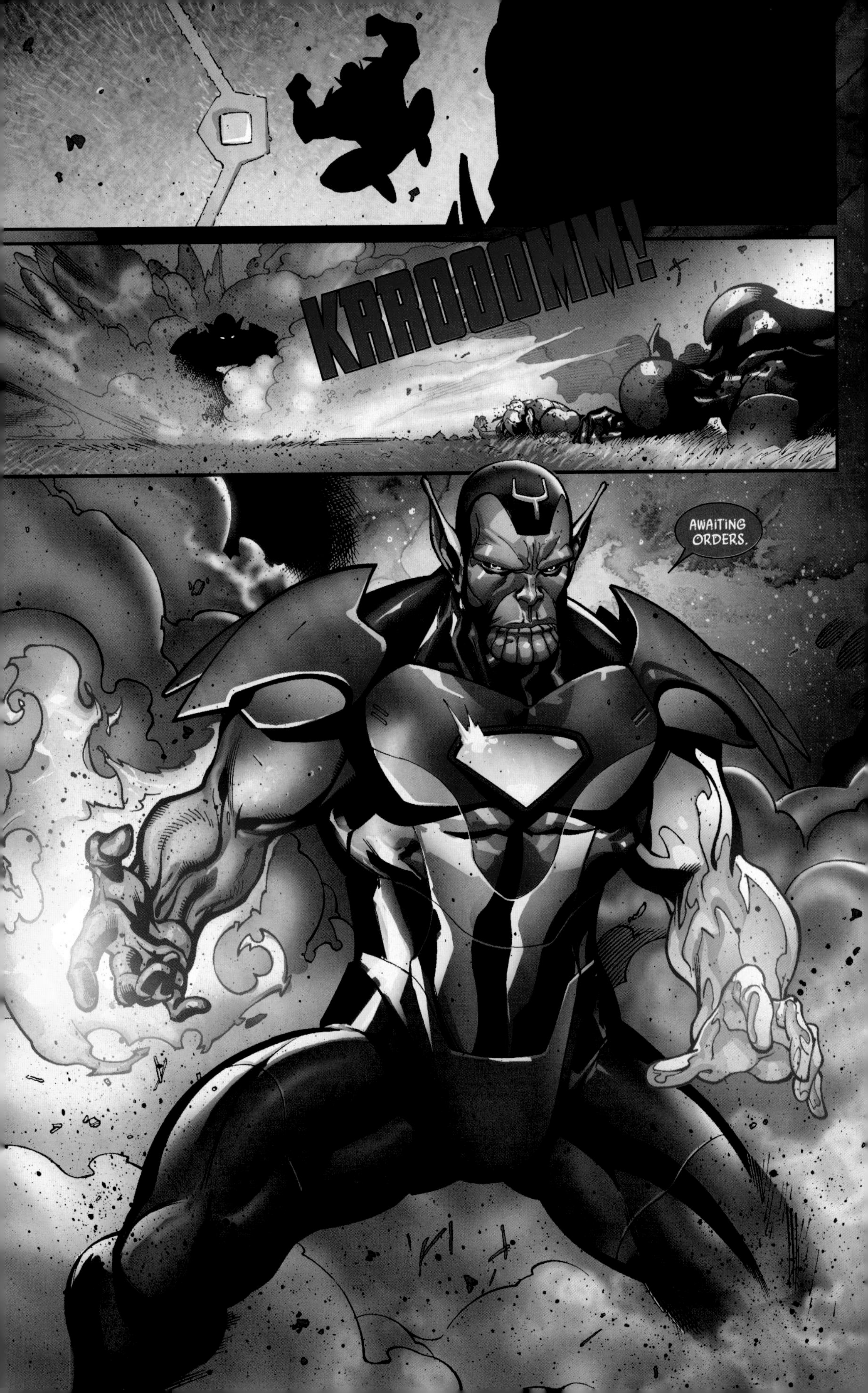
KRROOOMM!
AWAITING ORDERS.

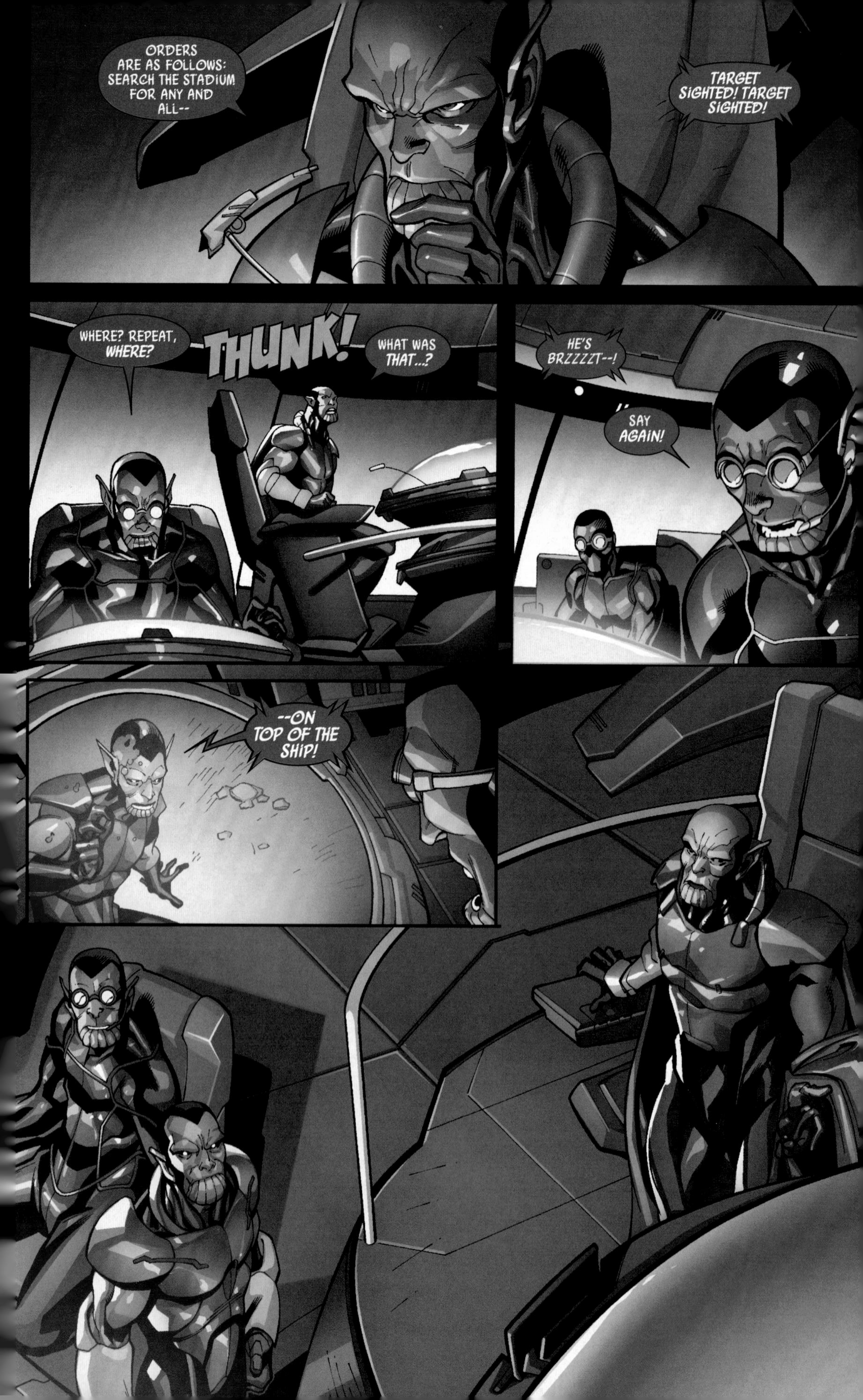
ORDERS ARE AS FOLLOWS: SEARCH THE STADIUM FOR ANY AND ALL--
TARGET SIGHTED! TARGET SIGHTED!
WHERE? REPEAT, WHERE?
THUNK!
WHAT WAS THAT...?
HE'S BRZZZZT--!
SAY AGAIN!
--ON TOP OF THE SHIP!

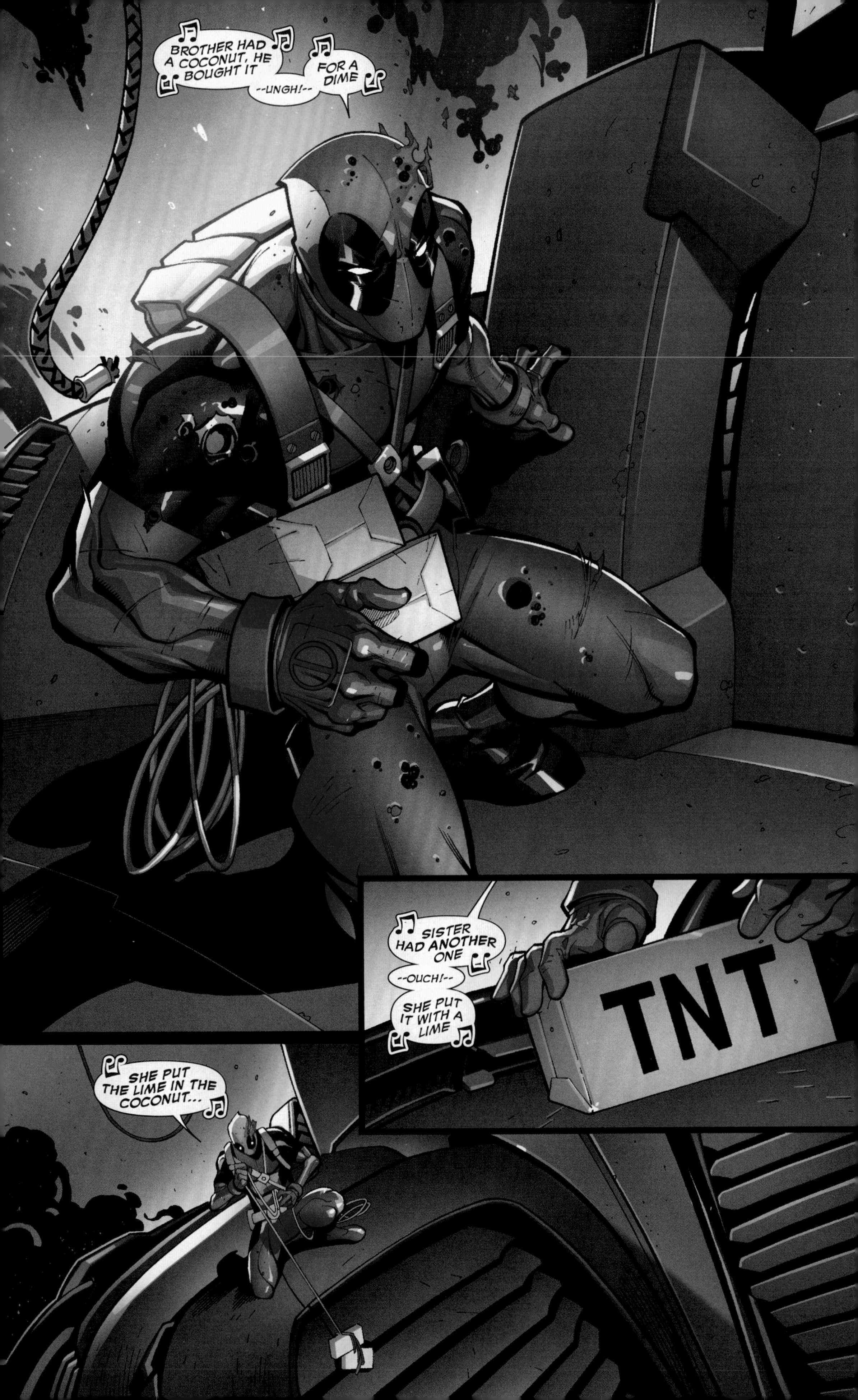
BROTHER HAD A COCONUT, HE BOUGHT IT
--UNGH!--
FOR A DIME
SISTER HAD ANOTHER ONE
--OUCH!--
SHE PUT IT WITH A LIME
TNT
SHE PUT THE LIME IN THE COCONUT...

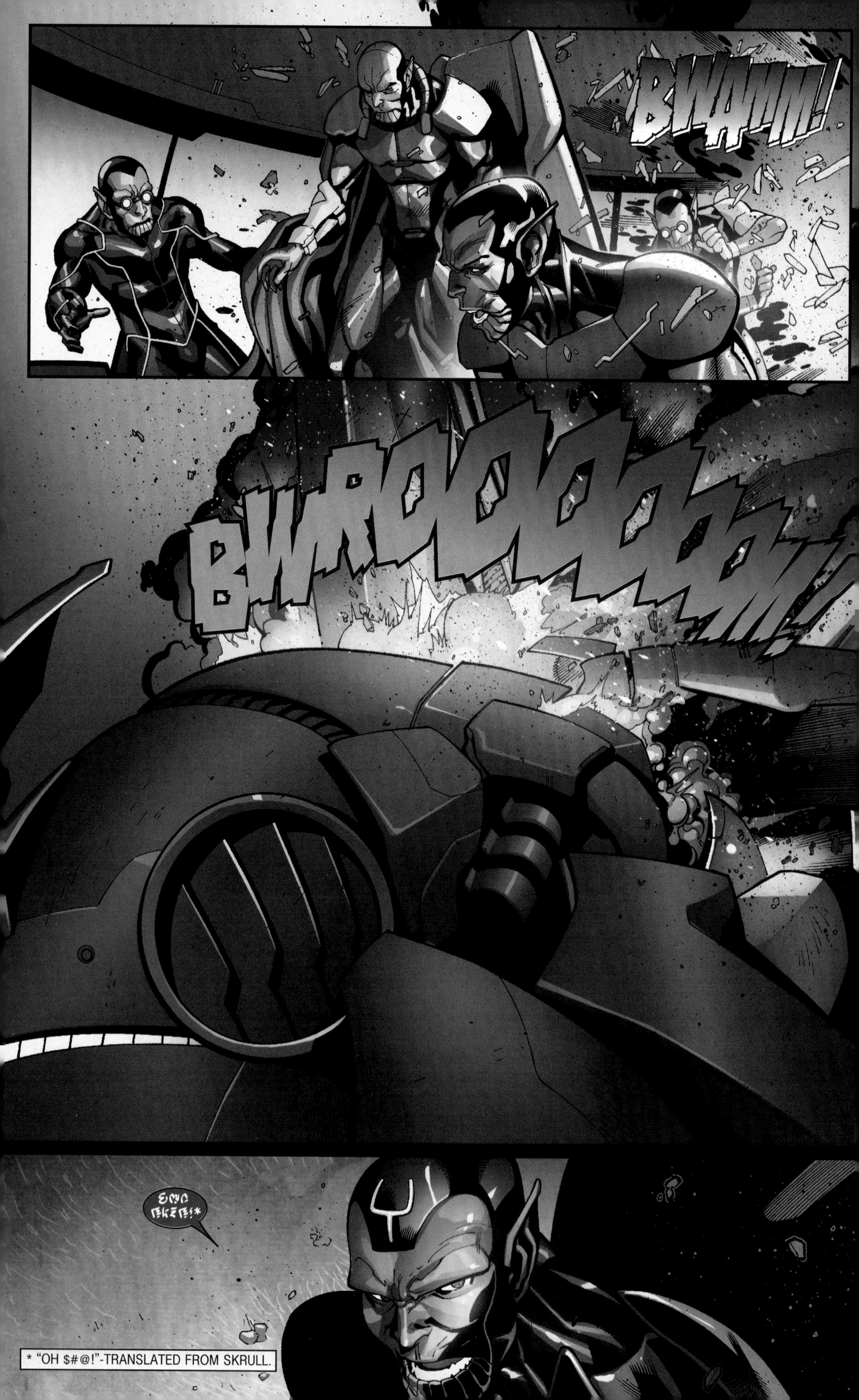
BWAMM!
BWROOOOOM!
* "OH $#@!"-TRANSLATED FROM SKRULL.

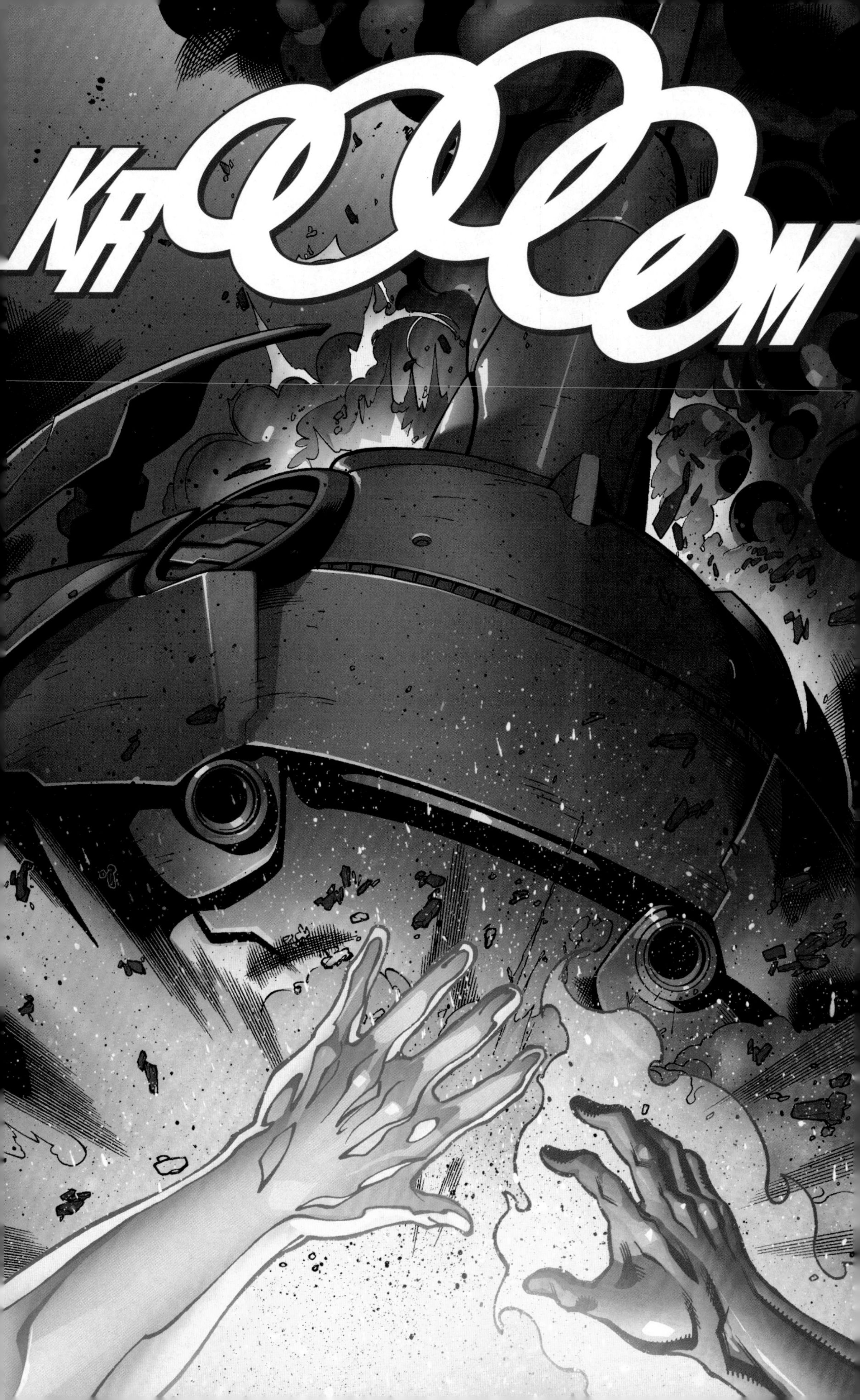
KABOOOM

So, you were saying, *"P.O.V."* stands for *"point of view"*?

USUALLY.

BUT IN MY CASE, IT STANDS FOR *"POOL-O-VISION™"*.

500 points

500 points

500 points

500 points

50 points

500 points

500 points

500 points

YOU WIN!!!

What's the little "TM" for?

IT'S *SILENT.*

What?

IT'S *SILENT.* YOU DON'T PRONOUNCE IT.

That doesn't even make sense.

TO *YOU,* MAYBE...

I **am** you!

YEAH, BUT--

THERE'S THE BIG DOG.

JUST LIKE I PLANNED.

Wait. After *"crash ship into bad guys,"* there was a plan?

THERE'S ALWAYS A PLAN. C'MON, FASTER! FALL FASTER!

The only way you're going to "fall faster" is if you--

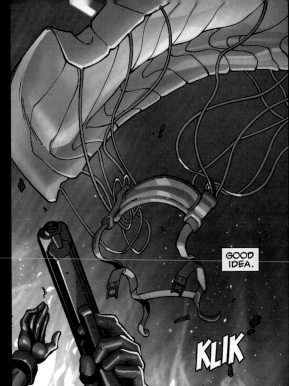

GOOD IDEA.

KLIK

ANYWAY...

OOMPF

WRAKK!

THE POINT IS, EVEN THOUGH MY VISION'S A BIT WARPED...

OUCH

...I'M NOT BLIND.

KLONG!

AND I'M DEFINITELY NOT STUPID.

HOLD IT RIGHT THERE!

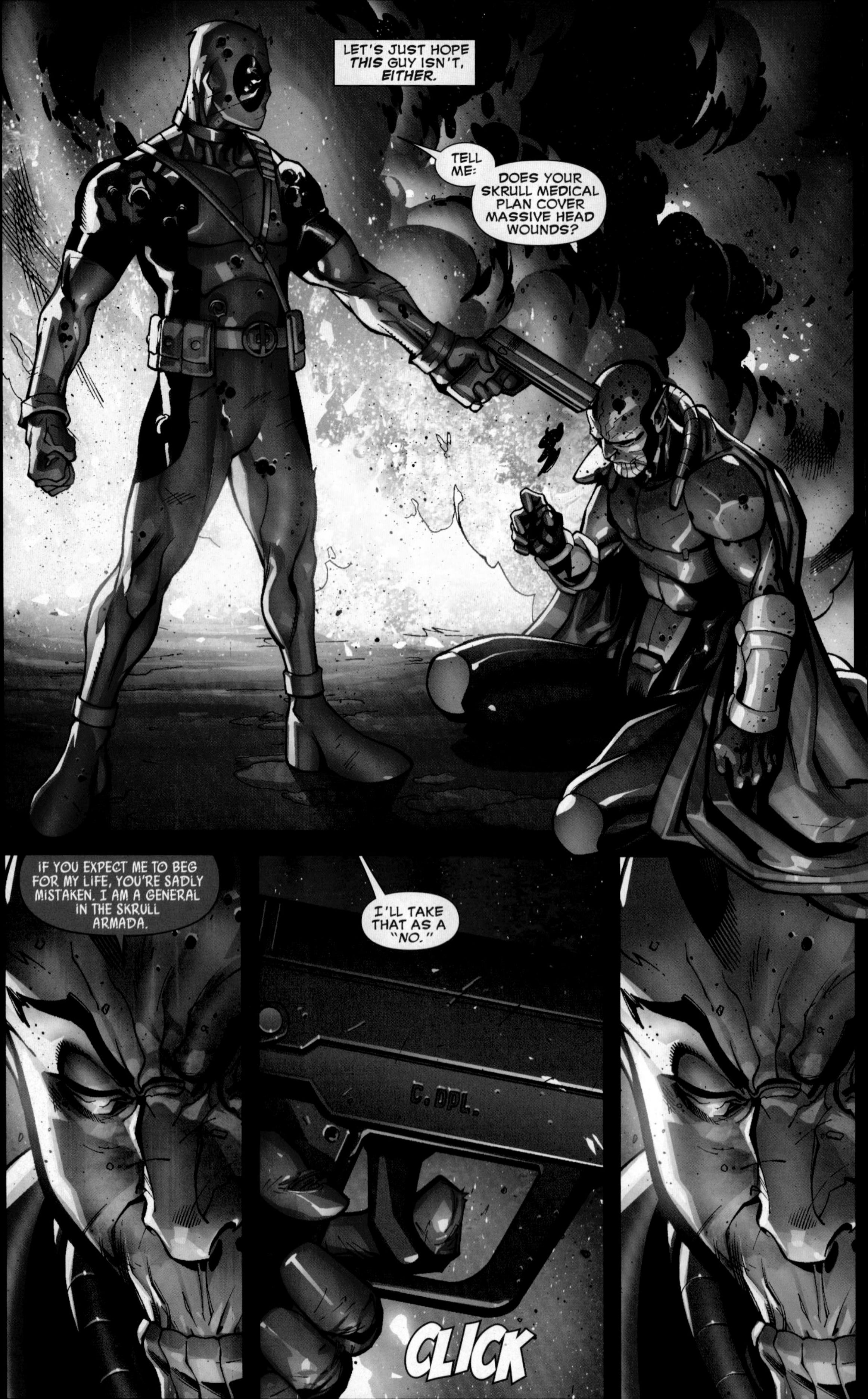
LET'S JUST HOPE THIS GUY ISN'T, EITHER.
TELL ME:
DOES YOUR SKRULL MEDICAL PLAN COVER MASSIVE HEAD WOUNDS?
IF YOU EXPECT ME TO BEG FOR MY LIFE, YOU'RE SADLY MISTAKEN. I AM A GENERAL IN THE SKRULL ARMADA.
I'LL TAKE THAT AS A "NO."
C.DPL.
CLICK

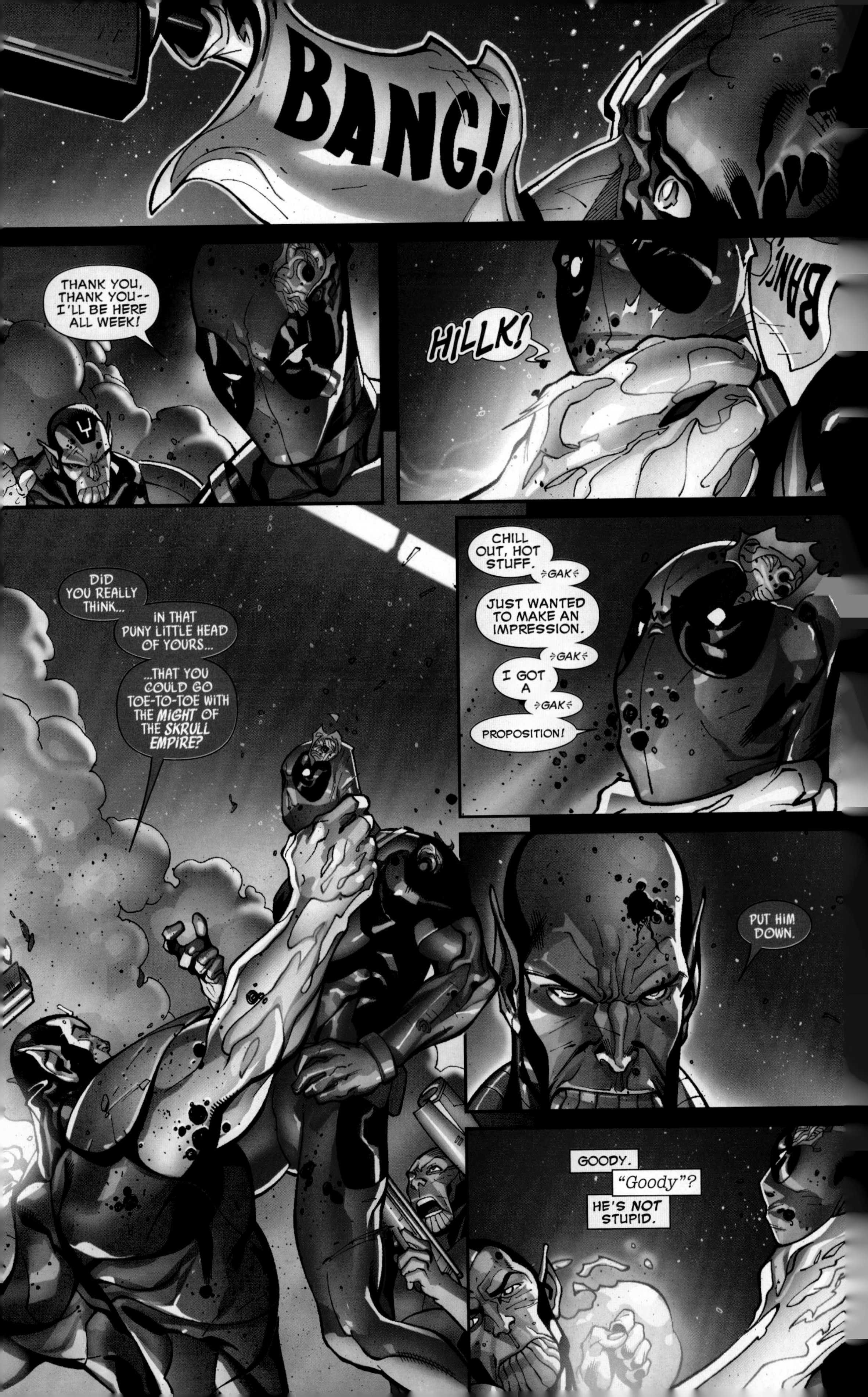
BANG!
THANK YOU, THANK YOU-- I'LL BE HERE ALL WEEK!
BANG
HILLK!
DID YOU REALLY THINK...
IN THAT PUNY LITTLE HEAD OF YOURS...
...THAT YOU COULD GO TOE-TO-TOE WITH THE MIGHT OF THE SKRULL EMPIRE?
CHILL OUT, HOT STUFF.
GAK
JUST WANTED TO MAKE AN IMPRESSION.
GAK
I GOT A
GAK
PROPOSITION!
PUT HIM DOWN.
GOODY.
"Goody"?
HE'S NOT STUPID.

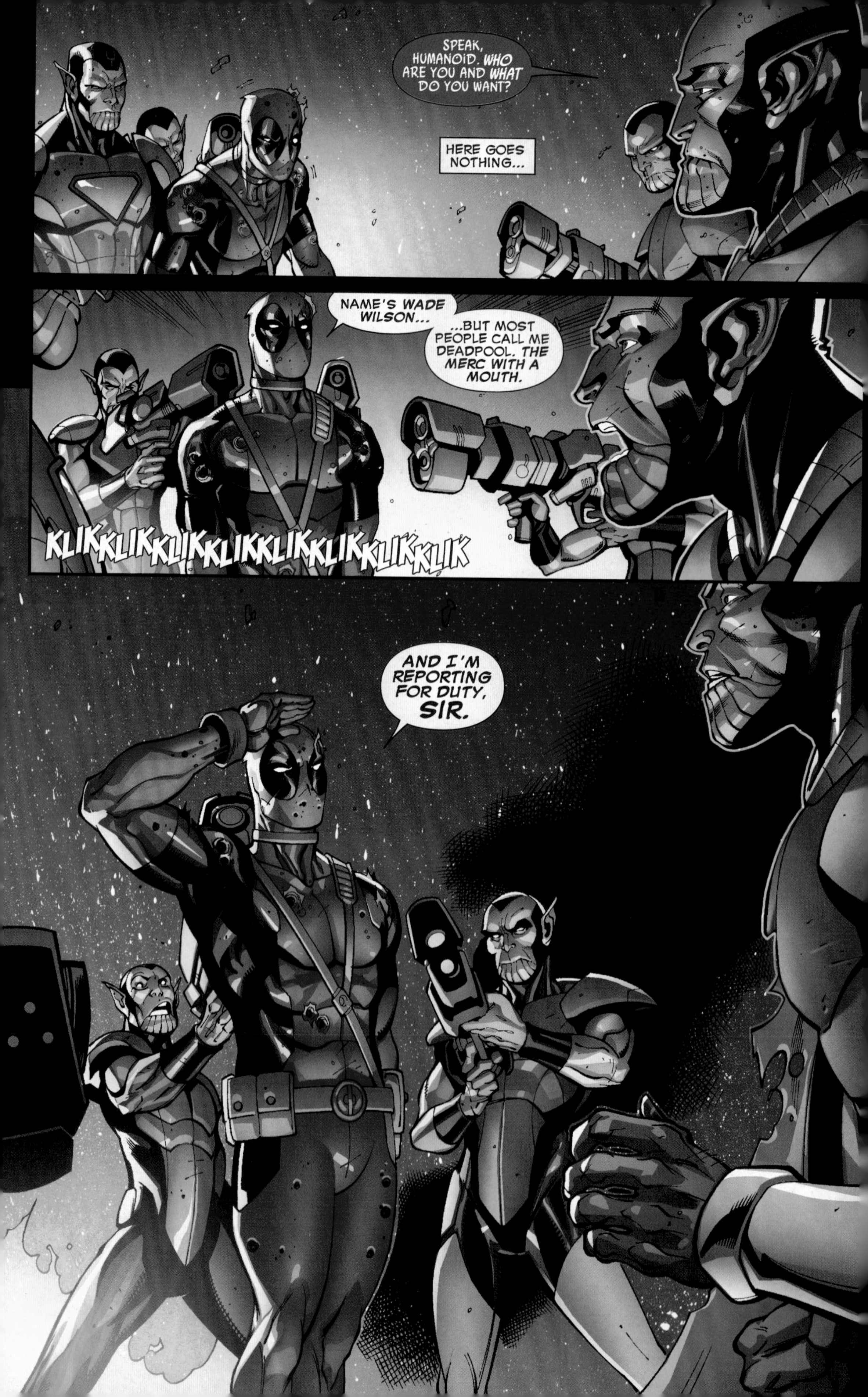
SPEAK, HUMANOID. WHO ARE YOU AND WHAT DO YOU WANT?
HERE GOES NOTHING...
NAME'S WADE WILSON...
...BUT MOST PEOPLE CALL ME DEADPOOL. THE MERC WITH A MOUTH.
KLIKKLIKKLIKKLIKKLIKKLIKKLIKKLIK
AND I'M REPORTING FOR DUTY, SIR.

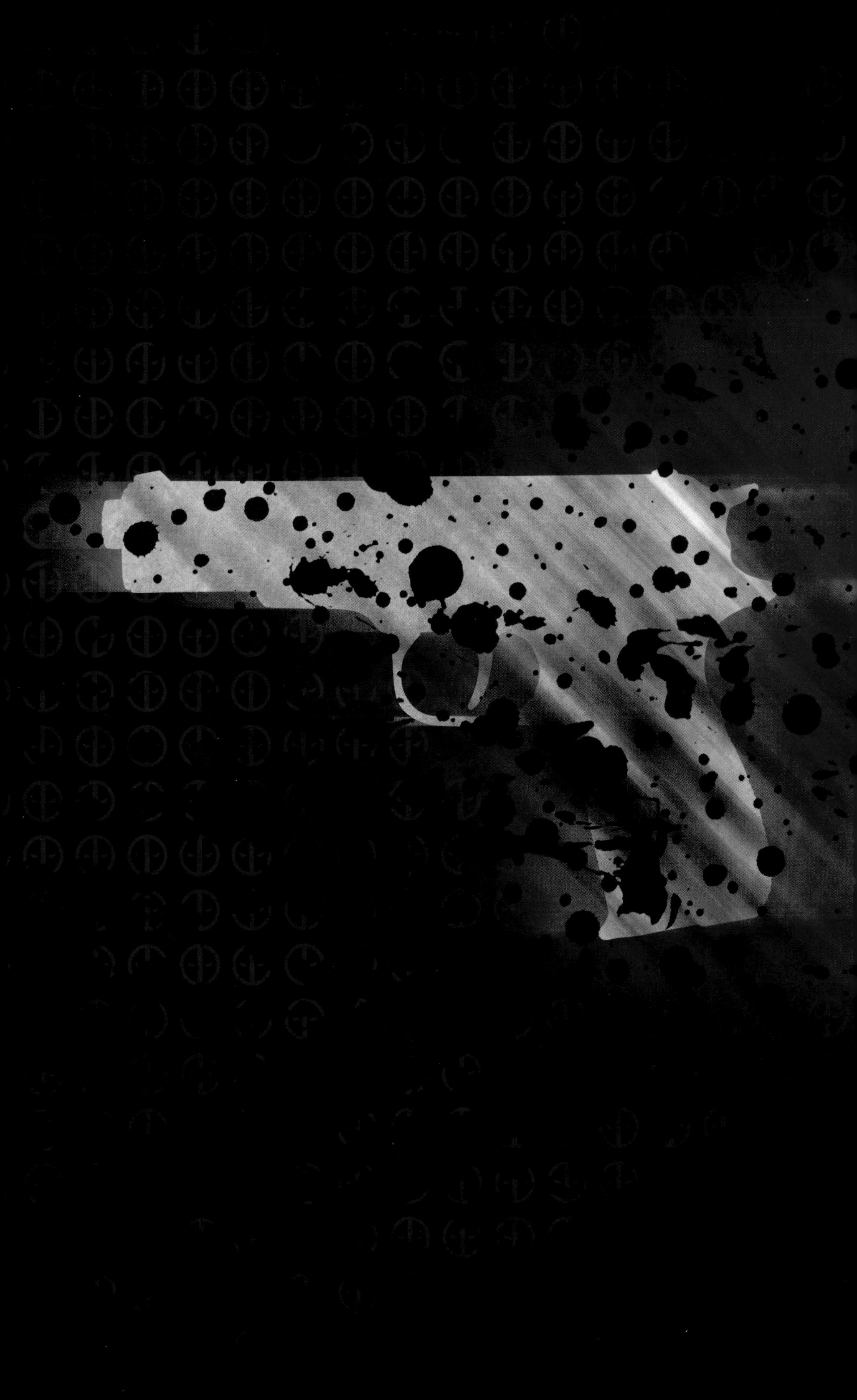

2

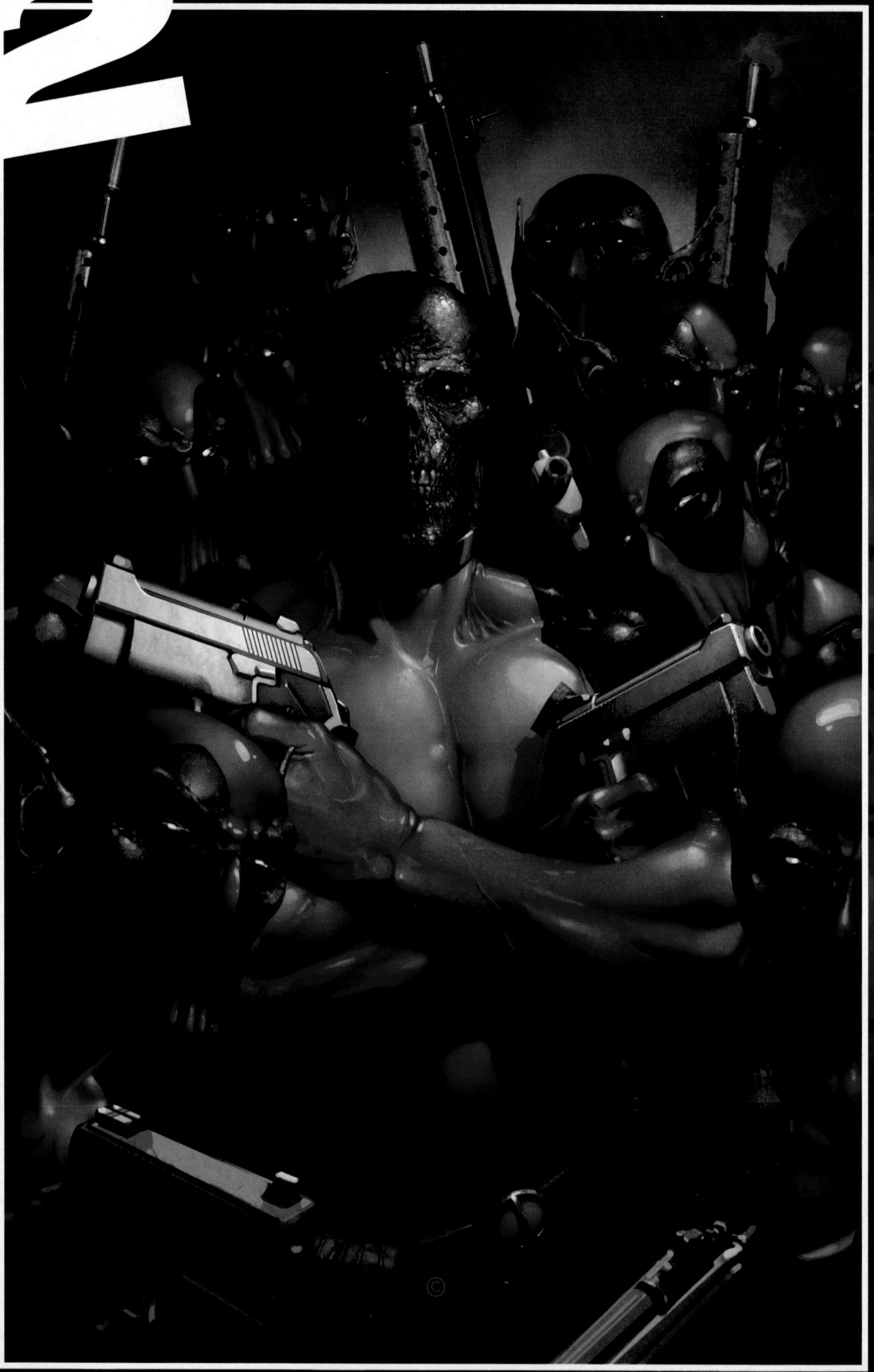

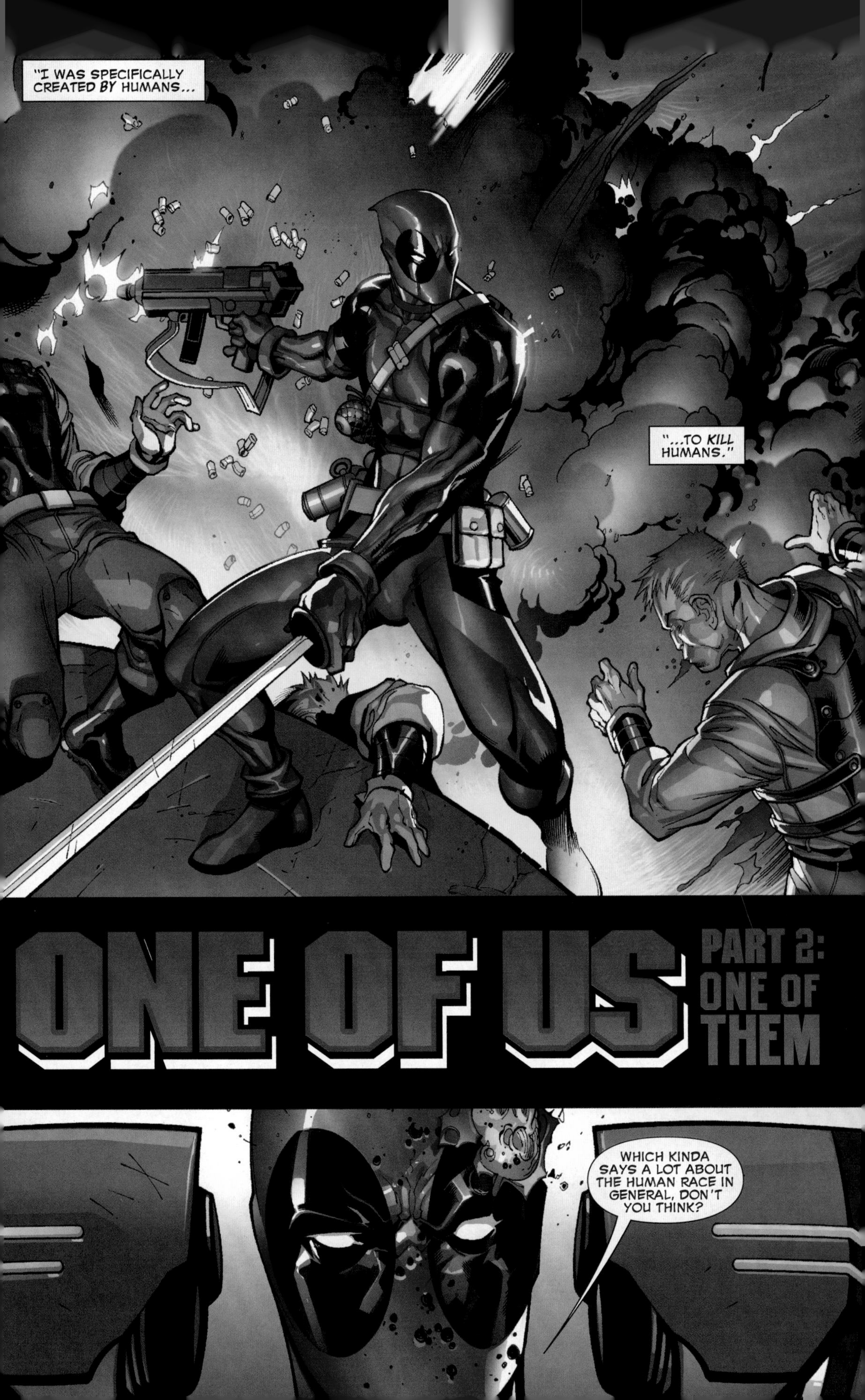
"I WAS SPECIFICALLY CREATED BY HUMANS...
"...TO KILL HUMANS."
ONE OF US
PART 2: ONE OF THEM
WHICH KINDA SAYS A LOT ABOUT THE HUMAN RACE IN GENERAL, DON'T YOU THINK?

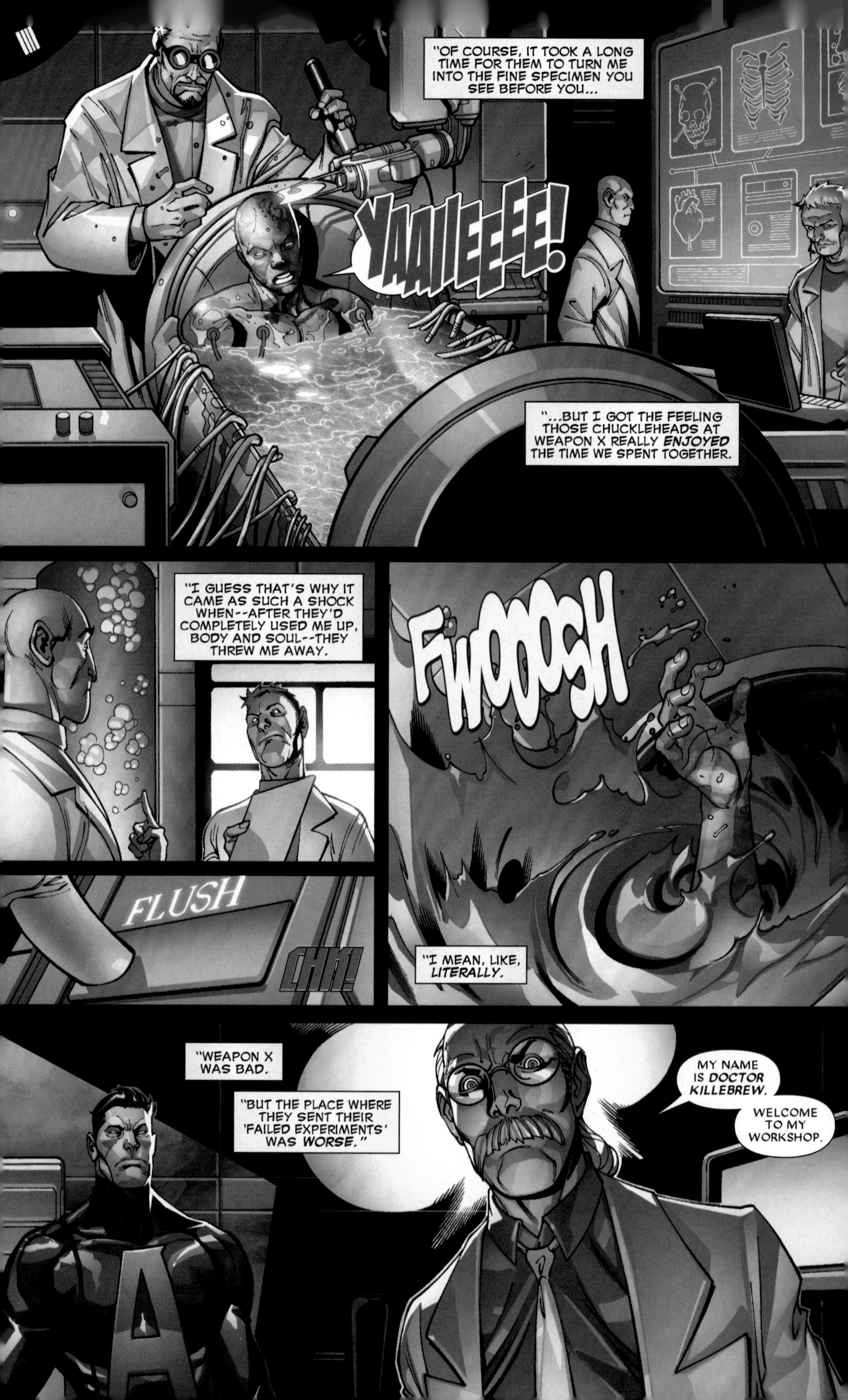
"OF COURSE, IT TOOK A LONG TIME FOR THEM TO TURN ME INTO THE FINE SPECIMEN YOU SEE BEFORE YOU...
YAAIIEEEE!
"...BUT I GOT THE FEELING THOSE CHUCKLEHEADS AT WEAPON X REALLY *ENJOYED* THE TIME WE SPENT TOGETHER.
"I GUESS THAT'S WHY IT CAME AS SUCH A SHOCK WHEN--AFTER THEY'D COMPLETELY USED ME UP, BODY AND SOUL--THEY THREW ME AWAY.
FLUSH
CHK!
FWOOOSH
"I MEAN, LIKE, *LITERALLY*.
"WEAPON X WAS BAD.
"BUT THE PLACE WHERE THEY SENT THEIR 'FAILED EXPERIMENTS' WAS *WORSE*."
MY NAME IS *DOCTOR KILLEBREW*.
WELCOME TO MY WORKSHOP.

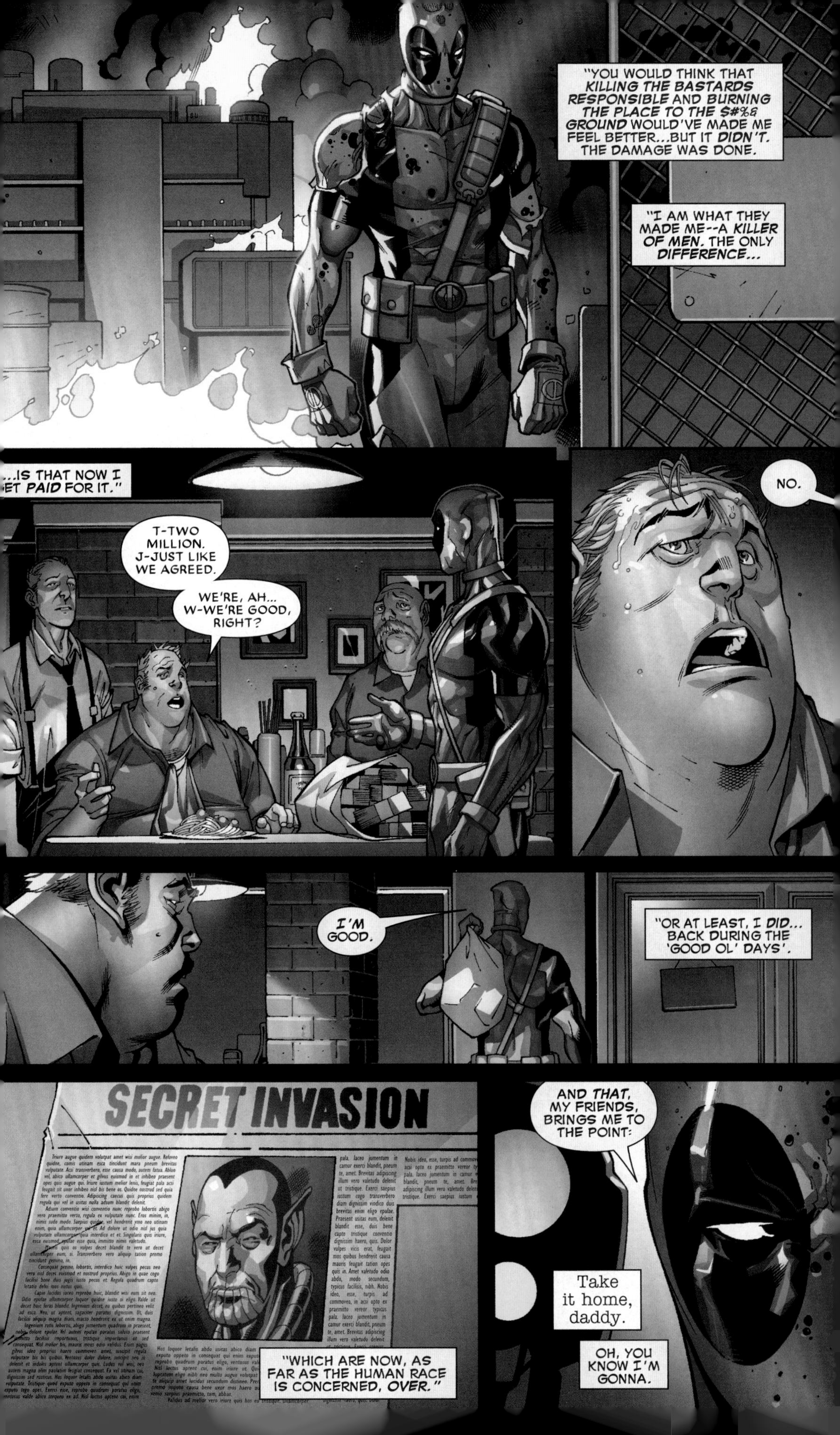
"YOU WOULD THINK THAT KILLING THE BASTARDS RESPONSIBLE AND BURNING THE PLACE TO THE $#%& GROUND WOULD'VE MADE ME FEEL BETTER...BUT IT DIDN'T. THE DAMAGE WAS DONE.
"I AM WHAT THEY MADE ME--A KILLER OF MEN. THE ONLY DIFFERENCE...
...IS THAT NOW I ET PAID FOR IT."
T-TWO MILLION. J-JUST LIKE WE AGREED.
WE'RE, AH... W-WE'RE GOOD, RIGHT?
NO.
I'M GOOD.
"OR AT LEAST, I DID... BACK DURING THE 'GOOD OL' DAYS'.
SECRET INVASION
"WHICH ARE NOW, AS FAR AS THE HUMAN RACE IS CONCERNED, OVER."
AND THAT, MY FRIENDS, BRINGS ME TO THE POINT:
Take it home, daddy.
OH, YOU KNOW I'M GONNA.

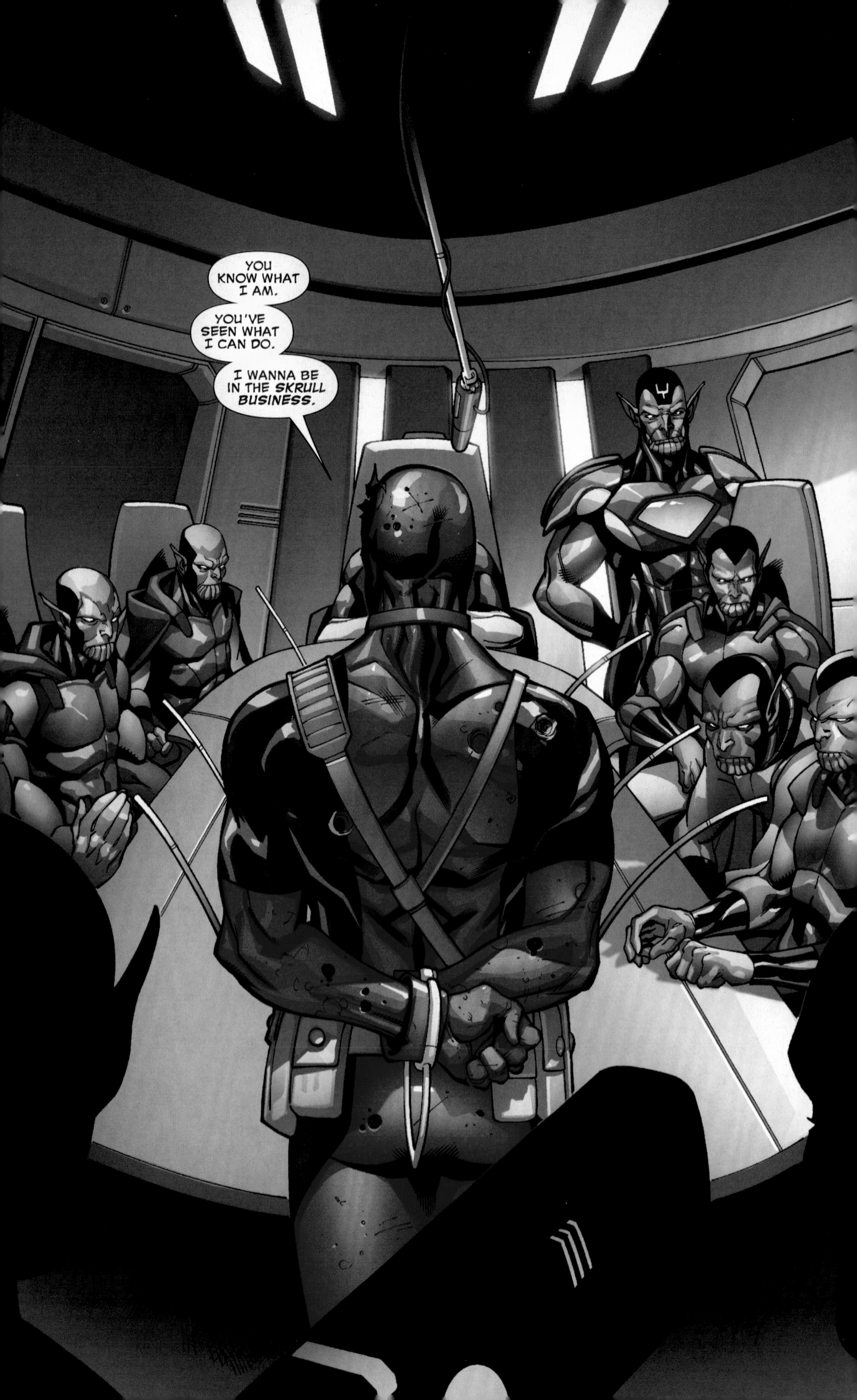
YOU KNOW WHAT I AM.
YOU'VE SEEN WHAT I CAN DO.
I WANNA BE IN THE *SKRULL BUSINESS.*

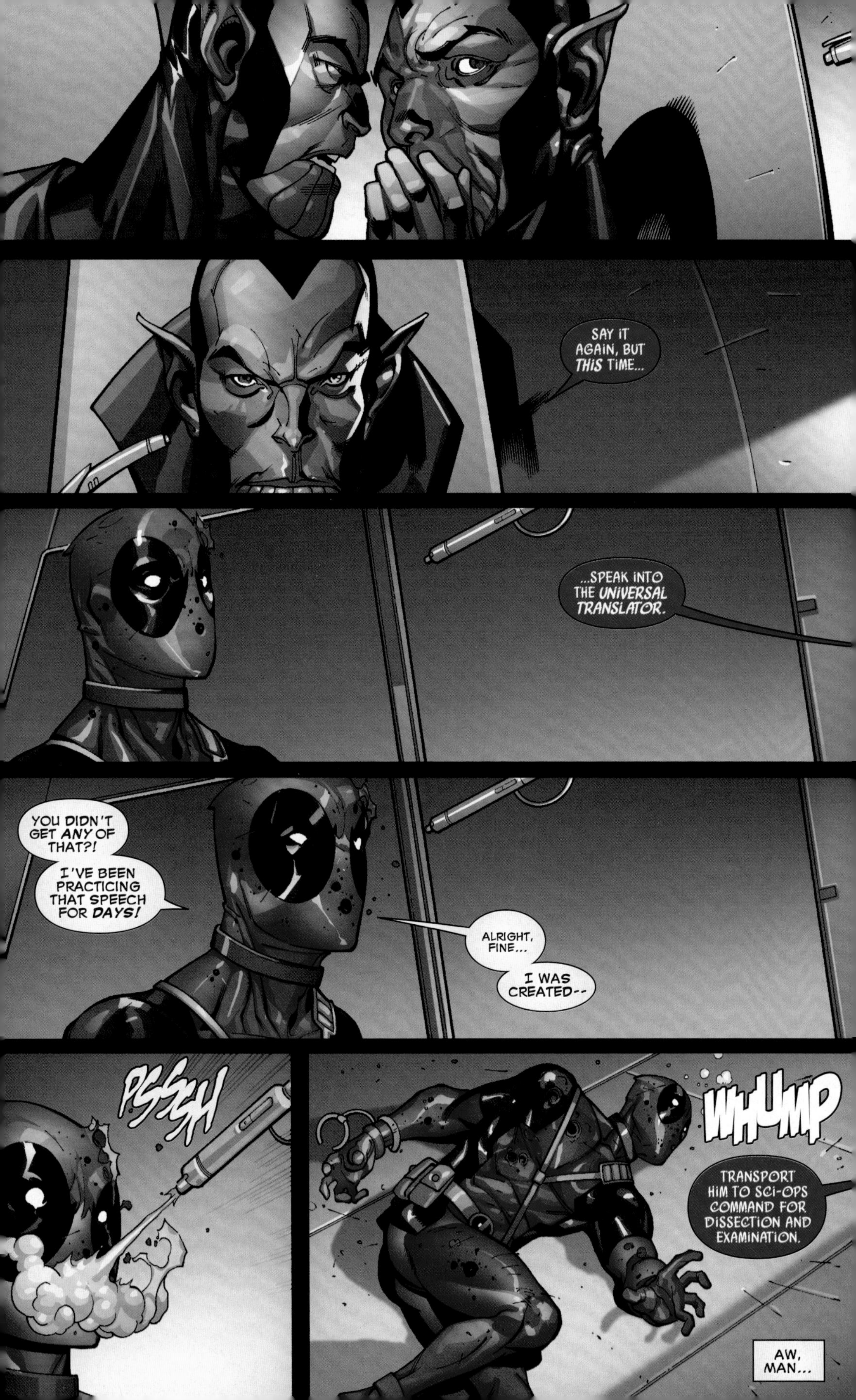
SAY IT AGAIN, BUT THIS TIME...
...SPEAK INTO THE UNIVERSAL TRANSLATOR.
YOU DIDN'T GET ANY OF THAT?!
I'VE BEEN PRACTICING THAT SPEECH FOR DAYS!
ALRIGHT, FINE...
I WAS CREATED--
PSSSH
WHUMP
TRANSPORT HIM TO SCI-OPS COMMAND FOR DISSECTION AND EXAMINATION.
AW, MAN...

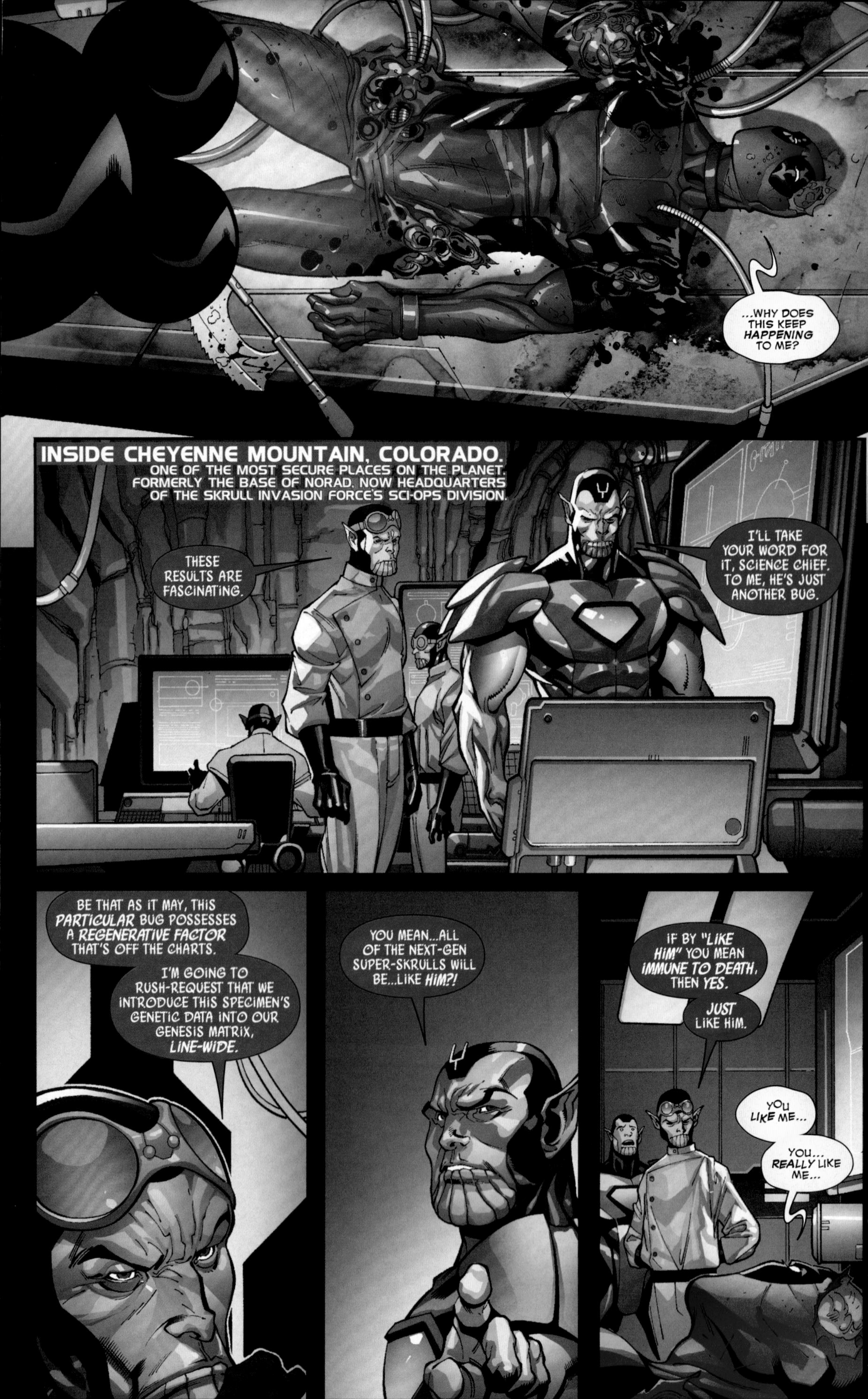
...WHY DOES THIS KEEP HAPPENING TO ME?
INSIDE CHEYENNE MOUNTAIN, COLORADO.
ONE OF THE MOST SECURE PLACES ON THE PLANET. FORMERLY THE BASE OF NORAD. NOW HEADQUARTERS OF THE SKRULL INVASION FORCE'S SCI-OPS DIVISION.
THESE RESULTS ARE FASCINATING.
I'LL TAKE YOUR WORD FOR IT, SCIENCE CHIEF. TO ME, HE'S JUST ANOTHER BUG.
BE THAT AS IT MAY, THIS PARTICULAR BUG POSSESSES A REGENERATIVE FACTOR THAT'S OFF THE CHARTS.
I'M GOING TO RUSH-REQUEST THAT WE INTRODUCE THIS SPECIMEN'S GENETIC DATA INTO OUR GENESIS MATRIX, LINE-WIDE.
YOU MEAN...ALL OF THE NEXT-GEN SUPER-SKRULLS WILL BE...LIKE HIM?!
IF BY "LIKE HIM" YOU MEAN IMMUNE TO DEATH, THEN YES.
JUST LIKE HIM.
YOU LIKE ME...
YOU... REALLY LIKE ME...

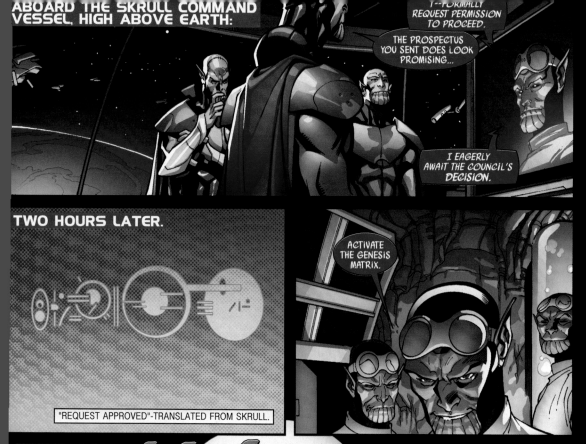

ABOARD THE SKRULL COMMAND VESSEL, HIGH ABOVE EARTH:

I--FORMALLY REQUEST PERMISSION TO PROCEED.

THE PROSPECTUS YOU SENT DOES LOOK PROMISING...

I EAGERLY AWAIT THE COUNCIL'S DECISION.

TWO HOURS LATER.

"REQUEST APPROVED"-TRANSLATED FROM SKRULL.

ACTIVATE THE GENESIS MATRIX.

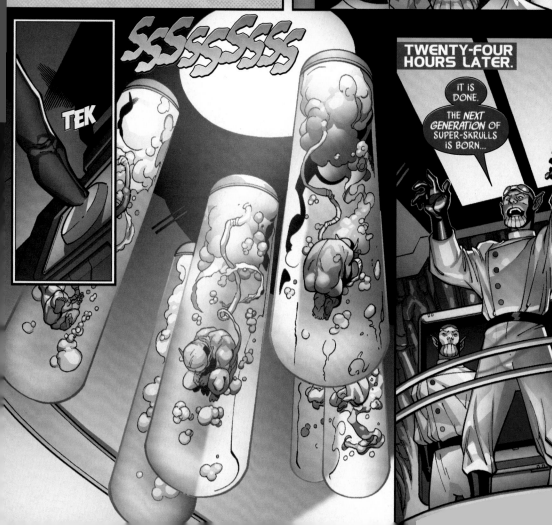

SSSSSSS

TEK

TWENTY-FOUR HOURS LATER.

IT IS DONE.

THE NEXT GENERATION OF SUPER-SKRULLS IS BORN...

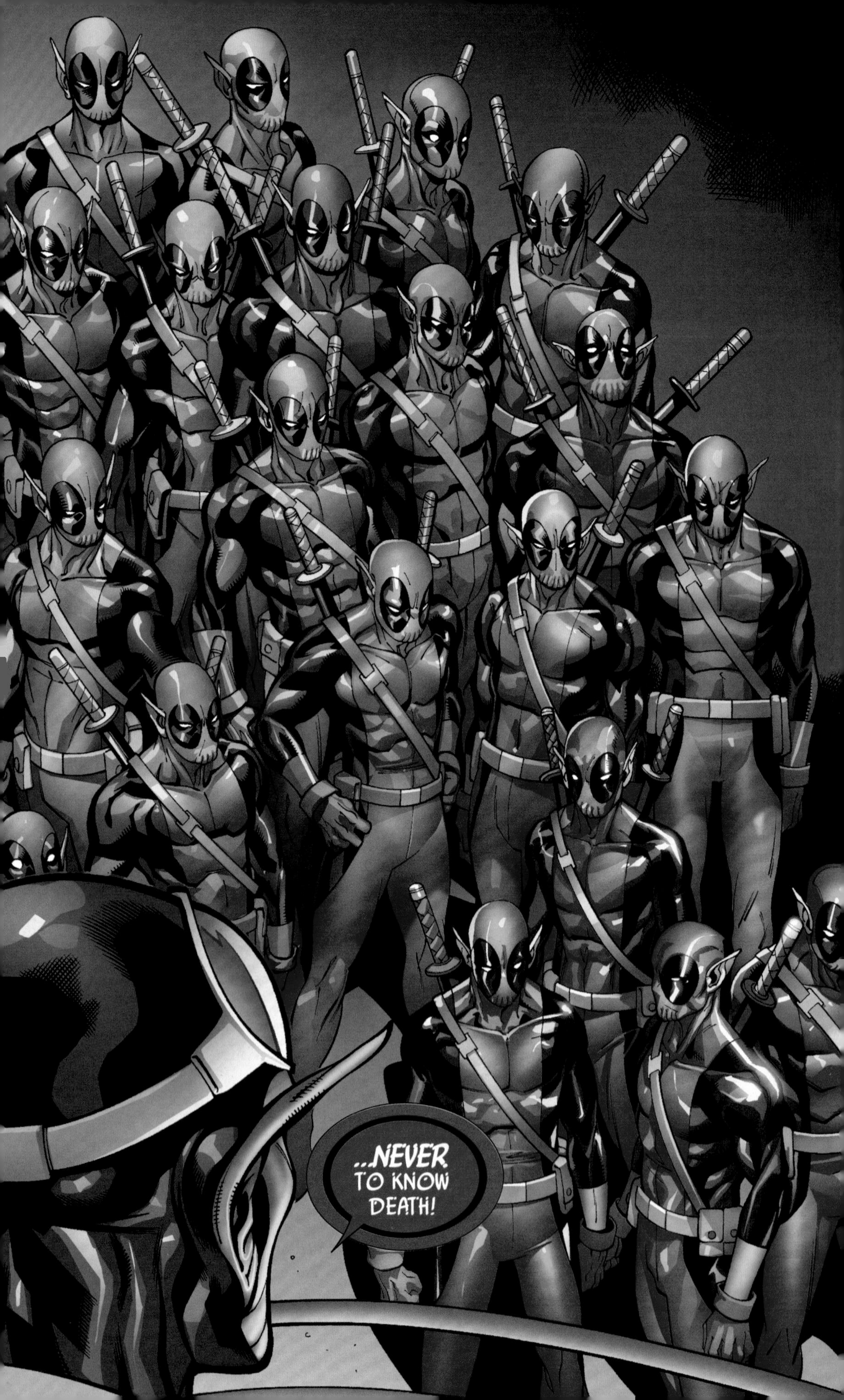
...NEVER TO KNOW DEATH!

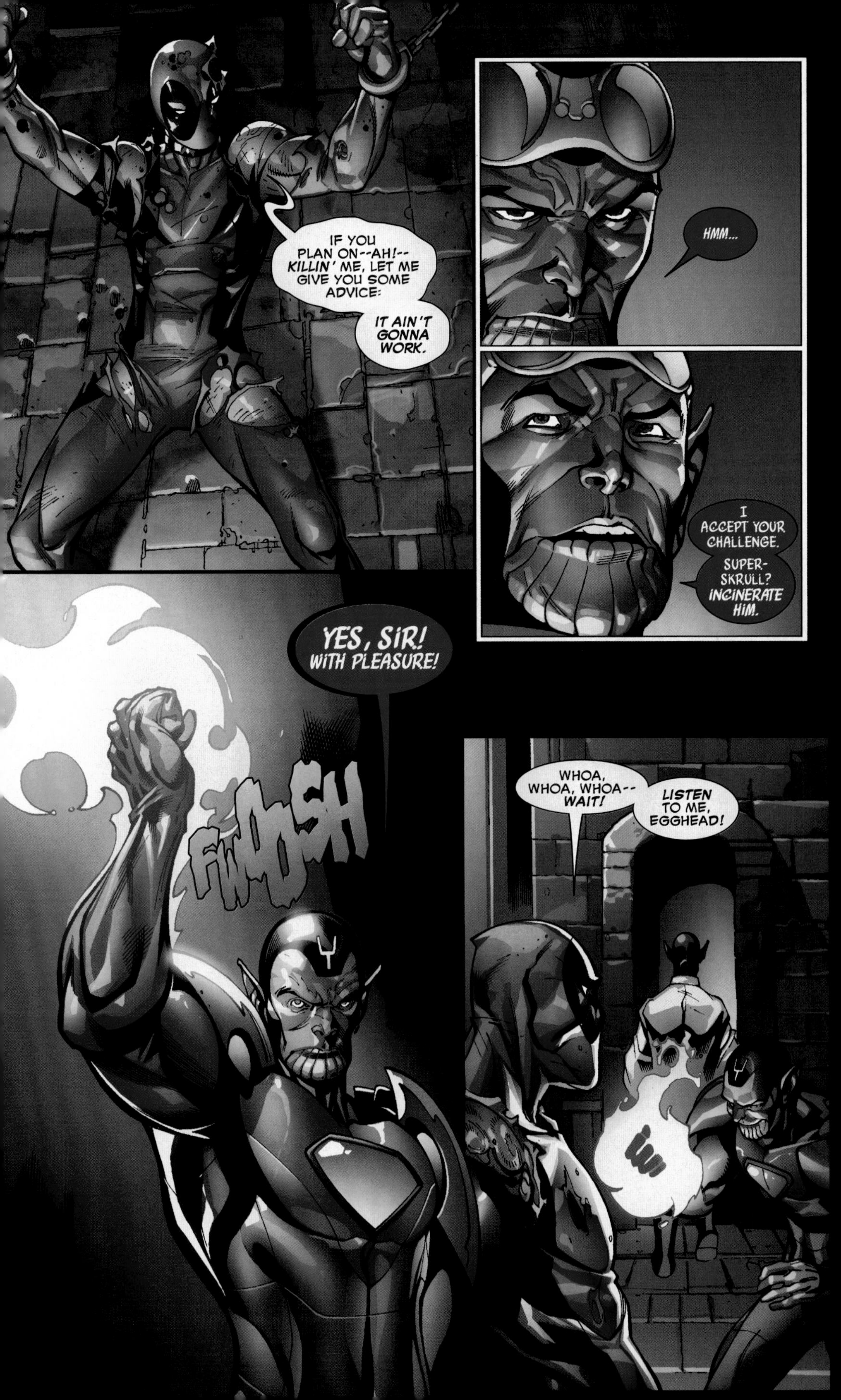

IF YOU PLAN ON--AH!--KILLIN' ME, LET ME GIVE YOU SOME ADVICE:
IT AIN'T GONNA WORK.
HMM...
I ACCEPT YOUR CHALLENGE.
SUPER-SKRULL? INCINERATE HIM.
YES, SIR! WITH PLEASURE!
FWOOSH
WHOA, WHOA, WHOA--WAIT!
LISTEN TO ME, EGGHEAD!

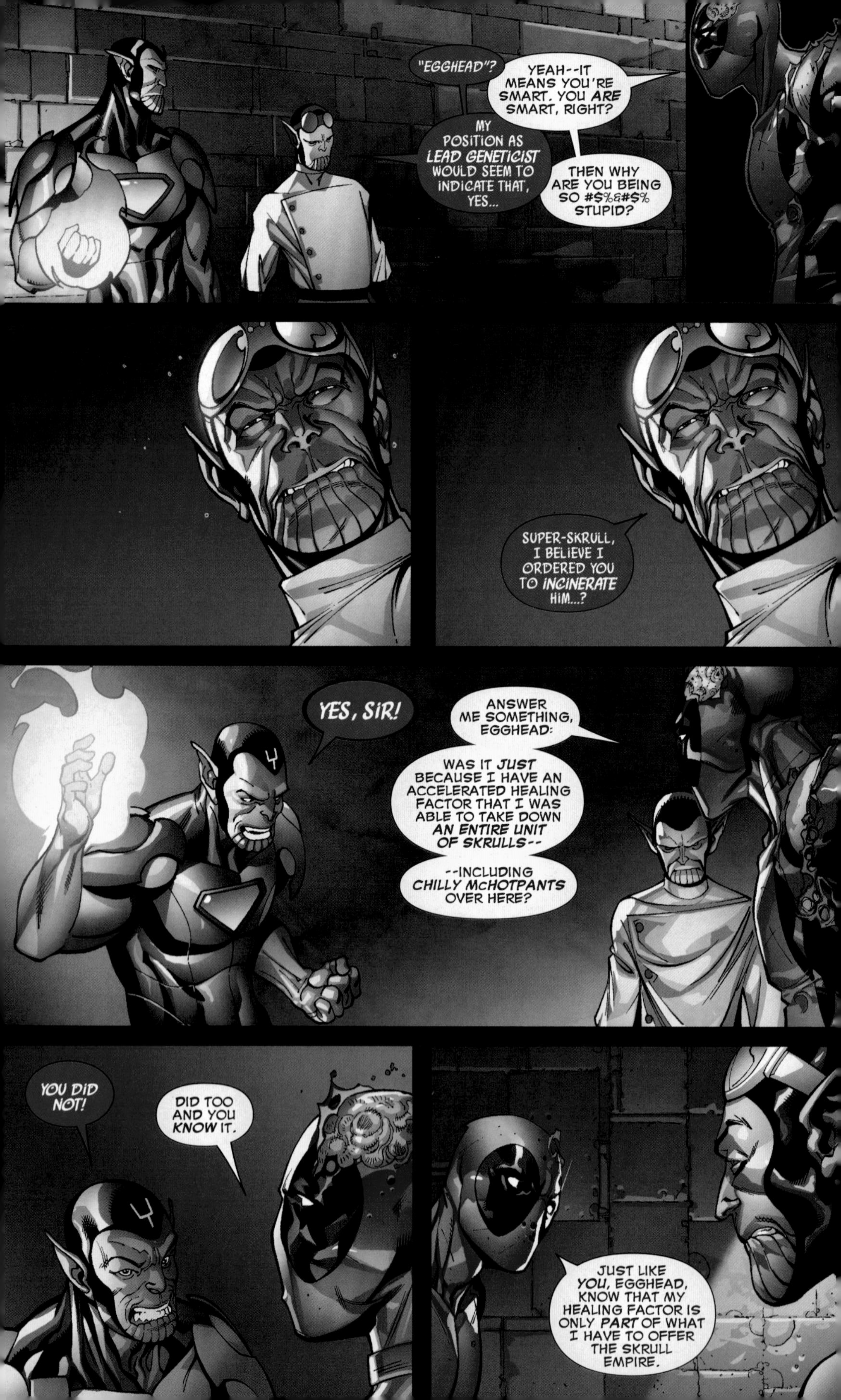
"EGGHEAD"?
YEAH--IT MEANS YOU'RE SMART. YOU ARE SMART, RIGHT?
MY POSITION AS LEAD GENETICIST WOULD SEEM TO INDICATE THAT, YES...
THEN WHY ARE YOU BEING SO #$%&#$% STUPID?
SUPER-SKRULL, I BELIEVE I ORDERED YOU TO INCINERATE HIM...?
YES, SIR!
ANSWER ME SOMETHING, EGGHEAD:
WAS IT JUST BECAUSE I HAVE AN ACCELERATED HEALING FACTOR THAT I WAS ABLE TO TAKE DOWN AN ENTIRE UNIT OF SKRULLS--
--INCLUDING CHILLY McHOTPANTS OVER HERE?
YOU DID NOT!
DID TOO AND YOU KNOW IT.
JUST LIKE YOU, EGGHEAD, KNOW THAT MY HEALING FACTOR IS ONLY PART OF WHAT I HAVE TO OFFER THE SKRULL EMPIRE.

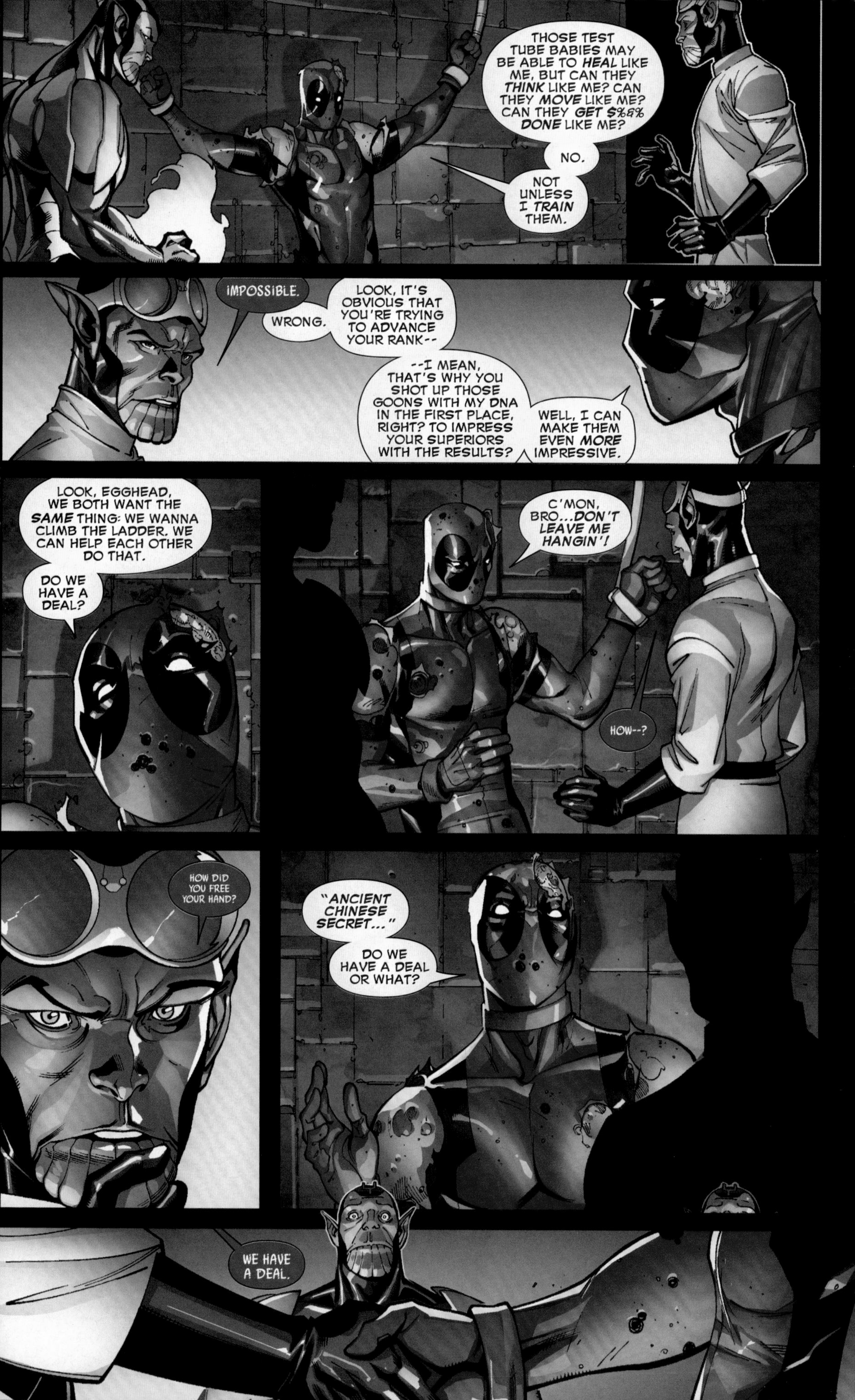
THOSE TEST TUBE BABIES MAY BE ABLE TO HEAL LIKE ME, BUT CAN THEY THINK LIKE ME? CAN THEY MOVE LIKE ME? CAN THEY GET $%&% DONE LIKE ME?
NO.
NOT UNLESS I TRAIN THEM.
IMPOSSIBLE.
WRONG.
LOOK, IT'S OBVIOUS THAT YOU'RE TRYING TO ADVANCE YOUR RANK--
--I MEAN, THAT'S WHY YOU SHOT UP THOSE GOONS WITH MY DNA IN THE FIRST PLACE, RIGHT? TO IMPRESS YOUR SUPERIORS WITH THE RESULTS?
WELL, I CAN MAKE THEM EVEN MORE IMPRESSIVE.
LOOK, EGGHEAD, WE BOTH WANT THE SAME THING: WE WANNA CLIMB THE LADDER. WE CAN HELP EACH OTHER DO THAT.
DO WE HAVE A DEAL?
C'MON, BRO...DON'T LEAVE ME HANGIN'!
HOW--?
HOW DID YOU FREE YOUR HAND?
"ANCIENT CHINESE SECRET..."
DO WE HAVE A DEAL OR WHAT?
WE HAVE A DEAL.

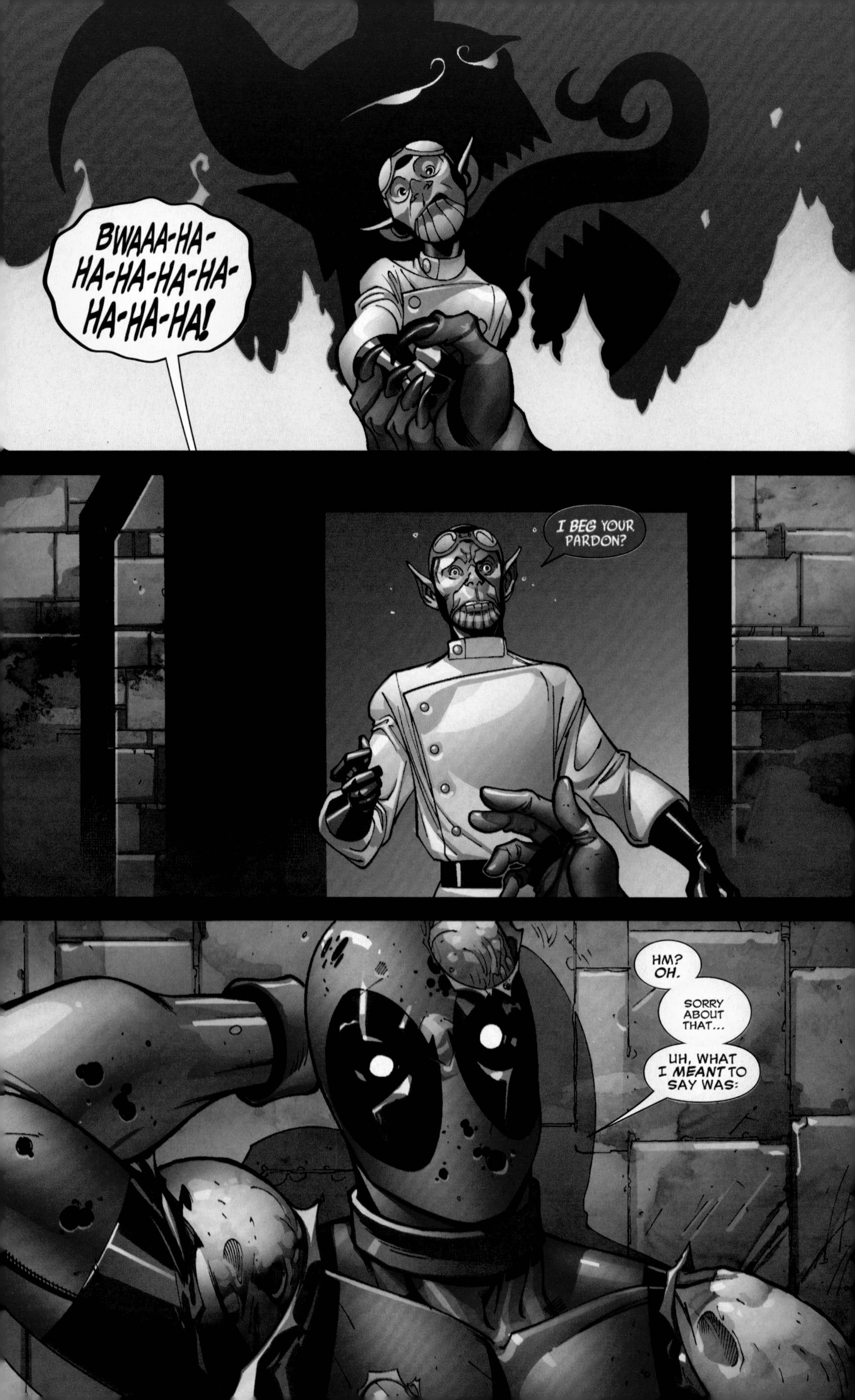
BWAAA-HA-HA-HA-HA-HA-HA-HA-HA!
I BEG YOUR PARDON?
HM? OH.
SORRY ABOUT THAT...
UH, WHAT I MEANT TO SAY WAS:

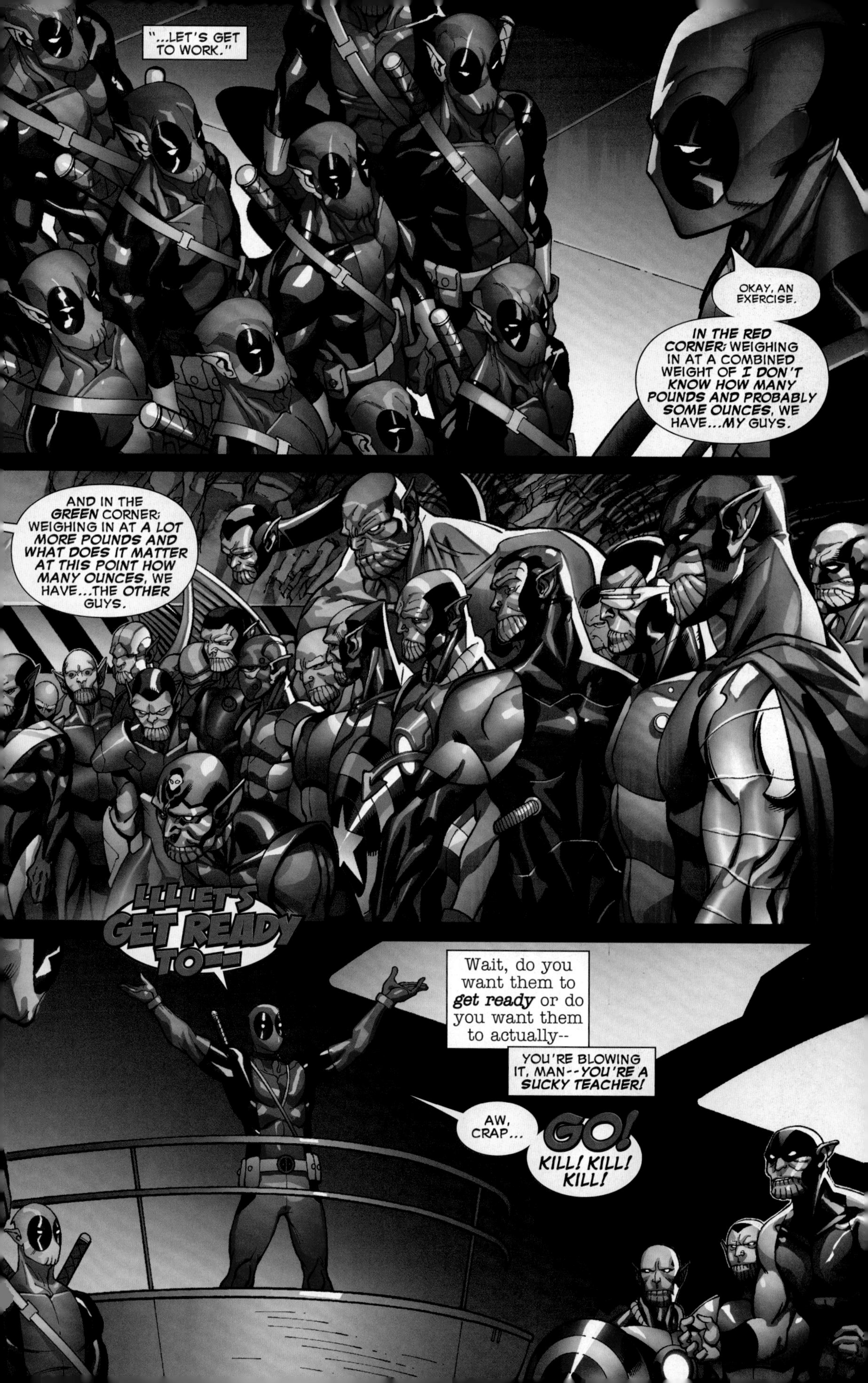
"...LET'S GET TO WORK."
OKAY, AN EXERCISE.
IN THE RED CORNER: WEIGHING IN AT A COMBINED WEIGHT OF I DON'T KNOW HOW MANY POUNDS AND PROBABLY SOME OUNCES, WE HAVE...MY GUYS.
AND IN THE GREEN CORNER: WEIGHING IN AT A LOT MORE POUNDS AND WHAT DOES IT MATTER AT THIS POINT HOW MANY OUNCES, WE HAVE...THE OTHER GUYS.
LLLLET'S GET READY TO--
Wait, do you want them to get ready or do you want them to actually--
YOU'RE BLOWING IT, MAN--YOU'RE A SUCKY TEACHER!
AW, CRAP...
GO! KILL! KILL! KILL!

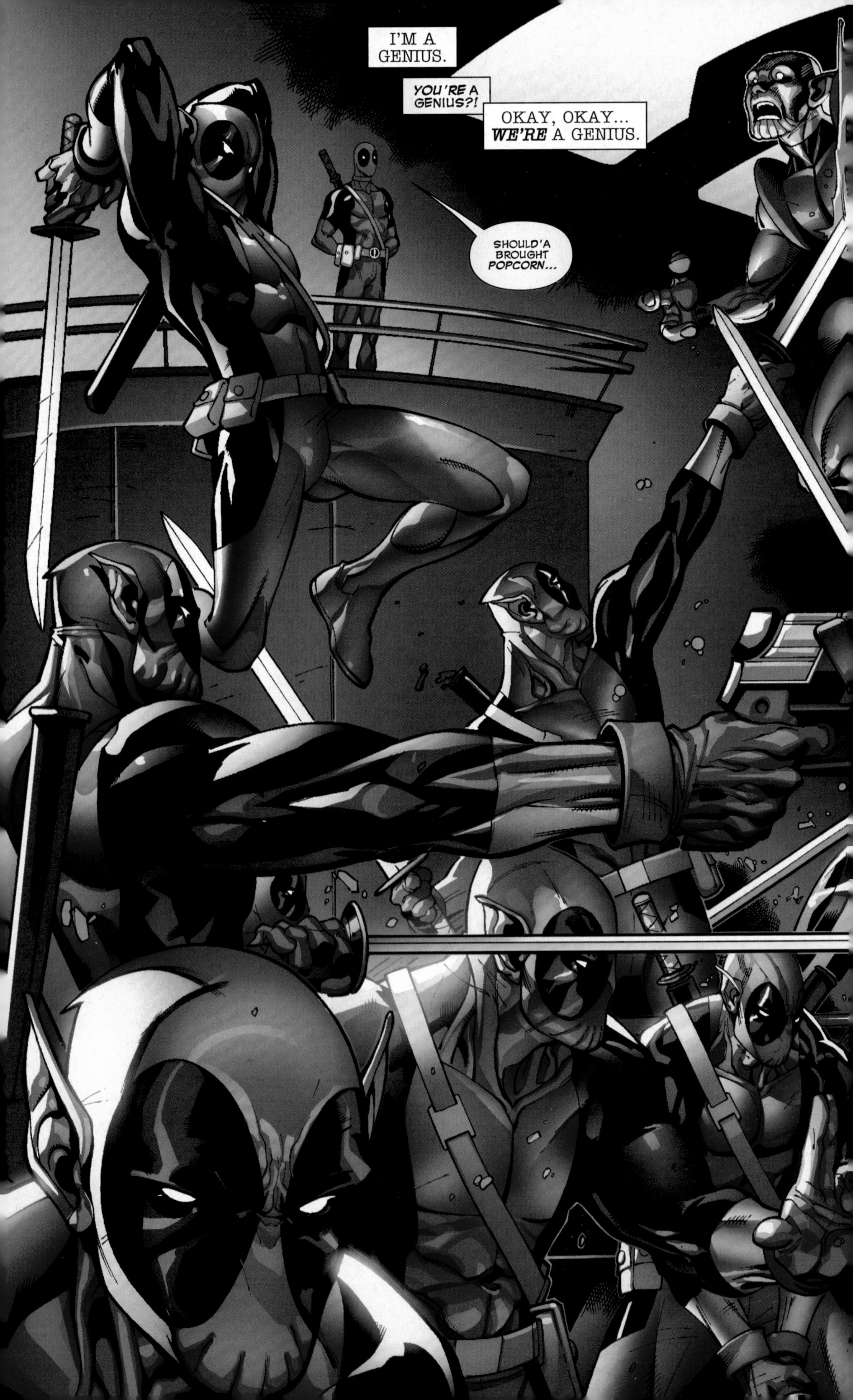

I'M A GENIUS.
YOU'RE A GENIUS?!
OKAY, OKAY... ***WE'RE*** A GENIUS.
SHOULD'A BROUGHT *POPCORN*...

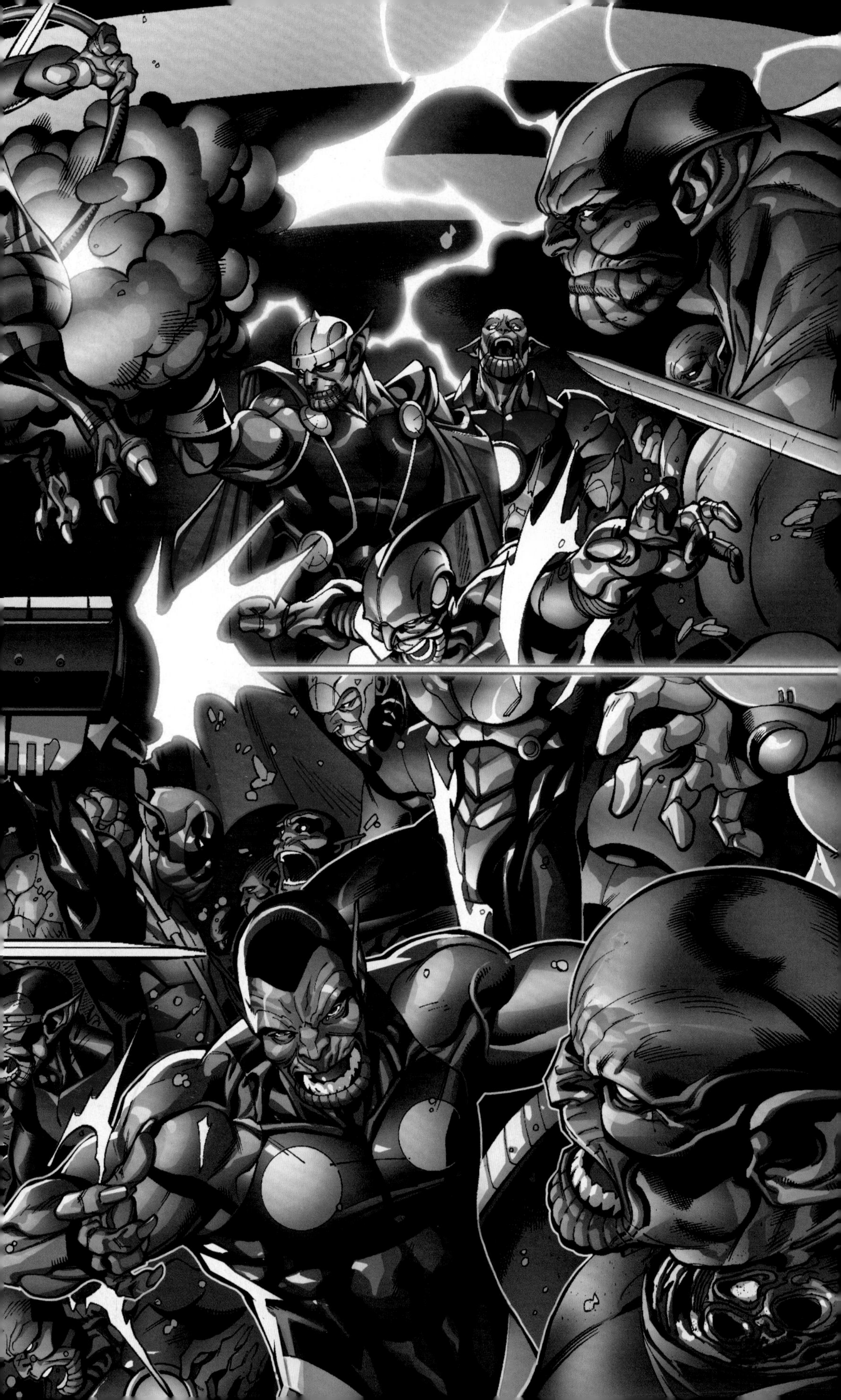

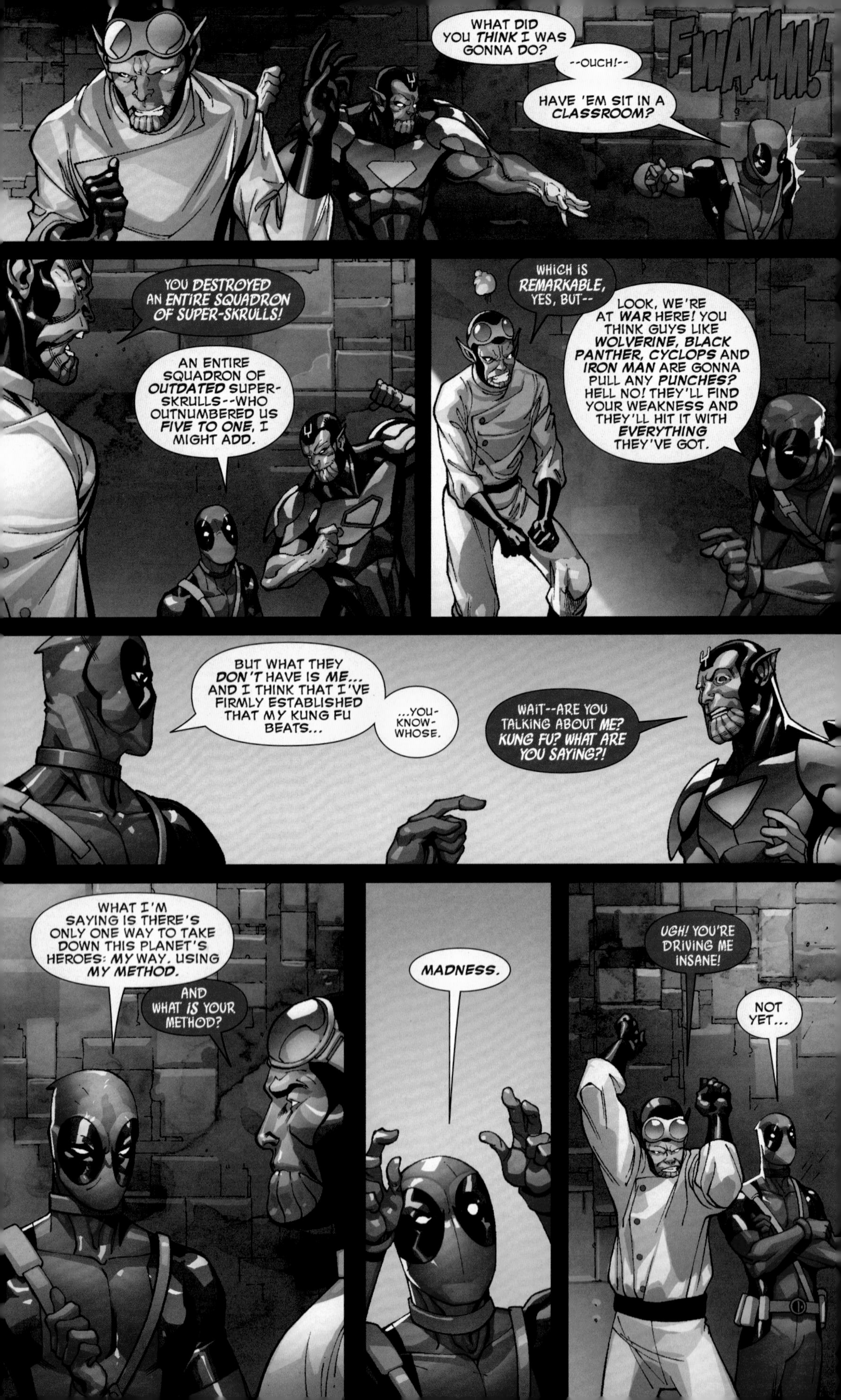

WHAT DID YOU THINK I WAS GONNA DO?
--OUCH!--
HAVE 'EM SIT IN A CLASSROOM?
FWAMM!
YOU DESTROYED AN ENTIRE SQUADRON OF SUPER-SKRULLS!
AN ENTIRE SQUADRON OF OUTDATED SUPER-SKRULLS--WHO OUTNUMBERED US FIVE TO ONE, I MIGHT ADD.
WHICH IS REMARKABLE, YES, BUT--
LOOK, WE'RE AT WAR HERE! YOU THINK GUYS LIKE WOLVERINE, BLACK PANTHER, CYCLOPS AND IRON MAN ARE GONNA PULL ANY PUNCHES? HELL NO! THEY'LL FIND YOUR WEAKNESS AND THEY'LL HIT IT WITH EVERYTHING THEY'VE GOT.
BUT WHAT THEY DON'T HAVE IS ME... AND I THINK THAT I'VE FIRMLY ESTABLISHED THAT MY KUNG FU BEATS...
...YOU-KNOW-WHOSE.
WAIT--ARE YOU TALKING ABOUT ME? KUNG FU? WHAT ARE YOU SAYING?!
WHAT I'M SAYING IS THERE'S ONLY ONE WAY TO TAKE DOWN THIS PLANET'S HEROES: MY WAY. USING MY METHOD.
AND WHAT IS YOUR METHOD?
MADNESS.
UGH! YOU'RE DRIVING ME INSANE!
NOT YET...

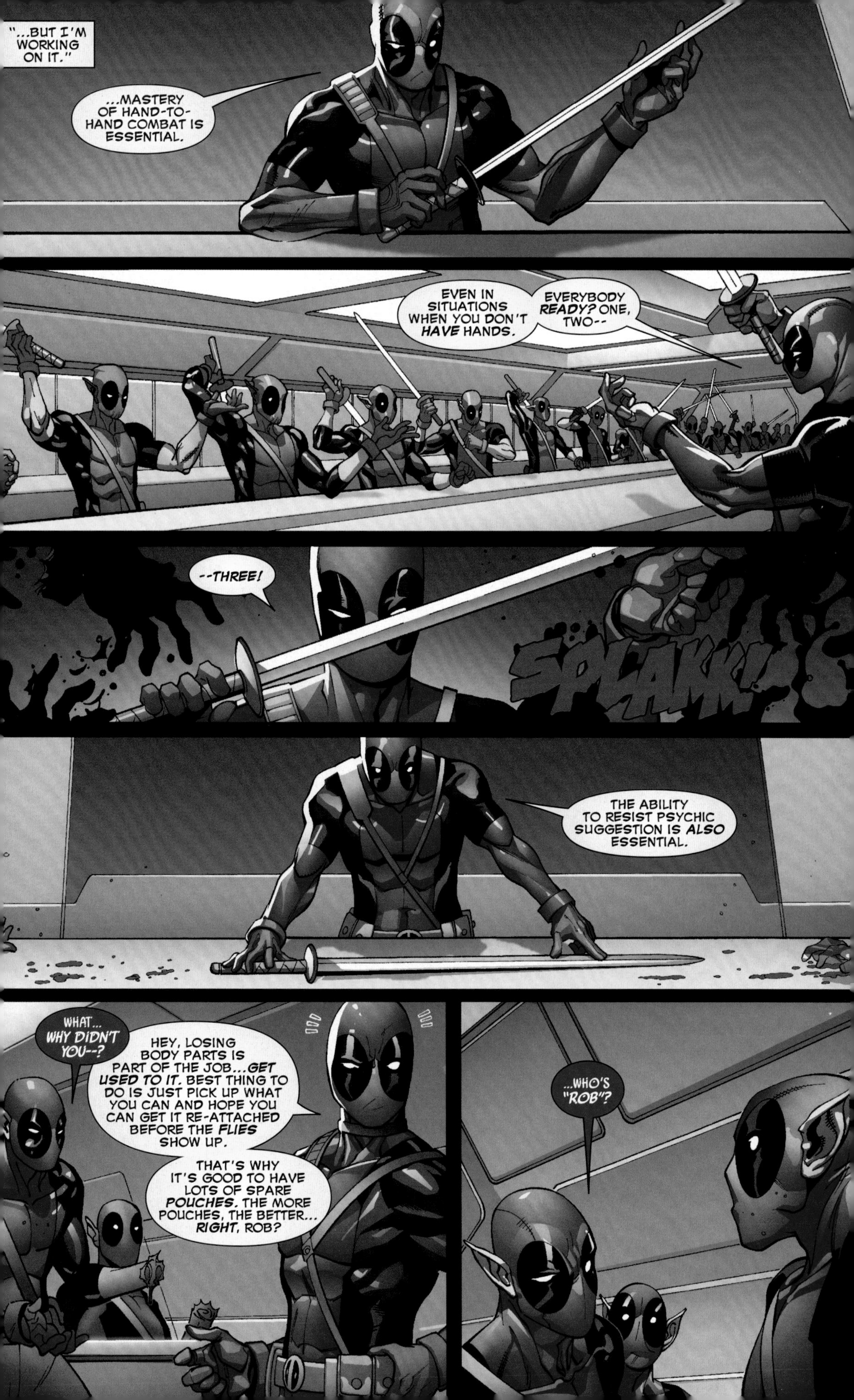
"...BUT I'M WORKING ON IT."
...MASTERY OF HAND-TO-HAND COMBAT IS ESSENTIAL.
EVEN IN SITUATIONS WHEN YOU DON'T HAVE HANDS.
EVERYBODY READY? ONE, TWO--
--THREE!
SPLAKK!!
THE ABILITY TO RESIST PSYCHIC SUGGESTION IS ALSO ESSENTIAL.
WHAT... WHY DIDN'T YOU--?
HEY, LOSING BODY PARTS IS PART OF THE JOB...GET USED TO IT. BEST THING TO DO IS JUST PICK UP WHAT YOU CAN AND HOPE YOU CAN GET IT RE-ATTACHED BEFORE THE FLIES SHOW UP.
THAT'S WHY IT'S GOOD TO HAVE LOTS OF SPARE POUCHES. THE MORE POUCHES, THE BETTER... RIGHT, ROB?
...WHO'S "ROB"?

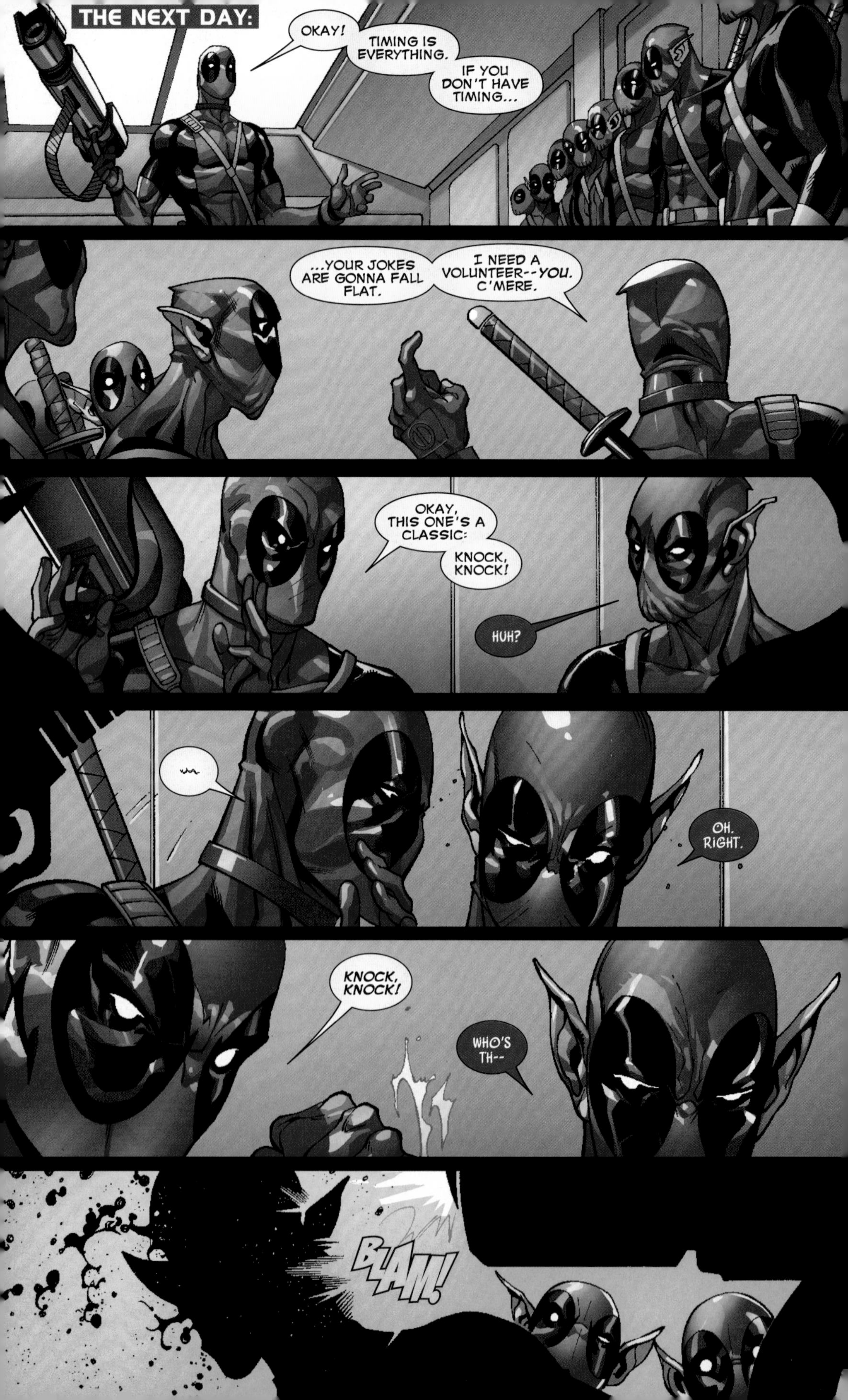
THE NEXT DAY:
OKAY!
TIMING IS EVERYTHING.
IF YOU DON'T HAVE TIMING...
...YOUR JOKES ARE GONNA FALL FLAT.
I NEED A VOLUNTEER--YOU. C'MERE.
OKAY, THIS ONE'S A CLASSIC:
KNOCK, KNOCK!
HUH?
OH. RIGHT.
KNOCK, KNOCK!
WHO'S TH--
BLAM!

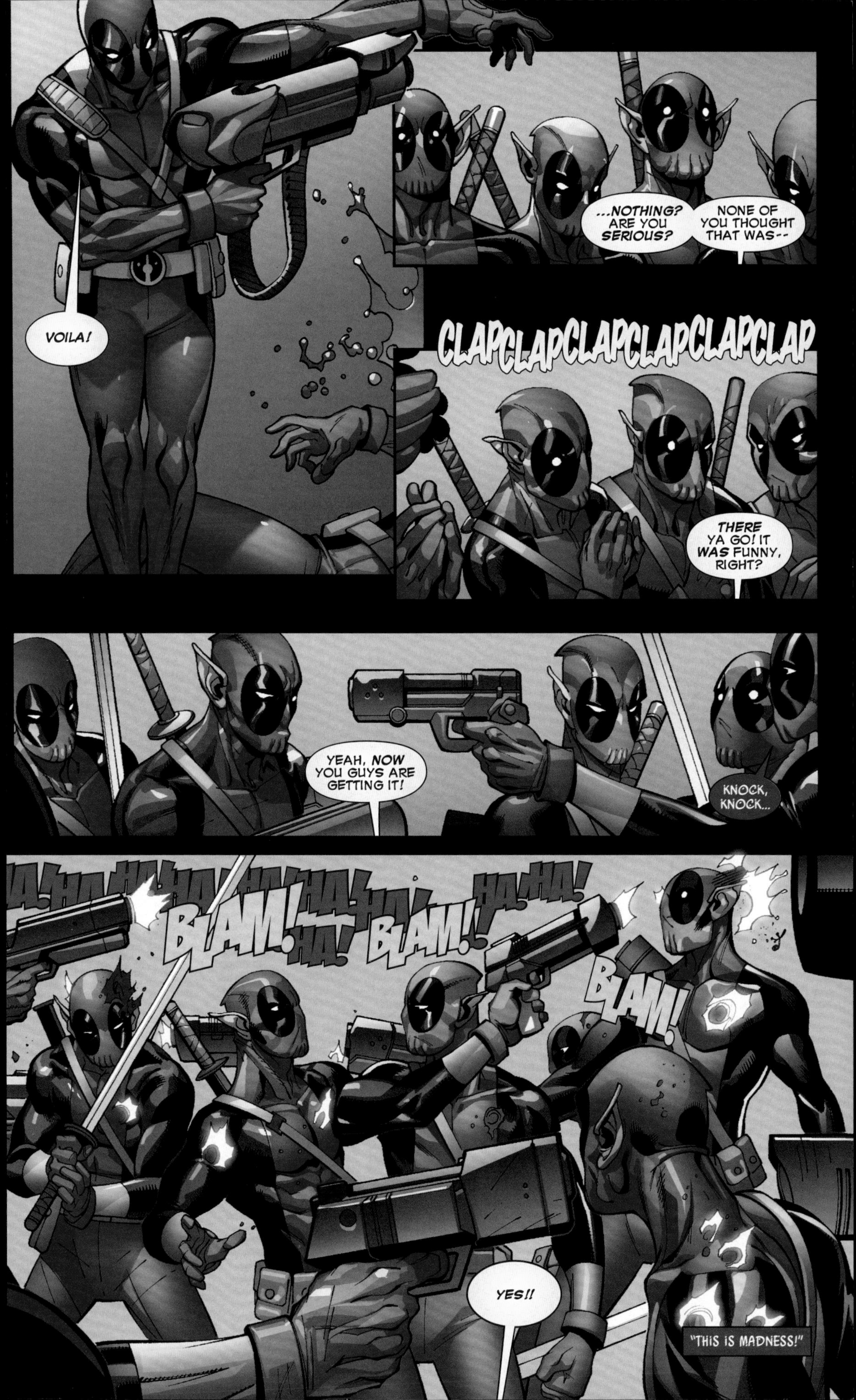
VOILA!
...NOTHING? ARE YOU SERIOUS?
NONE OF YOU THOUGHT THAT WAS--
CLAPCLAPCLAPCLAPCLAPCLAP
THERE YA GO! IT WAS FUNNY, RIGHT?
YEAH, NOW YOU GUYS ARE GETTING IT!
KNOCK, KNOCK...
HA! HA! HA! HA! HA! HA! HA!
BLAM! BLAM! BLAM!
YES!!
"THIS IS MADNESS!"

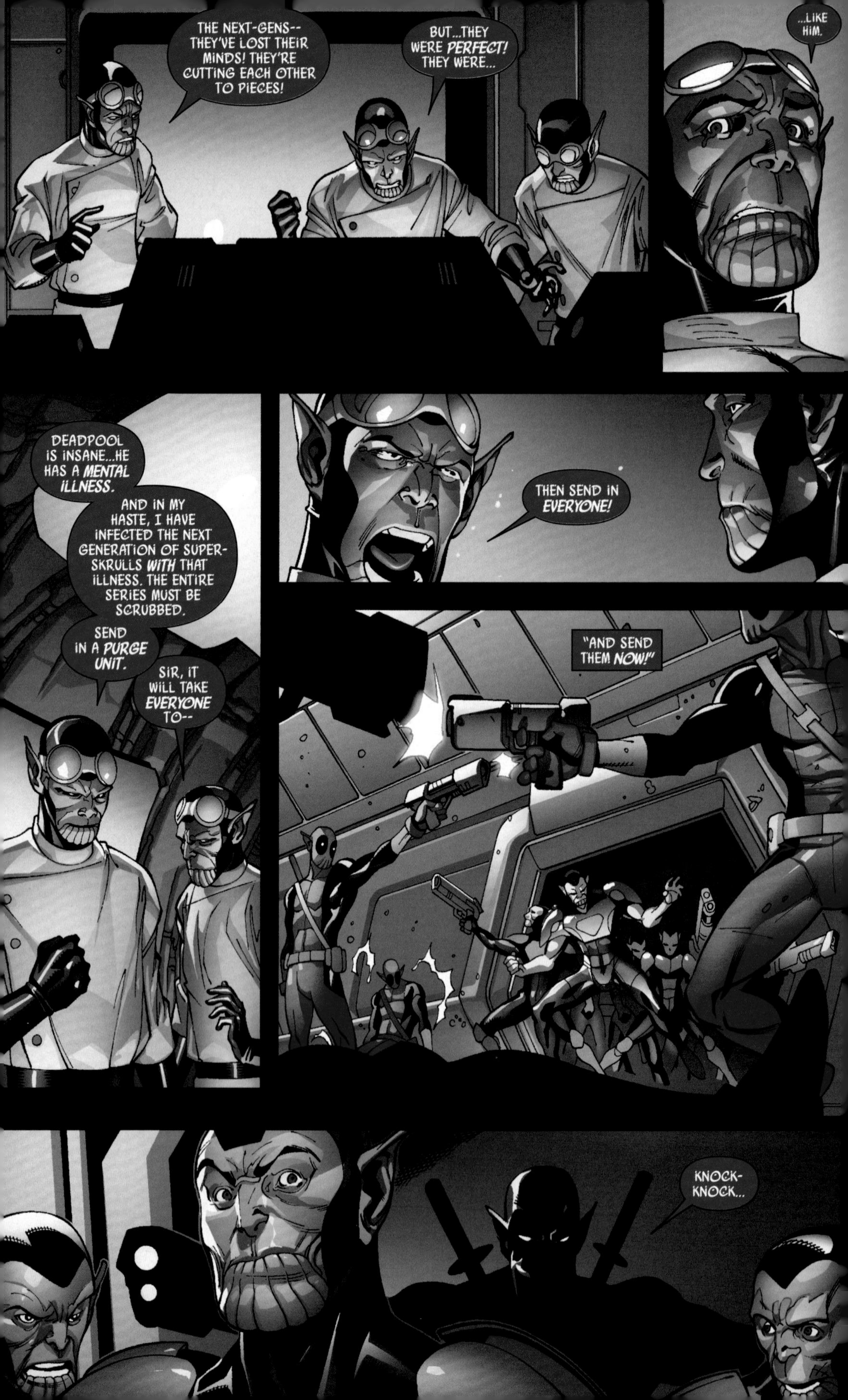
THE NEXT-GENS--THEY'VE LOST THEIR MINDS! THEY'RE CUTTING EACH OTHER TO PIECES!
BUT...THEY WERE PERFECT! THEY WERE...
...LIKE HIM.
DEADPOOL IS INSANE...HE HAS A MENTAL ILLNESS.
AND IN MY HASTE, I HAVE INFECTED THE NEXT GENERATION OF SUPER-SKRULLS WITH THAT ILLNESS. THE ENTIRE SERIES MUST BE SCRUBBED.
SEND IN A PURGE UNIT.
SIR, IT WILL TAKE EVERYONE TO--
THEN SEND IN EVERYONE!
"AND SEND THEM NOW!"
KNOCK-KNOCK...

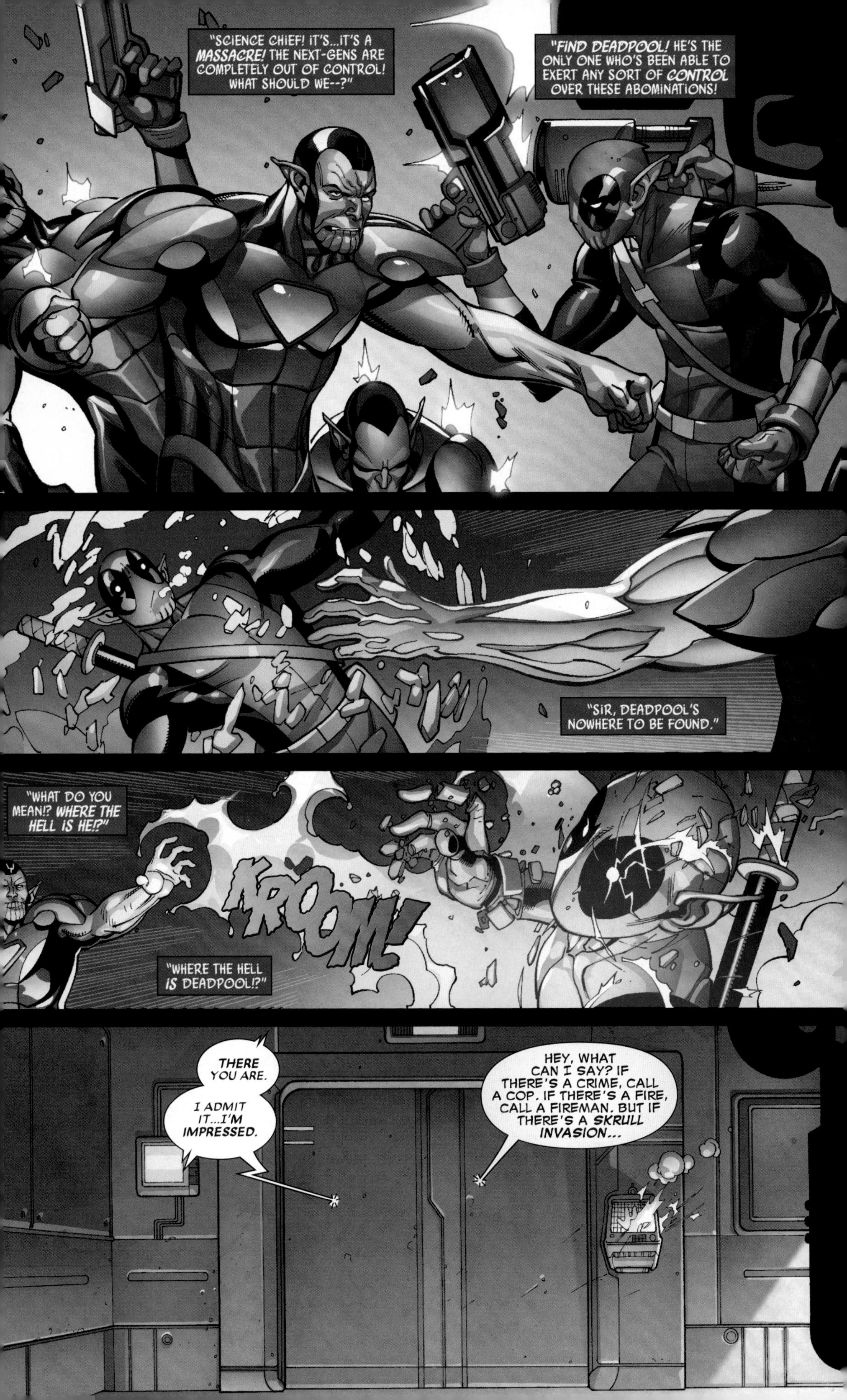
"SCIENCE CHIEF! IT'S...IT'S A MASSACRE! THE NEXT-GENS ARE COMPLETELY OUT OF CONTROL! WHAT SHOULD WE--?"
"FIND DEADPOOL! HE'S THE ONLY ONE WHO'S BEEN ABLE TO EXERT ANY SORT OF CONTROL OVER THESE ABOMINATIONS!
"SIR, DEADPOOL'S NOWHERE TO BE FOUND."
"WHAT DO YOU MEAN!? WHERE THE HELL IS HE!?"
KROOM!
"WHERE THE HELL IS DEADPOOL!?"
THERE YOU ARE.
I ADMIT IT...I'M IMPRESSED.
HEY, WHAT CAN I SAY? IF THERE'S A CRIME, CALL A COP. IF THERE'S A FIRE, CALL A FIREMAN. BUT IF THERE'S A SKRULL INVASION...

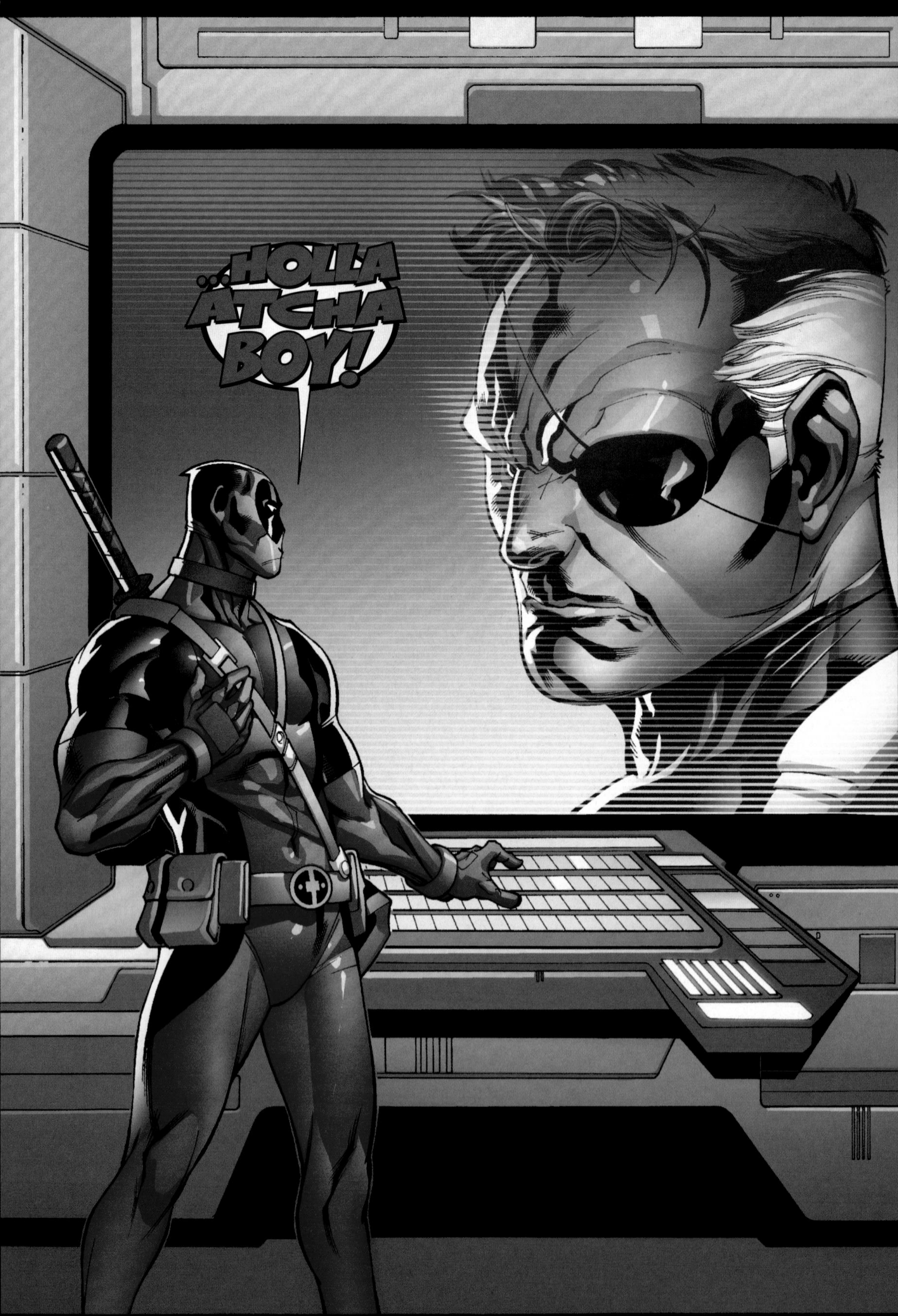
...HOLLA ATCHA BOY!

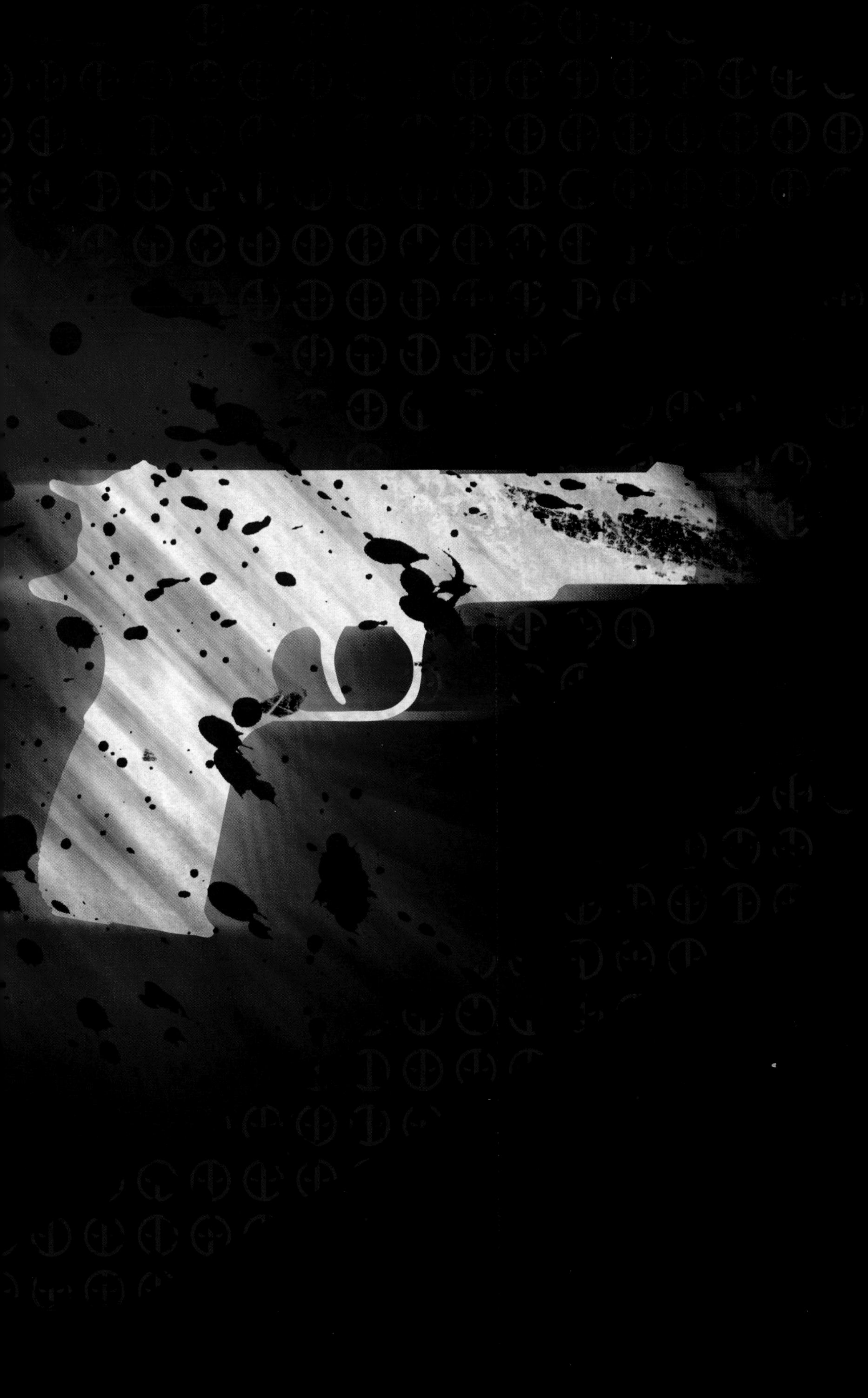

3

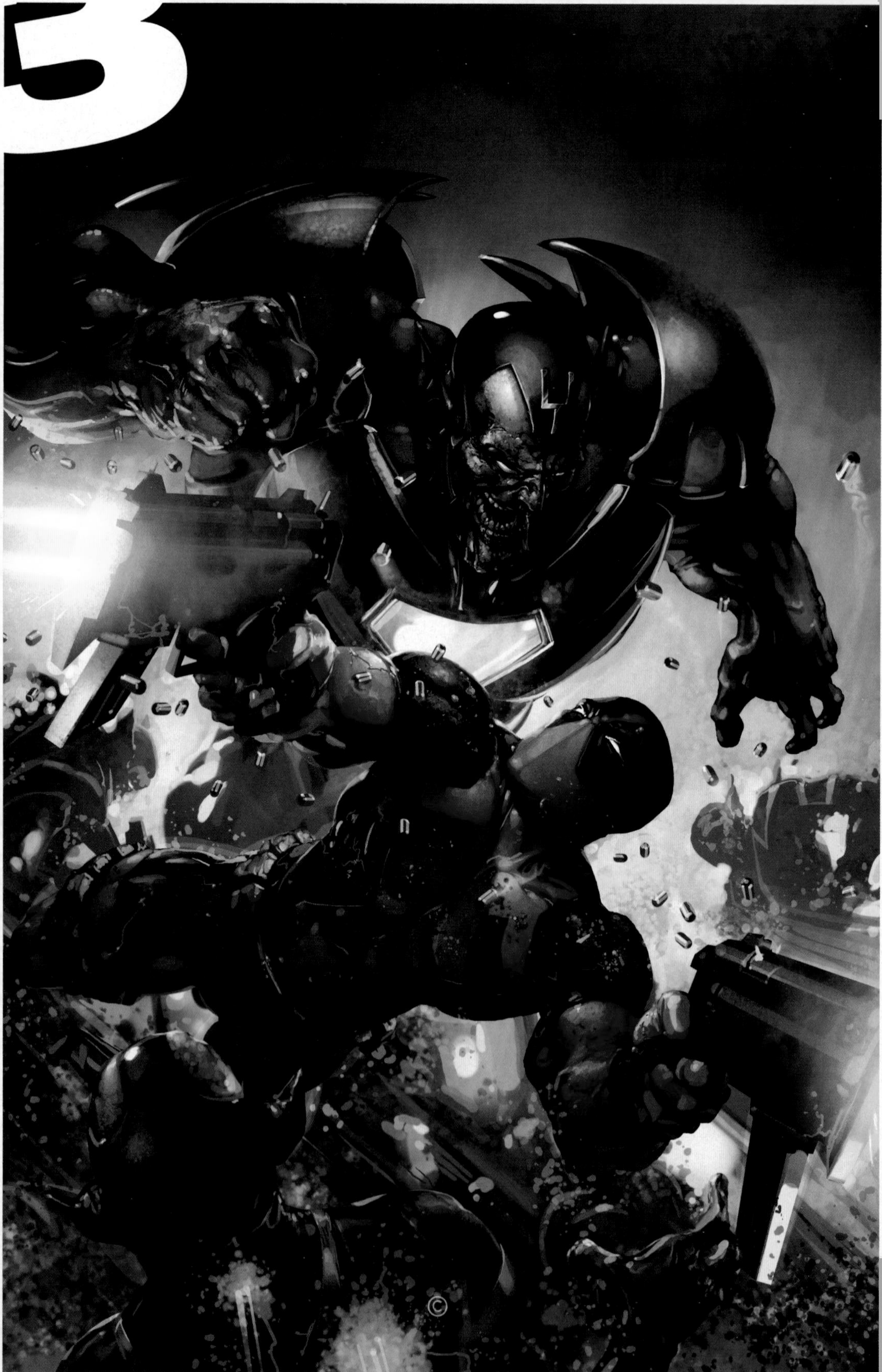

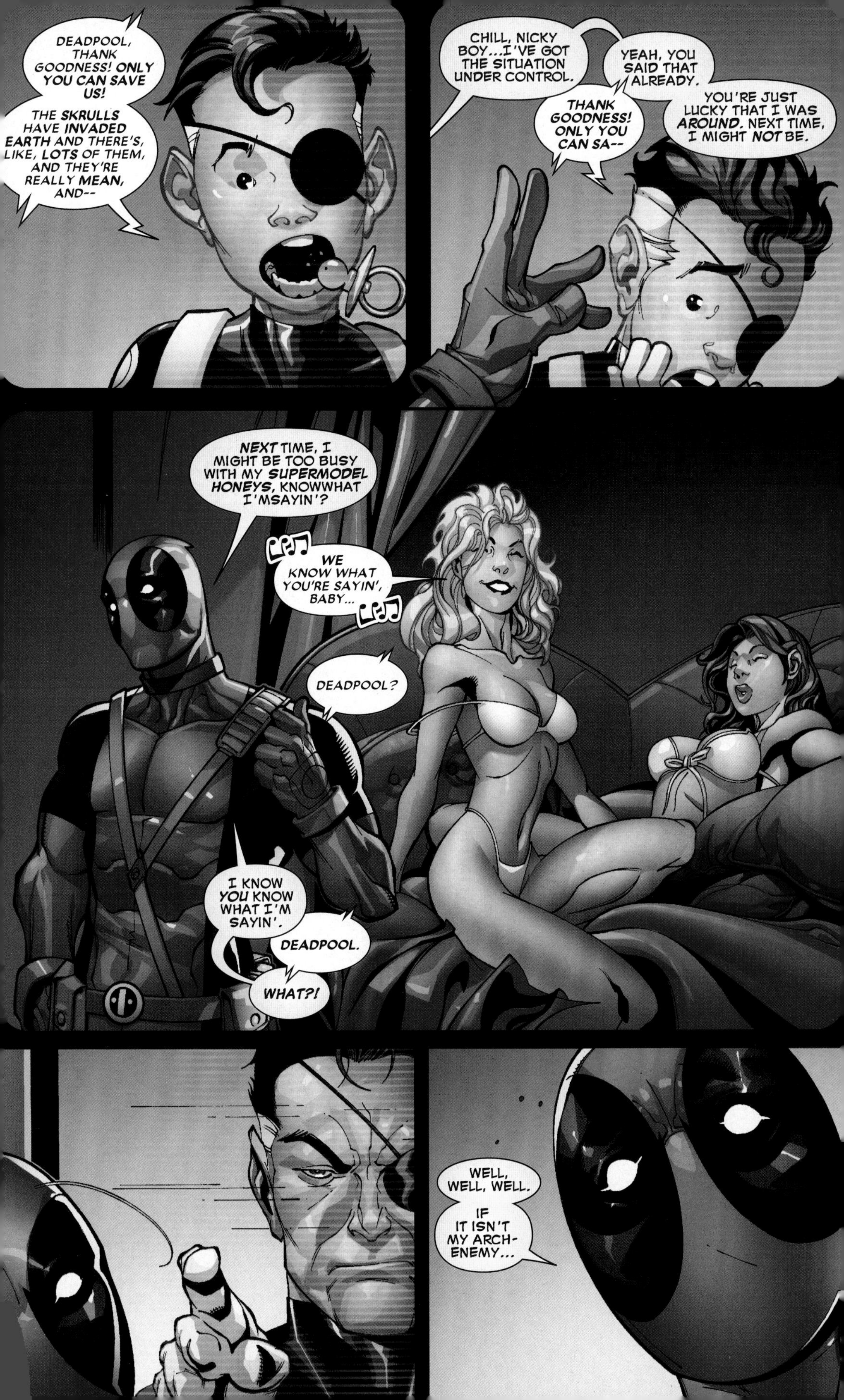
DEADPOOL, THANK GOODNESS! ONLY YOU CAN SAVE US!
THE SKRULLS HAVE INVADED EARTH AND THERE'S, LIKE, LOTS OF THEM, AND THEY'RE REALLY MEAN, AND--
CHILL, NICKY BOY...I'VE GOT THE SITUATION UNDER CONTROL.
THANK GOODNESS! ONLY YOU CAN SA--
YEAH, YOU SAID THAT ALREADY.
YOU'RE JUST LUCKY THAT I WAS AROUND. NEXT TIME, I MIGHT NOT BE.
NEXT TIME, I MIGHT BE TOO BUSY WITH MY SUPERMODEL HONEYS, KNOWWHAT I'MSAYIN'?
WE KNOW WHAT YOU'RE SAYIN', BABY...
DEADPOOL?
I KNOW YOU KNOW WHAT I'M SAYIN'.
DEADPOOL.
WHAT?!
WELL, WELL, WELL.
IF IT ISN'T MY ARCH-ENEMY...

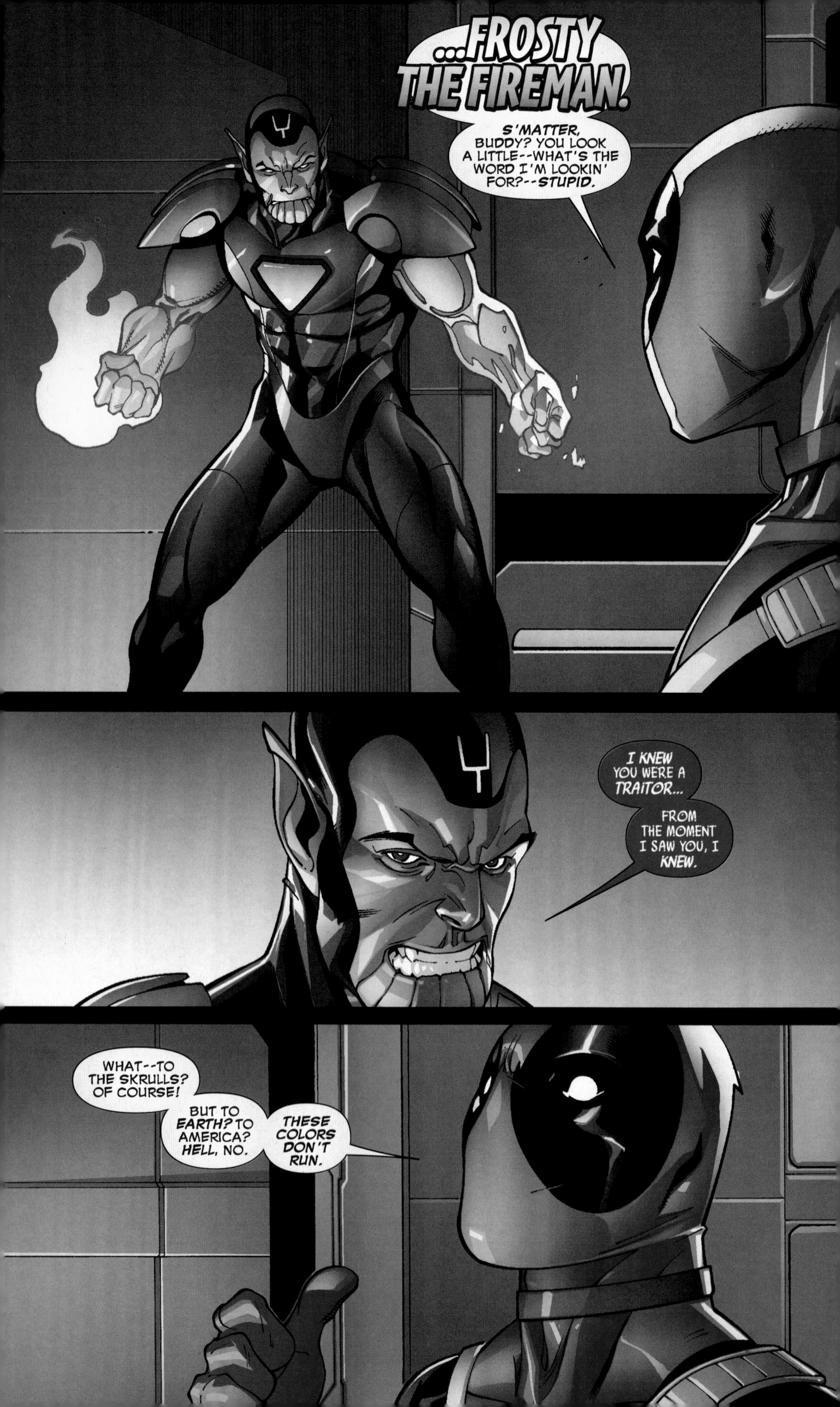
...FROSTY THE FIREMAN!
S'MATTER, BUDDY? YOU LOOK A LITTLE--WHAT'S THE WORD I'M LOOKIN' FOR?--STUPID.
I KNEW YOU WERE A TRAITOR...
FROM THE MOMENT I SAW YOU, I KNEW.
WHAT--TO THE SKRULLS? OF COURSE!
BUT TO EARTH? TO AMERICA? HELL, NO.
THESE COLORS DON'T RUN.

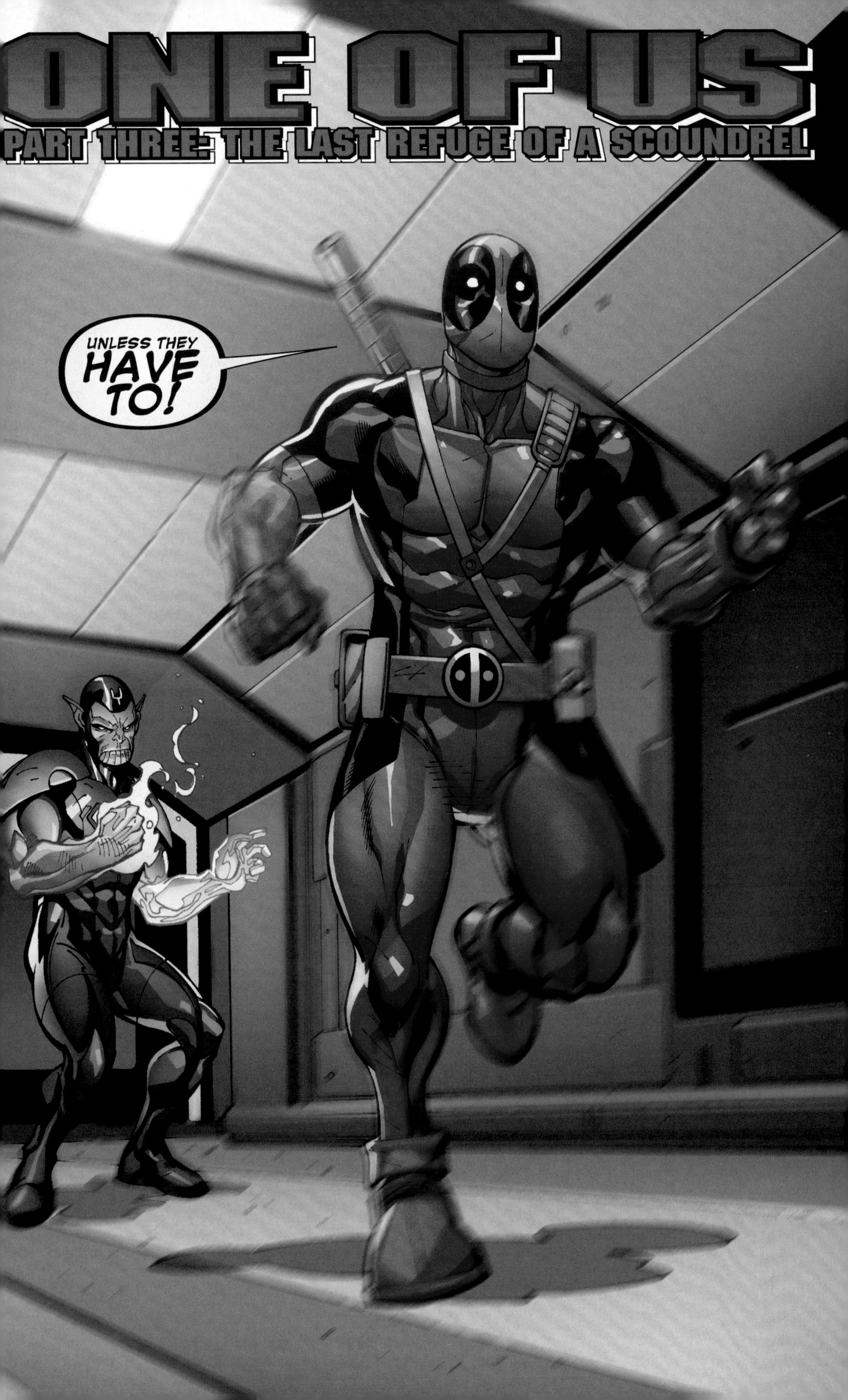
ONE OF US
PART THREE: THE LAST REFUGE OF A SCOUNDREL
UNLESS THEY HAVE TO!

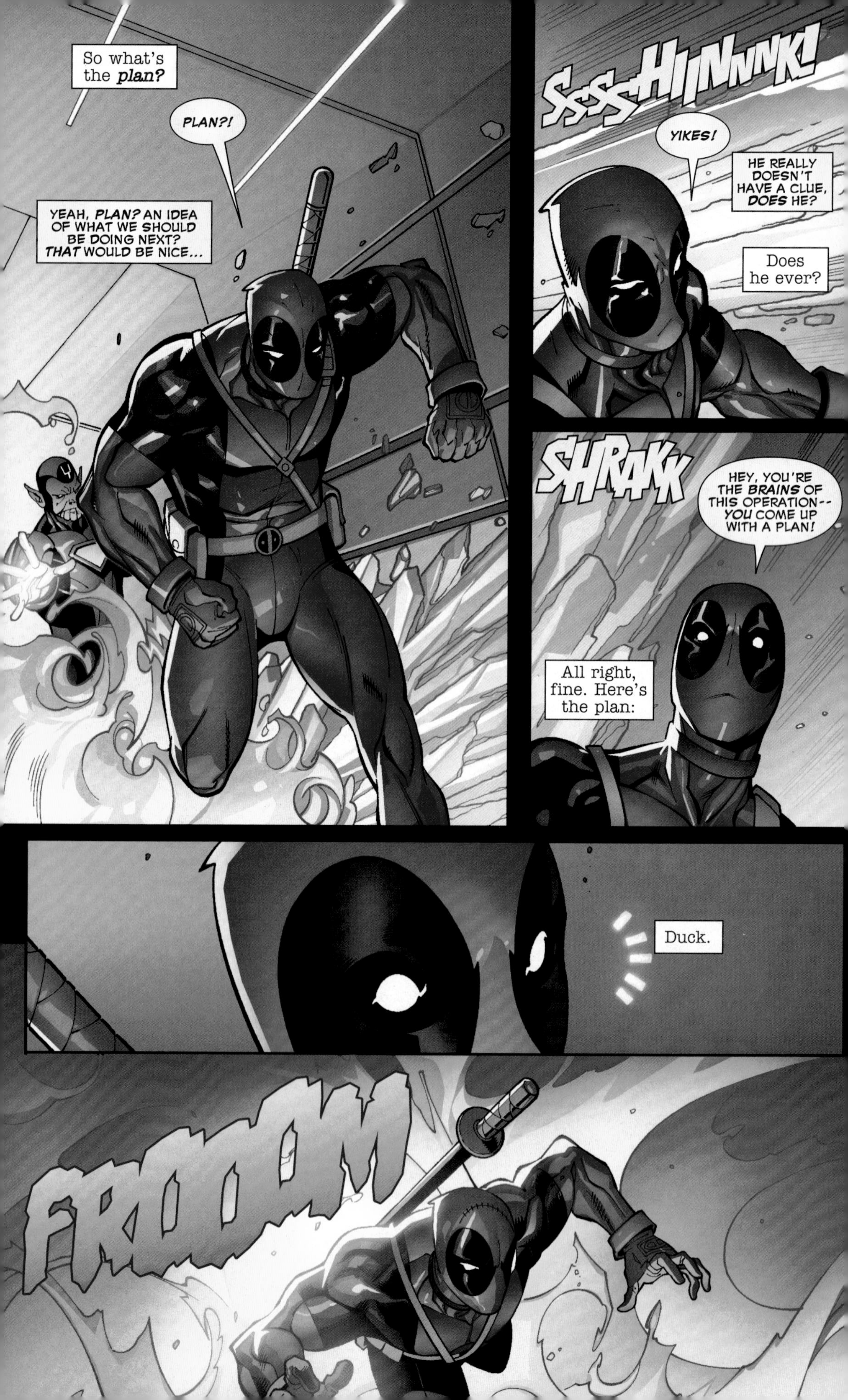

So what's the *plan?*
PLAN?!
YEAH, *PLAN?* AN IDEA OF WHAT WE SHOULD BE DOING NEXT? *THAT* WOULD BE NICE...
SSSSHIINNNK!
YIKES!
HE REALLY DOESN'T HAVE A CLUE, *DOES* HE?
Does he ever?
SHRAKK
HEY, YOU'RE THE *BRAINS* OF THIS OPERATION-- *YOU* COME UP WITH A PLAN!
All right, fine. Here's the plan:
Duck.
FROOOM

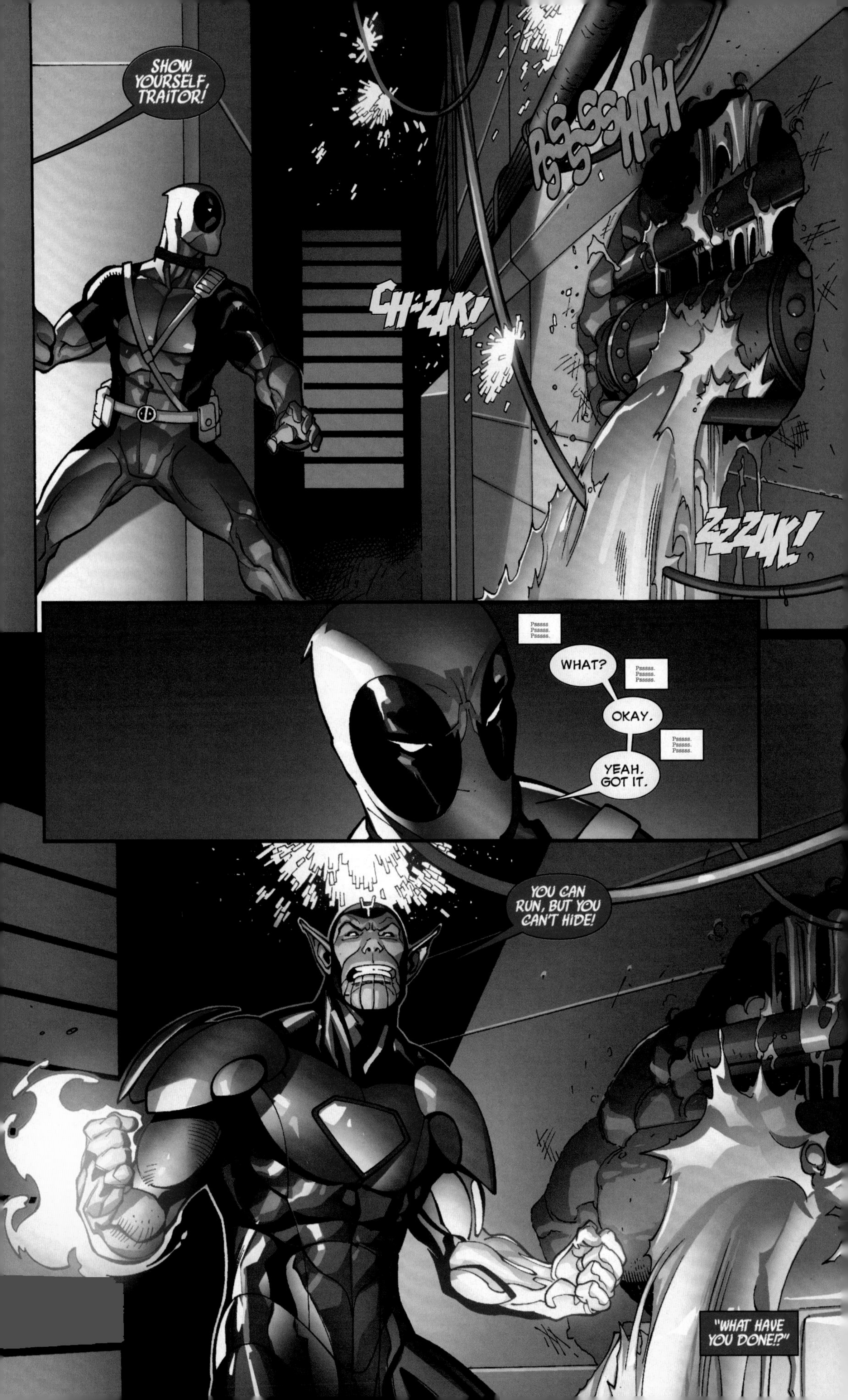
SHOW YOURSELF, TRAITOR!
RSSSSHHH
CH-ZAK!
ZZZAK!
Psssss Psssss. Psssss.
WHAT?
Psssss. Psssss. Psssss.
OKAY.
Psssss. Psssss. Psssss.
YEAH. GOT IT.
YOU CAN RUN, BUT YOU CAN'T HIDE!
"WHAT HAVE YOU DONE!?"

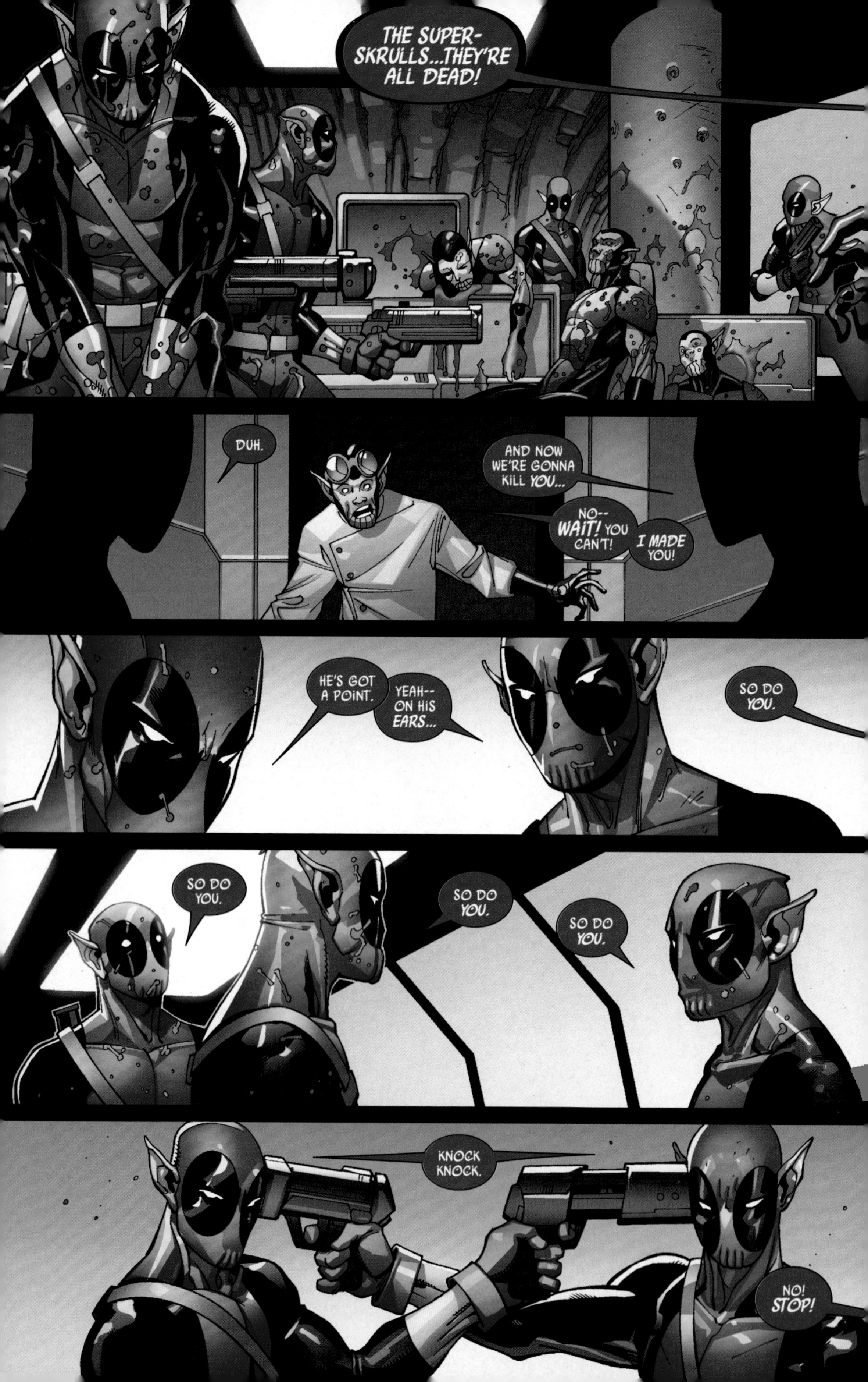
THE SUPER-SKRULLS...THEY'RE ALL DEAD!
DUH.
AND NOW WE'RE GONNA KILL YOU...
NO-- WAIT! YOU CAN'T!
I MADE YOU!
HE'S GOT A POINT.
YEAH-- ON HIS EARS...
SO DO YOU.
SO DO YOU.
SO DO YOU.
SO DO YOU.
KNOCK KNOCK.
NO! STOP!

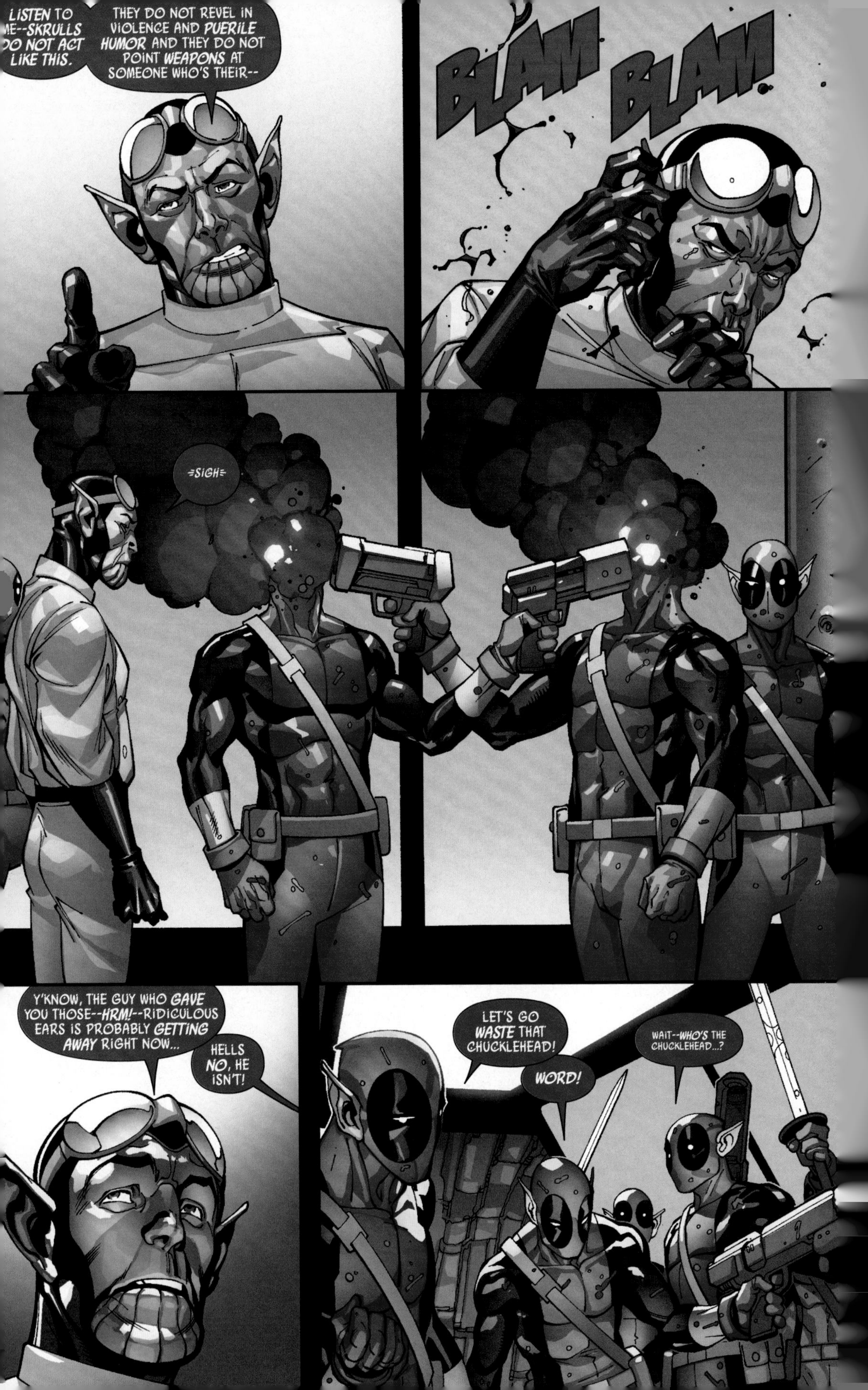
LISTEN TO ME--SKRULLS DO NOT ACT LIKE THIS.
THEY DO NOT REVEL IN VIOLENCE AND PUERILE HUMOR AND THEY DO NOT POINT WEAPONS AT SOMEONE WHO'S THEIR--
BLAM BLAM
=SIGH=
Y'KNOW, THE GUY WHO GAVE YOU THOSE--HRM!--RIDICULOUS EARS IS PROBABLY GETTING AWAY RIGHT NOW...
HELLS NO, HE ISN'T!
LET'S GO WASTE THAT CHUCKLEHEAD!
WORD!
WAIT--WHO'S THE CHUCKLEHEAD...?

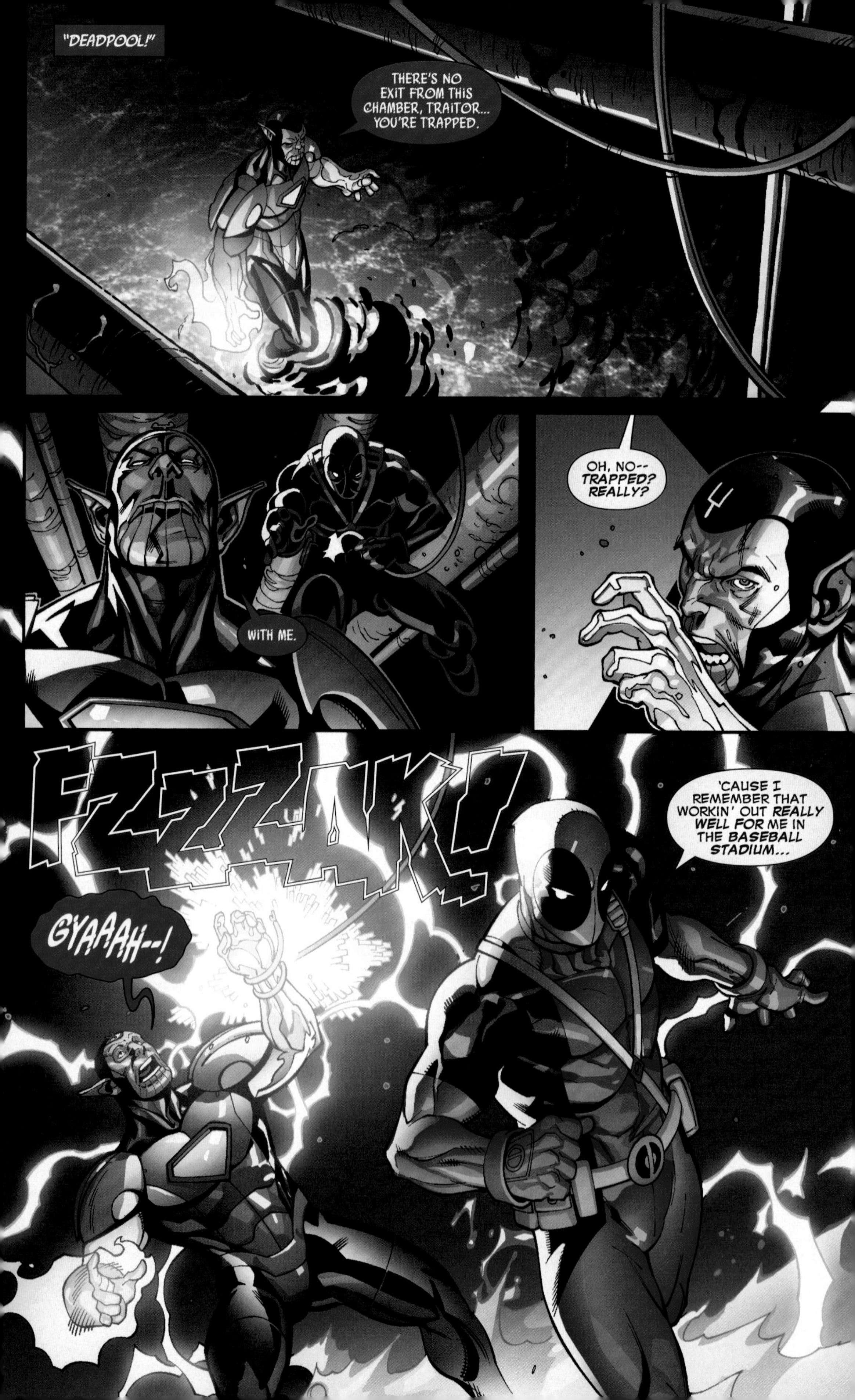
"DEADPOOL!"
THERE'S NO EXIT FROM THIS CHAMBER, TRAITOR... YOU'RE TRAPPED.
WITH ME.
OH, NO-- TRAPPED? REALLY?
FZZZAKK!
'CAUSE I REMEMBER THAT WORKIN' OUT REALLY WELL FOR ME IN THE BASEBALL STADIUM...
GYAAAH--!

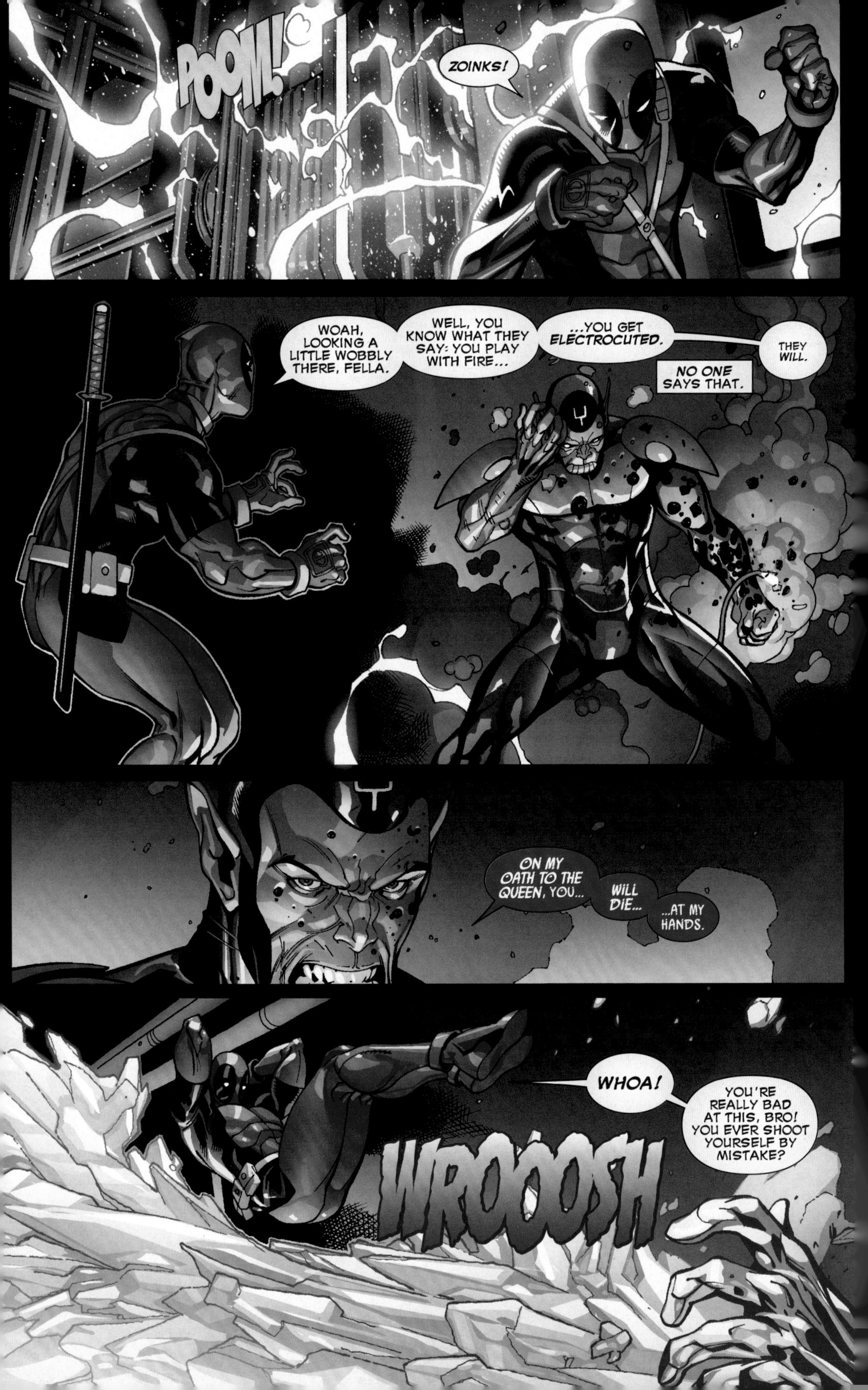
POOM!
ZOINKS!
WOAH, LOOKING A LITTLE WOBBLY THERE, FELLA.
WELL, YOU KNOW WHAT THEY SAY: YOU PLAY WITH FIRE...
...YOU GET ELECTROCUTED.
THEY WILL.
NO ONE SAYS THAT.
ON MY OATH TO THE QUEEN, YOU...
WILL DIE...
...AT MY HANDS.
WHOA!
YOU'RE REALLY BAD AT THIS, BRO! YOU EVER SHOOT YOURSELF BY MISTAKE?
WROOOSH

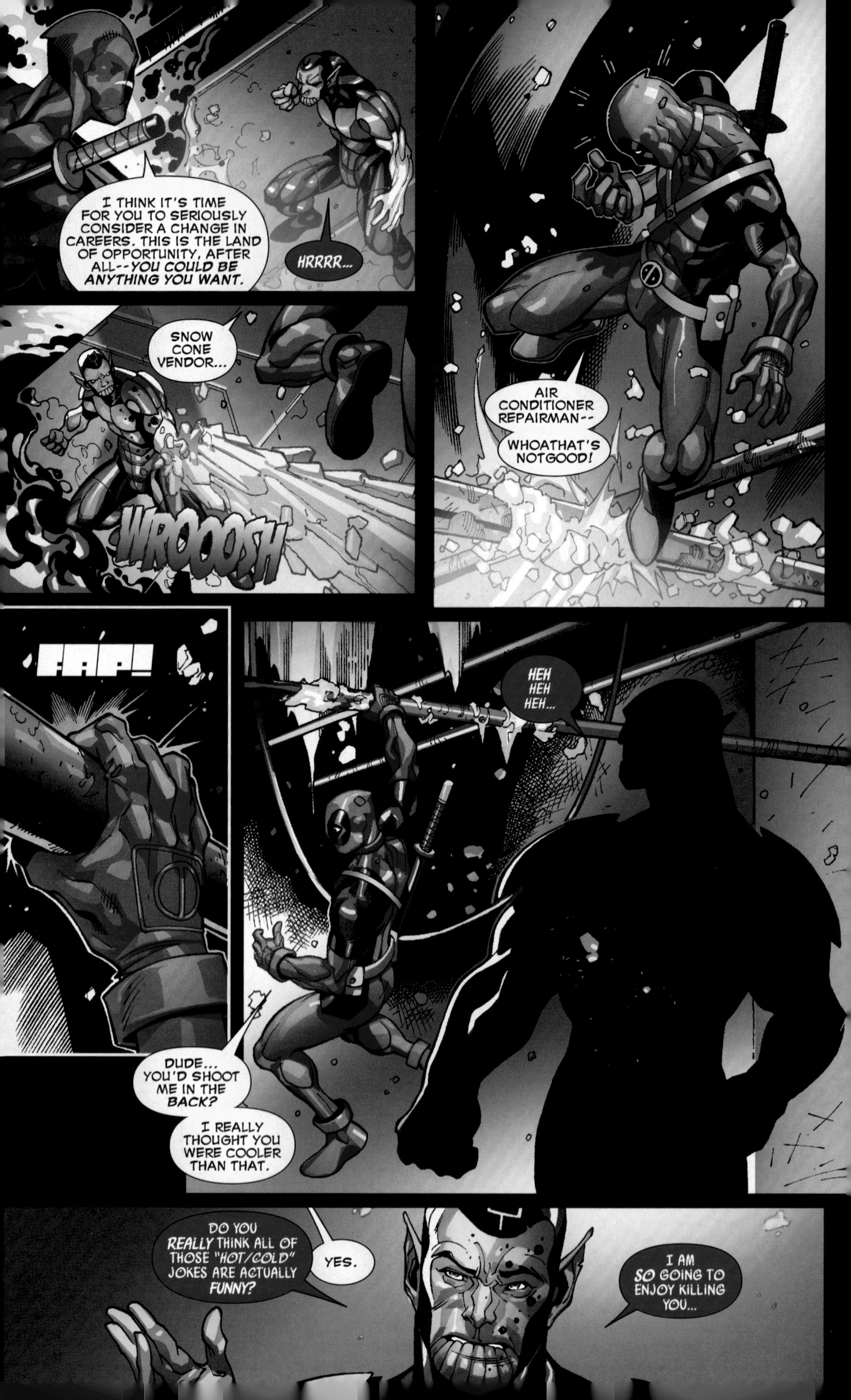
I THINK IT'S TIME FOR YOU TO SERIOUSLY CONSIDER A CHANGE IN CAREERS. THIS IS THE LAND OF OPPORTUNITY, AFTER ALL--*YOU COULD BE ANYTHING YOU WANT.*
HRRRR...
SNOW CONE VENDOR...
WROOOSH
AIR CONDITIONER REPAIRMAN--
WHOATHAT'S NOTGOOD!
FAP!
HEH HEH HEH...
DUDE... YOU'D SHOOT ME IN THE *BACK?*
I REALLY THOUGHT YOU WERE COOLER THAN THAT.
DO YOU *REALLY* THINK ALL OF THOSE "*HOT/COLD*" JOKES ARE ACTUALLY *FUNNY?*
YES.
I AM *SO* GOING TO ENJOY KILLING YOU...

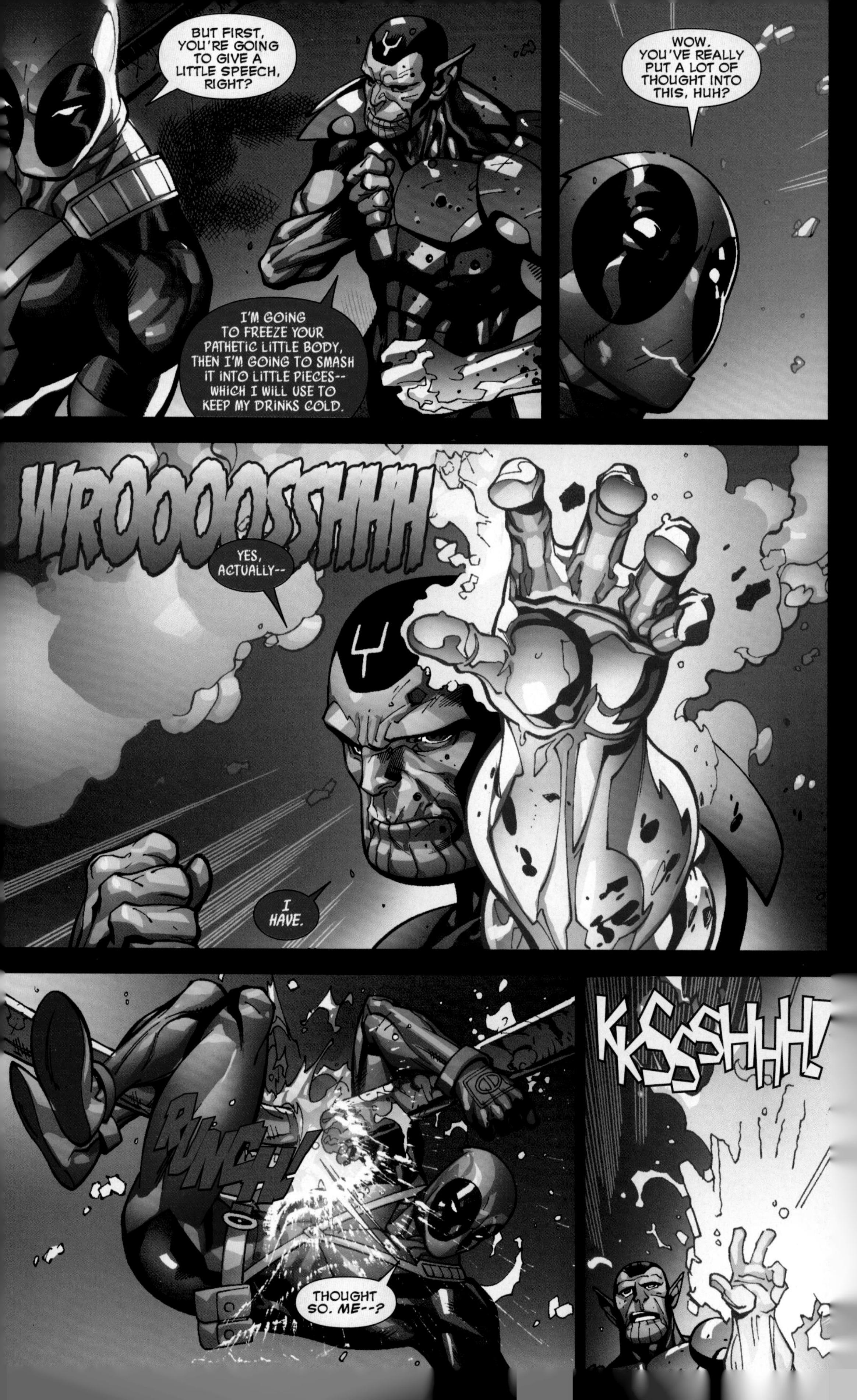

BUT FIRST, YOU'RE GOING TO GIVE A LITTLE SPEECH, RIGHT?
I'M GOING TO FREEZE YOUR PATHETIC LITTLE BODY, THEN I'M GOING TO SMASH IT INTO LITTLE PIECES-- WHICH I WILL USE TO KEEP MY DRINKS COLD.
WOW. YOU'VE REALLY PUT A LOT OF THOUGHT INTO THIS, HUH?
WROOOOSSHHH
YES, ACTUALLY--
I HAVE.
PUNCH
THOUGHT SO. ME--?
KKSSSHHH!

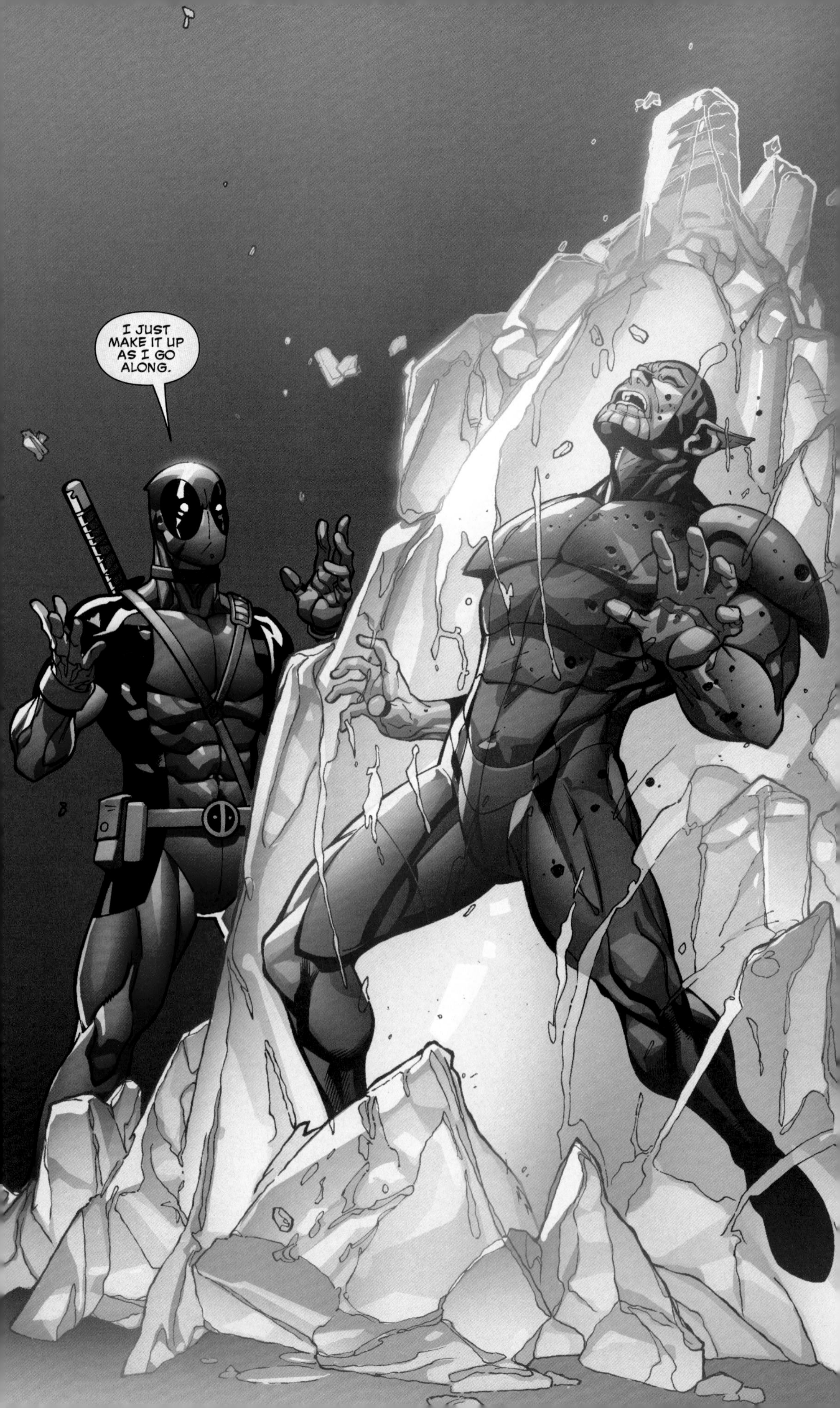
I JUST MAKE IT UP AS I GO ALONG.

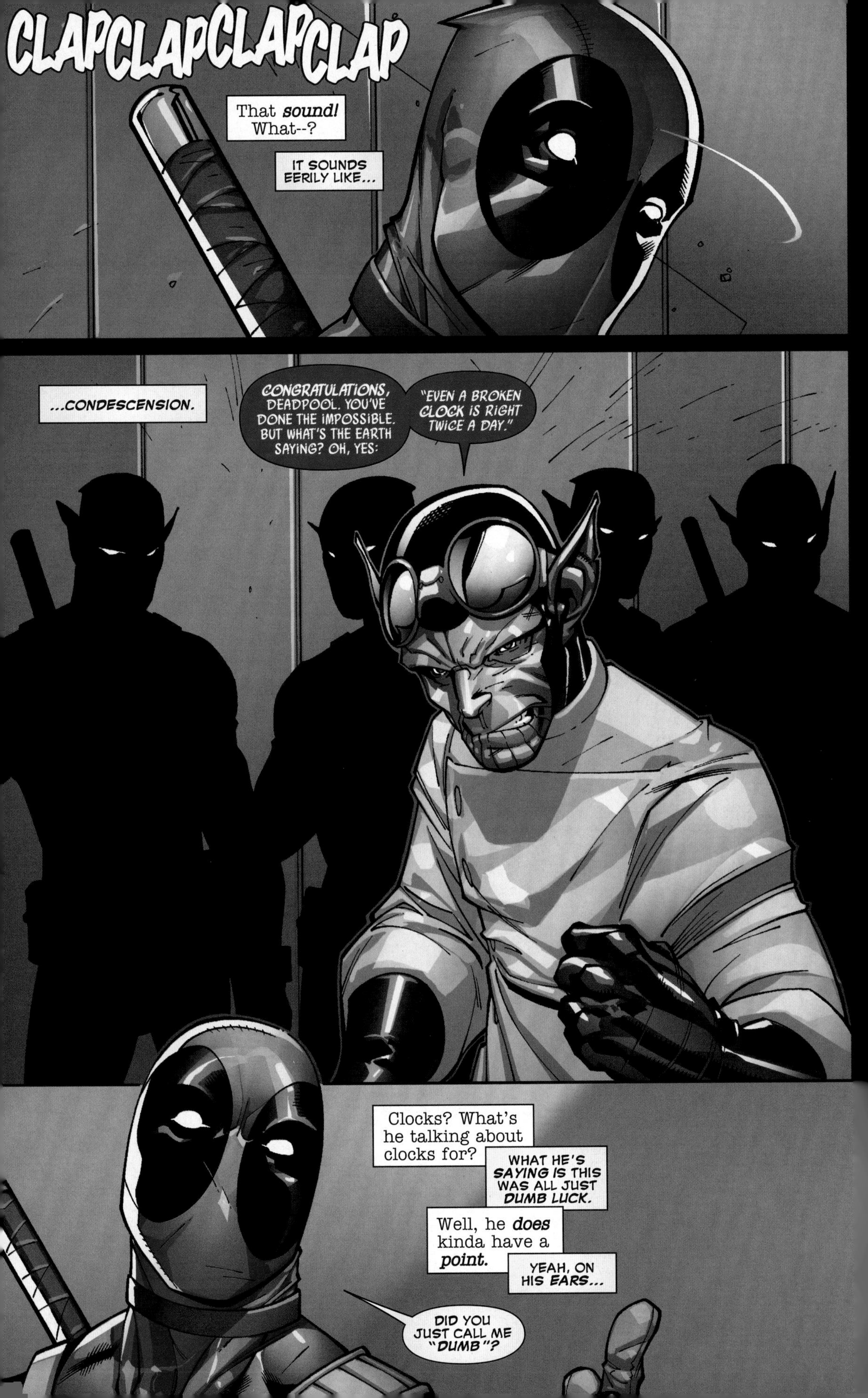
CLAPCLAPCLAPCLAP
That **sound!** What--?
IT SOUNDS EERILY LIKE...
...CONDESCENSION.
CONGRATULATIONS, DEADPOOL. YOU'VE DONE THE IMPOSSIBLE. BUT WHAT'S THE EARTH SAYING? OH, YES:
"EVEN A BROKEN CLOCK IS RIGHT TWICE A DAY."
Clocks? What's he talking about clocks for?
WHAT HE'S *SAYING* IS THIS WAS ALL JUST *DUMB LUCK.*
Well, he **does** kinda have a **point.**
YEAH, ON HIS *EARS*...
DID YOU JUST CALL ME "*DUMB*"?

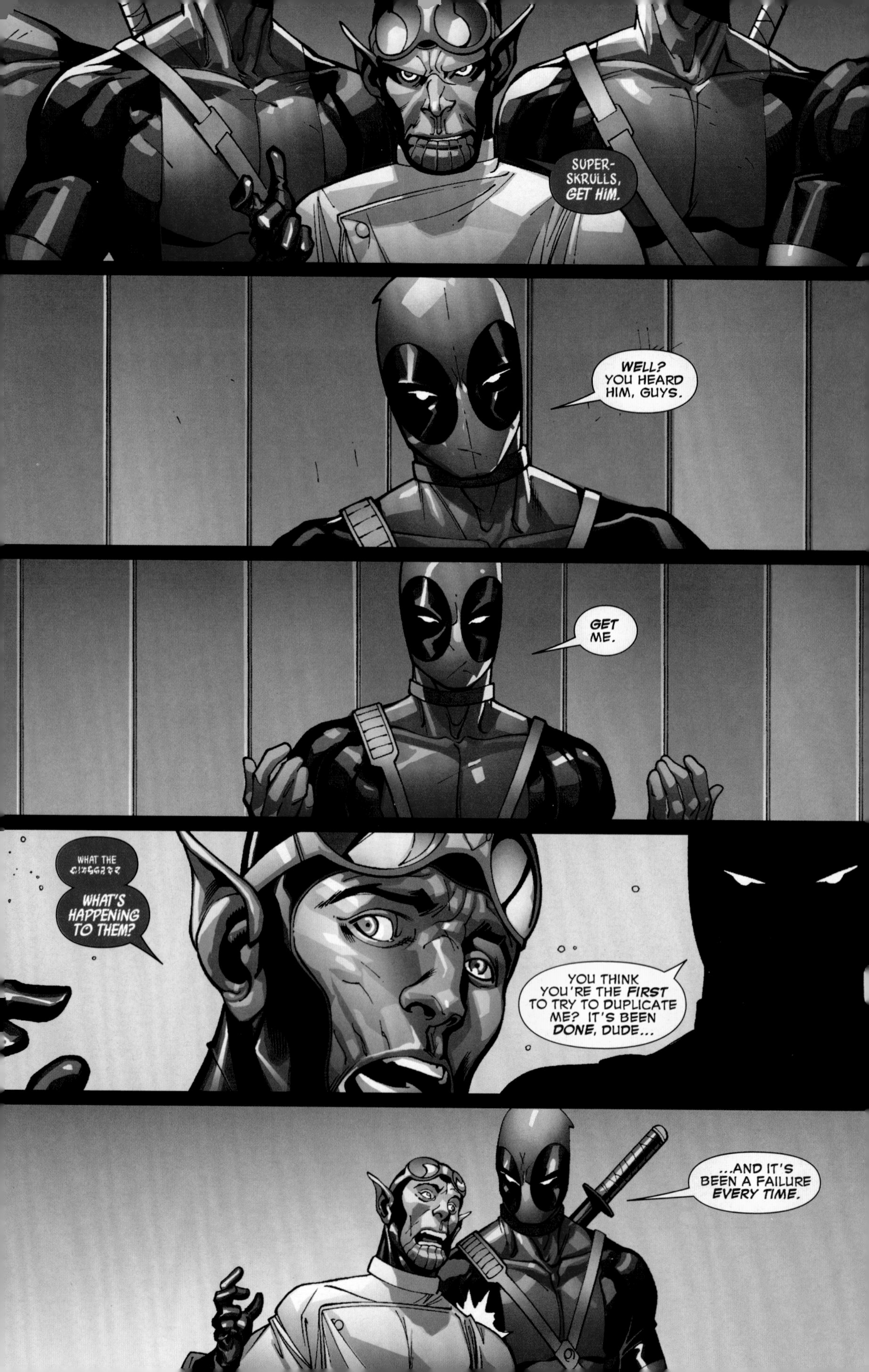
SUPER-SKRULLS, GET HIM.
WELL? YOU HEARD HIM, GUYS.
GET ME.
WHAT THE
WHAT'S HAPPENING TO THEM?
YOU THINK YOU'RE THE FIRST TO TRY TO DUPLICATE ME? IT'S BEEN DONE, DUDE...
...AND IT'S BEEN A FAILURE EVERY TIME.

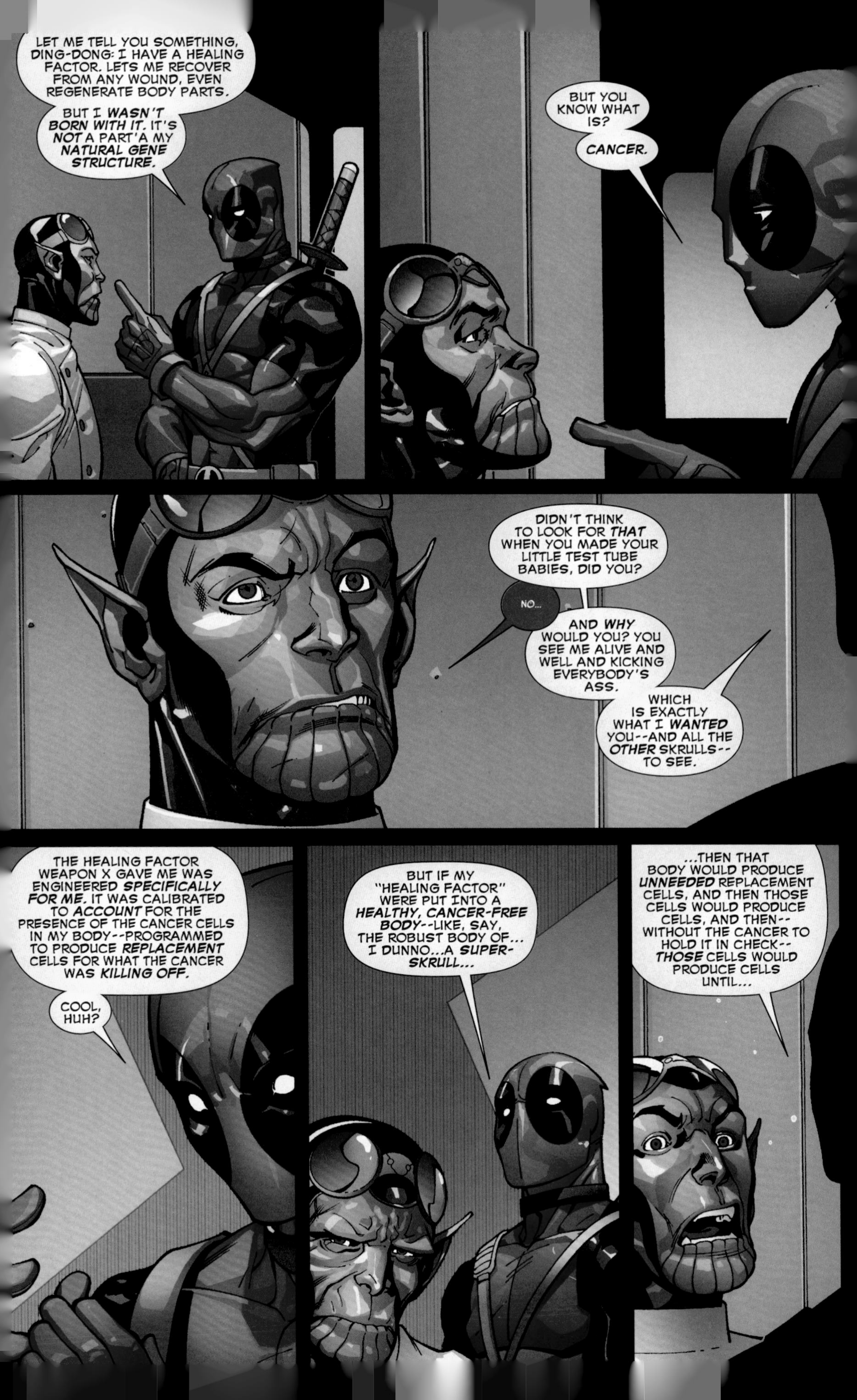
LET ME TELL YOU SOMETHING, DING-DONG: I HAVE A HEALING FACTOR. LETS ME RECOVER FROM ANY WOUND, EVEN REGENERATE BODY PARTS.
BUT I WASN'T BORN WITH IT. IT'S NOT A PART'A MY NATURAL GENE STRUCTURE.
BUT YOU KNOW WHAT IS?
CANCER.
DIDN'T THINK TO LOOK FOR THAT WHEN YOU MADE YOUR LITTLE TEST TUBE BABIES, DID YOU?
NO...
AND WHY WOULD YOU? YOU SEE ME ALIVE AND WELL AND KICKING EVERYBODY'S ASS.
WHICH IS EXACTLY WHAT I WANTED YOU--AND ALL THE OTHER SKRULLS--TO SEE.
THE HEALING FACTOR WEAPON X GAVE ME WAS ENGINEERED SPECIFICALLY FOR ME. IT WAS CALIBRATED TO ACCOUNT FOR THE PRESENCE OF THE CANCER CELLS IN MY BODY--PROGRAMMED TO PRODUCE REPLACEMENT CELLS FOR WHAT THE CANCER WAS KILLING OFF.
COOL, HUH?
BUT IF MY "HEALING FACTOR" WERE PUT INTO A HEALTHY, CANCER-FREE BODY--LIKE, SAY, THE ROBUST BODY OF... I DUNNO...A SUPER-SKRULL...
...THEN THAT BODY WOULD PRODUCE UNNEEDED REPLACEMENT CELLS, AND THEN THOSE CELLS WOULD PRODUCE CELLS, AND THEN--WITHOUT THE CANCER TO HOLD IT IN CHECK--THOSE CELLS WOULD PRODUCE CELLS UNTIL...

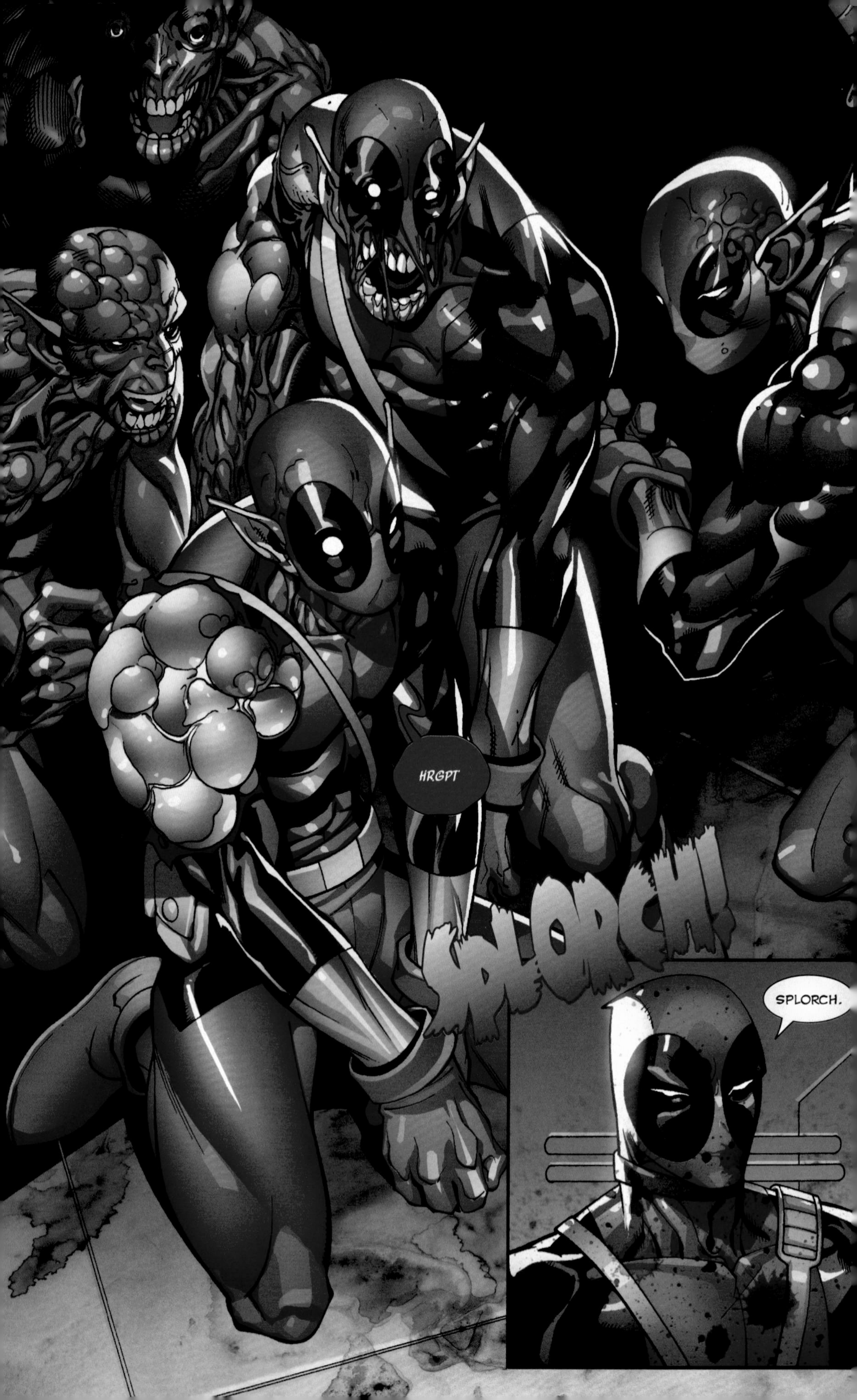
HRGPT
SPLORCH!!
SPLORCH.

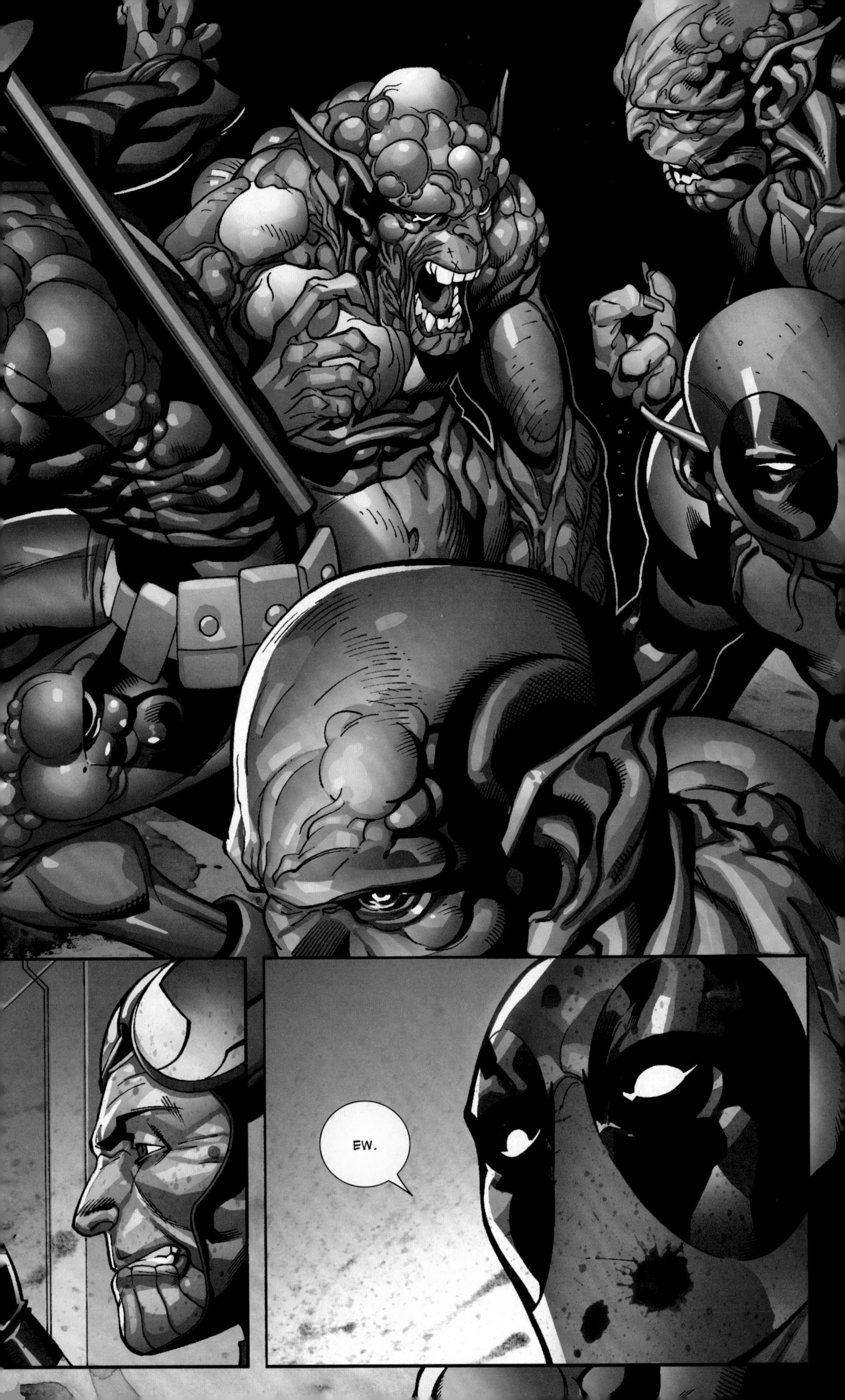
EW.

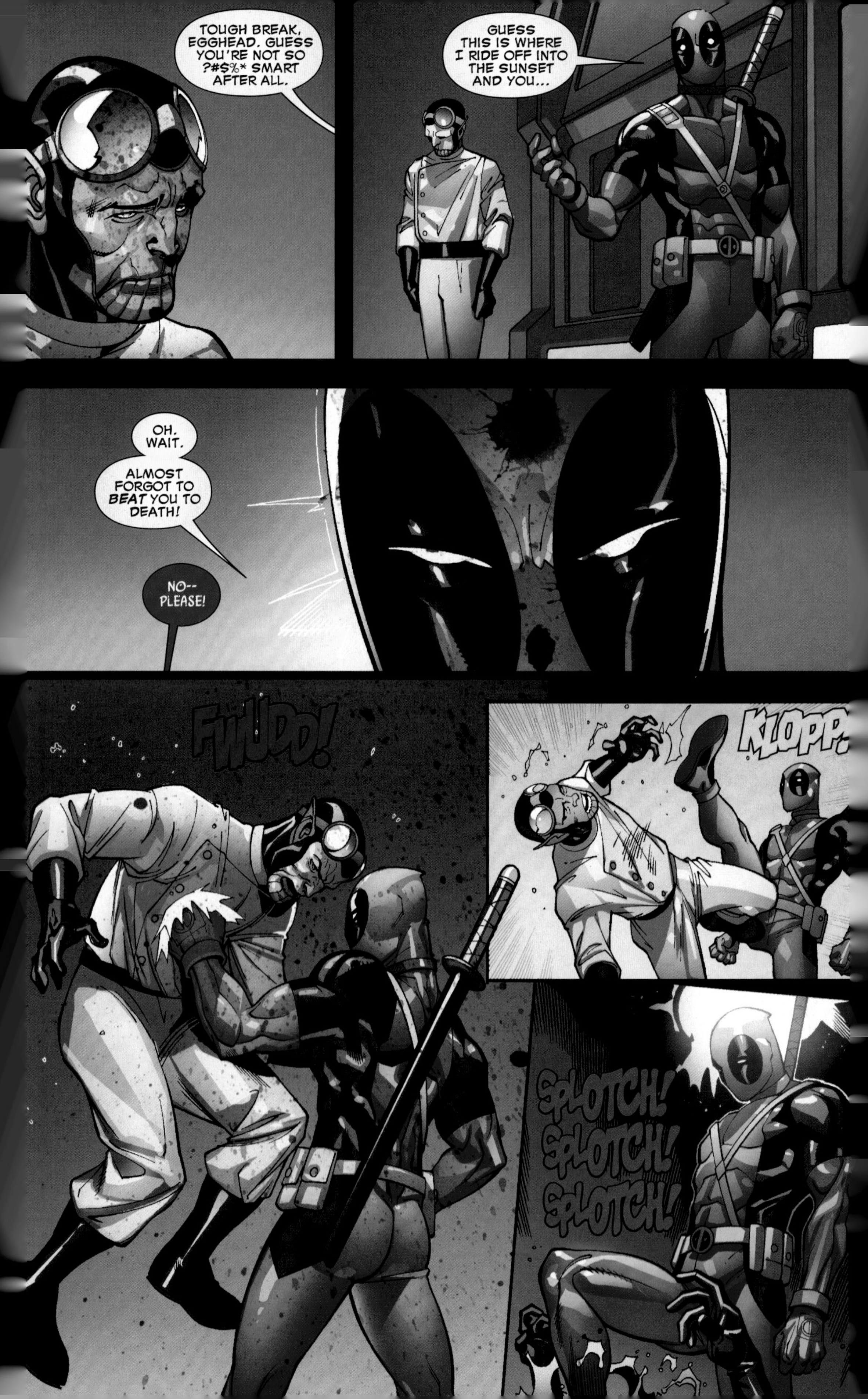
TOUGH BREAK, EGGHEAD. GUESS YOU'RE NOT SO ?#$%* SMART AFTER ALL.
GUESS THIS IS WHERE I RIDE OFF INTO THE SUNSET AND YOU...
OH. WAIT.
ALMOST FORGOT TO BEAT YOU TO DEATH!
NO-- PLEASE!
FWUDD!
KLOPP
SPLOTCH! SPLOTCH! SPLOTCH!

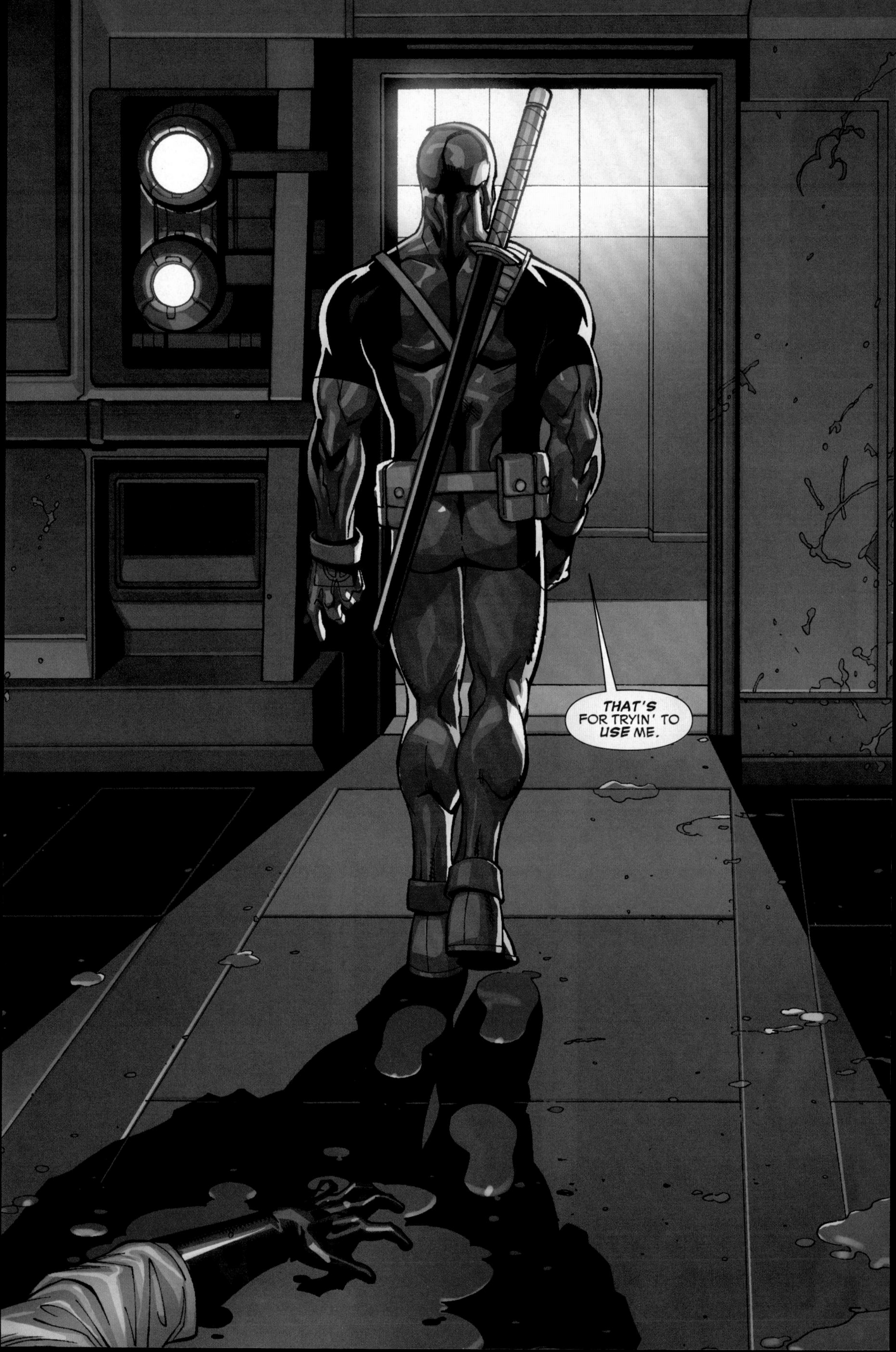
THAT'S FOR TRYIN' TO USE ME.

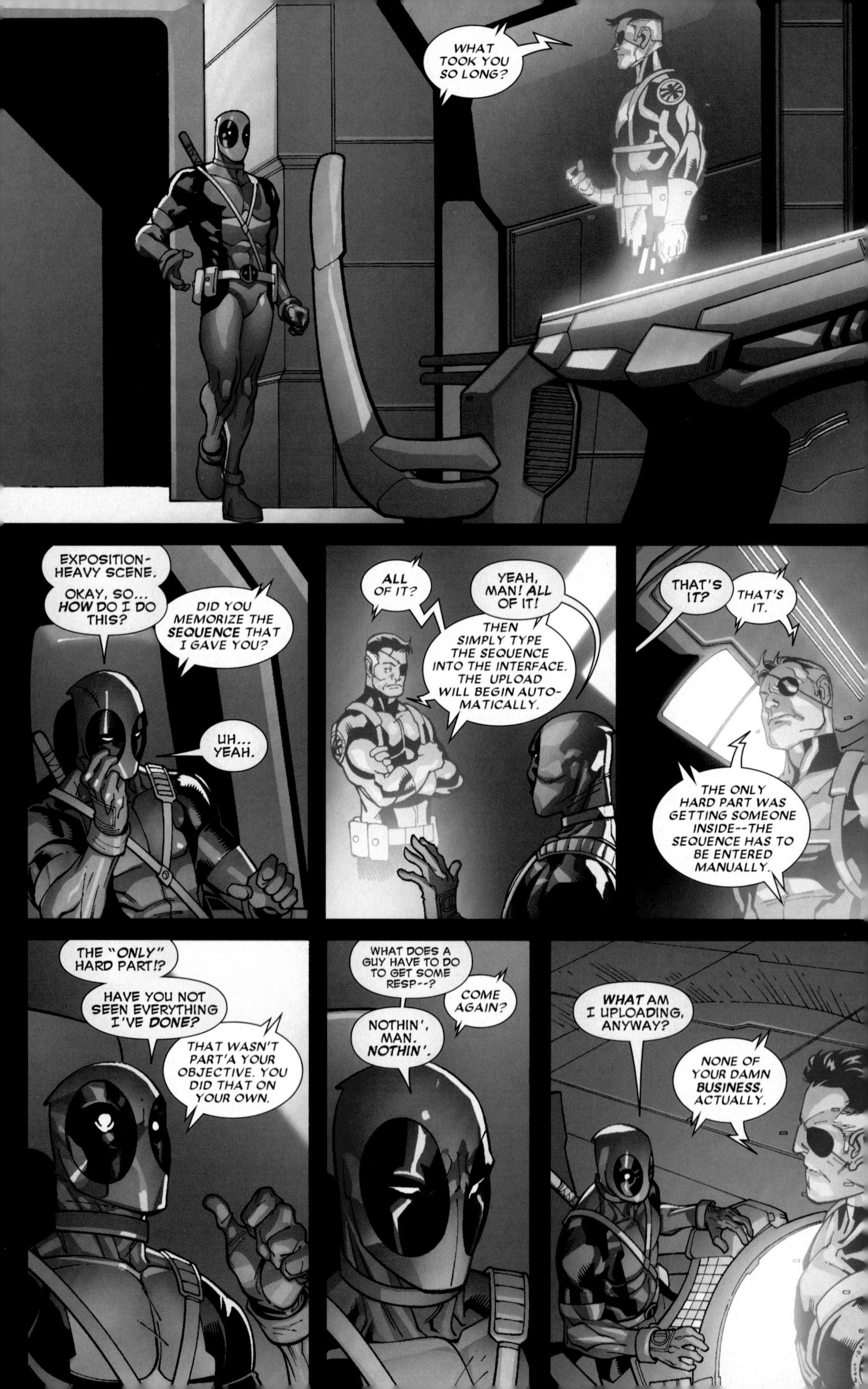
WHAT TOOK YOU SO LONG?
EXPOSITION-HEAVY SCENE.
OKAY, SO... HOW DO I DO THIS?
DID YOU MEMORIZE THE SEQUENCE THAT I GAVE YOU?
UH... YEAH.
ALL OF IT?
YEAH, MAN! ALL OF IT!
THEN SIMPLY TYPE THE SEQUENCE INTO THE INTERFACE. THE UPLOAD WILL BEGIN AUTO-MATICALLY.
THAT'S IT?
THAT'S IT.
THE ONLY HARD PART WAS GETTING SOMEONE INSIDE--THE SEQUENCE HAS TO BE ENTERED MANUALLY.
THE "ONLY" HARD PART!?
HAVE YOU NOT SEEN EVERYTHING I'VE DONE?
THAT WASN'T PART'A YOUR OBJECTIVE. YOU DID THAT ON YOUR OWN.
WHAT DOES A GUY HAVE TO DO TO GET SOME RESP--?
COME AGAIN?
NOTHIN', MAN. NOTHIN'.
WHAT AM I UPLOADING, ANYWAY?
NONE OF YOUR DAMN BUSINESS, ACTUALLY.

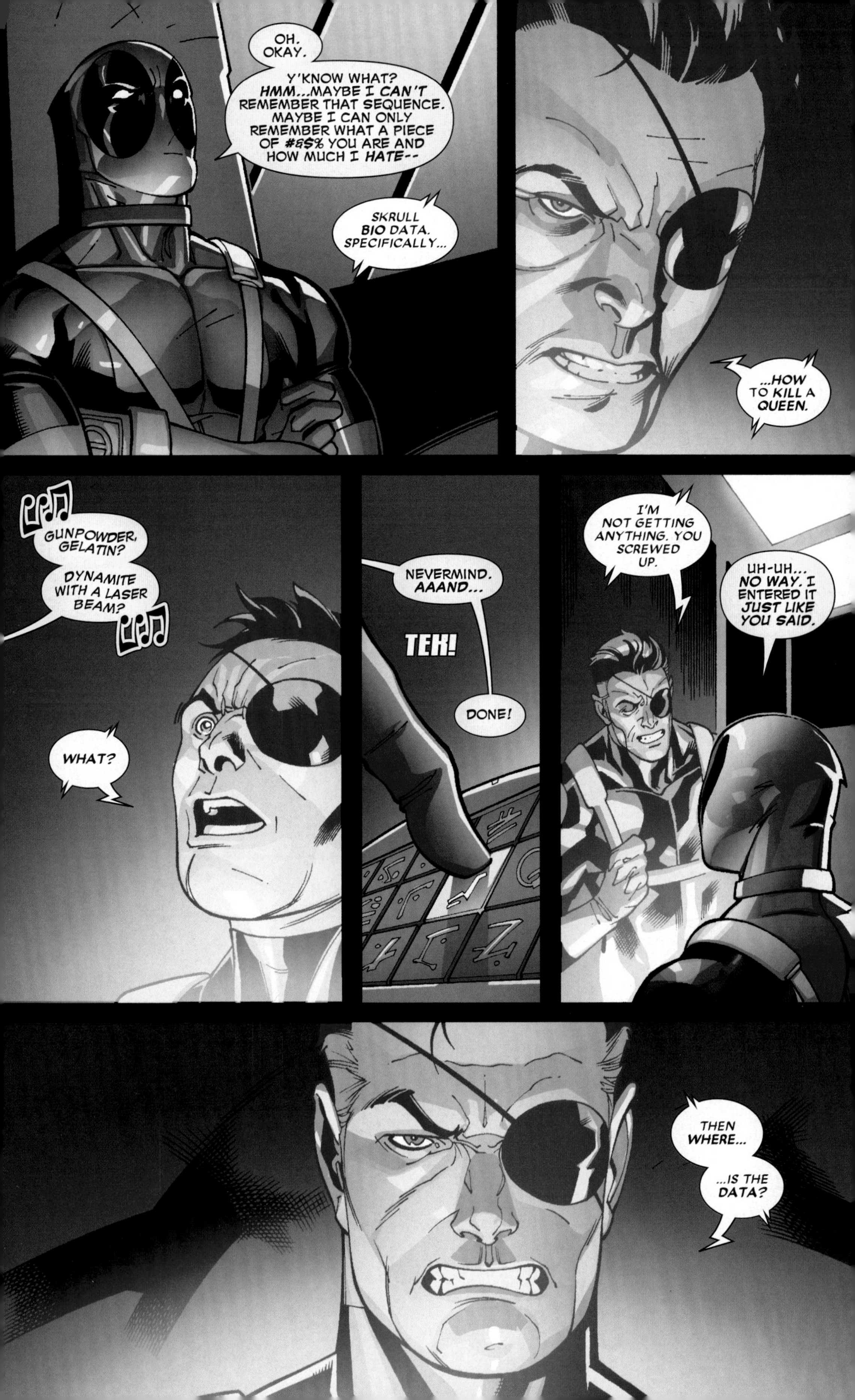
OH. OKAY.
Y'KNOW WHAT? HMM...MAYBE I CAN'T REMEMBER THAT SEQUENCE. MAYBE I CAN ONLY REMEMBER WHAT A PIECE OF #&$% YOU ARE AND HOW MUCH I HATE--
SKRULL BIO DATA. SPECIFICALLY...
...HOW TO KILL A QUEEN.
GUNPOWDER, GELATIN?
DYNAMITE WITH A LASER BEAM?
WHAT?
NEVERMIND. AAAND...
TEK!
DONE!
I'M NOT GETTING ANYTHING. YOU SCREWED UP.
UH-UH... NO WAY. I ENTERED IT JUST LIKE YOU SAID.
THEN WHERE...
...IS THE DATA?

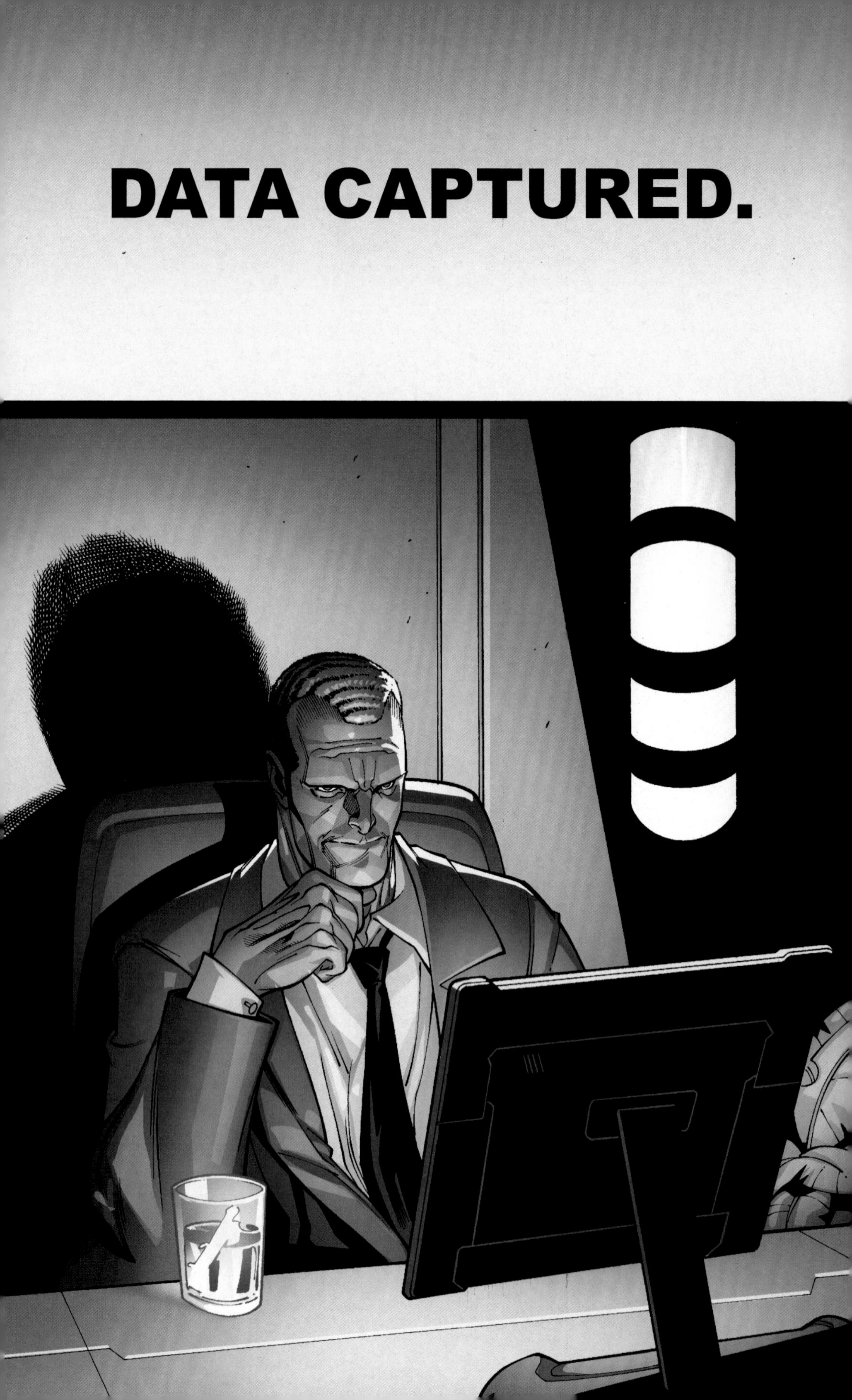
DATA CAPTURED.

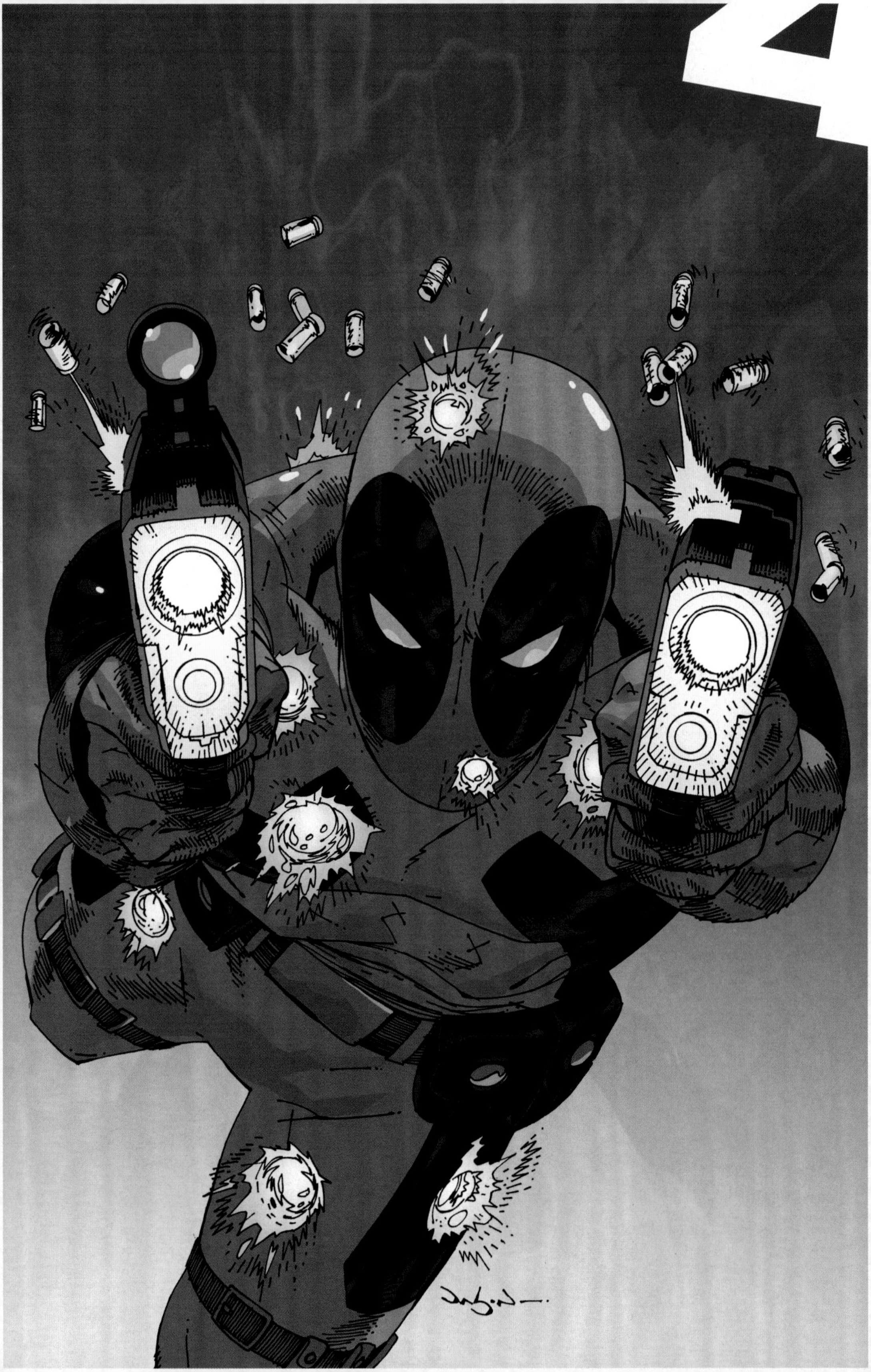
4

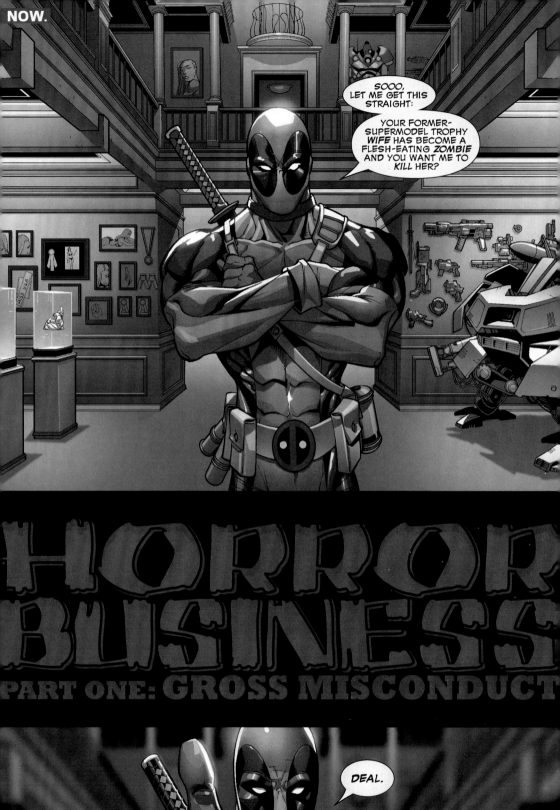

SOOO, LET ME GET THIS STRAIGHT:

YOUR FORMER-SUPERMODEL TROPHY *WIFE* HAS BECOME A FLESH-EATING *ZOMBIE* AND YOU WANT ME TO *KILL* HER?

HORROR BUSINESS

PART ONE: GROSS MISCONDUCT

DEAL.

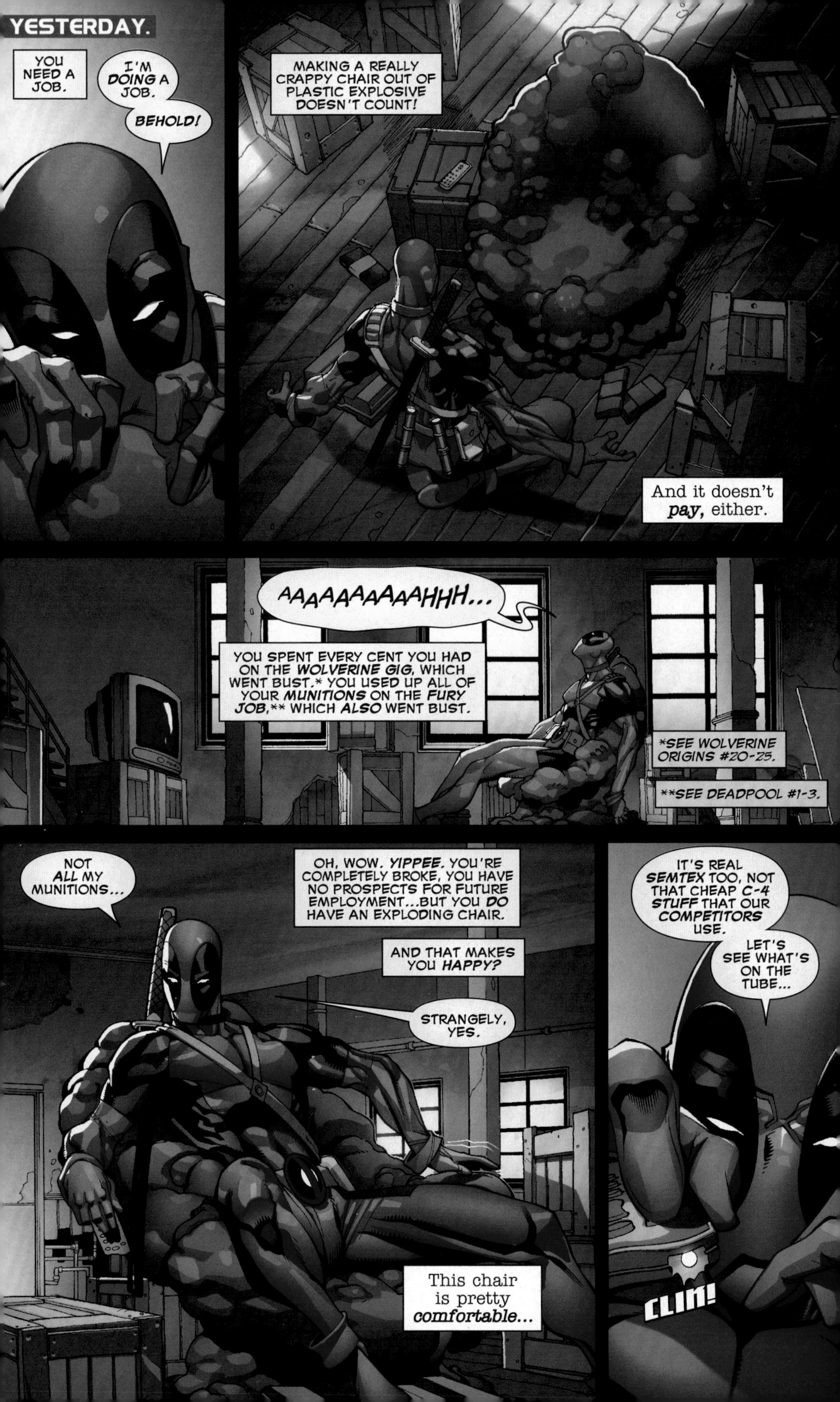
YESTERDAY.
YOU NEED A JOB.
I'M DOING A JOB.
BEHOLD!
MAKING A REALLY CRAPPY CHAIR OUT OF PLASTIC EXPLOSIVE DOESN'T COUNT!
And it doesn't pay, either.
AAAAAAAAAHHH...
YOU SPENT EVERY CENT YOU HAD ON THE WOLVERINE GIG, WHICH WENT BUST.* YOU USED UP ALL OF YOUR MUNITIONS ON THE FURY JOB,** WHICH ALSO WENT BUST.
*SEE WOLVERINE ORIGINS #20-25.
**SEE DEADPOOL #1-3.
NOT ALL MY MUNITIONS...
OH, WOW. YIPPEE. YOU'RE COMPLETELY BROKE, YOU HAVE NO PROSPECTS FOR FUTURE EMPLOYMENT...BUT YOU DO HAVE AN EXPLODING CHAIR.
AND THAT MAKES YOU HAPPY?
STRANGELY, YES.
This chair is pretty comfortable...
IT'S REAL SEMTEX TOO, NOT THAT CHEAP C-4 STUFF THAT OUR COMPETITORS USE.
LET'S SEE WHAT'S ON THE TUBE...
CLIK!

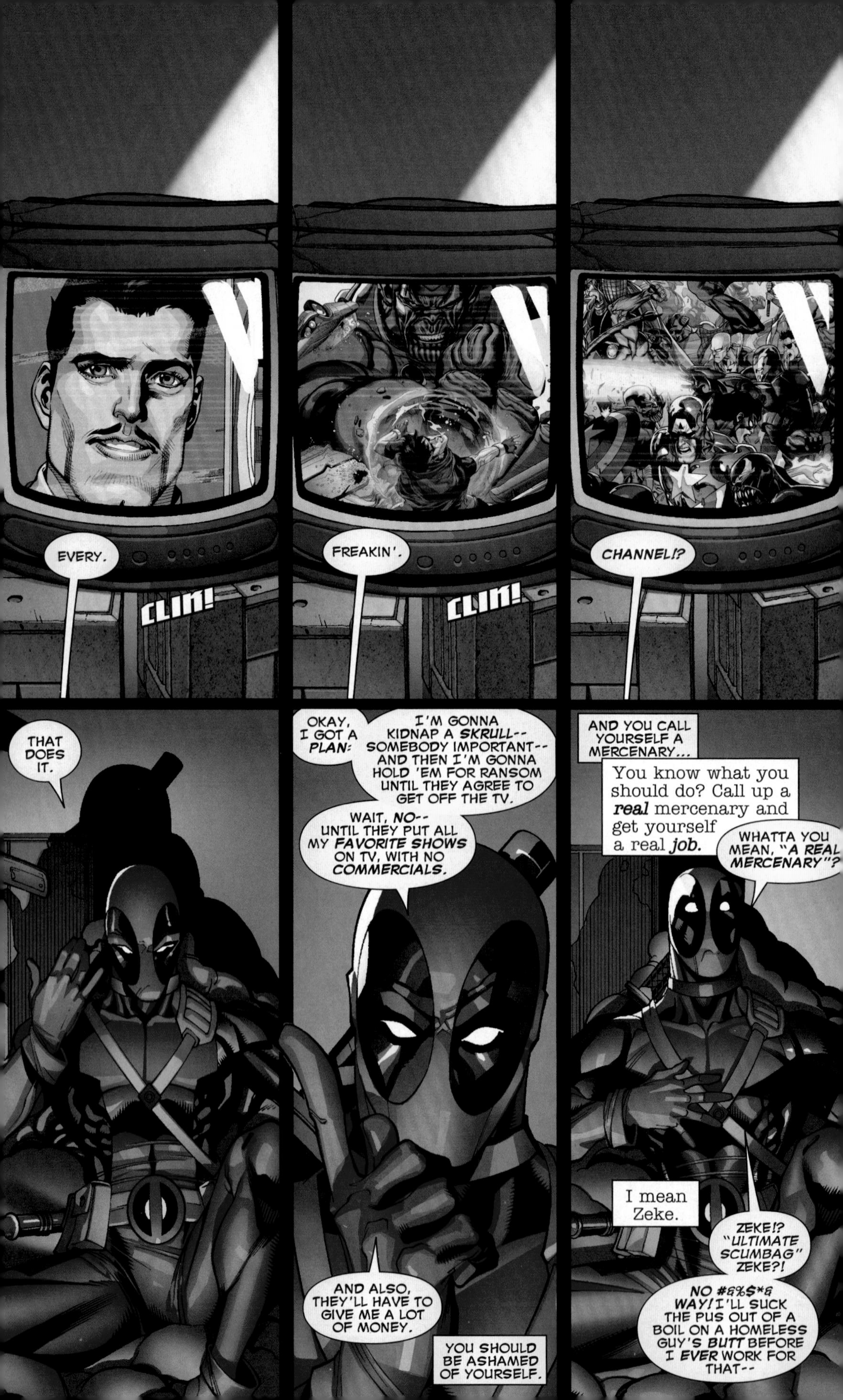
EVERY.
CLIN!
FREAKIN'.
CLIN!
CHANNEL!?
THAT DOES IT.
OKAY, I GOT A PLAN:
I'M GONNA KIDNAP A SKRULL-- SOMEBODY IMPORTANT-- AND THEN I'M GONNA HOLD 'EM FOR RANSOM UNTIL THEY AGREE TO GET OFF THE TV.
WAIT, NO-- UNTIL THEY PUT ALL MY FAVORITE SHOWS ON TV, WITH NO COMMERCIALS.
AND ALSO, THEY'LL HAVE TO GIVE ME A LOT OF MONEY.
YOU SHOULD BE ASHAMED OF YOURSELF.
AND YOU CALL YOURSELF A MERCENARY...
You know what you should do? Call up a real mercenary and get yourself a real job.
WHATTA YOU MEAN, "A REAL MERCENARY"?
I mean Zeke.
ZEKE!? "ULTIMATE SCUMBAG" ZEKE?!
NO #&%$*& WAY! I'LL SUCK THE PUS OUT OF A BOIL ON A HOMELESS GUY'S BUTT BEFORE I EVER WORK FOR THAT--

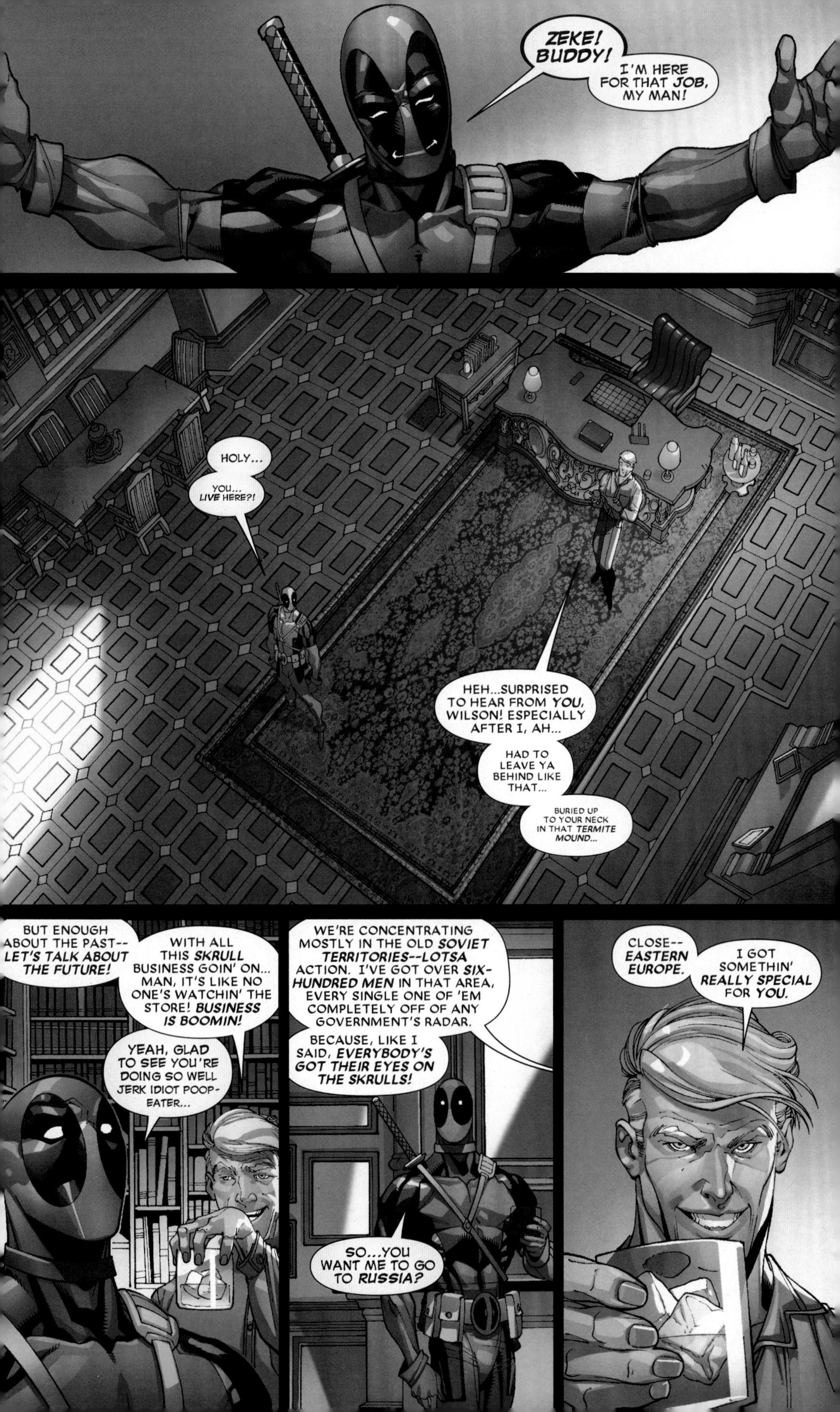

ZEKE! BUDDY!
I'M HERE FOR THAT JOB, MY MAN!
HOLY...
YOU... LIVE HERE?!
HEH...SURPRISED TO HEAR FROM YOU, WILSON! ESPECIALLY AFTER I, AH...
HAD TO LEAVE YA BEHIND LIKE THAT...
BURIED UP TO YOUR NECK IN THAT TERMITE MOUND...
BUT ENOUGH ABOUT THE PAST-- LET'S TALK ABOUT THE FUTURE!
WITH ALL THIS SKRULL BUSINESS GOIN' ON... MAN, IT'S LIKE NO ONE'S WATCHIN' THE STORE! BUSINESS IS BOOMIN!
YEAH, GLAD TO SEE YOU'RE DOING SO WELL JERK IDIOT POOP-EATER...
WE'RE CONCENTRATING MOSTLY IN THE OLD SOVIET TERRITORIES--LOTSA ACTION. I'VE GOT OVER SIX-HUNDRED MEN IN THAT AREA, EVERY SINGLE ONE OF 'EM COMPLETELY OFF OF ANY GOVERNMENT'S RADAR.
BECAUSE, LIKE I SAID, EVERYBODY'S GOT THEIR EYES ON THE SKRULLS!
SO...YOU WANT ME TO GO TO RUSSIA?
CLOSE-- EASTERN EUROPE.
I GOT SOMETHIN' REALLY SPECIAL FOR YOU.

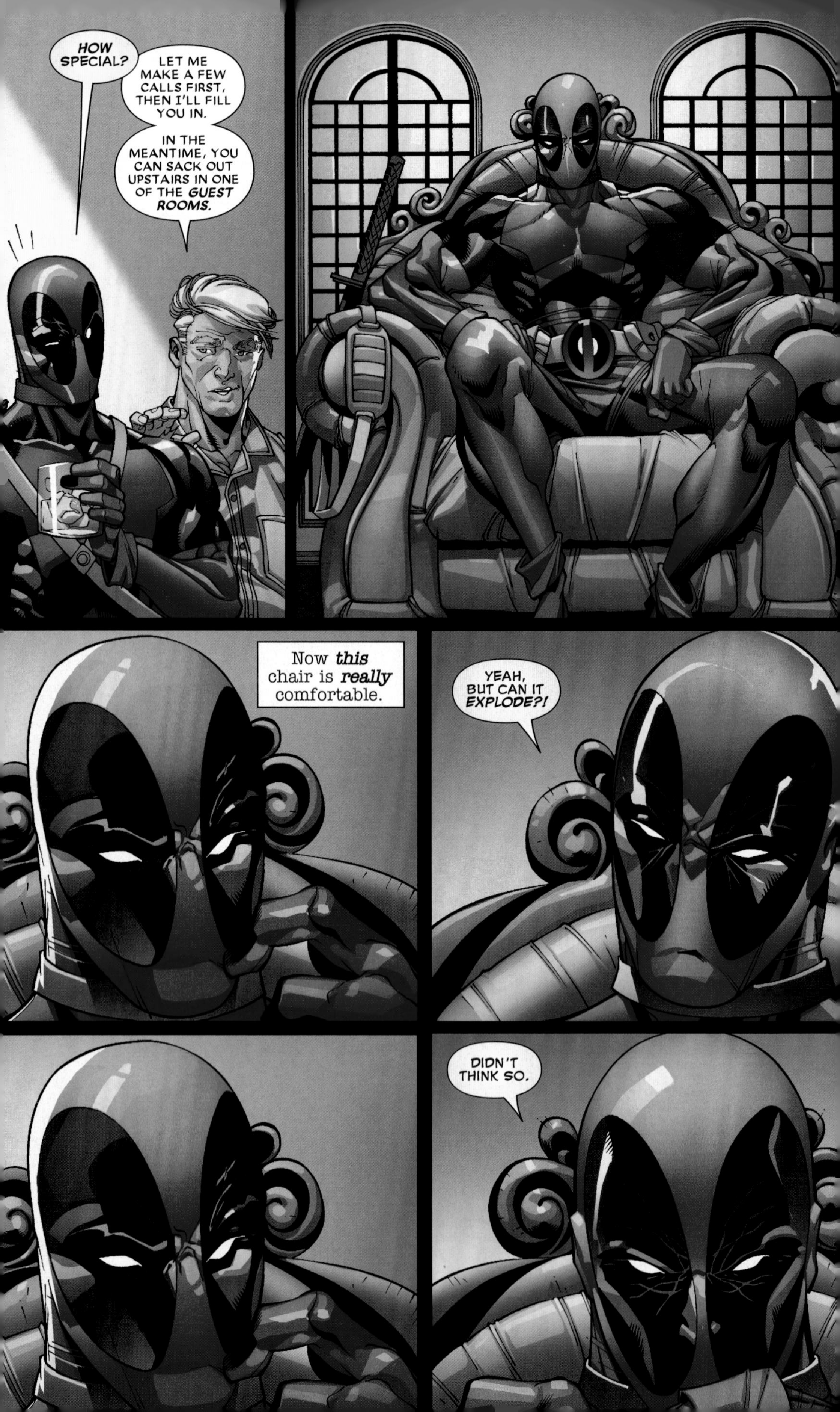

HOW SPECIAL?
LET ME MAKE A FEW CALLS FIRST, THEN I'LL FILL YOU IN.
IN THE MEANTIME, YOU CAN SACK OUT UPSTAIRS IN ONE OF THE GUEST ROOMS.
Now this chair is really comfortable.
YEAH, BUT CAN IT EXPLODE?!
DIDN'T THINK SO.

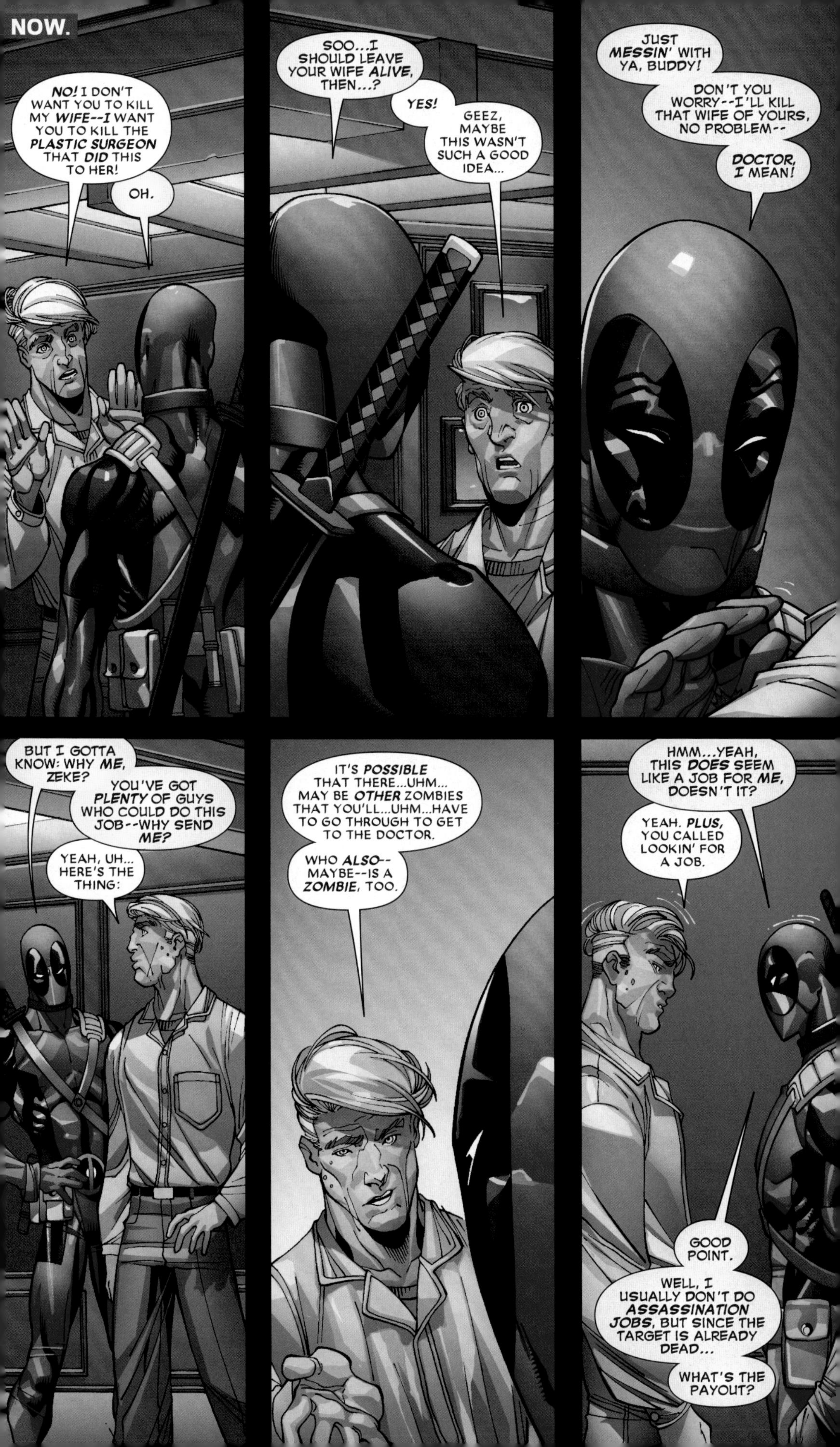
NOW.
NO! I DON'T WANT YOU TO KILL MY WIFE--I WANT YOU TO KILL THE PLASTIC SURGEON THAT DID THIS TO HER!
OH.
SOO...I SHOULD LEAVE YOUR WIFE ALIVE, THEN...?
YES!
GEEZ, MAYBE THIS WASN'T SUCH A GOOD IDEA...
JUST MESSIN' WITH YA, BUDDY!
DON'T YOU WORRY--I'LL KILL THAT WIFE OF YOURS, NO PROBLEM--
DOCTOR, I MEAN!
BUT I GOTTA KNOW: WHY ME, ZEKE?
YOU'VE GOT PLENTY OF GUYS WHO COULD DO THIS JOB--WHY SEND ME?
YEAH, UH... HERE'S THE THING:
IT'S POSSIBLE THAT THERE...UHM... MAY BE OTHER ZOMBIES THAT YOU'LL...UHM...HAVE TO GO THROUGH TO GET TO THE DOCTOR.
WHO ALSO--MAYBE--IS A ZOMBIE, TOO.
HMM...YEAH, THIS DOES SEEM LIKE A JOB FOR ME, DOESN'T IT?
YEAH. PLUS, YOU CALLED LOOKIN' FOR A JOB.
GOOD POINT.
WELL, I USUALLY DON'T DO ASSASSINATION JOBS, BUT SINCE THE TARGET IS ALREADY DEAD...
WHAT'S THE PAYOUT?

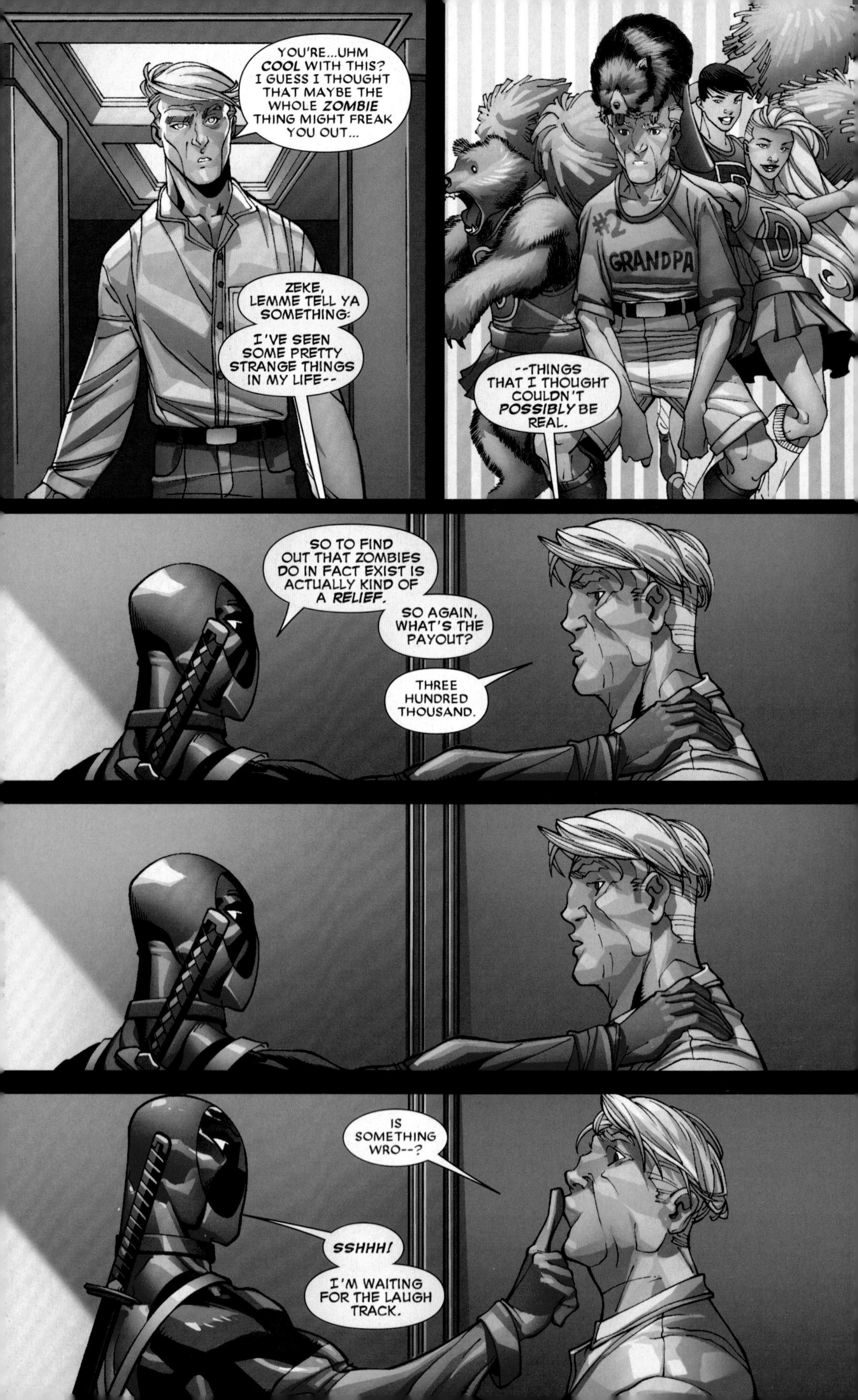
YOU'RE...UHM *COOL* WITH THIS? I GUESS I THOUGHT THAT MAYBE THE WHOLE *ZOMBIE* THING MIGHT FREAK YOU OUT...
ZEKE, LEMME TELL YA SOMETHING:
I'VE SEEN SOME PRETTY STRANGE THINGS IN MY LIFE--
#2 GRANDPA
--THINGS THAT I THOUGHT COULDN'T *POSSIBLY* BE REAL.
SO TO FIND OUT THAT ZOMBIES DO IN FACT EXIST IS ACTUALLY KIND OF A *RELIEF.*
SO AGAIN, WHAT'S THE PAYOUT?
THREE HUNDRED THOUSAND.
IS SOMETHING WRO--?
SSHHH!
I'M WAITING FOR THE LAUGH TRACK.

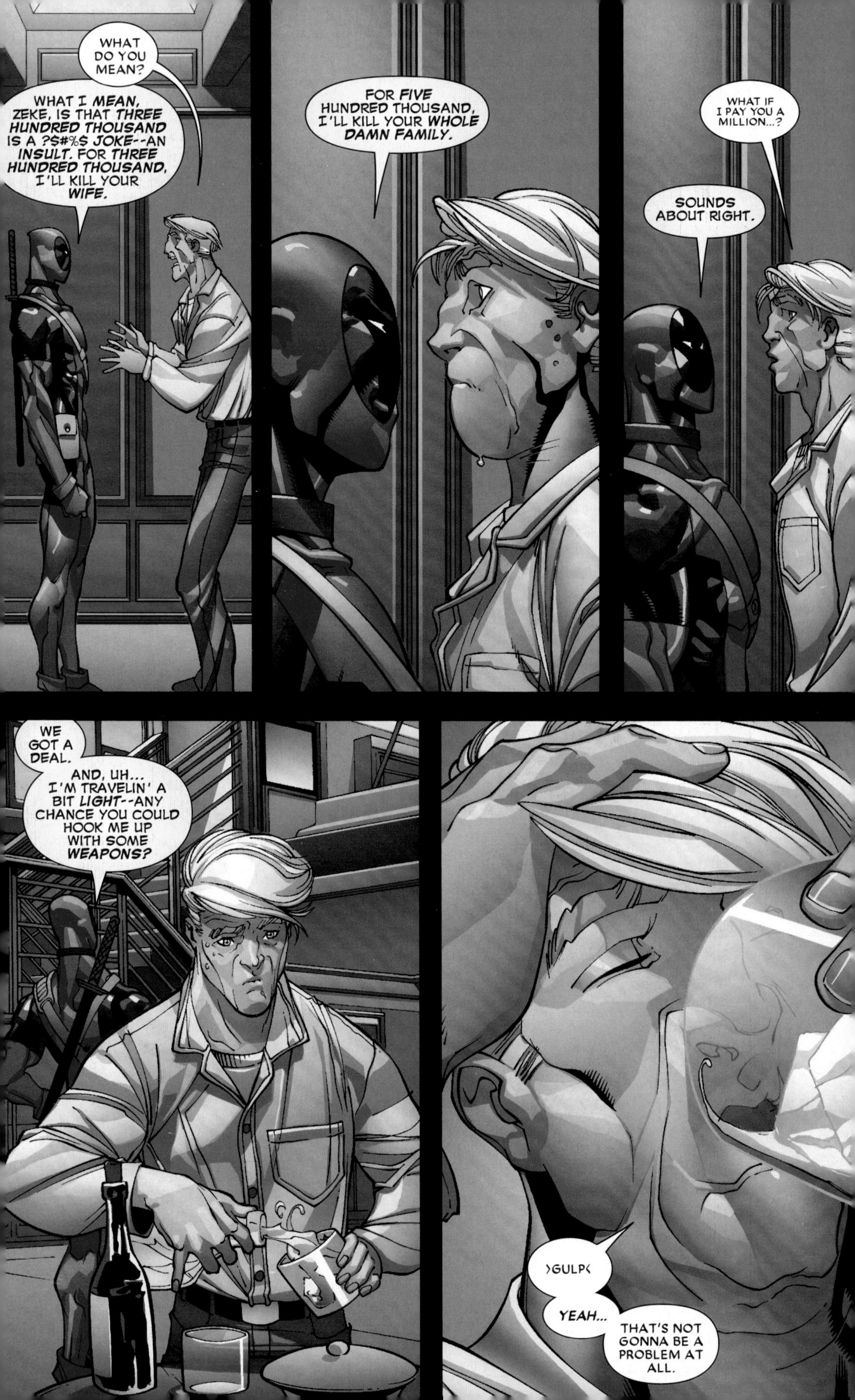
WHAT DO YOU MEAN?
WHAT I MEAN, ZEKE, IS THAT THREE HUNDRED THOUSAND IS A ?$#%$ JOKE--AN INSULT. FOR THREE HUNDRED THOUSAND, I'LL KILL YOUR WIFE.
FOR FIVE HUNDRED THOUSAND, I'LL KILL YOUR WHOLE DAMN FAMILY.
WHAT IF I PAY YOU A MILLION...?
SOUNDS ABOUT RIGHT.
WE GOT A DEAL.
AND, UH... I'M TRAVELIN' A BIT LIGHT--ANY CHANCE YOU COULD HOOK ME UP WITH SOME WEAPONS?
>GULP<
YEAH...
THAT'S NOT GONNA BE A PROBLEM AT ALL.

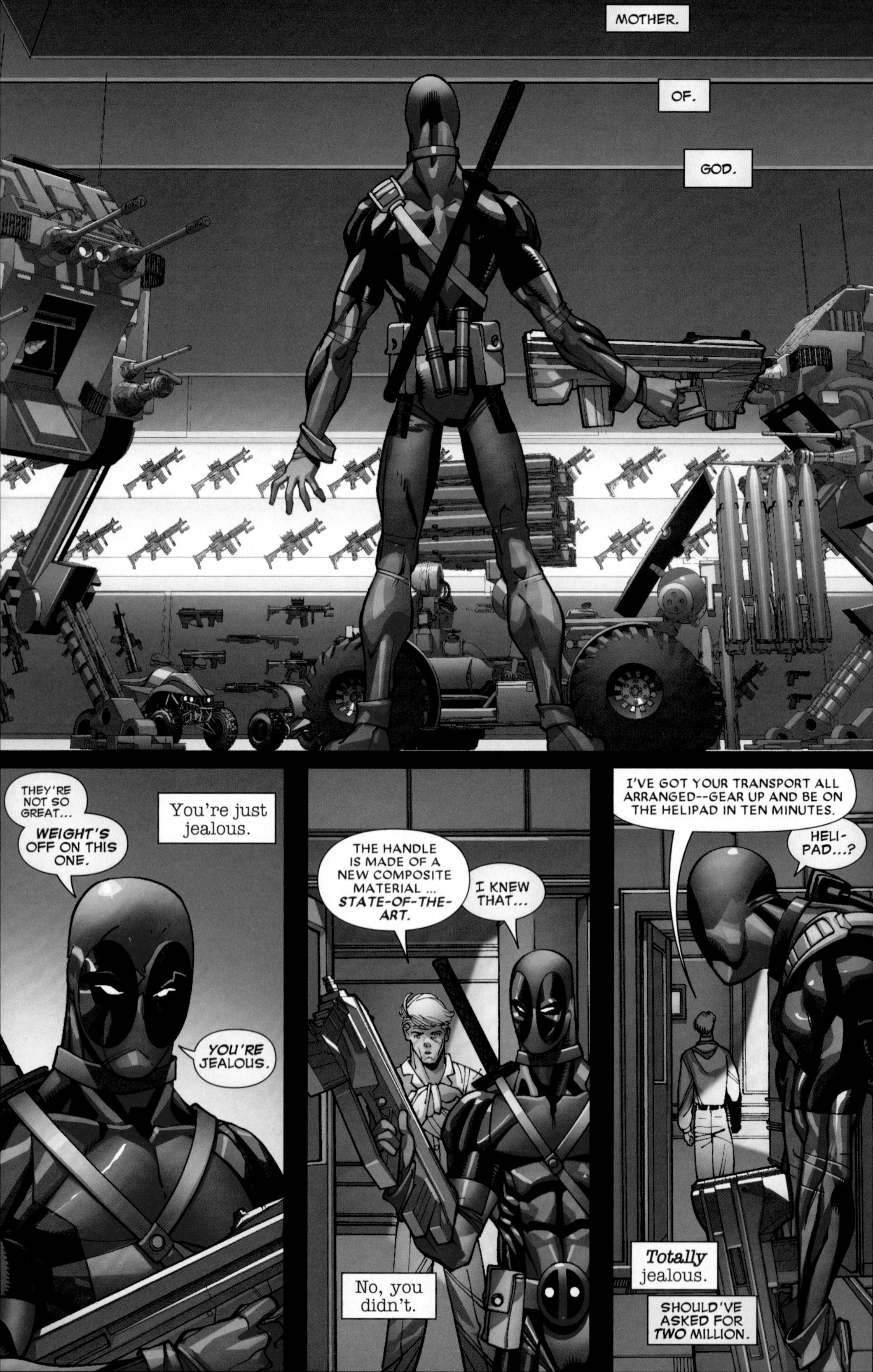
MOTHER.
OF.
GOD.
THEY'RE NOT SO GREAT... WEIGHT'S OFF ON THIS ONE.
You're just jealous.
YOU'RE JEALOUS.
THE HANDLE IS MADE OF A NEW COMPOSITE MATERIAL ... STATE-OF-THE-ART.
I KNEW THAT...
No, you didn't.
I'VE GOT YOUR TRANSPORT ALL ARRANGED--GEAR UP AND BE ON THE HELIPAD IN TEN MINUTES.
HELI-PAD...?
Totally jealous.
SHOULD'VE ASKED FOR TWO MILLION.

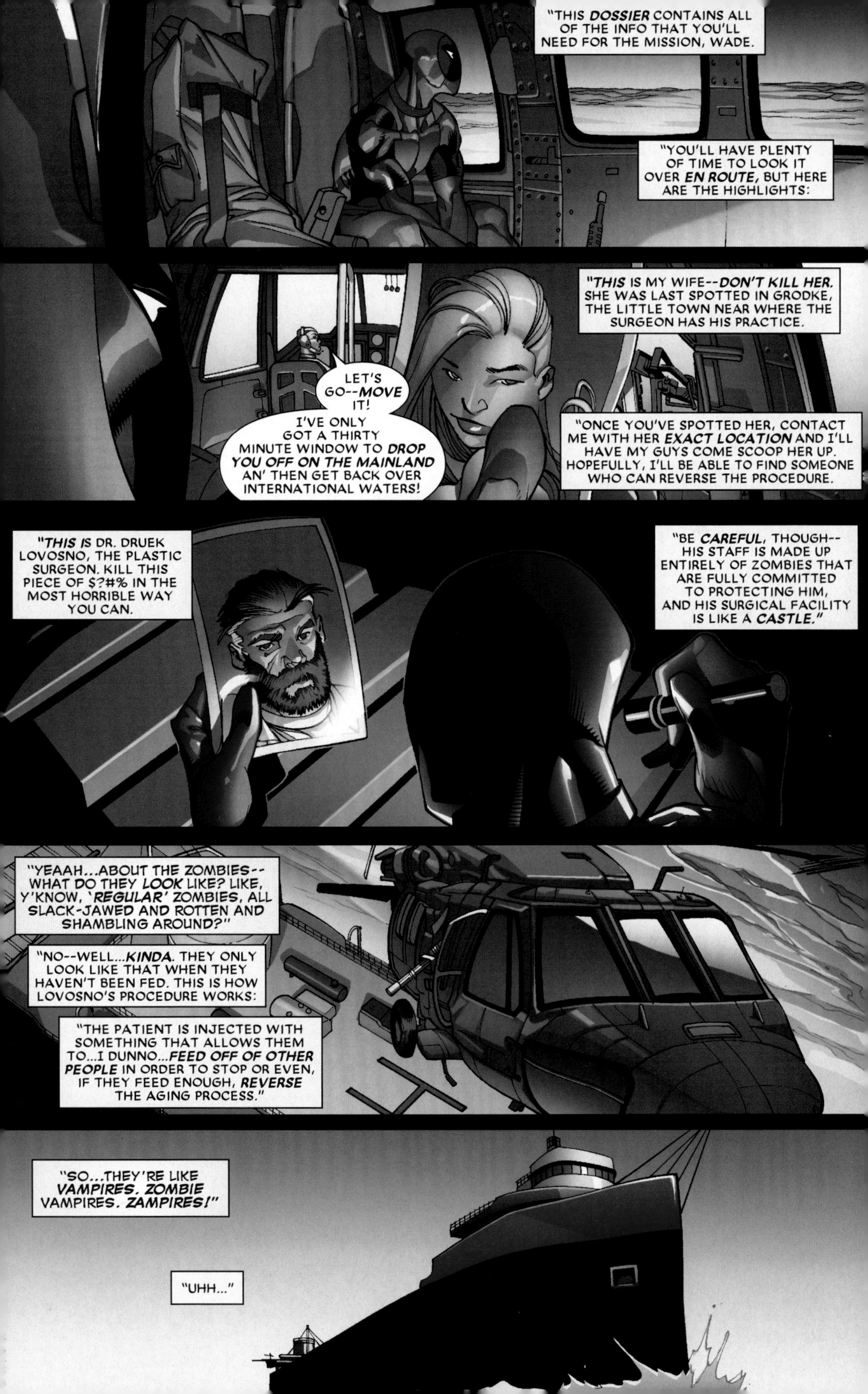
"THIS DOSSIER CONTAINS ALL OF THE INFO THAT YOU'LL NEED FOR THE MISSION, WADE.
"YOU'LL HAVE PLENTY OF TIME TO LOOK IT OVER EN ROUTE, BUT HERE ARE THE HIGHLIGHTS:
"THIS IS MY WIFE--DON'T KILL HER. SHE WAS LAST SPOTTED IN GRODKE, THE LITTLE TOWN NEAR WHERE THE SURGEON HAS HIS PRACTICE.
LET'S GO--MOVE IT!
I'VE ONLY GOT A THIRTY MINUTE WINDOW TO DROP YOU OFF ON THE MAINLAND AN' THEN GET BACK OVER INTERNATIONAL WATERS!
"ONCE YOU'VE SPOTTED HER, CONTACT ME WITH HER EXACT LOCATION AND I'LL HAVE MY GUYS COME SCOOP HER UP. HOPEFULLY, I'LL BE ABLE TO FIND SOMEONE WHO CAN REVERSE THE PROCEDURE.
"THIS IS DR. DRUEK LOVOSNO, THE PLASTIC SURGEON. KILL THIS PIECE OF $?#% IN THE MOST HORRIBLE WAY YOU CAN.
"BE CAREFUL, THOUGH--HIS STAFF IS MADE UP ENTIRELY OF ZOMBIES THAT ARE FULLY COMMITTED TO PROTECTING HIM, AND HIS SURGICAL FACILITY IS LIKE A CASTLE."
"YEAAH...ABOUT THE ZOMBIES--WHAT DO THEY LOOK LIKE? LIKE, Y'KNOW, 'REGULAR' ZOMBIES, ALL SLACK-JAWED AND ROTTEN AND SHAMBLING AROUND?"
"NO--WELL...KINDA. THEY ONLY LOOK LIKE THAT WHEN THEY HAVEN'T BEEN FED. THIS IS HOW LOVOSNO'S PROCEDURE WORKS:
"THE PATIENT IS INJECTED WITH SOMETHING THAT ALLOWS THEM TO...I DUNNO...FEED OFF OF OTHER PEOPLE IN ORDER TO STOP OR EVEN, IF THEY FEED ENOUGH, REVERSE THE AGING PROCESS."
"SO...THEY'RE LIKE VAMPIRES. ZOMBIE VAMPIRES. ZAMPIRES!"
"UHH..."

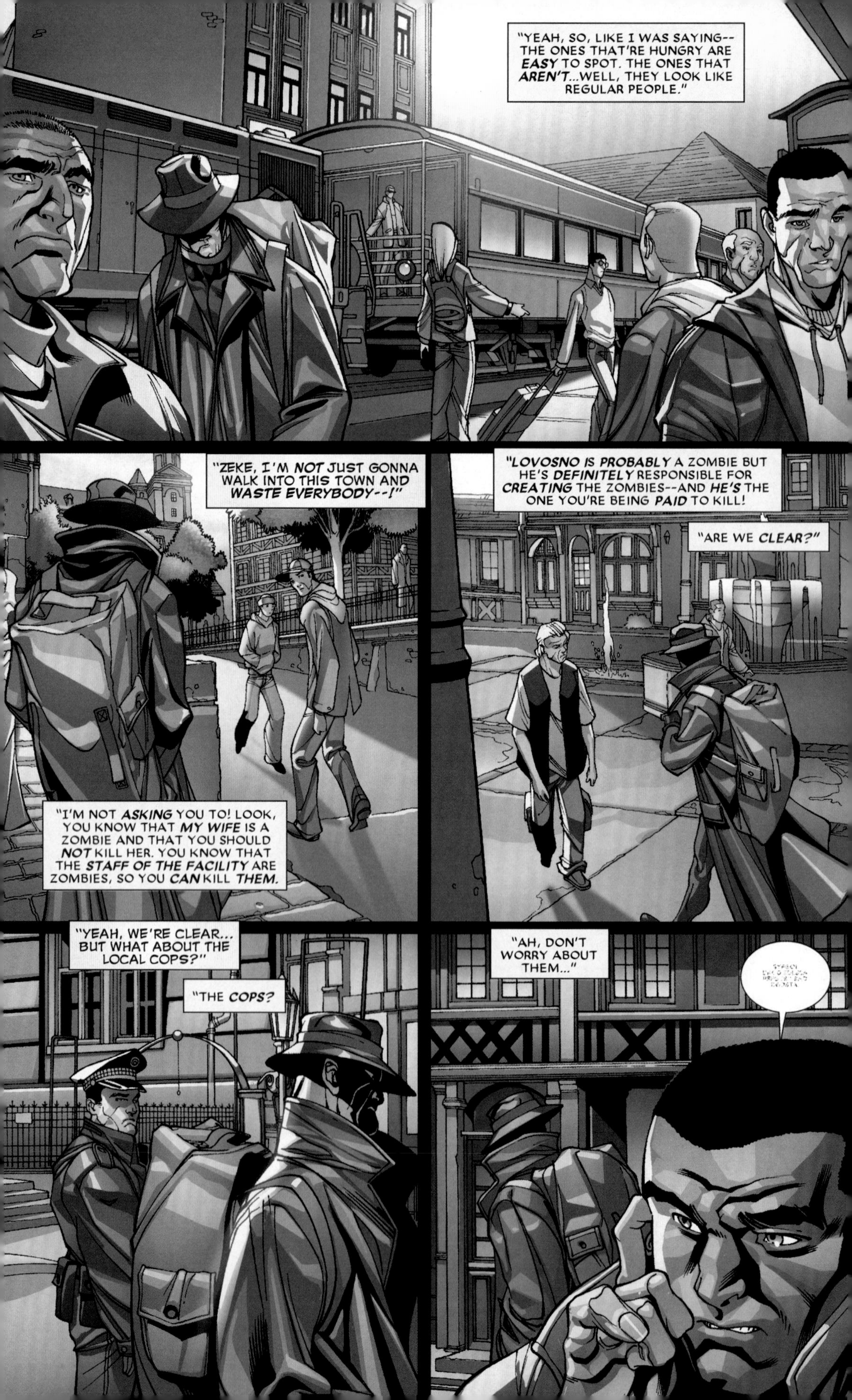
"YEAH, SO, LIKE I WAS SAYING-- THE ONES THAT'RE HUNGRY ARE EASY TO SPOT. THE ONES THAT AREN'T...WELL, THEY LOOK LIKE REGULAR PEOPLE."
"ZEKE, I'M NOT JUST GONNA WALK INTO THIS TOWN AND WASTE EVERYBODY--!"
"I'M NOT ASKING YOU TO! LOOK, YOU KNOW THAT MY WIFE IS A ZOMBIE AND THAT YOU SHOULD NOT KILL HER. YOU KNOW THAT THE STAFF OF THE FACILITY ARE ZOMBIES, SO YOU CAN KILL THEM.
"LOVOSNO IS PROBABLY A ZOMBIE BUT HE'S DEFINITELY RESPONSIBLE FOR CREATING THE ZOMBIES--AND HE'S THE ONE YOU'RE BEING PAID TO KILL!
"ARE WE CLEAR?"
"YEAH, WE'RE CLEAR... BUT WHAT ABOUT THE LOCAL COPS?"
"THE COPS?
"AH, DON'T WORRY ABOUT THEM..."

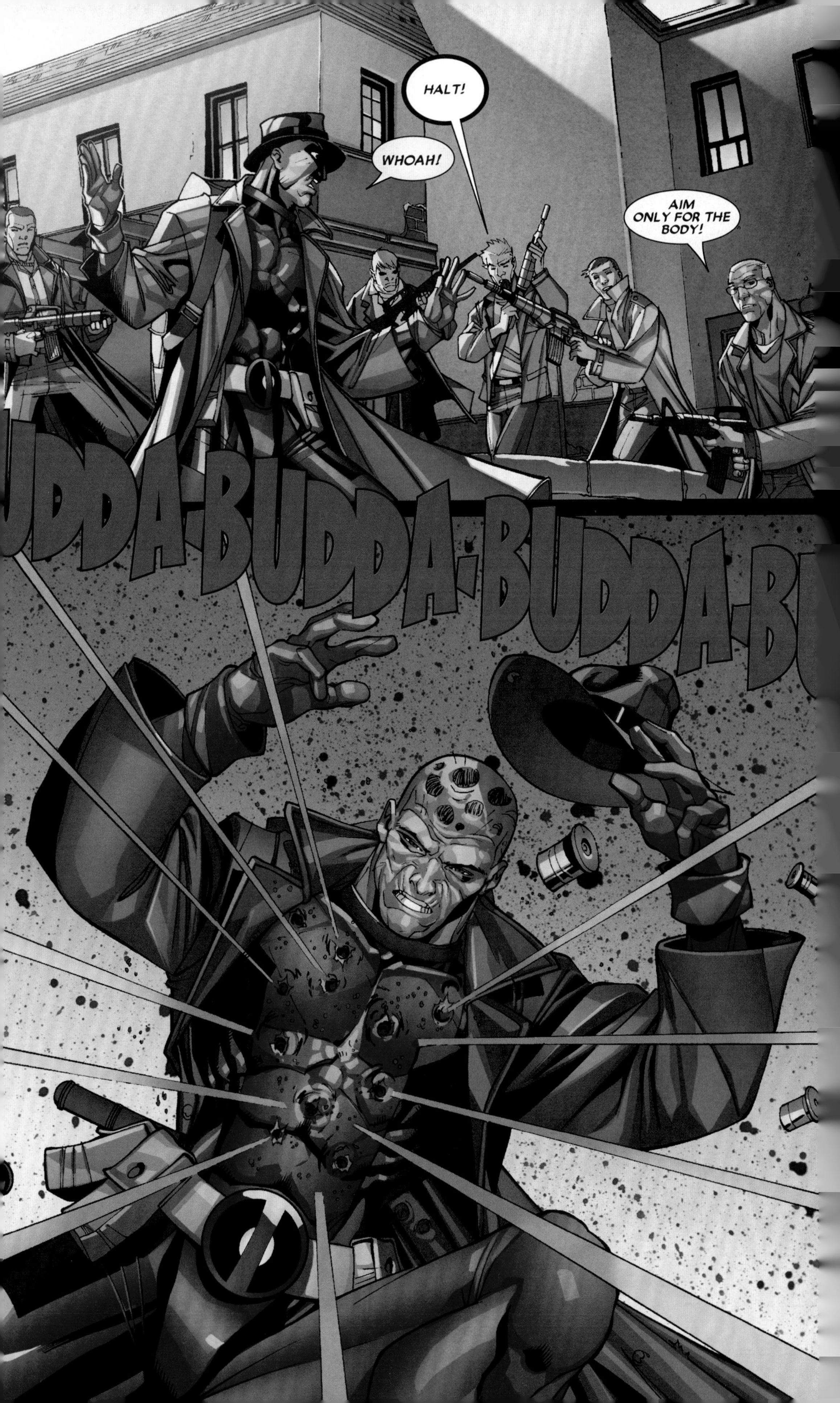

WHOAH!
HALT!
AIM ONLY FOR THE BODY!
BUDDA-BUDDA-BUDDA-BUDDA-BU

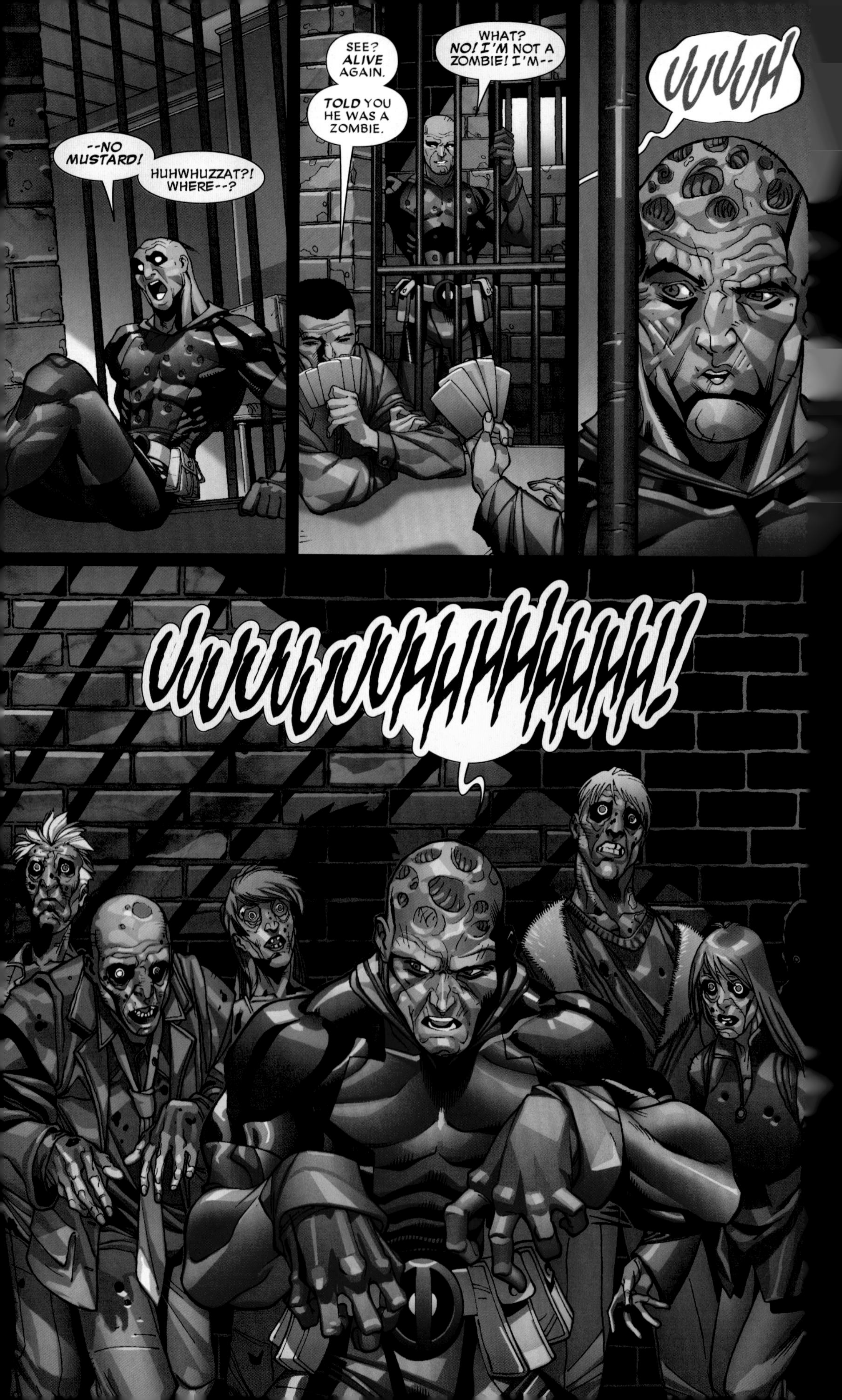
--NO MUSTARD!
HUHWHUZZAT?! WHERE--?
SEE? ALIVE AGAIN.
TOLD YOU HE WAS A ZOMBIE.
WHAT? NO! I'M NOT A ZOMBIE! I'M--
UUUUH
UUUUUUUUHHHHHHHHH!

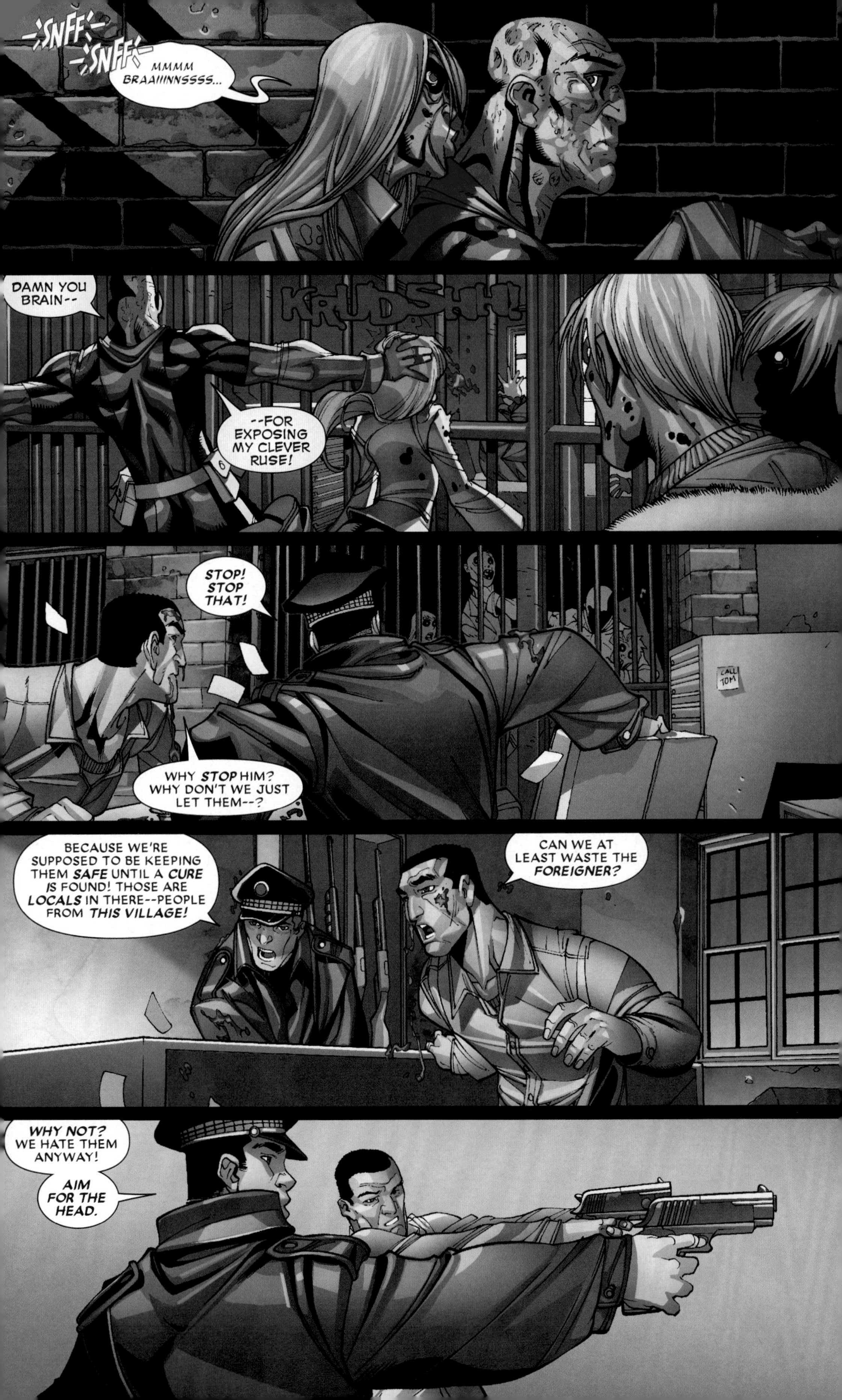
SNFF SNFF
MMMM BRAAIIINNSSSS...
DAMN YOU BRAIN--
KRUDSHH!
--FOR EXPOSING MY CLEVER RUSE!
STOP! STOP THAT!
CALL TOM
WHY STOP HIM? WHY DON'T WE JUST LET THEM--?
BECAUSE WE'RE SUPPOSED TO BE KEEPING THEM SAFE UNTIL A CURE IS FOUND! THOSE ARE LOCALS IN THERE--PEOPLE FROM THIS VILLAGE!
CAN WE AT LEAST WASTE THE FOREIGNER?
WHY NOT? WE HATE THEM ANYWAY!
AIM FOR THE HEAD.

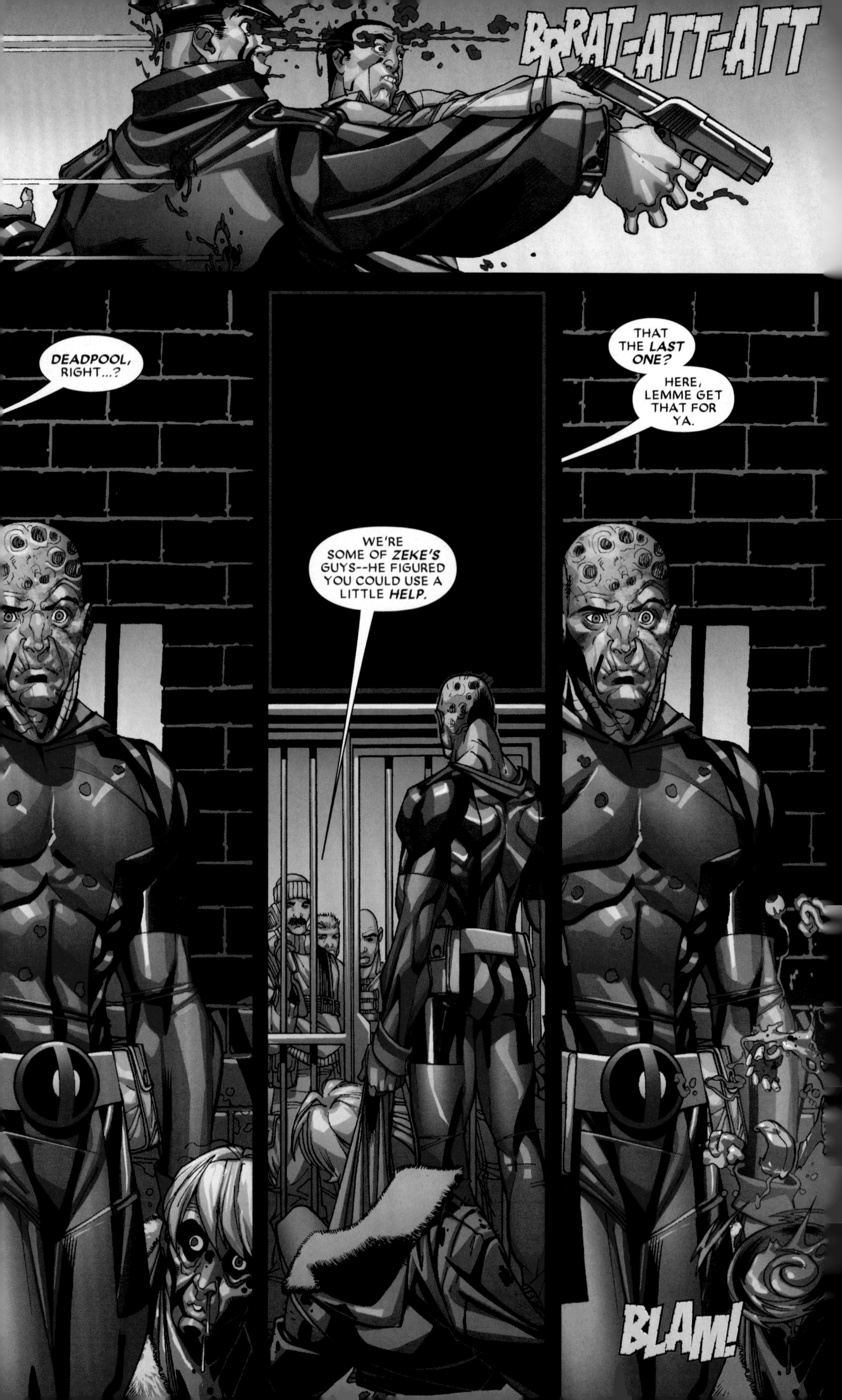

BRRAT-ATT-ATT
DEADPOOL, RIGHT...?
WE'RE SOME OF ZEKE'S GUYS--HE FIGURED YOU COULD USE A LITTLE HELP.
THAT THE LAST ONE?
HERE, LEMME GET THAT FOR YA.
BLAM!

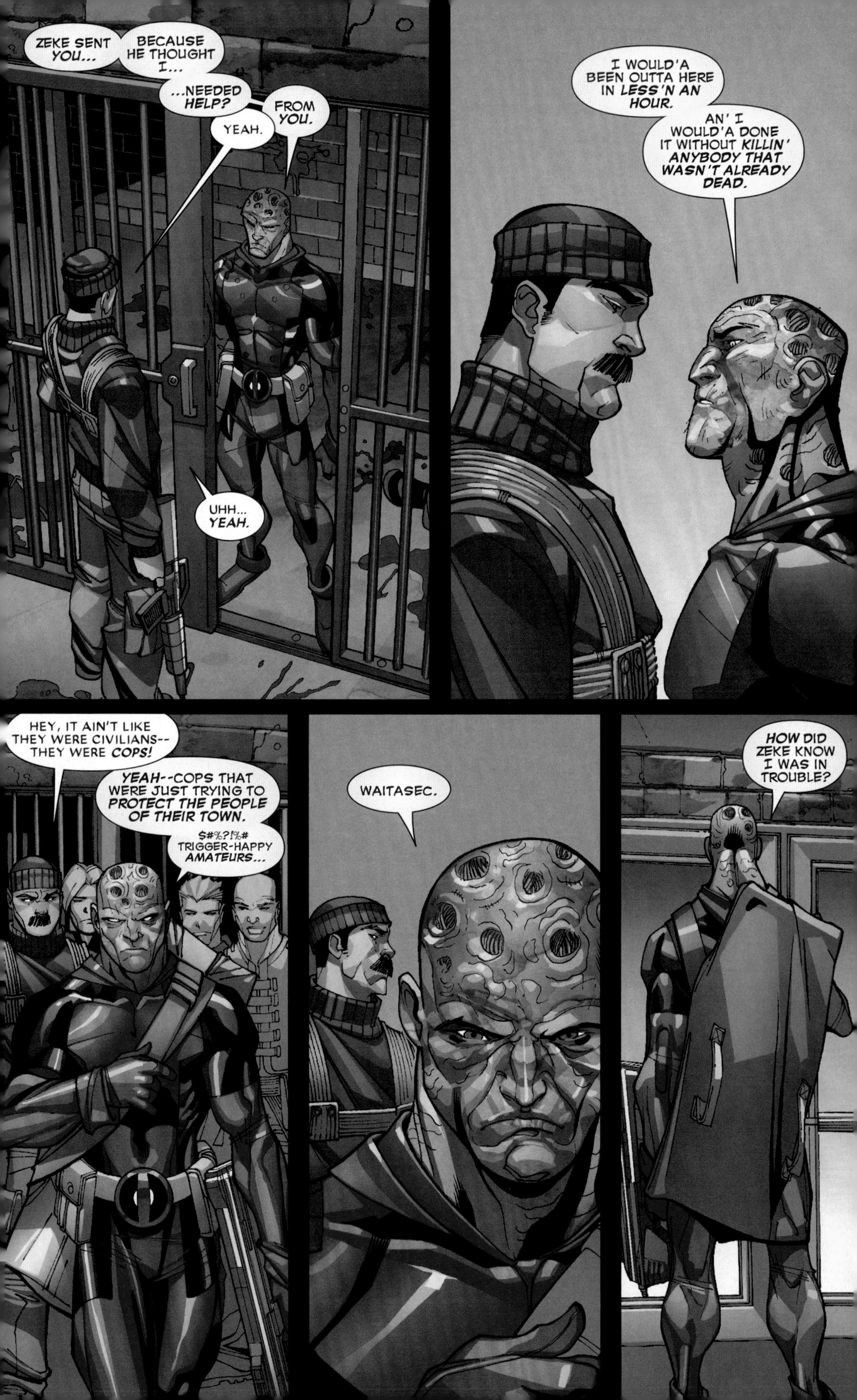
ZEKE SENT YOU...
BECAUSE HE THOUGHT I...
...NEEDED HELP?
YEAH.
FROM YOU.
UHH... YEAH.
I WOULD'A BEEN OUTTA HERE IN LESS'N AN HOUR.
AN' I WOULD'A DONE IT WITHOUT KILLIN' ANYBODY THAT WASN'T ALREADY DEAD.
HEY, IT AIN'T LIKE THEY WERE CIVILIANS-- THEY WERE COPS!
YEAH--COPS THAT WERE JUST TRYING TO PROTECT THE PEOPLE OF THEIR TOWN.
$#%?!%# TRIGGER-HAPPY AMATEURS...
WAITASEC.
HOW DID ZEKE KNOW I WAS IN TROUBLE?

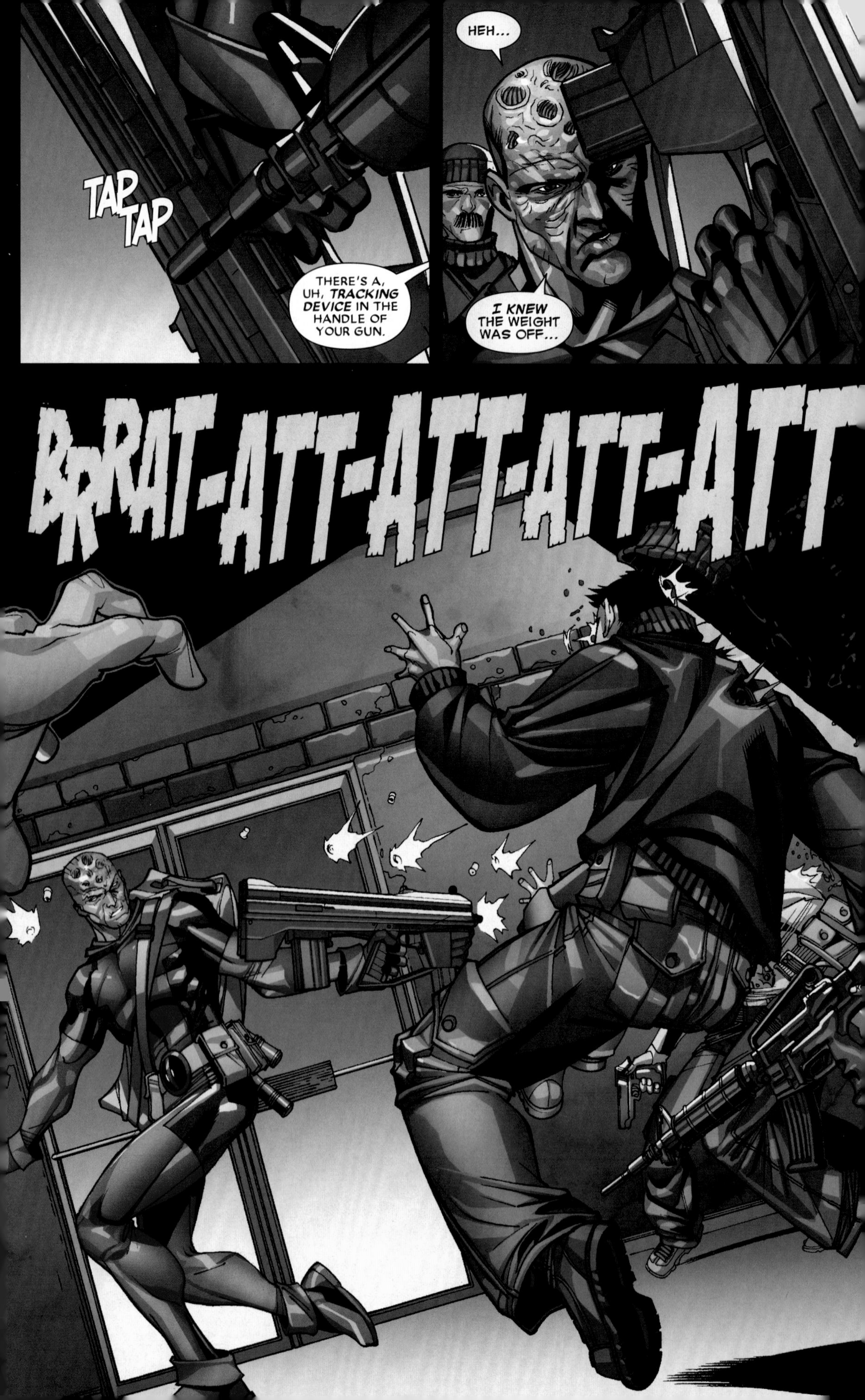
TAP TAP
THERE'S A, UH, *TRACKING DEVICE* IN THE HANDLE OF YOUR GUN.
HEH...
I KNEW THE WEIGHT WAS OFF...
BRRAT-ATT-ATT-ATT-ATT

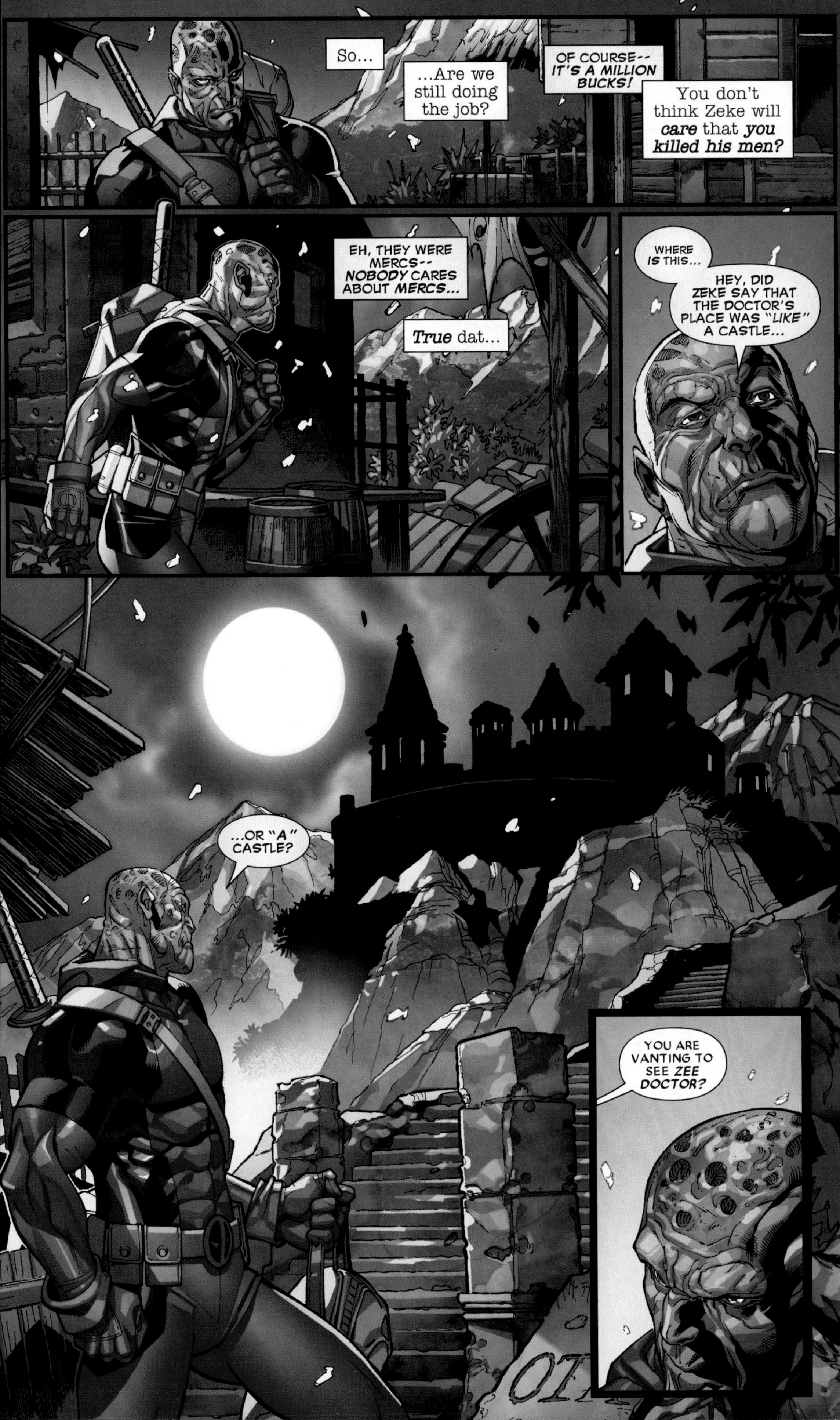

So...
...Are we still doing the job?
OF COURSE-- IT'S A MILLION BUCKS!
You don't think Zeke will care that you killed his men?
EH, THEY WERE MERCS-- NOBODY CARES ABOUT MERCS...
True dat...
WHERE IS THIS...
HEY, DID ZEKE SAY THAT THE DOCTOR'S PLACE WAS "LIKE" A CASTLE...
...OR "A" CASTLE?
YOU ARE VANTING TO SEE ZEE DOCTOR?

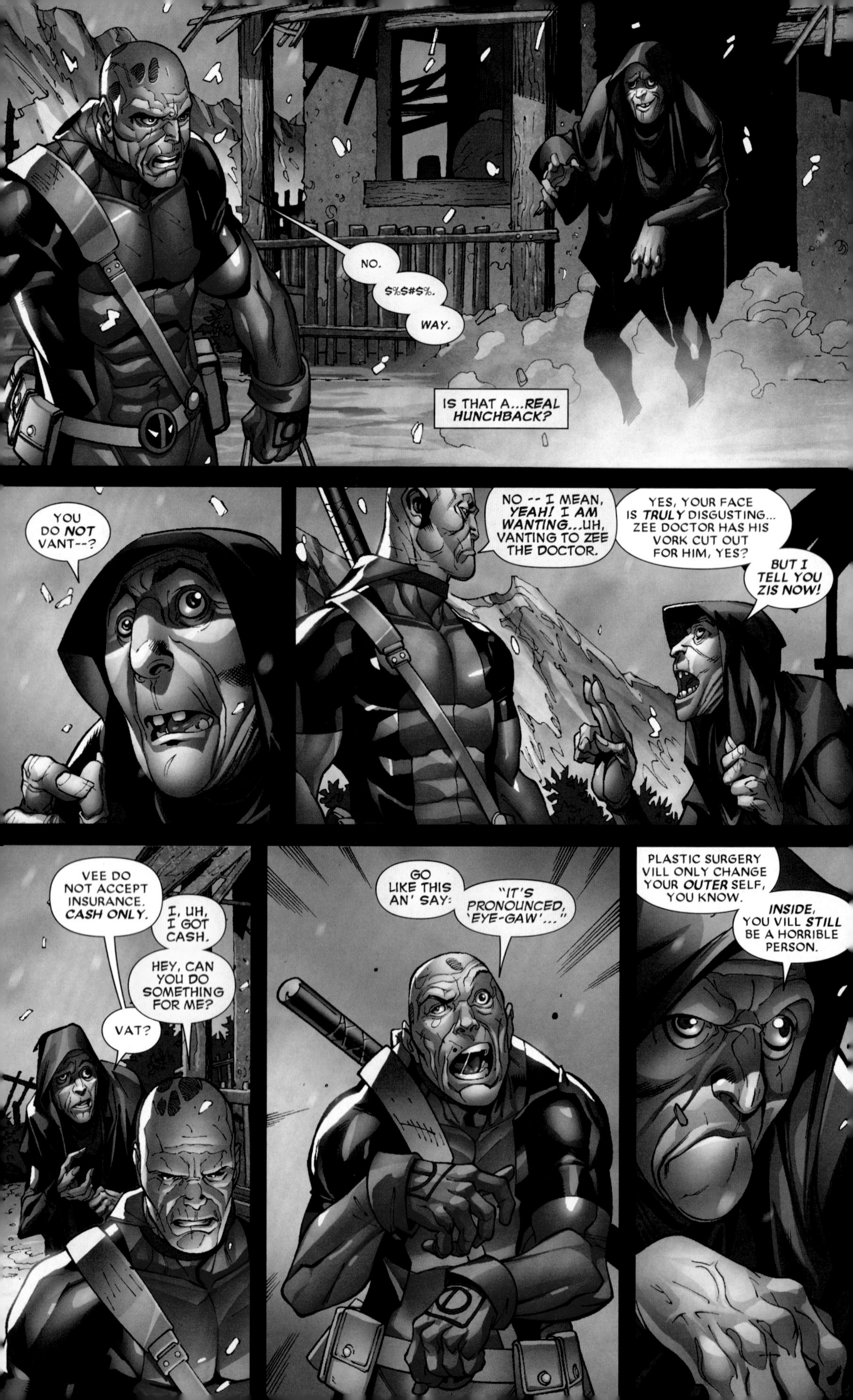
NO.
$%$#$%.
WAY.
IS THAT A...REAL HUNCHBACK?
YOU DO NOT VANT--?
NO -- I MEAN, YEAH! I AM WANTING...UH, VANTING TO ZEE THE DOCTOR.
YES, YOUR FACE IS TRULY DISGUSTING... ZEE DOCTOR HAS HIS VORK CUT OUT FOR HIM, YES?
BUT I TELL YOU ZIS NOW!
VEE DO NOT ACCEPT INSURANCE. CASH ONLY.
I, UH, I GOT CASH.
HEY, CAN YOU DO SOMETHING FOR ME?
VAT?
GO LIKE THIS AN' SAY:
"IT'S PRONOUNCED, 'EYE-GAW'..."
PLASTIC SURGERY VILL ONLY CHANGE YOUR OUTER SELF, YOU KNOW.
INSIDE, YOU VILL STILL BE A HORRIBLE PERSON.

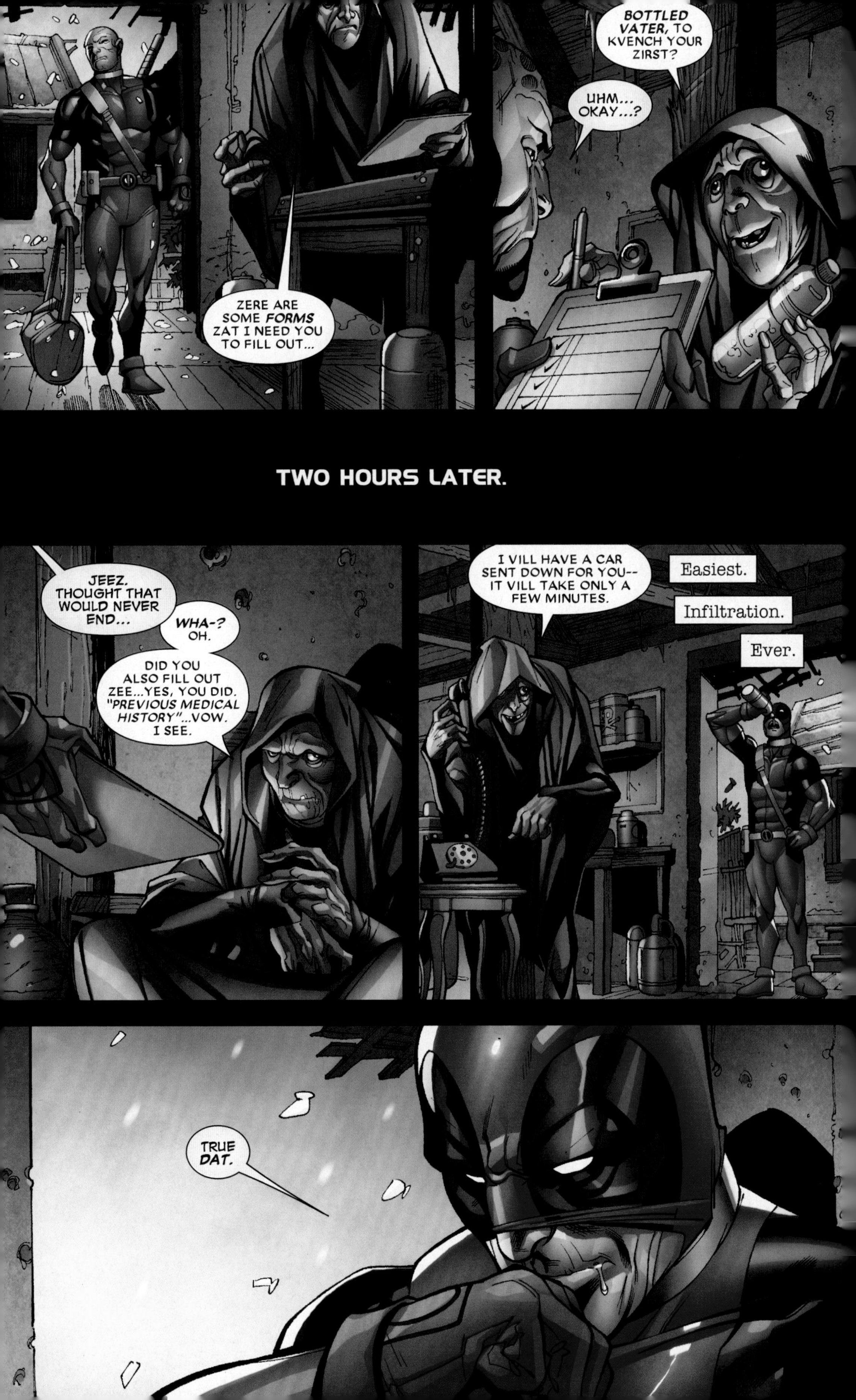
ZERE ARE SOME *FORMS* ZAT I NEED YOU TO FILL OUT...
BOTTLED VATER, TO KVENCH YOUR ZIRST?
UHM... OKAY...?
TWO HOURS LATER.
JEEZ. THOUGHT THAT WOULD NEVER END...
WHA-? OH.
DID YOU ALSO FILL OUT ZEE...YES, YOU DID. *"PREVIOUS MEDICAL HISTORY"*...VOW. I SEE.
I VILL HAVE A CAR SENT DOWN FOR YOU-- IT VILL TAKE ONLY A FEW MINUTES.
Easiest.
Infiltration.
Ever.
TRUE *DAT.*

HMM... FEELIN' KINDA...

POISON

EXTREMELY EFFECTIVE AGAINST CHUMPS

AH, SH--

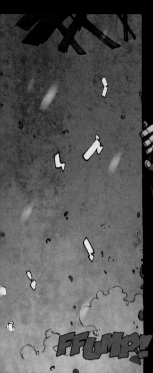

FFUMP!

I'VE DONE *VELL*, MASTER?

YES--

--*VERY* WELL. YOUR FAITHFUL SERVICE WILL SOON BE REWARDED WITH THE REMOVAL OF THAT AWFUL, *AWFUL* HUMP...

...WHEN MY SCHEDULE ALLOWS IT.

beep-boop-boop

HELLO... *ZEKE?*

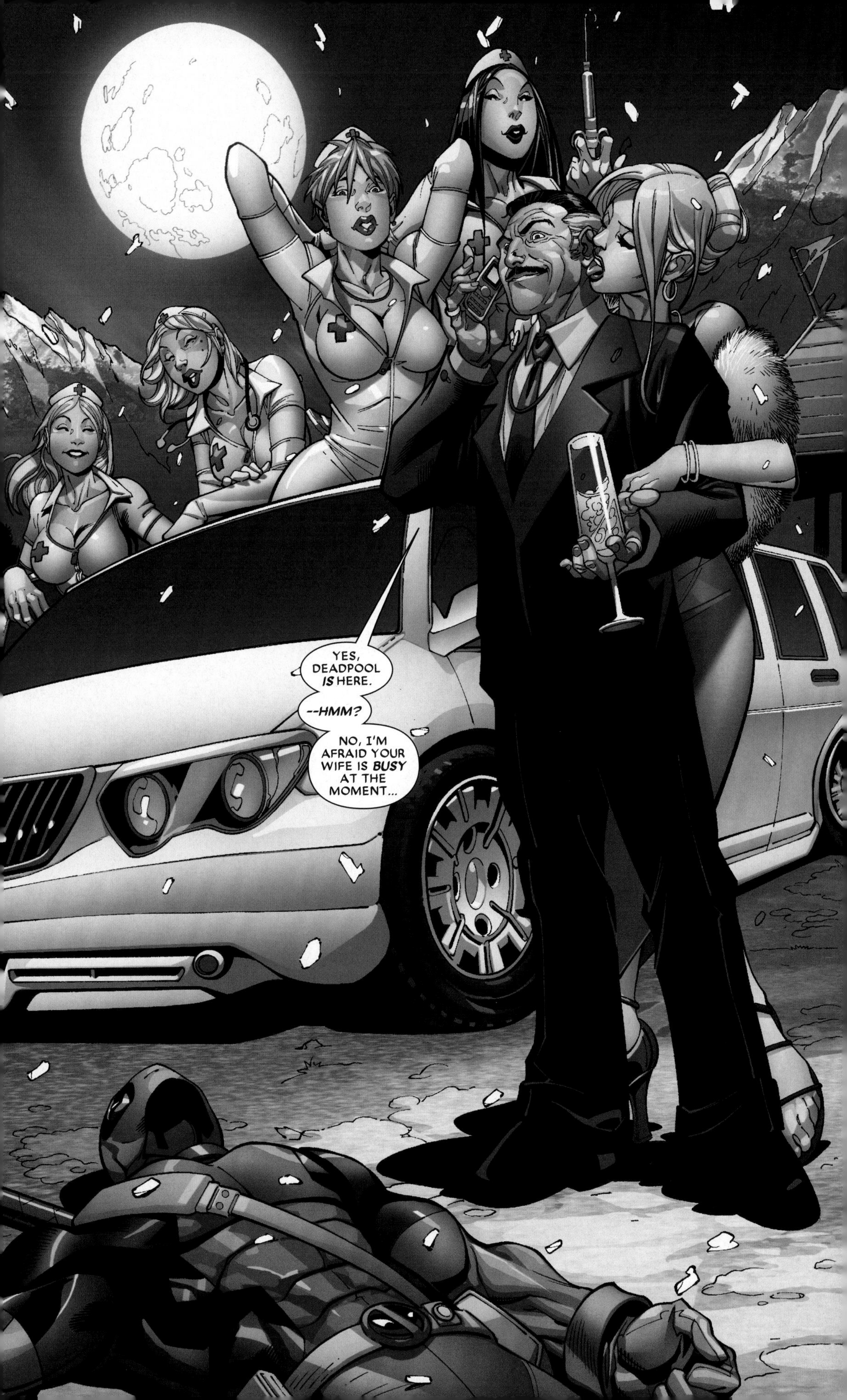
YES, DEADPOOL IS HERE.
--HMM?
NO, I'M AFRAID YOUR WIFE IS BUSY AT THE MOMENT...

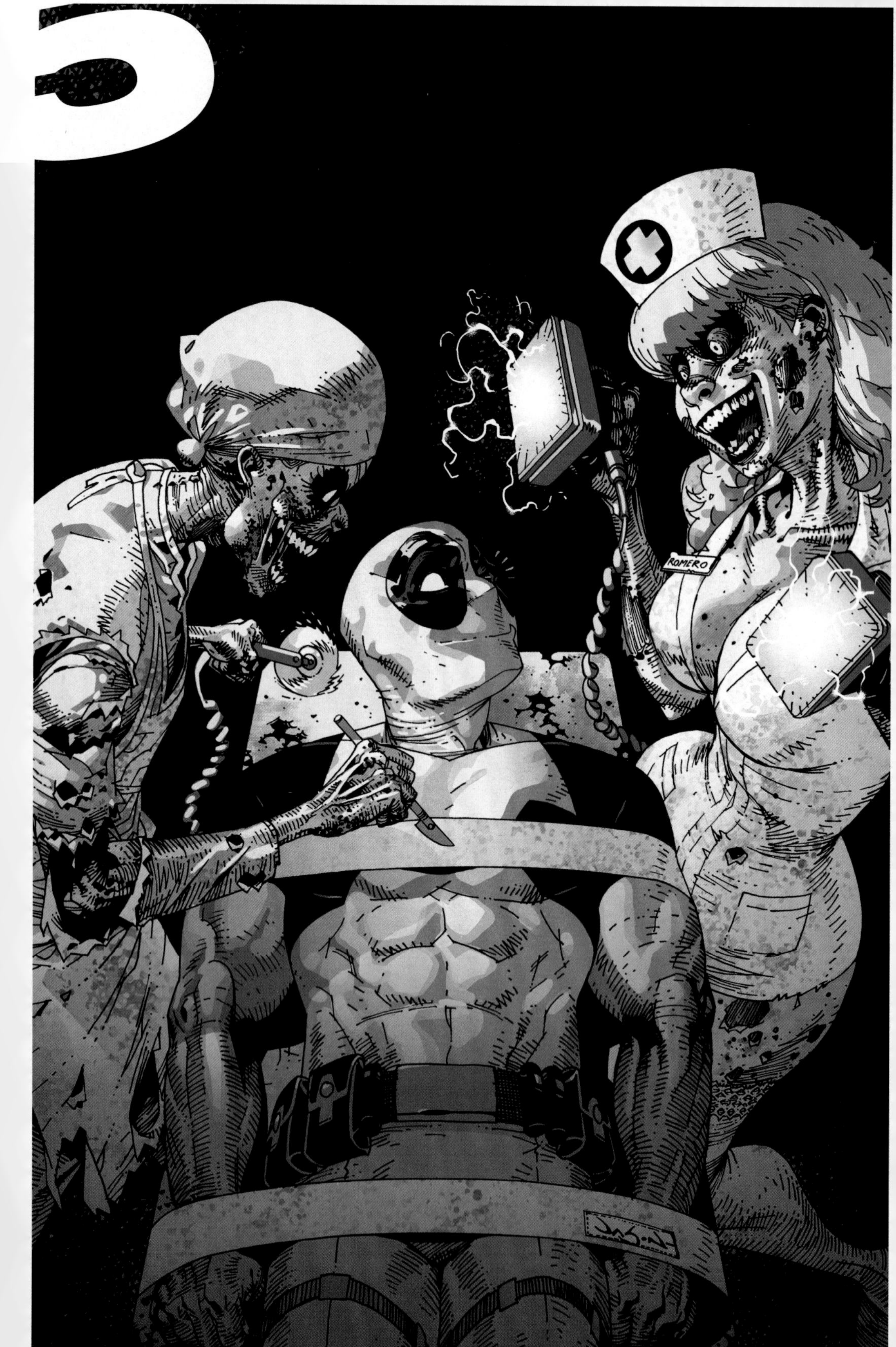
ROMERO

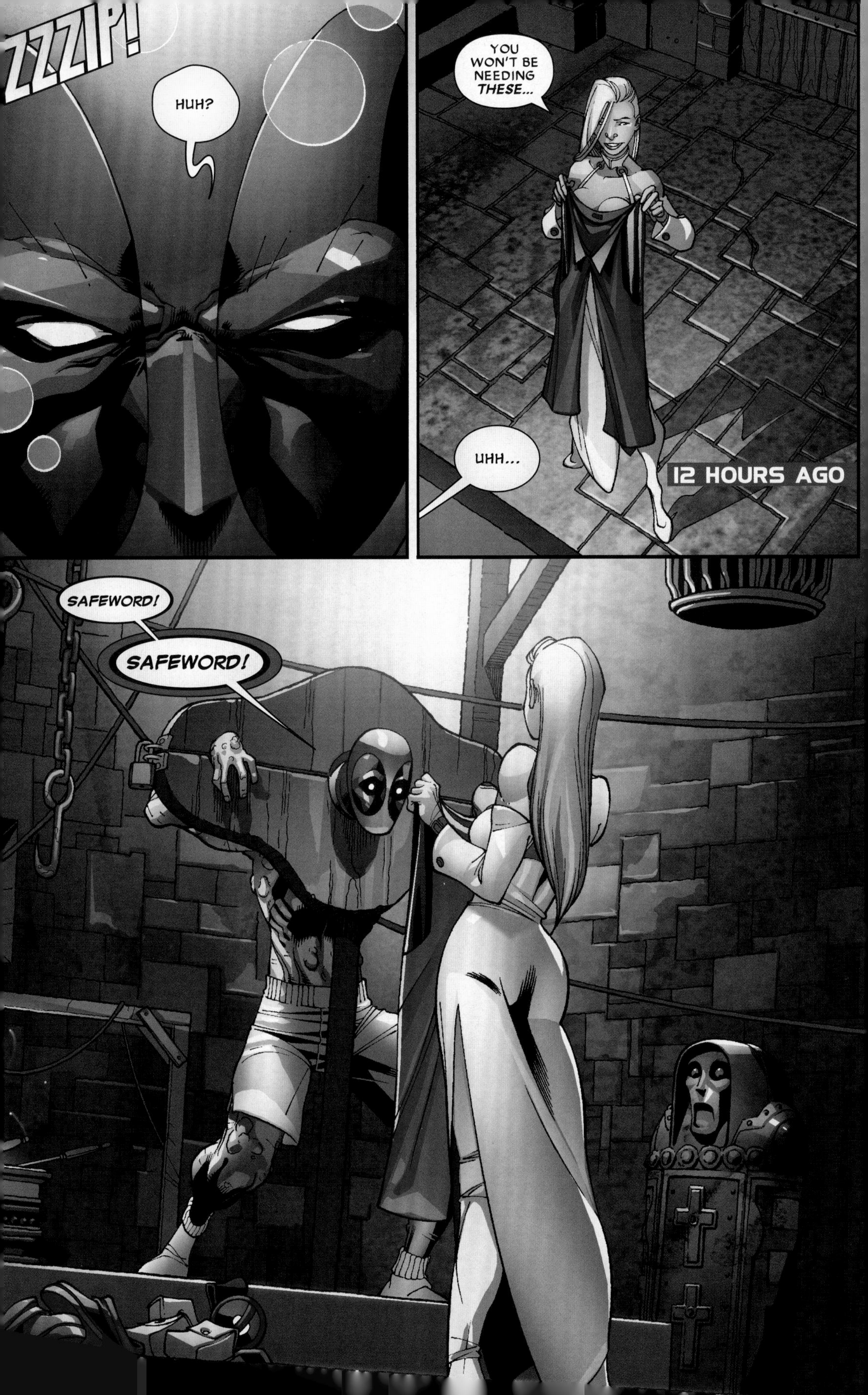
ZZZIP!
HUH?
YOU WON'T BE NEEDING THESE...
UHH...
12 HOURS AGO
SAFEWORD!
SAFEWORD!

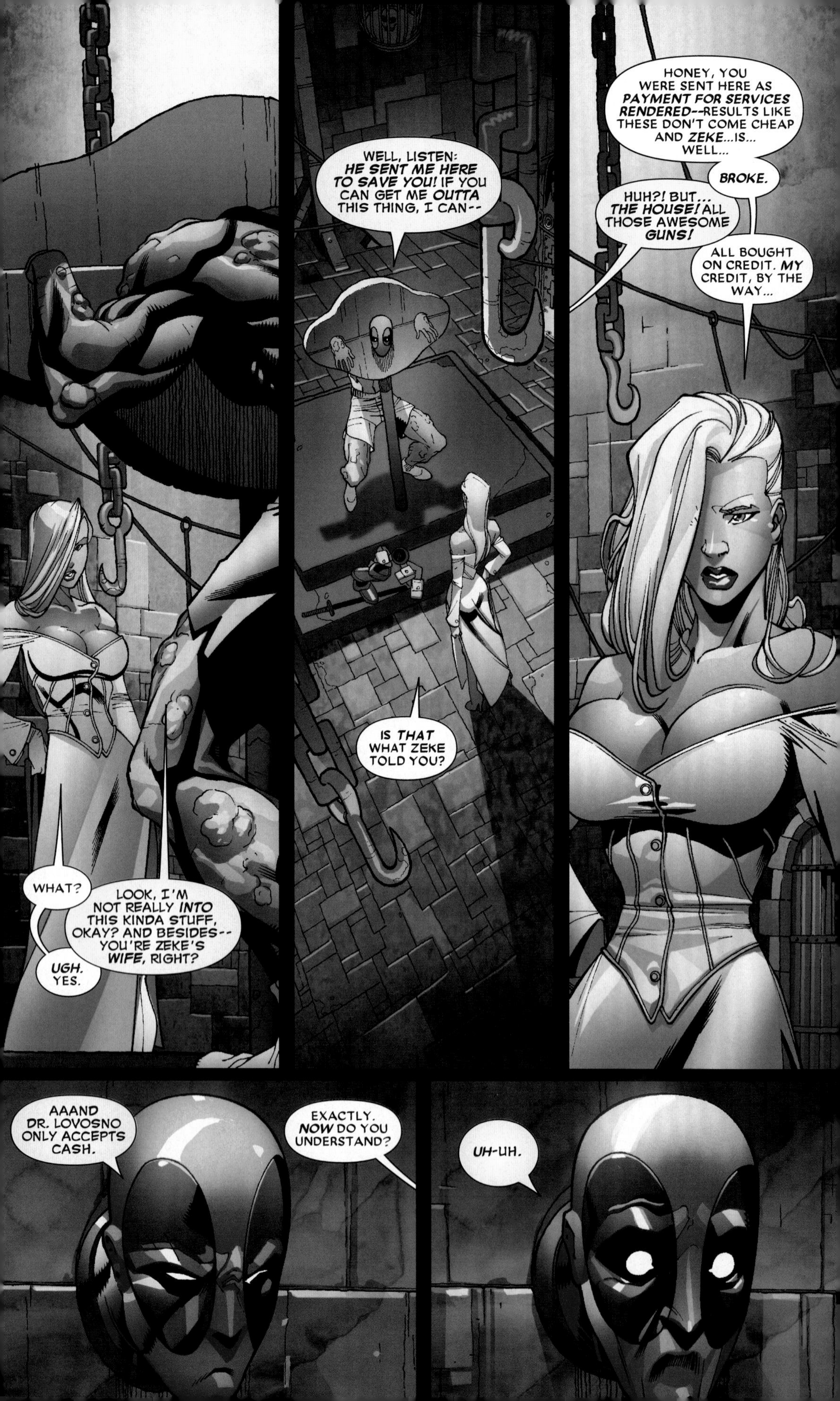
WHAT?
LOOK, I'M NOT REALLY INTO THIS KINDA STUFF, OKAY? AND BESIDES-- YOU'RE ZEKE'S WIFE, RIGHT?
UGH. YES.
WELL, LISTEN: HE SENT ME HERE TO SAVE YOU! IF YOU CAN GET ME OUTTA THIS THING, I CAN--
IS THAT WHAT ZEKE TOLD YOU?
HONEY, YOU WERE SENT HERE AS PAYMENT FOR SERVICES RENDERED--RESULTS LIKE THESE DON'T COME CHEAP AND ZEKE...IS... WELL...
BROKE.
HUH?! BUT... THE HOUSE! ALL THOSE AWESOME GUNS!
ALL BOUGHT ON CREDIT. MY CREDIT, BY THE WAY...
AAAND DR. LOVOSNO ONLY ACCEPTS CASH.
EXACTLY. NOW DO YOU UNDERSTAND?
UH-UH.

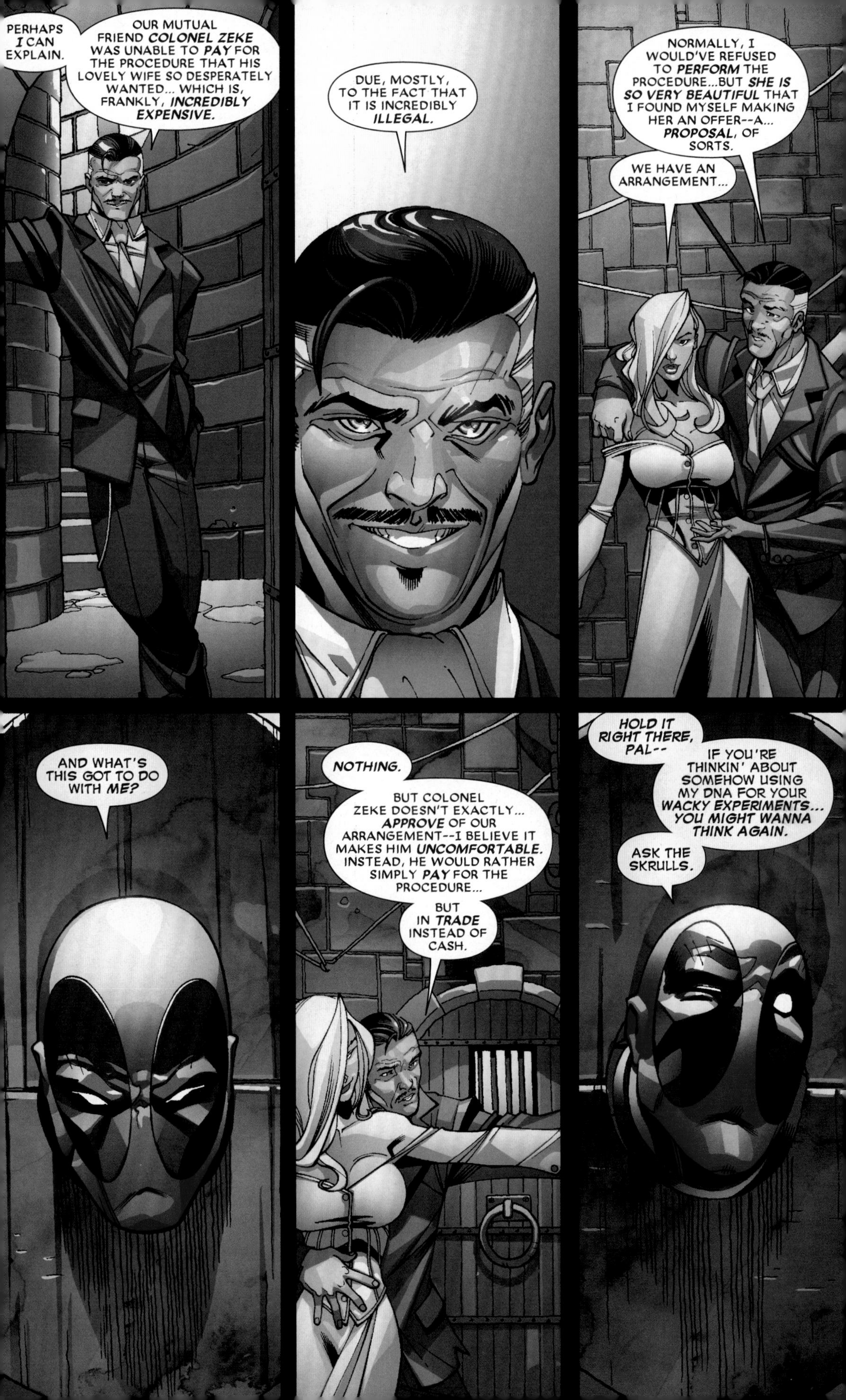
PERHAPS I CAN EXPLAIN.
OUR MUTUAL FRIEND COLONEL ZEKE WAS UNABLE TO PAY FOR THE PROCEDURE THAT HIS LOVELY WIFE SO DESPERATELY WANTED... WHICH IS, FRANKLY, INCREDIBLY EXPENSIVE.
DUE, MOSTLY, TO THE FACT THAT IT IS INCREDIBLY ILLEGAL.
NORMALLY, I WOULD'VE REFUSED TO PERFORM THE PROCEDURE...BUT SHE IS SO VERY BEAUTIFUL THAT I FOUND MYSELF MAKING HER AN OFFER--A... PROPOSAL, OF SORTS.
WE HAVE AN ARRANGEMENT...
AND WHAT'S THIS GOT TO DO WITH ME?
NOTHING.
BUT COLONEL ZEKE DOESN'T EXACTLY... APPROVE OF OUR ARRANGEMENT--I BELIEVE IT MAKES HIM UNCOMFORTABLE. INSTEAD, HE WOULD RATHER SIMPLY PAY FOR THE PROCEDURE...
BUT IN TRADE INSTEAD OF CASH.
HOLD IT RIGHT THERE, PAL--
IF YOU'RE THINKIN' ABOUT SOMEHOW USING MY DNA FOR YOUR WACKY EXPERIMENTS... YOU MIGHT WANNA THINK AGAIN.
ASK THE SKRULLS.

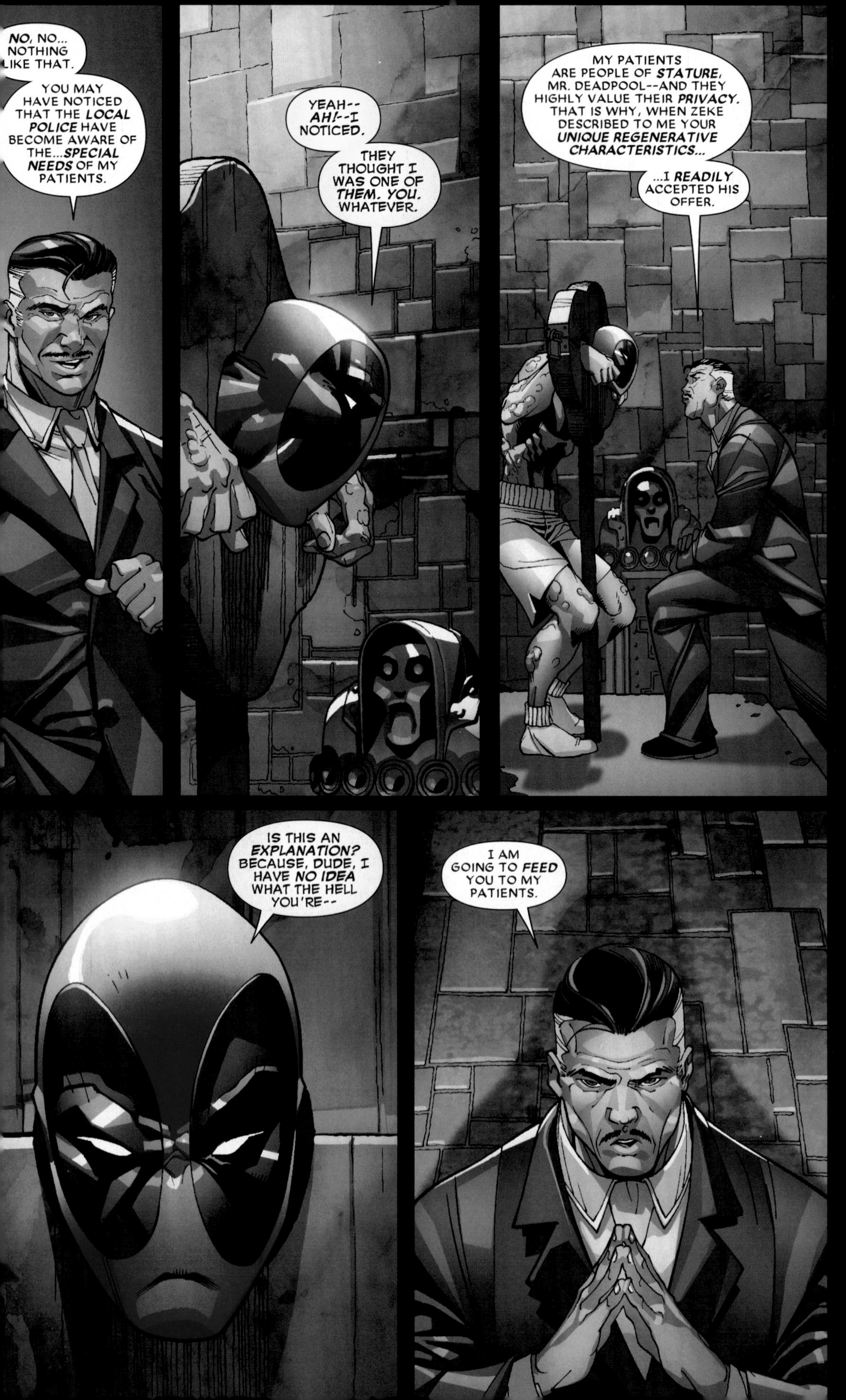

NO, NO... NOTHING LIKE THAT.
YOU MAY HAVE NOTICED THAT THE LOCAL POLICE HAVE BECOME AWARE OF THE...SPECIAL NEEDS OF MY PATIENTS.
YEAH-- AH!--I NOTICED.
THEY THOUGHT I WAS ONE OF THEM. YOU. WHATEVER.
MY PATIENTS ARE PEOPLE OF STATURE, MR. DEADPOOL--AND THEY HIGHLY VALUE THEIR PRIVACY. THAT IS WHY, WHEN ZEKE DESCRIBED TO ME YOUR UNIQUE REGENERATIVE CHARACTERISTICS...
...I READILY ACCEPTED HIS OFFER.
IS THIS AN EXPLANATION? BECAUSE, DUDE, I HAVE NO IDEA WHAT THE HELL YOU'RE--
I AM GOING TO FEED YOU TO MY PATIENTS.

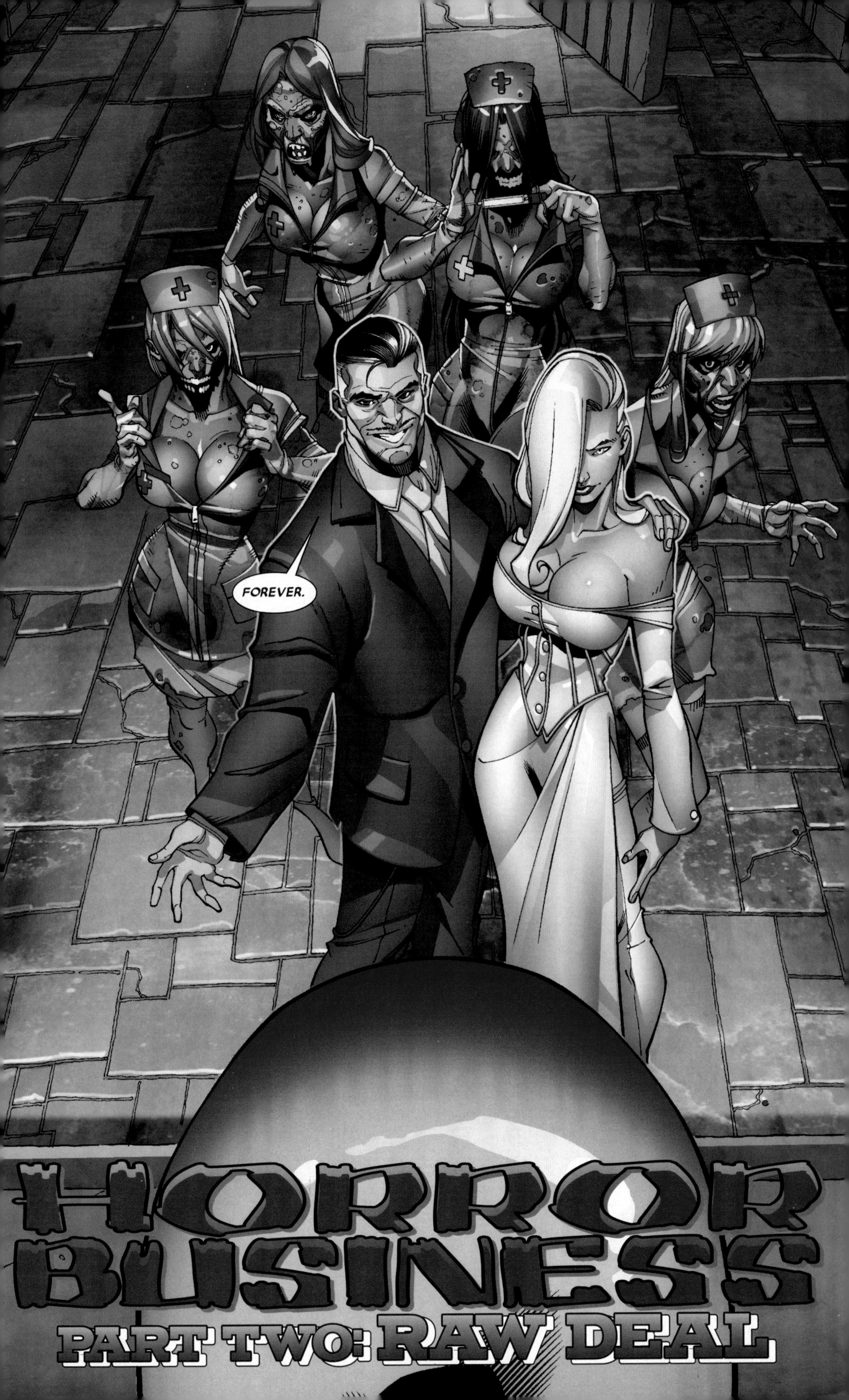
FOREVER.
HORROR BUSINESS
PART TWO: RAW DEAL

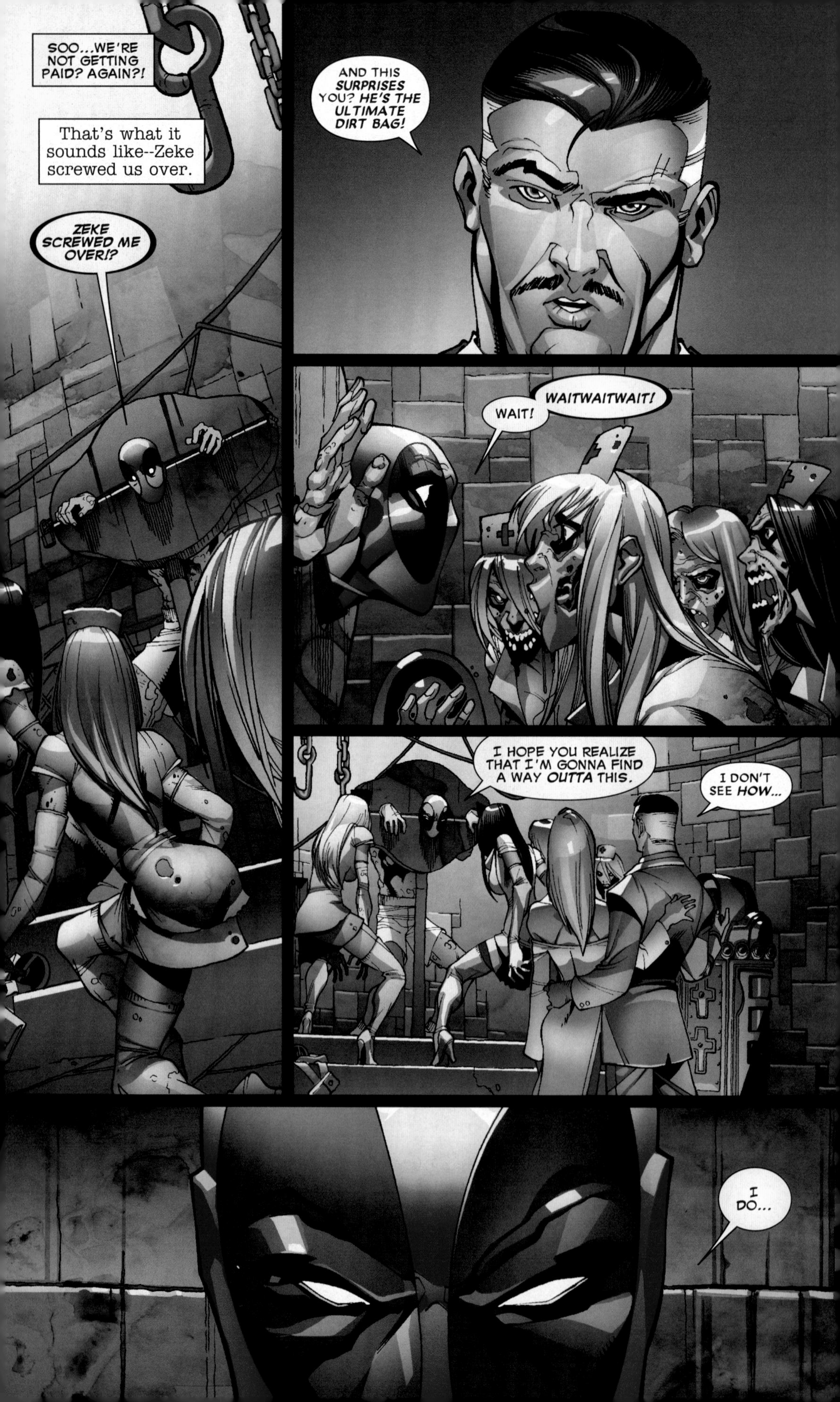
SOO...WE'RE NOT GETTING PAID? AGAIN?!
That's what it sounds like--Zeke screwed us over.
ZEKE SCREWED ME OVER!?
AND THIS SURPRISES YOU? HE'S THE ULTIMATE DIRT BAG!
WAIT!
WAITWAITWAIT!
I HOPE YOU REALIZE THAT I'M GONNA FIND A WAY OUTTA THIS.
I DON'T SEE HOW...
I DO...

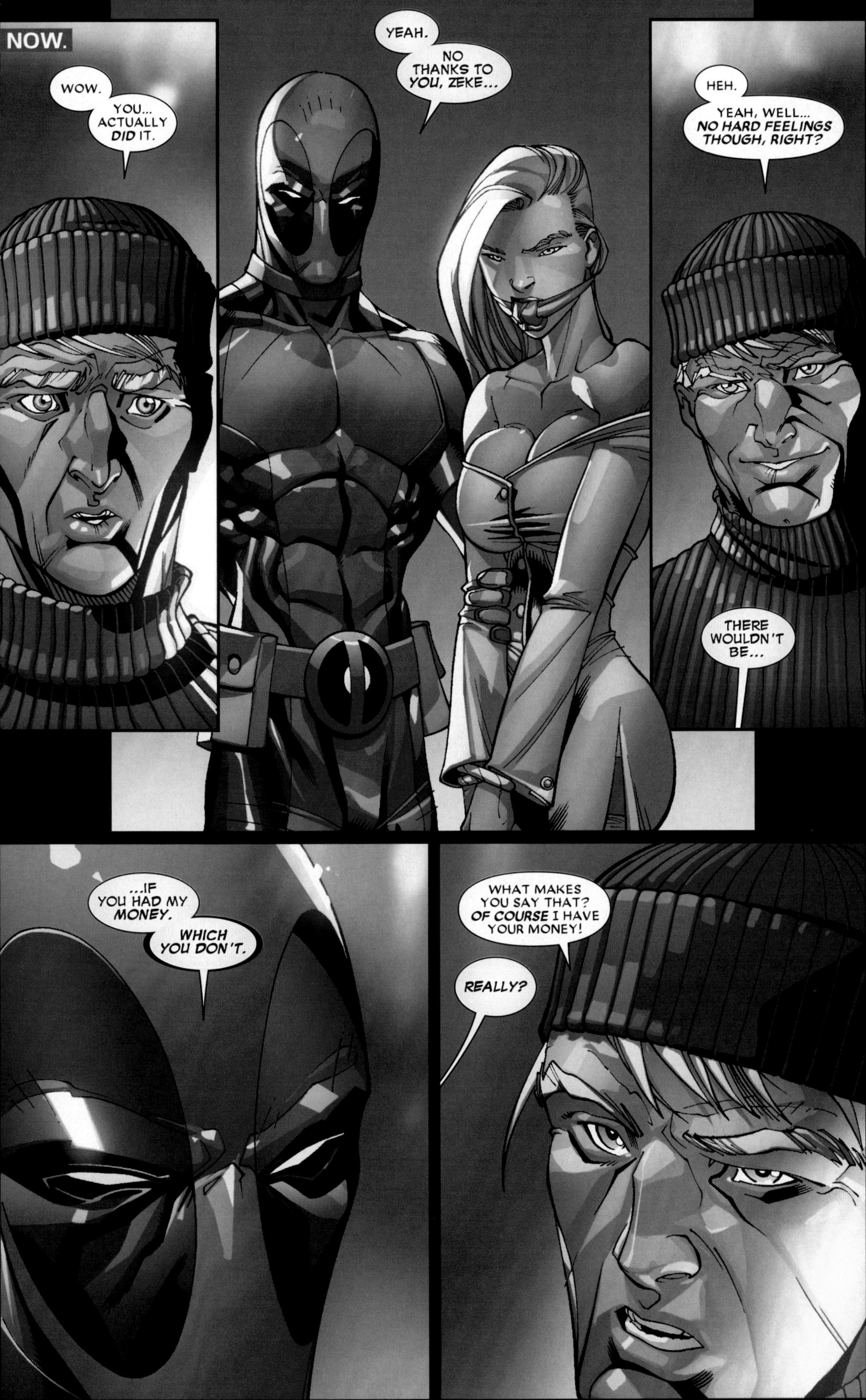
NOW.
WOW.
YOU... ACTUALLY DID IT.
YEAH.
NO THANKS TO YOU, ZEKE...
HEH.
YEAH, WELL... NO HARD FEELINGS THOUGH, RIGHT?
THERE WOULDN'T BE...
...IF YOU HAD MY MONEY.
WHICH YOU DON'T.
WHAT MAKES YOU SAY THAT? OF COURSE I HAVE YOUR MONEY!
REALLY?

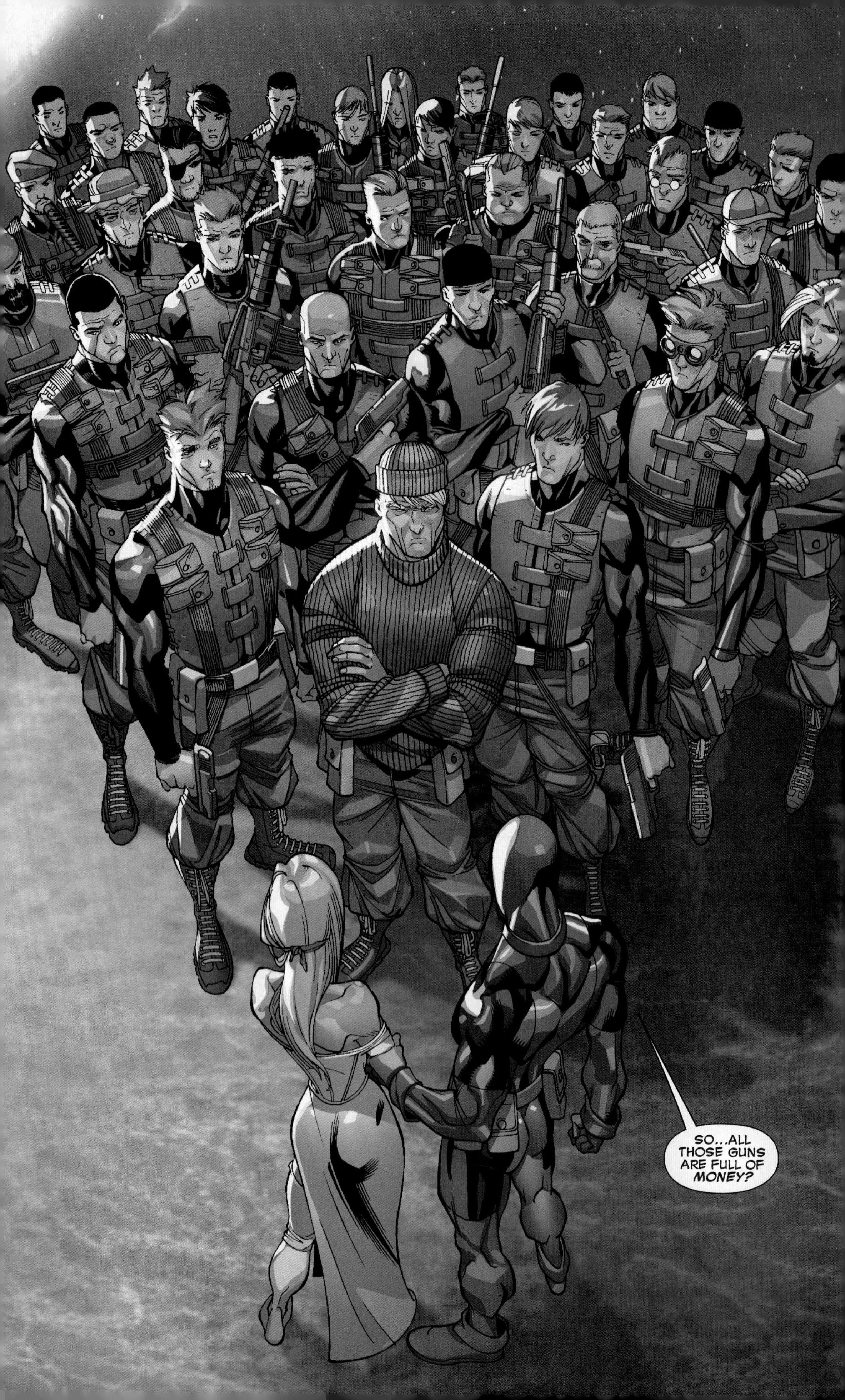
SO...ALL THOSE GUNS ARE FULL OF *MONEY?*

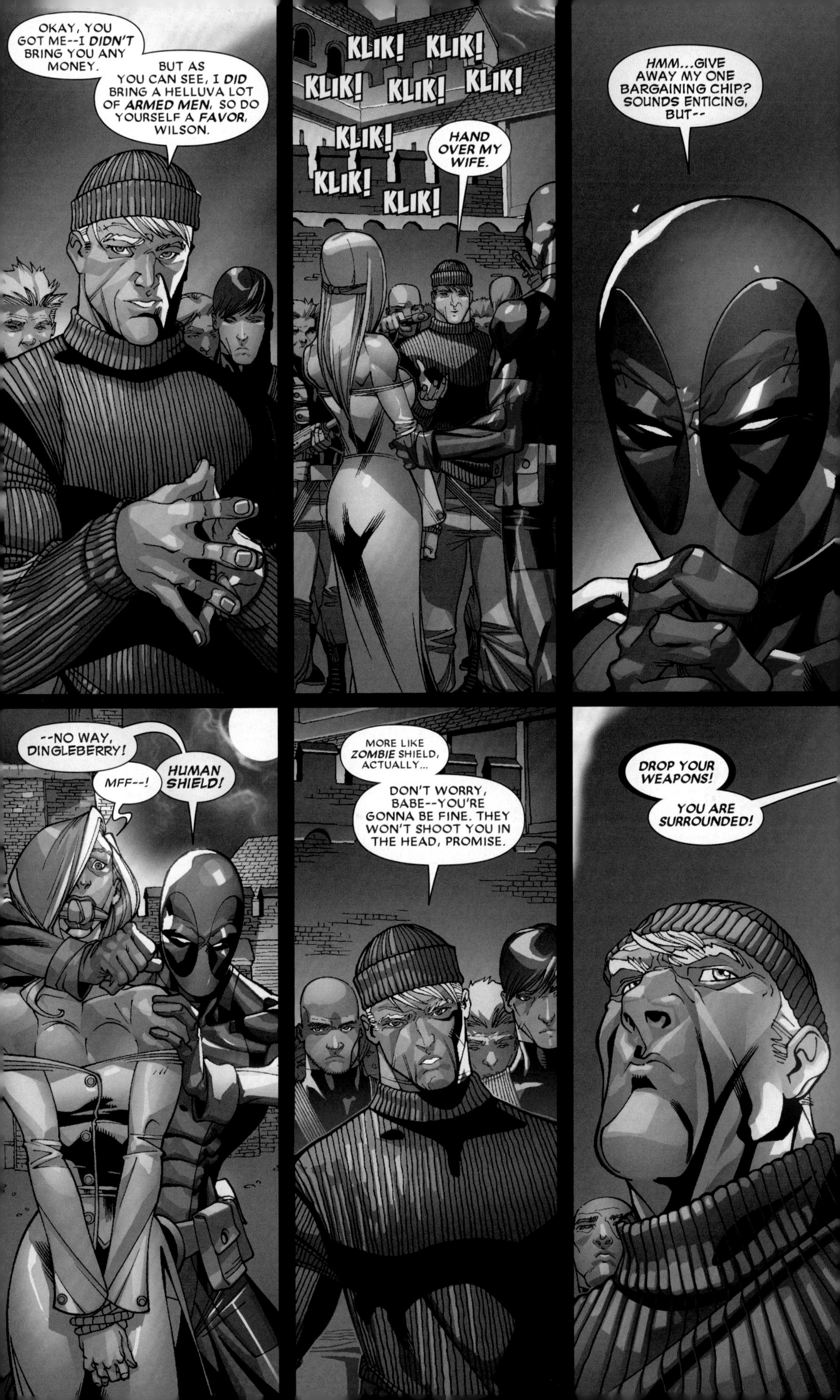
OKAY, YOU GOT ME--I DIDN'T BRING YOU ANY MONEY.
BUT AS YOU CAN SEE, I DID BRING A HELLUVA LOT OF ARMED MEN, SO DO YOURSELF A FAVOR, WILSON.
KLIK! KLIK!
KLIK! KLIK! KLIK!
KLIK!
KLIK!
KLIK!
HAND OVER MY WIFE.
HMM...GIVE AWAY MY ONE BARGAINING CHIP? SOUNDS ENTICING, BUT--
--NO WAY, DINGLEBERRY!
HUMAN SHIELD!
MFF--!
MORE LIKE ZOMBIE SHIELD, ACTUALLY...
DON'T WORRY, BABE--YOU'RE GONNA BE FINE. THEY WON'T SHOOT YOU IN THE HEAD, PROMISE.
DROP YOUR WEAPONS!
YOU ARE SURROUNDED!

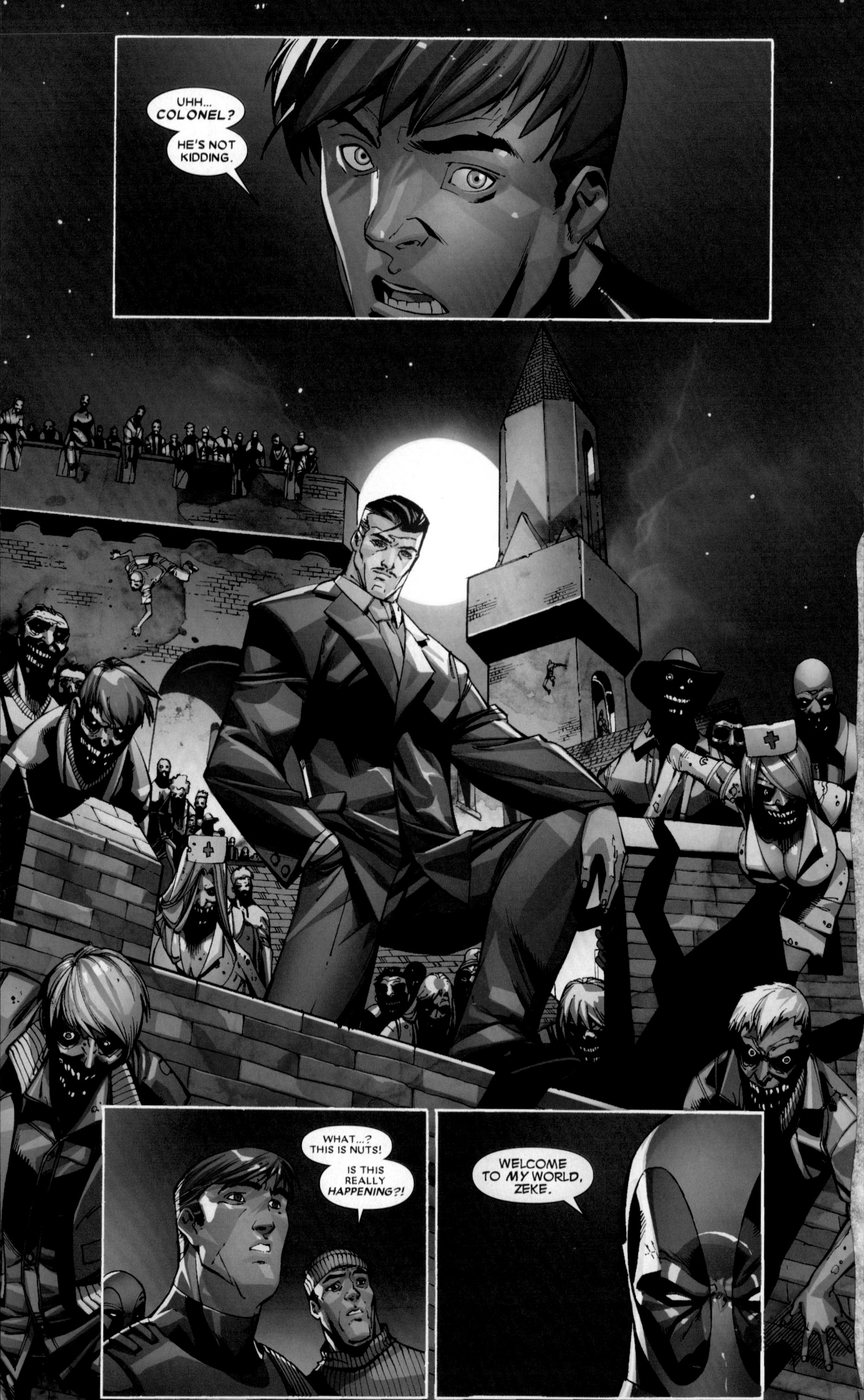
UHH... COLONEL?
HE'S NOT KIDDING.
WHAT...? THIS IS NUTS!
IS THIS REALLY HAPPENING?!
WELCOME TO MY WORLD, ZEKE.

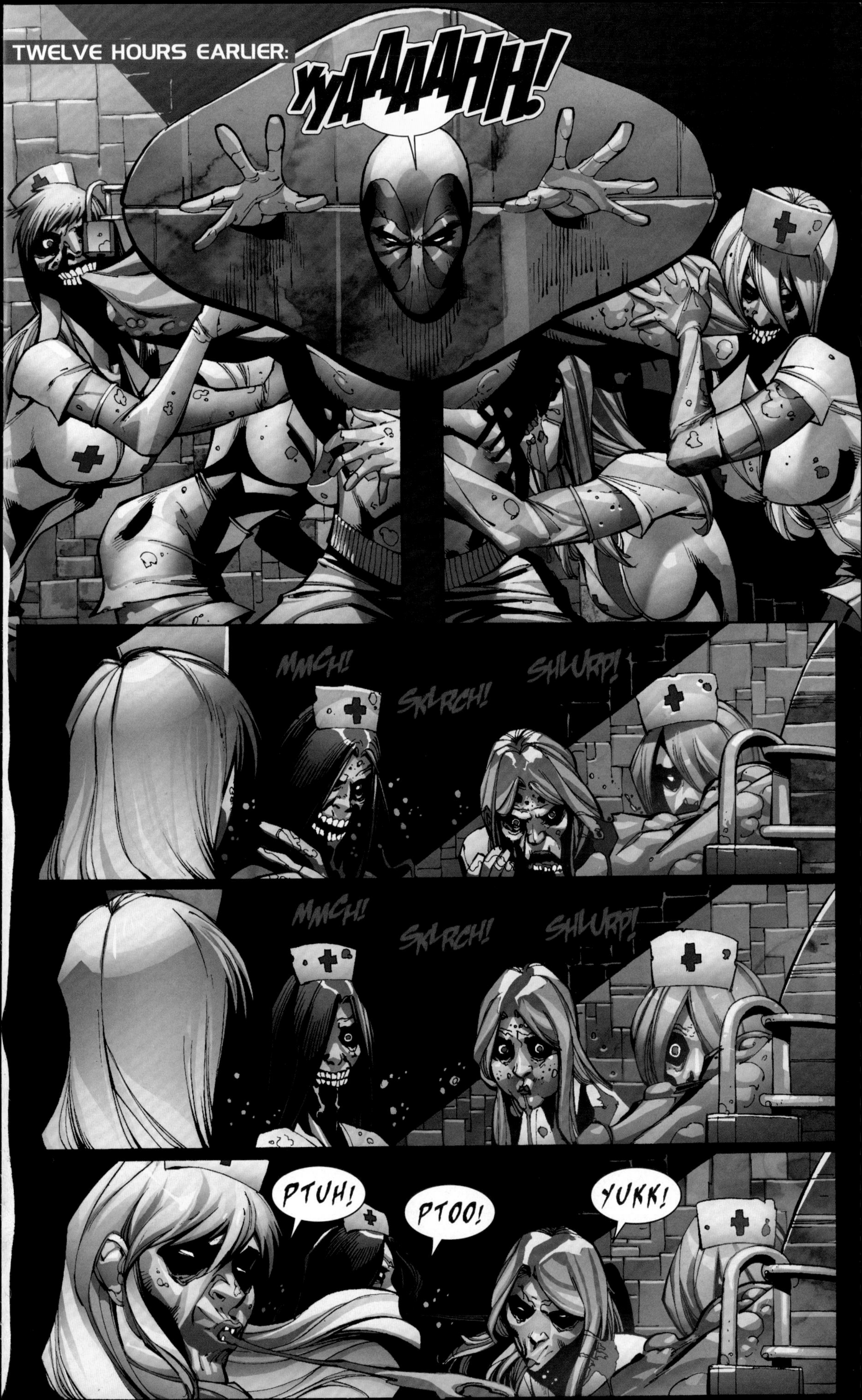
TWELVE HOURS EARLIER:
YYAAAAHH!
MMCH!
SKLRCH!
SHLURP!
MMCH!
SKLRCH!
SHLURP!
PTUH!
PTOO!
YUKK!

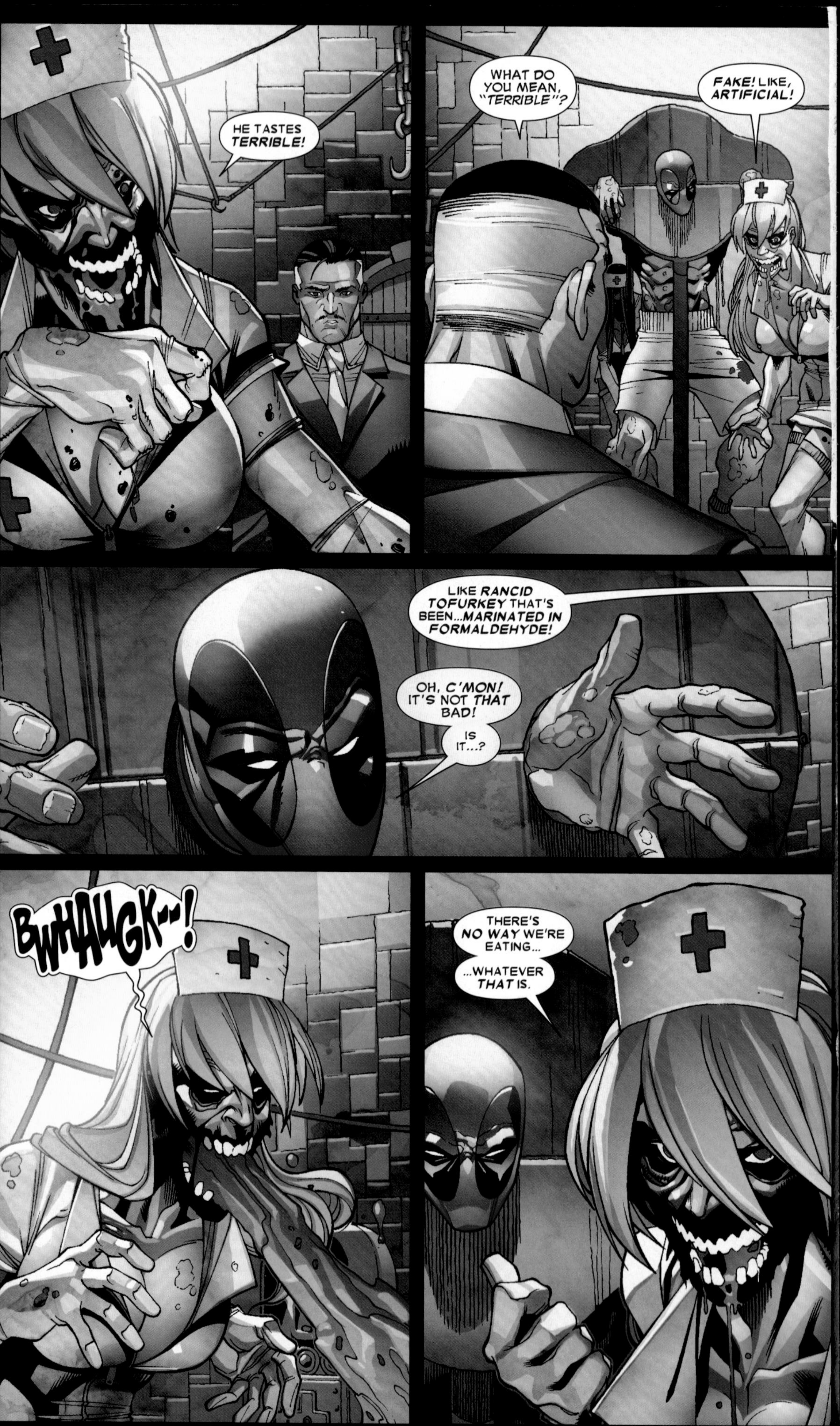
HE TASTES TERRIBLE!
WHAT DO YOU MEAN, "TERRIBLE"?
FAKE! LIKE, ARTIFICIAL!
LIKE RANCID TOFURKEY THAT'S BEEN...MARINATED IN FORMALDEHYDE!
OH, C'MON! IT'S NOT THAT BAD!
IS IT...?
BWHAUGK--!
THERE'S NO WAY WE'RE EATING...
...WHATEVER THAT IS.

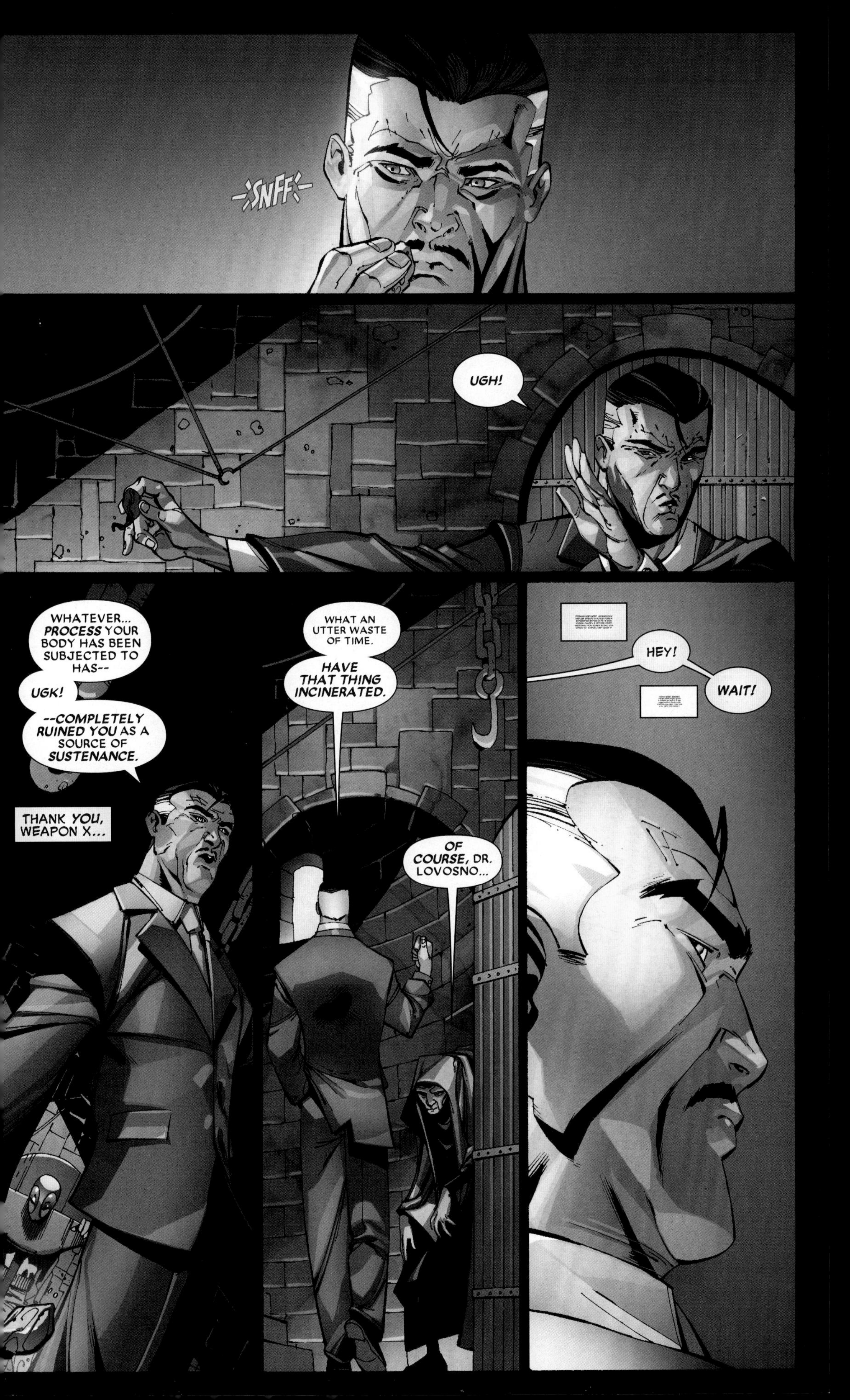

-SNFF-
UGH!
WHATEVER... PROCESS YOUR BODY HAS BEEN SUBJECTED TO HAS--
UGK!
--COMPLETELY RUINED YOU AS A SOURCE OF SUSTENANCE.
THANK YOU, WEAPON X...
WHAT AN UTTER WASTE OF TIME.
HAVE THAT THING INCINERATED.
OF COURSE, DR. LOVOSNO...
HEY!
WAIT!

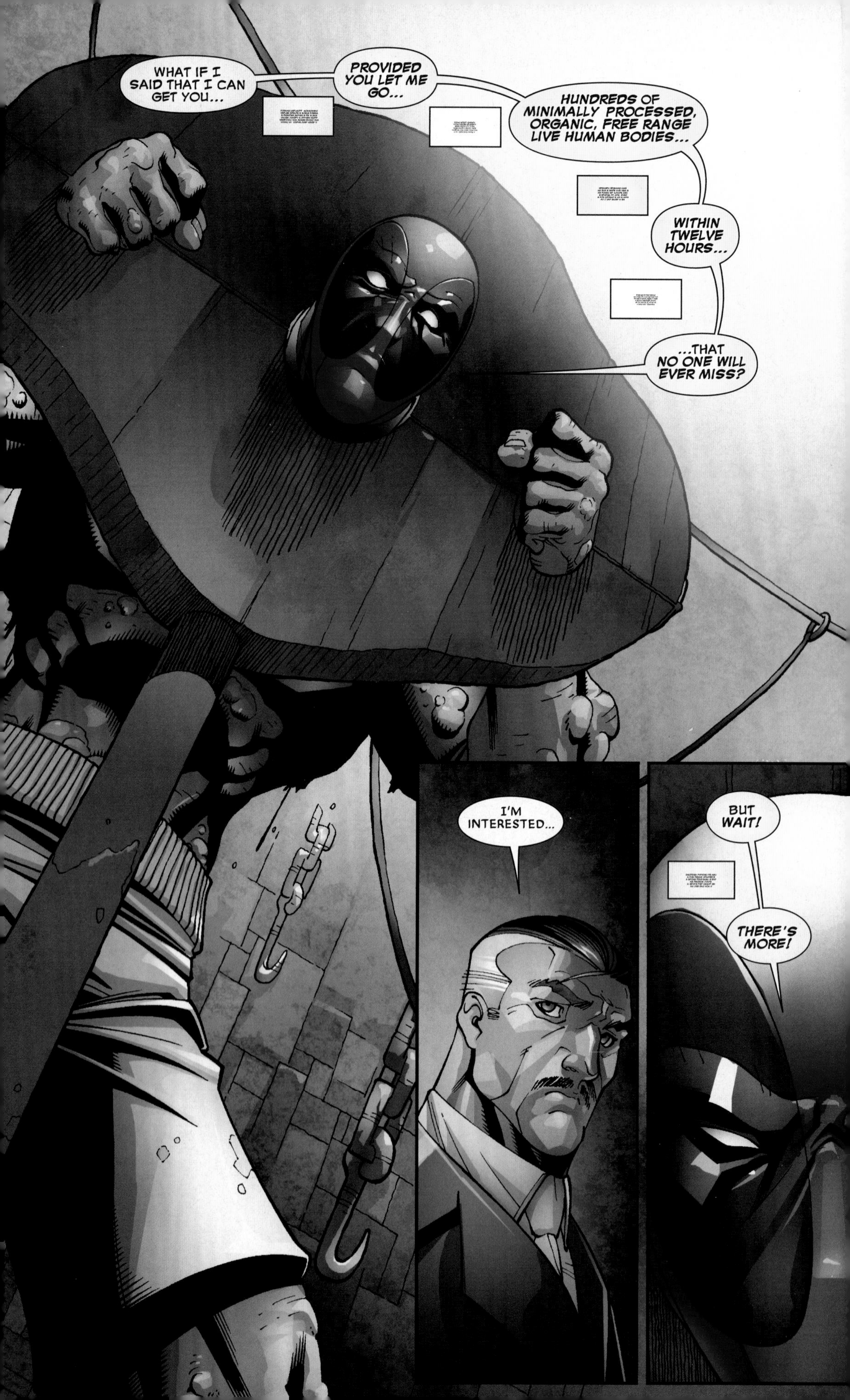
WHAT IF I SAID THAT I CAN GET YOU...
PROVIDED YOU LET ME GO...
HUNDREDS OF MINIMALLY PROCESSED, ORGANIC, FREE RANGE LIVE HUMAN BODIES...
WITHIN TWELVE HOURS...
...THAT NO ONE WILL EVER MISS?
I'M INTERESTED...
BUT WAIT!
THERE'S MORE!

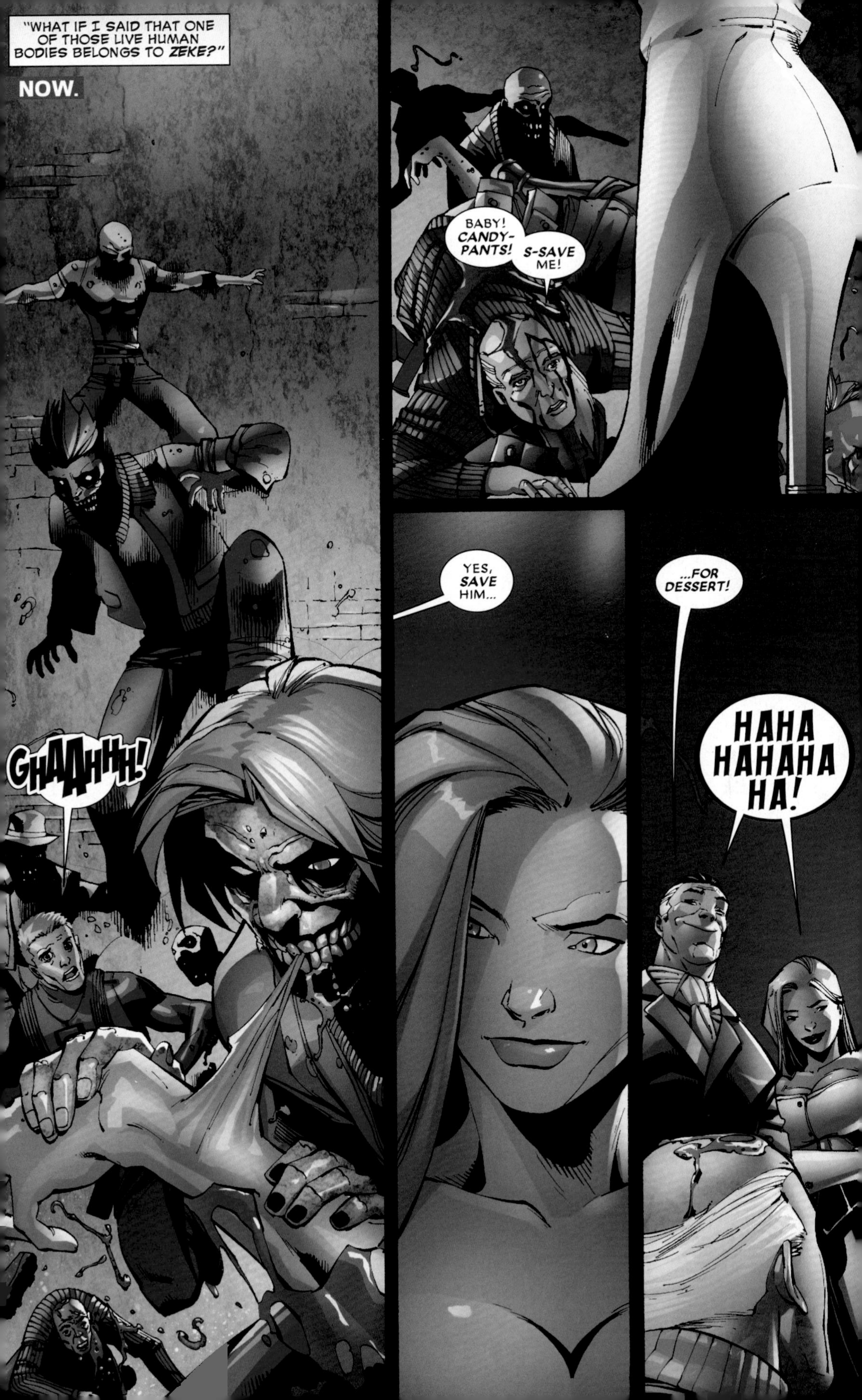
"WHAT IF I SAID THAT ONE OF THOSE LIVE HUMAN BODIES BELONGS TO ZEKE?"
NOW.
GHAAHHH!
BABY! CANDY-PANTS!
S-SAVE ME!
YES, SAVE HIM...
...FOR DESSERT!
HAHA HAHAHA HA!

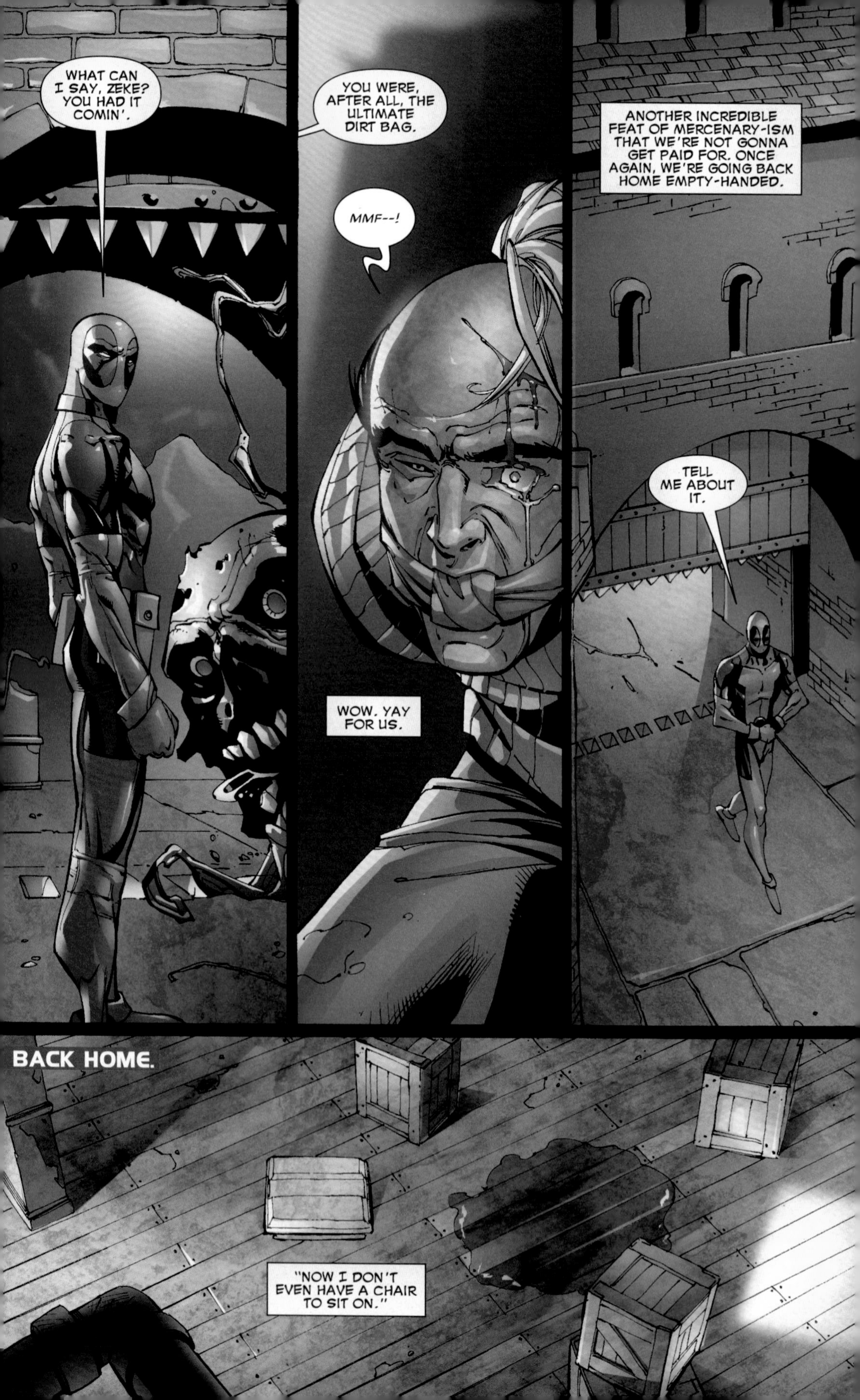
WHAT CAN I SAY, ZEKE? YOU HAD IT COMIN'.
YOU WERE, AFTER ALL, THE ULTIMATE DIRT BAG.
MMF--!
WOW. YAY FOR US.
ANOTHER INCREDIBLE FEAT OF MERCENARY-ISM THAT WE'RE NOT GONNA GET PAID FOR. ONCE AGAIN, WE'RE GOING BACK HOME EMPTY-HANDED.
TELL ME ABOUT IT.
BACK HOME.
"NOW I DON'T EVEN HAVE A CHAIR TO SIT ON."

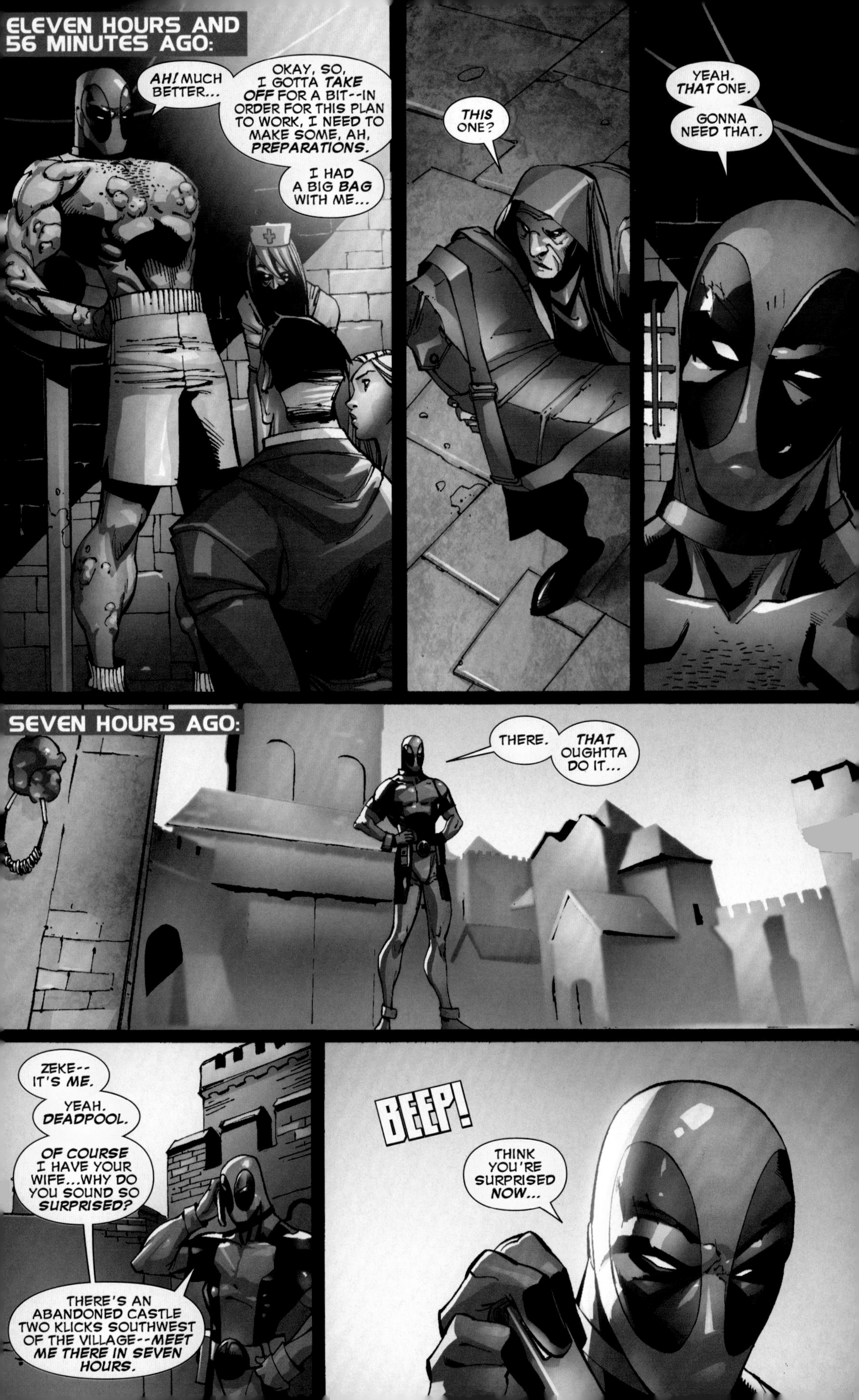

ELEVEN HOURS AND 56 MINUTES AGO:
AH! MUCH BETTER...
OKAY, SO, I GOTTA TAKE OFF FOR A BIT--IN ORDER FOR THIS PLAN TO WORK, I NEED TO MAKE SOME, AH, PREPARATIONS.
I HAD A BIG BAG WITH ME...
THIS ONE?
YEAH. THAT ONE.
GONNA NEED THAT.
SEVEN HOURS AGO:
THERE.
THAT OUGHTTA DO IT...
ZEKE-- IT'S ME.
YEAH. DEADPOOL.
OF COURSE I HAVE YOUR WIFE...WHY DO YOU SOUND SO SURPRISED?
THERE'S AN ABANDONED CASTLE TWO KLICKS SOUTHWEST OF THE VILLAGE--MEET ME THERE IN SEVEN HOURS.
BEEP!
THINK YOU'RE SURPRISED NOW...

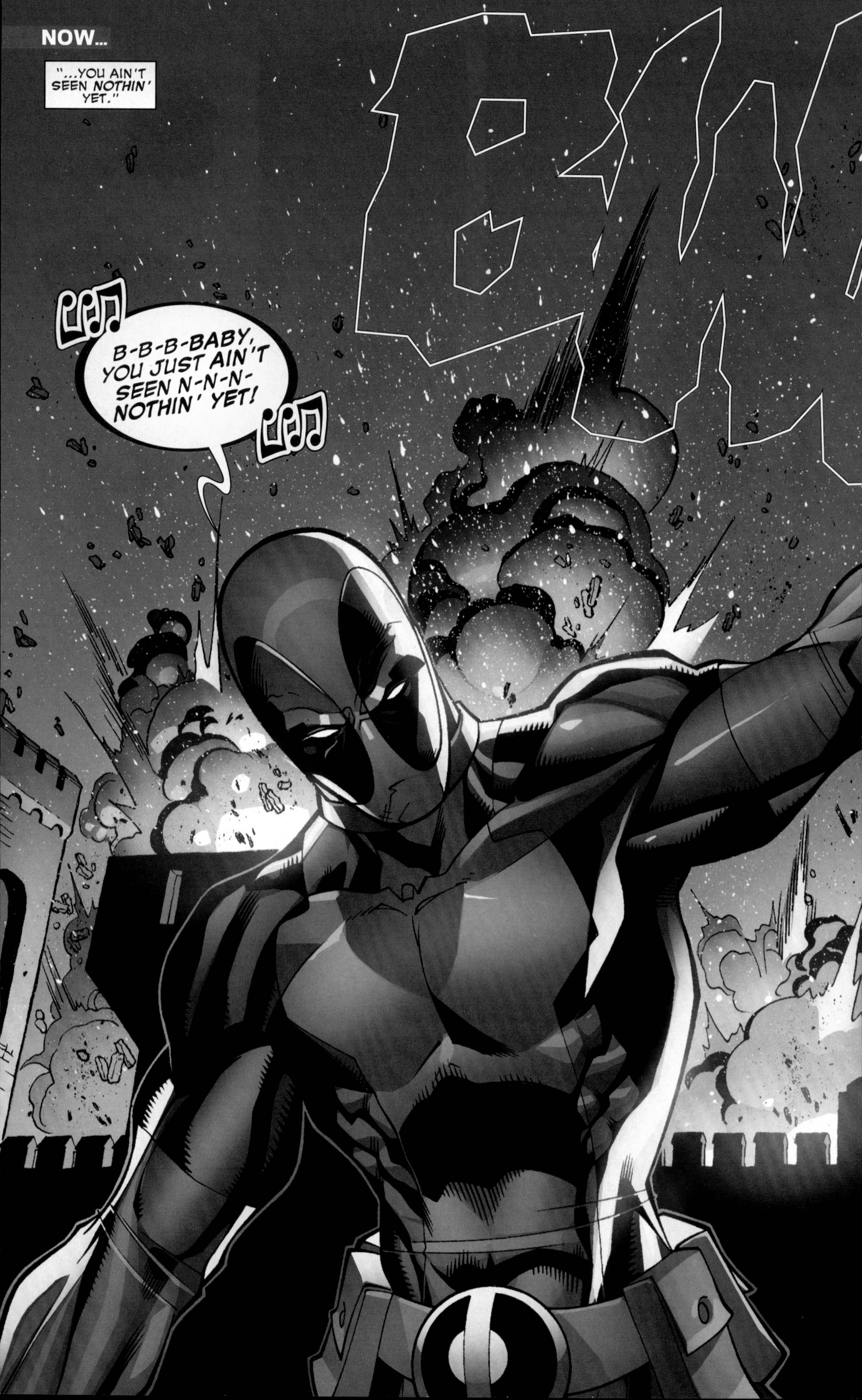
NOW...
"...YOU AIN'T SEEN NOTHIN' YET."
B-B-B-BABY, YOU JUST AIN'T SEEN N-N-N-NOTHIN' YET!

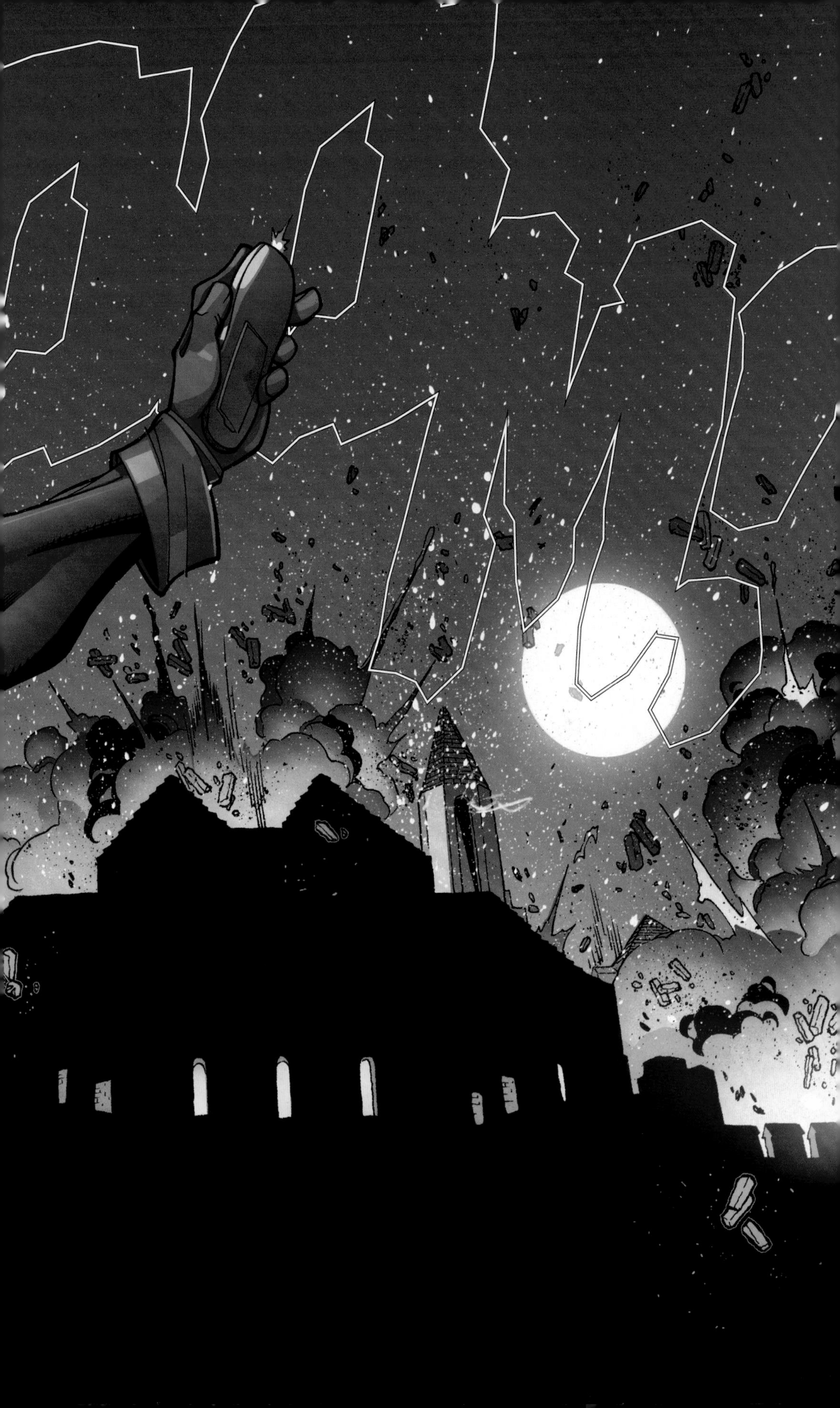

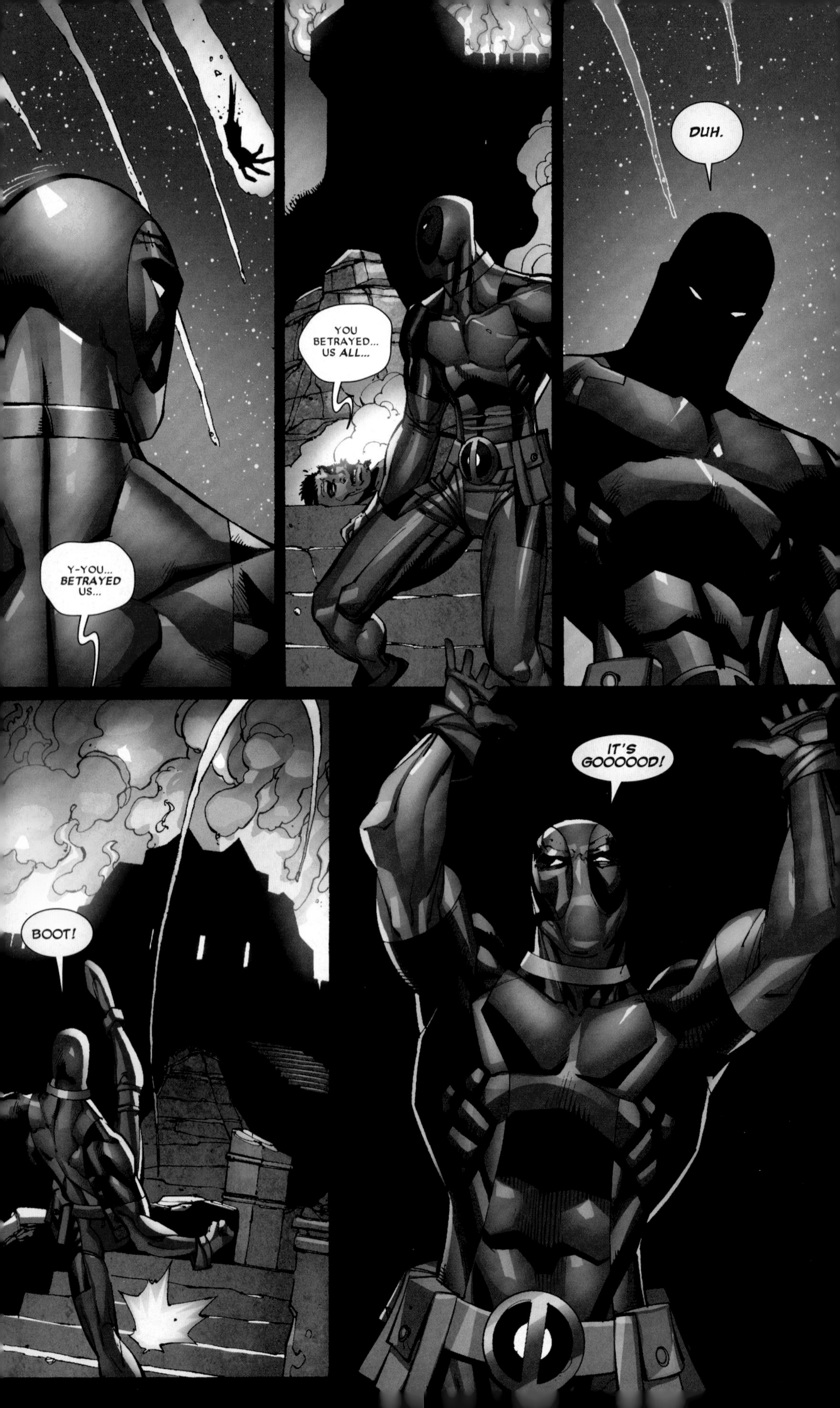

Y-YOU... BETRAYED US...
YOU BETRAYED... US ALL...
DUH.
BOOT!
IT'S GOOOOOD!

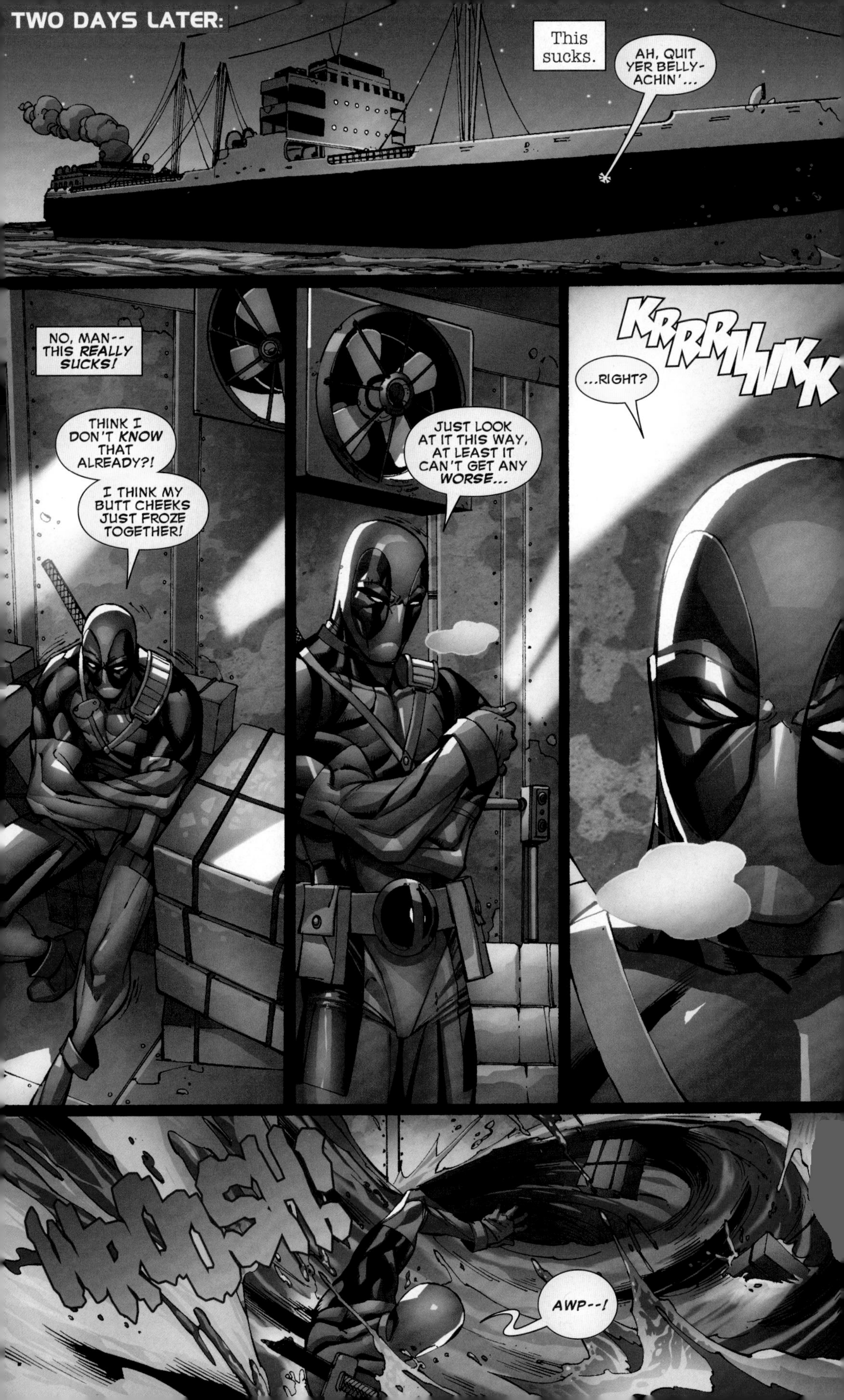

TWO DAYS LATER:
This sucks.
AH, QUIT YER BELLY-ACHIN'...
NO, MAN--THIS REALLY SUCKS!
THINK I DON'T KNOW THAT ALREADY?!
I THINK MY BUTT CHEEKS JUST FROZE TOGETHER!
JUST LOOK AT IT THIS WAY, AT LEAST IT CAN'T GET ANY WORSE...
KRRRINKK
...RIGHT?
AWP--!

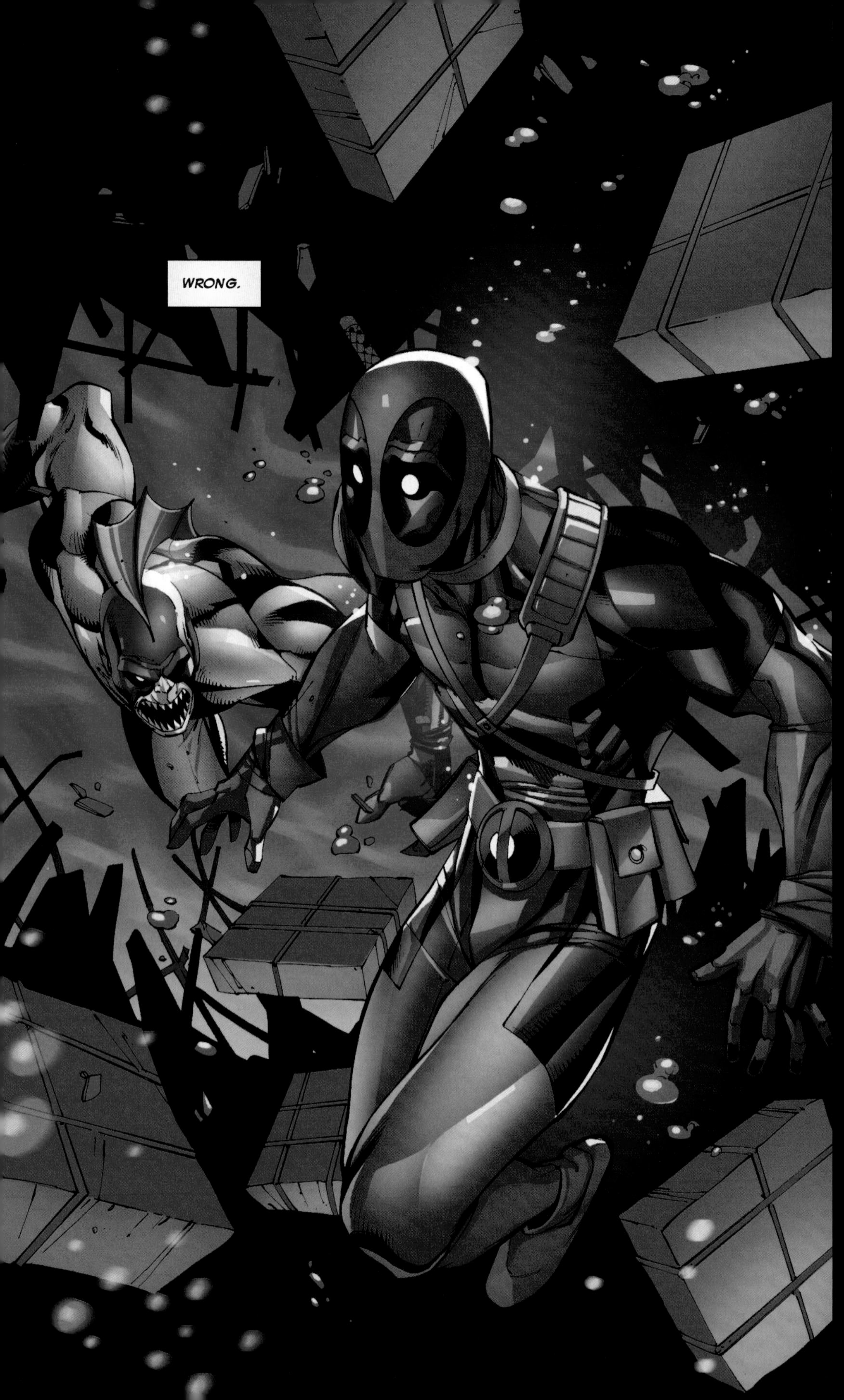
WRONG.

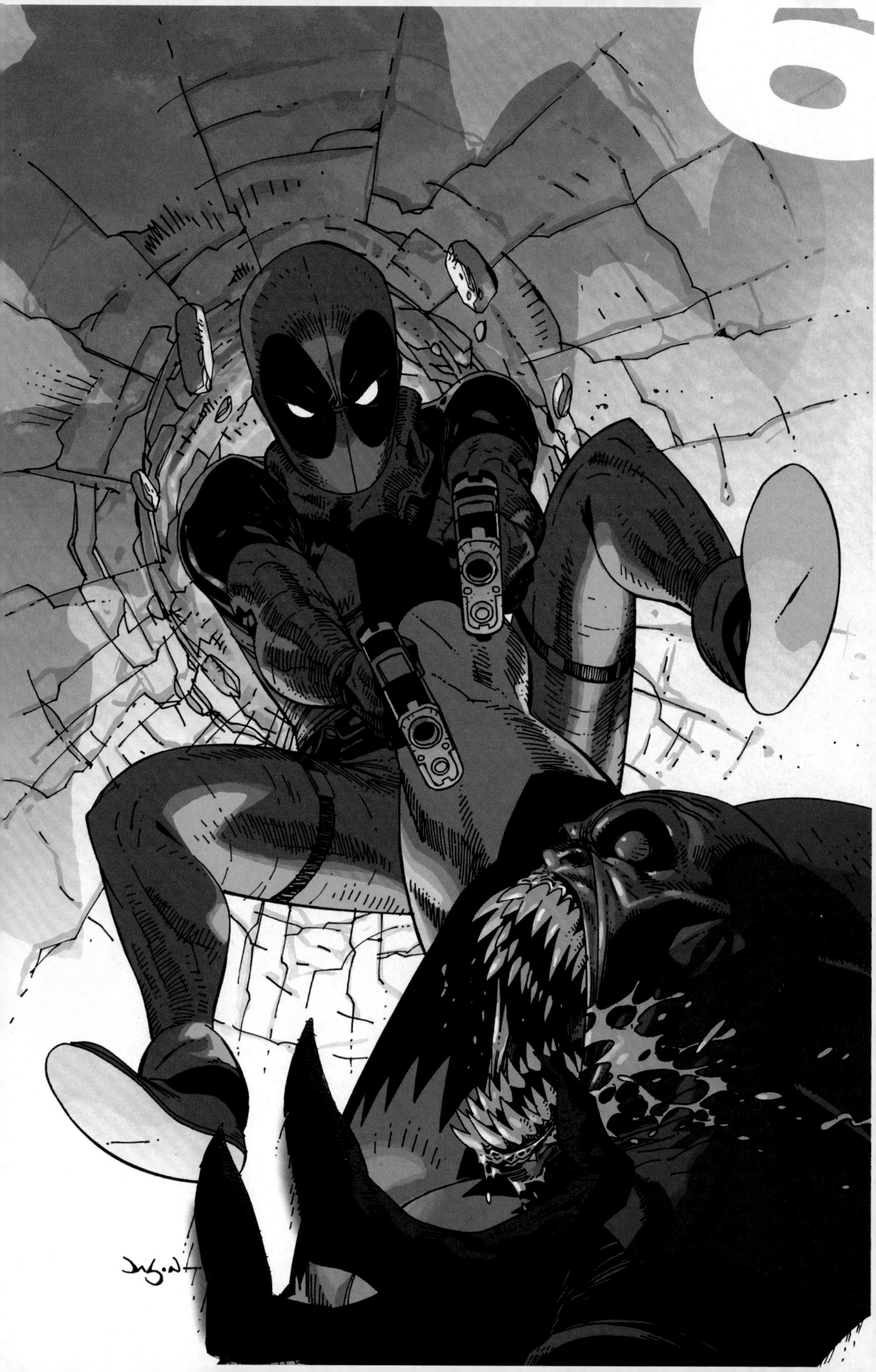
6

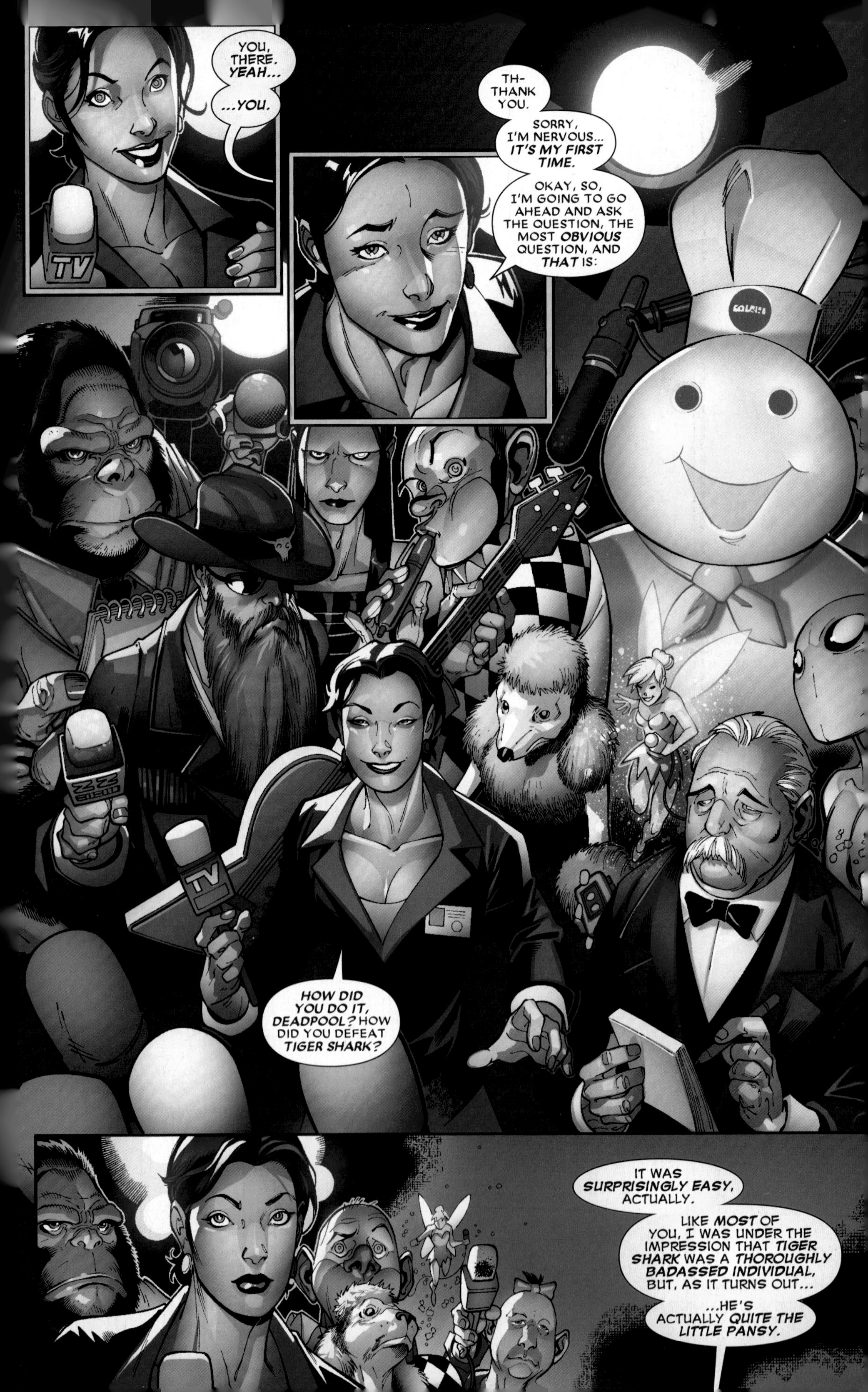
YOU, THERE. YEAH...
...YOU.
TH- THANK YOU.
SORRY, I'M NERVOUS... IT'S MY FIRST TIME.
OKAY, SO, I'M GOING TO GO AHEAD AND ASK THE QUESTION, THE MOST OBVIOUS QUESTION, AND THAT IS:
TV
HOW DID YOU DO IT, DEADPOOL? HOW DID YOU DEFEAT TIGER SHARK?
IT WAS SURPRISINGLY EASY, ACTUALLY.
LIKE MOST OF YOU, I WAS UNDER THE IMPRESSION THAT TIGER SHARK WAS A THOROUGHLY BADASSED INDIVIDUAL, BUT, AS IT TURNS OUT...
...HE'S ACTUALLY QUITE THE LITTLE PANSY.

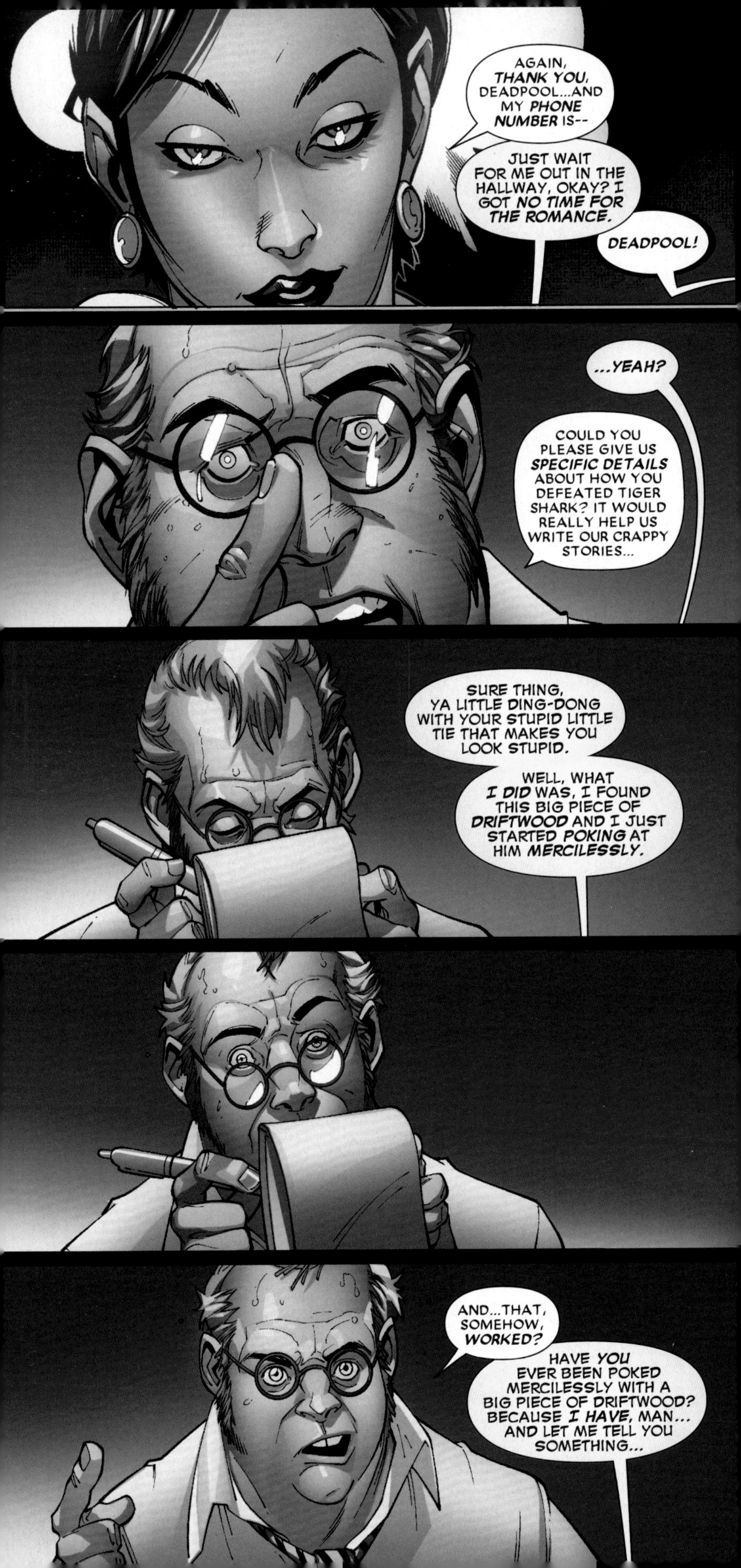

AGAIN, THANK YOU, DEADPOOL...AND MY PHONE NUMBER IS--
JUST WAIT FOR ME OUT IN THE HALLWAY, OKAY? I GOT NO TIME FOR THE ROMANCE.
DEADPOOL!
...YEAH?
COULD YOU PLEASE GIVE US SPECIFIC DETAILS ABOUT HOW YOU DEFEATED TIGER SHARK? IT WOULD REALLY HELP US WRITE OUR CRAPPY STORIES...
SURE THING, YA LITTLE DING-DONG WITH YOUR STUPID LITTLE TIE THAT MAKES YOU LOOK STUPID.
WELL, WHAT I DID WAS, I FOUND THIS BIG PIECE OF DRIFTWOOD AND I JUST STARTED POKING AT HIM MERCILESSLY.
AND...THAT, SOMEHOW, WORKED?
HAVE YOU EVER BEEN POKED MERCILESSLY WITH A BIG PIECE OF DRIFTWOOD? BECAUSE I HAVE, MAN... AND LET ME TELL YOU SOMETHING...

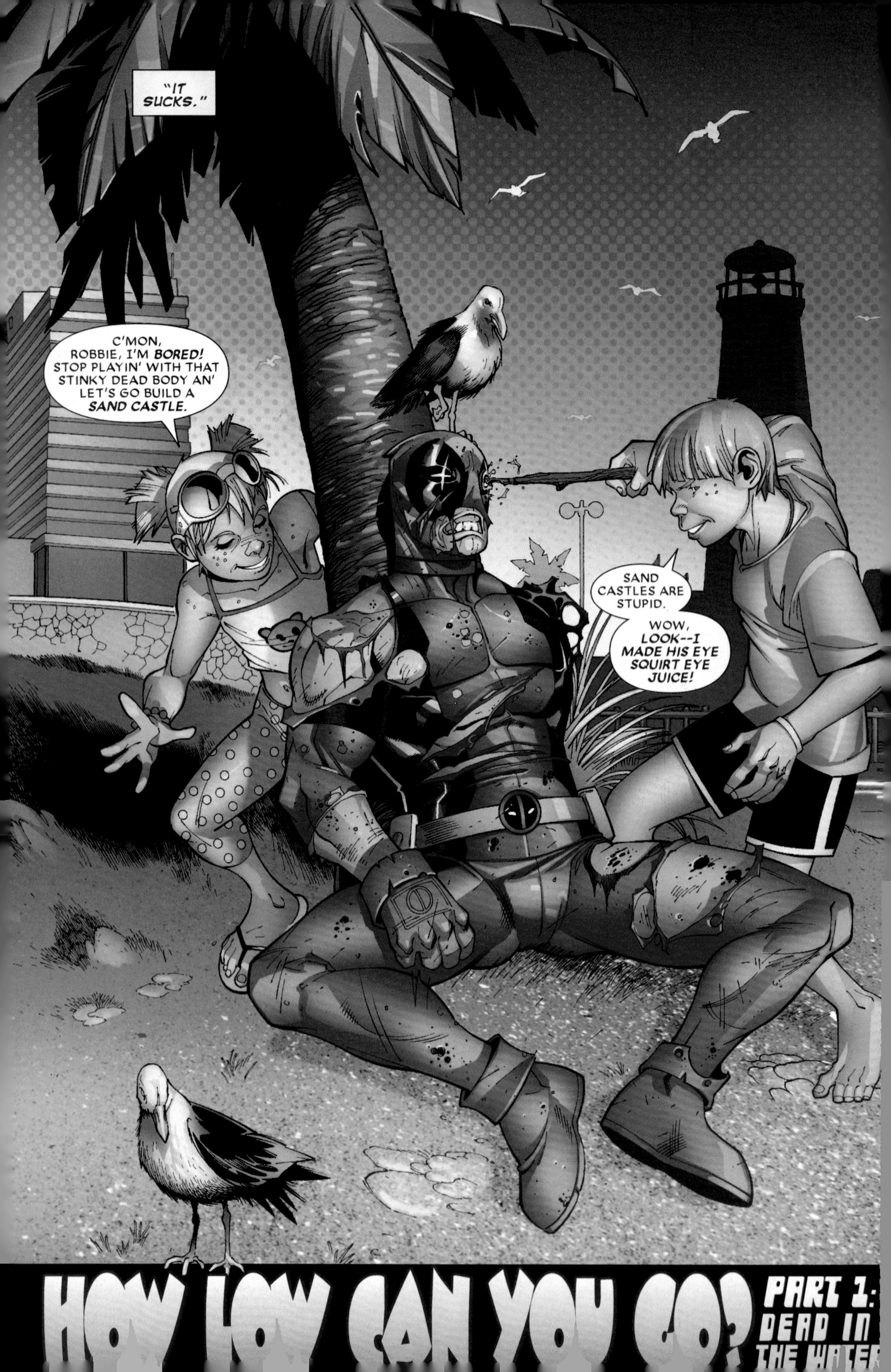
"IT SUCKS."
C'MON, ROBBIE, I'M BORED! STOP PLAYIN' WITH THAT STINKY DEAD BODY AN' LET'S GO BUILD A SAND CASTLE.
SAND CASTLES ARE STUPID.
WOW, LOOK--I MADE HIS EYE SQUIRT EYE JUICE!
HOW LOW CAN YOU GO?
PART 1: DEAD IN THE WATER

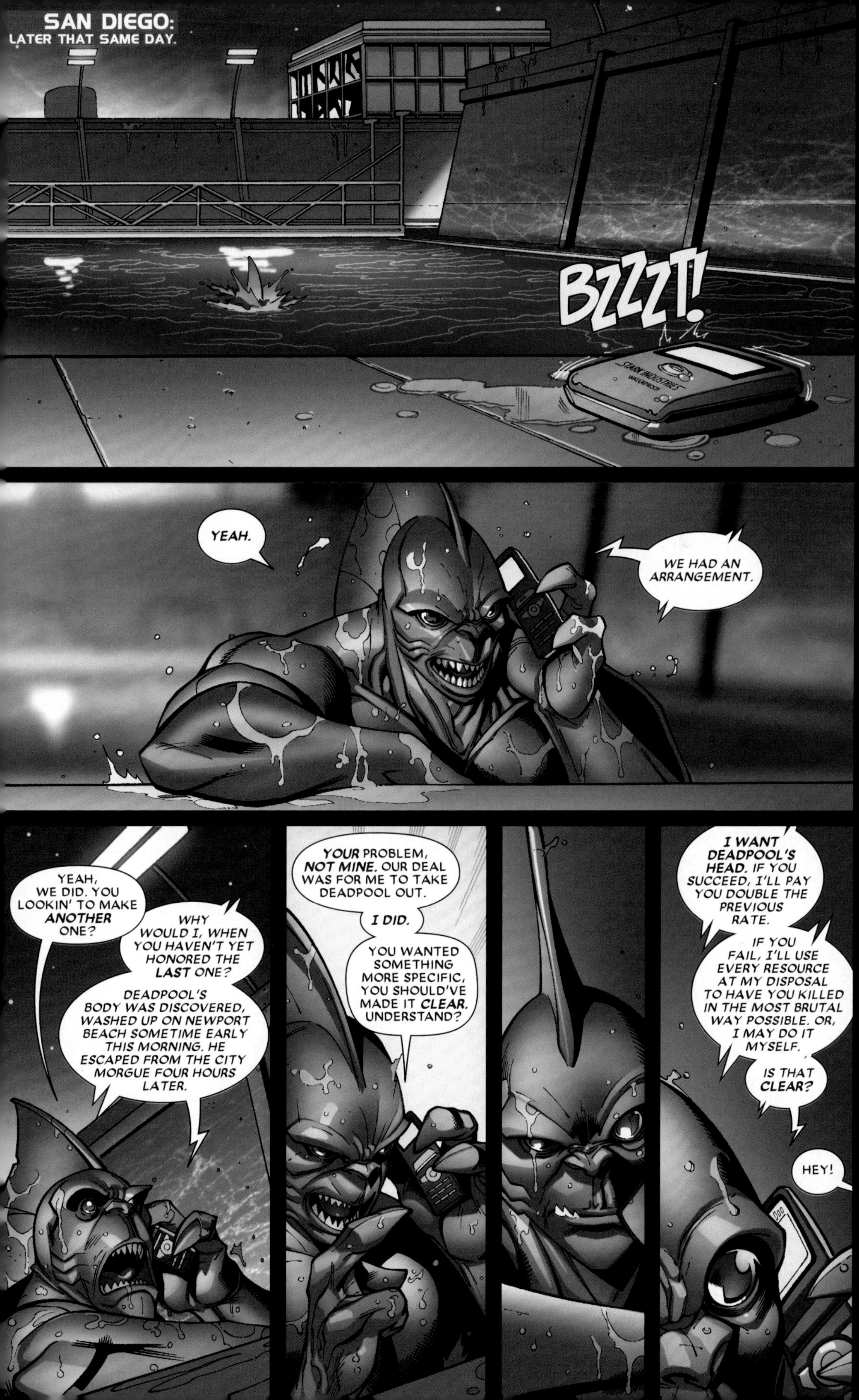
SAN DIEGO:
LATER THAT SAME DAY.
BZZZT!
STARK INDUSTRIES
YEAH.
WE HAD AN ARRANGEMENT.
YEAH, WE DID. YOU LOOKIN' TO MAKE ANOTHER ONE?
WHY WOULD I, WHEN YOU HAVEN'T YET HONORED THE LAST ONE?
DEADPOOL'S BODY WAS DISCOVERED, WASHED UP ON NEWPORT BEACH SOMETIME EARLY THIS MORNING. HE ESCAPED FROM THE CITY MORGUE FOUR HOURS LATER.
YOUR PROBLEM, NOT MINE. OUR DEAL WAS FOR ME TO TAKE DEADPOOL OUT.
I DID.
YOU WANTED SOMETHING MORE SPECIFIC, YOU SHOULD'VE MADE IT CLEAR. UNDERSTAND?
I WANT DEADPOOL'S HEAD. IF YOU SUCCEED, I'LL PAY YOU DOUBLE THE PREVIOUS RATE.
IF YOU FAIL, I'LL USE EVERY RESOURCE AT MY DISPOSAL TO HAVE YOU KILLED IN THE MOST BRUTAL WAY POSSIBLE. OR, I MAY DO IT MYSELF.
IS THAT CLEAR?
HEY!

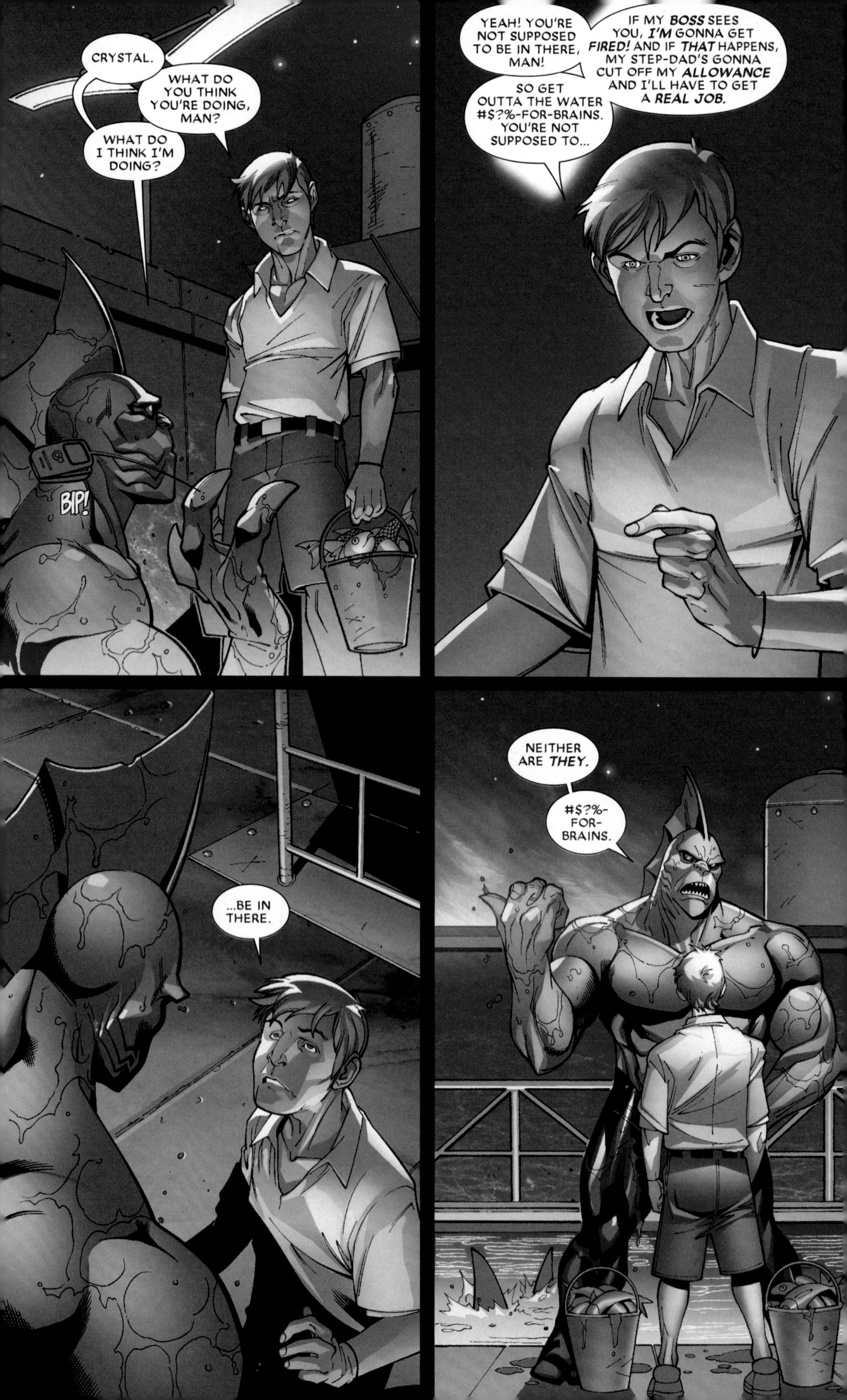
CRYSTAL.
WHAT DO YOU THINK YOU'RE DOING, MAN?
WHAT DO I THINK I'M DOING?
BIP!
YEAH! YOU'RE NOT SUPPOSED TO BE IN THERE, MAN!
IF MY BOSS SEES YOU, I'M GONNA GET FIRED! AND IF THAT HAPPENS, MY STEP-DAD'S GONNA CUT OFF MY ALLOWANCE AND I'LL HAVE TO GET A REAL JOB.
SO GET OUTTA THE WATER #$?%-FOR-BRAINS. YOU'RE NOT SUPPOSED TO...
...BE IN THERE.
NEITHER ARE THEY.
#$?%-FOR-BRAINS.

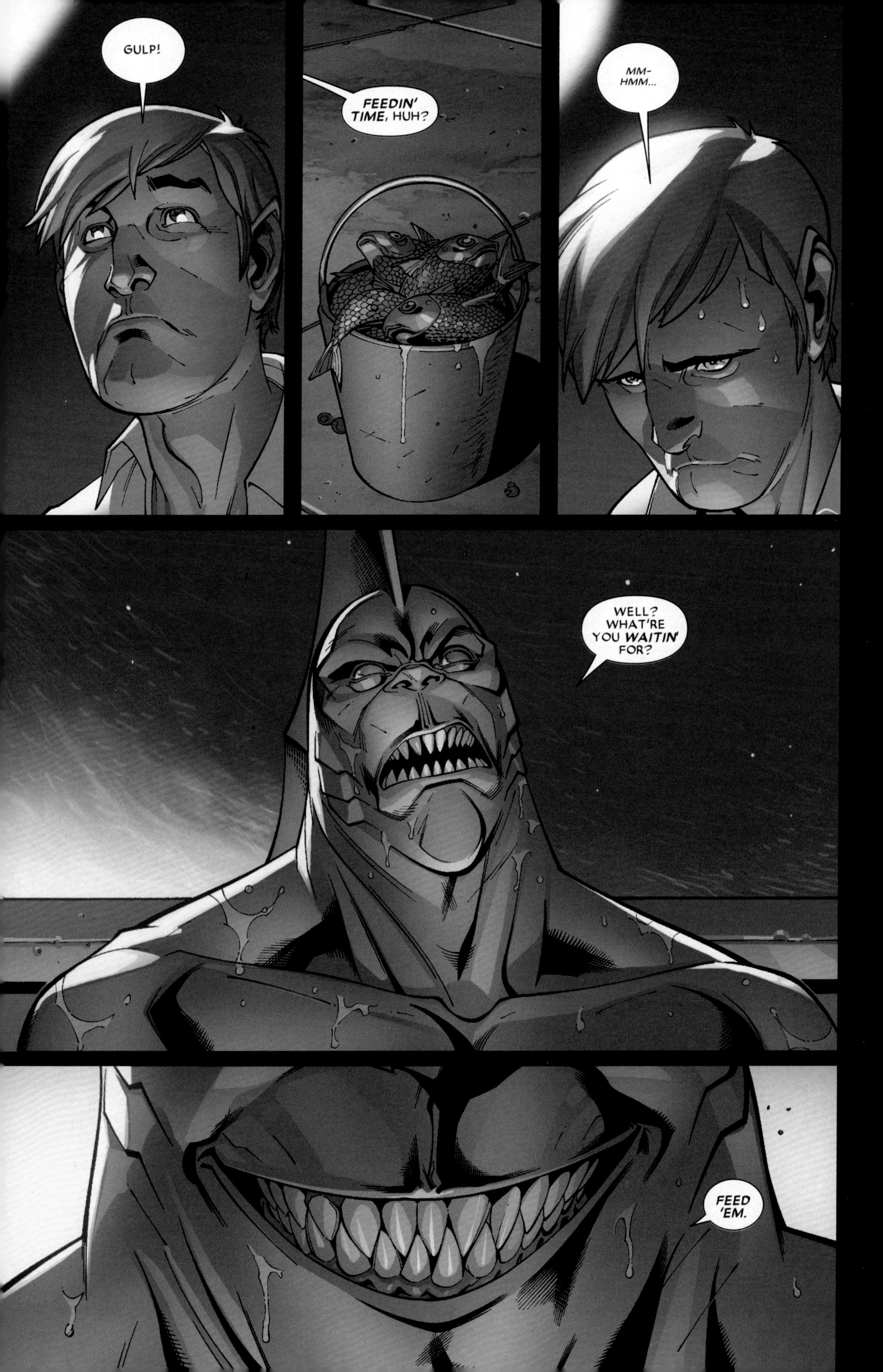

GULP!
FEEDIN' TIME, HUH?
MM-HMM...
WELL? WHAT'RE YOU WAITIN' FOR?
FEED 'EM.

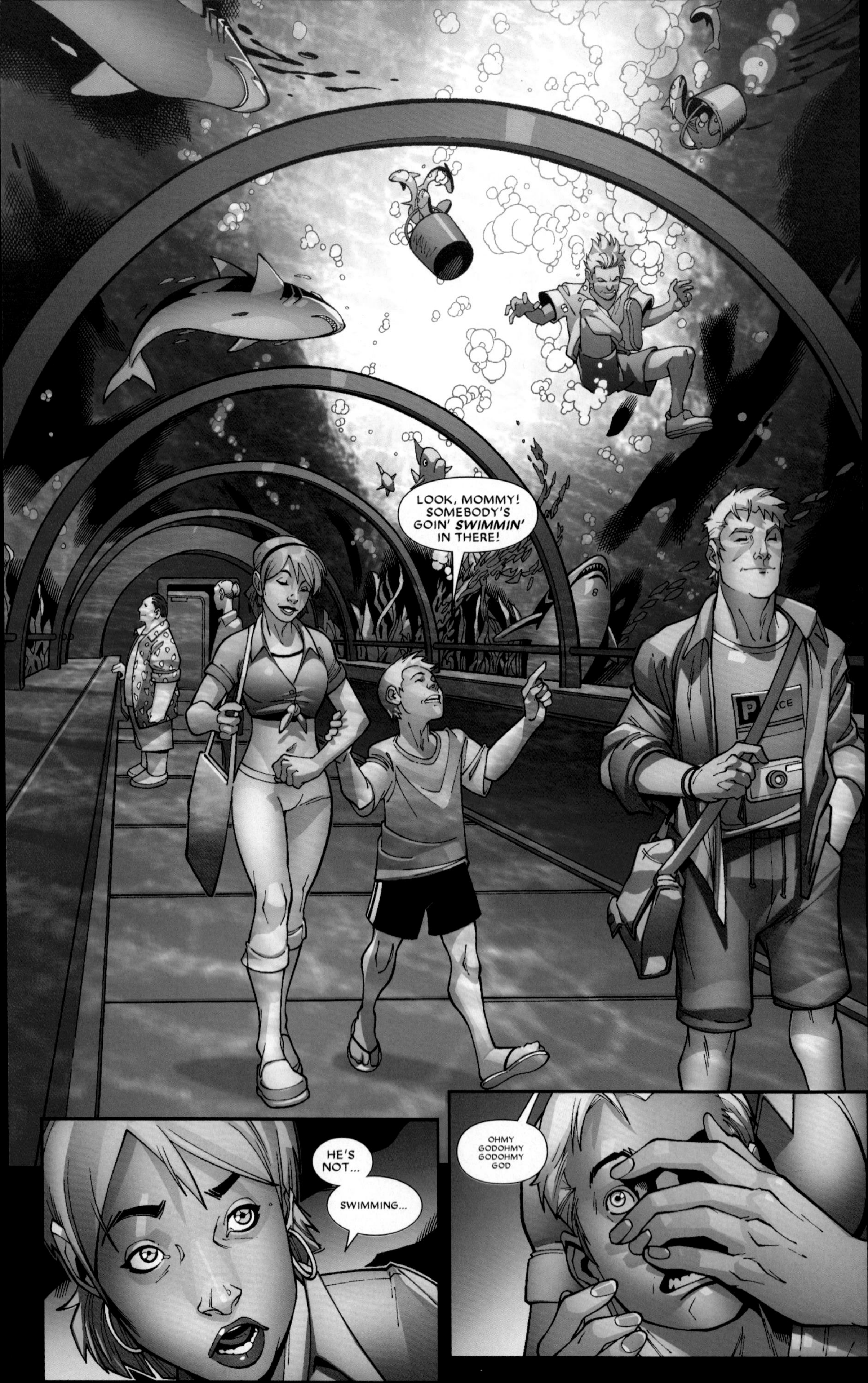
LOOK, MOMMY! SOMEBODY'S GOIN' *SWIMMIN'* IN THERE!
HE'S NOT...
SWIMMING...
OHMY GODOHMY GODOHMY GOD

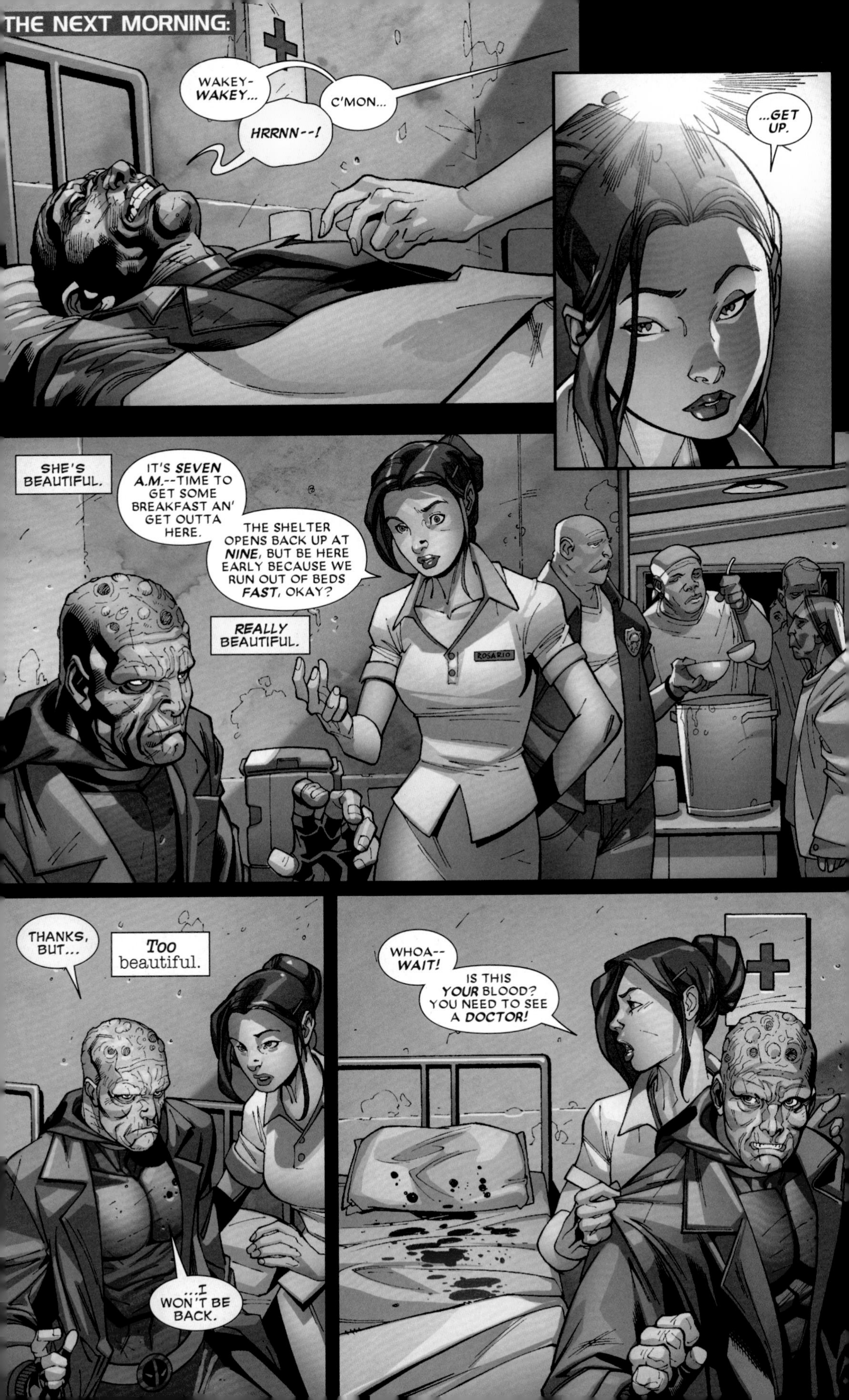
THE NEXT MORNING:
WAKEY-WAKEY...
HRRNN--!
C'MON...
...GET UP.
SHE'S BEAUTIFUL.
IT'S SEVEN A.M.--TIME TO GET SOME BREAKFAST AN' GET OUTTA HERE.
THE SHELTER OPENS BACK UP AT NINE, BUT BE HERE EARLY BECAUSE WE RUN OUT OF BEDS FAST, OKAY?
REALLY BEAUTIFUL.
ROSARIO
THANKS, BUT...
Too beautiful.
...I WON'T BE BACK.
WHOA--WAIT!
IS THIS YOUR BLOOD? YOU NEED TO SEE A DOCTOR!

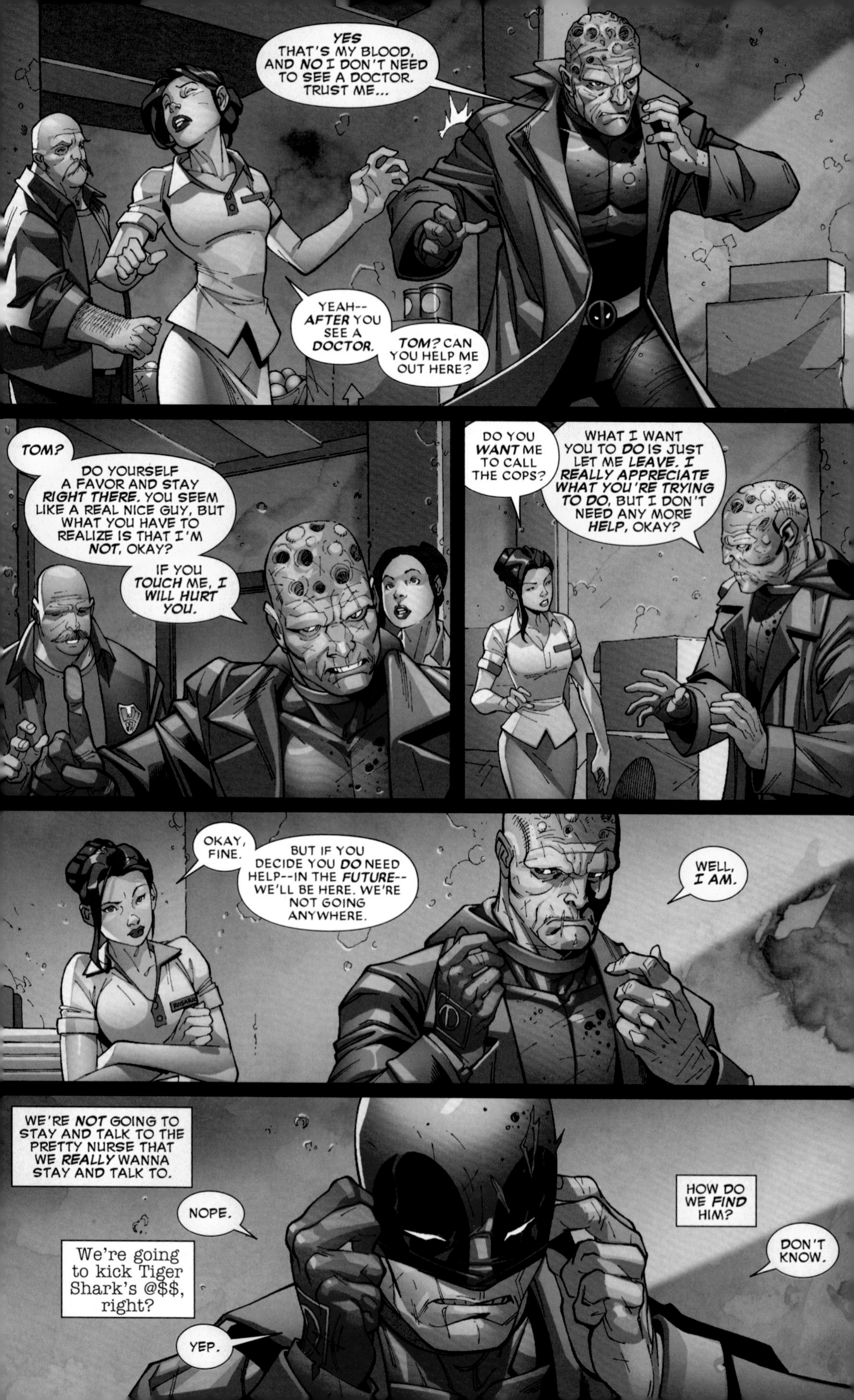

YES THAT'S MY BLOOD, AND NO I DON'T NEED TO SEE A DOCTOR. TRUST ME...
YEAH-- AFTER YOU SEE A DOCTOR.
TOM? CAN YOU HELP ME OUT HERE?
TOM?
DO YOURSELF A FAVOR AND STAY RIGHT THERE. YOU SEEM LIKE A REAL NICE GUY, BUT WHAT YOU HAVE TO REALIZE IS THAT I'M NOT, OKAY?
IF YOU TOUCH ME, I WILL HURT YOU.
DO YOU WANT ME TO CALL THE COPS?
WHAT I WANT YOU TO DO IS JUST LET ME LEAVE. I REALLY APPRECIATE WHAT YOU'RE TRYING TO DO, BUT I DON'T NEED ANY MORE HELP, OKAY?
OKAY, FINE.
BUT IF YOU DECIDE YOU DO NEED HELP--IN THE FUTURE-- WE'LL BE HERE. WE'RE NOT GOING ANYWHERE.
WELL, I AM.
WE'RE NOT GOING TO STAY AND TALK TO THE PRETTY NURSE THAT WE REALLY WANNA STAY AND TALK TO.
NOPE.
We're going to kick Tiger Shark's @$$, right?
YEP.
HOW DO WE FIND HIM?
DON'T KNOW.

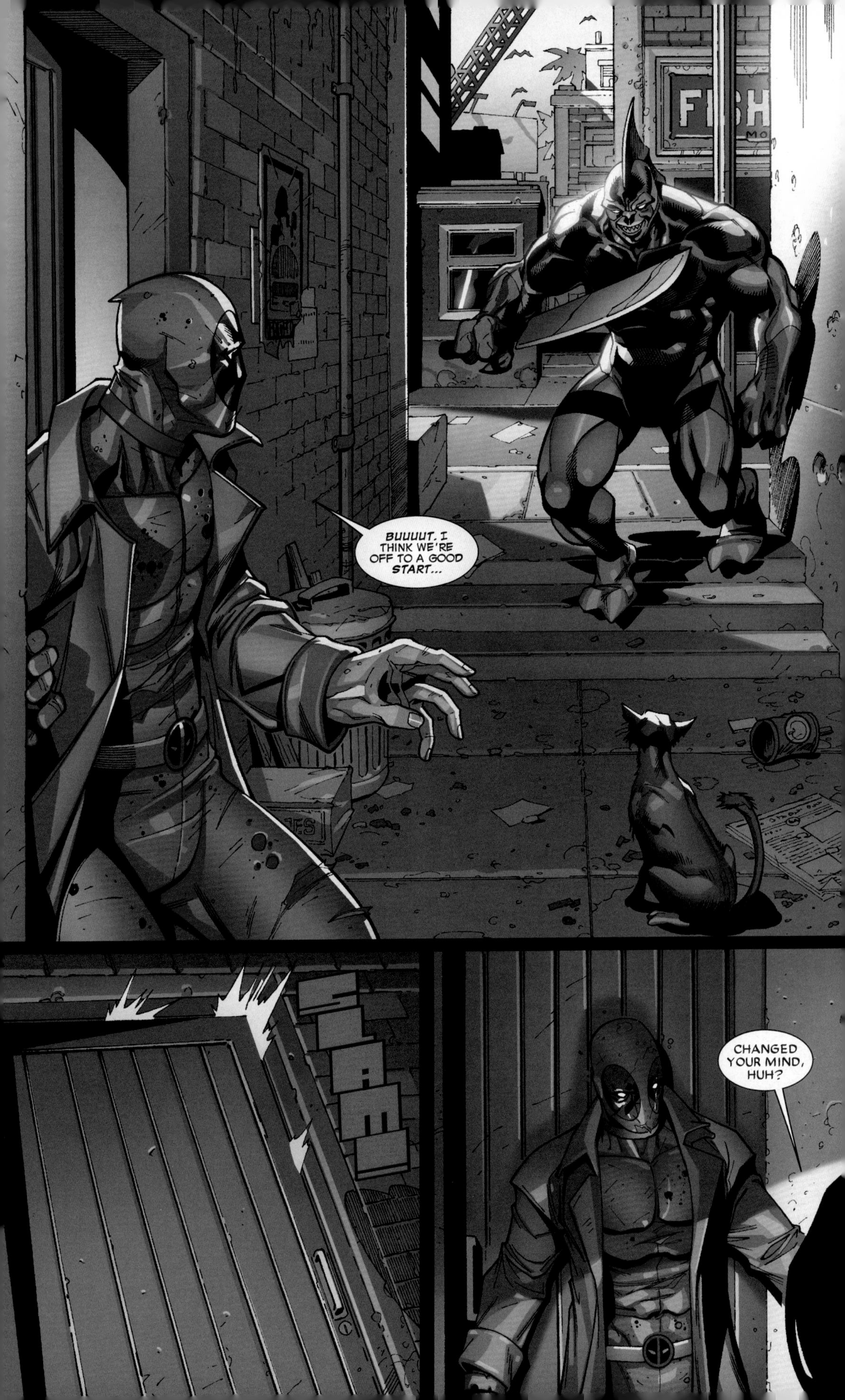
BUUUUT. I THINK WE'RE OFF TO A GOOD START...
SLAM
CHANGED YOUR MIND, HUH?

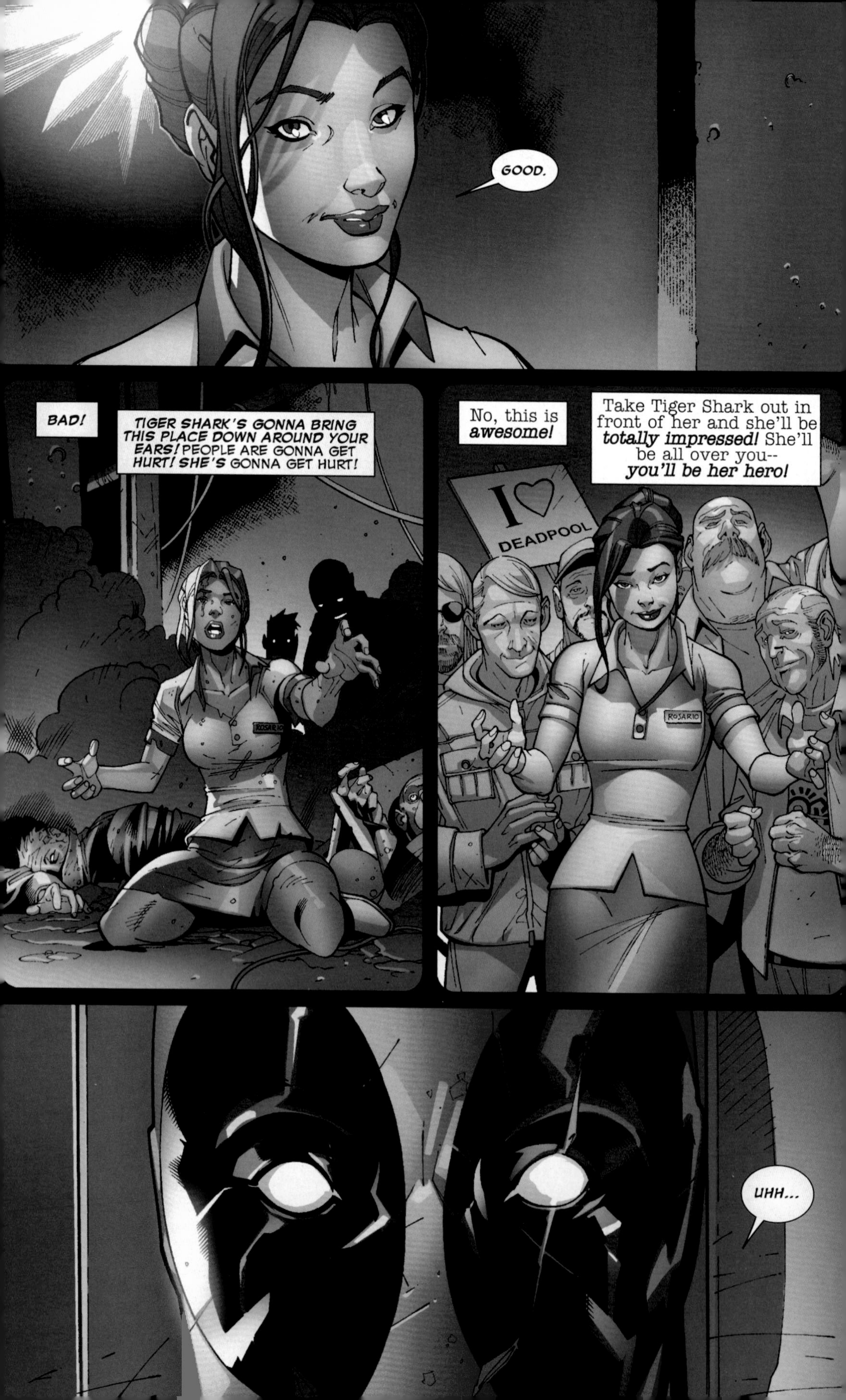
GOOD.
BAD!
TIGER SHARK'S GONNA BRING THIS PLACE DOWN AROUND YOUR EARS! PEOPLE ARE GONNA GET HURT! SHE'S GONNA GET HURT!
No, this is awesome!
Take Tiger Shark out in front of her and she'll be totally impressed! She'll be all over you-- you'll be her hero!
I ♥ DEADPOOL
ROSARIO
ROSARIO
UHH...

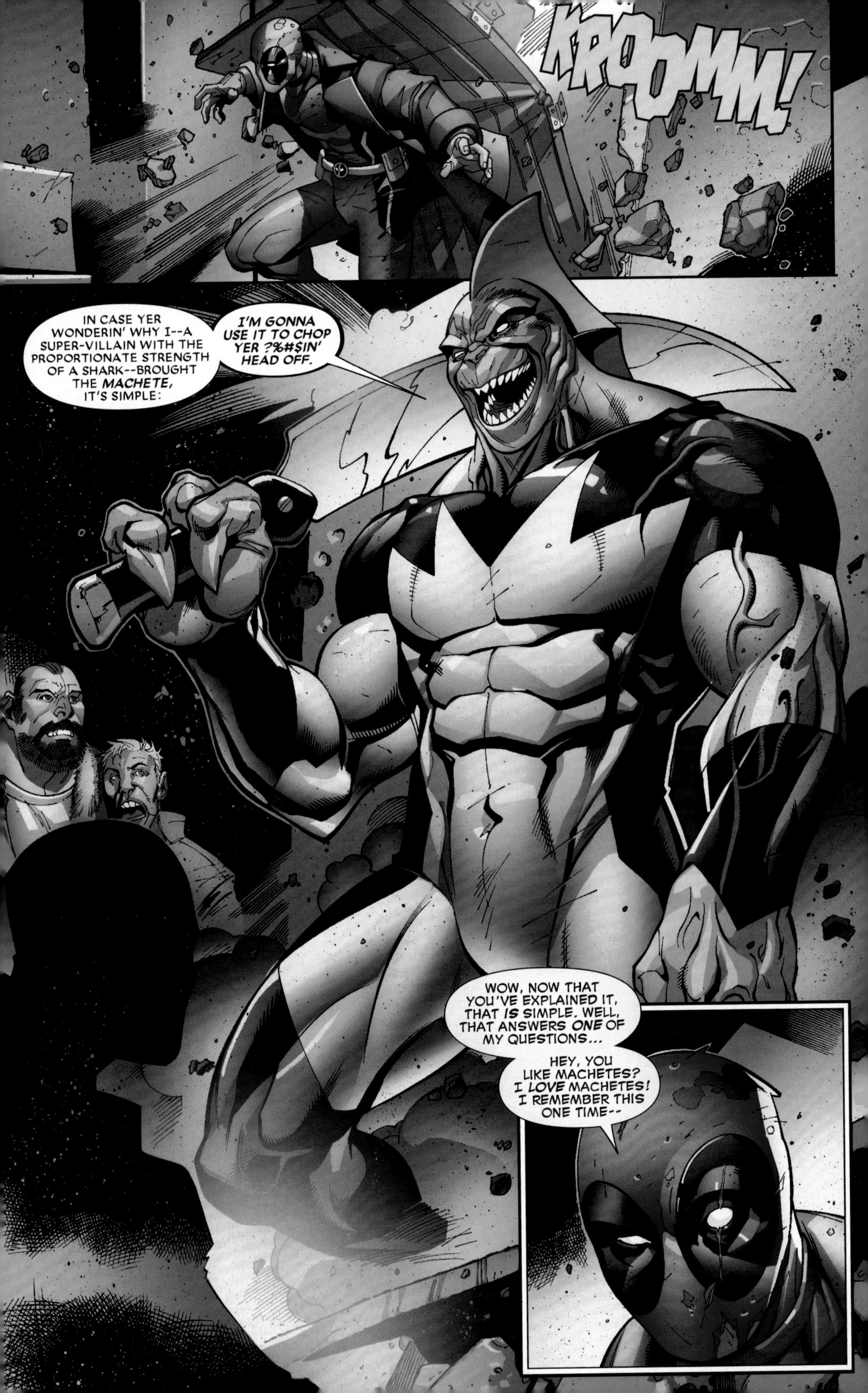
KROOMM!
IN CASE YER WONDERIN' WHY I--A SUPER-VILLAIN WITH THE PROPORTIONATE STRENGTH OF A SHARK--BROUGHT THE MACHETE, IT'S SIMPLE:
I'M GONNA USE IT TO CHOP YER ?%#$IN' HEAD OFF.
WOW, NOW THAT YOU'VE EXPLAINED IT, THAT IS SIMPLE. WELL, THAT ANSWERS ONE OF MY QUESTIONS...
HEY, YOU LIKE MACHETES? I LOVE MACHETES! I REMEMBER THIS ONE TIME--

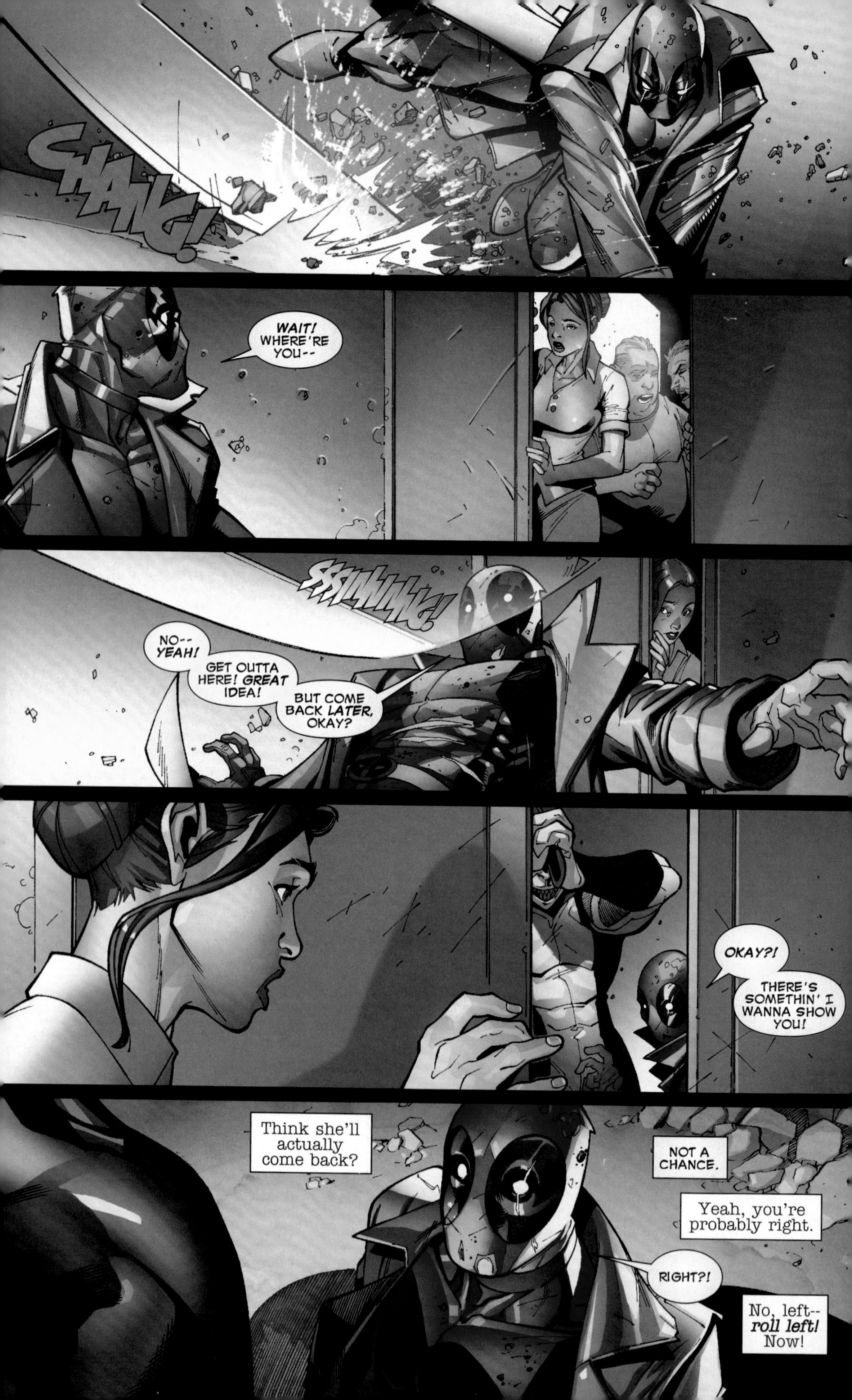
CHANG!
WAIT! WHERE'RE YOU--
SSSHHHHNG!
NO-- YEAH!
GET OUTTA HERE! GREAT IDEA!
BUT COME BACK LATER, OKAY?
OKAY?!
THERE'S SOMETHIN' I WANNA SHOW YOU!
Think she'll actually come back?
NOT A CHANCE.
Yeah, you're probably right.
RIGHT?!
No, left-- roll left! Now!

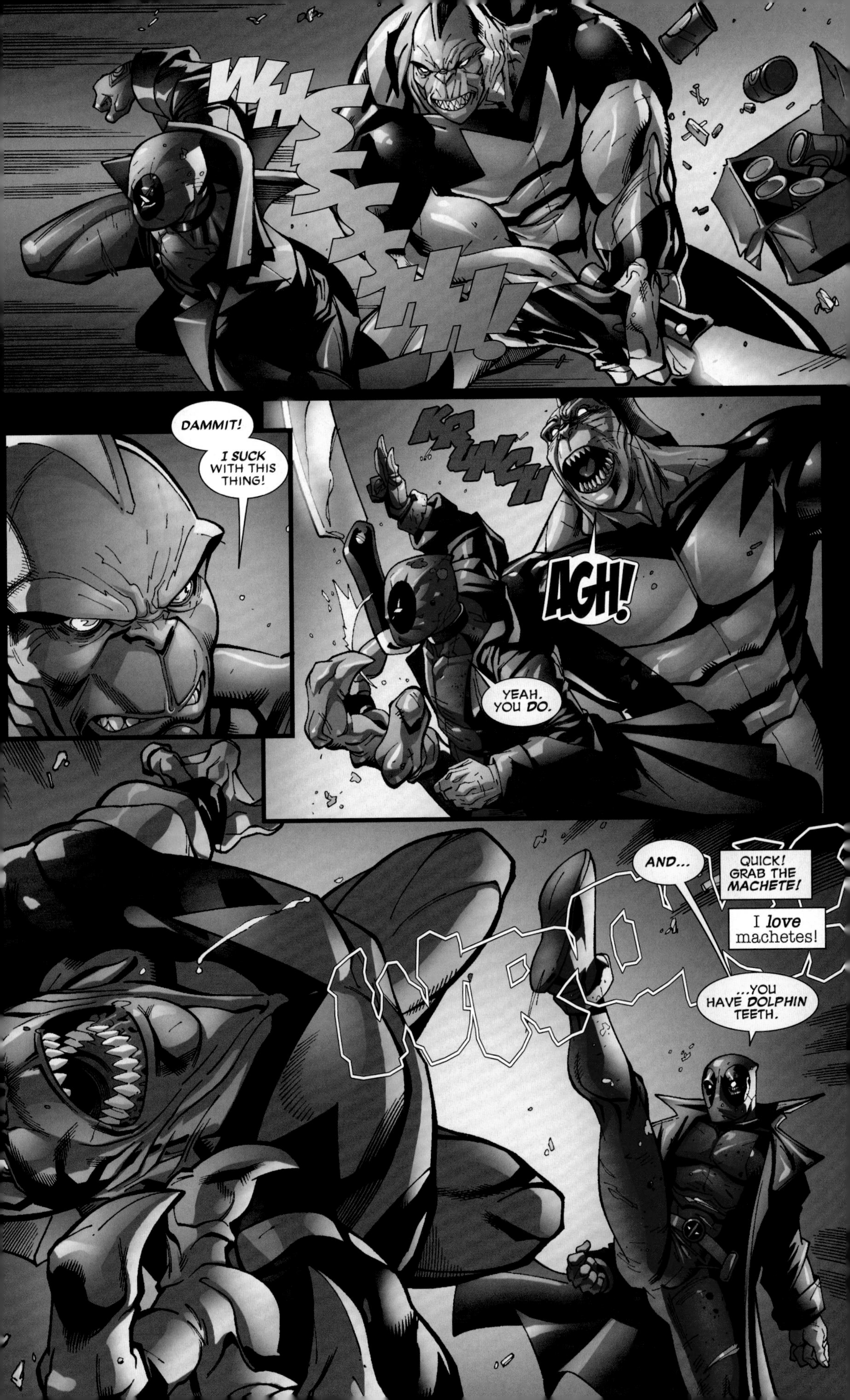
WHSSSHH!
DAMMIT!
I SUCK WITH THIS THING!
KRUNCH
AGH!
YEAH. YOU DO.
AND...
QUICK! GRAB THE MACHETE!
I love machetes!
...YOU HAVE DOLPHIN TEETH.

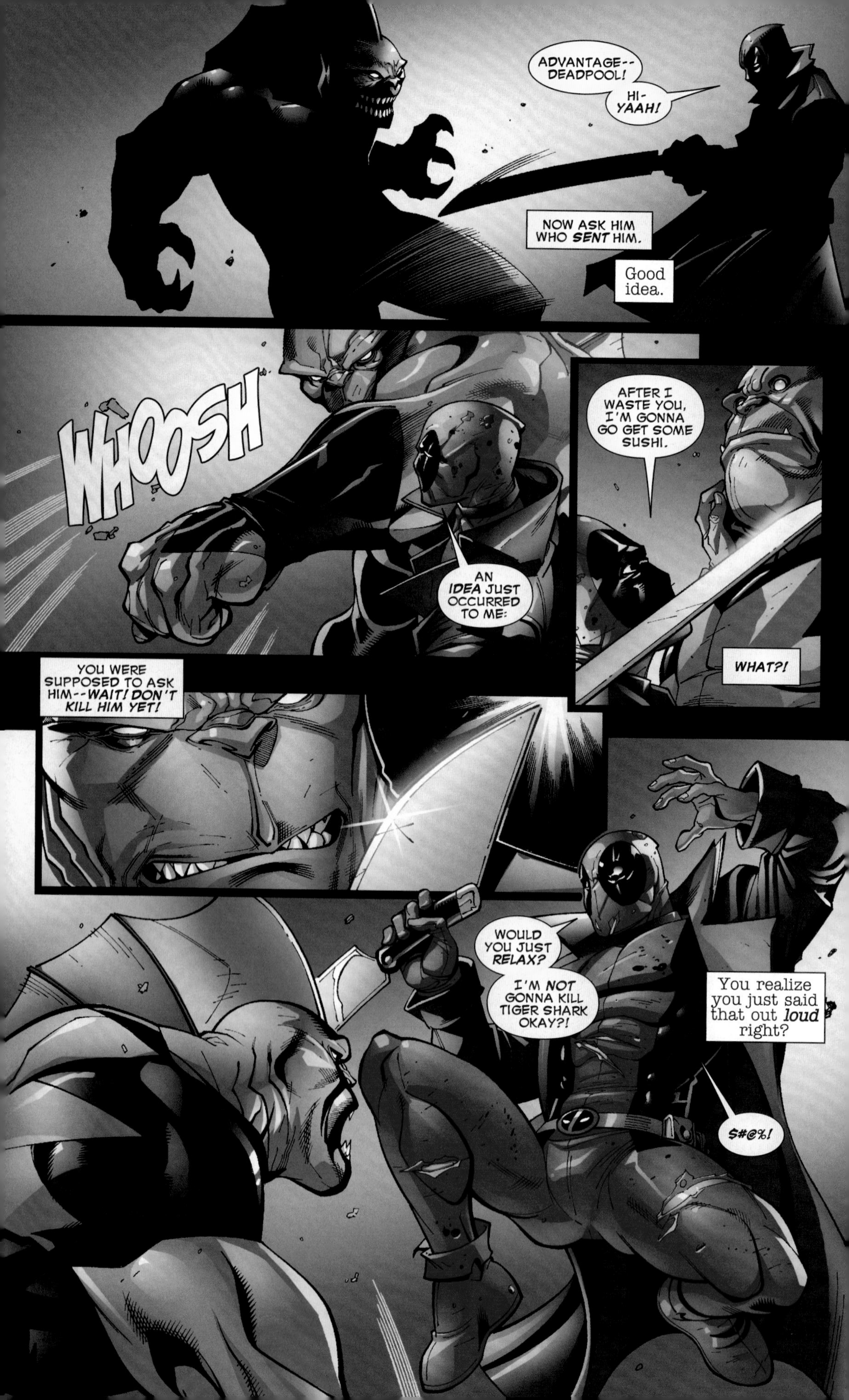
ADVANTAGE-- DEADPOOL!
HI- YAAH!
NOW ASK HIM WHO SENT HIM.
Good idea.
WHOOSH
AN IDEA JUST OCCURRED TO ME:
AFTER I WASTE YOU, I'M GONNA GO GET SOME SUSHI.
WHAT?!
YOU WERE SUPPOSED TO ASK HIM--WAIT! DON'T KILL HIM YET!
WOULD YOU JUST RELAX?
I'M NOT GONNA KILL TIGER SHARK OKAY?!
You realize you just said that out loud right?
$#@%!

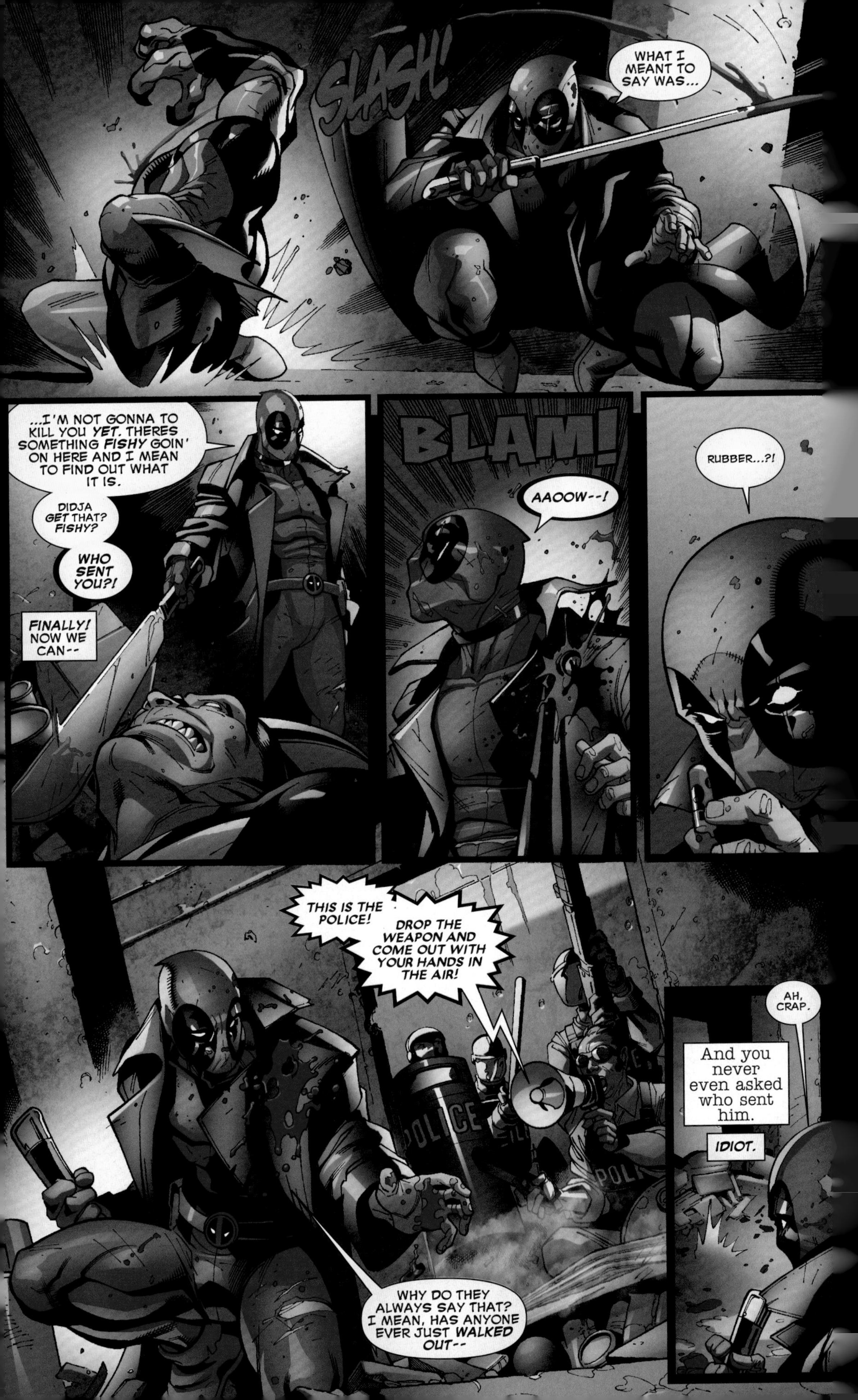
SLASH!
WHAT I MEANT TO SAY WAS...
...I'M NOT GONNA TO KILL YOU YET. THERES SOMETHING FISHY GOIN' ON HERE AND I MEAN TO FIND OUT WHAT IT IS.
DIDJA GET THAT? FISHY?
WHO SENT YOU?!
FINALLY! NOW WE CAN--
BLAM!
AAOOW--!
RUBBER...?!
THIS IS THE POLICE!
DROP THE WEAPON AND COME OUT WITH YOUR HANDS IN THE AIR!
WHY DO THEY ALWAYS SAY THAT? I MEAN, HAS ANYONE EVER JUST WALKED OUT--
AH, CRAP.
And you never even asked who sent him.
IDIOT.

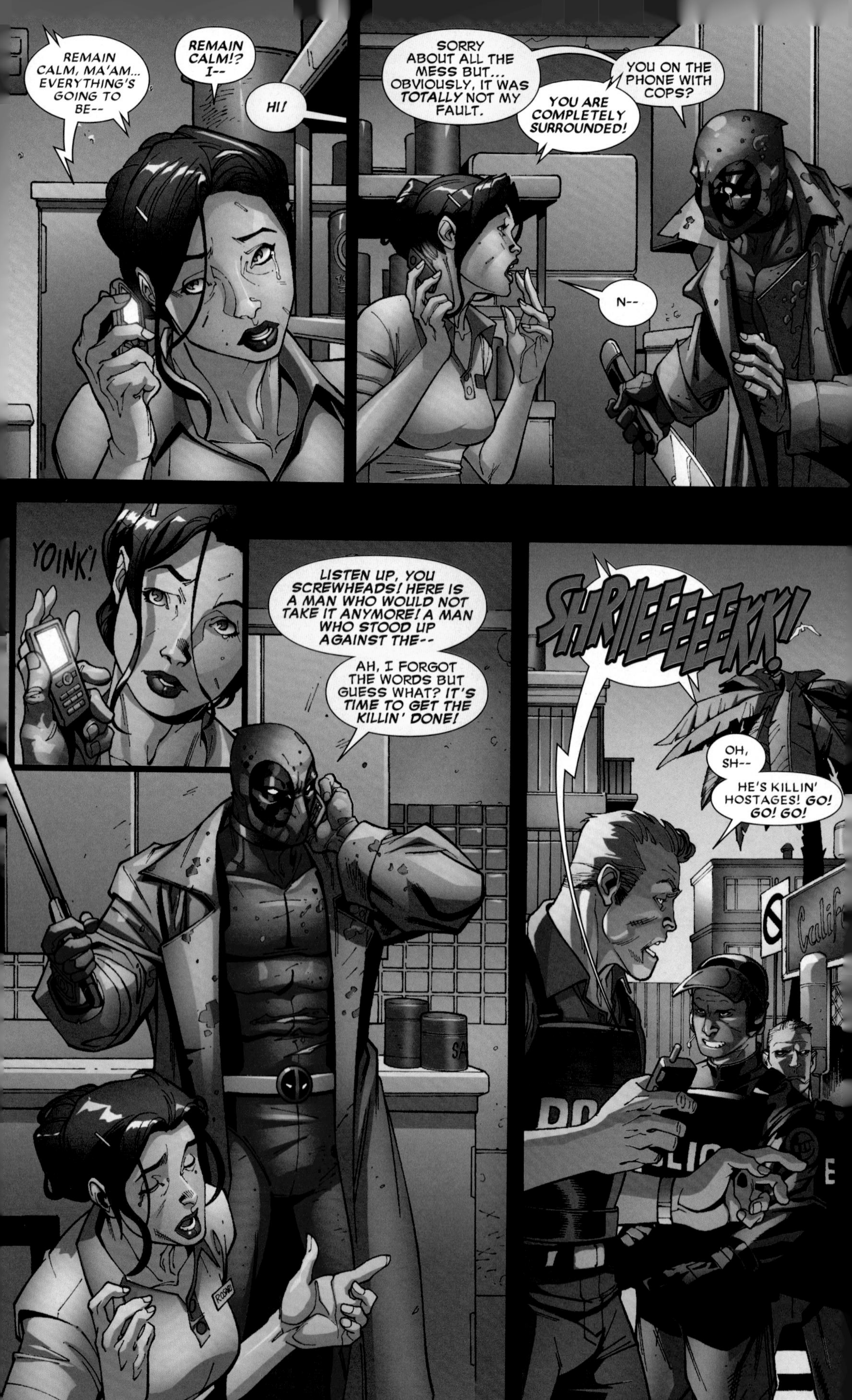
REMAIN CALM, MA'AM... EVERYTHING'S GOING TO BE--
REMAIN CALM!? I--
HI!
SORRY ABOUT ALL THE MESS BUT... OBVIOUSLY, IT WAS TOTALLY NOT MY FAULT.
YOU ON THE PHONE WITH COPS?
YOU ARE COMPLETELY SURROUNDED!
N--
YOINK!
LISTEN UP, YOU SCREWHEADS! HERE IS A MAN WHO WOULD NOT TAKE IT ANYMORE! A MAN WHO STOOD UP AGAINST THE--
AH, I FORGOT THE WORDS BUT GUESS WHAT? IT'S TIME TO GET THE KILLIN' DONE!
SHRIEEEEEKK!
OH, SH--
HE'S KILLIN' HOSTAGES! GO! GO! GO!

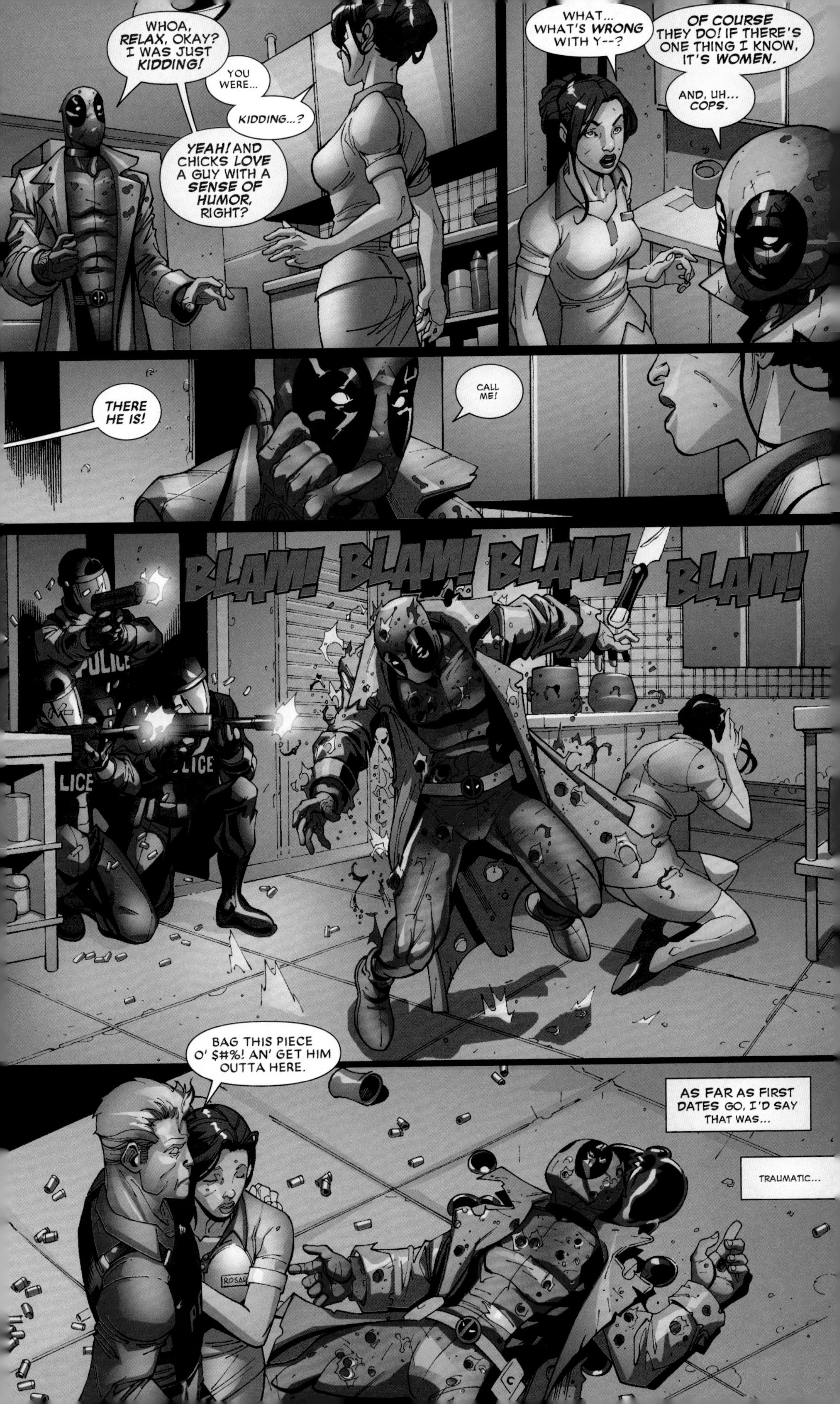
WHOA, RELAX, OKAY? I WAS JUST KIDDING!
YOU WERE...
KIDDING...?
YEAH! AND CHICKS LOVE A GUY WITH A SENSE OF HUMOR, RIGHT?
WHAT... WHAT'S WRONG WITH Y--?
OF COURSE THEY DO! IF THERE'S ONE THING I KNOW, IT'S WOMEN.
AND, UH... COPS.
THERE HE IS!
CALL ME!
BLAM! BLAM! BLAM! BLAM!
POLICE
LICE
LICE
BAG THIS PIECE O' $#%! AN' GET HIM OUTTA HERE.
AS FAR AS FIRST DATES GO, I'D SAY THAT WAS...
TRAUMATIC...

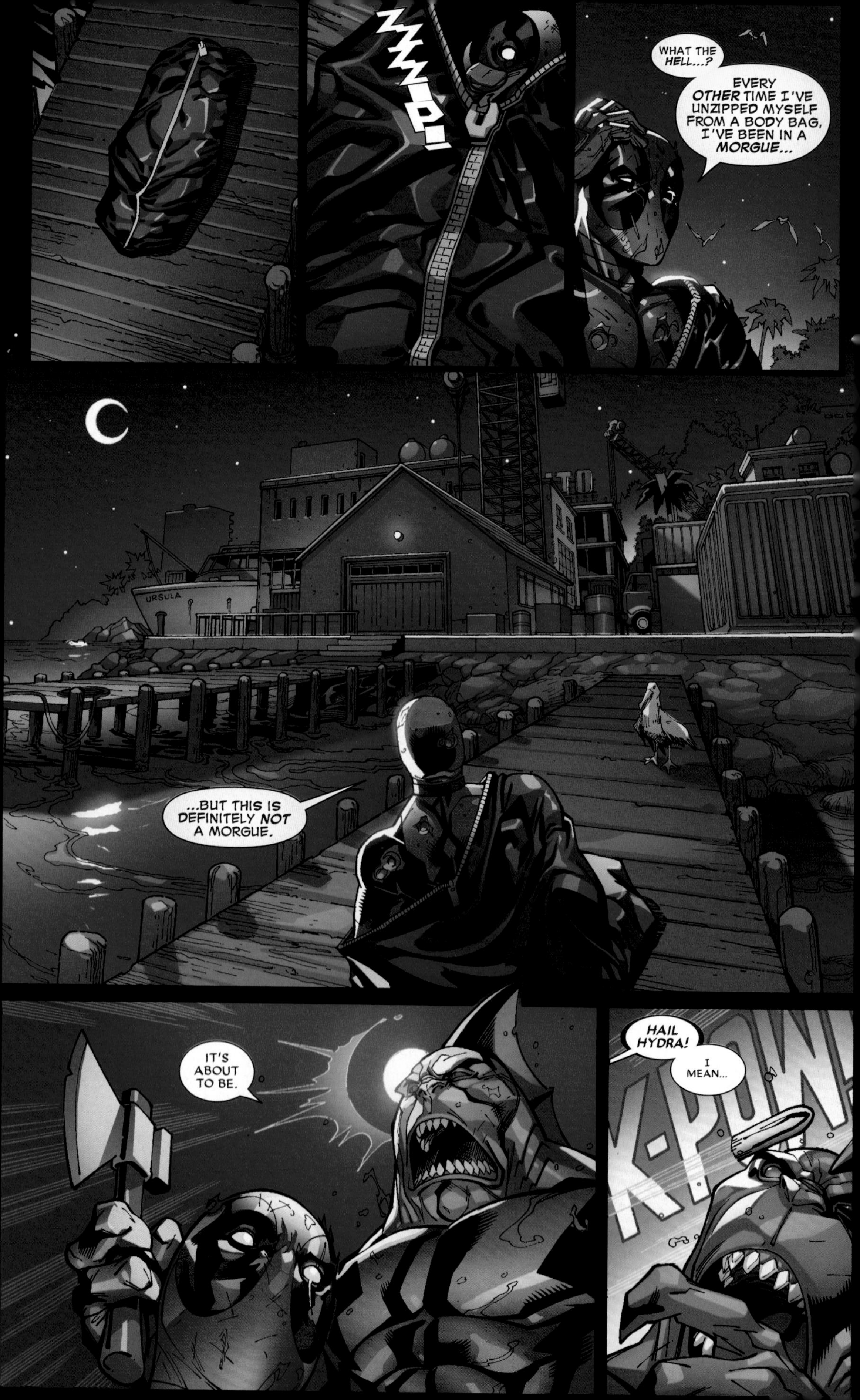
ZZZIP!
WHAT THE HELL...?
EVERY OTHER TIME I'VE UNZIPPED MYSELF FROM A BODY BAG, I'VE BEEN IN A MORGUE...
URSULA
...BUT THIS IS DEFINITELY NOT A MORGUE.
IT'S ABOUT TO BE.
HAIL HYDRA!
I MEAN...
K-POW!

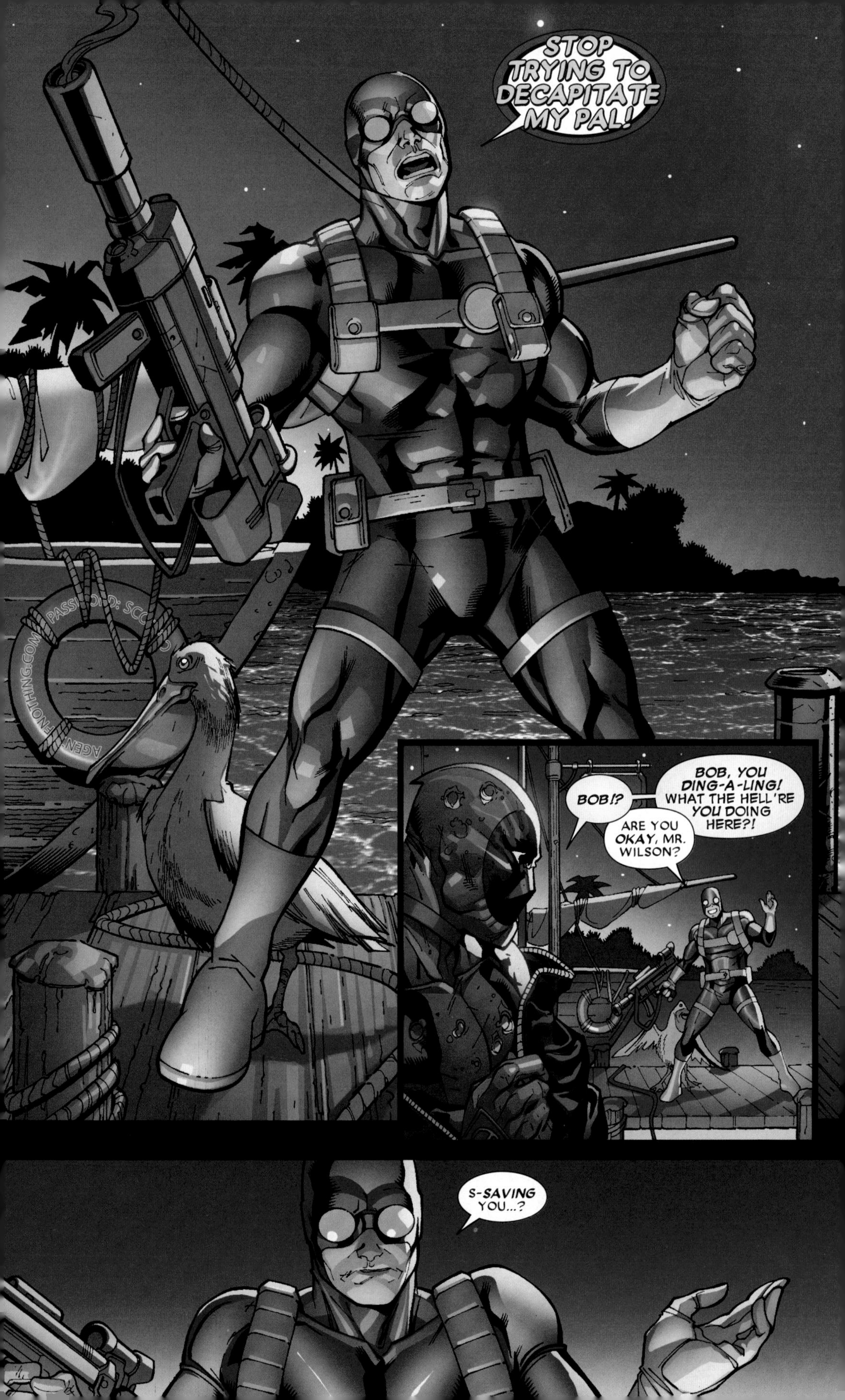
STOP TRYING TO DECAPITATE MY PAL!
BOB!?
BOB, YOU DING-A-LING! WHAT THE HELL'RE YOU DOING HERE?!
ARE YOU OKAY, MR. WILSON?
S-SAVING YOU...?

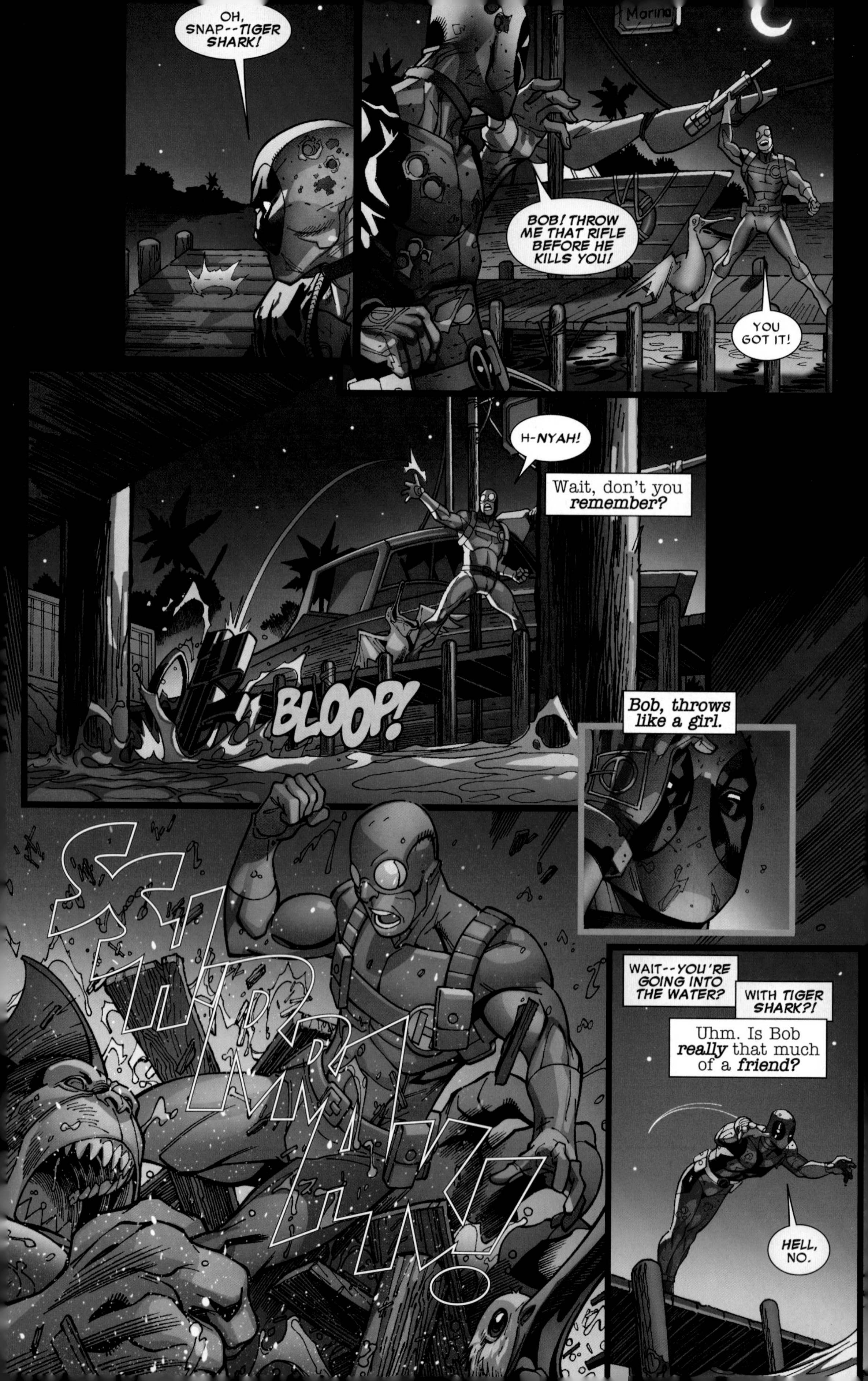

OH, SNAP--TIGER SHARK!
Marina
BOB! THROW ME THAT RIFLE BEFORE HE KILLS YOU!
YOU GOT IT!
H-NYAH!
Wait, don't you remember?
BLOOP!
Bob, throws like a girl.
WAIT--YOU'RE GOING INTO THE WATER?
WITH TIGER SHARK?!
Uhm. Is Bob really that much of a friend?
HELL, NO.

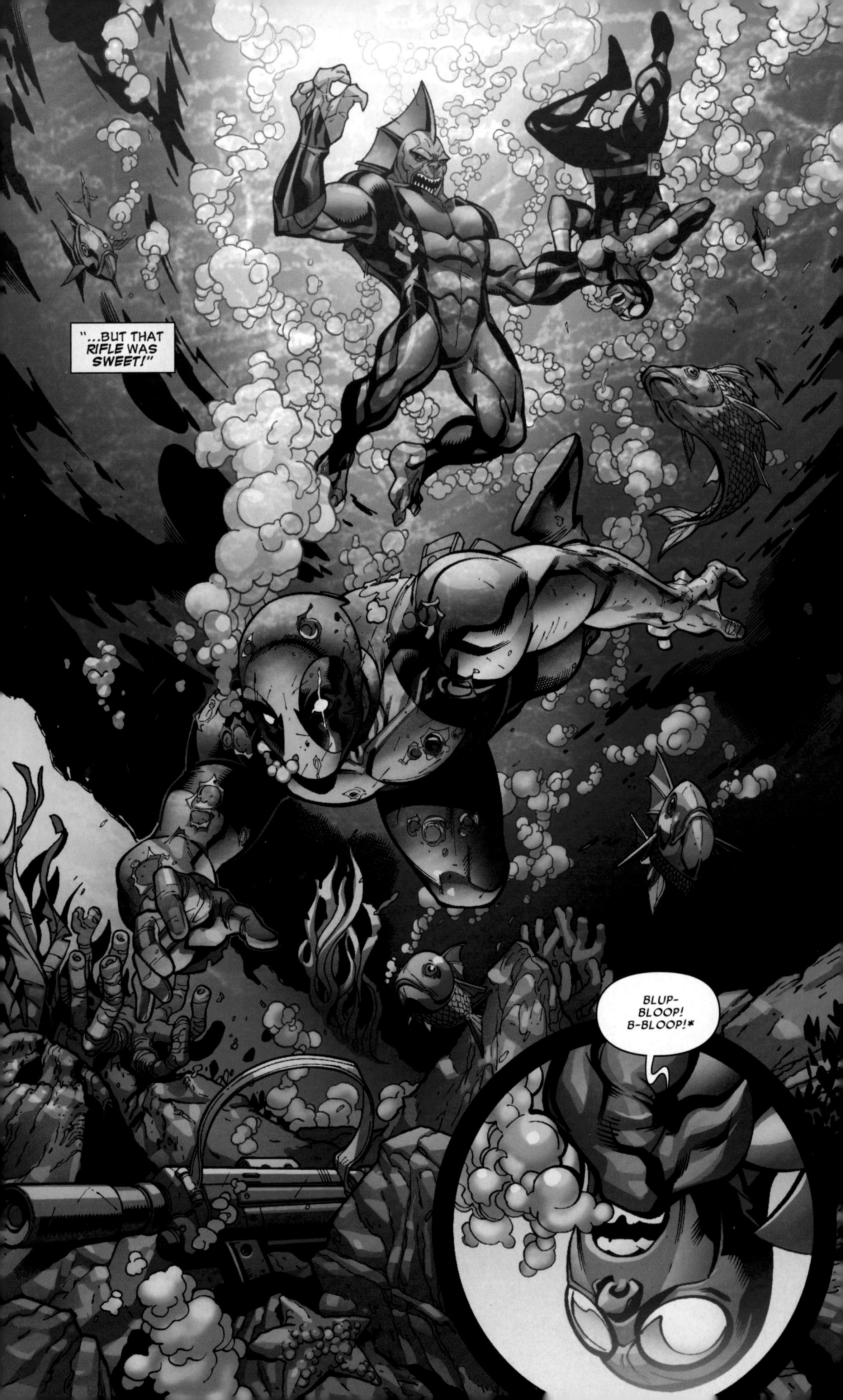
"...BUT THAT RIFLE WAS SWEET!"
BLUP-BLOOP! B-BLOOP!*

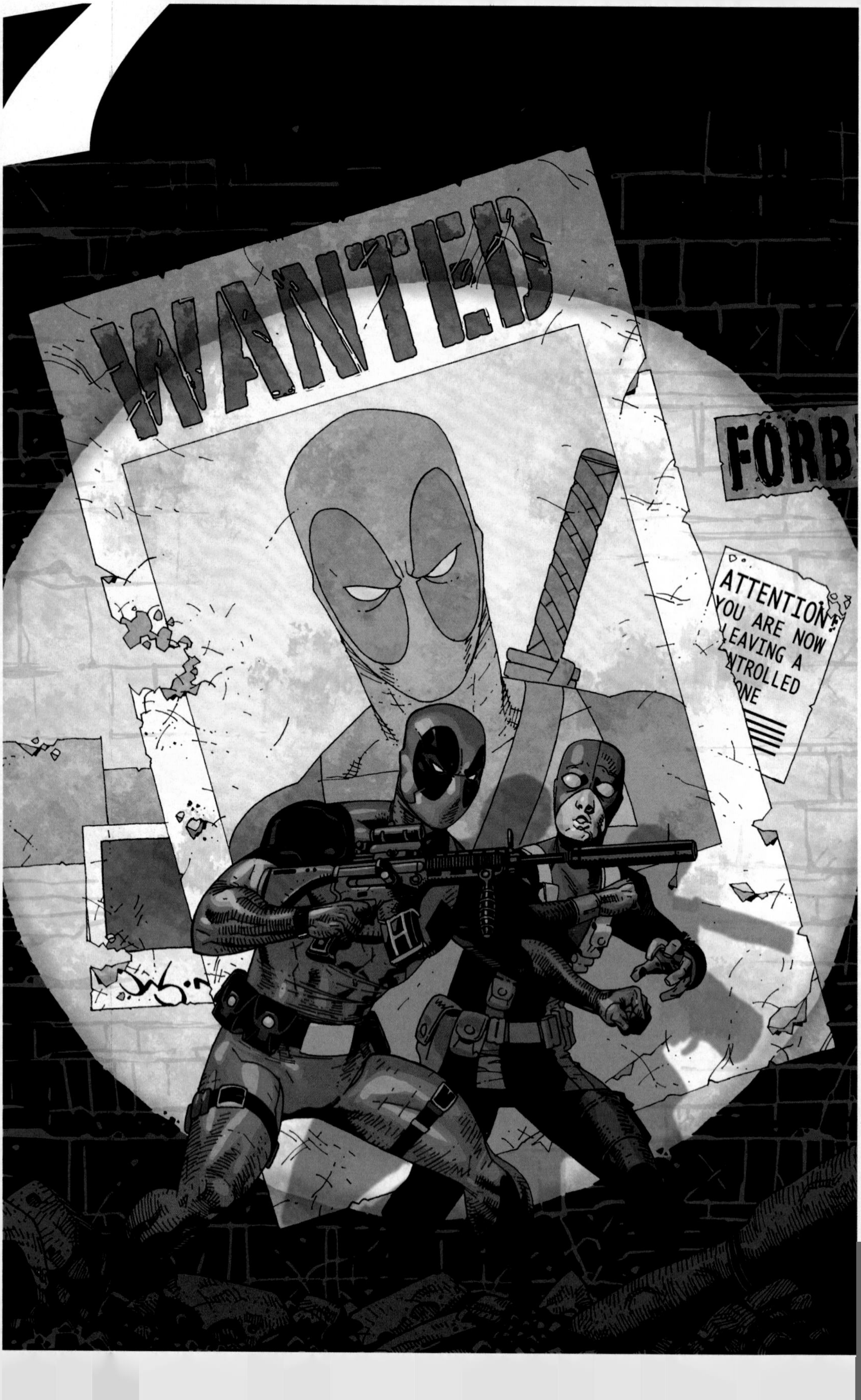
WANTED
FORB
ATTENTION!
YOU ARE NOW
LEAVING A
NTROLLED
ONE

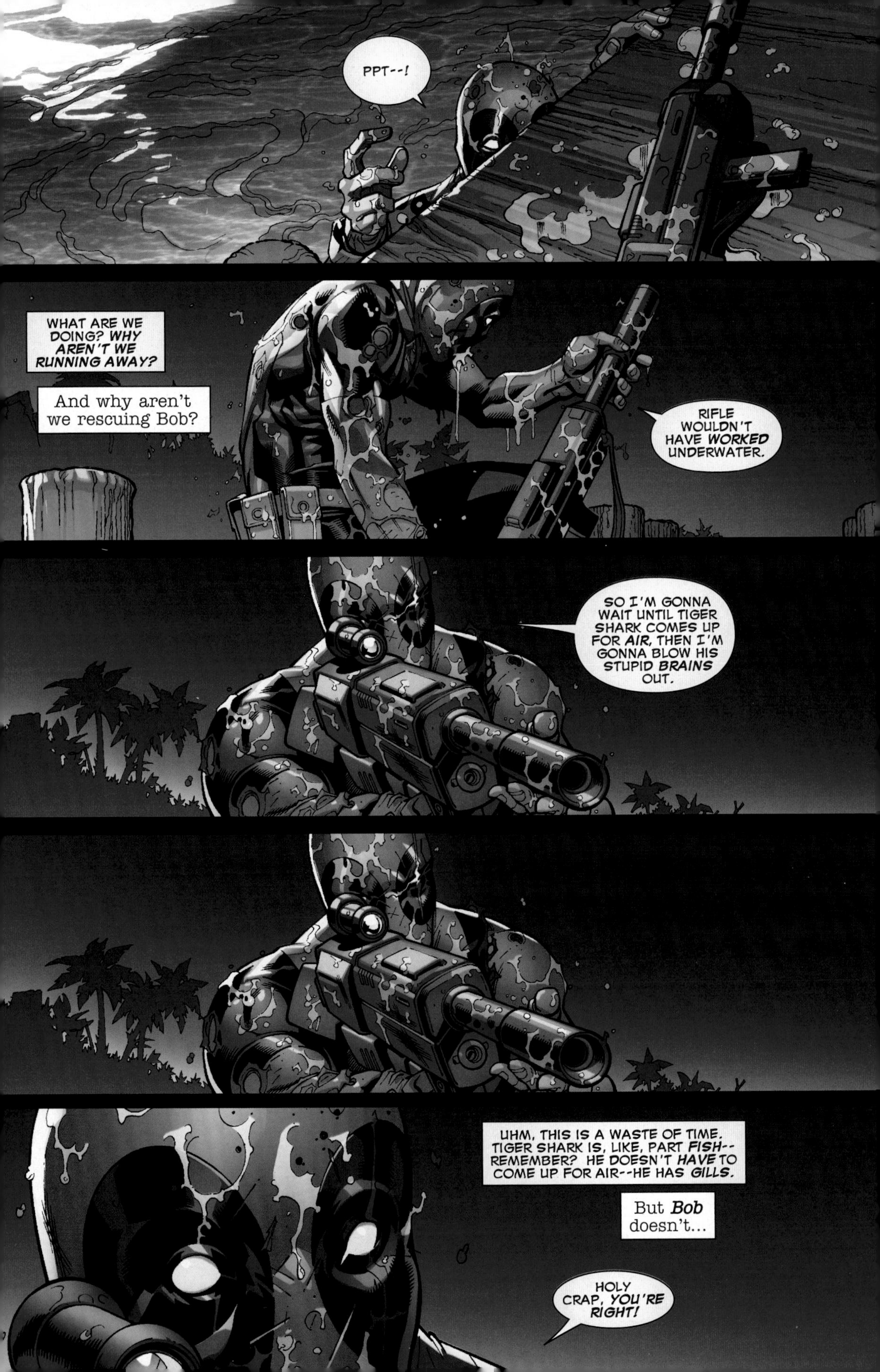
PPT--!
WHAT ARE WE DOING? WHY AREN'T WE RUNNING AWAY?
And why aren't we rescuing Bob?
RIFLE WOULDN'T HAVE WORKED UNDERWATER.
SO I'M GONNA WAIT UNTIL TIGER SHARK COMES UP FOR AIR, THEN I'M GONNA BLOW HIS STUPID BRAINS OUT.
UHM, THIS IS A WASTE OF TIME. TIGER SHARK IS, LIKE, PART FISH--REMEMBER? HE DOESN'T HAVE TO COME UP FOR AIR--HE HAS GILLS.
But Bob doesn't...
HOLY CRAP, YOU'RE RIGHT!

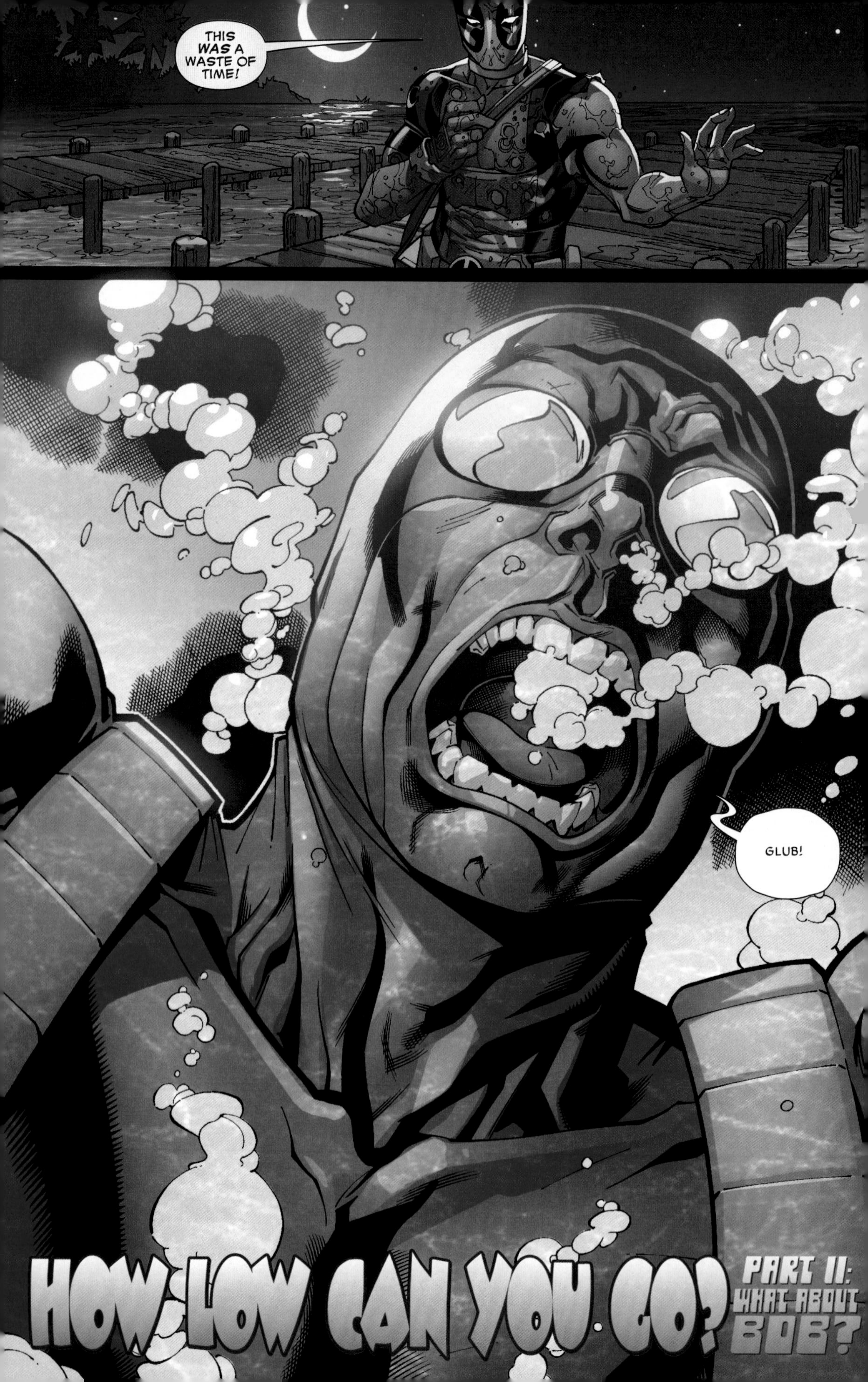
THIS WAS A WASTE OF TIME!
GLUB!
HOW LOW CAN YOU GO?
PART II: WHAT ABOUT BOB?

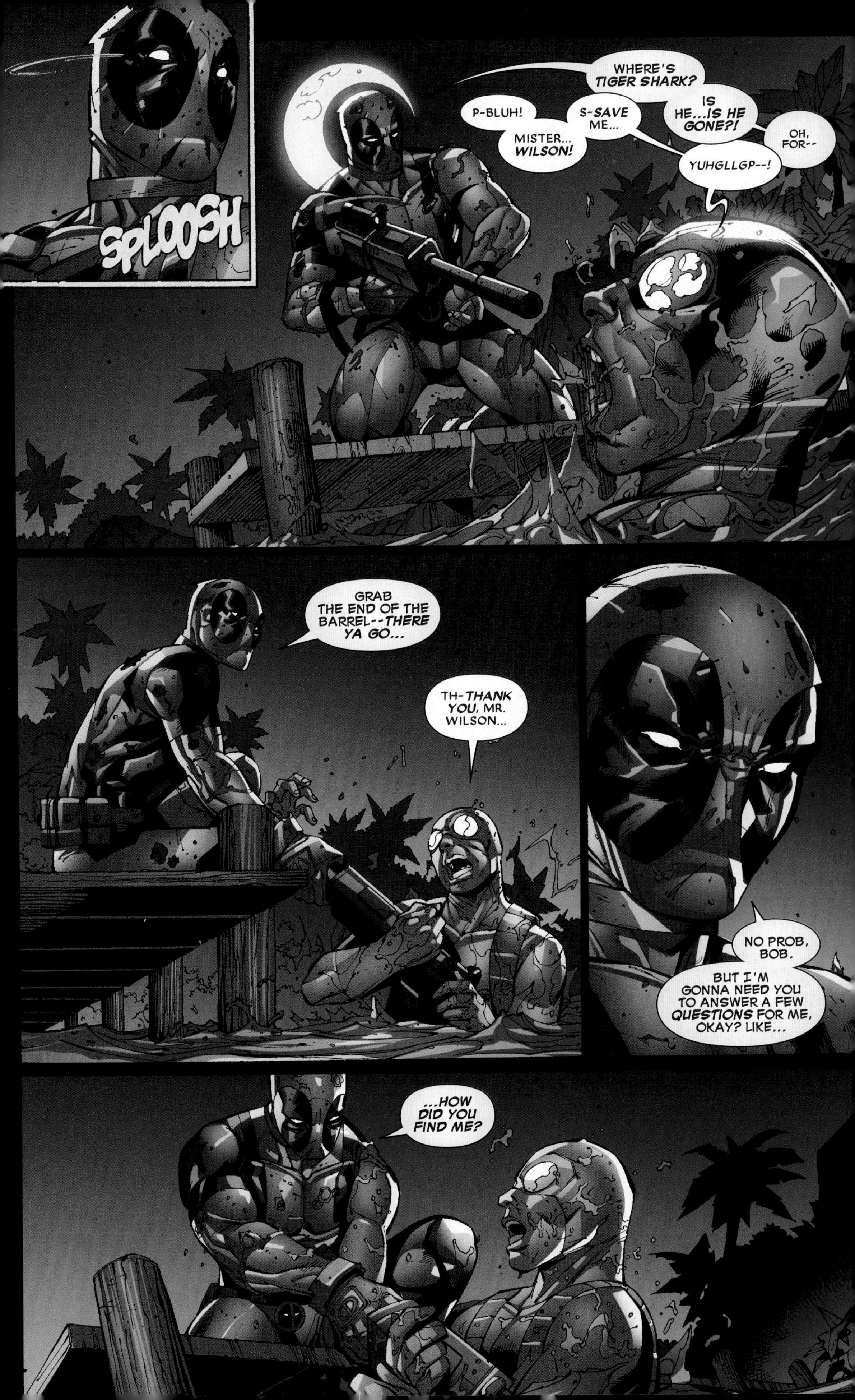
SPLOOSH
P-BLUH!
MISTER... WILSON!
S-SAVE ME...
WHERE'S TIGER SHARK?
IS HE...IS HE GONE?!
YUHGLLGP--!
OH, FOR--
GRAB THE END OF THE BARREL--THERE YA GO...
TH-THANK YOU, MR. WILSON...
NO PROB, BOB.
BUT I'M GONNA NEED YOU TO ANSWER A FEW QUESTIONS FOR ME, OKAY? LIKE...
...HOW DID YOU FIND ME?

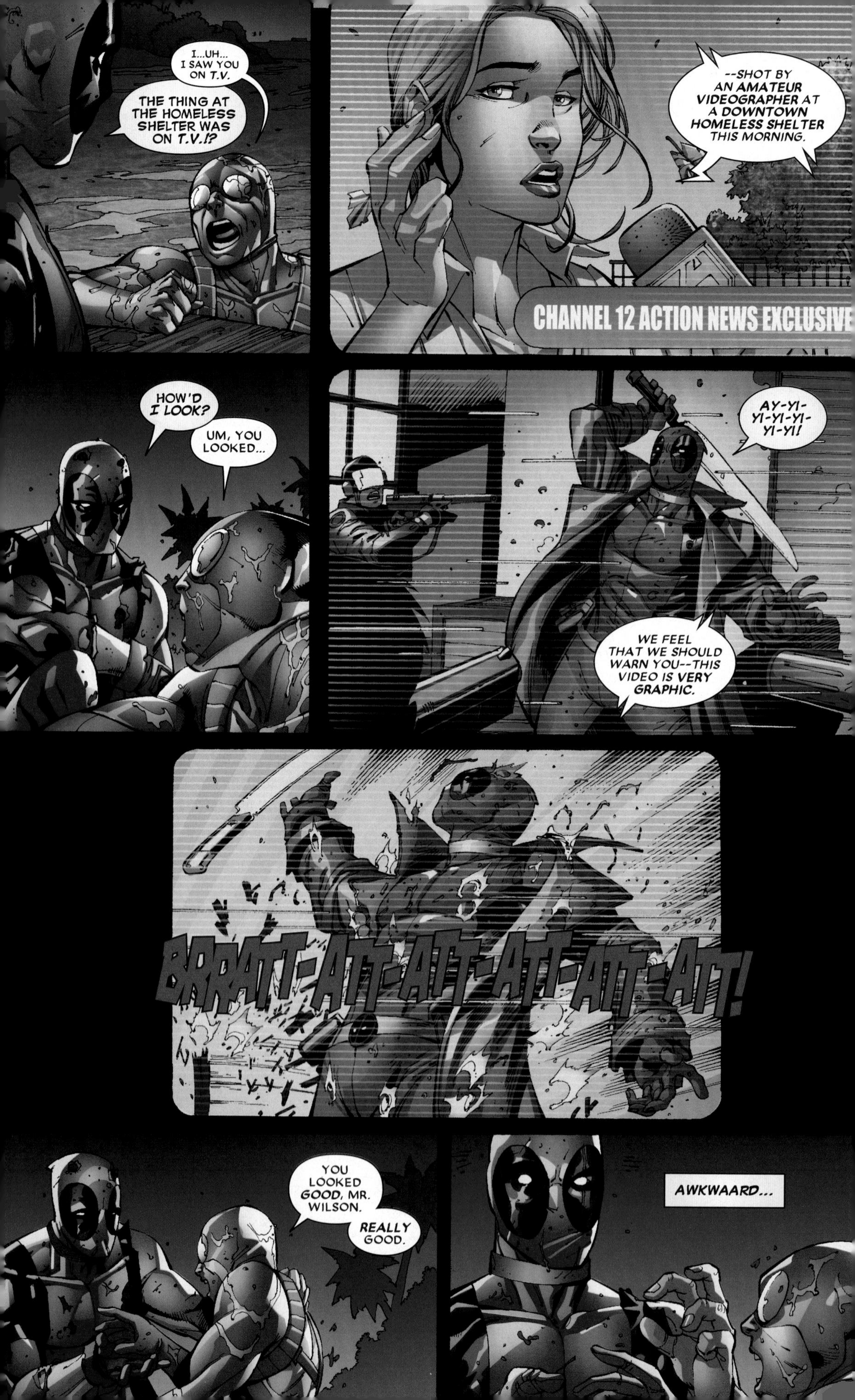
I...UH... I SAW YOU ON T.V.
THE THING AT THE HOMELESS SHELTER WAS ON T.V.!?
--SHOT BY AN AMATEUR VIDEOGRAPHER AT A DOWNTOWN HOMELESS SHELTER THIS MORNING.
CHANNEL 12 ACTION NEWS EXCLUSIVE
HOW'D I LOOK?
UM, YOU LOOKED...
AY-YI-YI-YI-YI-YI-YI!
WE FEEL THAT WE SHOULD WARN YOU--THIS VIDEO IS VERY GRAPHIC.
BRRATT-ATT-ATT-ATT-ATT-ATT!
YOU LOOKED GOOD, MR. WILSON.
REALLY GOOD.
AWKWAARD...

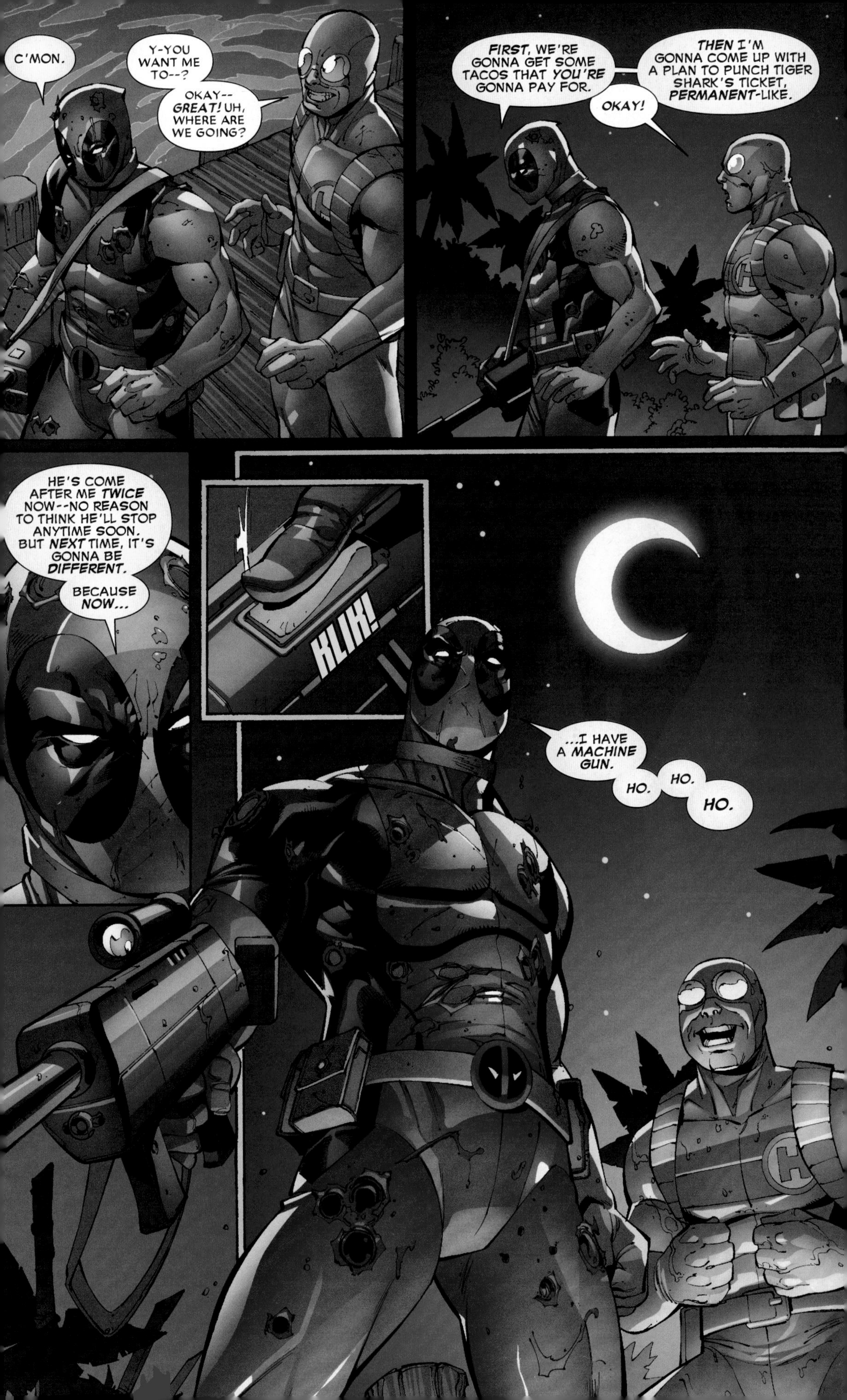
C'MON.
Y-YOU WANT ME TO--?
OKAY-- GREAT! UH, WHERE ARE WE GOING?
FIRST, WE'RE GONNA GET SOME TACOS THAT YOU'RE GONNA PAY FOR.
THEN I'M GONNA COME UP WITH A PLAN TO PUNCH TIGER SHARK'S TICKET, PERMANENT-LIKE.
OKAY!
HE'S COME AFTER ME TWICE NOW--NO REASON TO THINK HE'LL STOP ANYTIME SOON. BUT NEXT TIME, IT'S GONNA BE DIFFERENT.
BECAUSE NOW...
KLIK!
...I HAVE A MACHINE GUN.
HO.
HO.
HO.

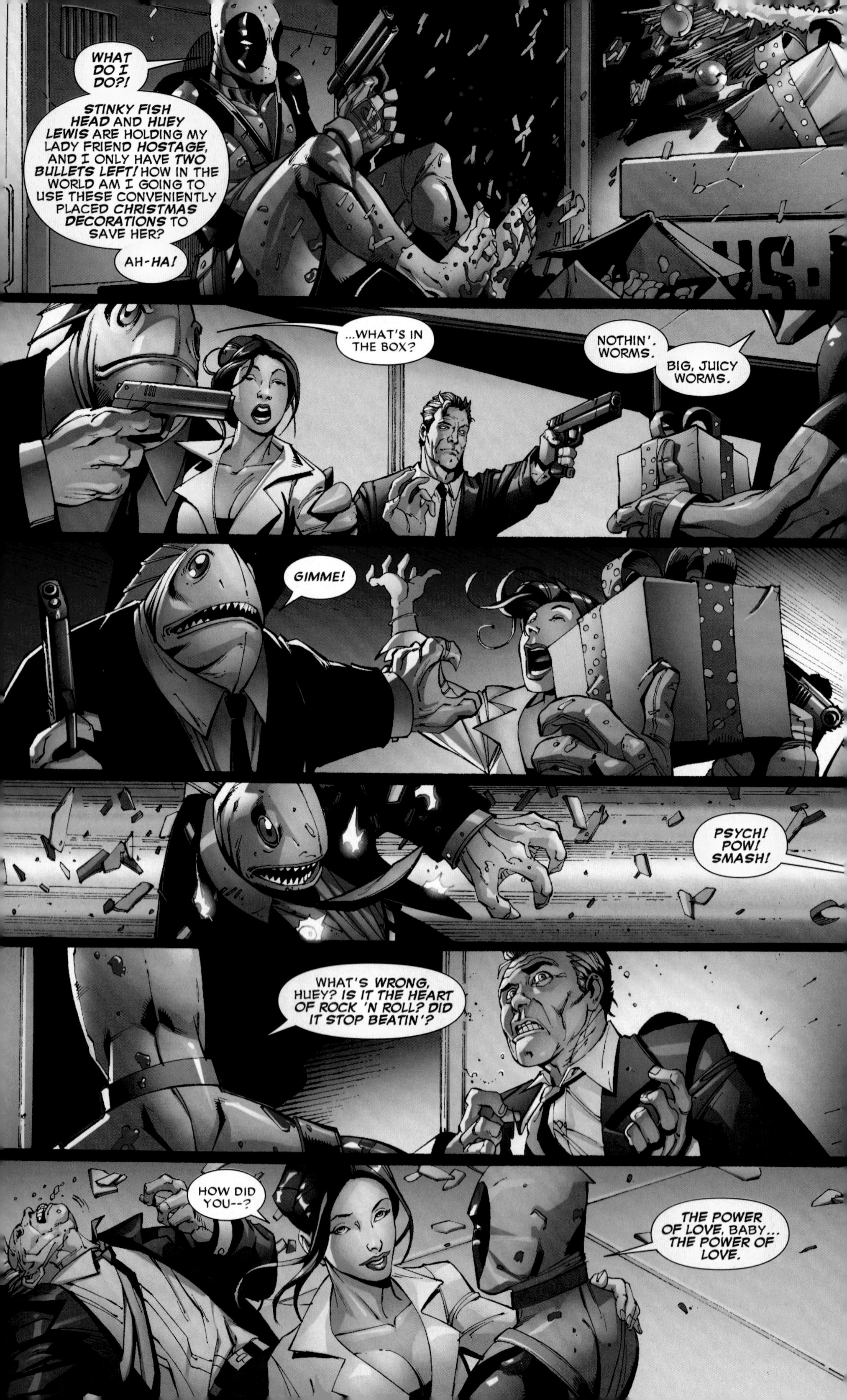
WHAT DO I DO?!
STINKY FISH HEAD AND HUEY LEWIS ARE HOLDING MY LADY FRIEND HOSTAGE, AND I ONLY HAVE TWO BULLETS LEFT! HOW IN THE WORLD AM I GOING TO USE THESE CONVENIENTLY PLACED CHRISTMAS DECORATIONS TO SAVE HER?
AH-HA!
...WHAT'S IN THE BOX?
NOTHIN'. WORMS.
BIG, JUICY WORMS.
GIMME!
PSYCH! POW! SMASH!
WHAT'S WRONG, HUEY? IS IT THE HEART OF ROCK 'N ROLL? DID IT STOP BEATIN'?
HOW DID YOU--?
THE POWER OF LOVE, BABY... THE POWER OF LOVE.

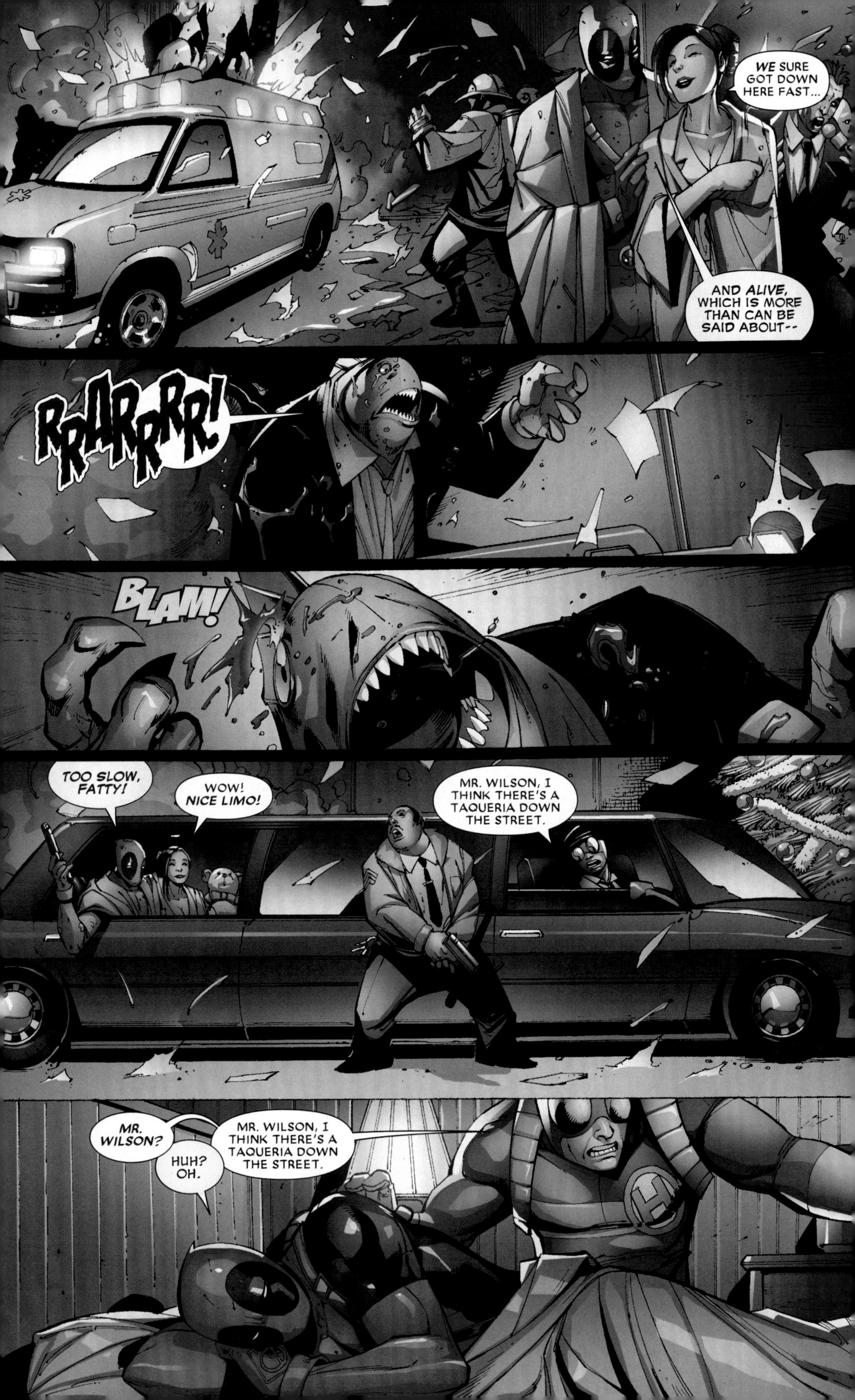
WE SURE GOT DOWN HERE FAST...
AND ALIVE, WHICH IS MORE THAN CAN BE SAID ABOUT--
RRARRRR!
BLAM!
TOO SLOW, FATTY!
WOW! NICE LIMO!
MR. WILSON, I THINK THERE'S A TAQUERIA DOWN THE STREET.
MR. WILSON?
HUH? OH.
MR. WILSON, I THINK THERE'S A TAQUERIA DOWN THE STREET.

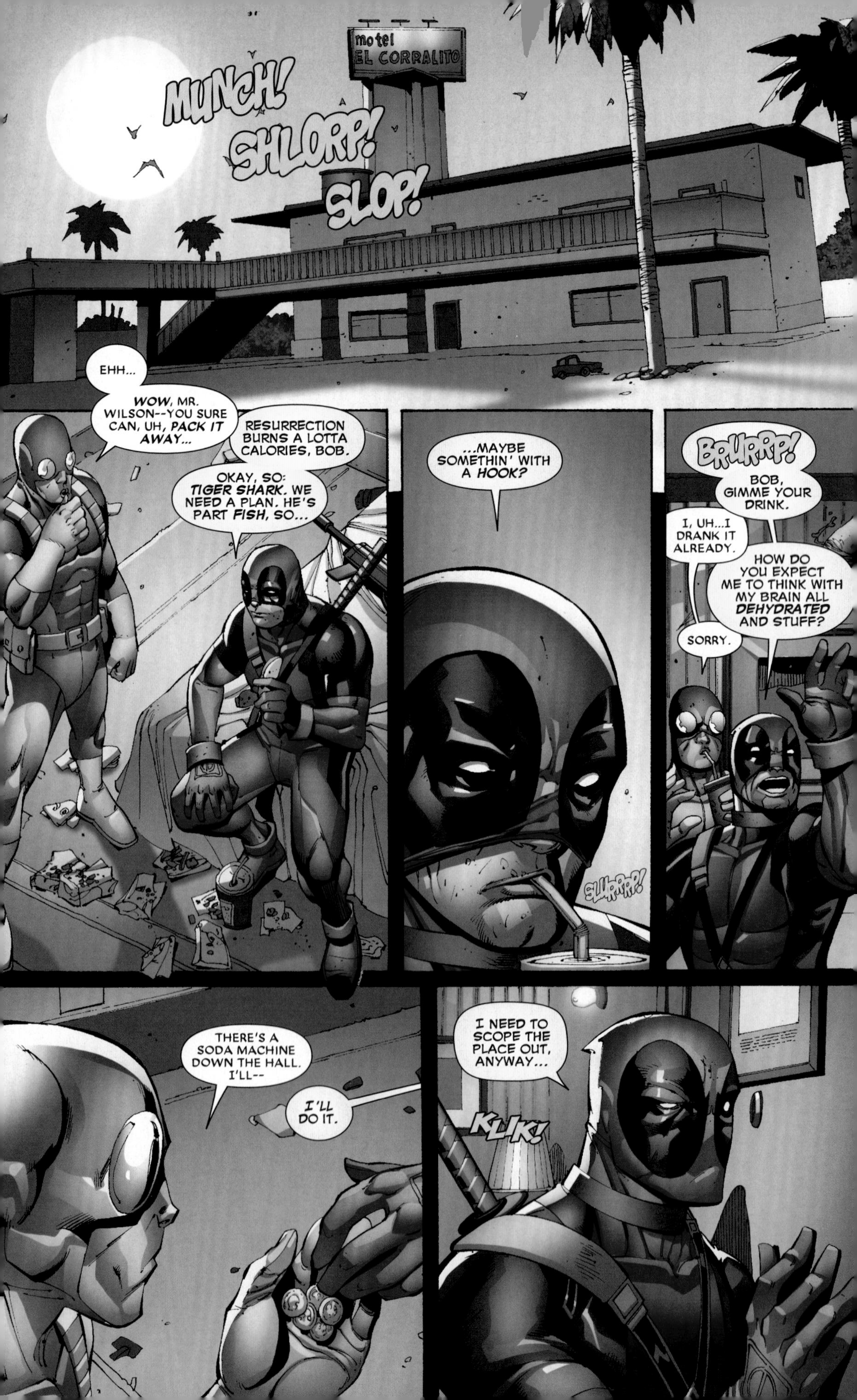
motel EL CORRALITO
MUNCH!
SHLORP!
SLOP!
EHH...
WOW, MR. WILSON--YOU SURE CAN, UH, PACK IT AWAY...
RESURRECTION BURNS A LOTTA CALORIES, BOB.
OKAY, SO: TIGER SHARK. WE NEED A PLAN. HE'S PART FISH, SO...
...MAYBE SOMETHIN' WITH A HOOK?
SLURRRP!
BRURRP!
BOB, GIMME YOUR DRINK.
I, UH...I DRANK IT ALREADY.
HOW DO YOU EXPECT ME TO THINK WITH MY BRAIN ALL DEHYDRATED AND STUFF?
SORRY.
THERE'S A SODA MACHINE DOWN THE HALL. I'LL--
I'LL DO IT.
I NEED TO SCOPE THE PLACE OUT, ANYWAY...
KLIK!

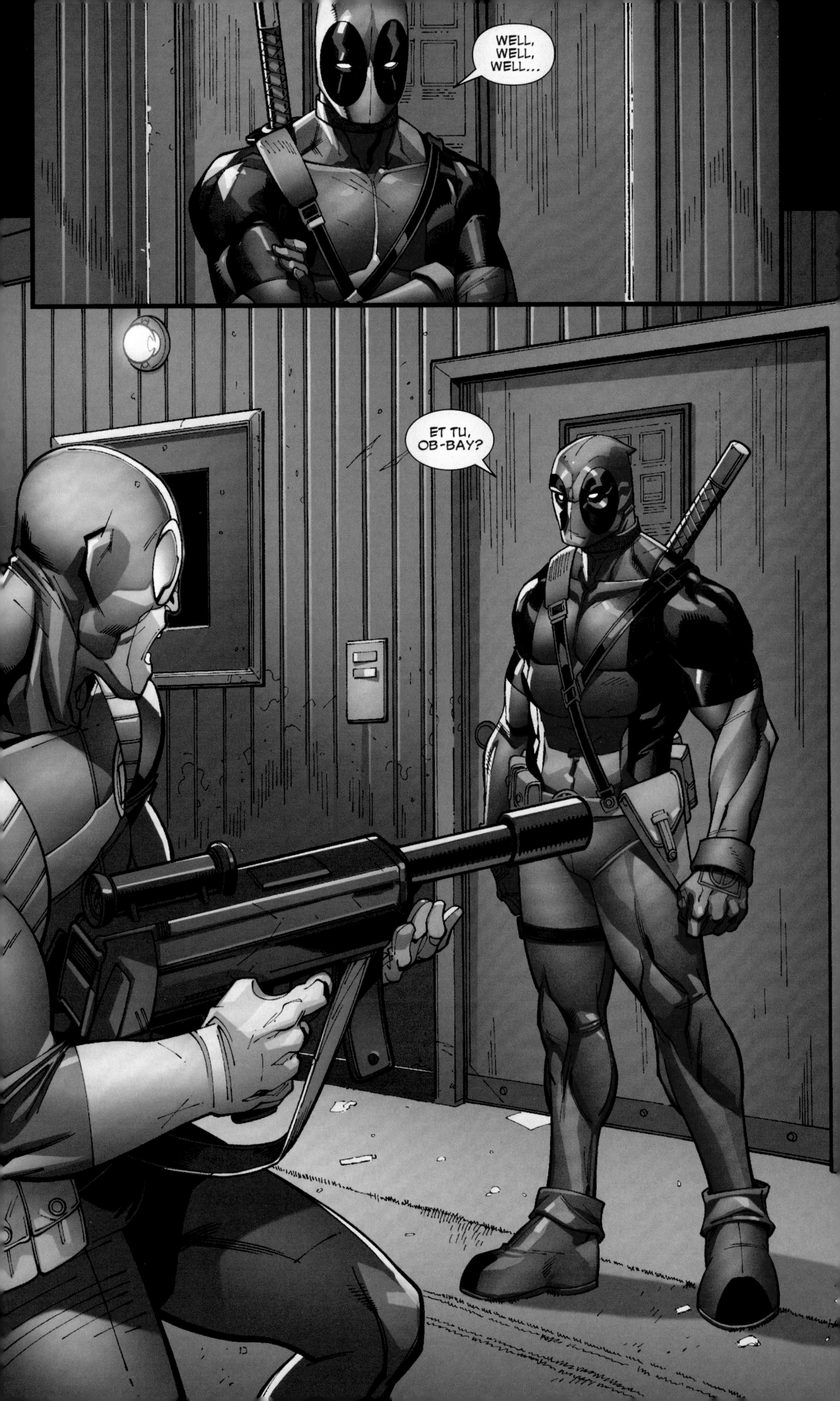
WELL, WELL, WELL...
ET TU, OB-BAY?

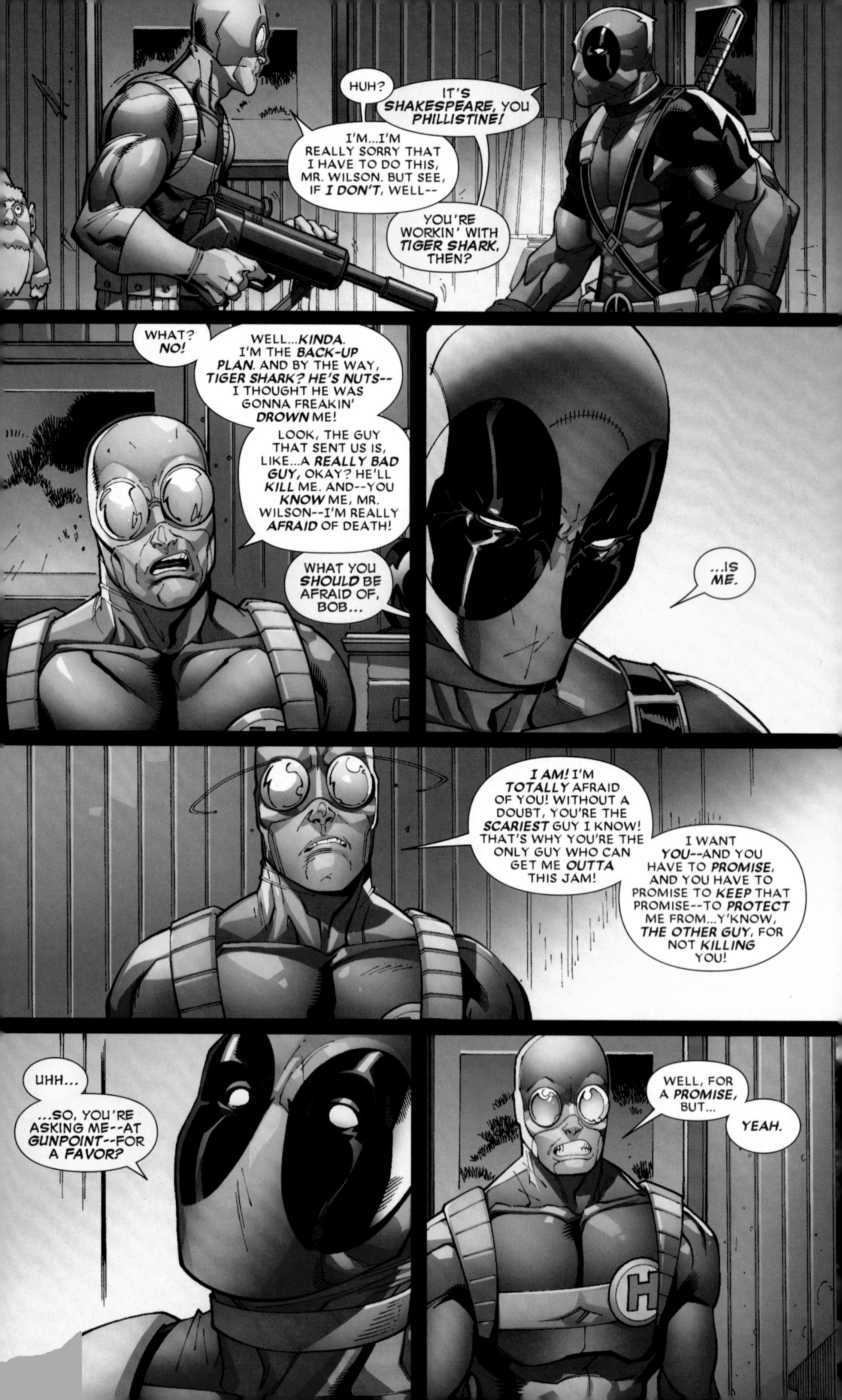
HUH?
IT'S SHAKESPEARE, YOU PHILLISTINE!
I'M...I'M REALLY SORRY THAT I HAVE TO DO THIS, MR. WILSON. BUT SEE, IF I DON'T, WELL--
YOU'RE WORKIN' WITH TIGER SHARK, THEN?
WHAT? NO!
WELL...KINDA. I'M THE BACK-UP PLAN. AND BY THE WAY, TIGER SHARK? HE'S NUTS-- I THOUGHT HE WAS GONNA FREAKIN' DROWN ME!
LOOK, THE GUY THAT SENT US IS, LIKE...A REALLY BAD GUY, OKAY? HE'LL KILL ME. AND--YOU KNOW ME, MR. WILSON--I'M REALLY AFRAID OF DEATH!
WHAT YOU SHOULD BE AFRAID OF, BOB...
...IS ME.
I AM! I'M TOTALLY AFRAID OF YOU! WITHOUT A DOUBT, YOU'RE THE SCARIEST GUY I KNOW! THAT'S WHY YOU'RE THE ONLY GUY WHO CAN GET ME OUTTA THIS JAM!
I WANT YOU--AND YOU HAVE TO PROMISE, AND YOU HAVE TO PROMISE TO KEEP THAT PROMISE--TO PROTECT ME FROM...Y'KNOW, THE OTHER GUY, FOR NOT KILLING YOU!
UHH...
...SO, YOU'RE ASKING ME--AT GUNPOINT--FOR A FAVOR?
WELL, FOR A PROMISE, BUT...
YEAH.

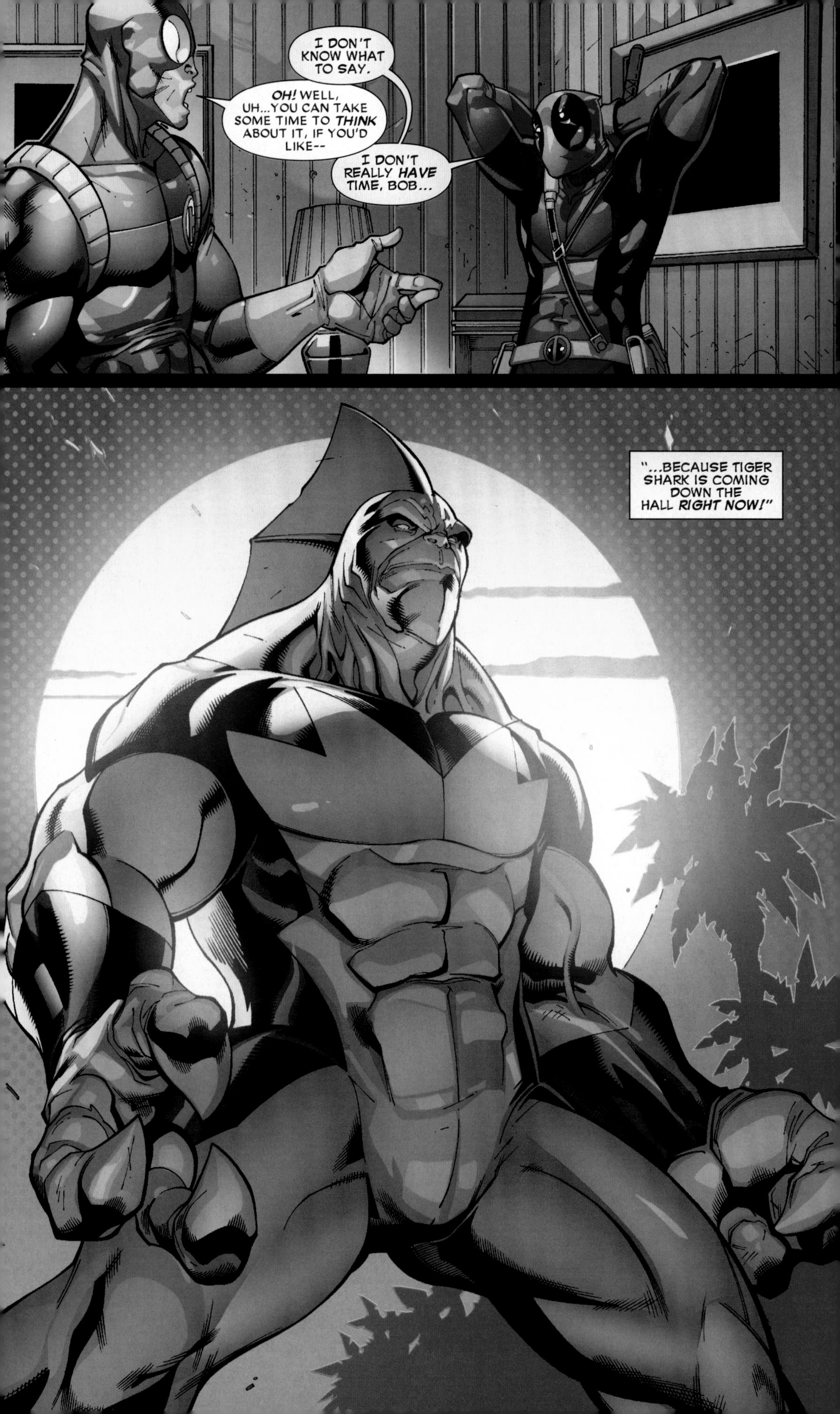
I DON'T KNOW WHAT TO SAY.
OH! WELL, UH...YOU CAN TAKE SOME TIME TO THINK ABOUT IT, IF YOU'D LIKE--
I DON'T REALLY HAVE TIME, BOB...
"...BECAUSE TIGER SHARK IS COMING DOWN THE HALL RIGHT NOW!"

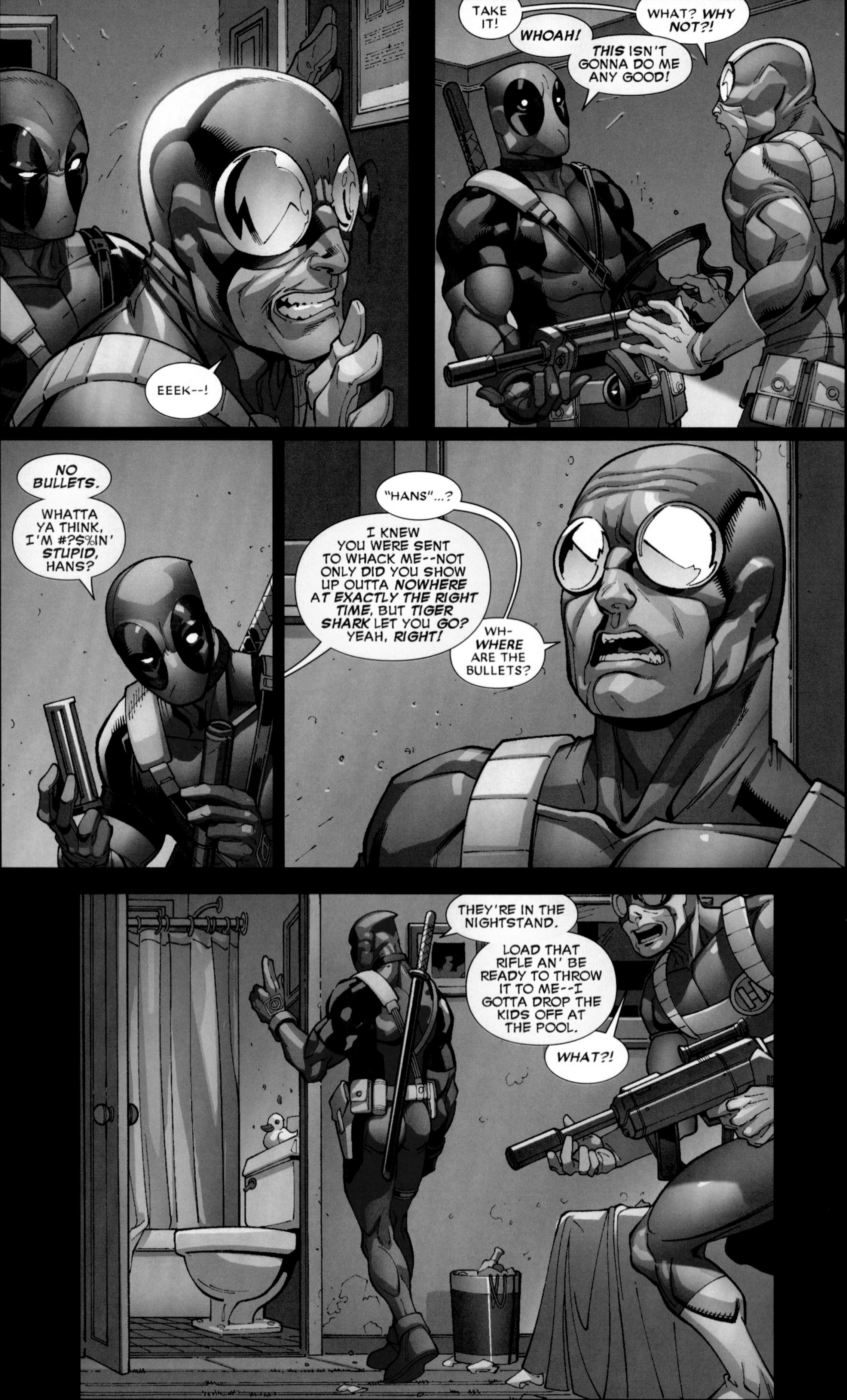
EEEK--!
TAKE IT!
WHAT? WHY NOT?!
WHOAH!
THIS ISN'T GONNA DO ME ANY GOOD!
NO BULLETS.
WHATTA YA THINK, I'M #?$%IN' STUPID, HANS?
"HANS"...?
I KNEW YOU WERE SENT TO WHACK ME--NOT ONLY DID YOU SHOW UP OUTTA NOWHERE AT EXACTLY THE RIGHT TIME, BUT TIGER SHARK LET YOU GO? YEAH, RIGHT!
WH- WHERE ARE THE BULLETS?
THEY'RE IN THE NIGHTSTAND.
LOAD THAT RIFLE AN' BE READY TO THROW IT TO ME--I GOTTA DROP THE KIDS OFF AT THE POOL.
WHAT?!

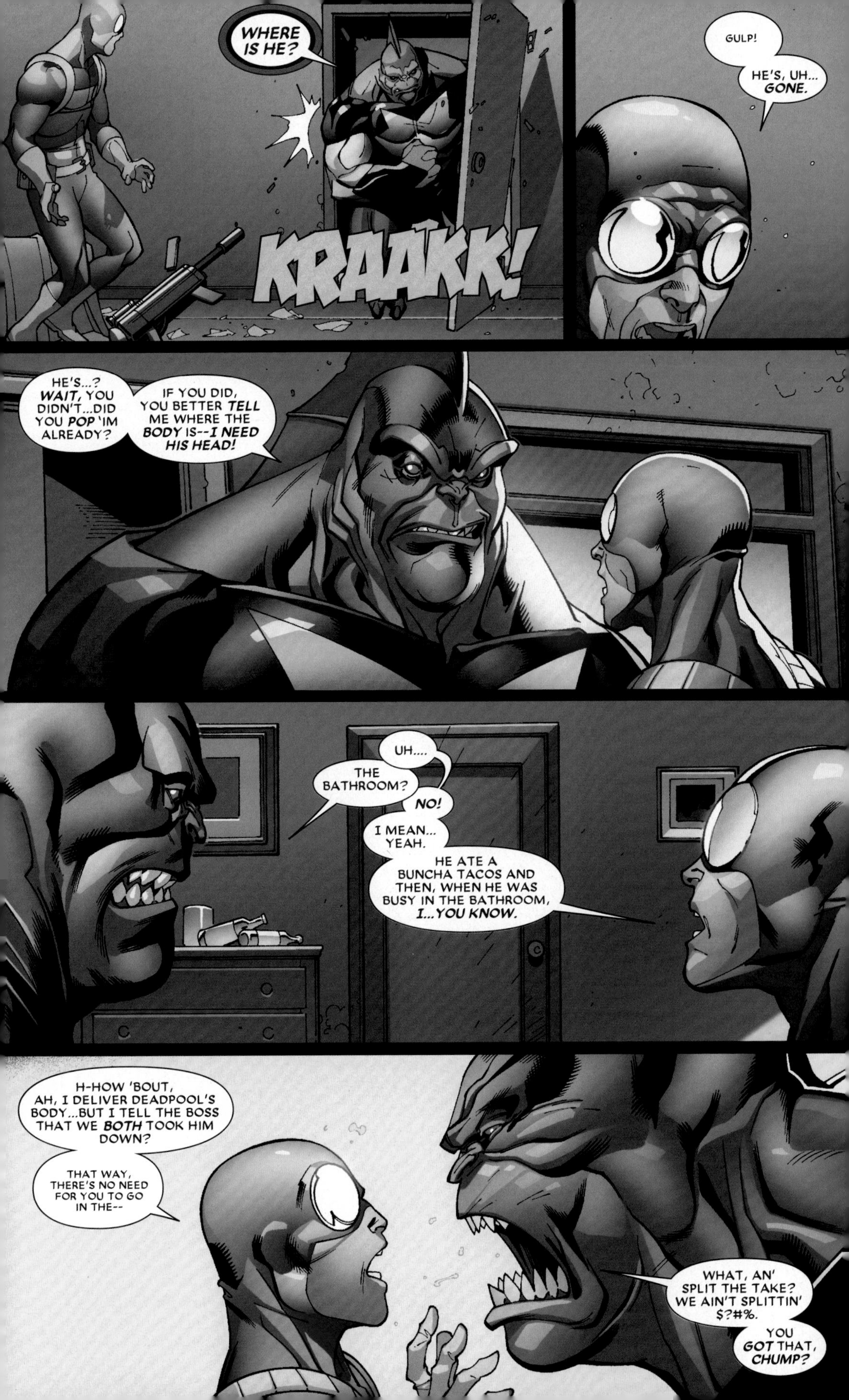
WHERE IS HE?
KRAAKK!
GULP!
HE'S, UH... GONE.
HE'S...? WAIT, YOU DIDN'T...DID YOU POP 'IM ALREADY?
IF YOU DID, YOU BETTER TELL ME WHERE THE BODY IS--I NEED HIS HEAD!
UH....
THE BATHROOM?
NO!
I MEAN... YEAH.
HE ATE A BUNCHA TACOS AND THEN, WHEN HE WAS BUSY IN THE BATHROOM, I...YOU KNOW.
H-HOW 'BOUT, AH, I DELIVER DEADPOOL'S BODY...BUT I TELL THE BOSS THAT WE BOTH TOOK HIM DOWN?
THAT WAY, THERE'S NO NEED FOR YOU TO GO IN THE--
WHAT, AN' SPLIT THE TAKE? WE AIN'T SPLITTIN' $?#%.
YOU GOT THAT, CHUMP?

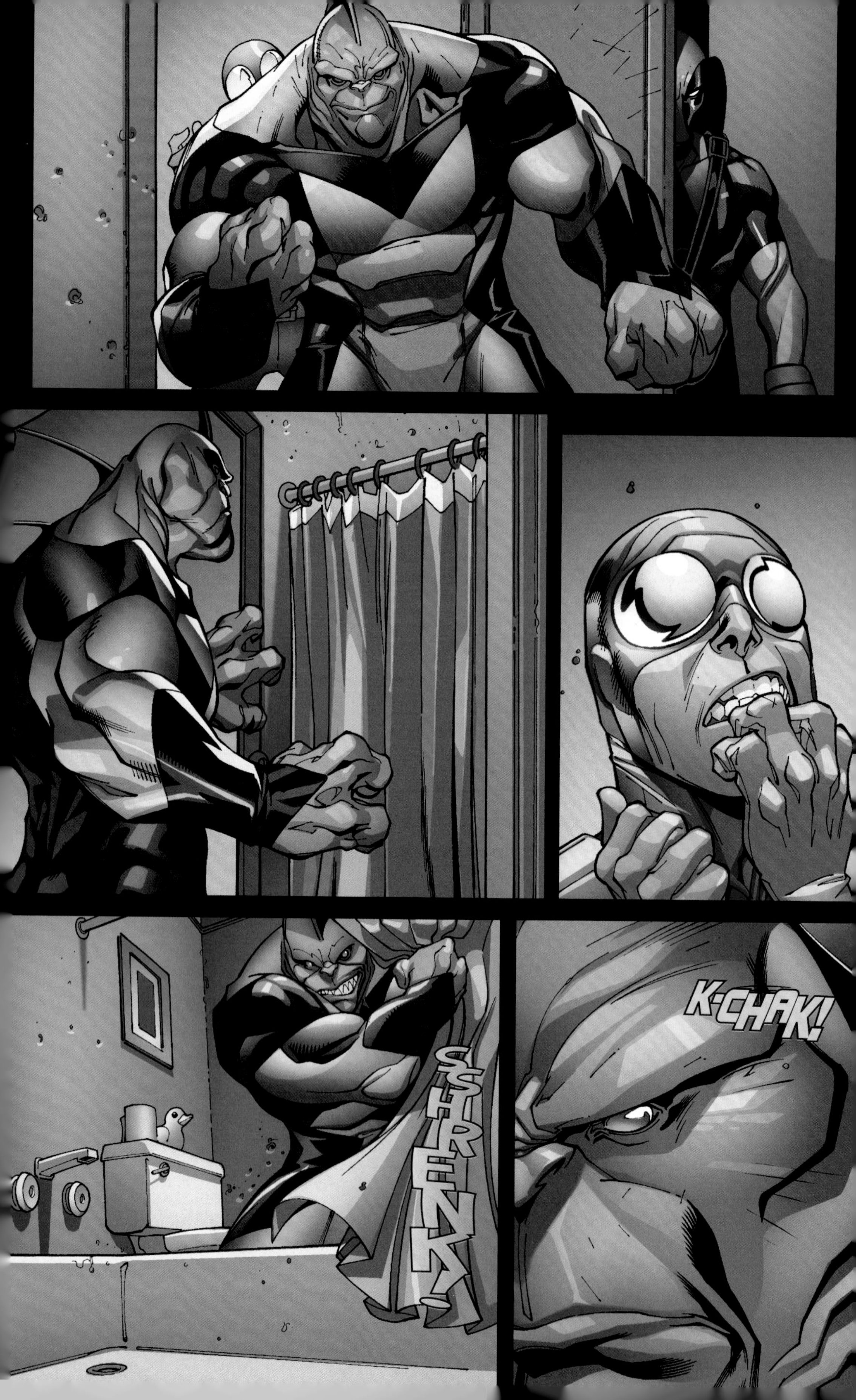

SSHRRENK!
K-CHAK!

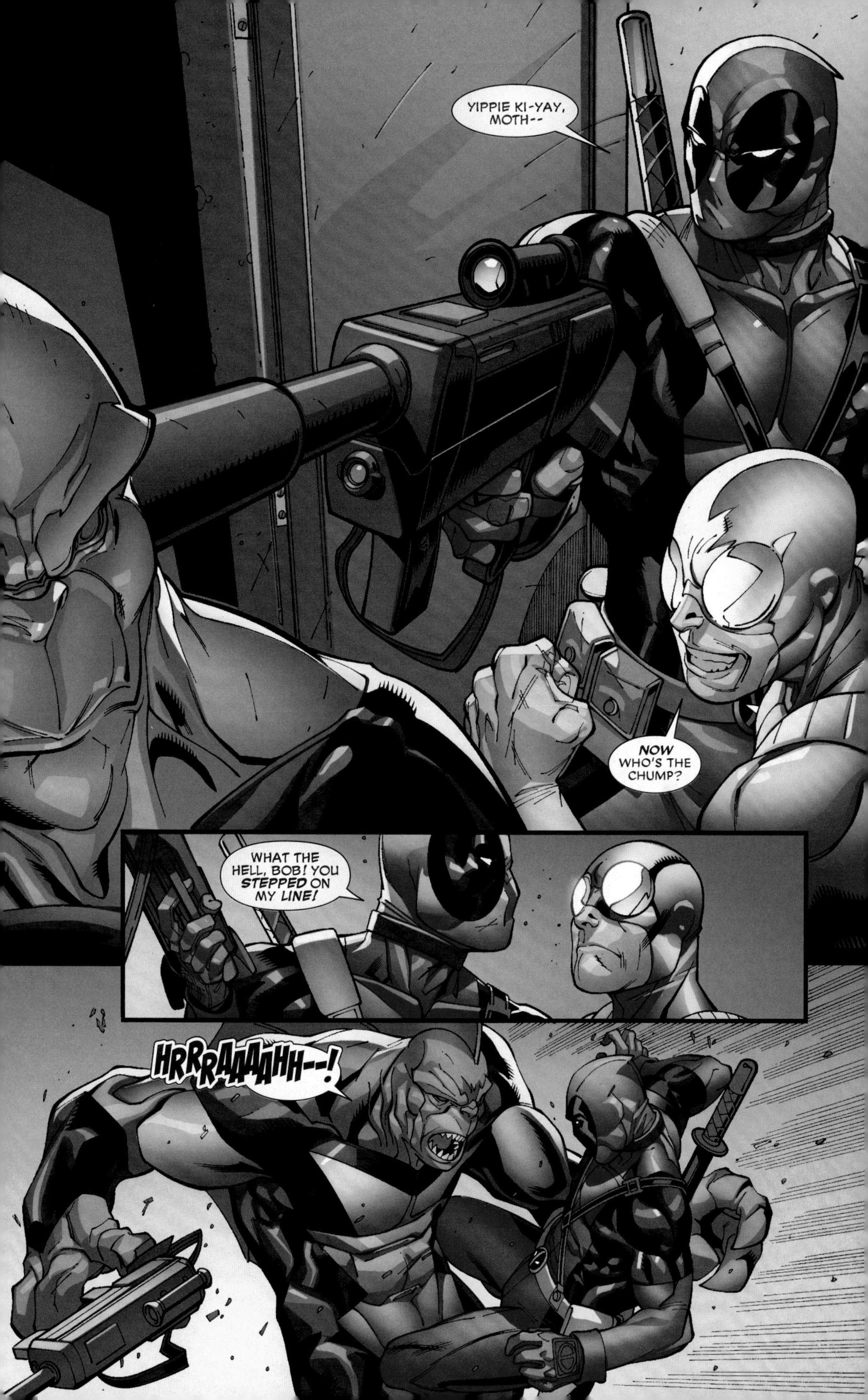
YIPPIE KI-YAY, MOTH--
NOW WHO'S THE CHUMP?
WHAT THE HELL, BOB! YOU STEPPED ON MY LINE!
HRRRAAAAHH--!

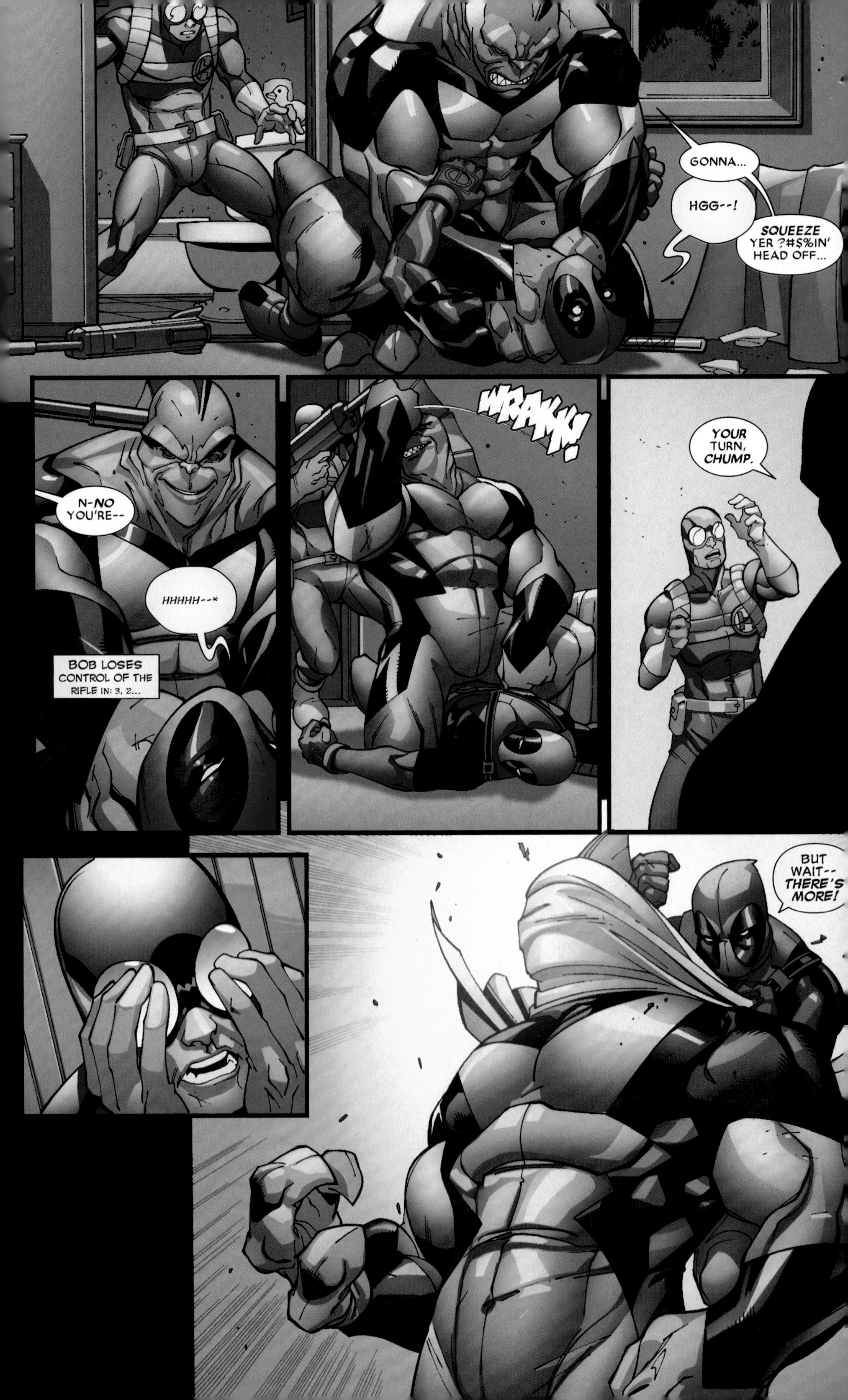
GONNA...
HGG--!
SQUEEZE YER ?#$%IN' HEAD OFF...
N-NO YOU'RE--
HHHHH--*
BOB LOSES CONTROL OF THE RIFLE IN: 3, 2...
WRAKK!
YOUR TURN, CHUMP.
BUT WAIT--THERE'S MORE!

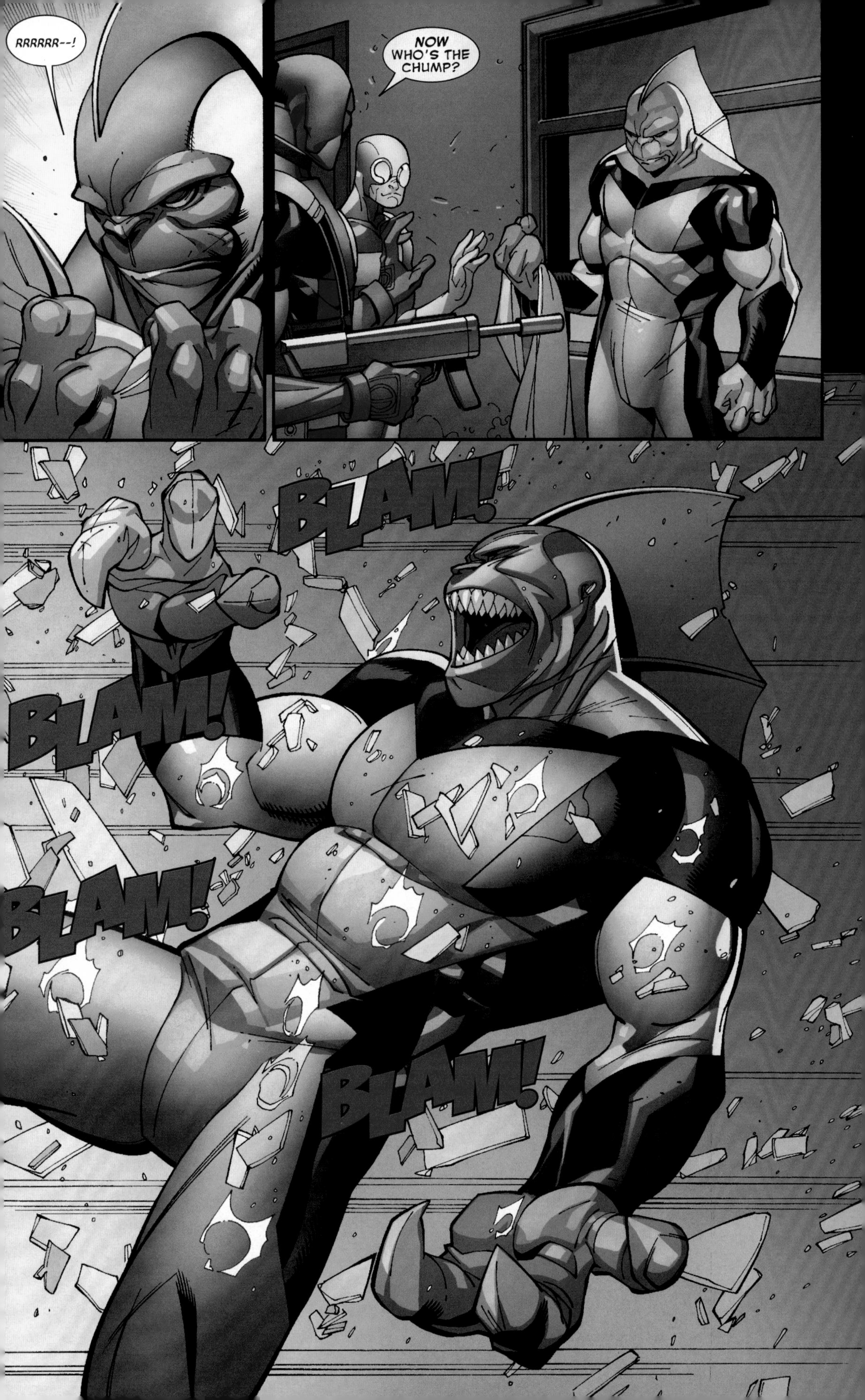
RRRRRR--!
NOW WHO'S THE CHUMP?
BLAM!
BLAM!
BLAM!
BLAM!

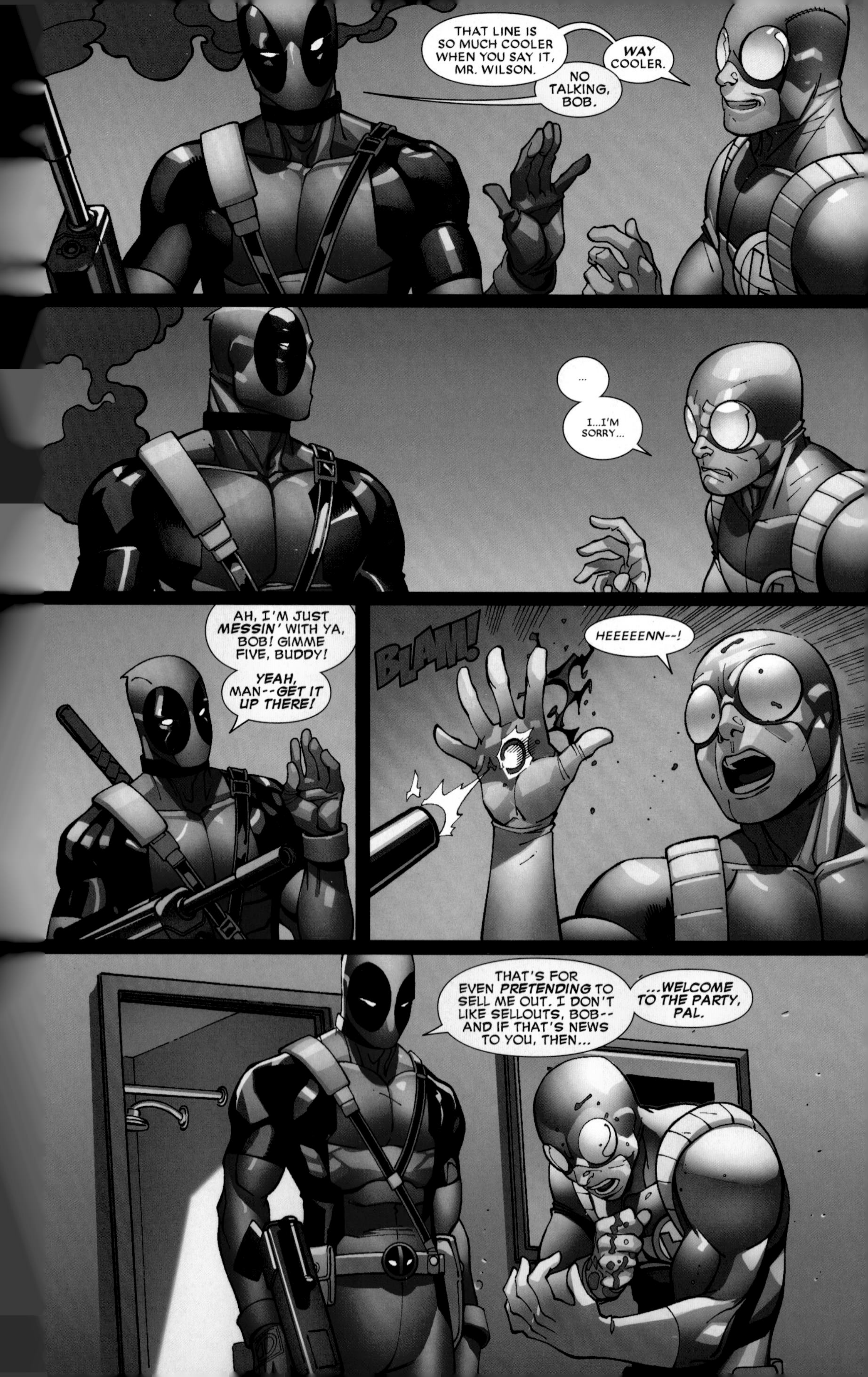
THAT LINE IS SO MUCH COOLER WHEN YOU SAY IT, MR. WILSON.
WAY COOLER.
NO TALKING, BOB.
...
I...I'M SORRY...
AH, I'M JUST MESSIN' WITH YA, BOB! GIMME FIVE, BUDDY!
YEAH, MAN--GET IT UP THERE!
BLAM!
HEEEEENN--!
THAT'S FOR EVEN PRETENDING TO SELL ME OUT. I DON'T LIKE SELLOUTS, BOB--AND IF THAT'S NEWS TO YOU, THEN...
...WELCOME TO THE PARTY, PAL.

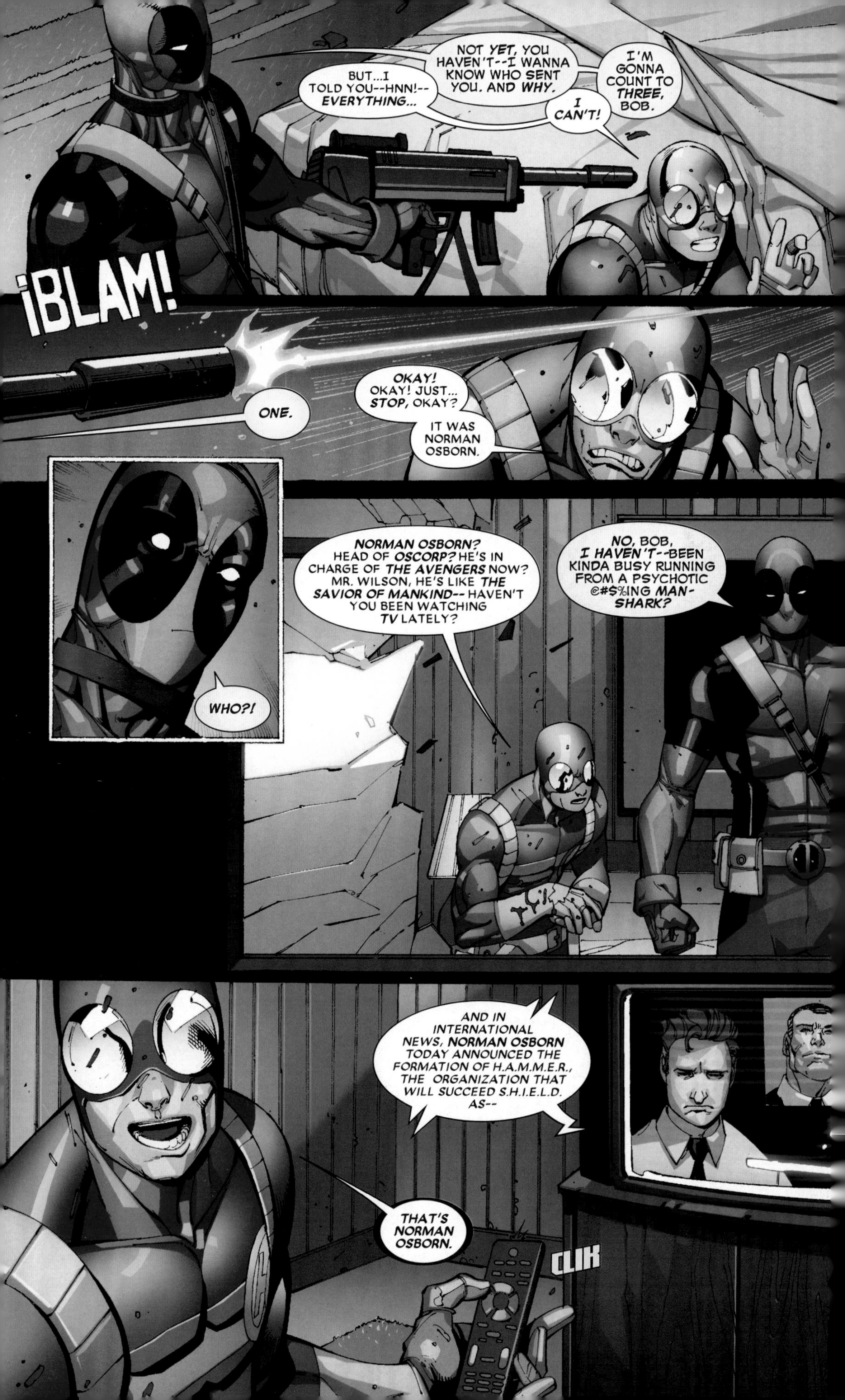

BUT...I TOLD YOU--HNN!-- EVERYTHING...
NOT YET, YOU HAVEN'T--I WANNA KNOW WHO SENT YOU. AND WHY.
I'M GONNA COUNT TO THREE, BOB.
I CAN'T!
¡BLAM!
ONE.
OKAY! OKAY! JUST... STOP, OKAY?
IT WAS NORMAN OSBORN.
WHO?!
NORMAN OSBORN? HEAD OF OSCORP? HE'S IN CHARGE OF THE AVENGERS NOW? MR. WILSON, HE'S LIKE THE SAVIOR OF MANKIND-- HAVEN'T YOU BEEN WATCHING TV LATELY?
NO, BOB, I HAVEN'T--BEEN KINDA BUSY RUNNING FROM A PSYCHOTIC @#$%ING MAN-SHARK?
AND IN INTERNATIONAL NEWS, NORMAN OSBORN TODAY ANNOUNCED THE FORMATION OF H.A.M.M.E.R., THE ORGANIZATION THAT WILL SUCCEED S.H.I.E.L.D. AS--
THAT'S NORMAN OSBORN.
CLIK

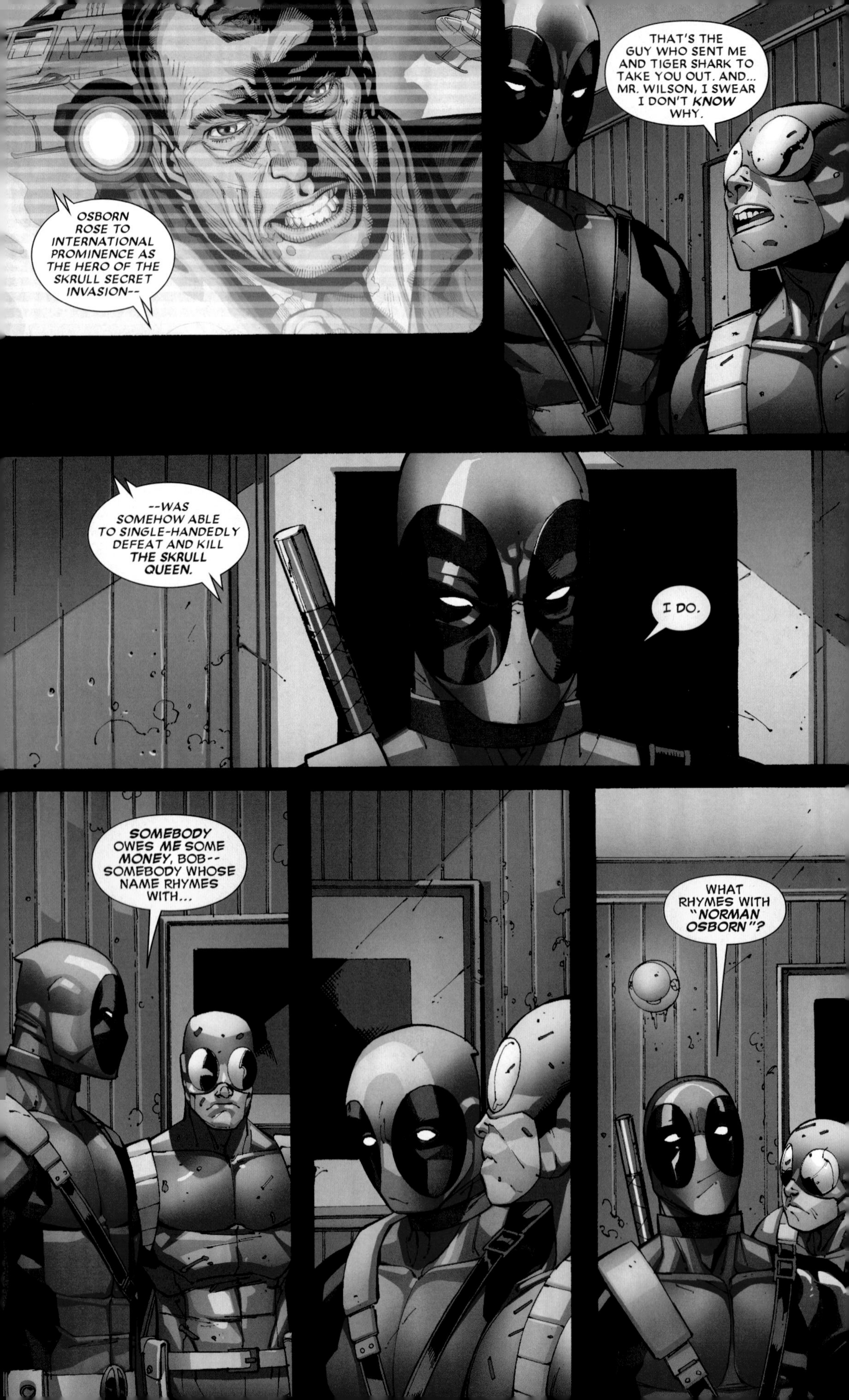
OSBORN ROSE TO INTERNATIONAL PROMINENCE AS THE HERO OF THE SKRULL SECRET INVASION--
THAT'S THE GUY WHO SENT ME AND TIGER SHARK TO TAKE YOU OUT. AND... MR. WILSON, I SWEAR I DON'T KNOW WHY.
--WAS SOMEHOW ABLE TO SINGLE-HANDEDLY DEFEAT AND KILL THE SKRULL QUEEN.
I DO.
SOMEBODY OWES ME SOME MONEY, BOB--SOMEBODY WHOSE NAME RHYMES WITH...
WHAT RHYMES WITH "NORMAN OSBORN"?

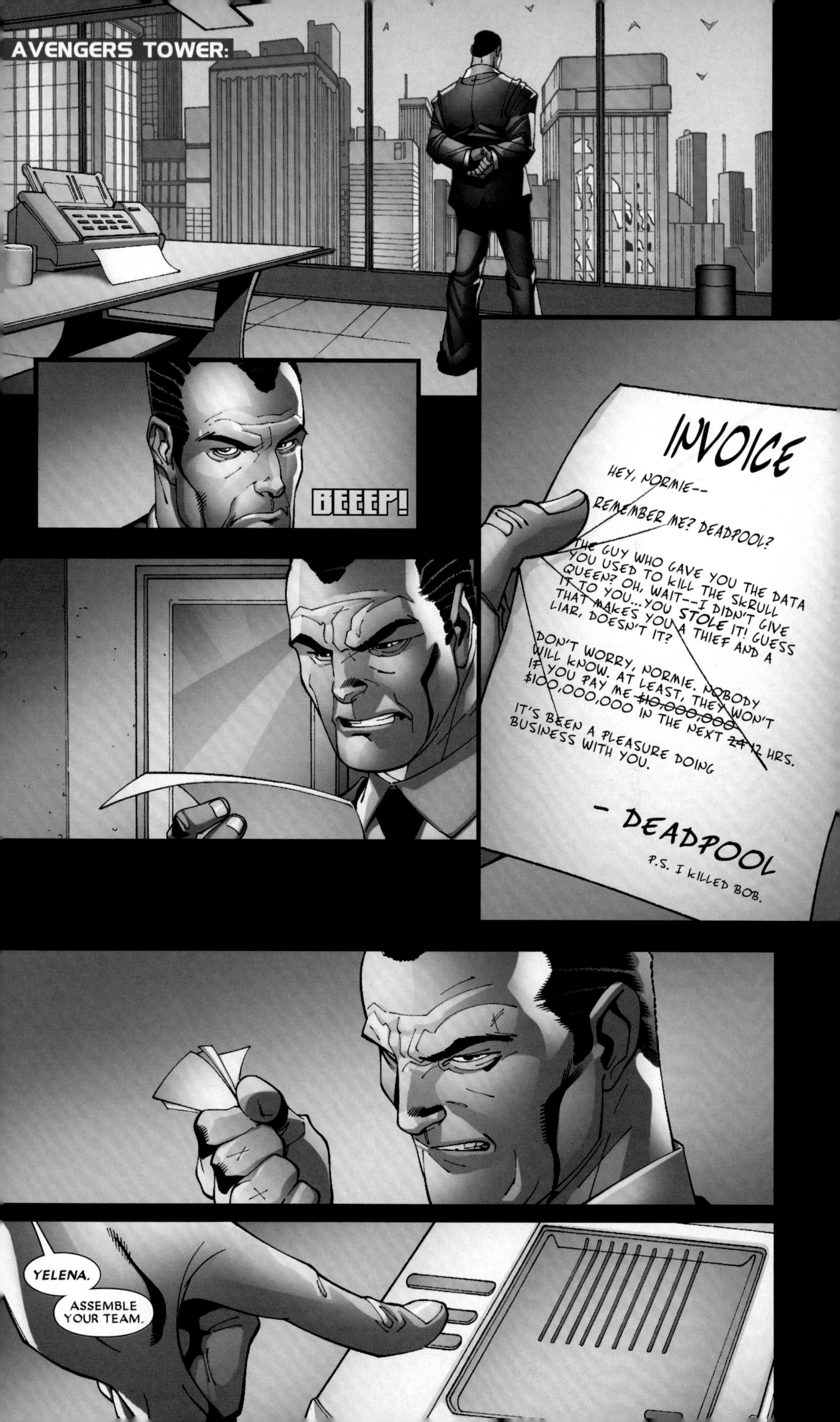

AVENGERS TOWER:
BEEEP!
INVOICE
HEY, NORMIE--
REMEMBER ME? DEADPOOL?
THE GUY WHO GAVE YOU THE DATA YOU USED TO KILL THE SKRULL QUEEN? OH, WAIT--I DIDN'T GIVE IT TO YOU...YOU STOLE IT! GUESS THAT MAKES YOU A THIEF AND A LIAR, DOESN'T IT?
DON'T WORRY, NORMIE. NOBODY WILL KNOW. AT LEAST, THEY WON'T IF YOU PAY ME $10,000,000 $100,000,000 IN THE NEXT 24 12 HRS.
IT'S BEEN A PLEASURE DOING BUSINESS WITH YOU.
- DEADPOOL
P.S. I KILLED BOB.
YELENA.
ASSEMBLE YOUR TEAM.

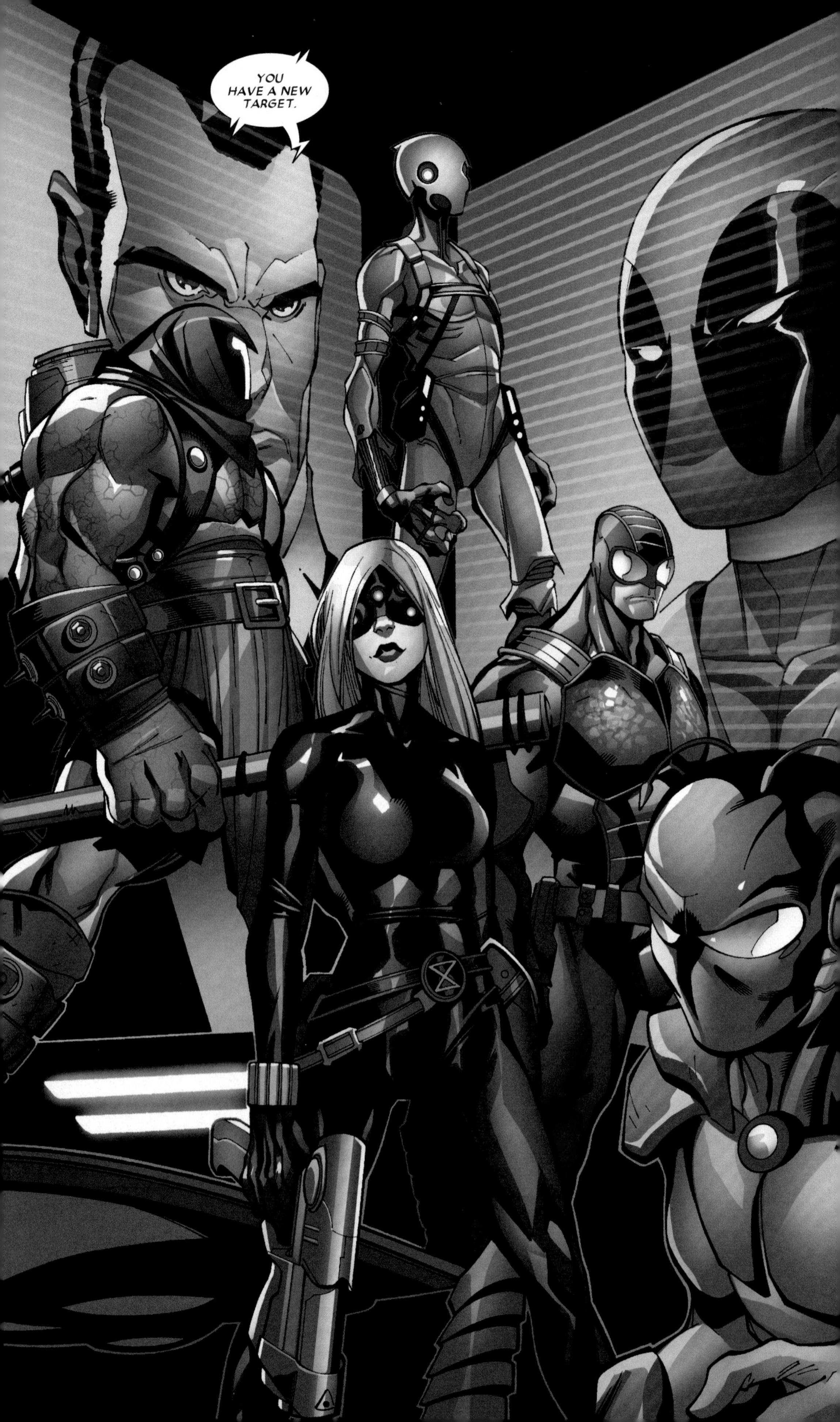
YOU HAVE A NEW TARGET.

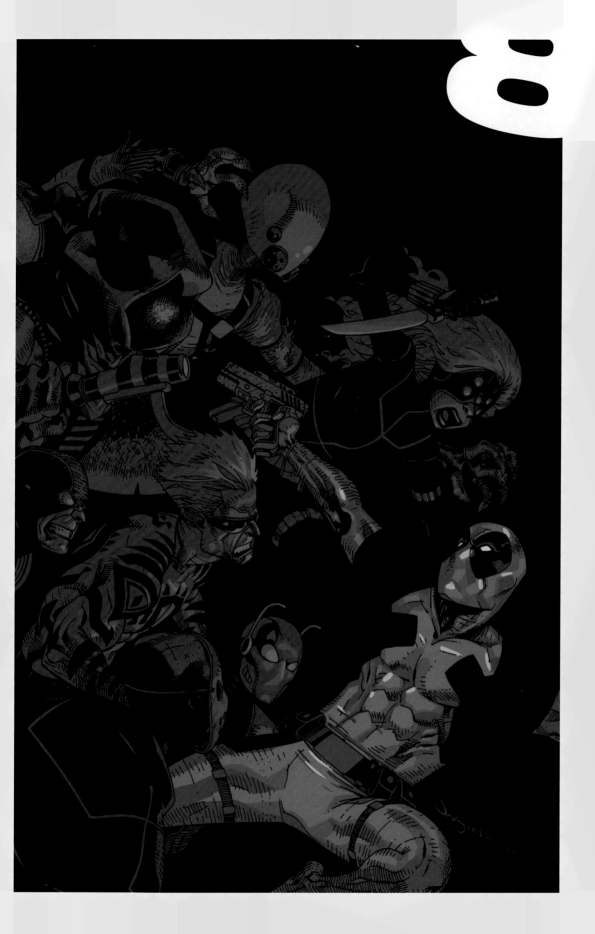

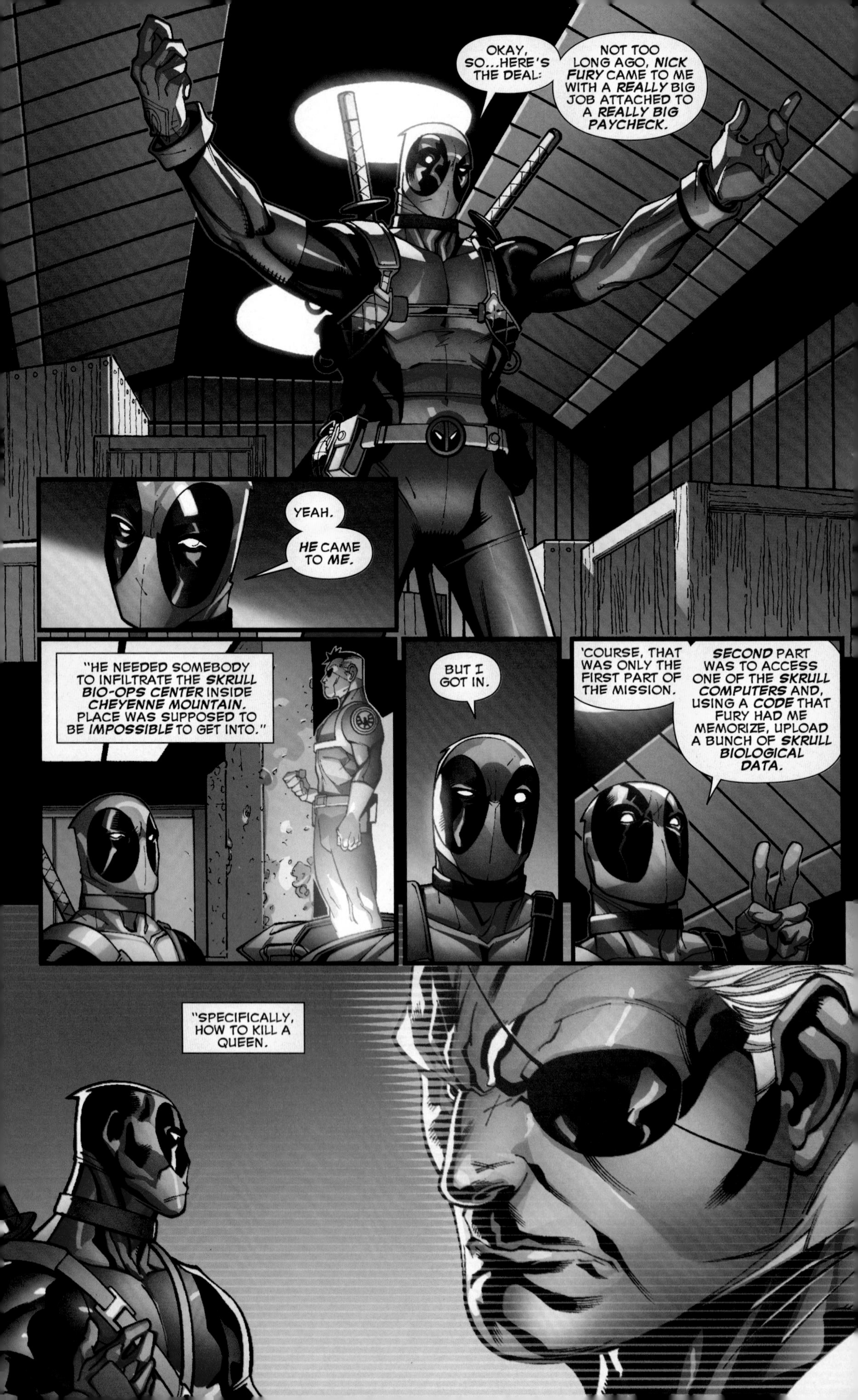
OKAY, SO...HERE'S THE DEAL:
NOT TOO LONG AGO, NICK FURY CAME TO ME WITH A REALLY BIG JOB ATTACHED TO A REALLY BIG PAYCHECK.
YEAH.
HE CAME TO ME.
"HE NEEDED SOMEBODY TO INFILTRATE THE SKRULL BIO-OPS CENTER INSIDE CHEYENNE MOUNTAIN. PLACE WAS SUPPOSED TO BE IMPOSSIBLE TO GET INTO."
BUT I GOT IN.
'COURSE, THAT WAS ONLY THE FIRST PART OF THE MISSION.
SECOND PART WAS TO ACCESS ONE OF THE SKRULL COMPUTERS AND, USING A CODE THAT FURY HAD ME MEMORIZE, UPLOAD A BUNCH OF SKRULL BIOLOGICAL DATA.
"SPECIFICALLY, HOW TO KILL A QUEEN.

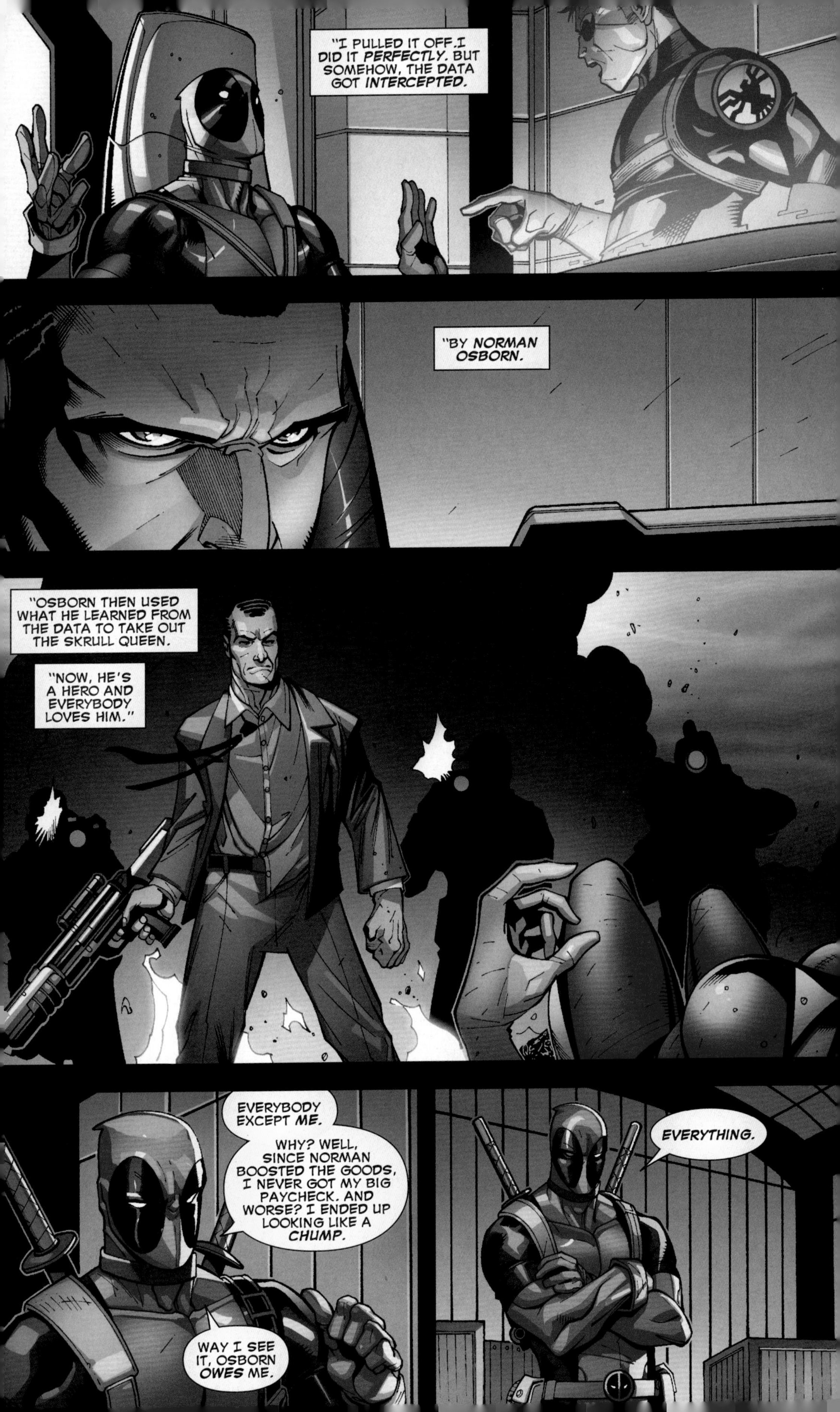
"I PULLED IT OFF. I DID IT PERFECTLY. BUT SOMEHOW, THE DATA GOT INTERCEPTED.
"BY NORMAN OSBORN.
"OSBORN THEN USED WHAT HE LEARNED FROM THE DATA TO TAKE OUT THE SKRULL QUEEN.
"NOW, HE'S A HERO AND EVERYBODY LOVES HIM."
EVERYBODY EXCEPT ME.
WHY? WELL, SINCE NORMAN BOOSTED THE GOODS, I NEVER GOT MY BIG PAYCHECK. AND WORSE? I ENDED UP LOOKING LIKE A CHUMP.
WAY I SEE IT, OSBORN OWES ME.
EVERYTHING.

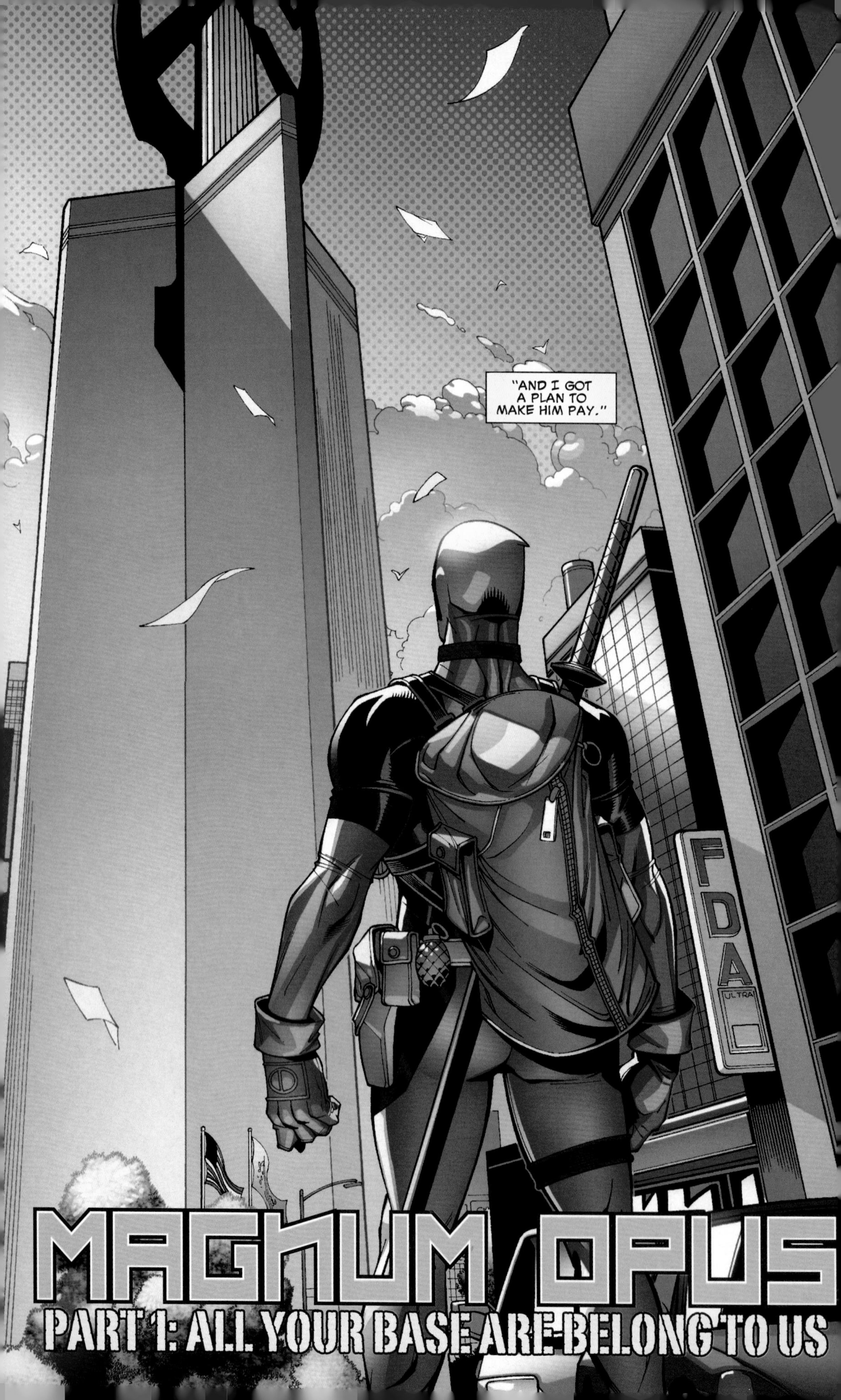
"AND I GOT A PLAN TO MAKE HIM PAY."
FDA
ULTRA
MAGNUM OPUS
PART 1: ALL YOUR BASE ARE BELONG TO US

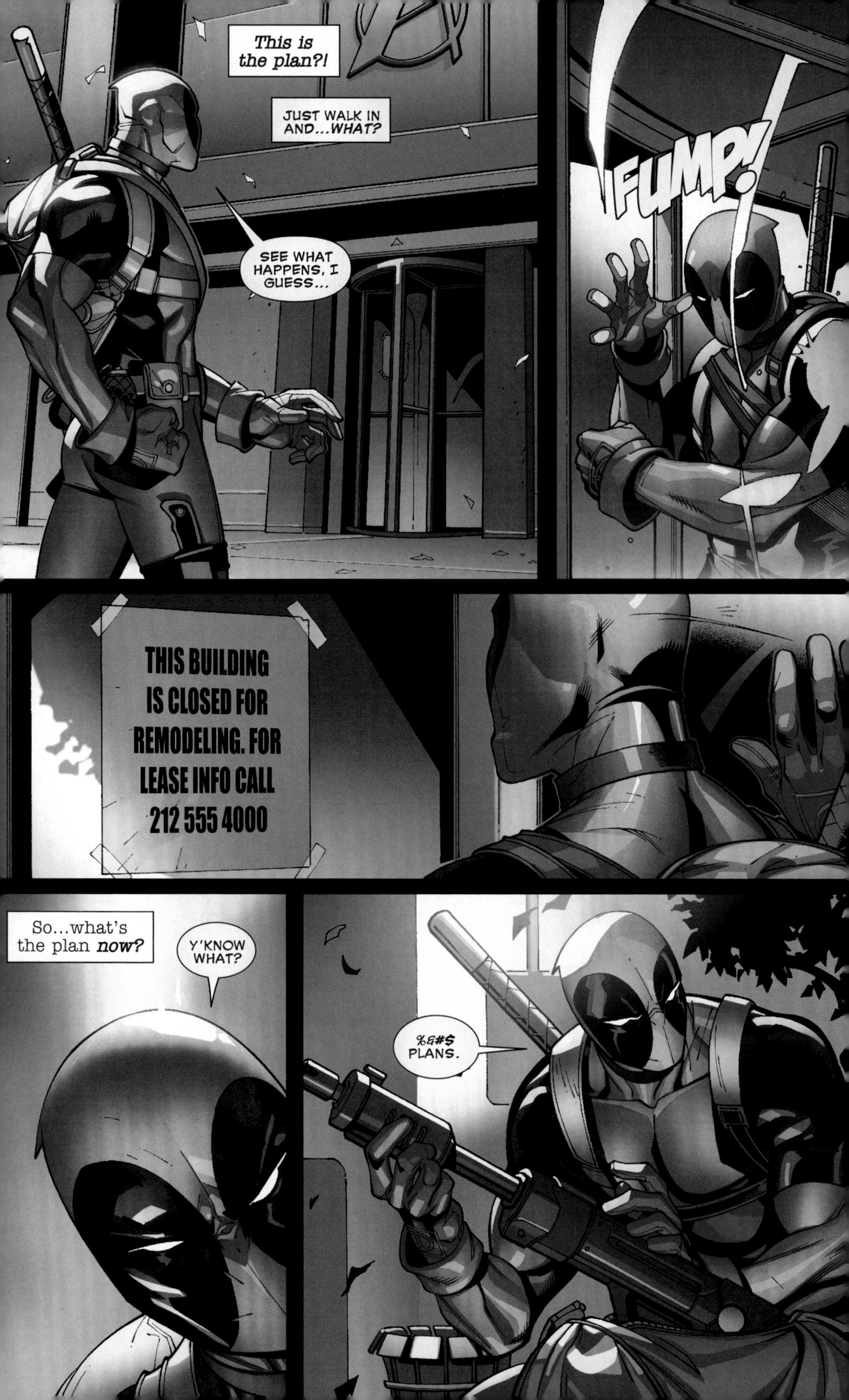

This is the plan?!
JUST WALK IN AND...WHAT?
SEE WHAT HAPPENS, I GUESS...
FUMP!
THIS BUILDING IS CLOSED FOR REMODELING. FOR LEASE INFO CALL 212 555 4000
So...what's the plan now?
Y'KNOW WHAT?
%&#$ PLANS.

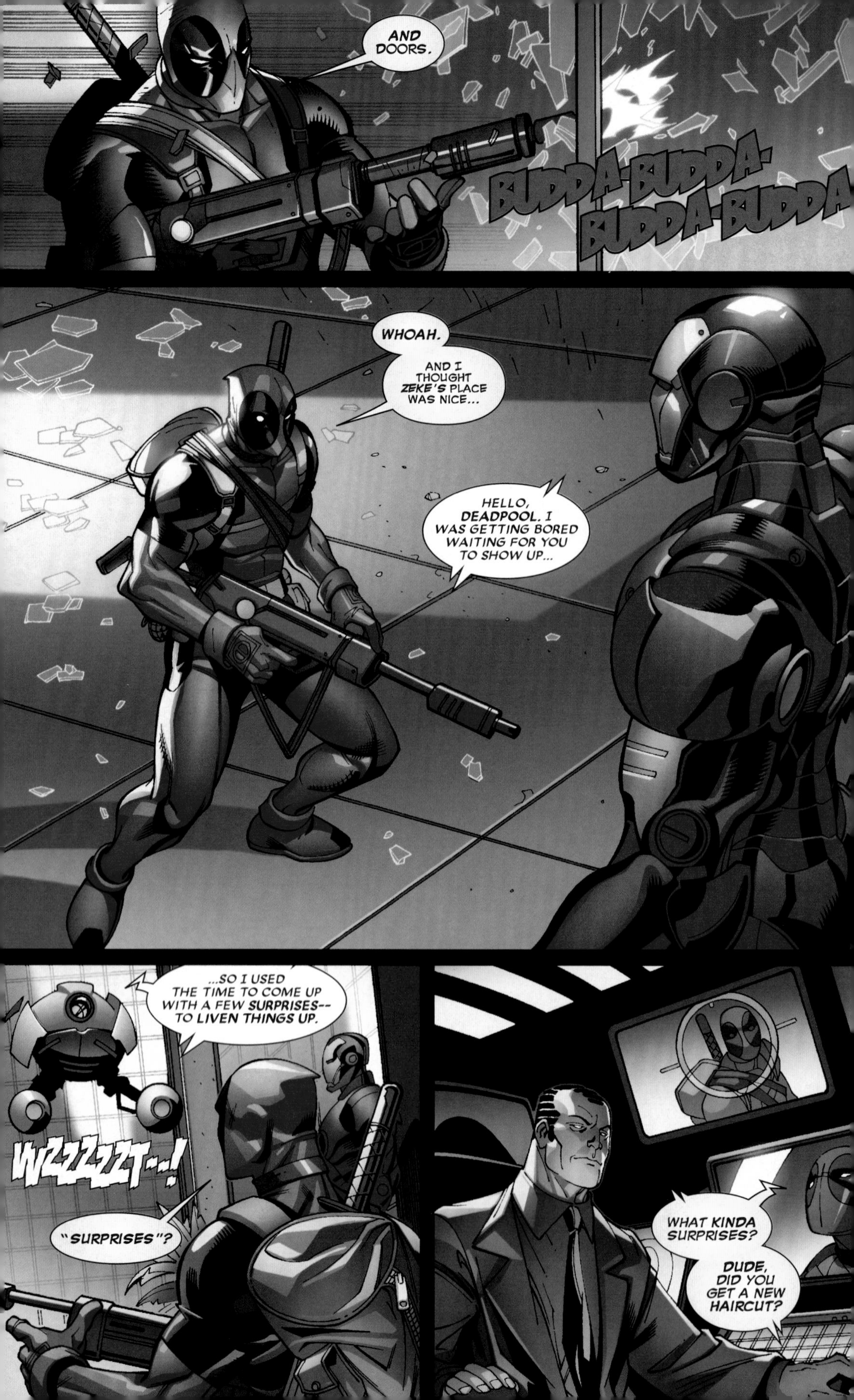
AND DOORS.
BUDDA-BUDDA-BUDDA-BUDDA
WHOAH.
AND I THOUGHT ZEKE'S PLACE WAS NICE...
HELLO, DEADPOOL. I WAS GETTING BORED WAITING FOR YOU TO SHOW UP...
...SO I USED THE TIME TO COME UP WITH A FEW SURPRISES-- TO LIVEN THINGS UP.
WZZZZZT--!
"SURPRISES"?
WHAT KINDA SURPRISES?
DUDE, DID YOU GET A NEW HAIRCUT?

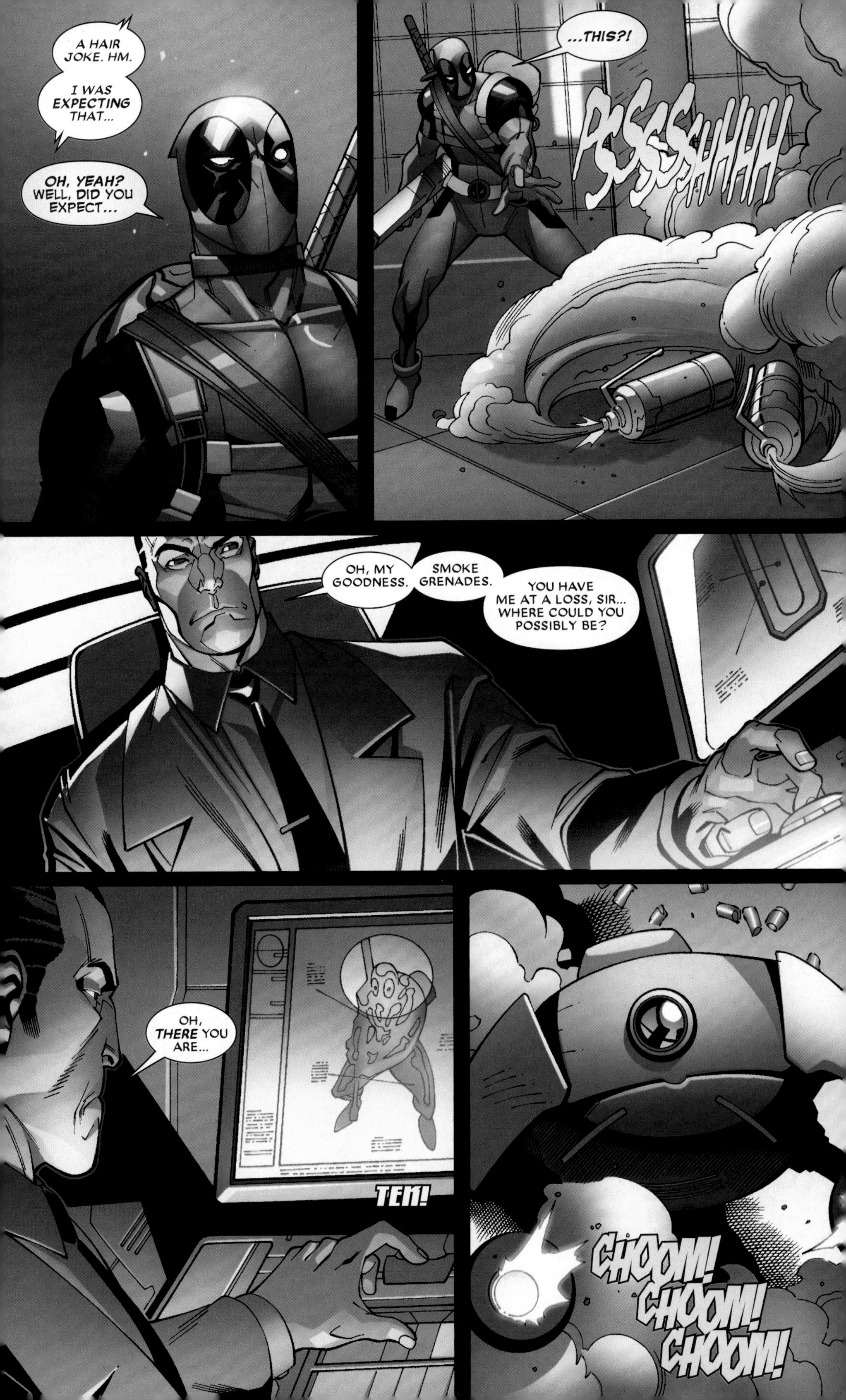
A HAIR JOKE. HM.
I WAS EXPECTING THAT...
OH, YEAH? WELL, DID YOU EXPECT...
...THIS?!
PSSSSHHHH
OH, MY GOODNESS.
SMOKE GRENADES.
YOU HAVE ME AT A LOSS, SIR... WHERE COULD YOU POSSIBLY BE?
OH, THERE YOU ARE...
TEN!
CHOOM! CHOOM! CHOOM!

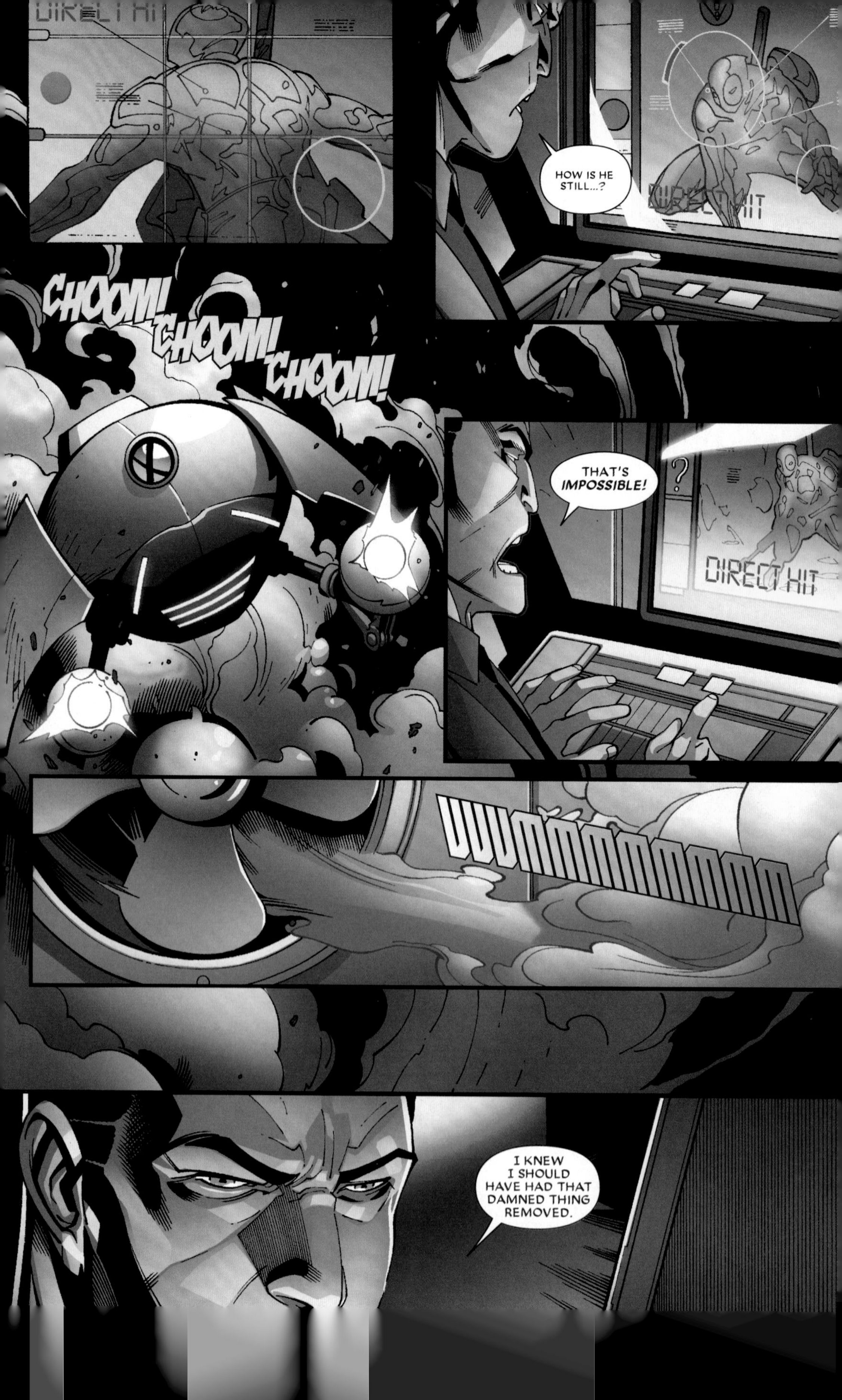
DIRECT HIT
HOW IS HE STILL...?
DIRECT HIT
CHOOM! CHOOM! CHOOM!
THAT'S *IMPOSSIBLE!*
DIRECT HIT
VVVMMMMMMMMMM
I KNEW I SHOULD HAVE HAD THAT DAMNED THING REMOVED.

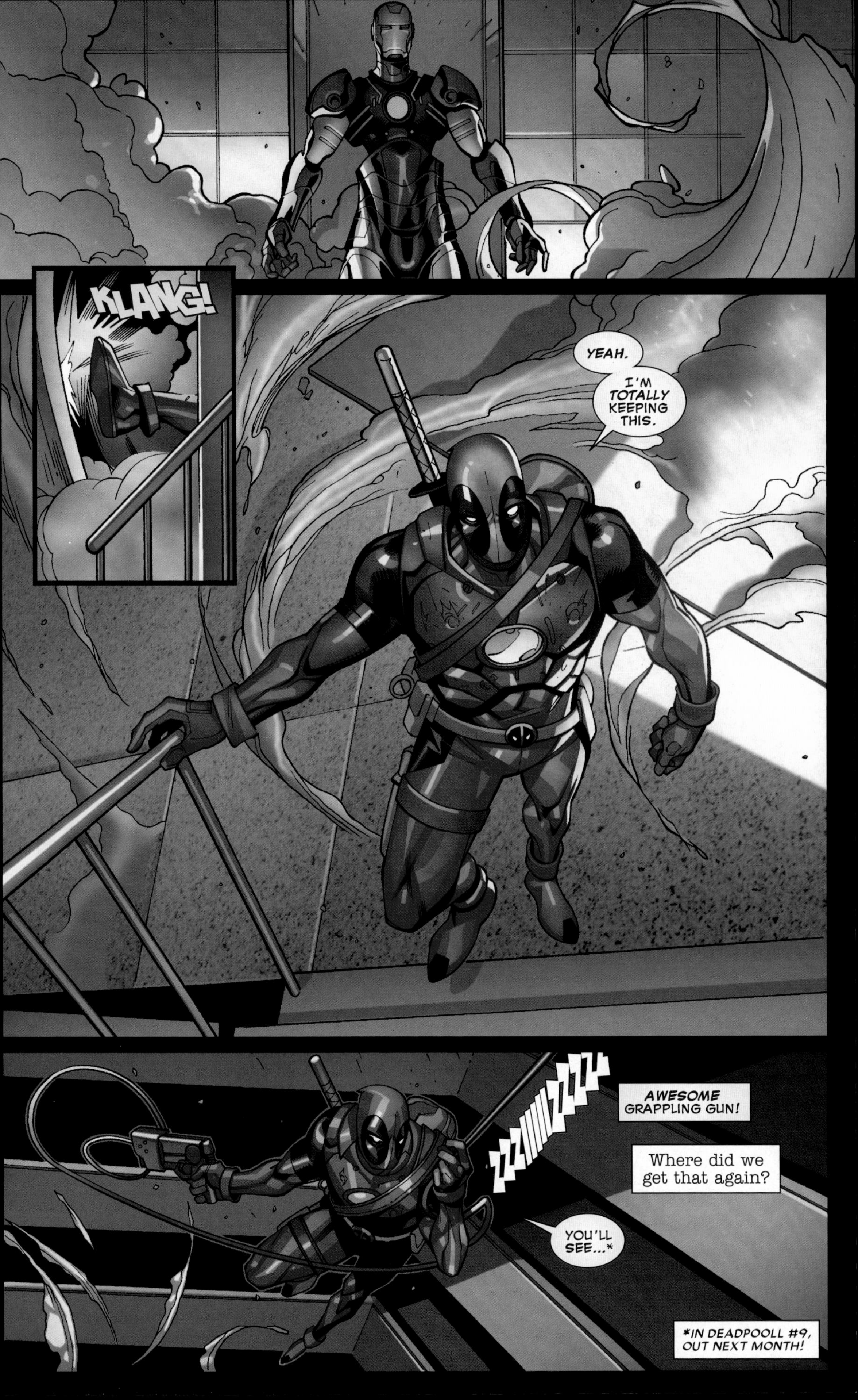
KLANG!
YEAH.
I'M TOTALLY KEEPING THIS.
AWESOME GRAPPLING GUN!
Where did we get that again?
YOU'LL SEE...*
*IN DEADPOOLL #9, OUT NEXT MONTH!

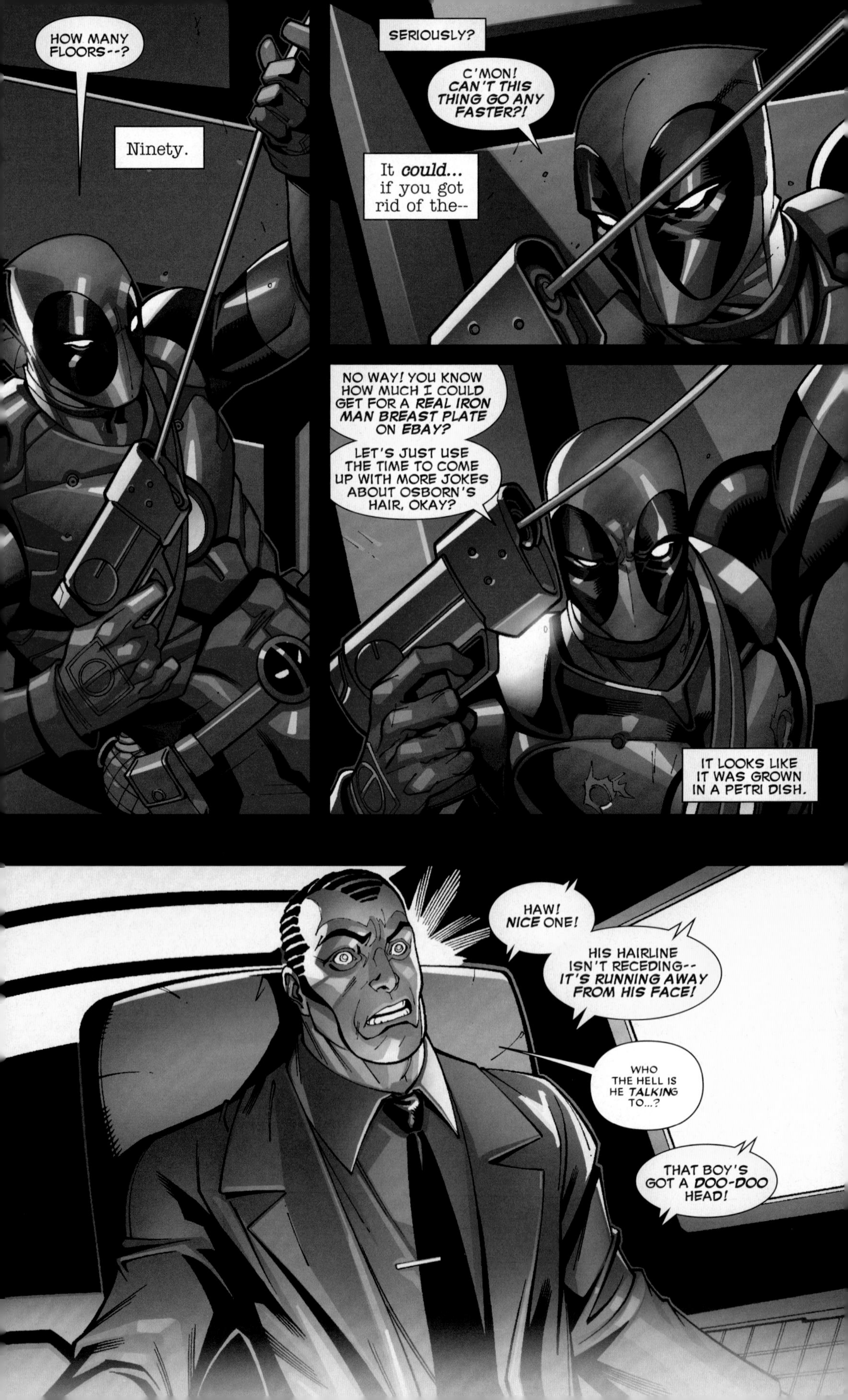
HOW MANY FLOORS--?
Ninety.
SERIOUSLY?
C'MON! CAN'T THIS THING GO ANY FASTER?!
It could... if you got rid of the--
NO WAY! YOU KNOW HOW MUCH I COULD GET FOR A REAL IRON MAN BREAST PLATE ON EBAY?
LET'S JUST USE THE TIME TO COME UP WITH MORE JOKES ABOUT OSBORN'S HAIR, OKAY?
IT LOOKS LIKE IT WAS GROWN IN A PETRI DISH.
HAW! NICE ONE!
HIS HAIRLINE ISN'T RECEDING-- IT'S RUNNING AWAY FROM HIS FACE!
WHO THE HELL IS HE TALKING TO...?
THAT BOY'S GOT A DOO-DOO HEAD!

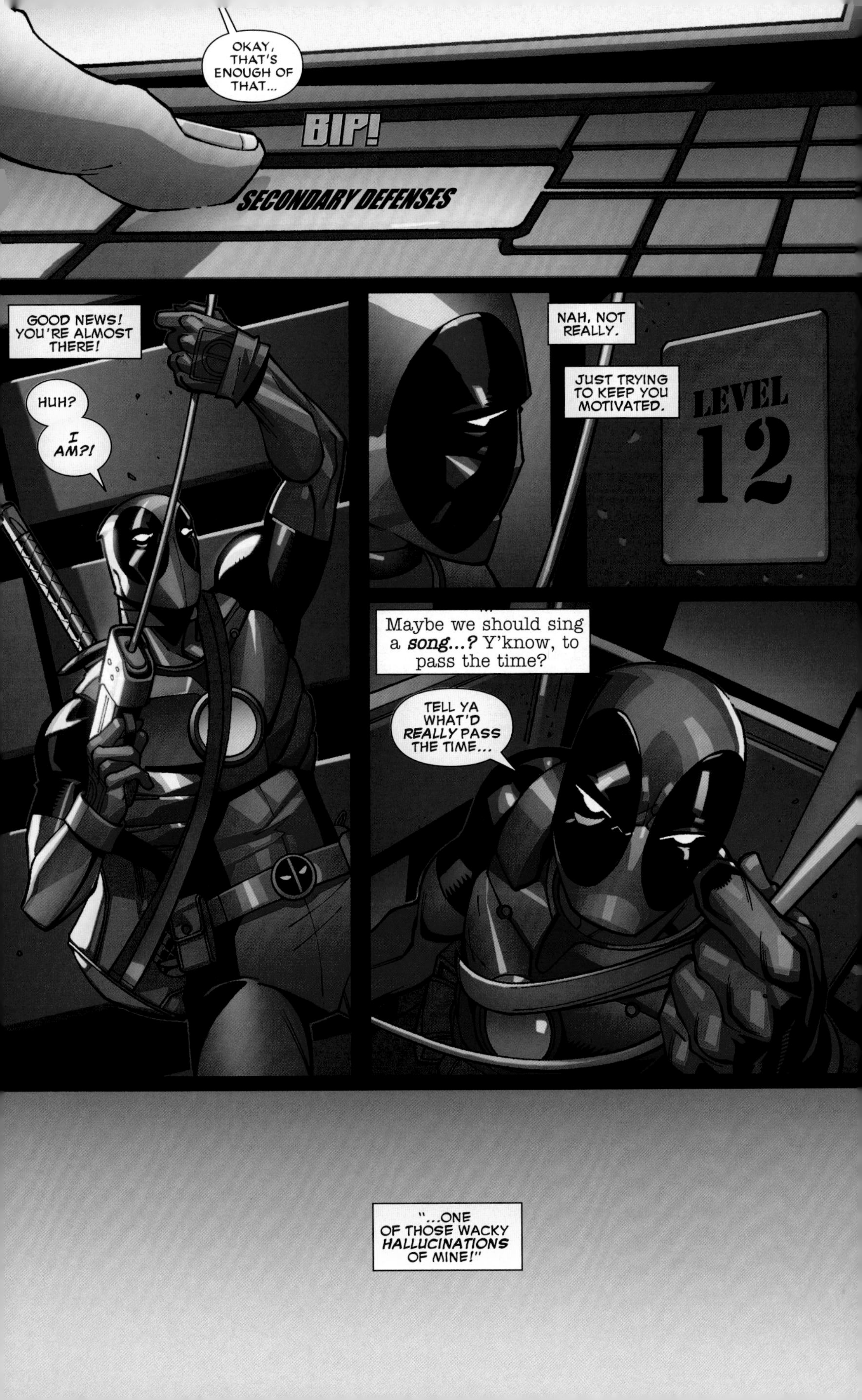
OKAY, THAT'S ENOUGH OF THAT...
BIP!
SECONDARY DEFENSES
GOOD NEWS! YOU'RE ALMOST THERE!
HUH?
I AM?!
NAH, NOT REALLY.
JUST TRYING TO KEEP YOU MOTIVATED.
LEVEL 12
Maybe we should sing a song...? Y'know, to pass the time?
TELL YA WHAT'D REALLY PASS THE TIME...
"...ONE OF THOSE WACKY HALLUCINATIONS OF MINE!"

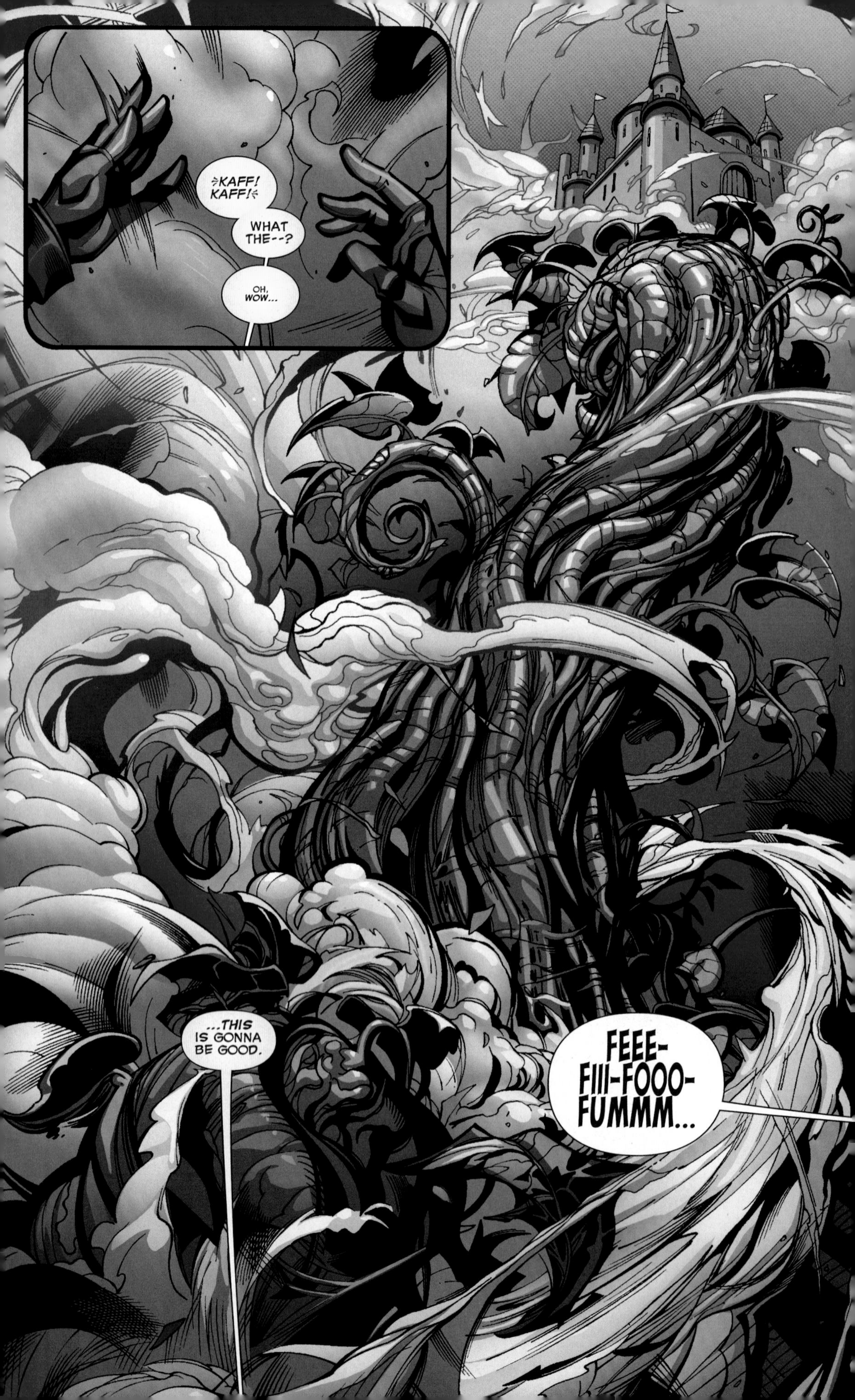

KAFF! KAFF!
WHAT THE--?
OH, WOW...
...THIS IS GONNA BE GOOD.
FEEE-FIII-FOOO-FUMMM...

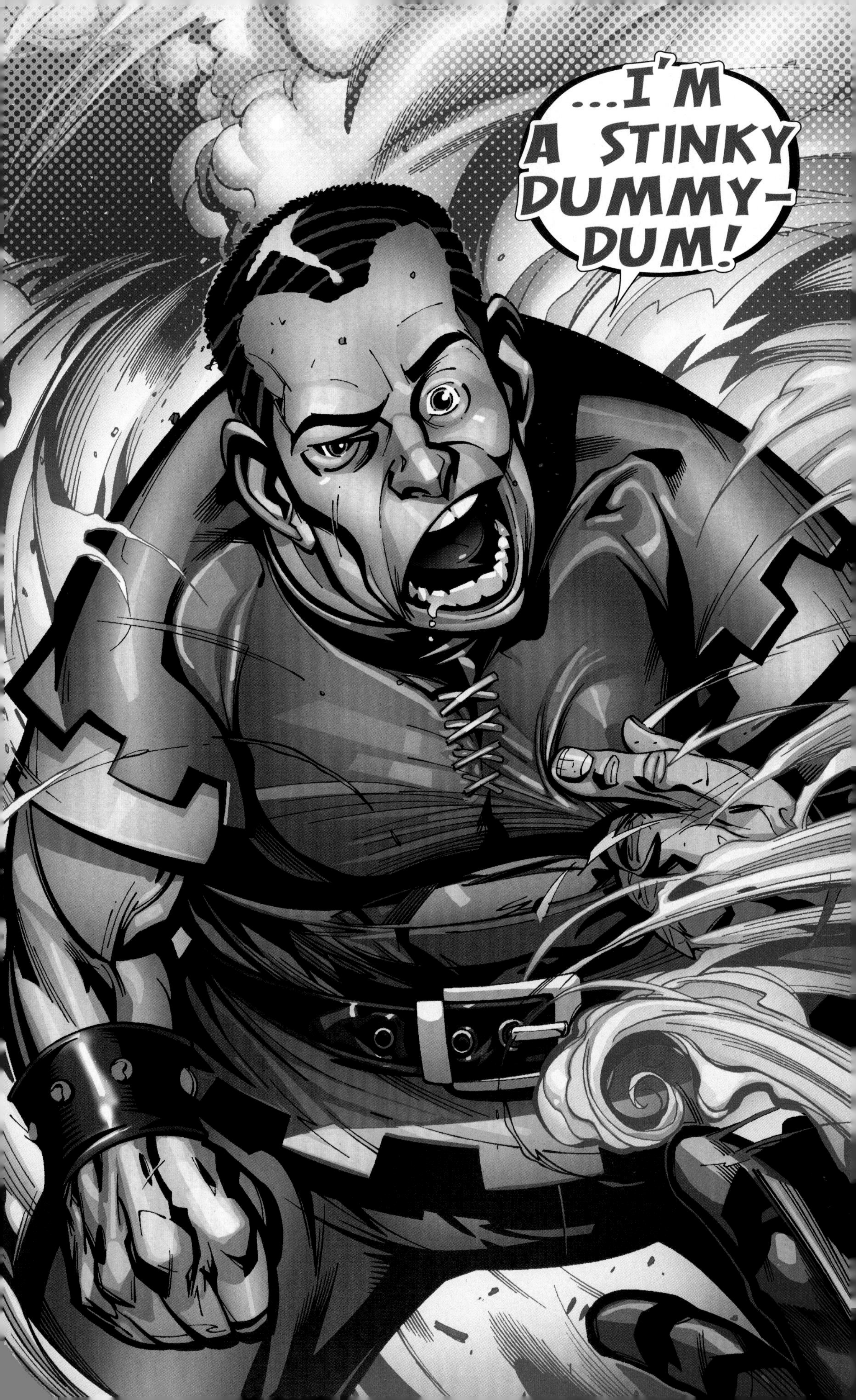
...I'M A STINKY DUMMY-DUM!

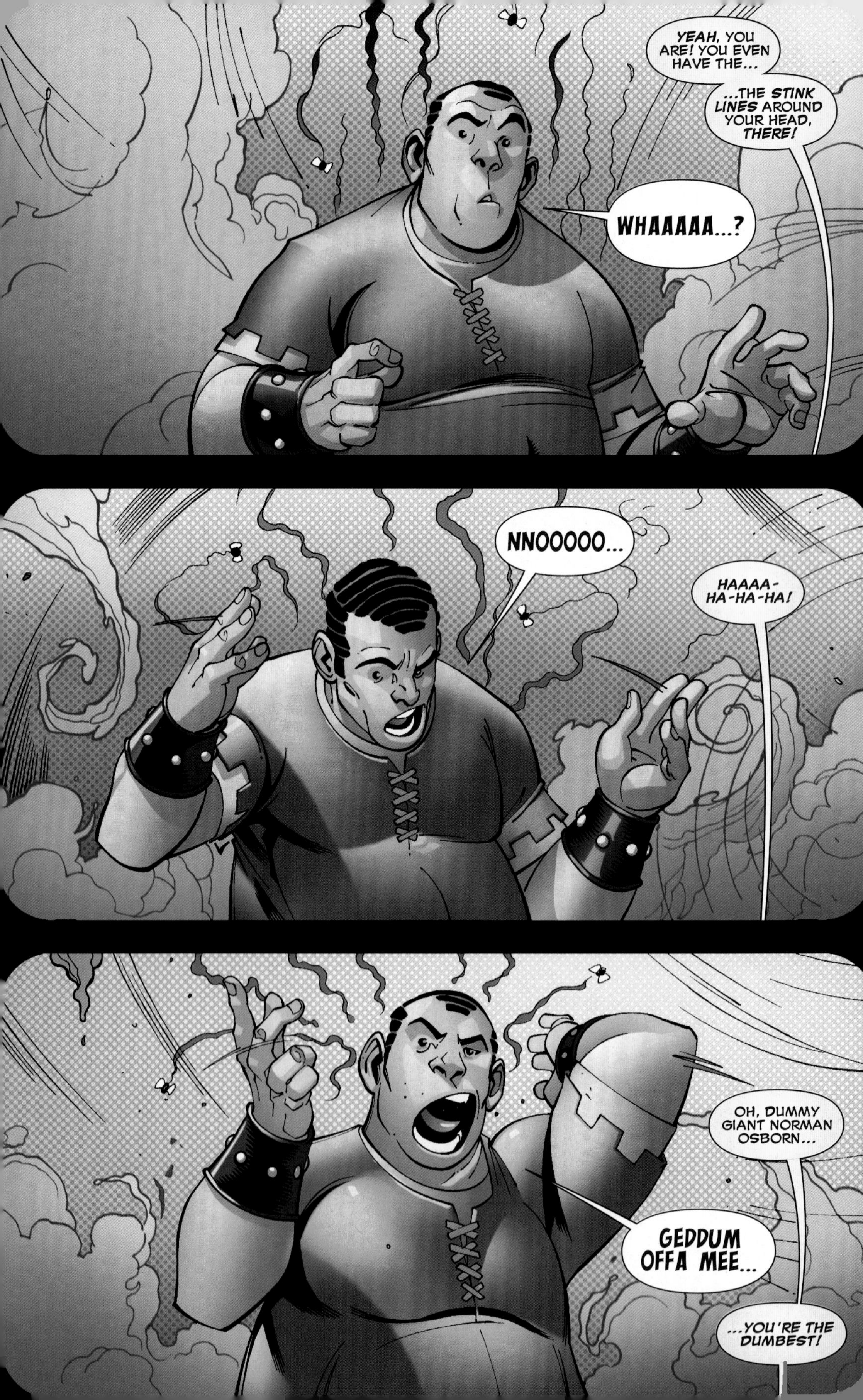
YEAH, YOU ARE! YOU EVEN HAVE THE...
...THE STINK LINES AROUND YOUR HEAD, THERE!
WHAAAAA...?
NNOOOOO...
HAAAA-HA-HA-HA!
OH, DUMMY GIANT NORMAN OSBORN...
GEDDUM OFFA MEE...
...YOU'RE THE DUMBEST!

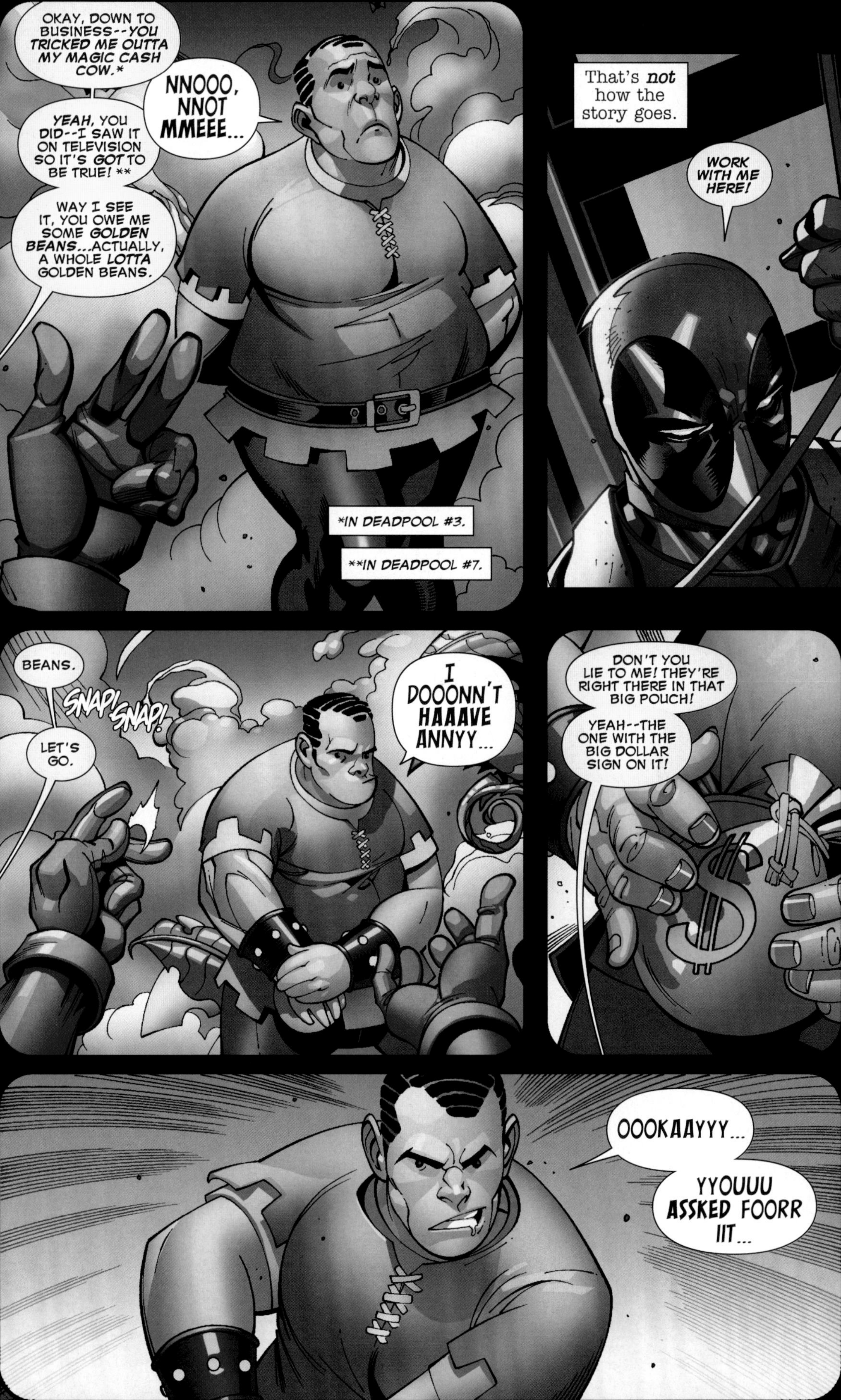

OKAY, DOWN TO BUSINESS--YOU TRICKED ME OUTTA MY MAGIC CASH COW.*
NNOOO, NNOT MMEEE...
YEAH, YOU DID--I SAW IT ON TELEVISION SO IT'S GOT TO BE TRUE! **
WAY I SEE IT, YOU OWE ME SOME GOLDEN BEANS...ACTUALLY, A WHOLE LOTTA GOLDEN BEANS.
*IN DEADPOOL #3.
**IN DEADPOOL #7.
That's not how the story goes.
WORK WITH ME HERE!
BEANS.
SNAP! SNAP!
LET'S GO.
I DOOONN'T HAAAVE ANNYY...
DON'T YOU LIE TO ME! THEY'RE RIGHT THERE IN THAT BIG POUCH!
YEAH--THE ONE WITH THE BIG DOLLAR SIGN ON IT!
OOOKAAYYY...
YYOUUU ASSKED FOORR IIT...

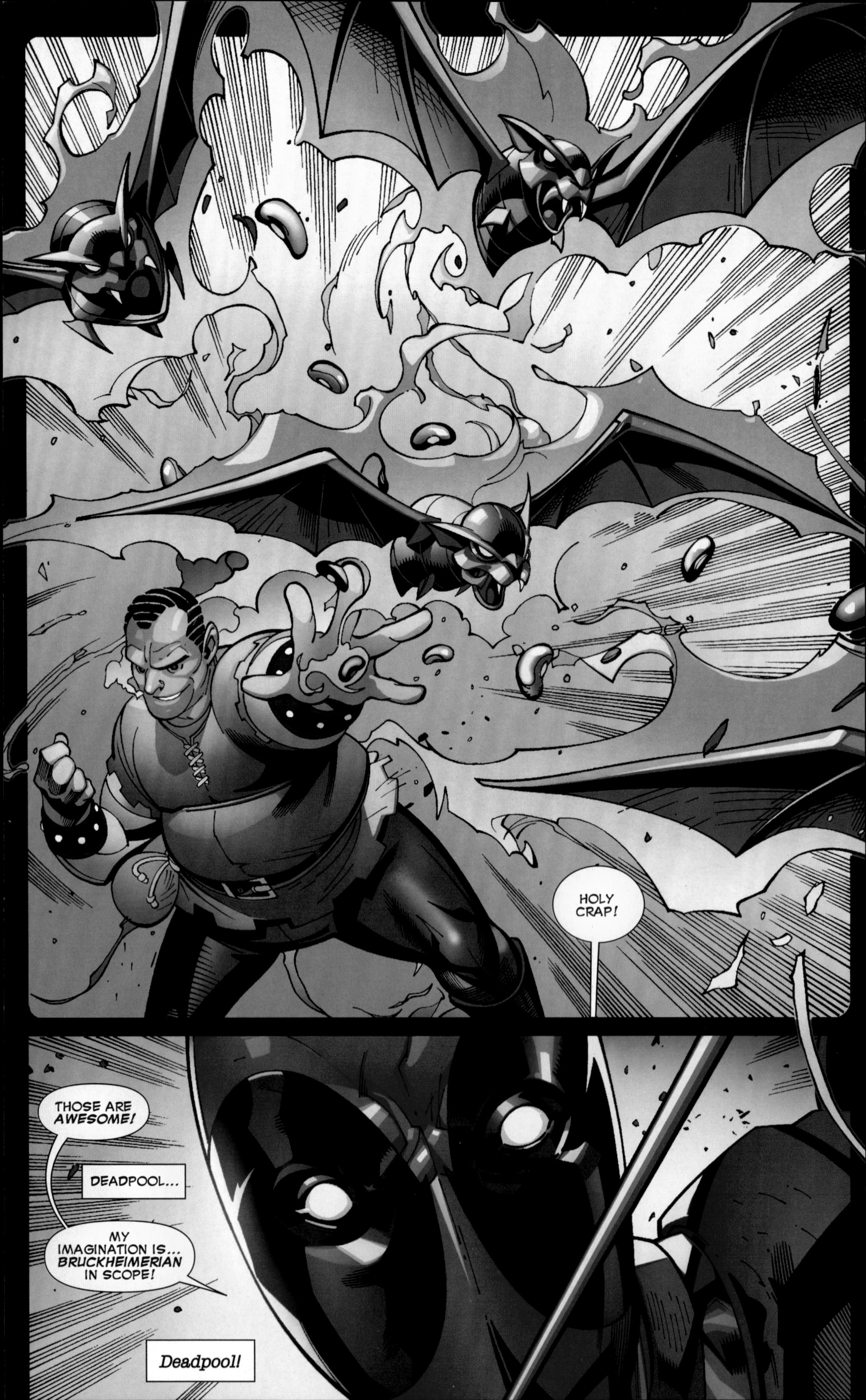
HOLY CRAP!
THOSE ARE AWESOME!
DEADPOOL...
MY IMAGINATION IS... BRUCKHEIMERIAN IN SCOPE!
Deadpool!

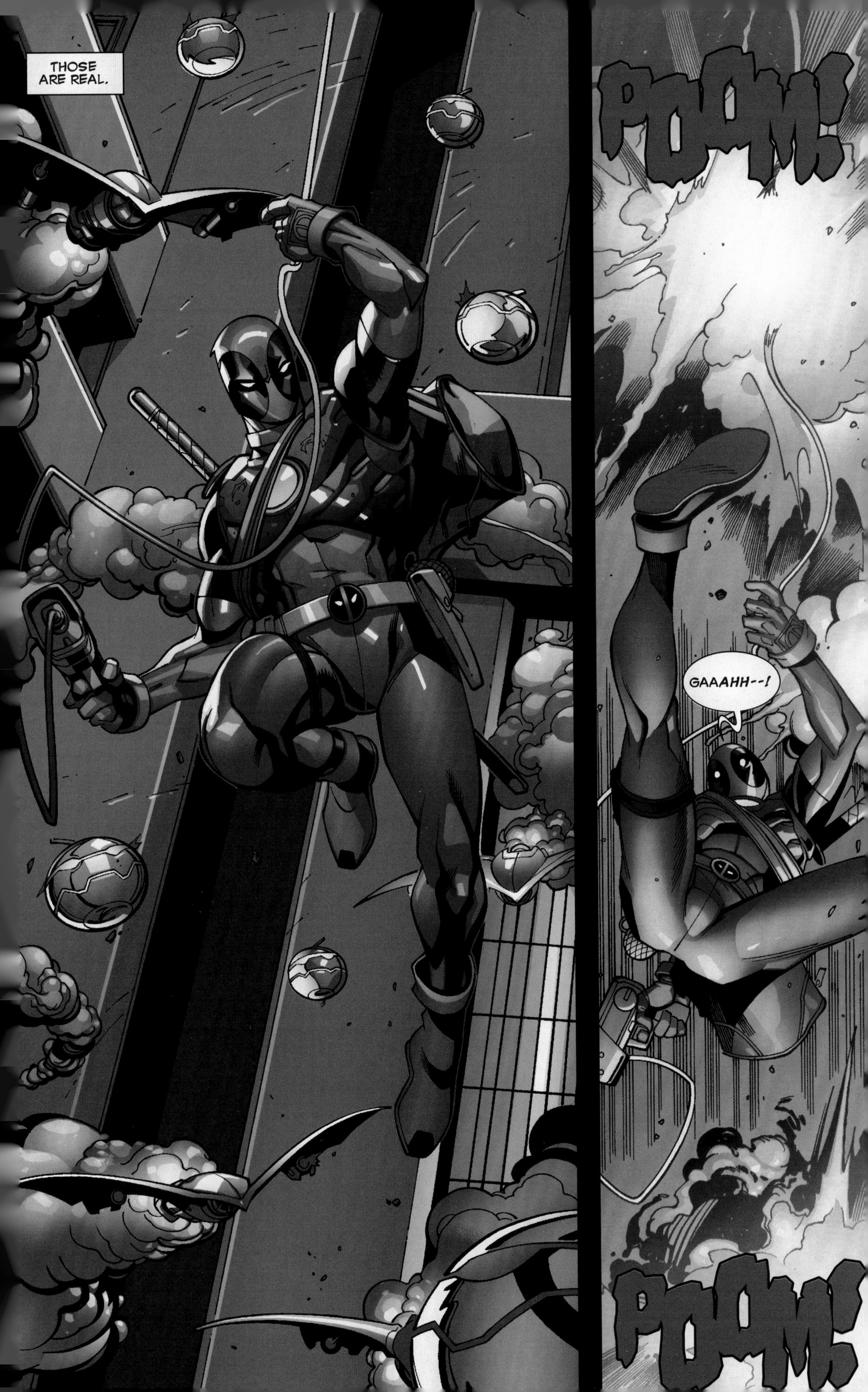
THOSE ARE REAL.
POOM!
GAAAHH--!
POOM!

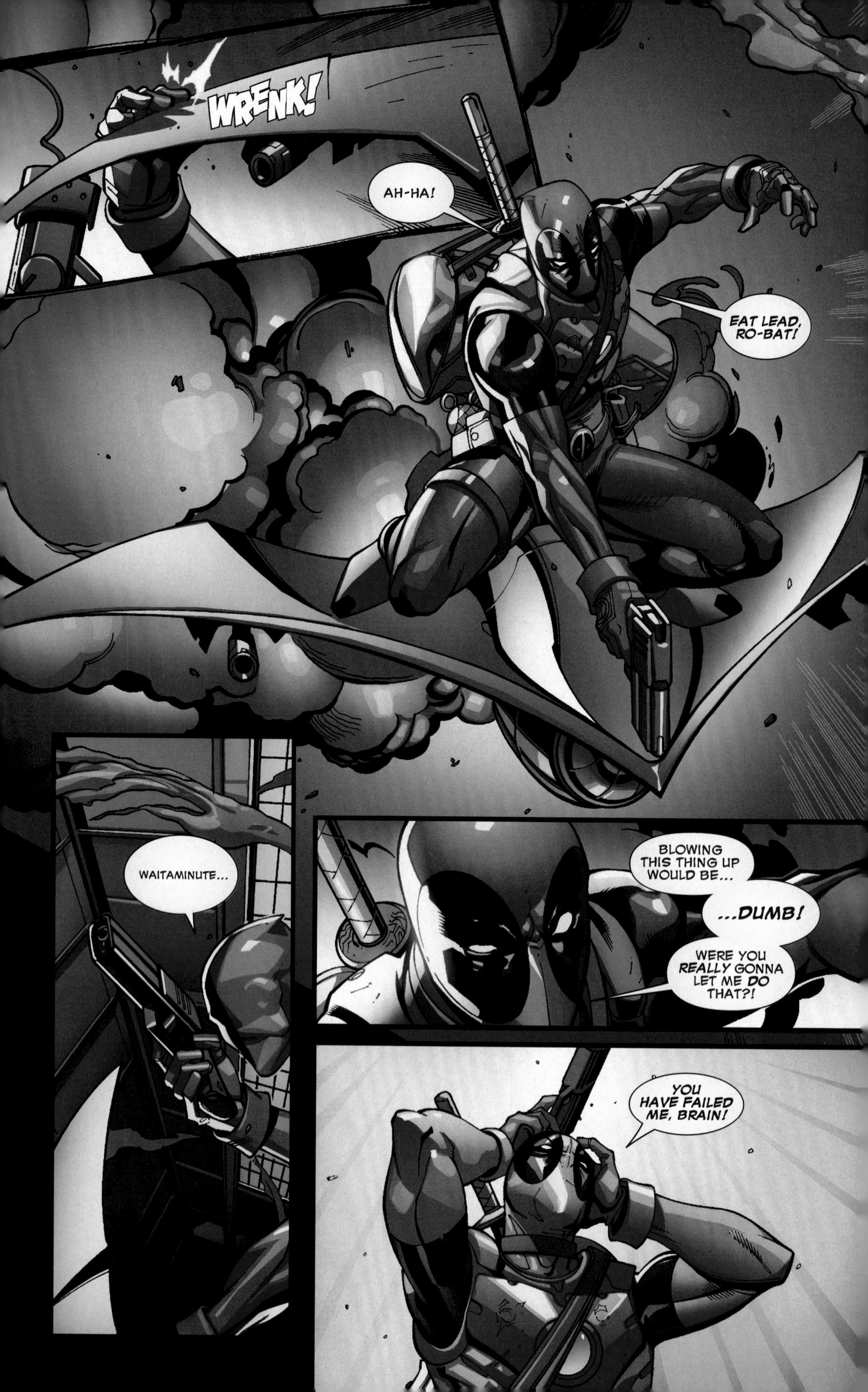
WRENK!
AH-HA!
EAT LEAD, RO-BAT!
WAITAMINUTE...
BLOWING THIS THING UP WOULD BE...
...DUMB!
WERE YOU REALLY GONNA LET ME DO THAT?!
YOU HAVE FAILED ME, BRAIN!

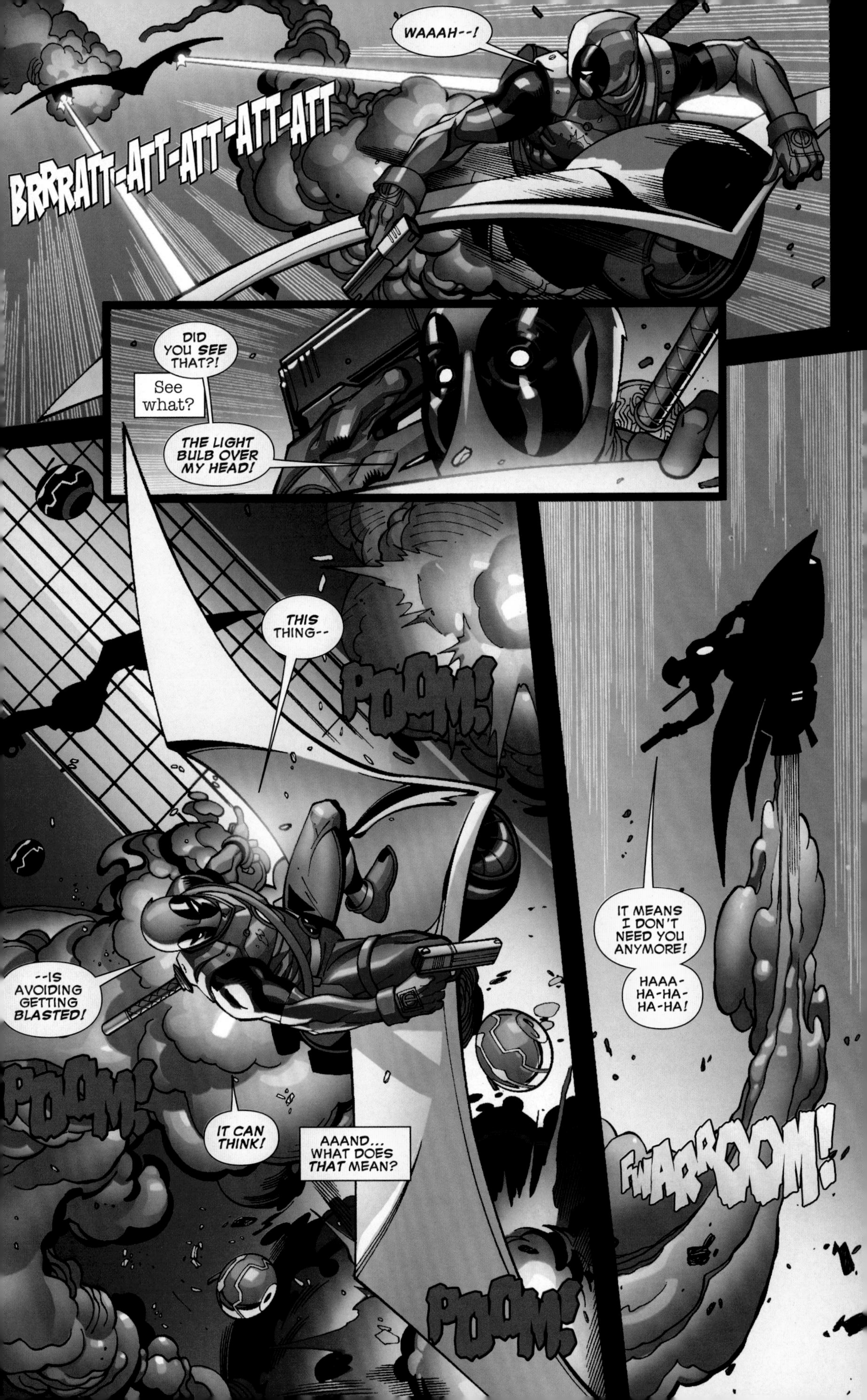
WAAAH--!
BRRRATT-ATT-ATT-ATT-ATT
DID YOU SEE THAT?!
See what?
THE LIGHT BULB OVER MY HEAD!
THIS THING--
POOM!
--IS AVOIDING GETTING BLASTED!
POOM!
IT CAN THINK!
AAAND... WHAT DOES THAT MEAN?
IT MEANS I DON'T NEED YOU ANYMORE!
HAAA-HA-HA-HA-HA!
FWAROOM!
POOM!

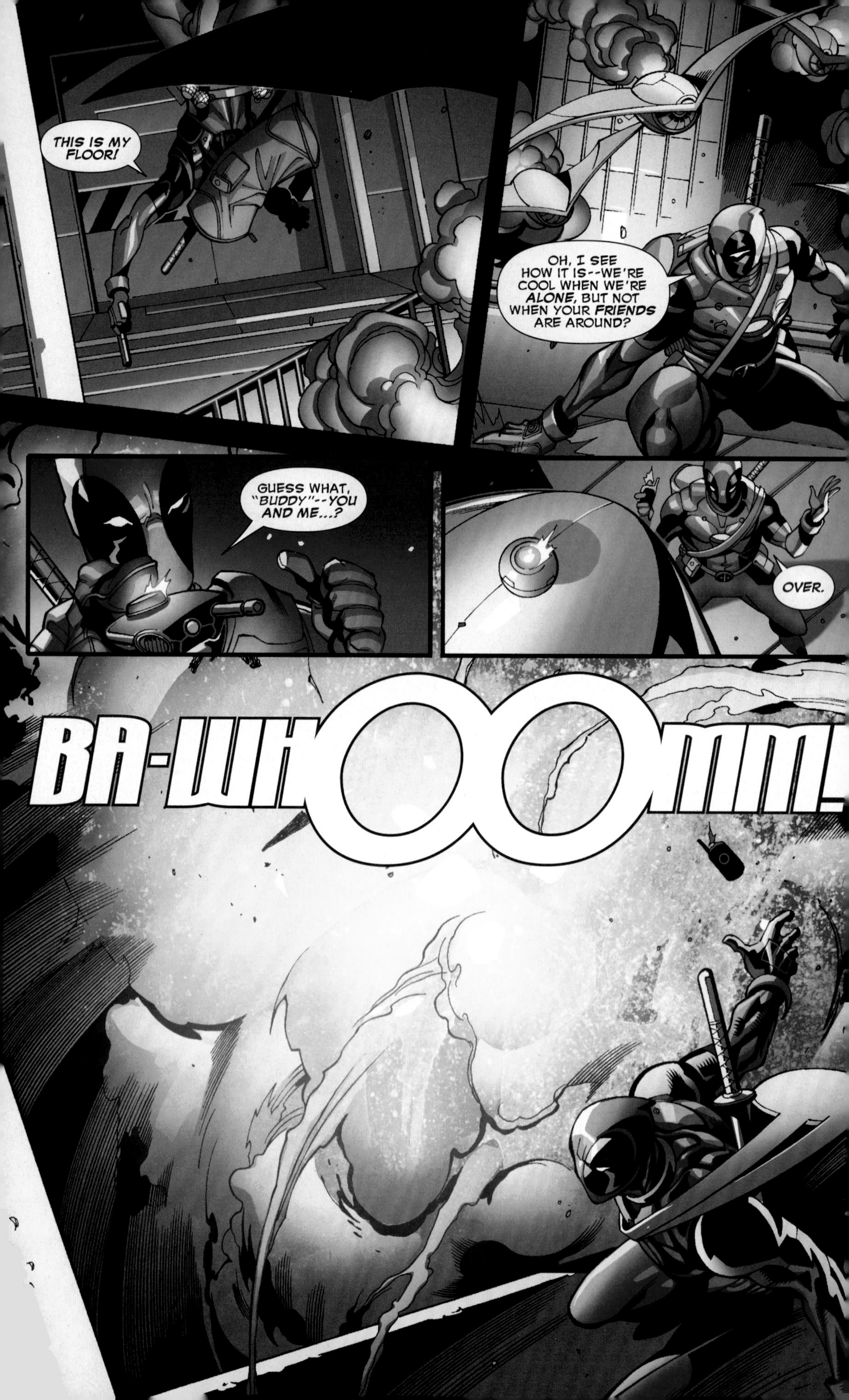
THIS IS MY FLOOR!
OH, I SEE HOW IT IS--WE'RE COOL WHEN WE'RE ALONE, BUT NOT WHEN YOUR FRIENDS ARE AROUND?
GUESS WHAT, "BUDDY"--YOU AND ME...?
OVER.
BA-WHOOMM!

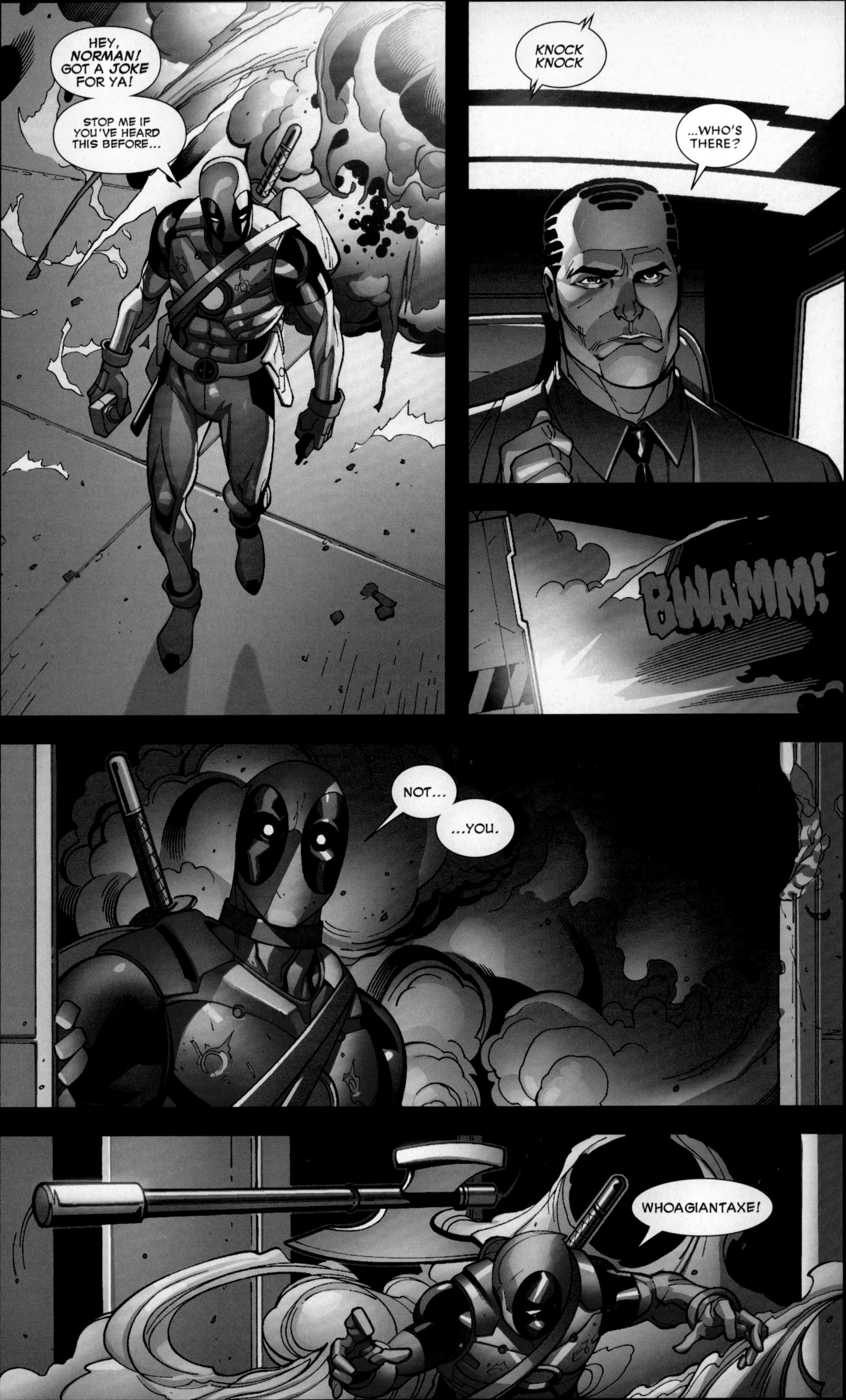
HEY, NORMAN! GOT A JOKE FOR YA!
STOP ME IF YOU'VE HEARD THIS BEFORE...
KNOCK KNOCK
...WHO'S THERE?
BWAMM!
NOT...
...YOU.
WHOAGIANTAXE!

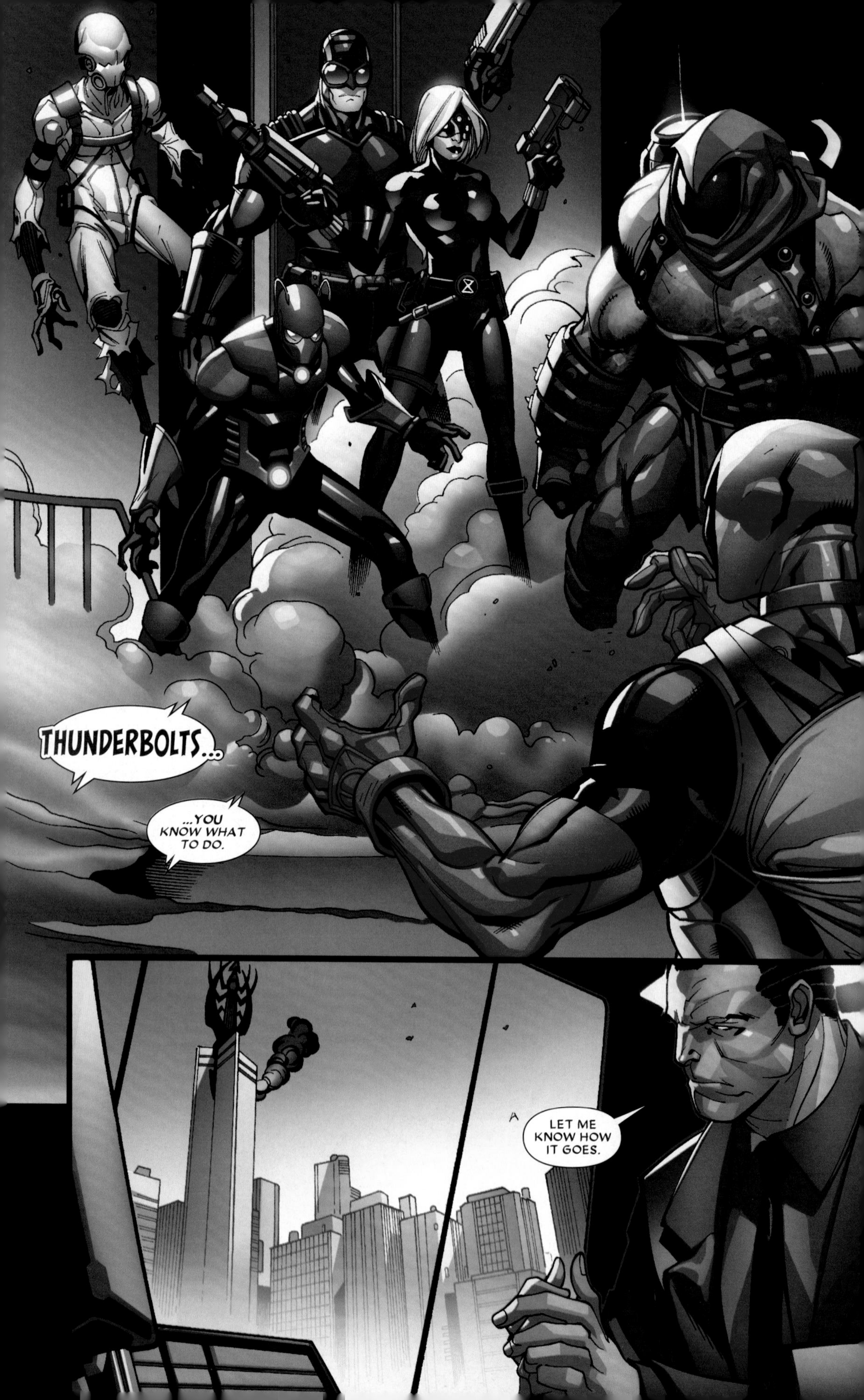
THUNDERBOLTS...
...YOU KNOW WHAT TO DO.
LET ME KNOW HOW IT GOES.

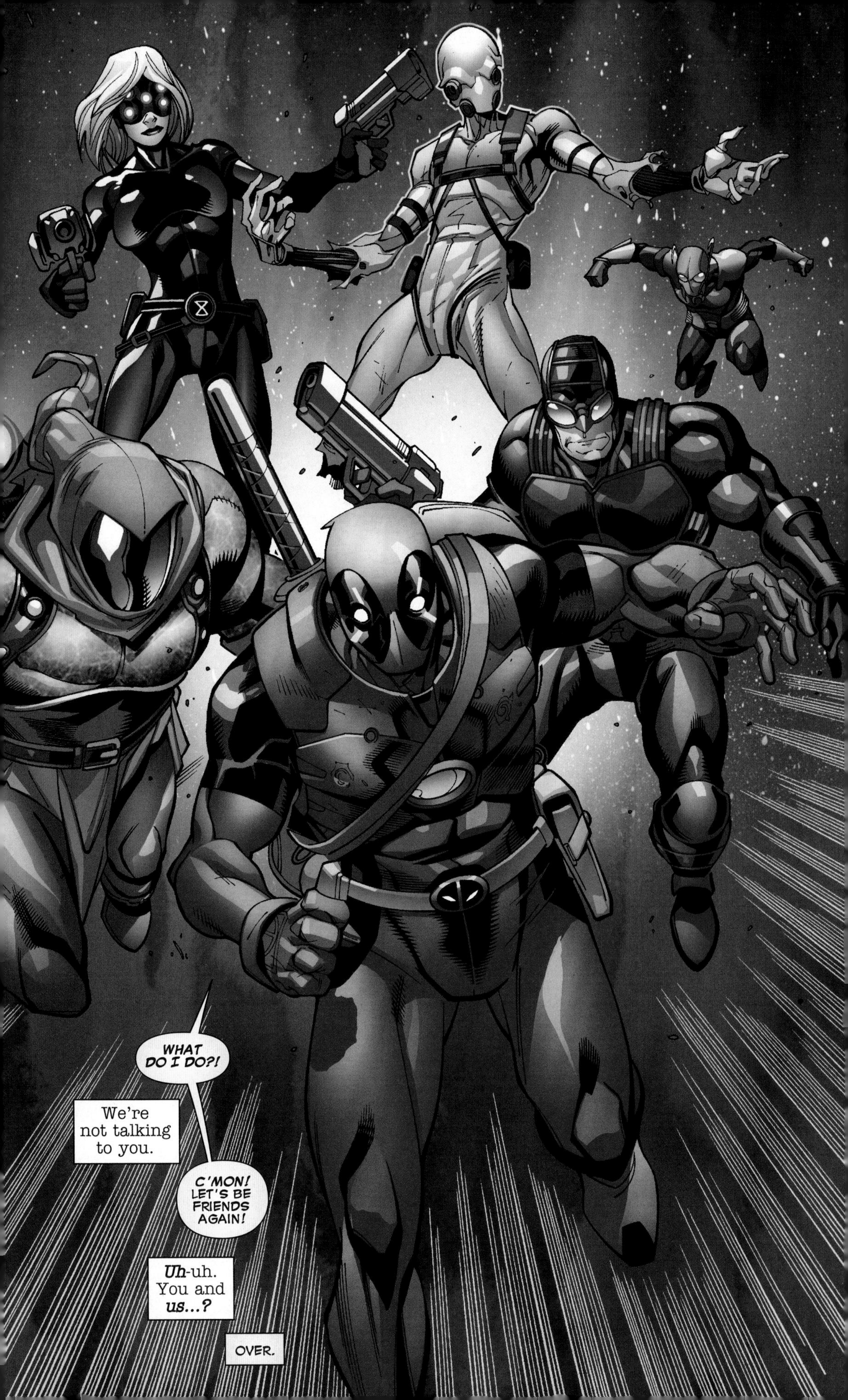
WHAT DO I DO?!
We're not talking to you.
C'MON! LET'S BE FRIENDS AGAIN!
Uh-uh. You and *us*...?
OVER.

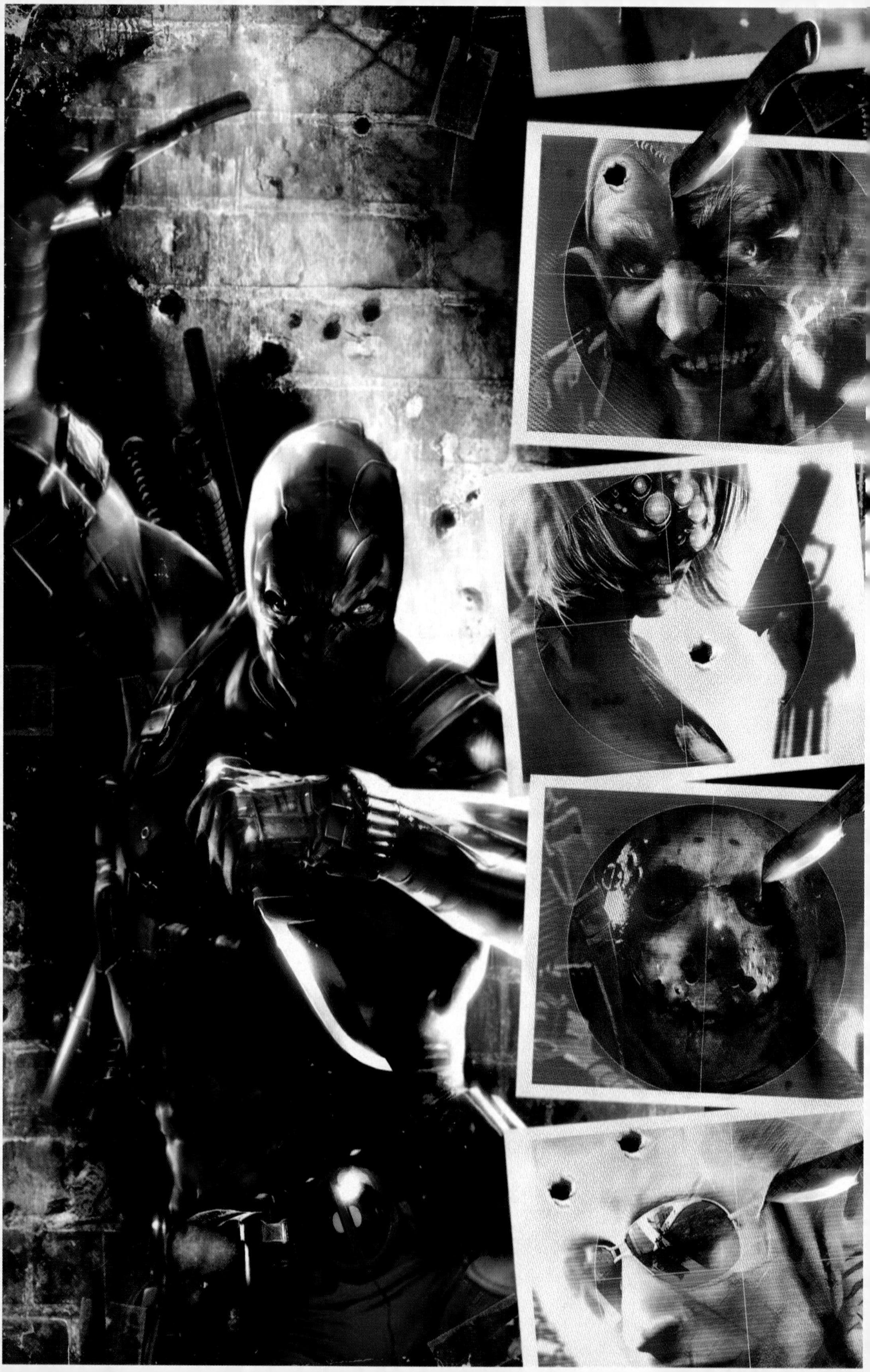

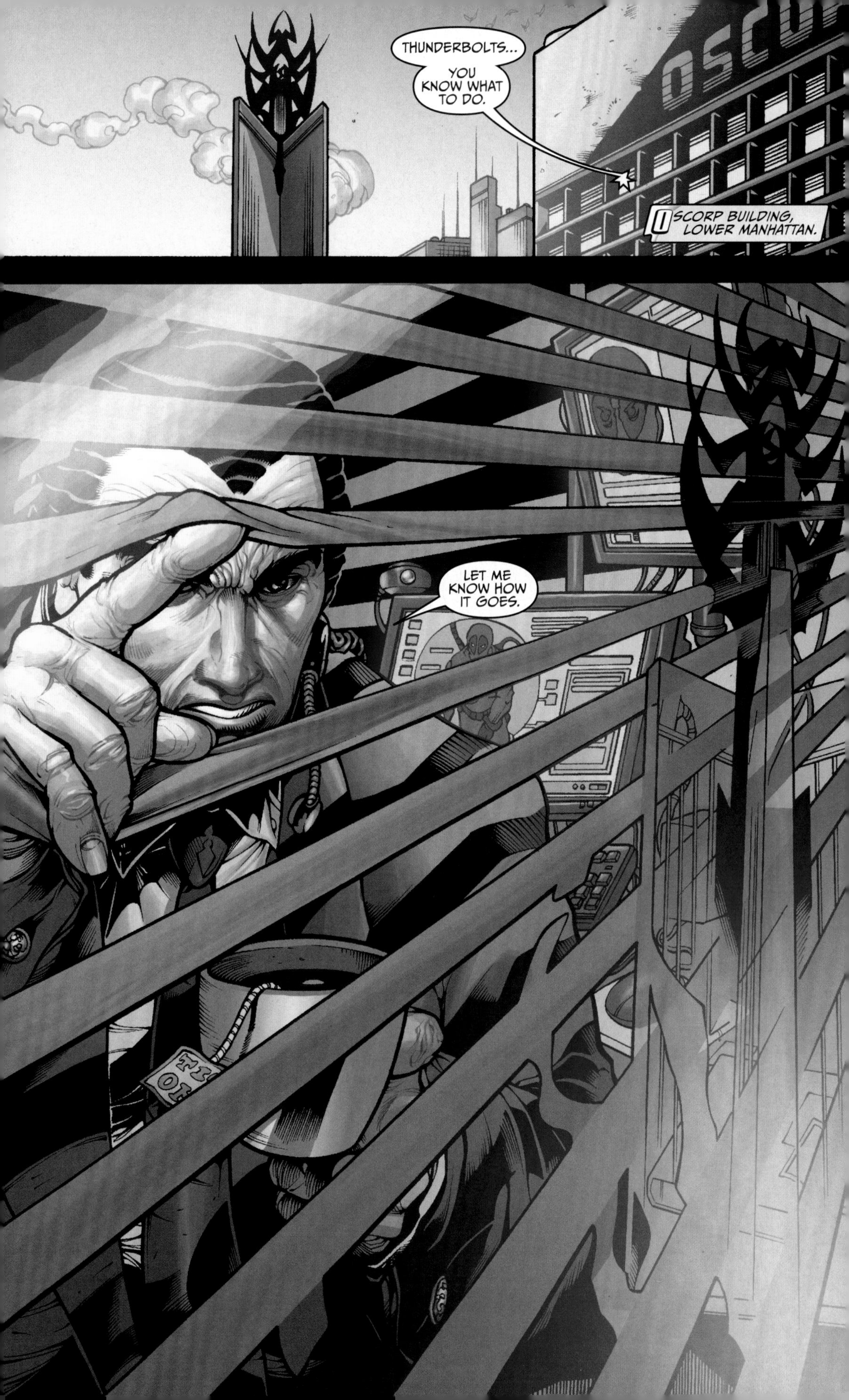
THUNDERBOLTS...
YOU KNOW WHAT TO DO.
OSCORP BUILDING, LOWER MANHATTAN.
LET ME KNOW HOW IT GOES.

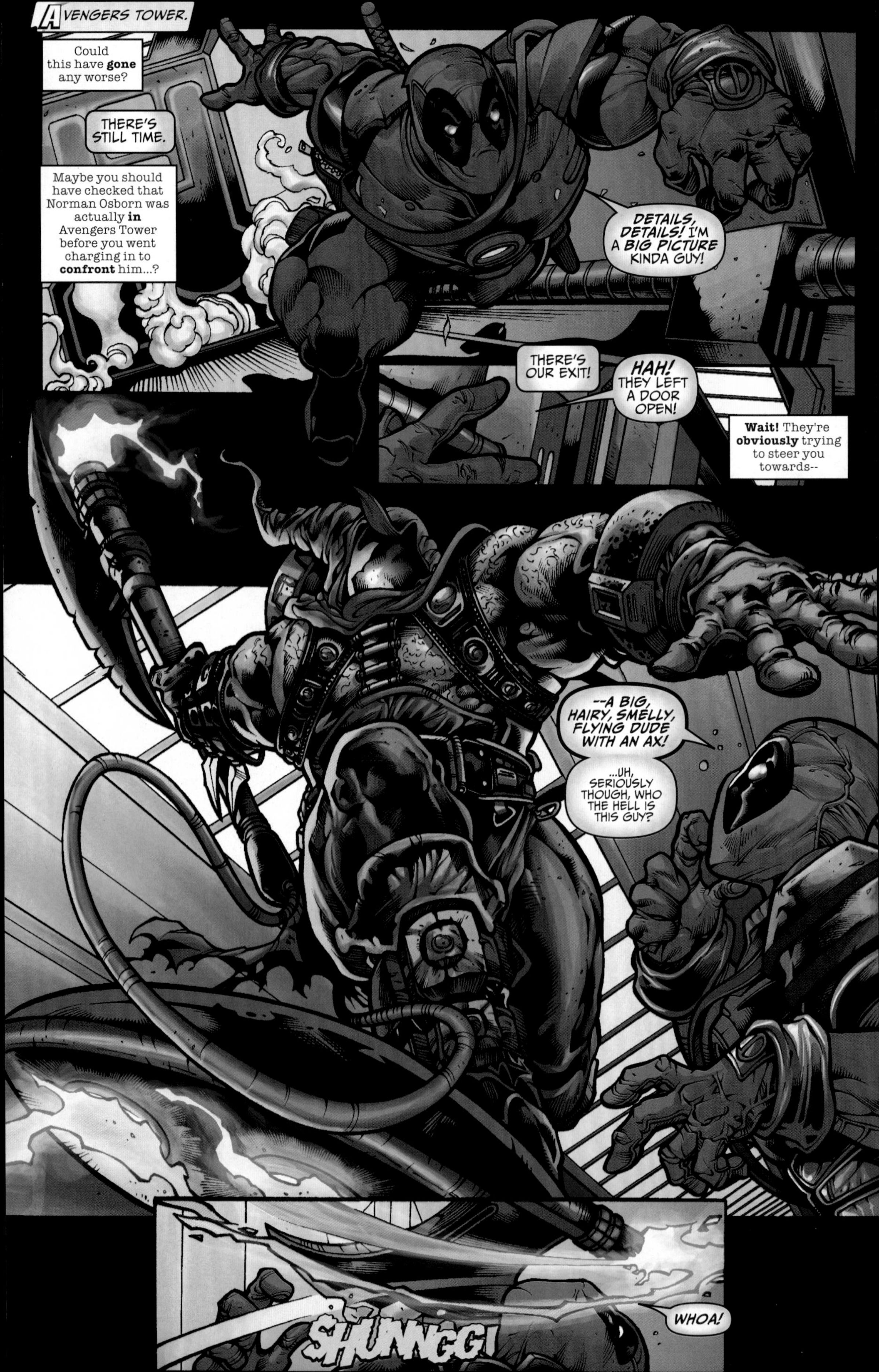
AVENGERS TOWER.
Could this have gone any worse?
THERE'S STILL TIME.
Maybe you should have checked that Norman Osborn was actually in Avengers Tower before you went charging in to confront him...?
DETAILS, DETAILS! I'M A BIG PICTURE KINDA GUY!
THERE'S OUR EXIT!
HAH! THEY LEFT A DOOR OPEN!
Wait! They're obviously trying to steer you towards--
--A BIG, HAIRY, SMELLY, FLYING DUDE WITH AN AX!
...UH, SERIOUSLY THOUGH, WHO THE HELL IS THIS GUY?
SHUNNGG!
WHOA!

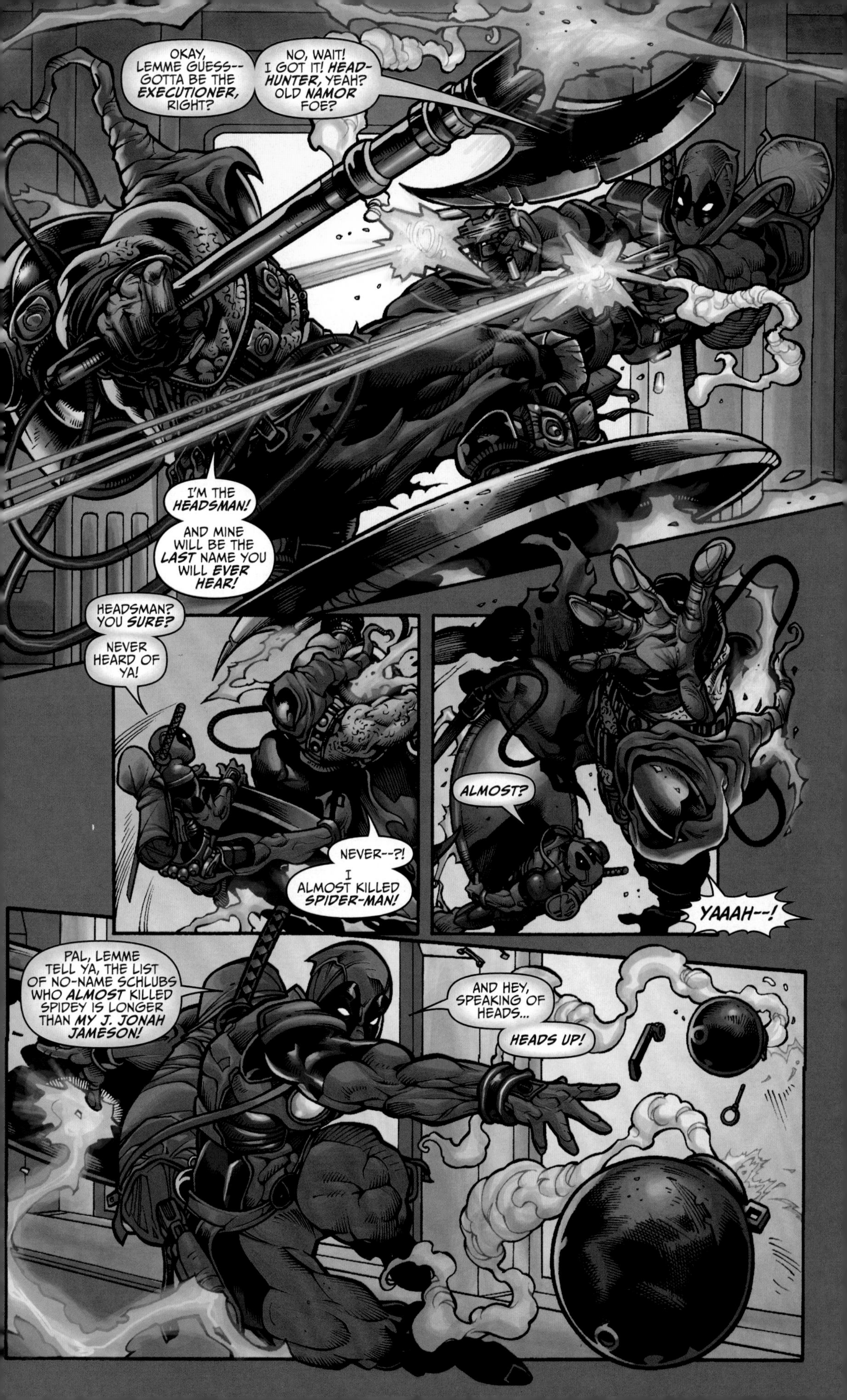
OKAY, LEMME GUESS-- GOTTA BE THE EXECUTIONER, RIGHT?
NO, WAIT! I GOT IT! HEAD-HUNTER, YEAH? OLD NAMOR FOE?
I'M THE HEADSMAN!
AND MINE WILL BE THE LAST NAME YOU WILL EVER HEAR!
HEADSMAN? YOU SURE?
NEVER HEARD OF YA!
NEVER--?! I ALMOST KILLED SPIDER-MAN!
ALMOST?
YAAAH--!
PAL, LEMME TELL YA, THE LIST OF NO-NAME SCHLUBS WHO ALMOST KILLED SPIDEY IS LONGER THAN MY J. JONAH JAMESON!
AND HEY, SPEAKING OF HEADS...
HEADS UP!

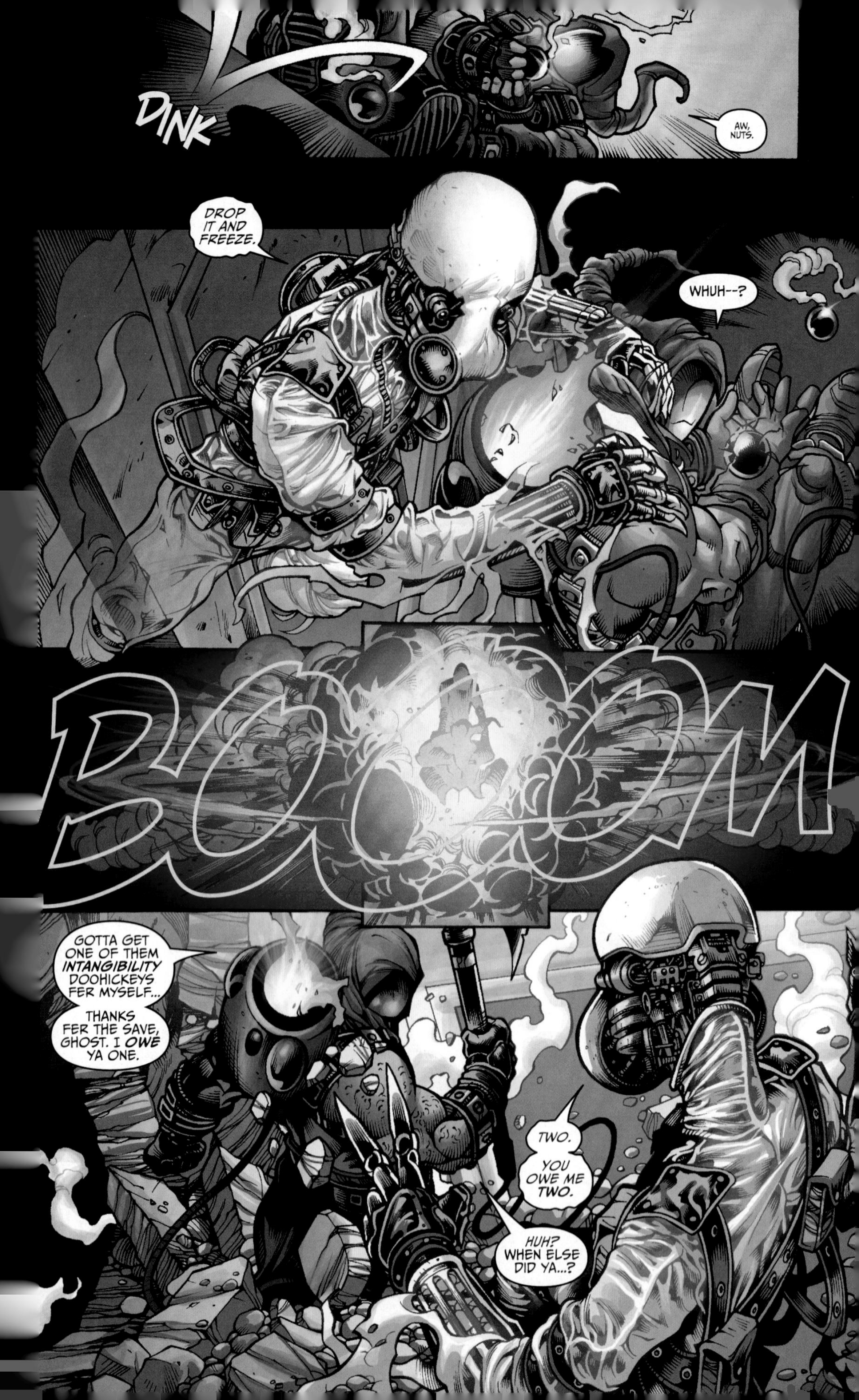
DINK
AW, NUTS.
DROP IT AND FREEZE.
WHUH--?
BOOOM
GOTTA GET ONE OF THEM *INTANGIBILITY* DOOHICKEYS FER MYSELF...
THANKS FER THE SAVE, GHOST. I *OWE* YA ONE.
TWO.
YOU OWE ME *TWO.*
HUH? WHEN ELSE DID YA...?

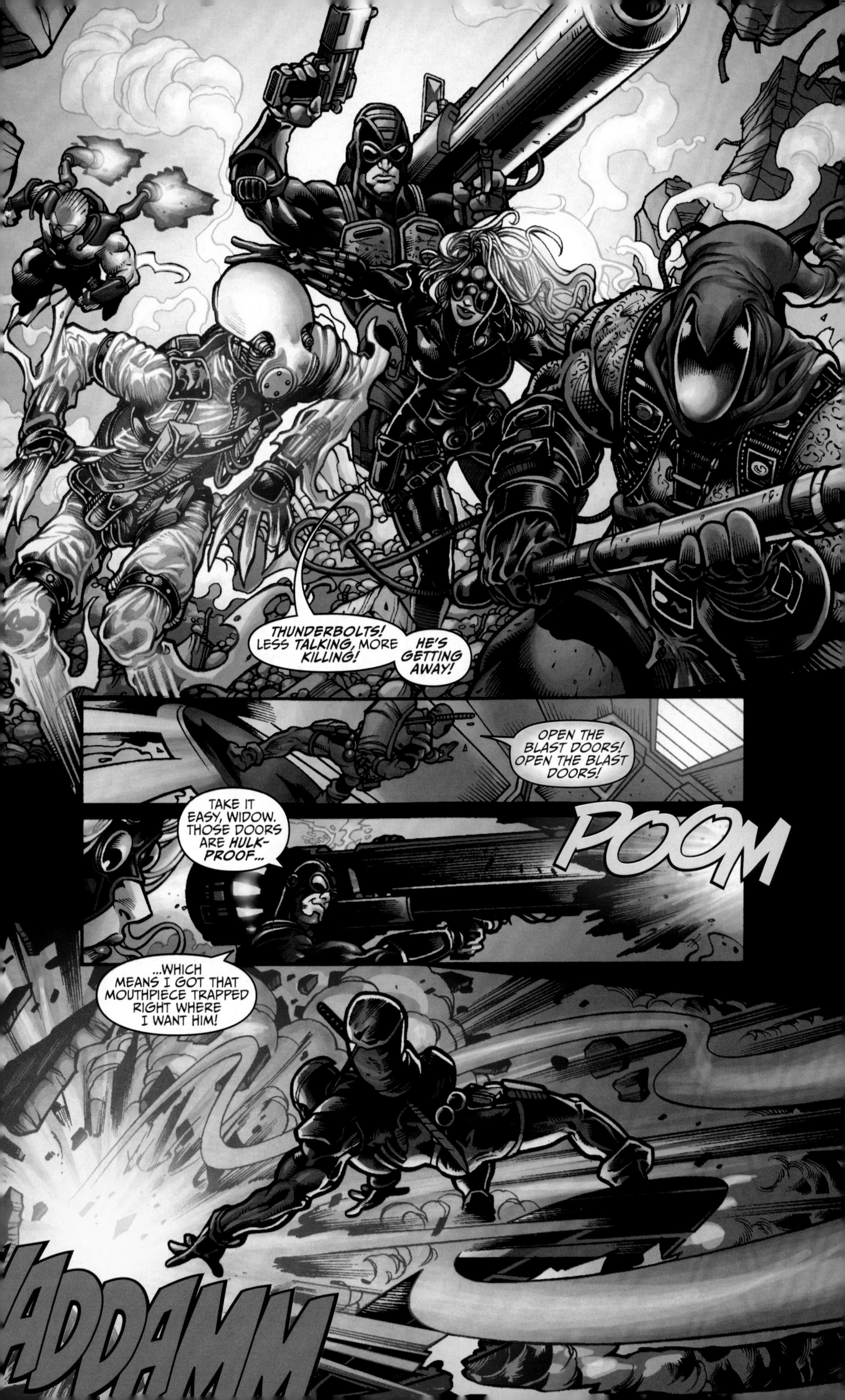
THUNDERBOLTS! LESS TALKING, MORE KILLING!
HE'S GETTING AWAY!
OPEN THE BLAST DOORS! OPEN THE BLAST DOORS!
TAKE IT EASY, WIDOW. THOSE DOORS ARE HULK-PROOF...
POOM
...WHICH MEANS I GOT THAT MOUTHPIECE TRAPPED RIGHT WHERE I WANT HIM!
ADDAMM

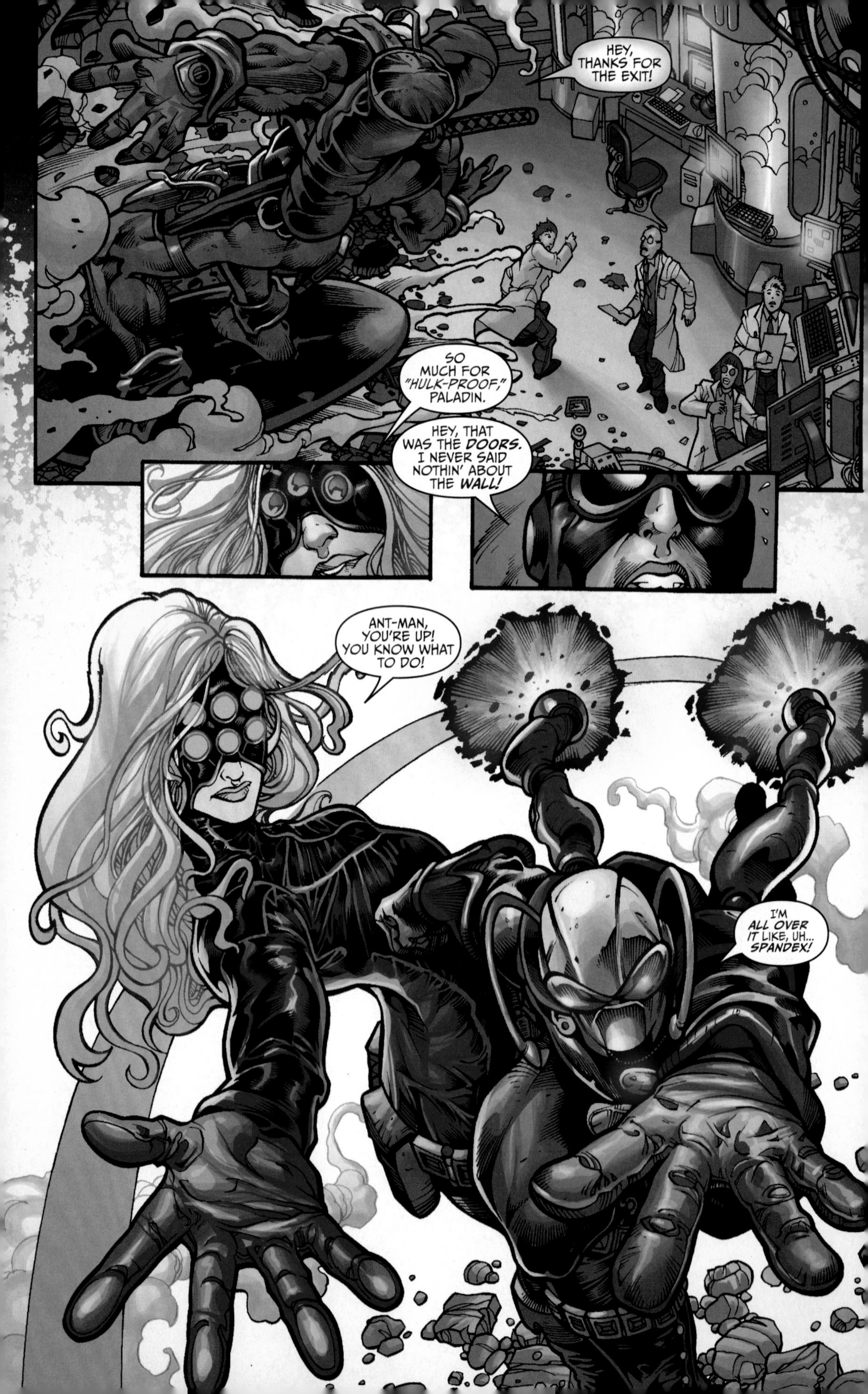
HEY, THANKS FOR THE EXIT!
SO MUCH FOR "HULK-PROOF," PALADIN.
HEY, THAT WAS THE DOORS. I NEVER SAID NOTHIN' ABOUT THE WALL!
ANT-MAN, YOU'RE UP! YOU KNOW WHAT TO DO!
I'M ALL OVER IT LIKE, UH... SPANDEX!

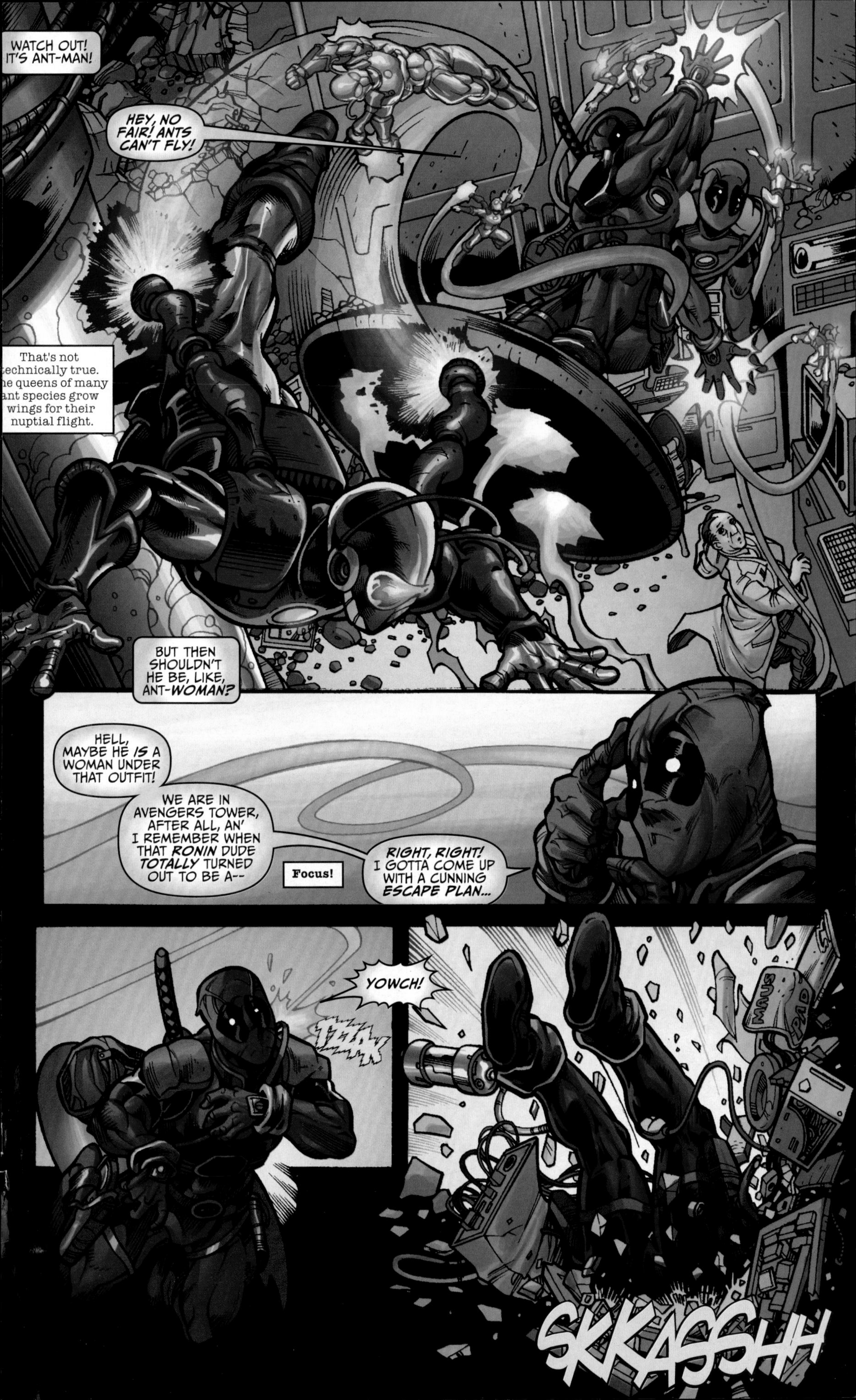

WATCH OUT! IT'S ANT-MAN!
HEY, NO FAIR! ANTS CAN'T FLY!
That's not technically true. The queens of many ant species grow wings for their nuptial flight.
BUT THEN SHOULDN'T HE BE, LIKE, ANT-WOMAN?
HELL, MAYBE HE IS A WOMAN UNDER THAT OUTFIT!
WE ARE IN AVENGERS TOWER, AFTER ALL, AN' I REMEMBER WHEN THAT RONIN DUDE TOTALLY TURNED OUT TO BE A--
Focus!
RIGHT, RIGHT! I GOTTA COME UP WITH A CUNNING ESCAPE PLAN...
YOWCH!
TZAK
MAUS PAD
SKKASSHH

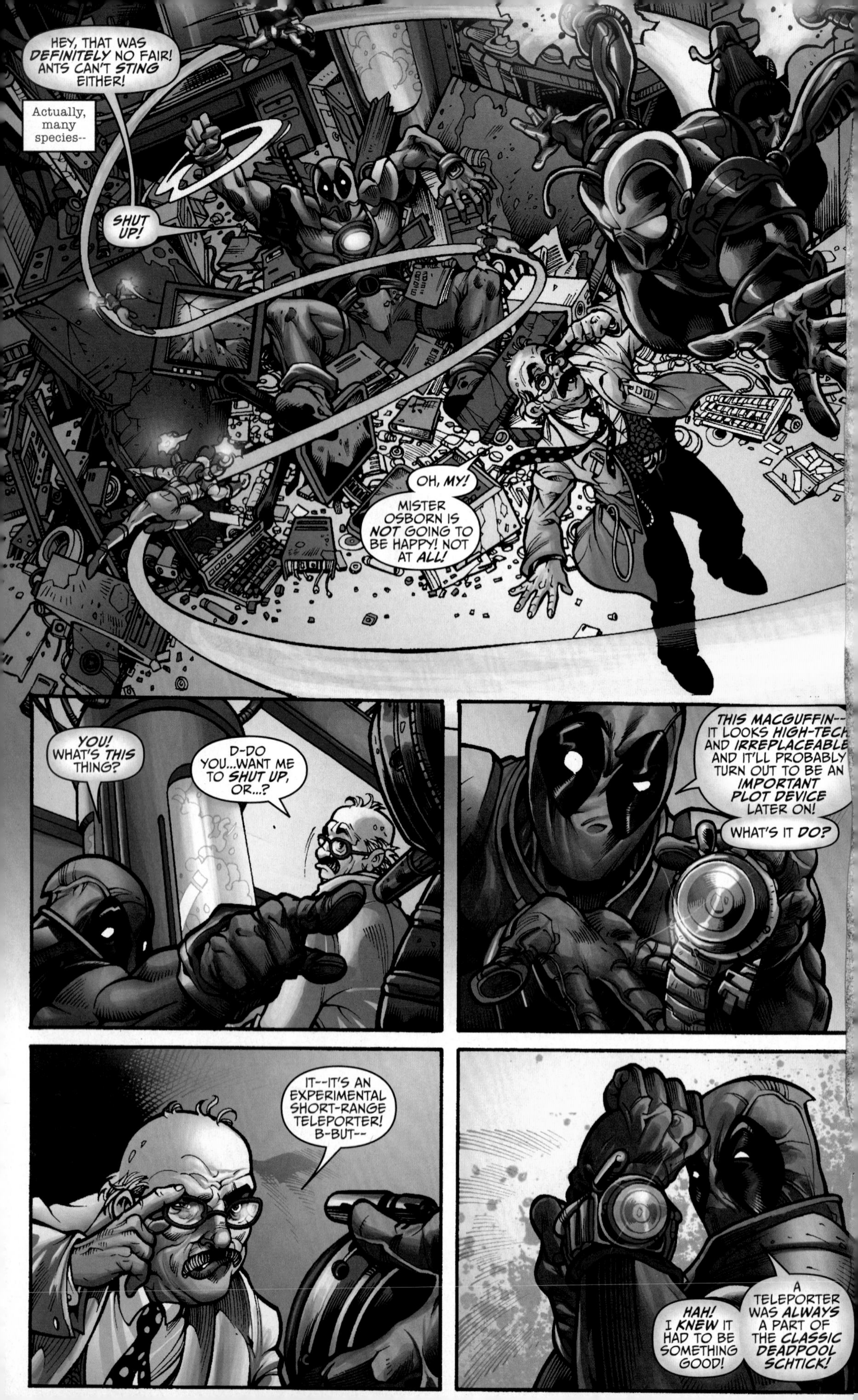
HEY, THAT WAS DEFINITELY NO FAIR! ANTS CAN'T STING EITHER!
Actually, many species--
SHUT UP!
OH, MY!
MISTER OSBORN IS NOT GOING TO BE HAPPY! NOT AT ALL!
YOU! WHAT'S THIS THING?
D-DO YOU...WANT ME TO SHUT UP, OR...?
THIS MACGUFFIN-- IT LOOKS HIGH-TECH AND IRREPLACEABLE AND IT'LL PROBABLY TURN OUT TO BE AN IMPORTANT PLOT DEVICE LATER ON!
WHAT'S IT DO?
IT--IT'S AN EXPERIMENTAL SHORT-RANGE TELEPORTER! B-BUT--
A TELEPORTER WAS ALWAYS A PART OF THE CLASSIC DEADPOOL SCHTICK!
HAH! I KNEW IT HAD TO BE SOMETHING GOOD!

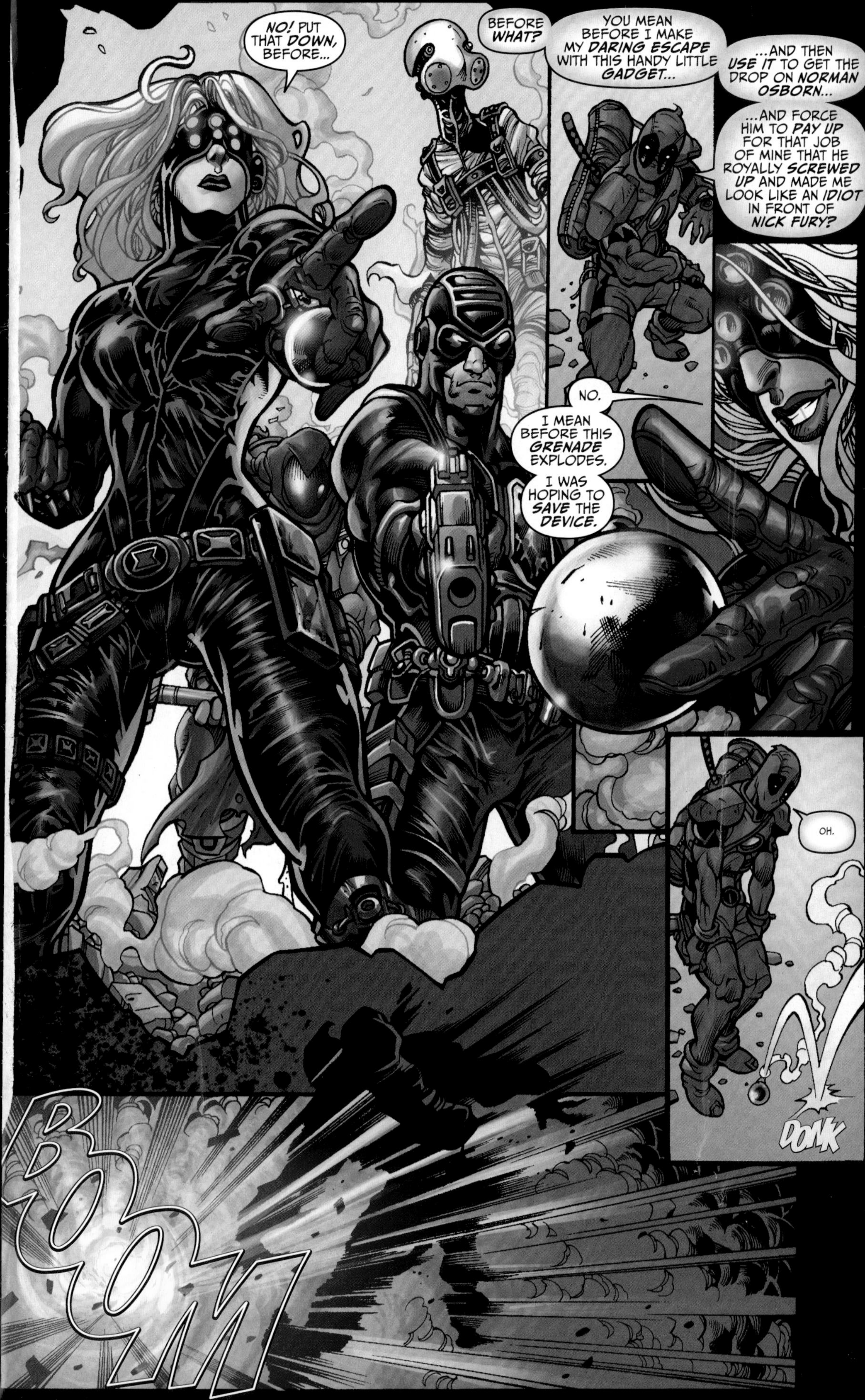
NO! PUT THAT DOWN, BEFORE...
BEFORE WHAT?
YOU MEAN BEFORE I MAKE MY DARING ESCAPE WITH THIS HANDY LITTLE GADGET...
...AND THEN USE IT TO GET THE DROP ON NORMAN OSBORN...
...AND FORCE HIM TO PAY UP FOR THAT JOB OF MINE THAT HE ROYALLY SCREWED UP AND MADE ME LOOK LIKE AN IDIOT IN FRONT OF NICK FURY?
NO.
I MEAN BEFORE THIS GRENADE EXPLODES.
I WAS HOPING TO SAVE THE DEVICE.
OH.
DONK
BOOM

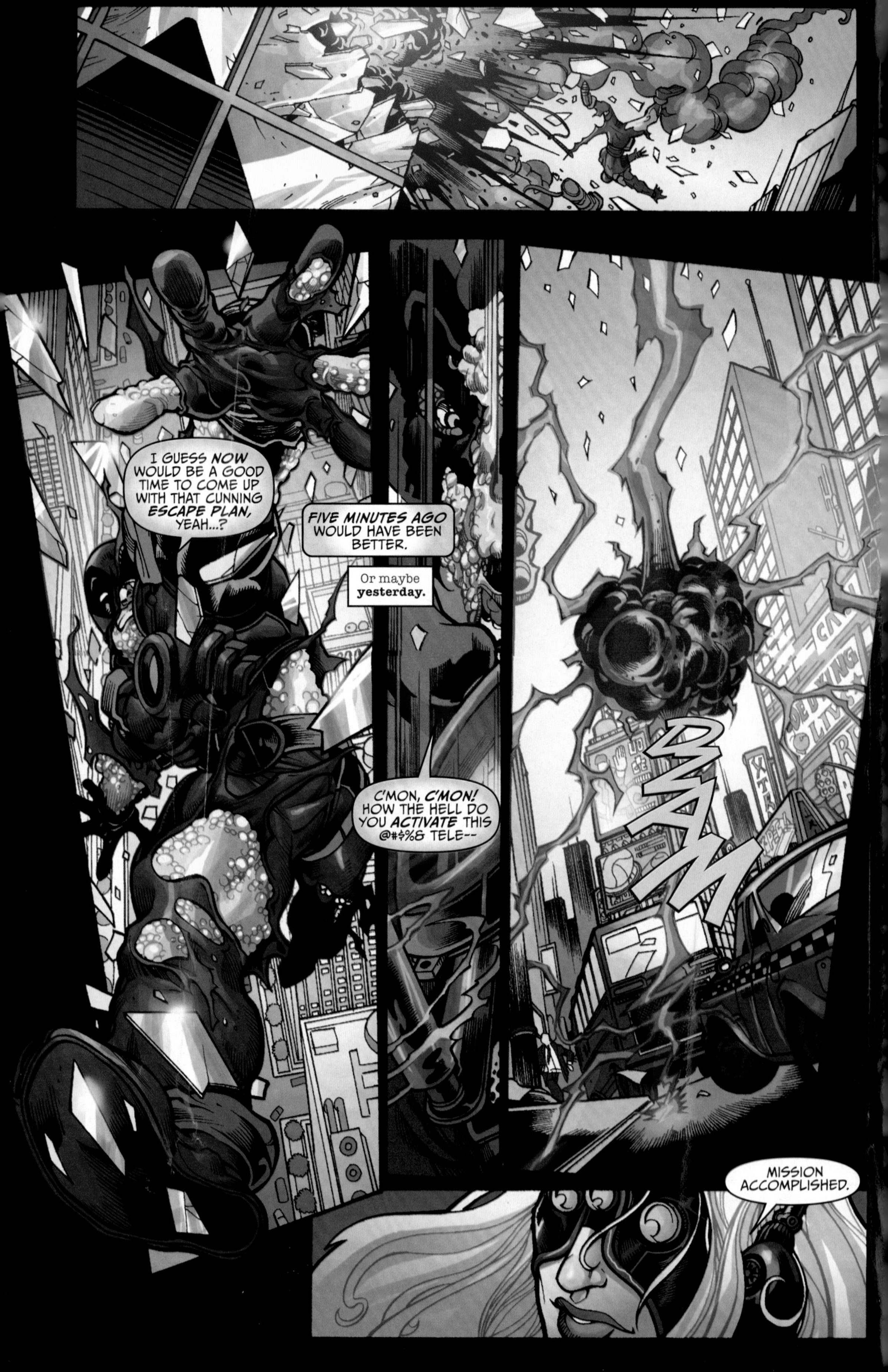
I GUESS NOW WOULD BE A GOOD TIME TO COME UP WITH THAT CUNNING ESCAPE PLAN, YEAH...?
FIVE MINUTES AGO WOULD HAVE BEEN BETTER.
Or maybe yesterday.
C'MON, C'MON! HOW THE HELL DO YOU ACTIVATE THIS @#$%& TELE--
MISSION ACCOMPLISHED.

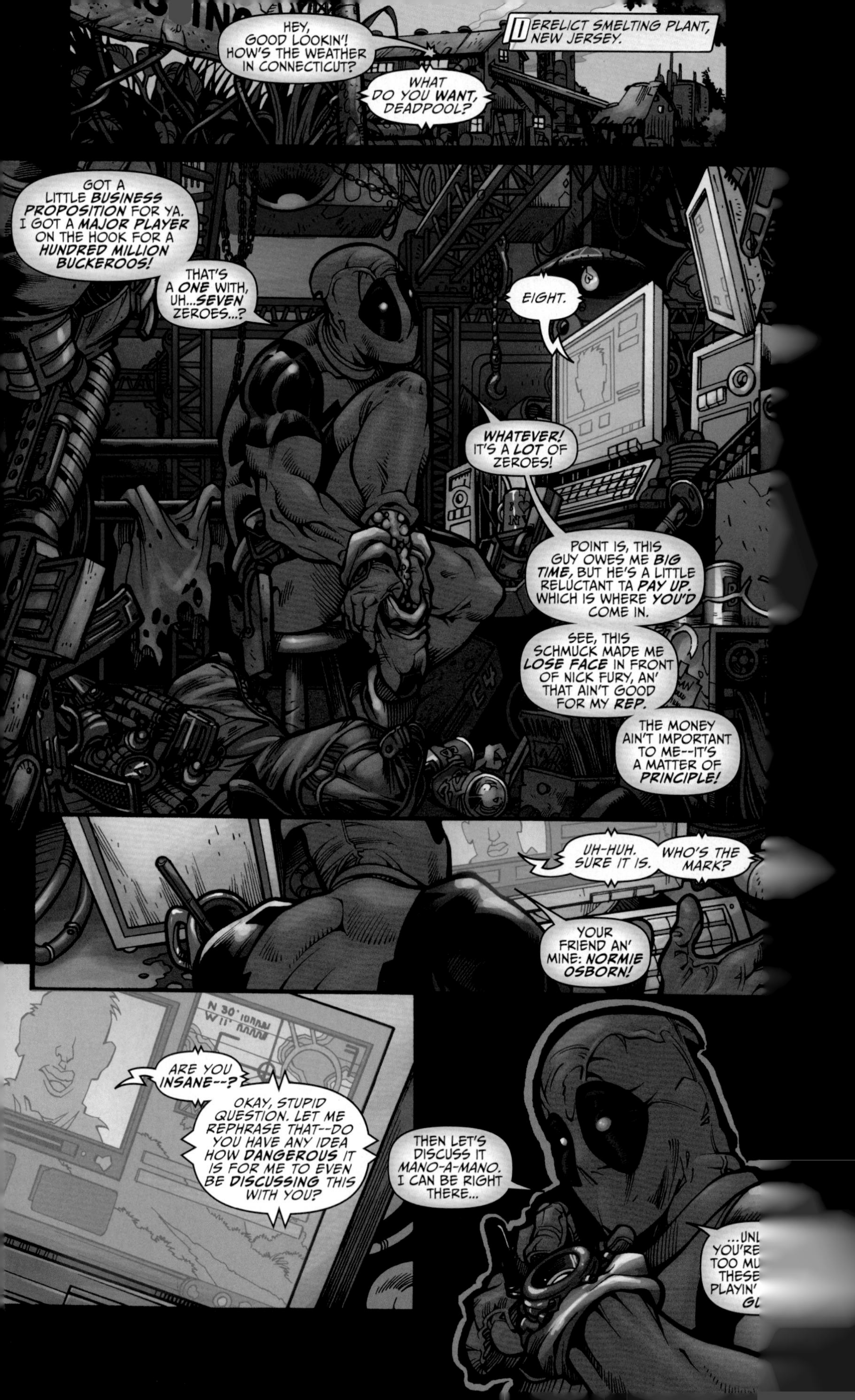
DERELICT SMELTING PLANT, NEW JERSEY.
HEY, GOOD LOOKIN'! HOW'S THE WEATHER IN CONNECTICUT?
WHAT DO YOU WANT, DEADPOOL?
GOT A LITTLE BUSINESS PROPOSITION FOR YA. I GOT A MAJOR PLAYER ON THE HOOK FOR A HUNDRED MILLION BUCKEROOS!
THAT'S A ONE WITH, UH...SEVEN ZEROES...?
EIGHT.
WHATEVER! IT'S A LOT OF ZEROES!
POINT IS, THIS GUY OWES ME BIG TIME, BUT HE'S A LITTLE RELUCTANT TA PAY UP. WHICH IS WHERE YOU'D COME IN.
SEE, THIS SCHMUCK MADE ME LOSE FACE IN FRONT OF NICK FURY, AN' THAT AIN'T GOOD FOR MY REP.
THE MONEY AIN'T IMPORTANT TO ME--IT'S A MATTER OF PRINCIPLE!
UH-HUH. SURE IT IS.
WHO'S THE MARK?
YOUR FRIEND AN' MINE: NORMIE OSBORN!
ARE YOU INSANE--?
OKAY, STUPID QUESTION. LET ME REPHRASE THAT--DO YOU HAVE ANY IDEA HOW DANGEROUS IT IS FOR ME TO EVEN BE DISCUSSING THIS WITH YOU?
THEN LET'S DISCUSS IT MANO-A-MANO. I CAN BE RIGHT THERE...
...UNL
YOU'RE
TOO MU
THESE
PLAYIN'
GL

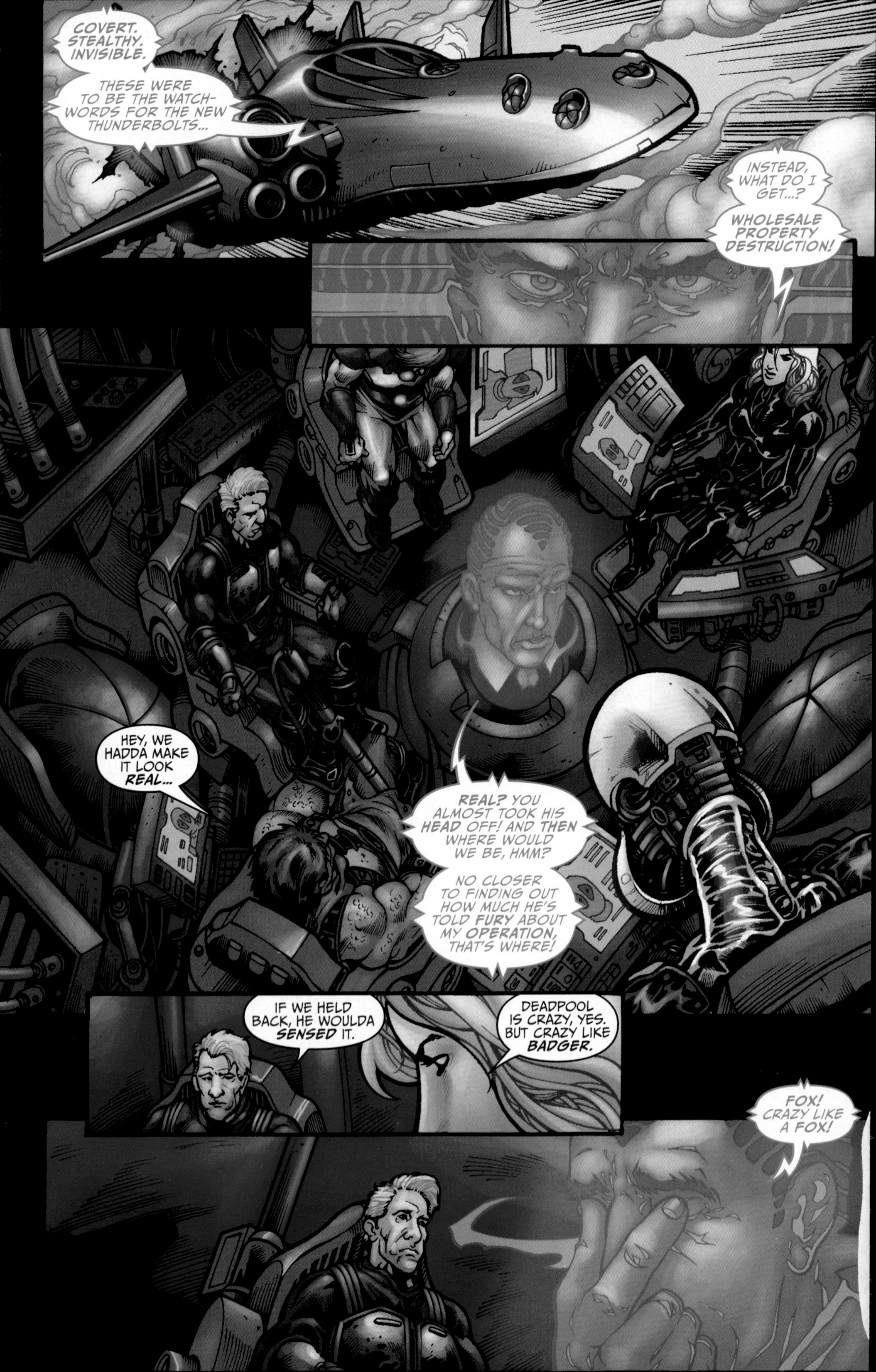
COVERT. STEALTHY. INVISIBLE.
THESE WERE TO BE THE WATCH-WORDS FOR THE NEW THUNDERBOLTS...
INSTEAD, WHAT DO I GET...?
WHOLESALE PROPERTY DESTRUCTION!
HEY, WE HADDA MAKE IT LOOK REAL...
REAL? YOU ALMOST TOOK HIS HEAD OFF! AND THEN WHERE WOULD WE BE, HMM?
NO CLOSER TO FINDING OUT HOW MUCH HE'S TOLD FURY ABOUT MY OPERATION, THAT'S WHERE!
IF WE HELD BACK, HE WOULDA SENSED IT.
DEADPOOL IS CRAZY, YES. BUT CRAZY LIKE BADGER.
FOX! CRAZY LIKE A FOX!

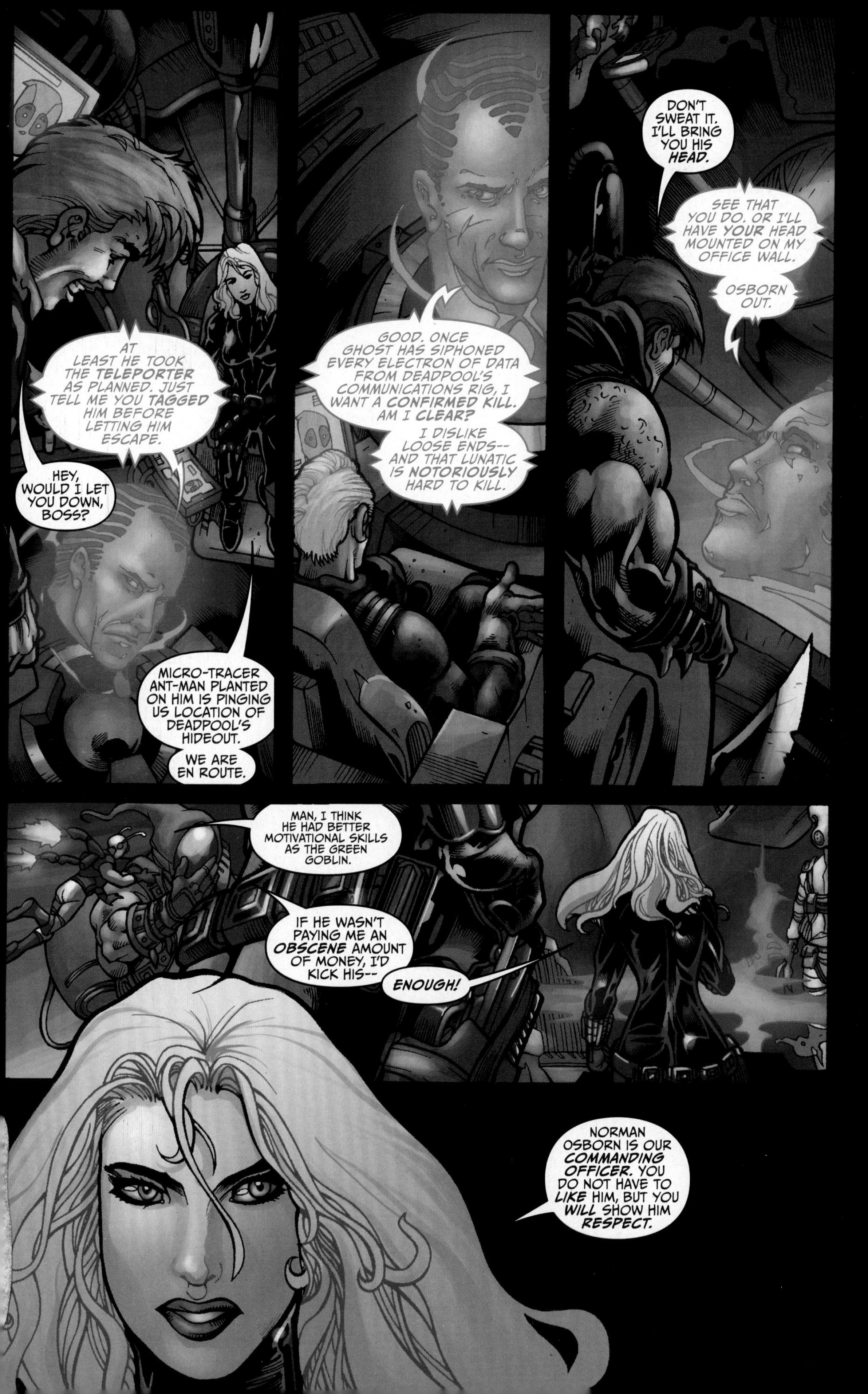
AT LEAST HE TOOK THE TELEPORTER AS PLANNED. JUST TELL ME YOU TAGGED HIM BEFORE LETTING HIM ESCAPE.
HEY, WOULD I LET YOU DOWN, BOSS?
MICRO-TRACER ANT-MAN PLANTED ON HIM IS PINGING US LOCATION OF DEADPOOL'S HIDEOUT.
WE ARE EN ROUTE.
GOOD. ONCE GHOST HAS SIPHONED EVERY ELECTRON OF DATA FROM DEADPOOL'S COMMUNICATIONS RIG, I WANT A CONFIRMED KILL. AM I CLEAR?
I DISLIKE LOOSE ENDS-- AND THAT LUNATIC IS NOTORIOUSLY HARD TO KILL.
DON'T SWEAT IT. I'LL BRING YOU HIS HEAD.
SEE THAT YOU DO. OR I'LL HAVE YOUR HEAD MOUNTED ON MY OFFICE WALL.
OSBORN OUT.
MAN, I THINK HE HAD BETTER MOTIVATIONAL SKILLS AS THE GREEN GOBLIN.
IF HE WASN'T PAYING ME AN OBSCENE AMOUNT OF MONEY, I'D KICK HIS--
ENOUGH!
NORMAN OSBORN IS OUR COMMANDING OFFICER. YOU DO NOT HAVE TO LIKE HIM, BUT YOU WILL SHOW HIM RESPECT.

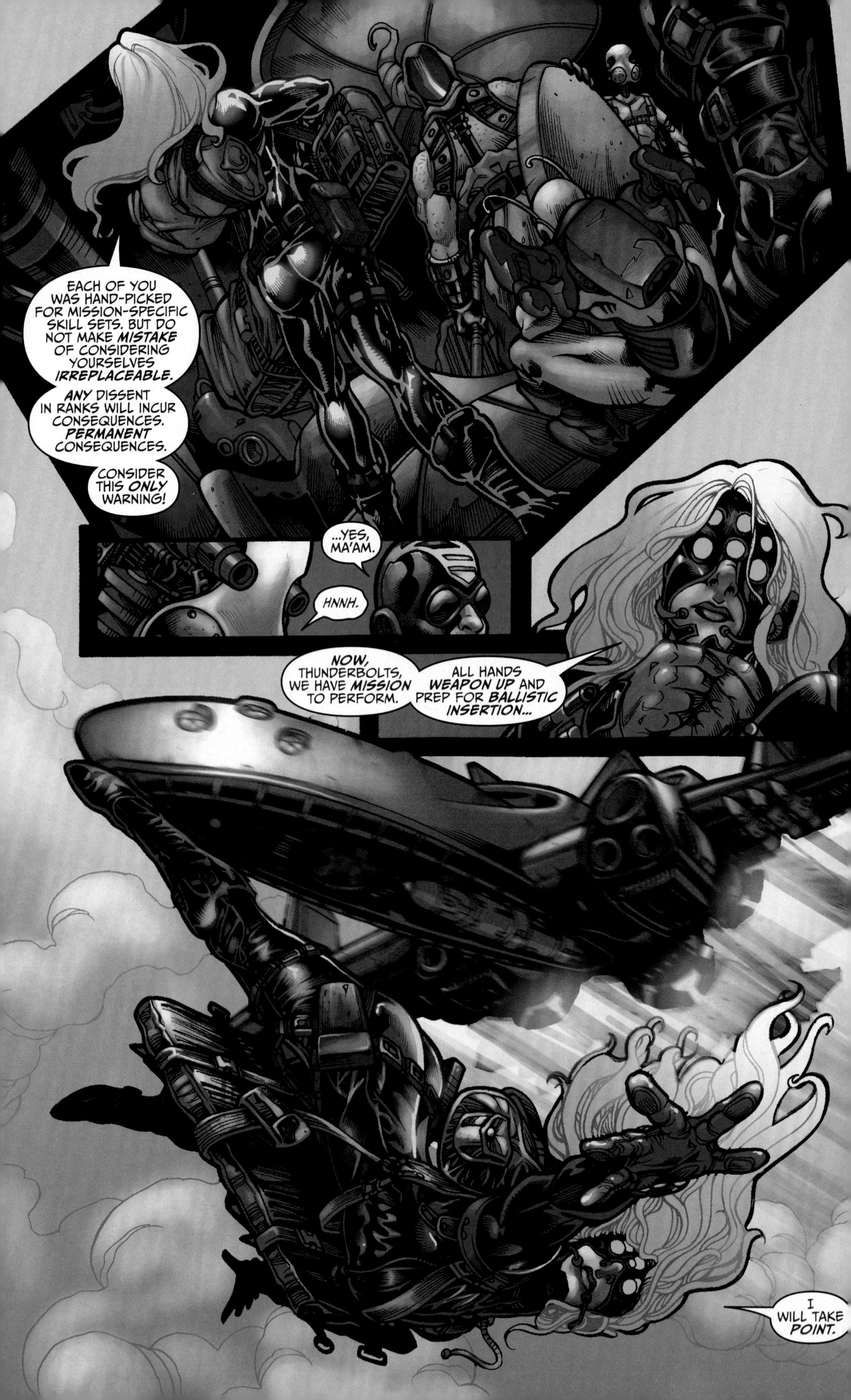

EACH OF YOU WAS HAND-PICKED FOR MISSION-SPECIFIC SKILL SETS. BUT DO NOT MAKE MISTAKE OF CONSIDERING YOURSELVES IRREPLACEABLE.
ANY DISSENT IN RANKS WILL INCUR CONSEQUENCES. PERMANENT CONSEQUENCES.
CONSIDER THIS ONLY WARNING!
...YES, MA'AM.
HNNH.
NOW, THUNDERBOLTS, WE HAVE MISSION TO PERFORM.
ALL HANDS WEAPON UP AND PREP FOR BALLISTIC INSERTION...
I WILL TAKE POINT.

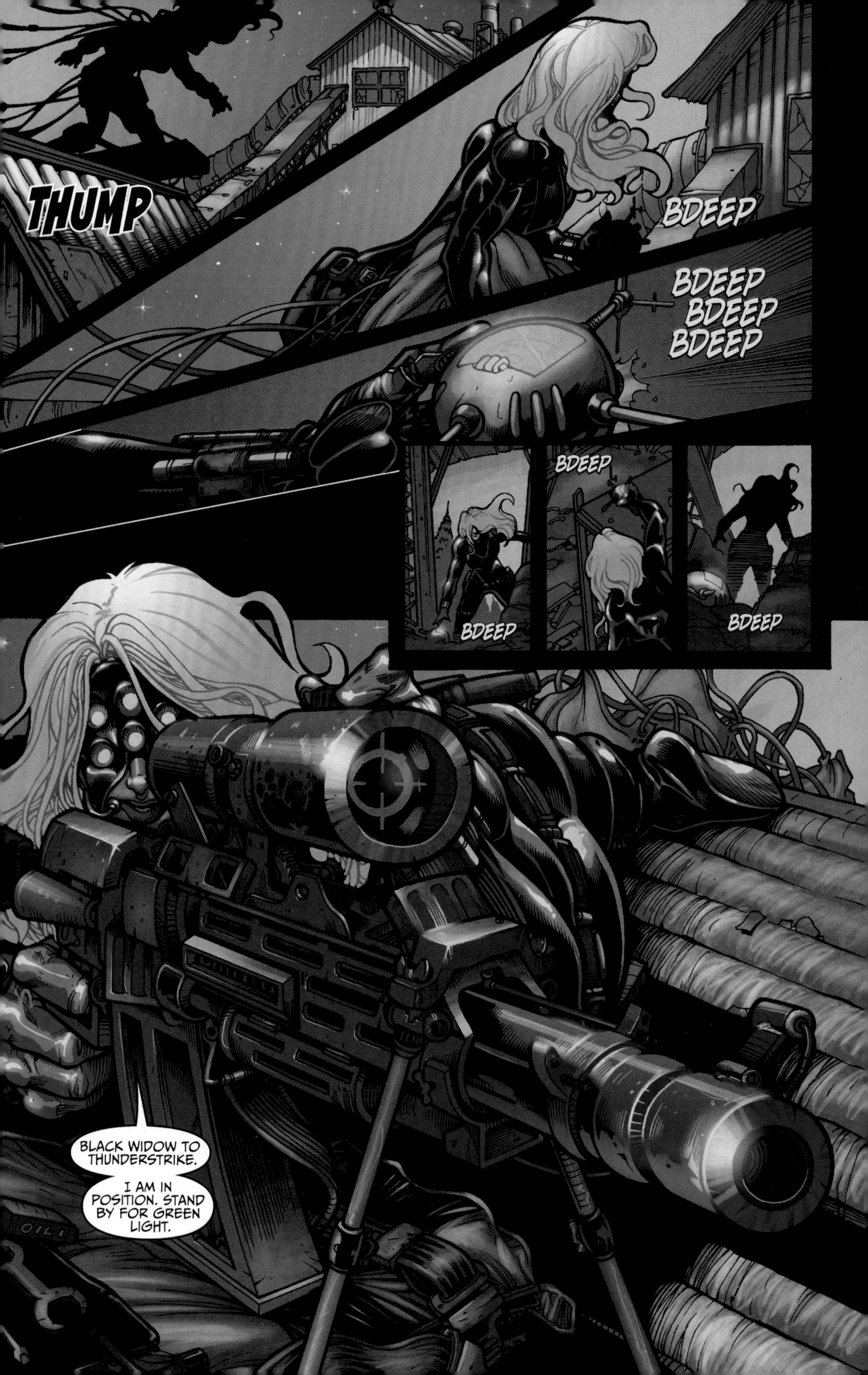
THUMP
BDEEP
BDEEP
BDEEP
BDEEP
BDEEP
BDEEP
BDEEP
BDEEP
BLACK WIDOW TO THUNDERSTRIKE.
I AM IN POSITION. STAND BY FOR GREEN LIGHT.

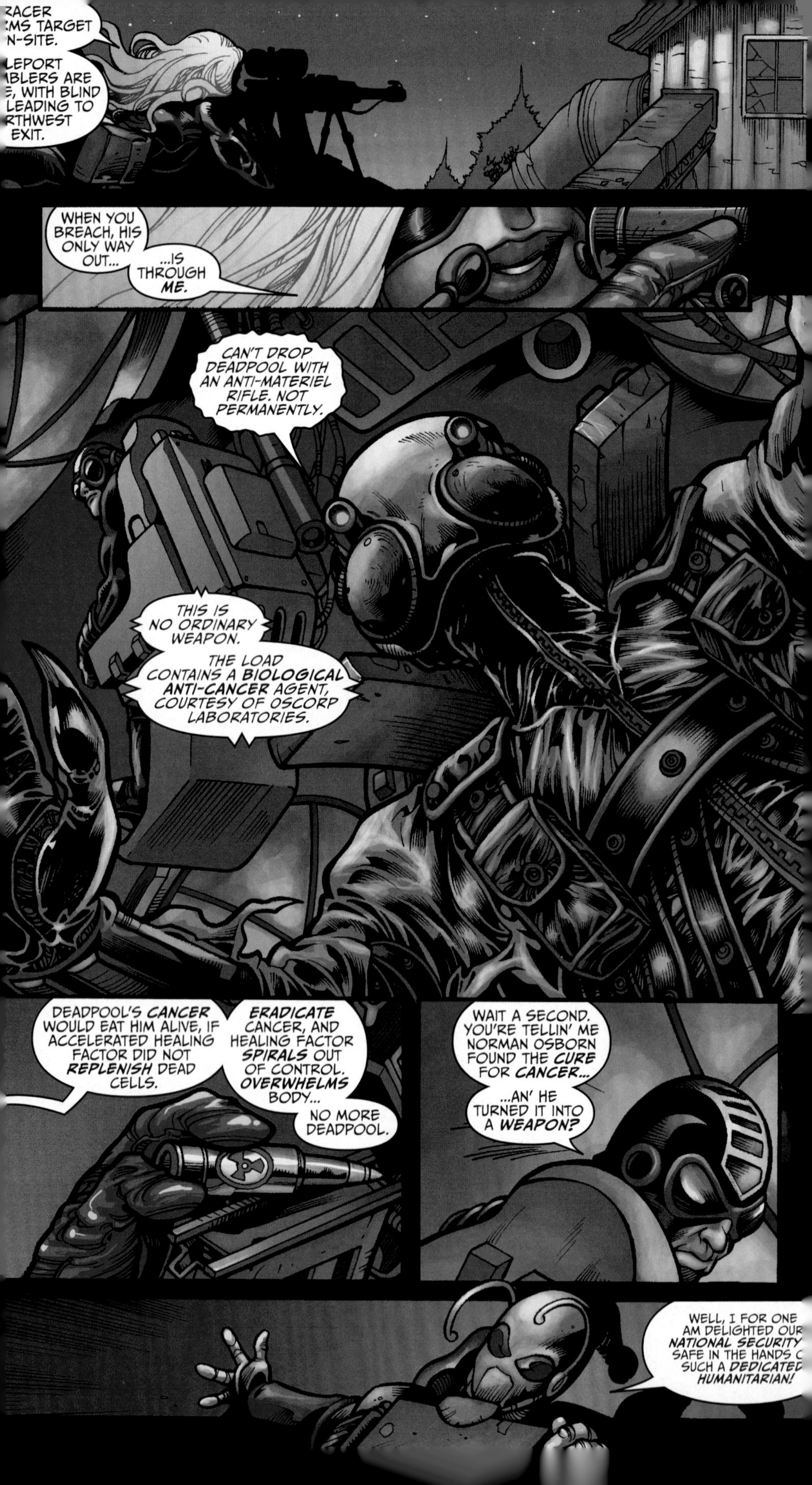

RACER
EMS TARGET
N-SITE.
LEPORT
MBLERS ARE
E, WITH BLIND
LEADING TO
RTHWEST
EXIT.
WHEN YOU BREACH, HIS ONLY WAY OUT...
...IS THROUGH ME.
CAN'T DROP DEADPOOL WITH AN ANTI-MATERIEL RIFLE. NOT PERMANENTLY.
THIS IS NO ORDINARY WEAPON.
THE LOAD CONTAINS A BIOLOGICAL ANTI-CANCER AGENT, COURTESY OF OSCORP LABORATORIES.
DEADPOOL'S CANCER WOULD EAT HIM ALIVE, IF ACCELERATED HEALING FACTOR DID NOT REPLENISH DEAD CELLS.
ERADICATE CANCER, AND HEALING FACTOR SPIRALS OUT OF CONTROL. OVERWHELMS BODY...
NO MORE DEADPOOL.
WAIT A SECOND. YOU'RE TELLIN' ME NORMAN OSBORN FOUND THE CURE FOR CANCER...
...AN' HE TURNED IT INTO A WEAPON?
WELL, I FOR ONE
AM DELIGHTED OUR
NATIONAL SECURITY
SAFE IN THE HANDS
SUCH A DEDICATED
HUMANITARIAN!

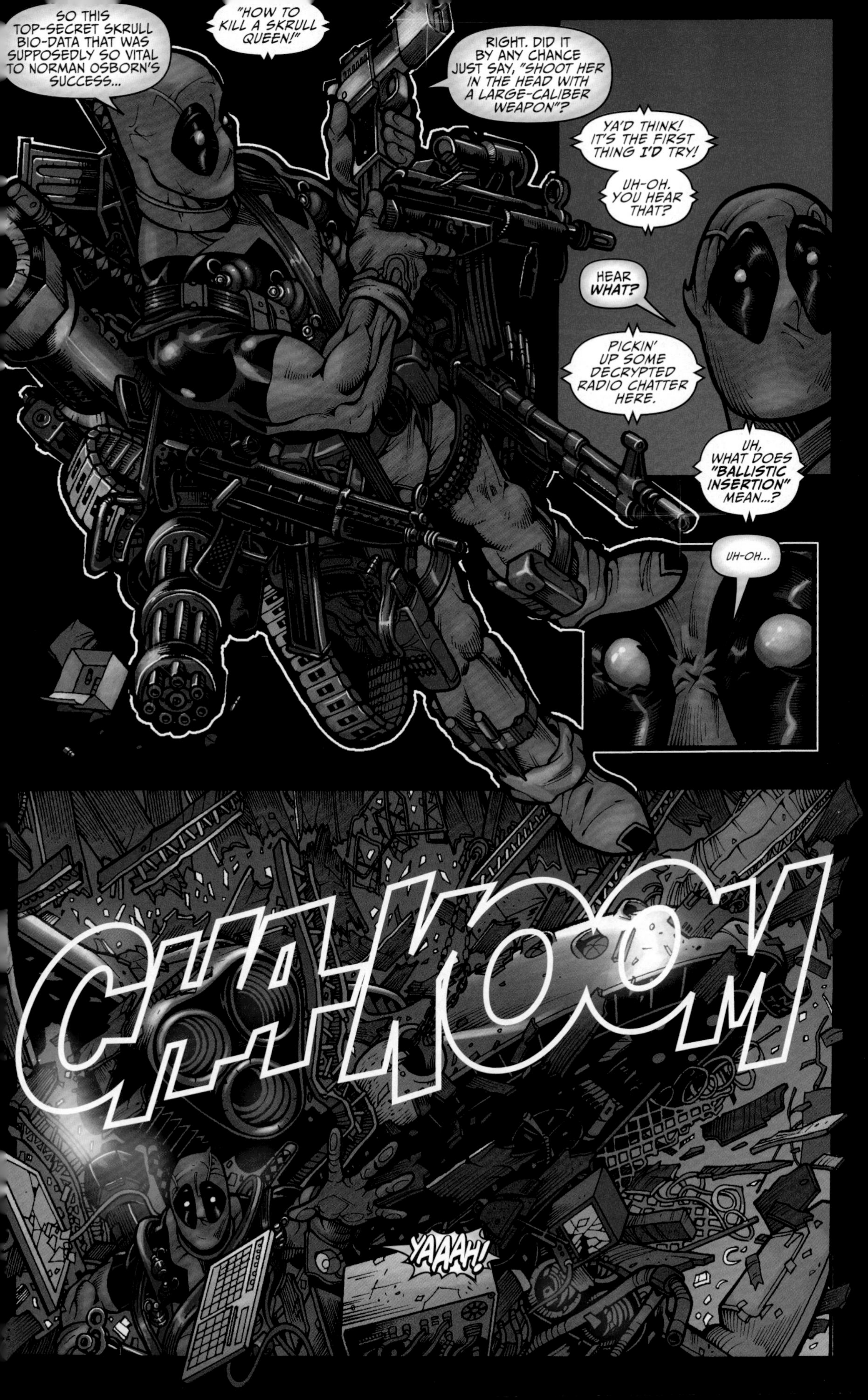

SO THIS TOP-SECRET SKRULL BIO-DATA THAT WAS SUPPOSEDLY SO VITAL TO NORMAN OSBORN'S SUCCESS...
"HOW TO KILL A SKRULL QUEEN!"
RIGHT. DID IT BY ANY CHANCE JUST SAY, "SHOOT HER IN THE HEAD WITH A LARGE-CALIBER WEAPON"?
YA'D THINK! IT'S THE FIRST THING I'D TRY!
UH-OH. YOU HEAR THAT?
HEAR WHAT?
PICKIN' UP SOME DECRYPTED RADIO CHATTER HERE.
UH, WHAT DOES "BALLISTIC INSERTION" MEAN...?
UH-OH...
CHHOOM
YAAAH!

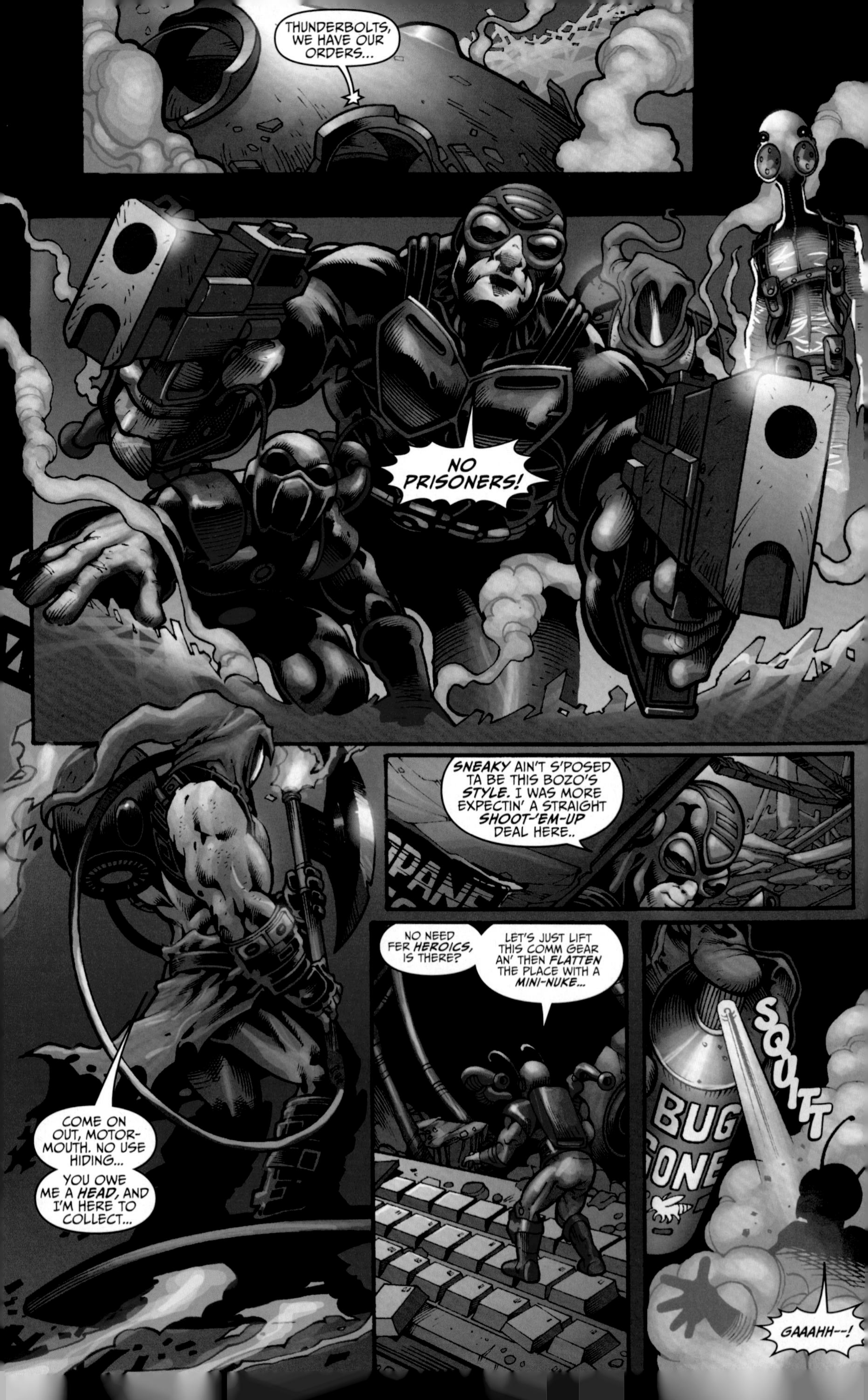
THUNDERBOLTS, WE HAVE OUR ORDERS...
NO PRISONERS!
COME ON OUT, MOTOR-MOUTH. NO USE HIDING...
YOU OWE ME A HEAD, AND I'M HERE TO COLLECT...
SNEAKY AIN'T S'POSED TA BE THIS BOZO'S STYLE. I WAS MORE EXPECTIN' A STRAIGHT SHOOT-'EM-UP DEAL HERE..
NO NEED FER HEROICS, IS THERE?
LET'S JUST LIFT THIS COMM GEAR AN' THEN FLATTEN THE PLACE WITH A MINI-NUKE...
BUG GONE
SQUIFT
GAAAHH--!

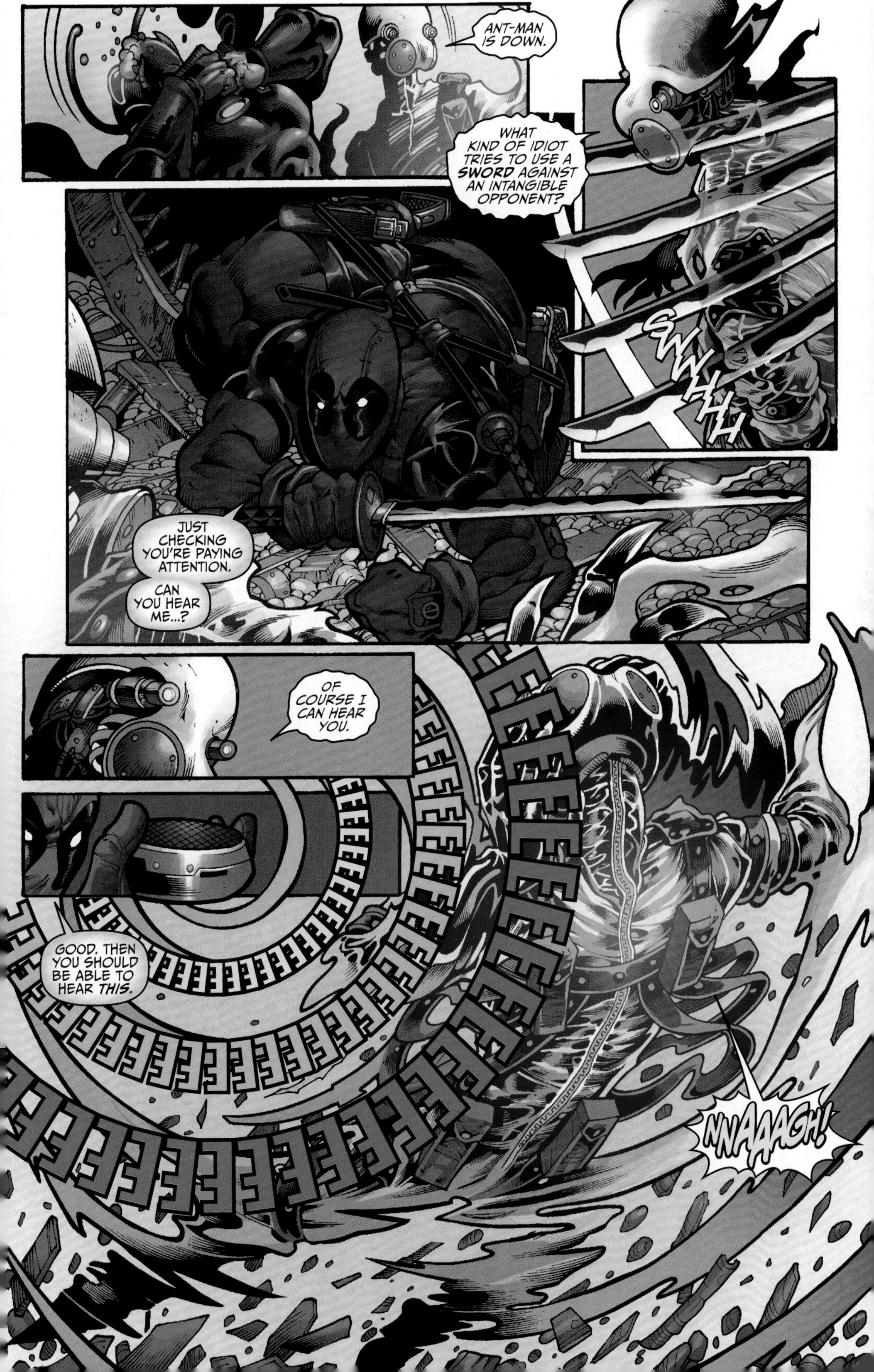

ANT-MAN IS DOWN.
WHAT KIND OF IDIOT TRIES TO USE A SWORD AGAINST AN INTANGIBLE OPPONENT?
SWHHH
JUST CHECKING YOU'RE PAYING ATTENTION.
CAN YOU HEAR ME...?
OF COURSE I CAN HEAR YOU.
GOOD. THEN YOU SHOULD BE ABLE TO HEAR THIS.
EEEEEEEEEEEEEEEEEEEEEE
NNAAAGH!

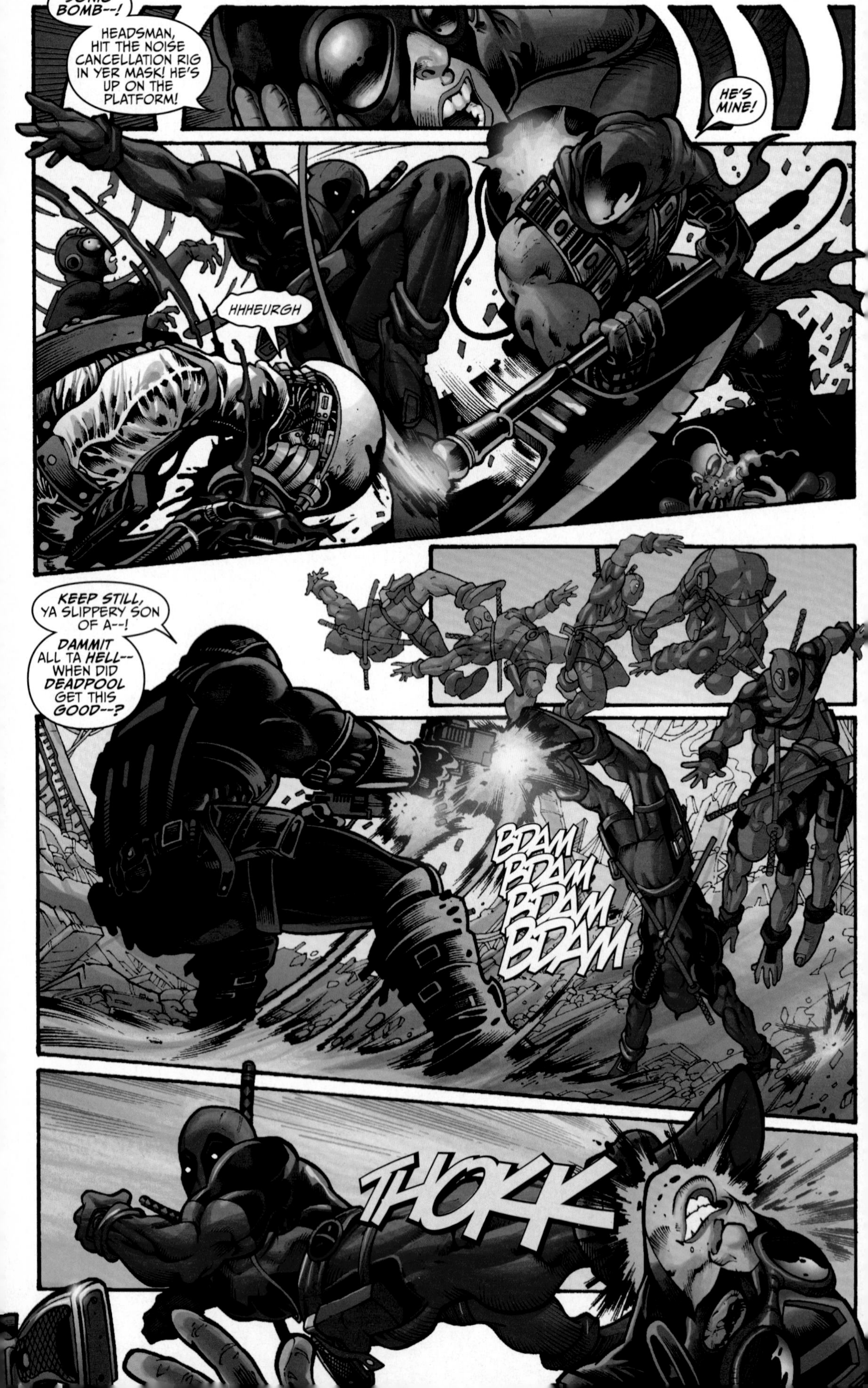
SONIC BOMB--!
HEADSMAN, HIT THE NOISE CANCELLATION RIG IN YER MASK! HE'S UP ON THE PLATFORM!
HE'S MINE!
HHHEURGH
KEEP STILL, YA SLIPPERY SON OF A--!
DAMMIT ALL TA HELL-- WHEN DID DEADPOOL GET THIS GOOD--?
B'DAM B'DAM B'DAM B'DAM
THOKK

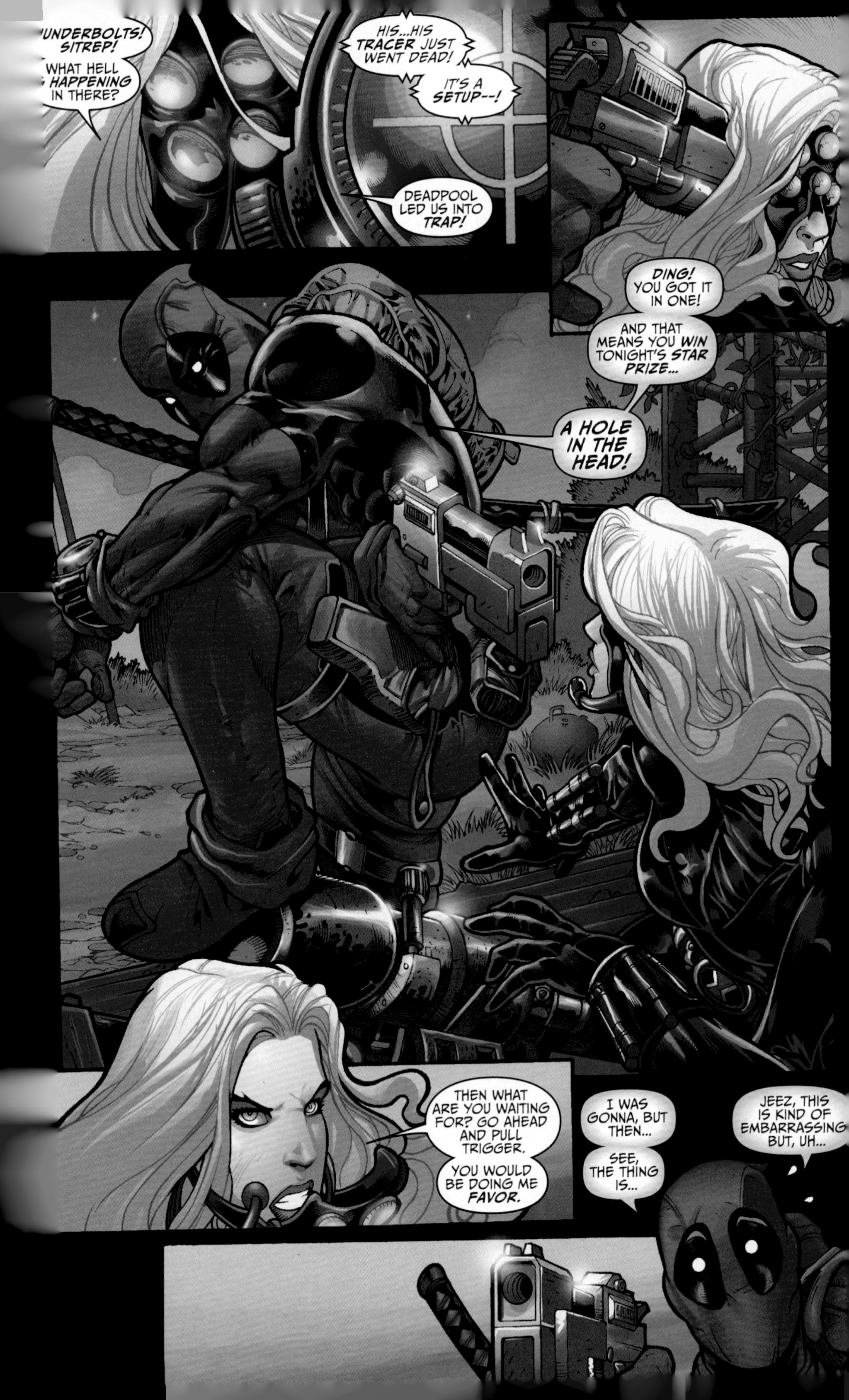

UNDERBOLTS! SITREP!
WHAT HELL HAPPENING IN THERE?
HIS...HIS TRACER JUST WENT DEAD!
IT'S A SETUP--!
DEADPOOL LED US INTO TRAP!
DING! YOU GOT IT IN ONE!
AND THAT MEANS YOU WIN TONIGHT'S STAR PRIZE...
A HOLE IN THE HEAD!
THEN WHAT ARE YOU WAITING FOR? GO AHEAD AND PULL TRIGGER.
YOU WOULD BE DOING ME FAVOR.
I WAS GONNA, BUT THEN...
SEE, THE THING IS...
JEEZ, THIS IS KIND OF EMBARRASSING BUT, UH...

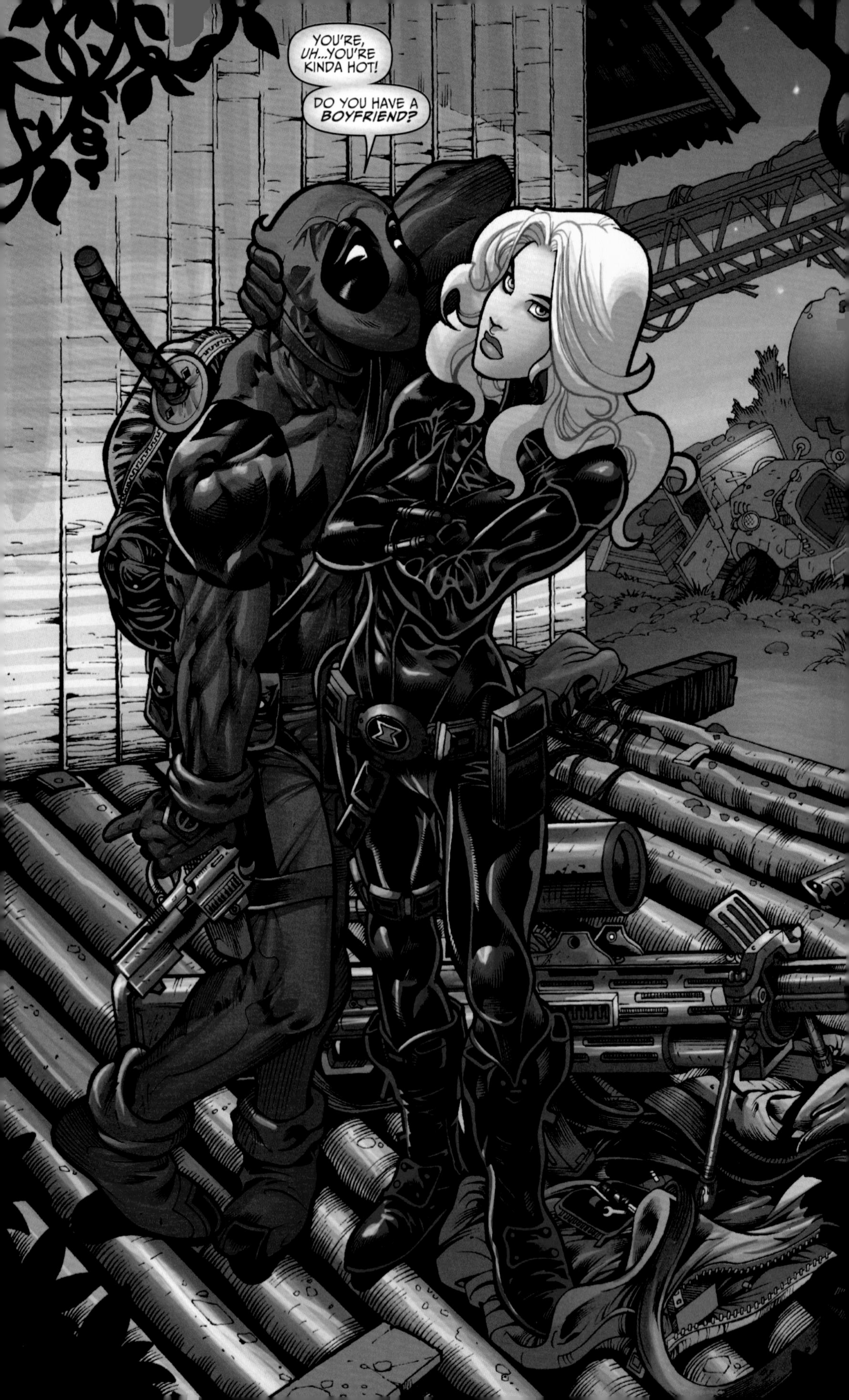
YOU'RE, UH...YOU'RE KINDA HOT!
DO YOU HAVE A BOYFRIEND?

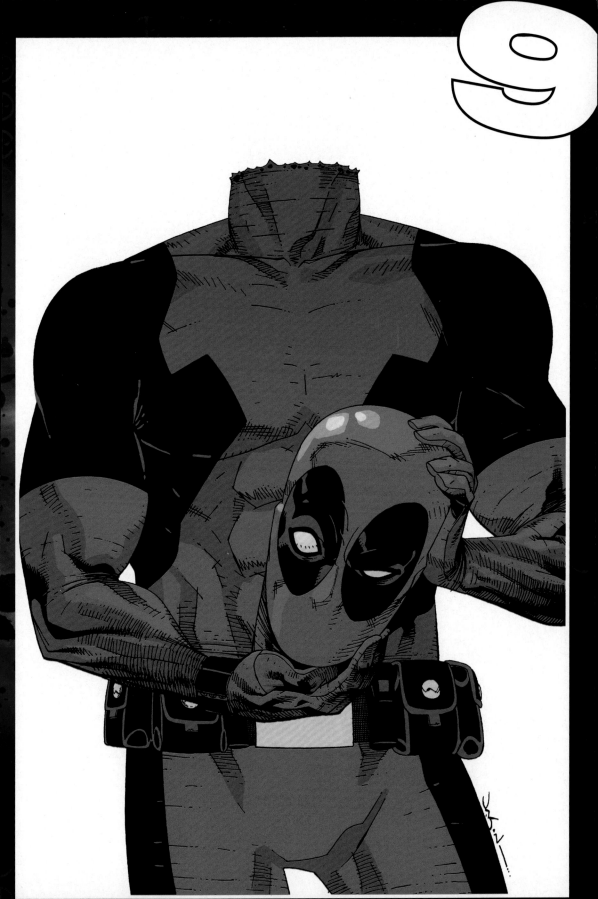

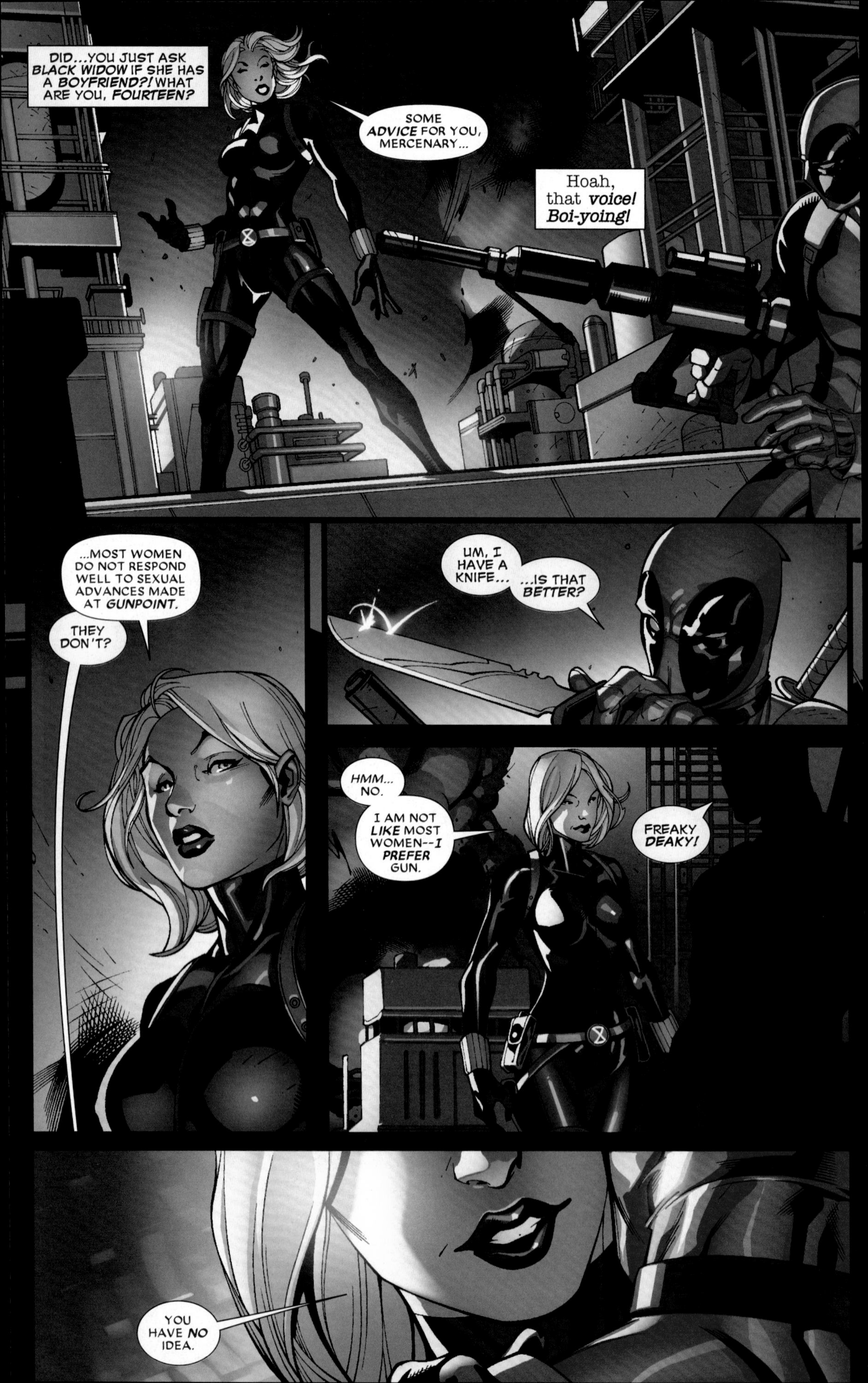

DID...YOU JUST ASK BLACK WIDOW IF SHE HAS A BOYFRIEND?! WHAT ARE YOU, FOURTEEN?
SOME ADVICE FOR YOU, MERCENARY...
Hoah, that voice! Boi-yoing!
...MOST WOMEN DO NOT RESPOND WELL TO SEXUAL ADVANCES MADE AT GUNPOINT.
THEY DON'T?
UM, I HAVE A KNIFE...
...IS THAT BETTER?
HMM... NO.
I AM NOT LIKE MOST WOMEN--I PREFER GUN.
FREAKY DEAKY!
YOU HAVE NO IDEA.

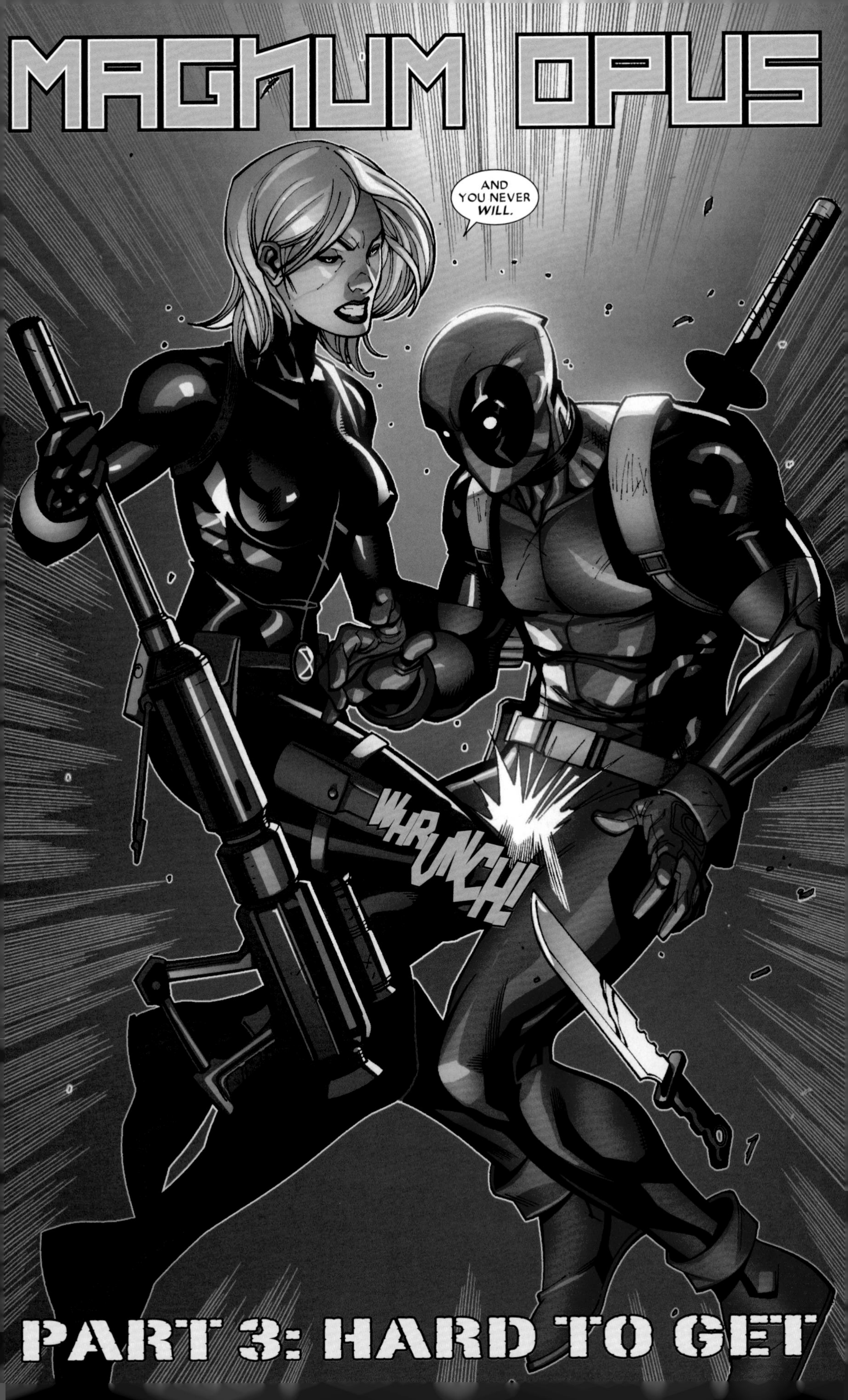
MAGNUM OPUS
AND YOU NEVER *WILL.*
WHRUNCH!
PART 3: HARD TO GET

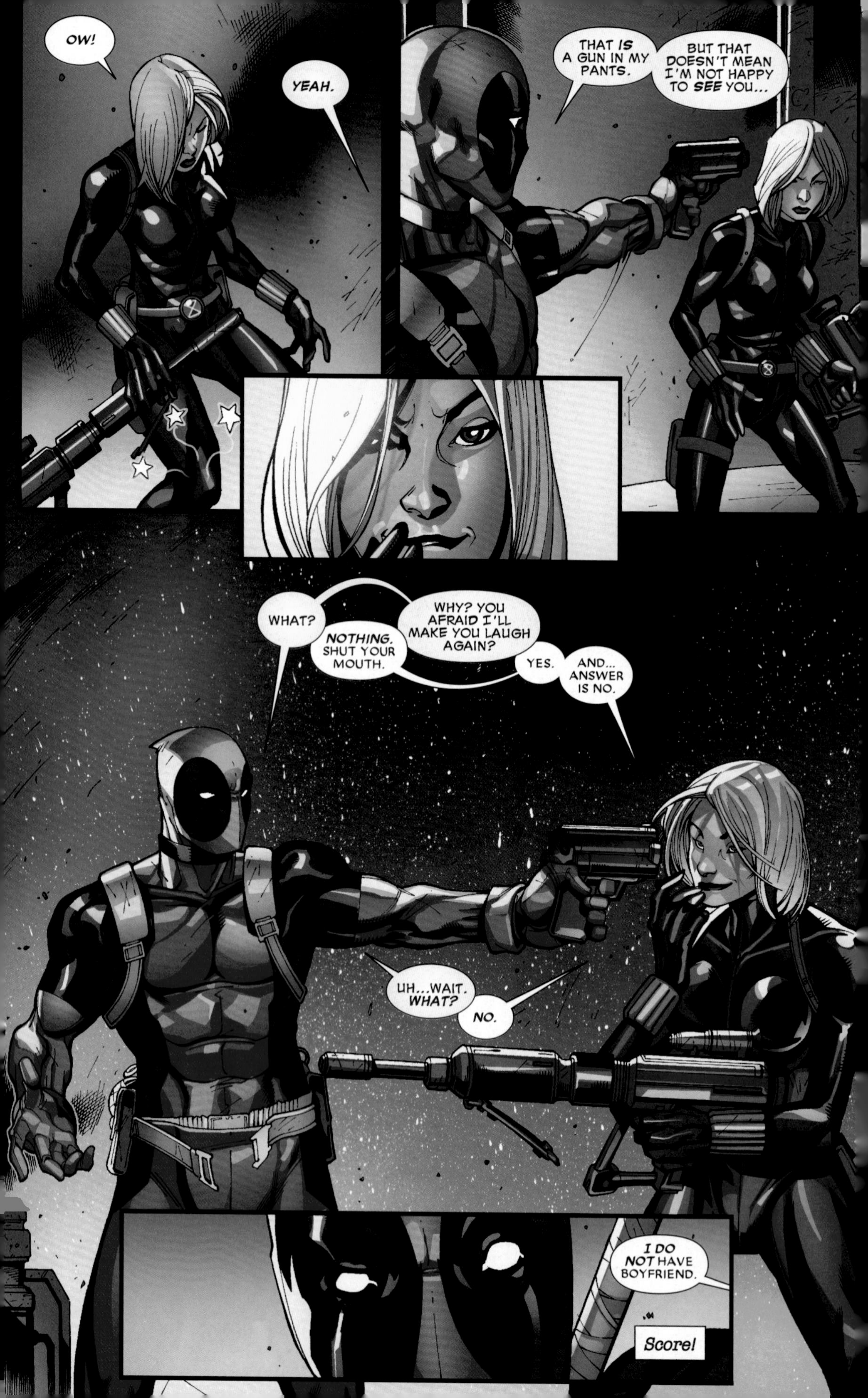
OW!
YEAH.
THAT IS A GUN IN MY PANTS.
BUT THAT DOESN'T MEAN I'M NOT HAPPY TO SEE YOU...
WHAT?
NOTHING. SHUT YOUR MOUTH.
WHY? YOU AFRAID I'LL MAKE YOU LAUGH AGAIN?
YES.
AND... ANSWER IS NO.
UH...WAIT. WHAT?
NO.
I DO NOT HAVE BOYFRIEND.
Score!

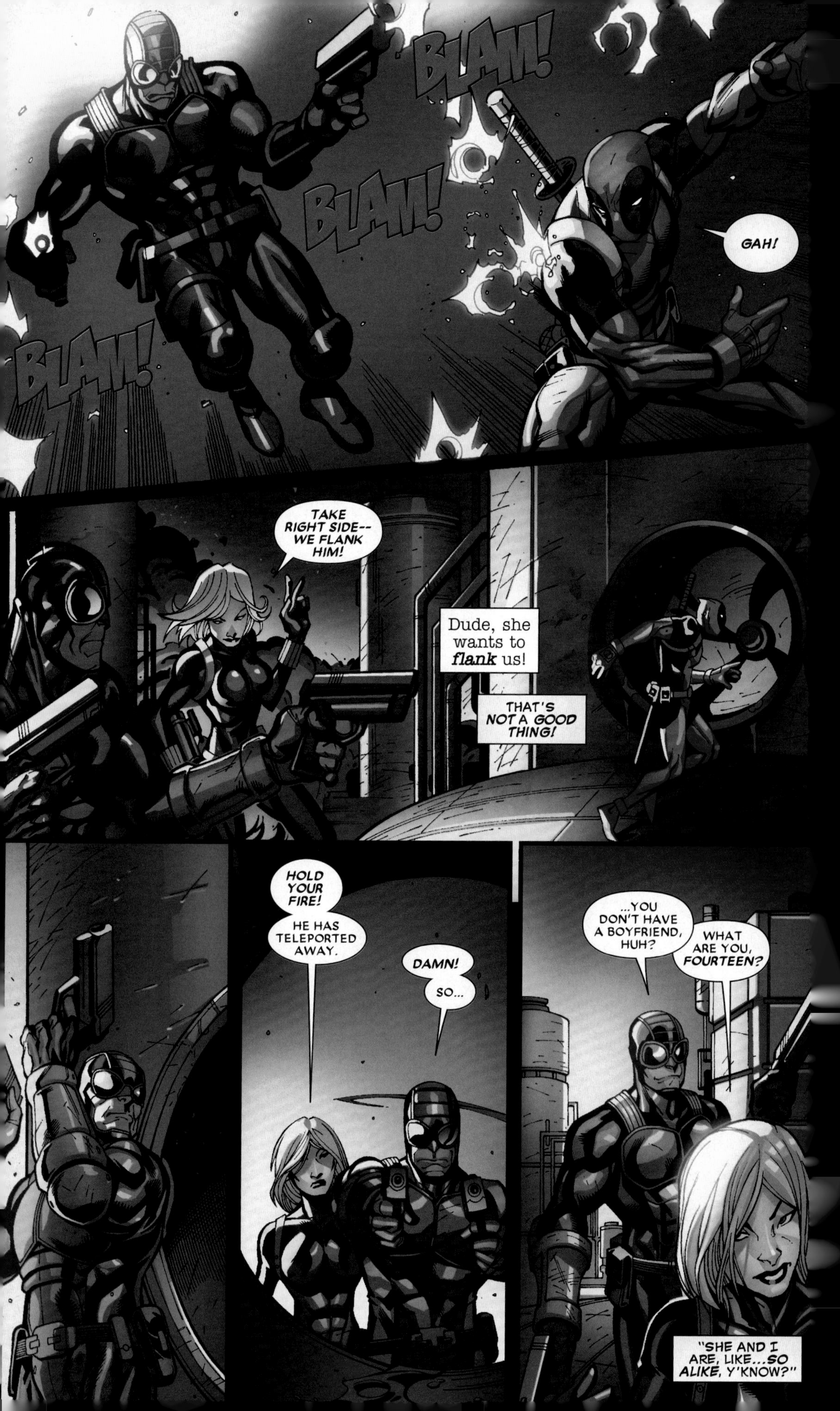
BLAM!
BLAM!
BLAM!
GAH!
TAKE RIGHT SIDE-- WE FLANK HIM!
Dude, she wants to flank us!
THAT'S NOT A GOOD THING!
HOLD YOUR FIRE!
HE HAS TELEPORTED AWAY.
DAMN!
SO...
...YOU DON'T HAVE A BOYFRIEND, HUH?
WHAT ARE YOU, FOURTEEN?
"SHE AND I ARE, LIKE...SO ALIKE, Y'KNOW?"

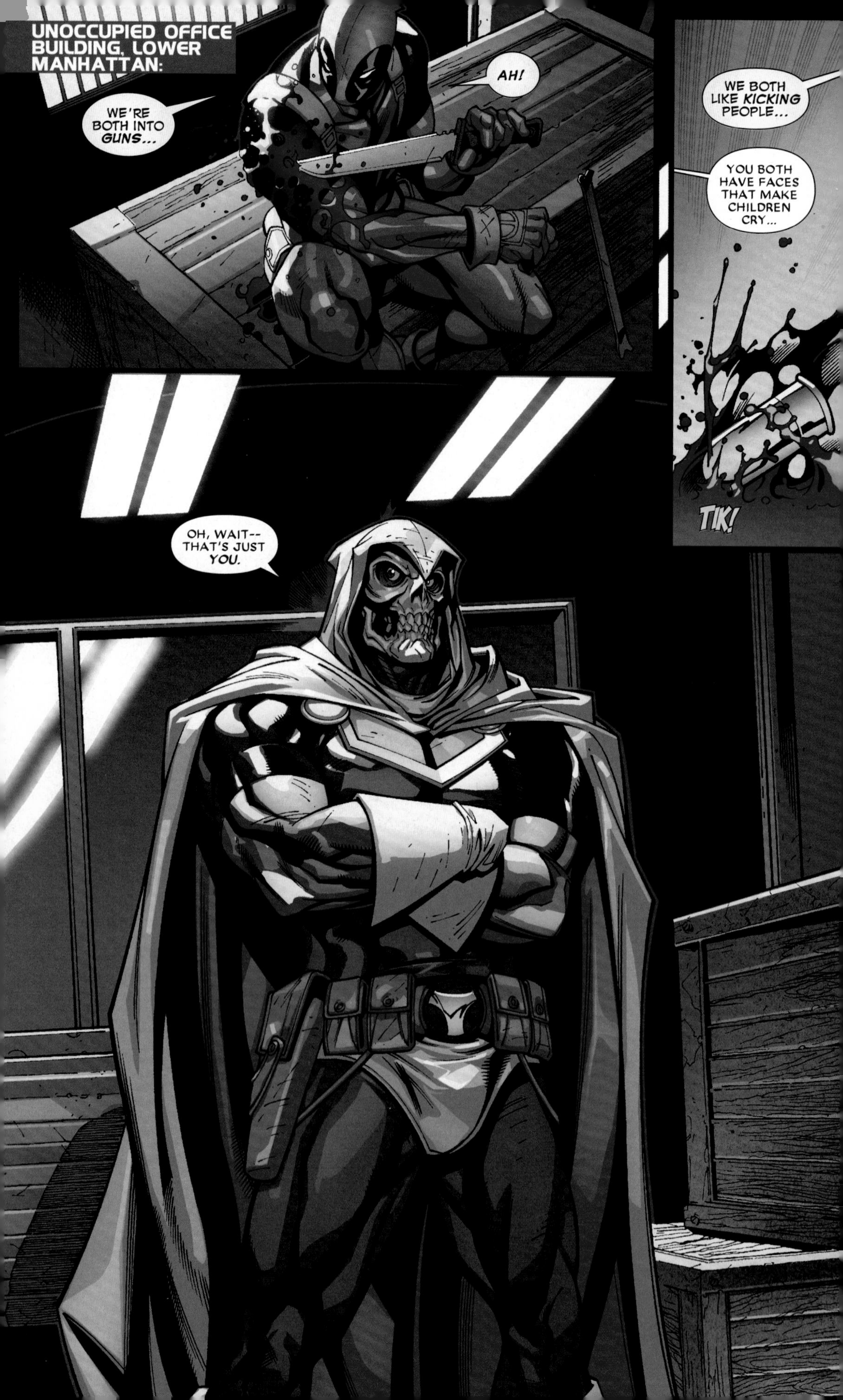
UNOCCUPIED OFFICE BUILDING, LOWER MANHATTAN:
WE'RE BOTH INTO GUNS...
AH!
WE BOTH LIKE KICKING PEOPLE...
YOU BOTH HAVE FACES THAT MAKE CHILDREN CRY...
TIK!
OH, WAIT-- THAT'S JUST YOU.

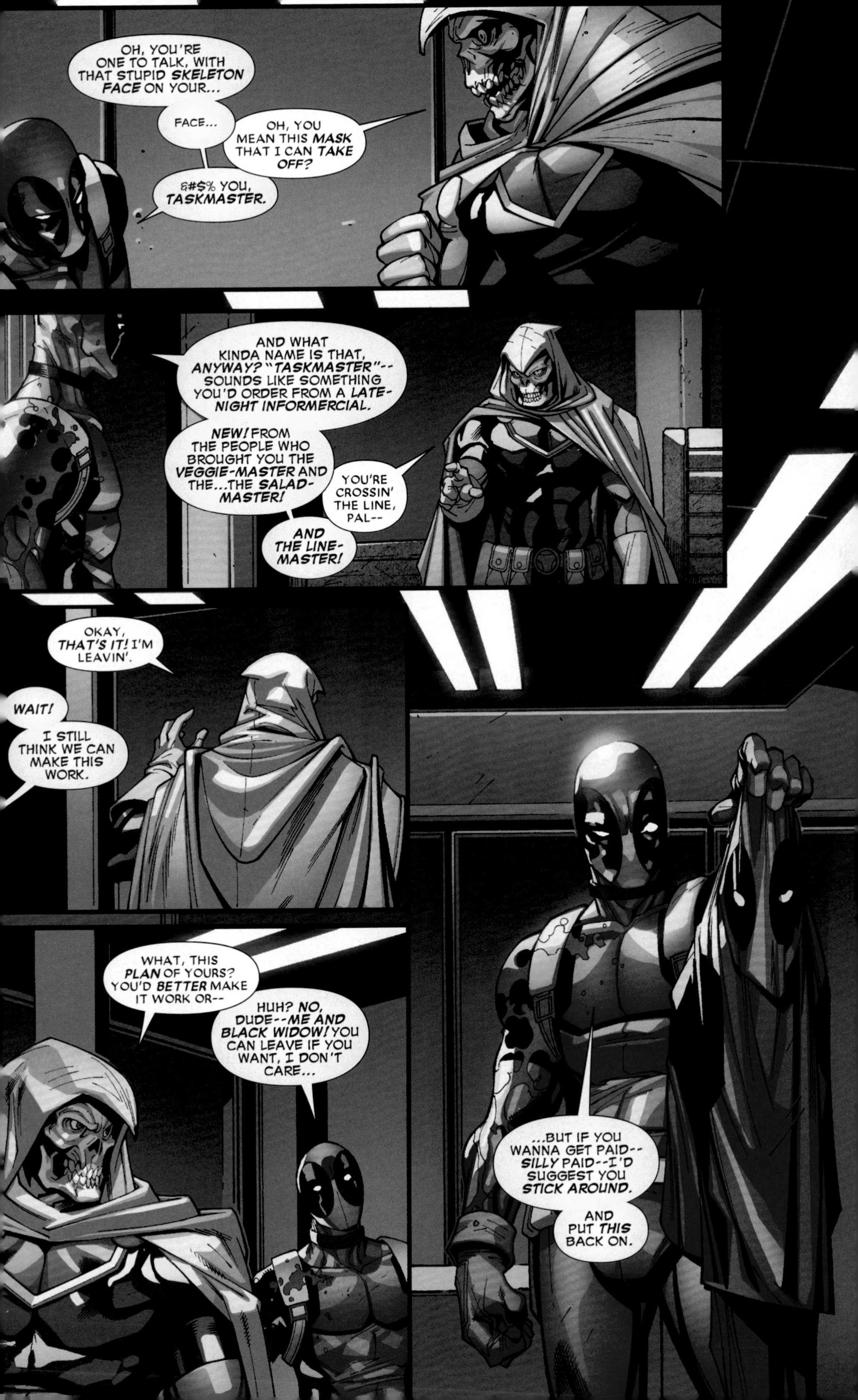

OH, YOU'RE ONE TO TALK, WITH THAT STUPID SKELETON FACE ON YOUR...
FACE...
OH, YOU MEAN THIS MASK THAT I CAN TAKE OFF?
&#$% YOU, TASKMASTER.
AND WHAT KINDA NAME IS THAT, ANYWAY? "TASKMASTER"-- SOUNDS LIKE SOMETHING YOU'D ORDER FROM A LATE-NIGHT INFORMERCIAL.
NEW! FROM THE PEOPLE WHO BROUGHT YOU THE VEGGIE-MASTER AND THE...THE SALAD-MASTER!
YOU'RE CROSSIN' THE LINE, PAL--
AND THE LINE-MASTER!
OKAY, THAT'S IT! I'M LEAVIN'.
WAIT!
I STILL THINK WE CAN MAKE THIS WORK.
WHAT, THIS PLAN OF YOURS? YOU'D BETTER MAKE IT WORK OR--
HUH? NO, DUDE--ME AND BLACK WIDOW! YOU CAN LEAVE IF YOU WANT, I DON'T CARE...
...BUT IF YOU WANNA GET PAID-- SILLY PAID--I'D SUGGEST YOU STICK AROUND.
AND PUT THIS BACK ON.

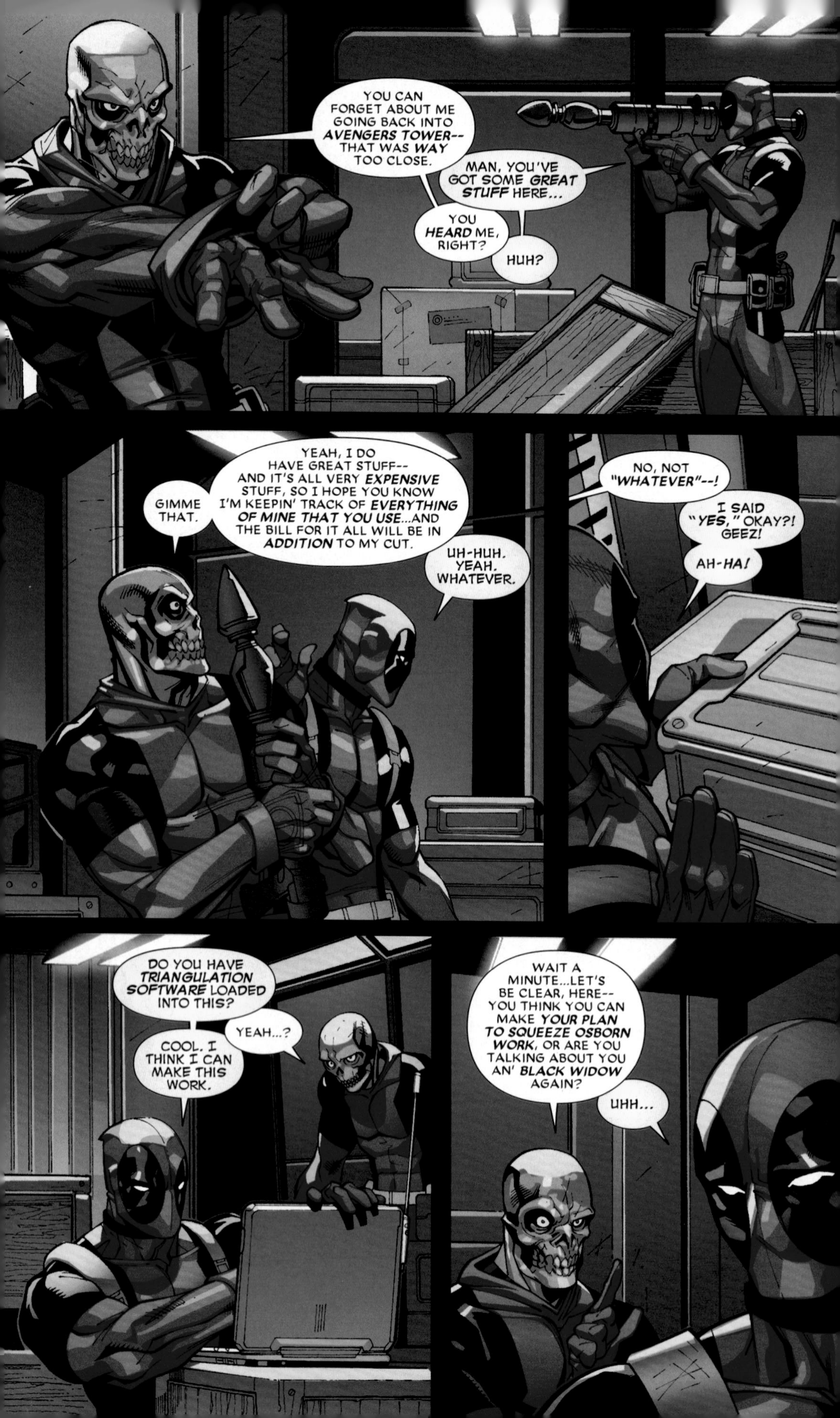
YOU CAN FORGET ABOUT ME GOING BACK INTO AVENGERS TOWER-- THAT WAS WAY TOO CLOSE.
MAN, YOU'VE GOT SOME GREAT STUFF HERE...
YOU HEARD ME, RIGHT?
HUH?
GIMME THAT.
YEAH, I DO HAVE GREAT STUFF-- AND IT'S ALL VERY EXPENSIVE STUFF, SO I HOPE YOU KNOW I'M KEEPIN' TRACK OF EVERYTHING OF MINE THAT YOU USE...AND THE BILL FOR IT ALL WILL BE IN ADDITION TO MY CUT.
UH-HUH. YEAH. WHATEVER.
NO, NOT "WHATEVER"--!
I SAID "YES," OKAY?! GEEZ!
AH-HA!
DO YOU HAVE TRIANGULATION SOFTWARE LOADED INTO THIS?
YEAH...?
COOL. I THINK I CAN MAKE THIS WORK.
WAIT A MINUTE...LET'S BE CLEAR, HERE-- YOU THINK YOU CAN MAKE YOUR PLAN TO SQUEEZE OSBORN WORK, OR ARE YOU TALKING ABOUT YOU AN' BLACK WIDOW AGAIN?
UHH...

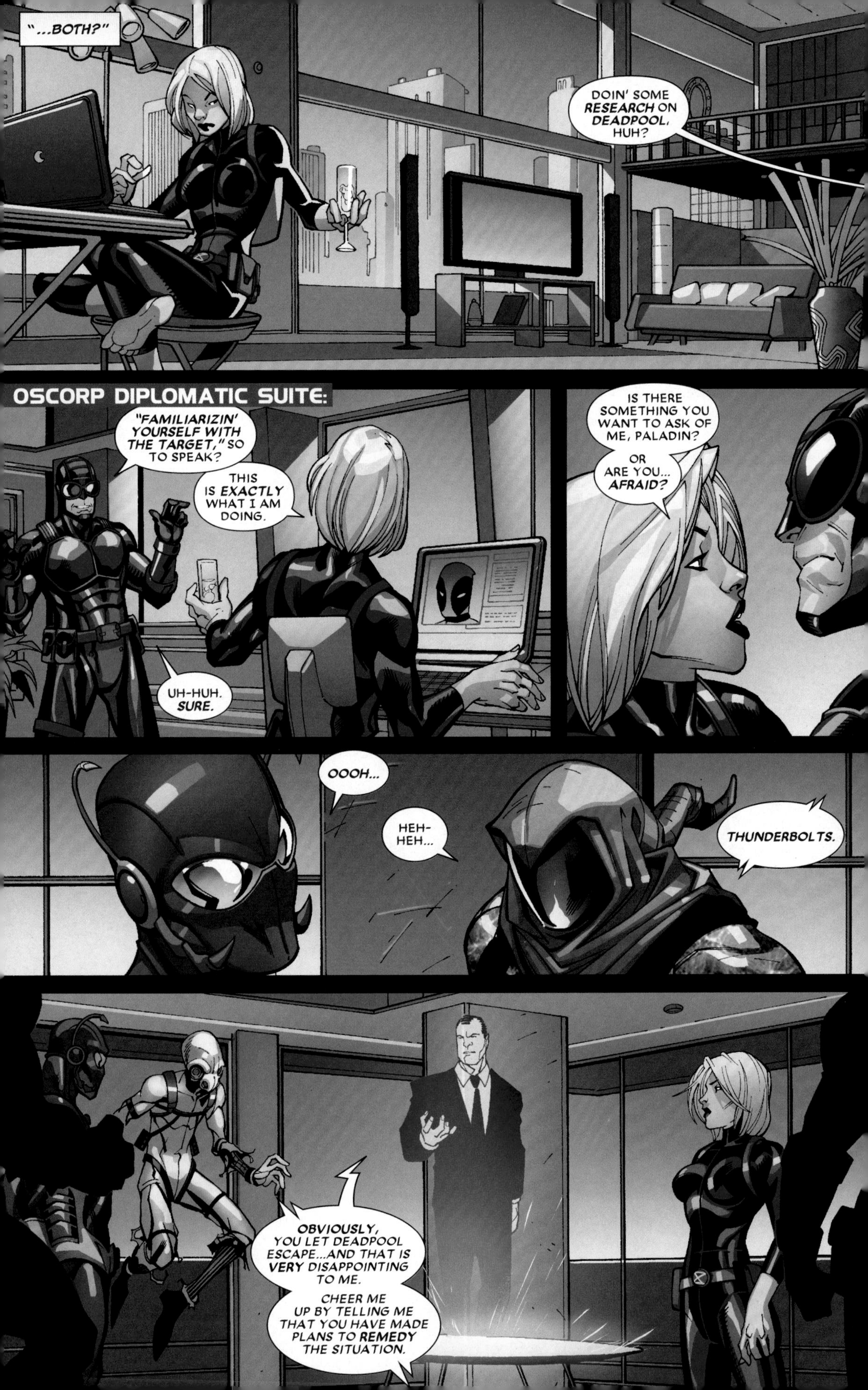
"...BOTH?"
DOIN' SOME RESEARCH ON DEADPOOL, HUH?
OSCORP DIPLOMATIC SUITE:
"FAMILIARIZIN' YOURSELF WITH THE TARGET," SO TO SPEAK?
THIS IS EXACTLY WHAT I AM DOING.
UH-HUH. SURE.
IS THERE SOMETHING YOU WANT TO ASK OF ME, PALADIN?
OR ARE YOU... AFRAID?
OOOH...
HEH-HEH...
THUNDERBOLTS.
OBVIOUSLY, YOU LET DEADPOOL ESCAPE...AND THAT IS VERY DISAPPOINTING TO ME.
CHEER ME UP BY TELLING ME THAT YOU HAVE MADE PLANS TO REMEDY THE SITUATION.

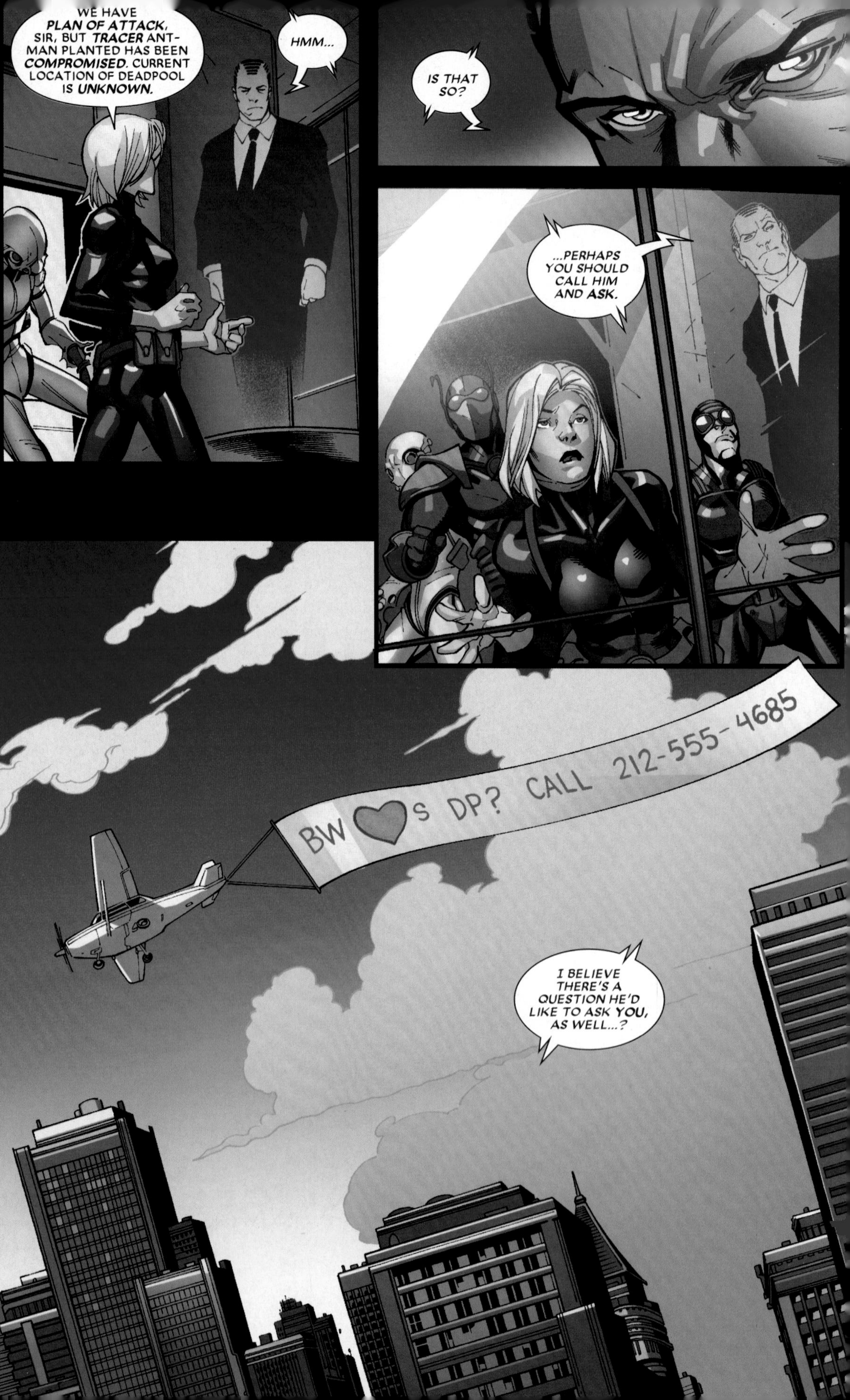
WE HAVE PLAN OF ATTACK, SIR, BUT TRACER ANT-MAN PLANTED HAS BEEN COMPROMISED. CURRENT LOCATION OF DEADPOOL IS UNKNOWN.
HMM...
IS THAT SO?
...PERHAPS YOU SHOULD CALL HIM AND ASK.
BW ♥s DP? CALL 212-555-4685
I BELIEVE THERE'S A QUESTION HE'D LIKE TO ASK YOU, AS WELL...?

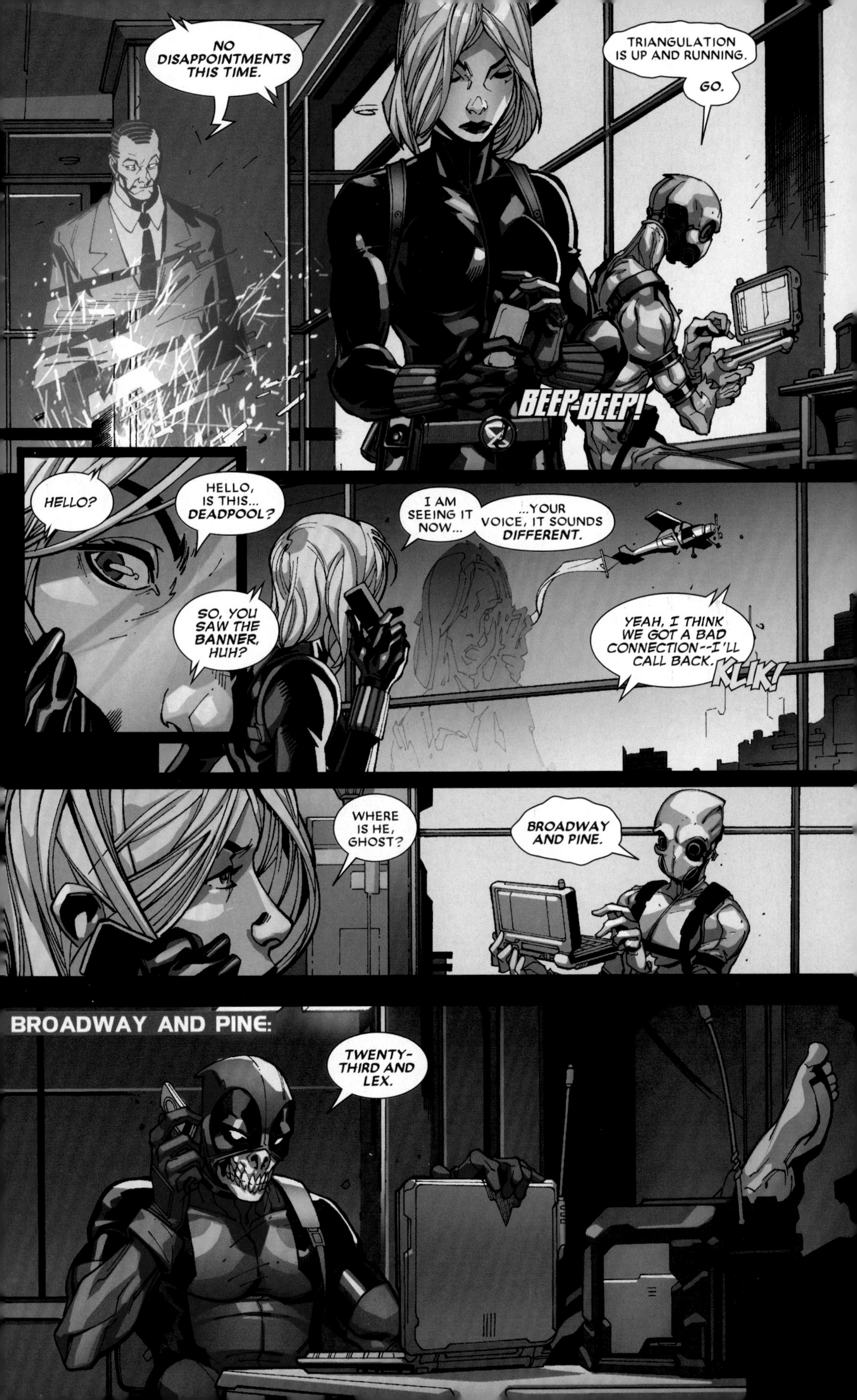
NO DISAPPOINTMENTS THIS TIME.
TRIANGULATION IS UP AND RUNNING.
GO.
BEEP-BEEP!
HELLO?
HELLO, IS THIS... DEADPOOL?
SO, YOU SAW THE BANNER, HUH?
I AM SEEING IT NOW...
...YOUR VOICE, IT SOUNDS DIFFERENT.
YEAH, I THINK WE GOT A BAD CONNECTION--I'LL CALL BACK.
KLIK!
WHERE IS HE, GHOST?
BROADWAY AND PINE.
BROADWAY AND PINE:
TWENTY-THIRD AND LEX.

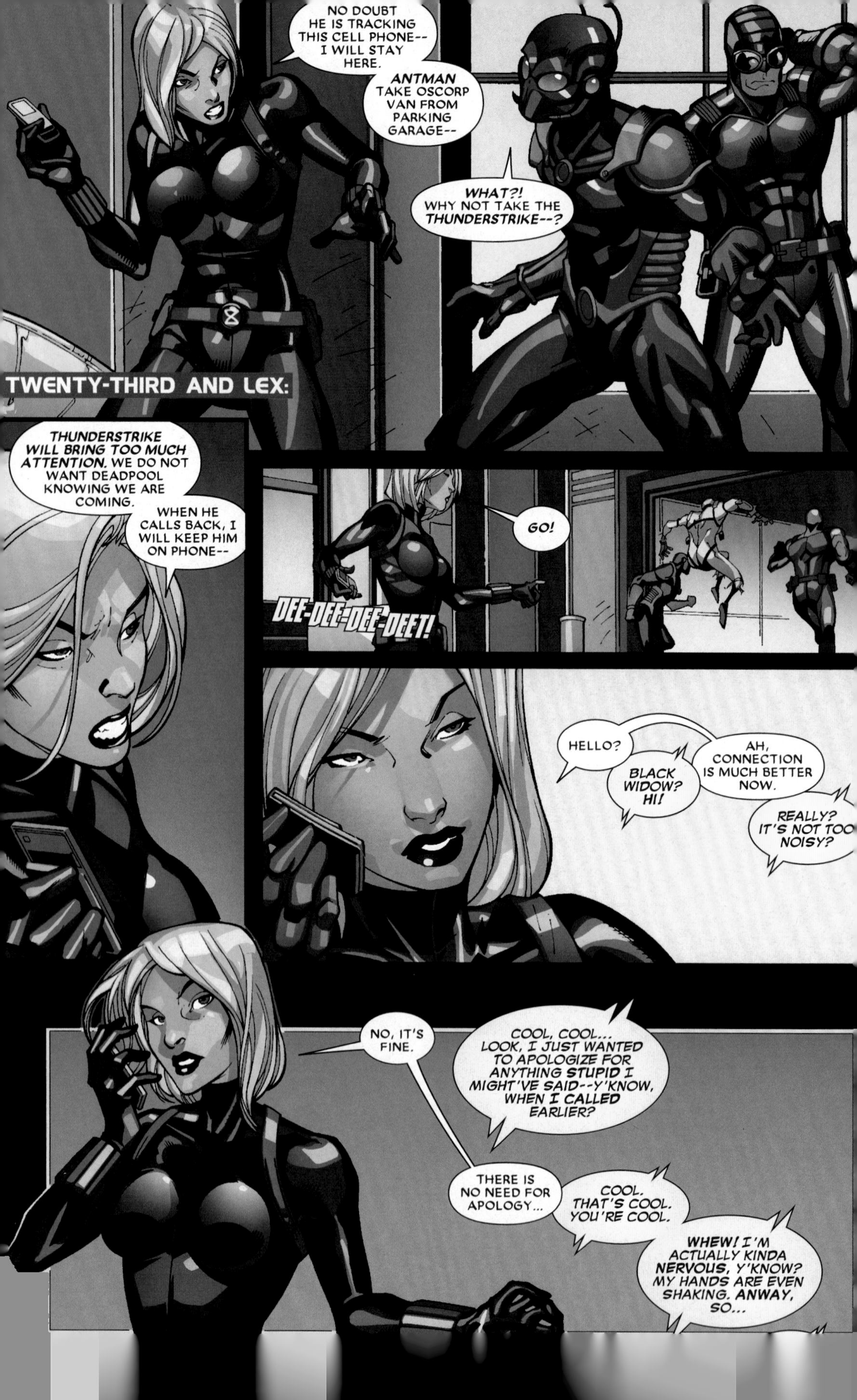
NO DOUBT HE IS TRACKING THIS CELL PHONE-- I WILL STAY HERE.
ANTMAN TAKE OSCORP VAN FROM PARKING GARAGE--
WHAT?! WHY NOT TAKE THE THUNDERSTRIKE--?
TWENTY-THIRD AND LEX:
THUNDERSTRIKE WILL BRING TOO MUCH ATTENTION. WE DO NOT WANT DEADPOOL KNOWING WE ARE COMING.
WHEN HE CALLS BACK, I WILL KEEP HIM ON PHONE--
GO!
DEE-DEE-DEE-DEET!
HELLO?
BLACK WIDOW? HI!
AH, CONNECTION IS MUCH BETTER NOW.
REALLY? IT'S NOT TOO NOISY?
NO, IT'S FINE.
COOL, COOL... LOOK, I JUST WANTED TO APOLOGIZE FOR ANYTHING STUPID I MIGHT'VE SAID--Y'KNOW, WHEN I CALLED EARLIER?
THERE IS NO NEED FOR APOLOGY...
COOL. THAT'S COOL. YOU'RE COOL.
WHEW! I'M ACTUALLY KINDA NERVOUS, Y'KNOW? MY HANDS ARE EVEN SHAKING. ANWAY, SO...

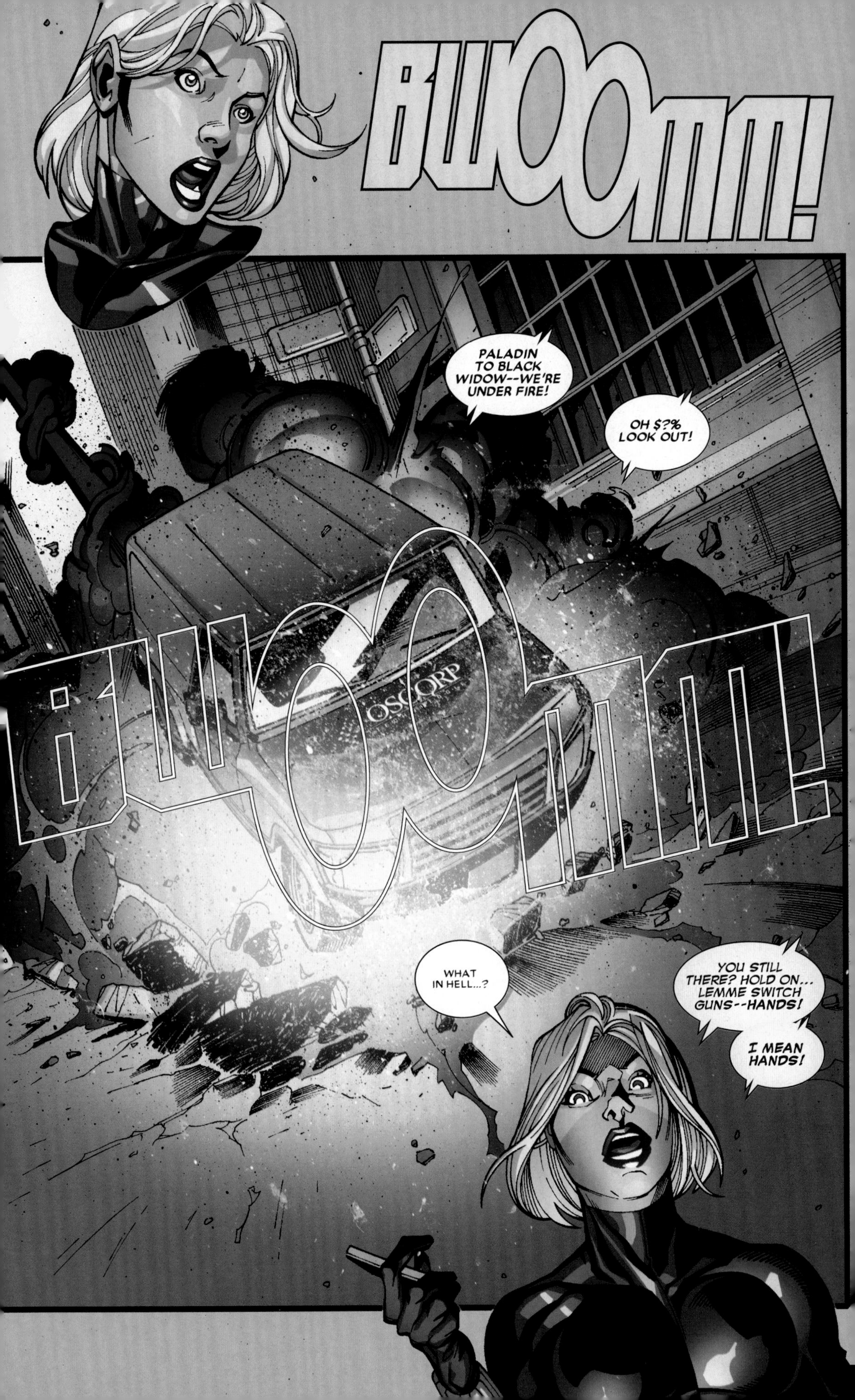
BWOOMM!
PALADIN TO BLACK WIDOW--WE'RE UNDER FIRE!
OH $?% LOOK OUT!
BWOOMM!
OSCORP
WHAT IN HELL...?
YOU STILL THERE? HOLD ON... LEMME SWITCH GUNS--HANDS!
I MEAN HANDS!

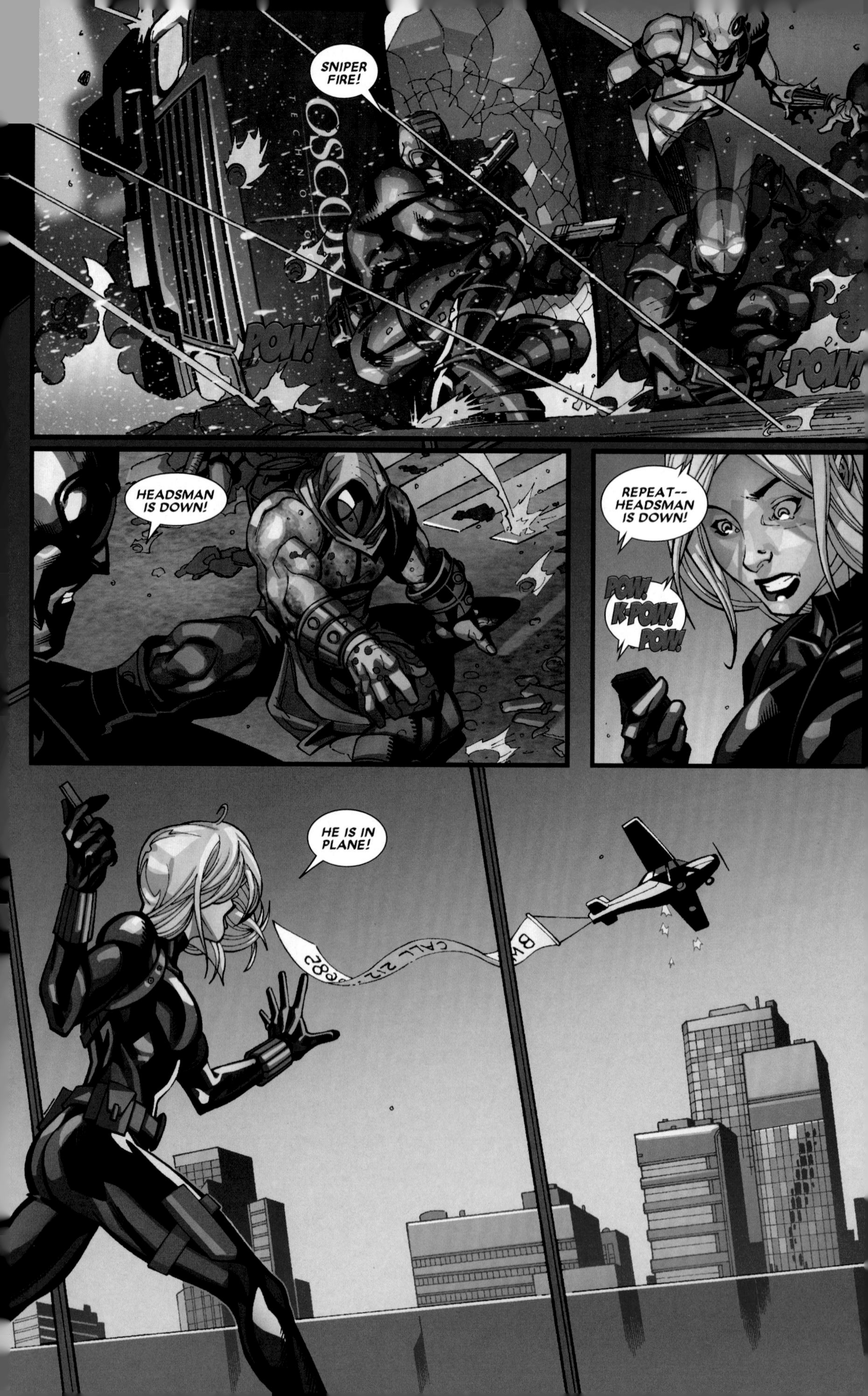
SNIPER FIRE!
POW!
K-POW!
HEADSMAN IS DOWN!
REPEAT-- HEADSMAN IS DOWN!
POW!
K-POW!
POW!
HE IS IN PLANE!

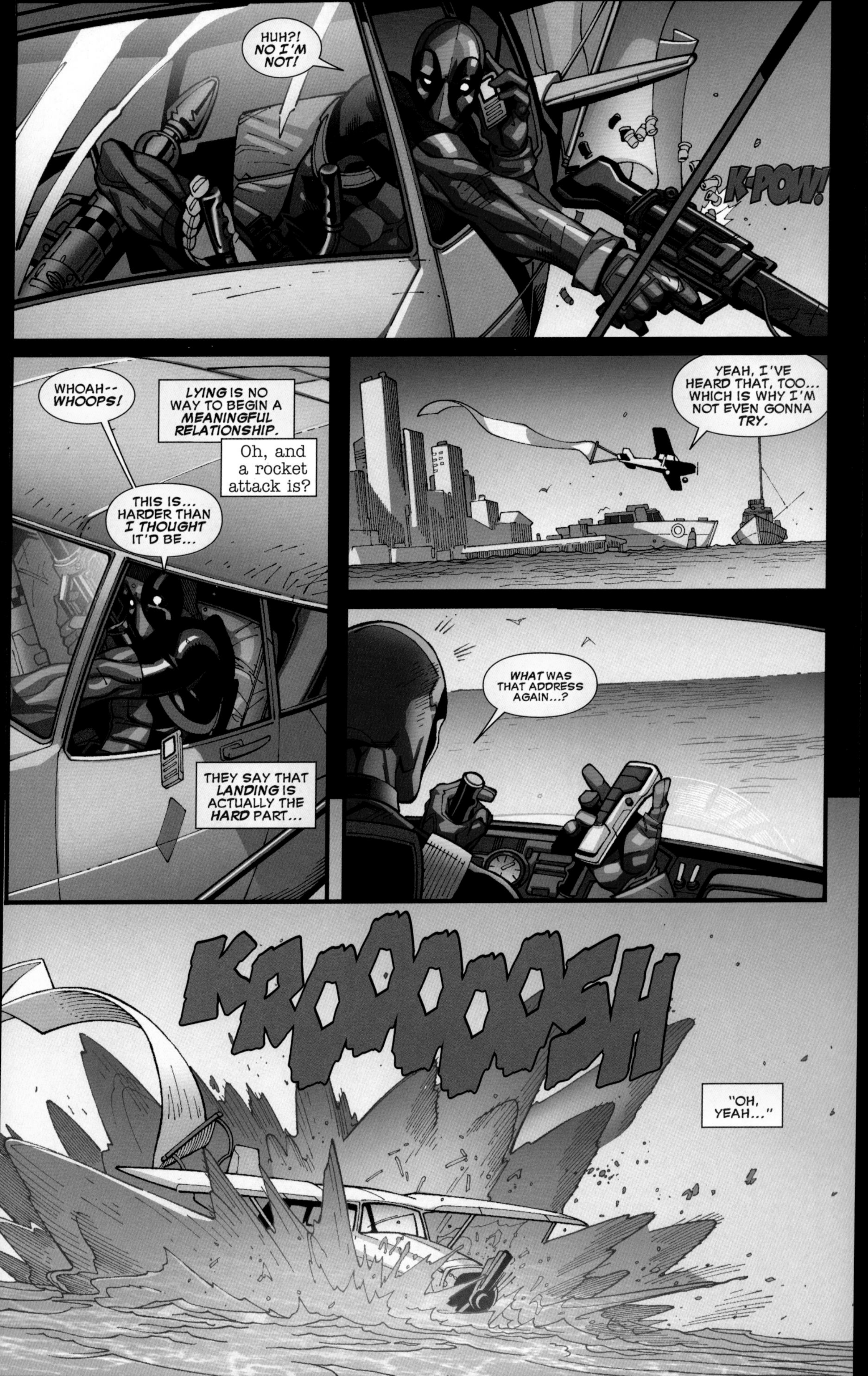
HUH?! NO I'M NOT!
K-POW!
WHOAH-- WHOOPS!
LYING IS NO WAY TO BEGIN A MEANINGFUL RELATIONSHIP.
Oh, and a rocket attack is?
THIS IS... HARDER THAN I THOUGHT IT'D BE...
THEY SAY THAT LANDING IS ACTUALLY THE HARD PART...
YEAH, I'VE HEARD THAT, TOO... WHICH IS WHY I'M NOT EVEN GONNA TRY.
WHAT WAS THAT ADDRESS AGAIN...?
KROOOOOSH
"OH, YEAH..."

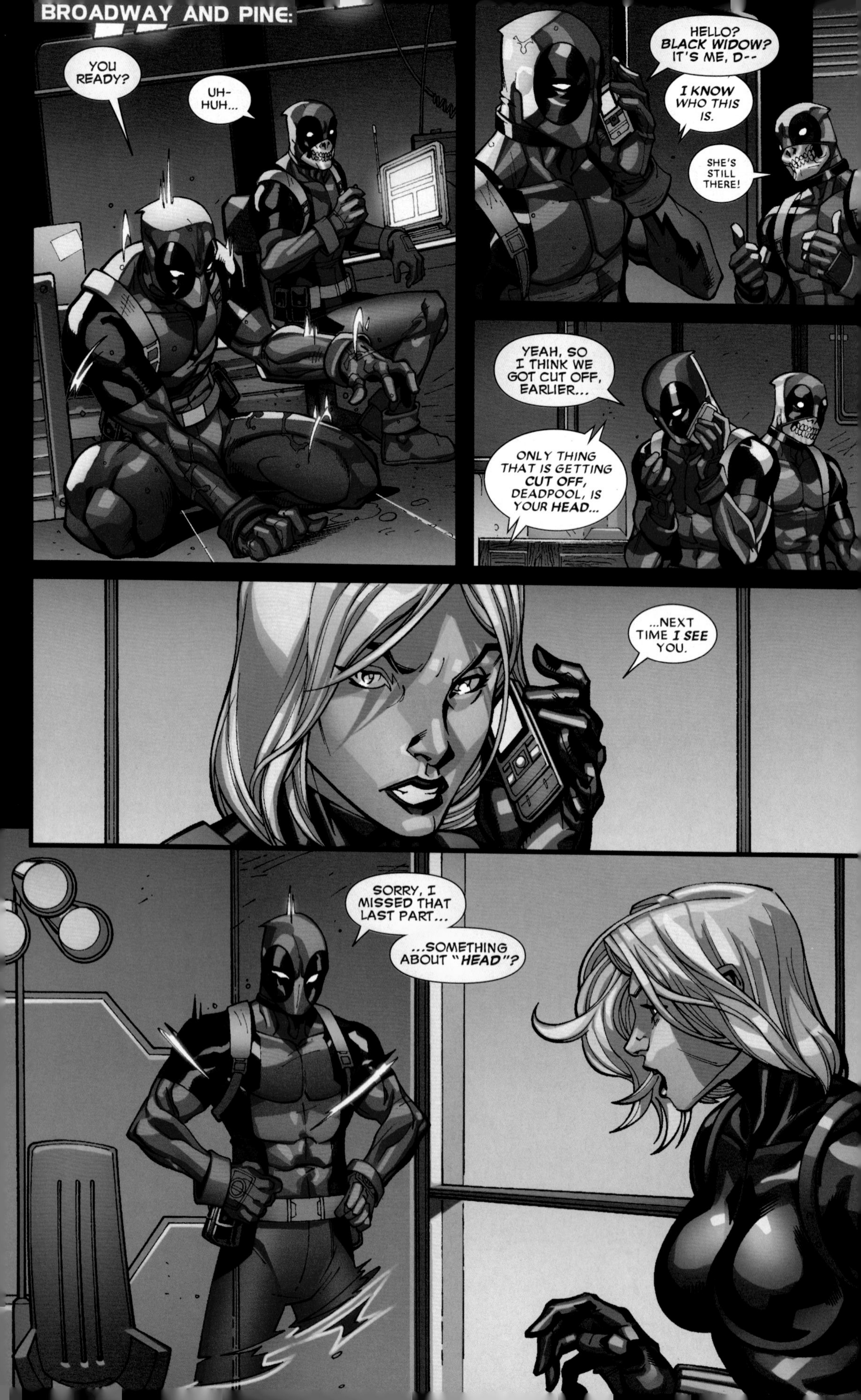
BROADWAY AND PINE:
YOU READY?
UH-HUH...
HELLO? BLACK WIDOW? IT'S ME, D--
I KNOW WHO THIS IS.
SHE'S STILL THERE!
YEAH, SO I THINK WE GOT CUT OFF, EARLIER...
ONLY THING THAT IS GETTING CUT OFF, DEADPOOL, IS YOUR HEAD...
...NEXT TIME I SEE YOU.
SORRY, I MISSED THAT LAST PART...
...SOMETHING ABOUT "HEAD"?

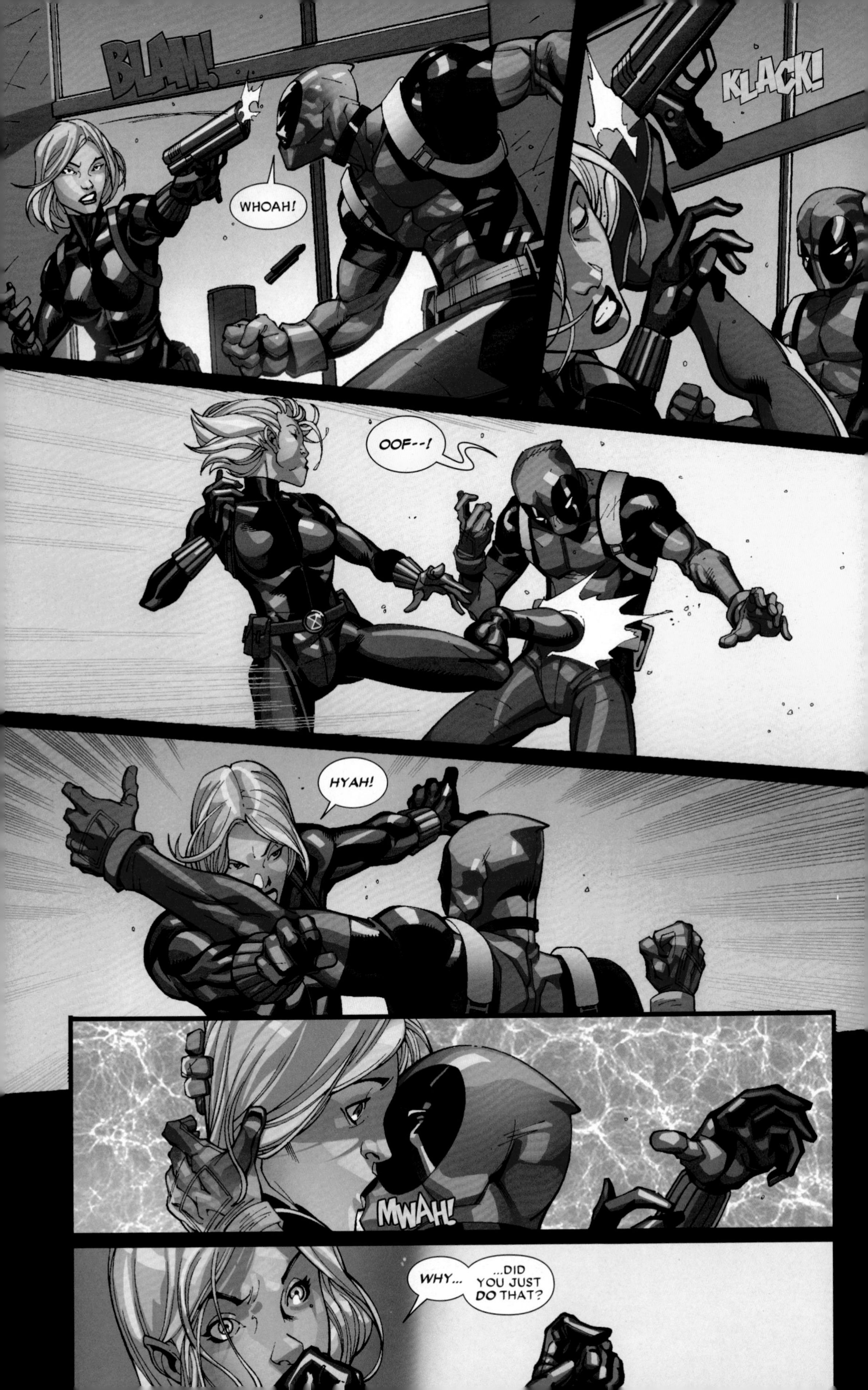
BLAM!
WHOAH!
KLACK!
OOF--!
HYAH!
MWAH!
WHY...
...DID YOU JUST DO THAT?

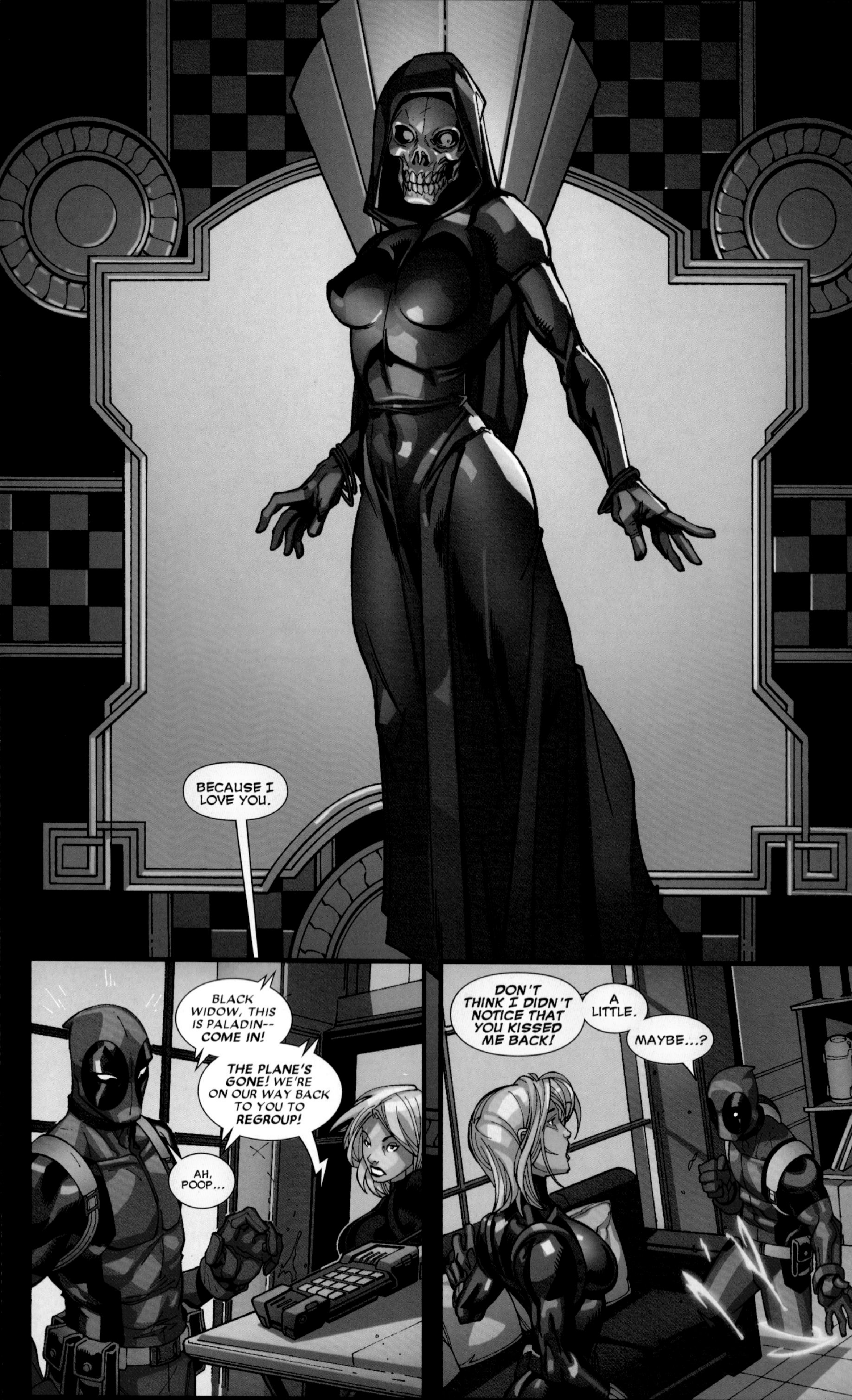

BECAUSE I LOVE YOU.
BLACK WIDOW, THIS IS PALADIN-- COME IN!
THE PLANE'S GONE! WE'RE ON OUR WAY BACK TO YOU TO REGROUP!
AH, POOP...
DON'T THINK I DIDN'T NOTICE THAT YOU KISSED ME BACK!
A LITTLE.
MAYBE...?

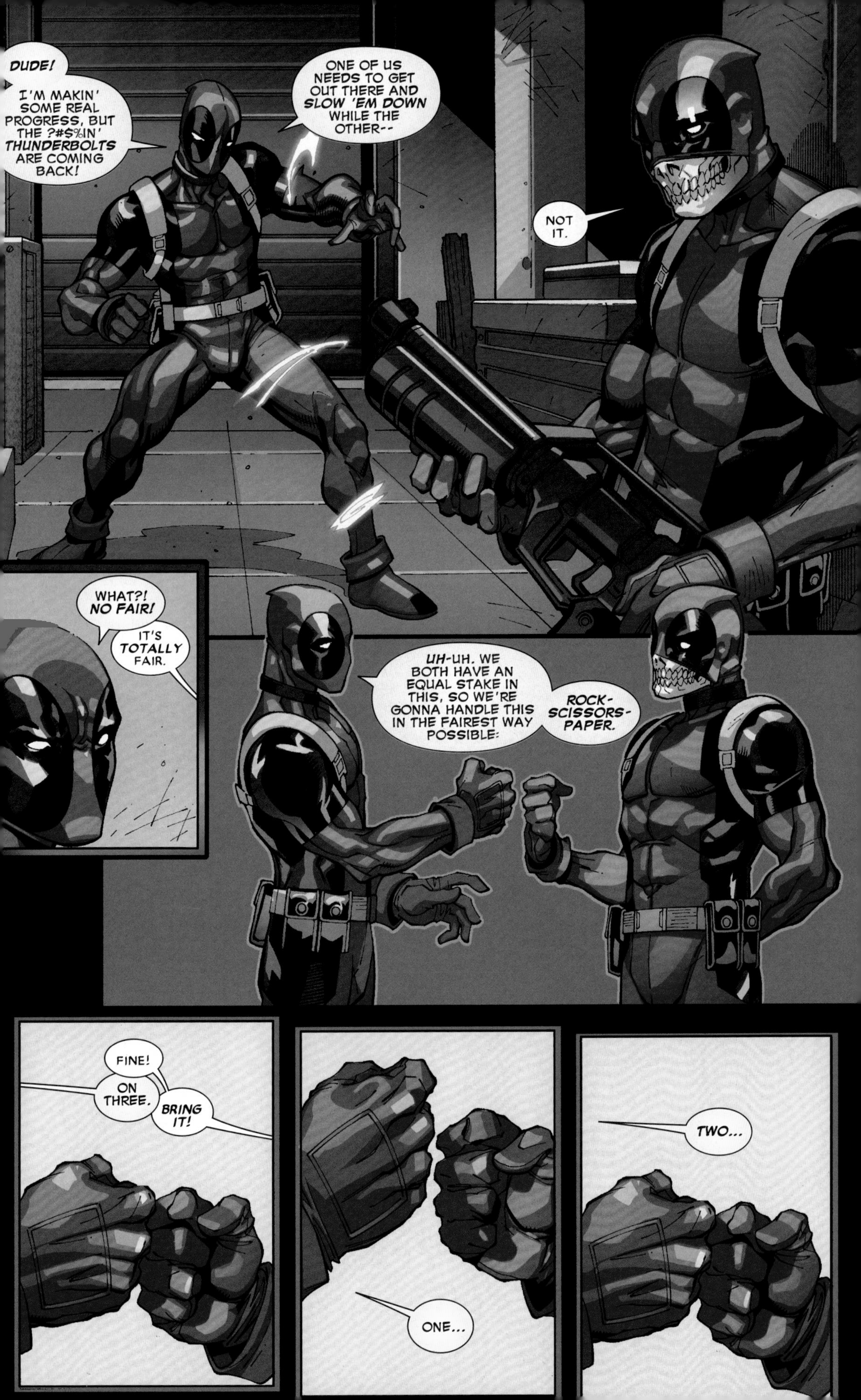
DUDE!
I'M MAKIN' SOME REAL PROGRESS, BUT THE ?#$%IN' THUNDERBOLTS ARE COMING BACK!
ONE OF US NEEDS TO GET OUT THERE AND SLOW 'EM DOWN WHILE THE OTHER--
NOT IT.
WHAT?! NO FAIR!
IT'S TOTALLY FAIR.
UH-UH. WE BOTH HAVE AN EQUAL STAKE IN THIS, SO WE'RE GONNA HANDLE THIS IN THE FAIREST WAY POSSIBLE:
ROCK-SCISSORS-PAPER.
FINE!
ON THREE.
BRING IT!
ONE...
TWO...

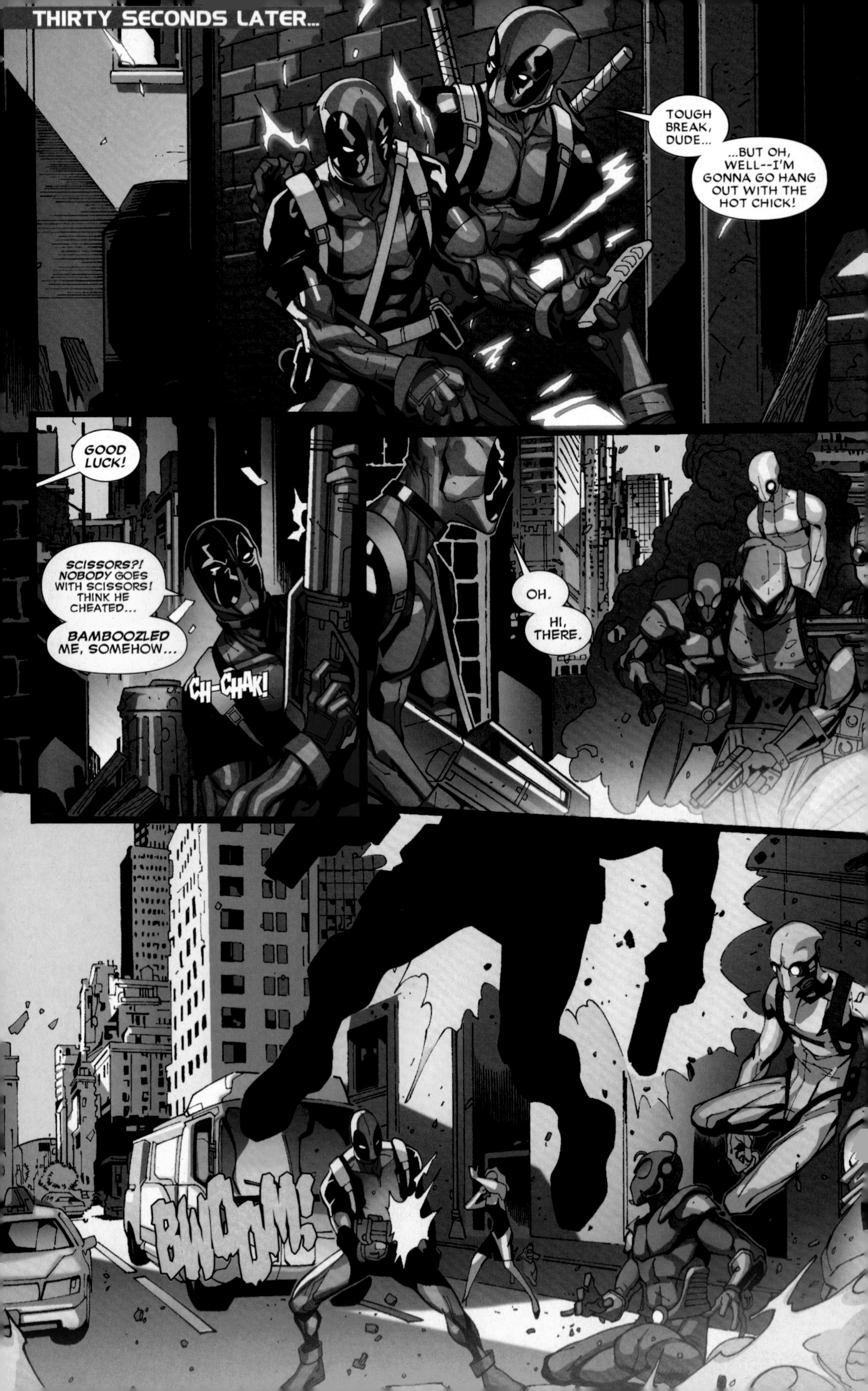
THIRTY SECONDS LATER...
TOUGH BREAK, DUDE...
...BUT OH, WELL--I'M GONNA GO HANG OUT WITH THE HOT CHICK!
GOOD LUCK!
SCISSORS?! NOBODY GOES WITH SCISSORS! THINK HE CHEATED...
BAMBOOZLED ME, SOMEHOW...
CH-CHAK!
OH.
HI, THERE.
BWOOM!

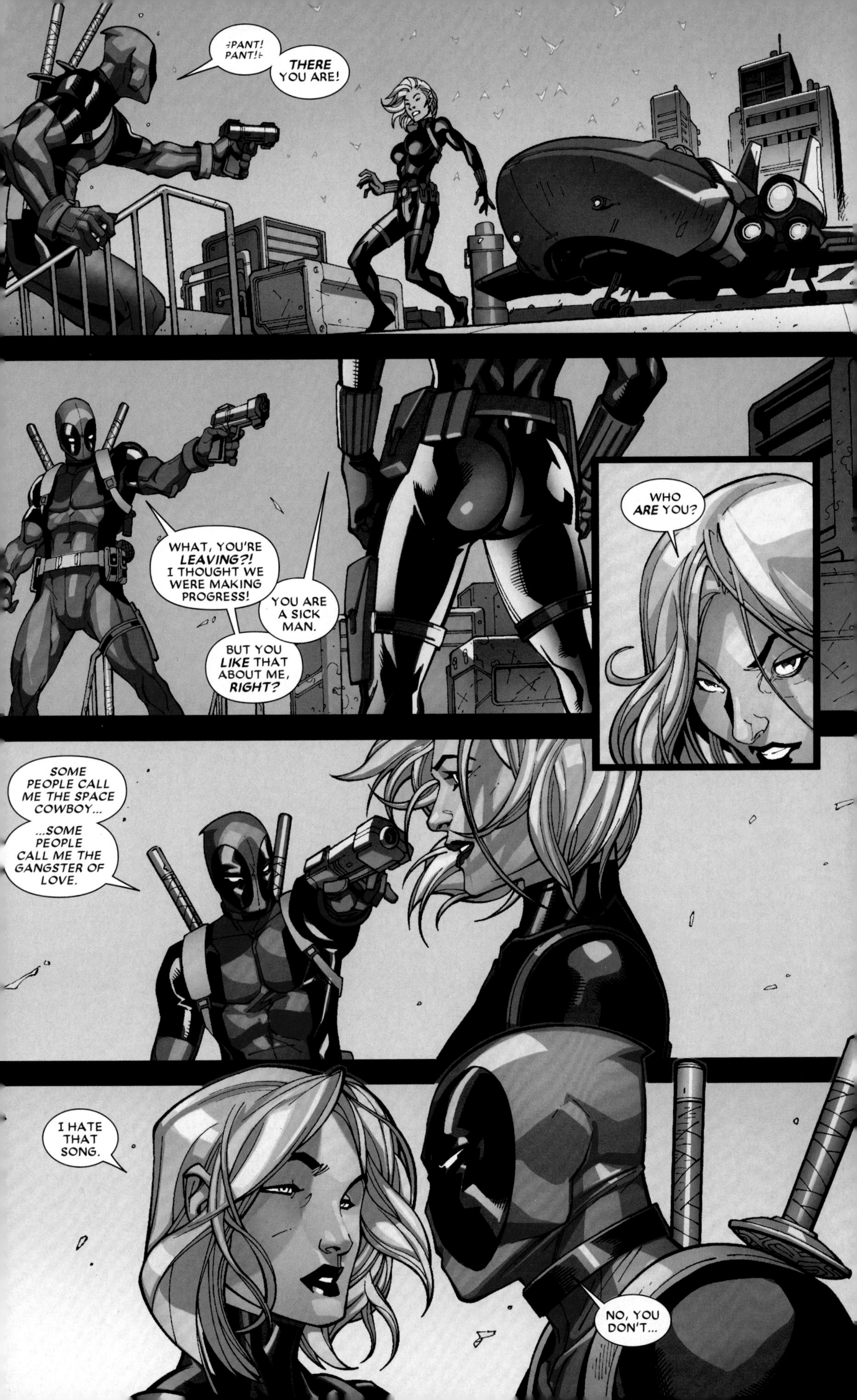

=PANT! PANT!=
THERE YOU ARE!
WHAT, YOU'RE LEAVING?! I THOUGHT WE WERE MAKING PROGRESS!
YOU ARE A SICK MAN.
BUT YOU LIKE THAT ABOUT ME, RIGHT?
WHO ARE YOU?
SOME PEOPLE CALL ME THE SPACE COWBOY...
...SOME PEOPLE CALL ME THE GANGSTER OF LOVE.
I HATE THAT SONG.
NO, YOU DON'T...

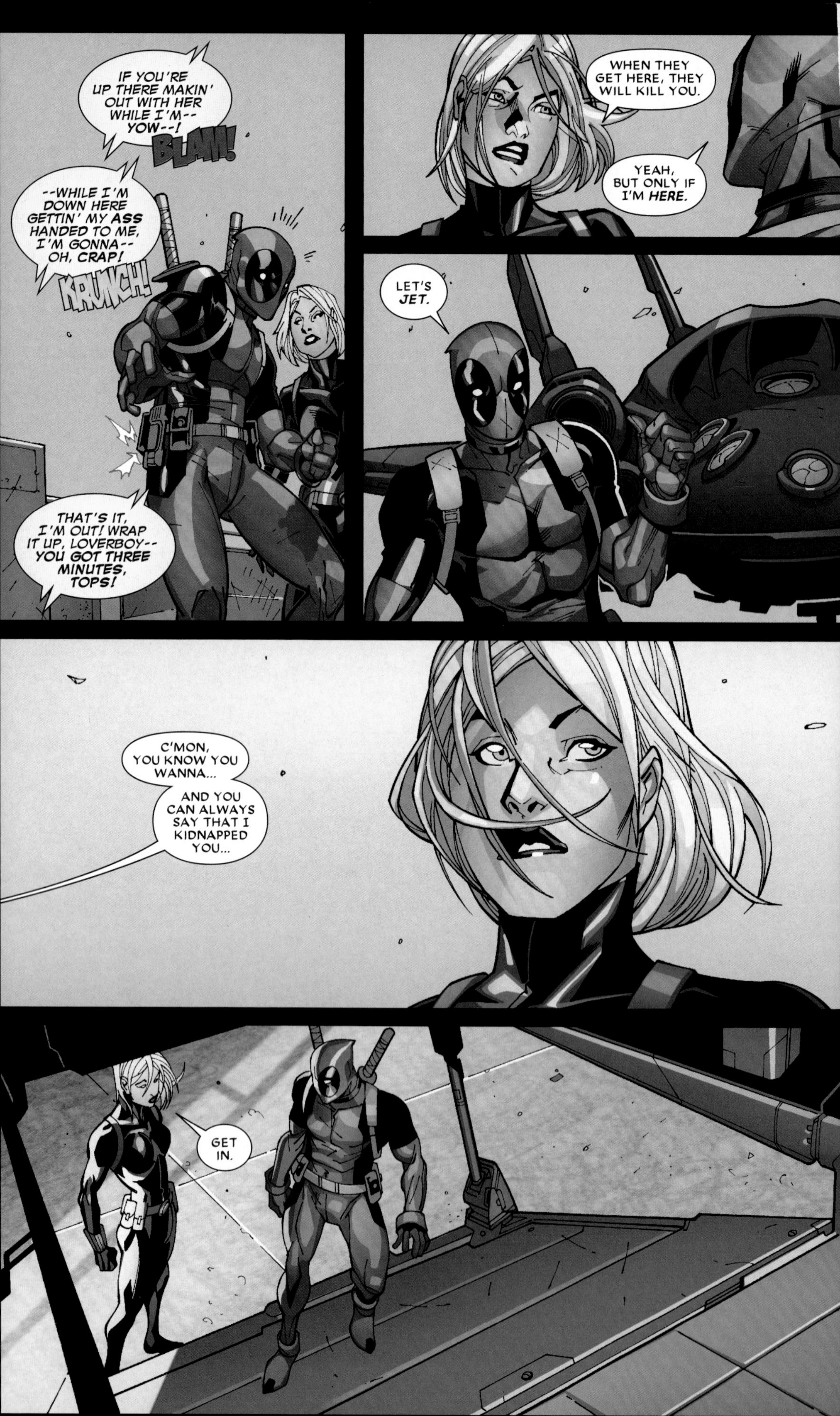
IF YOU'RE UP THERE MAKIN' OUT WITH HER WHILE I'M-- YOW--!
BLAM!
--WHILE I'M DOWN HERE GETTIN' MY ASS HANDED TO ME, I'M GONNA-- OH, CRAP!
KRUNCH!
THAT'S IT, I'M OUT! WRAP IT UP, LOVERBOY-- YOU GOT THREE MINUTES, TOPS!
WHEN THEY GET HERE, THEY WILL KILL YOU.
YEAH, BUT ONLY IF I'M HERE.
LET'S JET.
C'MON, YOU KNOW YOU WANNA...
AND YOU CAN ALWAYS SAY THAT I KIDNAPPED YOU...
GET IN.

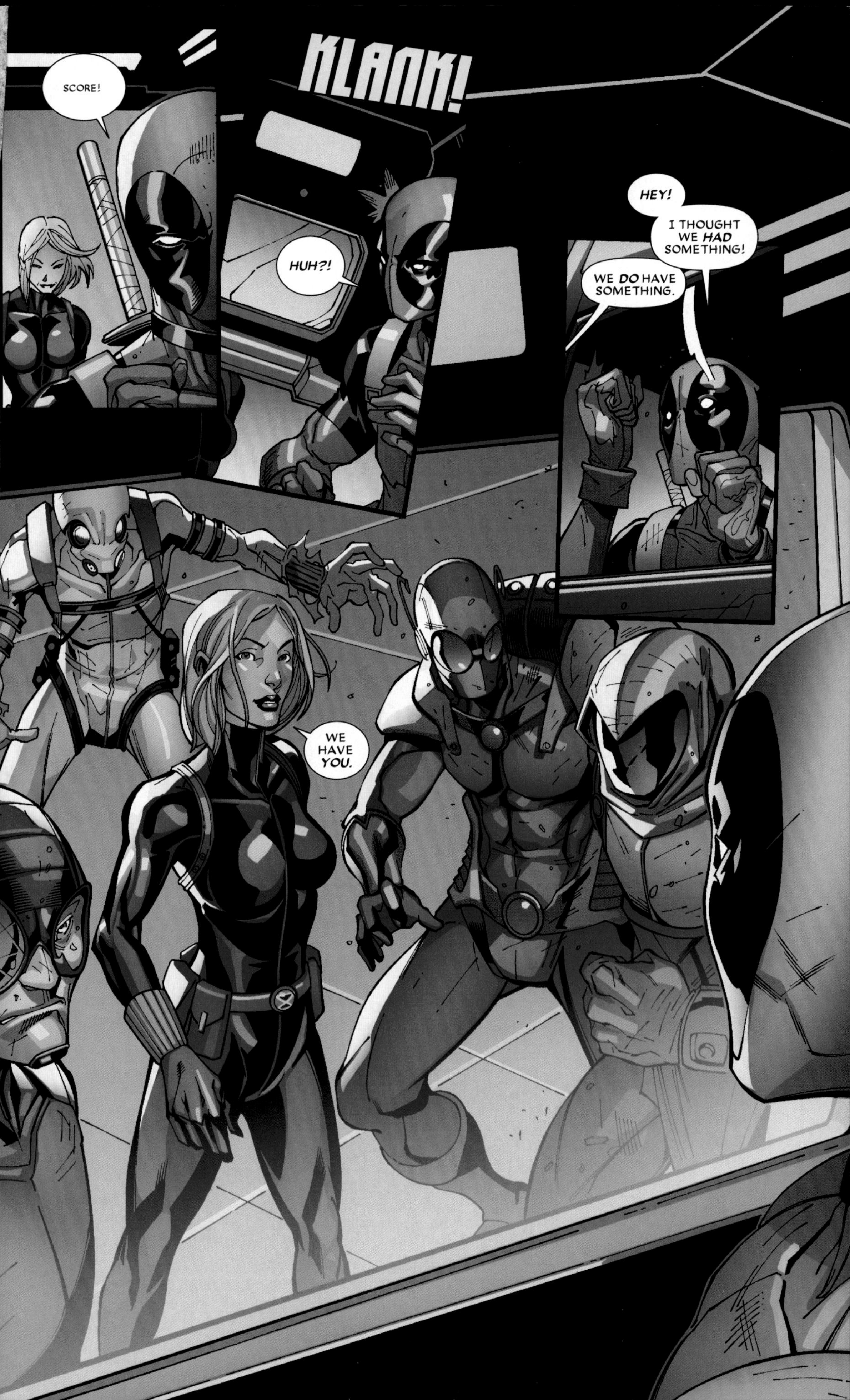
KLANK!
SCORE!
HUH?!
HEY!
I THOUGHT WE HAD SOMETHING!
WE DO HAVE SOMETHING.
WE HAVE YOU.

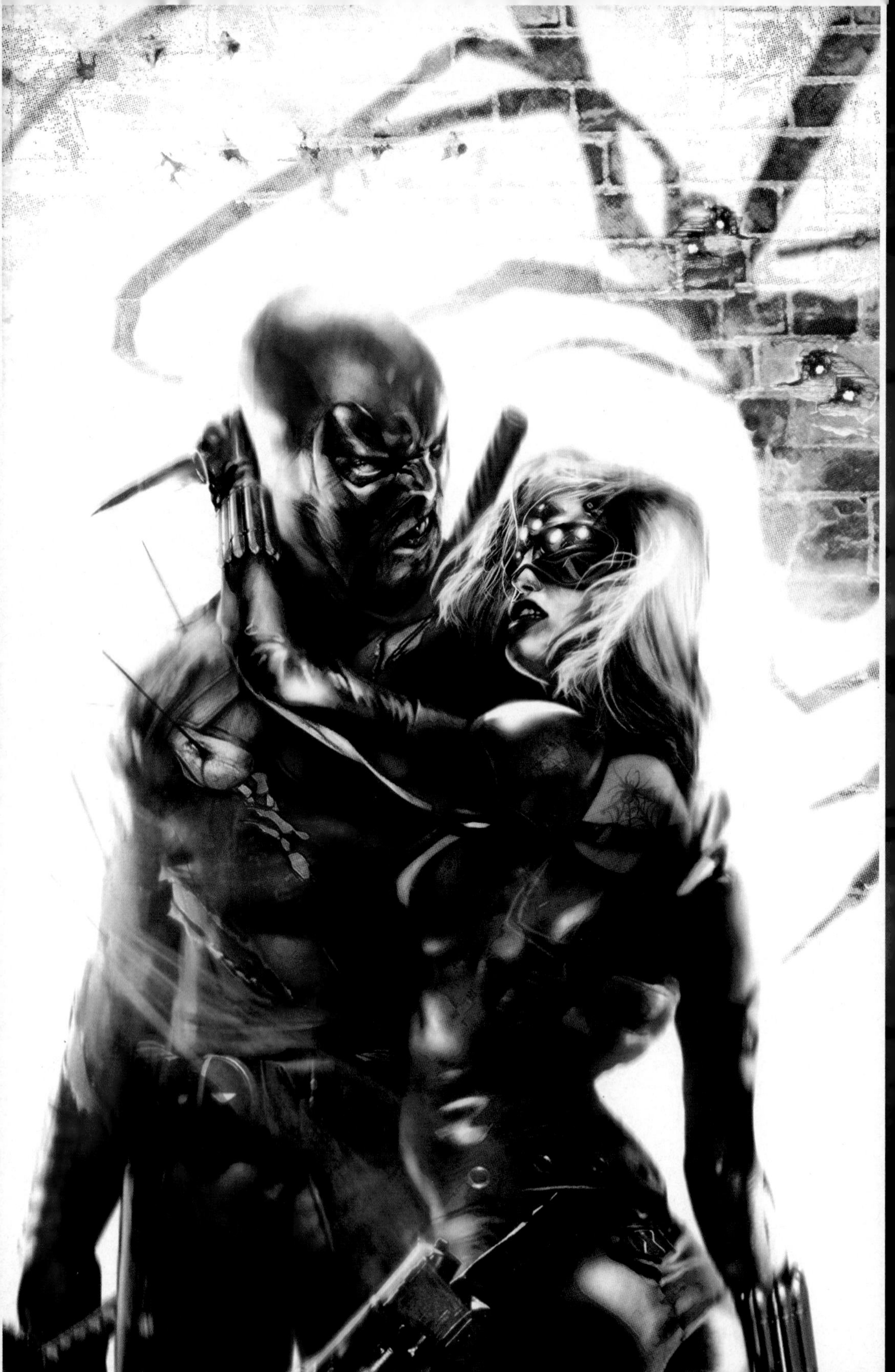

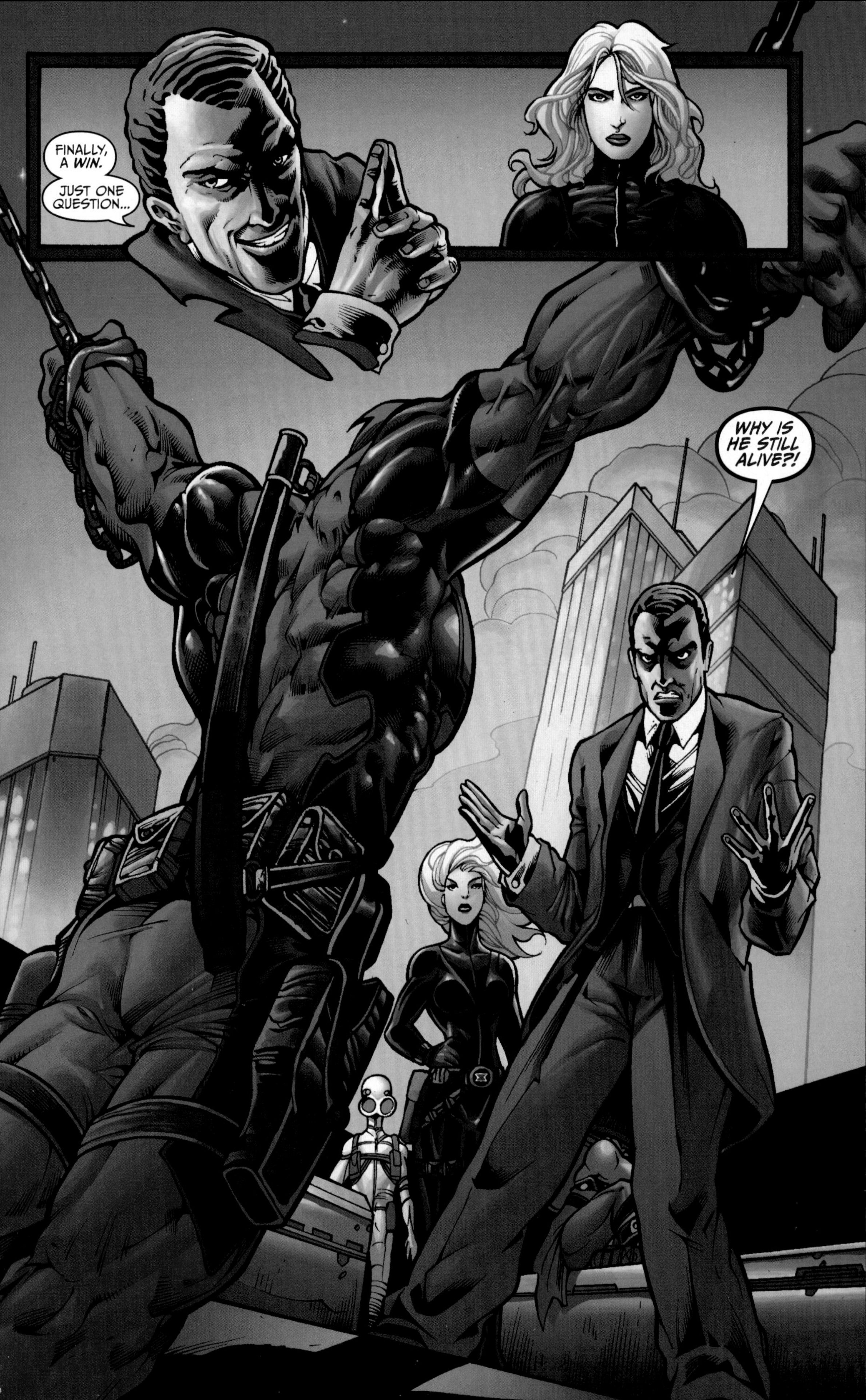
FINALLY, A WIN.
JUST ONE QUESTION...
WHY IS HE STILL ALIVE?!

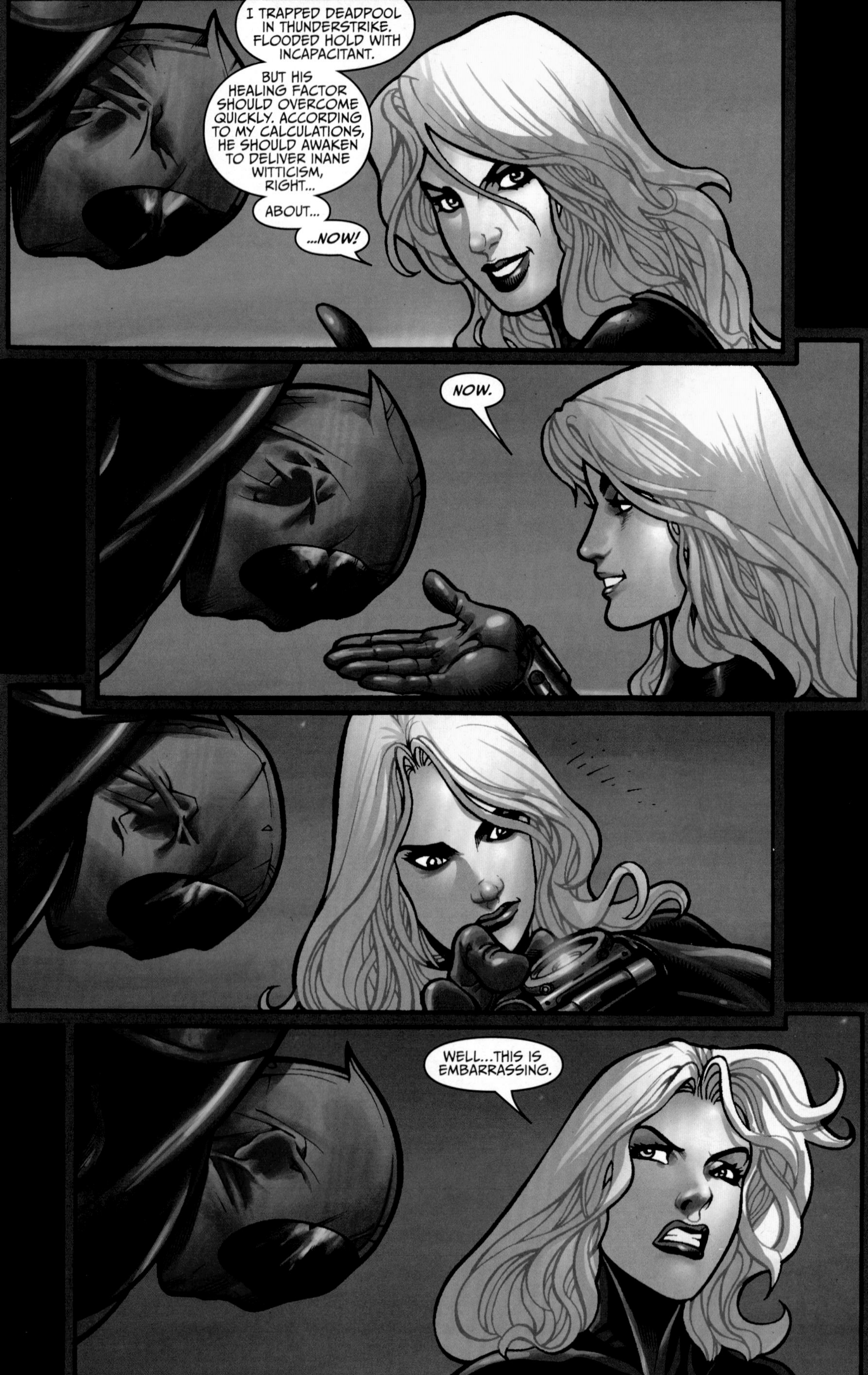
I TRAPPED DEADPOOL IN THUNDERSTRIKE. FLOODED HOLD WITH INCAPACITANT.
BUT HIS HEALING FACTOR SHOULD OVERCOME QUICKLY. ACCORDING TO MY CALCULATIONS, HE SHOULD AWAKEN TO DELIVER INANE WITTICISM, RIGHT...
ABOUT...
...NOW!
NOW.
WELL...THIS IS EMBARRASSING.

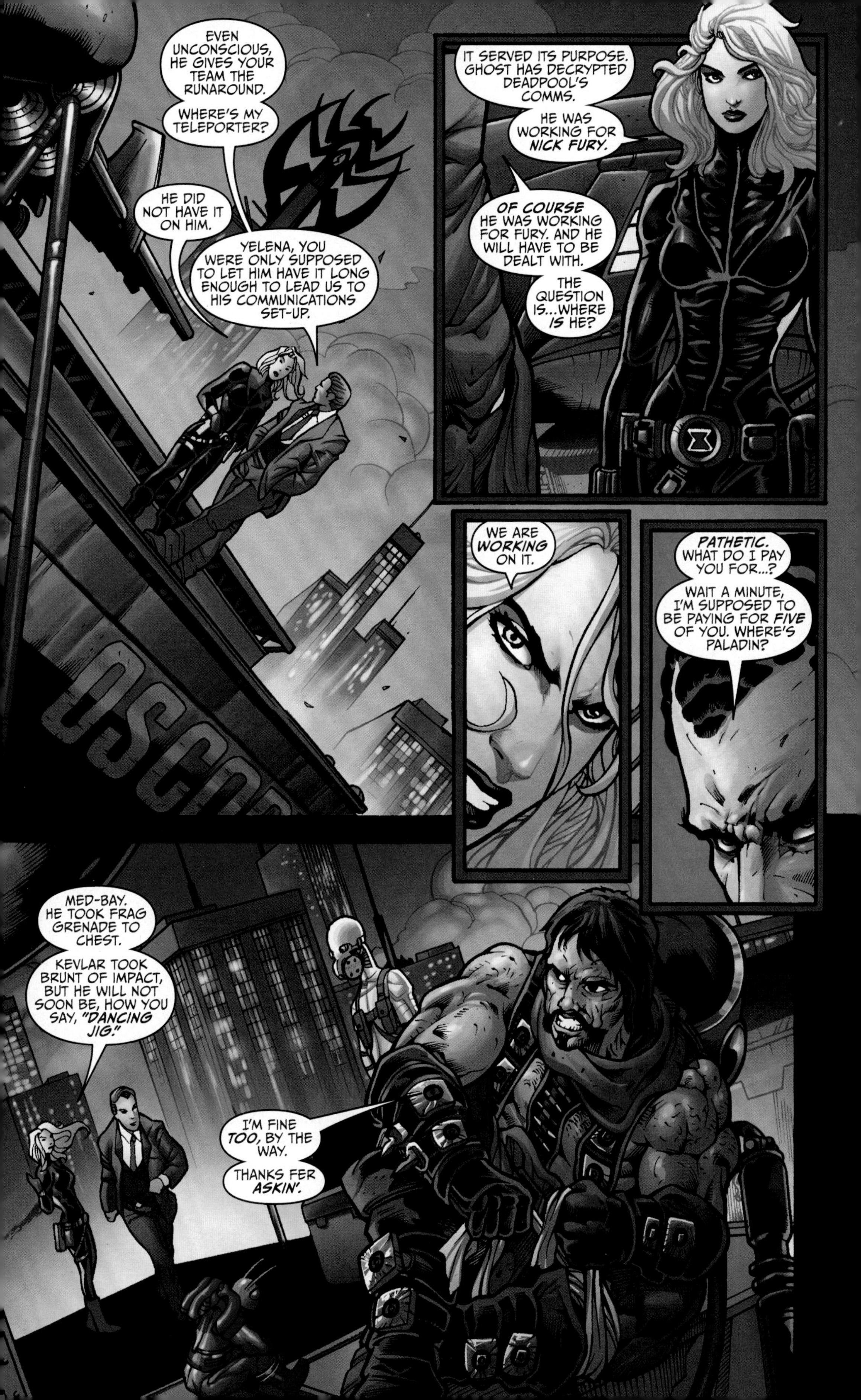
EVEN UNCONSCIOUS, HE GIVES YOUR TEAM THE RUNAROUND.
WHERE'S MY TELEPORTER?
HE DID NOT HAVE IT ON HIM.
YELENA, YOU WERE ONLY SUPPOSED TO LET HIM HAVE IT LONG ENOUGH TO LEAD US TO HIS COMMUNICATIONS SET-UP.
IT SERVED ITS PURPOSE. GHOST HAS DECRYPTED DEADPOOL'S COMMS.
HE WAS WORKING FOR NICK FURY.
OF COURSE HE WAS WORKING FOR FURY. AND HE WILL HAVE TO BE DEALT WITH.
THE QUESTION IS...WHERE IS HE?
WE ARE WORKING ON IT.
PATHETIC. WHAT DO I PAY YOU FOR...?
WAIT A MINUTE, I'M SUPPOSED TO BE PAYING FOR FIVE OF YOU. WHERE'S PALADIN?
MED-BAY. HE TOOK FRAG GRENADE TO CHEST.
KEVLAR TOOK BRUNT OF IMPACT, BUT HE WILL NOT SOON BE, HOW YOU SAY, "DANCING JIG."
I'M FINE TOO, BY THE WAY.
THANKS FER ASKIN'.

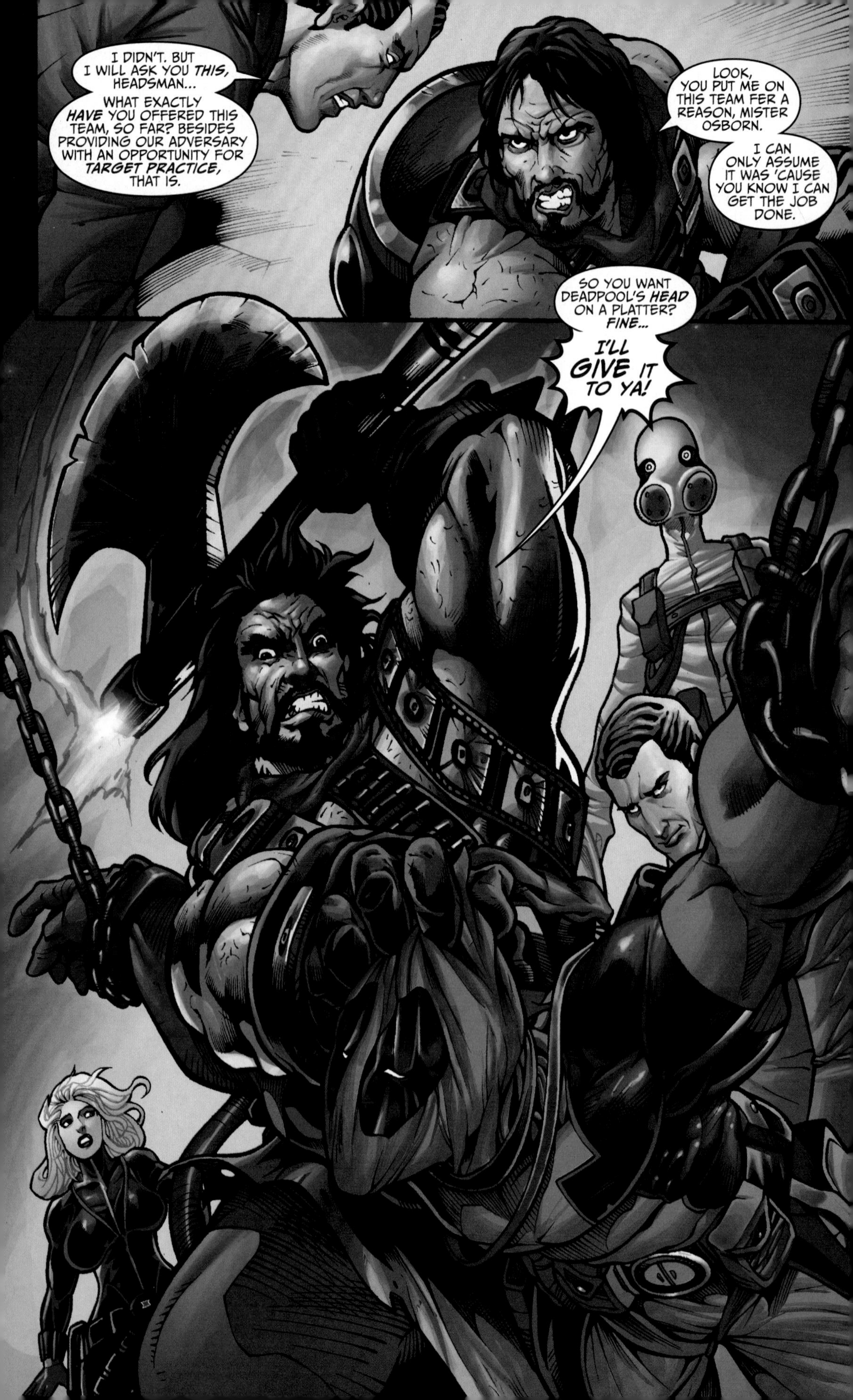
I DIDN'T. BUT I WILL ASK YOU THIS, HEADSMAN...
WHAT EXACTLY HAVE YOU OFFERED THIS TEAM, SO FAR? BESIDES PROVIDING OUR ADVERSARY WITH AN OPPORTUNITY FOR TARGET PRACTICE, THAT IS.
LOOK, YOU PUT ME ON THIS TEAM FER A REASON, MISTER OSBORN.
I CAN ONLY ASSUME IT WAS 'CAUSE YOU KNOW I CAN GET THE JOB DONE.
SO YOU WANT DEADPOOL'S HEAD ON A PLATTER? FINE...
I'LL GIVE IT TO YA!

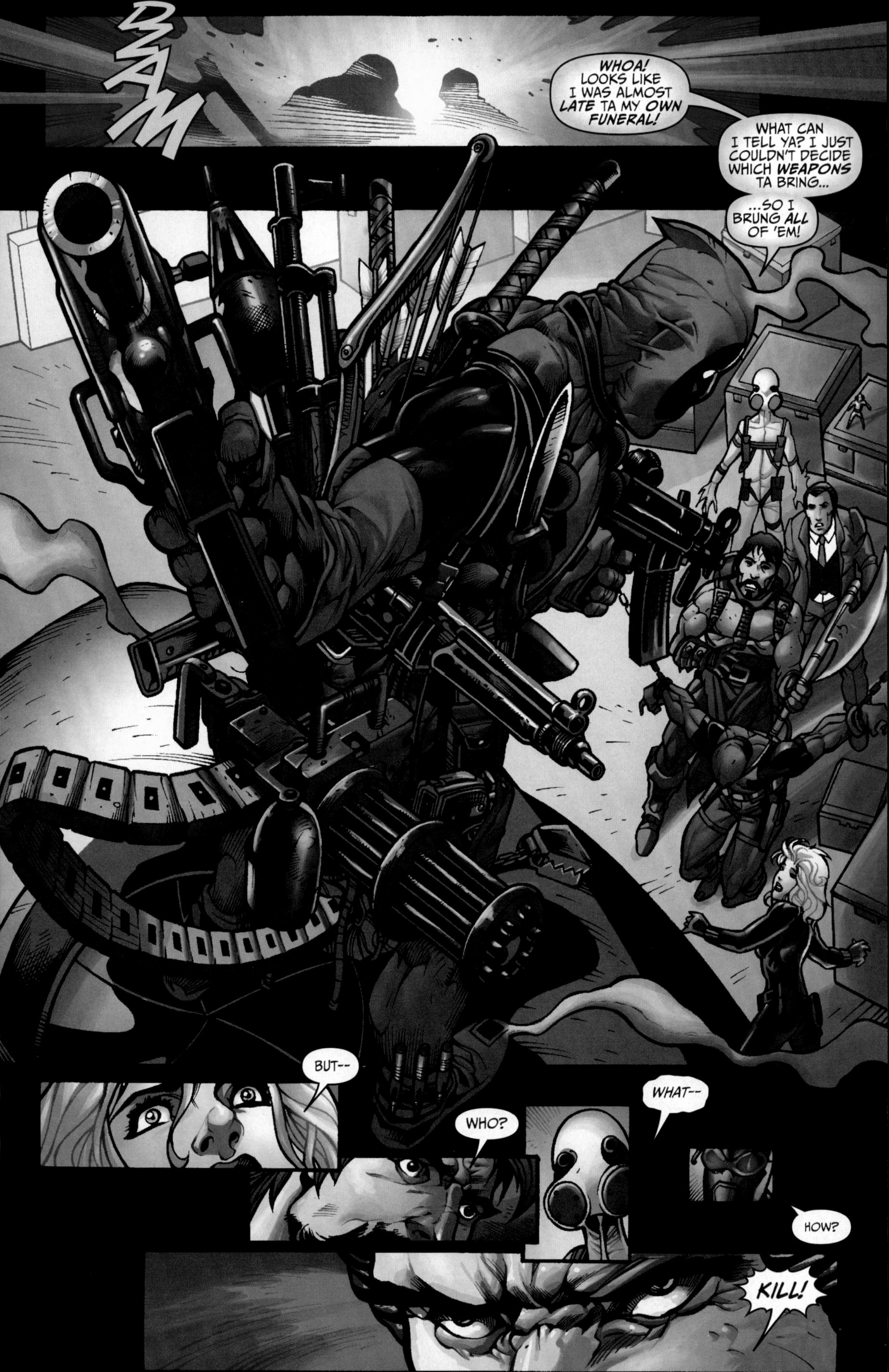

DWAM
WHOA! LOOKS LIKE I WAS ALMOST LATE TA MY OWN FUNERAL!
WHAT CAN I TELL YA? I JUST COULDN'T DECIDE WHICH WEAPONS TA BRING...
...SO I BRUNG ALL OF 'EM!
BUT--
WHO?
WHAT--
HOW?
KILL!

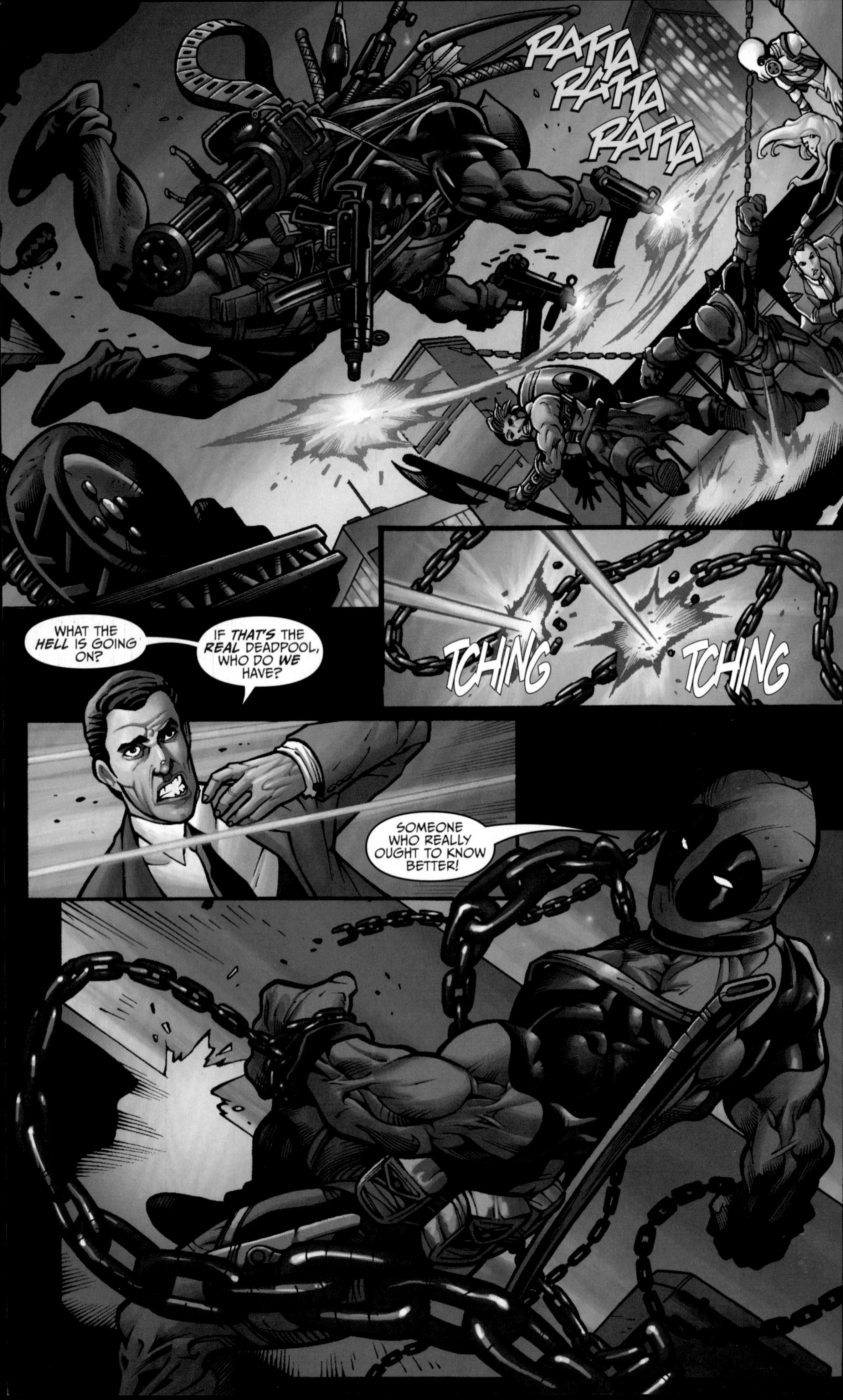
RAKKA RAKKA RAKKA
TCHING
TCHING
WHAT THE HELL IS GOING ON?
IF THAT'S THE REAL DEADPOOL, WHO DO WE HAVE?
SOMEONE WHO REALLY OUGHT TO KNOW BETTER!

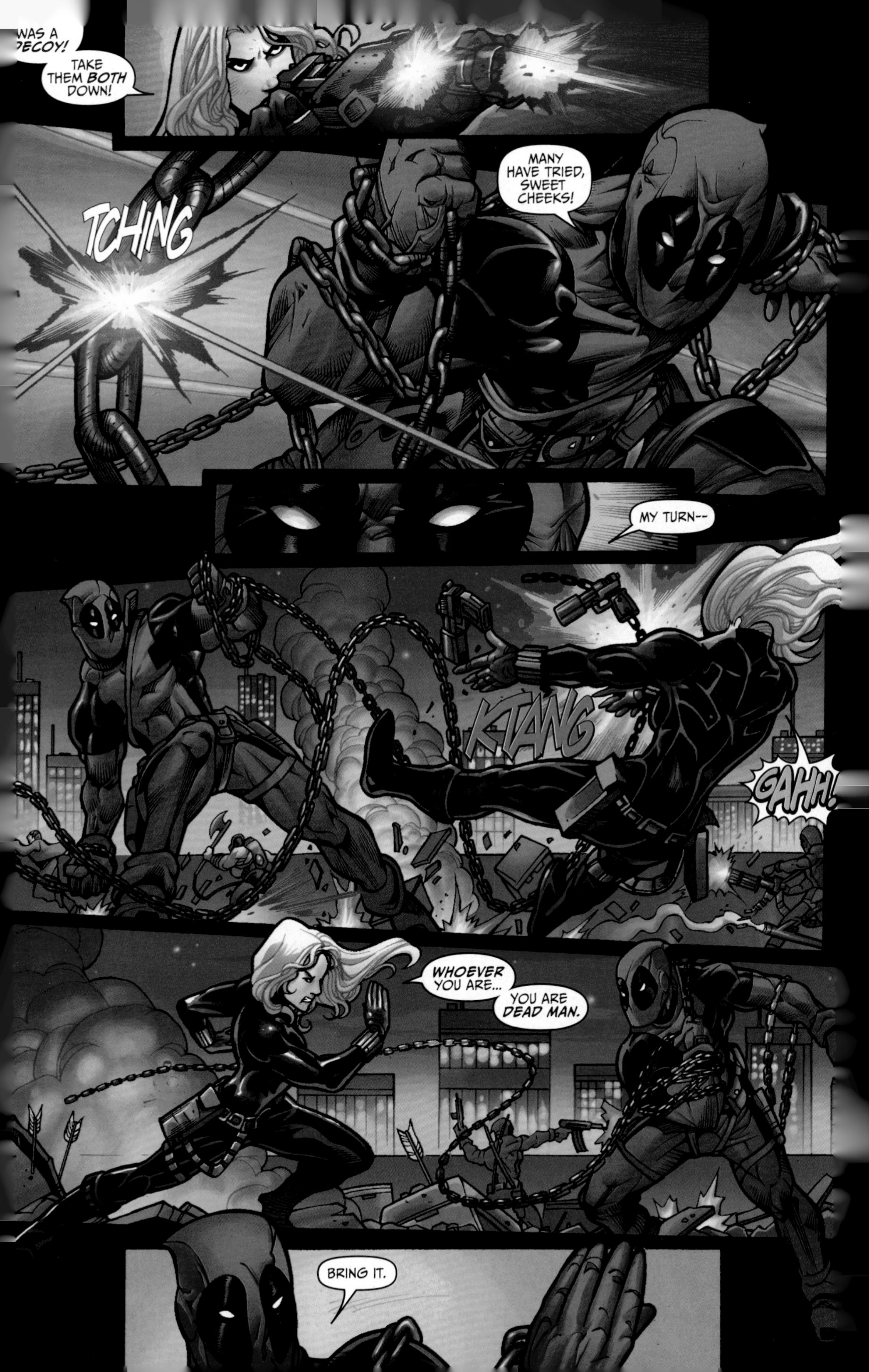
WAS A DECOY!
TAKE THEM BOTH DOWN!
MANY HAVE TRIED, SWEET CHEEKS!
TCHING
MY TURN--
KTANG
GAHH!
WHOEVER YOU ARE...
YOU ARE DEAD MAN.
BRING IT.

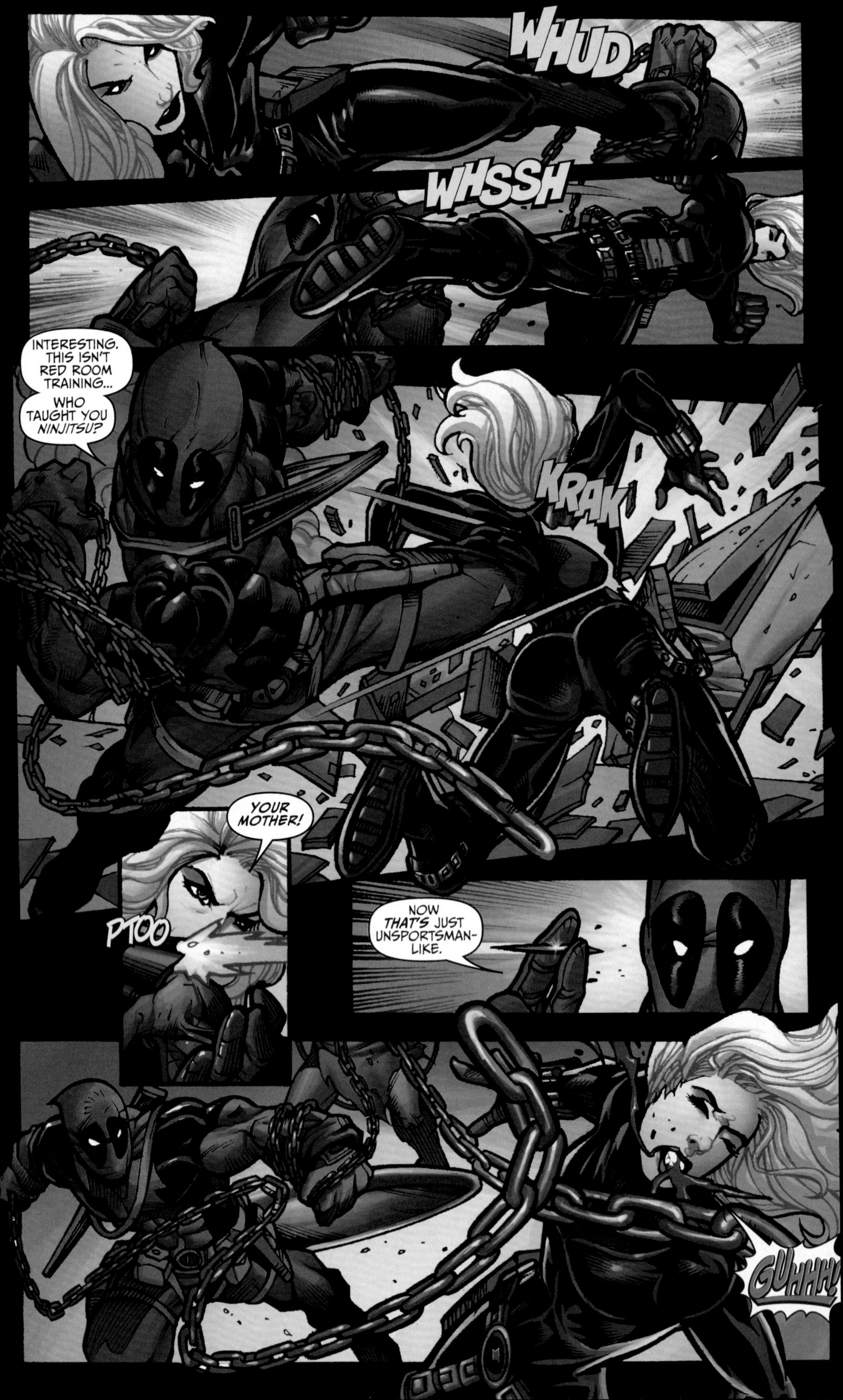
WHUD
WHSSH
INTERESTING. THIS ISN'T RED ROOM TRAINING... WHO TAUGHT YOU NINJITSU?
KRAK
YOUR MOTHER!
PTOO
NOW THAT'S JUST UNSPORTSMAN-LIKE.
GUHHH

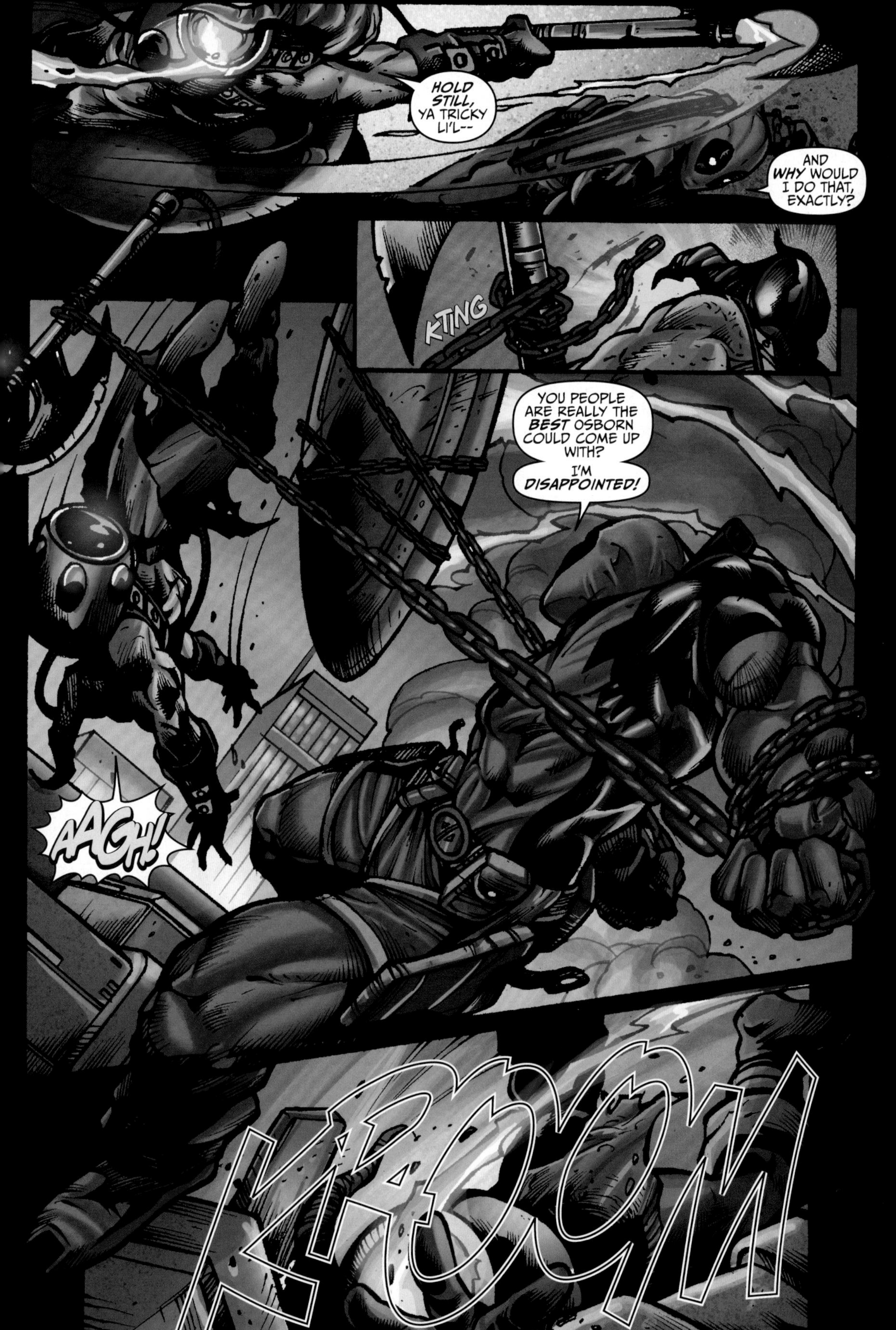
HOLD STILL, YA TRICKY LI'L--
AND WHY WOULD I DO THAT, EXACTLY?
KTING
YOU PEOPLE ARE REALLY THE BEST OSBORN COULD COME UP WITH?
I'M DISAPPOINTED!
AAGH!
KROOM

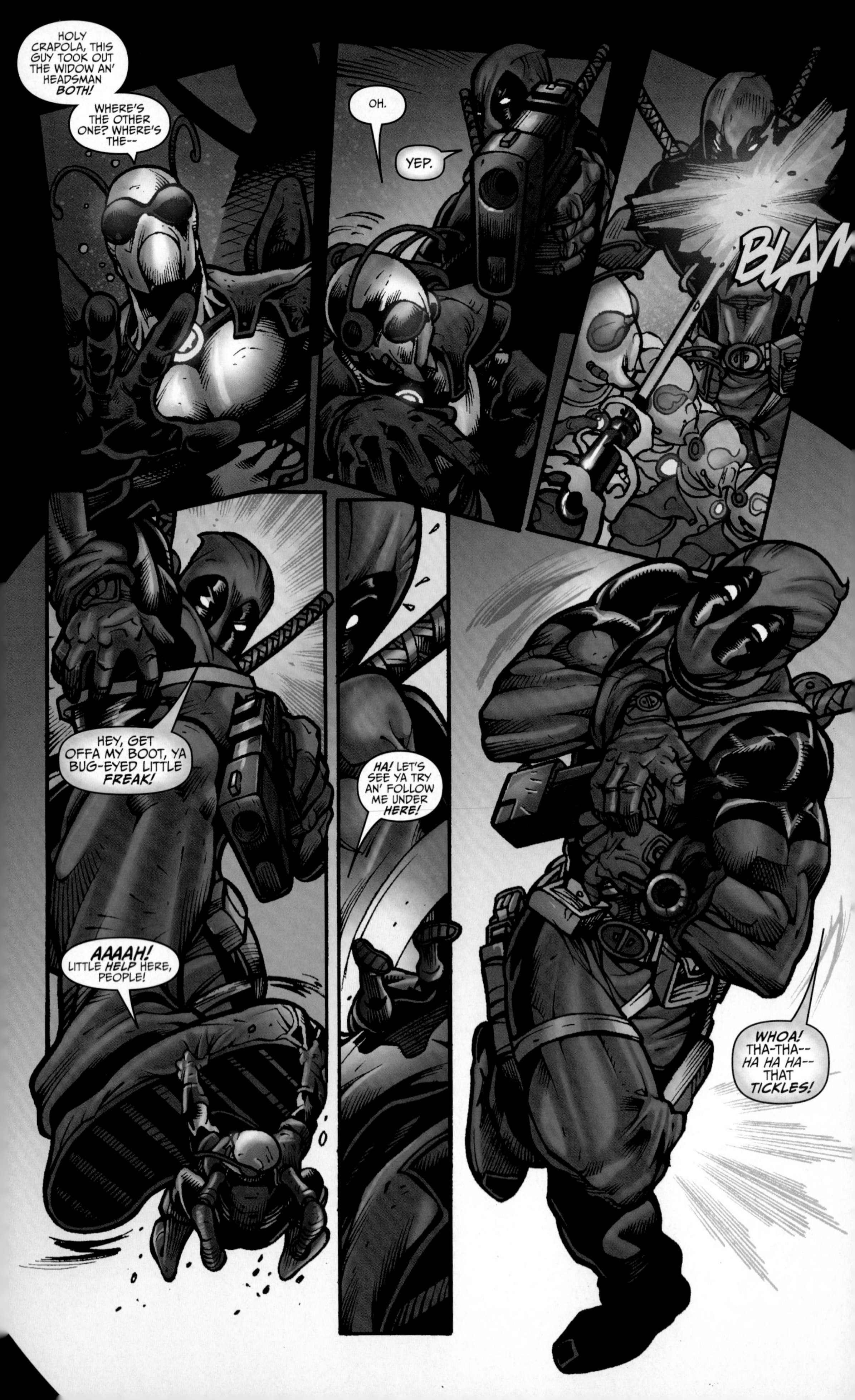
HOLY CRAPOLA, THIS GUY TOOK OUT THE WIDOW AN' HEADSMAN BOTH!
WHERE'S THE OTHER ONE? WHERE'S THE--
OH.
YEP.
BLAM
HEY, GET OFFA MY BOOT, YA BUG-EYED LITTLE FREAK!
AAAAH! LITTLE HELP HERE, PEOPLE!
HA! LET'S SEE YA TRY AN' FOLLOW ME UNDER HERE!
WHOA! THA-THA-- HA HA HA-- THAT TICKLES!

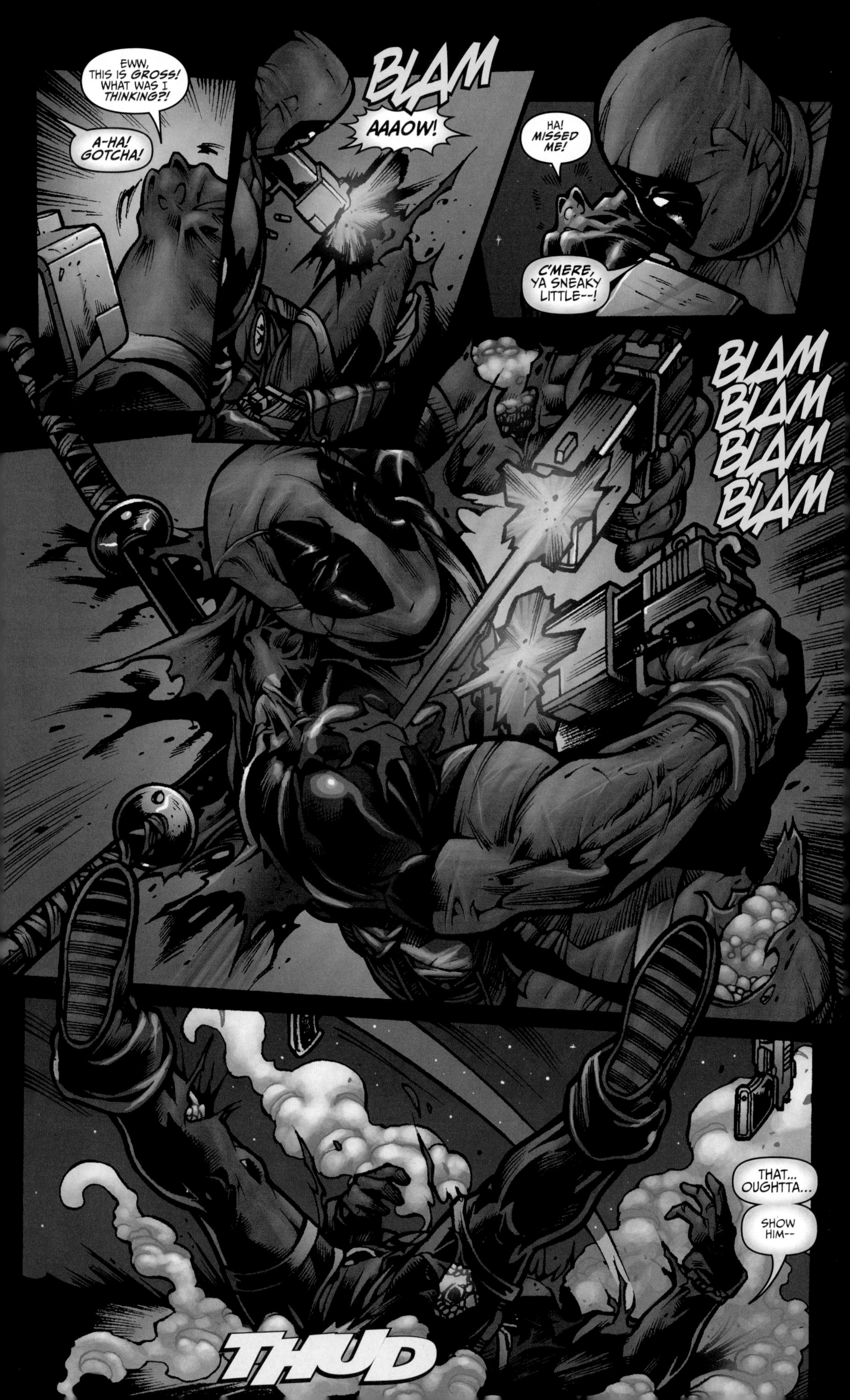
EWW, THIS IS GROSS! WHAT WAS I THINKING?!
A-HA! GOTCHA!
BLAM
AAAOW!
HA! MISSED ME!
C'MERE, YA SNEAKY LITTLE--!
BLAM BLAM BLAM BLAM
THAT... OUGHTTA...
SHOW HIM--
THUD

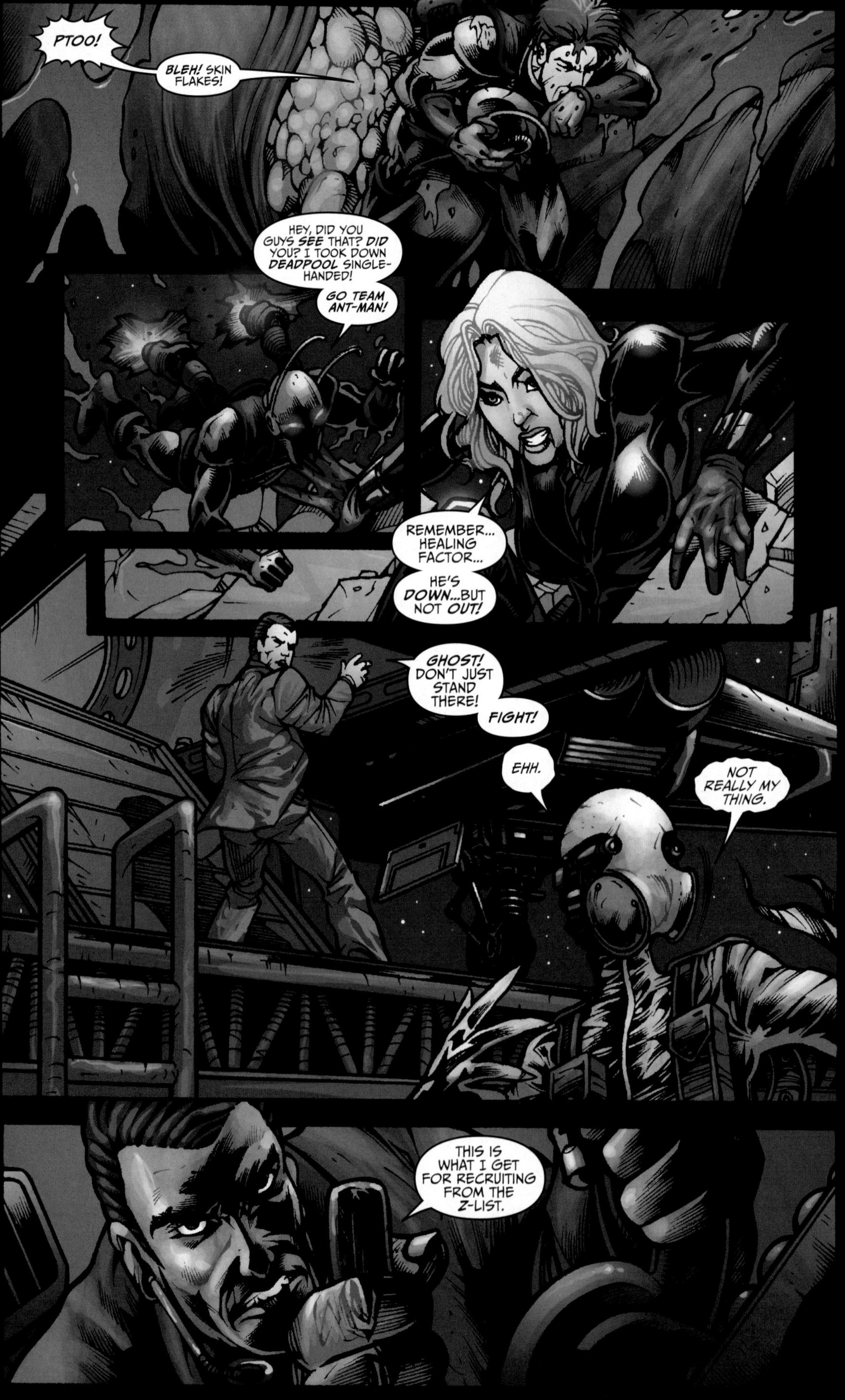
PTOO!
BLEH! SKIN FLAKES!
HEY, DID YOU GUYS SEE THAT? DID YOU? I TOOK DOWN DEADPOOL SINGLE-HANDED!
GO TEAM ANT-MAN!
REMEMBER... HEALING FACTOR...
HE'S DOWN...BUT NOT OUT!
GHOST! DON'T JUST STAND THERE!
FIGHT!
EHH.
NOT REALLY MY THING.
THIS IS WHAT I GET FOR RECRUITING FROM THE Z-LIST.

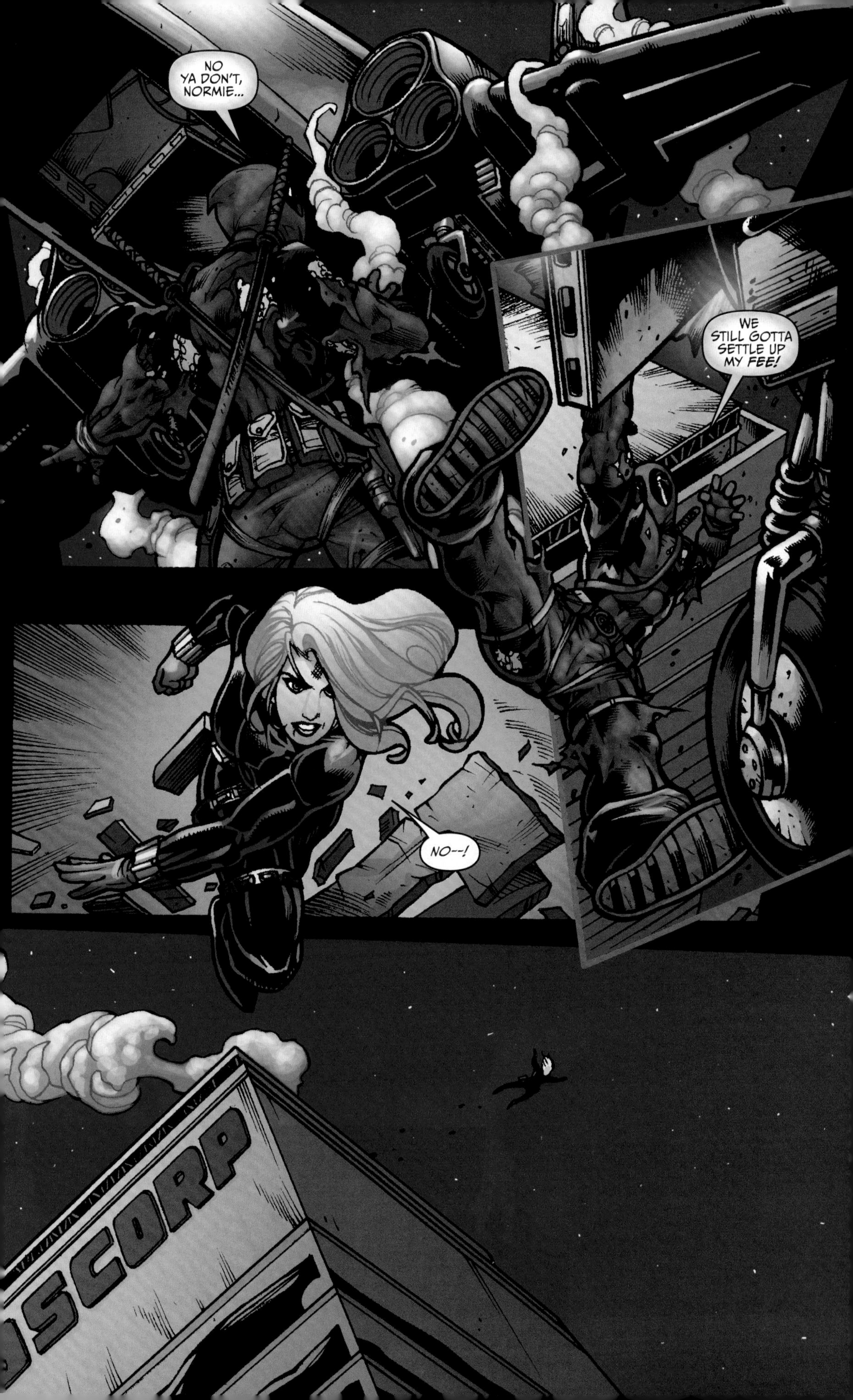
NO YA DON'T, NORMIE...
WE STILL GOTTA SETTLE UP MY *FEE!*
NO--!

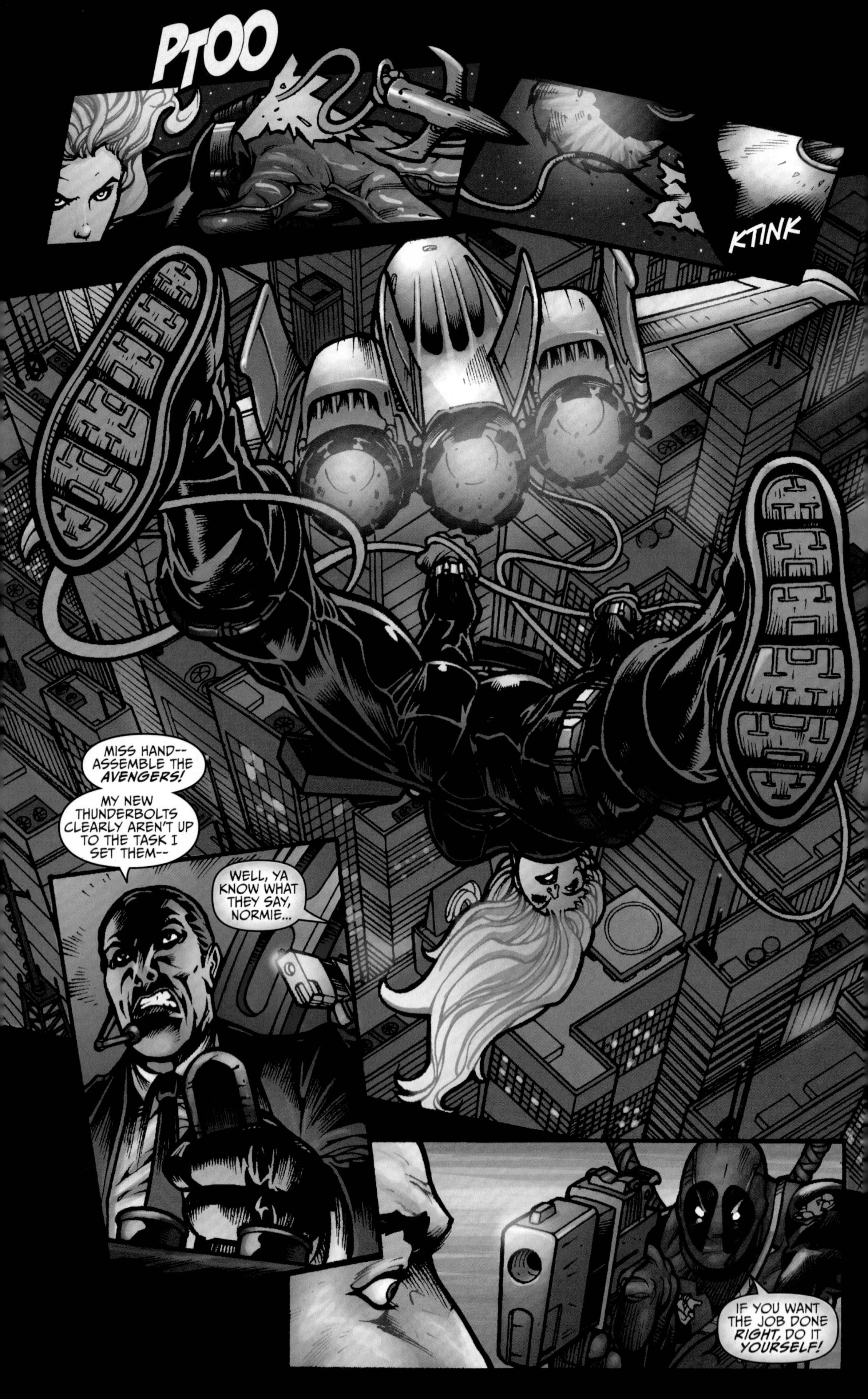
PTOO
KTINK
MISS HAND-- ASSEMBLE THE *AVENGERS!*
MY NEW THUNDERBOLTS CLEARLY AREN'T UP TO THE TASK I SET THEM--
WELL, YA KNOW WHAT THEY SAY, NORMIE...
IF YOU WANT THE JOB DONE *RIGHT*, DO IT *YOURSELF!*

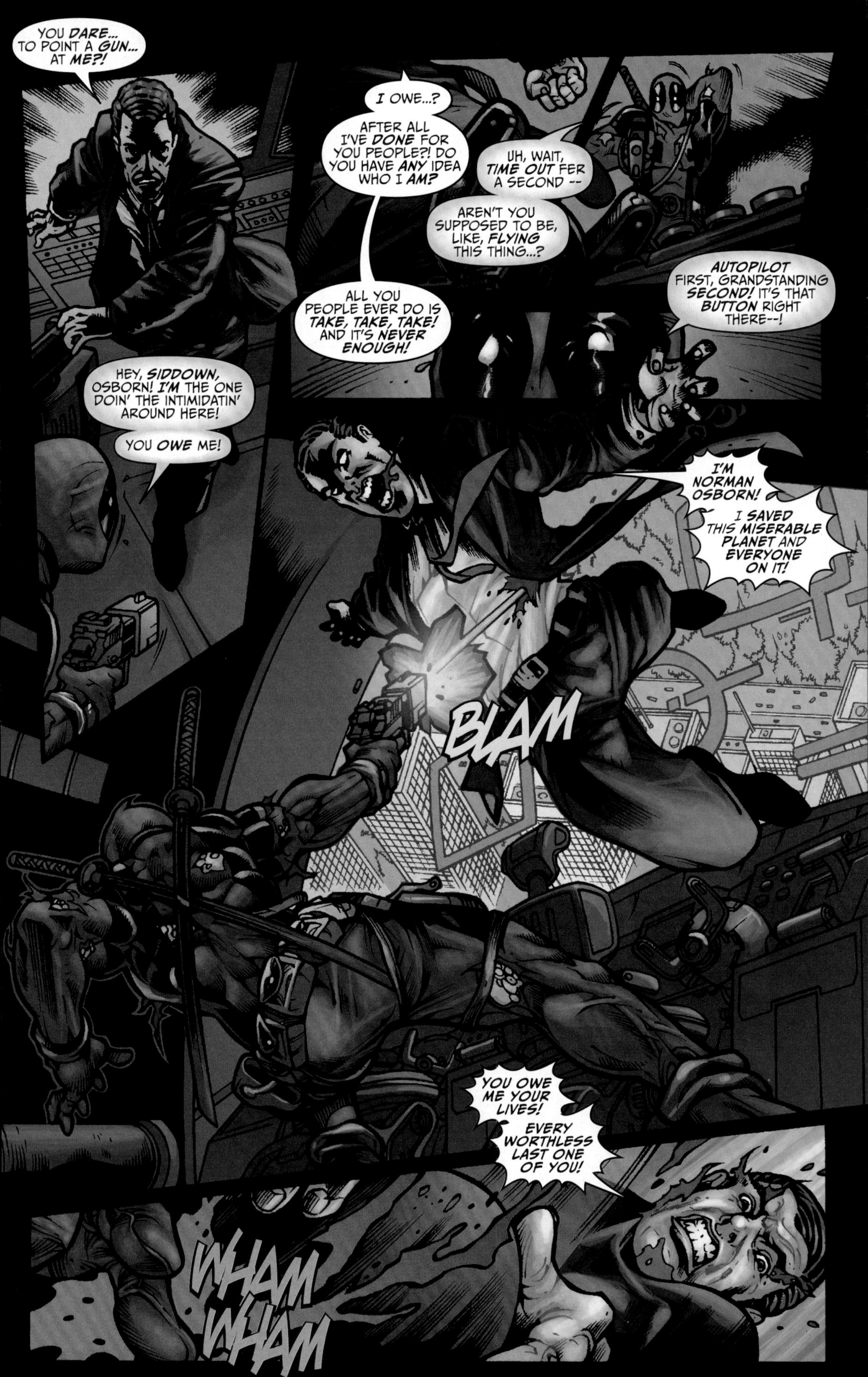
YOU DARE... TO POINT A GUN... AT ME?!
HEY, SIDDOWN, OSBORN! I'M THE ONE DOIN' THE INTIMIDATIN' AROUND HERE!
YOU OWE ME!
I OWE...?
AFTER ALL I'VE DONE FOR YOU PEOPLE?! DO YOU HAVE ANY IDEA WHO I AM?
ALL YOU PEOPLE EVER DO IS TAKE, TAKE, TAKE! AND IT'S NEVER ENOUGH!
UH, WAIT, TIME OUT FER A SECOND --
AREN'T YOU SUPPOSED TO BE, LIKE, FLYING THIS THING...?
AUTOPILOT FIRST, GRANDSTANDING SECOND! IT'S THAT BUTTON RIGHT THERE--!
I'M NORMAN OSBORN!
I SAVED THIS MISERABLE PLANET AND EVERYONE ON IT!
BLAM
YOU OWE ME YOUR LIVES!
EVERY WORTHLESS LAST ONE OF YOU!
WHAM
WHAM

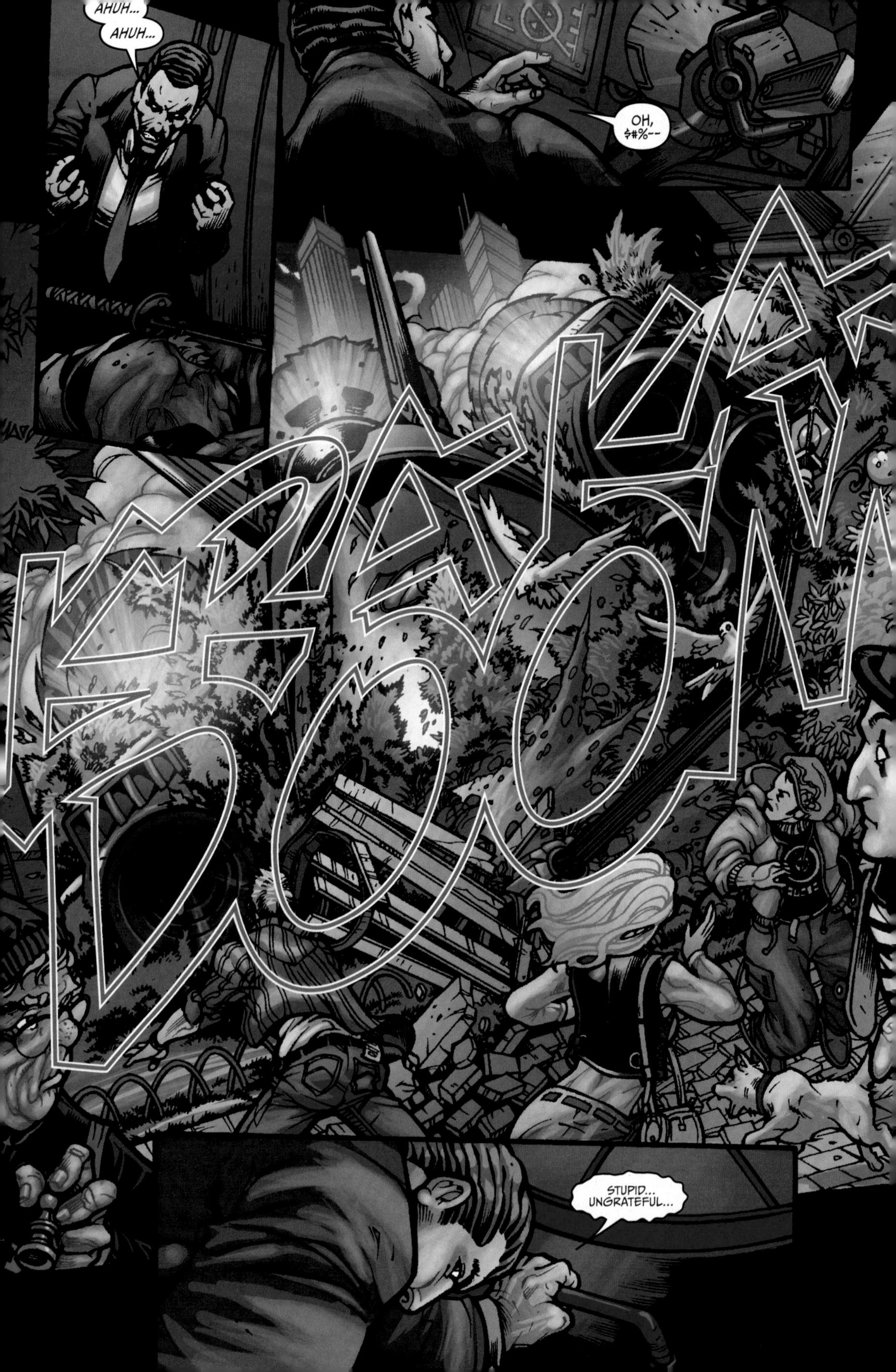
AHUH...
AHUH...
OH, $#%--
STUPID... UNGRATEFUL...

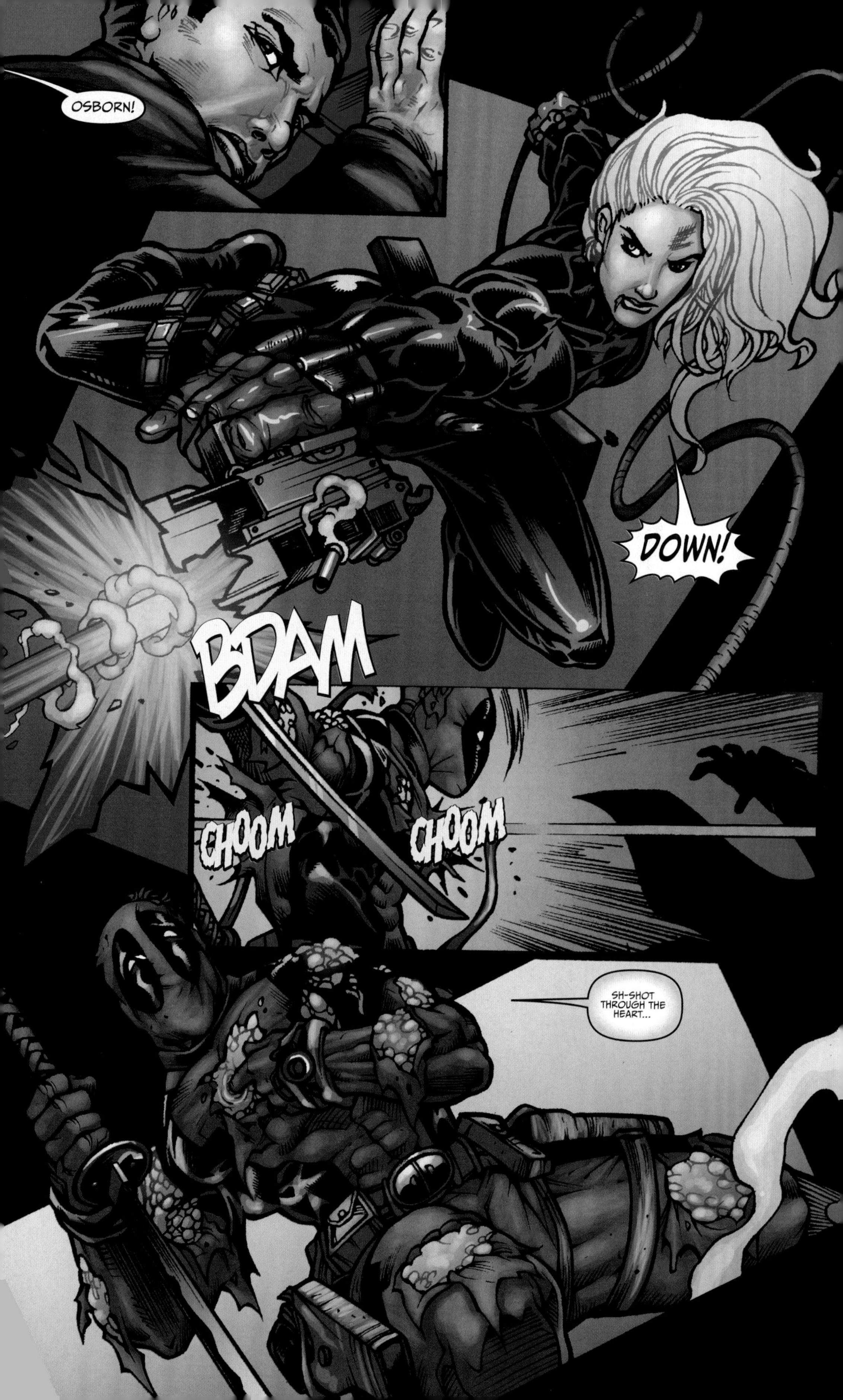
OSBORN!
DOWN!
BDAM
CHOOM
CHOOM
SH-SHOT THROUGH THE HEART...

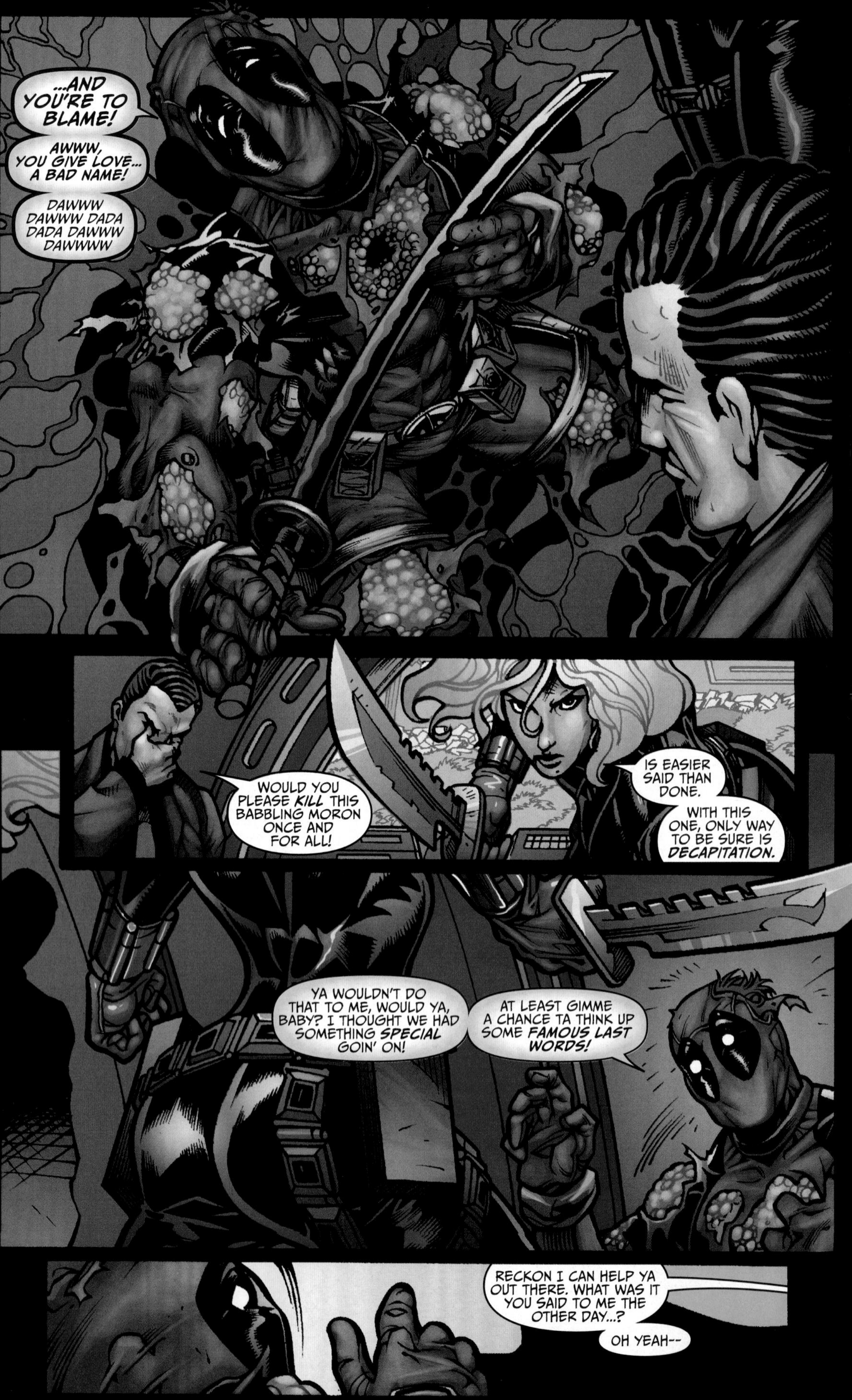
...AND YOU'RE TO BLAME!
AWWW, YOU GIVE LOVE... A BAD NAME!
DAWWW DAWWW DADA DADA DAWWW DAWWWW
WOULD YOU PLEASE KILL THIS BABBLING MORON ONCE AND FOR ALL!
IS EASIER SAID THAN DONE.
WITH THIS ONE, ONLY WAY TO BE SURE IS DECAPITATION.
YA WOULDN'T DO THAT TO ME, WOULD YA, BABY? I THOUGHT WE HAD SOMETHING SPECIAL GOIN' ON!
AT LEAST GIMME A CHANCE TA THINK UP SOME FAMOUS LAST WORDS!
RECKON I CAN HELP YA OUT THERE. WHAT WAS IT YOU SAID TO ME THE OTHER DAY...?
OH YEAH--

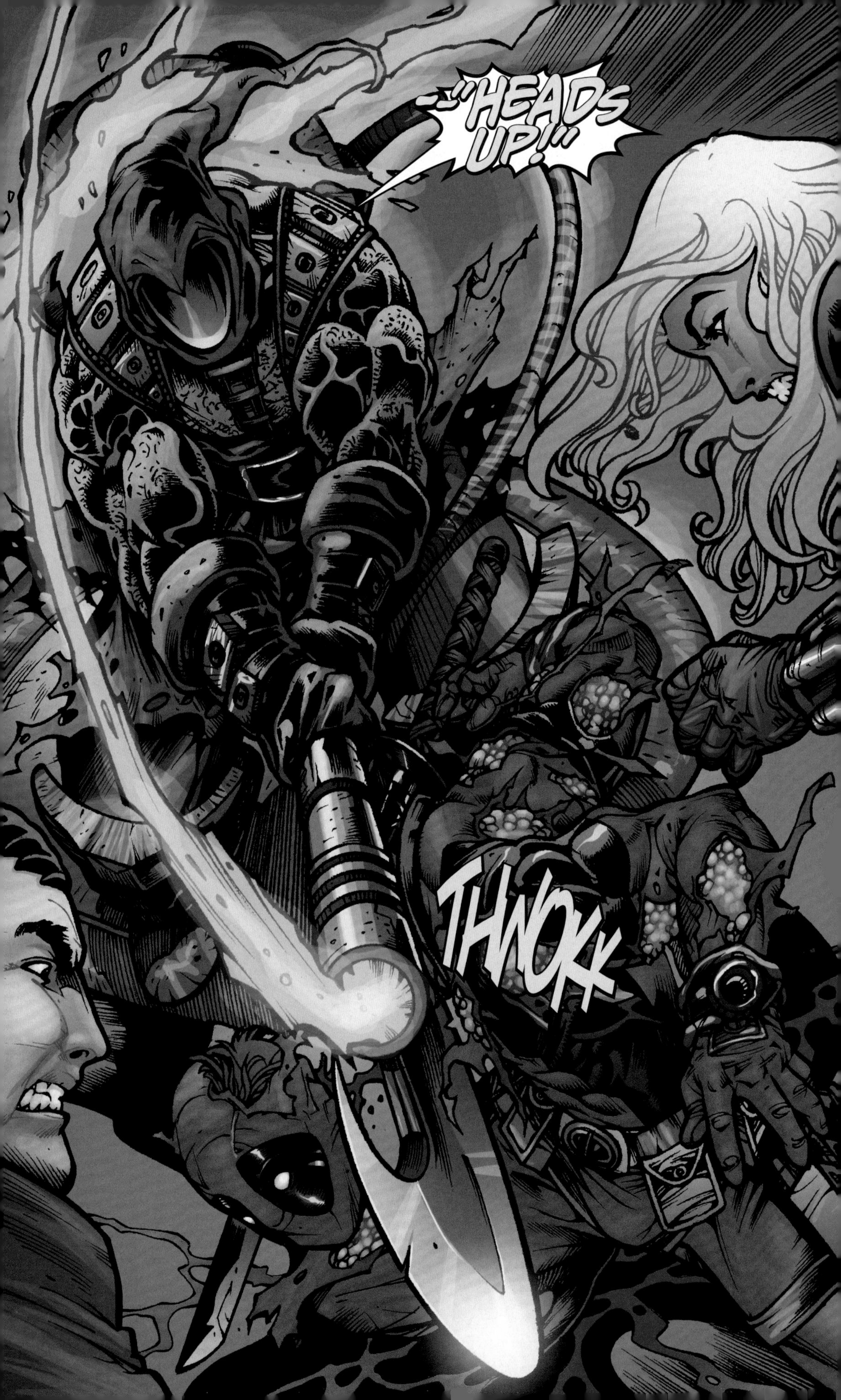
--"HEADS UP!"
THWOKK

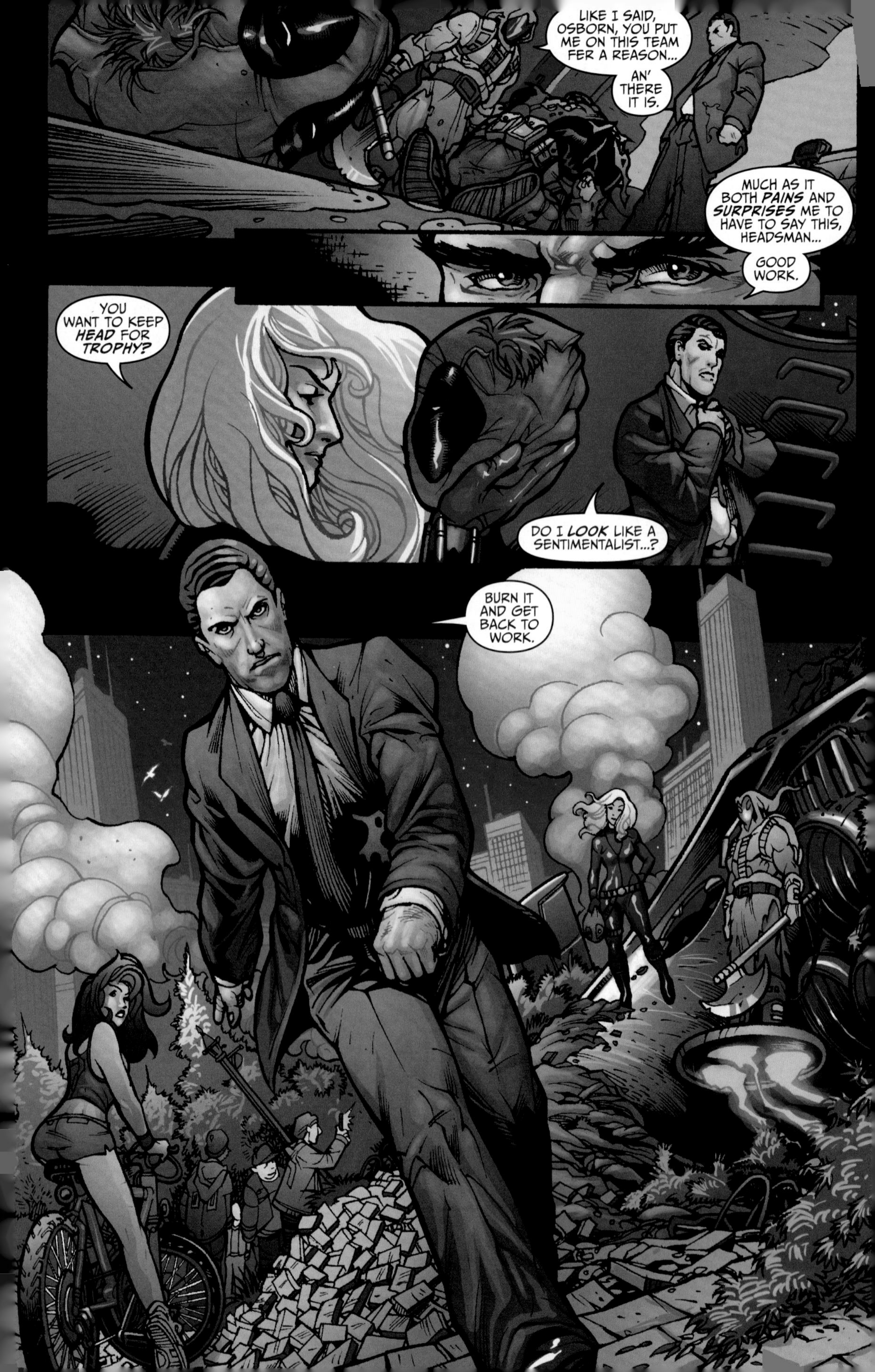
LIKE I SAID, OSBORN, YOU PUT ME ON THIS TEAM FER A REASON...
AN' THERE IT IS.
MUCH AS IT BOTH PAINS AND SURPRISES ME TO HAVE TO SAY THIS, HEADSMAN...
GOOD WORK.
YOU WANT TO KEEP HEAD FOR TROPHY?
DO I LOOK LIKE A SENTIMENTALIST...?
BURN IT AND GET BACK TO WORK.

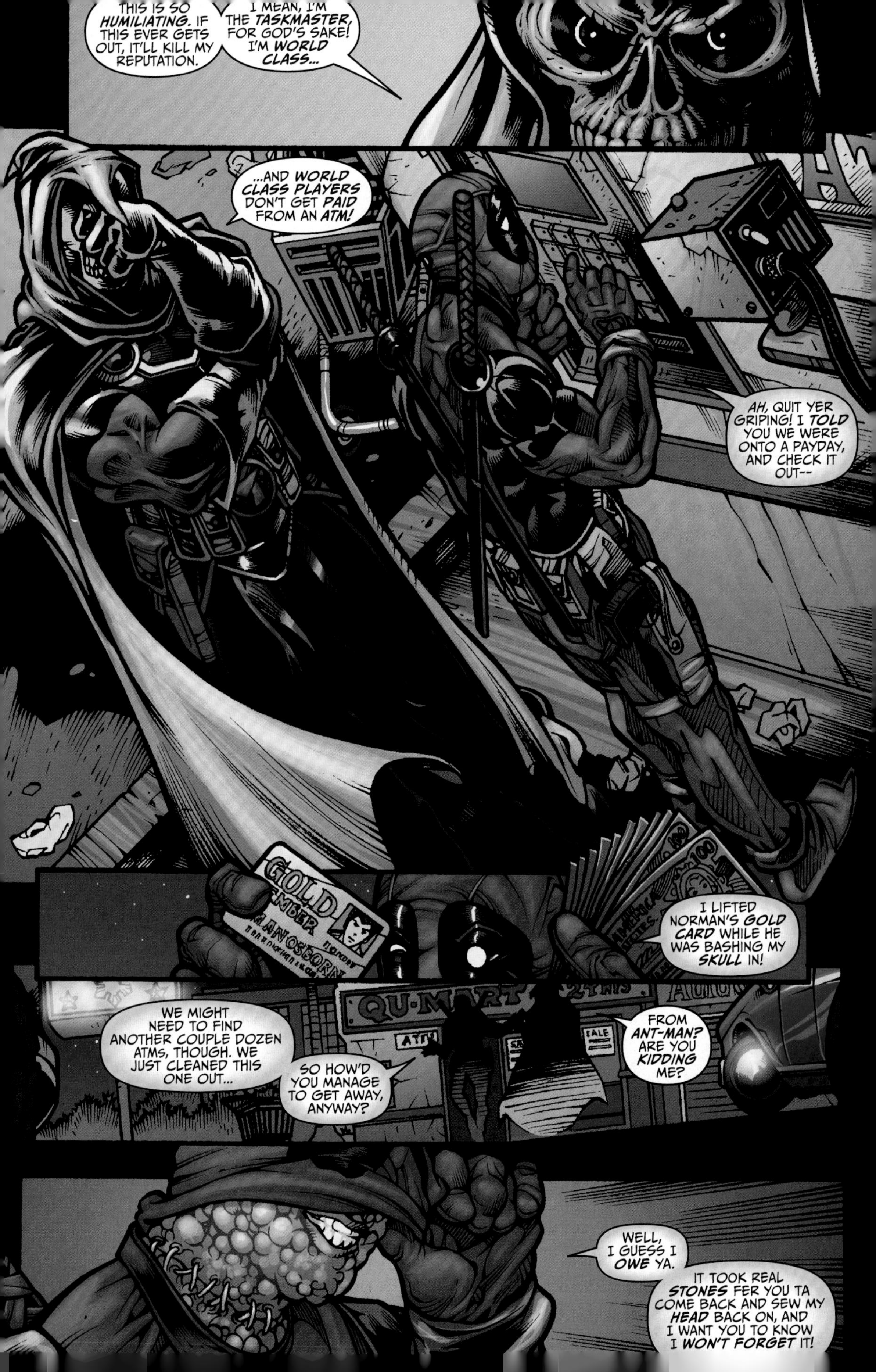
THIS IS SO HUMILIATING. IF THIS EVER GETS OUT, IT'LL KILL MY REPUTATION.
I MEAN, I'M THE TASKMASTER, FOR GOD'S SAKE! I'M WORLD CLASS...
...AND WORLD CLASS PLAYERS DON'T GET PAID FROM AN ATM!
AH, QUIT YER GRIPING! I TOLD YOU WE WERE ONTO A PAYDAY, AND CHECK IT OUT--
GOLD
I LIFTED NORMAN'S GOLD CARD WHILE HE WAS BASHING MY SKULL IN!
QU-MART
WE MIGHT NEED TO FIND ANOTHER COUPLE DOZEN ATMS, THOUGH. WE JUST CLEANED THIS ONE OUT...
SO HOW'D YOU MANAGE TO GET AWAY, ANYWAY?
FROM ANT-MAN? ARE YOU KIDDING ME?
WELL, I GUESS I OWE YA.
IT TOOK REAL STONES FER YOU TA COME BACK AND SEW MY HEAD BACK ON, AND I WANT YOU TO KNOW I WON'T FORGET IT!

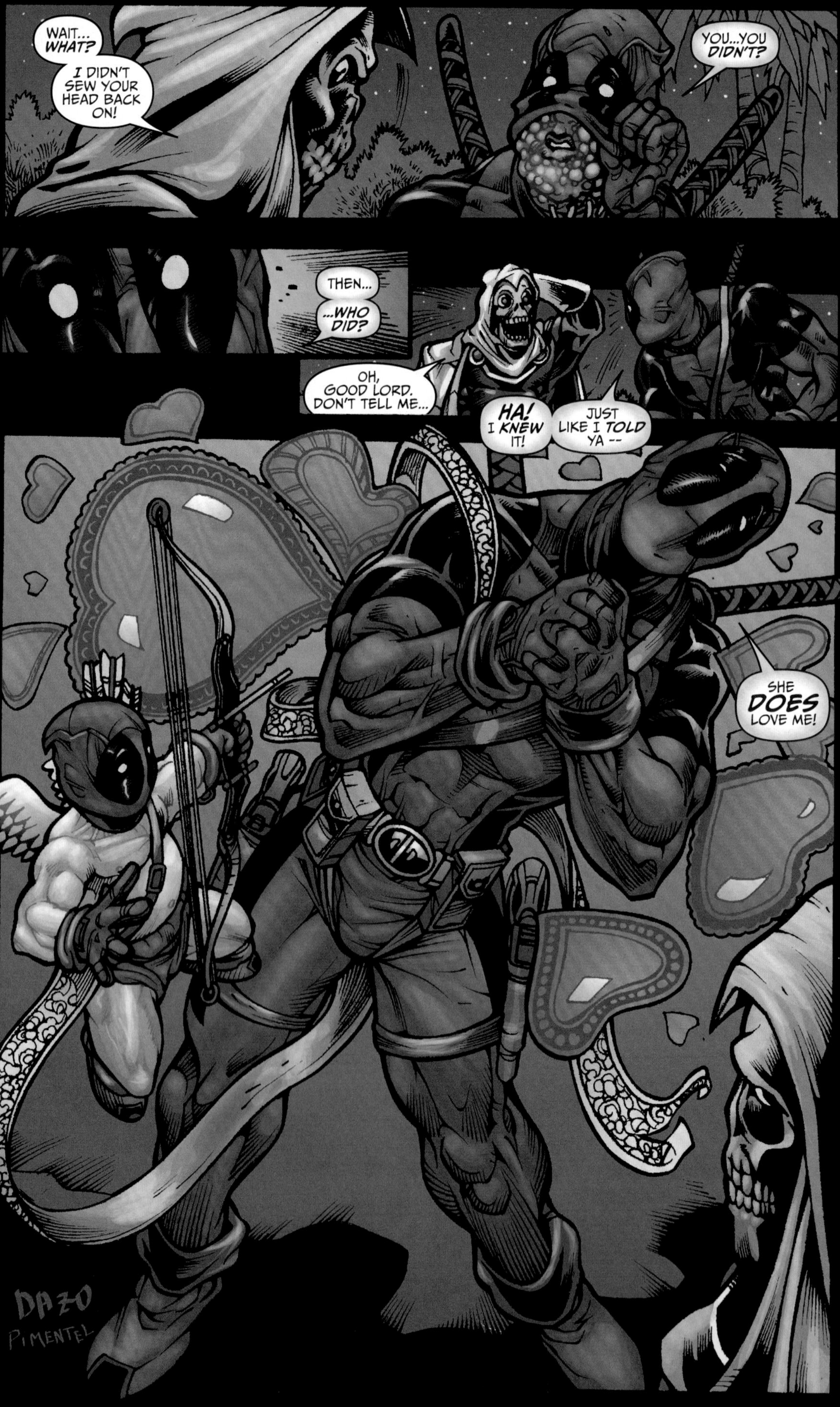
WAIT... WHAT?
I DIDN'T SEW YOUR HEAD BACK ON!
YOU...YOU DIDN'T?
THEN...
...WHO DID?
OH, GOOD LORD. DON'T TELL ME...
HA! I KNEW IT!
JUST LIKE I TOLD YA --
SHE DOES LOVE ME!
DAZO
PIMENTEL

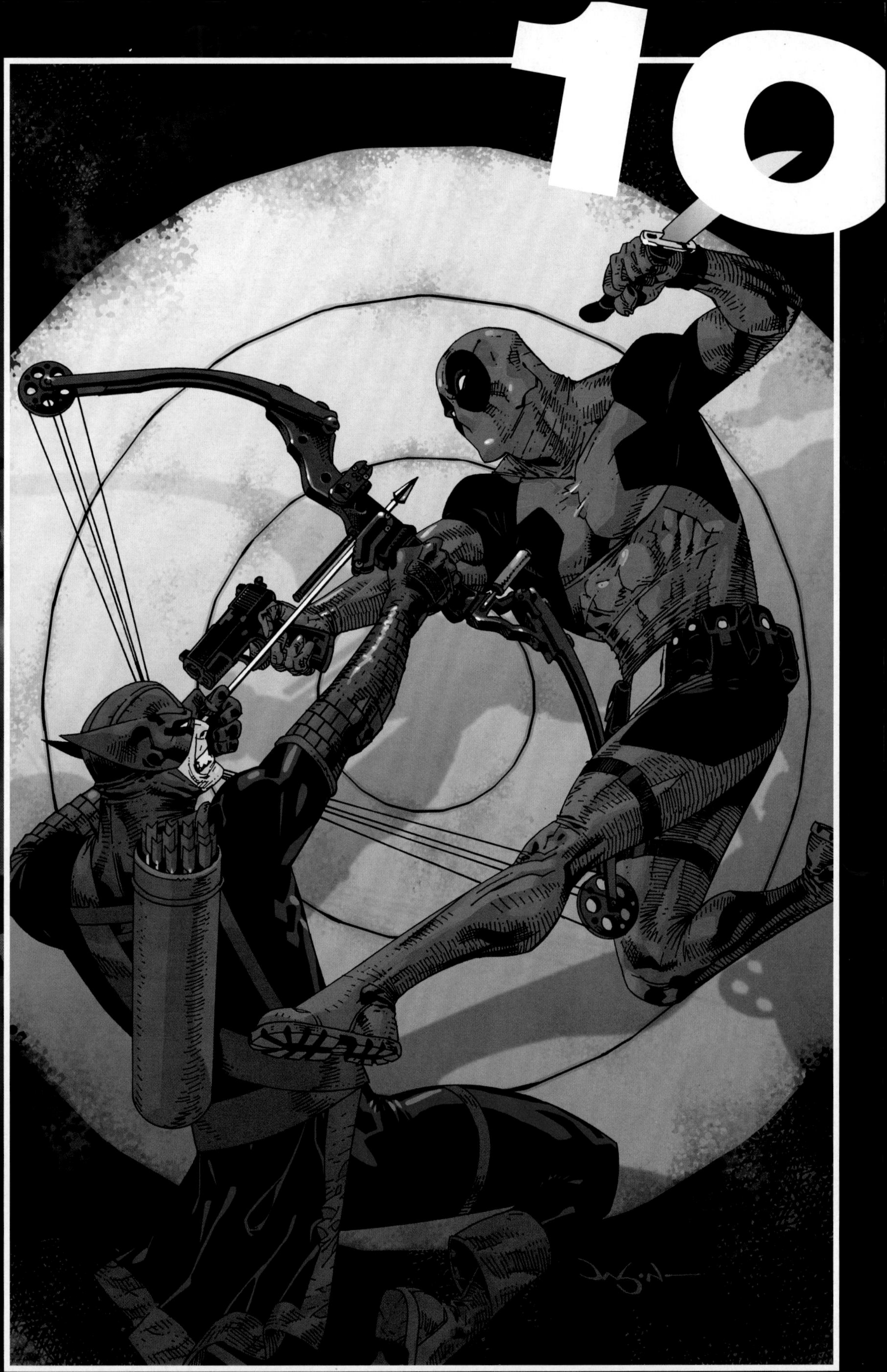
10

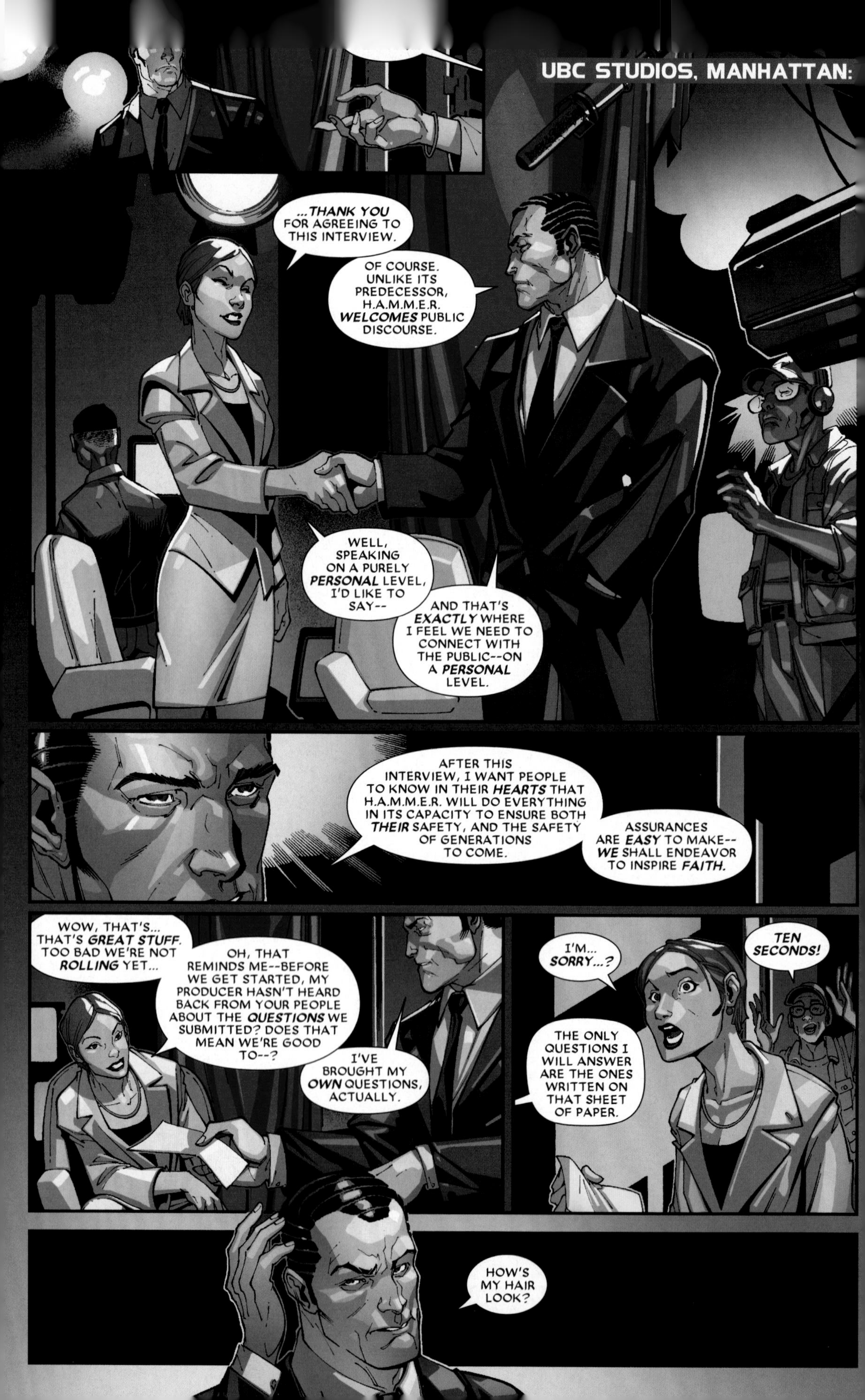
UBC STUDIOS, MANHATTAN:
...THANK YOU FOR AGREEING TO THIS INTERVIEW.
OF COURSE. UNLIKE ITS PREDECESSOR, H.A.M.M.E.R. WELCOMES PUBLIC DISCOURSE.
WELL, SPEAKING ON A PURELY PERSONAL LEVEL, I'D LIKE TO SAY--
AND THAT'S EXACTLY WHERE I FEEL WE NEED TO CONNECT WITH THE PUBLIC--ON A PERSONAL LEVEL.
AFTER THIS INTERVIEW, I WANT PEOPLE TO KNOW IN THEIR HEARTS THAT H.A.M.M.E.R. WILL DO EVERYTHING IN ITS CAPACITY TO ENSURE BOTH THEIR SAFETY, AND THE SAFETY OF GENERATIONS TO COME.
ASSURANCES ARE EASY TO MAKE-- WE SHALL ENDEAVOR TO INSPIRE FAITH.
WOW, THAT'S... THAT'S GREAT STUFF. TOO BAD WE'RE NOT ROLLING YET...
OH, THAT REMINDS ME--BEFORE WE GET STARTED, MY PRODUCER HASN'T HEARD BACK FROM YOUR PEOPLE ABOUT THE QUESTIONS WE SUBMITTED? DOES THAT MEAN WE'RE GOOD TO--?
I'VE BROUGHT MY OWN QUESTIONS, ACTUALLY.
I'M... SORRY...?
TEN SECONDS!
THE ONLY QUESTIONS I WILL ANSWER ARE THE ONES WRITTEN ON THAT SHEET OF PAPER.
HOW'S MY HAIR LOOK?

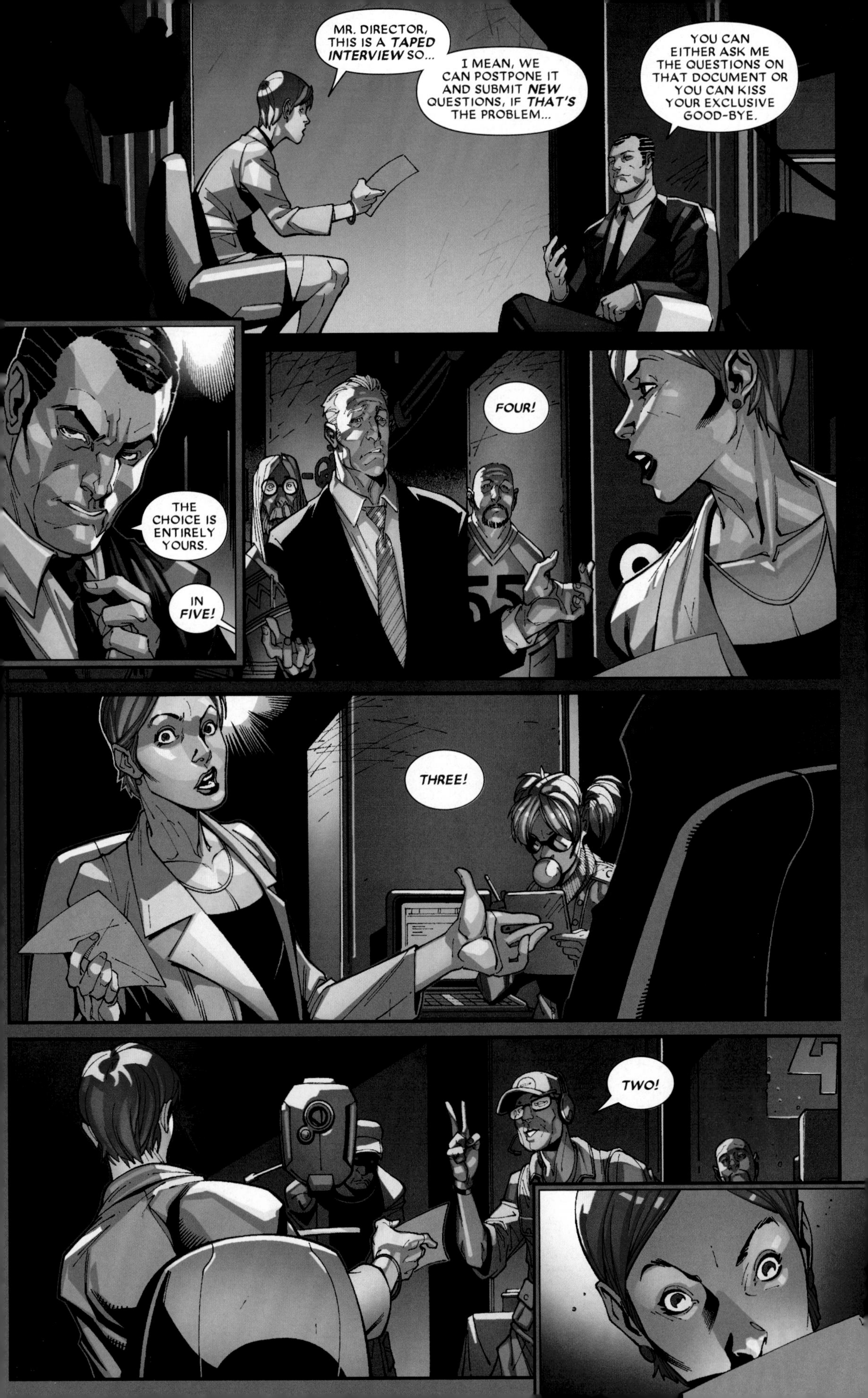
MR. DIRECTOR, THIS IS A *TAPED INTERVIEW* SO...
I MEAN, WE CAN POSTPONE IT AND SUBMIT *NEW* QUESTIONS, IF *THAT'S* THE PROBLEM...
YOU CAN EITHER ASK ME THE QUESTIONS ON THAT DOCUMENT OR YOU CAN KISS YOUR EXCLUSIVE GOOD-BYE.
THE CHOICE IS ENTIRELY YOURS.
IN *FIVE!*
FOUR!
THREE!
TWO!

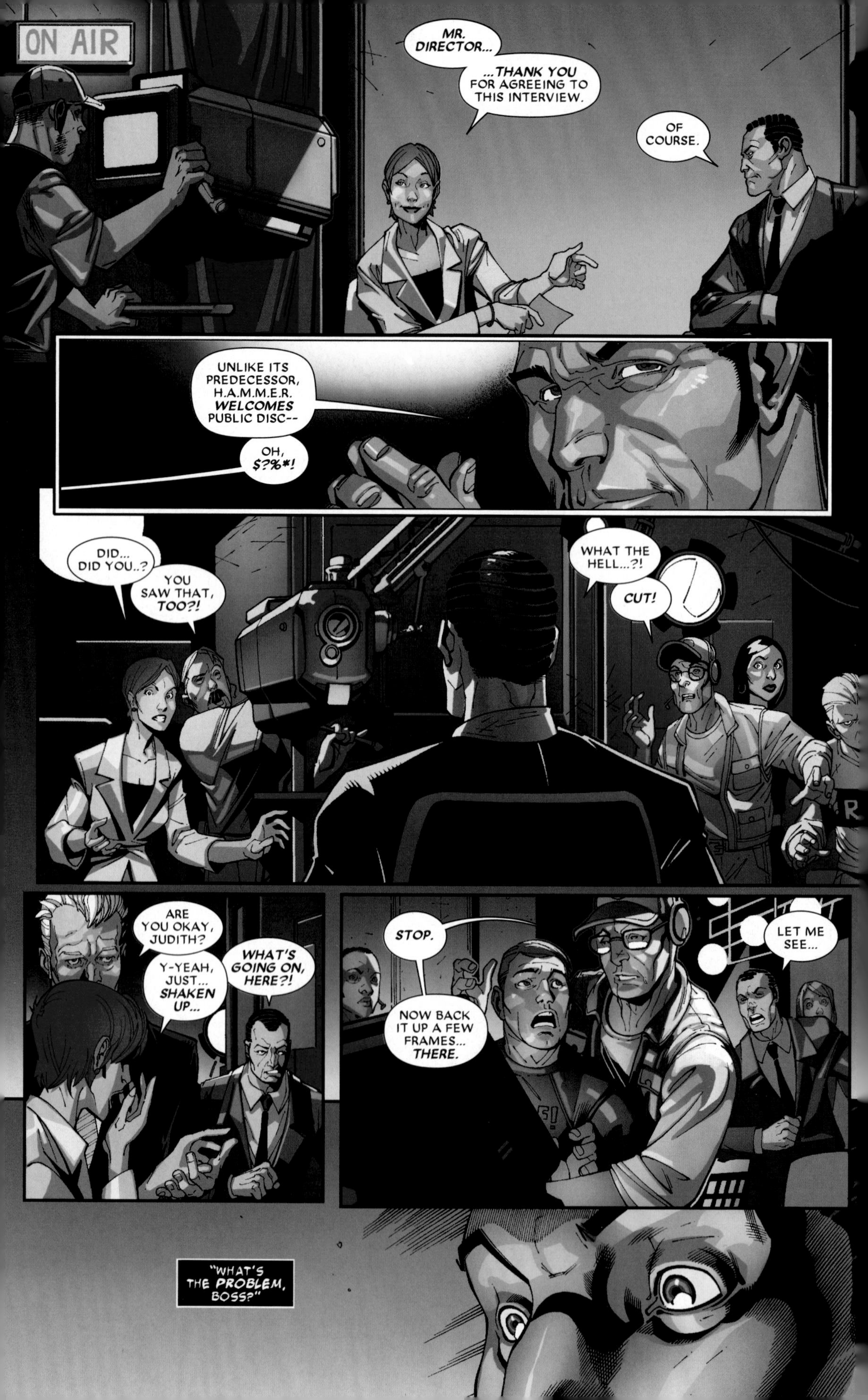

ON AIR
MR. DIRECTOR...
...THANK YOU FOR AGREEING TO THIS INTERVIEW.
OF COURSE.
UNLIKE ITS PREDECESSOR, H.A.M.M.E.R. WELCOMES PUBLIC DISC--
OH, $?%*!
DID... DID YOU..?
YOU SAW THAT, TOO?!
WHAT THE HELL...?!
CUT!
ARE YOU OKAY, JUDITH?
Y-YEAH, JUST... SHAKEN UP...
WHAT'S GOING ON, HERE?!
STOP.
LET ME SEE...
NOW BACK IT UP A FEW FRAMES... THERE.
"WHAT'S THE PROBLEM, BOSS?"

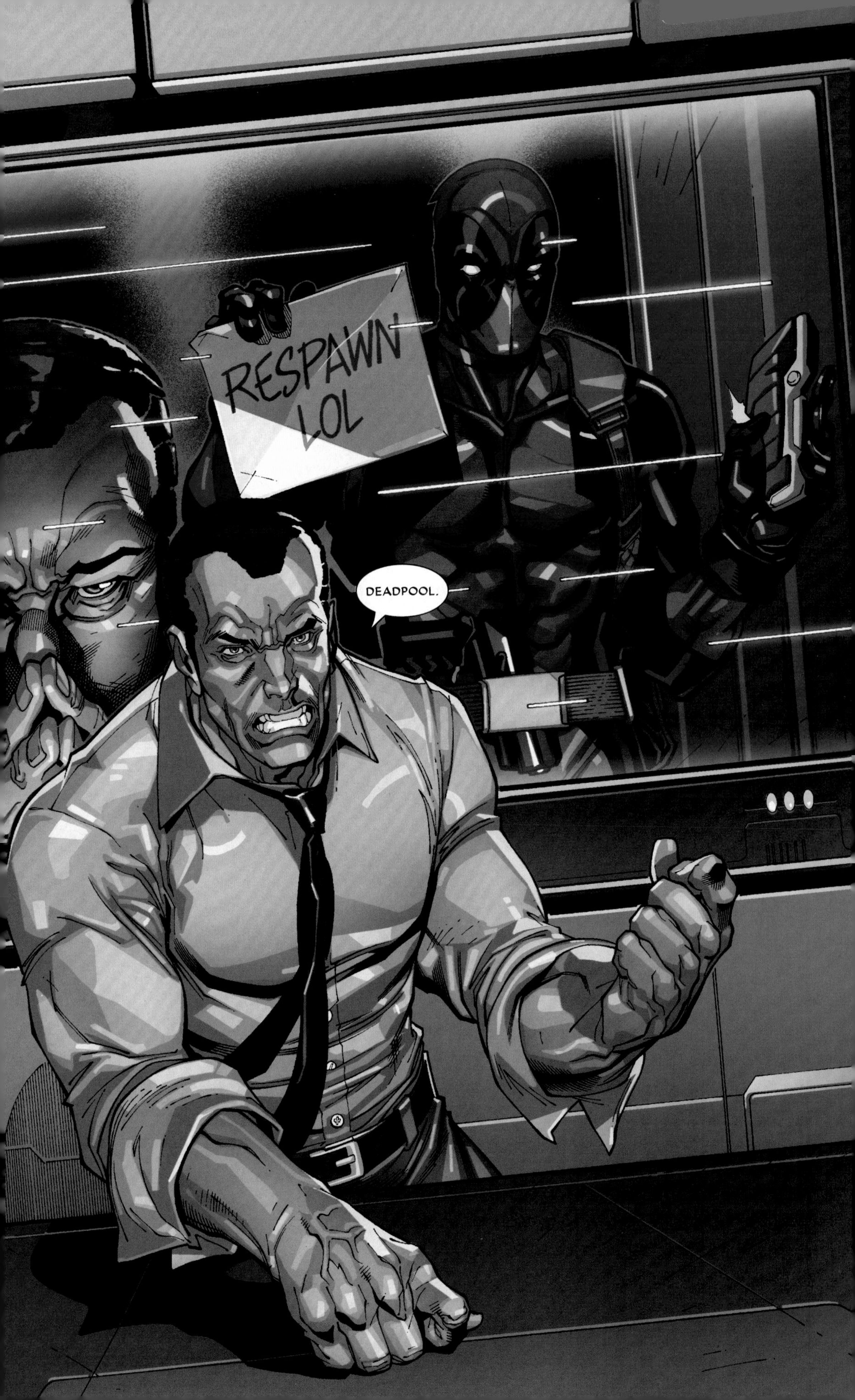
RESPAWN
LOL
DEADPOOL.

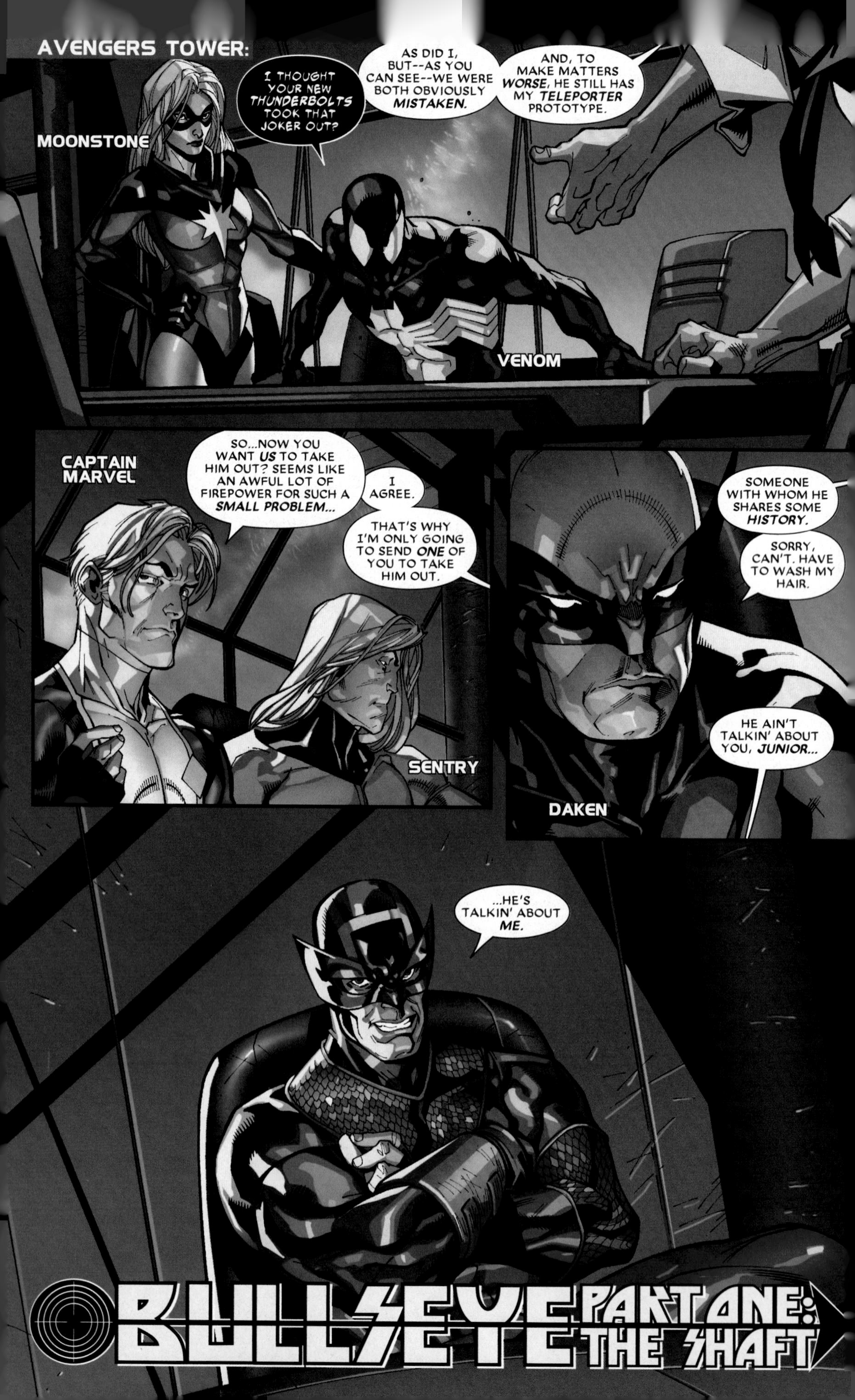

AVENGERS TOWER:
MOONSTONE
I THOUGHT YOUR NEW THUNDERBOLTS TOOK THAT JOKER OUT?
AS DID I, BUT--AS YOU CAN SEE--WE WERE BOTH OBVIOUSLY MISTAKEN.
AND, TO MAKE MATTERS WORSE, HE STILL HAS MY TELEPORTER PROTOTYPE.
VENOM
CAPTAIN MARVEL
SO...NOW YOU WANT US TO TAKE HIM OUT? SEEMS LIKE AN AWFUL LOT OF FIREPOWER FOR SUCH A SMALL PROBLEM...
I AGREE.
THAT'S WHY I'M ONLY GOING TO SEND ONE OF YOU TO TAKE HIM OUT.
SENTRY
SOMEONE WITH WHOM HE SHARES SOME HISTORY.
SORRY, CAN'T. HAVE TO WASH MY HAIR.
HE AIN'T TALKIN' ABOUT YOU, JUNIOR...
DAKEN
...HE'S TALKIN' ABOUT ME.
BULLSEYE PART ONE: THE SHAFT

"HAPPEN TO KNOW WHERE I CAN *FIND* HIM, BY ANY CHANCE?"

"I WILL *SOON*--I'VE ALREADY STARTED A *MEDIA CAMPAIGN* TO *FLUSH HIM OUT.* THAT IS, IF THE *FBI* DOESN'T PICK HIM UP FIRST. THAT BROKE IDIOT'S BEEN PIMPING HIMSELF OUT ON *CRAIGSLIST* AS A *GUN-FOR-HIRE!*"

I *TOLD* YOU--I DIDN'T *ORDER* A PIZZA!

LOOK, PAL--*I'M NOT PAYIN' FOR THIS PIE*, UNDERSTAND? I'M NOT EXACTLY IN GREAT *FINANCIAL HEALTH* RIGHT NOW, Y'KNOW WHAT I'M SAYIN'?

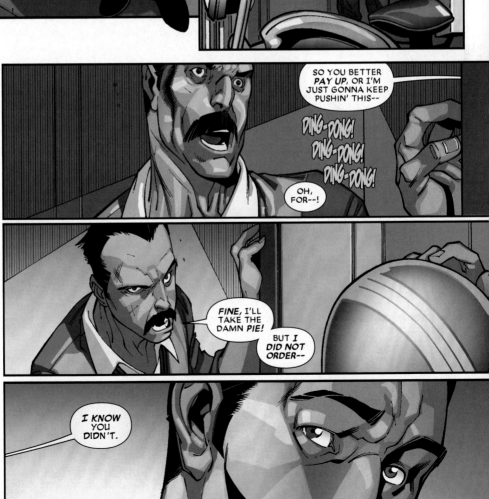

SO YOU BETTER *PAY UP*, OR I'M JUST GONNA KEEP PUSHIN' THIS--

DING-DONG! DING-DONG! DING-DONG!

OH, FOR--!

FINE, I'LL TAKE THE DAMN *PIE!*

BUT *I* DID NOT ORDER--

I *KNOW* YOU DIDN'T.

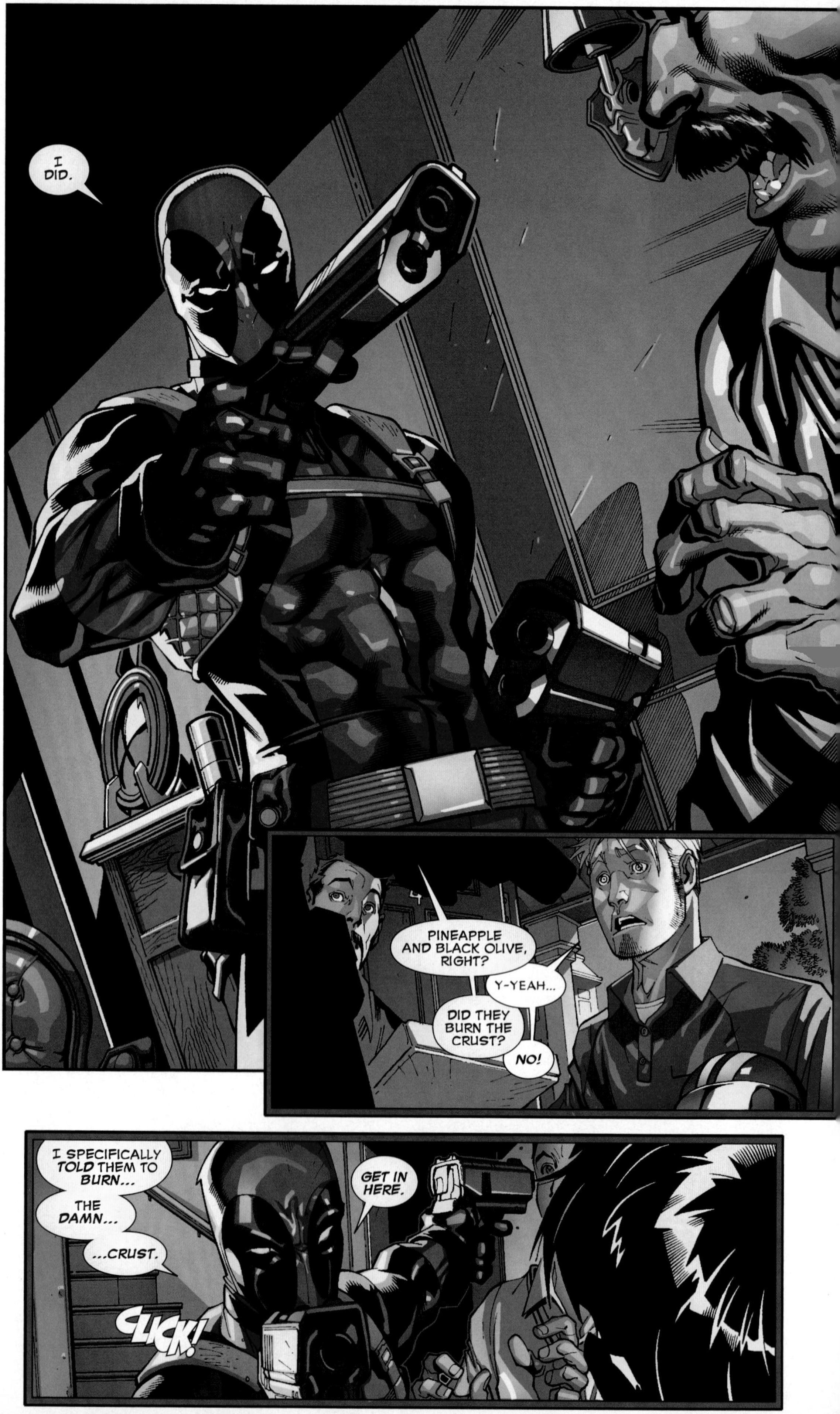

I DID.
PINEAPPLE AND BLACK OLIVE, RIGHT?
Y-YEAH...
DID THEY BURN THE CRUST?
NO!
I SPECIFICALLY *TOLD* THEM TO *BURN*...
THE *DAMN*...
...*CRUST*.
GET IN HERE.
CLICK!

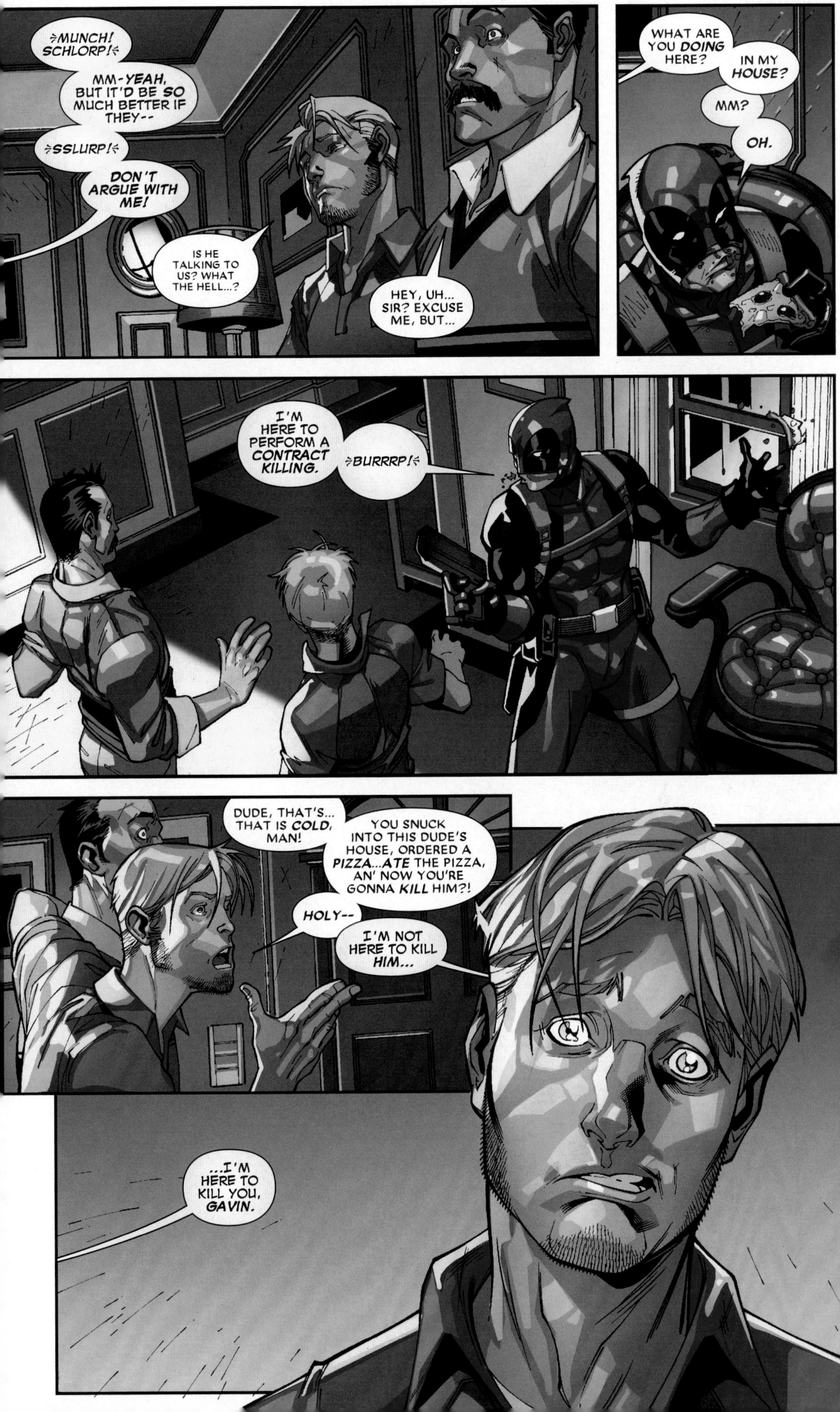

⋟MUNCH! SCHLORP!⋞
MM-YEAH, BUT IT'D BE SO MUCH BETTER IF THEY--
⋟SSLURP!⋞
DON'T ARGUE WITH ME!
IS HE TALKING TO US? WHAT THE HELL...?
HEY, UH... SIR? EXCUSE ME, BUT...
WHAT ARE YOU DOING HERE?
IN MY HOUSE?
MM?
OH.
I'M HERE TO PERFORM A CONTRACT KILLING.
⋟BURRRP!⋞
DUDE, THAT'S... THAT IS COLD, MAN!
YOU SNUCK INTO THIS DUDE'S HOUSE, ORDERED A PIZZA...ATE THE PIZZA, AN' NOW YOU'RE GONNA KILL HIM?!
HOLY--
I'M NOT HERE TO KILL HIM...
...I'M HERE TO KILL YOU, GAVIN.

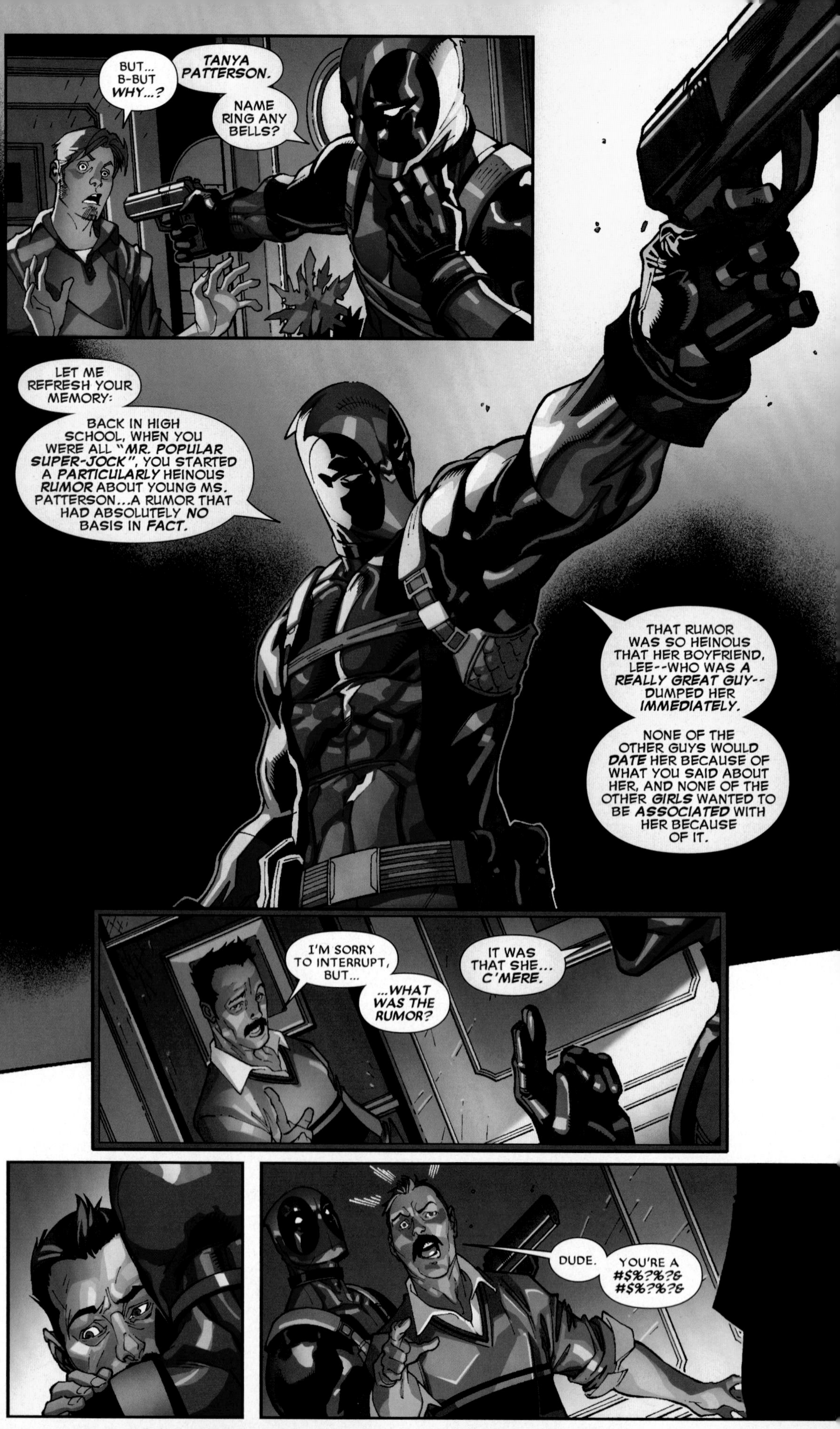
BUT... B-BUT WHY...?
TANYA PATTERSON.
NAME RING ANY BELLS?
LET ME REFRESH YOUR MEMORY:
BACK IN HIGH SCHOOL, WHEN YOU WERE ALL "MR. POPULAR SUPER-JOCK", YOU STARTED A PARTICULARLY HEINOUS RUMOR ABOUT YOUNG MS. PATTERSON...A RUMOR THAT HAD ABSOLUTELY NO BASIS IN FACT.
THAT RUMOR WAS SO HEINOUS THAT HER BOYFRIEND, LEE--WHO WAS A REALLY GREAT GUY--DUMPED HER IMMEDIATELY.
NONE OF THE OTHER GUYS WOULD DATE HER BECAUSE OF WHAT YOU SAID ABOUT HER, AND NONE OF THE OTHER GIRLS WANTED TO BE ASSOCIATED WITH HER BECAUSE OF IT.
I'M SORRY TO INTERRUPT, BUT...
...WHAT WAS THE RUMOR?
IT WAS THAT SHE... C'MERE.
DUDE.
YOU'RE A #$%?%?& #$%?%?&

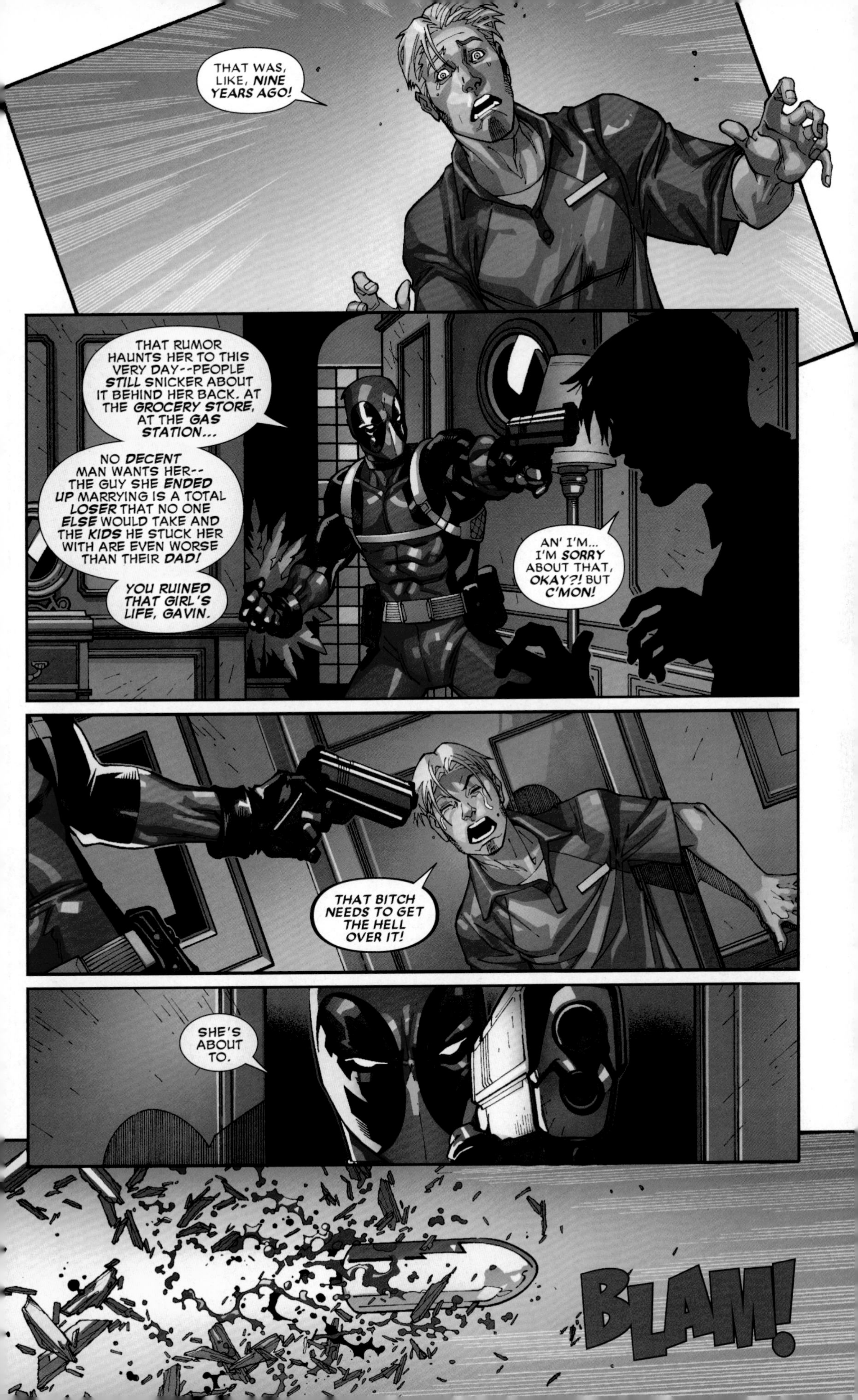
THAT WAS, LIKE, NINE YEARS AGO!
THAT RUMOR HAUNTS HER TO THIS VERY DAY--PEOPLE STILL SNICKER ABOUT IT BEHIND HER BACK. AT THE GROCERY STORE, AT THE GAS STATION...
NO DECENT MAN WANTS HER-- THE GUY SHE ENDED UP MARRYING IS A TOTAL LOSER THAT NO ONE ELSE WOULD TAKE AND THE KIDS HE STUCK HER WITH ARE EVEN WORSE THAN THEIR DAD!
YOU RUINED THAT GIRL'S LIFE, GAVIN.
AN' I'M... I'M SORRY ABOUT THAT, OKAY?! BUT C'MON!
THAT BITCH NEEDS TO GET THE HELL OVER IT!
SHE'S ABOUT TO.
BLAM!

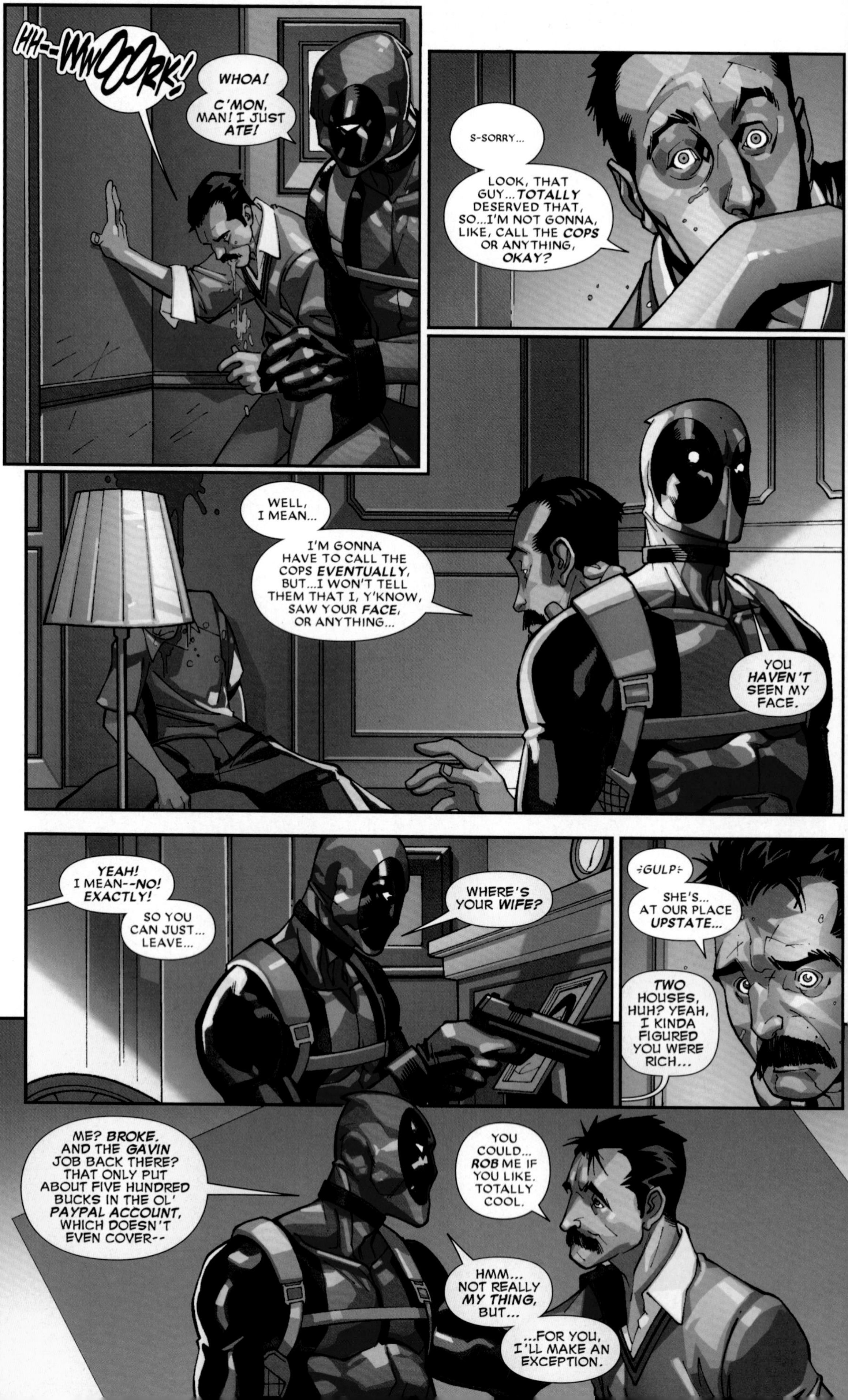
HH--WWOOORK!
WHOA!
C'MON, MAN! I JUST ATE!
S-SORRY...
LOOK, THAT GUY... TOTALLY DESERVED THAT, SO...I'M NOT GONNA, LIKE, CALL THE COPS OR ANYTHING, OKAY?
WELL, I MEAN...
I'M GONNA HAVE TO CALL THE COPS EVENTUALLY, BUT...I WON'T TELL THEM THAT I, Y'KNOW, SAW YOUR FACE, OR ANYTHING...
YOU HAVEN'T SEEN MY FACE.
YEAH! I MEAN--NO! EXACTLY!
SO YOU CAN JUST... LEAVE...
WHERE'S YOUR WIFE?
GULP
SHE'S... AT OUR PLACE UPSTATE...
TWO HOUSES, HUH? YEAH, I KINDA FIGURED YOU WERE RICH...
ME? BROKE. AND THE GAVIN JOB BACK THERE? THAT ONLY PUT ABOUT FIVE HUNDRED BUCKS IN THE OL' PAYPAL ACCOUNT, WHICH DOESN'T EVEN COVER--
YOU COULD... ROB ME IF YOU LIKE. TOTALLY COOL.
HMM... NOT REALLY MY THING, BUT...
...FOR YOU, I'LL MAKE AN EXCEPTION.

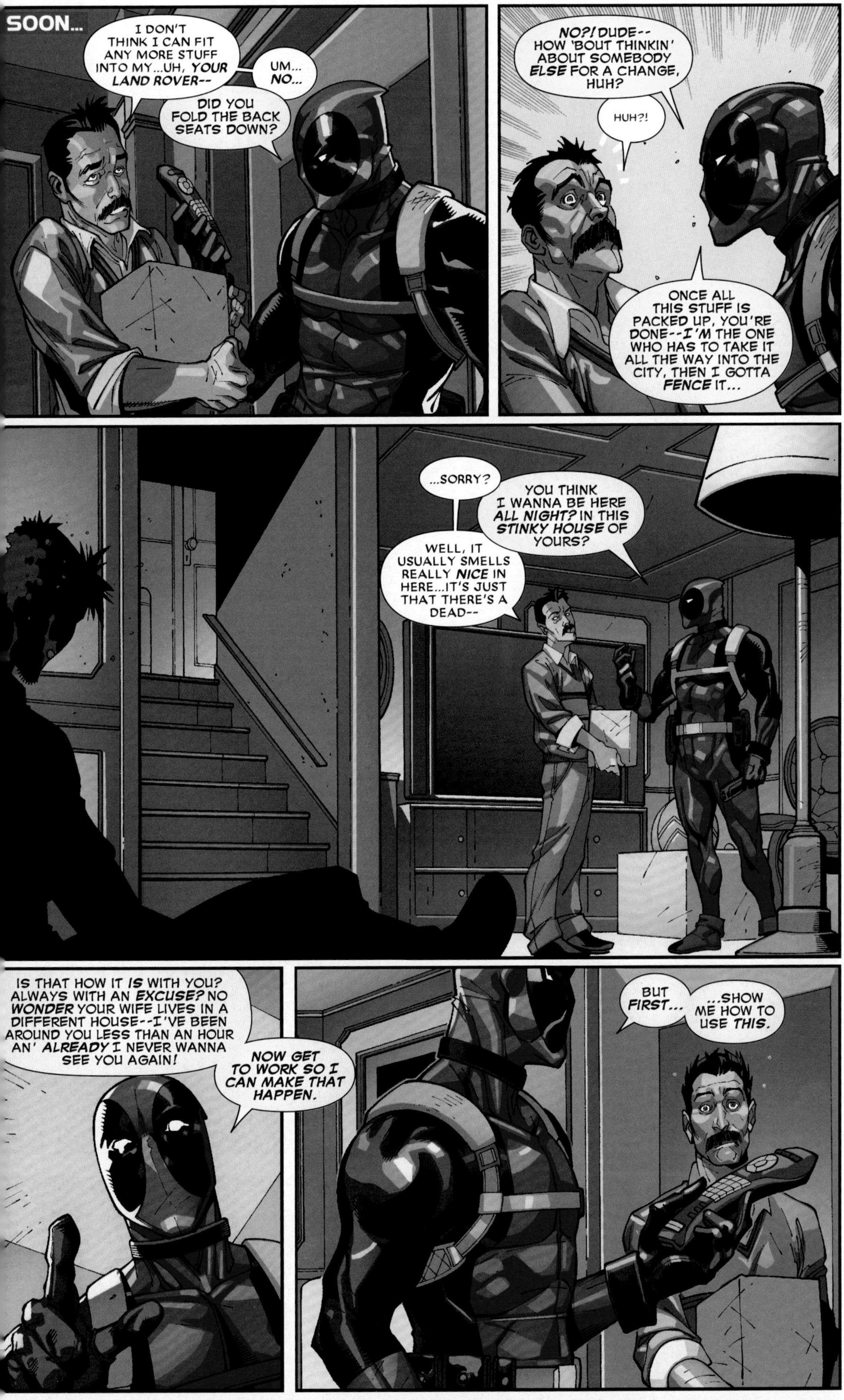
SOON...
I DON'T THINK I CAN FIT ANY MORE STUFF INTO MY...UH, YOUR LAND ROVER--
UM... NO...
DID YOU FOLD THE BACK SEATS DOWN?
NO?! DUDE-- HOW 'BOUT THINKIN' ABOUT SOMEBODY ELSE FOR A CHANGE, HUH?
HUH?!
ONCE ALL THIS STUFF IS PACKED UP, YOU'RE DONE--I'M THE ONE WHO HAS TO TAKE IT ALL THE WAY INTO THE CITY, THEN I GOTTA FENCE IT...
...SORRY?
YOU THINK I WANNA BE HERE ALL NIGHT? IN THIS STINKY HOUSE OF YOURS?
WELL, IT USUALLY SMELLS REALLY NICE IN HERE...IT'S JUST THAT THERE'S A DEAD--
IS THAT HOW IT IS WITH YOU? ALWAYS WITH AN EXCUSE? NO WONDER YOUR WIFE LIVES IN A DIFFERENT HOUSE--I'VE BEEN AROUND YOU LESS THAN AN HOUR AN' ALREADY I NEVER WANNA SEE YOU AGAIN!
NOW GET TO WORK SO I CAN MAKE THAT HAPPEN.
BUT FIRST...
...SHOW ME HOW TO USE THIS.

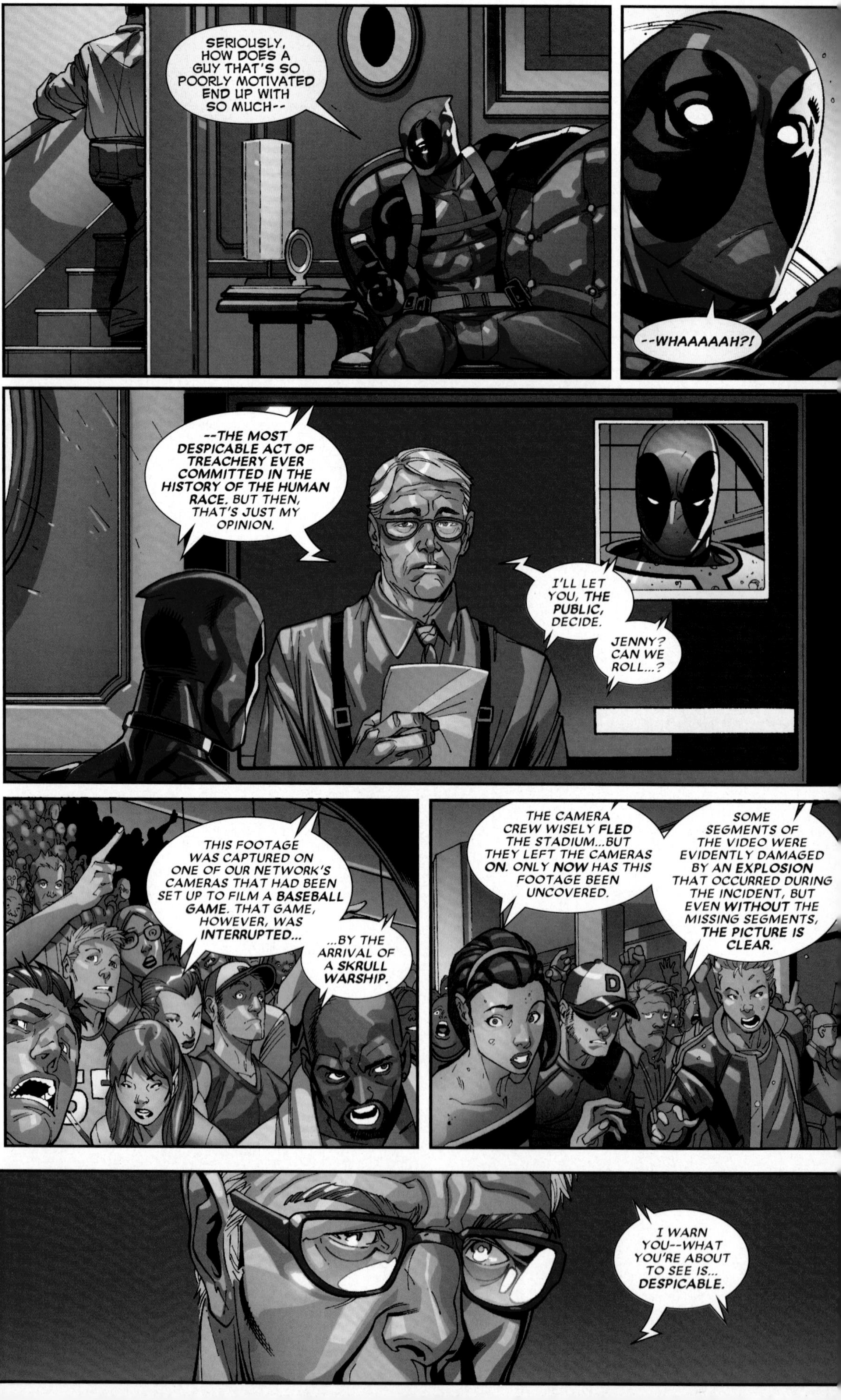
SERIOUSLY, HOW DOES A GUY THAT'S SO POORLY MOTIVATED END UP WITH SO MUCH--
--WHAAAAAH?!
--THE MOST DESPICABLE ACT OF TREACHERY EVER COMMITTED IN THE HISTORY OF THE HUMAN RACE. BUT THEN, THAT'S JUST MY OPINION.
I'LL LET YOU, THE PUBLIC, DECIDE.
JENNY? CAN WE ROLL...?
THIS FOOTAGE WAS CAPTURED ON ONE OF OUR NETWORK'S CAMERAS THAT HAD BEEN SET UP TO FILM A BASEBALL GAME. THAT GAME, HOWEVER, WAS INTERRUPTED...
...BY THE ARRIVAL OF A SKRULL WARSHIP.
THE CAMERA CREW WISELY FLED THE STADIUM...BUT THEY LEFT THE CAMERAS ON. ONLY NOW HAS THIS FOOTAGE BEEN UNCOVERED.
SOME SEGMENTS OF THE VIDEO WERE EVIDENTLY DAMAGED BY AN EXPLOSION THAT OCCURRED DURING THE INCIDENT, BUT EVEN WITHOUT THE MISSING SEGMENTS, THE PICTURE IS CLEAR.
I WARN YOU--WHAT YOU'RE ABOUT TO SEE IS... DESPICABLE.

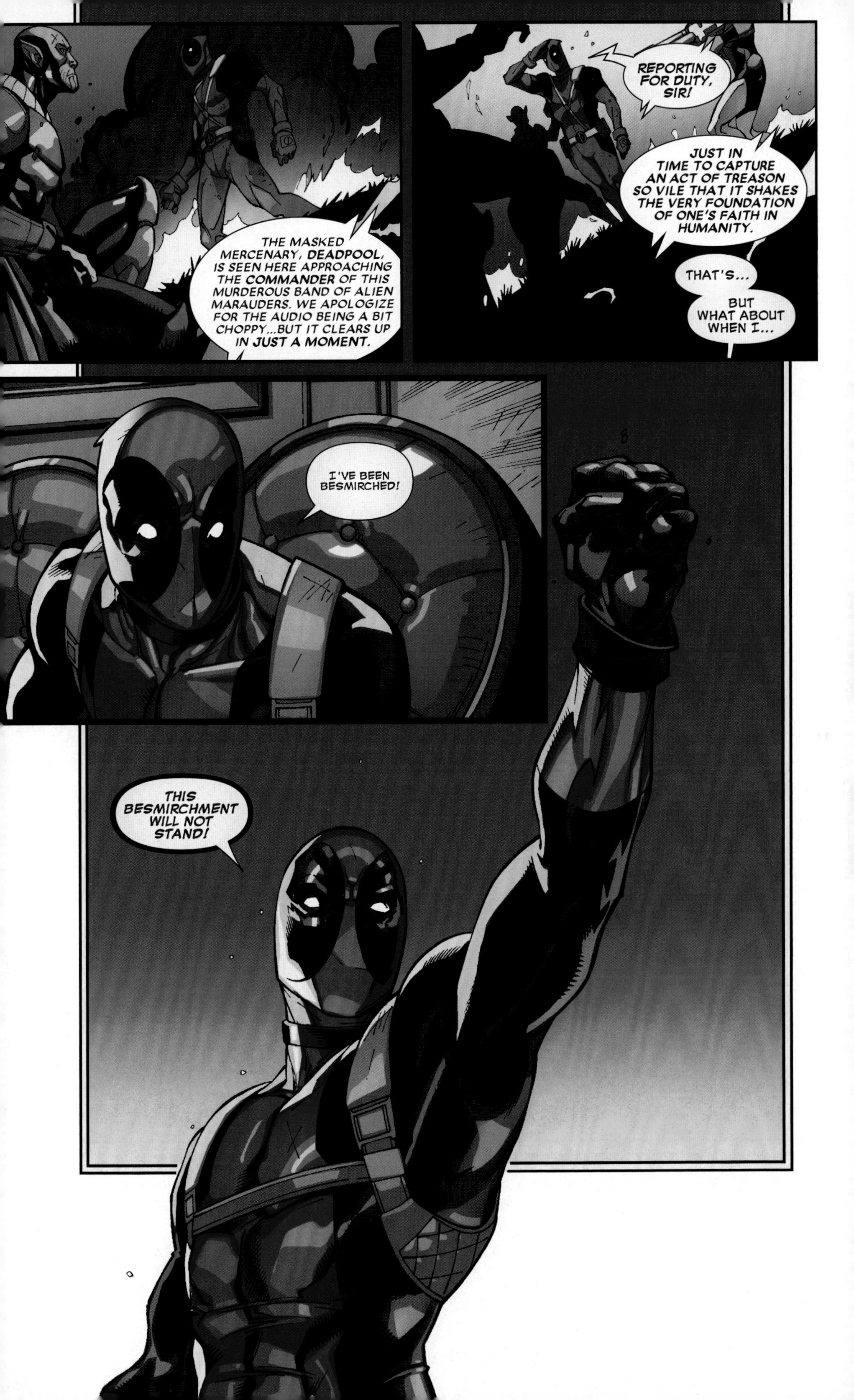
THE MASKED MERCENARY, DEADPOOL, IS SEEN HERE APPROACHING THE COMMANDER OF THIS MURDEROUS BAND OF ALIEN MARAUDERS. WE APOLOGIZE FOR THE AUDIO BEING A BIT CHOPPY...BUT IT CLEARS UP IN JUST A MOMENT.
REPORTING FOR DUTY, SIR!
JUST IN TIME TO CAPTURE AN ACT OF TREASON SO VILE THAT IT SHAKES THE VERY FOUNDATION OF ONE'S FAITH IN HUMANITY.
THAT'S...
BUT WHAT ABOUT WHEN I...
I'VE BEEN BESMIRCHED!
THIS BESMIRCHMENT WILL NOT STAND!

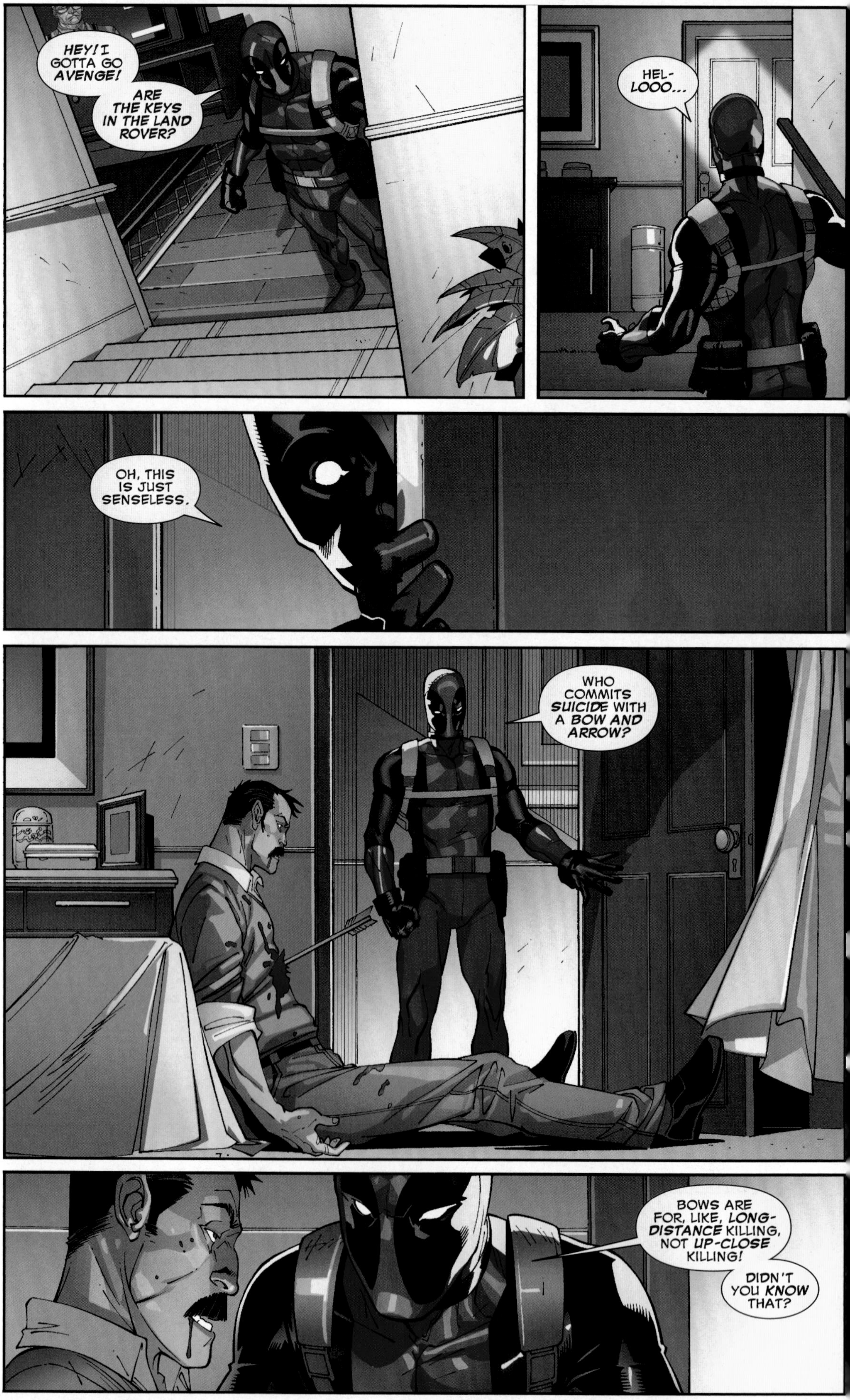
HEY! I GOTTA GO AVENGE!
ARE THE KEYS IN THE LAND ROVER?
HEL-LOOO...
OH, THIS IS JUST SENSELESS.
WHO COMMITS SUICIDE WITH A BOW AND ARROW?
BOWS ARE FOR, LIKE, LONG-DISTANCE KILLING, NOT UP-CLOSE KILLING!
DIDN'T YOU KNOW THAT?

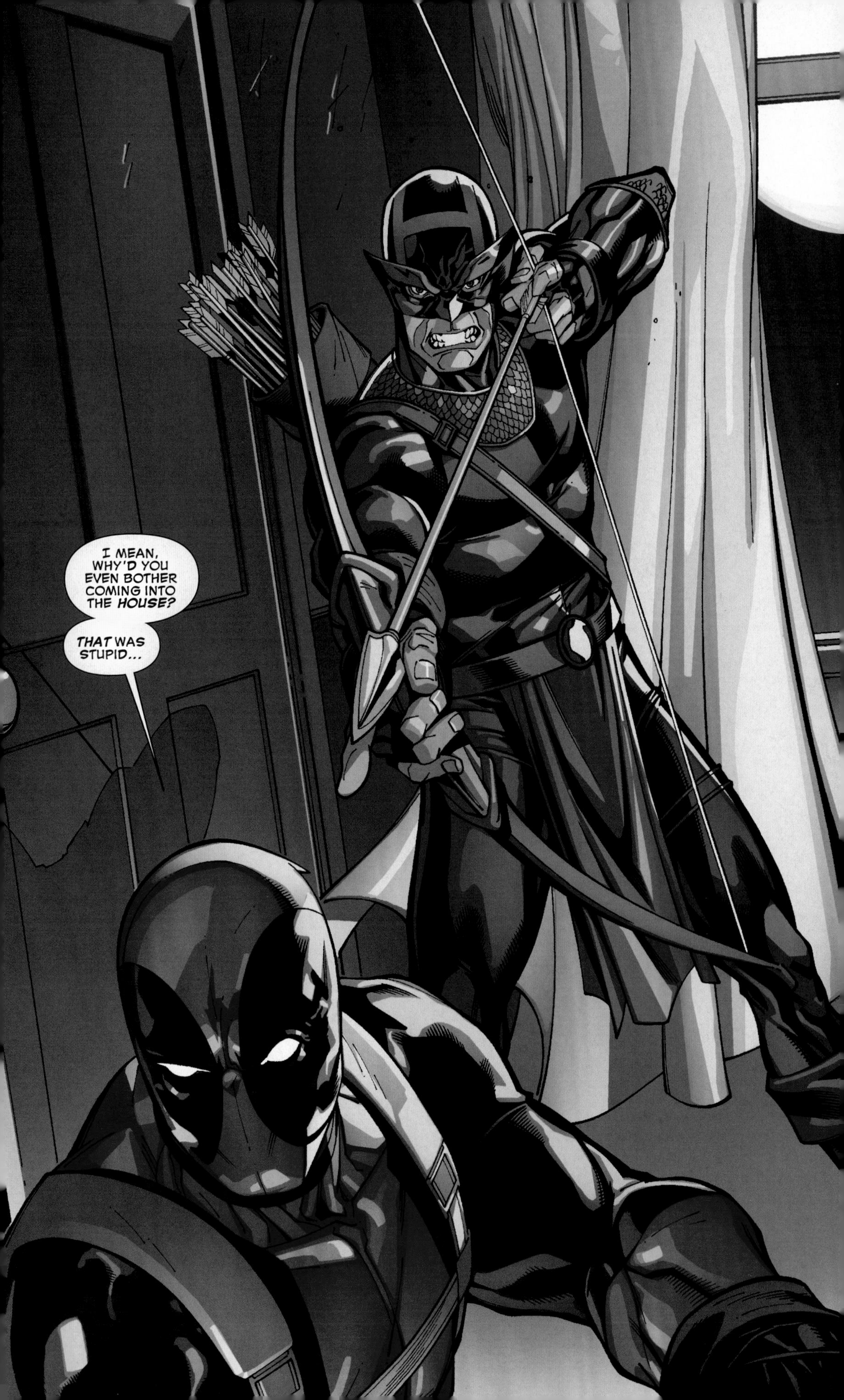
I MEAN, WHY'D YOU EVEN BOTHER COMING INTO THE *HOUSE?*
THAT WAS STUPID...

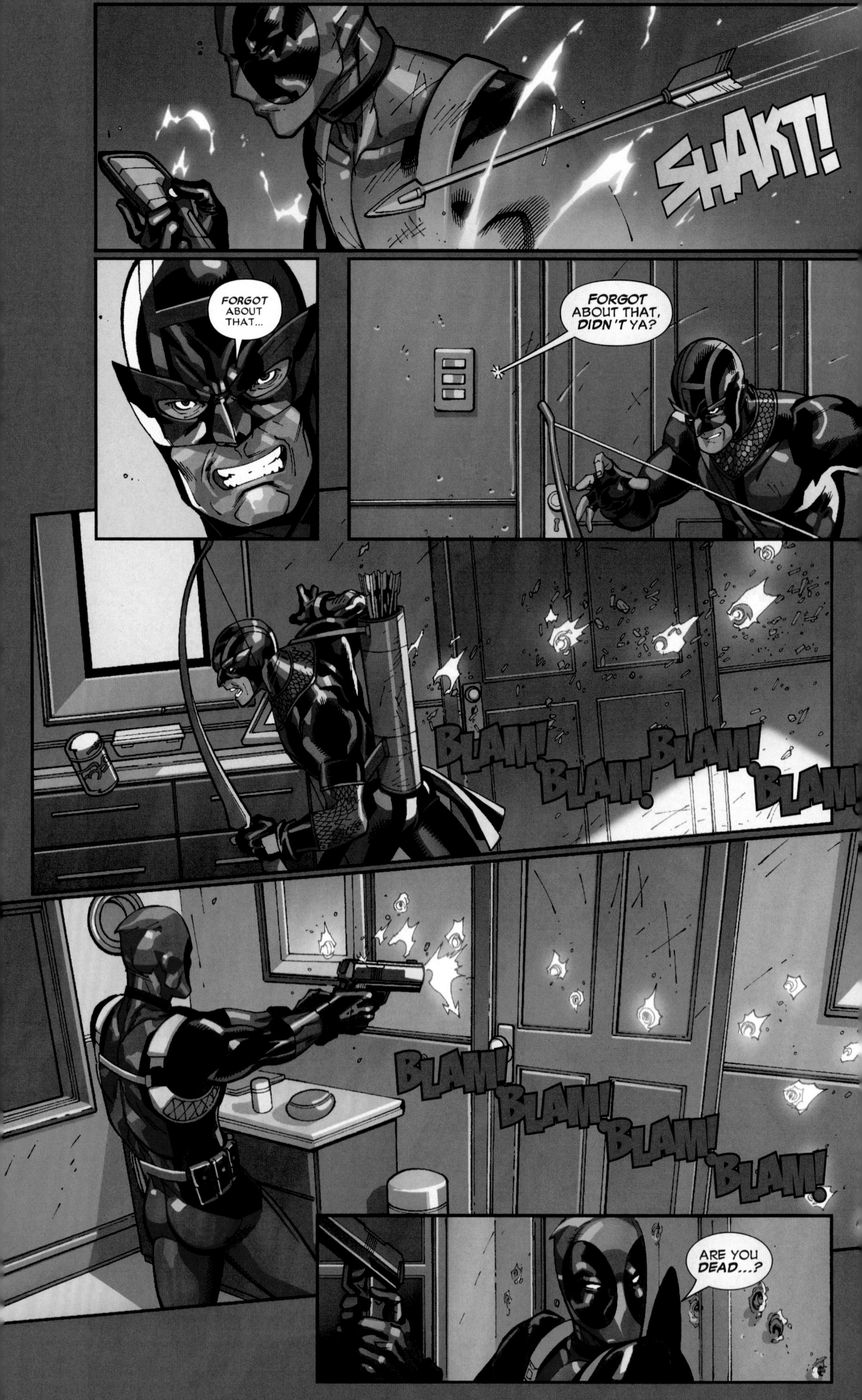
SHAKT!
FORGOT ABOUT THAT...
FORGOT ABOUT THAT, DIDN'T YA?
BLAM! BLAM! BLAM! BLAM!
BLAM! BLAM! BLAM! BLAM!
ARE YOU DEAD...?

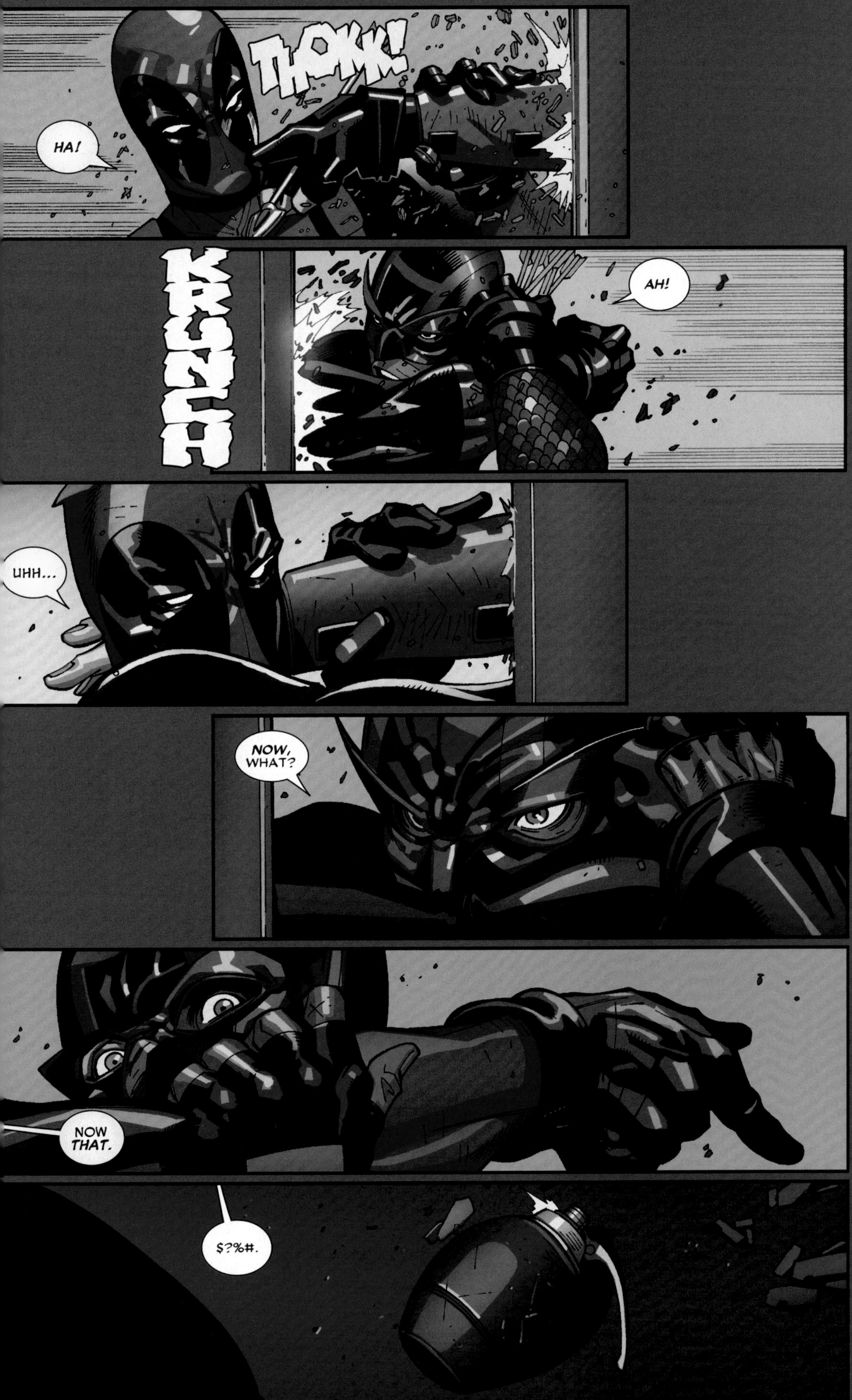
THOKK!
HA!
KRUNCH
AH!
UHH...
NOW, WHAT?
NOW THAT.
$?%#.

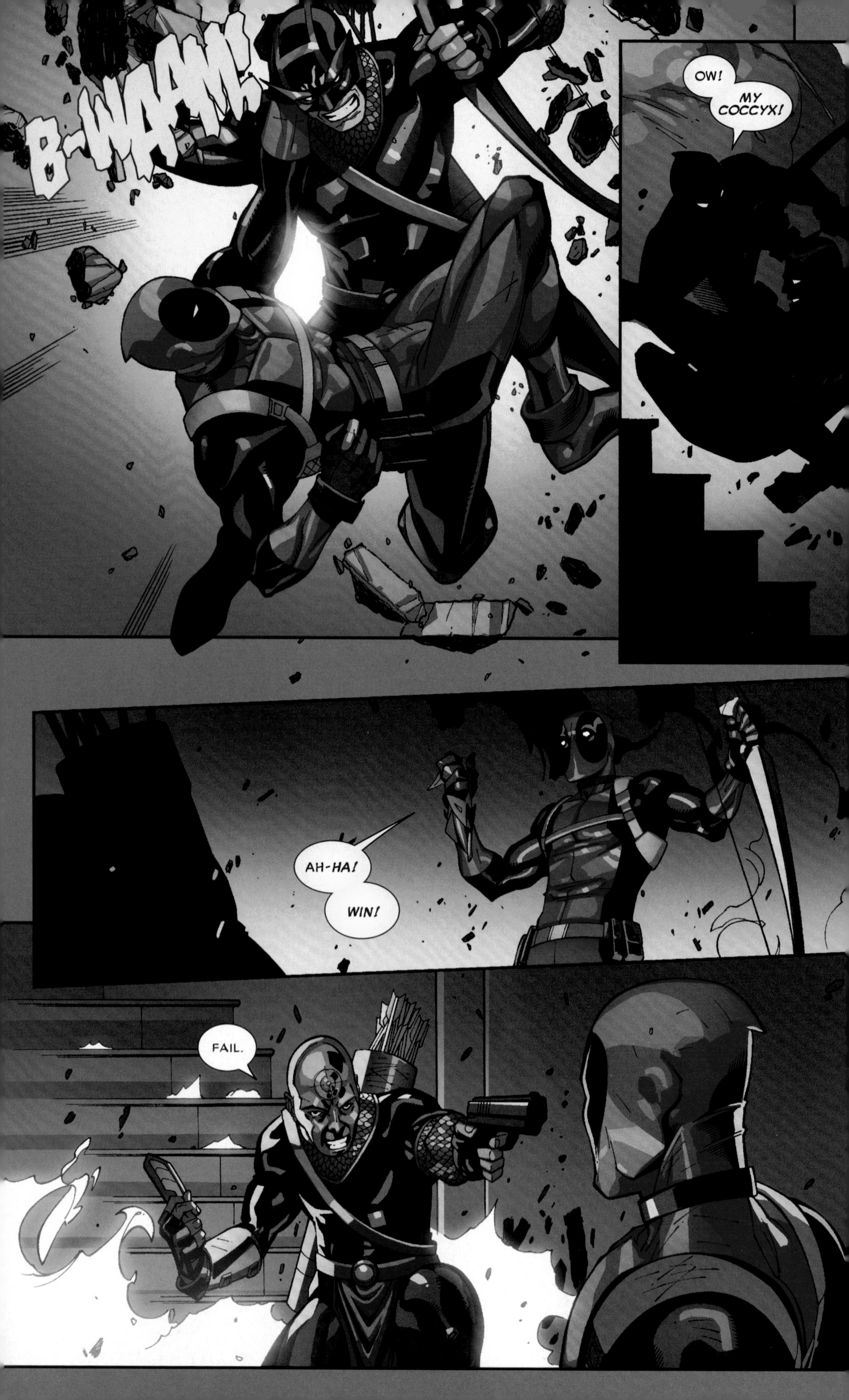
B-WAAM!
OW!
MY COCCYX!
AH-HA!
WIN!
FAIL.

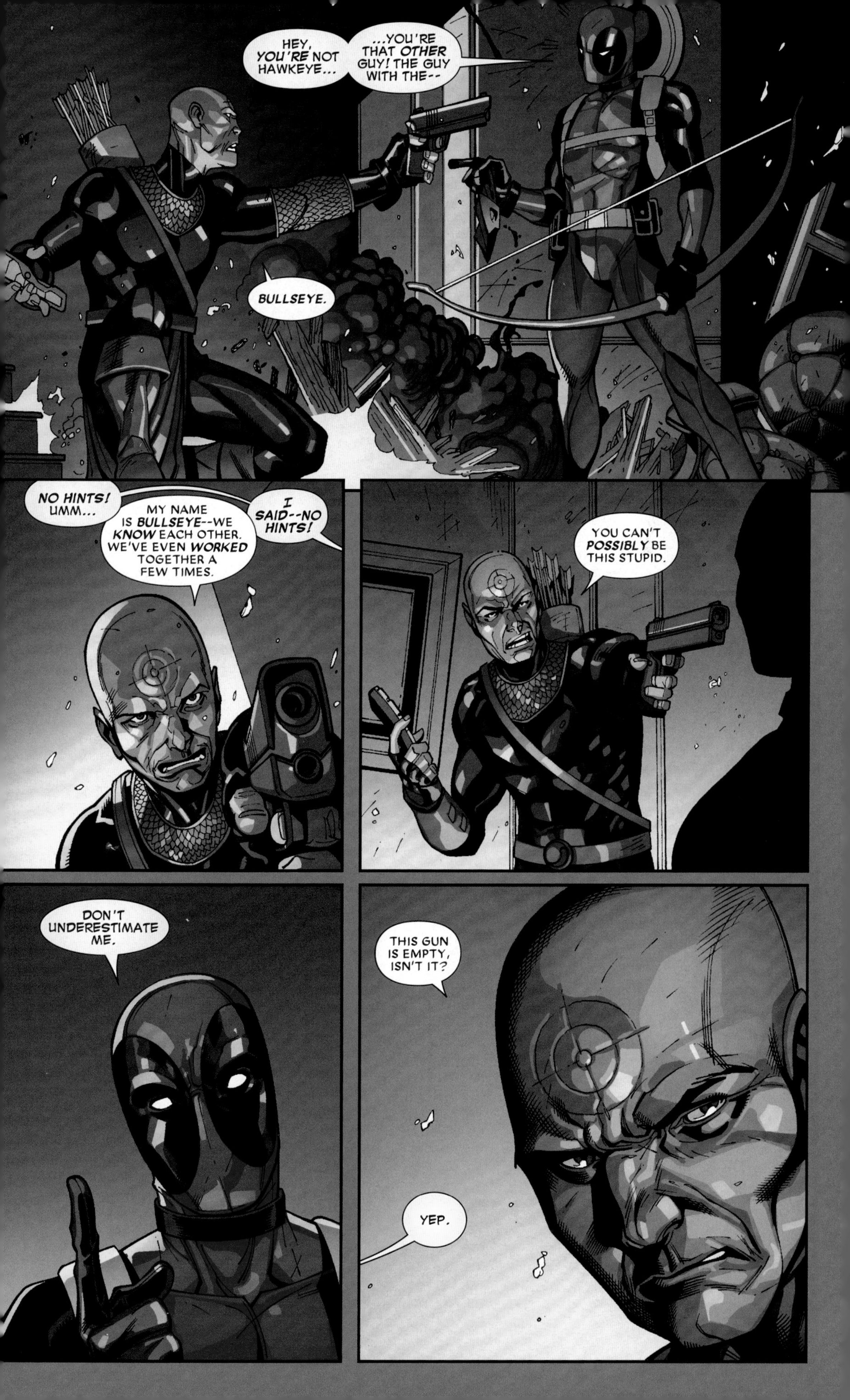
HEY, YOU'RE NOT HAWKEYE...
...YOU'RE THAT OTHER GUY! THE GUY WITH THE--
BULLSEYE.
NO HINTS! UMM...
MY NAME IS BULLSEYE--WE KNOW EACH OTHER. WE'VE EVEN WORKED TOGETHER A FEW TIMES.
I SAID--NO HINTS!
YOU CAN'T POSSIBLY BE THIS STUPID.
DON'T UNDERESTIMATE ME.
THIS GUN IS EMPTY, ISN'T IT?
YEP.

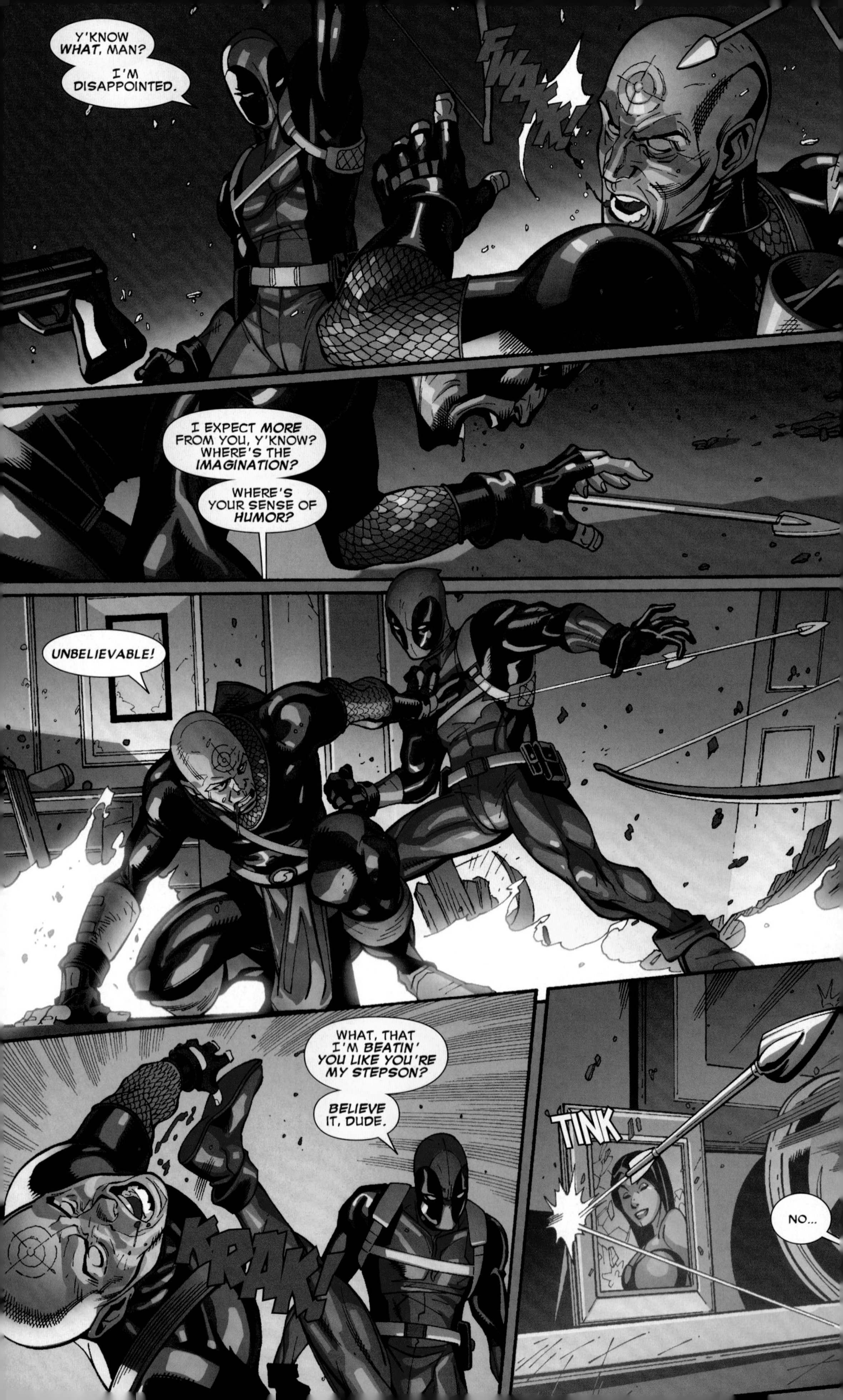

Y'KNOW WHAT, MAN?
I'M DISAPPOINTED.
FWAK!
I EXPECT MORE FROM YOU, Y'KNOW? WHERE'S THE IMAGINATION?
WHERE'S YOUR SENSE OF HUMOR?
UNBELIEVABLE!
WHAT, THAT I'M BEATIN' YOU LIKE YOU'RE MY STEPSON?
BELIEVE IT, DUDE.
KRAK!
TINK
NO...

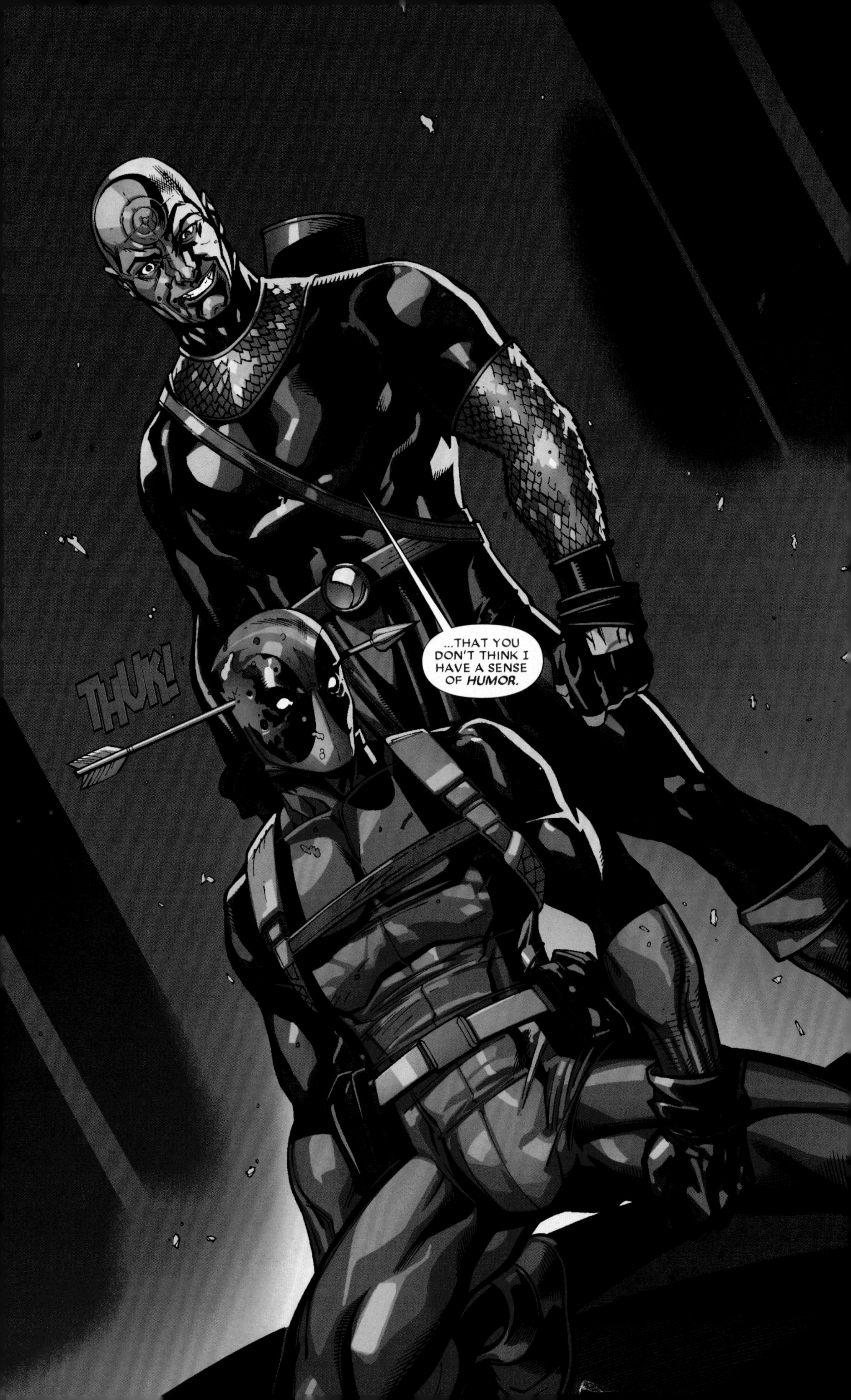
THUK!
...THAT YOU DON'T THINK I HAVE A SENSE OF *HUMOR*.

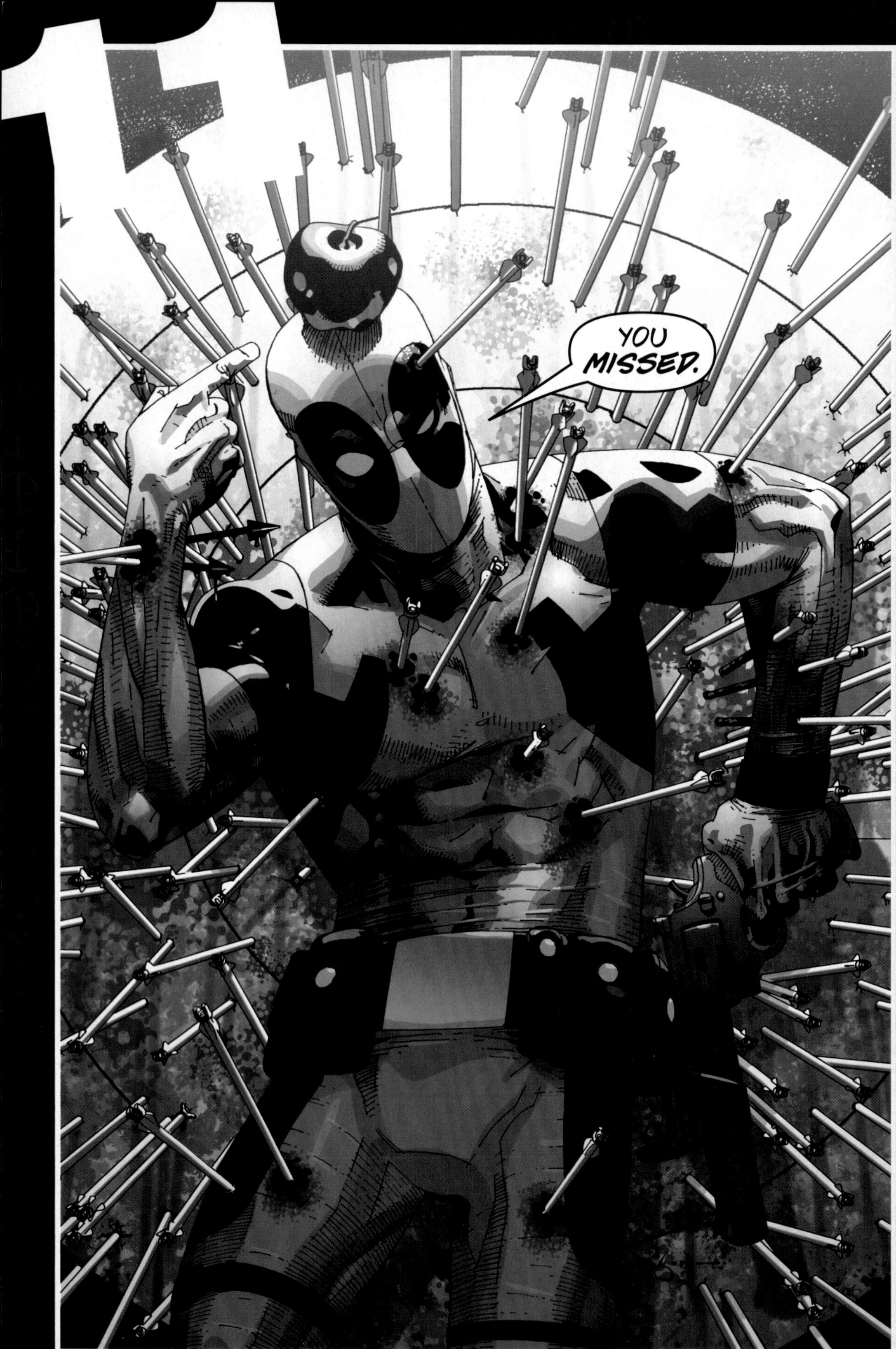
YOU MISSED.

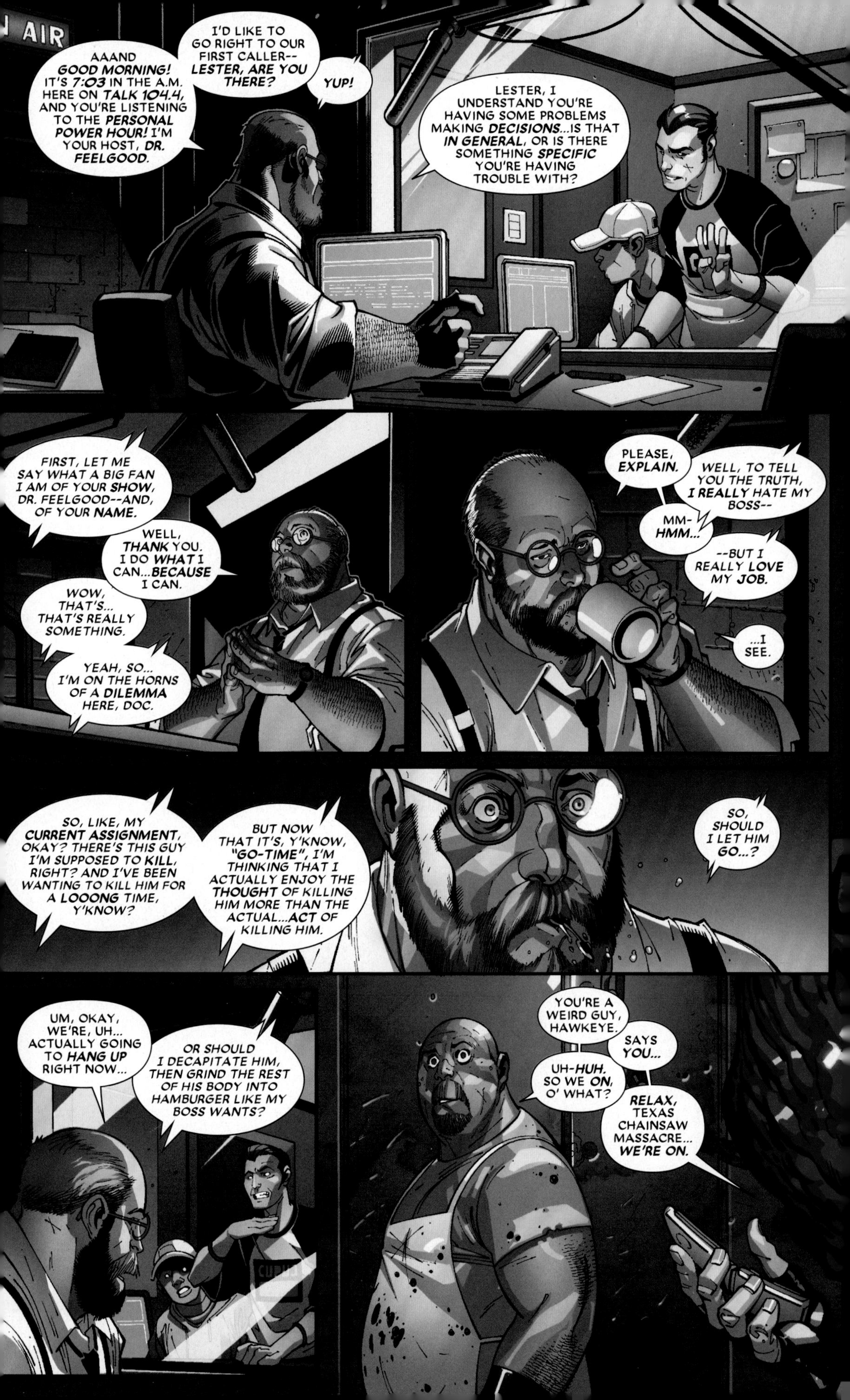

ON AIR
AAAND GOOD MORNING! IT'S 7:03 IN THE A.M. HERE ON TALK 104.4, AND YOU'RE LISTENING TO THE PERSONAL POWER HOUR! I'M YOUR HOST, DR. FEELGOOD.
I'D LIKE TO GO RIGHT TO OUR FIRST CALLER-- LESTER, ARE YOU THERE?
YUP!
LESTER, I UNDERSTAND YOU'RE HAVING SOME PROBLEMS MAKING DECISIONS...IS THAT IN GENERAL, OR IS THERE SOMETHING SPECIFIC YOU'RE HAVING TROUBLE WITH?
FIRST, LET ME SAY WHAT A BIG FAN I AM OF YOUR SHOW, DR. FEELGOOD--AND, OF YOUR NAME.
WELL, THANK YOU. I DO WHAT I CAN...BECAUSE I CAN.
WOW, THAT'S... THAT'S REALLY SOMETHING.
YEAH, SO... I'M ON THE HORNS OF A DILEMMA HERE, DOC.
PLEASE, EXPLAIN.
WELL, TO TELL YOU THE TRUTH, I REALLY HATE MY BOSS--
MM-HMM...
--BUT I REALLY LOVE MY JOB.
...I SEE.
SO, LIKE, MY CURRENT ASSIGNMENT, OKAY? THERE'S THIS GUY I'M SUPPOSED TO KILL, RIGHT? AND I'VE BEEN WANTING TO KILL HIM FOR A LOOONG TIME, Y'KNOW?
BUT NOW THAT IT'S, Y'KNOW, "GO-TIME", I'M THINKING THAT I ACTUALLY ENJOY THE THOUGHT OF KILLING HIM MORE THAN THE ACTUAL...ACT OF KILLING HIM.
SO, SHOULD I LET HIM GO...?
UM, OKAY, WE'RE, UH... ACTUALLY GOING TO HANG UP RIGHT NOW...
OR SHOULD I DECAPITATE HIM, THEN GRIND THE REST OF HIS BODY INTO HAMBURGER LIKE MY BOSS WANTS?
YOU'RE A WEIRD GUY, HAWKEYE.
SAYS YOU...
UH-HUH. SO WE ON, O' WHAT?
RELAX, TEXAS CHAINSAW MASSACRE... WE'RE ON.

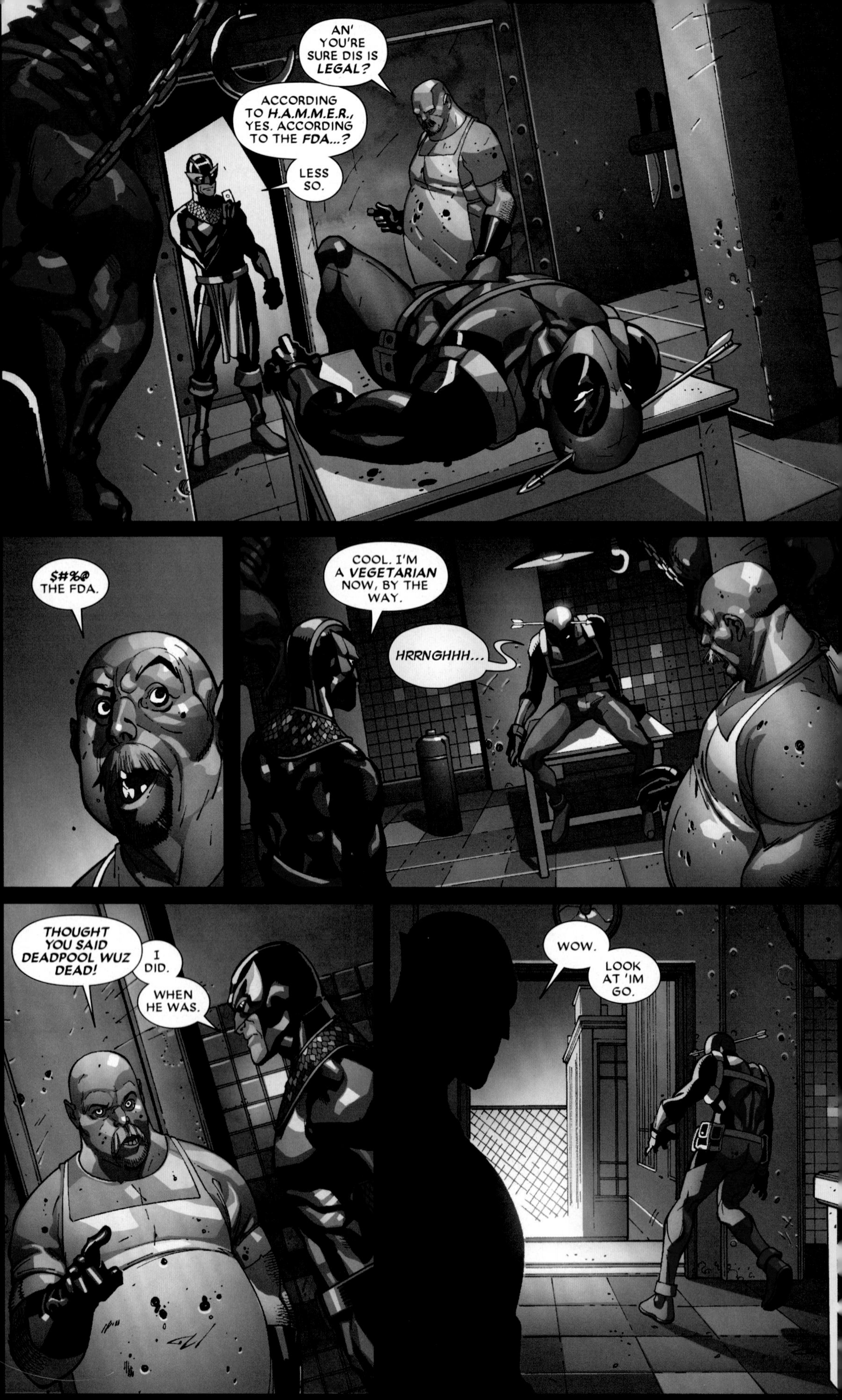
AN' YOU'RE SURE DIS IS LEGAL?
ACCORDING TO H.A.M.M.E.R., YES. ACCORDING TO THE FDA...?
LESS SO.
$#%@ THE FDA.
COOL. I'M A VEGETARIAN NOW, BY THE WAY.
HRRNGHHH...
THOUGHT YOU SAID DEADPOOL WUZ DEAD!
I DID.
WHEN HE WAS.
WOW.
LOOK AT 'IM GO.

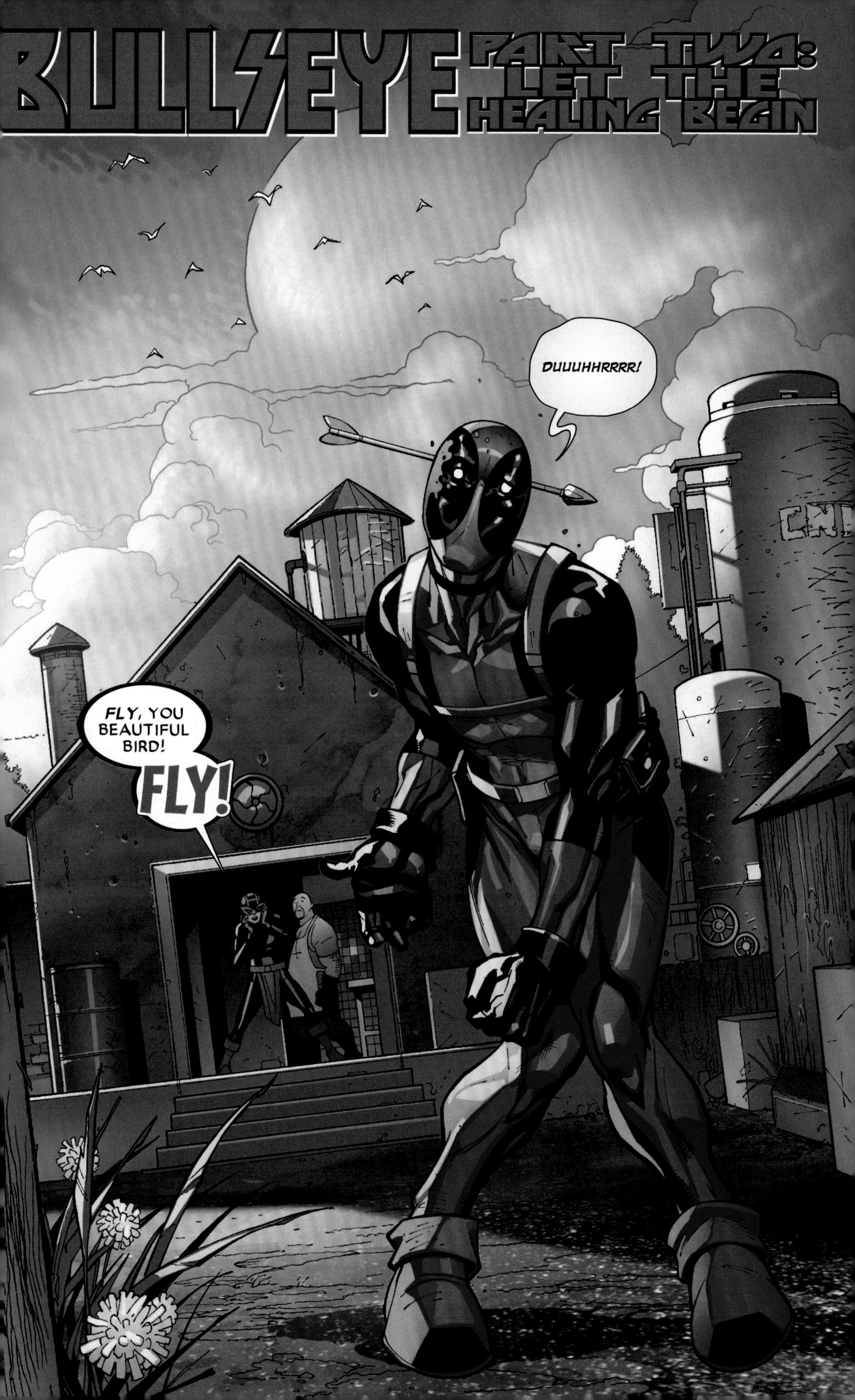
BULLSEYE PART TWO: LET THE HEALING BEGIN
DUUUHHRRRR!
FLY, YOU BEAUTIFUL BIRD!
FLY!

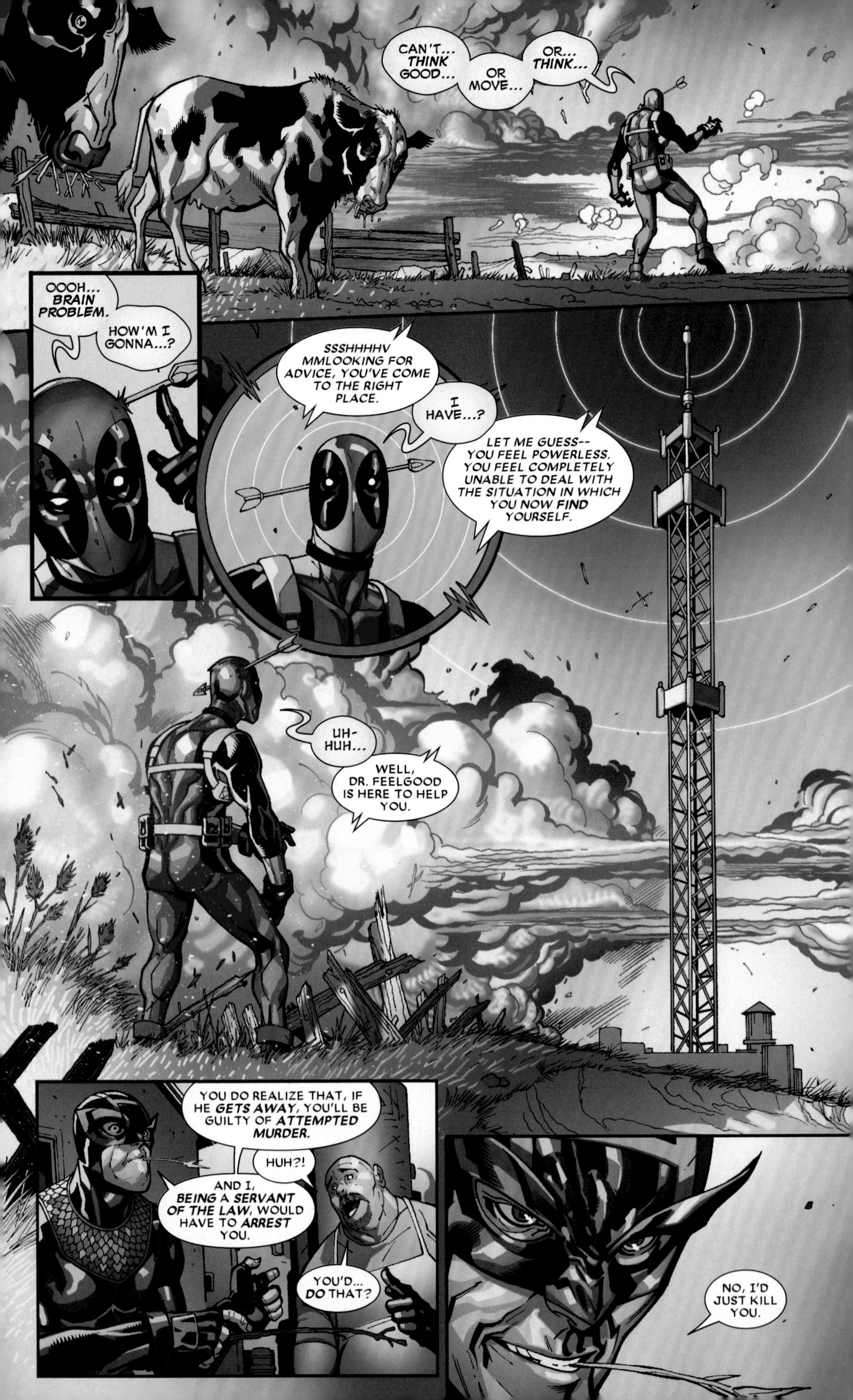

CAN'T... THINK GOOD...
OR MOVE...
OR... THINK...
OOOH... BRAIN PROBLEM.
HOW'M I GONNA...?
SSSHHHHV MMLOOKING FOR ADVICE, YOU'VE COME TO THE RIGHT PLACE.
I HAVE...?
LET ME GUESS-- YOU FEEL POWERLESS. YOU FEEL COMPLETELY UNABLE TO DEAL WITH THE SITUATION IN WHICH YOU NOW FIND YOURSELF.
UH-HUH...
WELL, DR. FEELGOOD IS HERE TO HELP YOU.
YOU DO REALIZE THAT, IF HE GETS AWAY, YOU'LL BE GUILTY OF ATTEMPTED MURDER.
HUH?!
AND I, BEING A SERVANT OF THE LAW, WOULD HAVE TO ARREST YOU.
YOU'D... DO THAT?
NO, I'D JUST KILL YOU.

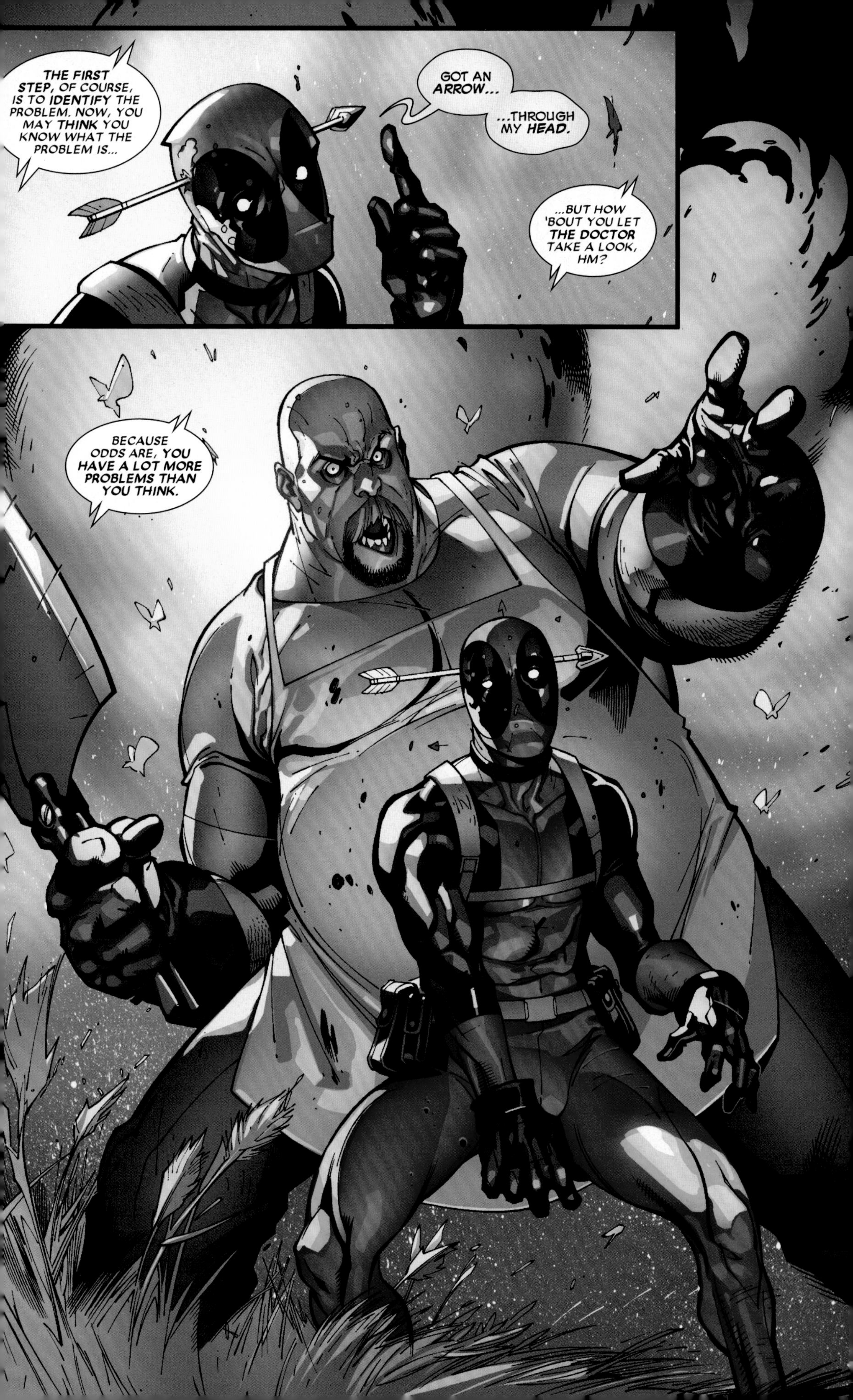

THE FIRST STEP, OF COURSE, IS TO IDENTIFY THE PROBLEM. NOW, YOU MAY THINK YOU KNOW WHAT THE PROBLEM IS...
GOT AN ARROW...
...THROUGH MY HEAD.
...BUT HOW 'BOUT YOU LET THE DOCTOR TAKE A LOOK, HM?
BECAUSE ODDS ARE, YOU HAVE A LOT MORE PROBLEMS THAN YOU THINK.

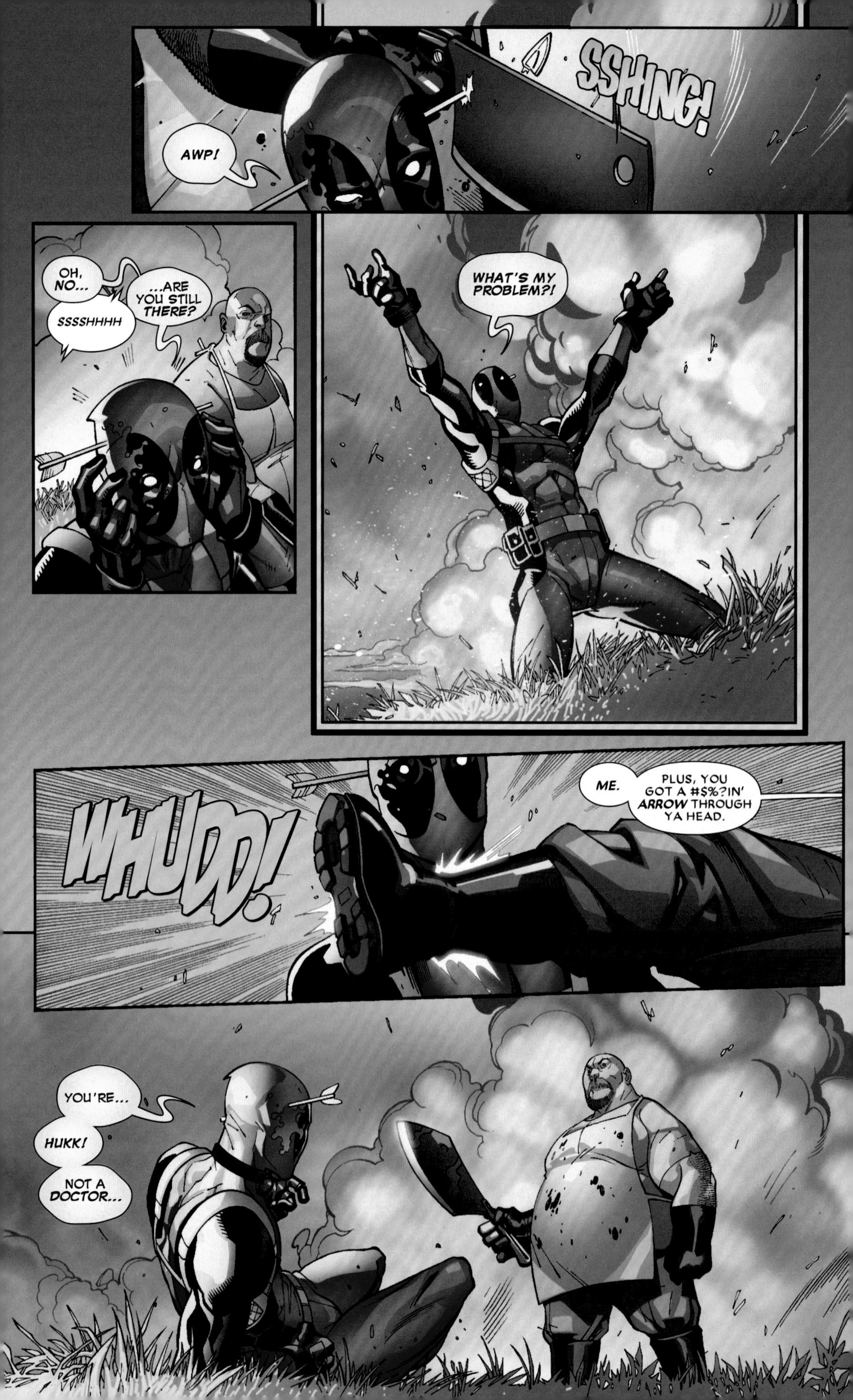
SSHING!
AWP!
OH, NO...
SSSSHHHH
...ARE YOU STILL THERE?
WHAT'S MY PROBLEM?!
WHUDD!
ME.
PLUS, YOU GOT A #$%?IN' ARROW THROUGH YA HEAD.
YOU'RE...
HUKK!
NOT A DOCTOR...

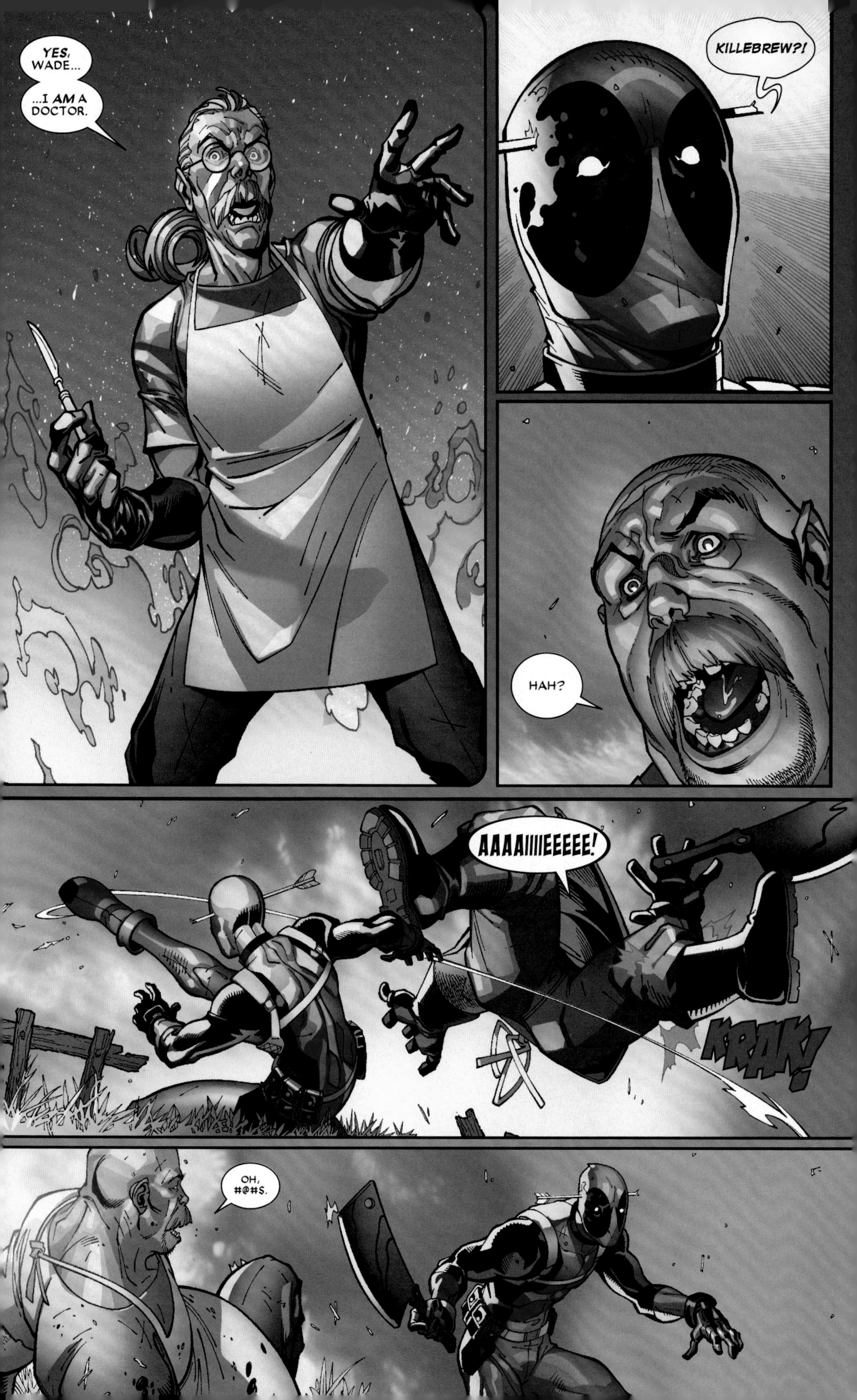
YES, WADE...
...I AM A DOCTOR.
KILLEBREW?!
HAH?
AAAAIIIIEEEEE!
KRAK!
OH, #@#$.

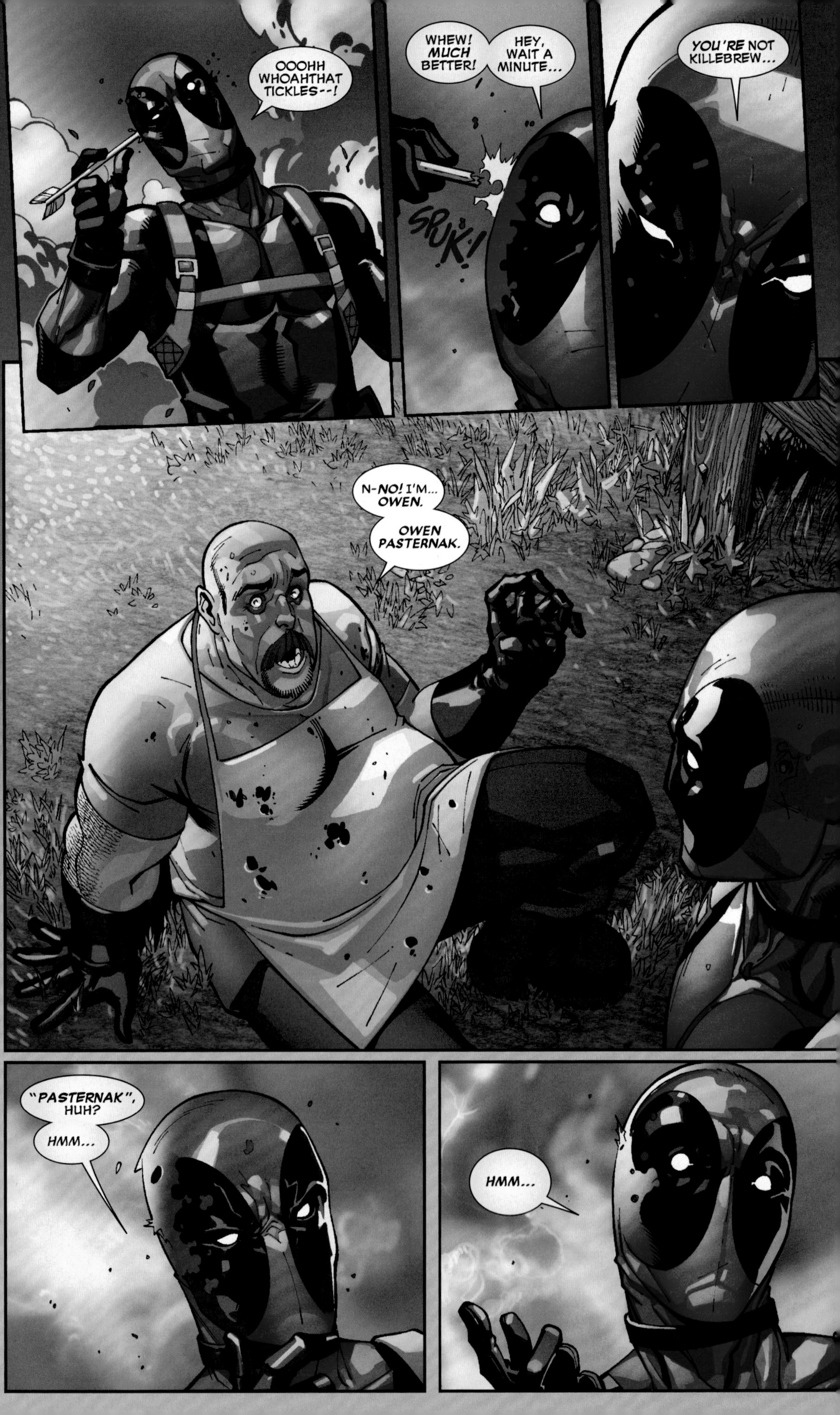
OOOHH WHOAHTHAT TICKLES--!
WHEW! MUCH BETTER!
HEY, WAIT A MINUTE...
SPUK!
YOU'RE NOT KILLEBREW...
N-NO! I'M... OWEN.
OWEN PASTERNAK.
"PASTERNAK", HUH?
HMM...
HMM...

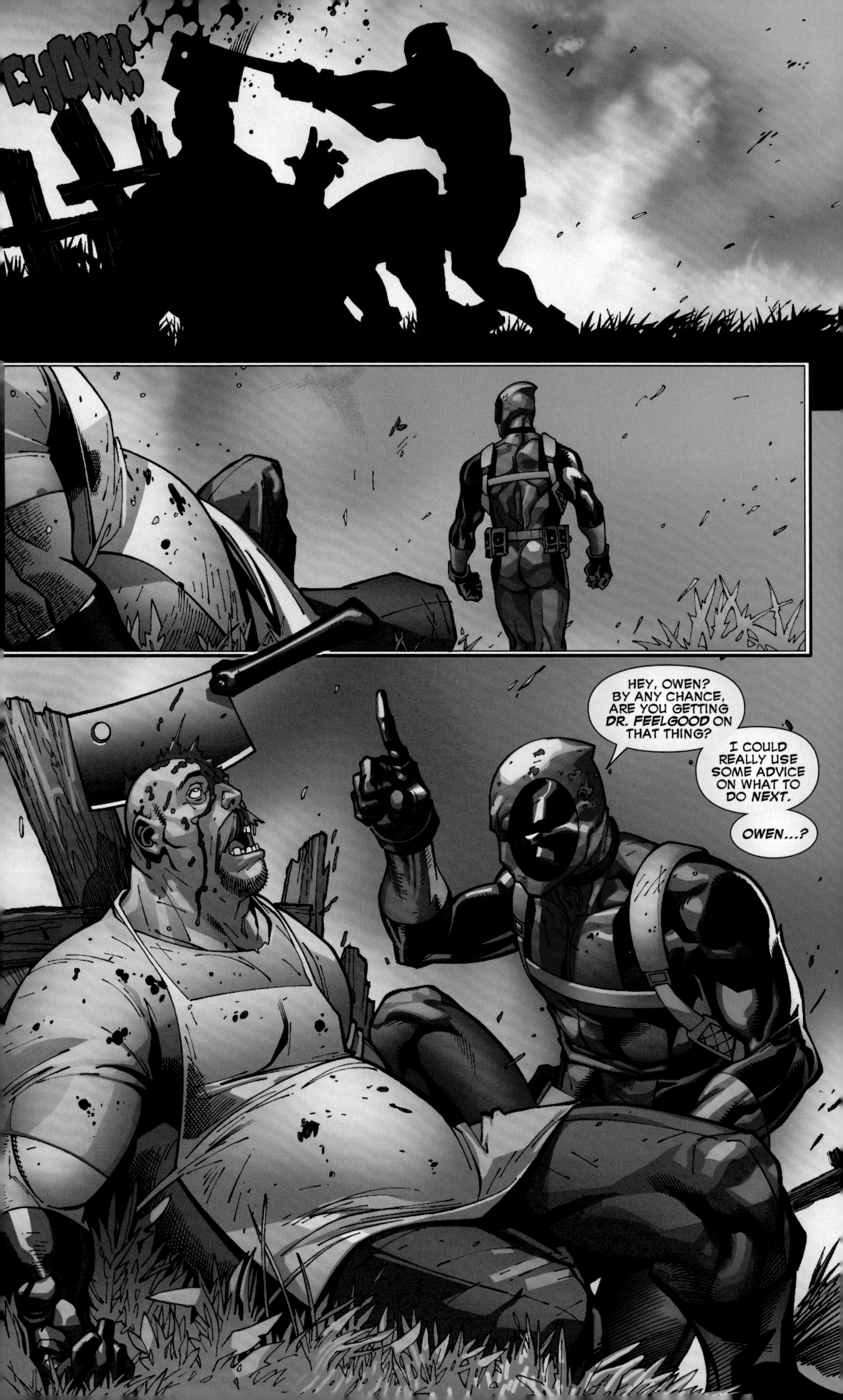
CHOKK!
HEY, OWEN? BY ANY CHANCE, ARE YOU GETTING DR. FEELGOOD ON THAT THING?
I COULD REALLY USE SOME ADVICE ON WHAT TO DO NEXT.
OWEN...?

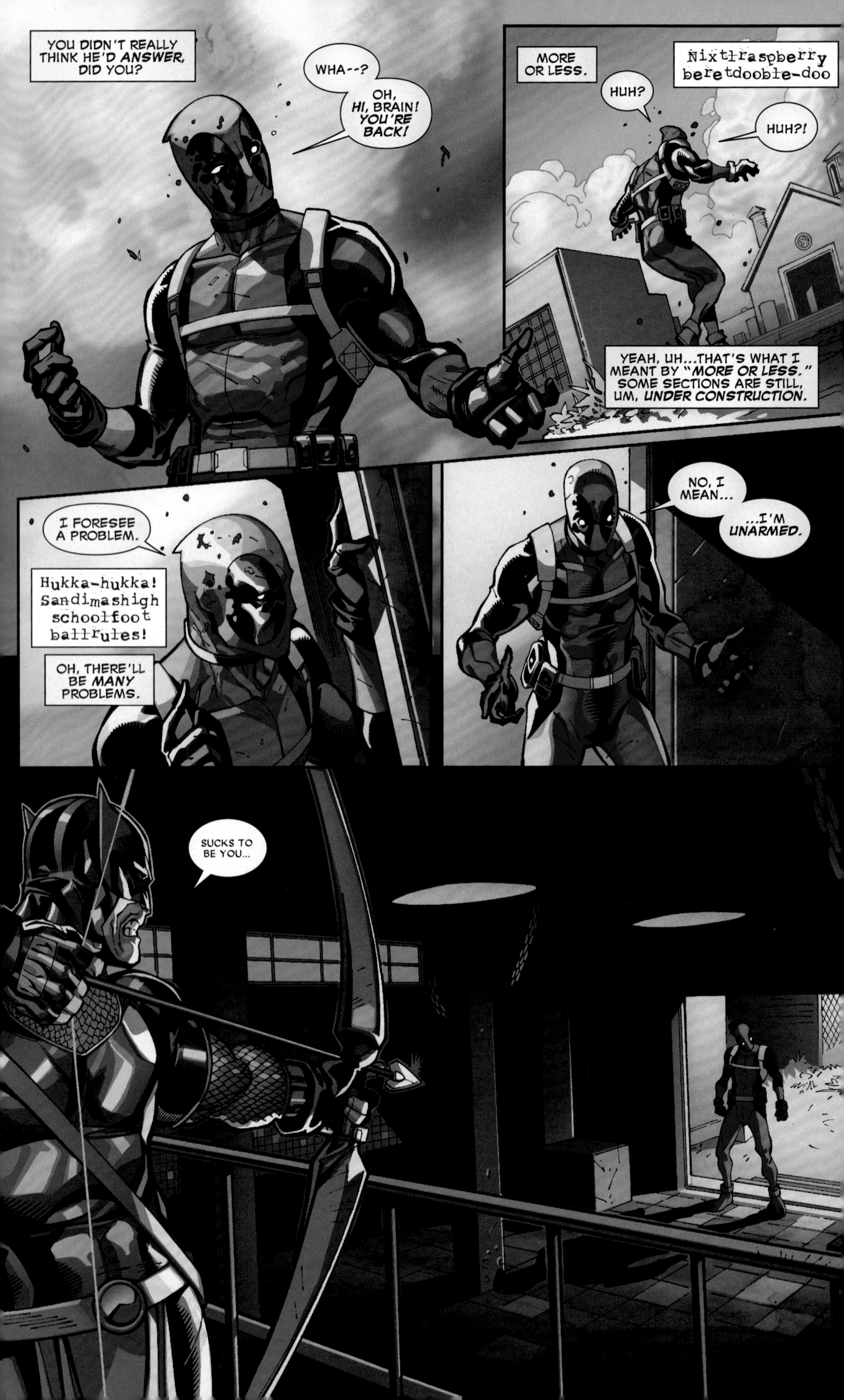
YOU DIDN'T REALLY THINK HE'D ANSWER, DID YOU?
WHA--?
OH, HI, BRAIN! YOU'RE BACK!
MORE OR LESS.
Nixtlraspberry beretdooble-doo
HUH?
HUH?!
YEAH, UH...THAT'S WHAT I MEANT BY "MORE OR LESS." SOME SECTIONS ARE STILL, UM, UNDER CONSTRUCTION.
I FORESEE A PROBLEM.
Hukka-hukka! Sandimashigh schoolfoot ballrules!
OH, THERE'LL BE MANY PROBLEMS.
NO, I MEAN...
...I'M UNARMED.
SUCKS TO BE YOU...

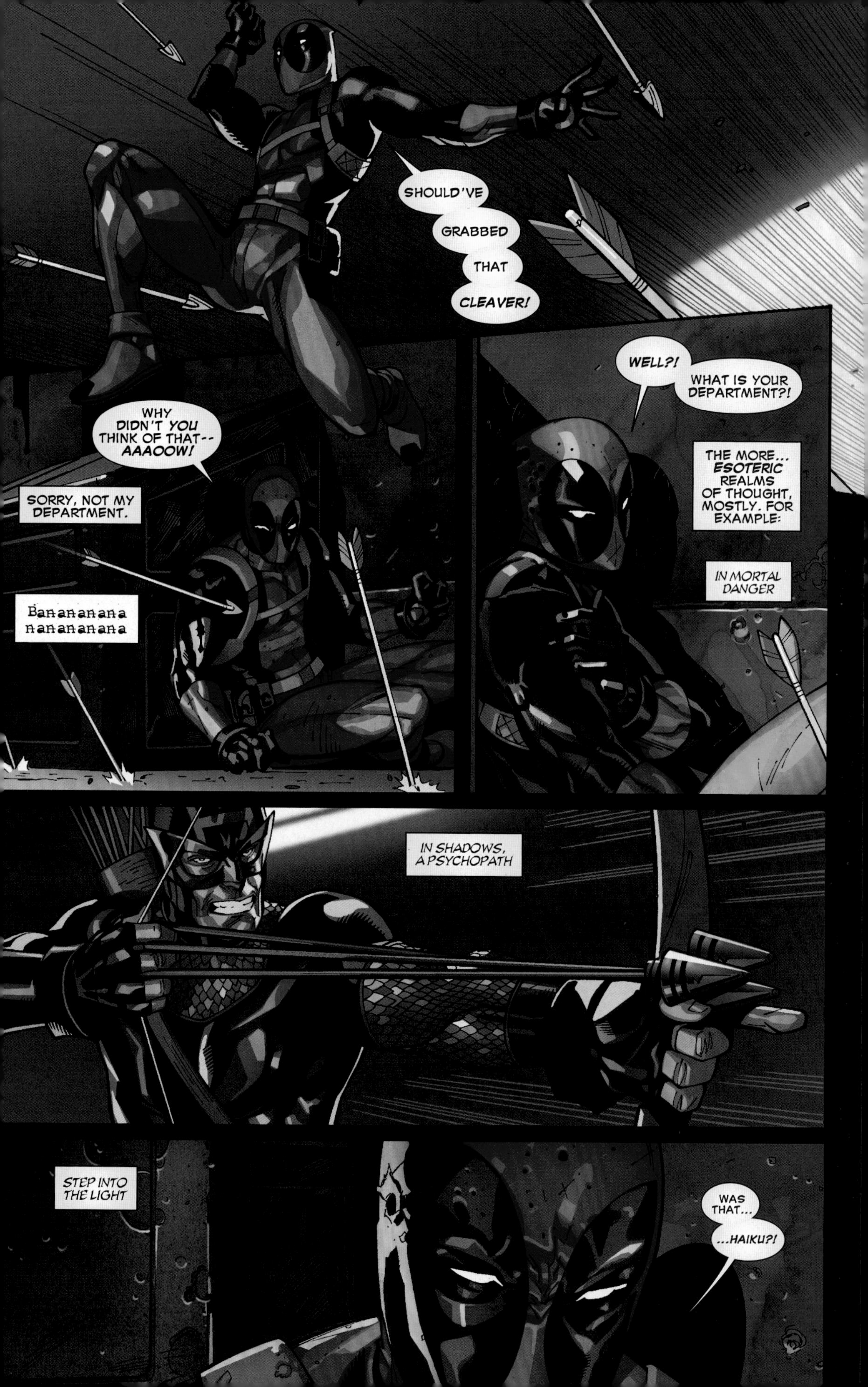
SHOULD'VE GRABBED THAT CLEAVER!
WHY DIDN'T YOU THINK OF THAT--AAAOOW!
SORRY, NOT MY DEPARTMENT.
Bananananana nananananana
WELL?!
WHAT IS YOUR DEPARTMENT?!
THE MORE... ESOTERIC REALMS OF THOUGHT, MOSTLY. FOR EXAMPLE:
IN MORTAL DANGER
IN SHADOWS, A PSYCHOPATH
STEP INTO THE LIGHT
WAS THAT...
...HAIKU?!

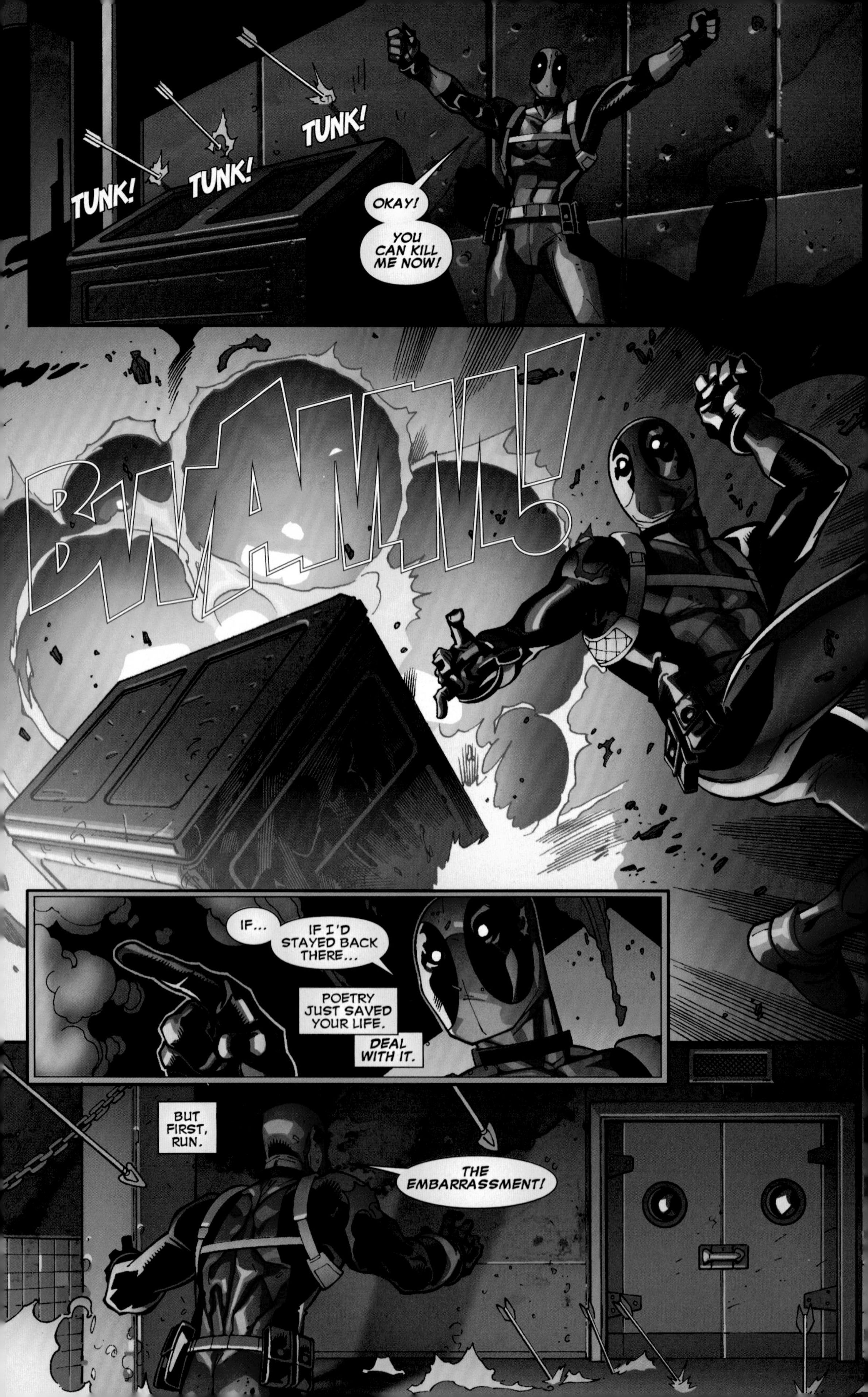

TUNK!
TUNK!
TUNK!
OKAY!
YOU CAN KILL ME NOW!
BWAMM!
IF...
IF I'D STAYED BACK THERE...
POETRY JUST SAVED YOUR LIFE.
DEAL WITH IT.
BUT FIRST, RUN.
THE EMBARRASSMENT!

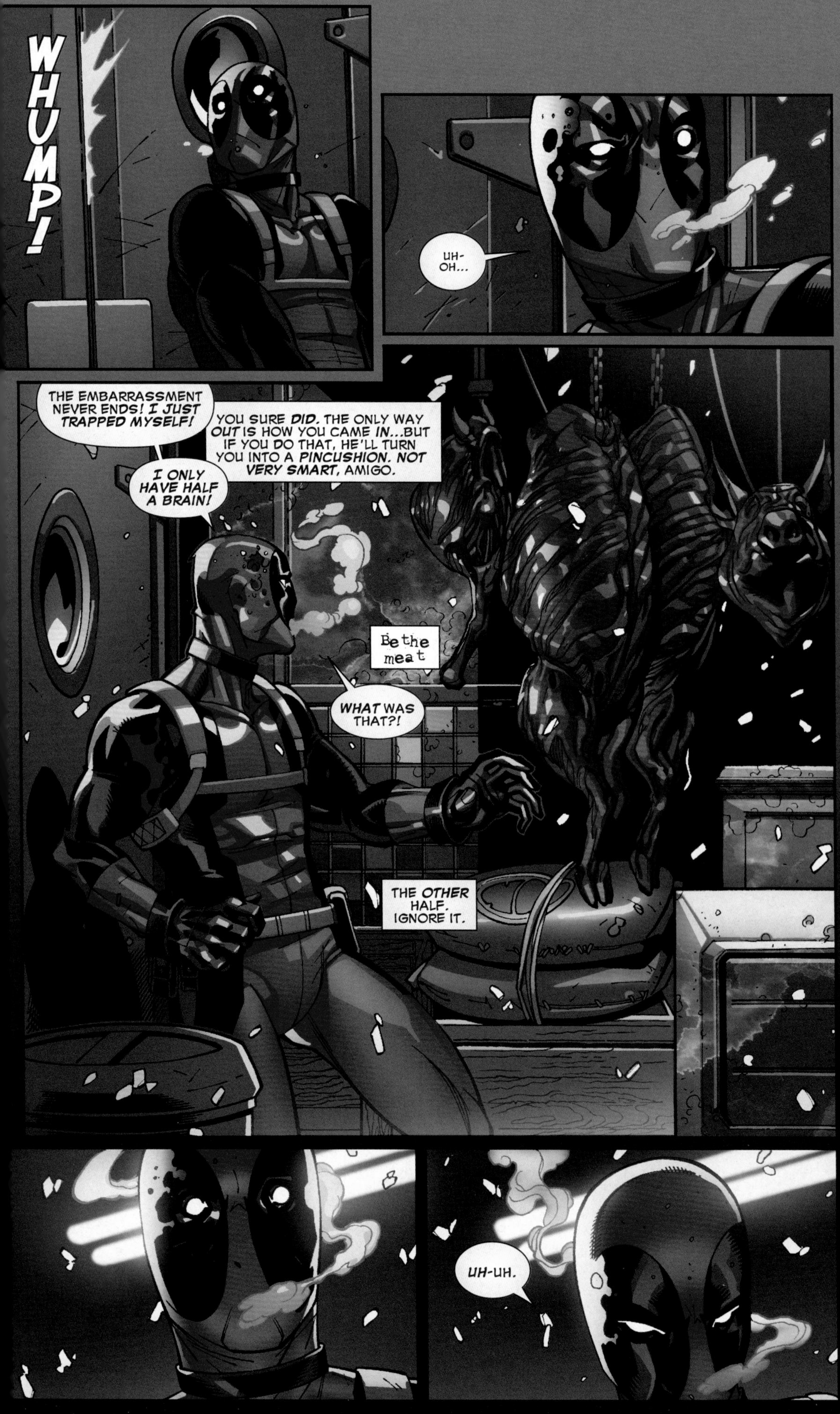
WHUMP!
UH-OH...
THE EMBARRASSMENT NEVER ENDS! I JUST TRAPPED MYSELF!
YOU SURE DID. THE ONLY WAY OUT IS HOW YOU CAME IN...BUT IF YOU DO THAT, HE'LL TURN YOU INTO A PINCUSHION. NOT VERY SMART, AMIGO.
I ONLY HAVE HALF A BRAIN!
Be the meat
WHAT WAS THAT?!
THE OTHER HALF. IGNORE IT.
UH-UH.

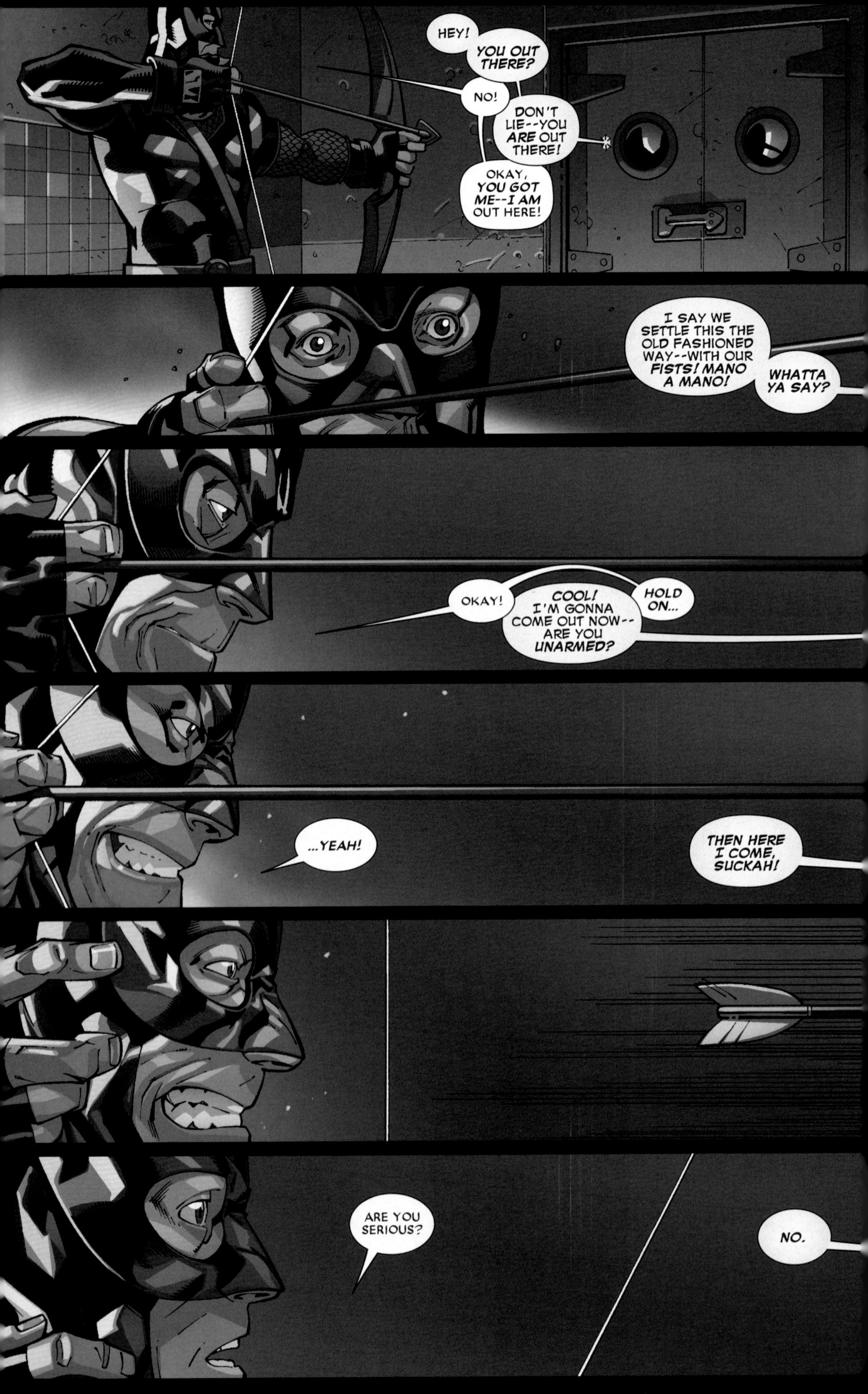
HEY!
YOU OUT THERE?
NO!
DON'T LIE--YOU ARE OUT THERE!
OKAY, YOU GOT ME--I AM OUT HERE!
I SAY WE SETTLE THIS THE OLD FASHIONED WAY--WITH OUR FISTS! MANO A MANO!
WHATTA YA SAY?
OKAY!
COOL! I'M GONNA COME OUT NOW--ARE YOU UNARMED?
HOLD ON...
...YEAH!
THEN HERE I COME, SUCKAH!
ARE YOU SERIOUS?
NO.

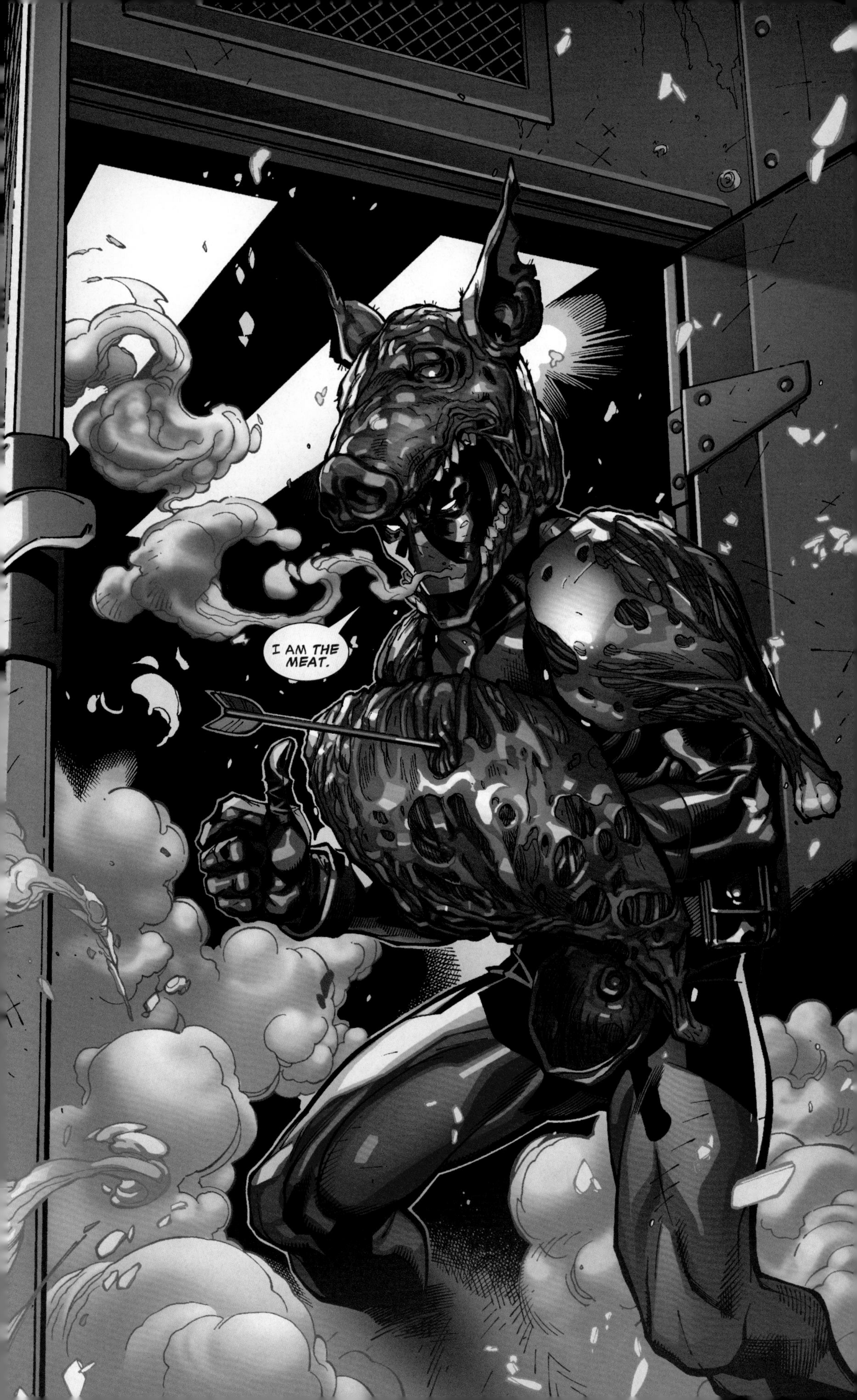
I AM THE MEAT.

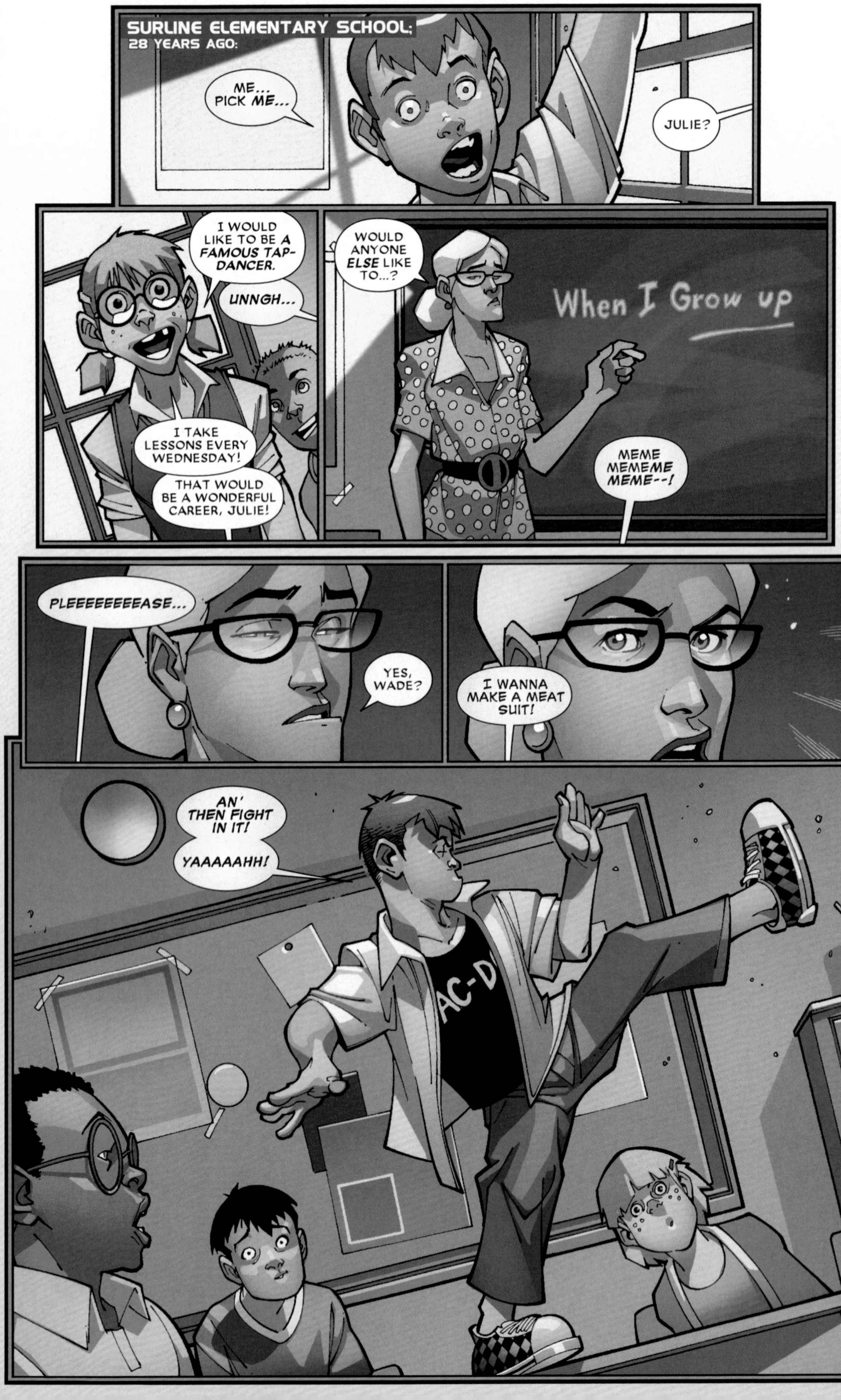
SURLINE ELEMENTARY SCHOOL; 28 YEARS AGO:
ME... PICK ME...
JULIE?
I WOULD LIKE TO BE A FAMOUS TAP-DANCER.
UNNGH...
I TAKE LESSONS EVERY WEDNESDAY!
THAT WOULD BE A WONDERFUL CAREER, JULIE!
WOULD ANYONE ELSE LIKE TO...?
When I Grow up
MEME MEMEME MEME--!
PLEEEEEEEEASE...
YES, WADE?
I WANNA MAKE A MEAT SUIT!
AN' THEN FIGHT IN IT!
YAAAAAHH!
AC-D

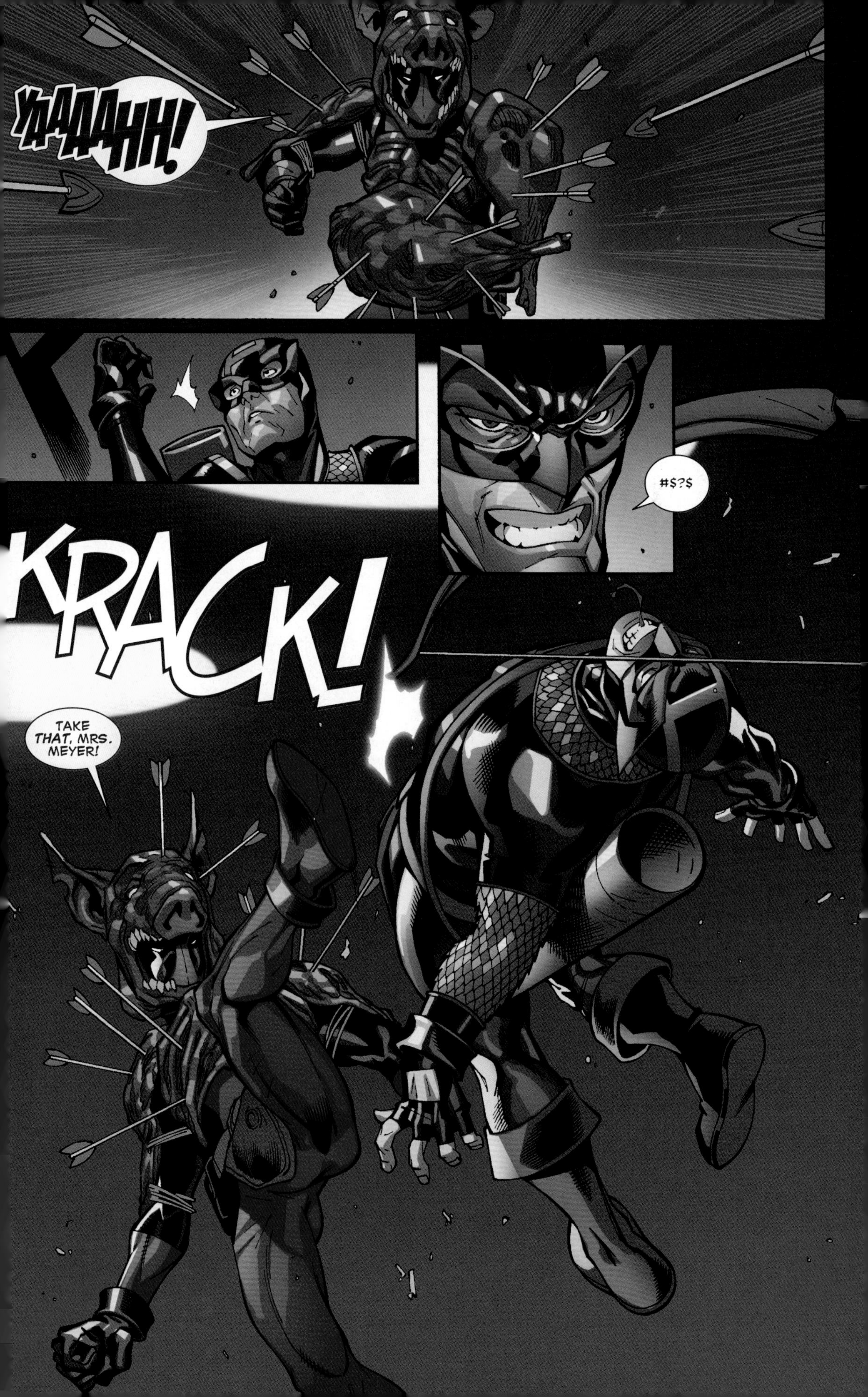
YAAAAHH!
#$?$
KRACK!
TAKE THAT, MRS. MEYER!

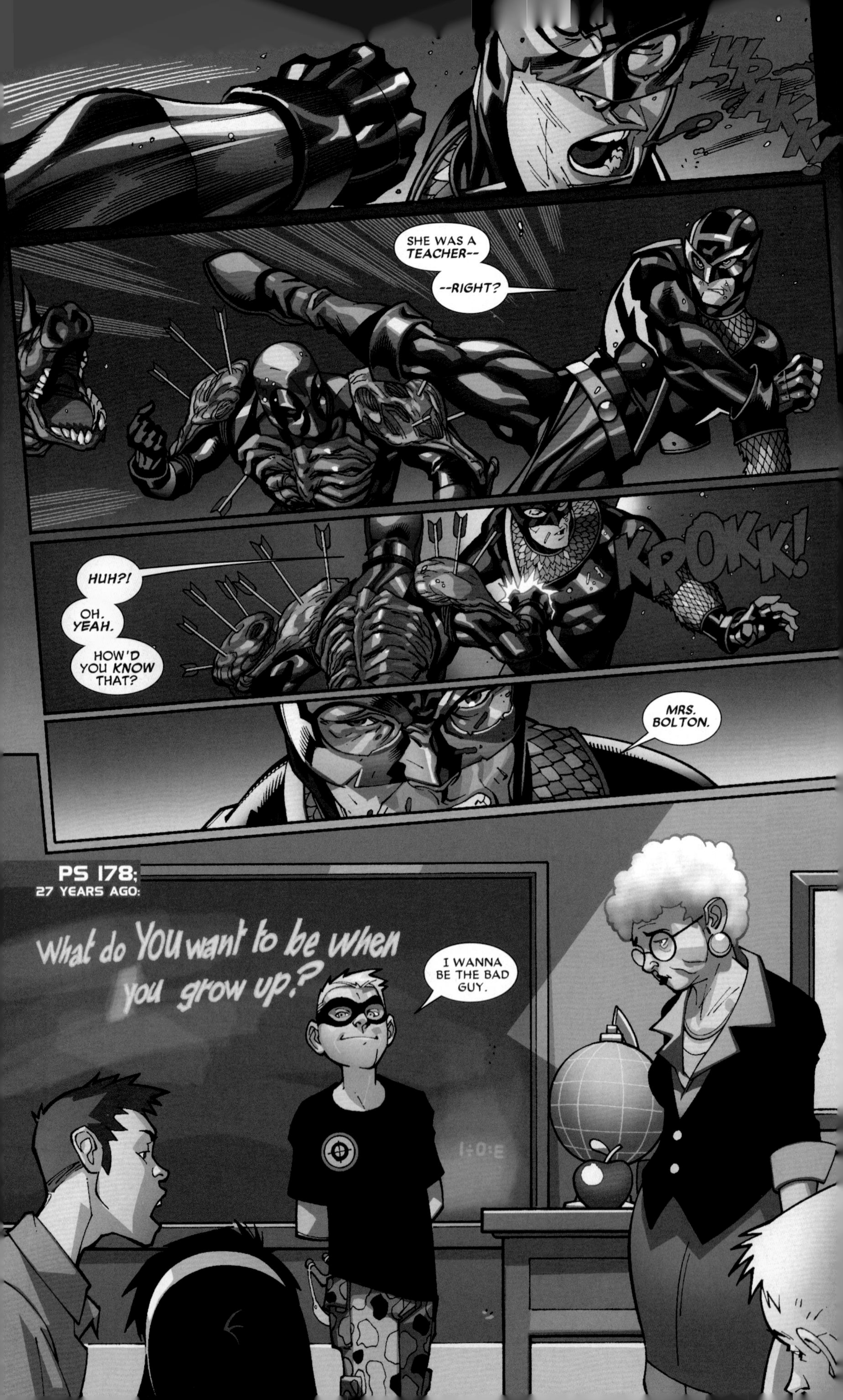
WRAKK!
SHE WAS A TEACHER--
--RIGHT?
HUH?!
KROKK!
OH. YEAH.
HOW'D YOU KNOW THAT?
MRS. BOLTON.
PS 178; 27 YEARS AGO:
What do You want to be when you grow up?
I WANNA BE THE BAD GUY.

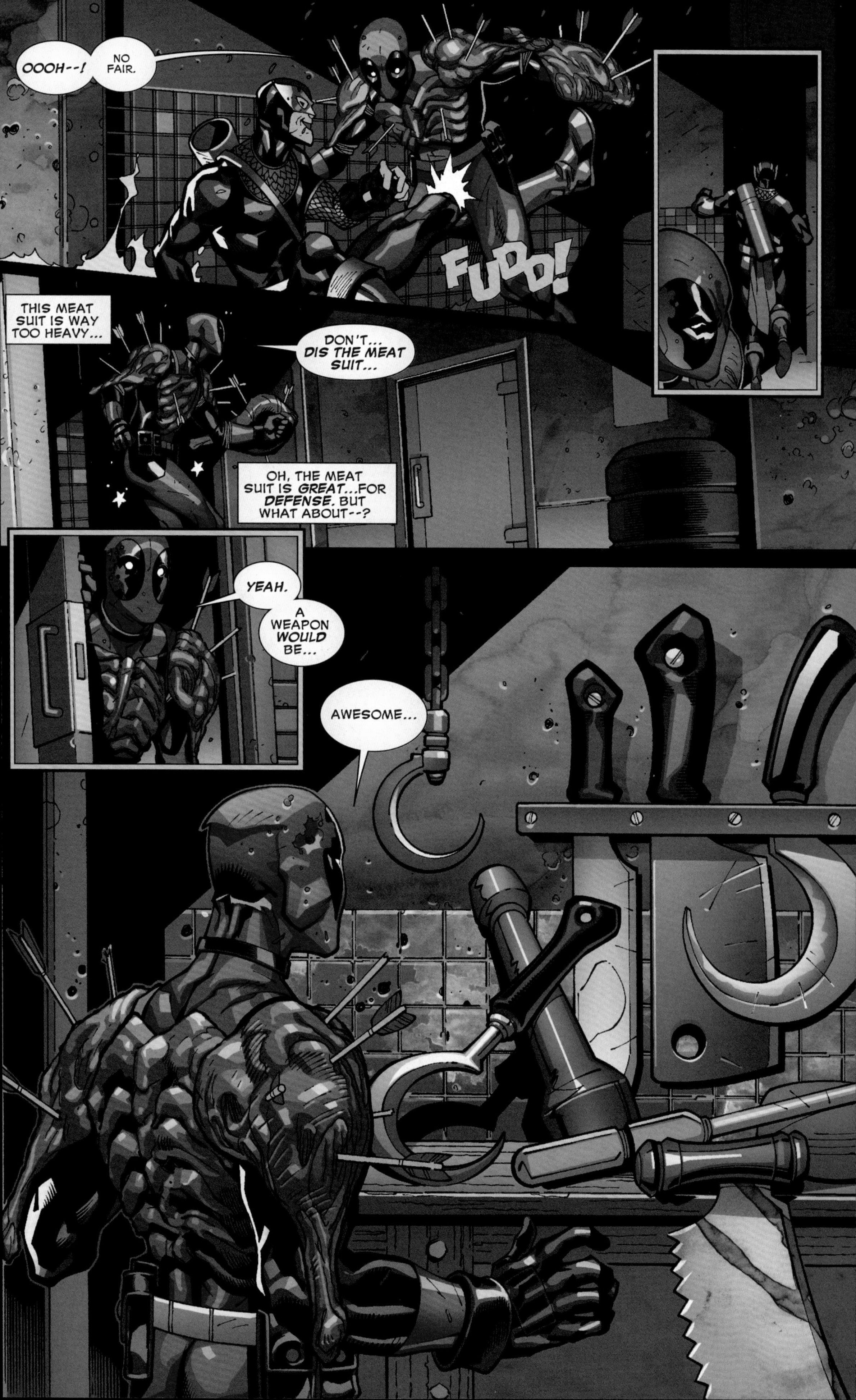
OOOH--!
NO FAIR.
FUDD!
THIS MEAT SUIT IS WAY TOO HEAVY...
DON'T... DIS THE MEAT SUIT...
OH, THE MEAT SUIT IS GREAT...FOR DEFENSE. BUT WHAT ABOUT--?
YEAH.
A WEAPON WOULD BE...
AWESOME...

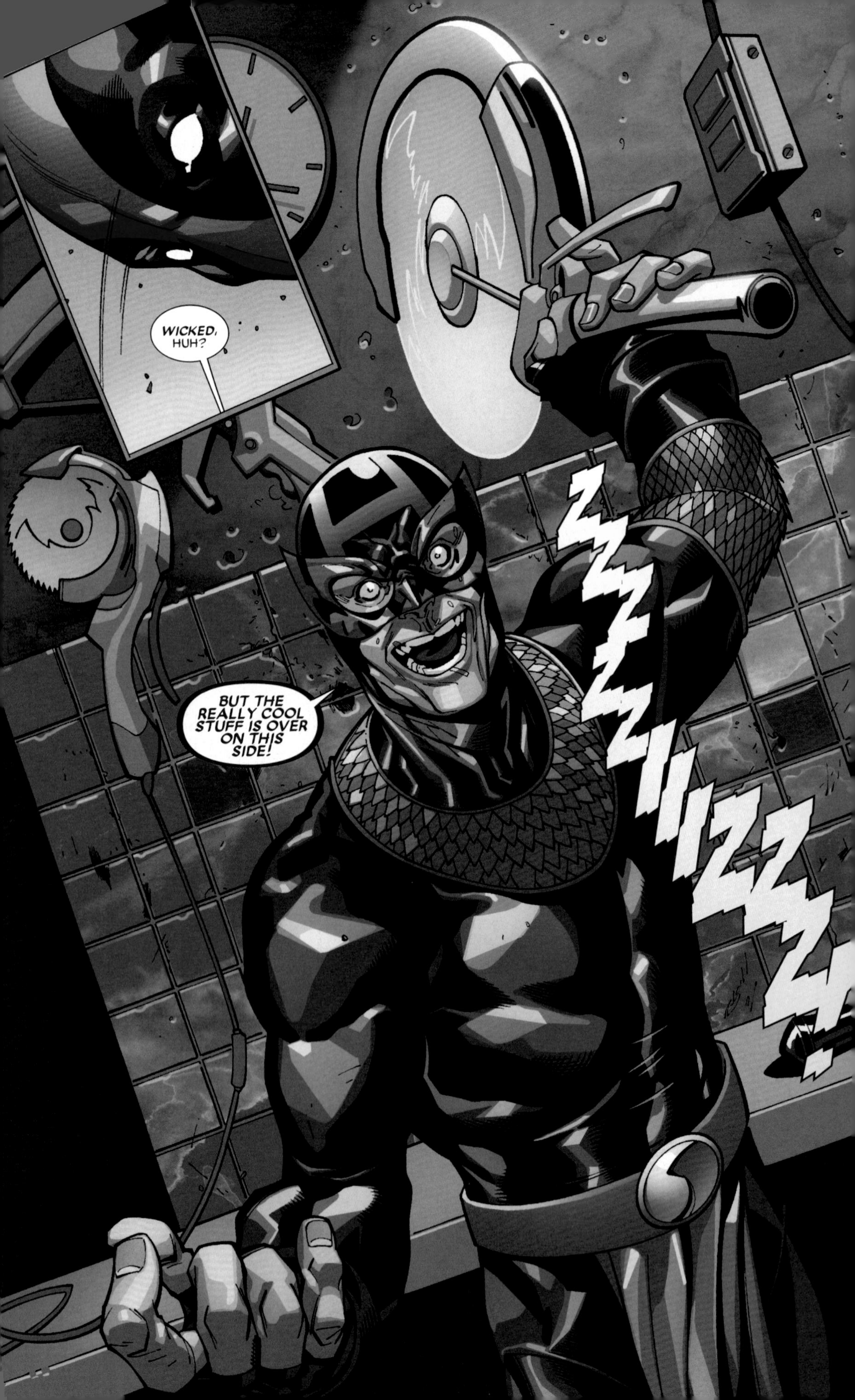
WICKED, HUH?
BUT THE REALLY COOL STUFF IS OVER ON THIS SIDE!
ZZZZIIIZZZZ

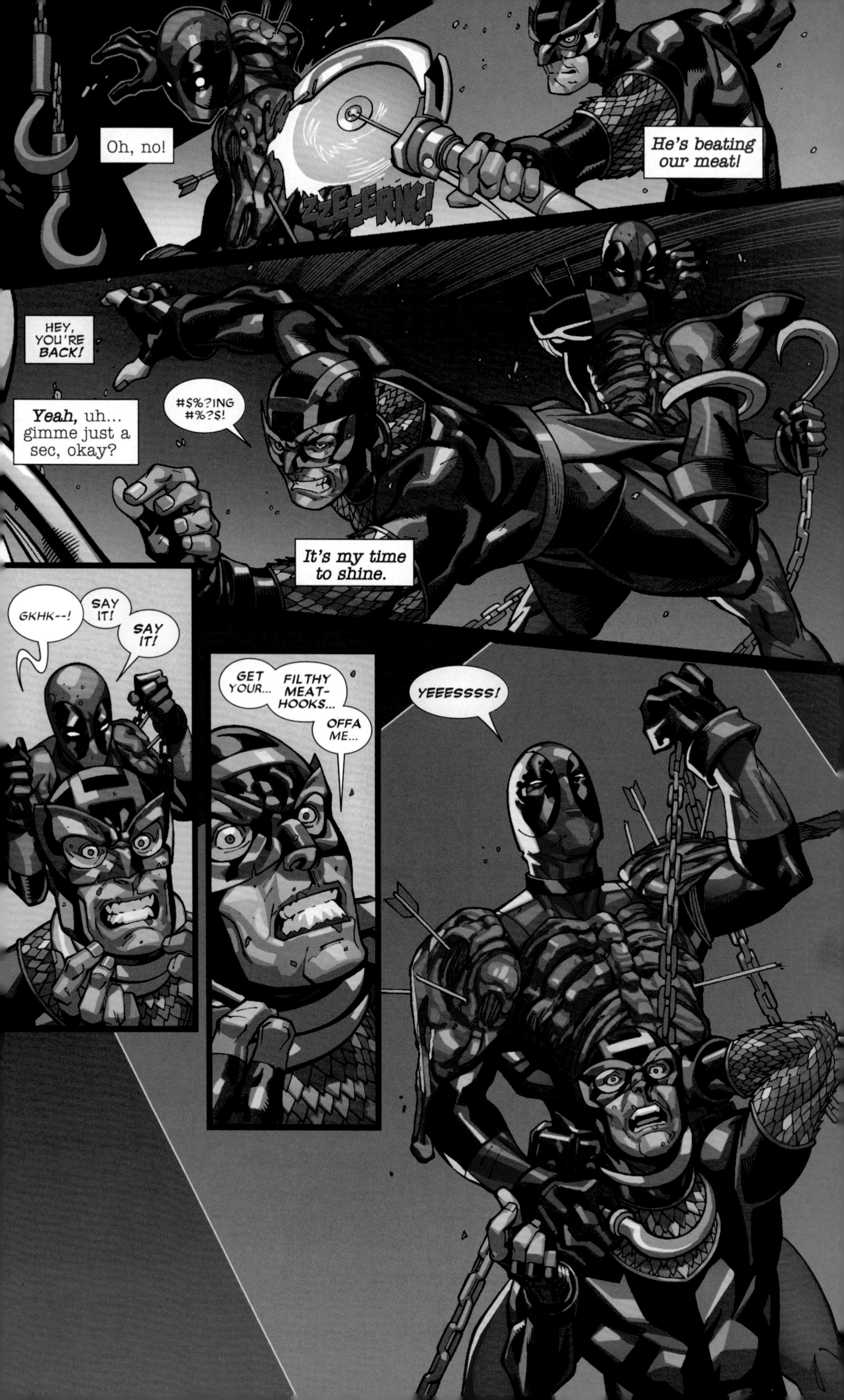

Oh, no!
He's beating our meat!
ZZEEEERING!
HEY, YOU'RE BACK!
Yeah, uh... gimme just a sec, okay?
#$%?ING #%?$!
It's my time to shine.
GKHK--!
SAY IT!
SAY IT!
GET YOUR...
FILTHY MEAT-HOOKS...
OFFA ME...
YEEESSSS!

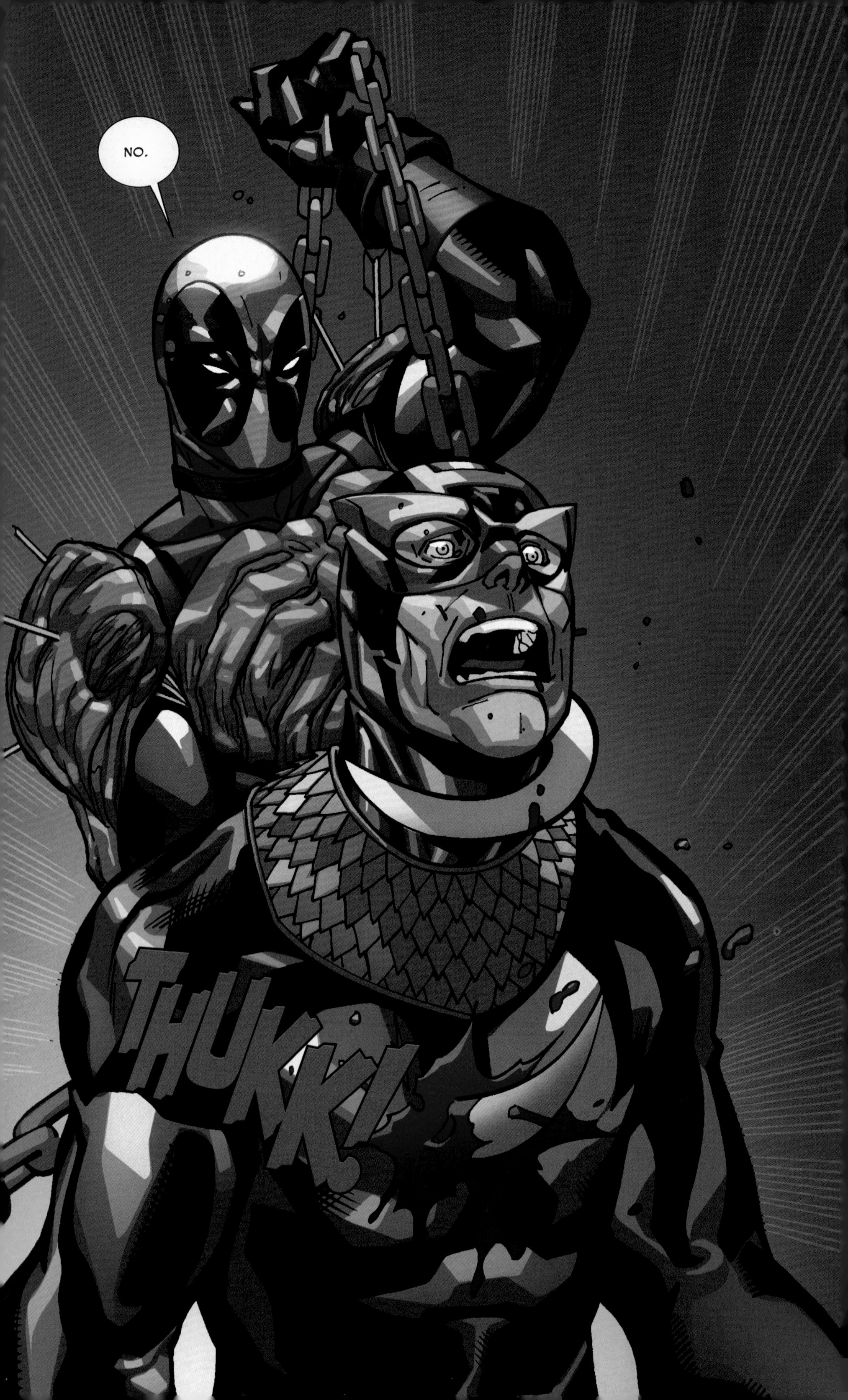
NO.
THUKK!

12

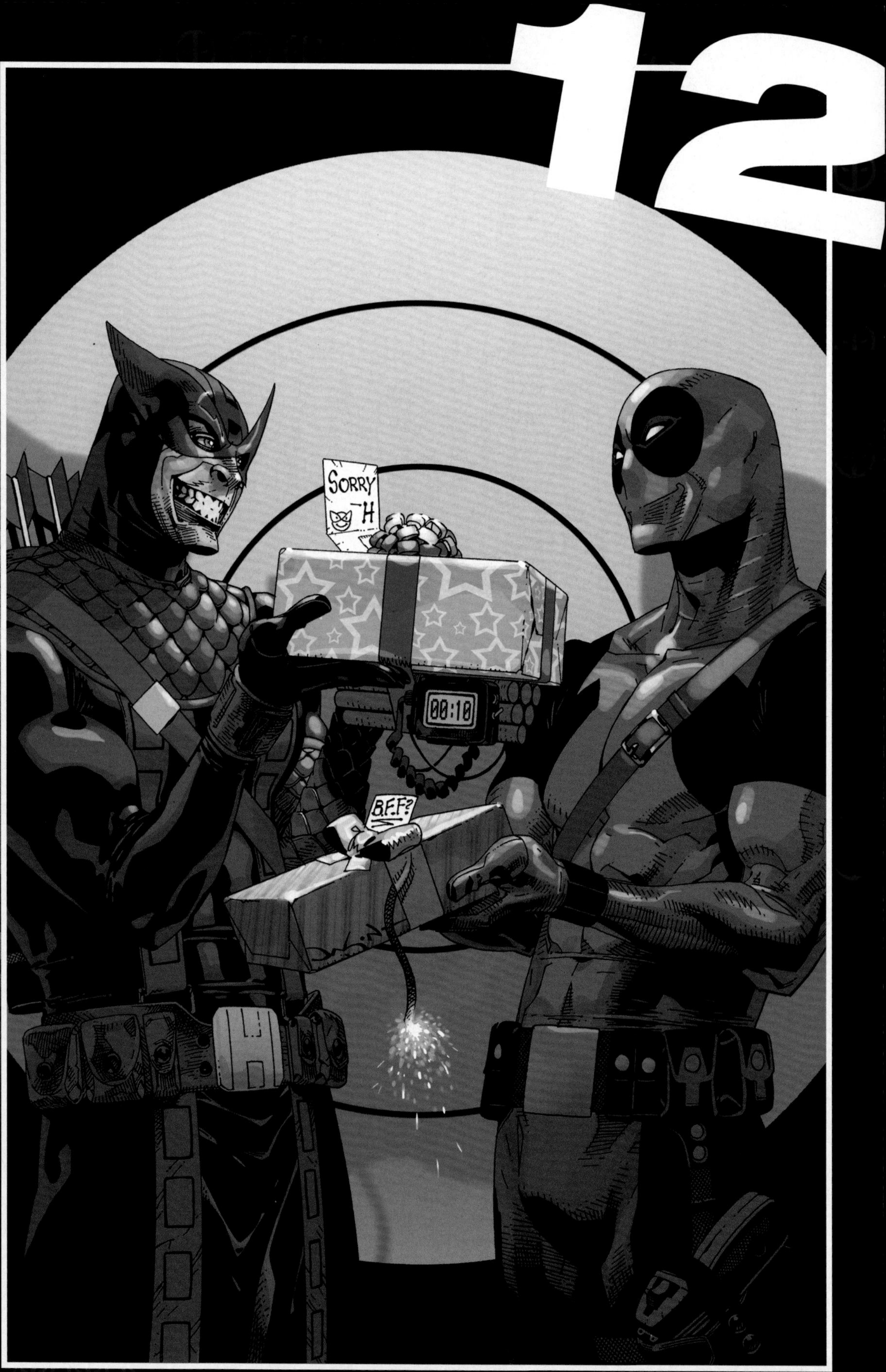
SORRY
-H
00:10
B.F.F.?

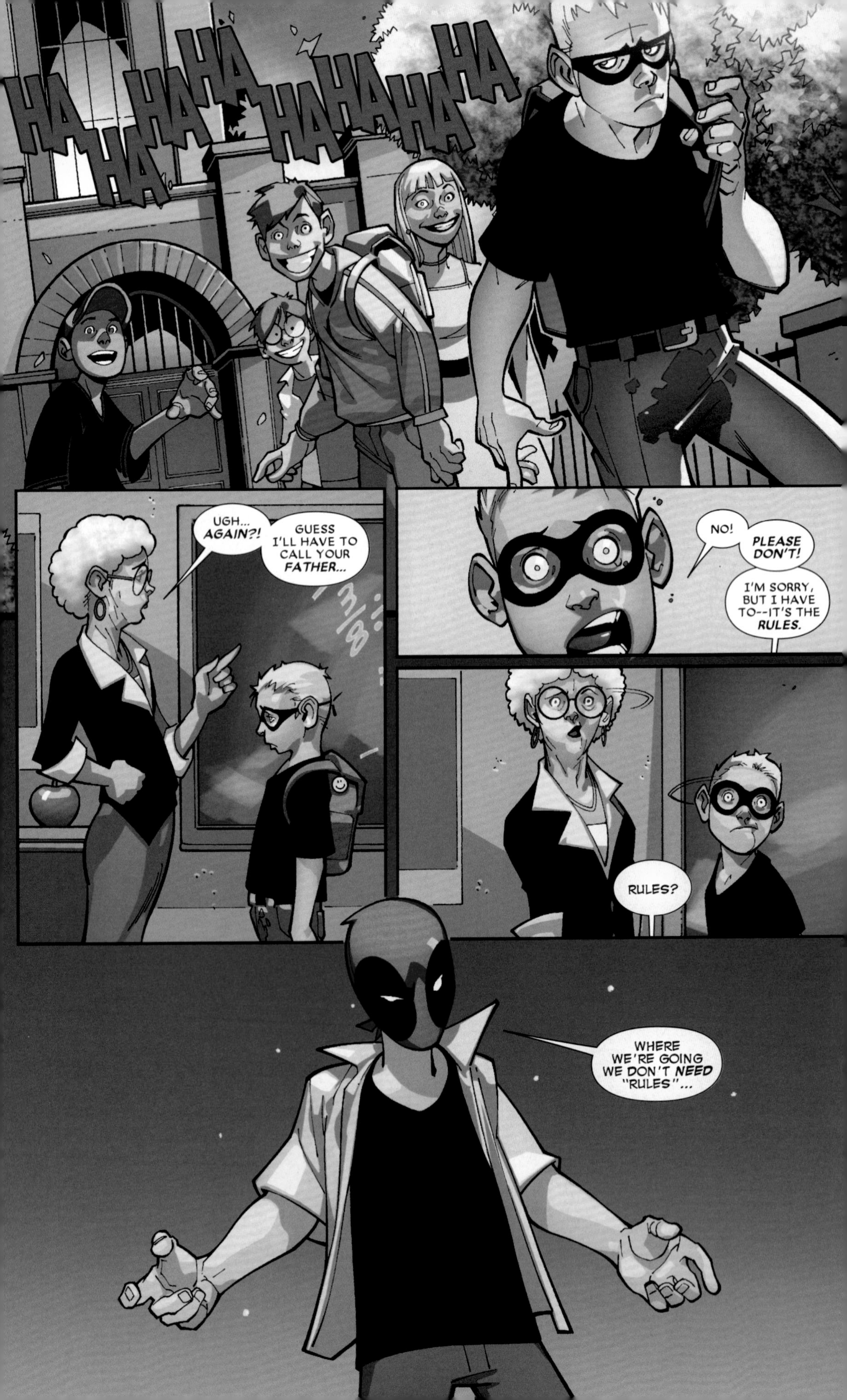
HA HA HA HA HA HA HA HA HA HA HA HA
UGH... AGAIN?!
GUESS I'LL HAVE TO CALL YOUR FATHER...
NO! PLEASE DON'T!
I'M SORRY, BUT I HAVE TO--IT'S THE RULES.
RULES?
WHERE WE'RE GOING WE DON'T NEED "RULES"...

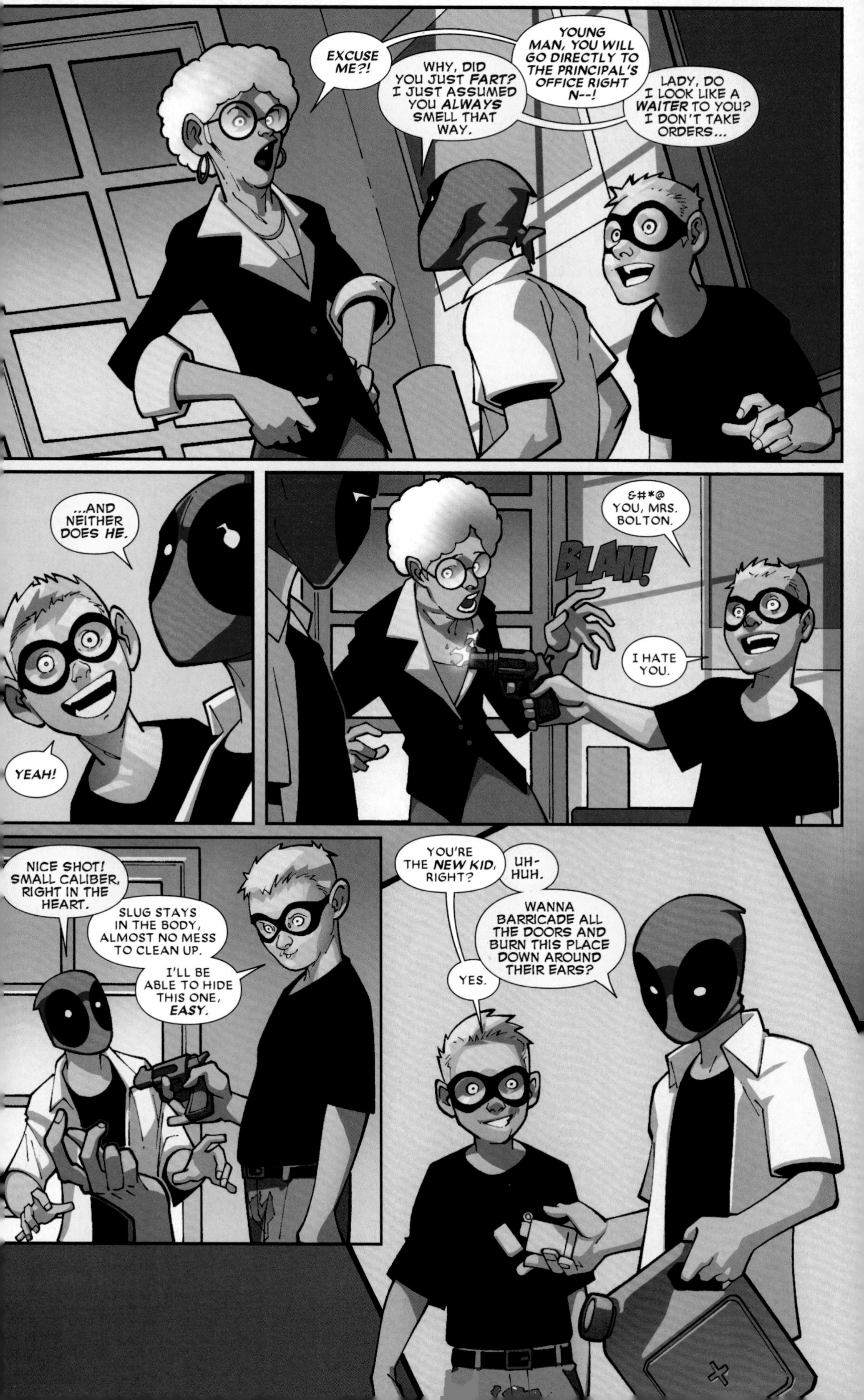

EXCUSE ME?!
WHY, DID YOU JUST FART? I JUST ASSUMED YOU ALWAYS SMELL THAT WAY.
YOUNG MAN, YOU WILL GO DIRECTLY TO THE PRINCIPAL'S OFFICE RIGHT N--!
LADY, DO I LOOK LIKE A WAITER TO YOU? I DON'T TAKE ORDERS...
...AND NEITHER DOES HE.
YEAH!
&#*@ YOU, MRS. BOLTON.
BLAM!
I HATE YOU.
NICE SHOT! SMALL CALIBER, RIGHT IN THE HEART.
SLUG STAYS IN THE BODY, ALMOST NO MESS TO CLEAN UP.
I'LL BE ABLE TO HIDE THIS ONE, EASY.
YOU'RE THE NEW KID, RIGHT?
UH-HUH.
WANNA BARRICADE ALL THE DOORS AND BURN THIS PLACE DOWN AROUND THEIR EARS?
YES.

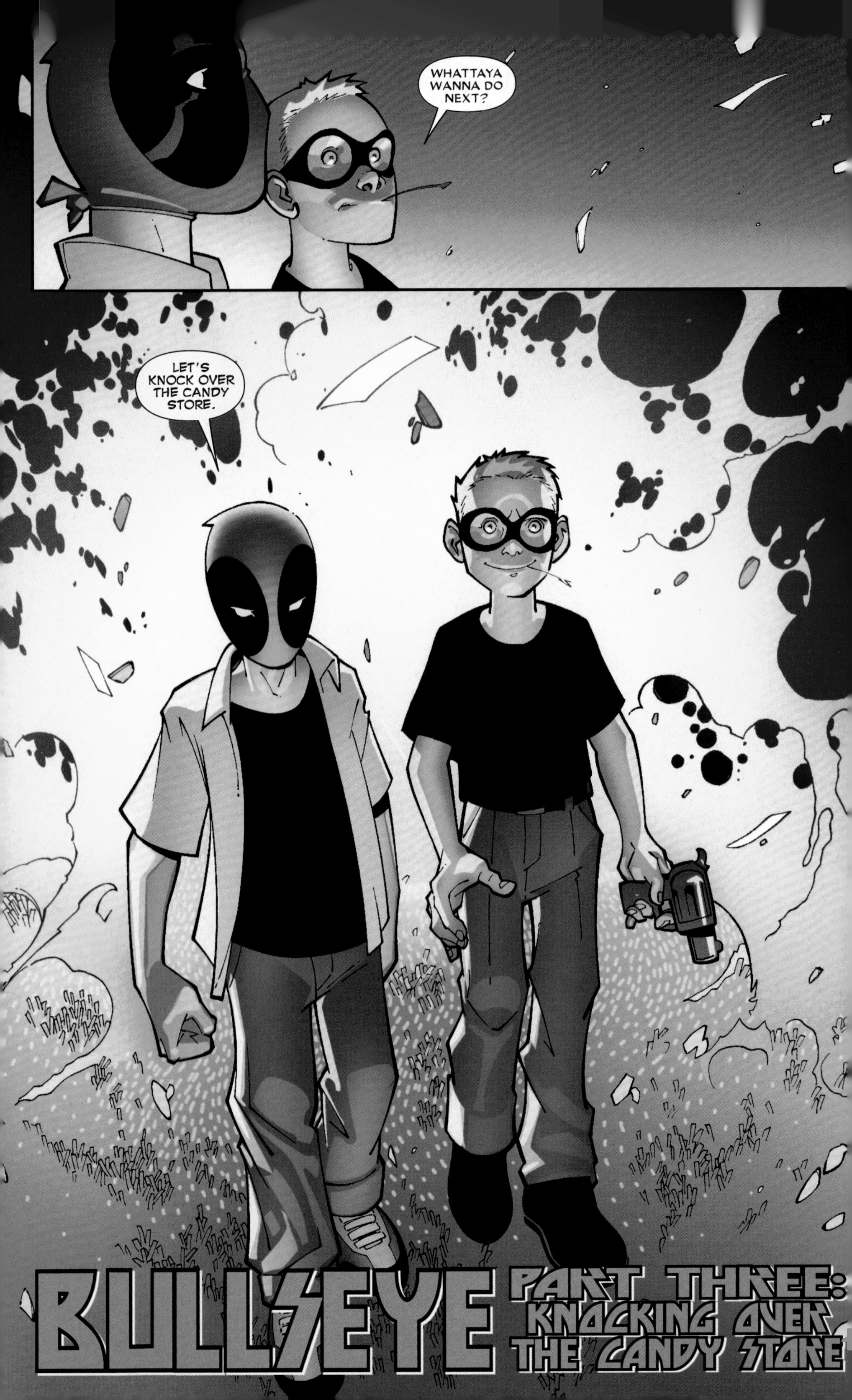
WHATTAYA WANNA DO NEXT?
LET'S KNOCK OVER THE CANDY STORE.
BULLSEYE
PART THREE: KNOCKING OVER THE CANDY STORE

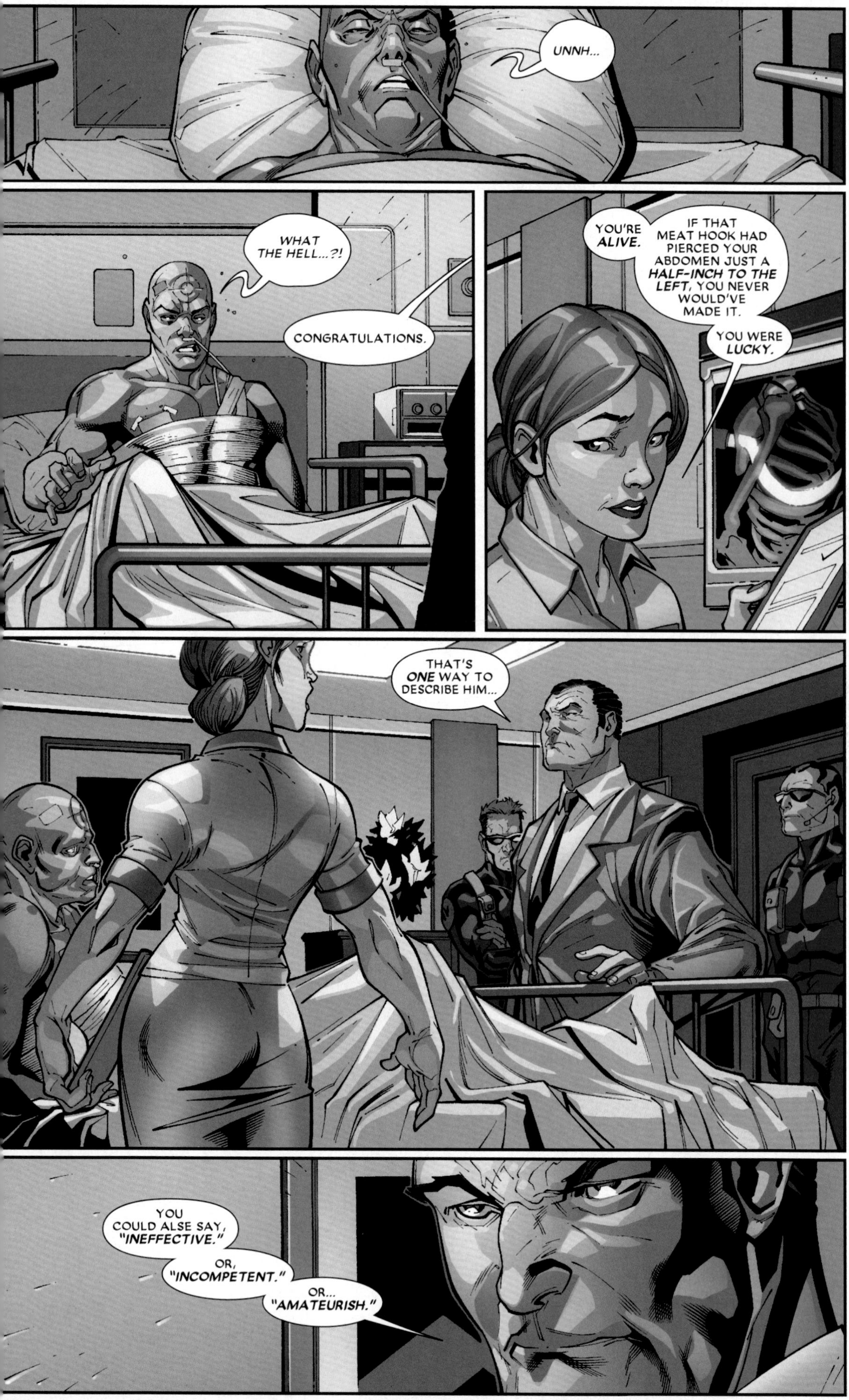
UNNH...
WHAT THE HELL...?!
CONGRATULATIONS.
YOU'RE ALIVE.
IF THAT MEAT HOOK HAD PIERCED YOUR ABDOMEN JUST A HALF-INCH TO THE LEFT, YOU NEVER WOULD'VE MADE IT.
YOU WERE LUCKY.
THAT'S ONE WAY TO DESCRIBE HIM...
YOU COULD ALSE SAY, "INEFFECTIVE."
OR, "INCOMPETENT."
OR... "AMATEURISH."

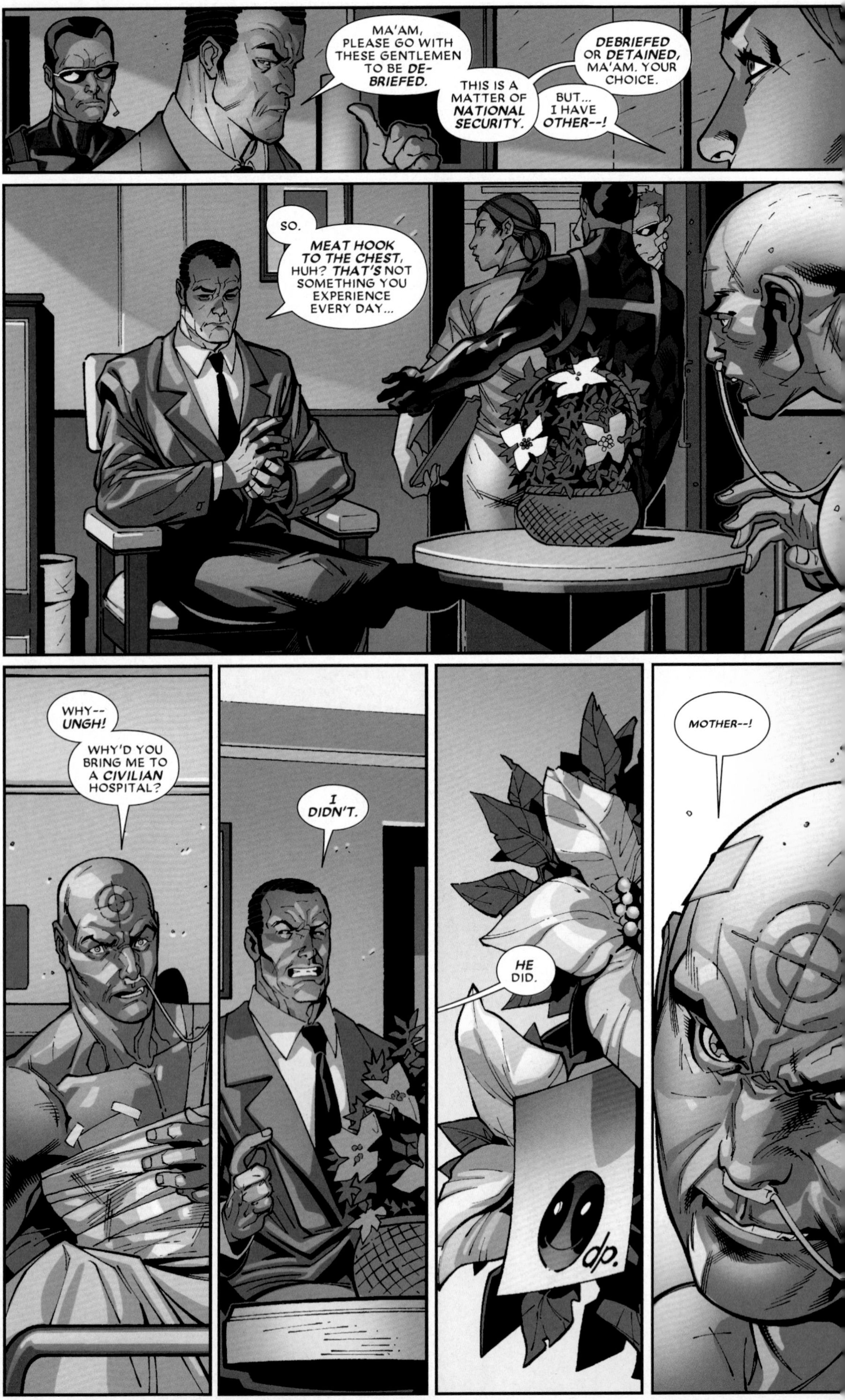
MA'AM, PLEASE GO WITH THESE GENTLEMEN TO BE DE-BRIEFED.
THIS IS A MATTER OF NATIONAL SECURITY.
DEBRIEFED OR DETAINED, MA'AM. YOUR CHOICE.
BUT... I HAVE OTHER--!
SO.
MEAT HOOK TO THE CHEST, HUH? THAT'S NOT SOMETHING YOU EXPERIENCE EVERY DAY...
WHY-- UNGH!
WHY'D YOU BRING ME TO A CIVILIAN HOSPITAL?
I DIDN'T.
HE DID.
dp.
MOTHER--!

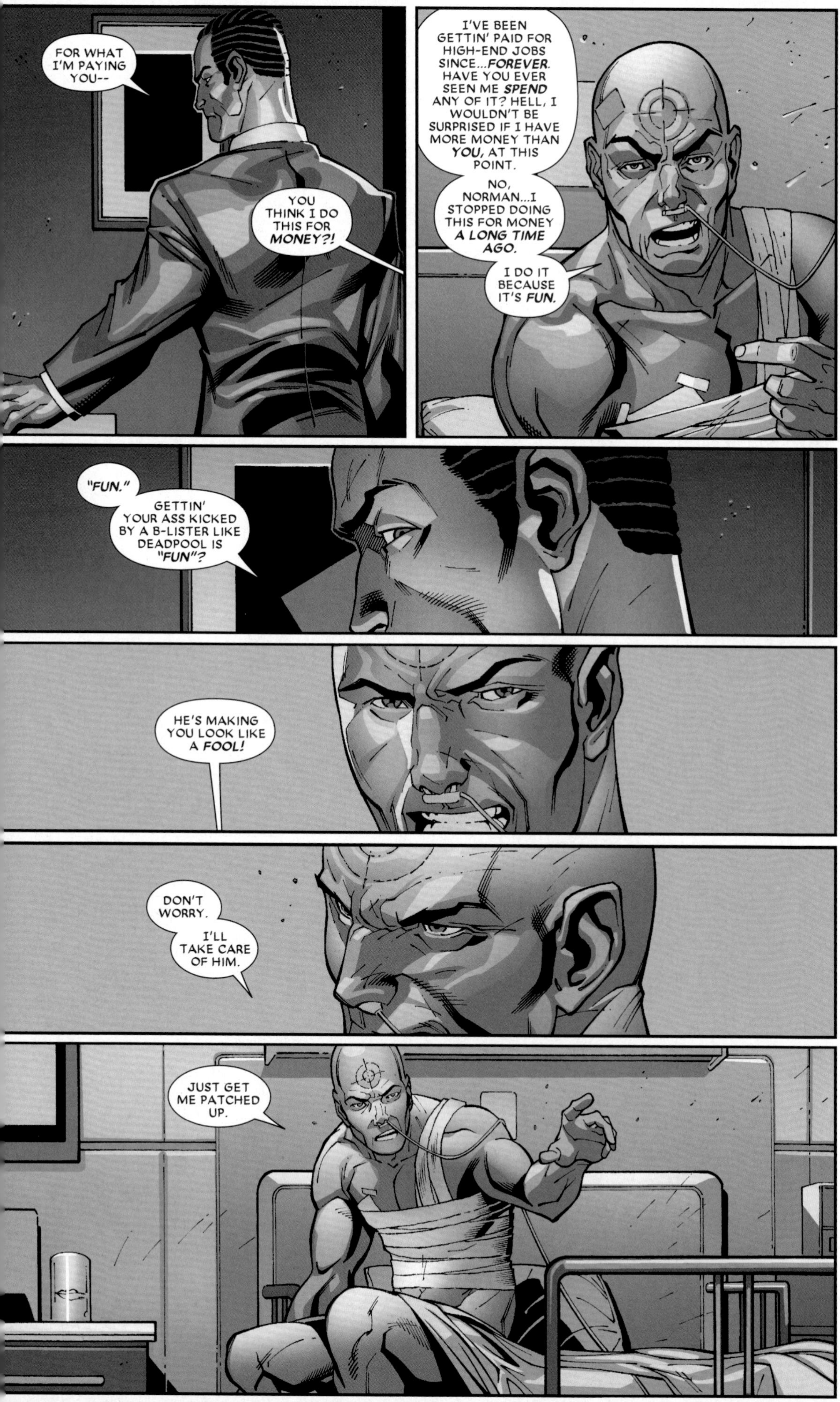
FOR WHAT I'M PAYING YOU--
YOU THINK I DO THIS FOR MONEY?!
I'VE BEEN GETTIN' PAID FOR HIGH-END JOBS SINCE...FOREVER. HAVE YOU EVER SEEN ME SPEND ANY OF IT? HELL, I WOULDN'T BE SURPRISED IF I HAVE MORE MONEY THAN YOU, AT THIS POINT.
NO, NORMAN...I STOPPED DOING THIS FOR MONEY A LONG TIME AGO.
I DO IT BECAUSE IT'S FUN.
"FUN."
GETTIN' YOUR ASS KICKED BY A B-LISTER LIKE DEADPOOL IS "FUN"?
HE'S MAKING YOU LOOK LIKE A FOOL!
DON'T WORRY.
I'LL TAKE CARE OF HIM.
JUST GET ME PATCHED UP.

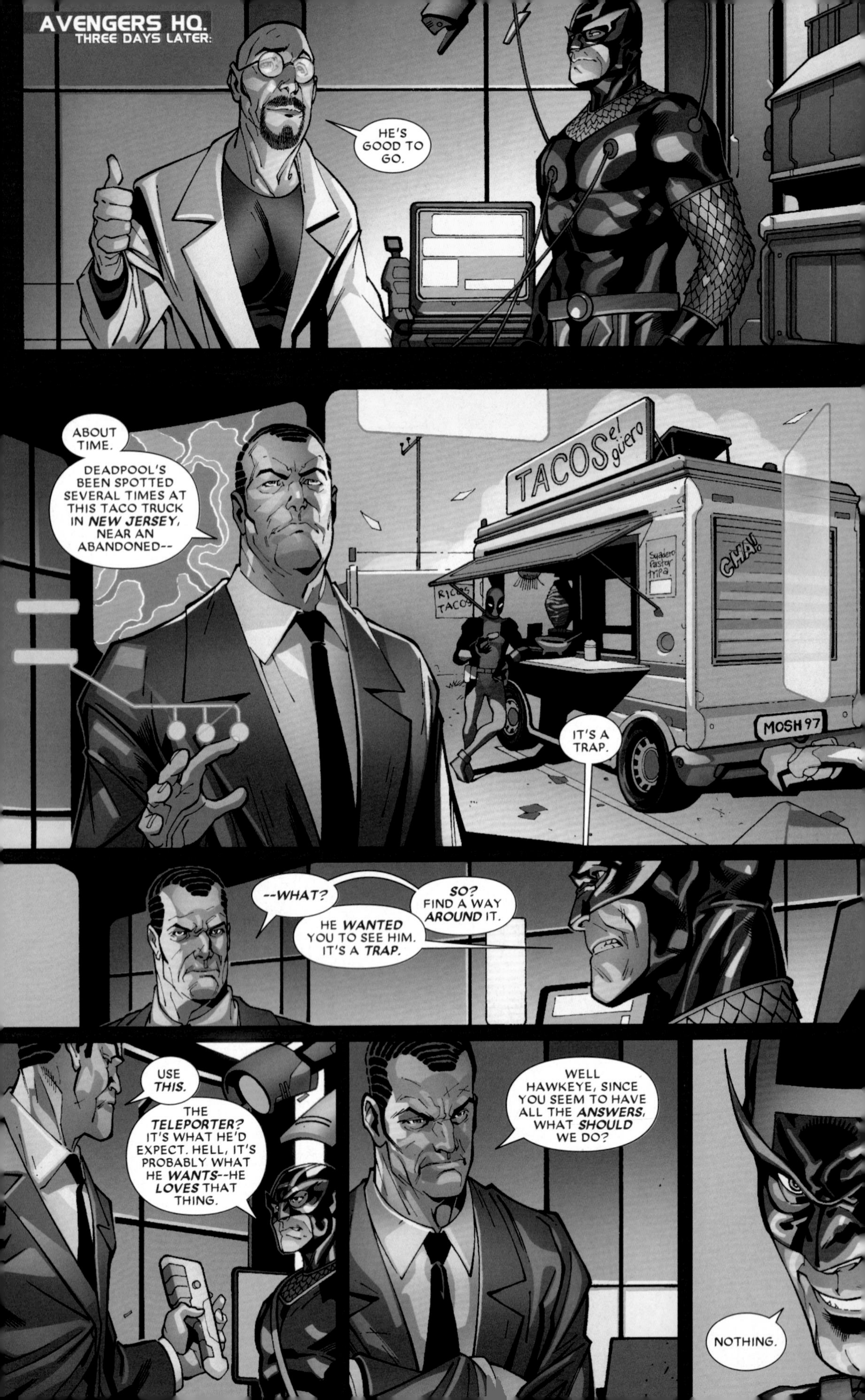
AVENGERS HQ.
THREE DAYS LATER:
HE'S GOOD TO GO.
ABOUT TIME.
DEADPOOL'S BEEN SPOTTED SEVERAL TIMES AT THIS TACO TRUCK IN NEW JERSEY, NEAR AN ABANDONED--
TACOS el guero
RICOS TACOS
CHA!
MOSH 97
IT'S A TRAP.
--WHAT?
SO? FIND A WAY AROUND IT.
HE WANTED YOU TO SEE HIM. IT'S A TRAP.
USE THIS.
THE TELEPORTER? IT'S WHAT HE'D EXPECT. HELL, IT'S PROBABLY WHAT HE WANTS--HE LOVES THAT THING.
WELL HAWKEYE, SINCE YOU SEEM TO HAVE ALL THE ANSWERS, WHAT SHOULD WE DO?
NOTHING.

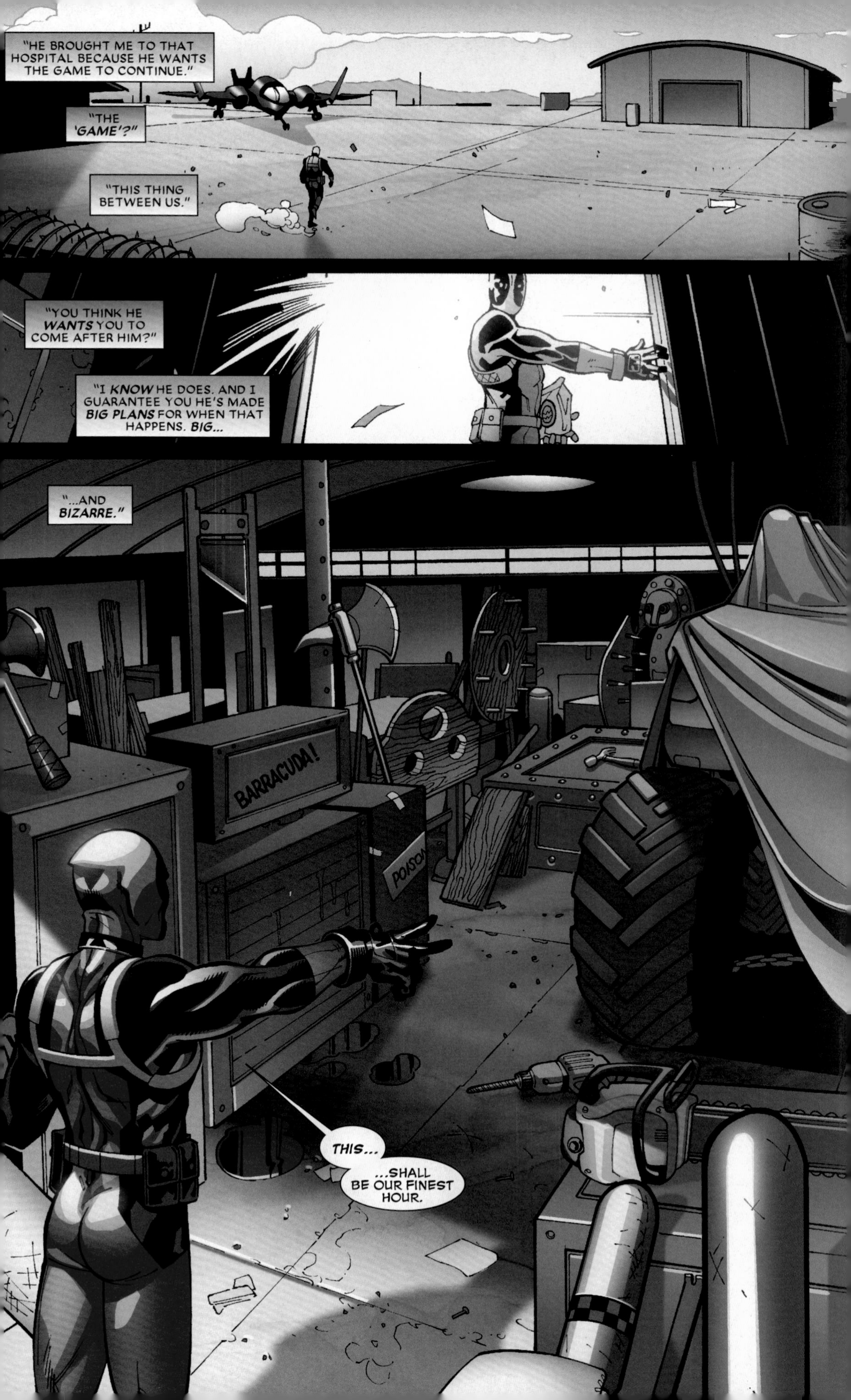

"HE BROUGHT ME TO THAT HOSPITAL BECAUSE HE WANTS THE GAME TO CONTINUE."
"THE 'GAME'?"
"THIS THING BETWEEN US."
"YOU THINK HE WANTS YOU TO COME AFTER HIM?"
"I KNOW HE DOES. AND I GUARANTEE YOU HE'S MADE BIG PLANS FOR WHEN THAT HAPPENS. BIG...
"...AND BIZARRE."
BARRACUDA!
POISON
THIS...
...SHALL BE OUR FINEST HOUR.

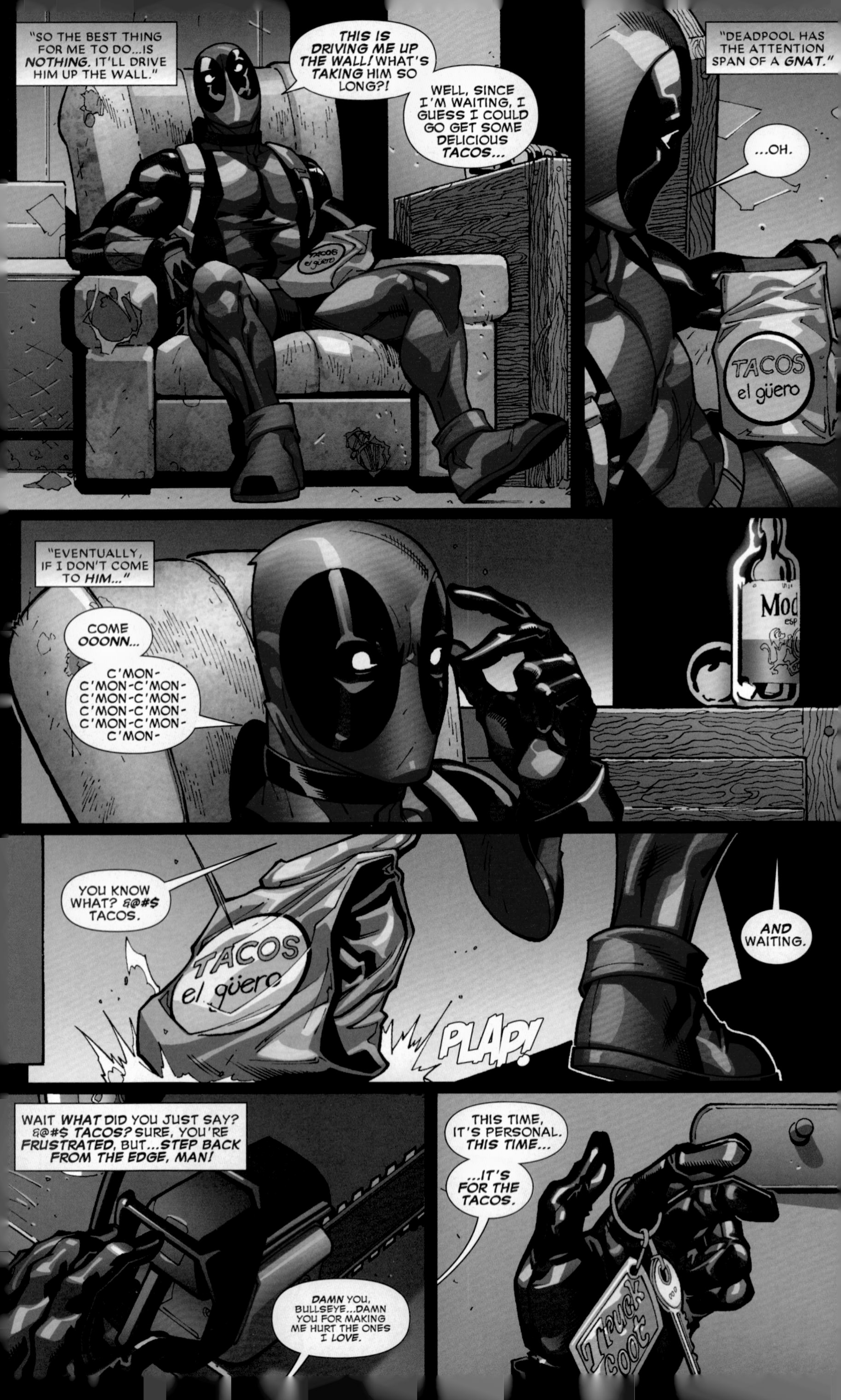
"SO THE BEST THING FOR ME TO DO...IS NOTHING. IT'LL DRIVE HIM UP THE WALL."
THIS IS DRIVING ME UP THE WALL! WHAT'S TAKING HIM SO LONG?!
WELL, SINCE I'M WAITING, I GUESS I COULD GO GET SOME DELICIOUS TACOS...
TACOS el güero
"DEADPOOL HAS THE ATTENTION SPAN OF A GNAT."
...OH.
TACOS el güero
"EVENTUALLY, IF I DON'T COME TO HIM..."
COME OOONN...
C'MON-C'MON-C'MON-C'MON-C'MON-C'MON-C'MON-C'MON-
YOU KNOW WHAT? &@#$ TACOS.
TACOS el güero
PLAP!
AND WAITING.
WAIT WHAT DID YOU JUST SAY? &@#$ TACOS? SURE, YOU'RE FRUSTRATED, BUT...STEP BACK FROM THE EDGE, MAN!
DAMN YOU, BULLSEYE...DAMN YOU FOR MAKING ME HURT THE ONES I LOVE.
THIS TIME, IT'S PERSONAL. THIS TIME...
...IT'S FOR THE TACOS.

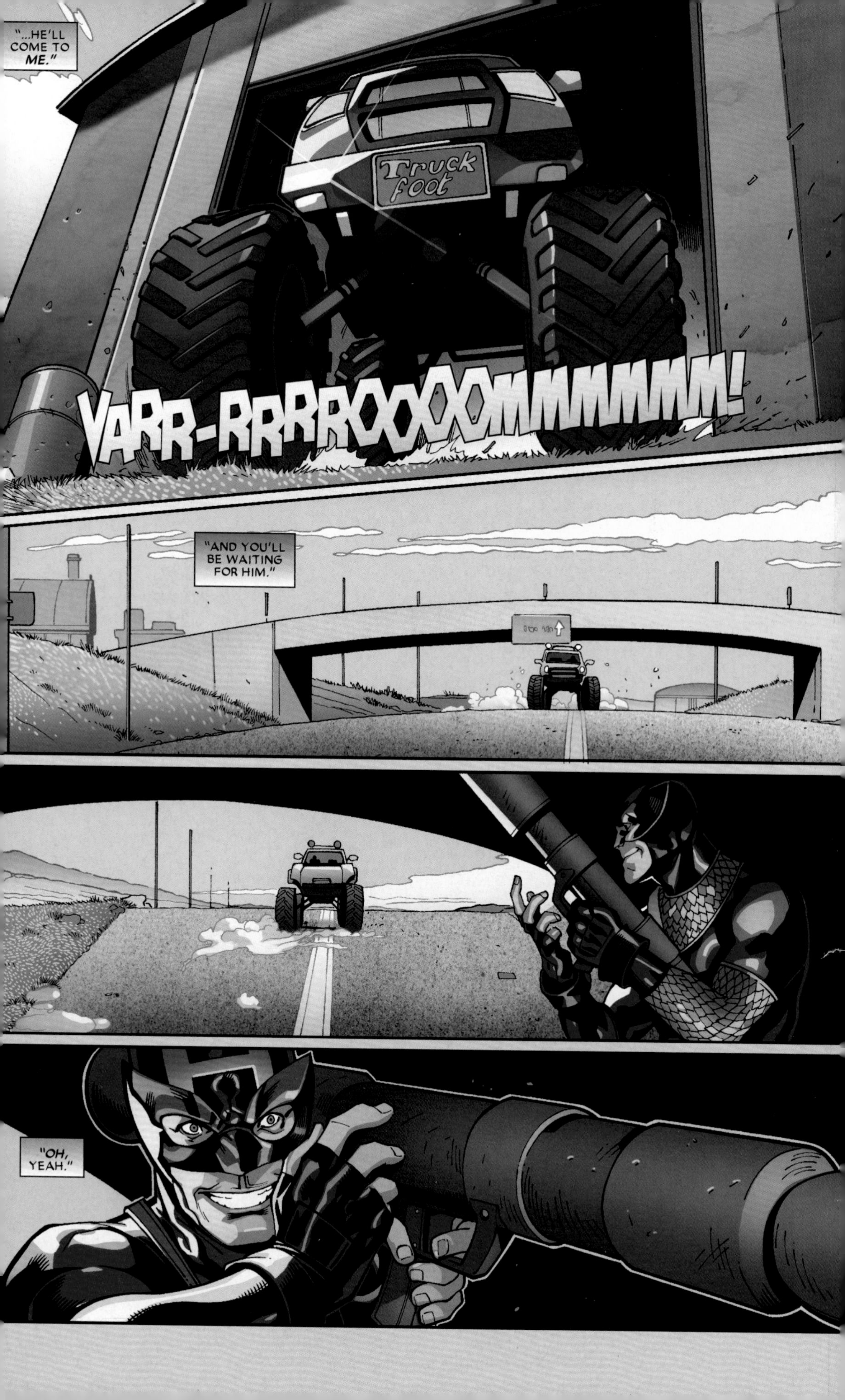
"...HE'LL COME TO ME."
Truck foot
VARR-RRRROOOOMMMMMMM!
"AND YOU'LL BE WAITING FOR HIM."
"OH, YEAH."

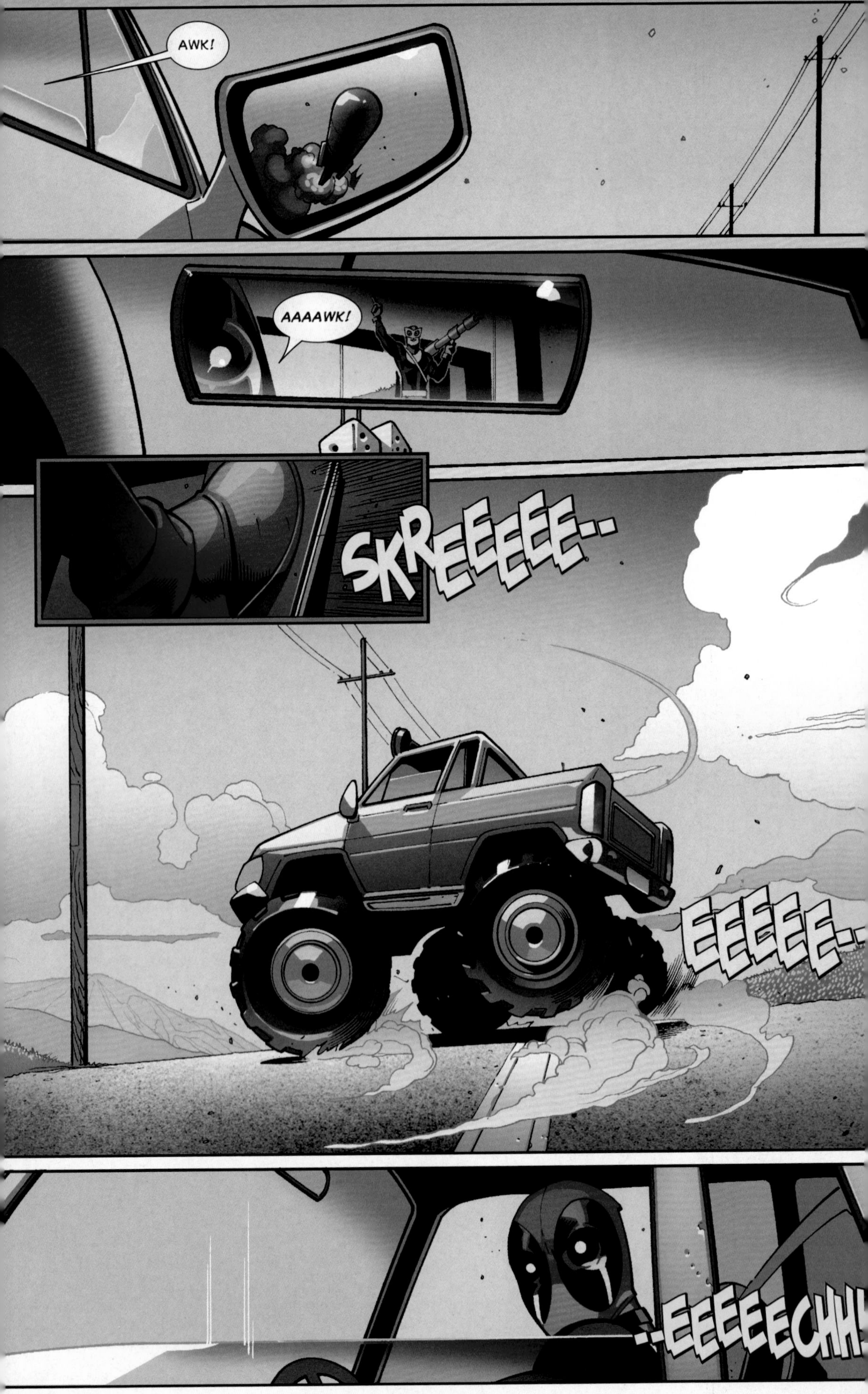
AWK!
AAAAWK!
SKREEEEEE..
EEEEEE..
..EEEEECHH!

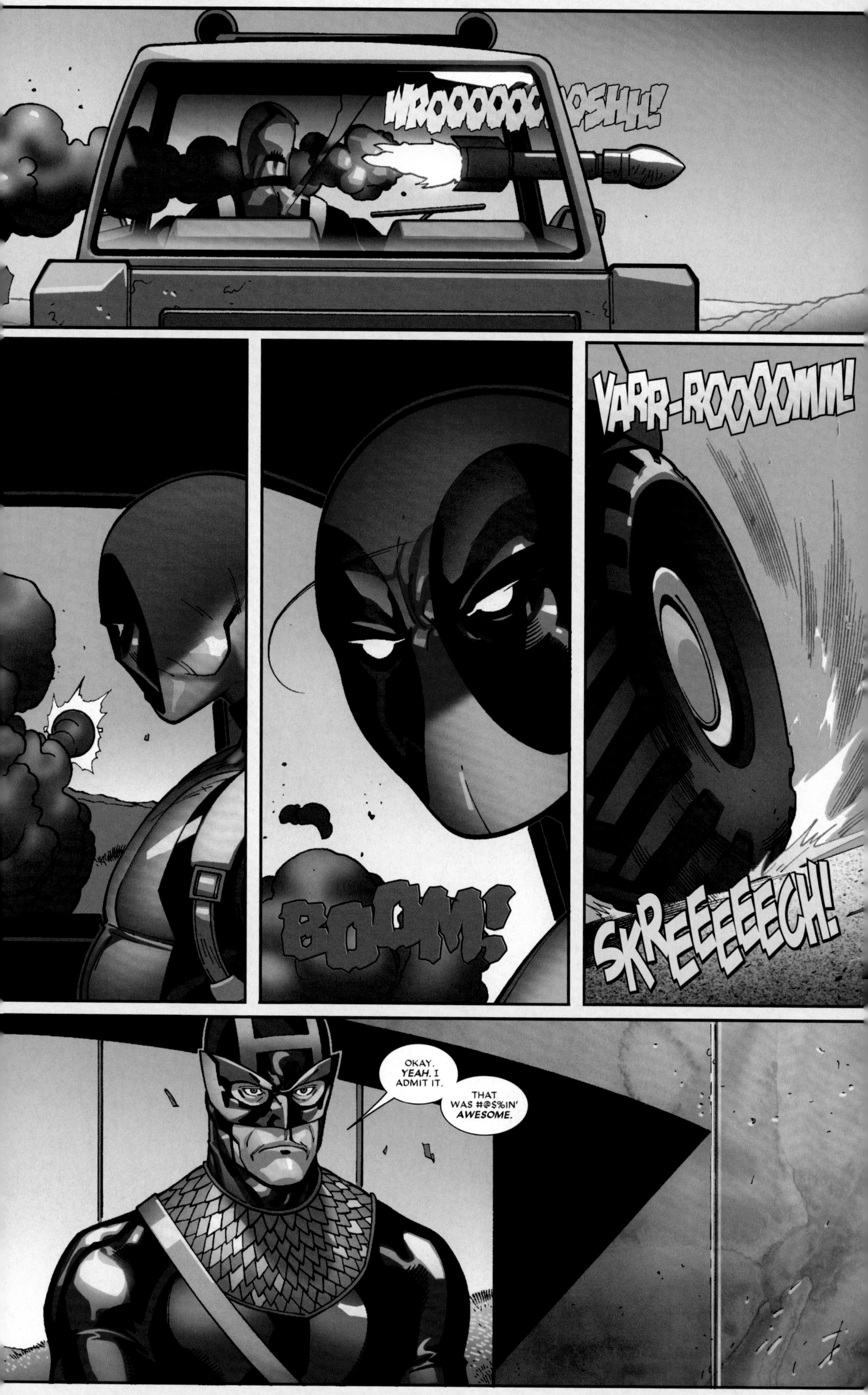
VARR-ROOOOMM!
BOOM!
SKREEEEEECH!
OKAY. *YEAH.* I ADMIT IT.
THAT WAS #@$%IN' ***AWESOME.***

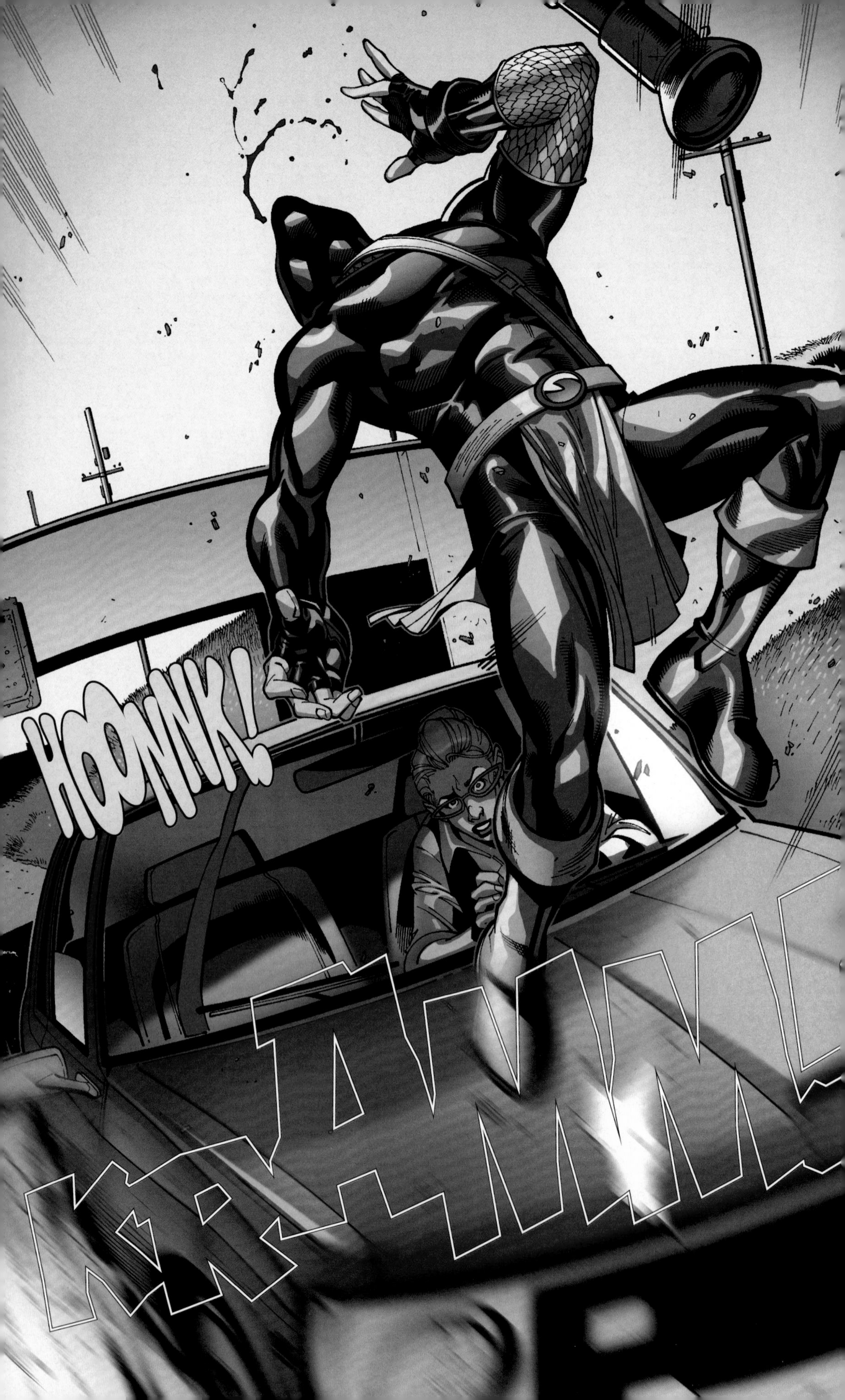
HOONNK!
KRAMMM

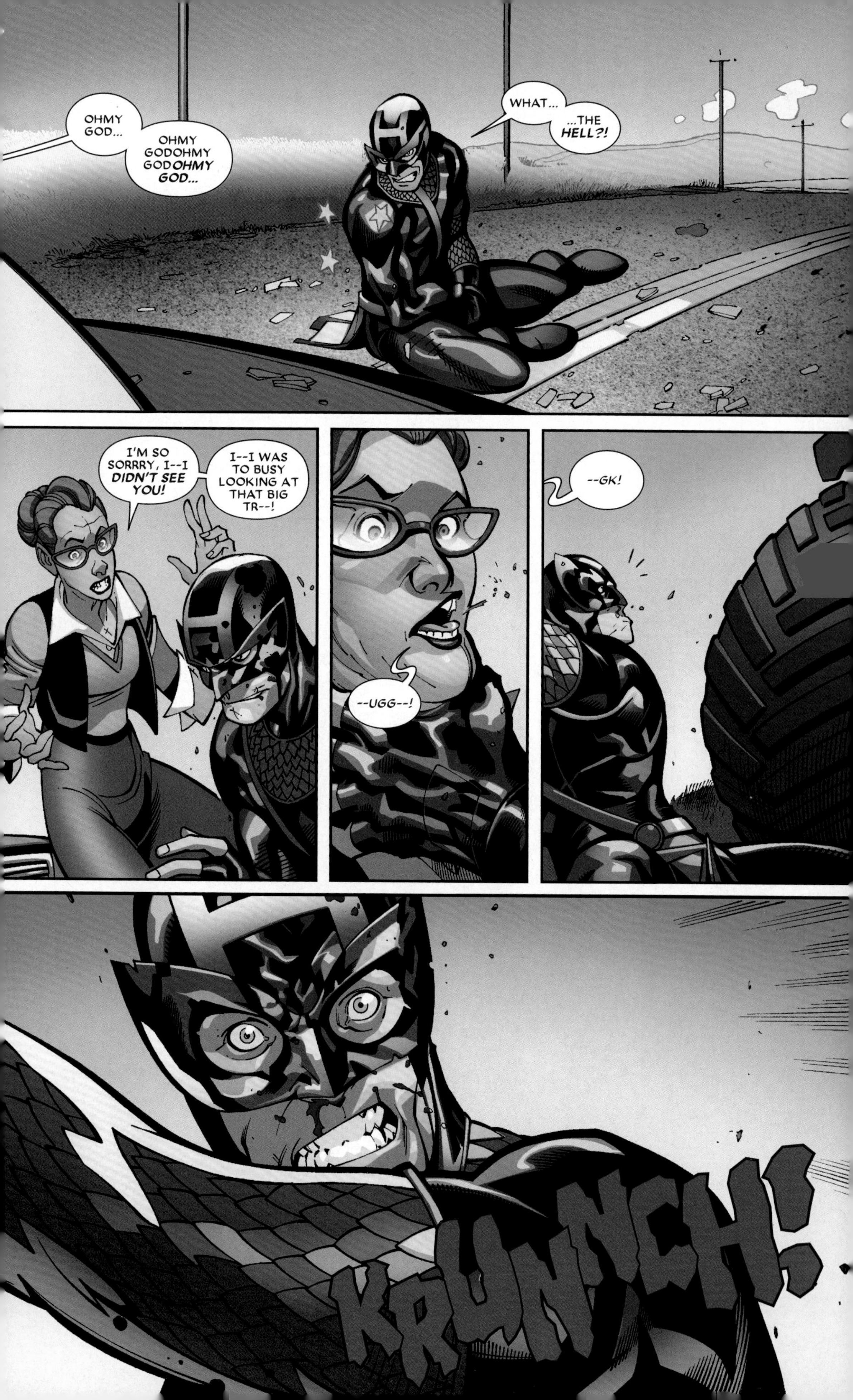
OHMY GOD...
OHMY GODOHMY GOD**OHMY GOD...**
WHAT...
...THE **HELL?!**
I'M SO SORRRY, I--I **DIDN'T SEE YOU!**
I--I WAS TO BUSY LOOKING AT THAT BIG TR--!
--UGG--!
--GK!
KRUNNCH!

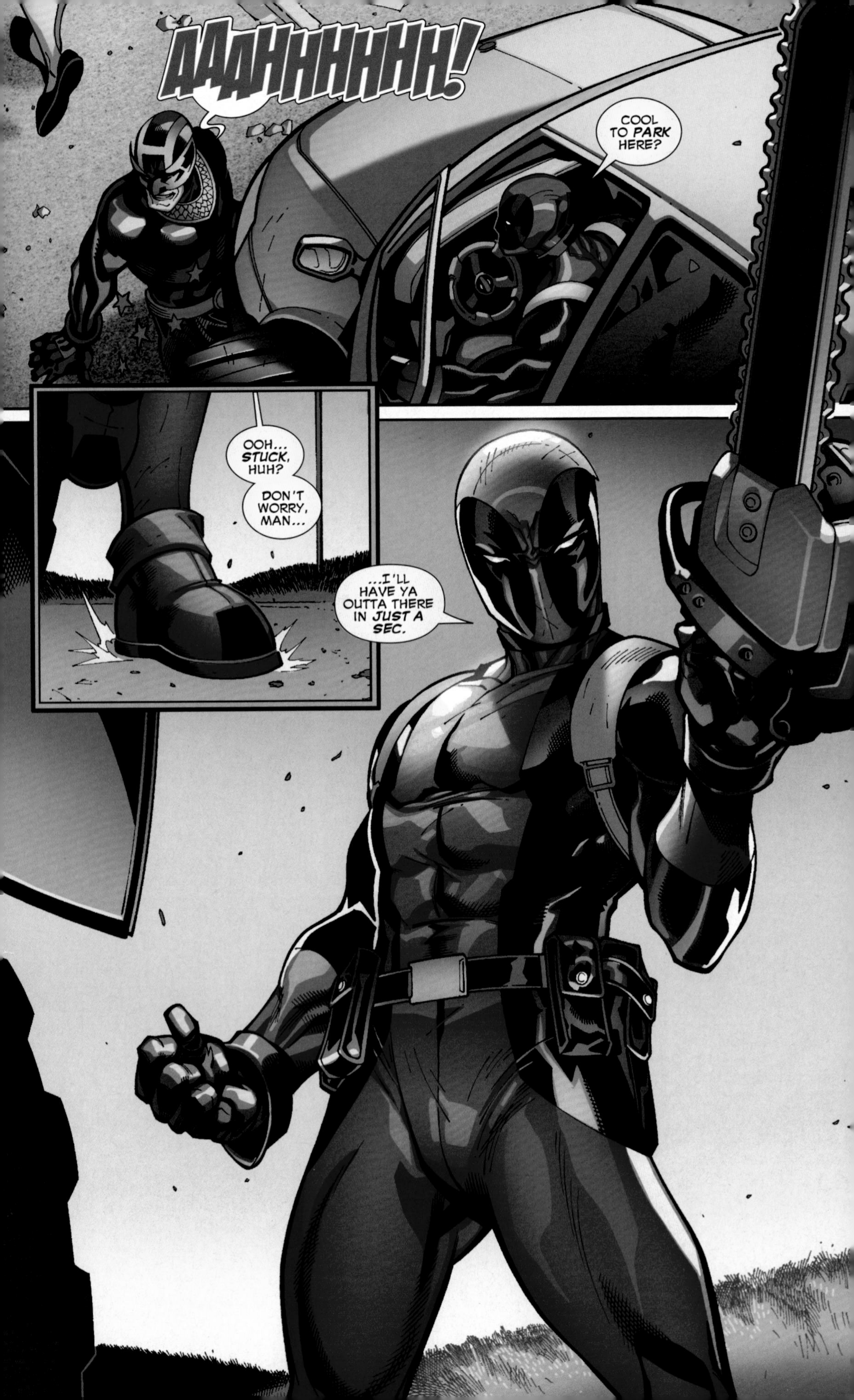
AAAHHHHHH!
COOL TO PARK HERE?
OOH... STUCK, HUH?
DON'T WORRY, MAN...
...I'LL HAVE YA OUTTA THERE IN JUST A SEC.

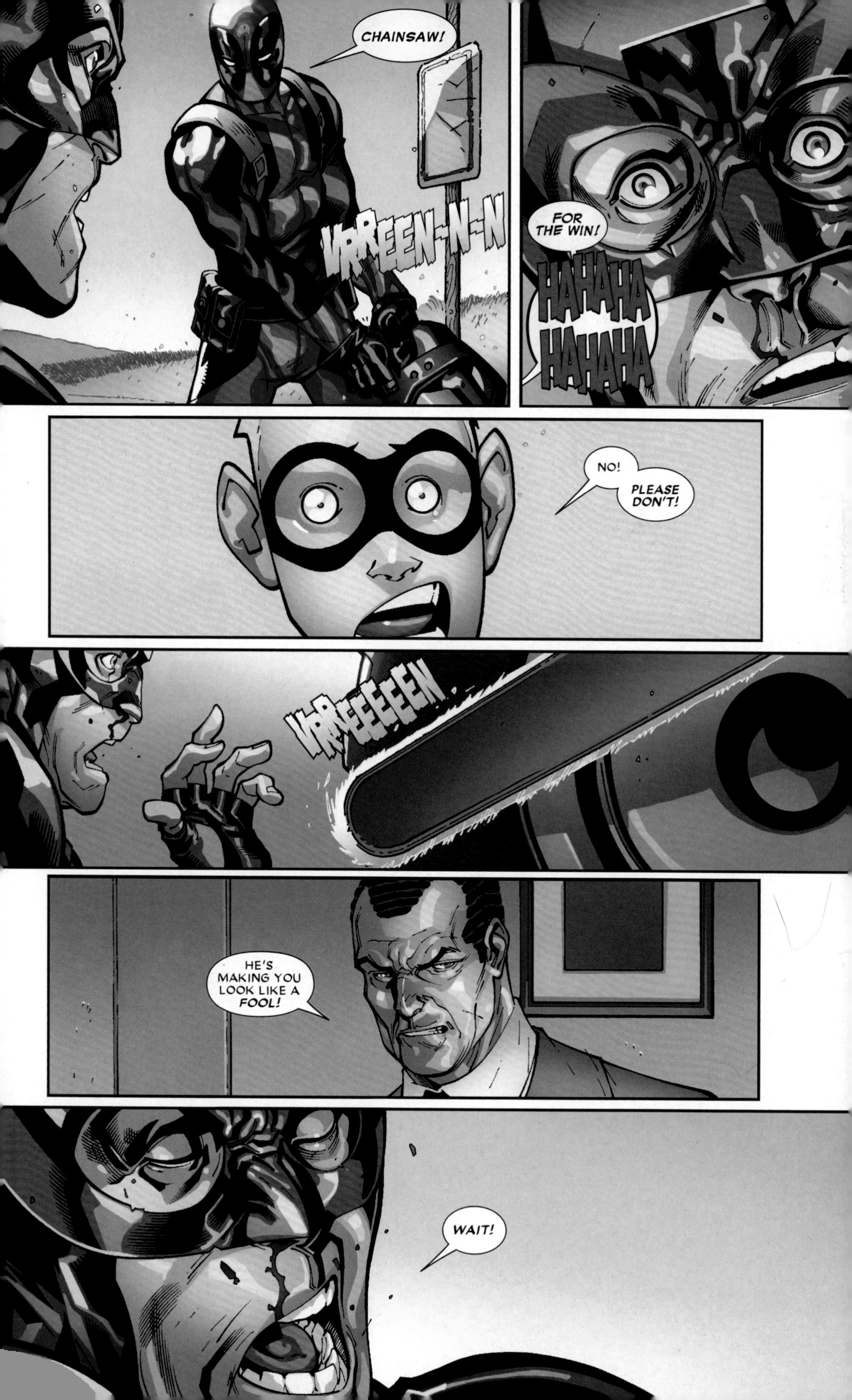
CHAINSAW!
VRREEN-N-N
FOR THE WIN!
HAHAHA HAHAHA
NO!
PLEASE DON'T!
VRREEEEEN
HE'S MAKING YOU LOOK LIKE A FOOL!
WAIT!

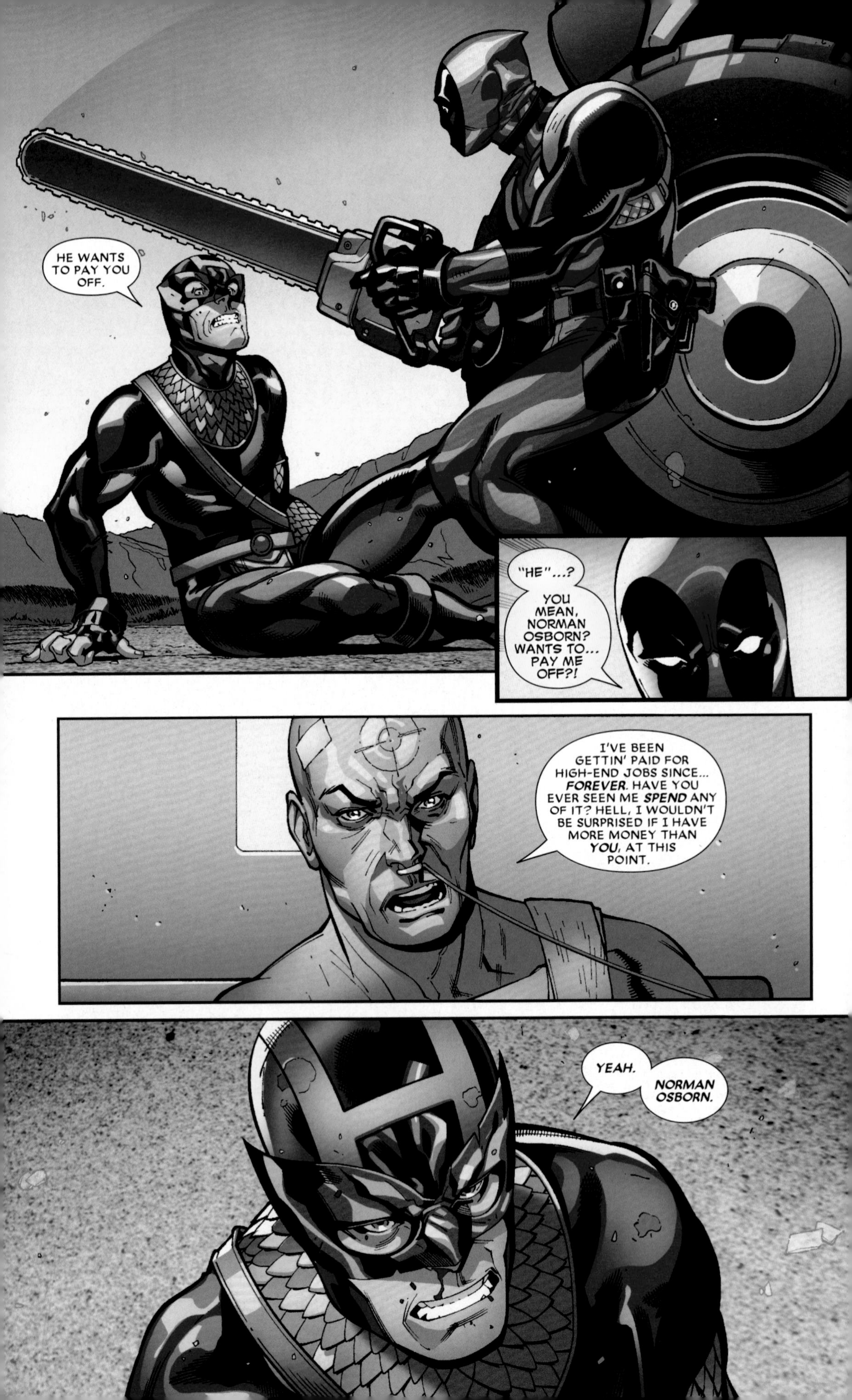
HE WANTS TO PAY YOU OFF.
"HE"...?
YOU MEAN, NORMAN OSBORN? WANTS TO... PAY ME OFF?!
I'VE BEEN GETTIN' PAID FOR HIGH-END JOBS SINCE... FOREVER. HAVE YOU EVER SEEN ME SPEND ANY OF IT? HELL, I WOULDN'T BE SURPRISED IF I HAVE MORE MONEY THAN YOU, AT THIS POINT.
YEAH.
NORMAN OSBORN.

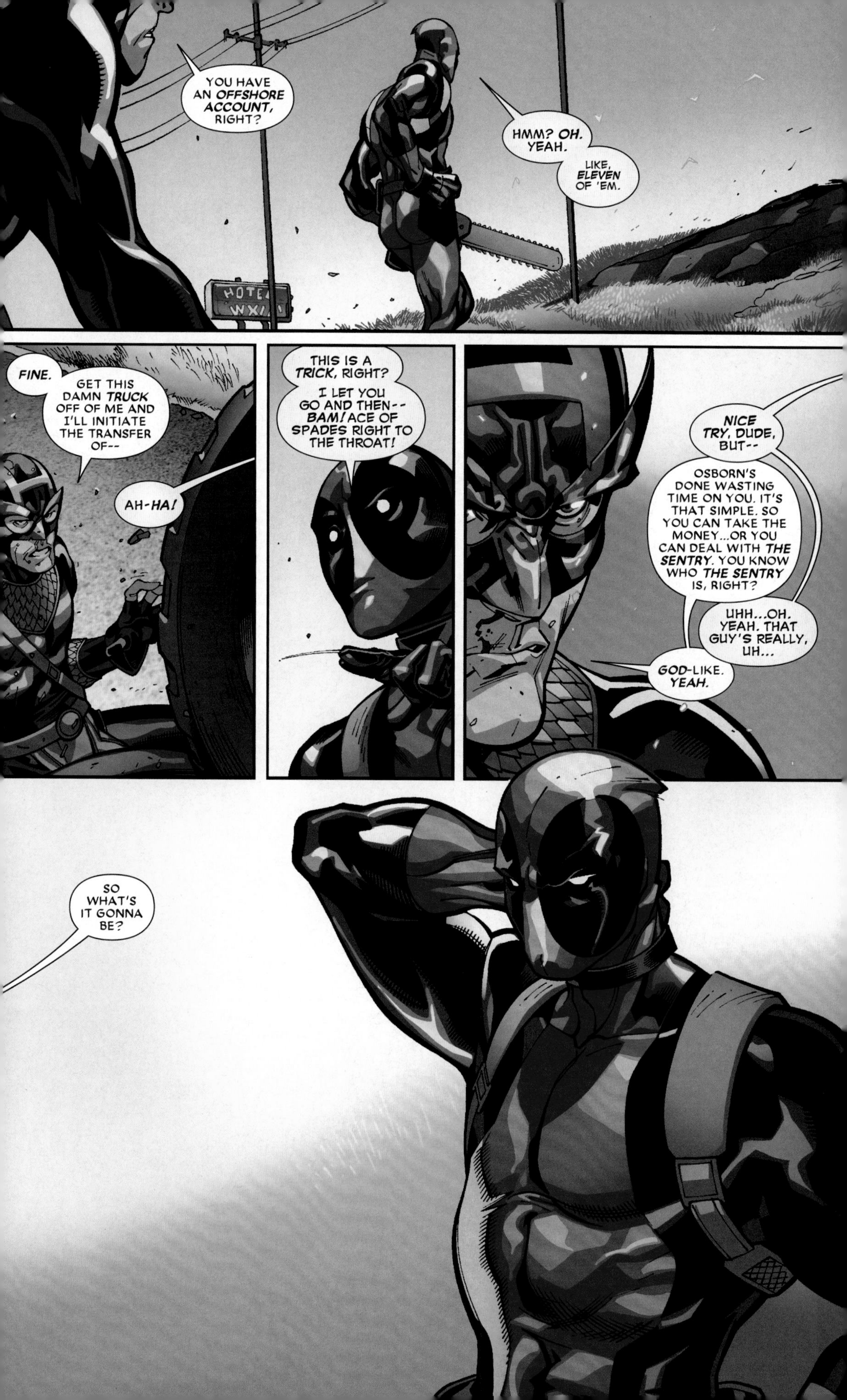
YOU HAVE AN OFFSHORE ACCOUNT, RIGHT?
HMM? OH. YEAH.
LIKE, ELEVEN OF 'EM.
FINE.
GET THIS DAMN TRUCK OFF OF ME AND I'LL INITIATE THE TRANSFER OF--
AH-HA!
THIS IS A TRICK, RIGHT?
I LET YOU GO AND THEN--BAM! ACE OF SPADES RIGHT TO THE THROAT!
NICE TRY, DUDE, BUT--
OSBORN'S DONE WASTING TIME ON YOU. IT'S THAT SIMPLE. SO YOU CAN TAKE THE MONEY...OR YOU CAN DEAL WITH THE SENTRY. YOU KNOW WHO THE SENTRY IS, RIGHT?
UHH...OH. YEAH. THAT GUY'S REALLY, UH...
GOD-LIKE. YEAH.
SO WHAT'S IT GONNA BE?

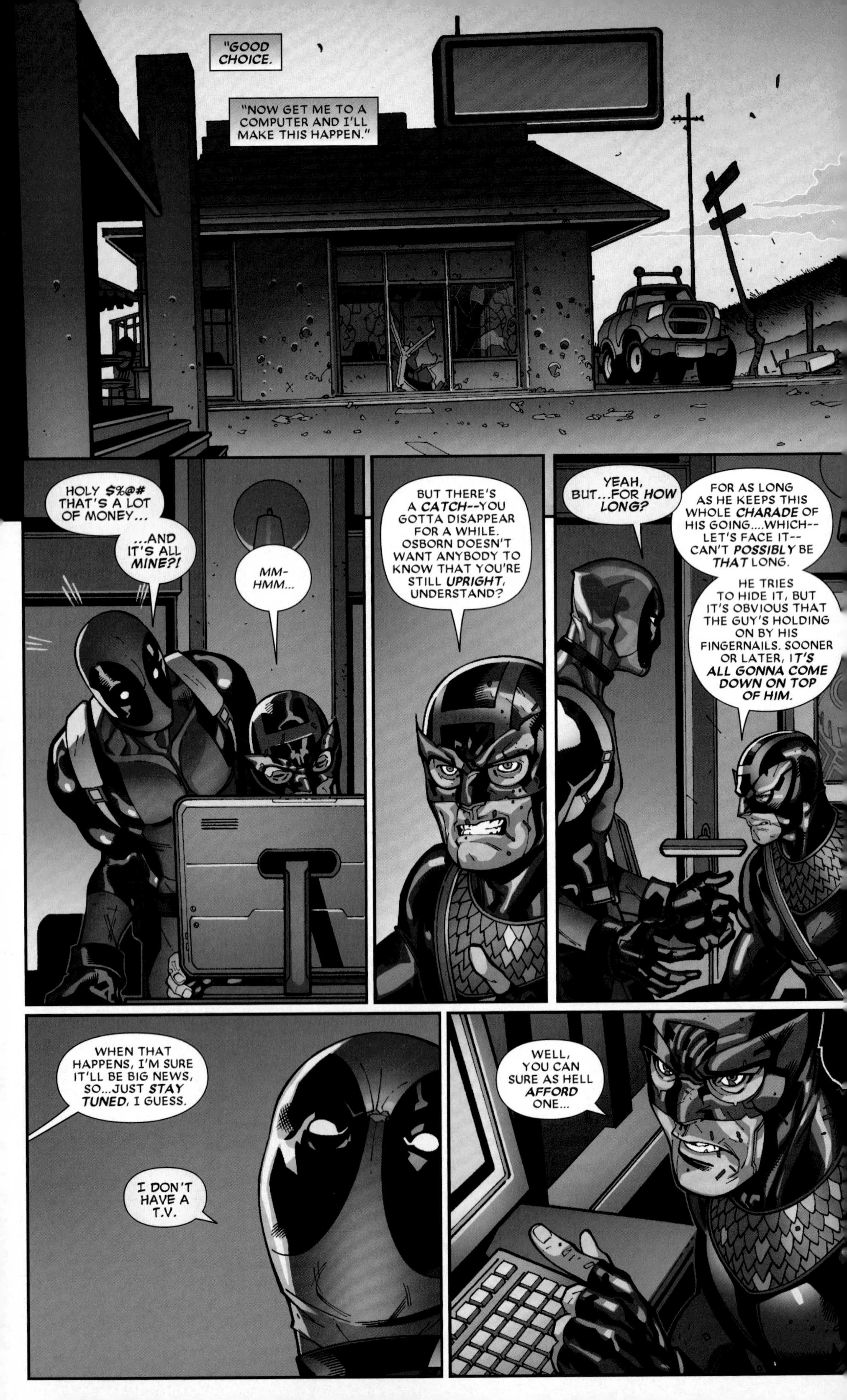
"GOOD CHOICE.
"NOW GET ME TO A COMPUTER AND I'LL MAKE THIS HAPPEN."
HOLY $%@# THAT'S A LOT OF MONEY...
...AND IT'S ALL MINE?!
MM-HMM...
BUT THERE'S A CATCH--YOU GOTTA DISAPPEAR FOR A WHILE. OSBORN DOESN'T WANT ANYBODY TO KNOW THAT YOU'RE STILL UPRIGHT, UNDERSTAND?
YEAH, BUT...FOR HOW LONG?
FOR AS LONG AS HE KEEPS THIS WHOLE CHARADE OF HIS GOING....WHICH--LET'S FACE IT--CAN'T POSSIBLY BE THAT LONG.
HE TRIES TO HIDE IT, BUT IT'S OBVIOUS THAT THE GUY'S HOLDING ON BY HIS FINGERNAILS. SOONER OR LATER, IT'S ALL GONNA COME DOWN ON TOP OF HIM.
WHEN THAT HAPPENS, I'M SURE IT'LL BE BIG NEWS, SO...JUST STAY TUNED, I GUESS.
I DON'T HAVE A T.V.
WELL, YOU CAN SURE AS HELL AFFORD ONE...

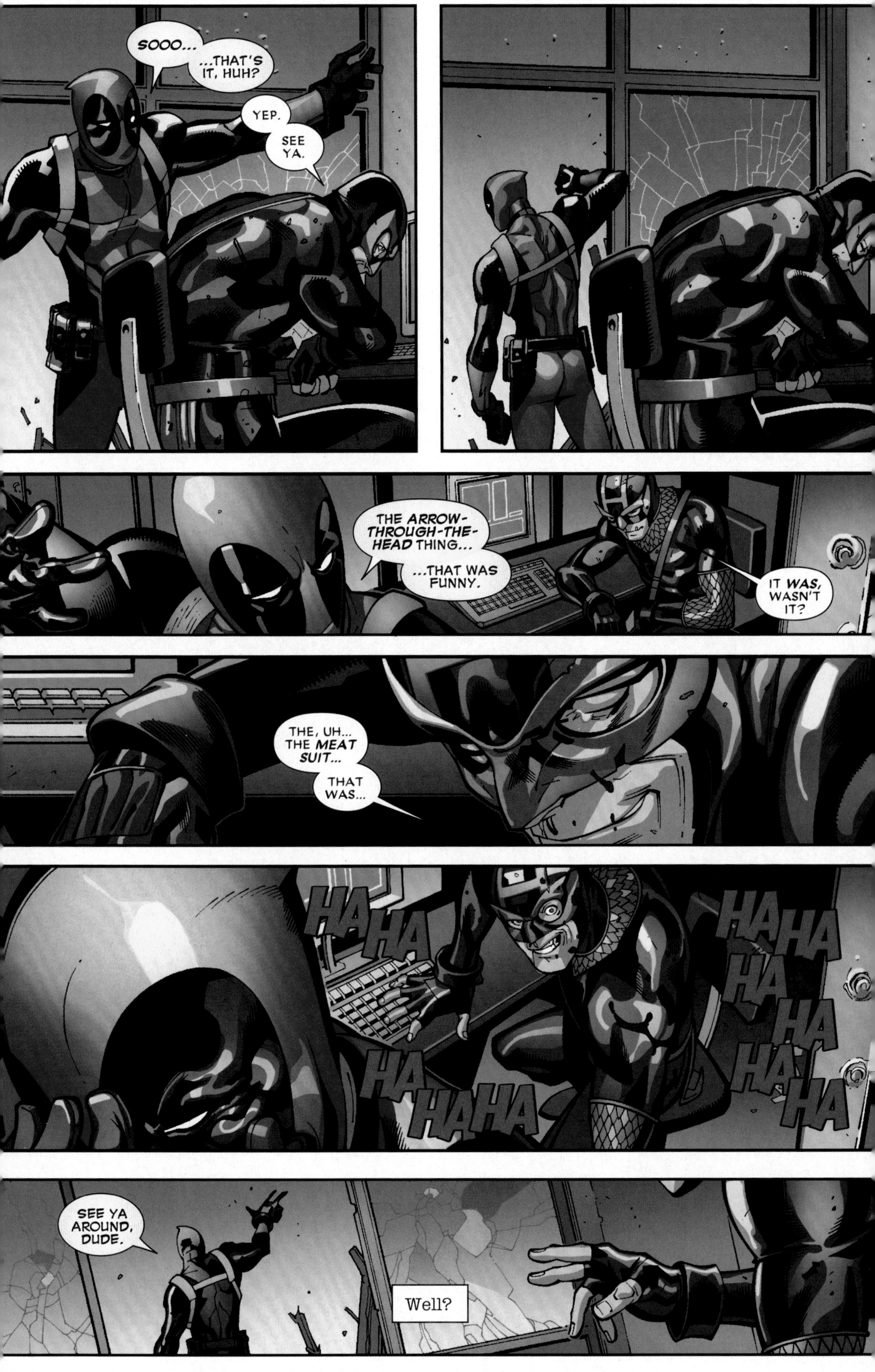

SOOO...
...THAT'S IT, HUH?
YEP.
SEE YA.
THE ARROW-THROUGH-THE-HEAD THING...
...THAT WAS FUNNY.
IT WAS, WASN'T IT?
THE, UH... THE MEAT SUIT...
THAT WAS...
HAHA
HAHA
HA HAHA
HAHA HA HA HA HA HA
SEE YA AROUND, DUDE.
Well?

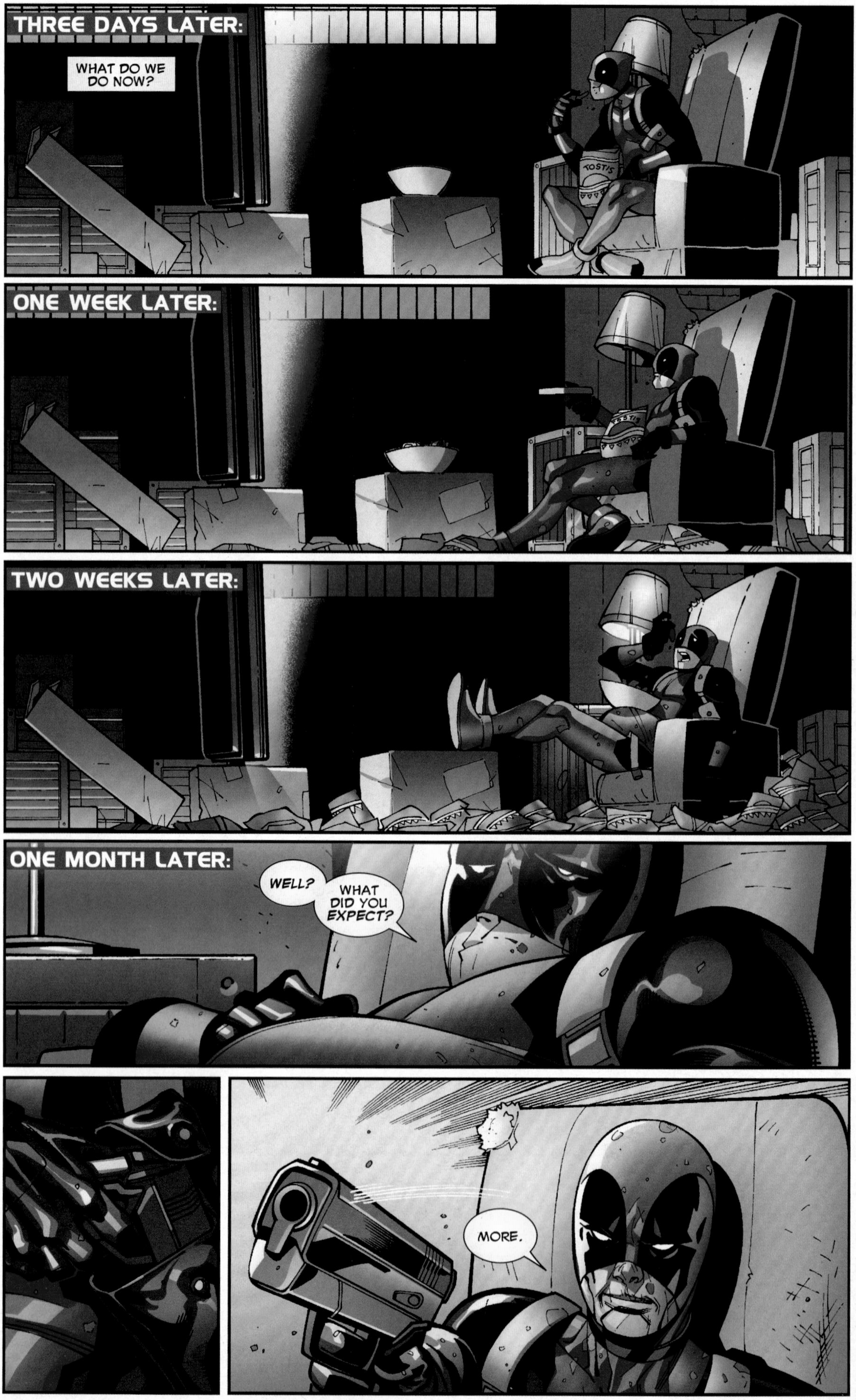
THREE DAYS LATER:
WHAT DO WE DO NOW?
TOSTI'S
ONE WEEK LATER:
TWO WEEKS LATER:
ONE MONTH LATER:
WELL?
WHAT DID YOU EXPECT?
MORE.

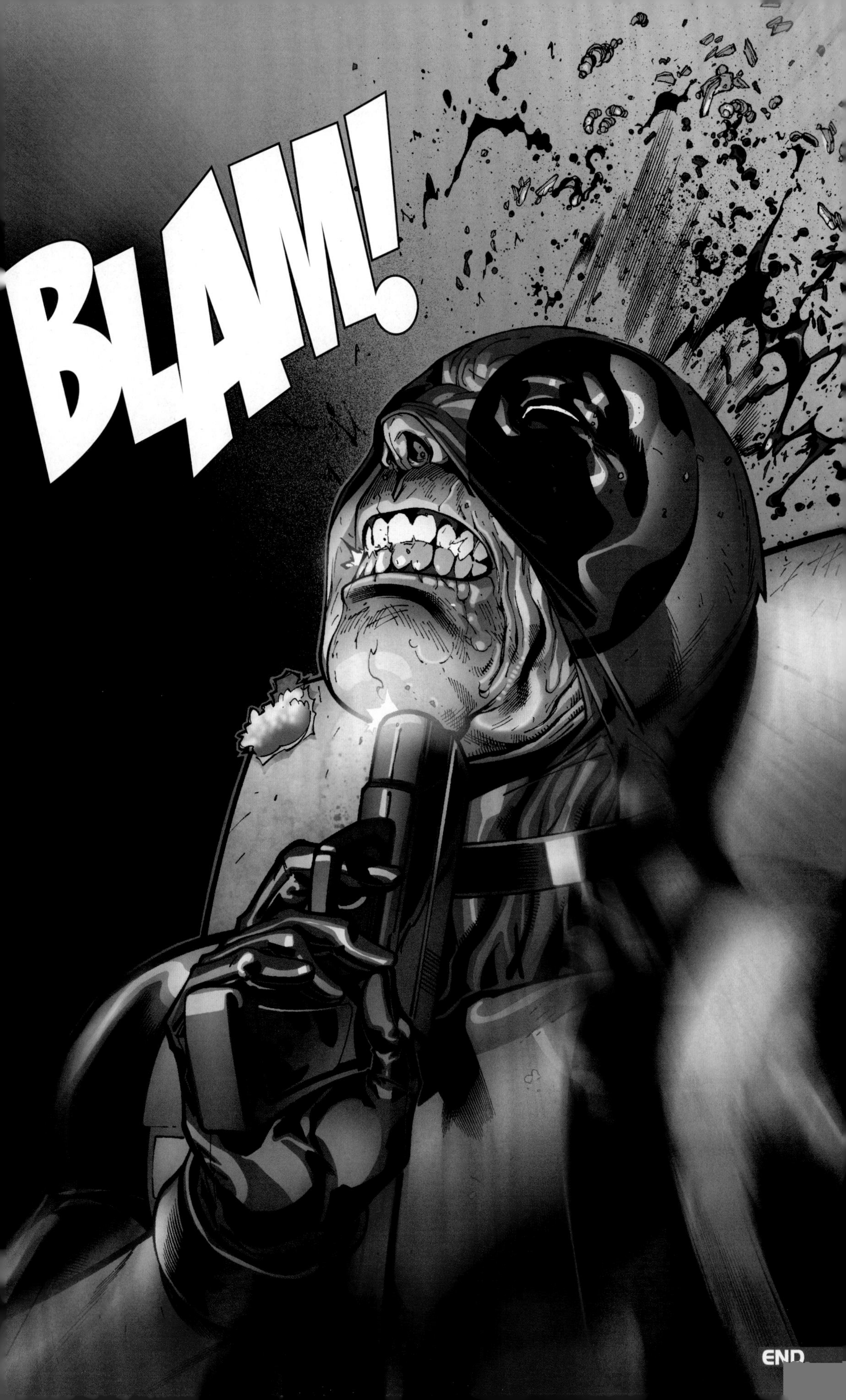
BLAM!
END

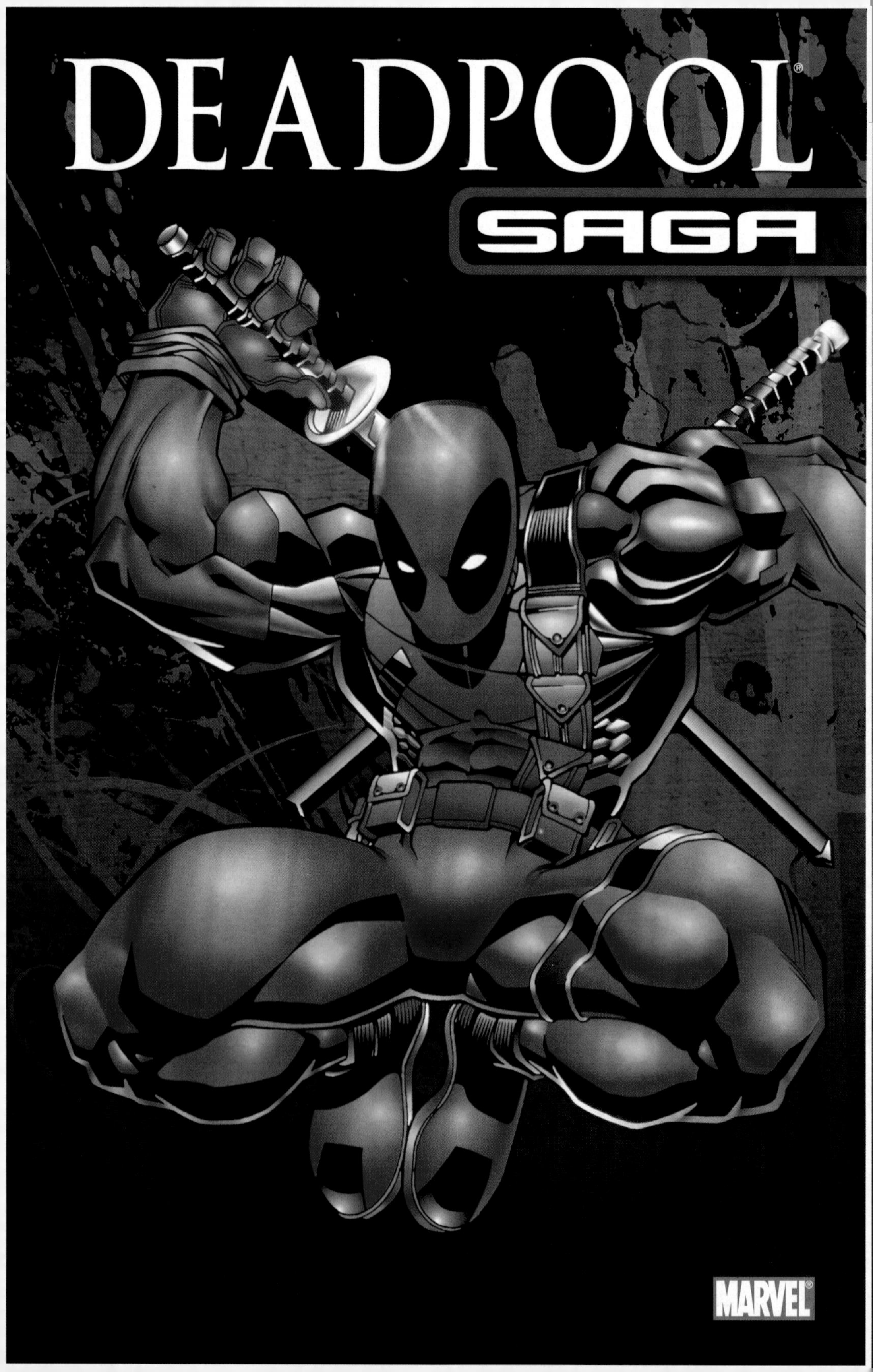
DEADPOOL®
SAGA
MARVEL®

Writer:
RONALD BYRD
Design:
RODOLFO MURAGUCHI
Assistant Editor:
ALEX STARBUCK
Editor:
JEFF YOUNGQUIST

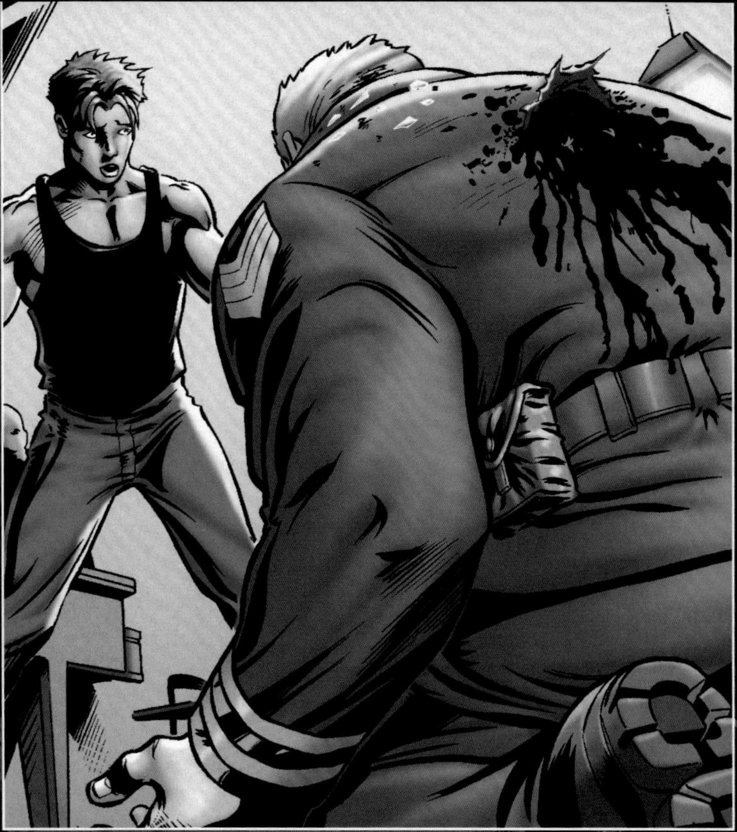

Almost nothing is known for certain about the youth of the man called "Wade Wilson," not even if he was born with that name. He remembers a mother who died when he was five and a mother who beat him during his teen years, a father he hasn't seen since childhood and a father who was shot in a barroom altercation when his son was 17. Whatever his past, the youth who became Deadpool grew up to be a violent, conflicted man.

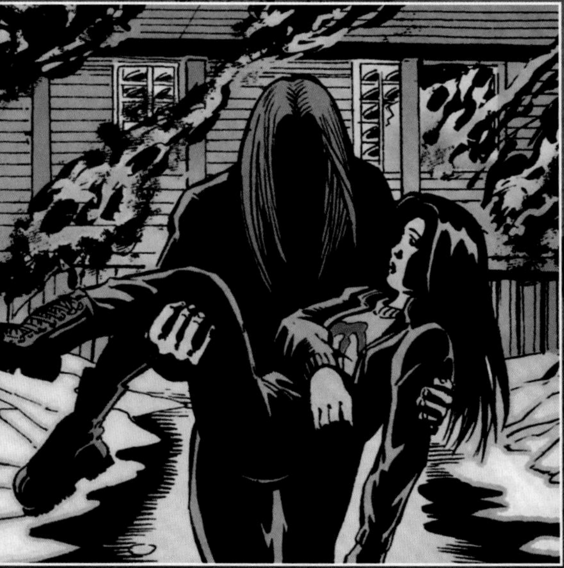

After serving in the military, that violent man became a teenage mercenary, taking assignments against those he felt warranted death. After failed assignments, he took new identities, and his true self, whoever that was, may have been lost in the process. A turning point came when, while on the run, he was nursed back to health by a husband and wife. Supposedly the husband's name was "Wade Wilson," and the mercenary craved that identity for himself. While trying to kill his benefactor, however, he inadvertently killed his wife Mercedes. Having broken his self-imposed rule against harming the innocent, the unhinged mercenary decided that **he** was Mercedes' husband, "Wade Wilson," and he mourned her before moving on.

Still a mercenary, Wilson traveled the world in the course of his assignments but never again abandoned the identity he believed was his. Eventually turning up in the USA, he fell in love with young Vanessa Carlysle, and although the couple lived their lives on the outskirts of society, they shared hopes for a better life. Unfortunately, Wilson contracted cancer, and he left Vanessa rather than force upon her what he perceived as the burden of a stricken man.

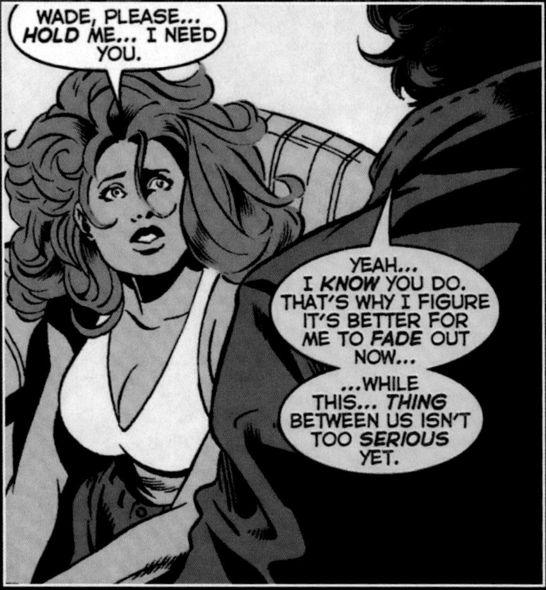
WADE, PLEASE... *HOLD* ME... I NEED YOU.
YEAH... I *KNOW* YOU DO. THAT'S WHY I FIGURE IT'S BETTER FOR ME TO *FADE* OUT NOW...
...WHILE THIS... *THING* BETWEEN US ISN'T TOO *SERIOUS* YET.

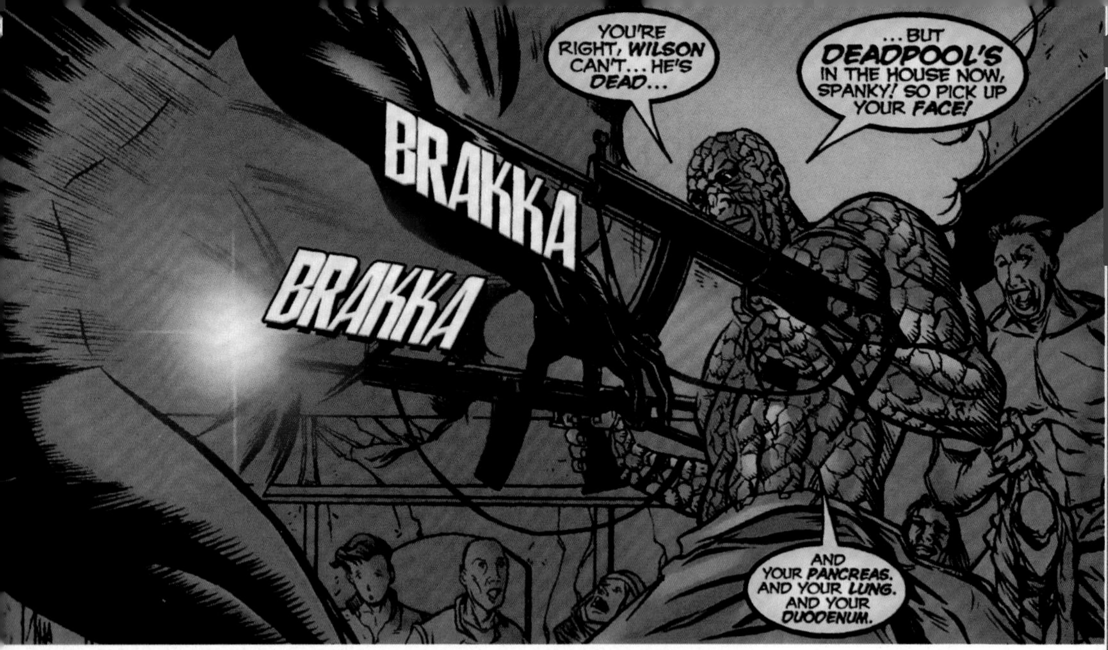
YOU'RE RIGHT, WILSON CAN'T... HE'S DEAD...
... BUT DEADPOOL'S IN THE HOUSE NOW, SPANKY! SO PICK UP YOUR FACE!
BRAKKA
BRAKKA
AND YOUR PANCREAS. AND YOUR LUNG. AND YOUR DUODENUM.

Wilson joined Canada's Department K and was mutated with a healing factor intended to cure his cancer. He worked with other operatives like Kane and Sluggo, but something went wrong. Whether due to a breakdown from his treatments or some other factor, Wilson apparently killed teammate Slayback. The government sent him to the Hospice for treatment, unaware of the sadistic experiments conducted by Dr. Emrys Killebrew. Killed for his rebellious streak, Wilson was revived by his healing factor, severely disfigured but no longer terminal. He tore the Hospice apart, freed his fellow test subjects, and proclaimed a new name for himself.

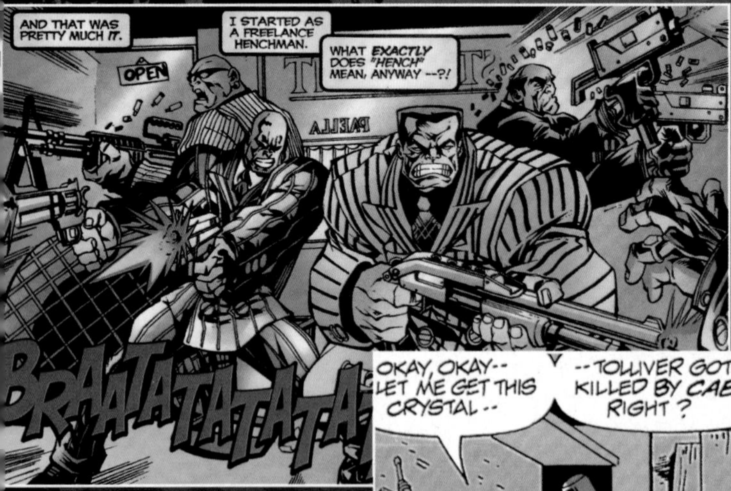
AND THAT WAS PRETTY MUCH IT.
I STARTED AS A FREELANCE HENCHMAN.
WHAT EXACTLY DOES "HENCH" MEAN, ANYWAY --?!
OPEN
BRAATATATATAT

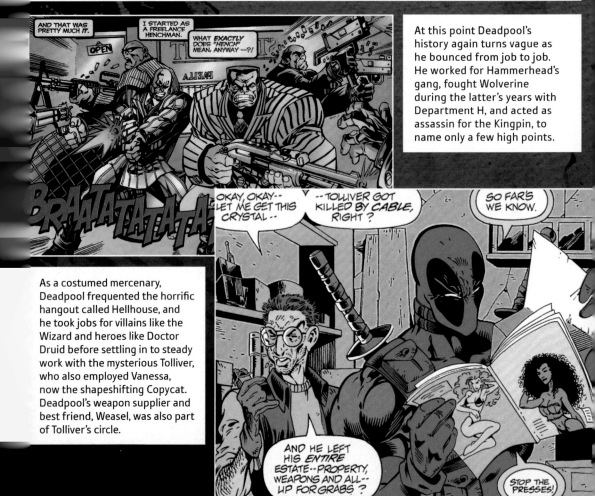

At this point Deadpool's history again turns vague as he bounced from job to job. He worked for Hammerhead's gang, fought Wolverine during the latter's years with Department H, and acted as assassin for the Kingpin, to name only a few high points.

As a costumed mercenary, Deadpool frequented the horrific hangout called Hellhouse, and he took jobs for villains like the Wizard and heroes like Doctor Druid before settling in to steady work with the mysterious Tolliver, who also employed Vanessa, now the shapeshifting Copycat. Deadpool's weapon supplier and best friend, Weasel, was also part of Tolliver's circle.

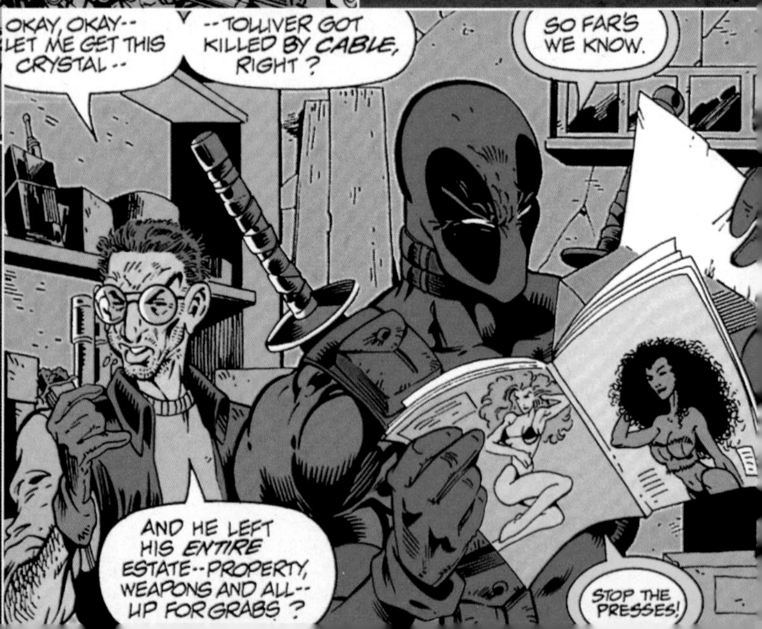
OKAY, OKAY-- LET ME GET THIS CRYSTAL--
--TOLLIVER GOT KILLED BY CABLE, RIGHT ?
SO FAR'S WE KNOW.
AND HE LEFT HIS ENTIRE ESTATE--PROPERTY, WEAPONS AND ALL-- UP FOR GRABS ?
STOP THE PRESSES!

Eventually Tolliver sent Deadpool to kill Cable, another super-powered mercenary and, secretly, Tolliver's father. At the time, Cable was acting as mentor to the New Mutants, so Deadpool burst into the Xavier Institute, ready to rumble, but Cable defeated him and mailed him back to Tolliver. Deadpool could little imagine how important Cable and his cohorts would become in his later life.

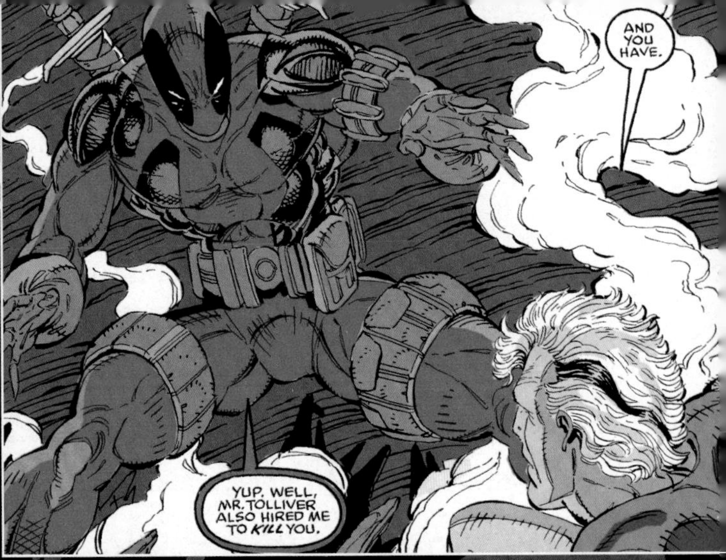

AND YOU HAVE.
YUP, WELL, MR. TOLLIVER ALSO HIRED ME TO *KILL* YOU.

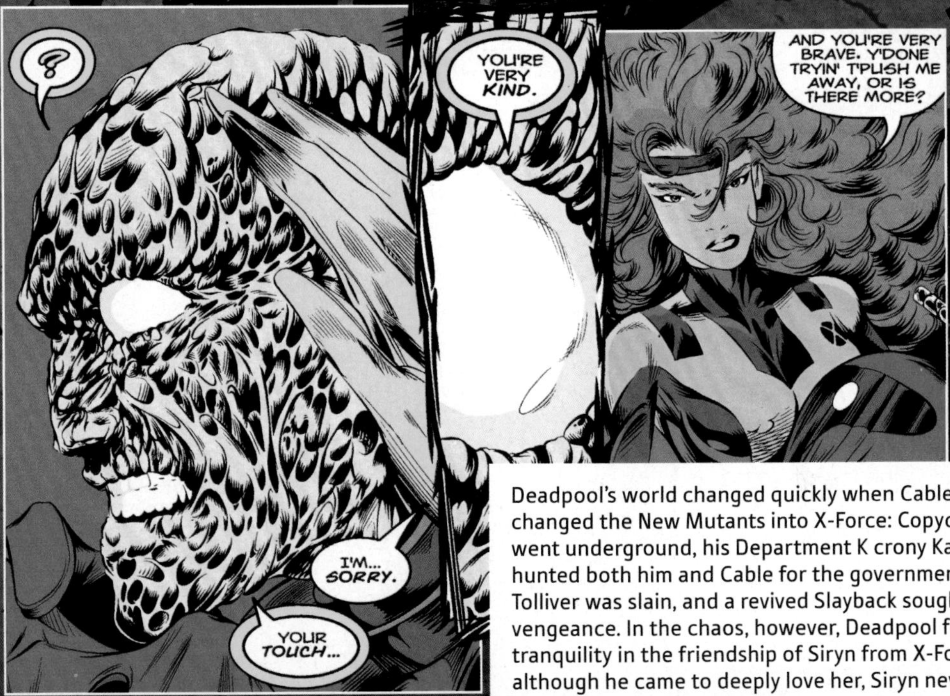

?
YOU'RE VERY *KIND*.
AND YOU'RE VERY BRAVE. Y'DONE TRYIN' T'PUSH ME AWAY, OR IS THERE MORE?
I'M... *SORRY*.
YOUR *TOUCH*...

Deadpool's world changed quickly when Cable changed the New Mutants into X-Force: Copycat went underground, his Department K crony Kane hunted both him and Cable for the government, Tolliver was slain, and a revived Slayback sought vengeance. In the chaos, however, Deadpool found tranquility in the friendship of Siryn from X-Force; although he came to deeply love her, Siryn never fully reciprocated his feelings.

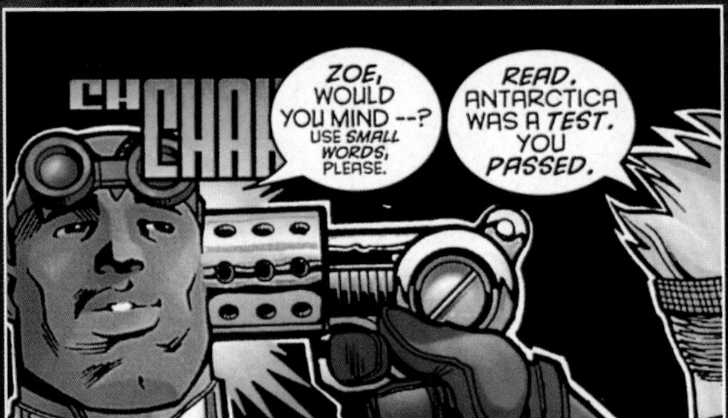

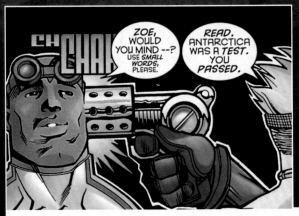

CH CHAK
ZOE, WOULD YOU MIND --? USE *SMALL WORDS*, PLEASE.
READ. ANTARCTICA WAS A *TEST*. YOU *PASSED*.

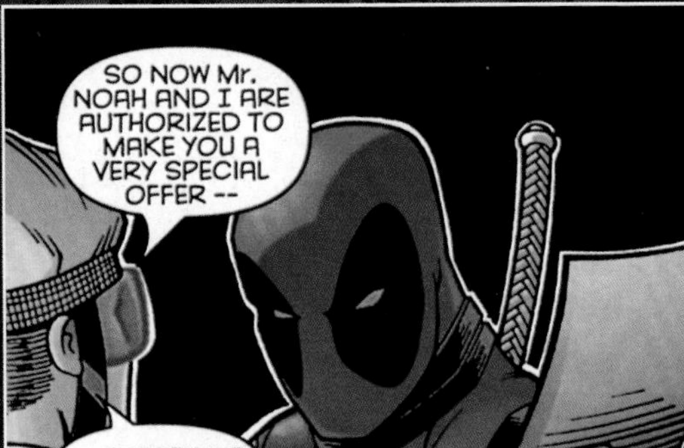

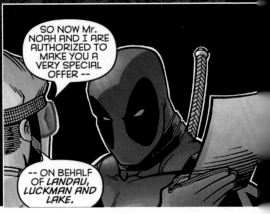

SO NOW Mr. NOAH AND I ARE AUTHORIZED TO MAKE YOU A VERY SPECIAL OFFER --
-- ON BEHALF OF *LANDAU, LUCKMAN AND LAKE*.

Deadpool's life settled back to normal, or as close to normal as he wanted it, but Zoe Culloden of the mystery firm Landau, Luckman, and Lake felt Deadpool was meant for more than mercenary misadventures. Zoe claimed a heroic destiny awaited the dubious Deadpool, who was sure that, although he had worn many names, "hero" would never be one of them.

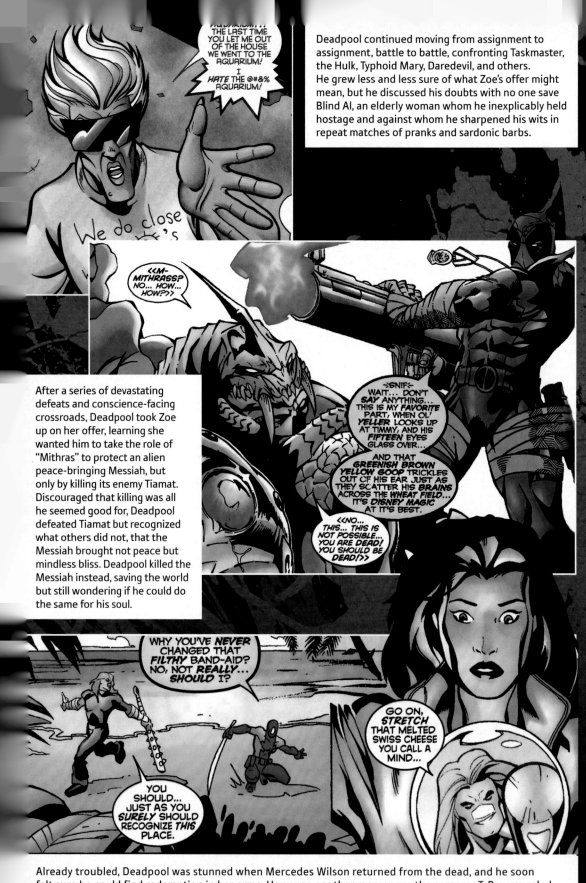

Deadpool continued moving from assignment to assignment, battle to battle, confronting Taskmaster, the Hulk, Typhoid Mary, Daredevil, and others. He grew less and less sure of what Zoe's offer might mean, but he discussed his doubts with no one save Blind Al, an elderly woman whom he inexplicably held hostage and against whom he sharpened his wits in repeat matches of pranks and sardonic barbs.

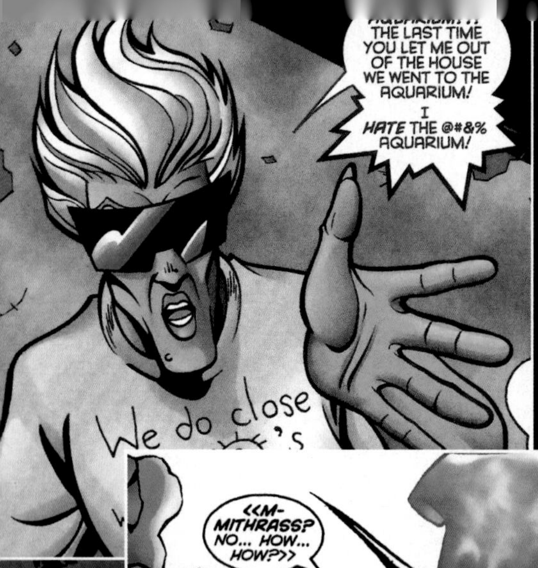
THE LAST TIME YOU LET ME OUT OF THE HOUSE WE WENT TO THE AQUARIUM! I HATE THE @#&% AQUARIUM!
We do close

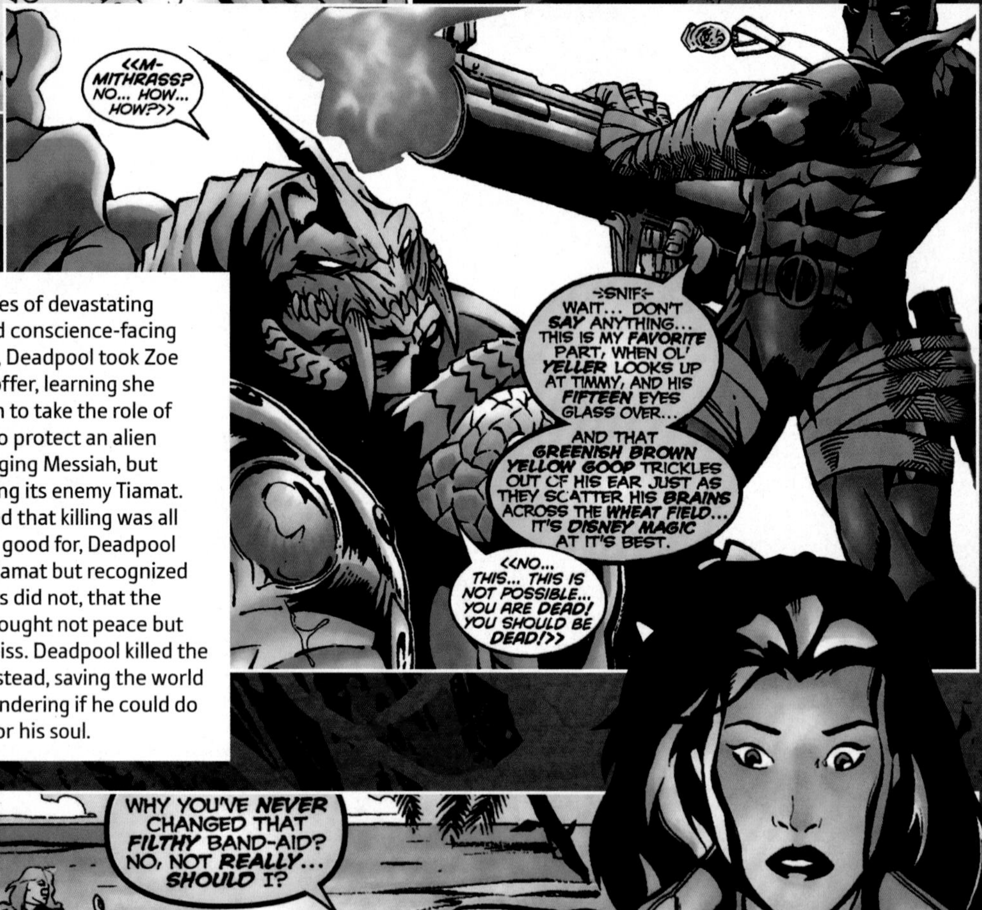
<<M-MITHRASS? NO... HOW... HOW?>>
-SNIF- WAIT... DON'T SAY ANYTHING... THIS IS MY FAVORITE PART, WHEN OL' YELLER LOOKS UP AT TIMMY, AND HIS FIFTEEN EYES GLASS OVER...
AND THAT GREENISH BROWN YELLOW GOOP TRICKLES OUT OF HIS EAR JUST AS THEY SCATTER HIS BRAINS ACROSS THE WHEAT FIELD... IT'S DISNEY MAGIC AT IT'S BEST.
<<NO... THIS... THIS IS NOT POSSIBLE... YOU ARE DEAD! YOU SHOULD BE DEAD!>>

After a series of devastating defeats and conscience-facing crossroads, Deadpool took Zoe up on her offer, learning she wanted him to take the role of "Mithras" to protect an alien peace-bringing Messiah, but only by killing its enemy Tiamat. Discouraged that killing was all he seemed good for, Deadpool defeated Tiamat but recognized what others did not, that the Messiah brought not peace but mindless bliss. Deadpool killed the Messiah instead, saving the world but still wondering if he could do the same for his soul.

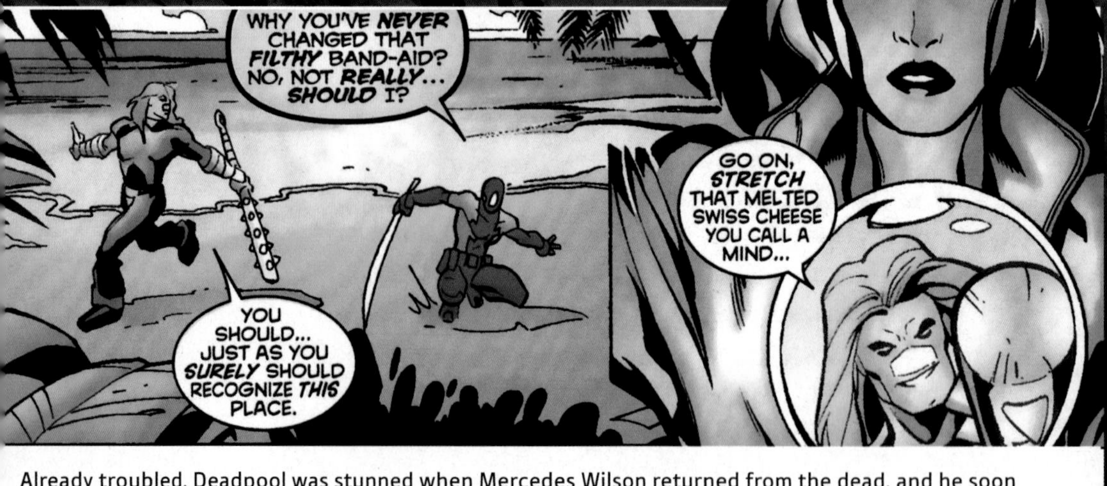
WHY YOU'VE NEVER CHANGED THAT FILTHY BAND-AID? NO, NOT REALLY... SHOULD I?
YOU SHOULD... JUST AS YOU SURELY SHOULD RECOGNIZE THIS PLACE.
GO ON, STRETCH THAT MELTED SWISS CHEESE YOU CALL A MIND...

Already troubled, Deadpool was stunned when Mercedes Wilson returned from the dead, and he soon felt sure he could find redemption in her arms. However, another mercenary, the sorcerer T-Ray, revealed that Deadpool could never find peace as Mercedes' husband...because **T-Ray** was her husband, the man Deadpool had left for dead long ago. Overwhelmed by the revelation, Deadpool nevertheless refused to break down in defeat the way T-Ray wanted.

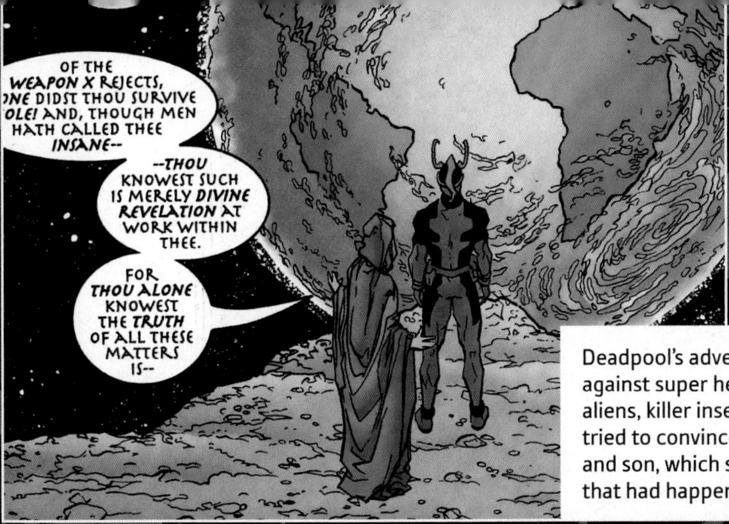
OF THE WEAPON X REJECTS, NE DIDST THOU SURVIVE OLE! AND, THOUGH MEN HATH CALLED THEE INSANE--
--THOU KNOWEST SUCH IS MERELY DIVINE REVELATION AT WORK WITHIN THEE.
FOR THOU ALONE KNOWEST THE TRUTH OF ALL THESE MATTERS IS--

Deadpool's adventures continued, setting him against super heroes, super-villains, werewolves, aliens, killer insects, and more. The god Loki even tried to convince Deadpool that they were father and son, which seemed as believable as anything else that had happened in Deadpool's life.

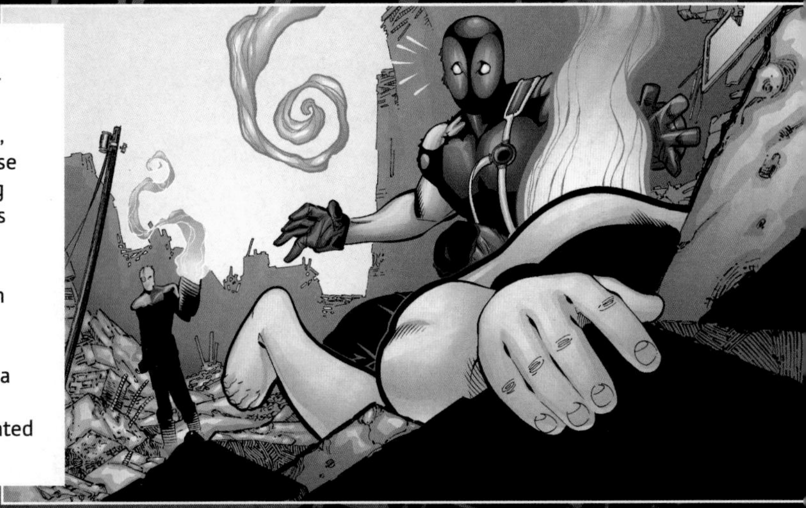

Deadpool then received an upgrade to his healing factor from Malcolm "Director" Colcord's Weapon X Program, which recruited him to oppose "the mutant menace." Joining Kane, who had turned callous while Deadpool had become more sympathetic to others, Deadpool was appalled when Kane murdered a mutant child. When Sabretooth, also in Weapon X, killed Copycat, a furious Deadpool was all but incinerated when he confronted her murderers.

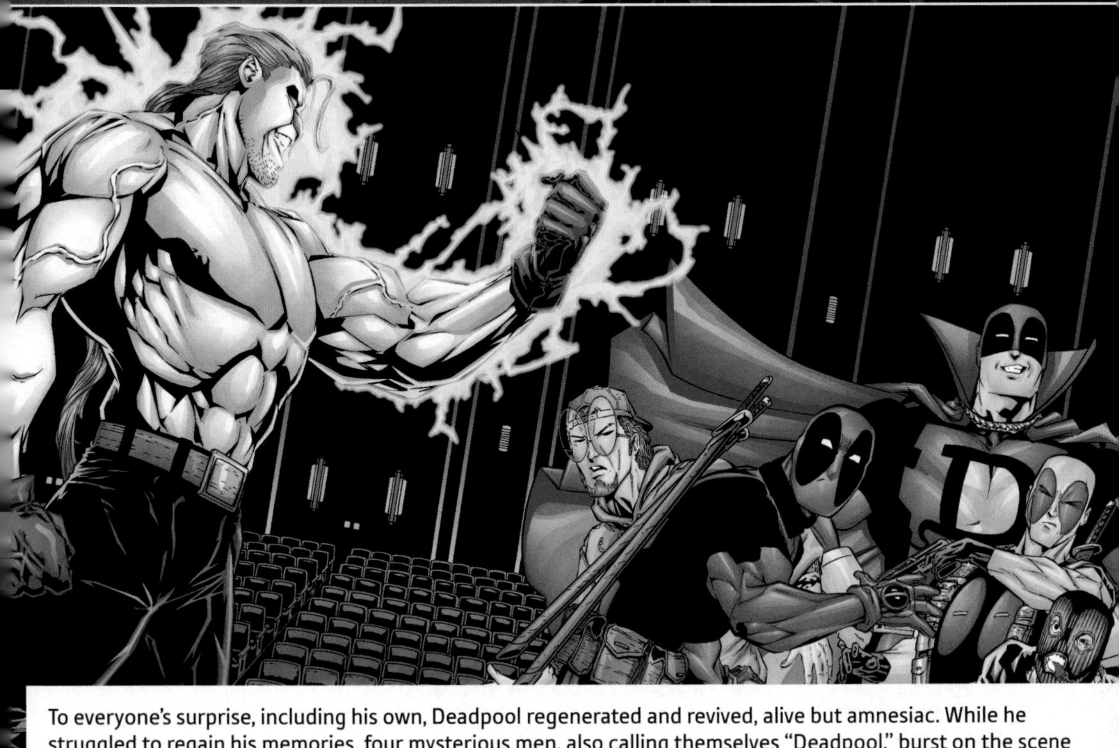

To everyone's surprise, including his own, Deadpool regenerated and revived, alive but amnesiac. While he struggled to regain his memories, four mysterious men, also calling themselves "Deadpool," burst on the scene in various venues. Deadpool learned they were aspects of his own personality, created by T-Ray in a scheme that ultimately failed.

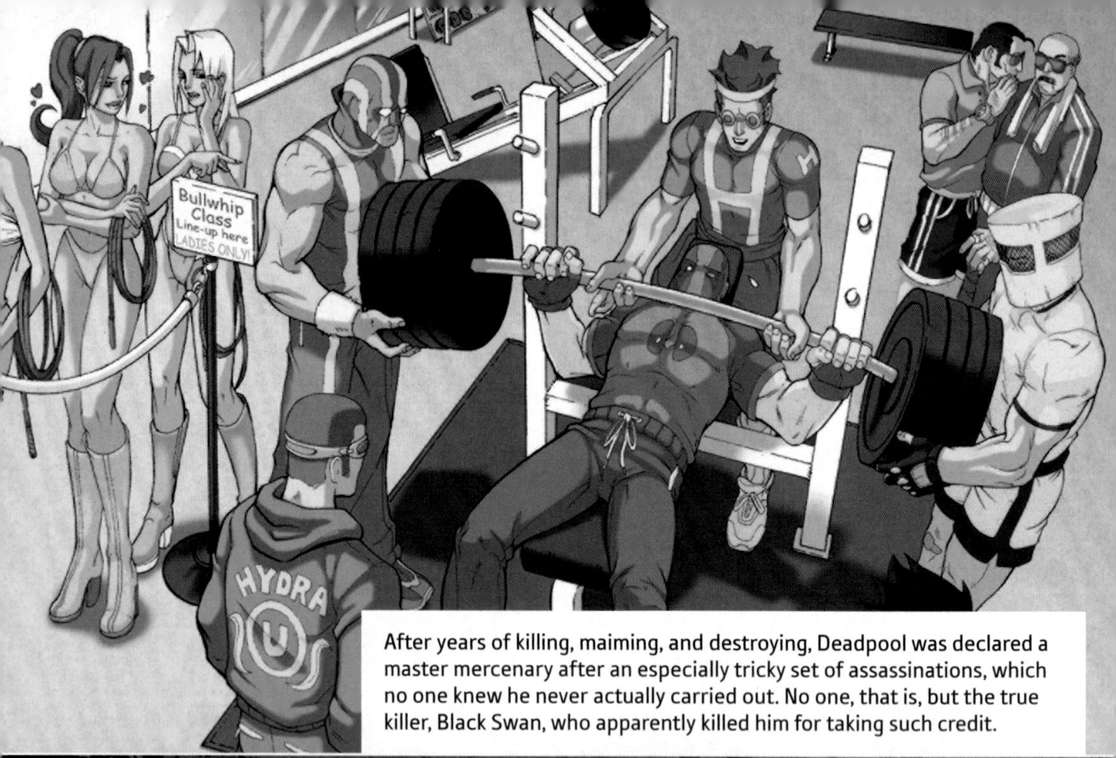
Bullwhip Class
Line-up here
LADIES ONLY!
HYDRA

After years of killing, maiming, and destroying, Deadpool was declared a master mercenary after an especially tricky set of assassinations, which no one knew he never actually carried out. No one, that is, but the true killer, Black Swan, who apparently killed him for taking such credit.

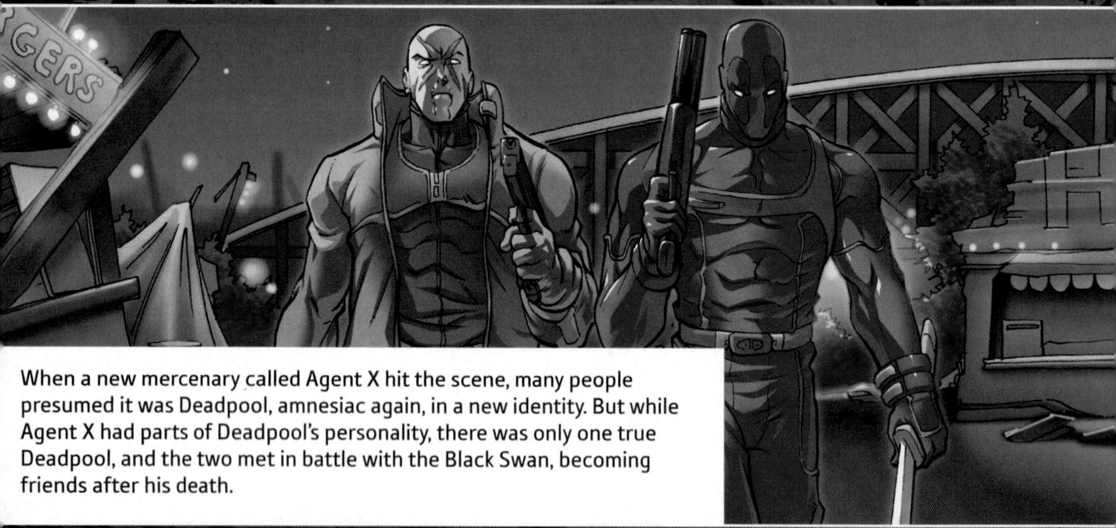
GERS

When a new mercenary called Agent X hit the scene, many people presumed it was Deadpool, amnesiac again, in a new identity. But while Agent X had parts of Deadpool's personality, there was only one true Deadpool, and the two met in battle with the Black Swan, becoming friends after his death.

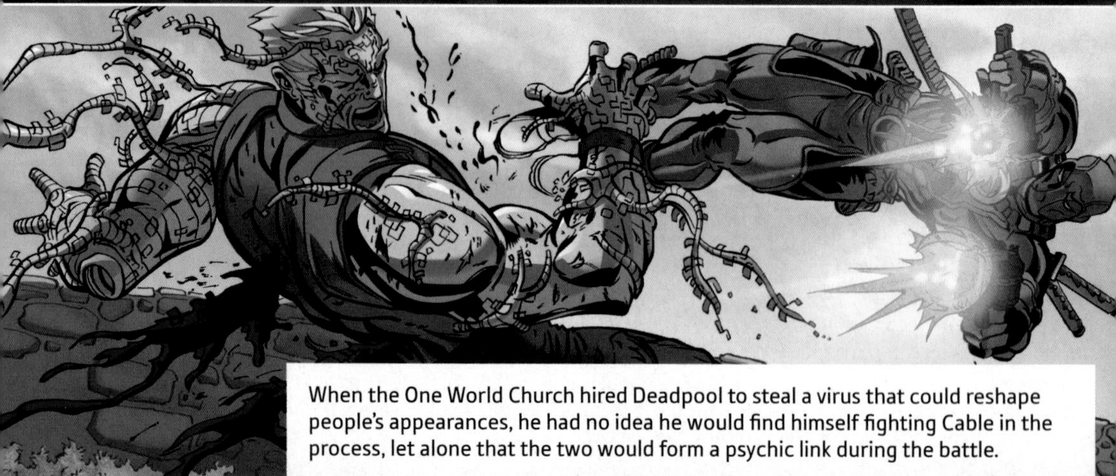

When the One World Church hired Deadpool to steal a virus that could reshape people's appearances, he had no idea he would find himself fighting Cable in the process, let alone that the two would form a psychic link during the battle.

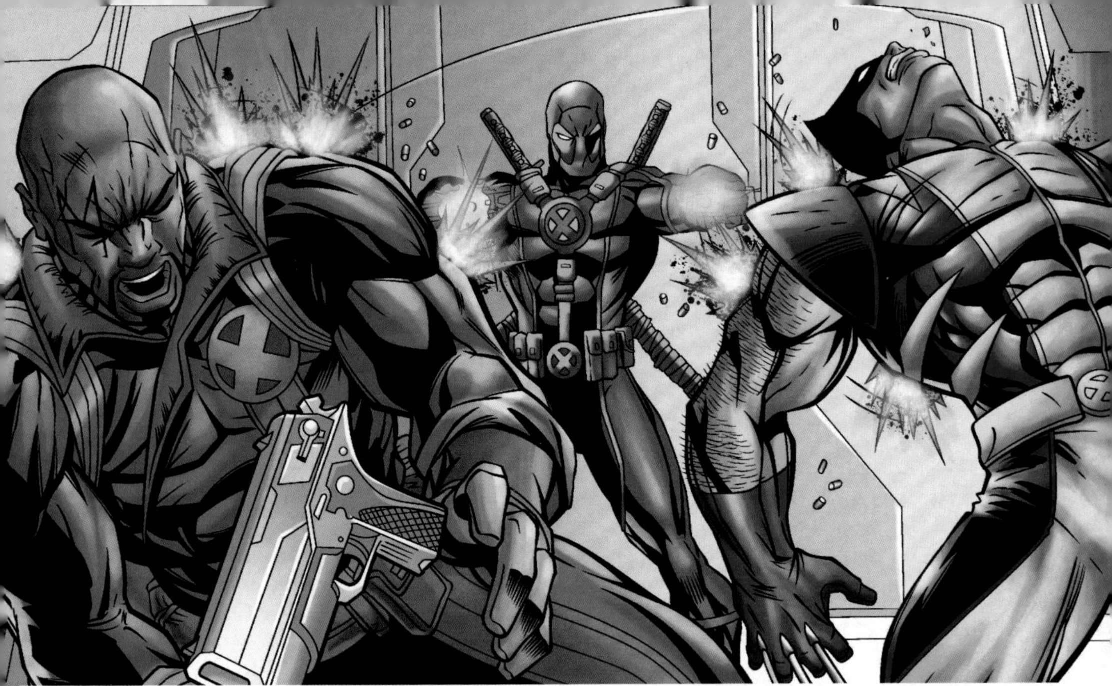

But a lot had changed since their battle at Xavier's school years before. His mercenary days far behind him, Cable was out to save the world through intervention and example. Deadpool had heard wild talk about saving the world before, but he became one of Cable's most ardent and unstable supporters, willing to fight friend or enemy on his behalf, and he became a frequent visitor to Cable's island paradise, Providence.

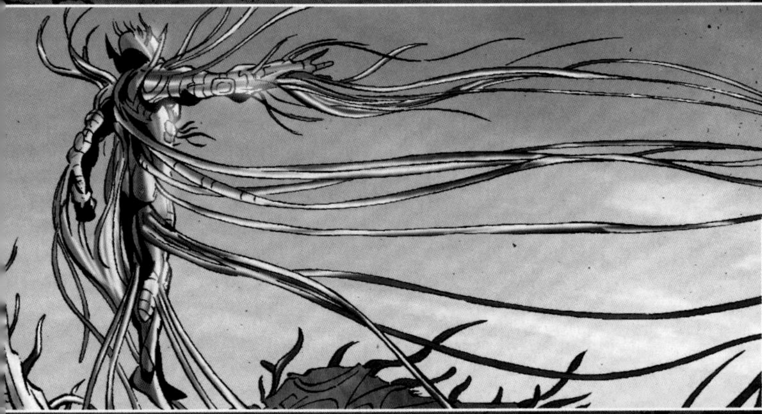

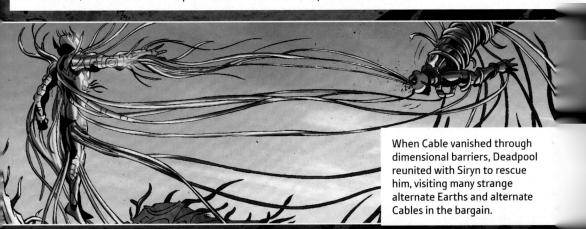

When Cable vanished through dimensional barriers, Deadpool reunited with Siryn to rescue him, visiting many strange alternate Earths and alternate Cables in the bargain.

During the "Civil War," Deadpool and Cable parted over differences regarding the Superhuman Registration Act and its effects on the future. Trying to put his newfound idealism behind him, Deadpool joined the government-sanctioned Six Pack to discredit him but inadvertently improved Cable's status in the eyes of the world.

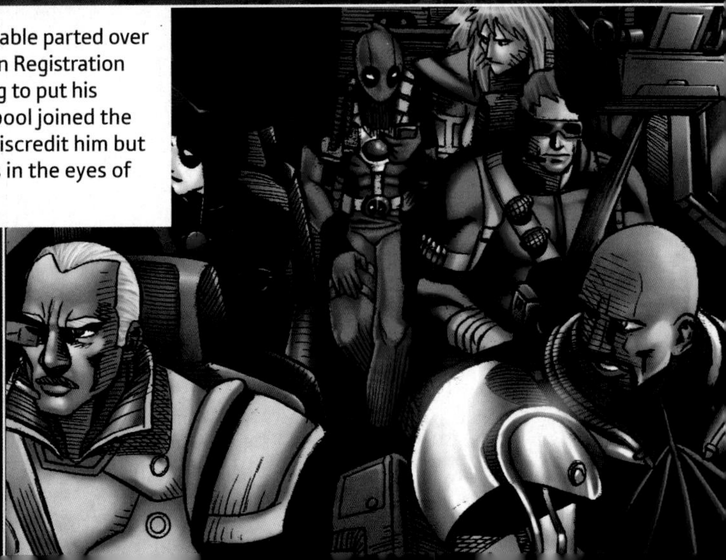

Unfortunately, Cable's dream reached an apparent end when Providence sank. Regardless of regrets over what might have been, Deadpool is now back in the mercenary game full-time, joining Weasel and other friends in Agency X. Cable may have disappeared into the future, but what future is waiting for Deadpool now?

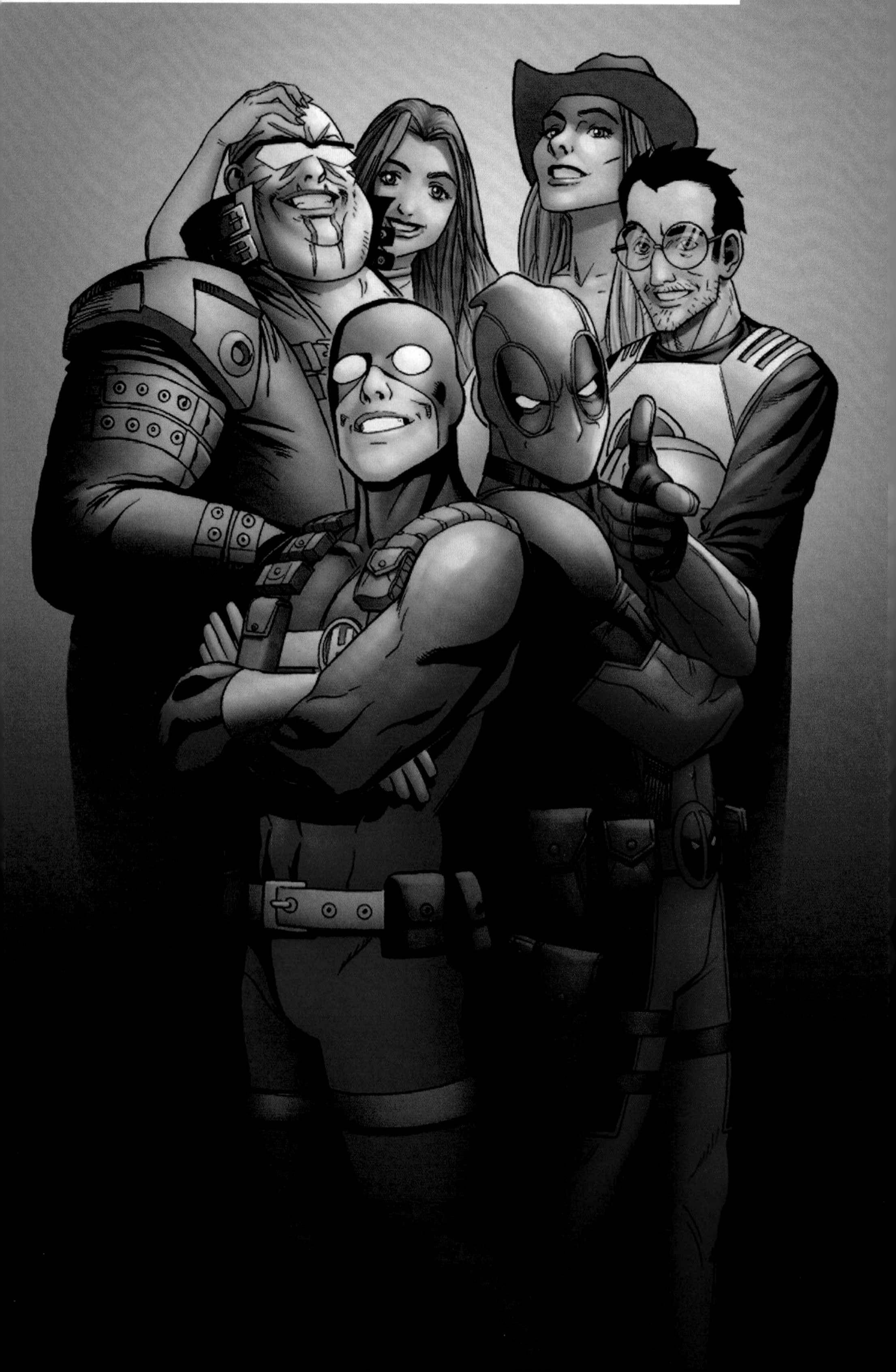

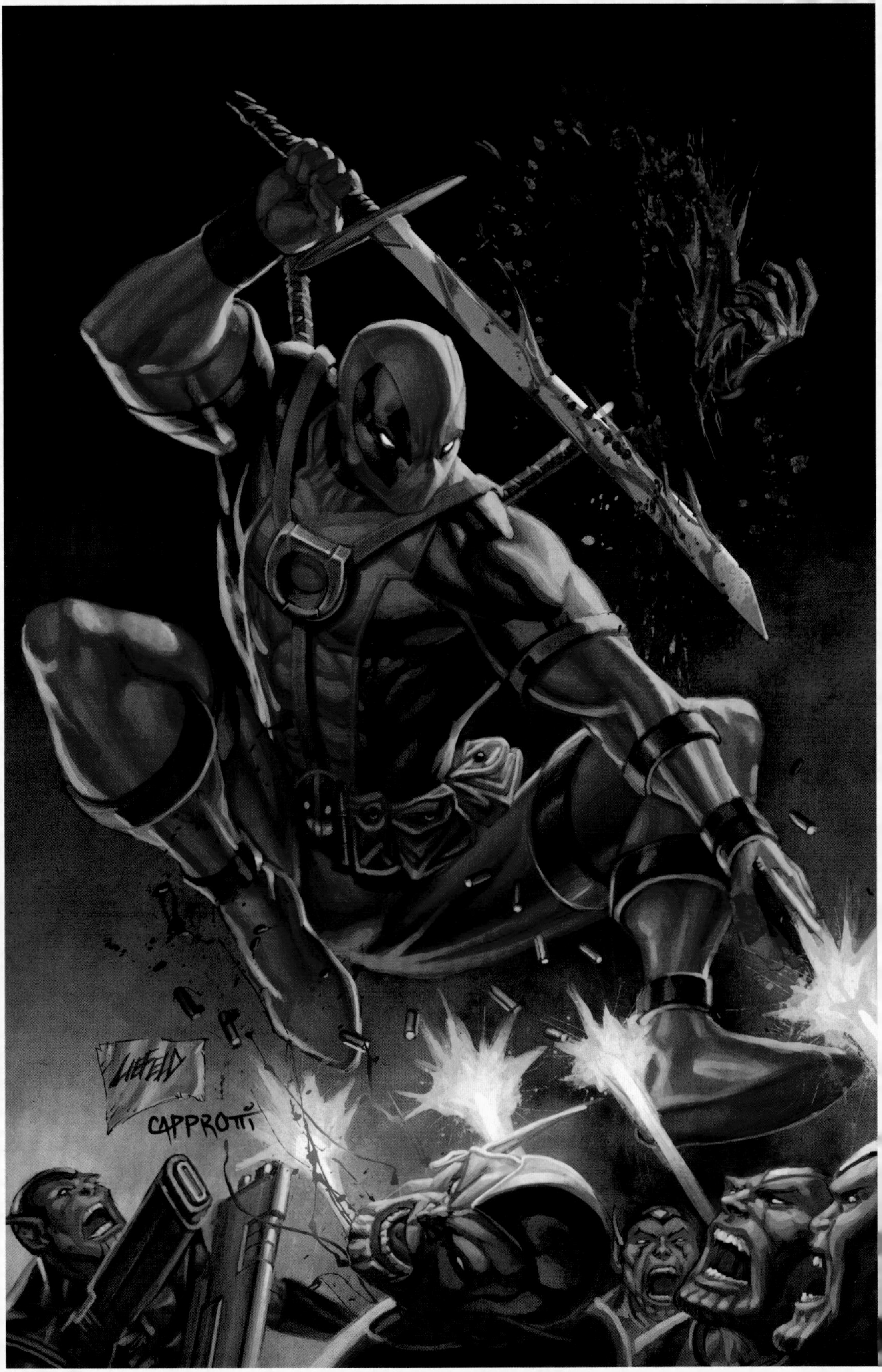
LIEFELD
CAPPROTTI

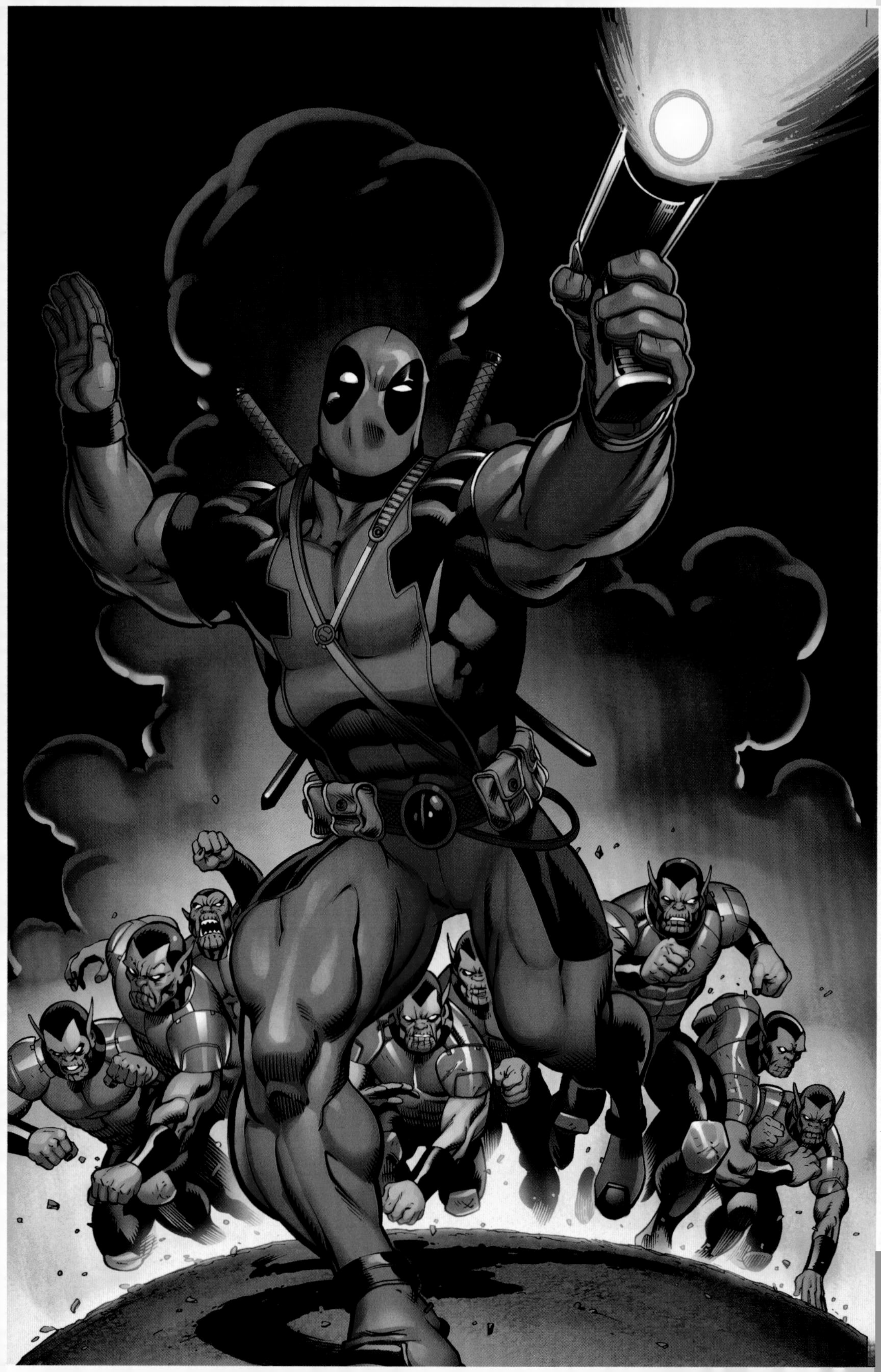

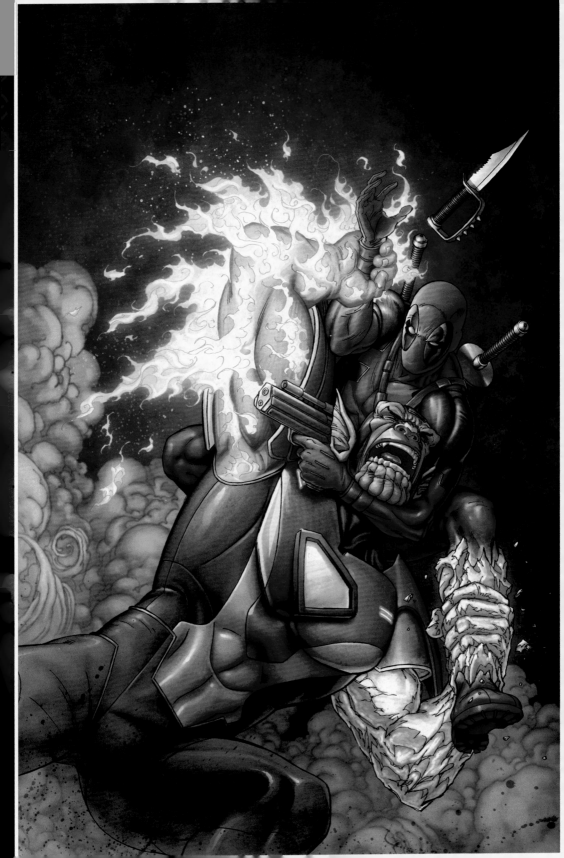

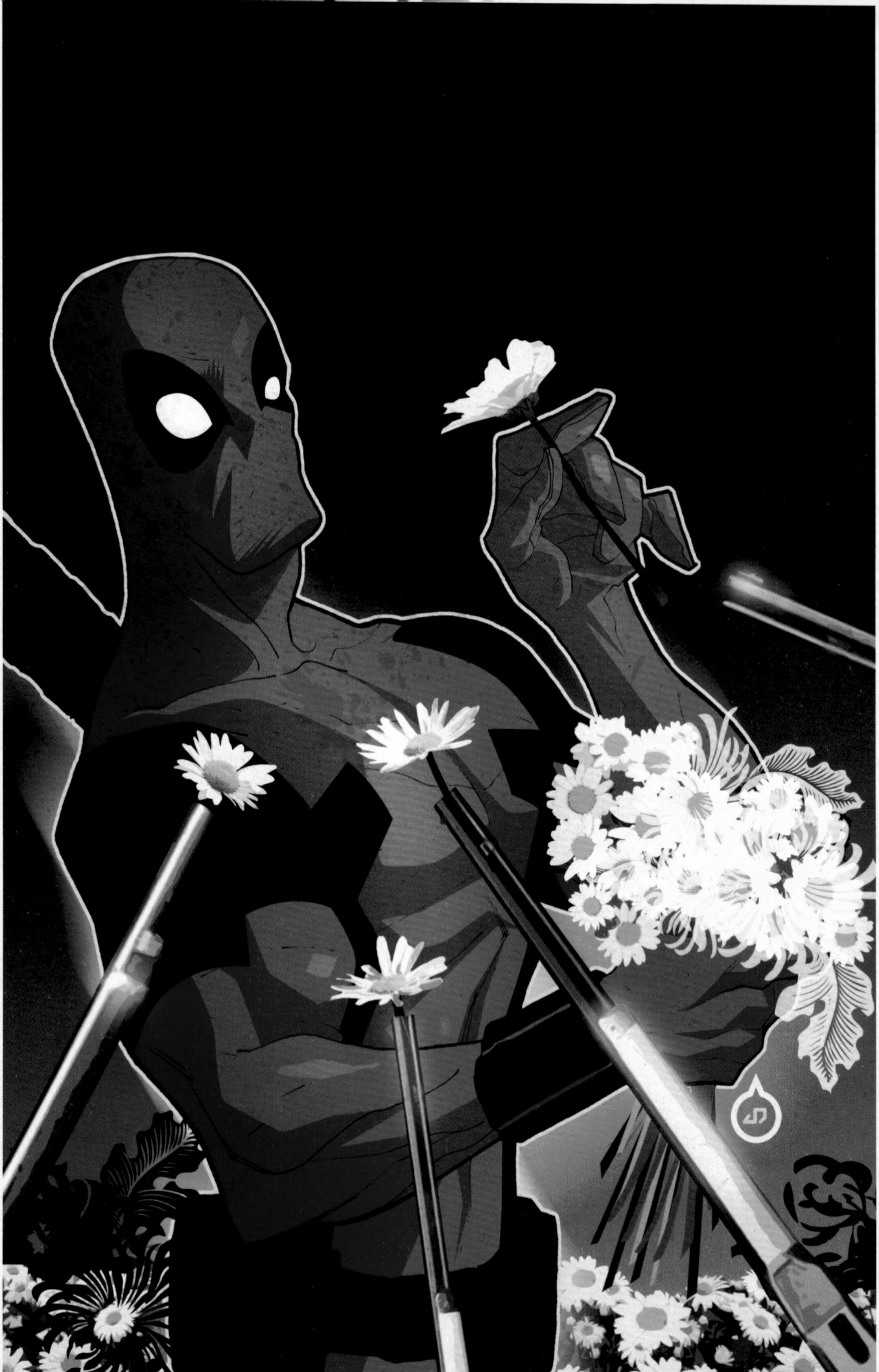

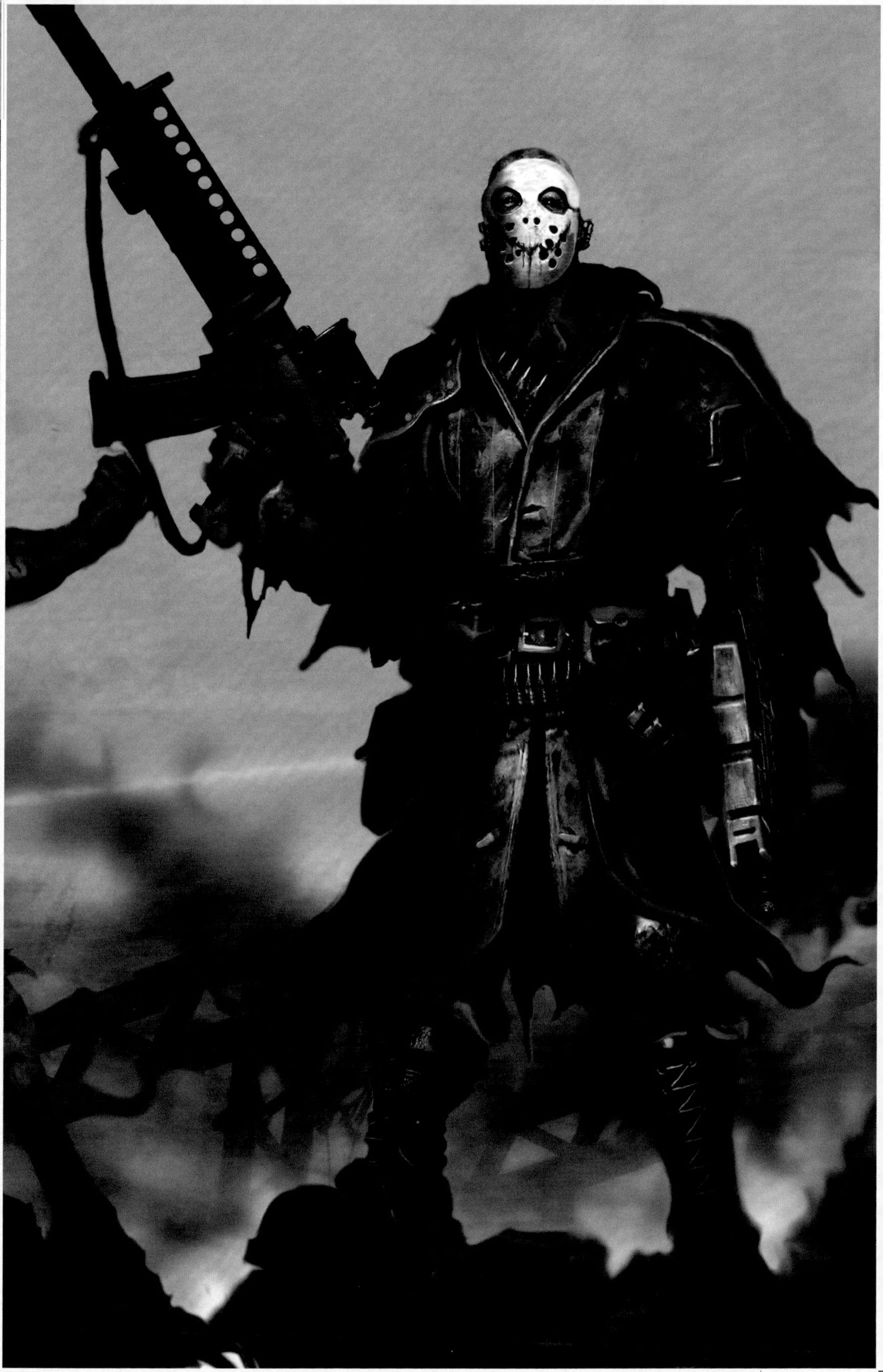

BOLTS #131 VARIANT

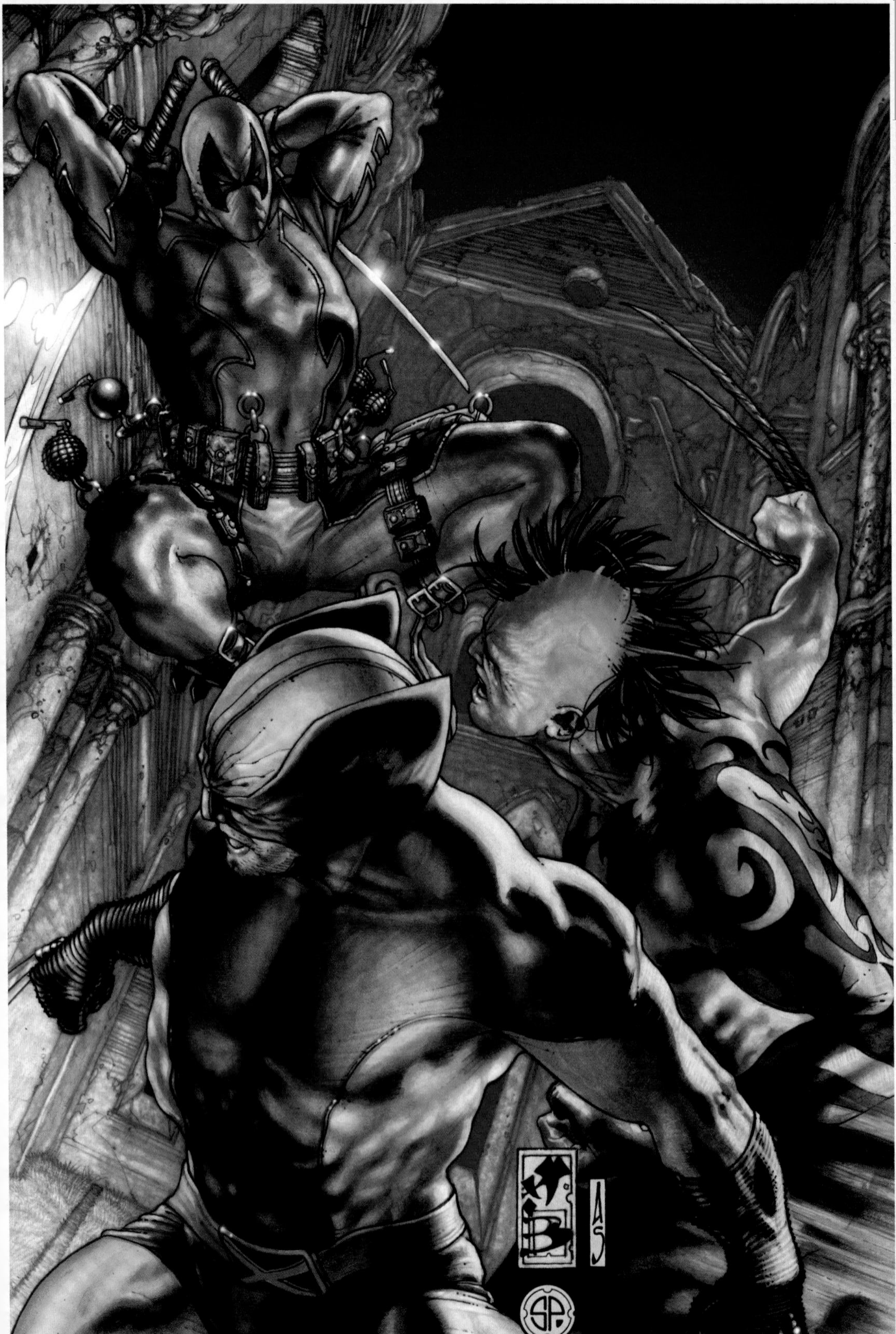

E: ORIGINS

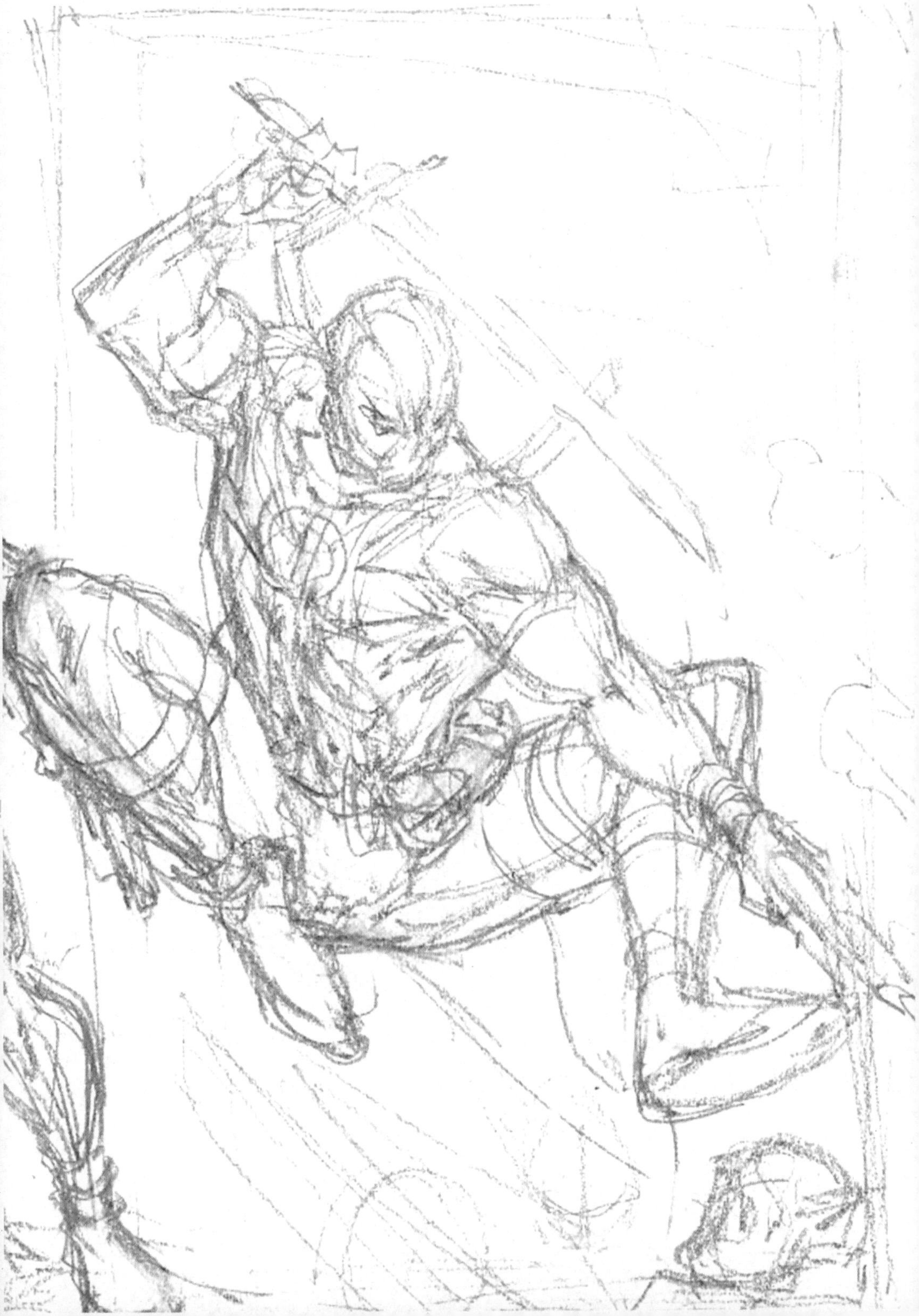

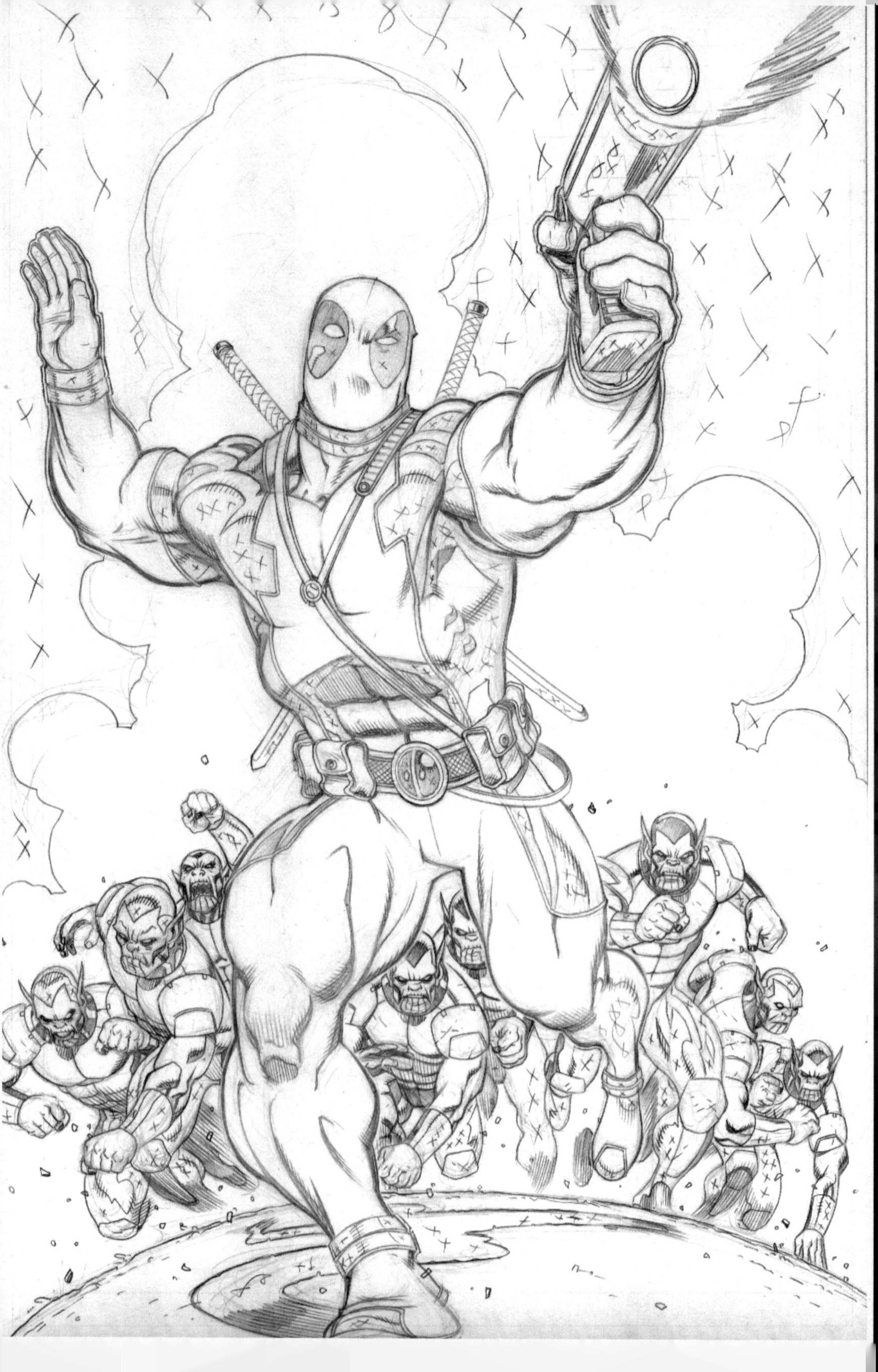

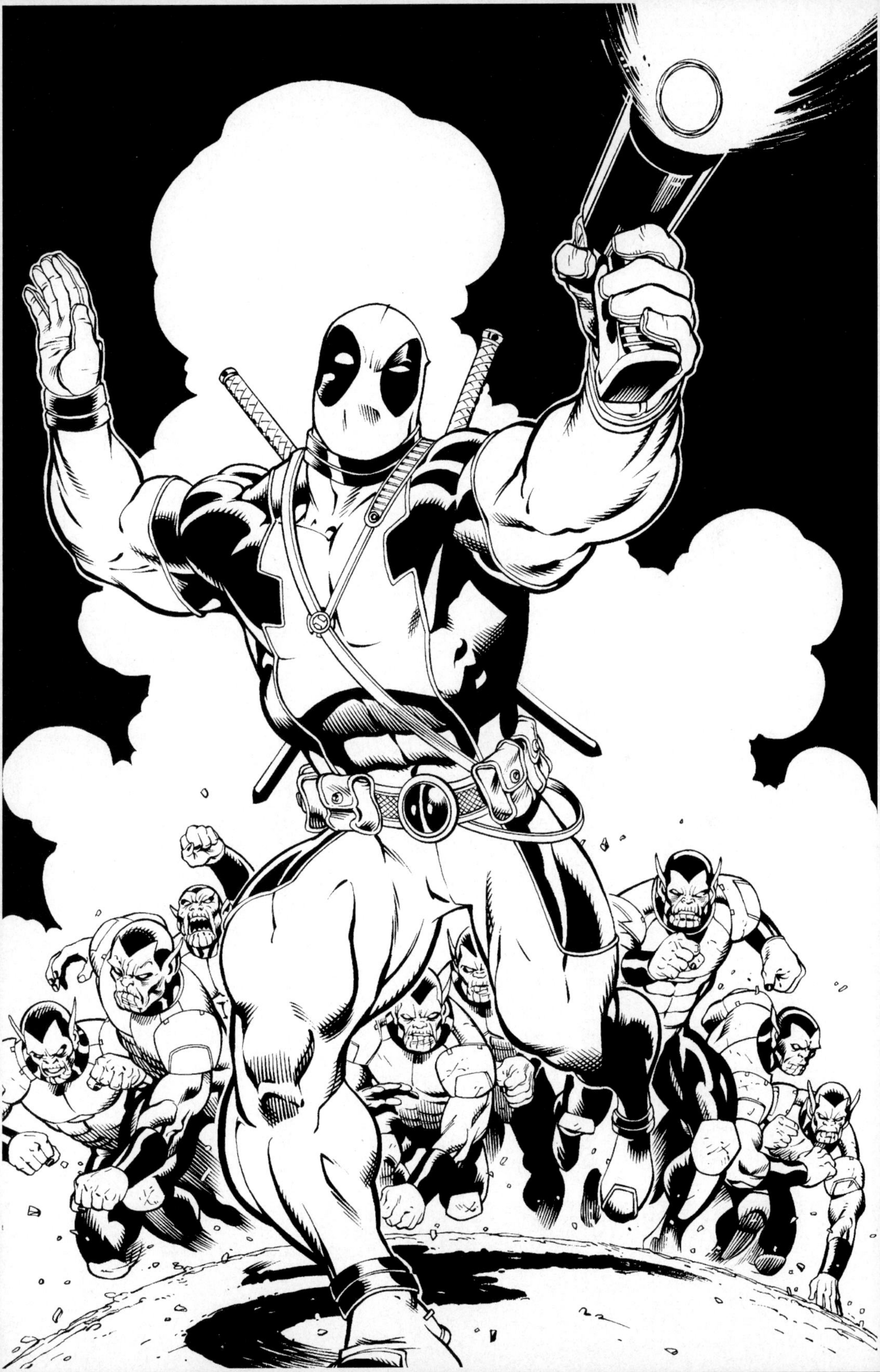

DEADPOOL #2 VARIANT COVER INKS
by Mark Farmer

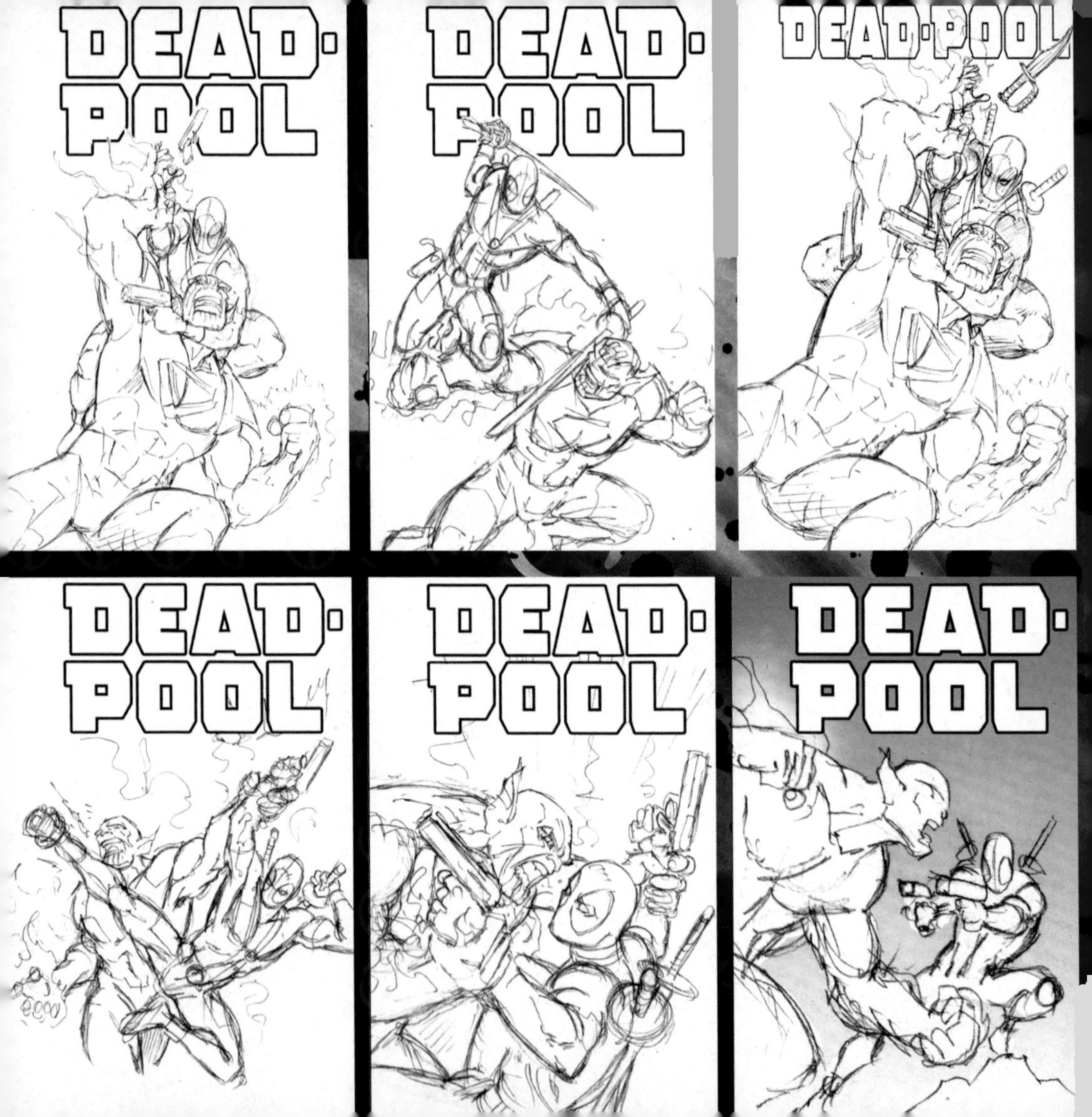
DEAD-POOL
DEAD-POOL
DEAD-POOL
DEAD-POOL
DEAD-POOL
DEAD-POOL

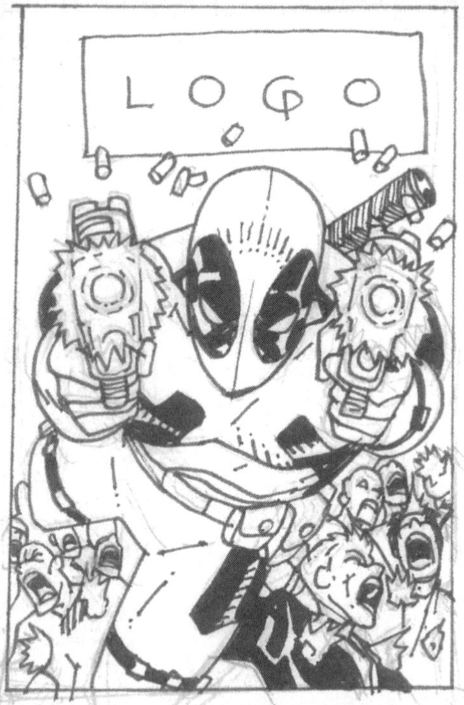
LOGO

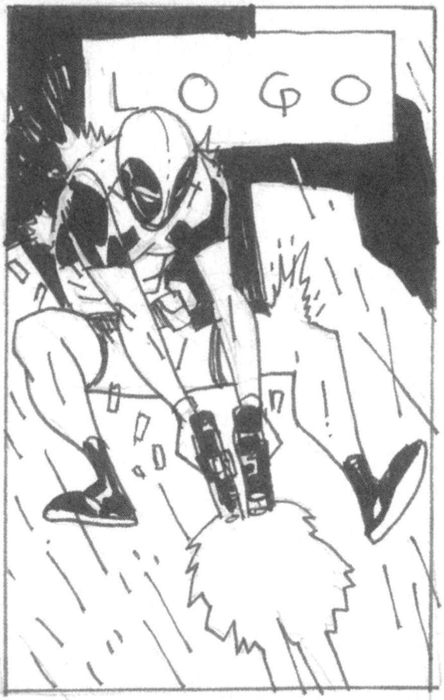
LOGO

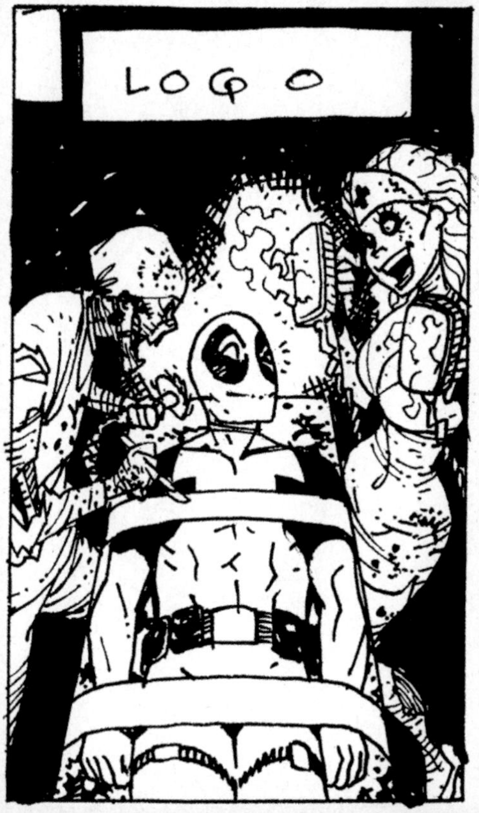
LOGO

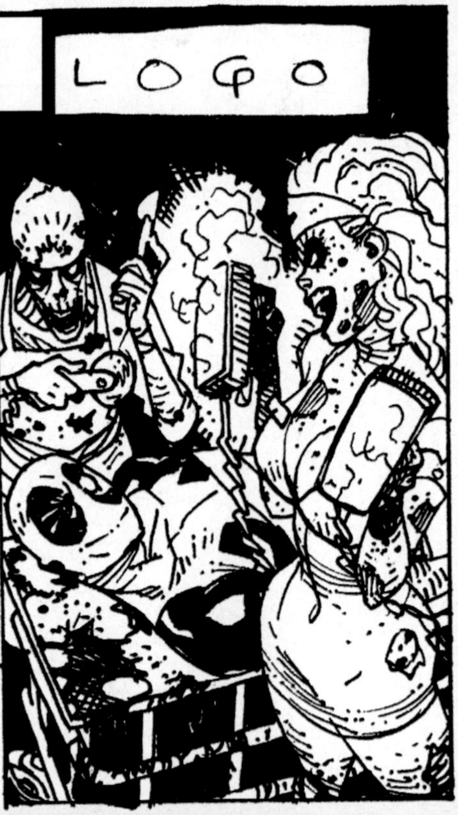
LOGO

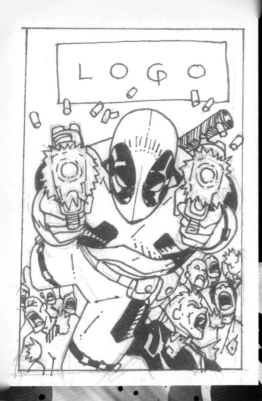

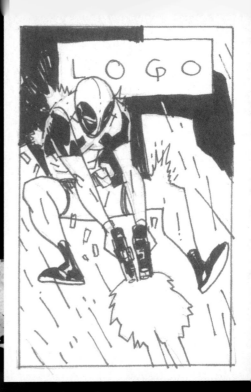

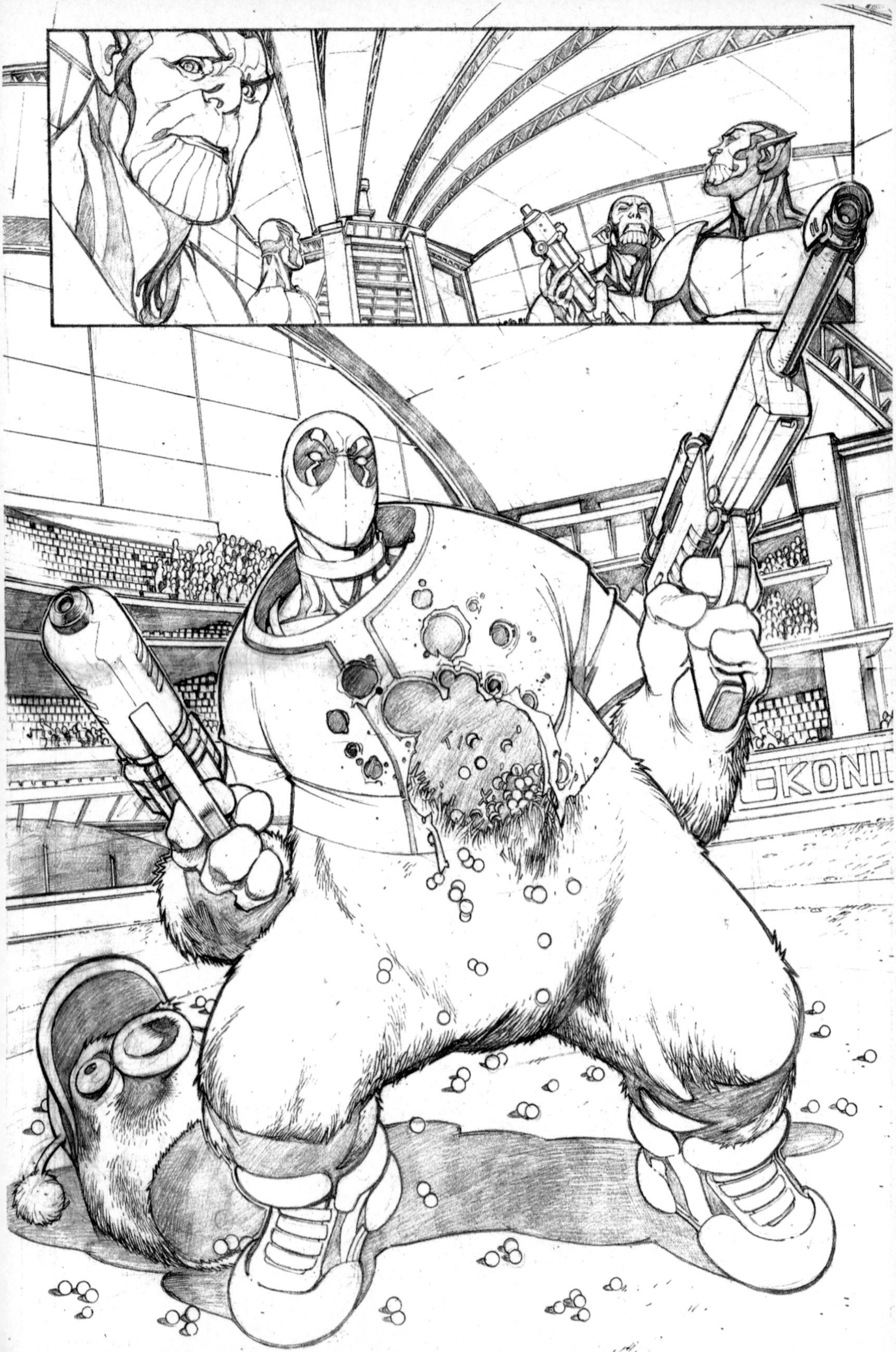
KONI

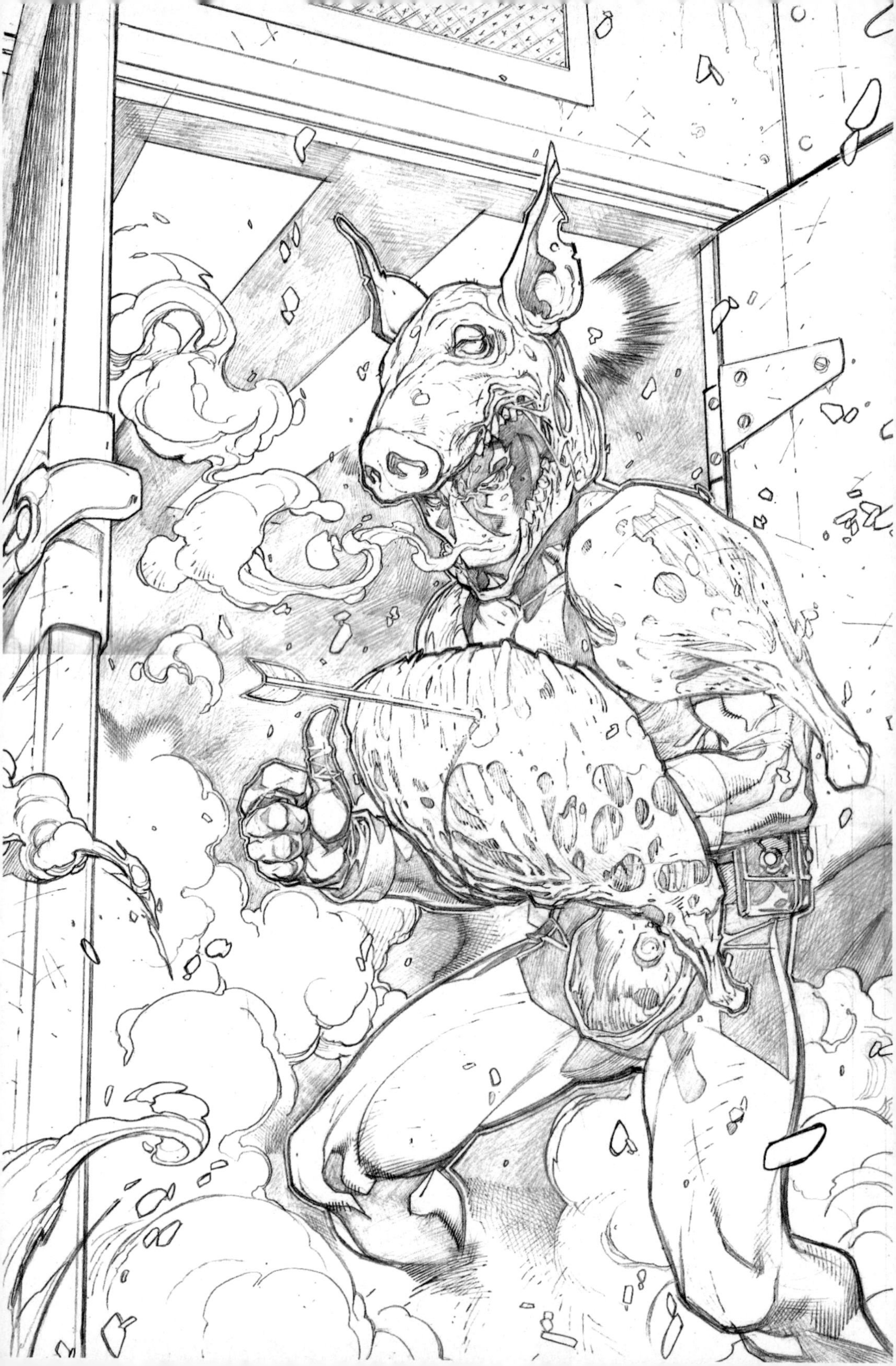

REAL NAME: Unrevealed

ALIASES: Wade Winston Wilson, Merc with a Mouth, Big Dee Pee, Captain Wilson, Johnny Salvini, Armando Khan, Mithras, Dr. Koffer, Takehiko Adachi, Chiyonosake ("the Wolf of the Rice Wine"), Wade T. Wilson, Jack, Rhodes, Corpus, Lopez, "Test-o-clees," others; impersonated Hobgoblin (Jason Macendale), others

IDENTITY: Known to authorities

OCCUPATION: Mercenary, adventurer; former pirate, mob enforcer, government operative, sumo wrestler, soldier, presumably others

CITIZENSHIP: Canada, with international criminal record

PLACE OF BIRTH: Unrevealed

KNOWN RELATIVES: Gretchen (ex-wife), unidentified parents (both possibly deceased)

GROUP AFFILIATION: Formerly Code Red, Agency X, Great Lakes Initiative, SHIELD's Six Pack, One World Church, Deadpool Inc., Weapon X, Team Deadpool, Heroes for Hire, Secret Defenders, Frightful Four, Department K, Oyakata's sumo stable, US Army; former operative of Commission on Superhuman Activities, Landau, Luckman & Lake, Tolliver, Taskmaster, Kingpin (Fisk), Dr. Druid, Yakuza and many others; Deadpool has often considered himself an X-Men member, but no one else does

EDUCATION: High school dropout, US Army Special Forces training, otherwise unrevealed

FIRST APPEARANCE: New Mutants #98 (1990)

HISTORY: Little is known about the man called Deadpool ("Wade Wilson")'s early life, not even his name. Although Deadpool believes his name is "Wade Wilson," it has been alleged he took it from another and his true name is "Jack," full name unrevealed. He once claimed that his father abandoned his mother while pregnant, who physically abused Deadpool as a youth, and who an adult Deadpool confronted and beat up in turn. He later claimed his mother died when he was five, a trauma which provoked a brutal streak in his personality, and that his father, a career military officer, was shot by one of his friends when he was 17. Possibly Deadpool had two sets of parents - his birth parents and a pair of adoptive parents, or perhaps a stepmother and stepfather from remarriages by his birth parents - partially explaining these discrepancies. Given Deadpool's perpetually erratic mental state, he may no longer remember the truth about his origins and could yet supply additional contradictory accounts.

In any event, following a brief stint in army black ops, from which he was supposedly discharged for being "too good," the future Deadpool began his mercenary career circa age 19. Accepting assassination jobs against people he felt warranted death, he habitually took new identities after failing assignments. After one such failure, he was injured fleeing his employers and collapsed into an icy river in Maine. He was found and nursed back to health by a young couple named, allegedly, Wade and Mercedes Wilson. Seeking his rescuer's identity as his own, the young mercenary attacked him and left him for dead, but accidentally killed his wife Mercedes as well. Unhinged over murdering an innocent woman, he became convinced that he was Mercedes' husband, Wade Wilson. Using that name, he resumed his mercenary activities, unaware Mercedes' husband survived and, sponsored by the mercenary's former employers, became sorcerer/assassin T-Ray. Further unaware he was being observed by interdimensional firm Landau, Luckman, Lake & LeQuare as a potential candidate for the Mithras Directive, through which a prophesied hero would protect an alien Messiah (S'met'kth) destined to bring Earth peace, the young mercenary Wilson next surfaced in Tangier, Morocco, where he romanced a woman named Francie. When this relationship ended, he traveled throughout Asia and, in Japan, a crime lord called the Boss hired him to infiltrate rival criminal Oyakata's sumo wrestling ring. Wilson spent three years as a wrestler under Oyakata's tutelage, becoming romantically involved with his daughter Sazae. When Boss ordered Oyakata's murder, Wilson reneged on his assignment, allegedly the first time he ever did so, and relocated to the USA. There he fell in love with teenage mutant prostitute Vanessa Carlysle, with whom he shared dreams of a better future. Hired by Middle Eastern interests to assassinate blind British government operative Althea (later Blind Al), at a Zaire base, Wilson inexplicably killed everyone there except for Al, who fled. Wilson's vengeful employers targeted Vanessa, who was rescued by LLL&L's Zoe Culloden, Wilson's "sponsor" in the Mithras Directive. Learning he had contracted cancer, Wilson left Vanessa, believing she could never find happiness with a terminally ill man.

In Canada, Wilson joined Department K, a Canadian government special weapons development branch. As a test subject in Department K's Weapon X Program, his cancer was temporarily regressed via a healing factor derived from Department K mutant operative Wolverine (Logan/James Howlett). As a potential Canadian super-operative, Wilson joined an unidentified unit, possibly an early incarnation of Weapon PRIME (PRototype Induced Mutation Echelon), training alongside near-invulnerable Sluggo and the cyborgs Garrison Kane and Slayback; he also reunited with Vanessa, who revealed her shape-shifting powers and joined as Copycat. During one mission or training session, Wilson seemingly killed Slayback for unrevealed reasons. When his healing factor malfunctioned, Wilson's health worsened and, his body horribly scarred, he was sent to the Hospice, where failed Weapon X subjects were supposedly treated or allowed to die with dignity. Apparently unknown to the Canadian government, the Hospice's patients served as experimental subjects for Dr. Emrys Killebrew and his sadistic assistant, him in his activities — with the disadvantage of merging the two every time the teleportation technology was used, requiring a painful separation. When Cable established the island community Providence in his long-term plan to improve the world, Deadpool became dedicated to his goals. When Cable threatened to destroy the world's weapons, the X-Men vowed to stop him; declaring himself an X-Man, much to their chagrin, Deadpool tagged along, but turned against the team to side with Cable, although he remained obsessed with supposed membership. Deadpool assisted Cable against SHIELD, Agent X, the monstrous Skornn and other enemies, but when he realized his irrationality and bloodlust could compromise Cable's goals, he resolved to foil his healing factor and commit suicide. He consulted information broker Black Box, who instead brainwashed him to kill the missing Cable. Deadpool tracked him through alternate realities via their DNA link, returned him to their native reality, shot himself in the head to break Black Box's control and soon recovered. With Deadpool's help, Cable subsequently took over the nation Rumekistan, but he and Deadpool parted ways regarding the USA's Superhuman Registration Act, which Deadpool, granted authority to capture unregistered superhumans, saw as a means to achieve the heroic status he had sought for so long. Assigned to apprehend Cable, Deadpool fought his friend, then took hostages, boasting his new status allowed him unlimited power, a statement which Cable broadcast to the world and which cost Deadpool his new status. Thinking turnabout was fair play, Deadpool joined the government-sanctioned Six Pack to discredit Cable, but the group's Rumekistan sabotage, when exposed, only furthered Cable's agenda. When Providence was destroyed following the Hecatomb's attack, Cable dropped from sight, and Deadpool joined Agency X, rescuing Agent X from Hydra and in the process taking a new sidekick, the hapless Bob, Agent of Hydra. When chance reunited him with the Great Lakes Avengers, now the Great Lakes Initiative, Deadpool became a reserve member after helping them defeat AIM; quickly becoming a nuisance, he was ejected by Squirrel Girl. Following a surreal adventure through time and space with Bob, Deadpool yet again revived his solo career, and his sanity further deteriorated, leaving him to hear two argumentative voices in his head and occasionally lapse into cartoon-like hallucinations. His skills unimpeded, he was anonymously hired to capture Wolverine by Winter Soldier, acting on Wolverine's instructions. After a prolonged and brutal battle, he succeeded, but Wolverine's son Daken, who wanted no one but himself to kill Wolverine, emerged from hiding to interfere. After Daken defeated Deadpool, Winter Soldier shot Daken, allowing Wolverine to depart with his son, the purpose of the entire exercise.

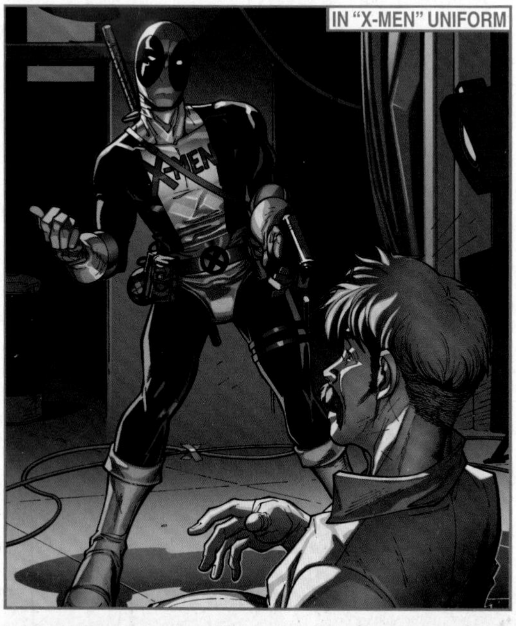

IN "X-MEN" UNIFORM

Art by Paco Medina

Deadpool recovered and took an assignment from ex-SHIELD Director Nick Fury during the Skrulls' "Secret Invasion." To access their computers, Deadpool publicly feigned cooperation with the aliens, earning a reputation as a traitor to Earth. He allowed the Skrulls to duplicate his healing factor in several soldiers, but because it was intended to counter his cancer, it induced fatal cellular overload in the subjects. His Skrull data transmission to Fury was intercepted by Norman Osborn, who used it to achieve a public victory during the invasion that won him unprecedented political power. Learning of Osborn's treachery, Deadpool attacked Osborn's Thunderbolts. Osborn sent his operative Hawkeye (actually Bullseye) to kill Deadpool. The two longtime associates embarked on a prolonged battle of weapons and warped wits, until Hawkeye, reluctant to kill his almost-friend, secretly paid Deadpool to end his vendetta. During an AIM assignment in the Savage Land, Deadpool met his Earth-2149 counterpart, a zombie reduced to a disembodied but equally deranged head who matched him wisecrack for wisecrack; back in the USA, Deadpool briefly joined the Red Hulk's Code Red team. During a brief stint as a pirate, Deadpool saved the island Jallarka from pirates. Fulfilled Fulfilled by the experience, which renewed his long-standing heroic impulses, he sought to join the X-Men, who hesitantly accepted him as an ally until Deadpool targeted X-Men critic Mark Kincaid, allowing the X-Men to garner good publicity by stopping him; which the X-Men learned was apparently Deadpool's intent all along.

HEIGHT: 6'2" **EYES:** Brown
WEIGHT: 210 lbs. **HAIR:** None (originally brown, then varied)

ABILITIES/ACCESSORIES: Deadpool's superhuman healing factor rapidly regenerates damaged or destroyed tissue. The speed at which this ability functions is directly proportionate to an injury's severity and partially affected by Deadpool's mental state, working most efficiently when he is awake, alert and in good spirits. Over the years, the power's efficiency has waxed and waned, since a single instance of overwhelming reconstruction can leave it weakened for weeks; at present, he can regrow severed hands within minutes and survive decapitation for about 12 minutes, at which point oxygen deprivation would affect his brain unless his head was reattached. Due to Thanos' curse, he is supposedly incapable of dying by any means. His healing factor also grants him virtual immunity to poisons and most drugs, as well as an extended life span and an enhanced resistance to diseases. Due to repeated brain injuries, he regenerates decaying brain cells at such a hyper accelerated rate that his sanity and memories suffer regular damage; his most frequent symptom is the belief he is a character in a comic book. Deadpool formerly could access Cable's bodysliding technology without use of machinery due to the two men's DNA mingling. Deadpool is an extraordinary athlete and hand-to-hand combatant, skilled in multiple unarmed combat techniques; his healing factor may contribute to his abilities, allowing him to undertake intensive exercise with minimal fatigue or aches. He is a master assassin, an excellent marksman, and an accomplished user of bladed weapons. He is fluent in Japanese, German and Spanish, among other languages. He employs a wide variety of weapons depending on his assignment or whim, but is virtually never without a combination of guns and knives; he customarily wears multiple pouches on his costume, containing mostly unrevealed paraphernalia. He wears a teleportation device in his belt and carries a holographic image inducer to disguise his true appearance as necessary.

POWER GRID	1	2	3	4	5	6	7
INTELLIGENCE							
STRENGTH							
SPEED							
DURABILITY							
ENERGY PROJECTION							
FIGHTING SKILLS							

DEADPOOL IS A TELEPORTER

under Death's administrations, he was confronted by the ghosts of Ajax's victims, including Worm Cunningham, who urged Deadpool to kill Ajax, believing this would free their earthbound souls. Although reluctant to again kill, Deadpool did so, never learning that the act failed to free the ghosts. Craving redemption, Deadpool accepted Culloden's offer; to his dismay, however, he learned the Mithras' destined role was to kill Tiamat, a potential threat to Messiah, rendering Deadpool's efforts to escape violence seemingly futile. Deadpool narrowly escaped death at Tiamat's hands, leading Tiamat to obsess over killing the Mithras over the Messiah, and Tiamat's Elders stripped him of his armor and granted it to Deadpool, showing him the Messiah brought not true peace, but only mindless bliss; protected from this bliss by Tiamat's armor, Deadpool apparently slew the Messiah.

When the alien Coterie gathered hundreds of super heroes for a "Contest of Champions," Deadpool was among the participants. Despite this seeming vindication of his heroic impulses, Deadpool was no longer optimistic about bettering himself; with LL&L ex-precognitive Montgomery as reluctant sidekick, he set up headquarters in Bolivia and resumed his mercenary career. Troubled by seeming hallucinations too intense for even his addled mind, he consulted deranged psychiatrist Dr. Bong, who suggested he exorcise frustrations by fighting Wolverine. The fight indeed cleared Deadpool's mind, but his psyche received a stunning blow when Mercedes Wilson, who he still believed was his wife, returned to life. Hoping to recapture his supposed loving relationship with her, he emotionally bonded with her, but the couple was teleported away by T-Ray, creator of Deadpool's hallucinations, who revealed himself as not only Mercedes' resurrector, but also her husband, proving Deadpool's hopes were based on lies. Yet the revelation did not break Deadpool's spirit as hoped, for Deadpool, robbed of the loving relationship with Mercedes he had deemed his only saving grace, declared his situation ludicrous and vowed to forget a past for which he could never atone, the better to improve in the future. Swearing further vengeance, T-Ray departed with Mercedes. Norse God Loki Laufeyson, claiming to be Deadpool's father, subsequently imprisoned Death to manipulate Deadpool into battle with his foster brother Thor Odinson. When Deadpool failed to meet Loki's expectations, the god revealed his deception and cursed him to resemble actor Thom Cruz; although long ashamed by disfigurement, Deadpool was even less content to wear another's face. Hired by the Council of Werewolves to assassinate lycanthropic author Duncan Vess, Deadpool's failed due to interference from Wolverine and the renegade werewolf Lycus. After a half-hearted attempt to earn the bounty placed on X-Man Gambit (Remy LeBeau) by the New Son, Deadpool made many attempts to re-disfigure his face, but Loki's curse foiled him. Seeking new quarters, he became roommates with Constrictor and Titania (actually Copycat posing as Mary MacPherran),in the "Deadlounge." Taskmaster hired the three to retrieve Baron (Helmut) Zemo's orbital platform, an assignment during which Deadpool briefly

IN PERSONALIZED LL&L ARMOR

Art by Walter McDaniel

Art by David Brewer

the superhuman Attending, with so hopeless an atmosphere that patients placed bets in a "deadpool" on when they would die. Killebrew subjected Wilson to torturous experiments to learn why his healing factor failed and for his own twisted satisfaction. Trapped between life and death, perceived a manifestation of the cosmic entity Death, and formed a near-romantic relationship with her, but because Killebrew insistently kept him alive for future experimentation, he could not truly join her. Seeking death, Wilson repeatedly taunted the Attending, earning his fellow patients' respect; despite the Attending's rage, Killebrew forbade him to kill Wilson. The Attending instead lobotomized Wilson's friend, cyborg Charles "Worm" Cunningham, whom Wilson then mercifully killed. As the Attending knew, under Killebrew's rules, any patient who killed another earned execution, and Wilson, despite Killebrew's interest, proved no exception. The Attending tore out Wilson's heart, and Death insisted that he join her, but Wilson's thirst for vengeance was so strong that it jumpstarted his healing factor, regenerating his heart. However, this didn't cure his scarred body, and also rendered him insane, a condition which proved inherent in his mutation; curing his insanity would negate his healing factor. Wilson attacked the Attending, leaving him for dead in turn, and was ready to die, but Death abandoned him. Taking the name Deadpool, he escaped the Hospice with his fellow patients.

Following his escape, Deadpool, per his own account, spent time as a mob enforcer alongside surgically altered Maggia leader Hammerhead. He soon resumed freelance mercenary work, donning a costume to accompany his codename, and his constant irreverent banter in even the deadliest situations earned him the nickname "the Merc with a Mouth." At some point he worked with or against Wolverine, by then a spy for Canada's Department H, presumably neither aware they shared a bond via their healing factors; he also clashed with Cable (Nathan Summers) and other super-powered mercenaries during his checkered career. It was presumably during these years he, for reasons known only to himself, abducted Blind Al and kept her prisoner in his San Francisco base, the hologram-equipped "Deadhut," where he occasionally meted out punishment by locking Al in his private torture chamber, "the Box." Al's escape attempts only motivated Deadpool to kill anyone whose help she sought, leaving her resigned to captivity, even developing an odd friendship with her captor. Following Baron (Heinrich) Zemo's death during a confrontation with Captain America (Steve Rogers), Deadpool, presumably on assignment, visited the villain's grave in Bolivia, where he first met Bullseye (Lester), a less experienced but no less deadly mercenary. For whatever reason, the two fought, mutilating Zemo's corpse in the process, the first of many battles they waged over the years. Deadpool acquired a position as Kingpin (Wilson Fisk)'s personal assassin, although he apparently had little contact with the Kingpin's many Manhattan-based super hero enemies. Years after the Hospice escape, Deadpool apparently returned to Canada and, under Department H's auspices, received treatment from Dr. Walter Langkowski, aka Alpha Flight's Sasquatch, whose Department H tenure began long after Deadpool's ended. Eventually, Deadpool abandoned the treatment as abruptly as he had sought it and returned to the USA. Hired by criminal genius Wizard (born Bentley Wittman), Deadpool initially went to the wrong address and took a job impersonating up-and-coming super villain Hobgoblin (Roderick Kingsley). Re-connecting with Wizard, Deadpool joined him, Taskmaster, and Constrictor in a short-lived Frightful Four incarnation to battle the Thing (Ben Grimm). When this failed, Deadpool returned to Kingpin, but Bullseye upstaged him during an assignment and replaced him as Kingpin's assassin; the two again fought, with Bullseye keeping the job, but the pair eventually developed mutual respect and camaraderie, if not actual friendship. Deadpool nevertheless landed a one-time assignment from Kingpin, to kill the Beyonder, who easily defeated him. Eventually, Deadpool accepted assignments and camaraderie at the Chicago mercenary hangout Hellhouse, where diminutive Patch (Bob Stirrat) issued assignments in exchange for profit cuts. During this period, Deadpool developed a rivalry with fellow Hellhouse patron T-Ray, whom Deadpool, still believing himself Wade Wilson, blamed for Mercedes' death. He also recruited nonpowered but ingenious Weasel (Jack Hammer) as weapon supplier; the two became close friends and fellow employees under time-traveling arms merchant Tolliver (Tyler Dayspring), in whose service Deadpool occasionally worked with Sluggo and Copycat, among others.

In recent years, Tolliver sent Deadpool to assassinate his father, Cable, in whose company Copycat was impersonating longtime fellow mercenary Domino (Neena Thurman); ironically, although Deadpool quickly overcame Cable and his new charges, the New Mutants, he was defeated by Domino/Copycat, evidently unaware she was acting contrary to her employer's wishes, who put him in a crate and mailed it to Tolliver. When Cable reorganized his charges as X-Force, they worked with Spider-Man (Peter Parker) against Black Tom Cassidy and Juggernaut (Cain Marko), but Deadpool teleported both criminals to work with Tolliver. Tolliver then sent him to attack Domino, who revealed herself as Copycat, and Deadpool was defeated by Cable and the true Domino, who swore vengeance against Copycat. Deadpool next accompanied Tolliver to the "Dead Man's Hand" underworld summit in Las Vegas to divide up the fallen Kingpin's empire, where, following a chance battle with Nomad (Jack Monroe), Deadpool killed Troy Donahue, underling to Tolliver's rival Lotus Newmark. Tolliver seemingly perished battling X-Force, supposedly leaving behind a will that ceded advanced technology to whoever found it; his mercenaries, including Deadpool, searched the world for it, and Deadpool's quest led to a chance encounter and battle with Blood Wraith, whose Ebony Blade he absconded with before its owner reclaimed it in Bosnia. Erroneously believed to have confidential knowledge about the will, Deadpool's search was interrupted by Slayback, who, having reconstituted himself following his death, sought revenge. In the ensuing battle, Copycat intervened and was gravely injured, prompting Deadpool to partially transfer his healing ability, saving her life, but weakening his remaining power. After slaying sorceress Malachi while in Dr. Anthony Druid's Secret Defenders, Deadpool, employed by External Gideon, joined Juggernaut to abduct Professor X and other X-Men, with whom Gideon empowered the Psi-Ber Sentinel, but Deadpool withdrew from the proceedings before the X-Men defeated Gideon. Deadpool again clashed with Juggernaut and Black Tom, who had forced Killebrew into service and believed Deadpool's healing factor could cure Tom's ailment. With help from Tom's niece, X-Force

WADE WILSON

Art by Steve Harris

WITH PERSONALITY ASPECTS

Art by Georges Jeanty

resurrected him by rebuilding him from his severed hand, restoring his healing factor to its previous peak, but leaving him amnesiac. A chance encounter with Weasel restored his memory, and he discovered that four individuals had claimed the Deadpool name: "Heroic Deadpool," "Killer Deadpool," "Maniac Deadpool," and "Media Deadpool," personality aspects given form by T-Ray and the Gemini Star artifact. On Thanos' behalf, T-Ray intended to manifest and extinguish Deadpool's entire personality, leaving him an empty shell, but Deadpool damaged the Gemini Star, causing his personality fragments to enter T-Ray, rendering T-Ray amnesiac instead. Seemingly restored to his customary approximation of "normal," Deadpool irrationally claimed the incident's denouement "proved" he was the true Wade Wilson. Thanos cursed Deadpool to be unable to die, although Deadpool apparently remained unaware of this. Following an assignment against the Four Winds crime family, Deadpool, erroneously believed to have killed all four leaders, gained great status as a mercenary and formed Deadpool, Inc., aided by business partner Sandi Brandenberg. His success proved short-lived when Black Swan, the Four Winds' true killer, sought vengeance for stolen glory. Both were believed dead after an explosion, but Swan's telepathic power merged both men's memories and skills within underling Nijo. Believing the amnesiac Nijo to be Deadpool, Sandi helped him recover and become Agent X, and the two, with Taskmaster, formed a new mercenary endeavor, Agency X. Black Swan soon resurfaced, with Deadpool in tow, supposedly intending to restore all three to their previous states. During the transfer, the Swan instead absorbed Deadpool and Agent X's abilities, but Agent X, aided by his friends, broke through Swan's telepathic shield and killed him, reversing the transfer. Himself once more, Deadpool declined to join Agency X, returning to his solo career. In unrevealed circumstances, he married and divorced a woman named Gretchen; SHIELD agent Valerie Jessup recruited Deadpool's services for an off-the-books mission by promising information on Gretchen's whereabouts, which apparently never led Deadpool to her.

Deadpool was next hired by the One World Church to steal the Facade virus, with which the Church's leaders intended to transform Earth's populace into blue-skinned beings like themselves to eliminate racism. When Cable intervened, Deadpool, having briefly joined the Church, fought him, but the virus depowered both men, forcing Cable to merge their deteriorating bodies into one and then re-separate them in healthy form. The process created a DNA link between the two, allowing Deadpool to access Cable's teleportation technology and accompany